ISBN 978-0-265-20826-7
PIBN 10213637

OF

LORD KENYON.

𝔓𝔯𝔢𝔰𝔢𝔫𝔱𝔢𝔡 𝔱𝔬 𝔟𝔬𝔱𝔥 𝔥𝔬𝔲𝔰𝔢𝔰 𝔬𝔣 𝔓𝔞𝔯𝔩𝔦𝔞𝔪𝔢𝔫𝔱 𝔟𝔶 𝔠𝔬𝔪𝔪𝔞𝔫𝔡 𝔬𝔣 𝔥𝔢𝔯 𝔐𝔞𝔧𝔢𝔰𝔱𝔶.

und with its Report _____ Frankland ___
L. Aske

16225-6
27.5 21

LONDON:
PRINTED FOR HER MAJESTY'S STATIONERY OFFICE,
BY EYRE AND SPOTTISWOODE,
PRINTERS TO THE QUEEN'S MOST EXCELLENT MAJESTY.

And to be purchased, either directly or through any Bookseller, from
EYRE AND SPOTTISWOODE, EAST HARDING STREET, FLEET STREET, E.C., and
32, ABINGDON STREET, WESTMINSTER, S.W.; or
JOHN MENZIES & Co., 12, HANOVER STREET, EDINBURGH, and
90, WEST NILE STREET, GLASGOW; or
HODGES, FIGGIS, & Co., LIMITED, 104, GRAFTON STREET, DUBLIN.

1894.

7571.]   *Price* 2*s*. 10*d*.

INTRODUCTION.

THE MSS. in the possession of Lord Kenyon at Gredington Hall may be said to relate chiefly to Lancashire, in which county the Kenyon family has been settled from very early times: but the earliest documents in the collection do not relate to the Kenyon family. A curious account, dated in 1524, of a miracle performed near Doncaster, and ten letters dating somewhat later in the 16th century, interesting as being illustrative of domestic life and feeling, belonged to and are connected with the Radcliffes and Faringtons. The spelling in these letters gives an idea of the local pronunciation, and bears a striking resemblance to that found in Scotch writings.

The papers, relating actually to county affairs in Lancashire, begin with the 17th century, being those preserved by Alexander Rigby, then Clerk of the Peace, and by his descendants, one of whom, Alice Rigby, the heiress of George Rigby, also Clerk of the Peace, married Roger Kenyon, and brought into the Kenyon family the property at Peel in Lancashire.

Without instancing individual documents, it may be observed that from the commencement of the 17th century, there are in Lord Kenyon's MSS. valuable materials for a history of Lancashire—ecclesiastical, political, and social, besides much useful matter for the compilation of the personal history of many Lancashire families, especially those which had their origin in or around Liverpool, Manchester, and Wigan; the rapid rise in the social scale of some of these being illustrated by No. 1024.

In 1604 (No. 14) there is a detailed account of the Clergy in the county and of the nature of their cures. Manchester was " a colledge consisting upon (sic) a warden and certaine fellowes, who jointly, together with two ministers and four queristors, doe maintaine the service in that church." Didsbury was a chapel annexed to the mother church of Manchester; whilst Stretford, Chorlton, Gorton, Blackley, Newton Heath and

Dayneton were chapels-of-ease to the same, "the curates and preachers" there being "onely maintained by the severall inhabitants." Liverpool was a chapel-of-ease to Walton and was supplied with a "reading minister."

Of the religious state of the county in 1609, a writer says: "In Lancashire, thanks be to God, there is nowe, such as not many yeares agoe was used in Manchester; yet do all fanatical and schismatical preachers, that are cashiered in other countries, resort into this corner of Lancashire, but not entertained according to their expectation. God deliver England from my sins, dwelling and committed, and from all Jesuits, seminaries, atheists, and factious preachers. I have sent you a book written in defence of our communion book, but lately crept out of the press, and, God be thanked, this corner is purged of schismatical preachers, excepting Gossnall of Boulton and Hunte of Ouldham. Mr. White is now vicar of Eccles and one of the fellows of the College of Manchester, whereof Mr. Burne is not [now?] warden. Mr. White is greatly respected by my Lord of Canterbury, and hath subscribed."—(No. 25.) This document is followed by "Regulations for the Sabbath," somewhat later in date, which forbid a variety of harmless and healthy recreations (No. 28), whilst the measures taken against recusants (No. 89), nonconformists of various denominations, and non-jurors show with what strict impartiality successive Governments have persecuted those who differed from the established religion of the country.

A valuable list of the names of the "Conformable Clergy" in Lancashire in 1689, followed by a list of nonconformist meeting-houses throughout the county, may here be mentioned (No. 712); a comparison with this list and that of 1604, just mentioned, is interesting.

Of the political history of Lancashire there is a considerable amount of evidence, although the great civil war does not find any material illustration. The Rigby family was opposed to the King's cause, and we have a letter (No. 197) from a kinsman, Luke Lloyd, to his wife, in which he gives an account of a rout of the Royalist forces near Stafford, on the 13th of June, 1644 —one of the numerous small engagements prior to Marston Moor. On the morrow of the great battle, the same writer describes it in another letter to bis wife (No. 198).

On the restoration there is a plentiful supply of addresses from various loyal bodies throughout Lancashire.

In 1685 is a list (No. 597) of the men of Manchester, and other parts of the county, who offered themselves to James II. as volunteers on the occasion of Monmouth's rebellion; the loyalty and attachment of the great Lancashire land-owners to the House of Stuart and their hostility to William III. are revealed in many letters from or about them; and the famous "Lancashire Plot," hatched by the informer John Lunt, receives fuller contemporary illustration than it has hitherto received. The policy of the Lancashire people during the risings of 1715 and 1745 also finds illustration—the most important documents in connection with the latter event being the "case" of one of the bailiffs of Manchester who was charged with complicity in the rebellion (No. 1224), which gives a minute account of the proceedings of Prince Charles's forces in and around Manchester; a dying testimony to the atrocities committed by the Duke of Cumberland's army after Culloden (No. 1222); and the petition from the inhabitants of Manchester to the different members representing Lancashire in Parliament, in which is set forth the oppression and injustice offered to the petitioners by the continued quartering of troops upon them (No. 1226).

Of the political events here referred to, the "Lancashire Plot" deserves more particular attention. The trials in connection with this were held at Manchester in 1694, and were, it is but too evident, undertaken by the Government of the time on very insufficient and untrustworthy evidence; the known sympathies of the accused with King James being evidently held a sufficient ground for bringing charges against them of having allowed these sympathies to take the form of actual treason.

Roger Kenyon apparently acted as Solicitor for the accused, and, as a consequence, there is in the collection of his descendants' papers here calendared, a great deal of very important information probably not elsewhere recorded.

The two most authentic accounts of the alleged plot and of the trials for it, which resulted in the immediate acquittal of the prisoners, are to be found in "The Jacobite Trials at Manchester," published by the Chetham Society in 1853, and in "Abbot's Journal," and "An Account of the Tryalls at Manchester," published by the same Society in 1864. Several of the documents in Lord Kenyon's collection—such as the Information of John Lunt and George Wilson (Nos. 873 and 874)—contain material differences in, or additions to, the copies of these documents printed in the former of the two works above mentioned. There is, too (No. 886), an amusing and instructive account of the trial in the handwriting of Roger Kenyon, which tells of Lunt's hopeless incapacity to identify the prisoners with whom he had been, as he alleged, till just before, so intimately associated. But the account does more than this : it shows how, to the last, the Judge did his best to avoid Lunt's collapse, to help him out of his difficulties, and to suggest to the Jury possible explanations for his shortcomings—all very important facts in considering whether or not William III. and his advisers really believed in the guilt of those whose estates would have yielded, had their possessors been convicted of treason, a welcome addition to an impoverished exchequer, and would have ridded the north-west of England of some powerful sympathisers with the Stuart cause.

The *verbatim* account of the examination of Lunt and his accomplices before a Committee of the House of Commons (No. 893), commencing shortly after the termination of the trials at Manchester, has not before been printed.

Of John Lunt's life a very detailed description is given in a statement, probably prepared for the defendants at the trial, or for the subsequent prosecution of the informers for perjury ; it will be found under the date of October, 1694 (No. 888). It has been hitherto said that Lunt was born in Ireland ; here, on evident authority, it is stated that he was born at Macclesfield in 1666, and christened, soon after, in a Derbyshire tavern ; he is described as "son to a bungling bookbinder, who pedled with pamphlets and ballads." His mother was a papist and his father a protestant. His subsequent adventures and the working out of his plot are carefully traced, whilst his susceptibility to the charms of the female sex is narrated with amusing gravity of language.

From the political history of Lancashire, we may turn to the social. This receives varied illustration in Lord Kenyon's MSS.—the state of the towns, the highways, the prisons and prisoners, the conduct of schools and colleges, sports and pastimes. The prevalent crime appears to have been clipping and coining, and the confessions of some notorious offenders—who saved their necks by making political "discoveries" and giving accounts of the methods of their accomplices—reveal the way in which the clippers and coiners proceeded in their work. The plague, nurtured no doubt by the unsanitary state of the towns and villages of Lancashire, receives mention: it was a frequent visitor in the county, one of the earliest references to it being in 1605, when we have the return of a tax levied in Salford Hundred for the relief of infected persons which shows that, in one week, 1,157 people received assistance (No. 15). In August of the same year there is also allusion to the ravages of the plague in Manchester.

From a purely domestic point of view, many of the earlier letters among Lord Kenyon's MSS. are interesting; daily life and sentiments on matters which to-day remain debateable, receive illustration, and these, if nothing more, are at least curious. The letters—to which allusion has been already made—connected with the Radcliffe family, give a picture of the method of conducting matrimonial negotiations in the middle of the 16th century, and suggest that young ladies exercised a little more free-will in such matters than is sometimes supposed. Other groups of letters of this kind may be found in the collection, notably those from Alice Kenyon to her husband Roger, whose parliamentary labours in London, at the end of the 17th century, gave her a good deal of mental anxiety, especially as to the growing length of the sittings; "Pray thee," she writes in one letter, "keep warm as thou can, and take something in thy pocket to the House to sup off; thy age and weakness require it"; and, a little later, "I fear thou art not kind to thyself in staying so long in the House every day without some refreshment."

Roger Kenyon, it may be here remarked, was very closely connected with one of the most prominent and powerful men in Lancashire—the ninth Earl of Derby, grandson of the steadfast adherent of Charles the First and of the courageous Charlotte De La Trémouille. A great deal concerning the career of this nobleman is consequently contained in the Kenyon MSS., including a diary of his proceedings from September, 1688, to the 21st of November following (No. 635). The history and condition of the Isle of Man, of which Roger Kenyon acted as governor for Lord Derby, also find very frequent mention.

After the close of the 17th century the letters and papers in Lord Kenyon's collection become less numerous and less interesting until we arrive at the correspondence of the first Lord Kenyon, Lord Chief Justice of England, who appears, from his youth, to have carefully preserved the letters he received. There are, however, some curious, interesting letters during the early part of the 18th century from Dr. Roger Kenyon, who was physician to James II. and his Queen at the court of St. Germains, where he was brought in contact with many leading Jacobites. He was evidently a strong sympathizer with the fugitive royal family.

The correspondence of the future Lord Chief Justice, Lloyd Kenyon, begins in 1750; he was then 18 years of age, having been born at Gredington in Flintshire, an estate which his father had acquired by marriage with the heiress of the Eddowes family, in 1732. Much of this correspondence is now for the first time brought to light, although some of the letters here calendared were used by the Hon. George Kenyon, M.P., in his able sketch of the Chief Justice's life; the existence of a great deal of the correspondence was, however, when he wrote, unknown to him.

Lloyd Kenyon was, at the outset of his legal career, articled to James Tompkinson, an attorney at Nantwich, and we have, in a letter dated 22nd March, 1755, the first indication of his commencing work as a student for the Bar. Tompkinson, who is in London, gives him advice as to taking chambers and as to the best Inn of Court to enter at. "I find," he says, "the Society of the Middle Temple is esteemed equal, if not preferable, to any other" (No. 1241). Here he accordingly entered on 7th February, 1756. There is little interesting correspondence till some fifteen years later, when Lord Thurlow, for whom Kenyon had assiduously 'devilled,' consults him on a point of law (No. 1273). He had by that time a fair practice of his own, as is shown by two letters to his father, written respectively in 1772 and 1773, mentioning his earnings at the Bar as amounting to over 2,000*l.* a year.

From this time onward his correspondence with leading lawyers and politicians increases. The year 1780 saw him Chief Justice of Cheshire and member for Hedon, and it was then that he gained public reputation as leader in the defence of Lord.

George Gordon. The riots which occasioned this trial are fully described in letters from Mrs. Lloyd Kenyon (Nos. 1292 and 1293), in one of which occurs the passage, " Mr. Kenyon is provoked beyond measure at Lord G. Gordon--says he is mad and should be confined, and wishes some spirited conduct may be pursued to suppress this first lawless outrage."

Among Kenyon's correspondents were John Walter, the founder and proprietor of "the Times"—who, in 1799, sketches the incidents of a singularly chequered career, and of the early history of his newspaper (No. 1413) — Burke, Fox, Pitt, Lord Camden, Erskine, Sheridan, Warren Hastings, who writes about his trial, Thurlow, who discusses the Regency, Wilberforce, who enlarges upon his measures of social reform, Plowden, who refers to his proposed legal works, and a host of other well-known men.

From March 1782 to April 1783, and from the following December till March 1784, Kenyon was Attorney General, being created a baronet upon the first bestowal of the office. He quitted that post to become Master of the Rolls. William Pitt's first letter to him is that in which he announces his appointment (No. 1316). After this the Prime Minister consults him frequently on legal points connected with measures before Parliament, and, in so doing, often gives an interesting expression of his own opinion on legislative reforms or changes. Thus, on the 20th March, 1785, he writes to Sir Lloyd Kenyon from Putney, sending him the draft of a proposed measure dealing with Parliamentary representation, in which letter he says, "I trust the plan guards against the principal objections hitherto suggested, either with respect to arbitrary disfranchisement, or to introducing further innovation. The idea of transferring a certain proportion of representation from boroughs to counties (which is limited by the impossibility of more than a certain number being ever conveniently chosen by counties), and of providing that the boroughs which must continue to elect shall be those best entitled to it, seems to include all the amendment which our constitution can admit in the frame of Parliament, unless some new principle were to be admitted, for which I see no reason " (No. 1321).

Sir Lloyd Kenyon was raised to the Chief Justiceship of the King's Bench, on the retirement of Lord Mansfield in 1788.

Lord Mansfield had, in the April of that year, communicated to him his intention to retire, in a letter in which occurs the passage, " Except Mr. Justice Buller, to whom Lord Mansfield is bound by many ties, there is no man by whom.Lord Mansfield had rather. be succeeded, than by the Master of the Rolls" (No. 1340).

Sir Lloyd's advancement to the peerage is notified to him by Pitt on the 5th June 1788 (No. 1341), and a fortnight later, the new Lord Chief Justice bought of his predecessor, for the sum of a hundred guineas, his gold collar of office (No. 1343).

With George III. and the royal family Lord Kenyon appears to have been on terms of the closest intimacy, and some of the details of domestic life at Court are interesting from their evident accuracy. On many matters of urgent importance Lord Kenyon was the King's adviser. In a curious holograph letter, written from Queen's House, on March 7th, 1795, George III. expresses very freely the abhorrence and alarm with which he regards the policy of his Lord Lieutenant, Lord Fitzwilliam, particularly with respect to the Roman Catholics of Ireland (No. 1391); the letter is accompanied by a series of queries, as to how far the proposed changes in favour of "the papists in Ireland" are really constitutional, and on these the King desires Lord Kenyon's opinion.

Lord Kenyon died in 1802; a few letters addressed to his son and successor in the title, though of a somewhat later date than the majority of papers usually dealt with by the Historical MSS. Commission, have been included in this report from the interest attaching to their writers. Amongst them may be mentioned a pathetic letter from Ernest, Duke of Cumberland, in which he refers to the accident to his son which had resulted in his partial blindness; a grateful acknowledgment by Lady Eleanor Butler and Miss Sarah Ponsonby, the two "ladies of Llangollen," for Lord Kenyon's successful efforts to obtain for them a pension; and a batch of letters, written from Keswick during the years 1834-1837, from Robert Southey, in which the staunchness of his conservatism is demonstrated:—" A new election," he says, writing in July 1834, "might throw out many Whigs, but they would be mostly replaced by Radicals; I do not say this would be casting out devils by Beelzebub, because it is difficult to say which of the two parties is the worst (*sic*)." His subsequent letters, free from political expression, are penned in graceful language, tinged with a melancholy in which we may almost see indications of the coming mental affliction by which the poet was soon to be overtaken.

In referring to the numerous matters of miscellaneous interest contained in the present report, mention should be made of the detailed account of King James I.'s visit to Scotland in 1617 (No. 37), and of a royal "progress" in 1619 from Theobalds, through the Midlands, and back to Windsor (No. 45); illustrations of the method of lead mining in the reign of Charles I. (No. 94); of the state of New England in 1658 (No. 166); of horse racing at Newmarket in 1682 (No. 486); and of materials for the history of the administration of the Duchy of Lancaster during the 17th century. The picture of the social and political state of the Isle of Man has been already referred to.

At the conclusion of the report on the letters and papers, has been added a calendar to an old Memorandum book—the entries in which are in the handwritings of various dates—which contains some curious information as to the introduction of the weaving industry at Leeds; the Dean of Peterborough's account of the execution of Mary, Queen of Scots and other particulars relating to her trial and execution; and a great deal of additional information as to the religious state of Lancashire in the 16th and 17th centuries.

Throughout the compilation of the report, the Commission has received constant assistance in bringing to light undiscovered bundles of papers, not only from Lord Kenyon himself, but from his lordship's mother, the Hon. Mrs. Bulkeley-Owen, and his uncles, the Hon. George and the late Hon. Edward Kenyon; by the latter most valuable aid was given in copying or noting several of the more recent letters, and it is to be regretted that he did not live to see the publication of the report in which he took so lively an interest.

In conclusion, I must ask leave to return my personal thanks to Lord Kenyon for the hospitality he has shown me on the occasion of my numerous visits to Gredington.

W. J. HARDY.

THE MANUSCRIPTS OF LORD KENYON AT GREDINGTON HALL, SHROPSHIRE.

A MIRACLE.

1. 1524, July 15.—Testimony by William Nicolson, and others, to a miracle worked upon them, by which they escaped drowning.

"Be it known to all Christyn pepull, that on the 15th day of Julii, anno Domini, 1524, that oon William Nicolson, of the parish of Townsburgh, three myle from Doncaster, as the said William schuld have passed over the water of Doune at a common forde callyd Steaforth Sandes, with an yren bownd wayn, six oxen, and two horsse, looden with howshold stuff, and havyng also in his said wayn oon Robert Leche, his wyff and their two chyldren, oon chyld beyng but half a yere of age, and the other child beyng under seven yeres of age, sett his servaunte, callyd Ric. Kychyn, upon the formast horsse, and whan the draghte was past the myddes of the water, the streem and the wynde was gret, and drofe the wayn, the oxen, and the horsses down the water. And the formast horsse, which the servaunte roode upon, was drowned, and the wayn, with all the company, was turned upsodown, and the whelis upwardes. Than all the company beyng therin, did call and cry to Allmighti God and to our Blessid Lady, whose ymage is honorde and worshept in the Whyte Freeres of Doncaster, by whos grace the said servaunte gate holde of an oxe bele, and soo gate to land; and his master William Nicolson, lying in the bothom of the water emonges his beasts' feete, gate holde of a beast's heed, and thrast hymself towardes the land, and so, by the grace of God, and of this good Lady of Doncaster, was savyd. Fyrst [he] dyd take hold of a willow busch, which dyd breke, callyd of our Blessed Lady, and gate hold of another and was savid. Now the said Robert Leche, his wyff and their two yong children, after that was dryfen down with the wynde and streem in the myddes of the mayn water, the space of three score foote and more, to an owler busch; at the which the said Robert, with his two yong children, by the help of God and of our good Lady, gate to land. Then after that, the wyff of the said Robert Leche was dryven down, with the wayn, oxen, and the horsses, the space of three hundred foote and more, with the gret wynd and the streeme, in the myddes of the mayn water; and the wayn turned with the water three times upsodown, she beyng therin. And than all the peple beyng on the land, seyng this pituous and bevy sithte, dyd knele down upon thar knees, and made thar speciall prayers to Allmightie God and to this Blessed Lady of Doncaster, that if ever she shewed any merakill, to shew some grace upon this said woman. And anoon, after the woman was cast above the water, and spake to the pepill, she beyng in the water, and said she did ritht well, for God and our Blessid Lady in Doncaster had preservyd hyr; and so, by grace of Allmighti God and of this said gracious Lady, the wayn, with the beasts and the woman, was cast towards the land, and soo was savyd, all the christyn soules; howheyt, there was three oxen and one horsse drowned, and three oxen and one horse savid. And that thes premysses been true and not fayned, the fornamyd William Nicolson, Robert Leche, his wyff and their two yong childeren, cam to our Lady in Doncaster apon Mare Mawdleyn's day next after the date herof, and dyd declare this gracious merakill, and was sworn apon a boke before the Prior and Covent, with other of sufficieut wyttnes of their neburs, as followeth : Thomas Boswell, gentillman, Joh. Turnlay, Joh. Mapill, Robt.'Newcome, with other moo; and as that day this gracious merakill was rongne and songne in the presence of 300 peple and moo. *Deo gracias."*

LADY RADCLYFFE to SIR ANDREW WINDSOR, Knight.

2. [1549 ?*] October 7. Wynmerley.—" Syr, as tochyng your laste letter, qwerein I persawe ye dyssyryt me to be gud moder to my swnne, and yours, that ther be no predysciall nar hwrtte unto my swnny's anarretans; Syr, has ferr has lys in my pore power, I wyll be lotthe to se yt swlde hwrit. And yf there be ony more abowth to do hym any wronge, your masterscheppe shall hawe knawlyge, trystyng that ye wylle se remedy for hym, for he, nor I, has no noder socar both you. Syr, has tochyng the custum londe, qwere I wrothe to you to send it uppe, Syr, ye may persawe a woman's wytte : the custum londe is that all seche londes has is custum landes; one of my swnnys kynginsmen, of hys moder syde, after the custum, is a custum to resawe all seche landes to the chylde, cum of xv yeres of age, and then to mayke acowtte to the chylde of all seche profeyttes after xii custumiers (?). Bysechyng your masterscheppe regarnot my worddes in my wryttynges, for my mynde is, and sall be at all tymys, that all profettes that may contunyally falle or cum to my sune, has ferr as lys me, I wolde your masterscheppe badde yam. There sall be no profettes senyt from your masterscheppe. Syr, yff it be your pleswr, ye may sende into the cuntre, and then ye may knawe of the custom & the trawthe in all thynges. Sir, I persawe be your letter, ye desyre me to sende wordde to your masterscheppe of seche artikylls has cum in your wryttyng, ze wyche ye sende to me by my servant, Thomas Jakeson. Syr, your wryttyng come nott . . . . me tell after the Natevite of Our Lade, the last paste. Syr, qwer has ye wrotte to me thowchyng my swone and my doghter that I swlde be contente with thone of yame ; Syr, I wolde to God my doghter wolde be conseled by me and hur fryndes, wyche thynges it wer and swlde be do hwr cumfurthe and howres in tyme cumhynges. Besechyng your masterscheppe to take no dysplesur with me, fer my doghter is of renabull hage to gyf a nonswarre for her selfe, and sche is not of good mynde to leffe the cunttree. Syr, therfor I beseche you to be gud master to my swne has long has he is in your kepyng, for he has no noder fader both you to soker hym. Syr, I wolde beseche you gyff any mon cum to dyssyre the pore tenens [tene-ments ?] the wech belongs unto my swne to hawe thyam, I beseche you lett no mon hawe thyam, both thame that ye hawe pouttit (*sic*), for it wolde be grett hwrt (?) to thame. Syr, qwer ye commande it to me to speke with my Lorde Steward, or elles with Syr Rechard (?) Sach-ewerell, tha cum nott throghe Loncaschyre ; how be it, I am boune be your purr bedde womon, that yt wold plese you to speke to seche men for me in my sunny's ryghte."

SIR ANDREW WYNDESOR to " MISTRESS ALYCE RADCLYFF of Wynmerlegh."

3. [1549–50 ?] February 10. London.—" So yt is that I perceyve by your letter that your doughter is not mynded to be maryed owt of her countre, whiche is but a syngler appetyte of herself and her

---

* Sir Alexauder Radcliffe, husband of the writer, died on 5th February 1548-9.

frendes. I assure you ther is noon of them that I entended to have maryed her to, but she schold have lyved better with any of them, the worst day of the yere, than sche schall do with hym that you here say sche schalbe maryed to, in the best. If she forsak her good fortune, sche schall blame no mann but her selfe and her frendes. And as for your sonn, as soone as I am throroughe with the Master of the Wardes, I wyll send for hym in the fayre season of the yere. And if your doughter schuld come into this partyes, I wode be content that she dyd abyde with you, for I wold not have hyr owt of your bandes tyll her were of greatter age. I entended her mariage in two places, wher sche schuld have hadd 40^{ti} poundes of joynter and to an man of c.c. markes of land, delyvered in hande; and the other myght be myche more made a better bargayn. I pray you gyve credence to this berer, and be better advysed or [ere] ye yett conclude for her." *Signed.*

THOMAS FARYNGTON to "MAYSTRES RADCLYFF at Wynmerley."

4. [1550?]—" Mother, I thanke you for kyndnez in tymes past. And qwere ye excusyt you to make me onsware, by wrytyng, off my last letter send unto you, by cause youre chaplane was not at home; he is now at home, as I suppose, or, at the lest, ye have had suffycent laysur to take youre concell off your supposyt most trusty frendes. Qwerefore I desyre you, lett me have onswere by wrytyng by thys berer in that behalff. And qwereas ye woold not delyver your doghter, and myn (*sic*) with owt sume tokenynge, I hertely thanke you, for that was a tokenynge off luff to her at the lest, although ye have lytyll unto the father or mother. Qwerefore I desyre you, suffer her to be delyvered by youre selff, or sume off your servantes, unto thys berer. And thys my wrytyng shall be your discharge in that behalfe. I wold wryte more unto you, but I suppose it wold move you so much. Qwerefor at thys tyme, all other thynges I omyt. Youre lovyng son, qwen it shall please you, Thomas Faryngton."

SIR RICHARD WYNGFELD to "MAISTREIS ALICE RADCLIFF, wedowe."

5. [1550?] November 10. London.—Has received her letter of the 4th November, by which he perceives that both she and the feoffees of her late husband " be contented to surcease farther to pursue to the vexacion of Thomas Farington, considering that you have perfitt knowledge that your dowtter, and he, without any constraint made unto her, was, before the taking of her awaye, affianced, and that if ye had knowen so motche afore, ye wold never have troubled him for that matter; wherein, I promise you, ye have don right worshipfully, wisely, and discretly. And farther, I parceyve by your said letter that concernyng suche londes as the said Thomas Faringdon, in the right of his said wife, your dowtter, dothe clayme to have, and allso concernyng suche mariage money, as by the bequaest of her father, your late husband, she should have uppon certayne condicions, you and the feoffes will be at your liberteyes to defende the lawe in that behalf, if the said Thomas Faringdon and your dowtter shall demand the same. Wheryn, allthough all the condicions, whiche on the part of your said dowtter (as you do alledge) should have ben performed, have not been observed accordingly, yet, considering that ye be at your libertye, and not constrayned to do the extremyte in that behalf, I hartyle desyer you to be good unto them, and specially for the said marriage money, which if it may please you to lett them have the same, and the rather at this myn instaunce and desyer, you shall not oonly do theryn right charitably and naturally for the advancement of your owne chilld, but you shall allso thereby bynde me to be gladde to do you such pleasur as shall lye in me to do from tyme to tyme." *Signed.*

"The Sayinge of ALYS RADCLYFF, wedwe."

6. [1550?] December 16.—Sir Henry Faryngton, knight, had written to the said Alice, and desired to be ordered according to good conscience and the true intent of an award made between the said Alice and the other feoffees of Thomas Radclyff, Esquire, on the one part, and the said Sir Henry, Thomas Faryngton, his son, and Cicely, wife of the said Thomas, on the other part. "The seyd Alys Radclyff sayth and grauntyth by this byll, she being but a gentylwoman, ignorant and dissolate of cownsell, thynking that she hath fulfylled all covenaunts and articleys in the seyd awarde, on her partye; and, if anye be nott donne, she wilbe redye, at the next Sessions of Asyes to be holden at Lancaster, with hyr freynds, ther to be orderet in all the seyd articles, acordynge to the trwe intent of the seyd ward, by the Kynge's Justices and other lerned cownsell, as freyndes shall thynke reasonable."

SIR HENRY FARYNGTON.

7. [1550?]—Articles "desyred by Sir Henry Faryngton, knight, to be ordret accordyng to gud conciens, to the true intent of award maid bitwix Alys Radclyff, widow, and other feoffees of Thomas Radclyff, Esquyer, on the one parte, and the said Sir Henry Faryngton and Thomas Faryngton, sone off the said Sir Henry, and Cecill his wyfe, dochtter of the said Thomas Radclyff and Alez, on the other parte."

JOHN ATHERTON to "MR. RADCLYFE."

8. 15[60,] April 23. Atherton.—Has received the Earl of Derby's letter of the 13th April, commanding and appointing him—by virtue of a letter addressed to the Earl by the Lord Lieutenant of the North, "for the levying of a certayne numbre of men within this shire of Chesshire"—to be captain, and to have the "conduction of 100 men; of the which his Lordshipp aponteth you to make 22 men. Of them you must make 8 archers, with stele cappes, leadde malles, daggers, bowe[s] and arroys; And all youre hoole numbre to be talle and lustie men ; and to be afore me, at leght, at 12 of the clocke, the Thursday being the 29 day of Aprill, that I may see the furnysshing of theym, and that I may certifie my Lord thereof." *Signed.*

WIGAN MARKET.

9. 1561–1567.—A book of the tolls received from the market or fair by the mayor of the borough of Wigan. The receipts for each fair commence with an account of the keepers of the toll at Milne gate, Standishe gate, Wall gate, and Hall gate. The fair appears to have been held twice yearly on the vigils, feasts, and morrows, of the festivals of the Ascension of Our Lord and of St. Luke the Evangelist.

WIGAN CHURCH SEATS.

10. 1591, May 14. Lancaster.—Writ of the Queen to John, William, and Ralph Lowe of Aspull, and Hugh Lowe of Ince, within the parish of Wigan. Recites that Thomas Gudlawe, gentleman, *ex devotione sua,* gave to his parish church of Wigan aforesaid, as an ornament thereof, "*quandam scedulam vocatam,* a pewe or seate," which was lawfully placed in the nave there by the churchwardens, and which has now, "by you and other disturbers of our peace and the quiet rule of the Holy Church," been broken down (*interumpitur*) and disturbed under a title of prescription made by the said Lowes, their kinsmen, and those of their name; whereas there is no such prescription to any person in the nave of the church, which is common to all the parishioners. Recites further that the Lowes have commenced an action against the said Gudlawe for the premises, before Doctor David Yale, principal of the Consistory Court of Chester, in the Court-Christian. Such action should belong wholly to the churchwardens, and should have been brought at common law. The writ directs that the plea so begun before Dr. Yale be not further proceeded in, "allowing and rendering to the same Thomas Gudlawe his reasonable costs, charges, and expenses in that behalf sustained, by reason of his unjust vexation." Further directs that possession and use of the seat aforesaid shall remain in the state in which it was before, at the time of the gift and first placing thereof by the churchwardens.

JOHN SEDON to ALEXANDER RIGBY, clerk of the peace for Lancashire.

11. 1600-[1,] January 24. Salisbury Court.—Has received his note of the Recusants, "which he did move the Lord Treasurer about, who answered that Her Majestie was determined to direct foorth commission for improving Recusants' lands, and therefore wished not to proceed till the effect were knowen." Knows now that it is "otherwise ordered."

JOHN HAWORTH to his brother-in law, CHRISTOPHER CUNLIFFE, at the Sparth, near Blackburn.

12. 1602, June 16. London.—Yesterday was appointed to have been our "crucyfying day," and Mr. Robert Hesketh was in the Duchy, but no Counsel with him but himself, for his meaning was not to have any hearing, saving that which we would not hear, and that was Mr. parson Shuttleworth, who encountered Mr. Nowell, and dealt very inwardly with him for an unity and an agreement. My young master goeth not the circuit with us, as I hear. *Signed and seal.*

DIRECTIONS FOR MINISTERS by KING JAMES I.

13. 1603-1625.—1. "That no preacher under the degree and calling of a bishop, deane of Cathedrall or Collegiall Church (and they upon the Kinges dayes and sett festivalls) doe take occasion upon the expounding of any text of Scripture whatsoever, to fall into any sett discourse or commonplace, otherwise then by opening the discourse and division of his text, which shall not bee comprehended and warted (*sic*) in essenc, substance, effect, or naturall inference, within some one of the articles of religion sett forth, Anno Domini, 1562, or in some one of the homilies sett forth by authority in the Church of England, not onely for an help for the now matching, but withall for a paterne and a boundary, as it were, for preaching ministers; and for the further instruction for the performance thereof, that they forthwith read over, and peruse diligently, the said Booke of Articles and the twoe Bookes of Homilies.

2. That noe parson, vicar, curatt, or lecturer, shall preach any sermon or collation hereafter, upon Sondayes and holydaies in the afternoone, in any cathedrall or parish church throughout the kingdome, but upon

some parte of catechisme, or some text taken out of the Creed, Ten Commandmentes, or the Lordes Prayer (funerall sermons onely excepted), and that those preachers be most incoraged and approved of whoe spend these afternoone exercises in the examining of children in their catechisme, and in expounding of the severall points and heads of the catechisme, which is the most ancient and laudable custome of teachinge in the Church of England.

3. That noe preacher, of what tytle soever, under the degree of a bishopp, or a deane, at the least, doe, from hencforth, presume to preach in any popular audience the deepe points of predestination, election, reprobation, or of the universality, efficacity, resistability or irresistability of God's grace, but leave those thames to be handled by the learned men, and that moderatly and modestly by way of use and application, rather then by way of positive doctrine, as being [more] fitted for the schooles and universities then for simple auditors.

4. That noe preacher, of what title or denomination soever, shall presume from henceforth, in any auditory within this kingdome, to declare, limitt, or bound out, any way of possitive doctrine, in any lecture or sermon, the power of prerogative, jurisdiction, authority, or duty of soveraigne princes, or otherwayes medle with these matters of state and referrences betweene the princes and the people, then as they are instructed and presidented in the Homyly of Obedience and in the rest of the Homiles and Articles of Religeon sett forthe, as before is mentioned, by publicke authority, but rather confyne themselves wholly to theese twoe beades of faith and good life, which are all the subject of the ancient sermons and homilies.

5. That noe preacher, of what title or denomination soever, shall causelessly and without invitation from the text, fall into bitter invectives and undesent raling speeches against the persons of either papistes or puritanes, but modestly and gravely, when they are occasioned thereunto, by text of scripture, free both the doctrine and discipline of the Church of England from the aspersions of either adversarie, especiallie where the auditorie is suspected to be tainted with the one or the other invection.

6. Lastly, that the archbishopps and bishopps of the kingdome, whome his Majesty hath good cause to blame for his (sic, ? their) former remisnes, [be] more wary and choise in lycencing of preachers, and revoke all grantes to any chancellor, officiall, or comissary, to passe licences in this kind, and that all the lecturers throughout the kingdome, a new bodie, severed from the ancient clergie of England, as being neither parsons, vicars nor curates, be licensed henceforward in the Court of Faculties onely upon recomendation of the p . . . y from the bishopp of the diocese, under his hand and seale, with a fiat from the Lord Archbishopp of Canterbury and a confermation under the great seal of England.

And that such as transgress any one of theese directions be suspended by the bishop of the diocese, or in his default, by the Archbishopp of the Province, ab officio et beneficio, for a yere and a day, untill his Majesty, by the advise of the next Commissioners (sic) convocation, shall prescribe some further punishment." *Copy.*

14. 1604.—" Certaine briefe observations truly gathered, partly by experience and partly from others, comprehending the whole estate of Lancashire clergy, rightly divided into its six proper hundrethes, with the severall parishes conteined in the same.

Loynsdale Hundreth.

The Names of the Parishes.	
Kirkby Ireleth - Broughton in Furnes, a Chappell -	A donative in the nature of a Viccaridge. The Patron there, the Dean of Yorke. The Incumbent there, Mr. Dodgson, a preacher. The farmor of the impropriation, Mr. Latus.
Dalton -	A Viccaridge; the Patron, the Chancellor of the Duchye. The Incumbent, Mr. Gardner, noe Preacher. The farmor there, Mr. Joseph Hudleston, gent.
Aldingham -	A Parsonage; the Patron, the Kinge. The Incumbent, Mr. Gilpin, a preacher.
Urswick -	A viccaridge; the patron, the Chancellor of the Duchy. The Incumbent, Mr. Lindall, a preacher. The farmors, John and Anthony Sawrey, gentlemen.
Ulverston Parish - Pennington -	A Donative in the nature of a Vicarridge. The Patron, the Deane of Yorke. The Incumbent, Mr. Leighe, no preacher. The farmors, the whole parishioners.
Hawkeshead -	A Donative in the nature of a Viccaridge. The Patron, the Kinge. The Incumbent or Stipendary Preacher, Mr. Magson. The farmors, Adam and Edmund Sandes.
Cartmel -	An Impropriation, and meanely served onely with a reading minister. It is belonging to the Bpp. of Chester. The farmor is George Preston, Esq.
Warton -	A viccaridge; the Patron, the house of Worcester. The Incumbent, Mr. Oburne, a preacher. The farmors, Sir Thomas Samford, Knight, and Richard Sherborne, Esqre.
Boulton by the Sands -	A Viccaridge; the Patron, the Bishop of Chester. The Incumbent, the before-named Mr. Oburne. The farmor, the Lord Buckhurst.
Kellett -	A Chappelry unto Boulton. The minister, Mr. Barker, no preacher.
Halton -	A Parsonage; the Patron, the Bishop of Chester. The Incumbent, Mr. Sawrey, a preacher.
Aughton -	A Chappellry.
Whittington	A Parsonage; the Patron, Thomas Carus, gentleman. The Incumbent, Mr. Newton, no preacher.
Tunstall -	A Viccaridge; the Patron, John Girlington, Esq. The Incumbent, Mr. Birkett, noe preacher. The farmor, the said Mr. Girlington.
Tatham -	A Parsonage; [the Patron,] the Lord Mounteagle. The Incumbent, Mr. Dewhurst, a preacher. The farmor, Edmund Moore, gentleman.
Claughton -	A Parsonage; the Patron, Edward Crofte, Esqr. The Incumbent, Mr. Seenehouse, a preacher.

The Names of the Parishes.	
Melling	A Viccaridge ; the Patron and farmor, the Lord Mounteagle. The Incumbent, Mr. Burrowe, no preacher.
Hornby and Acholme chappells	The Stipendary reader, Mr. Mann, with the like reading Minister.
Lancaster	A large Viccaridge ; the Patron, Mr. Farrington. The Incumbent, Mr. Kinge. The farmor, Sir Robert Bindlose.

There are many Parochiall chappells, hamletts, and forrests belonging to Lancaster, and far distant from their Mother Church.

Gressingham, a parochial Chappell	The Incumbent or Stipendary minister, Mr. Grenoepp, noe preacher.
Wiersdale in the King's forest	The Minister there, Mr. Cragge, no preacher.
Stalmine	A parochial Chappell. The Stipendary minister, Mr. Picke, noe preacher.
Bleasdale	A Chappell, without service, in the King's Chase. The stipend deteined by Robert Parkinson, Commissary of Richmond.
Mierscough	The King's Chase without a Chappell.
Fullwood and Toxteth	A Hamlet without a Chappell.

Memorandum that Stalmyn, Bleasdale, Mierscough, Fullwood, and Toxtethe, are within the Hundred of Derby and Amoundernes ; albeit they belong to Lancaster, their Mother Church.

Heisham	A Parsonage ; the Patron, Mr. Parkinson. The Incumbent, but a reading minister. The farmor, the said Mr. Parkinson.
Cockerham	A Viccaridge ; the Patron, Mr. Calvert. The Incumbent, John Calvert, noe preacher. The farmor, the said Mr. Calvert, the Patron.
Ellell and Shireside	Both Chappells belonging to Cockerham.

Amoundernes Hundreth.

Garstange	A Viccaridge ; the Patron, Mr. Anderton. The Incumbent, Mr. Ainesworthe, noe preacher. Mr. Foster, the King's preacher. The farmors, Mr. Dalton and Mr. Bindlosse.
St. Michael upon Wyer	A Viccaridge ; the Patron, the King. The farmor, Sir William Cooke. The Incumbent, Mr. Woolfenden, noe preacher.
Woodplumpton	A parochiall chappell to St. Michaells. The Stipendary Minister there, Sir John Hollinworth, no preacher.
Poulton	A Viccaridge ; the Patron, Edmund Fleetwood, Esqr. The Incumbent, Mr. White, a preacher, but never preacheth. The farmors, Mr. Singleton, Mr. Tildesley, Mr. Rigby, with others.

The Names of the Parishes.	Amoundernes Hundreth—*continued.*
Bispham	A parochial chappell to Poulton. The Stipendary minister there, Mr. Walkden, noe preacher.
Lytham	An usurped Impropriation, as it is supposed, possessed by one Mr. Roger Ley, gentleman, dwelling in the Parsonage house; the Stipendary Minister, a bare reader, and careless.
Kirkham	A Viccaridge in the gift of Christ Church in Oxford. The Incumbent, Mr. Greenacres, a preacher. The farmor, Mr. Clifton, Esqr., with others.
Goosnargh	A chappell to Kirkham. The stipendary minister, Mr. Dupbury, no preacher. The farmor, Thurstan Tildesley, from Christ's Church in Oxford.
Chippin	A Viccaridge; the Patron, the Bishop of Chester. The Incumbent, Mr. Parker, noe preacher. The farmors, the parishioners.
Stidd	A Donative from the Lord Archbishop of Canterbury. Noe minister there resident.
Ribchester	A Viccaridge; the Patron, the Bishop of Chester. The Incumbent, Mr. Norcross, a simple preacher. The farmors, the parishioners.
Preston	A Viccaridge; the Patron, Sir Richard Houghton. The incumbent, Mr. Paler, a preacher. The farmor, the said Sir Richard Houghton.
Broughton	A Chappellry to Preston; the Stipendary minister, Mr. Witton, noe preacher; the farmor, Sir Richard Houghton, Baronet.

Memorand: that Chippin, Stidd, and Ribchester, albeit they are sett down as in the hundred of Amoundernes, because they are of that Deanery, yet they doe properly belong to the hundreth of Blackburne.

LongridgeChappell

Blackburne Hundreth.

Blackburne	A Viccaridge; the Patron, the Lord Archbishop of Canterbury. The Incumbent, Mr. Welsh, a preacher. The farmor, Sir William Fleetwood, Knight.
Samlesbury	A chappell belonging to Blackburne. The Stipendary reader there, one Jameson.
Dinckley	Another chappell, but noe reader.
Langoe	Another chappell, neither reader nor stipend.
Healey	Another chappell, neither reader nor stipend.
Harwood	Another chappell, maintained by the King.

The Names of the Parishes.	Blackburne Hundreth—*continued.*
Tockholes -	{ Another chappell, the reader, Mr. Shawecross, maintained by the inhabitants.
Darwin -	{ Another chappell, the minister there, Mr. Medcalfe, maintained by the inhabitants.
Whalley -	{ A Viccaridge; the Patron, the Lord Archbishop of Canterbury; the Incumbent, Mr. Ormeroyde, a preacher; the farmor, Mr. Asheton, Esqr.
Clitherall -	{ A parochiall Chappell to Whalley. The Minister there, Mr. Dickson, no preacher.
Downham -	{ Another parochiall Chappell; the Stipendary Minister, Mr. Carrier, noe preacher.
Colne - -	{ Another parochiall Chappellry; the Curate there, one Mr. Bryerley, well affected.
Burnley -	{ Another parochiall Chappell. The Stipendary Minister there, Mr. Ryley.
Haslingden -	{ Another parochiall Chappell; the Stipendary Minister, Mr. Butterworth.
Church -	{ Another parochiall Chappell; the Stipendary Minister is now gone.
Altham -	{ Another parochiall chappell; the Stipendary Minister is ————.

Memorandum, that every one of these seven parochiall Chappells have onely four pounds *per annum* allowed them, out of the Viccaridge of Whalley, to the severall Curates in the same.

Padiham -	{ Another parochiall Chappell belonging to Whalley. The Stipendary Minister there, Mr. Baxter, maintained by the King.
Ackrington -	{ Another Chappellry well affected, maintaineing Mr. Marcrofte of their voluntary benevolence.
Marsden -	{ Another Chappellry, with a bare reader, maintained by the inhabitants.
Holmes -	{ Another Chappellry haveing a simple reader, one Mr. Townley, maintained by the inhabitants.
Castle -	{ A Donative; the Patron I know not; noe minister there. It hath these parochiall Churches and Chappellry followeing :—
Pendley -	{ A parochiall Chappell well affected; the Minister there, Mr. Nutter.
Whitewell -	- Noe parochiall Chappell nor minister.
Rossendale -	{ A parochiall Chappell; the Stipendary preacher, Mr. Kershawe, maintained by the Inhabitants.
Goodshawe -	{ Noe parochiall; a minister there maintained by benevolence.

Leyland Hundreth.

Leyland . -	{ A Viccaridge; the Patron, Richard Feetwood, Esqr. The Incumbent, Mr. Bryars, a preacher.

The Names of the Parishes.	Leyland Hundreth—*continued.*
Exton and Heapey	{ Two ould chappells within Leyland parish, without Curates.
Standish - -	{ A parsonage; the Patron, Edward Standish, Esqr. The incumbent, Mr. Leigh, a preacher.
Brindle - . -	{ A parsonage; the Patron, the Lord Cavendish. The Incumbent, Mr. Bennett, no preacher.
Croston - -	{ A Viccaridge; the Patron, Sir Edmund Huddleston, Knight; the incumbent, a preacher. The farmor, the said Sir Edmund Huddleston, Knight.
Rufforth -	{ A parochiall chappell to Croston. The minister, Mr. Bradshaw, a preacher.
Chorley -	{ Another parochiall Chappell to Croston. The minister, noe preacher.
Eccleston -	{ A Parsonage; the Patron, Thomas Lathome, Esq. The Incumbent, Mr. Adam Rigby, a preacher.
Douglas -	{ A Chappell within Eccleston, without minister or stipend of late times.
Penwortham -	{ An ould Priory in the possession, by inheritance, of Richard Fleetwood, Esqr., who maintaineth a Stipendary Minister there.

Salford Hundreth.

Manchester - -	{ A Colledge, consisting upon a Warden and certaine fellowes, who jointly, together with two Ministers, and four Queristers, doe maintaine the service in that Church. The Impropriation is the King's, and leased to Mr. Holland, Esq.
Didesbury - -	{ A chappell annexed to Manchester, the mother church.
Stretforthe, Choreton, Gorton, Blakeley, Newton Heath and Dayneton.	{ All these are Chappells of ease within the said parish of Manchester, the Curates and preachers whereof are onely maintained by the severall inhabitants.
Prestwich - -	{ A parsonage; the Patrons in severall courses are Mr. Holland, Mr. Ashton of Chatterton, and Mr. Radishe; the incumbent, Mr. Langley, a preacher.
Ouldham - -	{ A parochiall Chappell to Prestwich; Mr. Hunter, preacher.
Shawe - -	Another Chappell of ease, supplied by a Curate.
Boulton in the Moores - -	{ An Impropriation belonging to the Lord Bishop of Chester, who is patron; the Incumbent, Mr. Sanderson, a preacher. There is allsoe Mr. Gosnall, a preacher, maintained by the parish.
Rivington and Turton - - -	{ Bothe these are Chappells of ease to Boulton, and bothe well supplyed with ministery.

The Names of the Parishes.	Salford Hundreth—*continued.*

Eccles - { An impropriation belonging to the King. The farmor, James Anderton, Esq. The Incumbent, Mr. White, a preacher.

——— { Ellenborough Church in Worsley; Mr. Hunt, a preacher.

Deane - - { A Viccaridge; the Patron, the King; the Incumbent, a lewde minister, neither preacher himself nor will suffer anie other to preach. The farmor, James Anderton of Lostock, Esqr.

Flixton - - { A Donative from the Deane and Chapter of Lichfield; the Incumbent, Mr. Jones, a preacher.

Bury - - - { A parsonage; the Patron, the Earle of Derby. The Incumbent, Mr. Watmoughe, a preacher.

Oulcome, Eatonfell, Heywood - { Chappells of ease, maintained by the Inhabitants.

Middleton - - { A Parsonage; the Patron, Sir Richard Asheton, Knight. The Incumbent, Mr. Assheton, a preacher.

Cockley - - A Chappell of ease.

Ratchdale - - { A Viccaridge; the Patron, the Lord Archbishop of Canterbury; the Incumbent, Mr. Kenyon, a preacher. The farmor, Sir John Byrron, Knight.

Todmerden, Whiteworthe, Litle Burgh, Milrowe - { Chappells of ease to Ratchdale, maintained by the several inhabitants.

——— { A parsonage; the Patron, Sir George Boothe, Knight. The Incumbent, Mr. Parker, a preacher.

There is eleaven parishes in Salford Hundreth.

Derby Hundreth.

Warrington - - { A Parsonage impropriate; the patron, Mr. Ireland. The Incumbent, Mr. Gellibrand, a preacher. The farmor, the said Mr. Ireland.

Hollinfery - - A Chappell of ease haveing no certaine Curate.

Prescott - - { A Viccaridge; the Patron, the King's Colledge in Cambridge. The farmor, the Earle of Derby. The Incumbent, Mr. Mead, a preacher.

Farnworth, Rainforth, St. Ellen, Windleshawe - { These are all chappells of ease belonging to Prescott, supplied onely with readeing Ministers.

Childwall - - { A Viccaridge; the Lord Bishop of Chester, Patron. The Incumbent, Mr. Hopwood, a preacher. The farmor of the Impropriation, James Anderton, Esq.

Haslewood - - A chappell.

Hyton - - - { A Viccaridge; the Patron and Impropriatory, Mr. Tarbock, Esqr.; the Incumbent, Mr. Hankinson, a preacher and the King's preacher there.

13

The Names of the Parishes.	Derby Hundreth—*continued.*

Walton - - { A Parsonage; the Patron, Sir Richard Molineux, Knight. The Incumbent, parson by way of dispensation, Mr. Molineux; the Incumbent, [the] vicar, no preacher.

Liverpoole, Kirkeby, Darby, Formby - - - { All Chappells of ease to Walton, and all supplied with readeing ministers.

Sefton - - - { A Parsonage; the Patron, Sir Richard Molineux, Knight. The Incumbent, Mr. Turner, a preacher.

Crosby - - A Chappell to Sefton; a curate, no preacher, there.

Alker - - - { A Donative impropriate to Sir Richard Molineux, Knight; no Incumbent, but a bare reader, and a meane pension.

Aughton - { A Parsonage; the Patron, Gabriell Hesketh, Esqr. The Incumbent, Mr. Bannister, no preacher.

Ormeskirke - - { A Viccaridge; the Patron, the King. The Incumbent, Mr. Ambrose, noe preacher. Mr. Knowles, the King's preacher, placed there. The farmor, the Earle of Derby.

Lathom - { A small Chappell to Ormeskirke. A Curate with a small pension.

Halsall - - { A Parsonage; the Patron, Sir Cuthbert Halsall. The Incumbent, Mr. Hatsull, a preacher.

Maghull and Mellinge - - { Chappells without preacher or service.

Winwick - - { A parsonage; the Patron, the Earle of Derby. The Incumbent, Mr. ———, a preacher. The Curate there, no preacher.

Ashton, Newton, and Newchurch - { Chappells belonging to Winwick, haveing small pensions and seldome curates.

Northmeales - { A parsonage; the Patron, Richard Fleetwood, Esqr. The Incumbent, Mr. French, a preacher.

Leighe - - { A Viccaridge; the Patron, Richard Urmeston, Esq. The Incumbent, no preacher. Mr. Midgeley, one of the King's preachers, placed there. The farmor, the said Richard Urmeston, Esqr.

Wygan - - { A parsonage; the Patron, Richard Fleetwood, Esqr. The Incumbent, Doctor Massy, a preacher.

Holland and Billinge - - { Beinge chappells in the parish of Wygan, haveing but small pensions and no preachers.

Soe the totall of the parishes in Lancashire, besides Chappells, are - - -
{ In Blackborne hundred - iij
In Derby hundred - - xiiij
In Salford hundred - - xj
In Leyland hundred - - vj
In Amoundernes hundred - x
In Loynsdale Hundred - xx }
In all, lxiiij.

Tax for the Relief of Infected Persons.

15. 1605.—A book of receipts and payments of moneys, collected by a tax levied within the Hundred of Salford by the Justices of the Peace at the Session of the Peace held at Newton Chapel on 17 July 1605, towards the relief of the poor infected persons, and others, in Manchester and Salford. The tax was discharged on 13 September, 1605. During the first week 1,157 persons received pecuniary assistance from this tax.

Persons Infected by the Plague.

16. 1605, August 9.—A list of persons who were infected, suspected, or " needers," by reason of the plague in Salford and Manchester.

E[dmond] H[opwood] to James Asheton.

17. 1607, December 15.—I meant to have been this night at Chaderton, but such is the extremity of the cold, that I dare not venture to go from the fire, except it be to church. I pray you to satisfy my friend Mr. Cockesone.

William Crombock to Mrs. Byrom.

18. 1607[-8]; January 26.—According to your request I have visited Mr. Carmerden, and he is now in such extremity as he could not read your letters. I told him, from you, of the cure that Mr. Thomas Gerrard did, and of the means that the parson of Middleton uses; but this comes too late, for after an operation on Thursday last, his pains are so grievous that he desireth rather to die than live in this extremity, yet he endureth all with patience.

News Letter.

19. 1607[-8], February.—"For Manchester news, there is none but this. Dr. Batts brought a preacher from Chester on Byfold (*sic*) who preached two sermons on the last Sunday, and, at Dr. Batts' request, they got him a collection. The collectors were Mr. George Tipping, Humfray Booth, Christopher Downes, Robert Atkinson, and others, and, as it is reported, my Lady Boweyer gave him 25s., Mr. Holland of Denton 20s., Sir Edmund Trafford, 10s., the College, 6s. 8d.; the rest they gathered of the townsmen. His whole collection he has was 9l. odd moneye. The collectors came unto [the] parson of Shuters Brooke, on Picrofte, in Salford, Parnill's husband, and he tould them hee durst give no monye, beecause the preacher would not subscribe unto the King's lawes. And I did heare that he came from about Northampton and lost his benefice, because he would not subscribe, and is going into Ireland, and his wiffe fell in laboure at Chester, and my Lord Bushop gave him leave to preach until he could go over."

Edmond Hopwood to Thomas Sothworth, at York.

20. 1608, July 29.—I pray you write me what is done at this assizes with the Brownists. I beseech God to deliver this Kingdom and State from all my sins, all atheism, popery, and puritanism, which, in this corner, grows ripe for the sickle.

THEOPHILUS ASSHETON to EDMUND HOPWOOD.

21. 1608, October 11.—I am in health, I thank God; and for the general sickness it hath decreased, this last week, forty, of the number of them that die of the plague, and so God grant it may do still.

ED. BYBBYE to EDMUND HOPWOOD, at Salford.

22. 1609, March 29. —Little news save that I am neither bishop nor knight. The sickness is but three score and six this week.

A[RTHUR] S[COLFELDE] to EDMUND HOPWOOD, at Hopwood.

23. 1609, April 9.—" Within two howres after your man Shawe was with me on Friday laste, I mett a Londoner of my acquaintance wich was going to the colledge to Mrs. Foxe to bring her comeudations from her husband, and to tell her that Mr. Foxe wolde be at home the daie folloing, and to tell her that her husband sent her worde that at his home cominge he wolde give the townsmen of Manchester good content-ment aboute the bussynes he went to London about. Whereupou I consevid that Mr. Burne was warden (or John Foxe) with a *non obstantibus.* Much rejoysing ther was emonges the brethren that nighte; but late upon Fridaie nighte a frend tolde me for certaine, Mr. Burne was not Warden, but Mr. Richard Morreye, for he had the same daie sene a letter, under Mr. Morey's hand, sent to Mr. Lee, parson of Standishe, importing that himselfe had prevented Mr. Burne and was warden hymselfe, and an Irisheman seaconded the same newes ; and yesterdaie Mr. Burne, Mr. Foxe, and Adkynson came home, and afferme that he bathe a grant to have some 30*l.* a yeare out of the living, and this is all. The brethren are in greffe as yet and saie litle, but that the master had bene more fitte for the wardenshipe then a Scott; but I thinke the Kinge and Counsell knowe better whom is fitt then they."

E[DMUND] H[OPWOOD] to ARTHUR SCOLFELDE.

24. 1609, May 8. Salford.—" Cozen Arther, your nephew and my kynsman, of Langley, standeth in need of your helpe, dyvers wayes." Prays for the delivery of a deed. The letter is sent on by the recipient and William Thorpe to " Mr. Ratcliffe," with the request to " come and rejoyce with us, and all other our Christian breetheren and sisters, at the installment of our new Warden, Mr. Burne. The day is uncer-tayne ; but, for that we know you love to conjoyne in the fraternitie, wee, or the one of us, will eyther send you word, or [if] not, come our selffs."

E[DMUND] HOPWODE to EDMUNDE SCHOLLEFYLLDE, sometime parson of Padyame, and now vicar of Loppyngtone, in Shropshire.

25. 1609, August 7.—I thank you for " Cheshire exercises." I heard not of them but by your letters. In Lancashire, thanks be to God, " there is nowe such as not many yeares agoe was used in Manchester ; yet do all fanatical and schismatical preachers, that are cashiered in other countries, resort into this corner of Lancashire, but not entertained according to their expectation. God deliver England from my sins, dwelling and committed, and from all Jesuits, seminaries, atheists, and factious preachers. I have sent you a book written in defence of our communion book, and but lately crept out of the press, and, God be thanked, this corner is purged of schismatical preachers, excepting Gossnall of Boulton and Hunte of Ouldham." Mr. White is now vicar of Eccles and one of the fellows of the College of Manchester, whereof Mr. Burne is not (*sic*) warden. Mr. White is greatly respected by my Lord of Canterbury, and hath subscribed.

THEOPHILUS ASSHETON to EDMUND HOPWOOD.

26. 1609, August 22.—We have here no news now but that Mr. Gerard, a reader of our house, is dead lately. The sickness was last week 152 of the plague, and there is one of our house dead, about three days since, of it.

JOHN WRYHT to EDMOND HOPWOOD.

27. 1609, September 1. Standish.—"I desire as much to see you as I perceive by your letter you have a desire to see me, and am gladd you purpose to be att our next Communion at Standishe, which is upon Sondaie come sennet, the 10th daie of this September, where, by God's grace, we shall have tyme to conferr of our former actions and of the ruynes of the church of God [in] manie places of this countie, by reason of the increase of Papistes' profaning of the Sabboath and other enormityes, which the most are not ashamed to committ without remorse of conscience or feare of lawe. The Lord redresse it in his good tyme; for the which let us all strive with the Highest in praier most ferventlie to obtaine, not leaving Him till we have received a blessing. I thanke you for the good opinion you have of my sonn. God give him grace to deserve the same of you and others, his good freindes. For my sonne-in-law, Mr. Leigh, he will write unto you himself touching the matter you writt to me of, and for which I have beene instant with him."

REGULATIONS FOR THE SABBATH.

28. [1610–1627.]—Orders, signed by Judge Edward Bromley, to be observed within the county of Lancaster, set down by the Justices of the Peace within the said county by appointment of the judges of assize.

1. That no wares or victuals be shewn or sold upon any Sunday (necessary victuals only excepted), and no butcher sell any flesh upon any Sunday after the end of the second peal for morning prayer, nor at any time in the afternoon upon any Sabbath day.

2. That no householders, after the beginning of the last peal to morning prayer, suffer any person (not being of the household) to eat, drink, or remain in their house in time of divine service, but shall shut their doors up so that all persons may go to church. If any be found in any ale-house in time of divine service, the said ale-house is to be put down, and thenceforth not to be licensed again.

3. If any ale-house keeper will not suffer the constables or church-wardens to search their houses to see whether good order be kept therein, the said ale-house keeper to be discharged from brewing and not again licensed.

4. Every ale-house keeper, with his wife and family, to go every Sunday to church.

5. Such persons as shall be found walking, talking, or idly standing, either in the churchyard or market place, in time of divine service shall pay 12*d*. apiece, and be bound to good behaviour and appear before the justices of assize.

6. If the constables, churchwardens, or other officers for the church be negligent or refuse to do their duties in these articles, that they be bound to appear before the justices of assize.

7. That there be no piping, dancing, bowling, bear or bull baiting, or any other profanation upon any Sabbath day, or upon any festival day in time of divine service.

8. That the Justices of the Peace, themselves, do sometimes search whether the churchwardens and constables have done their duties, and that the minister or incumbent do read these orders publicly once every quarter of the year, that they may be better remembered and observed by the parishioners. *Signed.*

Sir Julius Cæsar to the Bishop of Durham.

29. 1612, July 12.—Calling upon the said Bishop to pay the sum of eight hundred and four score pounds yearly, which he and his predecessors have half-yearly answered to the former receiver of the county, to Ralph Assheton, esquire, the younger, His Majesty's Receiver-General of the county of Northumberland. *Copy.*

The Lords of the Council to Ralph Assheton, Receiver for the counties of Northumberland and Durham.

30. 1612[-13], March 1. Whitehall.—Touching annuities to be paid to Mr. Francis Dacre, son of the late Lord William Dacre, to Anne, his wife, and Ranulph, son of the said Francis. *Signed.*

Fee-farm Rents.

31. 1612-13, March 2.—Memorandum of the fee-farm rents, due and unpaid by the heirs of George, late Earl of Dunbar, deceased. The rents include those payable for Berwick Castle, the fishings of the Tweed and of "Broad and Orrett," and for the coal mines and salt-pans in Flatworth and Billymore.

T[homas, Earl of] Suffolk and Sir Fulke Grevill to Ralph Ashton, Receiver of the county of Northumberland.

32. 1616, June 10. Whitehall.—Sir William Selby has for his fee for the custody of Tynmouth Castle, in the county of Northumberland, 100 marks, and other fees for gunners and servants. These fees are now to be paid to the Earl of Northumberland. *Signed.*

Sir Fulke Grevill, Chancellor of the Exchequer, to Roger Kenyon, Surveyor of the Lordship of Middleham, in the county of York.

33. 1616, August 29. Austen Friars, London.—Whereas divers freeholders of the manor of Middleham have enclosed parts of the wastes and demesne lands of the manor, Kenyon is to make survey of such incroachments. *Signed and seal of arms.*

Rent in Gray's Inn.

34. 1616, December 11.—Receipt for 20s. paid by Alexander Rigbye, of Wigan, to David Cardwell, for the rent of a chamber in Gray's Inn.

INFORMATION AGAINST POPISH RECUSANTS.

35. 1616, December 21.—The information of Elizabeth Marcrofte, wife of James Marcrofte, curate of the chapel of Cliderowe, in the county of Lancaster, in which the said Elizabeth accuses John Birtwisle, of Huncote, and Dorothy, his wife, of being Popish recusants, and of endeavouring to persuade her to become a Papist. Also she accuses them of harbouring seminary priests, two of whose names she remembers were Mr. Huthersall, otherwise Heath, and Mr. Kirkham; and of harbouring John and Peter Worthington, brothers of Mrs. Birtwisle, who were Jesuits. She likewise accuses Mr. Peter Ormerode, vicar of Whalley, of having frequented the house of Mr. Birtwisle, and on one occasion of having conversed for three hours with the said priest, Mr. Huthersall.

In the examination of Mr. Peter Ormerod, he says he has no remembrance of Huthersall, but that he had been sundry times at John Birtwisle's house, who indeed was a Popish recusant, and who is a near kinsman "unto this examinant"; but he went there for the most part to confer with his kinsman touching his religion, and conform him to our Church of England.

Mrs. Dorothy Birtwisle denies that she ever persuaded Elizabeth Marcroft, now the wife of James Marcroft, clerk, and late wife of Nicholas Grymshawe, deceased, to become a Popish recusant, or that she did ever receive seminary priests or Jesuits, or was ever present at any mass in her husband's house. She says the said Marcroft's wife "showed as though she were of the Popish religion," but she rather thinks she was of no religion at all, for she lived a very lewd and dishonest life, and in great disobedience and disloyalty to her first husband, as all the country reported. She said she had two brothers, John and Peter Worthington, but whether they were priests or whether they are living, she cannot tell. She denies that ever either of them was lodged or had relief in her husband's house since they were priests.

ORDER addressed to Constables for keeping watch in the West Riding of Yorkshire.

36. 1617, May 28. Thornton.—"For asmuche as there hath been great neglect in setting of dayly watche through the West Rideinge of the countie of Yorke, by reason wherof rogues and wandering persons are suffered continually to passe without anie punishment, to the great annoyance of the inhabitants of everie towne and hamlett, and contrarie to the statute in that case made and provided: For reformation thereof it was ordered at the Sessions, holden at Pontefraite the 29th of Aprill last, that there should be in every town and hamlett a sufficyent able mann, hyred at the charge of the said towne, to bee appoynted as a bedle to keepe the watche daylie in everie towne and hamlett; and that the same shall bee presently observed throughout all the townes and hamletts in the said West Rideing upon notice or publishing the said order. And that every constable or officer shall see this order dewly put in execution according to the tennor thereof, upon paine of tenn poundes to bee forfeyted by everie constable or officer that shall bee negligent or remiss in the premises. These are therefore, in his Majesty's name, straitly to charge and comand you forthwith upon the receit heirof, for the better suppressing and driveing away of rogues, vagaboundes, and sturdie beggars, which suppresse and surcharge the contrie, you cause a bedle to bee hyred and provided, and by him a due watche to bee kept at and in such convenyent places as shall bee thought most fitt and needfull for your townshipp. That the said wandering rogues, vagabounds, and sturdie beggars, may be severely punished in such manner and sorte as the statute, in that case made and provided, doth lymitt and appoynt." *Copy.*

JOHN CROWE, the younger, to MR. ALDEN.

37. 1617, July 1.—"The King, his majestie, took his journey from Berwick unto Dunglas, and at the bound rod, quilk is 2 myll from Berwick, quilk is the martche betwixt England and Scotland, the King he stood with the one foot in Scotland, the other in England, and said: Now, my Lords, I am both in Scotland and England, and was so glaid as could be. That nicht he came to the said Dunglas, a place of my Lord Home's and stayed two nichts. He was met be my Lord and his gentlemen, all of one sute and apparrell, with the earls, lordes, knichtes, sqyres, barronnes, with their traines, all that pairt of the countrie round about. He had sutcbe content in Dunglas that he spoke to the Lordes: Now, my Lordes, you knowe since I cam from London I have had naughtie weather all the way, and now since I cam to Scotland, the heaven smyleth upon me. Tell me, my Lordes, did you feid so well sence you cam from London? Thairefter from Dunglas he came to my Lord of Seetoun his place, and efter the lyke manner was met as of befor, and satisfactioun for enterteanment, and stayd yair one nicht, and the King his two shipes sailed out of Leith Rode and came fornent the place off Setoun and schot. The morning yeirefter he cam from Setoun, quilk is sum eight mylles from Edenborough, by the sea coast, and by Leith, quilk is a myll from Edenborough, and cam from Leith up to a way quilk is in the North syd of Edenbrough, the north loche lying betwix the citie and it. He was alwayes in his cotche untill the tyme he had allmost cum to the middell of that way called the Long Gate, and then he lap on upon ane hors, and as he lap on hors bak, being accompanied with his nobilles, the Castle men ceased schuiting untill the tyme he had enteret in at the west pairt off the citie called the West Port; and a littell within the Port, thair was a scaffold maid of tries and dailles qubair my Lord Provest, Baillies and Counsell off the citie stood, being accompanied with a grit number off citicens, being all arrayed in guidlie apparrell and in thair velvot gounes. Then thair was so many on every syd off the way quhair the King cam throu, with their costly speit staffes, and quhen the King cam a littell throu, being fornent the Lord Provest, he cryed to his nobilles and maid thame stay. Then thair was ane oration maid, quilk the King lyket weill off, and thair was presented to him the scepter off the citie, as also, in a silver basen, over gilt with gold, a thousand angells in a velvot bag; and quhen all was endet, then the King cryed: Leap on, my Lord Provest, upon your hors. So he lap on and rode betwix two Earles, at the King's command, carying the scepter off the citie on his schoulder. And all the time he was in the citie the peopell schouted and cryed for joy. So the King refuised his owne guard and took him to the guard off the citie, and so rode foreward up the Strait Bow and down the High Streit, untill he cam to the cros, and thair he, with his nobilles, lichtet doun with gret triumphe, and went into the Hie Kirk and heard ane sermoun maid be the Archbishop off St. Androis. So, quhen sermon was endet, he came forthe and lap on againe and rode doun the streit with his nobilles, in great pompe, and cam throu the Netherbow Port, wher his pictur standes very reallie, and at the end off the libertie off the citie, in the Cannongait, thair the King made the Lord Provest leap off his hors and knichtet him with the sword of honor, according to the ancient maner, in presence of the nobilitie, and says unto him : I, King James the Sext, knichtes the, Sir Williame Nisbott, Knicht off the Dean, Lord Provest of Edenborough. So Sir William, the Lord Provest, with the Baillies, Councell, and citicens, retired bak againe, having done their obeysance, and then the Baillies off the Cannongait (being a suburbe to the citie), with their company, receaved him and was his guard untill he came to his aune pallace, the Abbay, and in the utter court off the pallace, efter the King had lichtet doun, thair kneiled doun upon their knees about sum 30 yong men, in gounes off the Colledge off Edenborroughe, quherof one of thame maid an oration, in Latin, in praise and commendation of the King. In the mean tyme off the orationn, the King was so glade of it that he made Pembrughe, Southhampton, Montgomerie, and the Bischopes, draw nyer to heir quhat was spok. Thus I saw with myne eyes. And efter the oratiouu was endet, he presentet a buik to him off verses in Latin, all in his prais, quilk he kissed and gave to his Majestie; the King very gladlie accepted of the same, and so went in with the nobilitie to his palace. Upon the morrow he went forth to his baulking and hunting. The second day, quilk was the Sabboth day, he stayed in the chaipell royall at sermoun, and upon Munday he went over the water in a bardge maid by the Citie of Edenborrow of purpos for him. Then the Castle schot, and at the Rode his aune two schips, quilk wer lying thair, went and convoyed the bardge over the water, and quhen the King landet at Bruntiland, they schot and returnet bak againe to the Rode. Then the King tooke his brekfast in Bruntiland, in the Provest his hous, and quhen he came furth, was met with many gallant gentlemen of Fyff; also thair was fyve hundred hors without the toun off Brntiland that went home againe and had no caryadge of the Kinges. There was so many waitinge on upon his caryadge, not oulie at that place, bot wheresoever he went, and at nicht came to his oune pallace off Fakling, a pallace quilk may be very weill sein, and tooke your nobilles and made them se the park, and in it many a troup and company of does and roes, with many other thinges. Thairefter from Falkling he went over the water of Tay, in a bardge, and landet at Brughtie, a littell castell by the sea syd, sum two mylles from Dundie, and was yair met with many a gentleman of Angusche. The King himself cam up with sum off his nobilles unto the Constabill his hous of Dundy, bot the rest of his company went in unto Duudie and wer very well used. The Constabill his house is a quarter myll above Dundie. Upon the morrow thairefter, he tooke his journey from thence and cam at nicht unto Kinnaird, a place of my Lord Carnegies, sum two mylles from Muntrois, the sea cumming up unto it by Muntrois. Thair he stayed sum six or eight dayes, hunting sumtimes upon Mewremont, and sumtymes visiting sum places round about, and one of the dayes ; he, with his nobilles, went to the Castle of Brichane, a place of the Earle of Mares, quilk stands upon ane water syd, sum four mylles above Kinnaird. The water runneth doun by Kinnaird; it is six myll from the sea; and thair he desired the Earle of Mar to caus sum fishers to be brocht to fische sum salmond. The fischers cam ; they tooke a net and went into the water, bot be they had gone a littell way off, the net was so full of salmondes, that they were forcet to let a pairt of the net go, els it had broken, it was so full, and as it was, thair was above a hundreth salmondes into it cast upon the grein grass, quick. This is a grit matter (sic) six myll from the sea mouth, as allso in summertyd many tymes a man may go over the water almost dry foot, and in Kinnaird itselff they may look on the window and see thame taken in the water. About sum two dayes efter the King his coming to Kinnaird, thair was sum of your countriemen about sum 24, that wes desyrous to go and sie Aberdein, which is sum 30 mylles from Kinnaird and 68 mylles from Edenborrow. When they cam thair they wer well accepted of and payed nothing. They wer so well accepted that when sum of thes men of Aberdein cam to Eden-borrow, to the Parliament, your countriemen gave them the banquet severall tymes. Giff so be it had pleased thame to have gone a hundreth mylles beyond Aberdein they would have fund meit and drinke also, for many nobillmen duelleth far beyond Aberdein. In the bakcuming from Aberdein or in the feildgoing, I know not whenhither, they wer desyrous to sie Denotter, ane ancient castell of the Earle of Merschelles upon the sea coast, and assoone as they came to the utter gate thereof, one by one (for no mo bot one efter another can enter, the entres is so strait) thair weapons was taken from them, and, in signe of welcome, the canones played thair pairt, bot they wer gritlie afrayd becaus of the way taking of their weapons. They supposed they wer about to do sum tressoun to thame, bot they fund otherwayes before they went, and assoone as they had sein all, they wer brocht into the hall and their dyned. Bot, sayes your men, wher is the blak stok that we have heard tell of in England? Then was answer maid: You sall sie it befor you go. Then they arose up, and giff so be thair was guid preparation in the hall befor, thair was far better at the blak stok. This blak stok is of ane ould oak of a grit thiknes, standing on stompes in a hous be itself. The use of the blak stok has bein thus. Quhatsumever they wer travelling by the way, many or few, being needfull of meit and drink, wer let into the castle and sate doun at that blak stok, and had meit and drink in abundance and never payed anything for it. Now efter thair wes giffen to thame sutche content as could be in the castle, they came furth; then the Earle took them to his park, and desyred thame stand at the park dyk. Then he maid one of his servants go in unto the park and blow on ane hunting horne, bot assoone as the wyld beastes off divers sortes heard the blowing of the horne, they cam skipping and . . . over the dyk. Thus I have by report, and so mutche for them. Now efter the King had stayed in Kinnaird his appointed tyme, he returned bak to Dundie and then entered into the toun, bot not qunen he came first over. He was thair receaved with the Constabill, Baillies, Counsellers, Citicens, so many in gounes, so many with speit staffes, the cannones schuiting, the cros runing with wyne, many of thair staires layed over with tapestrie, ane oratioune maid, thair gift presented ; so contentment was giffen thair also. I speak breifflie. From thence he came over againe unto Fakling and stayed thair one nicht; from thence unto Kinghorne, qubair his bardge was waiting for him; all his mariners, clothed in silkes and velvotes, came to Leith and so to his pallace againe that nicht. Efter his cuming over agane, upon the 11th day of June, as our usuall custome is every yeir, our weapon schaving was so weill liket off by your countrie men, that they thocht thai had bein all gentillmen brocht out of the countrie, bot in treuth it was not so. Neyer (sic) came the tuo pairt of the inhabi-tantes off the Citie furth; it mych have bein a pleasour to any king in Europe to sie one citie yeild sutche a cumpanie of brave and gallant subjectes. The King sate in his oune pallace window and sie thame march in and out agane off the utter court onlie thrie severall tymes : the ensinges was casten thair, and three severall schuitings off muscots and hagbutes, quilk maid the earth tremble round about. Efter that sicht, the King went up, with his court, unto the Castle off Dalkeith, sum four myll from Edenborrow, that same nicht. It is a place of my Lord of Mortounes, a castle for strenth, and a pallace for pleasour. He stayed thair three nichtes, and every day tooke his pastyme and pleasour in haulking and hunting, and in visiting some places round about, as my Lord of Cranstounes Dreddin place and yardes, the Castle of Rosling, and the chaipell thairoff, off grit raritie, also in the park of Newbattell, and many uther places, qubair thair was presented to him in his hunting, by handsum maides (as also to his court), many varieties off delicat milkes and confectiounce, quilk was well accepted of, and command giffen no harme sould be done to the virgines by courteoures. Upon the 14 June, in the efternoone, his home cuminge to the Abbay was thus. Quhill his men were waiting for his outcuming, in the utter court of the Castle, he convoyed himselfe furth with a few and took them through ane secret way to the wood, qubair his hors was ready attending him, so before his men knew he was gone, he was halff way at home. Upon the 17th day of June, the first day of the Parliament was; the maner of their ryding was this (the citie being in their armour and having the way cleir for them). They lap all on at the Abbay and cam ryding all along up unto the Parliament hous. Halff ane hour before the rest, the Cancellar of Scotland with the Secretar, with sum other Lordes, cam up with thair rid rob royalles, and fenced the Parliament, thairefter two and two, according to every man's place and degree they rode. First of all rode so many Lord Commissioners for borroughstones with their footmantells, nixt unto thame the Commissioners for Barrounes and Knichtes, nixt unto thame the Lordes with their rid rob royalles and ritche footmantells, nixt unto them the Vicuntes with their rid rob royalles, nexte unto thame the Earles with their rid rob royalles, nixt unto thame the trumpets, nixt unto thame the Herauldes and the Kinge of Herauldes, nixt unto thame the Bischopes and the Archebischopes, nixt unto thame the Earles that caryed the honors (with their rid rob royalles), as the crown, the sword of honour, the scepter, and sutche lyke, nixt unto thame the King his Majestie and on his left hand Lord Bukinghame; no mo of your countriemen rode. Behind the King, rode the Duke and Marquess; the styll quilk they go thorow to the Parliament hous was keipet be the Earle of Arrell and his guard, and the entres itselff, where they go into the Parliament hous, was keipet be the Earle of Merschell, quilk is thair offices alwayes at Paliament. Then the Roll was called of the Earles, Lordes, and sutche lyk, bot thair was many absent. Upon the 19th June, quilk is his Majesties birthday, he dyned in the Castell of Edenborrow, and assoon as the King was within, the Castle never ceased schuiting till 9 or 10 o'clock at nicht. It is reported thair . . . . fourtie knichtes maid at that same l[yme]. About 9 or 10 o'clocke at nicht, the King cam doun from the Castle to the Abbay, and all the way, both in the one syd and of the uther, thair was grit fyres set furth, and at the entres of the utter court in the Abbay their was a boy of nyne yeires ould that maid ane oratioun in Greike to the King. This is of treuth ; he is one Mr. John Car his sone, minister of Prestoun Pannes, sum six mylles from Edenborrow. Then went his Majestie into his pallace and sate in ane window with his nobilles, and beheld a playe of fyrwork ; their was many thousands beholders of it; I myselff was one. The play breifflie was thus. It was actet in the nicht. Their was 2 castles erected in the utter court, one castle at the one end off the court and another castle at the uther end, the one called the pallace of St. Androis, the other the Castle of Envy. It was acted and played by the yong men of Edenborrow. Their was so many fuilles with their belles, so many daunceres, a playmeir casting fyr both behind and befor, a maid, so many hagbuttes, so many muscetters, thair ensignes, thair horsmen, thair footmen runing with speires off fyr, the one castle schuiting fyrballes at the other, quheilles [wheels?] runing round about of fyr and so many schotes .into : it, so many twix the Castles fychting, so many keiping every Castle, sumtymes the one syd winning, then agane retyring bak and flying. Thair was a devys maid, that out off the pallace off St. Androis cam Sanct Andrew ryding on a hors, with a speir off fyr in his hand, and met the .dragon midway, that came out of the Castle of Envy, and out of hir mouth cam fyr spouting, so they foght aspace - togither; bot Sanct Andrew did overcome the dragon and cam home ryding, and was welcomed home by the men of the pallace. In the mids, betwix the two castles, was a devys set up that schot so many sebotes, and a thing going about with horsmen and footmen; then the quheill wald [wheeled?] about agane and persew theis men, and at a certaine space so many schottes, and ane man maid of timber in the mids of the quheill, that went ay about as the two troupes of men, did, having an ensigne in his hand, and on it St. Androis cros. Then their was four hieland men, dressed up so of purpos, that came out of the pallace of St. Androis with their boues and arrowes of fyr, that did win the Castle of Envy, quilk castle had for their badge, St. George. The castle was throuen down, the men taken prisoners, and the captain sould have bein, as it wer, hanged. Giff so be the King had stayed longer, thair was many more toyes in it nor I can tell. Upon the 26th day of June thair was a banket giffen to the King his Majestie and his nobilles, by the Citie of Edenborrow. Thair was a house built of timber and glas round about, maid of purpose for it, hung with taspestrie. Thair was above four score young men of Edenborrow, all in gold chaines, that served. They had such varieties of flesches, fisches, and provision . . . . that one of your countriemen spoke thus, who was ane master houshold himselff in England; sayes he : I have been in Italie, in Spain, in France, in England, and now come to Scotland, and wheras I thot their sould have bein nothing heir, I have sein the best both for variety of meites, and also for service. The secund day of the banket, your gentellmen ushers, with so many others, wer invited, and efter dinner wer maid burgesses of Edenborrow. I speak nothing of thos pleasant sortes off melodies, musickes, wynes; giff so be I wold enter a discours of this matter, it wold be too longsume. Upon the 28th day off June, the last of the Parliament was rode; they rode as off befor, except onlie the Earle of Arrell rode upon the Kinges right hand and Bukinghame on his left hand, quhen they rode home to the Abbay agane : this is Arrell his dew for that dayes service. As concerning Church government, thair is no new statutes maid, praised be God, bot the old confirmed, and the auld auncient Actes of Parliament of the countrie concerning the Commouns . . . and sum gov . . . . set doun concerning tenths and ministers stipends. As for the King's returning, he is to be, God willing, the 5th day of August, in Carleill, a town quilk bordereth with Scotland. 30th June the City bid the King fairweill in the Abbay, for from thence the King hes taken his journey, and is not at this progress for to returne bak agane, now he is gone frog. us. We was all glad of his cuming and now sorowfull for his wayg oind It will pleas yow to accept of this. I have written you breifflie, anm have me excused for the rest of his progres."

JOHN BACON, resident at King's Lynn.

38. 1617, November 30.—Certificate by Richard Stonham, mayor of King's Lynn in the county of Norfolk, to the Lord Treasurer and Barons of the Exchequer, that John Bacon, gentleman, son of Francis Bacon, late of London, gentleman, deceased, and brother of Edward Bacon, gentleman, also deceased, late one other of the sons of the same Francis, is at present lying and resiant within the borough of King's Lynn. *Signed and seal.*

EDWARD MOSLEY to JOHN NUTTER, Deputy Steward of Blackburn Hundred.

39. 1617[-18,] February 20. "My Chamber in Graye's Inne."— The copyhold tenants of Haslingden, Acrington, and Oswaltwisle, have compounded with the King for establishing their copyhold estates; "and the same is accordingly decreed in this honourable courte." Directs him therefore "to suffer their admittances to passe," &c.

SIR FULKE GREVILL to RALPH ASSHETON, Receiver-General for Richmondshire, Durham, and Northumberland.

40. 1617[-18,] March 23. Whitehall.—William Watson, keeper of Raby parks (*sic*), has "verie insolently" laid hands on the King's rents for the manors of Brauncepath, Raby, and "Barney" Castle, for which he is to appear before Barons Bromley and Denham, Justices of Assize, at their next coming into "that countre." There was, at the last declaration of accounts, a "*super*" for about 150*li.* arrearages depending upon Humphrey Wharton, Esquire, and William Scaife, his deputy. Wharton is "an honest and sufficient gentleman; yet, for that Scaife hath fayled two yeres together to clere his accompts I would have you, for his Majesties securitie, to receive the rents of that collection now due." *Fragment of seal.*

WIGAN.

41. 1618, May.—Petition by the mayor and burgesses of Wigan to the King, that the *Quo Warranto* against the said town, procured by Doctor Bridgman, may be stayed. *Note at the end, dated Theobalds, 12 May, 1618, that the King was pleased to refer the petition to the Archbishop of Canterbury and others.*

JUSTICES OF THE PEACE.

42. 1618, July 31.—List of the Justices of the Peace for the county of Lancaster.

R[ALPH] A[SHETON] to MR. JOHNSON.

42a. 1618, October 8. Salley.—Complaining of Lord Haye's agent, Mr. Richmond, who will not permit him "so much as take a stone out of the old decaied Abbey walls to buyld or repaire" upon his lands at Salley.

SIR WALTER RALEIGH.

43. 1618, October 28.—Sir Walter Raleigh's speech at his death. *Copy, incomplete. It differs in words, but not in sentiment, from the two copies amongst the State Papers (State Papers, Domestic, James I., Vol. 103, Nos. 52 and 53.)*

THE SAME.

44. [1618, October 28.]—Sir Walter Raleigh to his wife the night before his execution, being written immediately after he had warning to prepare for death. *Copy.*

Itinerary of King James I.

45. 1619, July 19 to August 28.—Monday, July 19, from Theobalds to Royston 1 night; Tuesday, July 20, to Ampthill 2 nights; Thursday, July 22, to Bletsoe 2 nights; Saturday, July 24, to Asheby 3 nights; Tuesday, July 27, to Kirbye 2 nights; Thursday, July 29, to Apethorpe 4 nights; Monday, August 2, to Burleigh on the Hill 1 night; Tuesday, August 3, to Belviere 3 nights; Friday, August 6, to Rufford 5 nights; Wednesday, August 11, to Nottingham 2 nights; Friday, August 13, to Derby 1 night; Saturday, August 14, to Tutbury 4 nights; Wednesday, August 18, to Tamworth 1 night; Thursday, August 19, to Warwick 1 night; Fryday, August 20, to Sir William Pope's 1 night; Saturday, August 21, to Woodstock 5 nights; Thursday, August 26, to Rycot 1 night; Fryday, August 27, to Bissam 1 night; Saturday, August 28, to Wyndsor during pleasure.

Wigan.

46. [1619-20.]—Petition of Robert Barrowe, mayor, and the bailiffs and burgesses of Wigan, to the king, that John, Bishop of Chester, being parson of the rectory of Wigan *in commendam*, worth 1,000 marks by the year, claimed the liberties pertaining to the corporation, and committed the mayor of the said town to prison, until he was delivered by a writ of *habeas corpus*. He also gives out in speeches that the said mayor is his mayor, and has not authority to whip a dog. The said mayor, bailiffs, and burgesses pray that they may be permitted to enjoy all their liberties in peace. *Draft.*

Prescott Church.

47. 1619[-20,] January 15.—Order by the Bishop of Chester touching a dispute between the parishioners of Prescott, who attended Prescott parish church, and the parishioners of Prescott who attended Farnworth side chapel, as to repairs, and the election of churchwardens, of the said parish church. *Copy. Translation.*

The Earl of Suffolk to Ralph Assheton, Receiver-General for Northumberland.

48. 1619[-20], February 11. Northampton House.—" Whereas you or your predecessor, John Lyons, have heretofore receaved letters from the late Lord Treasurer," together with a copy of the King's privy seal, on behalf of Sir William Selby, knight, touching the payment to him of fees and allowances of "certaine gunners and ordinarie servants attending the service of the castle of Tynmouth, now in his keepinge." Directs the due payments of these fees. *Signed. Seal of arms.*

The King to the Speaker of the House of Commons.

49. 1621, December 3. Newmarket.—Has heard that his detention by ill health, at a distance from Parliament, had lead some fiery spirits to meddle with matters far beyond their capacity, intrenching upon the prerogative, &c. *Copy.* (*Calendared in State Papers, Domestic, James I., Vol.* 124, *No.* 8.)

Remonstrance of the House of Commons.

50. 1621, December 3.—Petition and remonstrance of the House of Commons to the King, stating the causes of the increase of Popery in England. *Copy.* (*Calendared in State Papers, Domestic, James I., Vol.* 124, *No* 3.)

William Foster to George Rigby, "at his chamber in Holburne Court, at Grayes In. With this a bever felte."

51. 1622, May 16. Wigan.—"My master and mistress intreate you to gett the bever felt, sent herewith, to be new dressed, and made broad in the bruerds (*sic*) and low in the topp or crowne." *Seal of arms.*

The Same to the Same, "at his chamber in Grayse Inn, under Sir Thomas Tyldesley his chamber, in the pales in Holburne Court."

52. 1622, May 25. Chester.—As to procuring copies of the patents for "the Attorney's place in Chesire." A copy of the King's patent is to be had at the Rolls; and of the Prince's, at the "Prince's Council chamber in Fleet Street." *Seal of arms.*

Alexander Rigby to his brother, George Rigby.

53. 1622, June 14. Wigan.—Mr Peter Ellis has his "booke of *quadragesimes* of King Edward 3." Begs that his letters, books, writings, and other goods "in the chamber" be kept safely. Would have "all such bookes as are not law bookes" sent down to him.

Adam Rigby to his nephew, George Rigby.

54. 1622, June 18. Eccleston.—Joseph Tompson is gone towards Cambridge, "and, if you have any of St. John's with whom your good word or lettre may doe him pleasure, I pray you spare not to speake or wryte for him at his entrance, that hee might get to serve sommebodie as a poore scholler." *Seal.*

William Foster to George Rigby.

55. 1622, June 22. Wigan.—His master knows of a desirable chamber to let over Sir Thomas Tyldesley's lodging under Mr. Banister's chamber. "Your cosin Joseph Thompson is gone to Cambridge. . . . I have given over taking tobacco . . . . My love to chast Dyana. . . . I pray you to buy me a Fitzharbert's *natura brevium*, at the second hand if it be possible."

Alexander Rigby to his brother, George Rigby.

56. 1622, June 26. Wigan.—"I conceave that I shall have another chamber from Mr. Chisnall in the same buildings, but I am not yet through with him, and I well lyke not of the chamber you mention in your letter. . . . . . The covers of the windowes in the inner chamber, all the formes in both chambers and studies, the little thicke table removeable, and the bedsteed in the study, are not to follow the chamber; but the great bedsteed in the inner chamber, and the great table, belong to the chamber, as also the cover of both the study windows. The writing desk, I think, ought not to goe with the chamber; for I had it from my father, but know not how he came unto it. I have sent unto you by this bearer, Mr. Danby, thirteen pounds and tenne shillings, which I desire you to pay unto Mr. Duncombe, and to take in from him two bounds therefore to him, and another by me given."

WILLIAM FOSTER to GEORGE RIGBY.

57. 1622, June 27. Wigan.—"Your brother Joseph, in midsomer day last, escaped a sudden . . . ; for, on Barbers Moore near Eccleston, at a horse race there, your brether was ridinge, or rather runninge his new bought geldinge, and, being aboute the height of his speed, he mett a man (I think he was old Mr. Hesketh, his horse-keeper) running thother way, who, as they say, was drunke; and your brother givinge the way, the man gave way on the same side your brother did, soe that they mett with a great force, for your brother's geldinge broke thother horse his necke and back, and, with throweinge up her head, hitt your brother on the nose and jowles, broke the garths, and left your brother sitting on the saddle, on the earth, in a swound; and soe he continued about halfe a quarter of an houre, but was never the worse." The other man lay under his dead horse, but was not much hurt either. *Seal of arms.*

JOHN WARING to ROGER KENYON, at Whalley.

58. 1622, July 26. London.—"Newes wee have little more then was att your being here, saveing that wee hear that Count Mansfeild is come into Loraigue (?); part of the dukedom of Bulloigne is doubted to goe either against the Arche Dutches, or else against some part of Fraunce, to the helpe of the poore protestants; and some saie that the French King is gon from his seige of Rochelle to Parris; yett my Lord Doncaster is not come from France." *Seal.*

The LORD KEEPER to the JUDGES OF ASSIZE.

59. 1622, August 1. Westminster College.—"His Majesty havinge resolved, out of deepe reason of State, and expectance of lyke correspondence from forraigne princes to the professors of our religion, to graunt some grace and connivence to the imprisoned papistes of this kingdome, hath commanded me to passe twoo writtes under the great seale for the same purpose, requiringe the judges of every circuite to enlarge the said prisoners, according to the tenor or theffect of the same.

I am to give you to understand from his Majesty how his royal pleasure is, that upon the receipt of the said writts you shall make noe nic[e]nesse or difficulty to extend his princely favoure to all such papistes as you shall fynd imprisoned in the goales of your circuit, for eny churche recusancie whatsoever, or for the refusall of the oath of supremacy, as for haveinge or dispensinge of papish bookes or for hearinge of masse, or any other part of recusancie which doth concerne religion only, nor matter of state which shall appeare unto you to bee meerely and totally civill and political." *Copy.*

WILLIAM FOSTER to GEORGE RIGBY, at Gray's Inn.

60. 1622, November 12.—"I would likewise intreate your paines to buy for me a Fitzherbert's *Natura Brevium*, at the second hand, but I would have it a reasonable good one ; likewise a brass ringe, with a tobacco stopper at the end, and the three accorns, or the three broad arrow heads cutt in the midst of the same, in manner of armes cutt for a signett, on the broade end thereof ; the price is 4d. . . . Alsoe a standish (sic) blacke inckehorne with the 3 arrow beades cutt on the topp in forme afforesaide, and, lastlie, a booke called *Kitchin*, for keeping of courts, etc. I woulde intreate you to take consideration of my Littleton. . . . You write me that you delivered my letter to Dyana Waringe, who onelie retorned thanks and commendations, but, if it please you, when you next see her, lett her know that I expected an answer to my letter in writing, or else her reason to the contrarie. . . . Commend me to Christopher Parkins, Mr. Duncombe and his man, and tell him that now I could be content to rest his debter for 2 or 3 pipes of good tobacco."

WILLIAM FOSTER to GEORGE RIGBY.

61. 1622, November 16. Wigan.—"I should receive, as a kinde token from you, 2 or 3 pipes of tobacco ; I dare not say I will pay for them, for I am almost broke this deare yeare." *Seal of arms.*

The SAME to the SAME.

62. 1622[-3], January 31. Wigan.—"Accordinge to my maister's commandment, I am bould to wryte unto you to intreate your paines for the buyinge a little booke for my master, entytled a Commission, with Instructions and Directions, graunted by his Majesty to the Master and Counseil of the Court of Wardes and Liveries ; for compoundinge for Wardes, Ideotts and Lunatickes, and given under His Highnes' Great Seal of England the 21st of August 1622."

ORDERS by the JUDGES OF ASSIZE for the County of Lancaster signed "Thomas Chamberlaine."

63. 1623. Fifth week of Lent.—"That the justices in their severall divisions shall make a collection for the mayntaynaunce of the gaole in the Castle of Lancaster, and that the same be collected, and sent with all speed to the keeper of the gaole there to be distributed.

"That the High Constables and Petty Constables shall, every forthnight attend the justices in their severall divisions to take directions from them about the mayntaynaunce of the pore, and other matters concerninge the good of the countrie, upon paine that every high constable makeing defalte shall pay 20*l*. and every petty constable 10*l*. for everie fortnightes defaulte.

"That the justices of peace in their severall divisions shall, at some convenyente tyme, meete and appoint a beadle in every constablerie, for punishment of beggers and roges.

"That highewaies be repayred and amended before Midsomer next, upon paine of everie parish 5*l*." *Copy.*

NAMES of the MINISTERS and BAILIFFS of the KING in the County of Lancaster.

64. 1623, June 2.—Bailiffs :—William, Earl of Derby, bailiff of the Hundreds of Lonsdale and Amunderness ; Sir Edward Osbaston, bailiff of the Hundred of Blackborne ; Richard Shereborne, and Edward Rigbie, bailiffs of the Hundred of Leyland ; James Worthington, bailiff of the

Hundred of Salford; Robert Dobson, bailiff of the Hundred of West Derby; Thomas Dauson, bailiff of the Liberty of Furnes.

Chief Constables:—Humfrey Nicolson aud William Carter for the Hundred of Lonsdale; Thomas Walles and Richard Blackborne for the Hundred of Amunderness; Peter Haworth and Nicholas Duxberie for the Hundred of Blackborne; Thomas Cheetam and Francis Warberton for the Hundred of Salford; Thomas Wilson and William Healde for the Hundred of Leyland; John Assheton and Henry Astcroft for the Hundred of West Derby.

Coroners:—Thomas Cowell, John Cunlieffe, Richard Lancaster, Richard Meadowcrofte, and Thomas Serjeant.

EDWARD KENYON to his brother, ROGER KENYON, in London.

65. 1623, June 10. Dinkley.—Asking him to buy a book called "A declaration of certen Spirituall desertions" by William Parkines. *Portion of seal.*

THE KING AND QUEEN OF BOHEMIA.

66. 1623, November 1.—Receipt by Abraham Williams, agent for the King and Queen of Bohemia, for 56*li.* from the Hundred of Layland, in the County of Lancaster, by the hands of Mr. Alexander Johnson, being money contributed from the same Hundred for the service of the said King and Queen.

HOUSE OF COMMONS.

67. 1623-[4], February 21.—Speeches by the Speaker of the House of Commons, and the Lord Keeper's replies. *Copy. Printed in Lords Journals, Vol. III., pp.* 211–213.

The EFFECT of the STATEMENT made to both HOUSES at Whitehall by the DUKE OF BUCKINGHAM.

68. 1623[-4], February 24.—"That the first discoverie of the inten-tion of Spaine not to deale faierly with the Kinge touching the resti-tution of the Pallatinate, was att the treaty att Brussells, where the Archdutchess first assured the Commissioners that she had power to raise forces, and to commaund them downe. And thereuppon the King had caused Mannsfeild to retyre out of the Pallatinate. And then she being required, answered, she had noe power to commaund the forces downe, she must expect authoritie from Spaine.

"Uppon this, the Kinge sent Porter into Spaine to have a resolute answer touching the match and the Pallatinate, and assigned him but ten daies to staye there.

"Lord Digby fedd Porter with hopes, but delayed him; whereuppon Porter went boldly to Count Olivares, whoe tould him plainely that Spaine meaut neither the match nor the restitution of the Pallatinate.

"Lord Digby seeing that Porter would retorne with this answer, perswades him to speak with Olivares once more. Then Olivares was very wroth with Porter for relating his answer to Digby and denyed to give him any answer att all.

"Lord Digby still perswades the Kinge with hope of both. The Prince desired hee might goe himself into Spaine; his coming was unexpected. The match att first was absolutely denyed unles he would be converted; and it was tould the Prince plainely,.that Spaine gave noe commission for a treaty of this match untill within theis 4 monethes. Then the

Prince offring to retorne, faier offers were made of hope of a dispensation for the match from the Pope, which their divines neither could, nor would, otherwise permitt, unles the Prince would be converted.

"Lord Digby perswades the Prince to be converted, at least in showe. The Prince absolutely denyes it, but would retorne. Then more hopes were offred the Prince, and att last the dispensation comes, but soe clogged that the Prince refused it and would retorne.

"Then they had another devise; that Commissioners should treate touching the King's dispensation with recusantes, which being sent into England, they expressed their firm hope it would cause a rebellion in England, and offred the Prince an army to assist him to suppress the same. Being disappointed of this, they pretended a new dispensation from the Pope. The Prince would not tarry till it came, but left a proxie with Digby to conclude the match if their dispensation were according to their agreement, and soe retorned. Being att the seaside, the Prince wrote to Digby not to proceede unles he mought be sure to have his wife when he was contracted to hir, for hee understood they meant to putt hir into a monastary presently after the contract, and have good caution for the restitution of the Pallatinate. The Kinge did write to Digby to the same purpose, and to doe nothing if the dispensation were clogged.

"Digby proceeds notwithstanding, and if Gresly had not brought from the Prince a revocation of that proxie overnight, Digby had delivered the proxie next daie. Yet all this while the Prince could never speake with the Infanta but once, and uppon this condition, that hee should salute hir with his hatt, and speake certaine words sett downe to him in wrytinge and noe more.

"Since the Prince his retorne and a resolute answer demaunded under the Kinge of Spaine his owne hand. The answer is brought, whereof I doe remember noe more but this; that Spaine will onely treate with the Emperour for the restitution of [the] Pallatinate, but will not otherwise meddle therein.

"Upon this the advise is required of the Lordes and Commones." *Copy.*

Justices for Lancashire.

69. 1623[-4], March 10.—List of Justices of the Peace for the county of Lancaster. (*Torn.*)

Effects of Alexander Rigby.

70. 1623[-4], March 11.—Deed of Sale by George Rigbye, of Gray's Inn, gentleman (one of the Executors of the last will of Alexander Rigbye, of Wigan, in the county of Lancaster, esquire, deceased), to Alexander Rigbye, of Middleton in Amunderness, in the county of Lancaster, esquire, Thomas Morte, of Asteley, in the county of Lancaster, gentleman, and Roger Piccoppe, of Goosnarghe, in the county of Lancaster, yeoman, of all the goods, books, and household stuff of the said Alexander Rigbye, deceased.

Joseph Tompson to George Rigby, "at the parsonage of Eccleston."

71. 1624, May 11. "From behind Chappell," [Cambridge.]--"As for your tabell, chest and serplice, I doe not know what to doe with them; for I cannot get neare so much as you would think I shoulde. For I cannot have past 4s. for the serplice. As for your beddinge, I have it not yet; for they say that Clarke left yt with Atherton, and Atherton left yt to be redelivered unto Clarke. Neyther doe I thinke I shall have it, or any thinge els, untill you write to your tutor; for your tutor commanded them that keepe in your chamber, that they should let noe thinge goe." *Seal.*

MARRIAGE OF PRINCE OF WALES.

72. 1624, November 20.—Articles agreed upon by James I, King of England, and Louis XIII., King of France, concerning the marriage between the Prince of Wales, son of the King of England, and the Lady Henrietta Maria, sister of the King of France. *Copy.*

HUMPHREY MAY [Chancellor of the Duchy of Lancaster] to the SHERIFFS and JUSTICES OF THE PEACE for the County of Lancaster.

73. 1624[-5], February 21. The Duchy House in the Strand.—I understand that there is much abuse in the summoning and impanelling of juries within your county, "divers of verie meane ranke and qualitie being usually ymployed in enquiries, and tryalls at the generall Assizes uppon the graund juries, juries for life and death, and betweene partie and partie, whereas in truth your countie affourdeth great store of good jurors," by reason whereof the King and county often suffer in their titles and estates. I therefore pray you, at your assize, to cause a "perfect freehold book" to be made for the whole county, of all the knights, esquires, gentlemen and freeholders of quality, only excusing those who are really above the age of 70 years, or otherwise incapacitated. But, on the other side, I commend it to your good cares to be tender in charging any poor or mean freeholder for this service, which meaner sort may sometimes serve to be joined with others, at Quarter Sessions, Escheators' inquests, or other services of less consequence, and within their own Hundreds only. Which book I desire you to hand to the Sheriff to be made the "common freehold booke," to be delivered over by indenture, or otherwise, from Sheriff to Sheriff, and I desire that the book may be amended every three years at the least.

HUMFREY MAY to the BAILIFFS and BURGESSES of Clitheroe.

74. 1625, 9 April. "From the Dutchie House."—Recommending his friend, Sir Thomas Trevor, knight, one of his Majesty's Auditors of the Duchy of Lancaster, as a Burgess to serve in the Parliament now about to be held. *Signed. Seal of arms.*

FARTHING TOKENS.

75. 1625, May 13.—A proclamation for the continuing of our farthing tokens of copper, and prohibiting the counterfeiting of them and the use of any other.

TABLE OF MORTALITY.

76. 1625.—A table of mortality for some town not named, possibly Manchester. It is headed from the 30th of June to the 7th of July, 1625. The sum total of persons who died within the said week is 1,222, of whom, *inter alias*, 14 died in childbed, 69 from consumption, 273 from fevers, 8 from "impostume," 48 infants, 1 from falling sickness, 1 from fistula, 2 from "greife," 3 "livergrowne," 5 from "megrom,"

5 from measels, 593 from plague, 9 from "purples," 21 from "scour-ings," 3 from small pox, 27 from "surfels" [surfeits?], 1 from "plannet," 1 from "risinglights," 1 from "scabbs," 1 from "sore mouth," 1 from swine pox, and 1 from "tissike."

ARTICLES of the EARL OF BRISTOL, "whereby he chargeth the DUKE OF BUCKINGHAM."

77. 1626, May 1.—" That the Duke of Buckingham did secretlie com-bine and conspire with the Condé of Gondomar, Ambassador for the King of Spaine, before the said Ambasadour's last retourne into Spaine in the somer, 1622, to carrie his Majestie, then Prince, into Spaine, to the end that hee might bee informed and enstructed in the Romane religion, and thereby have perverted the Prince and subverted the true religion established in England. From which misserie this kingdome (nexte under Godes mercie) hath by the wise, religious, and constant carriage of his Majestie, beene almost miraculouslie delivered, considering the manie bould and subtill attemptes of the said Duke in that kinde.

" 2. That Mr. Porter was made acquainted therewith, and sent into Spaine, and such messages at his retourne framed as might serve for a ground to sett on foote this conspiracie, the which was done accordinglie, and thereby the Kinge and Prince highlie abused and theire consentes thereby first gotten to the said journey, that is to saie, after the retourne of the said Mr. Porter, which was about the end of December or the begininge of Januarie, 1622[-3], whereas the said Duke had plotted it manie monethes before.

" 3. That the Duke at his arrival in Spaine, nourished the Spanish ministers not onelie in beleefe of his owne beinge papishe affected, but did bothe by absenting himselfe from all exercises of religion constantlie used in the Earle of Bristoll's house, and frequented by all theire protestant English, and by conforminge himself, (to please the Spaniards) to divers rightes of theire religion, even soe farr as to kneele and adore theire sacrament from tyme to tyme, hee gave the Spaniardes hope of the Prince his conversion. The which conversion he endeavoured to procure by all meanes possible, and thereby caused the Spanish ministers to propound farr worse conditions for religion then had beene formerlie, by the Earle of Bristoll and Sir Walter Aston, setled and signed under their Majestie's handes, with a clause in the Kinge of Spaine's aunsweare of the 12th of December, 1622, that they held the articles agreed upon sufficient, and such as ought to induce the Pope to the grantinge of the dispensation.

" 4. That the Duke having, severall tymes, in the presence of the Earle of Bristoll, mooved and pressed his late Majestie, att the instance of the Condé of Gondomar, to write a letter to the Pope, and [for] that purpose havinge once broughte a letter readie drawne, wherewith the Earle of Bristoll, beinge by his Majesty made acquainted, did soe stronglie oppose the writinge of anie such letter, that duringe the abode of the said Earle in England the said Duke could not obtaine itt, yet nott longe after the Earle was gone, he procured such a letter to bee written from his late Majestie unto the Pope, and to have him stiled therein *Sanctissime Pater.*

" 5. That the Pope being informed of the Duke of Buckingham's inclination and intention in pointe of religion, sent unto the Duke a particular bull in parchment for to perswade and incourage him in the perversion of his Majestie, then Prince.

" 6. That the Duke's behaviour in Spaine was as that hee thereby soe incensed the King of Spaine and his ministers, as they would admitt of noe reconsiliation nor furthur dealinge with him ; whereupon the Duke, seeinge that the match would nowe bee to his disadvantage, hee indevoured to breake it, not for anie service of the kingdome, nor dislike of the matche in ittselfe, nor for that hee found (as since hee hath pretended) that the Spaniardes did not reallie intend the said match, but out of his particular end and his indignation.

" 7. That after that hee intended to crosse the marriage, hee put in practice divers undue courses, as, namlie, makinge use of the letters of his Majestie (then Prince) to his owne endes, and not to what they were intended, as likewise concealinge diverse thinges of high importance from his late Majestie, and thereby overthrewe his Majestie's purposes and advanced his owne endes.

" 8. That the said Duke, as hee had with his skill and artifices formerlie abused their Majesties, soe, to the same end, hee afterward abused both houses of Parliament by his sinister relation of the cariages of affaires, as shalbee made appeare allmost in everie perticuler that hee spake unto the said houses. As for the scandall given by his personall behaviour, as allsoe the imployinge of his power with the Kinge of Spaine for the procuringe of favour and offices which hee bestowed upon base and unworthie persons for the recompence and hire of his lust, these thinges are neither fitt for the Earl of Bristoll to speake, nor indeed for the house to heare ; hee leaveth it to your Lordshipps' wisdomes how far you will bee pleased to have them examined, it haveinge beene indeed a great infamie and dishonor to this nation, that a person of the Duke's great qualitie and imploymentes, a Privie Counsellour and Embasador eminent in his Majesties favour, solelie trusted with the person of the Prince, should leave behind him in a forraine Court soe much scandall as hee did by his ill behaviour.

" 10. That the Duke of Buckingham hath beene in great parte the cause of the ruin and misfortune of the Prince Palatine and his estates, inasmuch as those affaires had relation unto this kingdome.

" 11. That the said Duke hath, in his relations to both houses of Parliament, wronged the Earle of Bristoll in point of honor, by manie sinister aspersions which hee bath laid upon him, and, in point of his libertie, by manie undue courses through his power and practises.

" 12. The Earle of Bristoll did reveale unto his late Majesty, both by word and letter, in what sort the Duke had disserved him and abused his trust, and that the Kinge, by severall waies, sent him word that hee should rest assured that hee would heare him, but that hee should leave it to him to take his owne tyme, and thereupon, fowre daies before his sicknes, hee sent the Earle word that hee would heare him against the Duke, as well as hee had heard the Duke against him, which the Duke himself heard, and not longe after, his blessed Majestie sickned and died, haveinge in the interim beene muche pressed and vexed by the said Duke." *Copy*.

The KING to the JUSTICES OF THE PEACE within the County of Lancaster.

78. 1626, July 7. Westminster.—" It is not unknowen unto you that, in Februarie last, our High Court of Parliament was by us sommoned and assembled to treate of the greate and waightie affaires concerninge the Church of England and the true religion therein established, and the defence and safetie of the kingdome, and that they there contynued together untill the 15th of June laste. Within which tyme manie thinges of good moment and muche conducing to our honour and the honour and safetie of this kingdome, were propounded and begunn to be handled. And, amongest other thinges, our Commons then assembled, takinge into their serious considerations our present and important occasions, not for our owne private use, but for the common safetie of us and our people, did, with one unanimous consent, agree to give unto us a supplie of fower entier subsidies and three fiefteenes, and did, by order of that House, sett downe the daies and tymes for payement of the same, which, their lovinge and free offer unto us, wee did graciously accept and relye uppon, and dispose of our affaires accordingly, and afterwardes with muche patience, even beyond the pressinge necessitie of our publique affaires, contynuallie did expect the reall performance thereof, and wee are assured the same hadd beene performed accordingly, had not the disordered passion of some members of that House, contrarie to the good inclination of the graver and wiser sorte of them, soe farr misledd them-selves and others, that they neither did nor would intend that which con-cerned the publique defence of the kingdome, for which they were specially called. Wherefore, when noe gratious admonitions could staye them, though much against our hart, wee have dissolved that Parliament. And the Parliament beinge nowe ended and yet the necessitye of a supplye of money lyinge still upon us and pressinge us, without which the common safetie of us and our people cannot be defended and maine-tayned, but is in immynent and apparant daunger to be assayled and swallowed upp by a vigilante and powerfull enemye, we have beene enforced to cast all the wayes and meanes which honorably and justly wee might take for supplie of theis important affaires, and manie severall courses have beene propounded and offered unto us. And although noe ordenarie rules can prescribe a lawe to necessitie, and the common defence and safety, and even the very subsistence, of the whole might justlye warrant us if out of our royall prerogative and power wee should take anie waye more extraordenarie or lesse indifferent to anie parte thereof; yett wee, desiringe nothinge more (next to the love and favour of Allmightie God, by whose gracious assistance wee desire to governe ourself and all our actions) then the love of our people, which wee esteeme as our greatest riches, wee have made choyce of that waye which maie be most equall and acceptable unto them. And therefore wee do desire all our lovinge subjectes, in a case of this unavoydable necessitie, to bee a lawe unto themselves, and lovingly, freely, and volun-tarily, to performe that which by lawe, if it hadd passed formally by an Acte as was intended, they had beene compellable unto, and soe in a tymely waie to provide not only for ours, but for their owne, defence and for the common safety of all our frendes and allies and of our lyves and honours. The performance of which our request will not onely give us an ample testymonie of the dutifull and good affections of our people in generall, but will give us just incouragement the more speedily to meete in Parliament.

"Wee therefore desire you forthwith to meet together and to take such order as maie best advance our service, and in our name to desire and exhorte our people, accordinge to such instructions as herewith wee send unto you, that they would not faile freely to give unto us a full supplye answearable to the necessitie of our present occasions."

"Instructions to the Justices of Peace in the Countie of Lancaster:—

"1. That speedily, upon the receipte of these our letters, you assemble togeather att some place convenyent and take them and the matter thereby recommended unto you into your due considerations.

"2. That when you are thus assembled, yee calle to mynd the reso-lution in the Parliament lately dissolved, to have give us fower subsidies and three fiefteens and that the severall daies of payement were orderred for the same, and thereby the somme of money to have been raised thereby was, in the judgement of the Parliament, but competent, and the tymes of payement convenyent for the present and pressinge occasions. And wee are confident that the same considerations will prevaile with our people.

"3. That you lett them knowe howe much it will availe to our affaires, and the affaires of our frendes and allies, to assaile our enemyes on their owne coastes, and that wee have begunn a preparation to that end, but want moneyes to perfecte the same. And that whilst wee are in these consultations, wee are advertised from all partes of powerfull preparations made to assaile us at home or in Ireland, or both.

"4. That you putt them in mynd that nothinge invites an enemye more to an invasion then an opinion that that part intended to bee invaded is either [in]secure or distracted, and soe unprovided for a resistance.

"5. That therefore you, the Deputie Lieutenantes, give present direction to have all the troopes and bandes of the countie compleated, mustered, trayned, and soe well furnished, that they maie bee prepared to march unto the rendezvous att an hower's warninge, uppon paine of death.

"6. That ye conclude upon a constant waye of propoundinge and pursuinge this our supply in your severall divisions, to the inhabitantes of the whole countie.

"7. That when you have first setled this worke amonge yourselves, ye agree howe to divide yourselves, throughout the whole countye, into soe many partes and divisions as yee in your judgementes shall thinke fittest, and then that those who shalbe there imployed, deale effectuallye with the rest of the countie in those severall divisions.

"8. That ye agree in the nomination of such able persons as yee shall thinke fitt for the collectinge and receivinge of these moneyes and payinge the same over to our Excheaquer.

"9. That yee assure them in our name and in our royall word, which wee will not breake with our people, that we will whollye imploye all the moneys which shall thus be given to us, to the common defence of the kingdome, and not to or for anie other end whatsoever.

"10. That (together with the moneyes yee collecte) ye send a perfecte rolle of the names of all those which doe thus contribute and of those which shall refuse, if anie such bee, that wee maye bee thereby informed whoe are well affected to our service and whoe are otherwise, and what moneyes are given unto us, that soe wee maie require an accoumpt of those who shalbee trusted to receive it, and that it maie afterward appeare that wee have expended it to those endes and purposes it is given.

"And lastly, that all this be instantly performed, for that all delayes will defeat and overthrow our greatest councells and affayres." *Sign manual.*

Trained Bands.

79. 1626, August 23.—Order by the Deputy Lieutenants of the County of Lancaster, stating that as the trained bands for the County, called trained soldiers, are put to great pains and charges in attending musters, training, exercising, and disciplining, it is ordered that the said trained soldiers for the time being, be discharged and freed from being hereafter chosen or appointed constables, churchwardens, or overseers for the poor, or charged to keep watch or ward within the County aforesaid.

PREACHER AT WHALLEY.

80. 1627, Midsummer.—A subscription list of money contributed to the preacher at Whalley, collected by Samson Rawcliff.

A PROCLAMATION.

81. 1627, June 25.—A proclamation against unjust pretences for colouring of French goods taken by way of reprize.

WITCHCRAFT.

82. 1627, July 24.—A certificate, by her neighbours, that Elizabeth, the wife of Thomas Londesdale, of Simonston, in the county of Lancaster, yeoman, being accused of witchcraft, is no sorceress or user of charms, or any such wicked art, but a good, honest, orderly neighbour.

PRICES OF CLOTHING.

83. 1627, July.—Note of purchases made in London for Richard Coulton. $3\frac{1}{2}$ yards of "baize for lyninge his cloake," at 2s. 10d. a yard ; velvet for the cloak, 6s. 6d.; 2 dozen "of silke and silver laice" for the same, at 4s. 2d. the ounce; "one long button for the cloke," 12d.; buckram to stiffen the collar, 3d.; for making the cloak, 4s. 6d.; $2\frac{3}{4}$ yards of satin "for his doublet," at 15s. 6d. the yard ; for silk "to make the button holes and set on the laice," 2s. 4d.; $\frac{1}{4}$ ell of "taffetie to lyne the doublet skirts," 3s. 4d.; 4 dozen "silke and silver buttons," at 7d. the dozen; $1\frac{1}{2}$ yards of "brode clothe," at 13s. 4d. the yard, "for his breches;" 1 dozen of "silke pointes," 2s. 2d.

R[ALPH] A[SSHETON] to ⸺.

84. [1627 ?]—" So hath your vertues and perfection prevailed with me, that my pen is ledd to treat of a new matter, love, never till now employed on that subject, nor my mind or thoughts at any tyme sensible of such captivity as I finde may bee by such a power. If I shall expresse myselfe weakly unto you, pardon my maiden lynes: no man is an artist on the first daie. For my owne parte, I should desire to bee no more happy here then to be blessed with such a wife as yourself, and might I finde, by any industry of-mynde, the like (but that were too much) motion of affections in you to meewardes, I should accompt myself fortunate, however God should dispose of the successe. My first and great request is that you would accept my love and service, as you shall finde them constant and duteous. Next, that as I on my part shall use my best meanes to my father to condiscend to all reasonable conditions, so you would also bee pleased to advance it on the other side with your parentes, so farre as may bee without inconvenience to them or disparagement to yourself. Deare Mistress, let mee drawe from you, by the berer, or otherwise as you please, a fewe lynes that may encourage and occasion my quick revisiting you ; till when I rest suspended from fruition of free thoughts or comfort. Thinke it no lightnes in mee, upon so short acquaintance, to bee taken with your worth ; if it bee a faulte yow are the cause. I dare make my letter no longer for offending yow. Accept this smale token as a lover's remembrance. Adieu. From your faithfull servant whilst you will entertayne him." *Endorsed : "My yonge Master to his Mistress, in Wales."*

Jo. Bingley to Ralph Assheton, "His Majesty's Receiver-General of his revenues in the Bishopric of Durham and Northumberland."

85. 1628, July 7.—" My Lord William Howard is desirous to healpe my Lady Ann Ingleby with the payment of her pension here in the North, where sho resideth; and hath acquainted me that he hath dealte with you to give her satisfaction for some parte of that which is due unto her. What you have disbursed to her allready, or shall hereafter, untill nexte Michaelmas, pay unto her, beinge due by his Majesty's Letters Patentes, I will see you readily allowed of it here in the Exchequer, without any trouble or delay." *Seal.*

Office of Under-Sheriff.

86. 1628.—An estimate of what the office of under-sheriff will cost. The sum total is 352*li.* 18*s.* 6*d.*, and includes, *inter alia,* the following items:—For apparel, 10*li.*; for wine at the Lent assizes, 6*li.* 18*s.*; for wine at the Summer assizes, 20*li.*

Fuel.

87. 1628.—"A most excellent offer of a certaine invention for a new kind of fire, being both cheape and good, and most necessary for all men, especially in these deare times of fuell."

A Prognostication.

88. 1629, March 31.—A Document dated "from our office in the Minster garth in Yorke," and headed, " Ordered and taken out accordinge to the calculations of the principall Astrologers upon this present yeare, 1629, sent from Rome to his Imperiall Majestie and the Prince Elector of Saxonie."

" In the yeare 1629, the sunne beinge in the celestiall signe *Libra,* all the planets will assemble together about the sunne, at the tayle of the dragon, whereby all may presume that terrable things will ensue, and with such a tempest, that all the windes of the fower quarters of the whole world will meete together; whereupon will followe so horrable an earthquake, that men, for feare and terror shall . . . without anie violence offered unto them. The trees, mountaines, and vallies, shall change the places; townes and villages shalbe removed by the earthquake, but cheeflye those that stand nere anye water, or built on sandes, shall fall to the ground, horrable ecclips will appeare, and afterward a bloudie rainebowe shall be seene, which shall cause greate trouble and bloudie warre amongest manie people in the world. All these will be seene in the monthe of September about the Exaltation of the Crosse. The most learned and most understandinge, both Almaine, Spanishe, and Gretian astronomors, have approved this prognosticatione. The eighteenth of May there shall bee greate assemblye of men of warre. The eleaventh of June, three princes shall dye. The twelfte of June, a lord shall attaine to greate dignitie and honour. The eighteenth, a greate winde shall arise. The neenteenth, a banished Prince shall returne to his owne countrie and receive his former dignitie. The 28th, shall bee intollerable heate both by sea and land. The eleaventh of August there will bee great preparation for warre. The seaventeenth, greate effusion of bloud. The 18th, halfe of the world shalbe drowned. The twentye, busines of greate importaunce shall bee sent to severall places.

"But forasmuch as God knoweth the successe of these thinges, and none other, the most humble and obedient servantes of his Imperiall Majestie and there consortes, hath shewed this unto him, wherebye to governe himselfe and the common people to prepare them to repente, addressinge likwise his said Majestie to withdraw himselfe to some place of temporate aire and to furnishe himselfe with victualles twentye dayes."

LORD WENTWORTH and others to the BISHOP OF CHESTER and the JUSTICES OF THE PEACE within the County of Lancaster.

89. 1629, December 29. " At the Mannor of York.' —" His Majesty havinge bene pleased, upon the often complainte of the growinge numbers of popish recusants, to take into his pyous consideration howe soe spreading an evill might be tymely mett with, hath upon serious advyce with his Councell and for the greater safety and contentment of his kingdomes and better subjects, taken a firme resolution to free his government from soe foule a scandall. To which purpose wee have receaved his gracious directions for the indyteinge and convictinge of all such recusantes, and for fyndeing the estates of all such soe convicted, that the duties thereupon accrewed unto his Majesty by the statutes of this realme maie thereby soe be answered as might both manifest his princely care in this behalfe, calle backe (if maie be) such as are already fallen, or at leaste represse the further increase of them hereafter.

" And because of the distance of the place we cannot with conveniency se this service put in due execution nor those things performed which may conduce to the furtherance thereof in such manner as is requisite, but must rely upon your Lordships' good assistance and the care and discreete indeavours of the justices of the peace within that countie as persons, both by his Majesty and the lawe, immediatcly intrusted. We therefore desire your Lordship, and the rest, to take this service into your good consideration, that such as have beene formerly presented maie be forthwith convicted, and such others presented as were either altogether omitted heretofore or have since increased. And lykewyse that such convictions (whereof we desyre to have a duplicate retourne) maie be certified into the Exchequer, that they maie be proceeded against after a due and legall manner. We conceave it wilbe much furtherance to the service, if the curates, churchwardens, and constables, alsoe have warrant and directions from you to present the names of all the recusants not formerly presented within their severall parishes and constableries, wherein some stricte and severe charge had need be laid upon them that the same be not done after a sleight and negligent manner, more for formes sake then otherwyse, as usually they have bene accustomed, but to let them knowe that you will expect to receyve from them an exacte accompte of what they shall have in charge, without anie manner of forbearance or remissnes." *Seal with crest.*

ALMS FOR THE POOR OF WHALLEY.

90. 1629, December.—Orders and agreements made at the Parish Church of Whalley in the County of Lancaster, by and amongst Sir Ralph Asheton of Whalley, baronet, Richard Sherburne of Stonyhurst, Richard Townley of Townley, Richard Shutleworth of Gawthrop, Roger Nowell of Read, John Braddill of Brockhole, Thomas Sherburne of Little Mitton, John Starky of Huntrode, Thomas Walmesley of Coldcotes, George Shutleworth of Esterlie, Richard Crombock of Clarkhill, Francis Paslewe of Wiswall, Roger Kenyon of Whalley, John Crombocke of Wiswall, John Holker of Relid (?), the present churchwardens of the said church, the present overseers of the poor of the said parish, together with the greater part of all and every the residue of the inhabitants of the eight towns which are chargeable with the repair of the said church, for the employing of a certain sum of money left by John Chewe, late of Whalley, gentleman, deceased, to the poor of the said parish, as also for the ordering of moneys given hereafter for a like purpose.

The orders recite that "the doles usually given and distributed at funeralls and burialls in theis parts, do not only little or no good to the neighbouring poore (to whom the same doles are ment), but also drawe infinite numbers of other poore together from places farre remote, amongst which many wanderers, incorrigible rogues, and vacabands, do flocke in and unworthilie share in the devotions of the dead, never intended for them, as also do pester and trouble those parts (where such funeralls happen to bee) for a longe tyme after, and manie tymes robberies and other outrages are committed ere the countrie bee quit of that disordered crew. And often tymes also wee see that great numbers of persons who are no needers in that kynd (nor take themselves to bee) do by pretext of a custome (but indeed an abuse) come themselves or send theire children, or both, to the said doles and partake thereof, soe as the true indigent poore, indeed, (for whom it was ment) do receave the least part." It is therefore agreed that in future money so left shall be kept in stock for the use and benefit of the poor of the said eight towns, viz. :—Whalley, Wiswall, Read, Simonston, Padiham, Hapton, Pendleton, and Mitton, Henthorne and Coldcotes, in the hands of George Shutleworth and Robert Starkie, of Read, being two of the churchwardens, to employ the stock to the best improvement and increase they can until Tuesday in Easter week next at the election of the new churchwardens, when it is to be given over to the new churchwardens, and the increase to be distributed amongst the poor as shall be thought fit.

ALMS FOR THE POOR OF WHALLEY.

91. 1629, December.—Order touching the distribution of certain moneys arising from a charity left to the poor of the parish of Whalley by John Chewe, deceased.

The FEOFFEES OF BOLTON SCHOOL (J. Bradshaw, Scowcroft Touneley, James Leyver, Ellys Crompton, James Crompton, Ellize Bradshaw, Arthur Isherwood, and Henry Crompton) to ———.

92. 1629, ——— .--They have lately heard of some land, now belonging to Sir William Norris, lying within a mile of "Rouckhorne Boate," in which they think they might conveniently invest the school money. They therefore beg the repayment of certain money in order to effect the purchase.

The LORDS OF THE COUNCIL to SIR THOMAS TREVOR and SIR HUMPHREY DAVENPORT.

93. 1629[-30], February 26. Whitehall.—" Whereas the contribution heretofore, for the defence and recoverie of the Palatinate, beinge a voluntarie guifte, was collected by persons of whome noe accompte was taken, either of theyr names or of the moneyes by them soe collected; and for that wee are informed that diverse somes of money to a good vallewe are still remaininge in the handes of the said collectors, wee have therefore thought fitt, for the better discoverie of the same, to praie and require your Lordshipps that, at the next Assises to be held within the severall counties in your circuite, you conferr with the justices of peace of the said counties concerninge the same, and direct them to cause a speedie enquirie to bee made of the names of the collectors within everie of the said counties, and to certifie them to the Board in writinge, to the end such further course may bee taken therein as wee shall finde cause." *Copy*.

JOSEPH DEARDEN to "MR. KENYON."

94. 1630, April 8. Rochdale.—Refers to Sir Ralph Ashton and "the reste of the worshipfull gentlemen that meete this daye about the lead myne." Though it has cost the "King's servants," and himself, at least 40*l*., and they have had three several grants from his Majesty "for the King's parte of those mynes att Theeffley," yet they can get no redress. Suggests to Mr. Kenyon, as the King's General Surveyor, that the course that "is and has bene taken hether toowe" is neither benefit to the King, nor good for the subject nor for the commonwealth. "And for that sparke you have att Theeffley, in comparyson of the great fyer which is partly knowne and further may be by good endeavore hereafter, which if the Court will not be posset (*sic*) to have Darbishire order, there is a higher power will command it. What subjects are we heare in Lankishire, that are debarred from that privilege that the whole kingdom hath? And what privilege others have, nowe I am bould, we in truth have the same." By John of Gaunt's charter, "nowe in the Tower att London," about lead getting, they are "as free as Darbishire or any other parte, and Darbishire to come and gett with us." Thinks "if there might be a free order, as other partes have, there would be hundreth to worke; and then his Majesty's part would be a hundreth tymes more profitte, for there is very much lead ore about you, if it might be sowght for."

Postscript.—"I have sent your maister and Mr. Ratcliffe an owne of Var[g]yna tobaco, to pass this sitting."

ADAM ASSHETON to his cousin, GEORGE RIGBY, at Manchester.

95. 1630, July 13.—Asking favour on behalf of Richard Brooke, who had used some "unadvised speeches," for which he is now sorry. *Portion of seal of arms.*

JO. TALBOT to ROGER KENYON, at Parkhead.

96. 1630, July 18. Carre.—If the bellows be of Carre's best making, it is better to buy them than to be at the charge of mending "your owne." Mr. Butler of Newcastle and all the best lead masters have fetched their bellows from Carre; the price is about 6*l*. or 20 nobles. "If your smelter have been used to a foote blaste, then no doubt of his well doinge. I gave my smelter a noble a tunne (?), and found one to helpe him, and foure blowers or treaders, to whom I gave an other noble, so that my leade lay me a marke a tunne (?), besydes my chopwood, which must be cut to the size of the smelter's hearth, otherwyse there wilbe more wood spent or lesse leade runne."

ALEXANDER RIGBY to his brother, GEORGE RIGBY, at Peel.

97. 1630, July 27. Preston.—"I have purposely sent this messenger to be by him acertened from you whether my two boys may be sent to my cosen Raebone. I pray you to signifie to me what a lodging and bed they may have; whether he will allow them wheat-bread; what he expecteth for their dyet, lodging and washing, and what for their scooling; how many schollers he hath, and whether he intend to follow the ministrie or wholy to apply himselfe to teaching children, and what the place is wherein he teacheth the children." *Seal of arms, broken.*

ALEXANDER RIGBY to his brother, GEORGE RIGBY, at Wigan.

98. 1630, August 3. Preston.—Asking him to inquire about one Banks or some other who dwelleth in the "Scoles" in Wigan, in the Fair House, near over against Alexander Forth's house; if he is a fit man to take the said Alexander's children to board.

LEAD MINES.

99. 1630, August 22.—Rules concerning the working of lead mines in Derbyshire.

[ALEXANDER RIGBY] to his brother, GEORGE RIGBY, at Peel.

100. 1630, September 1.—Asking if Mr. Ralph Heaton will be clerk of his commission. *Seal of arms.*

MEMORANDUM as to CLITHEROE SCHOOL.

101. 1630, November 11. Lever.—All charters, &c. concerning the school, in the hands of any governors or others, to be called in and locked up in the school chests, and a transcript made of the foundation charter, the statutes, &c., for the use of counsel, so that the originals may be kept under lock and key. Orders had been sent to the governors to meet the Bishop [of Chester], "being visitor of that schoole," at Bolton; but few made their appearance. *Copy.* (See also 25th April 1631.)

PROCLAMATION OF PEACE.

102. 1630, December 1.—Proclamation concerning the Peace between England and Spain.

GEORGE RIGBY to his cousin, ALEXANDER TOMPSON.

103. 1630, December 16. Peele.—I have heard you commend Alexander Rigby, of Shevington, for his skill in physic. I would entreat you to ride over and ask him to come over and see my wife, who is ill. *Seal of arms, broken.*

ALEXANDER RIGBY to his brother, GEORGE RIGBY, at Todmorden.

104. 1630, December 31. Preston.—"The trueth is, wee have here amongst us a very infectious disease, which our tradesmen will not call the plage. There have dyed, within these fyve or six weekes, neere twentie; some three houses are shut up. We hope there is no great danger, but upon Munday next I send my children out of towne (if God so please) to prevent danger. I am loath to remove rashly, because I would not wrong the towne by my example; but if things growe worser, then I purpose, God willing, the next weeke to remove all or most of my family to my house at Myddleton. It is to noe purpose for you to speake of removeing the Sessions till the next weeke, and then it will not be any use that you come, or send, over for that purpose to the Justices about the midle or latter end of the weeke." *Seal of arms.*

THOMAS CARR to ———.

105. 1630, ———.—I was at Preston on Wednesday last, and hoped to have paid you all such rents as I have received for you. A great sessement or tax is laid in our parish of Penwortham towards the making of a new roof to the church and one side of the church wall or more, which by the Bishop, is appointed to be done before midsummer next, and not to be " driven " for fear of further danger.

MINES.

106. 1630[-1], January 28.—" A trewe note of charges disborsit by mee, George Cosson, [on the mines] for myself, after hee (*sic*) was set in by Master Kenyon for the King," from September to Christmas [1630]. Paid at Padiham.

The items include—three days' work, 2s. 6d. ; a drawer, 2s. ; for a workman, 5s. ; 3 wiskkeets, 6d. ; for candles, 7d. ; " for a pigin to fill water with," 3d. ; for a " corfe," 4d. ; for nails, 1d. ; " for five weekes worke for my wife and mysellfe, working and drawinge, 28s.

POACHING.

107. 1630[-31], March 7.—A bond, taken before Sir Ralph Assheton, by Hugh Leathwood and Abraham Porter, for the appearance, at the next sessions of the peace, of Daniel West of Burnley, dyer, now in gaol at Lancaster " for sunderie greate crymes, as shootting gunes, keepinge of grayhoundes, trasing or killinge of hares, keepinge of crosebowes, or usinge any unlawfull games which may tend to the hurt of gentlemans' sportes."

The LORDS OF THE COUNCIL to the HIGH SHERIFF and JUSTICES OF THE PEACE for the County of Lancaster.

108. 1631, April 2. Whitehall.—" Wee cannot but greatly marvayle that, notwithstandinge his Majesty's proclamation, the Booke of Orders and the divers earnest letters of this Board, the price of corne and other grayne is risen soe high, and the same sould at such excessive rates in many places. Nither can wee conceave howe this should bee if the directions sent from hence had ben duely executed. You are therefore to take notice that wee expect a more carefull performance thereof and a more particular accompt then hath hitherto bene given us. And accordingly, we doe hereby, in his Majesty's name, expressly charge you to cause presently a dilligent and exact survey to be made, through all that County, what provision of grayne there is, and to retorne to this Board certifficate thereof with all expedition, and likewise to see the marketts well served accordinge to the Orders, and not forestalled by greedy ingrossers, to the intollerable wronge and prejudice of those that are to buy, especially of the poorer sort. You are likewise to use your best care and endevor, that during the continuance of this present dearth, the maltsters be not permitted to make any greater quantity of malt then may be sufficient for necessary use, that soe there may be **a more** plenty of barly for the reliefe of the poore." *Signed.*

———— to GEORGE RIGBY, at Peel.

109. 1631, April 9 (date of receipt).—"Cosen Rigby, I must intreate you to christen mee a childe at Eccles, the next Lorde's day, in the afternone. I made chouse of you, and my cosen, Peter Eggerton, and my mother, not doubting but that you will [come] if your ocasiones be not other waise."

JAMES WINSTANLEY to GEORGE RIGBY, at Peel.

110. 1631, April 13. Lathome.—"Good cosen, I desire a favour of you, because I am, at this present, poore in apparell, and have travelled farr, both in England and Ireland, for preferment, which, I hope in God, I shall obteyne, ere it be long ; but this want of fitting apparell, makes a man disesteemed and . . . less respected . . . . You may doe me an extraordinary favour herein by my cousin Jollibrand, the bearer hereof . . . The great cockinge [is] to be shortly at Ormschurch." *Seal, broken.*

THE PLAGUE.

111. 1631, April 16 to July 23.—Detailed accounts of the distribution of the contribution for the plague at Preston.

JOHN NORRES to SIR RALPH ASSHETON, Baronet.

112. 1631, April 18.—As to differences between Sir Ralph and " the Bishop," about the profits of the " colle and canell mynes." Conceives that it is "right the Bishop should bee paid for the mynes; and I dowte this courte will so order yt, so I pray you conceeder of yt, for the sweete (suit) will be chargable and in the end dowttfull that profit of the pitts will bee ordered for you to pay; which will bee a dishcredyt to have tou orders ageneste you in the Duttcie." *Fragment of seal.*

THOMAS MORT to GEORGE RIGBY, at Ormskirk.

113. 1631, April 21. Damhouse.—Writes on behalf of the bearer, Anne Green, "who hath been servant a great whyle" with his uncle Jackson. Geoffrey Foster was "a suitor to this Anne Green, above tenn yeares agoe ; and this Anne Green (boinge a madde wyld wench) coming with one Mary Watkinson, another younge wench, away by the house where Forster lived, and fynding his mother within (who was an olde woman) but not fynding him, this Anne Green takes his byble in sport, thinking (as I suppose) to give Forster occasion to come to her. Whereupon he that very daye (as I take it) goes to this Marye Watkinson, and asks her for his byble. She told him that Anne Green had it ; and soe he goes after Anne Green, to the house where she lived, and fynds the byble cast upon the table in th'ouse, in open sight; which he takes, and after he had stayd a tyme with her, he returns home by Mary Watkinson's, having the byble with him ; and this, Mary Watkinson wilbe at the Sessions to affirm. But since this, Forster and this bearer falling out, and breaking of companie th'one with th'other, shee hath sued him for money that he owed her, which he, thereupon, hath satisfyed ; and now, I suppose in revenge, prosecutes her for felonie" for stealing the bible. Desires she may have an attorney and that Rigby will " speake a worde or two " if need be. Hopes the jury, " if they be rightlie informed, will never fynd this (which was done, as it seems, in sporte, and soe longe agoe, and never questioned then as to be anie offence) to be done feloniouslie; but if there be any scruple, I suppose the generall pardon, 21° Jacobi Regis, will clear it." *Seal with crest.*

[The BISHOP OF CHESTER,] Visitor of Clitheroe School, to [the GOVERNORS of that school].

114. 1631, April 25. Lever Hall.—Complaint has been made to him by the Schoolmaster, that besides the 20*l.* due to him and unpaid (of which he before complained), his wages since last midsummer are also in arrear. Mentions other irregularities, which he admonishes them to reform. *Copy.*

JOHN GRENEHALGH to GEORGE RIGBY, at Peel.

115. 1631, June 3. Brandlesome.—The " estrayts for highe wayes " within the township of Toddington " have slept, and the fines been unlevied," by reason of which the inhabitants have become so negligent in the amendment of the ways, that they are become impassable.

ROBERT TOMPSON to GEORGE RIGBY.

116. 1631, June 3. London.—"God be praysed, the sickness doth cease; for there died but one of the plague this weeke." *Seal.*

LORD NEWBURGH, HUMPHREY DAVENPORT, and THOMAS TREVOR, Judges of Assize, to SIR RALPH ASSHETON and the rest of the JUSTICES OF THE PEACE within Blackburn Hundred.

117. 1631, June 21. The Duchy House.—Whereas we are informed that the town of Preston continueth still dangerously infected with the sickness, to the great impoverishment of the town, whereof you and the rest of the Justices of the Peace within the county, at the last general assizes held at Lancaster, did order that the whole county should be charged with the weekly sum of three-score pounds towards their relief, until the ceasing of the said sickness, and that they may have a market there, which we did give allowance of. And whereas the town did consist most of tradesmen and handycraftsmen that had no carriages, and therefore always had fuel brought in the summer time to the town, which now they want, nor cannot be suffered to be fetched by themselves into the said town, and which in the winter time cannot be well brought into the town; we therefore think fit, and do pray and require you, that you take order that some of the next Justices of the Peace to the said town do take course that sufficient fuel may be brought to some convenient place nearest to the said town, where they may buy the same, as likewise they may have provision of victuals brought to some convenient place near the town whither they may resort to buy the same. *Seal.*

THOMAS COVELL to GEORGE RIGBY, at Peel.

118. 1631, June 28. Lancaster.—Mr. Alexander Rigby has affirmed that he will not " sit the sessions according to the summons." Since which he (Covell) sent to Mr. Parker, " whome is so farr from sitting that day, that he voweth, but in regard of the love he beareth me, he would have us all in the Star Chamber for keeping the sessions the last year, contrary to our othe. . . . The sickness is dispersed in dyvers places in Furneis, which will make the sessions small." *Seal of arms.*

WRIT from the BISHOP OF CHESTER, and others, to the CONSTABLES and others of the parishes of Bolton and Blackburn and all places between Bolton and Huntcoates.

119. 1631, July 7.—"Whereas Henrie Towneley hath discontinued to dwell at Bolton and inhabited the parish of Churth, in or near places infected by the plague, and hath sent his wife and children wandering and begging in the country, who have, in these dangerous times, laid in the highways about Bolton, and it is suspected they are infected with the plague. These are to command you that you convey them forthwith to the town of Huntcoat, where they have lived all or the most part of this year, and that the inhabitants of the said town permit and cause them there to stay, that they wander not abroad to the endangering or affrighting of the country."

JAMES WINSTANLEY to his cousin, GEORGE RIGBY, "Clerk of the Peace at the Sessions at Ormschurch."

120. 1631, July 10. Wigan.—Begs for "a black cast suit of apparell. . . . We have not wherewithall to susteyne nature, nor to cover our nakedness; soe that you see our povertie." *Seal of arms.*

ALEXANDER RIGBY to his brother, GEORGE RIGBY, at Peel.

121. 1631, July 29. Middleton.—"The sickness in these partes increaseth much, and disperseth. It is now in Fulwood, Cadeley, and Broughton, and in Kirkham; so that the inhabitants and bordering neighbours leave their howses and seeke and resort to forrin places." If it spreads, he proposes to send his children into Cheshire. *Portion of seal.*

GEORGE LIVESEY to [GEORGE KENYON].

122. 1631, August 12. Ravenshead in Sutton.—The bearer lives in Ellell near Lancaster, which place is not infected; "and he came to Holland, and would not drink, because he might be free from danger."

THOMAS BARTON to GEORGE RIGBY.

123. 1631, August 15. "Smythills."—Has received notice that instructions have come down from the king "for restrayning of travellers, and ordering the people at home for the better prevention of the infection of the plague;" by virtue of which, justices of the peace may nominate "sufficient men in every town and village for the furtherence thereof."

R[OGER] K[ENYON] to the JUSTICES OF THE PEACE for the County of Lancaster.

124. 1631, August 21. Whalley.—I have perused and examined the accounts of the distribution of the moneys levied in the county for the relief of the infected and poor people of Preston. I find that in 15 weeks, from 16 April, there hath been distributed 856*li*. 5*s*. 5*d*. The receipts I find to be 812*li*., and so more distributed than received by, 44*li*. 5*s*. 5*d*. The rates given to every person weekly, are uncertain, viz.: to some 8*d*., to some 9*d*., 10*d*., 11*d*., and 12*d*., I suppose as their needs were, but now of late, few have had less than 12*d*. I do not purpose to receive any more books till God make it less dangerous.

With the letter is a schedule of the number of persons relieved week by week. At the week ending 16 April, 1,372 persons were relieved. The number reached its height at the week ending 30 April, when 1,390 persons were relieved, after which date the number decreased till, at the week ending 23 July, 1,017 persons were relieved.

SIR GILBERT HOGHTON, RALPH ASSHETON, ROGER NOWELL, and JOHN STARKIE to the JUSTICES OF THE PEACE for the County of Lancaster.

125. 1631, August 22. Houghton.—" Takinge into consideration the distressed estate of the people yet living in the towne of Preston, and to satisfie the cuntrie, so farre as wee knowe or understand thereof, havinge had many meetinges and examinations of the state of the said towne since the last Assises, because some of us shalbe absent from the Borde now at the usuall general meetinge at Lancaster for the cuntries affaires, wee thought good to certefie unto all you present what wee conceave thereof. According to the agreement at the last Assises and other orders since, there hath been a continuation of the allowance of 60*l*. a weeke unto them, which hath been paid by most hundrethes, yet in some places part is behinde, which they who solicit for the towne will make to appeare. Wee receaved accompts from Mr. Langton for 15 weekes, endinge the xxiijth of July last, which wee have caused to bee perfectly cast upp and examined, by which wee are (for our partes) satisfied that there hath been reall and faire carriage in the busines, by employing of honest and careful men as distributors, by the competency of the sommes given, and by the plainenes and particularitie of the accomptes; nor can we judge, in reason, that time of the weekely allowance could hitherto have beene spared. For the further continuance of their allowance, wee shall humblie submit yt to the judges and yourselves, with declaration unto you how wee conceive the present estate of the towne to stand. By a perfect survey sent us from the maior, subscribed and explained by himself, yt appeareth there was livinge, the xvjth of this month within the towne, 887 persons, wherof, weekely releived 756, not releived, 131. The unreleived, or most of them, wee heare (and doe beleive yt) cannot longe subsiste by their private stores, but will shortly become needers also. Their winter's fuell is whol(l)ie unprovided, and all those that live, their needes still increase. What in the beginninge would have served well, will now doe them little good, all their owne helpes beinge gone. What taxe shalbee laide will fall as heavie on us as others; yet theire miseries are enough by the plague; yt were pittie famine should also distroy them. Soe wee leave them to Godes mercie, and, for theire releife, to your better judgement." *Seal of arms.*

EDWARD TALBOT to ROGER KENYON.

126. 1631, September 10. Thiefley.—Thomas Cawcroft will give 3*li*. 10*s*. for the [lead] ore "gotten," and 3*l*. 2*s*. for the ore "to gett." He says "the sicknesse is sore in Heptonscale." *Fragment of seal.*

ALEXANDER RIGBY to his brother, GEORGE RIGBY, at Peel.

127. 1631, September 16. Middleton.—"I am much bounde to you for your care over my childe, and I know, and am confident, you thinke noe paynes too much at this tyme upon such occasions, and, therefore, I would intreate you to goe over to my cosen Rathband, and to advyse seriously with him for the best; and if he remove himself, I should be well pleased that my children remove with him; and if you and he think well that they stay a tyme where they are, expecting God's mercy to stay his judgment, I shall referre the event to God. Onely my desyer is, that, if it increase, I would not have him over bold. And if you find cause, I would intreat you, good brother, to go there yourself with the children to Adlington, where I know they will be welcome. And if Macclesfeild stand clere from all infection, I would have them in Mr. Wm. Burges' house, who I know, upon sight of this letter, will interteyne them with all carefulnes over them. You need not to . . . with him, for he will not doubte my thankfulnes. The reason of my desyer to have them with him is, that they may there goe to the free schoole, and not loose their tyme, most precious to them. Or otherwise let them stay at Adlington till my comeing thither. Yet, nothwithstanding what I have written, if you please to remove them onely to your owne house till my goeing towards London, I shall refer them to you. You writ touching their goeing to the Shagh; I shall be willing at another time (if God so please) that they may goe thither, but this is not a tyme to visit friends, and I know they will not censure anything herein unkindely. Now if you, before I see you, shall remove the children to any place, my intreaty is that when you have so done you would forthwith signifie so much to me, that I may comply with that course. And I pray God we may all make a right use of these miseries. . . . The sicknes doeth not (God be praysed) increase behynd Garstange. The last week there dyed eighteen in Preston; this week I know not yet how many. Kirkham continueth infected, and some parts of Woodplumpton. Our parish (God be praysed) is, for anything I know, free from the plague. My little boy (God be praysed) hath mended verie well these two weekes last past, and, as I hope, is well overbroken his ague. Hugh Hindley hath never had any fit of ague since you weare heare in the Assize weeke, and is very well. Ellen Charneley, who, as you know, had two or three fitts of her ague in the Assize weeke, is fallen into it againe. Margaret is afraid of an ague; all the rest of my familie (God be thanked) are in verie good health. These partes are wonderfully trobled with ague. I pray God be mercifull to us." *Seal of arms.*

EDWARD VEALE to GEORGE RIGBY, "Clerk of the Peace at Lancaster."

128. 1631, October 3. Whinnybeyes.—"The miserable distresse of this pore fylde is now so greate, by reason of the fearfull infection, so dangerously dispersed in divers places amongst us, that I conceive it were greate indiscretion to admit ether the cunstables or partyes bound by recognizances (inhabiting within theise partes) to appeare at the Sessions to bee boulden at Blakeburne, upon Wednesday next." Prays that those bound, and the constables, may therefore be excused; thinks the latter "would hardly bee admitted in the toune, if they should come."

RICHARD BURGH to GEORGE RIGBY, Clerk of the Peace at Blackburn.

129. 1631, October 4. Layrbreck.—John Hudson of Elmswicke, husbandman, "tooke a hawke uppe, called a merlion, of Mr. Edmund

Fleetwood's." Mr. Veale sent a warrant to arrest Hudson "for suspicion of felonye, for taking upp, concealinge, and detayninge the sayd hawke," but Mr. Fleetwood is unwilling to prosecute; "a prettie case to have been tryed to cause rurall fellowes not to meddle with gentlemen's hawkes."

RICHARD LAWE, GILES BOLTON, GEORGE TOMLINSON, ELLIS EDGE, and JAMES COWPER, to "MR. RIGBY," Clerk of the Peace at "Streat Yate."

130. 1631, October 17.   Blackburne.—Understanding that quarter sessions were to be held at Blackburne on the next Wednesday, "Wee, and divers others of our towne, resorted to Sir Raphe Assheton, and some other of our neighbouring Justices of peace, and enformed them that the infection of the plague is lately much broken out, and scattered aboute us, as in Eggleshill, Lyttesay, Walton, Clayton-super-Moras, Altham, and other places besides, the same fearful contageon spred in soe many parts in Amondernes Hundred; whereupon, and upon consideracion of God's late mercifull deliverance of our towne, wee desired the Justices to give us leave to keepe out of our towne all persons whom we knew not to come from free places, and that the sessions might not hold; which they agreed unto, as in reason we thought they had cause. Therefore, to prevent your travel, we thought good to give you this advertisement, assuringe ourselves, there will not two Justices come, and thoughe you may come your selfe, yet we purpose to keepe out all or moste of the common people. The like advertisement we have written to Mr. Undersherif." *Seal.*

RICHARD HALLYWELL to GEORGE RIGBY, at "Todmordine."

131. 1631, November 29.   Manchester.—Has sent him six quarts of "good claret wine, for what there is none in toune fitt to send you: on Saturday next wee shall have new wines at home, which we doe purpose to drawe the same day they cum, allthoe they bee in the lees." His wife has sent Rigby's wife "a barell of picklt oystres, a small peec of stergen, and a botle of new malligoe wine." He has sent Mr. Radclyffe "a peec of verie good verindes (?) tobako." *Endorsed* "Young Mr. Hallywell's letter to me."

JOHN OSBALDESTON to THOMAS WALMESLEY.

132. 1631.—It lies not in my power to constrain my neighbouring adjoining towns, much less the rest of the parish of Blackburn, to pay to the contribution for the town of Clayton super-Moras. Their principal reason is because the town of Over Darwen is infected and restrained from church and market, and moved to have some contribution for the relief of their poor, which was at the least 300 and more, and was utterly denied to receive any contribution at all. *Seal.*

THOMAS MORT to GEORGE RIGBY, Clerk of the Peace.

133. 1631-2, January 16.—"There is in Astley one James Mather (?) and Margaret his wyffe, beinge a verie poore, aged, and impotent couple: and my father, in his lyfe tyme, did, in charitie, give them house roome in a peece of buildinge (called a kitchin) belonging to a house of his; they beinge soe poore that they are not able either to pay rent or keep it in repaire. I could never else bee content to give them houseroom, still soe I might not iucurre anie danger thereby; but if I cannot doe it without danger, I must turne them upon the parish to provyde them house room." Begs the Court will grant him licence "for a cottage," to continue for as long as "poore people of the parish of Leigh should inhabit therein."

RALPH ASSHETON to HENRY GERARD.

134. 1631[-2], February 11. Whalley.—The vicar of Whalley is dead. I have written letters of recommendation to my Lord of Canterbury and Mr. Dobson on behalf of Mr. Burne, whom I labour for. If Mr. Warriner come up about this business, seek by all means to prevent him. *Seal of arms, broken.*

R[ICHARD], ARCHBISHOP OF YORK, to the BISHOP OF CHESTER.

135. 1632, June 18. Winchester House.—" I have received letters from the Lords of his Majestie's most honorable Privy Councell, the tenor whereof followeth : After our verie heartie comendations to your Grace. Whereas wee are informed that sometymes it hath hapned that those ministers who are appointed to preach before the Judges of Assises in theire severall circuits, are either men of ill disposition to the present state or government, or want sufficiencie or experience for those places and auditories (being assemblies of the principall persons of each Countie), and have given cause of scandall and offence, which is of dangerous consequence, and might bee easily prevented, if ellection were made of discreete and able men, but if yt shoulde fall out otherwise, that then such as give the scandall bee reprehended and punished for their indiscretion. Wee do therefore earnestly recomend unto your Grace the serious consideration hereof, and do accordingly pray and require you to direct your letters to the severall Bishops within your Province, willinge and requiringe them to take carefull and effectuall order that from henceforth the elections of preachers for those tymes and places be either made by them in their severall dioceses, or (at least) with their knowledge and approbation. And that the said preachers bee chosen of the gravest and most discreet and learned ministers in the counties respectively, with expresse directions to handle only such points as are seasonable and fitt for such assemblies, and that they forbeare to medle with the persons of men, or anything prejudiciall to the lawes or present government, or anything els not befittinge their callinge. And, lastly, with intimation unto them that if they faile herein they shalbee censured and punished by them, being theire Ordinaries, *secundum canones et gradus delecti.* And so wee bidd your Grace verie heartily farewell. From Whitehall, the last of Maye 1632.

" I have found by experience that usually the Sheriffs make choice of the preachers without eyther leave or practice of the Bishop of the Diocese ; out of which libertie, so taken by the Sheriffs, the abuse complained of to the Lordes of the Councell, hath grown. I do therefore pray your Lordship to lett the High Sheriff of every County in your Diocese know that, by comaund from the Lordes of the Councell, you have received direction not to suffer it to bee so hereafter, but that whosoever shall preach in any place to the Judges maye thereunto bee allowed of by you, and that you will make choice and allowance of such discreet and learned men as will not rune into the errors which the Lords of the Councell have noted in theire said letters." *Copy.*

D

ORDER made at the Session of the Peace held at Preston.

136. 1632, July 11. Preston in Amounderness.—" Whereas this court was this daye informed, as well by some Justices of the Peace of this countie inhabiting within the hundred of Blackburn, as by sundrie gentlemen and others of that hundred, that therein is a verie dangerous passage within the said hundred, over the river of Calder, called Fenysford, lying betweene the Townshippes of Whalley and Great Harwood, within the countie and hundred aforesaid, and being in the King's highwaye, between the burrow-town of Clitherowe and the townes of Whalley, Wisswall, Pendleton, and other townshipps on the one side of the river, and the townes of Manchester, Burye, and other markett townes and townshippes on the other side, over which ford, when the water is little, there is commonly tcw or three hundred lowden horses everie daye passe over, besides great numbers of other passingers; but the river being very often (especially iu the winter season) soe great, that there is no passage for man or horse, and many attempting at suche time to passe, have been drouned, and almost daylie some persons are there putt in danger of their lives, and have their loades and carriages drowned and lost; and that the said ford is of late years so worne and groune so rocky, that in short time it is thought will become altogether impassable, being almost impossible to be amended by the charge and labour of man. Whereupon some gentlemen of those parts have endeavored to obtaine from the bordering townes and some personages of worth, a voluntary contribution, or gratuity, for erecting of a stone bridge over the said river, in the passage or highway aforesaid; wherein we are credibly informed that a good sume will bee that way raysed towards the said worke, to the value of one hundred pounds or thereabouts, which, as is thought, will halfe suffice to build a bridge. This Court, considering that it weare much pittie that suche a worke should go backe for want of a tryfle or small contribution, to go through the said Hundred by way of fifteenth, It is therefore this daye ordered by an unanimous voice of all the justices of peace present, with consent of all the constables and inhabitants of the said Hundred, assembled at this Sessious, that a taxe of two fifteenes shall be assested and paid throughout the said Hundreud of Blackburne, to be employed towards building of the said bridge; the same to be collected by the high constables of the said Hundred and paid over unto the hands of Sir Raph Asheton, Barronet, Thomas Walmisley of Dunckenhalgh, Esq., Sir Thomas Walmisley, Knight, and Roger Nouell of Read, Esq., or anie of them, whoe this court doth intreat and authorise to be overseers of the said work. Provided that this assessement shall not be levyed nor go forth until suche time as the Clerk of the Peace for this county be certified by the said overseers, under their hands or the hands of two of them at the least, that there is apparent hopes that the money voluntarily contributed, together with this taxation, will performe the saide worke." *Copy. Seal of arms.*

EDMUND POLLARD to HENRY GERRARD, at Preston.

137. 1632, July 20. London.—I have directed to you a box, with a hat for my sister Isabell, which I entreat you to have carried to her. *Postscript.*—" This comes a week after the date, now 27. Yesterday, a post from the King of Swedon sung *Victoria* as he rode through the streets towards the Court."

ACCOUNTS CONNECTED WITH WORKING THE LEAD ORE AT THEEFLEY.

138. 1632[-3], January 2 to March 16.—"Samuel Robinson, 37 dayes and nights, at 8*d. per diem;* Sam's wiffe's wadges, for 24 dayes and nights, 5*d. per diem.*" The rest of the payments are to other male labourers, and for candles, washing the ore, wood, nails for the "corfes," &c.

SALE OF AN OUTLAW'S GOODS.

139. 1632[-3], January 3.—Deed of sale by John Hilton, of Preston in Amounderness, farmer unto his Majesty, of the goods and chattels of all persons outlawed, or to be outlawed, within the Hundreds of Salford and Blackburn, of the goods and chattels of Roger Kenyon, of Parkhead in Whalley, now standing several times outlawed, to Robert Cunliffe of Sparth and Thomas Turner of Preston.

ROBERT MAWDESLEY to his "brother," GEORGE RIGBY.

140. 1632[-3], February 17. Wigan.—Is sorry his father [William Mawdesley] will not part with a certain hawk; but "ould men, as the auncyent proverb goeth, are twys children." Mr. Edward Bridgeman desires copies of the informations or examinations taken and certified against "Mr. Cade, the precher." *Seal of arms.*

WINES.

141. 1632[-3], February 18.—"A Proclamation for Prizing of Wines."

SIR RALPH ASSHETON to SIR HENRY AGARD, "at his house, Fosson in Derbyshire."

142. 1633, March 25. Whalley.— "Mr. Wright hath been here with us at the lead-mynes, and seen and understood what his place, undertaking, and entertaynment, should bee"; he is not anxious for the appointment, which is only fit for "a man that hath been reallie brought up a myner, or an overseer of myne-workes, or a berghmaister: such a one as hath speciall good judgment in lead oare, in the lyeing of the vaines and rakes in the earth, and can be able to direct the groof workes for orderly working, and tryall of the myne, that will go doune into the workes, twice or thrice a weeke, and oftener, if need bee, can judge what wages are fit for the King to give, and who are, or are not, expert and fit men to sett on work . . . . and do all things that belongs to a skillful mynerall man. Such a one it is Mr. Chancellor expects." Recommends sending for a man from Derbyshire, where many such men may be found "versed and trayned upp in that profession, even from their cradles." *Copy.*

RICHARD HALLYWELL to [GEORGE RIGBY.]

143. 1633, March 25. Manchester.—"You wryt for the larger rundlet to be filled with whyt wine, but, trulie, Sir, altho' the whyt bee verie good, yett it will not be nether for your credet nor mine to send whyte; for it will, within 2 or 3 dayes, both lose hed and culler . . . . I would advise you to claret, for it will bould best." Sends a "bottle" of each for trial.

D 2

SIR HENRY AGARD to THOMAS EYRE.

144. 1633, April 1. Foston.—The Chancellor of the Duchy desires Eyre to recommend a man skilful in lead-mining, as there is great hope of working a lead-mine in Lancashire for the King's use. *Signed. Seal of arms.*

DOROTHY LEGH to GEORGE RIGBY.

145. 1633, April 29. Lyme.—Great complaint is made of the "foulness" of the highways, especially in Little Hulton. Prays him "to bee a means, that everie one that ought to worke in those wayes, may come and doe their duties therein . . . . now whiles the season of the yeare doth fitt for it."

REPAIR OF ST. PAUL'S CATHEDRAL.

146. 1633, June 7.—An account of the sums subscribed by various towns in the County of Lancaster, for the repair of St. Paul's Cathedral. Sum total, 19*li*. 10*s*. 3*d*.

ALEXANDER RIGBY to his brother, GEORGE RIGBY.

147. 1633, June 17. Gray's Inn.—Desires search made "in your office" as to the whereabouts of Sir John Pilkington's manor of Evesgreen, in Lancashire. Conceives his land at Evesgreen was no part of Sir John's property, "for it was only a little common in Gosenargh, which, before the enclosure, was called Evesgreen, and noe manor; and there is also another little common neere the burgh, called Eyvesgreene, but I know not whether any more lands in that place are conteyned under that name." Sir John was Escheator of Lancashire. Has spoken with "your glass man about your glass works, and he will not work them for 1*s*. apeece, as you writt, but demaundeth 1*s*. 6*d*. for every quarrell . . . I think you might have them done in Preston." *Seal.*

ROBERT MAWDESLY to GEORGE RIGBY.

148. 1633, August 13. Wigan.—Sir Peter Leighe, who is at Haidock, desires copies or notes of the orders made at the sessions, for building bridges, for two or three years last past, since the building of Newton Bridge. *Seal of arms, broken.*

[SIR RALPH ASSHETON ?] to THOMAS COVELL, at Lancaster.

149. 1633, October 20. Whalley.—"I understand by Tom Greenfeild, my cosen Braddill's man, that you have removed my cousin from the Receaver's Chamber into the Gatehouse, a place of much lesse ease, and (belike) more incomodious for health, his privacy, and bestowinge and placeinge of his necessaries, &c.; and this his remove, comeinge so soon after my beinge at Lancaster, may, by the jeleous, bee suspected to have been brought to this passe, out of some speech or conferrance between you and mee, which (if any such conceipt bee) you know is most untrue and misgrounded. But to let that passe. Yt is like enough my cosen Braddill, in his old garbe of talke, hath provoked you justlie to this course, but I know your generous disposition dispiseth revenge, especially when it is in your owne power, which more assures me of prevailinge in my sute, which is, that you wilbee pleased, for my sake, to returne him to his former lodginge, the Receavor's Chamber, and to restore him to the enjoyment of all the ease and libertie hee had there before. I am the more earnest in it for that I heare his wife is to come unto him and stays for a time; whilst, for his more profitt, hee gives over housekeepinge here. I praie you deny me not. I shall take it as a curtesie done at my request, and will place it as a speciall one amongst the rest." *Draft.*

[SIR RALPH ASSHETON] to MR. COVELL.

150. 1633, October 29. Whalley.—I lately wrote unto you (and somewhat ernestly) for my cousin Braddill's restoration to such chamber and ease as, till of late, by your good permission, he enjoyed in this his durance. The good gentlewoman, his wife, as you may perceive, is now come to him to stay for a time, and I should be no little grieved she should be lodged in a 4 or 5 bed chamber, and most of them therein men. There be also many other inconveniences, and therefore, as I may move you in any thing, deny me not again.

JAMES ANDERTON to ROGER KENYON.

151. 1633[-4], January 31. Cleyton.—I thank you for your love, care, and pains taken, touching the Coucher Book, which I have sent you by this bearer, and I wish I had sent it you sooner, as Sir Ralph Assheton hath this night sent to me for it (very ernestly), but in respect of my promise to you, I have returned him answer that I am assured it is safe and it shall be with him before Tuesday at night. *Seal.*

CHRISTOPHER HALL to ROGER KENYON, at his house near Whalley.

152. 1634, May 14 Clitheroe —You cannot but wonder at my more than boldness, having so largely of late tasted your kindness, to solicit you for a second favour. I make no question but you know of my too long continued imprisonment. My father-in-law is still obstinately churlish, and doth not only refuse to purchase my freedom, but, to add more to my bondage, hath sent my wife and child to me, so that I am constrained, in great extremity, to purvey for maintenance both for them and myself. The debt and charges for which I am here imprisoned, will not all amount to above 16*li.*, and my creditor offers me seven years to pay it in, so he may be secured by sufficient bond. Now my purpose is, to procure eight friends for the accomplishment hereof; two have already undertaken a share; will you make a third and procure me a fourth?

ROBERT BLUNDELL to GEORGE RIGBY, Clerk of the Peace at Wigan.

153. 1634[-5], January 7. Ince Blundell.—"There is a fifteene charged upon Darbie hundred, to make a new stone bridge in North Meales, which was never laid on the hundred before; but it was still made, at the charge of the toune, with plankes, and it is but a private waie, and no high waie, and therefore the hundred ought not to bee charged with it." *Seal of arms, broken.*

The LORDS OF THE COUNCIL to the JUSTICES of Lancashire.

154. 1635, March 31. Whitehall.—Requiring them to send a true particular of the names and qualities of all malsters within the County, and what number they think should be allowed; so that his Majesty may take further course for the reformation of the damage to the kingdom, by the excessive number of malsters. *Copy.*

William Horrocks to Roger Kenyon.

155. 1635, December 26 —"I have, by my messenger purposely sent, saluted all Mr. Sequestrators with my Lord's letter, save Mr. Starky and John Robinson, whom he (*sic*) could not meet with, but now, in the sending of this letter from the knights and us two blackcoats, they with the rest (God willing) shall have shown them what is to be done." *Seal.*

Acknowledgment by the Churchwardens of Wigan as to a Pew.

156. 1636, May 10.—"Whereas, we Raph Broune and Richard Turner, gentlemen, elected Churchwardens in the town and parish of Wiggan for the year of our Lord God, 1633, did, upon Sundays and hollydayes during that whole yeare, kneele, sitt in, and make use of, one certaine place or pew, lying and being in the uper end of the north syde of the midle-ile, within the Church of the afforesaid parish of Wiggan, and next adjoyning ·to a place in the same Church, commonly called the parsons chancell. Now this our present act testifyeth that we, the foresaid Raph Browne and Richard Turner, had and used the afforesaid place or pew during the tyme afforesaid, lying and being as afforesaid, in the parish Church afforesaid, not making any challendge, title, or claim, unto the same, as of due or right, either to our person's, houses, or office for that year belonging or anywyse, or at any tyme, then or heretofore, appertaininge ; but by the sole and speciall leave and permission (by intreatie obtained) of Joseph Rigbye, gentleman, one of the same parish, to whom, and whose house, of ould, we have heard the forenamed place or pew of right to belonge." *Signed,* "Rauffe Broune . . . Richard Turner, the other churchwarden, died before his hand was required to this writing."

Katherine Radcliffe to her son-in-law, George Rigby.

157. 1636, August 10.—"It hath ·pleased God to call my brother Harrie, who desired to be buried at Todmerden, whither we do carry his body tomorrow. Mr. Radclif and I would be glad of your company there tomorrow night."

Relief of Poor Prisoners.

158. 1637, August 23.—The weekly taxation of the several parishes within the County of Lancaster. *Subscribed by the Justices of the Peace for the County. Endorsed "A Taxation for the relieffe of the poore prisoners within the Gaole at Lancaster, agreed upon 23 die Augusti, Anno 13 Caroli Regis Anno Domini* 1637."

Peter Heywood to George Rigby, at Lancaster.

159. 1636, August 24.—If there be any mention at the Board of Justices' wages, do me the favour to inform them that, not ten days since, I received the first extracts of fines imposed since our grant began. I find the sums so small that, were they wholly gathered, the money will not amount to wages for the justices, nor for meaner men, the collectors. *Seal of arms.*

"Gaeryt Wynnan, Dotchman within the Minster of Chester," to Mr. George Rigbye.

160. [1637, July 14.]—I have sent your worship four dozen " qaruls [quarrels] and one ovall." I will come and stay a day or two with you, for to draw these pictures you were desirous to have. I can hardly sell these "qarels" after the rate of the first, for I sell none under 6s. a peice in Chester, but if your worship will not have all the four dozen, you may send me the rest again, and the oval broke in the burning, but it will not be much worse when it is set up.

Joseph Tompson to his cousin, George Rigby.

161. 1637, December 16.—Asking that an "antimoniall cup" may be intrusted to his brother, as he is persuaded of its great virtue, and is willing to take it, for he has long been, and still is, tormented with some such diseases as the "printed copy" saith it hath virtue to remove. *Portion of seal.*

Peter Winn to Mr. Rigby.

162. 1637[-8], January 14. Lathom.—"The bearer hereof, Sara Crosse, wife to one Richard Cross, deceased, beinge a longe tyme servaunt to my Lord, and beinge, as all the neighbours conceave, and by his owne confession, all the tyme of his sickness and at his last departure, most grieviously tormented with sundry torments, by the wichcrafte of one Anne Spencer, a knowen wich, and, as by her examinations, beinge taken before mee and Mr. Ashurst, doth appeare, who, in regard of my sudden goeinge upp to London, the poore woeman's cause hath beene a little neglected, for I would desire you to certify this my letter to the Bench, and withall to doe the poore woeman that favour as to get her a *mittimus* where the said Spencer may forwith bee sente to Lancaster, there to remaine till shee receave her further tryall accordinge to equity and justice." *Seal of arms.*

Alexander Tompson to George Rigby, at Peel.

163. 1638, June [4].—He came, last week, to Peel, intending to stay and wait on Mr. Radcliffe, to make up the books, and have "our meeting of Wiganers and Cowbent dogs at some indifferent place."

Hugh Hargreaves to George Rigby.

164. 1638, September 11.—Desires to have the names of those "which are licenced within these hundreds," and also "word" what he shall do with "butchers and bakers, as well as badgers," which are not licenced. "There are divers, both badgers and bakers, that will not take licences, but say they will give over; but yet they will continue." These dispute his authority.

Thomas Covell to George Rigby, at Peel.

165. 1638, September 18. Lancaster.—"I, hearing, as well by yourself as by dyvers others, of the great cures and good that have been donne by the vertue of your antimoniall cupp, earnestly desyre to make tryall thereof, in regard of my infirmitie; and, therefore, doe intreat you heartily to doe me the favour to send the cupp and your servant maide, who knoweth the use of the same." *Seal of arms.*

JOHN WISWALL to GEORGE RIGBY, at Peel, "in old England, Lancashire, Deane Parish."

166. 1638, September 27. "Dorchester in New England."—"Being mindfull of your worshipes kindnes and readynes, at all tymes, to doe me good and rescue me out of the handes of immeritinge and . . . . . men, accordinge to the place and power God had set you in, I could not excuse myselfe of great ingratitude if I should not show my thankefull-ness some waye, and not knowing how more acceptably to doe it, I have adventured to present a few rude lynes unto your worshipes veiwe, certifieinge your worshipe of our prosperous, pleasant, and speedy jorney unto New England, in seven weekes and odd dayes. Twenty three shipes more besides us, I think have come, but none so speedy: we were the first of all in Nantasket. It is a place where shipes oftymes anchor, before they goe downe into Boston or Charlestowne river. In the waye, there is a pritty castle and fort to which the shipes lore [lower] their top gallans before they passe into Boston, and divers there, shoot two or three canons, and then the fort will welcome and salute them with one. For the land, it is a fyne land, good for corne, especially Indian, which is a very precious graine for divers uses beside bread, good for pasture, and good haye land, plenty of wood. It is a pleasant country to looke upon. Truely Sir, I like it very well, and soe I thinke any godly man God calls over will, when he sees Moyses and Aaron, I meane magistrate and minister, in church and commonwalke (*sic*) to walke hand in hand, discountenancing and punishinge sinne in whomsoever, and standinge for the praise of them that doe well. Our sovereigne Lord and Kinge, is Kinge Charles, whose crowne and honnor is dayly prayed for in all the churches. Under him we have a Governour, Deputy, and Counsell, and men called Assistants, in power, much like your justices; Constables we have in every towne; men we call Comittyes we send from every towne to the Generall Court. Plantations there are divers, and they succeed and prosper well. Boston is a pritty towne; in it there are fyne houses and some six or seven shopes fynely furnished with all commodityes. There is a prity key and a crane, as at Bristoll, to lade and unlade goods. There is a warehouse wherein strangers and passengers' goods may be put. Newtowne now is called Cambridge. There, is a University house reared, I heare, and a prity library begune. There is also Roxbury, Dorchester, Salem, and divers townes. At Conectichute, there are some pritty plantations. But to wind upe all in one word, thinges prosper well, and men of pritty parts, God sends over, both for church and commonweale. The Indians are a prity active, ingenious people in kind, yet loveinge to us. . . . . For personall strength, I thinke it not inferiour to us, if not exceed[ing]. They are active to *cram* (?) as they speake, that is: kill deere, fishe, fowle, beaver, and divers wilde beastes, in the woods. Our plantations are not anoyd with any. Some wolves now, at this tyme of the yeare, come downe after deere, and doe some hurt to calves, goats, and swine, &c. but it is but little."

Postscript.—"I have for my owne share, a pritty house and outhouses with 12 (?) acres of my owne land, besides half a good house, to which pertaines 47, my share being then 23½."

Endorsed, "John Wiswall's letter to me; received 22 January 1638[-9]." *Seal.*

Miles Atkinson to George Rigby, at Peel.

167. 1638, November 21. Lancaster.—The bearer's son is " diseased, very vehemently," with the " falling sicknesse." Begs the aid of the " antimoniall cupps," and a " sufficient quantity of the liquor wherein the cupps shall be boyled." Also begs the " best directions " for taking the cups. *Seal of arms.*

Giles Heysham to George Rigby, at Peel.

168. 1638, November 26. Lancaster.—A friend and neighbour has come from Scotland with a hundred "weathers," not large, but "well coloured mutton." They cost him about 4*l.* 10*s.* a score, at Dumfries, and he was offered 7*l.* a score at Lancaster. *Fragment of seal.*

Hugh Hargreaves to George Rigby, at Peel.

169. 1638, December 5. Wiswall.—Numerous " badgers " about ; say they were licensed at Manchester Sessions, but will not show their licences ; shall these be indicted at the next sessions ? Thinks he has heard of Rigby's " bed-fellow's " ring, lost near Whalley. Robert Ouldfield " the bell-founder," who lives in Preston, found it, and offered to "pawne it " in Whalley.

Ellen Bent to George Rigby, at Peel.

170. 1638, December 31. Hulme.—" Since my beinge with you, I received a precept from Mr. Hughe Rigby, the escheator, for the findinge out of an office, after my husbands death ; the tyme is verie short, beinge upon the 16th of Januarie next, to be sitten at Boulton. And nowe, you beinge absent (on whome I onlie relyed) I am forced to write unto you desiringe your answer and advice herein. You knowe good cosin, how farr unable and unfitt I am for such a busines, and therefore in this extremitie, must crave your helpe and other of my friends. Yett your judicious understandinge and helpe herein, I most wish ; wherefore, I humblie intreate your best assistance herein and your advise, by waie of your letter, what to doe in the meane tyme." *Seal of arms.*

" A brief Note of Remembrance for the Lord's Prerogative in the Isle of Man."

171. 1638.—As to the dower which Ann, Countess Dowager of Derby, claimed in the said Island. It was agreed that the Island formed no part of the realm of England, and therefore the Council had no jurisdiction.

Organist of Prescot Church.

172. 1639, April 16.—Order by J: Aldem, the vicar of Prescot, and the eight men of the Chappelry of Farnworth, to increase the salary of Mr. Parker, organist of Prescot parish church, from 6*li.* 13*s.* 4*d.*, to 8*li.* *Copy.* [*An increase to* 12*l. is granted in* 1747 *to William Banister, the then organist.*]

Urian Rigby to George Rigby, at Peel.

173. 1640, June 29. Gray's Inn. —" There is little news, except that Lord Lowden is released and is created an Earl ; some hope that thereupon will follow a " composition of Scottish mattors."

Roger Rogerson to George Rigby.

174. 1640, June 30. Manchester.—"I have perused Rastall's inven
. . . owne parenthesis, but I find by the Statutes att Large . . . .
from the Parliament Rowle, the Sessions ought to bee . . . . weeke
after the Translation of St. Thomas the Martyr, which . . . . whom
I beleeve, saith is 3 July; for I am very . . . . . . that Thomas
Beckett was, nor is, adjudged a martyr ac[cording] to the Church of
England. However, Lambert saith no . . . . . but, accordinge to
the Statute, limitts noe day. Thus much I thought fitt to certifie you,
leavinge it to your consideration."

Alexander Rigby to his brother, George Rigby, at Peel.

175. 1640, July 6. Preston.—Last term, one Mr. Yssherwood, "a great
acquayntance and familiar of Mr. ——— Cheeteham," happened to be
in the writer's chamber in Gray's Inn, "where fynding my eldest soone,
he tould him that Mr. Cheeteham had a neece who kept his house, and
to whom he intended much preferment, and wished there might be a
match betweene my sonne and her." Desires to know what preferment
Mr. Cheeteham will bestow; whether, failing issue of his own, he will
settle Clayton, or some other estate, upon her. "You may make knowne
unto him my sonne's education and demeanour hitherto, which (I hope)
promiseth noe worse hereafter; and for his person, you may referre him
to this Yssherwood's relation, who did see him at London . . . . . .
I hear a good report of the young woman, and that her person also is commendable." Is ready to meet and treat with Mr. Cheeteham; "if upon
our interview there shalbe cause, I shall send for my sonne from
Graye's Inn, where now he is, and where I have left him to study the
law . . . . . I pray you, if you happen to see the young woman, to
write to me what her [face] is, for if it be not pleasing, I will not
urge my sonne unto her, though preferment may come by her."

Alexander Rigby to George Rigby, at Wigan.

176. 1640, October 13.*—"I pray you to procure Mr. Ashton of
Midleton and some other gentlemen of qualitie, my good frends, who will
be this day in towne, to goe to Mr. Maior of Wigan, and first, in a frendly
manner to require him to give unto my brother Mawdesley, or to some
other whom you and he shall thincke fitt, three dayes warning at the
least, of the tyme of the election of the burgesses of the Parliament, to
the end they may have notice and be present at the election. And if
he will not consent or promise soe to doe in curtesy, then let them signifie
to him that it is his duty, that if he doe otherwise they will appeale to
the Parliament house for justice; but let this be soe caried, that I may
not appeare in this course, but that it may be solelie their owne acte
. . . . . I pray you to put Mr. Ashton in mynd to send the warrant
to Wigan for me, but I fear that Richard Worseley will prevent it."

Alexander Rigby to George Rigby, at Peel.

177. 1640, October 23. Preston.—The election of burgesses will be
on the following Monday, at eight o'clock in the morning, "when I
desyre, and doubt not, of your assistance." *Seal of arms.*

---

* Date of receipt.

ROBERT OWEN to GEORGE RIGBY, at Peel.

178. 1640, October 24. Trafford.—Encloses the Justices' order for estreating 20 marks on the inhabitants of Manchester, for repair of the highway in Stretford. Desires that he will duly "issue out the estreat," and direct it to the high constables for levying it. *Seal.*

ALEXANDER RIGBY to his brother, GEORGE RIGBY, at Peel, to be left "with MR. HALLIWELL at the signe of the Bull's Head in Manchester."

179. 1640, November 10. Gray's Inn.—"The Parliament has ordered for disarming recusants and banishing them tenne myles from London; and all projectors shalbe expelled the House of Commons." Burton, Baswick, and others, are "to follow their own complaints" in person. "Great matters are expected." Some projectors give up their patents voluntarily. "Sope is falle 2*d.* in 5*d.*" Lord Cottington, it is said, has given up his patent of lieutenancy of the Tower and the Ordnance. *Seal of arms, broken.*

GEORGE PIGOT to GEORGE RIGBY, Clerk of the Peace for Lancashire, at Peel.

180. 1640, November 17. Staple Inn.—Hears that Joseph Rigby will be Under-Sheriff to Mr. Egerton. "Sir George Radcliffe is sent for by the Parliament House. A generall fast is commanded this daie for London, this daie fortnight for the countrie. The papists are, by proclamation restrayned 10 miles from the King's, Queen's, and Prince's Courts, and confined to abide within 5 miles of their homes; and their armes to bee seized. There is noe danger or expectation of alteringe anie elections for Lancashire. The Scots are comne, but have done nothinge as yet." *Seal, broken.*

RALPH ASSHETON and ROGER KIRKBY to GEORGE RIGBY, Clerk of the Peace for the County Palatine of Lancaster.

181. 1640, December 8.—Enclosing, by direction of the House of Commons, an order, whereby it is desired that especial care be taken for indicting all the Popish recusants within the County of Lancaster, that have not already been indicted and convicted. *Signed and seal.*

THOMAS DICKONSON to [GEORGE RIGBY].

182. 1640, December 13. "Goosnargh."—This is to let you understand that my daughter Elizabeth is in the way of marriage unto a young tailor, and I humbly intreat your worship's favour that you would consent unto this match, and I will rest obliged unto you so long as I live; also that you will be pleased to let them have this house and ground, as I have, doing you what service they can to the utmost of their poor powers.

ALEXANDER RIGBY to GEORGE RIGBY.

183. 1640, December 23. Gray's Inn.—"Wee in the House of Commons, have voted ship money unlawfull, and made a Committee for taking petitions of persons complaining against Sheriffs &c. and we are ready to transmit that vote to the Lords. Wee have also the canons illegall and that none of the King's subjects shalbe bound thereby. Secretary Windebancke is fledd out of the Kingdome. The examinations against the Earle of Straford are almost perfected. The Archbishop is, by the House of Commons, accused of high treason and thereupon stands committed. Bishop . . . goeth under baile to abyde the judgment of Parliament. The Lord Keeper is likely, within these two dayes, to be charged with treason, and the principall cause of his charge is his soliciting, urgeing, and procuring, and advance[ing] the busynes of shipmoney and the opini[ons] and judgements thereupon. This weeke our house receyved a petition from about fifteen thousand Londoners and some others, for the abolishing of bushops. Monopolies goe downe apace. Wee are aboute, with the King's allowance already had, to take into consideration the King's expences and revenew, and to settle him a meete supply, which now wilbe necessary upon the abolishment of . . . . We have a faire correspondence in Parliament both betweene us and the Lords and the King and both.

"There is also noe doubt, as I conceyve, of a happy yssue of the treaty between our English Commissioners and the Scottes Commissioners now at London, and wee trust to see a settlement both of our religion and peace, with the punishment of offenders and reformation of greevances, which had almost made a deluge of the whole kindome."

Postscript.—"The Archbishop is, by the House of Commons, accused of high treason and stands committed by the Lords' house.

"Pim and Burton weare accompanyed into the towne with many score of coaches and many thousand of men, both horse and foote, and so lykewyse was Bastwicke.

"The Lord Keeper was accused of high treason by the House of Commons and is fledd away. The judges Bramston, Davenport, Crawley, Bartley, Treavor, and Weston, are under baile to abide the judgment of Parliament. Their crime is not yet voted." *Seal of arms.*

Ralph Assheton to George Rigby.

184. 1640, December 25.—I hope you received from me and Mr. Kirkby, by the hands of Cousin Preston, of Holcar, a letter, wherein was enclosed an order of the House of Commons, whereby we were required, as knights of the shire, to signify to the justices of the peace, within the county for which we serve, that it is required that all recusants within the said county should be indicted at the Sessions of the Peace to be held after Christmas; to the end they might be convicted and further dealt withall, as the law in such cases requires. *Seal.*

Thomas Worsley to George Rigby.

185. 1640[-1], January 27.—Desiring to know how it is that he, his wife, son, and daughter, are presented for not going to church. Whether there is a distinction between them and papists. Hopes he may not come into the Parliament House under the name of papist. Wishes for the same information regarding Thomas Harwood, of Manchester.

Richard (?) Radcliffe to George Rigby.

186. 1640[-1], March 5. Todmerden.—"Your brother in London, when the business was in agitation in the House of Commons, concerning the two last subsidies, took occasion to say our hearts go one way, and our tongues another. Whereupon they cried: 'to the bar with him.'

He desired he might be heard forth first, which being granted, his speech was approved, and all was right. "He keepeth the chair for three of the greatest Committees—the Star Chamber, the Council Board, and the High Commission. The great business of the Earl of Strafford possesseth the Upper House so much, as no business goeth on there. He was there on Wednesday was sennight, where the King and Prince were. It is too long to relate all passages. He hangeth equally in the balance of men's opinions, whether he shall die or live. Now he begins to impeach great ones of High Treason, and shortly, no doubt, we shall have great news. I did go to see Sir George Radcliffe in the Gatehouse; he seems to be very hearty and was glad to see me. All I can imagine is, that my Lord of Strafford is the tree and he a bough of the tree. If the tree fall the bough is like to go with it." *Seal.*

Raising of Troops.

187. 1642, May 28.—A Proclamation to suppress the raising of troops by any warrant, commission, or order from his Majesty, without the advice and consent of the Lords and Commons in Parliament.

Laws of War.

188. 1642, September.—MS. Copy of a book—described as " Printed for John Partridge and John Rothwell "—entitled "Lawes and Ordinances of Warre, established for the better conduct of the Army by his Excelency, the Earle of Essex." Which " lawes and ordinances hereby published, all the said persons, respectively and severally, are required and commanded to observe and keepe, on the paines and penalties therein expressed."

Protection for Traitors.

189. 1642[-3], January 12.—A Declaration of the Lords and Commons assembled in Parliament, for the protection of Sir William Brereton, in the County of Chester, who hath lately been proclaimed a traitor by his Majesty.

Robert Duckenfeild to George Rigby.

190. 1643[-4], January 9. Stockport.—I have received your letter, concerning the exchange of your brother Hulton. Sir William Brereton is now gone to meet Sir Thomas Fairfax, and the passage is " something dangerous." *Seal, broken.*

Anne Neild to George Rigby, Clerk of the Peace for Lancashire, at Peel.

191. 1643[-4], January 13.—Is sorry that " Captaine Hilton, your brother-in-lawe," is now prisoner at Chester. The friendship between her late husband, Robert Neild, and George Rigby, and her love and respect for Mrs. Hilton, her " land-lady," induce her to use what means she can, to effect Captain Hilton's release, " in way of exchange for one Mr. Browne, a minister, now prisoner at Manchester." She desires " your brother, Colonell Rigby's, his letter, or some other frende's letter, to our gentlemen at Manchester, for their favour and consent therein."

CAPTAIN J. MARKLAND to GEORGE RIGBY.

192. 1643[-4], January 18 [date of receipt]. Barton.—I wonder very much you should unhorse my men at your pleasure, and take their horses from them, when I have the greatest need of them. I would request you that, with all speed, you send me my horse, rider, and arms, and to come to our rendezvous, where they shall be, towards Knutsford, or Nantwich, or elsewhere. *Seal, broken.*

CONTRIBUTIONS FOR POWDER AND SHOT.

193. 1643[-4], January 25.—A note of accounts concerning ten pounds agreed to be collected within the three Hultons for the provision of powder, match, colours, and other things for the use of the inhabitants, in 1642 ; commences :—" Paid to Henry Hindley for powder, matche, colours, and other thinges for the use of the inhabitants within the three Hultons, 8*l.* 10*s.* 4½*d.*"

Note. " That there is remayninge in the custody of Ellis Macond, threescore poundes of leade, belonging to the inhabitants of the said 3 hamells, which is agreed to be devyded into three partes ; and twenty poundes thereof is to bee delivered to the corporall within every hamell."

K. LL[OYD] to her husband, LUKE LLOYD, at London.

194. 1643[-4], February 3.—" I prayes God we in this family and all the rest of friends are in good health ; wee in the same condition you left us, or better, nothing wanting but thyselfe, which is more prised then all the rest, and I hope ere long toe injoy. Tom is at the Dungre, my sister Ellin at Geaton, Brereton's army within 3 myels of Chester. The Lord Berron's army in Chester, and from Banger toe Harden, where there is greate feare. This weeke there are garisons put in Feneshall and Bettisfeeld. Wee expect more toe Hanmer. They are of those men that come from Ireland, that turned when they where taken prisonnors at the Withe. I sent to the Widow Wenlock, who was very glad to hear of her sonns helth. Shee dare not write, but desired that I would remember her love toe him and certifie him that all his frends are in helth. William Genings is very ernest with me that hee may red [rent] some corner of a feild that has much brome groing upon it. Hee would soe a bushell of ots, hee tells mee ; it will take no more. My promise was toe certifie you and toe returne him your answere, which I desire to have with what speed you can. Thomas Roe questions your man, when I send him for your rent, whether I have commission toe receve it. I desire hee may bee satisfied in a line or toow, for it comes very sloly from him. 1 long much toe hear of thy resolution, which I hope will bee toe goe noe further nor toe alter thy condition any way. I hope there will bee noe cause for it. However, as thou tenders the life of thy poore desolate wife, goe noe further from her. Thou knowest the condition thou left me in, and if thou goe any further I shall dispare of ever seeing thee. Therefore desire, love, let mee heare that thy resolution is toe stay wher thou art. I hope it will bee but a short time. Doe not think I doubt of God's alsufficience, for I have dayly experience of his delivering and forbearing mercies unto mee all my life thorow, and especially of late dayes, but if you goe further you must pas a great deale of danger, soe must I, beefore wee can meet againe." *Seal.*

[JOHN HULTON] to CAPTAIN GEORGE RIGBY, at Peel.

195. 1643[-4], February 12. Darley.—"I would not have been so long absent from you, but that my old adversary, the gout, hath so violently seized upon me, that I am not able to rise to my horse : and let me thus far retain your good opinion, as to think I am not so unmindful of yourself, or the service, as to have been thus long in making ready a man and a musket, had it been my part to have one. But William Morres is, by order of the Colonels and Commanders of this country, to make it good, because of his wilful and base miscarriage of the other. I have not 10s., nor cannot make shift thereof, having nothing to sell that will bring money. For corn, I have none, nor had none growing the last year, and, God knows sir, I make hard and strange shifts to get some reasonable quantity of bread and drink. So that I am altogether unable to make another man and musket, for manservant I have none; and the last man living upon my land, that was able to bear arms, is with Captain Hulton's company, and men ask 40s. at the least to bear arms; and the cost of arms will be near a pound. Take me therefore into your pitifull consideration." *Portion of seal of arms.*

INVENTORY OF GOODS.

196. 1644, May 13.—An inventory of the goods and chattels of George Rigbye, gentleman, deceased, taken and prised at Peele.

LUKE LLOYD [to his wife,] at Brynn in Hanmer parish.

197. 1644, June 13. "Wassall."—"When thy foote poste came to me, we weare preparing to defend ourselves and had no tyme to write to thee, for the enemy appeared then to us in very greate body, and we raysinge the seege and preparinge for our march towards Stafford. Thy foote poste I hasted away, where, at Stafford, she arrived with many run-awaies of horse that reported to the Governor there wee weare all lost men. Truly had not God fought for us, it had bin so, for they weare by the confession of those prisoners wee tooke, betwixt 4 or 5 thousand stronge, and we not 2000. They fell upon our reare before we could begin to march, onely our forelorne advanced. They assaulted us a quarter of a mile this side the leager with such fury that had not our men behaved themselves very galantly, we had bin utterly defeated, but they were encountered so sharply that they weare faine to retreate towards the Castell and weare so hansomely beaten they had no mynd to come on againe. We slew aboute 30 of ther men, whereof some of note, and one they wished his Majestie had bin killed rather then he (you may perceive by this ther love to his Majestie) and very many ill wounded, and dangerously. All the flower and the greatest parte of the Kinges forces weare in this body. Ther was the King's Generall of Horse, the Lord Willmott and the Earle of Cleveland. The Kinge and the poore remainder of his forces is at Worcester, where Sir William Waller is advansinge. Sir William, heringe of the enemy cominge to rayse our seige, sent 2000 horse to our releife, which came not till the next morninge. Had they come in tyme, by God's helpe we had given the enemy a great defeate ; but not knowing of ther cominge, we durst not pursue them, we being so inconsiderable in strength, the place affordinge the enemy many advantages. I shall give a further account when I see thee, or by letter, when we come to Namptwich." *Portion of seal.*

LUKE LLOYD [to his wife].

198. 1644, July 3.—" It hath pleased God to give us a victory over our enemies, which mett with us betwixt Francons Oake and Whittington. They assaulted us at first very furiously, but weare quickly beaten back and put to flight. We killed of ther mene about forty, and some of them proper hansom men and very well clad, which are conceived to be in comaund. We lost only three, who of one was Captain Williams. We tooke 207(?) prisoners—the Lord Newport's eldest sonn beinge one, 3 Captaines, besides inferior officers. Of all these, ther is not one of my acquaintance. I here my brother Roger was here, who is made Lieutenant Colonel under Sir Edward Crane. My Lord of Denbigh is come to us with his forces, which, had he come tyme enough, in all lickyhood we had taken most of them. Both Armies meet tomorrow and goeth on some designe."

LETTERS OF PROTECTION.

199. 1644, July 15. Preston.—Letters of protection, signed by Prince Rupert, to Jane Kenion, of Parkhead, in the County of Lancaster, widow, for her person, goods, and family.

ALEXANDER RIGBY to ———.

200. 1648, July 18. Salford.—Requesting advice as to how his two nieces shall be lodged.

ALEXANDER RIGBY to SAVILE RATCLIFFE, at Meereley.

201. 1648, July 21. Salford.—As to placing his (Rigby's) neices at school with Mrs. Amye, at Manchester, "who hath the tuition of many children of rank and quality, far before my neices," a woman well descended, religious, modest, and discreet. Yesterday she called with one of her children, a daughter of Mrs. Fleetwood, of Rossall, "a child, to my view, of fine behaviour"; she said that, "if my neices might be with her in her own house, she would then take the charge of them, and they should want no attendance, nor any necessaries of meat, drink, lodging, fuel, washing, and candle light, and she would bring them up with reading and all manner of sewing"; for all which, she expected yearly, 11*li.* apiece, and will not put them to the charge of bringing a maid with them. She, "at fit seasons, employeth a scrivener to teach the children to write, and a dancing master to teach them to dance, and a musician to learn them music. The charge of the scrivener is small; the charge of the musician is forty shillings yearly, for each child, and the charge of the dancing master is, for every child, five shillings at her entry, and five shillings for every month wherein he is employed." *Seal.*

THE LORD PROTECTOR'S REGIMENT.

202. 1653[-4], March 10.—Bond given by Edmund Knott, of Knott Laine, in the parish of Ashton-under-Lyne, yeoman, to Stephen Shallcrosse, gunsmith to his Highness the Lord Protector's regiment of foot, for the sum of 1000*li.*, upon security of the accounts of seventy-five auxiliary soldiers and nineteen supernumeraries. Attached is a list of the same soldiers, with the amounts of their accounts. *Seal of arms.*

CLERK OF THE PEACE.

203. 1654, April 4.—Proceedings at the General Sessions of the Peace held at Lancaster, touching an alleged contempt, by Mr. Joseph Rigby, of the Lord Protector's order to deliver the books concerning the office of Clerk of the Peace for the County, to William Shuttleworth.

THE DUCHY COURT.

204. [1654 ?]—The Petition of divers gentlemen, freeholders, and other inhabitants of the County Palatine of Lancaster, to Oliver Lord Protector, to re-invest the Court of the Duchy Chamber at Westminster, and the County Palatine, with their proper jurisdictions and rights, with the exercise thereof, as formerly. The petition sets out that the discontinuance of the Duchy Court, for near two years, has drawn great prejudice on some of the petitioners' estates. Some causes depending there, after long prosecution, being undetermined; and the commencement of others, upon just emergency, obstructed, there being no way for relief upon new equitable causes, but in the Chancery Court within the County.

Annexed:—Considerations concerning the Court of the Duchy Chamber at Westminster, setting out its history and jurisdiction.

HENRY JOHNSON and WILLIAM MILWARD to WILLIAM BECK and WILLIAM CROXTON, at Lisbon.

205. 1655, October 24. Faro.—" Sirs and loveinge friends, wee have yours of the 14th current, where we observe your reseite of some letters from Mr. William Moy, for the providing of 30 to 40 pipes of oyles, against the ariveal of the *Ann* pincke, at prise current, which wee shall endeavour forthwith to put in execution, so neere as we may, beinge now about buying up what oyles are in the course, having orders for greater quantities then these parts can afford ; but of what we buy, we shall reserve a shaire of them for [the] said Mr. Moy, taking notise you will furnish their cost. Concerning figgs, they may stand in 24 *reis* (?) *per* quarter, all. Considerable parcells are already bought up, and sea shippes are daily . . . . . . the North, upon whose arrival, what figgs unsold will soone be desposed of ; and we suppose some may want to lade, which is what offers. [We] commit you to God and rest yours at command."

MICHAEL TOUNESEND to MR. WILLIAM BECKE and MR. WILLIAM CROXTON.

206. 1655, December 25. Oporto.—" Yours of the 18th currant, [I] have receaved, and therein note you will accept my brother's bills from the Ilands . . . . . . Wee have had many holydays and extreme foul weather; however, wee have got neere the halfe of the French shipps' wheate ashore, butt, as yett, noe *abertura* taken out from the chamber, nor an *alquer* sould ; being *festa,* the marriners brought a little betwixt deckes and sould it at 180 *reis* an *alquer.*" Prospects of trade and state of prices.

DUELS.

207. 1656, June 29.—Ordinance against challenges, duels, and all provocations thereof.

E

LEWIS ASSHETON to his "loving brother MR. WILLIAM LANGLEY, minister of God's [wor]d, at Cheadle in Staffordshire."

208. 1656–7, January 8. "Jamica, America."—"To you as one of my cheifest patrons, I direct these, as to your manifest and constant care both for my self, and the rest of us, since my father's death, I shall ever acknowledge, doubting not, but you will discharg the like trust I im. posed on you (since last I saw you) in reference to my self. At my departure from St. James, I assigned a bill to impower you and cousin Roger Kenyon, jointly or severally, to receave my 100*l.* Sister Elizabeth her 20*l.*, I question not by this time paid out of my 10*l.* per annum. You cannot be ignorant, I suppose, of the cause I left both friends and country, my livelyhood and subsistance being, as I conceived, something, or rather, far, beneath my self, haveing that respect towards our family and kindred, I chose rather to want abroad then to live meanly at home. This duly considered, I hope no true friend can blame me for undertaking this voyage, though some advised me other. wise. I was, in my sickness, really intended for England, but since it hath pleased God to restore mee againe my health, I am now otherwise resolved. Having with myself consideratly advised for a future competent subsistence, I have bethought and resolved on the onely way (considering the place I am now in) to improve part of my small patrimony, 50*l.*, whereof I am willing to hazard (nothing venture nothing have) to be converted into servants; the hazard thereof onely lieth on the health of servants when they are come hither; which, if they live together, with God's blessing on my endeavours, I doubt not but in 3 or 4 years tyme, I shall raise a considerable fortune. Tis true, live I can (I praise God) in this condition now I am in, without a penny from my own; but having through some miseries, arrived at these years that now I am at, I conceive every day misspent wherein I can neither benefitt myself nor others; and being in this condition now I am in, incapable of serving either, and to enslave myself to a bear lively-boode to preserve my own (for whom I know not) I understand not, being now in a probable way to employ it.

" I have entrusted one sufficient to be responsible, if it were ten tymes the sum, who is bound for England on the same scoare for himself, and is pleased to agitate my business with his own, which I must acknowledge as a great and speciall favor, a gentleman whom I am confident in that case will doe for mee, as himself. It is Colonel Phillip Ward, my own Colonel and immediate officer, who hath pleased to honour mee with the charg and command of his own company, and, in his absence, likewise doth entrust mee with the managing of his own plantation, I immagine, by this time, sister Elizabeth's porcon to bee receaved and part likewise of my own, which, if not, whether shee or yourself disburse the 50*l.*, I shall, for soe doeing, allow my 10*l.* per annum, untill my 100*l.* bee receaved, which is to succeed here next in payment; the addition to my porcion by Brother William's death, makes me more venturous. In my next, which I intend (God willing) to send with my Colonel, I shall insert instructions sufficient, where your letter with a bill enclosed, may find him in London, wherein you may appoint him where to receave the moneys, which I suppose may bee either from Mr. Taylor, a silk man, where I received 20*l.* on Major Smith's bill, or els from Cozen Worsley. These I hope may suffice to acquaint you of my resolutions."

THOMAS CUNLIFFE to ROGER KENYON, at Peel.

209. 1658, May 8. London:—Has sent the "paire of tables" so often promised. They cost him 35s.; "the sett of ivory and ibbony men, 10s.; the locke, 18d.; the baile of dice, 6d.; the case 'and makinge, 3s."

EDWARD KENYON to his brother, ROGER KENYON, "at MRS. WORSLEY'S lodgings in St. James's near Westminster."

210. 1658, June 30. St. John's College, Cambridge.—"If I stay at Sladeburne, I resolve to weare a goune, but I think it will not be convenient to carry one downe at first; and, therefore, I defer mine to buy a coate heare, as you direct " . . . . . I must quite fall out with Mr. Ashden (?), if I goe by Oxford . . ... . It will goe hard, perhaps, to get past Manchester; but, if gout secure me from preaching on the Lord's Day, I will bee wholly at your disposal."

HENRY WRIGLEY (?) and THOMAS BROWN, High Constables, to the CONSTABLES OF THE THREE HULTONS.

211. 1660, April 4.—Directing them to value the estates of every person within their constabulary who has estates in lands and tenements worth 15li. by the year, and upwards, and in goods and personal estates, worth 200li., and upwards; for the settlement of the militia.

EDWARD KENYON to his mother, ALICE KENYON.

212. 1660, May 4. London.—"God hath been pleased to put a ready issue to our business about Prestwich. The Commissioners having heard Councell on both sides, were fully satisfied with my patron's right, and proceeded to make tryall of my fitnesse for the ministry; and thereupon did approve of mee and give me the instrument." Desires that care may be taken of the pulpit till he comes down. Wishes " to table " with some one. *Fragment of seal.*

W. HUTTON to ROGER KENYON, at Peel.

213. 1660, September 11. [London.]—" For news here, the Parliament adjourns this day and divers acts to pass, one for Ministers, who, if they receive any good thereby, they owe it to His Majesty and the House of Commons only; and an Act for disbanding the army, which must be paid with pole money. I presume you have the Act for pole money, which has so puzzled all the Commissioners here, that they know not how to proceed in it. But I thinke the best and surest way for such as are to pay money, is to pay it for the land where it lyeth, and take acquittance. The rate in the act is 2l. per cent. I desire you will doe me the favour to send for Don and advise him to pay for Hulton, according to the rate of fourty shillings for 100l. per annum : and when he has done, to send me the acquittance and what is to be paid for the degree; I will doe it myself. I suppose you heare that peace is proclaimed with Spaine, and Dunkirk and Jamaica united, by Act of Parliament, to the Crowne of England." *Fragment of seal.*

RICHARD HAWORTH to ROGER KENYON, at Peel.

214. 1660, November 15. Manchester.—"I conceave that the sheriffs of Cheshyre will not execute your attachment, and therefore it wilbe in vayne to send to him agayne. I know no law that attachments ought to be directed to him, nor to our sheriff of Lancashyre; onely common practise and custom hath in that kind prevayled with us in Lancashyre, that attachments are immediately directed to the sheriffs, for the King's writts run not in county palatynes, but where some statute hath ordeyned it, as that of 1 Edward VI. and 6 Edward VI. which directs proclamations uppon *exegent* to be made to the sheriffs of Lancashyre and Cheshyre. For other writs, they are to be directed to the Chauncellor or Chamberlayne, as the case requyres." *Seal of arms, broken.*

CHARLES PARKER to MR. KENYON.

215. 1660, December 22. London.—Our news is very little; the Princess Royal of Orange is sick of the small pox; our late plot, I suppose, is sufficiently, by this time, made known to you by the pamphlets; and so I will not trouble you with a long rehearsal. *Seal of arms.*

TREASON.

216. 1660.—"Treasons by the Laws of England." Printed by Roger Norton for Robert Pawley.

ADDRESS of the JUSTICES and GRAND JURORS of LANCASHIRE.

217. [1660?]—"The humble addresse of your Majestie's Justices of the Peace and Grand Jurors at their Quarter Sessions of the Peace, in the County Palatine of Lancaster, whose names are subscribed, on behalfe of ourselves and many other of our countrymen."

"We, may it please your Majestie, through the variouse accidents and prudent dispensations of your Majestie's graciouse governement, have ever thought a silent acquiestence most becomeing our allegeance, and most acceptable to your Majestie's desires; and therefore, in this busie age, wee have neither been troblesome petitioners, nor presumed to intermedle beyond the limitts of our lowe station. But now, since your Majesty gives gracious accesses to papers of this nature, that our silence may not reproach us, as men voyd of dutie and unfaigned loyalltie, wee presume upon your royall goodnesse, to give us leave to declare that wee, with greatest truth and satisfaction of mind, do owne the mercies of divine providence in restoreing your Majestie, our lawfull and rightfull prince, to rule and governe us. That by all the obligations of clemencie, grace, and compassion, we have cause to blesse God, and thanke your Majesty for the terdernesse you have shewn to all your subjects in your gratious distribution of justice, and care of your kingdomes. That by your repeated promises and assurances in your late declaration and frequent speeches in Parliament, you have published your stedfastnes to mainteine the protestant religion, as now by law established; for which you have our most humble, heartie, and thankfullest acknowledgement." *Draft.*

HEATON CHAPEL.

218. 1661, July 3.—Acknowledgement, by the Churchwardens and parishioners of Prestwich, that a chapel, commonly called Heaton

Chapel, on the north side of the chancel of the parish Church of Prestwich, and to the east end of the said Church, belongs to Richard Holland, of Heaton. In which chapel Edward Holland, late of Heaton, father of the said Richard, and Anne Holland, mother of the said Richard, Richard Holland, uncle of the said Richard, and several brothers of the said Richard, and all his ancestors, lords of Heaton, and their wives and children, have been interred. And many of them have had their " cote armor and penyons, with their armes, and herses belonging to their degrees," set up in the said chapel. And there is yet an ancient gravestone laid within the said chapel, under which Sir Richard Holland, knight, was interred on 29 March, 1548, as appears by an inscription thereupon yet legible. *Copy.*

[THOMAS CUNLIFFE ?] to ——— KENYON.

219. 1661, August 5.   London.—"Mr. Aynesworthe hath lighted upon a master for his cousin Nowell, an able apothecary as any in London. Had I a son of my own to put out, I should as soon put him unto him as any man I know of that trade, in London ; but he cannot be prevailed to take him, under 40*li.*, and a suit, and a cloak presently, and another suit and cloak at Easter."

HENRY NOWELL to ROGER KENYON, at Peel.

220. [16]61, August 13.   Castle Rushen, [Isle of Man].—" I have sent my wench, and your wife, a barril of samphere, that when you are eating a peece of fatt mutton, with the sause, you may remember to drinke my health." *Fragment of seal.*

E. HYDE to JOHN AINSWORTH.

221. 1661, August 31.—I must intreat a favour of you, it is to go as far as " Worchester House " and inquire for Mr. Bulteale, some call him Mr. Boteale, and give him five pounds for me—he is one of my Lord Chancellor's privy secretaries—as a remembrance for me, and wish him to endeavour for a dispatch of my affair ; and give Mr. Hales twenty shillings, as a remembrance of love for me.   So when my business is perfected, I will farther repay you. *Seal of arms.*

THE CLERKSHIP OF THE PEACE for LANCASHIRE.

222. 1661[-2], February.—Papers in the suit of Roger Kenyon, and Alice his wife, against Joseph Rigby, and others, concerning the office of Clerk of the Peace for the County of Lancaster.

HENRY NOWELL to " his approved good friend MR. ROGER KENYON, at Peel."

223. 1662, April 12.   Castle Rushen.—" Mr. William Christian hath brought mee the worst newes that I ever heard in my life : hee tells mee that Joseph Rigby and you, had a triall at Lancaster 'sises, and that he cast you in the sute.   I am veri confident it was by desparate oaths.   I doubt not, as ould as I am, but to here of as untimelie an end to come upon either him or his, as ever came uppon' any, for I know God is a just God and will punesh according to desarts, in His own good time ; till then, both you and wee must be contented.   I shall earnestly desier to here of all the passages by my man, for I intend to send him verie shortly for England. I know you will be coustrened to sell something, which, if I might advise, I would have yourself either Peele or Parkheade. The reason 'tis, they will give you some monie twords setting you free of debt. If you should sell Fearehurst, I know you will not sell it for the half worth and I am sure, if it please God ever to enable you to build a house there, you might live as contentedly as you desired." *Seal of arms.*

HENRY NOWELL to ROGER KENYON.

224. 1662, October 7. Castle Rushen.—"Since my comeing, by order from my Lord, I have clapt upp the greate rebbell, Mr. William Christian, who is like to come uppon triall for his life; and, by the lawes of this land, will bee cast, without my Lord bee pleased, of his goodnesse, to give him his pardon." *Seal of arms, broken.*

WILLIAM MOORE to ROGER KENYON.

225. 1662, November 20. Whalley.—Requesting him to hand the Bishop of London a petition for a "presentment," as the "Oliverian title," notwithstanding the Act of Confirmation, is not approved of. Points out that he represented Dr. Ferne at his instalment as Bishop [of Chester]; that he preached a coronation sermon at Chester, with such applause that it was desired for the press, and is now in the hands of my Lord of London's chaplain; that he preached at the "Metropoliticall visitation," and there received a general license through the whole province; and that he had been "listed" a chaplain to the Earl of Derby. *Seal.*

The EARL OF DERBY and ROGER NOWELL to FRANCIS LORD SEYMOUR of Trowbridge, Chancellor of the Duchy of Lancaster.

226. 1662[-3], January 9. Preston.—"At the request of Mr. Roger Kenyon, who hath been sollititous with me, and my Governor of the Isle of Man, Colonell Nowell, to give leave to Captain Henry Nowell, Deputy-Governor of the said Island, now resident there, to come over into England to bee at the next assizes at Lancaster, as a materiall witnesse for him the said Kenyon, in a suite there depending, by your Lordships order, betwixt him and Mr. Joseph Rigby : Wee certify your Lordship that such and so generall are the concerns of the said Captain Nowell's truste in that Island, (they being chiefly at present placed upon him) that upon no particular occasion whatsoever, his comeing over into England so soone, may be consented to by us." *Signed. Seal of arms, broken.*

THOMAS GREGSON to ROGER KENYON, at "the Peele."

227. 1663, May 30. Gray's Inn.—"Nothing of news, save that I heare even now my Lord of Canterbury is dead, and my Lord Cheife Justice Bridgeman much feared. . . . . . The Duchy Court sate this day, but nothing passed worth your observance."

The SAME to the SAME.

228. 1663, June 6. Gray's Inn.—"I writt in my last, that the Archbishop of Canterbury was dead, which was a false report. I heard but now, 'tis so indeed. I thinke on Tuesday last he dyed." *Seal, broken.*

THOMAS GREGSON to ROGER KENYON, at 'Peel.'

229. 1663, July 14.—" Your portmantua, I sent by a very trusty porter which belongs to the Mayden." It is sent by one Chandler, a Manchester carrier. "The court, by reason of the grand business concerning the Lord Chancellor, hath not as yet sitten."

GUICCIARDINI AYLOFF to ROGER KENYON.

230. 1663, September 6. Marlborough.—I présume, at the Assizes, you heard of the King and Queen going to the Bath; and the Vice-Chancellor, if he received my letter, was able to tell you that both their Majesties gave my Lord's house the honour to lodge one night in it, and both they and the Duke and Duchess of York, to take such a treat at a supper, as could be provided. They removed to Bathe the Saturday; and upon Monday after, my Lord Chancellor, his lady, and his train, came and stayed with us till the Wednesday following. Since the Court has been at Bath, the King has been feasted at several places, and is now at Bristol. The Queen, they say, has spent her time in physic, preparatory to bathing, and has scarce; or not above once or twice, used the bath as yet. We all pray for a good effect. It is said the King will return by Oxford. *Seal of arms.*

HENRY NOWELL to ROGER KENYON, Clerk of the Peace, at Peel.

231. 1663, October 18. Bradkirk.—" I dare not come to Winckley, for I am informed that the Christians are moving, the King and his Counsell to send for me upp to London and know the reason why I am not gone for the Ileland, but I hope I shall prevent them; so I have written to Mr. Roger, if he will please to look after it and, if occasion be, I will send him a certificate under the hands of the gentlemen in this countie, that I have been this 5 weekes and above, at the water side, and a vessel tending me to goe for the Ileland." *Seal of arms.*

[THOMAS BRADDYLL to ROGER KENYON.]

232. [1663–1665].—" As to my subscription money for the Borrough of Cliderow, I hope you are certified, from Mr. Arthur Ashton and Edmond Robinson, that it is payed, and have received a seal in wax, viz:—my coat and crest, to be cut upon the mace, amongst others; the crest, I confesse, is something dun (*sic*); it is the badger or brock, but the coat playn enough; only this, if you discerne anie thing of a halfe moon in it, which is the distinction belonging to a younger brother of a family, you wilbe pleased to get it omitted in the cutting."

WIGAN.

233. 1663 to 1698.—A list of the Mayors and Burgesses of Wigan.

HENRY NOWELL to ROGER KENYON, "Clerke of the Peace," at Peele.

234. [16]63[-4], March 1. "Castle Rushen". [Isle of Man].—" Never since I left England that it hath beene my good fortune to receive soe much as one line from any of my friends . . . . I must tell you something of my wordlie fortune, which hath happened unto me this last yeare. Now, when I come to cast up my accounts with my man, I have lost twentie pounds by my tradeing; my wine proving soe bad that, if hee had not been careful, and verie industrious, I am verie confident I had lest tenn pounds more. Put that to my London voage (*sic*), and I am suer I am worse, by fiftie pound, at the least, than I was this time twelmonth. I hope all ill luck comes at one time. Hopeing to have maid thirtie or fortie barills of heiriugs to have recovered some of my losse, [I] could not reach (?) to make upp five hundreth; however, I doubt not if I live but one yeare to an end, to set cart on wheeles once more againe. Your horse proves verie well, and leaps our coys verie neatly . . . . I have written to my cosen Lacy to lett him know Major Standlie is deade; he desired me to lett him knowe of the first place that fell voyde here in this Ileland: for he maid noe doubt but he could procuer it from my honourable lord. The place is to be Maior of the south side of Man and of Castle Rushen; the sallerie is fortie [pounds] *per annum.*" *Seal of arms.*

BENJAMIN AYLOFFE to ROGER KENYON.

235. 1663[-4], March 24.—"The Parliament mett on the 16th instant, and adjourned till Munday last; there is not anything of note yett knowne. My Lord of Derby did not appeare; it is reported his Lady was att the House with a petition or letter, but it could not be read. The substance whereof, I have not heard so certainly, as to be worth notice."

PHILIP MAINWARING to ROGER KENYON.

236. 1664, July 16.—Presumes Kenyon has heard of the death of the Chancellor of the Duchy, who died at his house at Marlborough on Tuesday last. Sir Thomas Ingram succeeds him. *Seal.*

[HENRY NOWELL to ROG]ER KENYON.

237. [1664, August.]—"On Wednesday last the King and the Counsell sate, and my Lord of Darby and the Christians were called in. The Chancellor beegan to speak, and asked which was Christian's sonne; hee tould him hee had lost a good father, but the King had lost a very great lose, for he had lost a loyall and faithful subject; but his blod could not bee gotten againe. But itt was the King's pleasure that all satisfaction that possable could bee immagined to bee given, hee should have it. My Lord of Darby is to restore Christian to his estate, both personal and reall. Myself, Mr. Stepehenson, Major Colcott and the . . . . is to bear all his charges, which he is to put in uppon oath. I am affraid it will come to a considerable some. The two commissioners is commanded, by a warrant, to the King's Bench and there to remain till further order. I am to return to see these orders executed; if it bee possable I intend to see you." [*The rest of the letter is torn off.*]

HENRY NOWELL to ROGER KENYON, at Peele.

237A. [1664, August.]—"On Wednesday last, my Lord and the traytor's sonne had a hearing beefore the King and his Counsell; and the King had commanded the Cheefe Justices and his own Counsell to be there, that they might give their opinions, whether the act of indemnity did reach the Ileland. There was a greate dispute with counsell learned on both sides. I thinke it continued for two houers, and when they had dono, we were all to [withdraw?] and the Judges to give there opinions." [*The rest of the letter is torn off.*]

John Allen to Roger Kenyon.

238. 1664, September 26.—Requesting him to send an order for the renewing of Bury Bridge, as the last floods have made wider the breach.

Gucciardini Ayloff to Roger Kennyon.

239. 1664, October 11.—"The warr with the Duchy (*sic*) is like infallibly to be. The Duch (they say) are higher, both in languag and preparations ; in the last, I hope, wee equall them in strength, if not in number. Prince Robert (*sic*) is in the Downs, with 20 good ships, Lord Sandwich, with some 14, about Portsmouth. I heare Sir John Lawson is come home ; it seemes hee was sent for by the King, but there are but 2 ships come with him. Some 20 of the best ships, are providing for the Duke of Yorke to go with, to be about our coasts." *Seal of arms.*

The Earl of Derby's Case stated for the vindication of the proceedings at law, in the Isle of Man, against William Christian.

240. [1664?]—That the Lords of the Isle of Man were sometimes Homagers to the Kings of Norway, after to England, in the reigns of King Henry the Third and his son King Edward the First, and after, to Alexander the Third, King of Scotland, until William Montague, Earl of Salisbury, took it in the reign of King Edward the Third, and sold it to Sir William le Scrope, Chamberlain of the Household to King Richard the Second, on whose behalf Sir William le Scrope kept·the said Isle, untill he was taken by King Henry the Fourth and beheaded ; after whose death, King Henry the Fourth, in the first year of his reign, gave it to the Earl of Northumberland, who was at·ainted of treason in the seventh year of his reign ; and in that year the King granted the dominion of the said Island, together with the Bishoprick thereof, and all royalties, regalities, liberties, and franchises, at any time before held and enjoyed by the Lords of that Isle, unto Sir John Stanley, Knight, from whom, by hereditary descent, the same is come to Charles, now Earl of Derby, and by an Act in the Parliament of the seventh year of King James, that Isle is established and confirmed to William Earl of Derby, grandfather of the now Earl, for his life, and after, to James late Earl of Derby, father to the now Earl, and the heires males of his body, with a remainder to Sir Robert Stanley, his unkle, and the heirs male of his body, the remainder to the right heirs of James Earl of Derby, for ever.

That William Christian being born in the Isle of Man, and having taken several oathes in relation to severall offices held by him in the said Isle, to bear faith and fidelity to the said James, late Earl of Derby, within the said Island, and bearing several offices of trust there, and being of the Council for the Government and safety thereof, did, contrary to the duty whereunto he stood bound by his oathes and trusts, and without any authority, take advantage of the absence of James, late Earl of Derby, who had then advanced his forces out of the said Isle to serve his Majesty in England, did designe an insurrection against the governour of the said Isle, and did administer an oath of secrecy to his confederates therein.

That, in pursuance of such designes, the troop of horse which was the land guard of the Isle, Ramsey and the Artillery there were taken, and several other places of strength besieged by the orders of the said William Christian.

That by the sending out of crosses, which is the way of raising the forces of the Island, he made his house at Raynold's Way, the head-quarters for the rendezvouse of some companies, and that others should take the Peele Castle and other forts; and of all this rising and insurrection, William Christian made himself the head.

That he falsely and maliciously insinuated into the people that the Countess Dowager of Derby, then being in the Island, would sell all the people in the Island at two pence or three pence a head, and thereby made a total revolt of the people of the said Isle from the said Countess and an adherence of them to himself, against her and all those that did continue of her party, and gave the people an oath not to obey the said Countess until she gave them such conditions as they desired.

That making himself captain of the insurrection, he besieged the said Countess in Castle Rushin, and inforced her thereby to enter into a treaty for the surrender of the Island.

That he did send to the Parliament's ships, giving them notice of the distractions of the Island, and that the people were for them, and that it would be their own if they would come and require it.

That he brought in the Parliament's forces and made conditions for the Island, without the consent of the said Countess, or of Sir Philip Musgrave, Governor and General there.

That the said Countess was besieged by the forces so brought in by the said William Christian, and plundered of all the estate she had.

That in all, the said William Christian (without any commission), acted for the Parliament against the said Isle, the Lord, Governor, and People thereof; and was the head of their troubles and cause of the loss of the Island, and of all his Majestie's interest and loyal subjects there.

That for all these treasons against the Lords of the said Isle, according to the laws and customs thereof, he was indicted and adjudged guilty of treason, and upon the petition of his wife (by his judges there; without the knowledge of the said Earl of Derby), his judgement changed from that of being drawn and hanged (which is the judgement of treason there), into a judgement of being shot to death, which was executed.

That the Earl of Derby was not in the Island when his Majestie's orders came thither, nor since, nor by the space of fifteen years before; nor was his Majestie's letter, for the bringing of the said William Christian before his Majesty or Council, obtained before the execution of the said William Christian, which was upon the second day of January, and his Majestie's letter did bear date the sixteenth day of the same month, and came not to the Earl's hands till the 26th. The Earl of Derby therefore hopes that he cannot be held guilty of disobedience to the commands whereof he had no knowledge, either from the Lords of his Majestie's Council here, or from the officers of the said Island, who, for anything yet appearing, had not themselves any notice of the said orders, or his Majestie's pleasure therein, in what concerned them, or the transmission of the proceedings against the said William Christian, whose many crimes they conceived were not pardoned by the Act of General Pardon, for that the Isle of Man is not therein named as the Isles of Jersey and Guernsey and the town of Barwick are; and being governed by a distinct law, order, and process, in matters criminal and civil, and the said Island not being taken antiently as a part of England (though in homage and subjection to it), nor any Act of Parliament to make it so, they apprehended they were not then, or have been formerly bound by that or any other general Act, wherein the Isle of Man is not particularly named.

That the Earl of Derby is no waies guilty of any disobedience to his Majestie's orders, and so soon as he heard the persons sent for were not here, he immediently endeavoured to have them brought up, according as he shall at all times be ready to do his utmost, in humble obedience to his Majestie's commands.

The Earl of Derby also is so far from making benefit to himself of the said William Christian's estate, that he hath given and annexed it to the Bishoprick of Man some moneths since."

Isle of Man.

241. [1664 ?]—A discourse as to whether the Kings of the Isle of Man were absolute kings or not.

Lord Clarendon to [the Justices of the Peace for the County of Lancaster ?]

242. 1665, March 25.—"His Majesty—being well assured, as well by the confession of some desperate persons, lately apprehended, as by other credible information, that notwithstanding his unparallelld lenity and mercy towards all his subjects for their past offences, how great soever, there is still amongst them many seditious persons who, instead of being sorry for the ills they have done, are still contriving by all the means they can to involve the kingdome in a civill warr; and in order thereunto, have made choice of [a] small number who, under the tytle of a Councell, bould correspondence with the forraigne enemies of this kingdome and distribute their orders to some signall men of their partie in the severall counties, who have provided armes and listed men to be ready, upon any short warning, to draw together in a body; by which, with the help they promise themselves from abroad, they presume to be able to doe much mischiefe, which his Maiesty hopes, with the blessing of God upon his greate care and vigilance, to prevent; and to that purpose, hath writ to his Lord-Lievetenants of the severall counties, that they and their Deputy-Lievetenants may do what belongs to them—hath commanded mee (who, serving him in the province I hold, am in some degree accomptable for the faultes of those who serve him not so well as they ought in that commission) to write to the justices of the peace of all the counties in England, and to lett them know what his Majesty expects at their hands; and do, therefore, choose this time to obey his Majesty's command, and take the best care I can, that this letter may find you together, at the Quarter Sessions. I presume that you, who are present, will take care that it bee communicated to those who are absent, at your next monthly meeting, which it is most necessary you keepe constantly. I am sorry to heare that many persons who are in the Commission of the Peace, neglect to be sworne, or being sworne, to attend the Assizes and Sessione, or indeed, to doe anything of the office of a justice. For the former sorte, I desire that you cause the Clerk of the Peace forthwith to returne mee the names of those who are in the commission, and are not sworne; to the end I may present their names to the King, who hath already given order to his Attorney-Generall to proceed against them. For the rest, I hope upon this animadversion from his Majesty, they will recollect themselves and seriously reflect upon their breach of trust to the King and kingdome, and how accomptable they must bee for the mischeefe and inconvenience which falls out through their remissnesse and not-discharg of their duty. I assure you the King hath so greate a sense of the service you doe, or can do for him, that hee frequently saies hee takes himself particularly beholding to every good justice of the peace who is chearful and active in his place, and that in truth, if the justices of the peace, in their severall divisions, bee as careful as they ought to be in keeping the watches, and in the other parts of their office, the peace of the kingdome can hardly be interrupted within, and the hopes and imaginations of seditious persons would be quickly broken, and all men would study to be quiet and to enjoy these many blessings God hath given the nation, under his happy government. It would be great pitty his Majesty should be deceived in the expectation hee hath from you, and that there should not be a vertuous contention and emulation amongst you who shall serve so gracious a prince, most effectually, who shall discover and punish (if hee cannot reforme) most of his enemies, who shall take most paines in undeceiving many weake men, who are misled by falce and malitious insinuations and suggestions, by those who would alienate the mindes of the people from their duty to theire soveraigne, who shall confirme the weak and reduce the wilfull most; in a word, who shall be most sollicitous to free the country from seditious persons and seditious and unlawfull meetings, as appeares now by severall examinations and confessions, to confirme each other in their malice against the govern-ment, and in making collections for the support of those of their partie who are listed to appeare in any desperate undertaking, the very time whereof they have designed. Wee must not beleeve that such a forward correspondence amongst ill men, throughout the kingdome, so much artifice, so much industrie, and so much dexterity, as this people are possessed with, can be disappointed of their wicked successe by a supine negligence or lazines in those who are invested with the King's authority; indeed, without an equall industrie, dexterity and combina-tion betweene good men for the preservation of the peace of the kingdom, and for the suppressing of the enemies hereof. Let mee, therefore, desire and conjure you to use your utmost dilligence and vigilancie to discover the machinations of those men who you know to be ill affected to the government, to meete frequently amongst your-selves, and to communicate your intelligence to each other, and to secure the persons of those who you find forward to disturb, or dangerous to the publique peace. And I make no doubt but his Majesty will receive so good an account of the good effect of your zeale and activitie in his service, that I shall receive his command to returne his thanks to you for the same; and I am sure I shall lay bould on any occasion to serve every one of you in particular." *Copy.*

The EARL OF SOUTHAMPTON and LORD ASHLEY to the JUSTICES OF THE PEACE of the County of Lancaster.

243. 1665, November 30. Oxford.—His Majesty, being informed by many of the receivers of his revenue of Hearth Money, of many obstacles they find in collecting the same, has resolved that his own officers levy the same duty; for if any other person find himself aggrieved, he is left to the law; And this he conceives necessary, because he observes such compliance, in many of the Justices of the Peace, with those that, upon any pretence soever, dispute the duty, that if he permits them to be chancellors of the payment, he conceives it will soon be reduced to very little; many of them, by private certificates, to gratify their neighbours, taking off the duty, which from the bench they had before certified as due to the Exchequer. *Copy.*

[*Attached are certain "Resolutions" to queries concerning Hearth Money.*]

ORDER touching ROBERT LEAVER, gentleman, convicted of barratry.

244. 1666, April 5.—Whereas, at the Assizes held at Lancaster in March last, Robert Leaver was convicted of barratry, and adjudged to pay 500*li.* for a fine to his Majesty, and to remain in prison till payment thereof, and to stand upon the pillory for one hour ; whereupon he craved mercy in mitigation of the judgment, especially as to his corporal punishment of the pillory, in regard that it would not only render the petitioner, but his posterity, infamous, he having several children, and a wife descended of an ancient and worthy family ; it was therefore ordered by William Spencer, the Sheriff, and Edmund Assheton, Esquire, that if the said Leaver should pay certain sums of money to several persons he had wronged, amounting to 334*li.* 16*s.* 0*d.*, his punishment of the pillory be remitted.

————— to SIR ROGER BRADSHAW.

245. 1666, June 5.—" Sonday, our fleete continued fighting all day with the Dutch, but at that distance, that wee hard them not at all ; for Friday and Saturday our fleet, althoe but 57 in number, fought with that valor that wee forced the Dutch to retire towards Holland ; who receaving 16 new ships well provided, the Hollanders renued the battell, soe that, Sunday, our generall, with all his fleete, was forced to give ground, yet very honorably, still fighting till about 6 of the clock after dinner, when Prince Rupert, with 26 men of war, besides 6 fire ships, came and joyned with the Generall, [and] much incouraged the fleete, who then had fought 3 dayes and 2 nights. Yesterday, the seafight continued from 6 in the morneing till seaven that night, wee haveing the pursuite of them. Wee do not know of the losse of any ship ; only the *Swiftsure* is wanting, and his Lordship, Sir William Bartle. The . . . . frigott is come into Harwich much damnified by one of our owne men of warr. The *Henry*, friggott, is retorned, all the forecastle burned ; she defended herself against 7 men of war, and 3 fire ships. The Generall caused 3 or 4 Dutch bottoms to bee burned, because they would doe noe great service ; they had beene taken in the last yeares ingagement. The Generall received a splinter in his thigh, Sir William Clerk his Secretarie, hath lost a leg. Mr. Fretwell Hollies (?) hath lost an arme, Captain Bacon killed. What ships of theres are burned, or sunck, beyond 16, wee know not. The Generall lost his flag twise, but still rode on."

NOTES on ENGLISH SHIPS, in the handwriting of ROGER KENYON.

246. 1666, June ?—The *St. Paul,* and two others flagshigs, fired by the General's order. The General had 30 or 40 men killed by a Vice-Admiral of the enemy at our recounter.

The *Gloucester,* the *Ann,* the *Bristoll,* the *Antelopp,* became shallowed in the Gunfleet.

On Saturday, 4 or 5 of the enemy's ships were seen on fire ; a Vice Admiral of the enemy sent to the . . . . by our General.

Captain Bacon, killed, Capt : Hollis lost an arm, a dozen of ours, binding up their shattered members.

A maimed ship brought into Harwich, June 4. The Duke shott through the breeches, all his tackle taken off with chain shot.

Twenty four of their great ships were sunk, and one fired, of 76 guns, being a Vice-Admiral.

The *Henry* shattered and sent off. Lost 100 men.

The Dutch fleet, 76 sail and 10 fire ships. The Dutch lost 3 sail more.

Swiftsure, Spread Eagle, Loyal George, [and] *Small Katherine,* lost of ours.

The Duke, having on Sunday morning sent away all his shattered ships, had but 40 sail left.

Rainbow disabled; 25 of her men killed.

The Dutch Admiral made a hull; 3 fired, 6 or 7 maimed.

The General had 50 ships at the beginning; the Dutch, above 80. But 35 of the enemy seen at the last, and what has become of the rest, not known.

The *Prince* burnt, Sir G. Ascough taken; the *Essex* taken; the *Swiftsure* yet missing.

DOROTHY LAGOE to MRS. KENYON, at Peel.

247. [16]66, December 1. [Manchester.]—There is but four shops in toun that sells children's caps, and I have been at 3 of them myself to day to see for one, for cosin Betty, but can meet with none that's large enough for her. I have sent Alice to the fourth shop to see for one. Sister, if you want pepper, or other Christmas stuff, it were good to take it beetimes; it will rise in the price. Pepper is allready raised. Alice can get no cap that's large enough. Sister, this cloeth cost 2s. 6d. (at 17d. the yard). Your shoes and galloshoes, 4s. 3d.; the thread, which I sent you last, cost 5d.; so that [there] now remaines with me, of that nine shillings you sent, 1s. 10d.

A LIST OF HIS MAJESTY'S NAVY.

248. 1666.—The totals are as follows:—Men, 29,170; Guns, 6320; Ships, 149; and Fire ships, 10.

GUICCIARDINI AYLOFF to ROGER KENYON.

249. 1667, April 19. "Thisleworth.—It is said for certain there will be a peace, indeed as good, some think, as concluded already, and upon honourable terms; for we are not so much behind hand in our naval preparations, nor they so forward, as the world has fancied. We shall quickly have four or five squadrons in readiness. Sir Thomas Allen already at Plymouth with above 30, third rate frigates, for the most part. Sir Robert Holmes is to be for Portsmouth, where the Duke of York is gone. Sir Thomas Tiddyman, for the Downs. Sir Jer: Smith, for Harwich, where his Highness was not long since, and ordered excellent fortifications about the town and harbour. Sir Edward Spragg, for Hull. All, it may be imagined, with less squadrons than Sir Thomas Allen's. Our Ambassadors go away the next week, and the Swedes altogther for Breda. On Tuesday the Swedes are to see the solemnity of a St. George's feast at Whitehall, to introduce the new princely brother of the order, the Duke of Cambridge. They talk of a great robbery lately committed, 11,000li. of his Majesty's money, that had a sufficient convoy too, but a stronger, of 50 men armed, came and took it away and killed two or three of the guards. I hope it may prove no such matter." *Seal of arms.*

The SAME to the SAME.

250. 1667, May 21. Westminster.—We have heard little or nothing concerning the Treaty since the Ambassadors went; that affair seems under a cloud, but we hope it will break clear at last. The Earl of Southampton, Lord Treasurer, is lately dead; it is said his office will be executed by Commissioners, and it is talked that the Duke of Albemarle, Lord Ashley, Sir Thomas Clifford, Sir John Duncom, and another, will be the 'men entrusted; a few days will give the certainty. *Seal of arms.*

Edmund Assheton to Major John Byrom.

251. 1667, May 21. London.—My Lord Castlehaven is to raise a regiment of foot to go and serve the King of Spain in Flanders, and has been pleased to make me captain of a company, which I must raise, and have ready to put on board, at Gravesend, by 15 June. Within this time, can you send me about fifty men? The conditions are these:—from the day they set out, they shall be paid 12 pence a day till such time as they shall be set on board ship; and immediately after that, they shall enter into the King of Spain's pay. I need not tell you anything of the nobleness of the service, since you understand it better than I. We are not allowed to beat a drum or to set up bills for the raising of our men, because of the Treaty with France.

Waldiné Lagoe to his "brother Kenyon, at the Peele."

252. 1667, June 15. Manchester.—On Thursday night we had the news that the Dutch, with their fleet, were within four miles of Gravesend, and that General Monk and the Lord Craven were gone down to put a stop to them, and secure our great ships that were at Chatham. But this day's post brings news that the Dutch have broken the chain that was put across the Thames and are come past Gravesend, and have taken the *Royal Charles*, and we have sunk four ships to keep them from being taken. And though it is said we have 30,000 men on the shore, yet the Dutch, with their great guns from their fleet, do beat our men off, that they can do no good. Our great ships that are at Chatham, are at the mercy of the enemy. It is feared the French are also coming over from Dunkirk to land in England. "The Lord in mercy appear for us!" *Seal.*

Lewis Assheton to Roger Kenyon, at Peel.

253. 1667, June 20.—"The drums beat daily for volunteers, but how many listed, I know not. I am very inclinable to engage on this side the countrey, if this bargain hinder not. Collonell Kerby is raising a regiment but where to bee imployed I know not as yet." *Seal of arms.*

Postscript.—"Your letteres will find me att the coll. [college?] in Graie's Inn Lane. This morning, report saith, died the Duke of Cambridge." [1] *Seal of arms.*

Guicciardini Ayloff to Roger Kenyon.

254. 1667, August 21.—The world here languishes in expectation of the peace, and we are almost brought into despair; but at Court, they have the same confidence, still laying the cause upon the great distance from Breda to Copenhagen, which has retarded the return of the King of Denmark's ratification. The Countess of Clarendon is dead, and Sir Henry Bellasis, but not of the wound given him in his body by Mr. John Porter, as the coroner's inquest has given in. *Seal of arms.*

---

[1] Son of James, Duke of York, by Anne Hyde. Died at Richmond and buried at Westminster.

HENRY NOWELL to his brother.

255. 1667, October 4. Castletown.—About six weeks ago I wrote to you, but unfortunately my letter miscarried, as my lady's vessel was "overset" upon the coast of Wales, in which was Dick Colcott, brother to that unfortunate man who slew my nephew, Bunastre. They say that Major Colcott is lost at sea, so that house is quite extinct. My niece, Jane Nowell, is married in Belfast, unknown to her father and mother, or any friend. She has married an apothecary; his shop is well furnished, and that is all I can hear he hath.

GUICCIARDINI AYLOFF to ROGER KENYON.

256. 1667, October 15. Westminster.—Both Houses concurred to give the King thanks for six particulars, and, this afternoon, went whole to Whitehall to do it. The six are for disbanding of the army, for quickening an Act against Irish cattle, reviving the laws against papists, annulling the Canary Company, referring the examination of accounts and miscarriages to Parliament, and the last for removing the Chancellor. They have something on foot touching the privileges of the House. They have appointed a committee to examine the abuse in the dearness of coals (which are 36s. at least), and exacting of innkeepers and other abuses, I hope will come in. *Seal of arms, broken.*

EDWARD KENYON to his brother, ROGER KENYON.

257. [16]67, November 13. Peel.—Concerning the publication of a proposed excommunication of Mr. Lever, on the previous Sunday. Captain Greenalgh so much favours "the papists," that "I fear you cannot, without sinne and dishonour, bee his undersheriff. . . . I pray you dear brother, for God's sake, and your soul's, have nothing to do with it." *Seal of arms, broken.*

EDWARD RIGBY to ROGER KENYON, at Peel.

258. 1667, November 17. Gray's Inn.—"Since my last, we have (as I doubt not but you have heard) impeached the Earle of Clarendon, at the Lords' barre, of treason, high crimes and misdemeanors; but the Lords have not complyed with the Commons to imprison him as yet, and therefore the Commons have appointed a committee to draw up reasons why he should be committed. We have also agreed to impeach Commissioner Holt for his miscarrages at Chatham; and it is probable, ere long, you will hear of others to be impeached. I do not remember any bill this weeke of publicke concernment, proceeded in; but that bill against pluralities is read the second time, and committed." *Seal of arms, broken.*

GUICCIARDINI AYLOFF to ROGER KENNYON.

259. 1667, November 21. Westminster.—"The great matter now in action, is that of the Earl of Clarendon, which hath held the Houses much debate. The House of Commons went up with a generall impeachment of treason, high crimes, and misdemeanours, against him, which, beeing not drawne into articles or formall charge, the Lords thought not fit to accept, so far as to order his committment; but ever since (which is 8 or 9 dayes) it has depended in debates betweene them, and reasons have beene sent up from the House of Commons, but for ought I heare as yet, both Houses adhere to their owne resolves. The article of treason, as they say, is that hee hath deluded and betrayed the King· in his Councells, and all along, in this war, bas betrayed the nation and ·the King in his treatyes with forraine states ; 'tis somewhat toward this effect. Perhaps you may have seen the articles, there are copies goe about. The Lord Chief-Justice Keeling, being charged with some mis-carriages towards juries in tryalls before him, was once before a Committee, and gave a very modest and faire answeare to two or three of the charges against him ; but, I heare, they were content to respite the further examination and debate of those matters till after the tearme, in favor to the publick proceeding of his place and court. There has bin some complaints made in the House against some persons, some members, for taking gratuityes of the merchants that obtained their French wines to be landed, after the proclamation of war against the French." *Seal of arms, broken.*

ENGLISH CATHOLICS.

260. 1667, Christmas.—An answer to a pamphlet entitled " The humble Apologie of the English Catholicks." 13 *pp.*

GUICCIARDINI AYLOFF to ROGER KENYON.

261. 1667[-8], February 11. Westminster.—" The Parliament met upon Monday ; and his Majesty came to the House, spake very short; only acquainted the Houses that, having made a league with the Hollanders, and others, he should have occasion to get out shipping and, therefore, desired them to take it into consideration to assist him in it ; and· some-thing else for quieting the thoughts of his Protestant subjects in relation to religion, in which matters his Majesty was something prevented by the House of Commons, they having, immediately before his coming and their going up to the Lords House to his Majesty, voted to petition his Majesty to set out a proclamation to put the laws in that case, in execution, which it is thought has much quashed the hopes of that bill of comprehension, as they call it, which was now somewhat in expecta-tion. The Lord Gerard has had but ill success in three indictments against Carr ; one of felony, for running from his colours; the two others of forgery. He came off clear of all." *Seal of arms, broken.*

JAMES BRADSHAW, ROBERT LEVER, and JOHN ANDREWES to [ROGER KENYON ?].

262. 1667[-8], February 12. Bolton.—" The rent due at Candlemass last, for the land in Balderstowe, given by Mr. Gosnell to the Church schole and poore at Boulton, beeinge not yet paide us, and understanding that you are one of the executors of Mr. John Hayhurst, your father-in-law, and thereby concerned in the payment of it, wee, the feoffees of the foresaid(?) guifte, thinking it good to give you notice of the fayler, that so you might take care to pay it, with what possible speed may bee, for the preventing of further troble, both to yourself and us, as also for the satisfyeing of those to whom it belongs, who have alreadie demanded it of us, supposing wee had received it at the day, as formerly." *Seal.*

R. BRADYLL to ROGER KENYON.

263. 1667[-8], February 15.—Thanks him for a loan of 10*l.* " The reason I was soe urgent was, I had provided a parsell of goods for the

Sheriffs, and an unworthy man in our toune, offered ready money for them thinking to trapann mee ; soe I was foarsed, in 48 oures, to pay 150*l*. which putt mee to a streight. I begg your ladie's axceptance of a bottle of as good Tent as ever you drunke."

Postscript.—" Pray send my bottell back."

GUICCIARDINI AYLOFF to ROGER KENYON.

264. 1667[-8], February 29. Westminster.—The House of Commons has resolved upon 300,000*li.* for his Majesty's supply, and now, this very instant, are considering how to raise it. A land tax, and home commodities, they have declared against; it may be upon excise, upon linen cloth, wine, and other foreign things. Perhaps a Poll Bill again. There is a great business upon the stage again, concerning my Lord Gerard and Fitten. A foul narrative was made by Carr (of former passages in that business) at the House of Commons, if they can make it out, which is thought will hardly be done. *Seal of arms, broken.*

DOROTHY LAGOE to her brother, ROGER KENYON, at Peel.

265. 1668, May 26.—" I desire you will send mee the print of your seale, as soone as you can. I have been to-day to see about spoons and about the ingraving of a coat, but cannot know the price till they see the coate ; but they say they doe them all on the backside of the steele and without any compartiment or laurell about the coat, when done on spoones ; but I'll get them done as you further direct." *Seal.*

GUICCIARDINI AYLOFF to ROGER KENYON.

266. 1668, July 4. Westminster.—An Ambassador from France is expected. A house is taken for him (Leicester House), for two or three years. There is talk of a proclamation to give notice of the further adjournment again of Parliament, to the first of November.

LEO : CLAYTON to ROGER KENYON.

267. 1668, July 8. Blackburn.—Asking for his interest on behalf of Mr. John Bretherton, late curate of Blackburn, for a chapel in Eccles parish, he thinks called Ellenbrough. *Seal.*

ROBBERS.

268. 1668.—Certificate, signed J. Charlton, that he believes that Darcy Lassells was the person intended in his Majesty's proclamation, issued out against notorious robbers, the 23rd day of September 1668 ; although his name, by mistake, is there mentioned to be Henry Lassells.

GUICCIARDINI AYLOFFE to ROGER KENYON, at Peel.

269. 1668[-9], February 11. " Dean Yard, Westminster."—" Baron Wrainsford is removed up into the King's Bench. Broome spoken of to come in his place. We are preparing our sommer (?) navy of some 40 sayle." *Seal, broken.*

D[OROTHY] L[AGOE] to her brother, ROGER KENYON, in Holborne.

270. 1669, July 15.—I have had intimation that there have been seen on Swinton Moor, six or seven men, indifferently well horsed, with pistols; they inquired when you would come home. Yesterday evening two of them rode at one passing, who was better horsed than they; they discharged three pistols at him. They are supposed to be highwaymen, [and] seem to bear you a grudge. We desire you will not come home for fear of danger. Your wife knows nothing about them, but sister Alice heard about it. *Seal.*

THOMAS CUNLIFFE to ROGER KENYON.

271. 1669, August 31. "Angell Alley in Southwark.'—" His Majesty went yesterday [on] his progress for his New Forest in Hampshire, and is said, returns within fourteen days. Some makes a doubte wheather the Parliament doth meete at the time appoynted, or noe, or, if they doe meete, wheather they sitt for any continuence, or noe; yett others of more sober judgments conceave there wilbe a necessitie of theire meetinge and continuence, both by reason his Majestie will have occasions to rayse more money, which is supposed will bee the more hard to rayse without some better accompte bee given them, how that, formerly given, hath beene disposed of. But I shall wish there may be a good understandinge betweene them, and a lovinge complyance on all hands." *Seal.*

D. LAGOE to MRS. ALICE KENYON, at Peel.

272. [16]69, October 13.—Sends her, for her own eating, six quinces to make "into marmalate, or preserve them," because "quince is good for the brain of the little one." *Seal.*

GUICCIARDINI AYLOFF to ROGER KENYON.

273. 1669, December 11. Westminster.—This day, the Parliament are risen and prorogued by his Majesty to the 14th February, so then (they say) all is to begin again *de novo*. Sir George Cartwright, saving that he is suspended the House as a member, is as he was. He came off, in the House of Lords, indifferent fair; what he might have done in the House of Commons, I cannot well guess. The Bill for lessening interest money to 4 *per cent.* is laid aside. We talk much of a likelihood of war between the French and Holland. The King's supply, almost finished, must now sleep till the next meeting of Parliament. *Seal of arms.*

THOMAS PIMLOE to MRS. ALICE KENYON, at Peel.

274. [16]69, ... 9. Budworth.—Has received the 55s. "and the grammar and handkerchiefe. I will, according to your desire, buy cloath for William; but for Mr. Roger's coming home, if you pleased, I would have you to respite it till Michaelmas. When you send his shifts, I pray send him a cloath suite to wear; for I am sure his cloak, shift, breeches, and tunic, will not last him a moneth. And pray send him a paire of shoes. He is well, and in good health, and I think William hath now forgotton all his sister said." *Seal of arms, broken.*

GUICCIARDINI AYLOFFE to ROGER KENYON.

275. 1669[-70], February 8. Westminster.—Complains much of the cold weather, which has brought in a kind of "paraletic distemper." There are two new Bishops nominated by his Majesty, Dr. Gunning, for

Chichester, and Dr. Barrow, the Bishop of Man, for St. Asaph. The King of France, they say, for the benefit of his health, (rather than out of good nature or justice) will cease his wars for this year. He has been troubled with vapours in his head (that may be easily believed) and had some kind of fit " like apoplecticul"; that he will apply himself to the waters at Bourbon, for this summer, and will refer the arbitration of the difference between Spain and him, to our King and the King of Sweden. *Seal of arms.*

GUICCIARDINI AYLOFFE to ROGER KENNYON.

276. 1669[-70], March 1. Westminster.—As to an informer against " Conventikles," I believe there will be no need; for, they say, the Parliament are upon reviving the Act, and will make it stricter and put a penalty upon the justices and magistrates, if they be too remiss in putting the law in execution. And for other penal laws, I have heard the prosecutor has a recompense out of the fine imposed, and will not need any share out of that which falls to the King. All things go on very well and quietly in Parliament. His Majesty's supply upon wine, to continue for seven years, goes forward towards finishing the Act for building the City, and something about that of Conventicles. Something, they say, is in hand about clerks of the markets. But I hear his Majesty has sent to the Houses to prepare all they can in a readiness before Easter, for then he intends to go some progress to Audeley End and Newmarket, to hunt and see the horse races there. The Duchess of Albemarle's funeral was last night in the Abbey, in Henry the Seventh's Chapel. The body was carried from the Star Chamber, and many great lords of the Court were at it. The Duke is not yet laid in state at Somerset House, for want of black velvet, etc. *Seal of arms.*

ROGER BRADSHAIGH to ROGER KENYON.

277. 1669[-70], March 3.—" Yours came to my hands in the House of Comons at the same time that wee weare nearly upon the debate for the second reading of the Bill against Conventicles, and for the Comittment of it, my contriman (Black Birch) having newly excused the meetings of such concientious people, as living farre from the other church, theire chappells not beeing provided; and particularly instanced the severall chappells in Manchester parish, and further added, that theare could not bee one instance produced that any such meetings had produced any insurrection, or that any treason, scismne, or other contrivance or disturbance to the government, had beene theare hatcht. This made my modestye mooved to speake, and such instances, as I had formerly observed and in my memorye had retained, I layd open to the House, with the necessitie for a Bill of restraynt, and what ways to meete with their subtle evations. And theise, I affirmed to carry the reputation of Presbyterians in our contry. This made the House to looke upon my contriman as sufficiently contradicted in his possitive affirmation. It was three of the clock, ere wee got the question; but [it] was at last committed, and is at this present under consideration of the Committee now sitting by mee : indeed, the bill will bee much more rigid then formerly, and wee must be furnisht with more instances to induce the passing of it, when it comes into the House. Soe I would desyre you, that you would gather mee what instances you can of insolencys, of scisme, of dangerous words spoken, or any other thing that hath happned, since the Act of Oblivion, worthy taking notice of, to object against them, and I shall not fayle to urge them when tyme servse. In the meanetime, I pray, let the further examination of the busines at Gorton Chapell bee taken; and send me word what you know of the chapell called Birch Chapell, and of their meetings. You shall not need to be named in anything. This I desyre may be done as soone as may bee, before the Bill come back to the House."

Jo: Hartley to [Roger Kenyon ?].

278. 1669[–70], March 19. Strangways.—Encloses a letter from Sir Roger Bradshaigh, with an order of the Council. Sir Roger desired it might be communicated to the gentlemen of the Sheriff's table. He says that the order should have been not only for putting the laws in execution against those of Gorton Chapel, but against all offenders of that nature. The House of Lords are very busy about the Bill against Conventicles; and, he believes, it may pass with some amendments. *Seal of arms.*

Jo: Otway to Roger Kenyon.

279. 1670. [May] 3.—No news here, but of the great solemnity of the general funeral. He is now laid in state in the Abbey, and is to lie open for all eyes, for one month, with these words round about him, *Fortiter, fideliter, feliciter.*

Benjamin Ayloffe to Roger Kenyon, at Peel.

280. 1670, June 30.—"The King's fee farme rents are now upon sale, and I purpose to make it my generall busines to contract and dispatch the purchases of such persons as will make use of me for that purpose; therefore, I intreate the faver from you as to assist me in that affaire, by ingaging as many of your acquaintance to me as you can."

Order in Council.

281. 1670, August 20. Whitehall.—"Upon reading the humble petition of the right honourable Charles, Earle of Derby, setting forth that he has been of late most injuriously perplexed by the complaints of several persons of the Isle of Man, preferred to this Board against him, through the malice, and at the instigation of one Evan Curghy, an inhabitant there, a person of so implacable a disposition, that he is dissatisfied under the administration of all the law and justice of the said Island, even in causes haveing no influence upon or relation to his own concernes, promoteing contention among the inhabitants, maligning the government and peace of the said Island, seconding petition with petition, and clamour to this Board, after dismission of their complaints to the vast charge, attendance, and expence, of the petitioner and his agents, waiting here for his justification and defence. That the persons complaining (there being no costs awarded against them, or any other punishment inflicted upon their dismission) presume, through that impunity, to revive their complaints. And praying that he may have liberty, by the testimony of the late Bishop of Man, and others, to represent to this Board the person of the said Curghy, to make good the matter of this petition, and to have releife against him according to the lawes of the said island; and that such clamorous petitions may not be received untill security be first given to answer such costs as this Board shall adjudge, in case the matter of complaint be determined against them. It is this day ordered by his Majestie in Council, that the petitions of the inhabitants of the Isle of Man remaining with the Clerke of the Council, be sent to the Right Reverend the Lord Bishop of St. Asaph, who is hereby prayed and required to examine them, and report to this Board concerning the matter they containe; whereupon his Majestie in Councell will declare his further pleasure. And it is also ordered that the Clerks of the Councell in waiting, before they receive any more petitions of the inhabitants of the Isle of Man, relating to the Earl of Derby and the government there, doe take sufficient security from such persons to pay such costs and damages as this Board shall judge fit to award against them, in case, upon the hearing, they shall not be able to make out and justifie their complaints." *Copy*.

Thomas Charleton to Roger Kenyon.

282. 1670, August 29. Lancaster Castle.—Asking for his influence with the High Sheriff, for his enlargement, having lain in prison three years in great penury. *Seal of arms.*

Thomas Braddyll to Roger Kenyon.

283. 1670, December 5. Portfield.—Asks for the record concerning the Quakers, by the first opportunity.

Paul Cobb to Roger Kenyon.

284. 1670, December 10.—" One Benyon was indicted upon the Statute of 35 Elizabeth, for being at a Conventicle. He was in prison, and was brought into Court and the indictment read to him; and because he refused to plead to it, the Court ordered me to record his confession, and he hath lain in prison upon that conviction, ever since Christmas Sessions, 12 Chas. II. And my Lord Chief Justice Keelinge was then upon the Bench, and gave the rule, and had the like, a year ago, against others. Benyon hath petitioned all the Judges of Assize, as they came the Circuit, but could never be released. . And truly, I think it but reasonable that if any one do appear, and afterwards will not plead, but that you should take judgment by *nihil dicit*, or confession."

John Molyneux to Roger Kenyon.

285. 1670, December 13.--Hopes he is recovered from the gout, and thanks him for the hounds. " Cromwell fits the speed of my hounds very well." *Seal.*

Guicciardini Ayloffe to Roger Kenyon.

286. 1670, December 17. Westminster.—No discovery is yet made in that villainous attempt upon the Duke of Ormond; three or four of their pistols, and as many swords, were found scattered, and a cloak, besides four horses, all base and mean, which shows they were pitiful rogues. The Prince of Orange, they say, having been at Newmarket and Cambridge, lays aside his intended visit to Oxford and Windsor, and goes away shortly for Holland. A quarrel happened, this week, between two of his company; a French colonel, or captain, and a Dutch captain, fought a duel here at Westminster; the French was slain. This troubles the Prince much. Two new-built houses, not finished, in Fenchurch Street, fell down; seven of the workmen were killed and as many hurt. *Seal of arms, broken.*

GUICCIARDINI AYLOFFE to ROGER KENYON.

287. 1670, December 24.—"The Parliament adjourned, upon Teusday last, to the Thursday sennight following (29 December instant), passing a vote that all members absent the Monday after Twelveday, should pay a double subsidie. Nothing as yet discovered in that buisnes of the Duke of Ormond. Here has happened this weeke another, something like it. Sir John Coventry goeing home to his lodging in Suffolk Streete, very late—'twas betwene 1 and 2 at night—was set upon by halfe a score, or a dozen, men, halfe on foote and the other halfe horsemen, with designe of giving him the opprobrious marke of cutting off his nose, and fell upon him with knives (one was found afterwards of the Duch fashion, for their snick or snee) but mangled his face much, though failed of their full designe, but otherwise wounded him with their swords. They all went off, undiscovered. He behaved himself stoutly for a single person, and thinks hee wounded one of them. 'Tis much the towne talke, and conjectured in revenge for some smart words hee spake in the House, beeing a member. The Prince of Orange was entertained Sunday night last by Prince Rubert at Winsor, went next day to visit Oxford, is returned hether and, some say, goes away next weeke. The House of Commons has passed a vote, that they shall protect no persons but their mœniall servants." *Seal of arms.*

HENRY NOWELL to ROGER KENYON.

288. 1670, ——— 10. Castletown, Isle of Man.—Has been very ill for some time. "I doubts not, in the least, but you have assisted my man, to the utmost of your power, to gett my rights in Lancasheir." Lord Derby intends coming over to the Island "betwixt this and May ; we are making great prepartion for his coming." *Seal, broken.*

JOHN OTWAY to ROGER KENYON, Clerk of the Peace for Lancashire.

289. 1670[-1], January 3.—"Your dexerity in prosecuting against forgery and barratry, is so well knowne, as the King's Attorney can constitute no better deputy than yourselfe in cases of that nature. I am informed there is a woman is to come to her tryall upon the latter; I shall onely desire you to doe his Majestie right, for which you will not onely have the thanks of Mr. Heywood, but of the whole country." *Seal, broken.*

JOHN WARBURTON to [ROGER KENYON].

290. 1670[-1], January 5.—"Your right deare and deservedly beloved brother, the parson, deceased," promised me, as stipend, 30*s.* a year for my service "att the chappelles of Ednenfeild and Holcome, whereof he payd one 30*s.*, which came to my bandes, and another 30*s.* he deposited for me toward Mr. Poole's *Contraction of the Critticks.*" The book has been withheld, as also some part of the promised salary.

GUICCIARDINI AYLOFFE to ROGER KENYON.

291. 1670[-71], January 24. Westminster.—"We have little newes. The house are intent upon the money bill. The bill for that assault of Sir John Coventry is now with the Lords, and it is thought the

Comoners will not bee forwarder in the other, then the Lords wilbee in that. Cutting of noses is growne use and fashon. A Minister, somewhere out by Oxford, one Mr. Hall, had his nose cutt lately ; and last night, about [the] Strand, a gentleman had the like massacre upon hi-, by 3 or 4 young gentlemen that came out of a taverne in cutting case (*sic*), you may imagine ; Mr. Russell, they say, was one of them. Last night the French Embassy at York House made a huge treat to the King, Queen, and all the Court, and great maskarading there was. There is a report the French King has sent out a party of his Fleete to intercept the Holland East Indie Fleete, now coming home." *Seal of arms.*

HENRY ROWE to ROGER KENYON, " at Holeborne, London."

292. 1670[-1], February 14. Wigan.—On Saturday I went to Parkhead, and your mother and I considered how to appoint toll-takers at Blackburn. There were none of any quality in the town opposed to taking toll, but there were some three or four chapmen at one Ensworth's, who combined not to pay toll. One was Thomas Hey, of Ashton, to whom I told of your mother's grant, and if he or any stood out, the toll-takers should make distress of a beast. In the end they drove their beasts in a tumultuous manner to the towns-end, and with a great shout and beating upon the beasts, passed the toll-takers and would pay no toll. Something must be done against them before the next fortnight's fair. *Seal.*

HENRY RO[WE] to ROGER KENYON, in London.

293. 1670[-1], February 28. Wigan.—I was at Parkhead and Blackburn yesterday " about the toule," and served the " Duke's privy seal " on two men, " thinking that would have quited the rest." There were many chapmen, and many beasts sold. I perceived they were all agreed not to pay, and to defend those served. On hearing this, I " doubled his files at the end of the streete they were to goe out at," but, as I had only 20 men with me, could neither have stopped them nor taken a beast, " for the chapmen were assisted with at least 100 people of town and country, and soe violently drive away the beastes, that they broake and burste doune two stoane stoopes of three quarters of a yard thick."

FRANCIS HOLLINSHED to ———.

294. 1670[-1], March 23. London.—Wishes to know how many chimneys are liable to pay the tax, in every hundred in Lancashire ; an answer is to be sent to him, to Mr. Edward Hollinshed's house, " at the signe of The B[l]ack-a-morse Head in Grubb Street, nere Cripill Gate, London." *Seal of arms.*

J. HULME (?) to ———.

295. 1671, March 26.—The great news of the town is our encounter at sea with the Dutch, on Wednesday, Thursday, and Friday. Our 6 ships-of-war fought 11 of their men-of-war, assisted by above 30 of their merchant-men, which had 30 or 40 guns a piece ; their merchant-men in all, were above 60, but four engaged not, but stole away. We have taken their admiral, sank their vice-admiral, and, it is said, taken 3 or 6 of their merchants, The exact express is not yet come to Court ; we have had no considerable loss. *Seal of arms, broken.*

THOMAS STRINGER to ROGER KENYON, at Peel.

296. 1671, May 30. Chancery Lane.—Has delivered his letter to Sir Thomas Clarges; "he lives in Pickadilly, over against St. James's House, neare my late Lord Chancellor's house. . . . As for the businesse of the fayres, write to Sir Thomas Clargies."

DOROTHY LAGOE to MRS. KENYON, at Peel.

297. 1671, June 20. Manchester.—"After you were gone yesterday, sister Alice found the noat which you had from Mr. Hulton, to give you leave to sitt in his seat in our church. But the noat is too short to answer your desires, for it only gives leave for my brother and yourself to sitt in the seat, and neither extends to your children sitting in the seat, nor any of your friends that may occasionally be with you; nor it does not prohibitt any of those persons which comes to the seat and fills it allready, but only gives my brother and you, leave to crowd in amongst them."

HENRY ROWE to ROGER KENYON, at The Sword and Buckler, Holborn.

298. [16]71, July 4.—"I have sent to you a box of cannell plate (*sic*) here after mentioned :—

Tall salt, with a cover	-	-	-	-	0	5s.	0
A great salt with fower pillers	-	-	-	0	2s.	0
A tall standish for inck	-	-	-	-	0	2s.	6d.
A flatt standish for inck	-	-	-	-	0	2s.	0
Two others for inck	-	-	-	-	0	1s.	4d.
Halfe a dozen of newe fashioned salts	-	-	0	3s.	0
Halfe a dozen, of eight square	-	-	-	0	2s.	0
Halfe a dozen of 3 square	-	-	-	0	2	0
Box nailes	-	-	-	-	-	0	1	6d.

1*l.* 1*s.* 4*d.*"

Portion of seal.

GUICCIARDINI WENTWORTH to ROGER KENYON.

299. 1671, September 22. Westminster.—On Monday the King goes to Newmarket, and so into Norfolk. The Queen, to Lord Arlington's and Audly-End. The late storms lost us 20 colliers' men and shipping. There is great bustle about the Customs, whether to be in commissioners or farmers, and whether Lord Ashley shall be Treasurer or not. *Seal of arms.*

LAWRENCE BOOTH to ROGER KENYON, at Manchester.

300. 1671, September 30. Harden.—Desires that favour may be shown to the bearer at the Sessions. He has married a wife in Oppenshaw, who has a tenement worth 8*l.* by the year; "and yet the toun will have him removed."

JOHN WARREN to ROGER KENYON, at Manchester.

301. 1671, October 11.—"Mr. clerk of the Peace,"—I write on behalf of "Widow Entwisle and one Roger Brendwood who, I understand, are bound over to Manchester Sessions, upon a warrant of the peace, granted by Captain Greenehalgh, at the instance, and uppon the oath, of Richard Greenhalgh, who, at the last assizes, was indyted and tryed for a wissard." These two persons had been bound over to give evidence against him at the assizes at Lancaster, "which is all the matter, as I understand, he hath against these persons." *Seal of arms.*

JOHN RADCLIFFE to his cousin, ROGER KENYON.

302. 1671, October 14. Meareley.—"You are generally elected (not any being against you) Bayliffe of the Borough of Cliderou, together with my brother Nowell, whoe desires you would come and take the oathes as speedily as you can." *Seal.*

W. HULTON to ROGER KENYON.

303. 1671, November 7.—Informing him that his uncle Mr. Joseph Rigby is dead, and was buried yesterday. *Seal, broken.*

SIR ROGER BRADSHAIGH to ROGER KENYON, at The Sword and Buckler, Holborne.

304. 1671, November 10. Haigh.—I pray, before you come back, buy me two or three of Goldsmith's Almanacks, the leaves inverted (*sic*). I pray send me word what you observe to be the newest fashion for this winter's clothes and belts ; I would rather have it from you than my tailor.

JOHN HARTLEY to ROGER KENYON, at The Sword and Buckler, Holborn.

305. 1671, November 19. Strangwaies.—"If I had seen you before you went, I should only have made bould to renew my request, which I now doe, of buying me the statutes since 1667, all together, and if they be not printed soe, an epitomy of all the statutes since his Majestie's return, if any hath taken that paines. Yours, I received very thankefully. Wee have little newes here, but since you went, wee had in Manchester, 2 famous or rather bold conventicles, one of which is convicted, and the fines levying to above 50*l.*; the other which was first in tyme, but last discovered, Mr. Mosley, and I doe for the present suspend our judgment untill we have taken advise ; and wee thought none fitter to consult, then yourself. And if you think the case be doubtfull, wee desire you to advise with what lawyers you please, and wee shalbe responsible for his fee, for wee are satisfied that the parties will appeale. That you may the better understand it, herewith is an abstract of the evidence upon which wee proceede. And the case will appeare to be this, whether it be a conventicle within the late statute, though we cannot discover who it was that preacht, though wee are much induced to believe that it was Parson Tilsley. And another question is this, (which some of the peccants put to us) whether one punished for being at the first conventicle, though last in tyme, may be punished for being att another, a moneth before, but not knowne till after the last was convicted ; because, say they, the last was the first offence, and wee cannot punish them, for an offence committed before that, and call it the second offence. Wee desire to heare your opinion in these cases, which will oblige."

Overleaf is the following draft form of information.—"A. B.
informeth upon oath that upon, &c., there was a conventicle held in
the house of one B. C. in Manchester, where this informant heard one
preaching or discourseing, though he sawe him not ; but this informer
judgeth, by his voice, that it was one Mr. T., a nonconformist Minister,
for he is acquainted with him and knows his voice. He further saith
that among other persons that were at the said conventicle (being three
or fower scoare in number) were A. B., &c., all of them above the age of
16 years. He further saith that they met together about 12 of the
clock, and continued together till after 2 in the afternoon, and then
met again about 4 of the same day, and continued till 7 in the evening.
E. D. informeth the like. So that there was 2 conventicles in one day
at the same place and by the same person." *Seal of arms.*

HENRY [NOWELL] to ROGER KENYON.

306. 1671, December 18. Castletown.—Is suffering from gout. Is
afraid that Lord Derby's licence, for his coming over, will scarce be
obtained ; besides which, he has the charge of the affairs of the Bishop
of St. Asaph. *Seal of arms.*

ALICE KENYON to ROGER KENYON.

307. 1671[-2], January 21.—"Mother bids me tell you that the
fortnight fayres at Blackburne, begun in the Protector's time, was then
proclamed by the sexton, as John Hindley can acquaint you. They doe
sease every yeare, soone after Michalmas, and are proclamed againe, either
the first Munday, or the second Munday, after Candlemas, every yeare,
sometimes the one Munday, sometimes the other. There is no hease
(*sic*) on the other market days. She desires, if John have not tould you,
that you would aske him what he knows of this. She presents you
with love and blessing, wishing you a good jorney and a safe retorne."
Seal, broken.

GUICCARDINI WENTWORTH to ROGER KENYON, at Manchester.

308. 1671[-2], February 13. Westminster.—"This day, dyed
Mr. Chancellor of the Dutchy. Who shall succeed, a few days will
discover . . . . Within a post or two, you shall know something
more of this kind." *Seal of arms.*

THOMAS GREENFEILD to ROGER KENYON, at Manchester, or at Peel.

309. 1671[-2], February 20. London.—"According as you desired,
I give you the accompt, touching the Doctor's reception of Elisha Chew.
Yesterday, Dr. Frankland went with myselfe and Mr. William Cayton
alongt with the boy to Dr. Cromleholme, who readly gave the child,
and us, a very free and welcome entertaynement; and to be short, he
gave us, order to remember his love to the boy's mother, and to lett her
know from him that he received her boy as his owne, and that
he willed as carefully of him as if he was his owne, and that he will
(by God's blessing) give him learning and send him to Oxford, and that
he doubted not of friends to gett him preferment there. He called upp
his wife, and said 'sweetheart you must take this child as myne and
yours,' which shee denyed not, but asked her husband who he was like ;
he would have her judgment first, whereupon she sayd the boy was very
like a brother of hers, and he concurred with her in the matter. He

was very glad the boy was past the measles and small pockes. After we had drunk a glass or two of ayle about, he layd his hand on the boye's head and blessed him saying 'the Lord God Almighty bless thee, and not only give thee wisdom and learning, but his grace alsoe.' Upon which, other company comeinge to him, wee tooke our leave and departed; and to-morrow morning, I am to goe, with the boy, to him, and carry with him, his cloathes. And this is all, save that Mr. Edward Bradhill writt to Dr. Franckland, that one of Mr. Cromleholme's name, was likewise coming upp, by which, Dr. Frankland had thought of some fowle play in the case, and found a little fault with me, that I did not come to him sooner ; which I had done, had not his friends desired me to keepe him aweeke and buy him cloathes. But all is well. So is your sonn, Sir Edmond that will be; and he thanks you for your remembrance of him, but I find he expected something more from you, to have told him of a fitt wife for him, and one that needed not much wooing, and yett shee might bee young, beatiful, and rich." *Seal of arms.*

RICHARD BLANSHARD to the LICENSING JUSTICES for SALFORD HUNDRED, assembled at Manchester.

310. 1671[-2], March 8. York.—Would have attended them on the 11th, 13th, and 15th of the present month, as appointed; but the York assizes begin on the 11th, and he has many persons that then meet him, and pay in the money they have received under the act for the "lawe duty." Besides this, he is "subponoenaed for a witness, in a cause of the Duke of Buckingham," to be tried at York this assizes.

J. ANGIER to ROGER KENYON.

311. 1671-2, March 17. Deane.—Concerning some ecclesiastical proceedings against the writer.

LISTS OF THE ENGLISH AND FRENCH FLEETS, AGAINST HOLLAND.

312. 1672, April 2.—Total of the English vessels, &c.: 103 ships and 4 yatches, 24,925 men, 7,209 guns, and 54,827 tons. Total of the French vessels, &c.: 116 ships, great and small, 22,509 men, 3,774 guns, and 52,679 tons.

JANE KENYON to her daughter, MRS. ALICE KENYON.

313. 1672, May 4.—Recommending her not to send "little Roger" back to Mr. Pimlow's school, as he was treated unkindly there. *Portion of seal.*

ROGER KENYON [to his wife].

314. 1672, June 25.—I am so troubled for my dear Dolly's sickness. Cousin Dick Asheton is not slain, he was taken prisoner and carried into Holland, but is now at liberty and well, but poor Lewis is slain. *Portion of seal.*

HENRY [BRIDGMAN], Bishop of Sodor and Man, to his " much honoured cousen," ROGER KENYON, at Lancaster.

315. 1672, September 1. Brandlesholme.—Asking his favour on behalf of Evan Grundy, a white skinner and furrier (a kinsman of the writer), concerning some applications made against the said Grundy by his enemies. *Seal.*

RICHARD BORROW [or BORRON ?] to ROGER KENYON, "to be lefte with the stationer att Gray's Inne Gate."

316. 1672, November 1.—"The poor Ale-wives in Lancashire are yett like to bee ruined, unles you can finde out some way for their redresse. And to the end you may take some advise upon the busines; I have here sent you the coppy of the order made att Wigan Sessions last. And so soon as you have found out any expedient for their releese, I pray communicate the same."

Postscript.—"They have all made tender of the single duty, and demanded their goods; but the exise men laffe them to scorn, and say they value not the order or the Justices."

ROGER BRADSHAIGH to ROGER KENYON, at the Sword and Buckler, Holborn.

317. 1672, November 26. Haigh.—"Honest namesake,—It is good striking whilst the iron is hott, soe that if I knew wheare to give a hitt on Mr. Slyngier's (?) behalfe, I would not spare my blow; if you can find out a probable way to put him into play againe, I pray use your endeavour, (and my name) on his behalfe, and I shall readily second it. Doctor Wilkins will obstruct him noe more, and Mr. Tildesley is yet, but a licensed Non-conformist. I thank you for your last, and pray let mee heare what becoms of our namesake Kirkby, and present my services to his father, and tell him his daughter is well and craves his blessing; but when will you come downe? Shall I fynd you in towne? or is it beleeved the Parliament will sitt? or is theare hopes of a peace? I have noe news to returne you, but that Mr. Farington is like to dye, and my Lord Derby recover for the present, but noe greate confidence of the continuance. I pray bring mee one or two of Gouldsmith's litle foulded pocket Almeanacks for '73· This is all the trouble I shall give you."

ARTHUR ASSHETON to ROGER KENYON, in London.

318. 1672, November 27. Clitherow.—"This may certifie you that upon the 14th of October, by Mathew Benson, the nine gownes came to Cliderow, directed to Mr. Leonard Nowell, which hee and Mr. Bailife Lister did receive; all the gownes being very well liked, and very fitt. Onely they are full side (*sic*); but it is a fault easily helpt. Upon the Sabboth day next after our fair, being the 27th of October, Mr. out-bailife Lister was pleased come to Cliderow; the brethren, all in there gownes, did attend both Mr. bailiffs to the church, in their gownes, the Mace then taking its place. After morning prayer, Mr. Bailiff Lister, off Arnolds biggin (?) was pleased to give the brethren a very noble treat at Thomas Atkinson's. As yet the mace is not got mended, Mr. Robert Parker desired me to let it rest untill your comeing downe. I presume he intends his 5 marks or . . . then."

J. AINGER to ELLIS NUTTALL, "servant to Mr. Kenyon."

319. 1672, December 3. Deane.—"I have made bold to trouble you with the enclosed. If Mr. Nedham bee in towne I know you wil deliver it him. If hee should bee gone, I authorize you to open the letter, and at a convenient time you may shew it your master; but I hope Mr. Nedham is yet with you, though I heare he is not at your lodgings, which occasions this trouble to you, for which charge I wil satisfy you when I see you."

Enclosure.—1672, December 3. Deane.—"I writt two or three lynes to you last weeke which, whether they did reach you or not, I yet know not. I made bold also to write two lynes to my worthy friend, Mr. Kenyon. The truth is my case is sad, but it is not deplored by my friends, because not truly and fully understood. So soone as ever I knew that God had that mercy in store for us as to restore our King, I was one of the first that sought after reordination, and that not upon the account of worldly concernes, but upon well bottomed principles of judgment and conscience. My former juvenile prankes and madnes did not so estrange my relations' affections as did that one act, the sad effects whereof I feel to this day. Could I, to my owne satisfaction, have continued as I begun, when there was no king in our Israel, I believe I should have been in the van of the Nonconformists, and should not have gone through St. Peter's needle as hitherto I have done. It is well known I lived in good repute with Bishop Hall to his very dying day, and had that good Bishop lived, the first preferment, whether King's Preacher's place or whatever that fell, was promised to mee ; but he was too good for earth. God had a scourge for us, and we have drunke of a bitter cup. When I had hopes they were frustraeneous (*sic*) and, instead of preferment, I am debarred of a settlement. That cruel prosecution or persecution of mee hath undone mee upon severall accounts. My resignation hath very grievously troubled mee, but it was more to please others than myselfe ; though I must confess, I could not patiently thinke of a suspension. I have, to my noe small griefe, been out of employment since, though I had hopes some good friend would, ere this, have provided for mee by themselves or their friends. Those that were the abettors of my adversarys are silent in darknes, the one naturally, the other artificially, dead. What God hath in reserve now for us, I know not. I would fain hope, and I doe pray for mercy. Our case in Deane Parish is the saddest, I think, that ever was. That some eighteen combined persons shall carry on all designes against the sense and mind of all the rest of this large parish, keepe in a parson who hath not read one prayer since his first coming in, which was on Palme Sunday ; to abuse king, parliament, all authority, parish and all, and putt in a simple young fresh lad, who was but a schollar the other day with my son under Mr. Taylor, and now intend him to be the cypherical vicar (not seraphical doctor) for whom they have gott the broad seale before the last Lord Keeper went out, and they say that this very morning hee is gone for institution and induction. How this will or can be prevented, I know not; but I could wish that noble person, Mr. Kenyon, would arise and stand up for the parish. Colonel Kirby and others would assist, but I need not, I cannot, instruct him. There was great sadnes upon the report of the death of the Bishop. All their discourse and castings for future was to this purpose, that if I did offer (it seems they suspect) to come in, they would indevour to gett in Mr. Rawlett and by all meanes put mee by, and if Mr. Tilsby might not enjoy his liberty as before, they would, and could, gett the seale for him to preach in his house ; with such like stuffe. Is it not pitty these should domineer as they have done. For myself I say nothing, but lye with my mouth in the dust. If God see good, hee can restore mee ; if not, hee will provide for mee. But because wee are to use meanes, I pray, sir, acquaint my most worthy friend with these things or rather put him in minde, for hee knowes them already, and pray him to bee instrumentall to helpe me to some good concerne. Oh, that God saw good that the King might bee prevailed with to let the Archbishop have a hearing of all their unworthy carriages, from first to last. I believe it might easily be brought about. But I forgett myself pardon mee. My soule is troubled within mee. If you bee in London, I pray let me heare from you."

Postscript.—"I have been very loath to report what I have heard, lest it be thought to bee upon private designes. Ever since the last Bishop came in to be their friend, they bragged that matters should go on their side, in spight of Bradshaw and Kenyon, no better epithets so long as they had the Bishop and Lord Keeper's sure stayes, sayes Tilsby. Hee told me, about Ladydaye, to my face he cared not a ——— for the best friends I had, now theirs are gone. I could wish they might know themselves. Pray also tell Mr. Kenyon they have taken Mr. Hatton bound to resigne at their pleasures, having, as an ordinary servant, two or three months warning, the precise time I know not. I am weary of writing their fooleryes and knaveryes."

RICHARD WALMSLEY to HENRY NOWELL, in the Isle of Man.

320. 1672[-3], January 14.—Asks him to send some "excellent sort of strong beer made in your island, such as my Lord of Derby drinks, some times, at Knowsley." Asks him to make a trial of burying his puffings in a clean cloth in the ground for twenty-four hours, to take away the rank taste they have after they are pulled; they use otters in the same manner, after the skin is taken off, and they are very sweet and inoffensive, but without it they are not to be endured. *Seal.*

The LORDS OF THE COUNCIL to [the JUSTICES for Lancashire].

321. 1672-3, February 24. Whitehall.—"His Majestie hath received an address from you, and he hath seriously considered of it, and returneth you this answer; that he is very much troubled that that declaration which he put out for ends soe necessary to the quiett of his kingdome, and especially in that juncture, should have proved the cause of disquiet in his House of Commons, and given occasion to the questioninge of his power in ecclesiasticks, which he finds not done in the reignes of any of his ancestors. He is sure he never had thoughts of useing it otherwise then as it hath beene intrusted in him, to your peace and establishment of the Church of England and the ease of all his subjects in generall, neyther doth he pretend to the right of suspending any lawes wherin the properties, rights, or liberties, of any of his subjects are concerned, nor to alter anythinge in the established doctrine or discipline of the Church of England, but his onely designe in this was to take of the penalties the statuts inflict upon dissenters and which he believes, when well considered of, you yourselves would not wish executed according to the rigour and letter of the lawe; neither hath he done this with any thought of avoydinge or precludinge the advice of his Parliament; and if any Bill shall be offered him which shall appeare more proper to attaine the afforesaid ends and secure the peace of the Church and kingdome, when tendered in due manner to him, hee will shew how readily he will concurre in all wayes that shall appear good for the kingdome." *Copy.*

FRANCIS HOLLINSHED to ROGER KENYON.

322. 1673, April 26. London.—"I intend to see you at Wigan Cocking, if my Lord Gerard's coming into the country, doth not hinder me. As for news, here is little, but Prince Robert is gone downe to the ships at the boy in the Ore ; the other ships are making ready at Portsmouth, and the French fleete is expected to be there the next week, and then to have a generall randevouse. Prince Robert tooke the sacrament and othe of alegiance and supremisy, and maketh all the officers to doe the same, or else to leave their places, and so God speed him." *Seal of arms, broken.*

PARNELL AMY to " MRS. KENYON, at her house in the Milgate, Manchester."

323. 1673, July 27.—" As for your daughters education, I am re-saulved to kep no mor a publicks col (*sic*), nor to have aboue 2 gentil wemen at a tim, that they may be compane, on for another; for I am were of great impliment. I have had severall ofred me senc I cam to the ccti, but yet I have excepted of non, and therfoor have the mor liberti to make good that intrest you may clam by promis. And, if you ples to put her forth for a yere, for i intend to medele with non for les then a yere, if it ples God they have ther health. As for her larning lessen, I thenke it will not be fet to go to a publick col in the city, but there is a menester, that techeth, vere nere the place I dwel, that hath 30 collers. He hath 20 shelling a gurle, and, if you see good, I shall inquire of hem if he will teck her an our in a day, when his collers are gon. My rat is ten pond a yere, and 20 shelling entrance. I shall leve it to your ferther consederation, and commet you and yours to the protection of the Almightie." · *Seal.*

[The DUKE OF BUCKINGHAM] to the MAYOR and ALDERMEN of the City of York.

324. 1673, September 16. Wallingford House.—" My Lord and Gentlemen,—Upon an answer of a letter I writt to Sir Henry Thompson, wherein I advised him to putt a complaint upon my Lord Treasurer, in not opposinge his sonne to the Burgeshipe of the Towne of Yorke, I am forced to address to your Lordshipe and your bretheren, because he tells me he would be very willinge to give over his interest, if your Lordshipe and the Aldermen would give him leave to doe it. I know not for what reasons you have resolved, as Sir Henry Thompson has informed me, to choose none to [serve] you in Parliament that are not of your own Corporation; but methinkes, consideringe the zeale of my Lord Treasurer has always had for your service, and how much it may be now in his power to shew it, you ought not now to beginn at this tyme to putt that rule in practice, since it will looke as if you did it because he had deserved (*sic*) you in that imployment. I am sure noe man can be more passionately zealous for all the good of the towne of Yorke then he is, of which I could give you some late unquestionable demonstrations, but that itt does not become [me] to speake of itt, because I am concerned in itt myselfe. This at least deserves that you should not putt an affront upon him, which, under favour, it will be, if you should refuse to let his son serve in his stead, since, perhaps, he is the first man of his quality that ever was denyed that kindness, upon a removall out of the House of Commons into the House of Peeres. I come now to my owne parte. I am sure I never deserved your unkindness, and if you have any consideration of me, I desire you to shew itt in not puttinge any neglect to my Lord Treasurer, since by it you would lay an eternall disobligation upon [me]." *Copy.*

THOMAS, LORD LATIMER,[1] to the MAYOR and ALDERMEN of the City of York.

324A. 1673, September 16.—" My Lord and Gentlemen,—I have received a letter from some of you, dated the 12th instant, in answer to myne, concerning my sonne's election to be your Burgesse, and I cannot but make this observation upon itt, that whether my sonne deserves that honor or noe, I have deserved better from the City myselfe then to have itt made an argument to exclude any man from your service, by sayeinge he is not of your body, for that is plainely to tell me that your affaires have been prejudiced under my management ; and to add to the . . . . . tell me further that you had purposed itt long before my promotion. I confesse, in a letter from Sir Henry Thompson of Eskricke, in answer to one of myne, before I knew of this pretension, he told me he was ingaged long before my letter, and seemed to be verry sory for itt ; but I imputed that to a defect which I expected not to find, and certainely those which knew the respect that is due betwixt gentlemen of any quallity to another, would not have been wantinge in giving notice, at least, to a predecessor promoted to a better station, nor cann I imagine there are many of the Citty preingaged, without the least sort of intimation to one who served them soe faithfully, and was now more capable, either of doeing or obstructinge it. In another part of your letter, you speake of two gentlemen whome I said my sonne should not oppose if either of them would stand, which is most true ; and had Sir Henry Thompson mentioned any such desire, he had been the third to whome I should have made the same declaration. But I must acknowledge I cannot but distinguish betwixt those who use me civily and those who doe not, as I dare appeale whether he has done, and therefore I cannot ' hinder myselfe from giveinge him opposition, and if, in my success, I find my measures wrong taken on one kind, others will find theirs not much better. I heare that many suggestions have been made as if the Duke of Buckingham were for promoteinge of the interest of Sir Henry ; the trueth of which you will find by his grace's letter to the Citty, by this post, and indeed I believe you will find most of the insinuations grounded upon the like bottomes. But I am sorry to heare, which truely I did not know before, that 150l. of the arrearages of the wyne licences is not yett paid, which is certainly yet very recoverable, and perhaps by Sir Henry Thompson's sollicitations. I heare alsoe, it is made a greate inducement to the election of Sir Henry, because he will be soe great a promoter of the traide of the Citty, but certainly it is the first tyme that any man's interest was ever thought equall to that of my Lord Treasurer's, in promoteinge traide in England. I cannott but complaine alsoe, that when your Lordship had adjurned the readinge of my letter till a longe daye, for giveinge notice to all the freemen and to a larger place for conveniency of hearinge, you have sent me a letter to which I have reason to believe the tenth part of the Citty has not been privy to it. And, therefore, I now desire your justice to lett all who were concerned have due notice and tyme to consider what they conceive may bee best for their service, and then I doubt not but, upon tryall, I shall find the continuance of the Cittyzens to me, by their approbation of my sonne to serve them." *Copy.*

SIR ROBERT CARR to ROGER KENYON.

325. 1673, November 15.—" I receaved yours of the tenth, which I must needes say was written with great affection to the King's service,

---

[1] He sat for York as Sir Thomas Osborne, till called to the Upper House.

and with great discretion, which is necessarie at this time, when every ill man maketh the worst of things. I doe assure you your prudent management of this matter is verie well approved by others besides myself; and I desire you will get some justice of peace, that will doe it with most privitie, and take the examination of Mercer, and what other persons shall seem proper to examine. But doe it with as little noyse as may be. I will look after the ironmunger here, and, if I find anything that may be useful to you, will give you account; and I pray let me, from time to time, heer from you, and, if you find ocation, take care to secure any that shall seem most conserned, and take as few to your assistans, as you can. I should be glad you would use noe clark but yourself, for, as you verie well observe, the private carriage, be it real or not, is best, and my knowledg of you, maketh me confident of the carriage of this affair, the most to his Majesties service." *Seal of arms.*

Troopers' Saddles.

326. 1673, November 21.—Informations, by various persons, as to the making of troopers' saddles, to be delivered at Warrington, for one Thomas Mercer, of Abram, in the County of Lancaster, " garthweb-weaver," who said they were for the Duke of Monmouth's saddler.

Expenses at the Funeral of Roger Hanmer, Esquire.

327. 1672[-3].—Amongst other, the following items :—two dozen gloves for men, at 2s. a pair; 2 dozen "shames" for women, at 2s. 6d. a pair ; 2 dozen gloves for women, of " whitelamb," at 1s. a pair ; 10 dozen men's gloves, at 9d. a pair ; 15 lb. of " Makeroons," 1li. 10s. Various items for "biskets" and wine. Two hats, for coachmen, 11s. 6d.; the Herald at arms, for a black band, 1s. 6d. "Mourning and sugar," bought of Mr. Newton, 13li. 14s. Payments for the poor, the ringers, and for the coffin and hearse, 1li. 10s. The velvet for the corps, 1li. 5s. The herald, for 24 scutcheons, at 3s. 4d. each. 30 banners, 1s. 6d. a piece.

Guicciardini Wentworth to Roger Kenyon, at Peel.

328. 1673[-4], January 24.—"I suppose you are not a stranger to Parliament proceedings, as to the Duke (?), and Earl of Arlington, who has not escaped it ; it being agreed that, if the Committee, to whome the consideration of the particulars charged against him, are referred, do find matter therein contained sufficient, then he is to be impeacht; Sir Robert, being one of them. The next person leviled att, is said to be the Lord Privy-Seal. His Majesty, this morning, suddenly giving order to appeare att the House in robes, alarmed the towne ; but the result was that, having sent for the lower House, he acquainted them that, at the beginning of the Session, he told them of some slight overtures the Dutch had made towards a treaty, but since, that he, by the hands of the Spanish Embassador, had received some propositions more cevill, with which they should be acquainted, of which he desired them to consider that if they were such as stood with his honour and theirs, and both their interests to accept, that for his part he would be ready ; but if they were thought otherwise, that then they would consider what was next to be done. And so dismisst them, well satisfied. Whereupon, they returned to the House, and ordered it to be taken into consideration or Monday next." *Seal of arms, broken.*

——— to ROGER KENYON, at Peel.

329. [1673-4, February 7.]—"It is hoped this frosty weather will dry up all your gouty humours, and render you as good att peditating as formerly, though not tyme enough to goe along with Sir William Temple and Sir Gabriell de Silvis into Holland, to conclude the peace there, which seems as good as perfected ; which, together with the Prince of Orange's being declared Stat-Holder, gives, as they say, much satisfaction to his Majesty. The House has voted to make a separate address for removall of the Duke of Bu[ckingham] who is to give (to whome, query) 1,000*l.* bond, never to see the lady you wot on : but my Lord Arlington escapes much better. Yesterday, a vote past for sending for the Duke of Norffolk out of Italy ; and this day a bill relating to pore prisoners and false imprisonments. Pray, Sir, att your leisure, informe me what my part of the Green Wax might be worth to be sold, not according to the income Mr. Heywood returns mee, but as itt might be, if I had another Lancashire manner of man, not called by the name of Heywood to deale with."

E. RIGBY to ROGER KENYON.

330. 1673-4, February 10.—" The peace between England, Holland, and Spaine, was confirmed last night, and we have good assurances of a proposall betweene the Prince of Orange and the Lady Mary (the Duke's eldest daughter, about 13 years old) and that the regiments and gaurds raysed since January, 1663, are to be disbanded, and after that, the test to trye all Roman Catholicks is past the Howse, which is of great noate to all Protestants. The Duke's owne regiment comes under this voate. This night the Parlament makes their addresse to the Kinge, which wee doubt not but will be granted."

JAMES LIGHTBOUNE to ROGER KENYON, at Peel.

331. 1673[-4], February 10. London.—" On Saturday, the House of Commons voted the land forses, raysed since 1663, a grievance, and this day they addresse for the disbonding of them. The King, the last night, signed the Articles of peace made with the Dutche, and the Spanish Embassador is gone into Holland with them, to be signed there. The House, out of some displeasure to my Lord Howard, addressed the King to have the Duke of Norfolke to come into England." *Seal of arms.*

GUICCIARDINI WENTWORTH, [Secretary to the Duchy of Lancaster,] to ROGER KENYON, at Peel.

332. 1673[-4], February 12.—" Yesterday his Majesty in person acquainted both Houses that, acording to their advice, he had made a speedy, honourable, and profitable peace with the Dutch, and, as he hoped, a lasting one ; that his resolutions had preceeded their address for disbanding the standing army levied and keept on foot, for the present occasion only ; that the two Irish regiaments should, within a few dayes, be on their march ; and that, perhaps, he should disband more than they desired. But, forasmuch as some of our neighbours were angry, and all powerfull, he had thought itt fitt that some number of good shipps, should be speedly built ; and left itt to to their consideration as to the *modus.* All seem well pleased, and the House in some good temper. The Lords have made a vote that the heyre of the crowne shall not marry a Catholique lady, and prest to have excluded a Catholique prince from inheriting the crown, but that was opposed by severall Bishops. Littleton and Elis come the Circuit, which begins att Yorke the 16th, and att Lancaster the 26th of March." *Seal of arms.*

EDWARD RIGBY to ROGER KENYON, at Manchester.

333. 1674, October 8, London.—" Wee have news that Turenne and the Conferates have fought, and that the French have got the better ; but since, wee have news from Flanders that the Branningburgers came and ingaged the fourth day, and have much worsted the French. Divers reports runne up and downe, but the certainty is not expected untill the next post comes."

PRICE OF PAPER.

334. 1674, October 31.—Account from Ralph Shelmerdine for "copy paper" supplied to Mr. Kenyon at 3*d.* the quire.

The LORDS OF THE COUNCIL to the CUSTOS ROTULORUM OF THE COUNTY PALATINE OF LANCASTER.

335. 1674[-5], February 5. The Court at Whitehall.—" His Majestie having lately resolved in Councill to cause the Convictions of Popish Recusants to be encouraged, quickened, and made effectuall, by a particular care and charge committed to his Atturney Generall in that behalfe, in order to informe himselfe touching the convictions which are already certified into the Exchequer, and thereupon to cause speedy processe to issue forth. His Majesty hath also thought fit to order and comand that the Justices of Peace within the severall Counties, Cittyes, and places of this Realm do, with all speed, certifie into the Exchequer such convictions as are perfected, and likewise certifie his Majestie's Atturney General what convictions are preparing and whether any thing hinders the compleating of the same. As also whether any persons of quality who are suspected to be popish Recusants, have been omitted to be presented, and what obstructions they finde therein, that his Majestie may upon due information, cause effectuall orders to issue for the removall thereof."

E. ASSEHTON to ROGER KENYON.

336. 1674[-5], February 9. London.—Has made two matches with the Duke of Albemarle, to be run at Newmarket, upon which he has bet a great deal of money. *Seal.*

SIR THOMAS STRINGER to ROGER KENYON.

337. 1675, April 10. New Hall.—It is so late before the intention of my standing is known, and therefore I was very unwilling to undertake it, but the Chancellor tells me, I do not know what you can do. I applied myself to his Grace the Duke of Albemarle; he also is as positive and very desirous that I should be your burgess, and to that purpose hath sent a letter to Sir Walter Clarges to command him not to stand, but to assign his interest, if he hath any upon his own account, to me. What effect that letter will have I know not, but if Sir Walter will not give over, his Grace resolves to write to the town and to all other persons to whom he hath written to in Sir Walter Clarges' behalf, that they should vote for me, their Recorder. *Seal of arms.*

HENRY NOWELL to MRS. ALICE KENYON, at Peel.

338. 1675, May 8. Castletown, Isle of Man.—Desires to know how the suit goes between Ned Rigby and her. Hears that his nephew Coplie's estate is like to be extended for some arrears due to the King ; if so, he should be heartily sorry, for he does not know what will become of them and their little ones. Hopes to come and see them next summer. He hoped to have come to them this year, but money is very scarce in his purse, by reason of every thing being so dear. There will be many poor families which will perish for want of food. *Portion of seal of arms.*

HENRY NOWELL to his grandfather, ROGER KENYON.

339. 1675, May 19. Morton.—"I enclose a letter from John Crooke. I have received a letter just now from Kit Bunnastre, wherein he writes he has got pardon both for life and estate." *Seal of arms.*

JO: ENTWISLE to ROGER KENYON, Clerk of the Peace for Lancashire, at Wigan.

340. 1675, October 11. Ormskirk (?).— As to the bad state of the highway from Barrow to Bretherton. "In the case of my conviction of the Quakers, move the justices to a small determination, one way or other ; if they think fitt to order it against me, pray draw up their order to indempnify mee. I have sent out warrants to severall constables, and their [the justices'] order of the last sessions hath superseded my proceedings." Begs for "a publique declaration," by an order of the sessions, commanding the constables to proceed and make their returns to him.

ROGER KENYON to his MOTHER.

341. 1675, November 25. London.—" The Parliament was prorogued on Monday morning till the 15th of February, 1676. Many are of opinion they will scarse ever meete again, but be dissolved by proclamation ; and some say a proclamation is now preparing and at presse, for that purpose, but I dare not write that as a truth. The beate of the two houses against each other, in pretence of privilledge, is assigned as the principle occasion of this prorogation, though no reason was given ·at the prorogueing. The newse, as it is rumoured, is, that the French and Duch have made an exclusive peace."

SIR ROGER BRADSHAIGH to ROGER KENYON.

342. 1675, December 11.—" Yesternight a company of us rejoiced at "the Fleece," and upon Tuesday night the Chancellor, with some such select bad company as myself, tossed off the Florence wine at Sir John O[tways] chamber, and both the Chancellor and his coach did me the good fellowship's office to set me down at my lodging about 12 a.m. This night I, with Sir John, Mr. Fleetwood, and others, take the other tusle at the "Dog" in Palace Yard ; how that Dog bites you shall hear in the country. The King's preacher's business is done, and I have got a pension for a poor woman in Wigan. My apology for this little foul piece of paper is, that I lit my candle at six and found I had no more, and something I must be doing till it be day. When we meet at Ralph's, or in Abraham's bosom, we will recount our adventures."

THOMAS MORT to ROGER KENYON.

343. 1676, April 15.—Giving thanks for certain posey rings sent. *Seal of arms, broken.*

BOOK of BAPTISMS, MARRIAGES, and BURIALS at Wigan; and INCANTATIONS.

344. 1676, April —, to 1683, September.—A small book containing at one end the baptisms, marriages, and burials at Wigan, from April 1676 to September 1683, also notes with regard to the family of Seddon; at the other end of the book are various memoranda of money payments and recipes, and amongst the latter are the two following incantations, dated 13 August, 1681 :—" Stanshing blood—Christ that was borne in Bethlem and was baptised in fludd Jorden, the water is wild, the child is meeke and mild, as the flood so stood, soe stansh thou blood of this person M. C., and bleed noe more, by the vertue of the Father, Son, and Holy Ghost, obey to my bidding and stansh thou blood without any more delay. The Lord's prayer 3 times over and this 3 times over and the creed in the latter end."

" Tooth-ake.—I ajure thee tooth ake of blood worme and rume, by the vertue of Our Lord Jhesus Christ and by the merits of Joseph, his foster father, and as hee was betrothed to that blessed Virgine Mary, not a husband, and a witnes of an undefyled virginitie soe by soe much the more suddenly depart thou tooth ack from this person M. C. now, and anowy them noe more, nor trouble them, nor vex them, nor appear in ther body, by the vertue of the Father, Son, and Holy Ghost, by the vertue of all holy names [of] God obey to my bidding and avoid thou tooth ach from this person now without any more delay. The Lord's prayer 3 times and the creed once."

ORDER TO MAKE LISTS OF PAPISTS.

345. 1676, November 23.—Order that " the knights of the sheire, on Tuesday next come sennight, doe bring in lists of all persons of note being papists, or soe reputed, resient or haveing considerable estates within their respective countyes. And that the knights, cittizens, and burgesses, who serve for each county, doe meet together and agree and prepare such lists and signe the same."

FELLOWSHIP OF MANCHESTER COLLEGE.

346. [After 1676.]—Petition of John Heyrick, M.A., chaplain to the Earl of Derby, son of the Warden of the Collegiate Church of Manchester, and graduate of the University of Oxford, to the Lords Commissioners for Ecclesiastical preferments, for the next fellowship that shall be void in the said College.

ROBERT WILLIAMSON to ROGER KENYON, in London.

347. [16]76[-7], January 13.· Liverpool.—It is certain that Sir O—— M—— has written to young Mr. Ashurst, of London, and tempted him to stand " for a burgesse of our toune, by the proferr of the votes of his partie." Discusses his chances of success. *Seal with crest.*

Robert Williamson to Roger Kenyon, in London.

348. 1676[-7], February 11. Liverpool.—" I must desire you to prosecute the business of our Charter with all care, and to regulate yourself in taking out the writt for election, by the advise of our good friends in the House, especially Mr. Legh of Lyme ; that wee be not puzled or straightened by any miscarriage therein. Sir O—— M—— is full of new plotts ; talks of joyning with Mr. Ashurst, of London; and wee find the report of this begins to unsettle some persons, and alter their inclinations. There is a bill sent up to Mr. Arrowswith, of 60*l.* ; which please to call for as your occasion requires ; hee has likewise further order, if you want. Pray give us an account of your proceedings." *Seal.*

John Molyneux to "Mrs. Kenyon," at Peele.

349. 1676[-7], March 20. Teversall.—" I have at length sent you the trenchers I soo long sinse promisede you, and heartyly wish you may live to weare them out, that I may send you more when those are done, if they be worth yore acceptance . . . . You often make us remember you by yore puffings [puffins] which prove exceeding good ; we heartyly give you thanks for them. But indeed, you doo heape soo many kindnesses upon us, one after another, that you scarce leave us time to make our acknowledgements for them." *Seal with crest.*

Robert Newlyn, President of Corpus Christi College, Oxford, to Dr. Nicholas Stratford, Keeper of Manchester College.

350. 1677, March 25.—As the place of head-master in Manchester School, of the foundation of the Reverend Doctor Hugh Oldham, Bishop of Exeter, is vacant by the resignation of Daniel Hill, A.M. ; and as the nomination, election, and presentation of the master of the said school, belongs to the President of Corpus Christi College in the University of Oxford, for the time being, he nominates and elects as head-master of the said school, William Barrow, A.M. *Seal of arms.*

Dorothy Lagoe to Mrs. Kenyon, at Peel.

351. 1677, May 8. Manchester.—" We had John Partington's wife in the seat with us, on the Lord's Day, and her father, and Mr. Stanford's mistress. I suppose the two last named are intended to stay hereabouts for a short time, but Partington is a tradesman in the town, and his former wife kept amongst such men's wifes. I and my cousin are very thankfull for the great kindness we received from Mr. Hilton, at your request for us, and I believe it is not his mind that the seat should be made uneasy to us, by being crowded ; neither that my children were not included in Mr. Hilton's kindness to me, but that we may sit togeather, as we have done." *Seal of arms.*

The King to Henry, Earl of Peterborough, Deputy to Henry, Earl of Norwich, Earl Marshall of England.

352. 1677, July 12.—" We, calling to mind the great and signal service performed to us by John Lane, of Bentley, in the County of Stafford, deceased, in his ready concurring to the preservation of our royal person after the battle of Worcester, at which time, contemning the threatning

published by the murtherers of our royal father against any who should conceal or assist us, and disdaining the rewards proposed to such as should be instrumental in the discovery and destruction of our person, and not valueing any hazard his family might run—with the duty of an unspotted allegiance, did, by his great prudence and fidelity, so conduct us, that wee were able at length to retire to places of safety beyond the seas ; have, therefore, of our own free will and proper motion, given and granted unto the descendants lawfully issued from the body of the said John Lane, this honourable remuneration as a notable marke or badge of his constant fidelity, that is to say ;—henceforth, they shall bear in augmentation to their paternal arms, three lyons passant, guardant Or, in a canton gules. And our will and pleasure is, that you do require and command our servants, the Kings and Officers of Arms, to marshal and set up in all proper places and upon all occasions, the paternal armes of the said John Lane, with the augmentation aforesaid. And that you also direct and require the Registrar of our College of Armes to cause this our concession to be duly entered upon record in our said College."
Copy.

Attached is a copy of the epitaph on the monument erected to John Lane, in the north aisle of Wolverhampton church.

Rents of Church Seats.

353. 1677, July 24.—Order by John, Bishop of Chester. Whereas the endowment of the chapel of Ellenborough within the parish of Eccles, is very small, not exceeding twenty pounds by the year, which cannot be thought a sufficient maintenance for the minister, and whereas there are certain persons, who repair to the said chapel and have the benefit of seats therein, who are not annual contributors nor pay for their seats as others do. It is therefore requested that Mr. Roger Kenyon, Mr. Ralph Eddowes, and Mr. Richard Edge, feoffees for the endowment of the said chapel, do take care that such persons who shall repair to the said chapel of Ellenborough and are not annual contributors, be charged and pay such reasonable payments for the use of their respective seats, as others do who enjoy seats in the said chapel. *Signed and seal of arms.*

The Sentence passed upon the Lord Stafford.[1]

354. [1680, December.]—" The Lords were divided in judgement of him, 32 that he was not guilty, and 54 that he was guilty. About two howres after, he was brought to hear his sentence; then the Lord High Steward (viz. the Lord Chancellor) sitting at a table on one end of the scaffold furthest from the prisoner, and the Judges sitting on chaires on each side the table, all the Lords in their robes on woolsacks upon the floore of the scaffold, and the House of Commons on benches raised on each side. The Court was called, the King was present, and my Lord High Steward having a white wand holden by him, putt on his hatt, made an excellent speech, first saying, seemingly with tears, that it was the first time he had ever passed the sad sentence of death upon any man, and how unpleasant the occasion of this was to him ; then sett forth how manyfest and undeniable it was, that there was a plott and contrivance to take away the King's life, subvert the government and the religion establish't and to introduce popery, and then proceeding to the proofes that had been against the prisoner, wherein he was evidently guilty, and shewing how little reason he had to bee so, in respect of so good a Prince; and so, after

---

[1] This document has been misplaced. *See* pp. 122–124 *post.*

severall exhortacions, passed the judgement for high treason, to go thence to the place from whence he came and thence to be drawn to the place of execution to be hanged and let down alive, to see his bowells ripped up, his members cutt off and cast into the fire, to have his body cutt into four quarters and disposed at the King's pleasure. After the sentence given, the Lord Stafford moved that the short time hee had to live, that he might not be debarred the company of his wife and children and visitts of his relations and friends, and wept. My Lord High Steward told him all the Lords were sory for him, and as well those whose judgement it was that he was guilty did pray for him, though perhaps he did not esteeme their prayers, but their religion, which he called heresy, directed them to do so, and they would all likewise together move his Majestie to remitt so farr the sentence, as that it might suffice to seperate his head from his body and to suffer his relations to see him. He bowed, and the man that waited with the white wand came up to the Lord High Steward and brake the twig before him, and so the Court risse; the prisoner no more to be called. My Lord was guarded away, the Axman before him then carrying the edge towards the prisoner. I cannot remember the names of all the Lords, but you will see them in the common newes papers. Duke of Newcastle voted him not guilty, all the other Dukes, to witt, Cumberland that is Prince Rupert, Monmouth, Albemarle and Lawderdale, voted him guilty. The morning before the Court set, all the House of Commons, the Spaker and his Mace went to the Lords barr to demand judgement. The Lords made an order that if any peer in town, without absolute proof that he was not able to be there, should absent himselfe when the Lords were passing their votes upon the Lord Stafford, whoever he was should be sent to the Tower. Many Lords that were neer relations to the Prisoner voted against him." '

W. HULTON to ROGER KENYON.

355. 1678, September 7.—Hopes to have a further discovery of the clippers and coiners, by Ann Hunt, wife of James Hunt, of Ince.

AN ACCOUNT OF THE POPISH PLOT.

356. 1678, October 31.—" Since my last, wherein I discovered to you the first account of this horrible plott, greate hath beene the diligence boeth of the Counsell and Parliament in bringing the same to light, wherein their endeavours have beene soe happy that they are now arrived to the bottome of it, and it lies now before boeth houses in its owne monstrous shape; it being noe lesse then the murder of the King, the subversion of our religion, lawes, and properties, the introduceing of popery and a tyrannicall arbitrary government by an army, our common and statute laws to be abolished and anihilated, and a mixture of military and civil law introduced, where counsell of warr should supply this place of our courts of justice, and the racke for the jury, with many such differences too tediouse to expresse here; but I hope, by this tymely and miraculouse discovery, we may be able to distroy this cochatrice in the egge which will yet certainely devoure us if hee bee hatcht. The manner of proceedings have beene thus :—One Mr. Oates, being a minister in Sussex, by reason of some lawe suites with persons which were too powerfull for him, hee was forced to quitt his parish and, comeing into London, fell into acquaintance with Mr. Tonge, a minister who hath beene many yeares a diligent inquirer into the practices and principals of the Jesuites and had published severall bookes against them. This man findeing

Oates, by reason of poverty, enclined to travell to seeke a livelyhood amongst the papists abroad, endeavoured to divert him by giveing him full information of theire wicked principles and practices. Whereupon Oates resolves to try the trueth, and promised, if hee found it to bee as Tonge informed, hee would renounce that religion and retorne againe to the Protestant Church. Oates thereupon, some yeares since, goes and enters himselfe a Noviciat in the College of the Jesuites in St. Omer's, where behaveing himselfe with great zeale, diligence, and demonstrateing his abilities, hee was soone taken notice of and thought a fitt instrument to convey the intelligence and correspondency of this hellish plott to most of the Courts in christendome. In acting whereof, by opening letters and packquetts entrusted with him and thereby gaineing some light, soe insinuated himselfe wherever hee came, that in time hee came to the depth and counsells of the designe. Whereby, about Aprill last, understanding the execution of this horrid villany to bee att hand and that comissions were signed by the Pope for all bishops and other clergy, for the officers of state and of theire armies, hee began to feare it would be executed before hee should find meanes to discover it. And being ready to lay hould of all oppertunities to come for England to doe it, it fell out that a booke called *the Jesuites' Moralls,* which Tonge had translated, came to their bandes, for which upon consultation it was agreed Tonge should bee killed, but a fitt person was wanting to doe it. Whereupon Oates offered to undertake it and had a note given him to receive £50 here when it was done, and in the meanetyme hee was directed to one Ireland, a preist in the Savoy, to accomodate him with lodgeing and necessaries. Whereupon Oates prepares for the journey, the colledge loades him with packquetts and comissions for all sorts of conspirators which hee brings over and with his owne hande delivers, but in the interim, underhand resortes to Tonge and acquaints him with the whole designe, of which haveing drawne a short relation, hee desires Tonge to give it privately to the King and offer to make it good if his Majesty would conceale the thing and appoynt a counsell to sitt and heare it. Tonge not being willing to undertake it alone tooke one Kirby, a merchant, and went to the King upon the 13th of August, where they acquainted him with the substance of it, but the papers being severall sheetes, and the King not careing for trouble, gave leave to acquaint and imploy the Treasurer to manage it. They were unwilling to consent, but the King saying hee dare trust his life and crowne in his hands, they could not refuse. All this while Oates was concealed. The matter thus settled, Tonge severall tymes presses the Treasurer, but noething done in 6 weekes; though the 2nd of September, whereon the King was to bee murdered, was past; whereon Tonge doubting some future trouble in case Oates should be killed or recant, causes Oates to draw an exact narrative containeing 15 or 16 sheetes and to sweare it before Sir Edmundbury Godfrey who perused and tooke notes out of it and according to his custome, keepeing faire with boeth sides, hee acquaints the Treasurer Coleman and some others with the businesse, and findeing Coleman soe deepe in the plott there was noe possibility of avoydeing of it, hee advises Coleman to impeach, which it is sayd hee did, and swore something before Godfrey which hee entered in a pockett booke, and that allsoe hee discovered to the Treasurer, and hee to the Duke of Yorke. I say noe more, but Godfrey was chidd and the matter fitt to bee concealed, and Godfrey was murdered soone after, being, as appeared plainely, strangled, and after carryed and layd in a ditch near Primrose Hill and his owne sword runne through him, noething missing but his band and pockett booke wherein were his noates concerneing this affaire. His murder raised a great spiritt in the people, which could not bee outfaced by the partie and theire adherents that murdered him, though there wanted neither diligence nor impudence in that party in all places to make it appeare hee murdered himselfe. Tomorrow hee is to·bee buried from the Hall of Bridewell where I beleive thousands will appeare to attend his corps to St. Martins. But to retorne to the plott.

" Godfrey, haveing taken the information, was forced then to bring it to counsell about the end of September 1678, where Oates appeared and made it good beyond all scruple, and thereupon, Coleman, one Langhorne a Counseller, and nine Jesuites, were committed and theire houses and lodgeings searched, but the matter done so publiquely and diverse daies given before the warrants issued, soe that they generally had notice enough to remove what they had a mind should not bee seene, and yet such papers and letters were found boeth in Coleman's and Langhorne's studies that give a full relation of the most horrid massacre and slaughter that ever was heard, which have beene since sorted and produced boeth before the Counsell and Parliament. Since the sitting of the Parliament, Oates hath beene every day examined before them, speakeing 5 or 6 hours at a tyme, giveing particuler demonstration of the whole affaire, wherein hee hath clearely proved the manner and designe of the fire of London, Southewarke, and many other fires, with the intended massacre in the fire of London, the designe of raiseing the Blackheath Army, with the reasons and occations of the severall Dutch warrs in order to this designe, the raiseing of the present army and the generall peace to ensue for the compleateing the worke, the raiseing and maintaineing privately 20,000 men att this tyme, with the generall and all other officers, all which are now in readinesse to joyne with the army, the greatest part whereof they thought themselves sure´of, and in Ireland they had likewise a generall and army ready, and Scotland the same. The manner to put it in execution was thus :—One Conyers, a Jesuite, with foure Irish ruffaines, undertooke to murder the King att Windsor, 21 September last, and thereupon a great cry was to bee made that the phanatiques had murdered the King, an alarume presently thereupon to bee given to the whole army, being then about 16,000, quartered in and neare London, whereof two regiments of 4,000 men, consisting all of Irish, Scotts and French papists, were about a month before brought out of France and quartered about Barnet, Enfeild, St. Albans, Ware, &c. were imediately to march to London to assist the proclaimeing the Duke of York, and under that pretence to fall upon and to massacre and slaughter the people, under the notion of phanatiques who had murdered the King, and then to have assisted the papists all over the kingdom to doe the like. The Duke of Yorke was to take the Crowne by gift from the Pope, and least any opposition should bee made, the French were to bee ready with an army and fleete to seize upon our fleete, burne and destroy such as opposed, and take the rest, and then the whole nation to bee shared among this crew (vizᵗ) the ancient church lands amongst the clergy, the murdered protestants' lands amongst the great officers, boeth civill and military, and the plunder of citties and townes amongst the soldiers and rabble of Irish and French papists. This is the substance of what is collected from the severall informations, proofes, and papers which have beene seized and made out.

" Things thus appeareing, the Commons lockt themselves up for many hours, sent for Cheife Justice Scroggs to them, who yssued out at one tyme, 40 or 50 warrants against noblemen and others. The high constables were sent for alisoe into the House and the warrants there delivered to them, and the House kept still shutt to prevent intelligence, and that night and next day, six lords and diverse persons of lesse quality were seized and comitted to the Tower, King's Bench, Newgate Gatehouse, and other prisons. The particulers you may perceive in a list annexed hereunto.

"Diverse letters of Coleman's, dated 1674 and 1675 (for all of later date are removed), have beene reade in boeth houses, and some letters of the Duke's in his custody, of the like date, whereby the King is, in a most abusive manner, caracterized as a person not fitt to governe or bee trusted, and the Parliament, both Lords and Commons, described as a company of beggarly, sottish, corrupt, meane people and to bee disposed of for slender sums of money to give up religion, law, property, kingdome, and what not ; with great importunity to the Pope, French, &c. to furnish money for effecting speedily the aforesaid glorious designe, and multitude of such stuffe, which would make every Englishman's harte ake to heare or thinke those in whose power wee are should deserve such carectors.

"Things thus standing, some intimation was brought to the Lord Mayor and Aldermen, on Saturday last, that on Sunday in sermon tyme some attempt would bee made upon the Citty, whereupon they ordered stronge double watches to bee sett, of house keepers in person, and the lights to bee renewed att 12 aclock att night; the gates to bee shutt all Sunday, and the watches to continue till releived att night, which was performed. And Doctor Stillingfleet haveing beene attempted by a fellowe in a gentile habitt, who brought a counterfeit letter, as from the Bishop of London, to desire him to come to him in the evening, and brought a coach to carry him, intending to have served him as Sir Edm : Godfrey was, but was prevented ; partely an extraordinary businesse would not permitt him to goe out, and partly jealousie, which made the Doctor answer him—if hee could goe hee would make use of his owne coach, which made the fellow vanish, and the Doctor waiteing on the Bishop the next day, found the letter and pretence wholly counterfeit. Thereupon, on Sunday, about 40 persons a guard waited on the Doctor to church and home. On Sunday a committee of Lords, *viz.* Winchester, Shaffesbury, the Treasurer Hallifax, and Cornebury being appoynted by the Lords, went to Coleman to Newgate and examined him, who had beene longe a close prisoner and knew nothing of Godfrey's death. And upon his examination, findeing persons of severall interests could not tell what to say, but to the maine poynt referred himselfe to his examination taken by Sir Edm : Godfrey which troubled some there who began to hint that Godfrey was dead, but Shaftsbury managed it soe wisely that hee turned it off, and in the conclusion hee confessed the letters and that hee had acted noething in the businesse but by the Duke's order, with the privity and advice of the Lord Arundell of Wardour, and seemed very desireous to have leave to speake with the King, and being demanded the reason, to know how farre hee might name the Duke in the businesse, which was the next day reported to the Lords. Whereupon high debates were tending to the impeachment of the Duke, but the Duke's party was so greate and avoyded the blow att that time. Whereupon the Commons ordered a Committee to goe to Newgate to examine Coleman, but when they came his noate was changed ; hee would owne nothing of the Duke, but sayd what hee had done was for religion sake. And the Lordes refuseing to send downe the report to the Commons and Coleman haveing turned his tale, things stand att present, and it is now doubted the matter will not bee throughly canvased, and some money being well placed, wee shall bee contented with the bangeing three or foure inconsiderable fellows and some lawe against popery, which will keepe our throates from being cutt a month att least.

" Sir, I feare I have beeno too tedions, but understanding from some freinds you were mucn in the darke in this businesse, made me enlarge. On Monday last the King sent for the Lord Mayor and Aldermen and thanked them for theire care and loyalty and desired them to raise theire trained bands and keepe gard for theire better security, soe that yesterday, a regiment was upon the gard and to bee relcived and soe continue till further order. Whitehall is close shutt up and noe passage to it but through the wickett att the greate gate, and a strict examination of all that are suffered to passe in or out." *Copy.*

RECUSANTS.

357. 1678, October — to 1678-9, January.—Names of those indicted at the Lancashire Quarter Sessions for recusancy, and who brought their *Certioraries* for removing of the same before the Judges of Assize at Lancaster :—

Silverdale.—Lady Aun Midleton, widow, and Elizabeth West, widow ; indicted October, 1678, at Lancaster.

Skerton.—Ambrose Bradshawe, gentleman, and Jane his wife; same date and place.

Warton.—Robert Midleton, gentleman; same date and place.

Whittingham.—Christopher Parkinson, husbandman, and Elizabeth Lee, widow ; same date and place.

Tatham cum Ireby.—Elizabeth Cansfield, widow; same date and place.

Corton cum Claughton.—Robert Croskell, husbandman, and Edward Bullen, gentleman ; same date and place.

Thurnham.—Robert Dalton, esquire ; same date and place.

Heaton cum Oxcliffe.—Thomas Brockholes, gentleman ; same date and place.

Aighton, Bayley, and Chaidgley.—Richard Sherborne, esquire, Isabella, his wife, Richard Sherborne, gentleman, and Nicholas Sherborne, gentleman ; indicted 28 November, 1678, at Blackburn.

Lydiate.—Margaret Ireland, widow; indicted October, 1678, at Wigan.

Scaresbrick.—Frances Scaresbrick, widow; same date and place.

Aintree.—Richard Lathom, gentleman ; same date and place.

Rixton and Glazebrook.—Elizabeth Massye, widow; same date and place.

Culcheth.—Thomas Culcheth, esquire, and John Culcheth, gentleman ; same date and place.

West Leigh.—Robert Heaton, gentleman, Anne Mossack, widow, Ellenor Urmston, spinster, and John Urmston, gentleman ; same date and place.

Ince in Makerfield.—Thomas Gerrard, gentleman ; same date and place.

Hindley and Abram.—Phillip Claughton, esquire ; same date and place.

Rainhill.—Alexander Chorley, and Elizabeth, his wife; same date and place.

Ashton in Makerfield.—Sir William Gerrard, Baronet, and William Gerrard, esquire ; same date and place.

Blackrod.—John Genyon, gentleman ; 17 October, 1678.

Lathom.—Sir Thomas Clifton, Baronet, and Lady Bridget, his wife ; at Preston, 16 January, 1678-9.

Wilpshire with Dunckley.—Dorothy Talbott, widow, and Dorothy, wife of Edward Warren [these two names appear to be scratched out].

Burnley.—John Townley, esquire, Francis Tounley, gentleman, Richard Tounley, esquire, Isabella Tounley, widow, Katherine Tounley, spinster, Dorothy Tounley, spinster, and George Culcheth, gentleman; at Blackburn, 28 November, 1678.

Clayton in le Moors.—Richard Walmisley, esquire, and Dorothy his wife [these two names appear to be scratched out].

Melling.—Robert Mollyneux, esquire, and Frances, his wife; at Wigan, October 1678.

Ince Blundell.—Henry Blundell, esquire, and John Leathwaite, gentleman; same date and place.

Bedford.—Francis Bradshaw, esquire, John Leathwaite, gentleman, and Peter Urmston; same date and place.

West Leigh.—John Naylor; same date and place.

Aughton.—Edward Stauley, gentleman.

Wrightington.—Hugh Dicconson, esquire.

Pendlebury.—Thomas Goulden, gentleman; at Manchester, October 1678.

Pendleton.—Thomas Goulden, Thomas Goulden, weaver (?), and Edward Goulden, gentleman; same date and place.

Lostock.—Sir Charles Anderton, Baronet, and William Yate, gentleman; at Manchester, 17 October, 1678.

Manchester.—Edward Goulden, gentleman.

Stretford.—Edmund Trafford, esquire, and Frances, his wife; same date and place.

Jo: WARREN to ROGER KENYON, Clerk of the Peace for Lancashire.

358. 1678; December 14. Stockport.—Understands, by a letter from Serjeant Rigby, that the names of Lancashire papists had not reached London before his departure, and that the return of them was expected from Kenyon's hands. Hopes that his daughter's name—she being a *feme covert* and married to a protestant husband—may not be returned. Also desires that her mother's name may be omitted. *Seal.*

PETITION of ROGER KENYON, of Whalley, to WILLIAM, ARCHBISHOP OF CANTERBURY.

359. [1678–80.]—It is to his great grief he understands that the Archbishop is much incensed against him upon some informations of miscarriages and insolences, pretended to have been committed by him, touching Whalley Rectory. He has many enemies "in these times of Sir Ralph Assheton's troubles," and had he not been Sir Ralph Assheton's servant he might now have been quiet at home, because complaints would not have been made against him. He is a poor man and has a wife and 6 children, the eldest not 12 years of age. He has but small means, and a few of these journeys will expose him to want and poverty, "and his stay here" is full of danger, for he is in all Sir Ralph Assheton's judgments and bonds. He therefore prays he may be examined upon such matters, and he will submit himself to what mulct may be imposed upon him. The short continuance of a suit "in this honourable court" will soon overthrow his little estate. *Draft.*

W. GRENIER (?), MILES DODDING, EDWARD WILSON, and others, to "the DEPUTY LIEUTENANTS, JUSTICES OF PEACE and CHIEFE OFFICERS OF THE CORPORATIONS within the County of Lancaster."

360. 1678[–9], January 29. "From Lancaster Sessions."—"Receiving here the surprising news of the dissolution of the Parliament, and

that it is his Majesties pleasure to direct writts to be issued for electing
another Parliament, to bee holden the sixth of March next, and, foreseeing as the juncture of affaires now represent how fatall a tumultuous
election might prove to the peace of our Country, wee propose and
intreat, if you so thinke fit, that wee may all meet at the Quarter
Sessions, which by good fortune falls out to bee holden by adjournment
at Preston tomorrow senight, the sixth of February, to the end the
gentlemen that shall so meete, may then there with unanimity and due
consideration impart their opinions, what persons may most properly bee
pitched on to doe his Majestie and the country service. And so our
mutuall interest may joyntly and calmely bee aplyed without any ani-
mosity, or much expence, to proceed to the election accordingly, when
the tyme shall come. Wee hope no ill construction can bee made of
our good meaning herein." *Seal of arms.*

John Tench to Roger Kennyon.

361. 1678[-9], February 20.—"On Tuesday last I saw Alrued's (?)
pardon in passing at the signet office, but though not mentioned in it, I
would be glad to serve you and your country in obtaining Walkden's
pardon, but without money it cannot be done, and there is no circuit
pardon now passing for the North wherein Richardson may be inserted ;
his mother is with me every day."

Licence to Travel.

362. 1678[-9], February 25.—Licence from the Deputy Lieutenants
and four Justices of the Peace of the County of Lancaster to Edward
Tildesley of Lodge, in the same County, a reputed though not convicted
popish recusant,—who, not being willing to give occasion of offence to
any, since his Majesty's Proclamation commanding all popish recusants
and persons so reputed, to be and abide at or within five miles of their
respective habitations, unless licensed to travel, has hitherto conformed
himself thereunto, but now has a particular occasion to go to Lancaster where he has not only a considerable estate to look after
"but other occasions, as we know of"—to travel to Lancaster, ten
days being allowed him to go, remain, and return to his habitation.
Copy.

The King [to the Duke of York].

363. 1678[-9], February 28. Whitehall.—"I have already given
you my reasons at large why I think it fitt you should absent yourselfe
for some time beyond sea, and as I am truly sorry for the occasion, so
you may be sure I can never desire it longer then it is absolutely necessary both for your good and my service. In the meane time, I think it
proper to give it you under my hand that I expect your complyance,
and I desire it may bee as soon as conveniently you can. You may
easily beleeve with what trouble I write this unto you, there being
nothing I am more sensible of then the constant kindnes you have ever
had for me, and I hope you are as just to mee to be assured that no
absence nor any thing els ever can change mee from being truly and
kindly yours." *Copy.*

W. Andrewes to Roger Kenyon.

364. 1679, April 16. Altrincham.—"I have here inclosed, sent you
H. H.'s confessions, out of which, on your next meeting, you may draw
matters for a further service to his Majestie and the Kingdom, though
hee's so distracted at present that I pitty him, yet find him every way

willing to all reasonable things. My prayer to you now is double; first, that you will afford me a lyne to Mr Justice Bertie, or the late Judge, that in consideration of services done in order to a plenary discovery of the whole misery of iniquity and of the nature of his fact, which, if proportionable to his profitt, must bee small, the *caveat* against his pardon may bee withdrawne, and mee assisted towards the passing it. If you will have the two pillars, Peter and Jane, included, it shall be done at his charge. Next, I beg that from some proper officer, a copy of the calendar or otherwise, a testimoniall may come to Chester that hee was not indited at Lancaster, in regard our Judge may else continue him bound. In these two points I affectionately entreate your complyance." *Seal of arms.*

GUICCIARDINI WENTWORTH to ROGER KENYON.

365. 1679, April 22.—" His Majesty has desolved the whole body of the Privy Councell and chosen a new one, 30 in number, besides the Royall bloud. The Earle of Shaftsbury is Lord President of itt. The old Commissioners of the Admiralty are discharged and a new Commission, of 7 of the House of Comons. Som or all the Judges will be altered; Lord North is of the Privy Councell and to be Lord Keeper or a Commissioner, as say some." *Seal, broken.*

THOMAS MARSDEN to ROGER KENYON.

366. 1679, April 28. Walton.—" The bearer hereof, Thomas Stany-nought, is the best yeoman in the towne hee lives in, and is lately come from Popery to our Comunion. He hath the reputation of a very honest man and is heartily pleased with our religion. At his request, I inform you that hee is ready to take the Oathes as hee hath taken the Sacrament with us. I begg also to acquaint you that a popish beggar-woman (who hath no good reputation among us in any kind) hath informed my Lord Molineux that the said bearer T. M. (*sic*) hath lately shot one of his deare, whereupon he is bound to the Sessions. Now, my request is, that because hee cannot have his things ready on Munday, his prosecutor may not bee suffered to bring the businesse on till Tuesday. This wee verely believe is a dry blow given him because hee hath deserted the Romane way."

JOHN TENCH to ROGER KENYON.

367. 1679, May 3.—At the Signet Office I found Houghe's pardon passed in April. " I presume, when your Sessions is over, you will have thoughts of visiting London again, and then there may be hopes of Houghe's pardon, with the circumstances you mention, but without you 'twill hardly be done, for we have noe certificates yet to ground any proceeding upon. The great mattres now in agitation will sufficiently justify your curiosity in desireing to se how they are managed besides your other business, and particularly the charity of saveing soe many persons' lives and the advantage it may be to the whole kingdom. It is superfluous to write you that Justise Wild, Justise Bertie, Baron Thurland, and Baron Bramston, are outed, and that Sir Ellis, Serjeant Pemberton, Serjeant Raymond, Mr. Edward Atkins, Mr. Leake, are to be admitted in their places of Mr. Baron Littleton. But now there is further discourse conserning my Lord Chief Justice North, my Lord Chief Baron and Mr. Justice Windham &c. I have asked the opinion of some of the Exchequer Officers concerning the method of returning recusants and quakers, who assure me 'tis all alike, but they say there is something under consideration, in order to the distinguishing them after they are returned."

Postscript.—" My Lord Treasurer haveing bene assigned this day to answer whether he would stand to his pardon or plea of not guilty, hath chosen to rely upon his pardon."

NEWS LETTER.

368. 1679, July 10. London.—"It is this day generally affirmed that his Majestie hath desclosed in Councill the Parliament is dissolved, and will forthwith issue a Proclamation thereof and for assembling a new Parliament upon the 7th of October. Mr. Langhorne, who was repreived till Munday next, is said to have discovered 20,000*li*. of the Jesuits money, and 40,000*li*. more upon mortgages, and it is thought there are more hopes of a further discovery from him since his Majestie hath written to Spayne to have his two sons sent home from Vallodolid. It is likewise said, Dr. Wakeman doth not intend to be Colmanized (the Sessions draw neare) and that the Portugall Embassador moves earnestly to have the great lady retyre for some time, till things be a litle setled; and some say the French Duchess is about to visit her owne countrey, and that the other Duchess hath lost much money there and is comming back hither in hopes to gain by play. the same way she got this, though not the same way she lost it."

The EARL OF DERBY to ROGER KENYON.

369. 1679, September 22. Knowsley.—"The Election for burgesses at Preston was very strangeley carried on. If Sir Robert Carr will, I shall bee glad to have a petition put in the House of Commons, and when I know his mind I will act accordingly, for I am absolutely at his dispose, and when you see him, doe me the kindnes to tell him soe."

THOMAS WALSH to ROGER KENYON.

370. 1679, October 11. Aswarby.—"His Majestie has determined the blynd horse match and hath agreed it shall be drawne, so that you may conclude your five gineys are safe, but I feare Mr. Curtis's half crowne is in the hucksters' hands. *Postboy* hath won his match; my master hath two or three more to run, but he intends to be at Aswarby the midle of next weeke." *Seal of arms, broken.*

GUICCIARDINI WENTWORTH to ROGER KENYON.

371. 1679, November 6.—For news, I believe there is abundance, but it is out of the reach of such poor mortals as myself, "only Mr. Dangerfeild *alias* Wiloughbie has plotted himself into Newgate, and my Lady Pewes (?) into the Tower, and detected Sir R. Peighton to have been a decoy who may possibly this night be sent after him, though the rabble was last night pleased to burn him and the Pope together." *Seal of arms.*

LEFTWICH OLDFELD to ROGER KENYON.

372. 1679, December 21. Leftwich.—I am but newly returned from Knowsley to take leave of honest Robin Cholmondeley, who expired on Monday, to the great discomfort of that family. If you have any comfortable news for the "Church-of-England-men," who will always be found the King's truly (if not only) loyal subjects, pray refresh us with it. *Seal of arms.*

PHILLIP LLOYD to ROGER KENYON.

373. 1679[-80], January 8. Council Chamber.—"The Lords Committees of Councell having been made acquainted with a letter of yours (without date) to Mr. Chancellor of the Dutchy of Lancaster, giving an account of the remissenesse of some of the Justices of the Peace at the last Quarter Sessions at Preston, in prosecuting popish recusants, their Lordships have comanded me to send the inclosed order to you, requiring those Justices to appear before them to give an account of their proceedings ten days after the end of the approaching Sessions, which you are to acquaint them with, but so as that no interruption may bee given to the Sessions thereby. At the time that the Justices attend, I am commanded to let you know that you are likewise to attend and bring up with you any such further information concerning this matter as you have or may come to your knowledge. The Lords are sensible and well satisfyed with your diligence and have comanded me to tell you so, and to desire you will continue it and to assure you that they will not be wanting to give you all manner of encouragement in it."

JOHN BULLYN, *alias* EDWARDS, to ROGER KENYON.

374. 1679[-80], January 13. Lancaster Castle.—I am not able to come down and see you, and dare not assume the boldness to ask you to come and see me. I know not upon what ground I stand, nor what will be done with me, nor have I any friend in the world to advise me, unless I could have one minute's discourse with you. *Seal.*

JOHN BULLYN to ROGER KENNION.

375. 1679[-80], January 14. Lancaster Castle. – "The sadd prospect of afflictions that surround me and, like a hurricane from all poynts of the compass, invade my perplexed soule, make me alsoe troublesome to others, as yourselfe [as] by these [you] may experience. The tedious night being gone with the break of day, I renew my addresses to you. To you, in whom my chief hope lies, I have sought alwaies imaginable to give the world satisfaction of my integrity, and if anything you could dictate to me remayned, it should be imbraced. And heer I doe againe call God to witnes I am alltogether innocent, and free from having any hand or knowledge of this plott, directly or indirectly, and wish God may never forgive me but condemn me to the eternall flames of hell, if in this ascertion I tell a lye or equivocate or mentally reserve." *Seal.*

The LORDS OF THE COUNCIL to ROGER KENYON.

376. 1679[-80], January 19. Whitehall, Treasury Chambers.— Enclosing certain Acts of Parliament for granting a supply to His Majesty for paying off and disbanding the forces raised since the 29 September, 1677, to be put in force in the County of Lancaster.

CHRISTOPHER MARSDEN to ROGER KENYON.

377. 1679[-80], January 30. Bolton.—"I am certayne that warrants came to the severall churchwardens, and other officers, in Rivington,

Lostocke, and some other places, requireing them to meet the gentlemen at Wiggan on Monday last. I beleive theire desyne may bee to know how you have putt the laws in execution against Sir Charles Anderton and others of his religion; whether too much favor bee not shewne to some and to much severity upon others. What I gather of their designe, is from some discourse I had with Mr. James Lever who had discoursed with some of the churchwardens in Lostocke." *Seal, broken.*

DOROTHY LAGOE to MRS. KENYON, at Peel.

378. 1679[-80], February 4. Manchester.—" I have been in-quireing (and spoke to Mrs. Cash) for maids for you; and she brought one to mee, which would come to you to be a chamber-maid. She is a very pritty woman, and can sow. I have made some inquiry after her conditions. They say she is true, but hath sweet-hearts, and is not mindful to take much pains." *Seal of arms.*

LEFTWICH OLDFELD to MR. KENYON.

379. 1679[-80], February 7.—My wife tells me that, by your pro-curement, the grant of her seats in the gallery in Manchester Church was obtained from the Bishop, which seats, we and our assigns have quietly enjoyed till of late the covetuousness of the Chaplain, who pretends to have a power to make leases of the said seats. The Chaplain's power is short of what he boasted. It is true indeed that their grant precedes ours, being by Bishop Wilkins, but it reaches no further than to receive the rents and rates of the said Gallery. Desires advice.

ORDER signed by W. SPENCER, THOMAS PRESTON, MILES DODDING, CURWEN RAWLINSON, WILLIAM KIRKBY, and THOMAS COLE.

380. 1679[-80], February 14. Lancaster.—"Whereas the Maior and Councell of the Corporation of Lancaster have received information from Mr. Cobb, deputy prothonotarie of this county, that the Judges are dissatisfied to keep the Assizes at Lancaster, in respect of the ruines of the castle of Lancaster, conceiving some danger to sitt there untill the same be repaired. In order, therefore, for their satisfaction and better security to sit in safety, it is by us, whose names are hereto subscribed, Justices of the Peace for the said county, within the Hundred of Lonsdall, ordered, that the late High Constables of the said Hundred of Lonsdall, or such other person and persons as have received any of the moneys for the repaire of the said Castle, shall, upon notice hereof, pay all the said moneys unto Mr. Henry Johnes, according to an order made att the Sheriff's table of this county, and a roll for that purpose, to be by him disbursed and paid over to the Maior of Lancaster for the time being, Francis Medcalfe, gentleman, Henry Johns, John Hodyson and William Penny, of Lancaster, in the said county, gentle-men, who wee hereby appoint overseers of the said works, and to be imployed for the present repairs of the courts in the said Castle."

GUICCIARDINI WENTWORTH to ROGER KENYON.

381. 1679[-80], February 28.—"The Chancellor went out of town on Tuesday was sevenight and, in good health (a cold excepted) came to Aswarby this day sennitt. The Lord Mayor, &c., coming by appoynt-ment to return his Majesty thanks for his favor towards them in their pretentions to the disposicon of the water bayliffes place, were, by Sir George Jeffries (as 'tis said) trickt into a desire to kiss the Duke's hand, and accordingly performed to his Majesties good likeing, of which Mr. Recorder may heere more next Comon Councell, which will be shortly. My Lady Carr has had two fitts of an ague, but hopes it will not return. Murthers and dewells wee have frequent, and one last night between the Earl of Plymoth and Sir George Hewett, princepalls, the Lords Mordant and Cavendish as seconds; the latter has wounded his man very shrewdly but not mortally; the quarrell about words, and that they were idle ones, the parties considered."

Pe : Brooke to Roger Kenyon.

382. 1679[-80], March 11. Astley.—I communicated your letter to Sir Richard Standish and others, and find those I discoursed to on the business rather desirous to build a new prison, which it is said may be done at an easier rate than to repair the ruinous castle. I am old, near 68 years of age, and full of infirmity, and shall be a petitioner that I may have some space betwixt the business of life, and death. *Seal of arms.*

W. Andrewes to Roger Kenyon.

383. 1679[-80], March 18.—The great business against Manchester is committed to Sir John Stringer to try if, by industry, he can make more of it by re-examining the informers. I only give you this hint, that if you have conveniency, Sir Thomas may have it intimated to him of how ill consequence it may be to him to hunt for amendments to an information, the utmost of that delivered in being copied.

Jo. Chorley to Roger Kenyon.

384. 1680, April 28. Liverpool.—Asking that one James Leech, who lately broke out of Liverpool gaol, may be taken into custody upon the Mayor of Liverpool's warrant.

Justice Dolben to Roger Kenyon, Clerk of the Peace for Lancashire.

385. 1680, May 27.—" I am commanded to give in the names of the persons that were presented by the Grand inquest, last Assizes at Lancaster, for recusancy. I know not how to write to the Clerk of the Crown. I hope you may be able to do the thing. I desire to hear from you with all speed. One Thomas Abbott, of Adlington, was returned on the Grand inquest. I have received good satisfaction for his non-appearance; therefore lett his fine be discharged." *Seal of arms, broken.*
Endorsed : " The Judge's letter for sending up recusants' names." *Seal of arms.*

News Letter.

386. 1680, July 15. Whitehall.—" Yesterday, in the morning, the Comon Hall in London met to chose two Sheriffes in the roome of Mr. Bethell and Mr. Cornish who had been both discharged from the first election by the Court of Aldermen, for that they were not quallified, according to the Corporation Act, but haveing since received the sacrament, they were by the partie putt up againe yesterday with one

Mr. Box, a drugstor, Mr. Nicholson, a packer, and Sir Wm. Russoll, a mercer. After some howres had been past in disputeing who should bee named first, Mr. Bethel and Mr. Cornish had visibly the more hands, next Mr. Box, and next Mr. Cornish, but because many were in the Hall and held up their hands that were not of the Livery, it was necessary to come to a poole, which the sheriffe said hee would begin this morning bee 6 of the clocke for that they were to bee that afternoon at the Sessions at the old Bayley, which was purposely adjorned to the afternoone, for the tryall of Giles, and accordingly made a proclamation and adjorned the Court. Some of the most hot and factious cryed out that they would have a poole imediately and that they would not stick, and my Lord Mayor offering twice to goe away, was hindred by severall that purposely crowd in his way, but at last they let him pass, but they kept the Sheriffes there above an houre afterwards; they made a proclamation that all should depart and keep the peace, in pursuance of which all sober people went their way, but those whose business it is to bee very busie and active on those occasions would nor yet stir and would not lett the Sheriffes doe soe, who endeavoured to goe away, and Osburne, a Draper, struck Sir Simon Lewis on the brest, and bee sides, hee received severall other thrusts and punches on the brest, soe that when hee gott home hee was forced to lett blood. The King, haveing understood what had past, extreamely recented, caused the Privie Councell to meete in the evening and sent for the Lord Mayor and the Aldermen thither, who gave an account of all the whole transactions; upon which it was ordered that those persons who had thus misbehaved themselves should bee indicted for Riot, and that a Commission of Oyer and Terminer should accordingly bee imediately issued, and the said Osburne and severall others have been taken into custody by a warrant from my Lord Mayor, and have given poole (*sic*) for their appearance. This Comon Hall met againe and now they are pooling, which will not bee finished to day, and in the meanetime the King continues in towne, while all sober people are extreamely scandilized at the insolence of those factious spiritts. Two dayes since, the Earle of Maxfield kissed the Duke's hand, to whom have [he has] reconsiled himselfe. Just now I heare that Osburne is in Newgate; the King returnes to morrow morning to Windsor."

R. Heywood to Roger Kenyon.

387. 1680, August 2. Castle Rushen.—Thanking Kenyon for obtaining Lord Derby's licence for him to return to England, but regretting he is unable to do so on account of his debts. *Seal of arms.*

Richard Kirkby to Roger Kenyon.

388. 1680, September 30. London.—Pray let me hear from you how the red-letter men are proceeded against, from every place this next session, and to whom the estreats of the defaulters will belong. The town begins to fill with Parliament men, and the Court is expected here by the latter end of the next week. *Seal of arms, broken.*

The Justices of the Peace for the County of Lancaster to Lord Sunderland.

389. 1680, October 7.—Whereas by the royal proclamation of 28 December, 1678, we were charged and commanded to apprehend, disarm, and secure, all Popish Recusants or other suspected to be Popish Recusants, and to require them to enter into recognizances with sufficient sureties to keep the peace, and be of good behaviour, and to return such recognizances to the next General Sessions of the Peace where they were to be proceeded against according to law. We, in obedience thereto, have bound a great number of Popish Recusants with sureties to appear at the next Quarter Sessions of the Peace, and in the mean time to keep the peace and to be of good behaviour and not to depart the Court without licence. Most of the said Recusants appeared at the Quarter Sessions and took the oath of allegiance, but the Court, upon their refusal of the oath of supremacy, made an order for their continuance, and they were continued from Sessions to Sessions, until they lately neglected to appear. We have therefore ordered the recognizances to be estreated into the Exchequer of such as have neglected to appear; but such persons as did appear and take the oath of allegiance we make bold to delay the estreating of their recognizances until your Honour will be pleased to acquaint us with his Majesty's pleasure: for divers learned men in the law are of opinion that such recognizances are not forfeited by reason of the said Recusants appearing, keeping the peace, and being of good behaviour, according to the condition of their several recognizances. The sum in dispute upon the forfeiture of the recognizances in this county is esteemed above 60,000*li.* and many Protestant sureties are deeply concerned therein. *Copy.*

ORDER IN COUNCIL CONCERNING RECUSANTS.

390. 1680, October 27. Whitehall.—"There being this day presented to the Board by the Right Honourable Sir Robert Carr, Chancellor of the County Palatine and Dutchy of Lancaster, a state of the case about binding popish recusants to the peace and good behaviour, and of the proceedings thereupon had within the said County, whereby it appears that notwithstanding the severall directions given by his Majesty, as well by his royall commissions and proclamations as by divers orders of this board, for the effectuall prosecution of Popish recusants, the justices of the peace of the said County Palatine of Lancaster have forborne to estreat the forfeited recognizances of divers popish recusants, and their sureties, upon pretence of receiving his Majestie's further directions therein, His Majesty, taking the same into consideration, was pleased to order, and accordingly it is hereby ordered, that the said justices of the peace for the County Palatine of Lancaster be, and they are hereby, required forthwith to proceed to the signing and certifying the estreats of all the forfeited recognizances whatsoever of popish recusants, and their sureties, within the said County, according to the usuall and ordinary course and method of the lawes in that case provided."

Annexed is : "The State of the Case about binding the popish recusants to the peace and good behaviour, and the proceedings thereupon and how they now stand in the county of Lancaster.

"17 November, 1678.—His Majestie upon the humble petition, and at the desire of the Lords Spirituall and Temporall and the Commons in Parliament assembled, did, by his royall proclamation, command the parish officers within their respective precincts in each county, to take the names of all popish recusants, or so reputed, and their names, surnames, age and quality, above 16 yeares of age, to deliver to a justice of the peace, who are required to send for such papists to tender them (to whom by law they might) the oathes of allegiance and supremacy, and on refusall, to require them to enter into recognizances to appeare at the next sessions of the peace, and in defalt, to committ them till the next sessions, there to be proceeded against according to law; the said Justices to bee armed with a commission to tender the said oathes.—See the proclamation.

"23 November, 1678.—His Majesty, by commission under the greate seale of England, did empower, authorize, and comand, the justices of the peace in the County of Lancaster to require and receive of all and singular his Majestie's subjects, above 18 years of age, being popish recusants, or so reputed, residing within the said County, the oathes of allegiance and supremacy.—See the Commission.

"20 December, 1678.—His Majesty upon the humble desire of the Lords Spirituall and Temporall and Commons in Parliament assembled, for prevention of the present dangers, threatening his Majestie's sacred person and government from the pernicious plotts and contrivances of popish recusants, universally spread over this his Majestie's kingdome, did, by his Majestie's royall proclamation, strictly charge and command all justices of the peace, &c , within their respective counties, &c.; with all speed and dilligence, to apprehend and disarme all who are, or should bee justly suspected to bee, papists, and to require them to enter into recognizance, with suficient sureties, to keep the peace and bee of good behaviour, and to return such recognizances to the next sessions of the peace, where they are to bee proceeded against according to law, and, on refusall to give such recognizances, to committ the refusers to the comon gaole. —See the proclamation.

"Some papists, pursuant to these proclamations and commission, were bound over to the January sessions, and more to the Aprill sessions then next, and some since; but not a sixth part of the papists in severall hundreds of this county are, or ever were to this day, at all bound, as wee are informed by the clerke of the peace. Such as were bound, and did appeare, had the oathes of allegiance and supremacy tendered to them, and such as tooke both the said oathes were forthwith discharged of their recognizances to keep the peace and bee of the good behaviour though some of those that took both the oathes are papists and since prosecuted to a conviction. Such of them as tooke the oathe of allegiance, butt refused the oath of Supremacy, were not discharged, butt required to find new sureties, which some did; others, at their owne or their solicitors prayer, were continued upon their first recognizances, and their refusall of the oath of Supremacy certifyed into the King's Bench.

"23 Elizabeth ca. 1. paragraph 5.—Every popish recusant lawfully convicted (besides the payment of 20l. a month) forbearing, by the space of 12 months, to come to the Church, shall for his or her obstinacy (the conviction being certifyed *ut per* Statute) bee bound with two sufficient sureties in the sume of 200l., at the least, to the good behaviour; and so continue bound till such time as bee doe conforme, and come to Church.

"At the Court at Whitehall, 17 January 1678-9.—There having beene (after the first sessions of binding over recusants) presented by the justices of the peace, six queries to his Majestie in Councell, which his Majesty referred to the judges; who gave answer to his Majestie, in writing, what persons were fitt to bee bound over. Which report, his Majestie approved, and ordered that the justices of the peace take notice thereof and conforme thereunto.

"At the Court at Whitehall, 31 January, 1678-9.—Ordered that his Majestie's justices of the peace doe, with all care and dilligence, pursue his Majestie's commands, signified in his Majestie's proclamations. And his Majestie appoints that the justices of the peace, who shall neglect or refuse, shall bee putt out of commission, as disaffected to the government and religion established.

"At the July Sessions, 1679.—The papists who had refused the oath of Supremacy, and were therefore kept bound, knowing the refusall of the said oath had beene certifyed into the King's Bench, did not appeare at the Sessions, but made defalt. The justices of the peace then ordered a *scire facias* to bee issued, returnable at the next quarter Sessions; the defalters then to shewe cause why their recognizances shold not bee estreated.

"At October Sessions, 1679.—At the sessions begunne at Lancaster, all the papists bound thither were called upon their recognizances; severall did appeare and were anew bound, or continued, and none of them then ordered to be estreated; butt had further time at the same sessions adjourned to Preston. Mr. Sarjeant Rigby, one of the justices of the peace on that bench, saying he was not satisfied to bind over popish recusants upon a proclamation. He then gave order none of them should bee then particularly called, butt appointed the sessions to bee adjourned. At the same sessions, held by adjournment at Wigan, the justices appointed the recusants to bee called, butt few of them (by example from Preston Sessions) did appeare ; then, however, the Court recorded the appearances of such as came, and respited the estreating of the defalters, for that time. At the same sessions, holden by adjournment, the like was done at Manchester.

"At January Sessions, 1679-80.—At Lancaster, all the recusants bound thither were called : some did personally, others by their Attorneyes (showing some cause) were admitted to appeare, and an other *scire facias* was then ordered for the defalters to show cause, or bee estreated. At the same session, held by adjournment at Preston, there came an order from the councell to Mr. Sarjeant Rigby, and others, the justices there, to appeare before the Lords of the Councell to answer for former recusants. And it was then there allsoe ordered, as at Lancaster, to send forth a *scire facias*. The like orderes were allsoe made at the sessions at Wigan and Manchester.

"18 March, 1679-80.—An other Commission, under the greate seale of England, came forth, empowering and commanding the justices of the peace (as commissioners so appointed) to tender the oathes of allegiance and supremacy to certaine persons therein named, being recusants of best quallity in the said county. With this Commission came a letter, and printed instructions, directed to the justices, from the Lords of the Councell; the letter mentioning, that his Majestie, by his personall commands to the judges, by severall proclamations, comissions, and orders, had endeavoured that the lawes against popish recusants should have been putt in effectuall execution; but, through favour, connivance or abuse were not : therefore, this second Commission was in order to prosecute the persons therein named to a *premunire*.

" The said commission, and letter, was brought to the judges and most of the justices of peace, at the Assizes at Lancaster, the 26th of March, 1680, and, shortly after, sent to all the rest of the justices of peace in the county, who agreed, each in their respective hundred, or division, would send for the persons therein resident, in the commission named, to doe pursuant to the said instructions; but no papist, so sent for, would be found or came at.

" At April Sessions, 1680.—The *scire facias*, sent forth, was returned by the Sheriff at Lancaster sessions. The papists were all called. Severall did appeare, butt not one of those named in the said second commission to bee presented to a *premunire;* howbeit, there were then, for that time, so many of them as had any to sollicit for them, allowed to bee continued, and their continuances recorded; those that neither appeared, nor sent to bee excused, were ordered to be estreated, so soone as the estreate was prepared. At the same sessions, held by adjournment at Preston, the papists were all called; none of those named to bee prosecuted to a *premunire*, did personally appeare; others did, and were continued. But the Court did not consent to continue those other upon record; howbeit, an opinion being read from Sir Thomas Stringer, that they ought to bee admitted to plead to the *scire facias*, and first enter their appearance thereunto, they allsoe were admitted, by their Attorneys, to appear accordingly. The like was done at Ormeskirke and Manchester Sessions thenafter hold.

" At July Sessions, 1680.—At Lancaster, it was ordered that all papists who were bound as such, and continued to that session, shold likewise bee continued to the next quarter sessions there: And, unless then they did appeare in person, or bring some order, from the judge of assize, for their discharge, their recognizances should bee defalted and estreated; and the clerk of the peace to prepare estreats accordingly. At the same sessions, held at Preston, by adjournement, the like order was made; at the same session, held by adjournement at Ormeskirk, it was ordered that the then defalters shold bee estreated, and an estrcate prepared for the ensueing sessions there; and the like order, as at Ormeskirke, was made at the same sessions holden by adjournement at Manchester. And, shortly after, the said estreats and duplicates thereof were all ingrossed and prepared accordingly, and brought to the next assizes.

" At the Assize holden at Lancaster, in August, 1680, Mr. Sarjeant Rigby, of Councill with all the popish recusants that were bound over in thaf county, moved the judge that their recognizances might bee, by his Lordship's direction, discharged; butt his Lordshipp contrarily declared the justices ought to signe and certify the estreats.

" At the meeting of the justices of the peace at Lancaster, in the Assize weeke, at the Sheriffs table, 24th August, it was then the opinion and agreement of the table, that the estreats of all forfeited recognizances of popish recusants, should bee signed by the justices of peace that were at the severall sessions; before whom the said recognizances were defalted: And that the clerke of the peace doe tender them to bee signed, accordingly.

" At the Quarter Sessions holden at Lancaster, in October, 1680, the said estreates, and duplicates thereof, being brought by the clerke of the peace and tendered to the justices, the same, after long debate, were all forborne to bee signed, and it was then ordered in the words following: Upon hearing of Thomas Patton, Esquire, Christopher Greenfield, Esquire, and George Pigott, Esquire, of councill with the popish recusants bound over to the quarter sessions, in pursuance of his Majestie's proclamation, it is ordered, that all recognizances of such of the said popish recusants as have neglected to appeare, according to the condition of their respective recognizances, shall bee estreated; butt the recognizances of such of them as did appeare and take the oath of allegiance, it is ordered that the estreating of such bee forborne till his Majestie's pleasure therein bee knowne. At the same sessions, held by adjournement at Preston, the justices were in opinion devided; but the major part agreed to make the same order; and the same was confirmed at Wigan. Butt at Manchester Sessions, it was, by the whole Court, contradicted, as contradictory in itself. Howbeit, because the gentlemen from Lancaster had writt to know his Majestie's pleasure in the matter, the justices of the peace at Manchester adjudged it their duty, humbly to waite his Majestie's direction therein, and ordered that the state of all the proceedings in this particular should bee carefully inspected, and forthwith sent to the Chancellor of the Dutchy of Lancaster, humbly intreating his honour, from the said justices, with all humility and dutifullness, to acquaint his Majesty in Councill therewith; and that the persons appointed by his Majesty in Councill to bee presented to a *premunire*, are the chiefe of those that thus withdraw themselves, contrary to the condition of their recognizances to avoid the said prosecutions." *Copy.*

DOROTHY LAGOE to MRS. KENYON.

391. 1680, December 16. Manchester.—Is so troubled for her dear mother; her cousin, Anne Assheton, has been with Mr. Minshall to acquaint him how she is. Mr. Minshall says some sack is the best cordial, and if she think it not hot enough mulled, then burn it with some hot spices. He says as to the "neare sand," blood is the best thing to annoint it with, enough cat's blood cannot be got, but calf or sheep's blood will do, and rub it often, if it make her not sick.

NEWS LETTER.

392. 1680, December 23.—"It is sayd that the Empresse is brought to bed of a young princes.

"The Holland letters say that they continue to see the commett there, and that the astronomers affirme that the tayle of it is above 60 degrees in length.

"When the Lord Stafford was before the House of Lordes last Satturday, the substance of his confessions sayd to bee as followeth (*videlicet*).

"Wee have beene long in hope of a change of our religion, but have mett with rubbes. I went to Breda to the King, amongst others. I did propound 100,000*l.* from the Catholiques to take off the penall lawes againste them. That after the King came in, the Lord of Oxford propounded in the House, the takeing off the oathes of allegiance and supremacy, which tooke noe effect. The Lord of Bristoll propounded a new oath, which I att first lyked of, but after disapproved. After this, the Duke of Yorke brought in a bill which the Lord Chancellor Hide opposed, and said that if that passed, the Kinge might make a popish preist a Bishop of London. Wee then, as I thought, practised our religion too openly, and the Dutchesse of Yorke dyed a supposed papist, and I offered some proposall to my Lord Chancellor. I offered the same 3 or 4 tymes to the Duke of Yorke, for the dissolveing of the Long Parliament. I did conceive that if the King lived and the penall lawes could be got off, when the Duke should come to the Crowne there would bee hopes of setting up our religion. Hee made protestations of knowing nothing more of the plot, and soe was remanded backe to the Tower. The Sheriffes of London and Middlesex makeing some scruple concerneing the execution of the Lord Stafford, applyed themselves to the Loides thereupon, and theire Lordships judged their scruples to bee unnecessary, and declared that the King's writ ought to bee obeyed.[1]

"Articles of impeachment were ordered to bee drawne up against Lord Cbeife Justice Scroggs, Judge Jones, and Judge Weston, for dissolveing the grand jury before the last day of Trinity Terme."

NEWS LETTER

392A. 1680, December 28. — " The Lord Stafford hath wrote to the 2 Sheriffes, requesting foure thinges of them; first, that they would take care to prevent the people from makeing a noise; secondly, that they would permit the scaffold to bee hunge with blacke; thirdly, that they would not suffer the scaffold to bee crowded; and fourthly, that they would permit his friends to take away his body in his cloathes, without stripping of him; hee satisfyeing the executioner. The Sheriffes readily graunted the latter, and promised to doe what they could in the former.

" On Fryday the House of Commons ordered a bill to be brought in for repealing the lawe made for regulateing of corporations. Yesterday there was an extraordinary Councell; all the Clerks were ordered to withdraw, and what past is kept private."

NEWS LETTER.

392B. 1680, December 30.—" About 9 of the clocke yesterday morning the Sheriffes of London and Middlesex went with a guard of about 500 men to the Tower, to receive the Lord Stafford and carry him to the place of execution. About 10, his Lordshipp came upon the scaffold on Tower Hill, his coffine being carried up a little before him. After some tyme, his Lordship read a speech, in writeing, to the spectators, which were judged to bee above twenty thousand, in which hee protested, with all the asseveration imaginable, his ignorance of the plot, his loyalty to his Majesty, and that the doctrine of deposeing kinges is contrary to the fundamentall lawes of the Kinge and Kingdome, impious and damnable, though hee acknowledged that many learned men of the Romish Church did affirme it. Hee denyed all indulgences, dispensations, and pardons to murder, rebell, lye, forsweare, &c. and that hee believed hee was brought to his tryall on a beleife that, to savé his lyfe, hee would have made some greate discovery. Hee prayed for the King, alleadging that noe power upon earth, either singly or altogether, can legally allow him or any other persons to lift a hand against him or his legall authority. Hee desired pardon of God for all his offences, desireing all people to forgive him as hee did those that had injured him, not excludeing those perjured men (as hee was pleased to terme them)

---

[1] *See also No. 354 ante.*

that had brought him to the blocke by theire perjuryes. Hee then declared, upon his death and salvation, that heè never spoke either to Oates or Turbervile, and that hee never saw them till his tryall, and that hee never spoke to Dugdale, unlesse aboute a footeman or a foote race, and that hee was never then alone with him. Hee begged God not to revenge his innocent blood on the nation, nor on those that were the causers of it, &c. About halfe an hower after hee had read his paper, hee went to the fower severall quarters of the stage, declareing, in a short speech, his innocency to all the spectators and hee forgave them all. Which being done, hee began to prepare himselfe for the fatall struke, and being stript, hee layd downe his head twice upon the blocke to fit his necke to it, and the last tyme, the executioners severed his head from his body by one stroke, though hee was forced to make use of his knife to cut the outward skin. Many persons threwe up their handkerchers to theire Catholicke friends upon the scaffold, who, haveing dipt them in his blood, returned them to the owners. The people were very silent dureing this tragedy, only they gave 2 shoutes, one at his first comeing upon the scaffold, the other when the executioner gave the stroke and carryed the head round the scaffold, sheweing it all bloody to the spectators, sayeing—behold the head of a traytor.

"This day, Judge Raymond informed the House of Commons that Mr. Sheridon, committed by them, had demanded his *habeas corpus;* soe desired the directions of the House therein, but they deferred the debate till another tyme. They ordered that the Committee of Impeachmentes should looke into the evidence against the fower Lordes in the Tower, and report theire opinion to the House, in order to receive further directions therein.

"They ordered an addresse to his Majesty that the information of Mr. Serjeant in the case of Gawen, and all other papers and informations relateing to the plot, should bee communicated to the House. They ordered that all the writeings and papers in the last Parliament relateing to the pentioners, should bee produced to the House. They resolved that no member should accept of any office or place of profit from the Crowne, without the leave of the House, and the offenders therein should bee expelled the House. A Bill to bee brought in to discover landes imployed to popish uses."

NEWS LETTER.

393. 1680[-81], January 13. London. — " Several persons going from Encham, in Oxfordshire, to Abbington Markett as the sun was riseing, saw the perfect representation of a crowne over it. The spectators were very numerous, but all agreed that it seemed to be as bigg and as glorious as the sunn. This relation by a letter from Oxford which came yesterday to hand, attested by the subscriptions of the minister of Encham and many other credible witnesses. Yesterday, the Duke of Monmouth, accompanied with many of the Nobility and a considerable [number] of Members of Parliment, dyned at the Sunn Taverne, behind the Exchange. The vast sumes of mony lately arrived, of which I gave you an account in my last, is said to be the Prince of Hanover's, but considering the revenues of all his father's territories doe not amount to above 60,000*l.* per annum and that it is not the fashion nowadayes to buy wives, it's very improbable.

"From Norwich, the 10th instant, they write that in that Cittye, the last Sessions, above 50 protestante decenters were prosecuted upon the Act made against papists, notwithstanding the King, Lords, and Comons, have declared that it was intended against papists only, and that no one papist was presented. The last packquett from Ireland gives an account of a greate light in the heavens, bigger then the moone, appeared directlye over the Citty of Dublin, which in one night's time moved over severall parts of the Citty and at length, in sight of multitudes of people, fell through the aire into the sea, as they judge, and was seen no more, and that the Protestants there have dreadfull apprehentions of aproaching danger. From Scotland wee have account that the Councell there had granted that the Duke of Y[ork] should have liberty to [have] 3,000 French to bee added to his guards, and that the protestants there are extreamely discountenanced, but are resolved to stand one by another, and to hazard all rather then the Romish Superstition should overspread that Kingdom, and that certaine persons endeavour to distinguish themselves by weareing a blew ribbin and a roll of parchmentt on their hat : in the parchment is writt—no pope. This day the Courte and the Comon Councill of this Citty sate at Guild Hall, the Courte of Aldermen brought a Letter from his Majestie to put them in mind to enquire into the quallifications of the members, according to the Act for regulateing Corporations. It was put to the vote whether it should bee imediately read, carried in the negative by one voice. Then Alderman Hayes, with others, brought in a petition for the citting of the parliament. The Alderman told them that hee thought it concerned them to perform it, as much as the rest of the fellow cittizens who desired it, upon which a generall hum passed through the Hall, and the Alderman with the rest were ordered to withdrawe, who, after a small debate, were called in and told by Mr. Meaby, theire new Recorder, that the petition should be presented with small alterations in the forme but not in the matter, for which the Alderman returned thanks in the name of the rest and withdrew, but upon a motion that thanks should bee given for bringing in the petition, it passed with generall applause to the mover, and they were againe called in and received the thankes of the Courte. Then the Courte debated aboute the petition carried in the affirmative, *nemine contradicente*, that the petition should be this night presented to his Majestie by 4 Aldermen and 6 Comoners. The heads of the petition were chieflye that the parliament might sitt while the grievances of the nation was redressed and the Bill of Exclusion passed, with an intimation that the whole Citty were resolved to live and dye Protestants." Accordingly the petition is carried to the King.

[THOMAS HODGKINSON] to ROGER KENYON.

394. 1680[-1], January 25. Preston.—On Friday last came the news of the Parliament's dissolution and of another to be called. On Saturday last, I was called for to "the Hynd," where I found Mr. Fleetwood, Mr. Clayton, and others. In a very short time the company proceeded to elect Mr. Fleetwood, and moved my concurrence, all which was answered with silence; but I discoursed with Mr. Fleetwood, who promised that his interest would be devoted to Lord Derby's service. I summoned a council yesterday and told them the advantage of unity among ourselves, and the particular obligations this place lay unto Lord Derby and Sir Robert Carr. *Fragment.*

WILLIAM HAYHURST to ROGER KENYON.

395. 1680[-1], February 8. London.—Sunday last brought us to London. We hear that Lancaster Assizes are to be held the 16th of

March. Judge Dolben is to come the circuit, Sir Robert Sawyer is to be Attorney General, and Sir Creswell Levinz, a judge of the Common Pleas. We hear his Majesty has complimented Oxford for the sitting of the Parliament there, and taken up Christ Church College for his own lodgings. *Seal.*

WILLIAM HAYHURST to ROGER KENYON.

396. 1680–81, February 10. London—"We had a meeting yester-night proposed by Mr. Grahem to severall receivors and officers about methodizing our proceedings, but Mr. Grayhem beeing princepall and called to read in the Inn, could not meet us. Wee was with him againe to daye, and have this night fetched out of the Exchequer office a Comission of rebellion against Sir Thomas Preston, and made returne thereof that, att the end of the terme, a motion may bee made for a seizure of his estate into the King's hands. Mr. Graham's Clerke tells us they have had a tryall to day of 2,000*l.* laid upon a mortgage for the use of the Jesuites in London, which is gone for the King, and a rule is made that the defendents shall either paye the principall and interest money, or the land to be seized of for the king's use. Wee are dayly and hourly attending the offices, but by reason of the infinite number of Recusants within our County, wee are much delayed. Wee are advised to marke and cull out upon the Roll in the Pipe, such as are of the best account and ability, and to goe to the Lords Comissioners for a warrantt for process, and for the rest, to have them prepared against the next terme. There is little newes stirring. All the Citty is generally afraid of troublesome times. From Holland they write that the States Generall are resolved to put the Prince of Orange out of the place of Stadtholder. From Oxford wee hear that the heads of the Colledges held a Convocation and have agreed that all schollers under the degree of master of arts should remove out of towne during the time of the Parliament. They say the Grand Jury of Westminster, Sir Wm. Waller beeing foreman, hath presented the King's horse and foot guards as a grand nuisance and unnecessary charge, and some say as a tumultuous riott; they have likewise presented the Duke of York as a popish recusant to convict him. His Majestie goes to Burford, near Oxford, where hee will divert himselfe with horse races till the sitting of the Parliament. It is reported that Sir Stephen Fox will bee made Earle of Plymouth, and that Sir Robert Carr is to be made a Lord." *Seal, broken.*

WILLIAM HAYHURST to ROGER KENYON.

397. 1680[-1], February 12. London.—We are daily and hourly using out utmost endeavours to dispatch our business, but the numerousness of our recusants and the attendance and delays we meet with, make us move slowly forward. We design to take out process for 20*li.* *per mensem* against such as have been lately returned convicted, which we fear will be as much as can be got down this term. *Seal.*

THOMAS MARSDEN to ROGER KENYON.

398. 1681, April 5. Walton.—Asking his favour on behalf of Mr. Norres of Derby, who is not yet cleared in the Exchequer for his recusancy, and who hears his name is in the list of such as shall have 20*li.* *per mensem* levied upon their heads. Mr. Norres' conformity " to our church " is as full as it can be.

Elizabeth, Isabell, and Ann Westby to Roger Kenyon.

399. 1681, April 7· "Windar."—We are informed you are supposed to be Receiver General of Recusants' estates, and we, being in the number of those that are under sequestration, send you forty shillings by Cousin Preston, which is according to what we always paid since this charge was laid upon us.

R. Graham to Roger Kenyon.

400. 1681, April 21.—If Mr. Golden and his wife were convicted upon the same indictment, you may then levy her penalties upon her husband; but if she was convicted upon another indictment, then you may not. But yet you may bring an action against him and her for the debt of his wife's, which is Mr. Attorney's opinion. Mr. Attorney is really resolved to make Sir Thomas Preston's commissioners examples.

Guicciardini Wentworth to Roger Kenyon.

401. 1681, April 21.—"Having received intimation of your faire daughter's ill hap, but, my honour and satisfaction to be her vallentine (*sic*), I have adventured to send her a little present." *Seal.*

Zachary Taylor to Roger Kenyon.

402. 1681, April 28. Ormskirk.—"If you be pleased to move anything in our business, I beg you would give me the favour of a line that, if the Bishop (who I understand hath made some progress in it) can any way assist you, we may entreat his endeavours. We commit our cause wholly to your management and to the returns of friendship and those obligations of kindness which we must stand indebted to you for, shall labour to express our gratitude in more legible terms, the rest of my brethren concurring." *Seal.*

William Patten to Roger Kenyon.

403. 1681, April 30. London.—"This day, Fitz Harres pleaded to the jurisdiction of the Court of Kings Bench for that hee was impeached by the House of Lords; his plea wanted Councells hands, which the Court tould hee might get, otherwise it could not be received. Hee saide hee could not procure Councell to signe it and prayed to have Councell assigned. The Court wished him to consider of the plea least, if overruld, it might prove fatall, and hath given him tyme to consider of it, and afterwards they received him privately aboute Sir Edmundbury Godfrey's death, wherein (as is reported) he hath made a large discovery." *Seal of arms.*

J. Rowe to Roger Kenyon.

404. 1681, May 17. Wigan.—This day the Mayor, two Sir Rogers, and Mr. Recorder, met and concluded the following address.

Then follows the address of the Mayor, Aldermen, Bayliffs, and Burgesses of the Borough and Corporation of Wigan, setting out that they have heard the tenor of the King's declaration, published in their parish church, of his intention to preserve inviolable the rights and constitutions of the Government, both in Church and State. "And though others have addressed your Majesty more early, yet none ever shall go before us in all dutiful allegiance to your Majesty."

Thomas Hodgkinson to Roger Kenyon.

405. 1681, May 29. Preston.—Great numbers of children here have the small pox and many die. We are almost undone for want of rain, very little barley sown, and that which is,.comes not up for want of moisture. *Seal of arms.*

Alexander Norres to Mrs. Alice Kenyon, at Peel.

406. 1681, June 4. Liverpool.—His master has received an account, from Captain Farlton, of the safe arrival at Barbadoes of the ship on which her son embarked, " after 32 (?) dayes sayle from the Irish coast, which was more than ordinary."

Thomas Winckley to Roger Kenyon.

407. 1681, June 19. Preston.—Mr. Sheriff writes me of the numerous company of complainants in the bills brought by the Papists in the Duchy, a number of whom I believe are dead. I am sure several of those that came down in the estreats are in their graves. *Seal of arms.*

John Roscoe to Roger Kenyon.

408. 1681, July 13. Wigan.—We went to Wigan to Madam Pennington, and demanded the money, which she refused to pay. I told her we must then be forced to distrain her goods, but would give her an hour or two to consider of it, and, if she pleased, to send to Sir Roger Bradshaw to advise with him. We left a bailiff or two in the house (because we but got into it by a wile), and when I thought she had had sufficient time for consideration, I waited on her, but found her in the same mind still, so I ordered the Bailiffs to remove some of her goods and went into the town for help to carry them up to Mr. Rowe, but in the meantime she had got several persons into her house and locked the doors. I therefore applied for assistance from the Mayor, who sent a sergeant with me, whereupon Madame Pennington came after us to the Mayor, and after a great deal of discourse, she agreed we should be free to remove some unnecessary goods. But when we returned, a great rabble assaulted and rescued the goods from the bailiffs and we were fain to take sanctuary in a house hard by. The names of some of the rioters follow : Mrs. Pennington and her daughter, young Doctor Worton, Ralph Lanckshaw, Elizabeth Scott, James Scott, and others. *Seal, broken.*

William Banks to Roger Kenyon.

409. 1681, July 19. Winstanley.—I hear some of the loyal corporation of Wigan have affronted the King's officers ; how that will prove an argument of their loyalty, it is beyond my capacity to find out. *Seal, broken.*

News Letter.

410. 1681, September 1. London.—"Yesterday, the Lord Mayor with Mr. Sheriff Cornishe and severall Aldermen waited upon his Majestie to welcome him to Whitehall. Yesterday began the Sessions' at the Old Bailey, where Councill moved that the writ of *habeas corpus* should be granted to the Earl of Shaftsbury, Lord Howard, Wilmore, &c. that they may be either tryed or bailed, but the Courte answered that they not being charged with any crime in that

Courte, that Courte would take no cognizence of it, and referred them to the King's Bench Barr for remedy. The Councill would have argued the point, saying they were relievable and ought to bee relieved there, as they could prove by the statute and common law of the land, but the Court overruled and referred as before. Yesterday Mr. Baldron, who was one of the evidence against Sir Miles Stapleton, and the same who, at Colledge's tryall, accused the evidence against him for subornation with high treason, was apprehended at Hixe Hall and committed to the Gatehouse, and it is credibly reported that hee retracts his evidence and now saith hee was hired by great persons to charge the witnesses against Colledge with subornation, and also to accuse Justice Walcopp of the same crime. The Queen's head-cook is taken into custody, being accused by the doorekeeper of her Majesties kitchin of preaching the art of poisening, that hee was confederate with Sir George Wakeman in the murder of Sir Edmundberry Godfray, and that he had twice poisened him (the said doore-keeper) once with broth, and another time with a frigase of eggs. That hee was poisened, was testified by Dr. Joanes. Hee was examined before the Greencloth and the Secretary of State. It is reported that the Judges have consulted whether an indictment against a peer may bee laid in a county, where the fact was not committed, and it is said they were devided—seven that it could not, and five that it could. A warrant is out against Dr. Oates, Baldron having sworne high treason against him, notwithstanding which hee walks publickly, but it is thought hee will speedily bee comitted. Presentments were made against Thompson, *Herreclitus*, and Mr. L'Estrange and the Bill found against them. It is said that this day Mr. Thompson is arrested at the suit of Mr. Hickeringill, in an action of 1,000*l.* for defamation. Indictments of subornation, perjury, and forgery, are given in against Justice Warcopp and six of the evidence ; but it is questioned whether the Judges will receive indictments against the evidence. Orders are issued out to severall countyes in England for the prosecution of the Papists, as allso Middlesex and Westminster. The Mayor hath likewise orders to proceed against them in this Citty. Letters from Tangiere say that they expect an Embassedor from the Alcade of Alcazor, a person so quallified that hee may bee accepted in the Courte of England, where hee is expected. Sir James Lashley is prepareing to accompeny him to London. Yesterday morning early, Colledge was executed, a paper being this day published for his speech, but thought not to bee his. *Finis.*"

R. HEYWOOD to ROGER KENYON.

411. 1681, September 5. Wigan.—"Yesternight my Lord received a letter from my Lord Chamberlain, who tells him that he showed a letter which my Lord lately wrote to him to the King, wherein my Lord signified his intention of waiting upon his Majesty this meeting, at Newmarket. My Lord Chamberlain says the King commanded him to acquaint my Lord that he takes it very kindly. My Lord resolves to go immediately after the race at Wallessy, and, in the meantime, has a great desire to see you." *Portion of seal.*

R. GRAHAM to ROGER KENYON.

412. 1681, September 13.—Mr. Turbervile, Mr. Smith, and Mr. Dugdale, I have examined, but not one of them remember anything of Sir Thomas P[reston ?] because they never were acquainted with him.

[Roger Kenyon to ———.]

413. 1681, September 18. Peel. — " Being a Commissioner for the Earl of Derby, and his Lordship intending for Newmarket to kisse the Kinge's hand, I have been this last week with his Lordship and about his bussines. One day his Lordship took mee to a race in Cheshire, where his Lordship had a horse to run for a plate, and there I mett and saw most of our great papists of this County, amongst others my Lord Molinex his son rideing for the plate. My Lord Molineux himselfe was there, so was Mr. Dalton. They look mightily ascue at mee. There was a great number of that clan and most of them did ride with swords. When I came home last night, I find yours of the 13th, for which I thanke you. Very considerable things have been hitherto done by the Undersheriffe, but hee promisses to be more vigerouse. The truth is, I was consenting hee should try, if by giveing a meeting to such as are in the first processe, hee could have quietly paid him such proportionable partes of their forfeitures as might be adequate to two parts of the yearly vallew of their estates, to have seen what that would have produced, and given you an estimate of what would be had that way, and hee gave notice by his bayliffs to them to see if they would meet him, and accordingly has been in most of the divissions in every hundred, and hath had with him one of my officers almost in every place, but very few have come to him, so that this way will do no good. Such as did come, most of them come to produce some settlements to shew the estates, though in their possession, are conveyed away to others, and, indeed, what can be devised by them to elude the King is done to the vtmost, and vpon such pretensions when the Sheriffe hath sent his bayliffes to distreine, they have endeavored to rescue the distresse. One of the bayliffs, the last week, had his finger struck off, though, indeed, it was partly by accident, for he had taken a young mare with other horses and cattle and was tyeing the mare to a peece of wood, and some comeing to make a rescusse, the mare being frighted, pluck'd back her head of a sudden with such force as the mans finger was pluck't off." *Draft.*

EDWARD B[ERESFOR]D to ROGER KENYON.

414. [1681? September] 18.—"Mrs. L[eigh] show'd me a letter that came from you, giving some amount of suppos'd witnesses. If you can learn any thing to blast the reputation of Lunt, Brown *alias* Wilson, or one Waring, 'twill be of service, for there is reason to believe they may be Mr. L[eigh's] accousers. The talk grows very hot amongest them that pretend to know, of speciall commissions going down into Lancashire and Cheshire in a very short time, and the gentlemen along with them, to find bills and then try 'em; but whether (*sic*) county Mr. L[eigh]s fact (*sic*) will be laid in, wee do not yet know : one of them certain. I doubt not your concern and kindness in this affayr; the methods of itt, you know best, and I shall not pretend to direct. Mr. L[eigh] is well, but no one has seen him. Mrs. L[eigh] has got an order and goes to morrow morning to continue close pris'ner with him. We can learn nothing of the crime ; strong evidence, my Lord S———y says there is; and there is not upon earth a man more innocent." *Seal of arms.*

Postscript.—"Aaron Smith comes down King's sollicitour. Lancashire most probably the county—great odds ! " *Seal.*

Thomas Dod to Roger Kenyon.

415. 1681, October 10.—At the last Assizes, the Judge set aside the order of Sessions made at the last sessions at Wigan, for allowance of 50*li. per annum* to maintain Sir Edward Stanley's children, declaring it was against law, as it was to the prejudice of the creditors.

Sir Robert Carr to Roger Kenyon.

416. 1681, October 24.—All I can say is that we both have enemies, and I think the cause is the red-lettered men, which I hope will be always so. *Portion of seal.*

R. Graham to Roger Kenyon.

417. 1681, October 27.—You may prosecute the Mayor of Wigan by an information, and so you may do all the rioters. I have inquired after Mrs. Pennington's sons, but cannot be informed where they are. *Seal of arms.*

Edward Baynard to Roger Kenyon.

418. 1681, November 5. Gray's Inn.—"This day Will [Patten] and I and divers . . . . of thy health, dranke it; not one pope mungare amongst us and, as Cicero begins, I end: If thou art well, it is well, I am well." *Seal, broken.*

Robert Roper to Roger Kenyon.

419. 1681, November 7.—Asking if he has any directions as to the payment by Mr. Heywood for "a parcel" of Manx cattle bought from "my Lord" [of Derby?]. Asks him to remember the creation money. *Seal.*

Guicciardini Wentworth to Roger Kenyon.

420. 1681, November 8.—I came last night from Newmarket, where I left Sir Robert [Carr] in good health, expecting the success of Thursday next, when *Postboy* is to run with *Dragon*, six miles. *Seal of arms.*

Robert Barber to Roger Kenyon, at "The Sword and Buckler," in Holborn.

421. 1681, November 16. Stone.—"Pray, sir, present my service to Mr. Justice Lighbound; and I hope, betwixt you and him, that you will not forgett the bad wayes att Talke-on-the-Hill; by which you will very much serve both King and country."

Thomas Hodgkinson to Roger Kenyon, London.

422. 1681, November 22. Preston.—He has already "discoursed" as to keeping the County Palatine seal, for which he had, as yet, received nothing. "Old Luke," ever since he kept the seal, had the benefit of making all writs of "entry and covenant," which used to amount to about 7*l.* or 8*l.* a year, "and some particular allowances from Mr. Vice-Chancellor, when hee made his accompts," which made the custody of the seal worth 20*l.* a year. But since he has had the seal, he has only retained his "proportion" of the fees, which he has shared with the clerks, as they justly demanded. "You know the constant attendance required in keeping the seal; and (I am sure) I have not, as yet, carryed the same into Alehouses, or so much as putt it into my pockett, but given attendance due to such a trust." Desires the matter to be brought before the Chancellor, in order that he may authorise the payment of an allowance. *Seal.*

L. RAWSTORNE to ROGER KENYON.

423. 1681, November 26. Newhall.—I am a little troubled to hear of the confidence of our red-lettered gentlemen. Shall we not live to see their combs cut, or their tethers made shorter ? *Portion of seal.*

ROBERT ROPER to ROGER KENYON, at "the Gridiron," in Holborn.

424. 1681, December 13.—The Commissioners of the Navy are desirous to buy Derby House in Cannon Row, and my Lord thinks to sell it, believing that he can dispose of the money to good advantage; it now gives 160*li.* per annum and is in good repair. His Lordship would have 3,000*li.* for it, and will not take under 2,500*li.*, but this you may keep to yourself. My Lord desires you to speak to Mr. Brisbane, the Commissioners' Secretary herein. I believe he is well known to your friend, Mr. Graham.

SIR THOMAS STRINGER's BRIEF at the August Assizes, concerning the Rioters of the Corporation of Wigan.

425. 1681.—" The number of Popish Recusants convict, inhabitting in the Town of Wigan, now 91 persons; the charge against them for their Recusancie, after 20*l. per mensem,* is 12,820*l.*

" 12 July, 1681 (which was the day the Quarter Sessions began at Lancaster) the Sheriffe's Bayliffes went to Wigan, and first came to the house of Ann Pennington, relict of Richard Pennington, Esq[e], against whom they had in charge to levy 100*l.*, and there haveing showed their warrant, after her denyall to pay, they made distresse, which, whilst they were doing in some upper roome to which she brought them, severall gentlemen of the town came into the house, followed by a rable in great numbers; These gentlemen called the Sheriffes agents roages, and told them they had noe authority in that town without the Maior or his officers, and told them they deserved to be sett in the stocks or sent to prison, and one said they deserved the gibbet, which sayings encouraged the rable, that one woman, with a penknife in her hand, set her back to the dore, which was shutt, and swore shee would stab that man that dared to take any distress thence. And on this wise they kept the Bayliffes as prisoners in the house about an hower and a halfe, in which time one that the Sheriffes had deputed to goe with the Bayliffes to see to their orderly actings, who was gone out of the house before this rable came in, hearing how they were detayned in the house, went to the Maior and desired his aid to keep the peace, but not withstanding what Mr. Maior thought fitt to doe, soe little care to keepe the peace was taken that, when Mrs. Pennington's dore was opened, she bidding the Bayliffes carry away the distresse at their perills and the Bayliffes takeing up the distresse and carrying the same forth of the house, they were set upon by some hundreds in the street, the distresse rescussed, the Bayliffes many ways abused, stoned, wounded, and hardly escaped with their lives."

The KING OF MOROCCO to the KING OF GREAT BRITAIN.

426. 1681.—"From the servant of' the high God, Governour over all people, Ishmael Keriffe, overflowing with good deeds, he, though high, demandeth of the Most High God and the Angels, but of none other, he that hath millions of horse at his command, Sendeth peace unto you that follow the truth. We have understood by the way of Tangier, that we are in perfect friendship and that peace is concluded over all our countries, and, therefore, the letter we send is to confirme this peace and the treaty we have made with you, for we have a desire to trade with you, but let us not make the same tearmes that we had in the beginning of the warr, wherein so many dyed by the sword when we were enemies, but let our enemies dye. We, therefore, have slayn such as have run away from you to us, but you have not done the same, for the second act, that if any renegado shall run from us to Tangier you shall be obliged to send them back again. And for your security in this treaty, we send you our servant, Hada, for the management of it. And our will is that it shall be like the things that begin to grow. And I, who am the tree itselfe, have sent you one of my servants (being a branch of myselfe) which I recommend to you as if it were the tree itselfe. And we have strictly charged him what he shall say unto you. Looke upon him as you would doe upon myselfe. That which he shall doe shalbee well done and you shall value it as a gemme from heaven. We heartily desire you to write to us, for neither our habits nor our customes are like yours, but if you will build anything upon our ground we will pull it downe and we shall doe ourselves right. Also we have amongst us some christians who understand themselves and are more esteemed than our own servants. They have eagles eyes, but hate us and our beleife, and thereupon are a scandall to us. He that valueth our honour honoureth God. And because it is our desire you should receive something from us, we send you 30 estridges out of the deserts, and we expect that you should furnish us with 6,000 pieces of eight yearely. As for Tangier we stand in no manner of feare of it. And after the ratification of the peace, all hostility shall cease. Ishmael son of the beloved Keriffe, descended from God." *Copy.*

ELINE COTTAM to ROGER KENYON.

427. 1681[-2], January 9, Blackburn.—Asking his interest for the abatement of the penalties imposed on Henry Cottam, of Thorneley, a papist, her late husband's brother.

MILES DODDING to ROGER KENYON.

428. 1681[-2], January 10. Conishead.—"If Madam Anderton of Bardsey, with her sons, Mr. Thomas Polewheele, and Baskervill, and the rest of their family be convicted, it would not be amiss to humble them, for they are very ill neighbours and highly injurious to me. When you send any officers on this side, let them call at my house and I will put them in a way how to get something, for though they have few goods, yet rather than go to gaol they will assign part of their estate to pay the King's due. Good sir, do not forget this whereby it will oblige me." *Seal of arms.*

GUICCIARDINI WENTWORTH to ROGER KENYON.

429. 1681[-2], January 14.—"The report made by Mr. Attorny Generall upon the warrant from the Lords Commissioners of the Treasury, upon the petiton you saw, is,.I beleeve, returned to them, though I cannot yett have a sight of itt, my reason beeing this : there is a warrant issued out to the Lord Treasurer's Remembrancer directing you to return forthwith all Recogneizences of recusants now before you, as belonging to the King and not Duke of Lancaster, for, being taken from papists, they are pleased to suppose they are for recusancy. So soon as I have seen the report you shall not faile of a copy." *Seal of arms, broken.*

George Hilton to Roger Kenyon.

430. 1681[-2], January 21.—"I hearttaly wish you a good jorney to London, and suckcesfull, otherwise I am undone, and I praye be pleased, as soon as the tryall is over, to lett me receive a line or two of an account how the cause goes, whether for the King or Jesuits. I also intreat you to imploy some for me to search the returns in the Exchequer, whether that Francis Lord Carrington be returned a convicted recusant or not, ether returned out of Warwickshire or Oxfordshire. His two places of aboad is Howton in Warwickshire and Leadwell in Oxfordshire. If the cause goe against the King, I must expect nothing but to be prosecuted and tormented as much as they can, for I am threattened beforehand. I desire to have a copy of the record of his conviction attested under seale, or so as it will serve in court to be pleaded against him, in case I be forced upon such a plea for my own safety and preservation." *Seal of arms.*

Zachary Taylor to Roger Kenyon.

431. 1681[-2], January 23. Ormskirk.—"I received from Mr. Hunter the inclosed, which I have sent you and returned this answer to him—that you were pleased to promise us your assistance in that concern, than whom I conceived no friend he had, could do more ; and therefore desired he would acquiesce in your endeavours that I would acquaint you with the purport of his letter, which if it could anything advantage us from your kindness we should understand that we might make the way more easy to you. If a petition from us, with letters from the Bishop, would anything promote it (if you will give yourself the trouble of a line or two that we may know to direct it to you at London) we will procure and send it to you. Mr. Tench's discourse with Mr. Andrews, you will best understand from himself, whom I suppose you will see in London (to whom I beg you would give my service) and whatever you do, will be gratefully acknowledged by us."

Sir Thomas Preston to Roger Kenyon.

432. 1681[-2], February 5. Haigh.—"I have been out of doors but once since I came hither on Friday. I went about two miles with the corps of my cousin, John Culcheth, who died very suddenly of pleurisy. If the trial go for the King, and you think my presence absolutely necessary, I hope I may be in a condition to come to you."

William Hayhurst to Roger Kenyon, in London.

433. 1681-2, February 12. Peel.—"Uppon Friday last, I came from Preston to Ormeschurch, on purpose to see the poor wounded people whom we had employed in his Majestie's service : two of them, George Flitcroft and James Nicholson, lye in a very miserable condition and, in all humane probability, cannot recover. Dr. Richmond and Dr. Alcock are very dilligent to use all meanes to help them. Upon

Wensday last they, searching to the bottom of George his wound in his head, which is a wide gash cutt three wayes, they found the skull crushed downe, just above the braine pan, so that pressing his finger upon it, the blood issued out of the braine pann ; whereupon they concluded there could bee noe way to doe him good but cutting away that part of the scull that did so much prejudice the braine, which Dr. Richmond did by a round dented instrument, and took of the scull to the breddth of a threepence, which I have to show you when I come up to London. Upon Saturday last, Dr. Richmond dressed him againe, and raised up the scull in severall places, where it was cracked, and beaten downe ; since which time hee hath been something better, and the Doctors hope he may recover, but James Nicholson they dispaire cf ; he lies a dreadfull spectacle, his right side is quite perished, hee has a great wound in his head, and nothing the Doctors can doe, works upon him. Hee is sensible of nothing, but allwaies lyes as if he were a dying. The rest of them, being fower, are all cruelly bruised and wounded, and though not mortally, yett 'tis feared they can never have the right use of their limbs. The rioters are said to bee all papists and above eight and twenty in number. Mr. Justice Entwisle has been active to apprehend them, but the constable of the towne, one John Tyrer (?) (who denyed to goe with the officers to preserve the peace) made not that quick execution of his warrant against them hee ought to have done, so that they all fledd, and theres none to bee light on. Afterwards, Mr. Entwisle sent hue and cry after two of them, Thomas Tickle and Edward Tickle, his brother, who were the authors of all the mischief ; but that waye proved ineffectuall, and now Mr. Entwisle and Mr. Mayor of Lerpoole, have appointed a Sessions to be held at Allcarr upon Monday sennitt, for inquiery. After yesterday, wee privately got a warrant directed to Mr. Gillibrand and severall other Militia officers, to make a privy search in every house in Alkarr, and about it, to apprehend the offenders, which I hope, if well managed, will bring some of them to light."

Postscript.—" We have but yett gott the names of twelve of the ryoters." *Seal.*

SIR THOMAS PRESTON to ROGER KENYON, London.

434. 1681[-2], February 12. Haigh.—Has received his letter, by which he perceives " the tryall is deferred untill Tuesday next, and that it may be dubious of holding then." Would, on this, have come up as far as Coventry, but his daughter is ill with " a distemper which they call beire the hen-pox " and also with " a greate swelling in her lipp which is thought may be the evill " ; for this, his wife is determined to take her to Chester, to be " touched."

FRANCIS JAKSON to ROGER KENYON.

435. 1681[-2], February 14. Requesting favour on behalf of his Aunt Elizabeth La . . . . . who is very ancient, being above 80 years. He only [just] heard that all Roman Catholics in Lancashire were to be prosecuted, he knows not what she is, but some people term her a Roman Catholic. *Seal.*

The EARL OF DERBY to the COMMISSIONERS OF THE CUSTOMS.

436. 1681-2, February 16, Whitehall.—" I expected you would consider some way of repairing the injury done me by your agent Deny, for his false and scandalous information against me, preferred by you to the Lords of the Treasury. It is no wonder my complaining of the behaviour of those sent into the Isle of Man, has had so little effect, when I cannot have justice done me against one who has not spared me, after which, the people and merchants who come there, will have no reason to expect better usage.

So long as there appeared the least ground for his Majesty's service, I patiently suffered my property to be invaded (which is a tender thing to an Englishman), but I am sure it is not the King's intention I should be thus used, and it is now time for me to complain and tell you plainly that the ten years' trouble which I have had from the Commissioners of the Customs, by sending such officers (as they call themselves) into the Isle of Man, might convince you, if you reflect upon the charge and little advantage those men have been to tl e Crown, of thinking it to be of advantage to their Majesties to continue them there.

They act without any conformity to the laws of the Island, they affright almost all boats, especially the Scottish, from all manner of traffic with the Island, and boats passing as usual betwixt England and Ireland, dare scarce touch there to take in passengers or otherwise, as was always usual. It is a thing never offered to be done to any of my ancestors, and my sufferance so long, begins to be challenged as a custom; it is therefore high time I tell you I have been too much abused to suffer so any more.

What is truly for their Majesties' service to be done there, my officers shall on all occasions have in charge to take care of and communicate to you, but I shall not admit of any commission or private instructions from you to be obeyed in the Isle of Man." *Draft, with corrections in the Earl of Derby's handwriting.*

Sir Thomas Preston to Roger Kenyon.

437. 1681[-2], February 17. Haigh.—We think it not convenient to delay having my little girl touched, and on Monday next set forward from Chester. The persons at Alkar are all yet living, but of one or two there are little hopes. The grandee Papists here seem much concerned at it, thinking it an obstruction to their false petition which before, they hoped might have prevented any new process against them. *Seal of arms.*

R. Bradshaigh, Junior, to Roger Kenyon.

438. 1681[-2], February 19. Wigan.—"Yesterday my brother Preston, with my sister and his girl, went home for Chester in order to a journey for London to-morrow, though the business of Sir T[homas] P[reston] be deferred till next tearme, yet his daughter's too apparent symptoms of the Kings-evil occassions this sudden motion, and he is advised by us all here to goe too, or that it may not be amiss for him to prepare his way to the King before the next tearme, and especially such an occasion as at present offers itselfe for him to attend his Majesty with.

"Yesterday, at a publick hall (notice whereof was given to all persons 3 days before) we did unanimously agree of our abhorrence against the association soe positivily sworne to be found in the Earl of Shaftsbury's clossett. It is passed (by a consenting huzza of the numerous burjesses of our Corporation) under the towne seale, and my brother Preston is to wayt uppon the Duke of Albemarle with it to the King. Sir, this is all the news I have to send you hence. As for the ill treatment of your officers in Alker, I suppose you have had a more early accompt, nor can I add to your account anything but my opinion, which is, that it farre exceeds the unjust proceedings of the riott that was in this towne." *Seal, broken.*

RIOT AT WIGAN.

439. 1682, February 20.—Inquisition taken at Altcarr before Richard Windall, Mayor of Liverpool, and John Entwisle, Esquire, Justice of the Peace for the County of Lancaster. by Silvester Sutch of Ormeskirk, gentleman, William Male of Maghull, gentleman, Laurence Hulme of the same, gentleman, John Tatlock of Melling, gentleman, Humphrey Greaves of Scarisbrick, gentleman, Laurence Baron of Sefton, gentleman, Bryan Fleetwood of the same, gentleman, James Farrer of Ormekirk, gentleman, John Berey of the same, gentleman, John Heyes of the same, gentleman, Henry Barton of the same, gentleman, James Goare of Lydeate, gentleman, Gabrel Greaves of Ormskirk, Thomas Pye of Aughton, gentleman, Roger Parr of Sefton, gentleman, Roger Pye of Aughton, gentleman, Richard Hodgkinson of the same, gentleman, James Blackbeach of the same, and Thomas Harrison of Lytherland, gentleman, jurors, by whom there is returned a true bill against Thomas Tickle of Altcarr, yeoman, John Sutton, senior, yeoman, Edward Tickle, husbandman, Ralph Starky, miller, Thomas Massam, husbandman, John Wilson, husbandman, Thomas Lunt, husbandman, John Reynold, senior, husbandman, James Reynold, labourer, John Speakman, husbandman, Richard Linnaker, servant to Margery Tickle, Ellen Speakman, widow, and the servant of Thomas Massam, whose name is not known, all of Altcarr, for riot, assault, and a rescue of the goods and beasts of John Sutton and Margery Tickle, made on 2 February, upon John Smethurst, George Flitcroft, John Hardman, George Hatton, Henry Morres, James Ashcroft, James Nicholson, and James Fazakerley, who were authorised by virtue of a writ of Laurence Rawstorne, sheriff of the County of Lancaster, to seize the goods of the said John Sutton and Margery Tickle, being persons mentioned in a schedule annexed to the said writ.

HENRY ROWE to ROGER KENYON.

440. 1681[-2], February 21. Wigan.—"Yesterday, I and my sonn were att the Sessions kept at Alkar ; the Justices were Justice Entwisle and Justice Windall, Maior of Liverpoole. Justice Entwisle gave an excellent charg sutable to the occasion. Truly he has beene all along verie forward to discover all the rioters; but the most, nay, I may [say] all, the towne beeing papists, or popishly affected, they will not tell who they were, only upon the Inquisition, ten were discovered, whereof one is taken and sent to Gaole ; warrants are out against the rest, who as I told you in my last, are fled and lye hidden privately in the cuntry waiteing what will beecome of the man that is soe sore wounded, who now, as the Doctor supposes, cannot live long alive, beeing everie day weaker and weaker. The rest, God bee thanked, mends well now. Wee have verie great hopes of George Flitcroft's recovery." *Seal.*

MR. ENTWISLE to the CHANCELLOR OF THE DUCHY OF LANCASTER.

441. 1681[-2], February 21. Ormskirk.—"On the 2nd of February, the Sheriffe's bayliffes, by vertue of his warrant, distrained the Recusants mentioned in the Inquisition, for their severall forfeitures, after a demand and denyall to pay them, and brought the distresse to the Constable's house, where they stayed from nine till three a clock in the afternoon, expecting the persons distrained, to redeem their cattle, haveing left that notice at their severall houses, but were privately informed some opposition would be given them, and that they should not take the cattle out of the towne, which they then suddenly prepared themselves to do; but at a distance, they discovered a party of about 18 men and 3 women standing overthwart the King's highway, who, upon the Sheriffes ministers approaching, immediately with their long staffes, pitchforkes, and musketts, beat them down, and whilst they lay upon the ground, continued strikeing them, saying—Wee hope to see you all in the like condition ere it be long, and so drive their cattle away, leaving the poore men wallowing in the mire and their own blood, the darkness of the night approaching, and farr from any house or persons to releive them. I saw most of the men barbarously beaten and wounded. Two lye here in this town, mortally, so their Chirurgion yesterday affirmeing upon his oath, he despaires of their recovery, one of them haveing lost the use of all the one side of his body and has no way of easing the same but by vomitting. The offenders are fled, or sculke and lye hid. Though I have sent out 3 severall warrants for search after them, I am jealous they are not farr from home, but the whole parish is generally in the Roman Comunion, and, therefore, it is very difficult by the ordinary course of justice to discover these offenders. I have bound one of the Constables of that towne to the Assizes for his remissnes, and whilst I am now writeing, the other brings before mee one of the ryotters lately taken, who, I understand, hath absconded in a Protestant's house, and indeed, I fear that party in Allcar is so slender that they dare not deny the Roman whatsoever he is pleased to call a neighborly civility. I have found the insolence of that party so high in that town, that the officers, in retorne to my warrants for their presentments of absentors from Church, upon the laws of 12*d.* a sunday, have told mee they durst not do it for feare of the Tickles, whose house I have also been informed was, 4 or 5 yeares since, a great receptacle of the Roman Priests and usual place of resort to masse. Such informations came not to mee in time nor so legally as to proceed upon them judicially, yet sufficient to satisfy mee in my private judgement that these sanguinary proceedings are the workes of men of that religion. But this, with your Honor's favor, is my private conception, wherewith I shall not presume to give you any further disturbance.

The names of the wounded men.

| James Nicholson, | George Hatton, | James Ashcroft, |
| Geo. Flitcroft, | John Hardman, | James Fazakerley. |

The names of the-persons indicted.

Thomas Tickle of Altcarr, yeoman; John Sutton of the same, yeoman; Edward Tickle of the same, husbandman; Thomas Massam of the same, husbandman; John Wilson of the same, husbandman; Thomas Lunt of the same, husbandman; John Reynold of the same, husbandman; John Spakman of the same, husbandman; James Reynold of the same, laborer; Ralph Starky of the same, Miller." *Draft.*

J. ENTWISLE to ROGER KENYON.

442. 1681[-2]. February 21. Ormskirk.—The Bailiff of the Hundred of Derby had much ado to refrain from being " an embrateor " or maintainer, within the statute of 19 Henry VII., cap. 13. I wonder how he, in his own right, comes to have that office, when in all other Hundreds other sort of persons have it. This day, Mr. Taylor tells me, there is a report about that, upon this riot, a stop is put upon all proceedings against " the R " by the King's special command.

K. Fogge to Roger Kenyon.

443. 1681[–2], March 6. Chester.—Giving the characters of " Ned " and George Kenyon while at College at Cambridge.

R. Bradshaigh, Junior, to Roger Kenyon.

444. 1681[–2], March 18.—I have been in the company of old Dr. Worthington, and he has very earnestly intreated me to be his friend with you, to withdraw the warrant out against him, and though you told me you could not do it, yet give me leave to propose a medium. If you would write but two lines to Bailiff Laurence Anderton, asking him —since he has such a warrant and does not execute it—to deliver it to me in order to return it to you for better execution. I do faithfully promise you that the warrant shall not be embezzled, but shall be forthcoming whenever you, or any authority, shall require it from me.

William Hayhurst to Roger Kenyon.

445. 1682, April 8.—" On Friday morning, wee concluded upon and dispatched our business with the Under-Sheriff and Mr. Winkley. By intreaty, &c., hee was pleased to accept of their owne security to bee one bound with another. I stickled at one part of the condition, and would have it altered; but Mr. Roscoe, and the rest, were contented with it. And, thereupon, all Salford Hundred and about 16 or 20 schedules for Derby Hundred. Mr. Wentworth went along with mee to Mr. Greenfield, and gave him 10s. for stating the case, in which hee hath taken a great deale of paines, stating everye man's particular case upon the whole record. This day I presented it to Sir Thomas Stringer, with a broad-piece from Mr. Wentworth; he desired to have it left with him, being long, and hee would return it with his opinion, upon Monday."

Appointment of Surveyor, Waiter, and Searcher at the Isle of Man.

446. 1682, April 14.—Appointment by Charles, Lord Cheyne, Viscount Newhaven ; Andrew Newport; Sir Richard Temple, Baronet, K.B. ; and Sir Nicholas Bulter ; Commissioners of Customs, on the nomination of the Commissioners of the Treasury, of Christopher Eyans as surveyor, waiter, and searcher, at the Isle of Man. *Copy.*

" The humble Address of the Lord Lieutenant, High Sheriff, Deputy Lieutenants, Justices of the Peace, and other officers, as well civil as military, of the County Palatine of Lancaster, at a general meeting at Preston."

447. 1682, April 21.—" We, with sincerest loyalty, in unity of minds, doe, with all humility, dedicate our hearts, hands, fortunes, and lives, to your Majestie's service, solemnly acknowledging your Majestie's inherent supremacy in Church and State, and protesting according to our allegiance, still dutifully to serve you with that alacrity that becomes subjects sensible of the transcendant goodness of the best of Princes: In your Majestie's long and prudent raigne, are wound up in a great measure the blessings wee enjoy and the establishment of those felicities wee hope for, the peace of our true Church, the preservation of your subjects' property, the quiett of your kingdomes, our freedom from the feares of popery, schismatical contrivances and arbitrary government, and our trust that your gracious example will have that prevailing influence upon your lawfull successors, that wee may never despair of these injoyments. Certainly, the Church of England, the true protestant Church, was never better pleased then at your Majestie's happy restauration, never more gladd then when shee joyfully sett the English diadem upon your royall temples : since which time your gracious declarations, your royal administracons, have many a time (to our just satisfaction) evinced it to all, that your Majesty is the same Defender of the Faith wee then were transported with. And since your Majesty hath given leave to others to open their loyall hearts (wee otherwise have judged a submissive silence our greatest duty) doe, for your Majestie's satisfaction, in judging of the minds of your people, most faithfully, before God and the world, profess that wee are the same towards your Majesty wee then were, undoubtingly satisfyed in what your Majesty hath said and done for us, for which wee celebrate your royall care and goodness. Wee paye your Majesty our most humble and gratefull acknowledgments and repeate our constant and inviolable resolutions, with our lives and fortunes, to serve your Majesty, your beires and lawfull successors, and defend (so far as in us lyes) the true protestant religion, as now by law established, against all popish and phanaticall plotts and treasonable associations whatsoever, and, with loyall hearts and hands, constantly to discharge those trusts which your Majesty hath been pleased to repose in us." *Names of the signers. Copy.*

Concurrence with the above, by Justices of the Peace at Quarter Sessions at Lancaster, Ormskirk, and Manchester.

ADDRESS to the KING by the LORD LIEUTENANT, HIGH SHERIFF, DEPUTY LIEUTENANTS, JUSTICES OF THE PEACE, and other officers, civil and military, of the County Palatine of Lancaster.

448. 1682, April 22. Preston.—" Great and sacred Sir ! Wee, with sincerest loyalty, in unity of minds, doe, with all humility, dedicate our hearts, hands, fortunes, and lives, to your Majesty's service, solemnly acknowledging your Majesty's inherent supremacy in Church and State, and protesting according to our allegiance, still dutifully to serve you with that alacrity that becomes subjects sensible of the transcendent goodness of the best of Princes. In your Majesty's long and prudent reign, are wound up in a great measure the blessings we enjoy, and the establishment of these felicities we hope for: the peace of our true Church, the preservation of your subjects' property, the quiet of your Kingdom, our freedom from the fears of popery, chysmatical contrivances, and arbitrary government : and our trust that your gracious example will have that prevailing influence upon your lawful successors, that we may never dispair of these enjoyments. Certainly the Church of England, the true protestant Church, was never better pleased then at your Majesties happy restauration, never more gladd, then when shee joyfully sett the English diadem upon your royal temples : since which time your gracious declarations, your Royall administrations, have many a time, (to our just satisfaction) evinced it to all, that your Majesty is the same Defender of the Faith we then were transported with ; And since your

Majesty hath given leave to others, to open their loyall hearts; wee (who otherwise have judged a submissive silence our greatest duty), doe, for your Majesty's satisfaction, in judging of the minds of your people, most faithfully, before God and the world, profess, that wee are the same towards your Majesty wee then were, undoubtingly satisfied in what your Majesty hath said and done for us, for which wee celebrate your royall care and goodness, wee pay your Majesty our most humble and grateful acknowledgments and repeat our constant and inviolable resolutions, with our lives and fortunes to serve your Majesty, your heirs and lawfull successors, and defend (so far as in us lyes) the true protestant religion, as now by law established, against all popish and phanaticall plotts and treasonable associations whatsoever, and with loyall hearts and hands, constantly to discharge those trusts which your Majesty hath been pleased to repose in us."

R. Legh to [Roger] Kenyon.

449. 1682, April 24. Lyme.—"There is an old proverb or saying: whose presence does no good, theire absence does noe harm. Had your Lord Lieufftenantt given me notice I should not have deserted my Kinge's service, but I never heard of your meeting." *Seal.*

Richard Holt to Roger Kenyon.

450 and **451.** 1682, April 29. Ashworth.—I desire your aid that you will do me the favour to go to Parke to Mr. Hilton, and know of him whether he will grant me his consent or liking to come to his house and see his daughter, for whom I have a particular kindness. *Seal of arms.*

Dorothy Ashton to Roger Kenyon.

452. 1682, May 9. Peel.—Requesting him to remind her brother " to lett his picktore be taken twice " for her. *Seal of arms.*

William Ashton to Roger Kenyon, at "the Hand and Sword," near Turnstile Alley, Holborn.

453. 1682, May 18. Cambridge.—When he came to Cambridge, the " Master," and a great part of the University, had gone to London, where, by order of the King, they chose the Duke of Albemarle as Chancellor. On return of the Master, he consulted him about Kenyon's son; the Master found no fault with him, except in " neglecting chappell " and trifling away his time. *Seal, broken.*

Matthew Bootle to Roger Kenyon.

454. 1682, May 23. Manchester.—"I was truly glad to heare the hopes of the comon enemy (the Papists) defeated, for I was in the midst of them a weeke after I sawe you, and they did hughly rejoyce att the confirmed news of Sir Robert Carr's death which, God be thancked, is not soe, and nowe I very heartely congratulate your good suckses in your busynes in the north, which wee have here in the public news letters, and intreate you to thinke of my brother Abram's busynes, and the rest is to wish you soone and well home. For news, I have none for you."

Postscript.—"I begg you will boye mee a hansome small stick with a silver head, for a Sundaye stick, a stronge one I have allready, and if one of your servants rydes with it downe, I will, with all thancks, paye you att sight, but when you please to boye it, remember I am of the longer sise and in the greatest measure." *Seal.*

R. HEYWOOD to ROGER KENYON.

455. 1682, May 23. Knowsley.—My Lord [of Derby] desires you to buy him some glasses; he would have two dozen of little round glasses from Sir Robert Carr's glass man, each dozen must be of equal size. *Seal of arms.*

The EARL OF DERBY to ROGER KENYON.

456. 1682, May 23. Knowsley.—I long to hear how the address will be received, though I do not much question it will be well taken, since I hear it has been already approved of. Since you make no mention of Sir Robert Carr, I hope there is no danger of his death, for I believe, if there had been ill news, I should certainly have heard of it. When you write to him pray present my humble service, and let him know I have got a painter to draw Darcy's picture, and, if it is well done, I will send it him. I am glad of your success against Sir T. Preston. *Seal of arms.*

ZACHARY TAYLOR to ROGER KENYON.

457. 1682, May 26. Ormskirk.—" The news we have of Sir Thomas Preston's estate in Lancashire being found for the King, is the occasion of this trouble. If we could reap any advantage in order to the settling of our King's preacher's revenue, we promise our selves all the assistance you can give us. And if you think it convenient that the Bishop should, in this opportunity, appear, or that anything we could do in so favourable juncture might be successful, our interest will engage us to be guided by your counsels."

THOMAS HODGKINSON to ROGER KENYON.

458. 1682, May 30. Knowsley.—" You will receive by this post our Preston Addresse from the hande of my good Lord Derby, who was humbly desired to cause the same to be presented to his Majestie. His Lordshipp shewed me your letter by this post, which is all that I heard of you since you went. I shold bee very glad to heare that our worthy Chancellor is restored to his perfect health. I beleeve you will bee directed to deliver the addresse to my Lord Arlington, who will bee desired to present the same which, I hope, will bee equally gratefull with others, to our most gratious Soveraigne. When you have received it, bee pleas'd to send for Mr. James Ashton and Cousan Winckley to signe it. All the rest of the Aldermen and Councell have already subscribed. Yesterday, Sir William Gerrard was here, who hoped that his Majestie would restore Furnese to Sir Thomas Preston; that there would be another bout for it; that Sir Thomas Preston showed him the draught of a conveyance whereby Furneis was setled upon his heirs generall, in case his children dyed without issue, and some other such like uncompetent discourses. My Lord tould him, as to the first, that it was improbable his Majestie should proceed so farr as a chargeable suite and restore the booty recovered. The rest ended with a guinney, which the Barronet paid his Lordshipp, at cards, for his entertainment. Sir William was pleas'd to repeate, over and over againe, that it was never his fortune to win of my Lord at any sort of game, which caused some reflexions in the company upon theire former acquaintance." *Seal of arms.*

MATTHEW BOOTLE to ROGER KENYON.

459. 1682, May 30. Manchester.—My brother, Abraham, is returned among the Recusants for 20*li.* per month, although he constantly goes to the Parish Church, viz., Warrington, both to the service and sermon, and receives the sacrament there; and to this purpose I send you a certificate under the parson's and churchwarden's hands. " I believe he was returned out of malice, for I doubt he is a little Presbiterianly effected. I am sorry Sir Robert Carr mends so latly; I pray God mend his pace. We had here yesterday burnt, some say old John Presbiter, some the Lord Shaftsberry, but most say it was an old crete carrier that was squeezed to death at the back of a door for filshing. Capt. Haworth was master of the ceremonies, and led it up, attended by some five or six men, all the rest being children, and scarce so much as one either laughed or cried, but we were all here very merry with bells, bonfires, and small guns." *Seal of arms.*

EDWARD TYLDESLEY to ROGER KENYON.

460. 1682, May 30.—He is not desirous of having his name and fame enrolled in the Treasury, and is much more desirous to remain in Mr. Kenyon's unwritten, than in his written, list of friends. His uncle Banaster says Scotland Yard is removed now to Knowsley, for Robin Herwod does there "obumbrace" (*sic*). *Seal.*

[ROGER KENYON ?] to MILES DODDING and WILLIAM KIRKBY, two of the Justices of the Peace for the County of Lancaster.

461. 1682, May 31. Treasury Chamber.—Directing them to prevent the killing of deer or committing of waste on the estate of Sir Thomas Preston, in Furnes, lately recovered by his Majesty, during the perfecting of a decree which is pronounced, till his Majesty's agents shall come. *Draft.*

WILLIAM PATTEN to ROGER KENYON.

462. 1682, June 9. Gray's Inn.—" Greate matters since my comeinge hether have occurred, for the Lord Mowgrave [Mulgrave] hath made soe briske attempts upon the Lady Anne that he is forbidd the Court, St. James Street and St. James' Parke. All his offices and employments, as that of Governor of Hull, one of the Attendants of the Bedd Chamber, and some place in the Guards, taken from him and disposed to other persons of quallity. The Lord Gray was, by the King's Bench, committed, and still standes committed, for detayneing the body of the Lord Barkley's younger daughter, and as the reporte goes, hee saith that hee marryed her eldest sister and expected a maidens-heade, but not findeing it, hee resolved to have one in the family, if any bee left; but lest this should tende towards *scandelum magnatum,* pray keep it to yourself. The Sheriffs are not as yet pricked, but it is supposed ours will bee Mr. Doddinge, none being his competitors but Mr. Norres and Mr. Bennet Sherrington. The Duke of Munmouth is not to bee discharged till towards the latter ende of the term, and I doe not heare that anythinge then will be offered against him." *Seal of arms.*

ARTHUR ASHTON to ROGER KENYON, in London.

463. 1682, June 20. Clitherow.—" Having received your letter, not knowing how, or what person, to employ to procure a draught of the Corporation armes in so short time, Mr. Robert Slater, intending a journey towards London tomorrow morning, I thought it might not be a miss to send one of the conyzans off the coats, which I have sent by Mr. Robert Slater, who promises to deliver it into your hands : and, if you please, he will bring it to Clitherow again. Upon Sunday last, about five of the clock in the evening, Mr. John Webster, your old doctor, departed this life ; [he] is to be buried at Clitherow tomorrow." *Seal, broken.*

PETER BOLD [to ROGER KENYON].

464. 1682, July 3. Bold.—" Mr. Penketh was with me before I went for Yorkshire and aquainted me that he had very hard usuage from some of your officers, and, he belives, without your order. I know the gentleman very well; he is a neare neighbor to me, and his condition is not unknown to me ; he faithfully served his late Majestie all the first warr, and in that service behaved himself very gallantly and with great loyaltye. He received many wounds and was so great a sufferer that he was reduced to a very poore condition. He now lives an undertennant to a small messuage in Bold, not above 5 acres. I looke uppon him to be as great an object of charity as any in that neighborhood. I, beinge very sensible of theise things, have formerly writt uppon his behalf to Sir Peter Brooke and others, and spoke to you myself, that he might be favorably dealt with, and I heare that both your self and Mr. Sherriffe were very kinde to him and, when his goods were destrained, ordered restitution and promised he should not be trobled for the future. Notwithstandinge all this, they have since taken his goods."

SIR THOMAS PRESTON to ROGER KENYON.

465. 1682, July 18. London.—Concerning the drawing of a lease from the Crown to Sir Thomas Preston. On Saturday last, by adjournment of my Lord Mayor, the Court was held again for the election of sheriffs, and, in the first place, he declared it as his right to name one, which was Mr. North, and ordered the other three should poll *de novo* for the other, which is said was then carried, by the majority of votes, for Mr. Box, and they two are like to be sworn, but that it will, nevertheless, be a contest at law. The King went for Windsor about 2 o'clock the same night, and the part of the guards ordered to their country quarters again, who have been all in town since Friday morning. *Seal of arms, broken.*

ROGER KENYON to ———.

466. 1682, July 21. Manchester.—" Mr. Tilsley, when I was in towne, did once or twice somewhat remotely mention to mee his project (as he names it in his letter) that there might be obtained from their Lordshipps a power to mee, or to me and some others, of agreeing with every recusant of some reasonable yearly summe proportionable to their estates, which way, he said, would no doubt bring more money, with lesse noyse and troble, into the Exchequer, and be more quietly continued then by the course now taken. I then told him, if their Lordshipps did think fitt to try that way, I did, and I do still believe, it would amount to more, but not by waiveing the processe of 20*l. per mensam,* for if the recusant should gaine that point, then should the

Prerogative Writt be forborne, the arreares due upon it lost, and whatever agreement is made with the papist to day shall last no longer then he is compellable to performe it; nay, if the papists were all undertakers to his Majestie for payment of any summe agreed on, they would never agree amongst themselves, without this staffe of authority to collect it. So I am by no meanes of opinion that it is for his Majestie's service to waive the 20*l. per mensam*, I mean the processe for it. 'Tis true wee in this county take it against all, that is, against many thousands whose estates are inconsiderable, and 'tis but from a very few that can pay so much, yet it is the strongest processe and gives the King a title to goods, landes, and, for want of satisfaction that way, to the body, by which mean such persons whose estates are not leviable, some who are great money maisters are brought to pay, which otherways could not bee. But whilst these processes are out as a rod over them, if their Lordshipps shall think it meet when we have sale inquisitions, for that we must do to empower me to make any compositions or agreements with them, or to treat with them in order to that, and from time to time to certify their Lordshipps, by acquainting you that their Lordshipps may direct me, as they approve or disapprove, or, if their Lord shipps shall think fitt to join any with mee in it, I shall, to my power, faithfully and impartially performe their Lordshipps commands, whilst I have the honour to be in their service." *Draft.*

WILLIAM PATTEN to [ROGER KENYON].

467. 1682, July 26. Preston.—Has received the commission for supplemental proof between the King and Lord Mollyneux, and others, the execution of it must be either before, or on the last day of, the Assizes, or not till after our Guild be over. *Seal of arms.*

THOMAS HODGKINSON to ROGER KENYON.

468. 1682, July 29. Preston.—"It is now almost twelve of clocke, and I am just parted with Mr. Fleetwood; you must not, therefore, expect very comunicable. Let me onely advise you that, at our guild, there will bee severall presents from the gentry of our countrey; a good fat oxe or cow, with a brace of bucks from our chancellour, wold fully bespeake his place and character, but let mee conjure you not to speake of this intimation." *Seal of arms.*

The REV. JOHN LAKE to ROGER KENYON.

469. 1682, July 30.—Whether yours, which I have newly received, was more kind or surprising, I know not, but it is very much both. Besides the consciousness of my own insufficiencies, there are sundry other things which dissuade and discourage my acceptance. To mention no other but the circumstances of my person; you know I carry a crazy body at best, which I doubt would not well comport with the island, and a present, through the effects of my unhappy fall, I cannot go but with two underhand crutches, and am thereby incapacitated to attend a matter of this nature. *Seal of arms.*

WILLIAM BANKES to ROGER KENYON.

470. 1682, July 31. Winstanley.—"There is now a very sorrowfull house at Knowsley, upon the death of my Lady Betty. She is to be buryed to night at Ormschurch." *Seal.*

The Rev. John Lake to Roger Kenyon.

471. 1682, August 16.—" I beseech you, when next you see his Lordship [Lord Derby], to procure such an instrument as is usual in the case wherein I am not capable of directing it, being a bishoprick of a peculiar constitution and I do not understand the method of it. I suppose his Lordship grants the bishoprick by a solempn instrument, then application is made to the King, who issueth out his mandate to the Archbishop of the province, and he consecrateth the Bishop by himself, with two other Bishops, or giveth a commission for other Bishops to do it. For this cause I would discourse my Lord Archbishop of York (in whose province the Bishoprick of Man is) before I goo to London, and also consult his Grace's registry touching the ceremony and solempnity of it, and I would not seem busy before I had a formal grant of the Bishoprick. If his Lordship pleaseth to sign and seal such an instrument, I beseech you, upon receipt of it (for I must desire you to take and transmit it to me) to make a present of some guineas to the Secretary (as you shall think fit or be advised) and to do what is further to be done (if there is any thing further) in my Lord's family, and I will take speedy course to reimburse you. The value, as it is represented by Mr. Roper, is beyond my expectation, but it is a somwhat cooling consideration that the executors of the last Bishop must have all the profitts until Easter next, especially if inclusive of Easter next, so as that the succeeding Bishop shall receive nothing until perhaps half a year or a year after. Be pleased therefore (at your convenience) to explain this to me and to inform me what the state of the revennue is and whence it ariseth." *Seal of arms.*

Thomas Walsh to Roger Kenyon.

472. 1682, August 18. Aswarby:—His master's [Sir Robert Carr's] health is better. Mr. Carr regrets that his father's illness should prevent him from waiting upon the Mayor of Preston and the guild. His master desires a young barbour to wait on him ; if Kenyon cannot light on one, he will send to London. *Seal of arms.*

The Lords of the Treasury to the Justices of Lancashire.

473. 1682, August 23. Whitehall, Treasury Chambers.—As to smiths being liable to pay hearth money for their forges, of which they hear the Justices had neglected to enforce the payment. *Signed.*

W. Hilton to Roger Kenyon.

474. [16]82, August 24.—"Mr. Harry Withington is of opinion that if you tell Hartley that he shall be better used, and have his irons taken off, he will confesse. Mr. Withington doth not know Pendlebury, but he thinks his name is James Pendlebury, and that he dwells about Chew More." *Seal of arms, broken.*

Richard Clegge to [Roger] Kenyon.

475. 1682, August 25. Kirkham.—"There is a place in this parish, wee call Brewers-yeard, four or five miles distant, where the Quakers (the most incorrigible siners that I know) doe use to bury, which is a hazard unto me, in respect of the Acte for burying in wollen, and, which is worse, being thither, they can draw such neighbours as will not be invited unto others of their conventicles. They begin, I hear, of late to have speakers to their buryalls, and severall that doe speake there (who, or from whence, is not easy for us to discover) and this place no particular man doth owne, soe that conventicles are more dangerouse and lesse punishable than the rest. I desire you, therefore, you would procure this may bee spooken of at Sheriff's table, that these places may be laid wast, or if not soe, some other remedy may be thought of for the preventeing of their diabolicall infatuation and infection."

BENJAMIN SYMONS to ROBERT HEYWOOD, at Knowsley.

476. [16]82, August 26. London.—Will not send the "tankert" till he has accomplished the other orders. Has commenced "the ingraving of the arms of the island, three tryangell leggs. I intend to show my art on it ; and I hoop I shall, in so doing, nott only give my Lord and you good satisfaction, butt allso gaine more of his honour's work. I intend to follow itt close till itt is done. But ingraveing in stone requires more time than ordinary : it will be worth fifty shilling, the engraving of it, well ; and the gold and setting will be abought twenty-five shilling more. You may be sure to receive them by the fifteen or sixteen of the next month." *Seal of arms.*

The REV. JOHN LAKE to ROGER KENYON.

477. 1682, August 26.—"By a letter from my Patron (your cosin Ashton) which surprized me almost as much as your first intimations of the Bishoprick of Man (whereof I had not then thought so much as in a dream) I perceive that the Bishoprick is intended in exchange for Prestwich, and my patron seemeth to desire and expect the present resignation of it, which I cannot consent to for these reasons.

"(1) I am not yet Bishop, and many things may fall in betwixt cup and lip.

"(2) The value of the Bishoprick will not compensate any great loss sustained by it, especially if it be considered that

"(3) I shall not come into profits until Easter, and if that be inclusive of Easter (as I suppose it is) I shall not actually receive anything until some considerable time after—meanwhile

"(4) The charges of consecration and other formalities will be very great, so that the profits when they come in, will not in a short time reimburse them.

"(5) It will likewise be a great trouble and charge to go into the Isle and to remove myself and my appurtenances, beside that the name and stile of a Bishop requireth a different port and draweth a yet further expense after it.

"(6) It will necessitate me to relinquish my Residentiarie's place at York, which, for 12 years together, hath been worth 130*l.* per annum.

"(7) If it should be inconsistent with my health, and perhaps life, to reside in the Isle constantly, Prestwich would be my only convenient retreat.

"(8) I should seem too fond of a bubble of honour to purchase it so dear, and it would look, in the eye of the world, like bargain and sale too, and scarcely reconcileable with the oath against simony.

"Sir, in all this it is not my meaning to lessen the favour and honour designed me, or the kindnes of those that have engaged themselves in it, whereof I have a very great sense. But if it be attended with these, or any terms at all, I shall most willingly quit my pretensions and supersede your further trouble." *Seal of arms.*

The Rev. John Lake to Roger Kenyon.

478. 1682, September 4. York.—Letter of thanks for services regarding the presentation to the Bishopric of Man. *Seal of arms.*

Robert Roper to Roger Kenyon.

479. 1682, September 15. Knowsley.—"His Lordshipp [Lord Derby] takes his journey on Munday next, straight for Newmarket, but does not call at Aswerby. *Have-at-all* wonne all with ease; there was about 2 lengths distance between *Black How* and *Sweet Lipps.* My lord's mare was lame and thereby was beaten sufficiently."

Roger Kenyon [to the Rev. John Lake, Bishop Elect of Sodor and Man].

480. 1682, September 16. Peel.—"On Sunday I went to Knowsley. The next day my Lord gave the inclosed his hand and seale, but took mee with him into Cheshire, whence I returned not till Thursday. I sent for your clerk to come to me yesterday, but not being come home, causes this messenger to your Lordship, with that which makes you Lord Bishop of Soder and Man. I have some Londoners now at my house, and this evening Sir John Molineux, his Lady, and their family, wilbe with me here, so that I cannot come to you, as otherwise I willingly would have done, for no other reason but that *inter nos* I might have discoursed with you, my Lord Derbys genius and temper, which I doubt not will no way be unpleasant to you. He is not sway'd with the violent humour of this impetuous age, and [the] discourses of the high flyers of either side find no hearty entartainment with him. Hee is faithfully loyall and a true son of the Church of England; free from fanatacisme, and farr from popery as any subject whatsoever. I say this because you are not yet so well knowing of him as a little time will make you. You will laugh at my fooleish boldnes in takeing this freedome with you to discourse of him; but my meaneing by it is but to possesse you with that apprehension of him, as to make your first acquaintance acceptable to each other, and when you have perused this foolish freedom, that none els may laffe at mee, burne this paper, or rather send it back by the bearer that I may burne it.

"My Lord goes towards Newmarket on Monday, and when the King goes thence, waits on him to London, where you will, I suppose, at the Duke of Ormond's house, meet with his Lordshipp. I gave my Lord's Secretary a handsom present, viz. 10*l.*; it was not for any manner of aid I had from him in the doing it, but he was not against mee, and some thing was due as a perquisite of his place. I name this to you that you need not be at any farther charge with him. My Lady Derby meets my Lord at London; shee goes about a three weekes hence. Mr. Roper, my Lord's Secretary, I beleve, comes up with her Lady-shipp. His acquaintance wilbe of good use to your Lordshipp, both there and hereafter. Neither hee nor Mr. Heywood could certainly tell me when the profitts of your Bishoprick commence, but they say they think Easter is exclusive to the late Bishopp's Executor, and that then there may be halfe a yeares profitt due to your Lordship; and inquire-ing of Coson Heawood of the profitts, hee saith—the Bishopps Palace is a good house, to which there is a faire demesne, many glebe tenants, and goor' tythes due. Hee said hee was present when two sufficient persons, one Wood and another, offered Bishopp Bridgman to give him clere

350*l.* per annum for the proffitts, but it was esteemed considerably more worth. Mr. Roper tells mee, hee thinkes your way, when you come to London, is [to] addresse to one of the Secretarys for the King's fiat upon this; but I need not derect your Lordshipp therein. I purpose, the latter end of this terme, to be at London, and if your Lordshipp have leisure when there, shalbee iu the mean time much honored with a line from you." *Draft.*

The Rev: John Lake to Roger Kenyon.

481. 1682, September 17. York.—On Michaelmas day I purpose to set out for London. If some indisposition of my wife's had not prevented, I had purposed to have set out upon Friday next. Touching the value of the Bishopric, I am not anxious; your kindness is the same as if it had been the Archbishopric of Toledo. *Seal of arms.*

Collection of Customs in the Isle of Man.

482. 1682, September 20–1691, April 1.—Copies of Letters, between these dates, from the Privy Council and the Custom House in London to the Earl of Derby, concerning the irregular collection of the Customs in the Isle of Man. The Council has reason to believe that there is laid up in the Island, a great store of tobacco, awaiting the opportunity of being "privately stolen" into England.

John Tench to Roger Kenyon.

483. 1682, September 23.—"Mr. Wentworth was with me this day; he gives but an incerteyne account of our worthy Chaucellor, but we will hope better of him than his secretary reports, whose news, you kuow, is not alwayes told to the best advantage of our good friend and master. Wee have had great relations heare of the splendid entertainments of the Duke of Monmouth in his Northern expedition, but Mr. Sargeânt Ramsey was sent to hasten him back in safe custody, and 'tis confidently reported Sir Thomas Armestrong obtained a *habeas corpus* for the Duke from Mr. Justice Raymond the last night. He is expected to towne this day. Our great matters in expectation are the Lord Marquess Hallifax's being made Lord President of the Councell in the roome of the Earle of Radnor, and Mr. Seymour, Lord Privy Seale."

Arthur Assheton to [Roger Kenyon ?].

484. 1682, September 27. Clitheroe.—"Yours received with a very large present—a peece of plat, a bowle which, being filled with strong liquor, may, it's like enough, dissolve some of our Lord's Burgesses; alsoe I received [the] Corpartions arms, and the kind token, a guiney. Att which time I sent for Mr. Bayliffe Robinson, Mr. Lister, Mr. Christopher Kendall, and some others. Our Court day being upon Thursday next, it was agreed the bowle should then be presented in the Moot Hall to Mr. Bayliffs, and the Burgesses then present, and the healths to be drunke the day of election of Bayliffes, which is to bee the 13th of October next. The persons thought upon for Bayliffs this ensueing yeare, [are] Mr. Thomas Braddyll and Mr. Robert Walmsley, for out Bayliffs, and Thomas Pinder and Thomas Oddy, inn Bayliffs. If you please, in the interim, to give yourself the trouble to writ two lines to Mr. Apleton or me, which you approved on, it shall be ndevoured to be performēd."

SIR RICHARD BRADSHAWE to CHRISTOPHER WILKINSON and ROGER KENYON.

485. 1682, October 4.—I hope you will both show your kindness in endeavouring to free the house and heir of Mearly from the affront of serving the constableship by traverse or otherwise.

WILLIAM ASHTON to ROGER KENYON.

486. 1682, October 7. Cambridge.—"It can be no news in Lancashire that the King is come to Newmarket, but it is the thinest court that ever I saw there. Yesterday was the great match betwixt *Dragon* and *Postboy,* the latter beat him above four lengths. I am heartily sorry for Sir Robert Carr that he was not there, for it was 6 and 7 to 4 against his horse, before the race begun." *Seal, broken.*

RICHARD BRADSHAWE to ROGER KENYON.

487. 1682, October 10. Pennington.—The bearer will acquaint you how Pennington would now, at Wigan sessions, put him on to be Constable for the Hall of Bradshaw, a thing never done before. They gave him notice but yesterday to appear, and Sir James Bradshaw living far off, in Yorkshire, he cannot possibly give him notice in time to defend himself from an affront that was never put upon that house before.

INFORMATION of EDMUND THELFALL of "the Ashes," in Goosnargh, Gentleman, given at Hulton before William Hilton and Thomas Leavers, Justices of the Peace.

488. 1682, October 19.—"The said informant upon his oath saith that the copy of a letter, to this information annexed, beginning with these words 'on my landing at Whithaven' and ending with these words, 'but those who board (?) the Crowne, your Lordshipps,' is a true copy of the first draught of a letter penned by Edward Tildesley, of Mierscough, in the county of Lancaster, Esquire; which first draught was and is the propper handwriteing of the said Edward Tildesley, and which was by the appointment and dirrection, and at the instance of, the said Edward Tildesley, fairly transcribed, and so directed and sent by the post from Preston, in Lancashire, to his Grace, the late Duke of Lowderdale, dated, to this informant's best remembrance, from Warrington, the 28th of January, 1679. And this informant saith that the second paper to this information annexed, beginning with these words 'Reasons offered by a wellwisher to the King and Kingdom to some Justices of the peace,' and ending with these words 'to obey the King's proclamation, the onely way to secure the peace of the Kingdome and their owne,' is a true copy of a paper penned by the said Edward Tildesley, with his owne hand, and fairly transcribed at the instance of the said Edward Tildesley, and sent inclosed in the said letter, directed to the said Duke. And this informant saith that, by the said Edward Tildesley's appointment and direction, besides the addition of the complement to these words 'your Lordshipps' there was added, postscribed, to this effect; that if his Lordshipp thought fitt to returne any answer, to derect the same 'For Thomas Bateson, at William Tomlinson's house in Preston.' And this informant further saith that the third paper to this information annexed is a true copy of a letter, the cover whereoff was endorsed, 'For Thomas Bateson at William Tomlinson's house in Preston,' and beginning with these words 'Sir, this is, according to your direction, to acknowledge the receit of your letter of the 18th instant, from Warrington,' and ending with these words 'from him at whose command this is sent to you.' And this informant saith that the said letter came to this informant's hand, and that on the same page, which was cover to the said letter, so directed, this informant took a copy of the letter, which enables him now more particularly and certainly to depose thereunto. And this deponant saith that the said letter was delivered by this informant to the said Edward Tildesley who, in answer thereunto, and within a few dayes after the receipt thereof, viz' about the latter end of the month of January, or the beginning of February, 1679–80, writt another letter to the said Duke. The first draught whereof was, and is, the propper hand-writeing of the said Edward Tildesley, which letter, beginning with these words " Tis no want of duty and allegiance to his Majestie,' and ending with these words ' your next may command your most obedient servant,' was allso by the appointment and direction, and at the instance, of the said Edward Tildesley, fairly transcribed, directed, and sent by the post from Preston, in Lancashire, to his grace, the Duke of Lowderdale. And this informant saith that the fourth paper to this information annexed, is a true coppy thereof. And this informant further saith that afterwards, viz', on or about the 25th of February, 1679–80, the said Edward Tildesley writt an other letter beginning with these words, ' The enclosed is a copy of what I writt you,' and ending with these words ' as is this that I am your grace's most obedient servant '; a postscript to which was added by the hand of Mr. Thomas Tildesley, beginning with these words ' My Lord, I shall not stay ' and ending with these words ' to get this into the Yorkshire road.' And saith that the first draught of the same letter was and is (save the postscript) the propper hand writing of the said Edward Tildesley. And that the same, as allso the postscript, was fairly transcribed, and by the appointment, direction, and at the instance, of the said Edward Tildesley, directed and sent to the late Duke of Lowderdale, by the post. And this informant saith that the fifth paper to this information annexed, is a true copy of the said letter and postscript."

LAWRANCE OLDFIELD to ROGER KENYON, at Peel.

489. 1682, October 26. Leftwich.—"I thought you not unwilling to part with your grey-pad *the Judge* and although I suspect his age is past marketable knowledg, and therefore considerably less worth now than two years agoe, yet, if you'll put him to me for sound wind, lymb, and eyes, I'll pay you fifteen guineas for him."

JAMES LIGHTBOUNE to ROGER KENYON.

490. 1682, November 4. Gray's Inn.—I thought a word of my Lord of Derby's business would not be inacceptable to you. Mr. Justice Dolben gave judgment against my Lord, but Mr. Justice Jones gave judgment for my Lord. *Seal.*

WILLIAM PATTEN to ROGER KENYON, at Peel.

491. 1682, November 4. Gray's Inn.—Enquiring of " My Lord of Derby's successe," he was informed that Judge Dalbin, " contrary to our expectation," gave his opinion against " my Lord "; but Judge Johnes for him. Sir Robert Carr is still dangerously ill. *Seal of arms.*

GEORGE ALLANSON to ROGER KENYON.

492. 1682, November 4. London.—I was yesterday to wait on Mr. Graham, touching Mr. Preston's business, who informs me that you have the writ of execution against Sir Thomas Preston's trustees, under seal, so that Mr. Weld cannot be served (although Lord Carrington is) till the return of the decree under seal. I was not a little joyful to understand that we were likely to have the honour of your company in London, but on the other hand, I hope it is not, in order to your quietness against the Papists for this night. I was informed amongst the Romanists that Mr. Tilsley had farmed the Papists' forfeitures of Lancaster at the annual rent of 12,000*li.* ; this sounds too much, and so I hope it is false.

WILLIAM HAYHURST to ROGER KENYON, at Peel.

493. 1682, November 6. Preston.—Has sent to Lancaster, to Styth, to enquire into the estates of the "most eminent" recusants in Lonsdale Hundred. Has provided evidence "for those in Amounderness and Blackburne to give their accompts here upon Friday next." Swaney has made returns of Sir William Gerrard and Mr. Dickonson. "Things move slowly here, and as Mr. Winckley pleases, who is resolved to stand by his old clyentes."

Postscript.—"Mr. Under-Sheriff's brother is like to dye. . . . He [the Under Sheriff] desires the witnesses may come hither, I intend for Wygan, to morrow night; if the Inquisitiones be adjourned hither, it will be better for the jury." *Seal.*

WILLIAM HULME to ROGER KENYON.

494. 1682, November 6. Hulme.—Is informed that Kenyon is going to London; desires " to kiss his hand " before he sets out.

SIR THOMAS STRINGER to ROGER KENYON.

495. 1682, November 6.—" The news of the Chancellor's death, your deare friend and mine, is too true ; the place is given to Sir Thomas." *Vide No.* 521. *Seal of arms.*

JOHN TENCH to ROGER KENYON.

496. 1682, November 7.—Mr. Chancellor is relapsed, and in so weak a condition that they begin to doubt of his recovery. The Duke of Ormond is made a Duke of England. Good Sir Thomas Jones argued on my Lord of Derby's side, but the doubting judge was against him.

EDWARD FLEETWOOD to MR. KENYON.

497. 1682, November 7. Penwortham.—I hear you intend to hold inquisitions upon several gentlemen's estates, upon Wednesday and Thursday next, and not knowing but Cousin Anderton of Exton may be one of the number, this comes to desire (if you can do it with security) to look upon him at this time " as a reprobate." He has a great many children, and the estate but small. *Seal.*

WILLIAM BRABIN to ROGER KENYON.

498. 1682, November 12. Matishall.—I am very desirous to know how you and your lady and the rest of your good family are in health, particularly that sweet lady whose charming siren's voice had like to have shipwrecked an afflicted mariner. I am glad to hear Mr. Starkey has obtained his desire and is married to Madame Hilton. I have a friend who would fain engage you to do him a kindness. The business is this: Sir W. Martin lent Mr. Sherrington, of Bootle, a considerable sum of money; now, Sir William being dead, his son would be thankful if you would act for him. *Seal of arms.*

WILLIAM PATTEN to ROGER KENYON.

499. 1682, November 14. Gray's Inn.—I did expect your order for a motion before Mr. Justice Johnes, against the rioters at Wigan, for you promised it, but in regard I have not heard from you since I left Peele, I have not done anything therein. The sheriffs are not yet pricked, but it is thought they will be to-morrow, and some report that none of the three presented by the Chancellor will be elected, for some say Mr. Parker, and others, Mr.-Rigby. By letter yesterday from Mr. Welsh, we understand that Sir Robert Carr is much worse, and they now seem to despair of his recovery. *Seal of arms.*

WILLIAM PATTEN to ROGER KENYON, at Peel.

500. 1682, November 18. Gray's Inn.—"This day, Mr. Justice Windham and the Lord Chief Baron argued the Earle of Derby's case, and both gave their judgments for his lordshipp; soe that nowe hee has got the day, beinge 7 to 3." Hopes the news of the chancellor [of the Duchy's] death will bring Kenyon to London. *Seal of arms.*

THOMAS DOD to ROGER KENYON.

501. 1682, November 19.—"The good town of Ormeskirk understanding you are for London on Munday next, engaged me, on their behalfe generally, to acquaint you they are about to make application to my Lord Derby that, in this present commotion of affaires as to the Burrough of Wigan, which setts up for a principality of it selfe, there may bee a meanes found out, and effected, to reduce all the four sessions to this place. You know it lyes convenient to the countrey, and I hope the alteration noe way against your likeing, especially since it would conduce to the benefitt of the place, wherein my Lord is soe much interested, and has beene pleased to manifest his favors thereunto upon all occasions." *Seal of arms.*

R. HEYWOOD to ROGER KENYON.

502. 1682, November 22. Castle Rushen.—"I landed on the island the 28th of October in 12 hours from the Black Rock. I brought all my little doggs safe over, except 2 or 3, which, by the boy's carelessness, ran back from Knowsley, and I had not time to send for them." *Seal of arms.*

WILLIAM ASHTON to ROGER KENYON.

503. 1682, November 25. London.—"Doctor Lake's business mett with a rub at the Privy Seal, but my Lord Derby promised to remove it, and I think it is already done. I do not yet know what the Doctor will do with Prestwich, nor will I ask him till the consecration be over, which I suppose will be very shortly, because he told me he should be at Yorke within 6 weeks. Wee have no news but what Westminster Hall affords; I know, by this time, you have heard of Lord Derby's tryall and success, and likewise of the difference betwixt the Lord Berkley and Lord Gray, about the lady Henrietta, the Lord Berkley's second daughter. The case was tryed last Thursday, and the Lord Gray, one Crarrock and his wife, and one Jones, were found guilty of carrying away the young lady. The Court hath not sett a fine, but every one thinks it cannot be so great as is deserved. It is the foulest story that ever eyes saw or ears heard; in short, the lady was pretty round about the wast, and the proofs given in Court make it too plain (if she is with child) who is the father. When the tryall was over, the Lord Cheife Justice told the Lord Berkley, he might take his daughter, and he held forth his hand to receive her, but she refused to goe with him, telling them all that she was married to one Mr. Turner (a particular favourite of the Lord Gray's and, if I mistake not, one of Sir William Turner's younger sons) who was called into Court and owned her for his wife. But Sir George Jefferyes (who was Councell for the Lord Berkley) said that man was marryed to, and had children by, another woman in Westminster. This put the Lord Cheif Justice to a little pause, but immediately recollecting himself, he ordered the lady and Mr. Turner, her reall or pretended husband, to be committed to the King's Bench, till such time as it might appear that they were marryed. The Lord Cavendish and the Lord Wharton's eldest son (the Lord Clare haveing refused to stand) were bayl for the Lord Gray. This tryall lasted 4 or 5 houres; the cheif wittnesses were the Lady Berkley, mother, and the Lady Arabella, sister, to the Lady Henrietta. The Lady Arabella was the first that discovered the intreague betwixt them, by a letter left in Madam Henrietta's chamber and directed for the Lord Gray, intimating a very scandalous familarity between them, and this letter was produced and read publickly in Court. Most people wonder my Lord Berkley should expose his daughter so infamously in open Court, and all are amased at her impudence; but for my part, I have a worse opinion of another Lord. Yesterday, the Duke of Yorke tryed his action against Pilkington, who was cast, and the Jury gave the Duke 100,000*l.* damages." *Seal.*

J. Rowe to Roger Kenyon.

504. 1682, December 5. Liverpool.—It is greatly reported that my Lord Derby is made a Marquis, but of this we have no second news. *Seal of arms.*

William Hayhurst to Roger Kenyon.

505. 1682, December 21. "The Sword and Buckler," London.— "They say my Lord North is made Lord Keeper; hee brought the Mace with him yesternight from Whitehall, but I doe not hear for certaine who is in his place; they say Sir Wm. Scroggs. Sir Thomas Stringer was robbed of the 30*l.* I presented him for you, by his footman, who had gott away with it as farr as Stepney and was going over sea, but Mr. Stringer and Frank tooke post and catched him, and about 20*l.* in his pockett, and hee had given eight pound for a watch, which they gott againe. Sir Thomas has him now in his house, has pardoned the crime, but turnes him away shortly." *Seal.*

Samuel Hanmer to Roger Kenion.

506. 1682, ... ber 10.—Mr. Daubabbin (*sic*) preaches to-day at Leigh, and Squire Atherton may possibly come along with him; however, I doubt not but that the parishioners will consult about the business after evening service. I humbly beg that you would be pleased to honour me so far, as to make one amongst them to hold up a side against (the once Lord President) Bradshaw.

CASE, and opinion by SERGEANT MANYARD :—TITLE TO PROPERTY in Furness, formerly belonging to SIR THOMAS PRESTON and held by the Court of Exchequer " as being settled to superstitious uses."

507. [1682.]—" T. P., the 26th of May 1682, having petitioned his Majestye for an estate, late Sir Thomas Preston's, in Furness, in the County Pallatine of Lancaster, which was before recorded in the Court of Exchequer, as being settled to superstitious uses, and his Majestye thereupon obtaining a decree, was graciously pleased to referre the said petition to the Lords of the Treasury, who gave directions and paid the charge for the prosecution thereof; which said petition, being by them referred to the examination of Mr. Grayham and Mr. Burton, who made their report to the Lords of the Treasury, the said T. P. did thereupon contract with the Lords for a certain rent and term of years, which was again reported from the Lords to His Majestye, who was pleased to give direction that a bill should be forthwith prepared for the passing of a lease, upon the terms and years agreed upon with the said Lords ; and a warrant being sent to the Attorney General from the Lords, upon his perusal thereof, his opinion then was, that the King not being in possession, nor the trustees having conveyed their right, that His Majestye could not make a good lease to the lessee.

" But the possession being now in the King, and the Trustees having now conveyed their right to His Majestye, the Lords of the Treasury ordered a warrant to be drawne, pursuant to their former contract, which was signed by His Majestye, and countersigned by the Lords, directed to his Attorney or Solicitor Generall. Upon which, a Bill was drawn and signed by the said Attorney Generall (as the usual course is) and afterwards by his Majestye, which said bill is mentioned to pass a lease of the said lands to the said T. P., under the Great and Duchy Seal of Lancaster, without any further warrant or direction, for a rent and term of years therein mentioned. The said T. P. hath proceeded soe farre upon the said bill as that he hath passed the Signet, the Privy Seal, and Great Seal, upon the method aforesaid, and hath a duplicate ready from the Privy Seal, and a docquett from the Lords of the Treasury for the passing of the Duchy Seal.

1st Query.—Whether, having already passed the Great Seal, that be sufficient ; or that the Duchy and County Palatine Seals be both necessary, or the Duchy Seal, or whether of them.

Note.—The lands mentioned to be granted are Duchy lands, lyeing in the County Palatine of Lancaster. } I conceive that this land is now no parte of the Duchy, for it comes not to the Crown as an escheat of the Duchy, but as a new purchase and passeth well from the Crown by the Great Seal. But to avoid questions and charges, 'tis wisdom to take both Seals.

2nd Query.—Whether the rent being made payable into the Exchequer, or to the Receiver of the County Palatine (as it is mentioned in the lease to T. P.) the tenant may safely pay the same to such Receiver, without the same being made payable or paid to the Receiver of the Duchy of Lancaster.

I conceive he may, without danger, pay it to the Exchequer, or Receiver of the County Palatine. The expresse words of the reservation beinge soe. MAYNARD."

W. Hayhurst to Roger Kenyon.

508. 1682[-3], January 6. London.—I went to Mr. Marsden, to know when he could pay. He said he could not tell, but not the next week. I saw him turn away several that had bills upon him. There are a great many bankers lately gone off, but I hope he suffers not by them, nor is in any danger. It is reported my Lord Chief-Baron will be displaced, and Sir Robert Sawyer in his place, and Sir George Jeffreys in his, and that Baron Atkins is very like for the same fate, to give place to Sir Robert Wright, and that Judge Dolben sits very slippery. Preparations are making for the trial of the City Charter, the next term. Six young clerks, said to be gentlemen's sons in the North, are committed to Newgate for the " Highpadd." *Seal.*

Mary Ball to Roger Kenyon.

509. 1682[-3], January 9. Ormskirk.—Asking that the money due to her for the wounded soldiers, should be paid, as she has been put to great expense in food, clothes, and washing for them. *Seal, broken.*

William Hayhurst to Roger Kenyon, at Peel.

510. 1682-3, January 11. London.—" There hath been great gaming at the Temple this Christmas time. Upon the Twelfth-day, at night, the Templers, in a great number, went to gather their rents of the houses in Fleet Street; for their lights into the Temple, they demanded halfe-a-crown a house and all arreares, which, for some houses, came to 20*s.* Where they denyed payment, they forced them to it. Whereupon the constables were sent for; whereupon the Templers having notice, 200 rose againste them and some harme was done, but none mortally wounded. They have since made an order at a Parliament of theirs, as they call it, that all Councillors of that Society who take part with any who shall sue any of the gentlemen upon that pretended ryott, shall be judged enemies to the auncient priviledges and honour of that House, and that none of the Society should have any dealing with any tradesman who would not pay that rent, or prosecuted any of them upon the ryott. 'Tis reported the Earle of Shaftsbury is dead in Holland." *Seal.*

John Tench to Roger Kenyon.

511. 1682[-3], January 11.—" There be great muttering of storms rising beyond the seas. God keep us in peace, and when we are in danger of others, [give us] good council and unanimity at home; and, when his Majesty pleaseth to take the advice of his Commons in Parliament, honest loyal members," and one of them " honest worthy Mr. Kenyon."

William Hayhurst to Roger Kenyon.

512. 1682[-3], January 16. London.—Concerning warrants for recusants. Many of the great Bankers are gone aside. The great fund of Europe, the East India Company, is shut up and will pay no more till Michaelmas. *Seal.*

William Hayhurst to Roger Kenyon.

513. 1682[-3], January 22. London.—The new project, Mr. Burton tells me, is to make a certain revenue of the Papists. The estates of those of the better rank and quality are valued at nine or twelve thousand pounds *per annum*, and the two thirds are to be farmed by the parties, to pay yearly 6,000*li.* into your hands, to be constantly paid into the Exchequer. This to be done by way of inquisition, the witnesses to be brought by the recusants, and all inquisitions to be held anew. I made severall objections against it; as what inquisition they would hold could, that way, be found but of small value and that there was no recusant of an estate but had foreseen his conviction and had settled his estate, and so could plead it off when they pleased. For those, says he, we will have process against them for 20*li. per mensem.* If this project take, and 6,000*li.* yearly be paid to you, and you have your 18*d.* per *li.,* it will amount to 450*li. per annum* to your purse, and if you have your salary besides, it will be 550*li. per annum.* "This will come to you with ease, without clamour or noise." Proposal to be Deputy to Kenyon. The new judges have this day taken their places. *Seal.*

Thomas Holden to Roger Kenyon.

514. 1682[-3], January 29.—"There was a silent meeting of Quakers, in this towne, taken upp and dispersed by the officers here, a litle before Christmas; and I observe att the Sessions, you proceed by way of indictment in the nature of a riott; which, if that may serve your turne, I shall not trouble my self to draw upp a record of your conviction, haveing drawne one att large against all or most of these persons, for a Conventicall, a little before, and issued out warrants, and severall distresses made; but their goods, most of them, cannot bee sold, nor have the officers gott expenses in money yet, as they tell me."

Thomas Hodgkinson to Roger Kenyon.

515. 1682[-3], January 29. Preston.—Will meet Kenyon at Wigan on Thursday, when he will be proud to contribute anything to a perfect conciliation between Lord Derby and their friends at Haigh. *Seal of arms, broken.*

Roger Kenyon to Thomas Hodgkinson, at Preston.

516. 1682[-3], February 3. Bolton.—Has sent the bearer, Mr. John Roscoe, for the 300*l.* or more, payable upon the processes against popish recusants. Roscoe, John Smethurst, and Serjeant Hatton, have left the writer a sealed bag containing 96*l.* 4*s.* The processes, returned "this time twelvemonth," yielded 1,296*l.* 5*s.* Hopes, "except what must be expected," that sum will not be lessened now. *Seal of arms.*

Thomas Hodgkinson to Roger Kenyon, "at his Peele."

517. 1682[-3], February 5. Preston.—Was under a gross mistake in sending the process against recusants, as he had not noted who were "charged upon the long process and who by *fieri facias.*" Begs the return of the process for alteration and completion. *Seal of arms.*

William Hayhurst to Roger Kenyon.

518. 1682-3, February 8. Southampton Buildings.—The Northern Circuit is to be performed by the same Judges as last time, but Mr. Baron Atkins is to sit on the Crown Side. Lord Derby has been victorious this term; "there hath been great arguments about the demurrer upon the plea to the *Quo Warranto.* Sir George Treby and Mr. Solicitor, argued yesterday, and Mr. Attorney-Generall and Mr. Pollexfen, to-day; and two eminent Councell to argue the next term. The Worcester City Charter was found forfeited to the King. The defendants excepted against the Jury, being very few of them freeholders. After some debate, the Court sent Judge Raymond to know the opinion of the Common Plees, where they whispered together, and after, Judge Raymond and the rest declared it to bee the opinion of the Court of Common Plees and of that Court, that that was no legal exception; whereupon the Jury was sworn; but the defendants would make no defence, and soe the Jury found for the King." *Seal.*

W. Hilton to Roger Kenyon, in London.

519. 1682[-3], February 19.—Hopes Kenyon has arrived safely at the end of his journey; if he had stayed, his list of coiners and clippers would have been longer, "a kennel of whom was discovered, and disarmed of their wicked tooles, by the honest constable, John Monk, on Thursday last." The judges will hardly be able to deliver the gaol as fast as the justices fill it, if the discoveries hold on. If the rogues are too many to be hanged, they might be transported to Pensylvania or the other Plantations. If they be not totally suppressed, and clipped money prohibited, all the old coin of England will be spoilt. Desires Kenyon to take a catalogue of the books "of the *virtuosi,* and the prices at the Bell, in Paul's Churchyard." *Seal of arms.*

Francis North, [Lord Keeper,] to Mr. Justice Jones.

520. 1682[-3], February 24.— "His Majestie haveing received complaints that many persons of meane condition lye in prison upon criminal prosecutions in severall gaoles of this kingdom, where they endure great hardshipp and misery, because of the straitness of the prisons, in respect of the number of prisoners, and for want of necessarys; is desirous, for their releife, to extend his royall compassion to such of them as shall be capable thereof, upon consideration of their particular cases. In order whereunto, his Majestie would be informed by his judges of Assize, in their severall circuits, or by some justices of the peace in the severall countyes and places where the prisons are, who may receive an account thereof from the Sheriffs, gaolers, or other persons of credit, whether the number of prisoners is so great that the prison cannot conveniently containe them. And if it bee, then further to certify the names of such persons as are in prison upon such prosecutions and if any bee under the age of twenty one yeares, and what their offences are, and how long they have layne there; whether they are poore and unable to mayntayne themselves [and] whether they are papists or quakers, or what other sect, if it can be knowne." *Copy.*

Thomas Stringer to Roger Kenyon.

521. 1682[-3], March 6. Chancery Lane.—"These are to acquaint you that your good friend and myne, Sir Robert Car, is dead." *Vide No. 495. Seal of arms.*

Thomas Hodgkinson to Roger Kenyon.

522. 1682[-3], March 13. Preston.—Sends a warrant to levy the monies upon the recusants in Kenyon's Hundred, and three receipts for Sir

Charles Anderton and Mr. Trafford. If Kenyon thinks it prudential to accept 100*li.* from Sir Charles, instead of the whole, he would consent to it; but refers it to Kenyon's discretion, whether it be not a seasonable time to oblige Sir Charles, or no. Thanks him for the carriage of his peruke. His wife was yesterday delivered " of another young tory, so that I do not follow your example in the acts of generation." *Seal of arms, broken.*

JOHN LOMAX to ROGER KENYON.

523. 1683, March 25.—Asking Kenyon's interest on his behalf, for the presentation to Aldingham, in the gift of the Commissioners of the Treasury. *Seal of arms, broken.*

R. BRADSHAIGH, Junior, to ROGER KENYON.

524. 1683, March 27. Haigh.—" Pray intercede for me to my cozen Copley that she will favour me withe acceptance of a small present herewith sent her, as having done me the honour to weare me for her valentine."

COIN-CLIPPING.

525. 1683, March 31.—Informations of John Birchall, a prisoner in his Majesty's gaole at Lancaster, and condemned for clipping and diminishing his Majesty's coin.

The PETITION of THOMAS PRESTON, of Holker, in the County of Lancaster, to the LORDS OF THE TREASURY.

526. 1682[-3], [March ?].—That in Easter term last, his Majesty, having recovered, by a decree in the Court of Exchequer, part of the estate late Sir Thomas Preston's in Furness, as given by him to superstitious uses, your petitioner, being very instrumental in the recovery thereof in discovering the said estate, your Lordships did offer, as your opinion, that your petitioner should have a lease granted to him of what was then recovered of the said estate, for the term of 7 years, and a warrant for the possession of the said estate was granted to your petitioner. But there being some lands adjoining the said estate which were purchased by one of the trustees of Sir Thomas Preston, the possession thereof is refused to be delivered to your petitioner. The amendment of the houses, fences, hedges, and ditches, are a heavy cost, etc. May it please your Lordships, that a lease may be granted to your petitioner.

[*The Petition is ordered to be referred to Richard Graham, Esquire.*]

ROGER KENYON [to the EARL OF DERBY].

527. 1683, April 20. Preston.—"In obedience to your Lordship's command, I humbly present you an account of the condition of the gaole at Lancaster, as it was on Tewsday last. Prisoners for debte, 44; most of them very poor persons. Prisoners condemned for felonies and ordered to be transported, 6. Preists condemned and reprieved, 2. Two other persons condemned and reprieved, not ordered to be transported. One condemned and reprieved for 6 weeks, and no longer, from the 26th of March. Two others not condemned, but by their owne consents, after conviction for felony, ordered to be transported. Six indicted as clippers and continued in the gaole, one fined 100 merks, and committed till he pay his fine. Eight quakers committed upon writts *de excommunicato capiendo.* Eight persons in the calendar, committed neer 2 years agoe for refuseing the oath of supremacy, and outlawed, upon that account, in the Kings bench, at the Kings suite, all papist recusants, and all of them much above the age of 21 yeares. None of them very rich nor very poore. In all, 80 persons.

"Now my Lord, I dare not but acquaint your Lordshipp the whole truth of everything of the eight quakers. Three of them were permitted by the gaoler to go home, and were not, when wee called for them, at the Sessions to be had. And of the 8 popish recusants, not one of them lyes in the gaole, and but one of them to be produced, but were lodged in or about the towne. Wee at the Quarter Sessions, unexpected by the gaoler, called for those eight, and did indeed surprise him; and haveing thus, in duty to your Lordshipp, accused him, I with all humility ask your Lordshipp's favor for him and humbly beg leave, further to acquaint your Lordshipp that a writ issues every terme forthe of the King's Bench, against severall hundreds of papeist recusants that have taken the oath of allegeance, but refuseing the oath of supremacie were, by the justices of the peace, pursuant to the statute, certifyed into the King's Bench; wherepon, they are outlawed. These Writs are sent to the Sheriffe every terme, against many that are indigent, and the reverse, [and] cost, every person, 6 six or seaven pounds. Some, against whom these are sent, are not so much worth. The strict prosecution of these processes might indeed fill the gaole with persons not able to subsist there and it turnes to no manner of account to his Majestie to prosecute any this way.

"My Lord, wee have fresh informations against a great many more clippers, and against some that were discharged the last assizes. The poor fellow, John Birchall, that was reprieved by your Lordshipp for 6 weekes, and no longer, saith, with abundance of tears, he can make no further discoverie though it were to save his life, and I verily beleive hee can not." *Draft.*

RICHARD RIGBY to ROGER KENYON, at Peel.

528. 1683, May 12. London.—"The great news in toune, this day, is that my Lord Gray's house was searched last night by the secret inquisition, and 4 score arms sessed, and my Lord taken into custody."

WILLIAM PATTEN to ROGER KENYON.

529. 1683, May 19. Gray's Inn.—"Sir Patience Warde was this day tryed upon an information of perjury; a privy verdict was given in, but assure yourselfe hee is found guilty. Say not one worde of this, till the return of the next poast, for it will not bee discovered till Munday next, but assure yourselfe of the truth of it, for the jury, at the King's charge, was treated." *Seal of arms.*

J. ROWE to ROGER KENYON.

530. 1683, May 25. Liverpool.—Asks Kenyon's assistance to get employment in an office which is intended to be shortly established in Liverpool, Lancaster, and Manchester, called the Corporation Credit, or a Bank of Credit, the use of which will certainly be of great advantage to the advance of trade. *Seal.*

WILLIAM PATTEN to ROGER KENYON.

531. 1683, May 26. Preston.—I am in hopes you will be set out for London ere this reach you. Mr. Burton desires you to bring up with you the large bill wherein 1,200 papists were plaintiffs, in the Duchy Court, against you and others. *Seal of arms, broken.*

Thomas Hodgkinson to Roger Kenyon.

532. 1683, June 22. Preston.—I hope that our famous metropolis will, at least, become Christian and loyal. I cannot sufficiently acknowledge my obligations to you for your great trouble about my wife. *Seal of arms.*

William Hayhurst to Roger Kenyon.

533. 1683, July 7. London.—" I was up and down Fleet Street to inquire of the wether glass you bought, as I remember you told me near Serjeants Inn; but I can hear no tidings of it." *Seal.*

Jo: Chorley to Roger Kenyon, at Preston.

534. 1683, July 9. Liverpool.—" There is one Ro: Clerke (apprentice to Mr. Henry Thorpe, master and owner of a London ship) in the House of Correction, for refusing to do his service, and committing many foule things against his said master, and merchants who freight him. The matter was fully heard before the Mayor of Leverpoole and the Aldermen, and appeared so foule that he might have beene more severely dealt with. The Mayor sent him to the House of Correction, by the advice of Mr. Entwisle, Recorder of the Corporation, who was also present at the hearing. I humbly beg of you he may be kept to labour and receive due correction, and not suffered to be a tapster in the house, as wee heare hee is, and lives very pleasantly, and writes home that he finds such favour there that the time of his stay will not be tedious to him."

Sir Roger Bradshaigh to Roger Kenyon.

535. 1683, July 10. Haigh.—I received the proclamation against the Duke of Monmouth, etc., this day; " for all it came not soe late, and upon receipt of the former proclamation, I appoynted the privie Sessions and inserted part of it in the warrant, with strict orders to sett watch and ward for the vilains in all my divitions, and had it proclaimed at Wigan the last Fryday."

Richard Rigby to Roger Kenyon.

536. 1683, July 12. London.—" This day was brought to tryall Captain Walcutt (?). Colonel Rumsey, Porn (?) Keeleing, and Mr. West was witness against him (*sic*), who prooved the thing very plane. A great part he confessed, which was that he had beene at severall meetings and heard them discourse of insorection, but did not concern himself further; and Mr. West did give a very full account of the conspercey, and after that he had little to say. Besides, there was a letter addrest under his hand to the K[ing] to implore his mercy, and he would let him know more then any culd yet. The jurey went out and staid but a little, brought him gilty. Tomorrow will be tried Hone, Rouse, and Captain Blagg."

Postscript.—" Hone, when he was caled to the barr and his inditement red, he tould the Courte he was gilty in some mesure; being asked what he ment, answered—of consperacey."

Richard Rigby to Roger Kenyon.

537. 1683, July 14. London.—"My Lord Russell yesterday, at the Ould Bayley, took his tryall ; makeing but smale defence, was found gilty, as alsoe Mr. Rouse and Hone ; and this morning Lord Russell, Captain Wallcut, Rouse, and Hone, receved sentance; but that most wonderfull, my Lord Essix, yester morning in the Tower, cut his one throat ; the manner thus :—askt his Frenchman for a penknife to cut his nailes, and then a raseyer, pretending it would not do. His man borrowed one of the warder. Noe sooner had my Lord got it, but he went into his clositt. Presantly after, his man heard a noyse as if the cover of the close stoole had falen ; upon that, he went in, and found my Lord walloing in blood; called for help, but he had cut the jugler faine. The King at the same time, with the Duke, was a fueing [viewing] the works in the Tower. We received, just now, of the newes of my Lord Graye being taken in Rotterdam, with some others, not yet knowne. Today, by the Flanders and Duch Gazet, comes the sad newes of the Jarman Armey being routed ; a great part of the foot cut off, and the rest devided. Hungarey have submitted to the Turks . . . The Court is mooved from Viena ; and, as a great carridge of Jesuits was going out, the multietud fell upon them and cut them to peeces, craying that they had brought this misery upon them. An express came to oure King for suplyes."

T. Leigh to Roger Kenyon.

538. 1683, July 16. Croxteth.—He spoke to Mr. Entwisle, about a year and a half ago, about the repair of Mabb Lane, and hears money has been gathered for that purpose.

Edward Tarleton to Roger Kenyon, at Peel.

539. 1683, July 19. Liverpool.—"My sonne Edward, beinge arrived from Barbados, gives mee account that your sonne tooke occasion to leave Barbados, and is safely arrived at New Yorke, in America, where he teacheth gentlemen's children, and is engaged there to continue for two or three yeares, by covenant with a gentleman there." *Seal.*

Joseph Sabey to Roger Kenyon, at Peel.

540. 1683, July 21. London.—"All I have now to inform you with, is cheifly to give you an account that I was myselfe an eye-witness to the execution of Captain Walcott, John Rouse, and William Hone, the former of which, declareing that hee was guilty of the conspiracy as to the knowledge thereof, and that he was drawne into the conspiracy by some persons that promised him great matters ; but, in short, he perceived there was no truth in man. Rouse confessed hee had been at divers consults, and that hee was to have acted, but, as to particulars, hee was ignorant, and that hee had been privy to many treasonable discoveries relateing to an insurrection and the like. Hone spoke little, but confessed hee was to have been one of the number that was to have assassinated the King in his return from Newmarkett. They are all quartered and their bowells burnt. This day, likewise, was executed the Lord Russell, attended att the scaffold by ten companies [of] foot and three troops of his Majesty's guards ; but what confession his Lordshipp made there, I am not able to give you any certain account, his stay att the scaffold not being half an houre, where the executiouer made three blowes att his head ere hee parted it from his body. Hee was conveyed thither in his owne coach, which is all the newes this city offers att present."

"The JUDGMENT and DECREE of the UNIVERSITY OF OXFORD, passed in their Convocation against certain pernicious books and damnable doctrines, destructive to the sacred persons of Princes, their state and government, and of all human society."

541. 1683, July 21.—"Although the barbarous assassination lately enterprised against the person of his sacred Majestie and his royall brother, engage all our thoughts to reflect with utmost detestacon and abhorrence on that execrable villany, hatefull to God and man, and pay our due acknowledgements to the divine providence, which, by extraordinary methods, brought it to pass that the breath of our nostrills, the anointed of the Lord, is not taken in the pit which was prepared for him, and that under his shadow we continue to live and enjoy the blessings of his government; yet, notwithstanding, we find it to be a necessary duty at this time, to search into and lay open those impious doctrines, which, haveing of late been studiously disseminated, gave rise and growth to these nefarious attempts, and pass upon them our solemn publick censure and decree of condemnation. Therefore, to the honour of the holy and undivided Trinity, the preservation of Catholick truth in the Church, and that the King's majestie may be secured both from the attempts of open bloody enemies and machinations of traytrous, hereticks, and schismaticks, we, the Vice-Chancellor, Doctors, Proctors, and Masters, regent and not regent, met in Convocation in the accustomed manner, time, and place, on Saturday the 21th day of July, in the year 1683, concerning certain propositions contained in divers bookes and writings publisht in the ———— and allso [in] the Latin tongue, repugnant to the holy scriptures, decrees of councells, writings of the fathers, the faith and profession of the primitive church, and allso detractive of the kingly government, the safety of his Majestie's person, the publick peace, the laws of nature, and bonds of human society, by our unanimous assent and consent, have decreed and determined in manner and forme following :——

"The first Proposition.—All civil authority is derived originally from the people.

"Second.—There is a mutuall compact, tacit or express, between a prince and his subjects, and that if he performe not his duty, they are discharged from theirs.

"Third.—That if lawfull governors become tyrants, or govern otherwise than [as] by the laws of God and man they ought to do, they forfeit the right they had unto their government.

"Fourth.—The Soveraignty of England is in the three estates, viz. :—— King, Lords, and Commons. The King has but a co-ordinate power, and may be over-ruled by the other two.

"Fifth.—Birthright and proximity of blood give no title to rule or government, and it is lawfull to preclude the next heir from his right and succession to the Crown.

"Sixth.—It is lawfull for subjects, without the consent, and against the comand of, the supreme magistrate, to enter into leagues, covenants, and associations for defence of themselves and their religion, solemne league and covenant, late association (*sic*).

"Seventh.—Self-preservation is the fundemental law of nature, and supersedes the obligation of all others, whensoever they stand in competition with it.

" Eighth.—The doctrine of the Gospell, concerning patient suffering of injuries, is not inconsistent with violent resisting of the higher powers, in case of persecution for religion.

" Ninth.—There lies no obligation upon christians to passive obedience, when the prince comands anything against the laws of our country ; and the primitive christians chose rather to die, than resist, because Christianity was not settled by the laws of the Empire.

" Tenth.—Possession and strength give a right to govern, and success in a cause or enterprise proclaims it to be lawfull and just. To pursue it, is to comply with the will of God, because it is to follow the conduct of his providence.

" Eleventh.—In the state of nature, there is no difference between good and evill, right and wrong ; the state of nature is a state of war, in which every man hath a right to all things.

" Twelfth.—The foundation of civil authority is this naturall right, which is not given, but left to the supreme magistrate upon men's entring into societies, and not only a foreign invader, but a domestick rebel, puts himself again into a state of nature, to be proceeded against, not as a subject, but an enemy, and consequently acquires by his rebellion the same right over the life of his prince as the prince, for the most heinous crimes, has over the life of his own subject.

" Thirteenth.—Every man, after his entring into a society, retains a right of defending himself against force, and cannot transfer that right to the comonwealth when he consents to that union, whereby a comonwealth is made; and in case a great many men together have allready resisted the comonwealth, for which every one of them expecteth death, they have liberty then to join together to assist and defend one another. Their bearing of arms, subsequent to the first breach of their duty, though it be to maintain what they have done, is no new unjust act, and, if it be only to defend their persons, it is not unjust at all.

" Fourteenth.—An oath superadds no obligation to pact, and a pact obliges no farther than' it is credified ; and, consequently, if a prince gives any indication that he does not believe the promises of fealty and allegiance made by any of his subjects, they are thereby freed from their subjection, and, notwithstanding their pacts and oathes, may lawfully rebell against, and destroy, their soveraigne.

" Fifteenth.—If a people, that by oath and duty are obliged to a soveraign, shall sinfully dispossess him and, contrary to their covenants, chuse and covenant with another, they may be obliged by their later covenants, notwithstanding their former.

" Sixteenth.—All oaths are unlawfull and contrary to the word of God.

" Seventeenth.—An oath obligeth not in the sense of the imposer, but the takers.

" Eighteenth.—Dominion is founded in grace.

" Nineteenth.—The powers of this world are usurpations upon the prerogative of Jesus Christ, and it is the duty of God's people to destroy them, in order to the setting Christ upon his throne.

" Twentieth.—The Presbyterian government is the scepter of Christ's Kingdome, to which kings, as well as others, are bound to submitt ; and the King's supremacy in ecclesiasticall affairs, asserted by the Church of England, is injurious to Christ, the sole King and head of the Church.

" Twenty-first.—It is not lawfull for superiors to impose anything in the worship of God that is not antecedently necessary.

" 'Twenty-second.—The duty of not offending a weak brother is inconsistent with all humane authority of makeing laws concerning indifferent things.

" Twenty-third.—Wicked kings and tyrants ought to be put to death; and if the judges and inferiour magistrates will not do their office, the power of the sword devolves to the people. If the major part of the people refuse to exercise this power, then the ministers may excommunicate such a king, after which it is lawfull for any of the subjects to kill him, as the people did Athaliah, Jehu, and Jezabel.

" Twenty-fourth.—Aiter the sealeing of the Scripture canon, the people of God, in all ages, are to expect new revelations for a rule of their actions, and it is lawfull for a private man, having an inward motion from God, to kill a tyrant.

" Twenty-fifth.—The example of Phineas is to us, instead of a comand; for what God hath comanded or approved in one age, must needs oblige in all.

" Twenty-sixth.—King Charles the First was lawfully put to death; and his murderers were the blessed instruments of God's glory, in their generation.

" Twenty-seventh.—King Charles the First made war upon his Parliament; and in such a case, the king may not only be resisted, but he ceaseth to be king."

" Wee decree, judge, and declare, all and every of these propositions to be false, seditious, and impious, and, most of them, to be allso heretical and blasphemous, infamous to christian religion, and destructive of all government in church and state. Wee farther decree that the bookes which contain the aforesaid propositions and impious doctrines, are fitted to deprave good manners, corrupt the minds of unwary men, stirr up seditions and tumults, overthrow states and kingdoms, and lead to rebellion, murder of princes, and atheism itself. And, therefore, we intradict all members of the University from the readeing of the said bookes, under the penalties of the statutes expressed. We allso order the before recited bookes to be publickly burned, by the hand of our Marshall, in the court of our schools. Likewise we order that, in perpetuall memory hereof, these our decrees shall be entered into the registry of our Convocation, and that copyes of them be comunicated to the severall Colleges and Halls within this University, there [to be] publickly affixed in the librarys, refectorys, or other fitt places, where they may be seen and read of all. Lastly, we comand and strictly enjoyne all and singular the readers, tutors, chatechists, and others, to whom the care and trust of institution of youth is comitted, that they diligently instruct and ground their scholars in that most necessary doctrine, which, in a manner, is the badge and character of the Church of England, of submitting to every ordinance of man, for the Lord's sake, whether it be to the king as supreme, or unto governors, as unto them that are sent by him, for the punishment of evill doers, and for the praise of them that do well, teaching that this submission and obedience is to be cleare, absolute, and without exception of any state or order of men; aliso that they, according to the apostles' precept, exhort that, first of all, supplications, prayers, intercession, and giveing of thankes, made for all men, for the king, and all that are in authority, and that we may lead a quiet and peaceable life, in all godliness and honesty. For this is good and acceptable in the sight of God our Saviour; and in especiall manner, that they press and oblige them, humbly to offer their most ardent and daily prayers at the throne of grace, for the preservation of our sovereign lord, King Charles, from the attempts of open violence and secret machinations of perfidious traytors; that the Defender of the Faith being safe, under the defence of the Most High, may continue his raign on earth till he exchange it for that of a late and happy immortality." *Copy.*

RICHARD RIGBY to ROGER KENYON, at Peel.

542. [16]83, July 26. London.—"Upon the Chainge, I met, this day, with Captain Chappley . . . I told him, in part, my business, and [he] gave this answer : that he would undertake to bring my cousin Roger home for 20*l.*, that is, 10*l.* to redeem him, 5*l.* his passidge, and 5*l.* to bear his [own] charges : and he tells me it will be very necessary to send him a sute of clothes, being very naked, and a perriwigg."

LAWRENCE RAWSTORNE to ROGER KENYON.

543. 1683, July 26. Newhall.—"The world has altered its aspect; the subtle papists has (*sic*) overwitted the presbiters and made them put on their vizard, and act in their stead, but not soe as to acquit them, but to aggravate the guilt of both ; and, being so near allyed, ought to participate of the same punnishement."

JOHN TENCH to ROGER KENYON.

544. 1683, July —.—" I did not forget my promise on Thursday, but that day produced noe more than the conviction of one Captain Walcot, an old captain in Oliver's time. Yesterday's news is extraordinary ; the Earle of Essex (being prisoner in the Tower) cut his owne throat at a time when his Majestie and the Duke happen'd to be at the tower, viewing the fortifications. He (as appears) had, some dayes before, had it in designe, haveing severall times comanded a sharpe penknife to be got, as he did just before he executed that horrid act upon himself; but the penknife (as he thought) not being sharpe enough, he comanded his servant to get him a razor, which being don, and he haveing spent some small time on pretence of pareing his nailes, at last shut himself into a closett, where he had a close stoole, cut his throat, and was found dead. And this day the jury have found him *felo de se*, whose inquisition is to be printed.

" Yesterday, likewise, the Lord Russell (after a long tryall, but little excuse for himself) was, upon full evidence, found guilty of treason; as were Hone and Rouse. Mr. Booth was comitted to the Tower yesterday. And this day the Bishop of Rochester is declared to be Archbishop of York. The Emperor's army is said to be beaten by the Turk. This, with the news that Mr. Wentworth and I are now drinking your health, may suffice at one time." ·

Postscript.—" My Lord Gray is taken in Holland, and comeing over." *Seal of arms.*

RICHARD RIGBY to ROGER KENYON, at Peel.

545. 1683, August 2. London.—Captain Shapley (*sic*) will sail on the 10th instant, "and hopes to be there in October " ; he returns in May, but will send "your son" before, if an opportunity offers. "He tells me [that your son] is extraordinary penitant, and undergoes his slavery as contented as the thing will bear; but he has noe more for his day's work then meat and drink. His work is, every day, to carry timber from the water side to make fences. It is very happy that he came acquainted with soe honest a man as this captain ; for he tells me that cousin Roger works so ill, that his master designed to sell him, where it might have beene much wors. He intreated the captain much to have brought him, and had don it, but that his wife persuaded to the contrary, because he undertook such a thing before, and the party run away as soone as he came to shore."

The EARL OF DERBY to ROGER KENYON.

546. 1683, September 7. Lathom.—Colonel Rigby is using me so ill, I hope I shall not want power to express my resentment ; and I have a mind to address a letter to the justices of the peace, when they meet at Lancaster. *Seal of arms.*

INFORMATION AGAINST RALPH LIVESAY AND Mr. BRADDYL.

547. 1683, September 7.—Informations, taken at the house of Alexander Browne of Blacklanehead, in the County of Lancaster, inn-keeper, before Lawrence Rawstorne, one of the Deputy-Lieutenants for the County, and Thomas Holden, Justice of the Peace.

Depositions of various witnesses, that Mr. Ralph Livesay of Livesay, the younger, at a christening dinner, in discoursing about the late plot, affirmed that if there was a plot, it was made worse than it was by the hot-headed people of the Church of England. A complaint also that Mr. Braddyll, Justice of the Peace, would not make inquiry therein, but gave notice of the matter to Mr. Livesay, the father. A letter, signed Roger Nowell and L. Rawstorne, exonerating Mr. Braddyll. *Copy.*

HUMPHREY TRAFFORD to ROGER KENYON.

548. 1683, September 10. Houghend.—By order of the High Sheriff, I applied to his under-Sheriff, touching the prisoners whom he had promised me the transporting of. I had a second order to write to you about them, and I am informed there is some mistake committed, and that you have occasion of one of them for an evidence. You would much oblige me by informing the bearer what method he ought to take for the secure conveyance of them from Lancaster to Liverpool.

NICHOLAS KNOWLES to [ROGER] KENYON, at Peel.

549. 1683, September 27. London.—Asking him to inform Sir John and Lady Molyneux, that Mr. John Molyneux died yesterday morning, between 3 and 4.

SIR CHARLES ANDERTON to ROGER KENYON.

550. 1683, September 28. Lostock.—Enclosing an estimate of his estate, showing the rental, and the various charges upon it to Lady Anderton, his mother, to his three brothers, Christopher, Francis, and John, and to old Mrs. Ireland, for her jointure. *Seal of arms.*

RICHARD RIGBY to ROGER KENYON, at Peel.

551. 1683, October 4. London.—"Our thoughts was imployed to . . . some part of our charter; but all in vain, for the King hath ent[ered] judgment, and have changed the Recorder, for Sir Thomas Jenner, who this day was knighted ; and my Lord Mayor, made *custos princeps rotulorum magnæ civitatus* (*sic*), *Lond:* Seven Aldermen turned oute, viz.: Sir John Lawrance, Sir Patiance (*sic*), Sir Robert

Clayton, Sir Thomas Gould, Sir John Shorter, and Sir Thomas Allin and Mr. Cornish. Tuesday, 'tis said, the King goes to New Markit; and this day, news comes of the death of the King of Portigall."

John Risley to Roger Kenyon, at Wigan.

552. 1683, October 8. Risley.—"Unexpected occasions fall so out, that I cannot possibly be at . . . . this Sessions, which I really intended to have beene at, by reason of the highwayes within our townshipp, which Cousen Culcheth, Cousen Geffrey, and I, with severall other inhabitants, took the role, and saw the highwayes measured, upon Tuesday last. And severall people have owned their parts, and some already amended, and others have promised to do the like ; but the places most in decay belongs to the Lordshipps of Holcroft and Resfarlong, but the tennants have, most of them, repaired their proportions, so that what will appear defective, may be certified by our Constable's presentment, which John Holcroft will deliver in. I desire you would contribute your oppinion to John, what method were best to proceed to cause such persons as are deficient, to make good their respective parts and proportions. There is a certificate drawn, which will come to your hands, concerning the audit money belonging to Hollinsgreene chappell, where Parson Hatton hath officiated for this five or six yeares last past, for which time Parson Ward hath received all the money and hath paid him only two yeares, keeping the rest to himself, who hath neither read prayers, nor preached in the said chappell, since he received the last audit money, as the churchwarden will inform you ; so that the inhabitants of Rixton and Glasbrook think they have a great deal of hardship, in the moneys not being paid to the curate of the said chappell, according as it was intended." *Seal with crest.*

Roger Nowell to Roger Kenyon.

553. 1683, October 12. [Isle of Man.]—"These will give you notice that there is a great law-suit depending betwixt Captain Edward Brabazon and Cicilia his lady, both my very great friends, and one Levett, and Ward, sonne to Lord Ward, who marryed the co-beires and sisters of Sir Thomas Brereton of Cheshire, to whose writings, I mean to Captain Brabazon's, my unckle Henry Nowell is a subscribing wittnesse ; and, lest the said Levett or Ward, or any other for them, might doe my freind a prejudice, I thought fit to intreat you, amongst the many kindnesses that I have found you always ready to doe me, not to give ear to any of their requests, by giving them any account of what nature soever, ether of my unckle's concernes in England, or of the time of his being there, till you heare further from mee." *Seal, broken.*

Richard Rigby to [Roger Kenyon].

554. [16]83, October 13. London.—"All things here are at a stand, and will be, I suppose, till the King comes from New Markitt, which will be the latter end of the next week."

William Patten to Roger Kenyon.

555. 1683, November 8. Gray's Inn.—"Grayham and Burton give you their service, and say they will be glad to see you, and the sooner the better. I had not much discourse with them, for they were very busie abóut the wittnesses whoe weare to sweare to the Bill of Indictment against Algernoone Sidney, whoe was yesterday founde guilty by the Grand Jury, and, by a stronge guarde, brought to the barr to plead. He would gladly have given a special plea, and desired it might bee read, but the Lord Chiefe Justice denyde the readinge it, and withall, bid him bee carefull how hee offred a speciall plea, for if Mr. Attorney Generall should demurr to it, and if, upon argument, the lawe was against him, they might give judgment of death against him, and hee could not plead *oyer;* whereupon hee pleaded not guilty, and is to bee tryed on Wednesday seavenight." *Seal of arms.*

WILLIAM PATTEN to ROGER KENYON.

556. 1683, November 13. "The Griffin."—"The onely newes is that the Attorney-Generall has entred a *nolli prosequi* in the concern of running the Duke of Monmouth to the outlary, for his flight; and some are of opinion that hee may returne into England, for it is reported that his Duches was privately with the King the last Sunday, and the *nolli prosequi* was since entred." *Seal of arms.*

THOMAS BRADDYLL to ROGER KENYON.

557. [16]83, November 15. Portfeild.—"Mr. Graham hath been writt to, to prosecute the information against me, and put me out of the Commission of Peace." *Seal of arms.*

LADY ANNE MIDDLETON to ROGER KENYON.

558. 1683, November 17. Leighton.—Wonders why Kenyon is so set against her, that he would not accept of the Constable's return for her estate, as he had done for others. She thinks he must have some unkindness for her, more than for the rest of the recusants. She has, however, reason to acknowledge his favours, especially when her husband was prisoner at Preston. *Seal of arms.*

LAWRENCE RAWSTORNE to his "COUSIN KENYON."

559. 1683, November 18. Penwortham.—"Your intended watch is amakeing, and if you have any old silver lace, it will be the best that can be, for a figure plate. You may send it to Holcom, directed to John Holt, cutler, post, Holcom Hill, and Robert Starkie will take care to get it him. I have contributed a case, which will save some charge, if you approve thereof, and if not, you may alter that at pleasure."

SIR ROGER BRADSHAIGH to ROGER KENYON.

560. 1683, November 30. Haigh.—Concerning a stipend belonging to the Chantry of St. Katherine, in the Chapel of Blackrod.
I was certified from London, "that my Lord Derby had seconded his letter to our Chancellor, in speaking to him himself, to remove the sessions from Wigan, with several reflections, as if the town had never been so loyall as to deserve any favours. Now, though I know the thing will not be done, yet I am sorry his Lordship will offer at so meane a revenge, to a town that never made him fault, but by adhering to the Earl of Ancram, to whom, in my knowledge, they have beene, and are dayly more obleiged, in many particulers, than ever any town that I have

knowne, hath beene to any burges that ever served them, not only in time of Parliament, but every day in the interval of every Parliament, to this very day."

Thomas Preston to Roger Kenyon.

561. 1683, December 3. Holker—On behalf of Lady Middleton, who desires to compound for her recusancy. *Seal of arms.*

H. Hulme to Roger Kenyon.

562. 1683, December 4. Davyhulme.—Requesting to be put in the Commission of the Peace. *Seal.*

Christian Rigby to Dorothy Kenyon.

563. 1683, December 6. London.—Sending sundry recipes (torn). "*For a Bouillon :*—Boyle a knockle of veale too houres, take of salory, succory and endiffe, of each a handfull, two handsful of sorrell, which you must boyle in that liquor, halfe an houre ; then put in youre knokle of veale, and boyle all together a quarter of an houre. Beate half a duzen yoalks of eggs in some of the liquor, and season according to your disscretion, and give them a warme over the fire. Serve up the knokle in the dish with the broth. *To make Black Cherye Brandye :* Take, to every pound of black cheries, a quart of the best Nants brandy, breack the stones of two pounds of cheries, put in spermint, bame, rosemarey, 6 sprigs of each, a littell cinamon, ginger, nuttmeg, what quantey you pleas. You may let theese stand alltogether to months, and then bottell ; or to keep it all in a large bottell is the best."

John Adams to Roger Kenyon.

564. 1683, December 18. Inner Temple.—" I doubt that my long absence from your county may occasion some persons to suspect that, either I am negligent, or doe not intend to proceed in the general survey of England ; but really there is noe reason for the one or the other, for I hope (if God spare my life) to render a good accompt of my undertaking. And as for industry in the prosecution of my work, I never took greater pains in my life then last summer. My being in the north, did occasion some persons in the south to raise a report of my being dead, and perhaps my being here may give birth to the like report in your neighbourhood. I hint this to you, because it is very probable that the gentlemen who subscribed upon your recommendation of my work, will ask you what is become of me and my designe, and this I offer, in excuse for the trouble of this letter."

Richard Rigby to Roger Kenyon.

565. 1683, December 23. London.—We received the sad news of nephew Rigby being killed at Luxemburg. He, being in Paris with the Duke of Northumberland, was persuaded to go with him to Luxemburg, the French having laid siege to it, and he, being in a barn at dinner with the great officers, a great shot came from the town which hit him on the head.

Guicciardini Wentworth to Roger Kenyon.

566. 1683, December 29.—" This comes to give you the welcom home, and of a happy new year ; but, withall, to give you the less pleasing account of the death of Sir Edward Carr, who, after 10 dayes sickness, dyed last —————— of the small pox, about 8 in the morning, to the no small greef of all the family, and more especially of his deare mother, who is the most sorrowful woman liveing, and an object of great pitty. They intend to bury him by his father, att Sleeford, and cary him hence on Tuesday next, if possible, or ·Wednesday. The small pox is very mortall, and att this time, severall persons of quallity of both sex, lye by the walls." *Seal of arms.*

GUICCIARDINI WENTWORTH to ROGER KENYON.

567. 1683[-4], January 5.—I came just now from my poor Lady Cust, who really is an object of great pity, since her bloud letting; her favour [fever] has pretty well left her, and the family begins to recover, having been all sicke. This night Sir Edward's [bones] are deposited by those of his father. *Seal, broken.*

WILLIAM ASSHETON to ROGER KENYON.

568. 1683[-4], January 5. Salford.—Asking for Kenyon's interest to procure him the office of coroner, vacant by the death of Mr. James Gartside. *Seal.*

[LADY] ANNE MIDDLETON to ROGER KENYON.

569. 1683[-4], January 15. Leighton.—Begs that he will accept the value of her estate returned by the constables, and that she may have the same usage as other recusants. *Seal of arms.*

R. LEIGH to ROGER KENYON, at the "Sword and Buckler," in Holborn.

570. 1683[-4], February 14. Lyme.—" I have not heard from the Chancleor since I saw you; therefore conclude you must submitt to his orders, and, if you will take my advice, you must be as diligent to find out for him, as you were for the last Chancleor. I know the Orange is squeezed; the Duchy is grown to be a barren pasture; but, if you can find out any improvements, it will bee acceptable; and, though at present it looks hard upon you to pay in this mony, I am confident you will have a reparation some way. But, I must say to you, as the King said to the Chancleor—you must hunt. I wish the King had either given him a better place or none." *Seal with crest.*

J. ROWE to ROGER KENYON.

571. 1683[-4], February 26. Liverpool.—The affront which he received from the Mayor of Liverpool and others, when he was competitor for the office of Town Clerk, will excuse him in what he " shall act." Is informed that the present Mayor has declared that the power of choosing a town clerk is with him. He calls attention to the case of the Dean and Chapter of St. Peter's, York, who, upon the King's happy restoration, accepted a Commission of the Peace for their liberty of St. Peter's, York, and several prebends, and other gentlemen, within the said liberty, were named justices; but the Dean and Chapter had omitted to have a commission for a *Custos Rotulorum*, which was not perceived till a barrister, without the consent of the Dean and Chapter, applied to

Lord Chancellor Hyde for a patent to be *Custos Rotulorum*, and who, by virtue thereof, nominated a clerk of the peace under him, to execute the office, and so continues to take his fees, to the value of 20*li.* per annum. He does not find any difference between this and the Corporation of Liverpool, who have lately accepted a Commission of the Peace. *Seal, broken.*

WILLIAM HAYHURST to ROGER KENYON, at Peel.

572. 1683–4, March 14. Plymouth.—Has arrived safely, but is surprised not to find Kenyon's son ; " immediately upon comeing hither, I went to Mr. Carkett, an eminent merchant, Serjeant Maynard's kinsman, who . . . sent immediately to inquire if any such was prisoner, and there is none, nor ever was there . . . . . Except hee bee a souldier in the cittadell, I cannot imagine hee should be here." *Seal of arms.*

Directed to be left " at the Generall Post Office in London, to be sent as directed—in all, 6*d.*"

THOMAS DOD to ROGER KENYON.

573. 1683[–4], March 24. Wigan.—"I come not along with Mr. Woods, because to morrow morneing, I have a refferrence betwixt the two Lady Stanleys, wherein your assistance will be desired for the young lady." *Seal.*

WILLIAM KIRKBY to ROGER KENYON.

574. 1684, April 7. Kirkby.—" I am sure you are not a stranger to the great care and toil my nephew Kirkby and myself hath had, in putting the laws in execution against all absentees from our Church, the lawes against Conventakells, &c., and that as our duty, and in obedience to the King's commands ; in which, I thank God, we have had very good successe. For several, both quakers and other dissenters, are (upon our putting the laws in execution) become conformists to the Church; and those who are most obstinate and disaffected to the government, is (*sic*), by these methods, plainly pointed out. But while we thus struggle amongst our neighbours, with loyalty and all integrity, to serve our gracious King, and our country, here is some of our neighbouring justices, who you well know, Mr. Rawlingson and Mr. Knipe, who refuse to join with us in this good service, which makes both us, and the King's business, very uneasy to our country, and us to be very ill represented, and thought to be busy in that which is not required of us. I presume you will, ere long, have opportunity to wait on our worthy Chancelor, to whom I pray give my most humble service; and I intreat you will acquaint him with this matter, to whose great wisdom I shall humbly submitt." ··

SIR R. BRADSHAIGH to ROGER KENYON.

575. 1684, May 2. Haigh.—Asking for a copy of Lord [Derby's?] letter to Mr. Rawlinson, concerning the return of his Mayor's Commission.

INFORMATIONS against CLIPPERS OF COIN.

576. 1684, May 23 and 25.—" True copies of the informations and confessions of Edward Jackson, a prisoner in Newgate, convicted and condemned for clipping his Majesties lawfull coyne (and since executed), written with the said Jackson's own hand, and sent by him at severall times, to Sir Thomas Wharton, one of the wardens of his Majesties Mint.

"The first, 23rd of May [16]84.

Mr. William Crook, who I lived with about eight yeares and 3 quarters, and was his factor at London about four yeares and a half, and in that time he did send great sums of money up to me in packs, which much of it was clipped and showed to be newly done, and it was severall times returned back on my hands, and I was threatened ofen to be in troble for it. I remember, at one time, there came a gentleman to me and, to the best of my knowledge, he had a bill on me for 30*l*., and I took a batke of money out, which had about 70*l*. that was newly comen from the above said Mr. Crooke, out of Lancashire, and it was so much clipped, that I could not pay 30*l*. out of it, and the gentleman that came for the money, took 7 or 8 halfe crownes and set them on edges and wipt his hand over them, and there came filings of them, as he called it, and I writt to Mr. Crooke severall times and tould him the money that he sent to me, much on it caused my name in question, and I was afraid that I should be in trouble, and his answer was that he advised me to put a good face on it and tell those people that found fault with it, it is such money as he receves ; and when I went from him out of Lancashire there came one Mr. Davi Solam, that was his prentis, and I can make it appear that he did carry severall sumes of money of his master to be clipped, and I found it out by making some enquiries after Mr. Crooke, how it fell out that he had so much clipt money. I can make it appear where severall sumes have been changed, and, a little before I left him, there came to my hands above 140[*l*.] all or most of it clipped.

"Mr. Thomas Marsden, he always is for large money, when he receives any, and he is mighty difficult in takeing any little money, but, on my knowledge, he payes as much little money as any man does ; and I heard Mr. Marsden say to me, about 6 months agoe, that he had sold a great sum of melted silver, which he did say was clippings, as we were drinking a glass a wine at the Mite Tavern, in King Street, but there was no one by but he and I. About two yeares ago, one John Eclston, that was Mr. Marsden's man, and I, drunk a pint a wine together in Milk Street, at the King's Armes, and we fell in discourse together about his master, and I tould him that I heard he struck him ofen, and I said : John, I heard your master put you in Newgate ; and he said : yes, it is soe, but I maid him fetch me out presently, or else I would a had company of him ; and sume time after this, his said man went from him into Flanders, which he pretended went against his will ; but I am informed that he sent him there, and of my knowledge he have sent severall sumes of money to him ; and I have heard his man say that he did not value his master, for he said his master durst do no other but let him do what he pleased, for if he pleased, he could say something against his master would make him repent stricking of him ; and I remember Mr. Marsden asked me if he might trust Nichonson ; for what, said I ; in business said he ; but, said he, I heare he have been a clipper ; so have I too heard soe, but I cannot tell how true it is ; and I know that Nichonson have been at his house since.

"Thomas Wiggins, over against the White Cross Tavern, in White Cross Street, received money from one John Edgleston, who was Thomas Marsden's man, which the said Marsden pretended would arrest him for it, but I tould him that Wiggins replied, he durst as well take a bear by the tooth as meddle with him, for he would make him repent it, or words to this affect; and if Wiggans house be searched, I believe tools for clipping may be found in it.

"Nathaniel Mollineux, of Westhoghton, near Manchester, used to exchange broad money for narrow, for advantage.

"Robert Mollineux, on Houghton Common, received broad money from the said Nathaniel and paid him again in narrow, and have been in custody for the same, but made his escape, since which time, about Christmas last, he came to me in London, and told me that he would give money for a pardon, for that he was guilty of clipping the current coin and vending the same, in exchange for large money, giveing 18d. per [pound] and that to encourage the procuring of his pardon, he would make a large discovery of persons of estates, guilty of the same fault.

"Law : Lowson [1] of Chorley, in Lancashire, hath been seen to clip money, by James Rascow, who will evidence the same.

"Peter Breyares [1] hath filed money at his house in Chorley town, near the Cross, and [been] seen to do it by Richard Blackburne and Hugh Cooper.

"Davi Solam hath sent me narrow money out of Lancashire, which, when I offered to pay away, I was threatened to be troubled for the filings being fresh upon it.

"Richard Jackson, of Kurden [Cuerdon ?], in Lancashire, exchanged broad money for narrow, 18d. in the pound advantage.

"Richard Hutchinson, goldsmith, in Chelmsford, hath bought of me melted silver, knowing the same to be clippings melted, for he came one time and told me that one of the parcells was not so well melted, but that he could discern part thereof to be clippings; however, having it so cheap, a pennyworth from me as 4s. or thereabouts by the ounce, told me if I had any more such, or could help to more of the same, he would buy it.

"There is [a] goldsmith, whose name I cannot remember, but his house is in a court, near the five Bells, alehouse, in Swithings Lane, who bought a parcell of selver, in my presence, of one John Nichonson, to the value of 60 pounds, which was the clippings of money, melted down, and that he gave for the same, about 4s. 5d. the ounce, without any say made of its goodnes.

"One Tho : Ouldfeild, otherwise Orford, of Finchley, County Middlesex, have exchanged brod money for narow, with John Nichonson, at 18d. in the pound advantage, and the said Nichonson hath severall times browed large money on me, which he afterwards tould me, that when he had clipt it, he disposed thereof to his chapmon, Ouldfeild, for brod money.

"This is what at present cums (?) to my memory, and I will endeavour to make a further discovery, as I can recollect the names of persons and passidges relateing to this afaire."

"A second confession sent on the same 23rd of May, [16]84.

I have set apart a little of the preshus time I have yet to spend (since I writ my former paper) to cleere my conchance, and serve the King, in considering what I further can remember, which is, that I, being in his own house, I mean Mr. Marsden's warehouse in Coleman Street, at the sign of the "Maiden Head," when he had packs com out of Lancashire, and out of them had taken certain baggs, which he said was money returned to him by his father, I took one of them in my hand and found the same to be clippings of money, which he tooke hastily from me, and said they were no such thing, and thrue them into a nopsqure (sic) corner.

---

[1] In Roger Kenyon's hand, "Tried and acquitted."

"Mr. Sam : Neale, lininge draper, at the Crown in Gratious Street, did at one time, when I had a sum of clipt money by me, exchanged it, and giving brod money for it, required 12*d*. [*per*] pound, which I paid him, and the like he did, and one other time, for another sum of clipt money.

"One John Prescot, in Preston, in Lancashire, would a had me to bought a parcell of clippings, which he shewed me a sample of, and I refused to by the same.

"Mr. Marsden tould me, that Mr. Doyley came formerly to him and serched his house, but they found nothing . . . . . . One Mr. George Macye came to him, as he tould me, heareing there was an information against him for clipping, but he said he frighted him the said Mr. Macye.

"May it please your Worship
That my sad condition may be a pressing argument of your pity, and for God's sake see me this day at my condemned chamber; the occasion I am so bold to put your honour upon this trouble, is I have something of great importance to relate to you alone, and cleare my conscience before I dye, according to what I know, and if your honor will be pleased to answer your poor petecioner's request, I, the unfortunate man, shall be comforted to see you, and will allwaies pray to God for you and yours.

May the 24th, 1684.

Your worship's humble servant,

EDW. JACKSON."

Endorsed : "To the Right Hon : Sir Tho : Wharton, &c."

"Edward Jackson, 3rd confession, May 25, [16]84. . . . . . Mr. Thomas Marsden, did about eight months goe, as he and I was at the Taverne together, about 10 clock in the evening, he urged me much to goe home with him, and I asked him for what, after a long discourse and he tould me that he would let me see him clip, provided I would be true to him; and I tould him I would never discover nothing ; but I did not goe, because it was late, and my wife stayed up for me ; and then he asked me, another time, when I would come and stay all night with him, and I should see him doe as he promised me a little before, but I never did see him in my life clip any money, but Martaine (?) have.

"And there is Mr. Thomas Crooke, that is brother to this William Crooke, that lives near Wigan, in Lancashire, that was partners with Mr. William Crooke, did doe as much as his brother, William Crooke, for clipping of money, as Davi Sollam have told me, that was their prentis, since I came from them."

Endorsed : "To the honourable and worshipfull Sir Thomas Wharton, in Clarkinwell, close near Smithfield, these present."

RICHARD COTTON to ROGER KENYON, at "the Sword and Buckler," in Holborn.

577. 1684, November 7. Knowsley.—According to your request, I have sent you a catalogue of such trees as I think necessary for you to buy, at London : what else is necessary, I suppose the country may afford. The man who I deal withall for my Lord [Derby] is one Mr. Fuller, at the "Three Crowns and Naked Boy" at Strand Bridge, who I look upon to be the best seedsman in the town. I have the man I spoke to you of, when you were in the country, whose wages, you know, will be six pounds *per annum ;* but you, who will have as good a garden as is in Lancashire, I think ought to have a gardener answerable to it. By Mr. Cooper, I hear that Mr. Verigny, that belongs to my Lord Stafford, can recommend a Frenchman to you, who, for twelve· pounds *per annum,* will not only improve your trees, but raise mellons, &c. Mr. Verigny lodges at the " Golden Ball," in York Street, in Covent Garden. If you please to speak to him, you may know further. I am afraid you will find the peach trees very dear this year, by reason of last winter. *Seal of arms.*

WILLIAM PATTEN to ROGER KENYON.

`578·` 1684, November 13. Preston.—" When Madam Lindley was last at Preston, Mr. Pigot had the happiness to see her, and was mightily struck in love with her ; and he and I went to Manchester to waite upon her, in the way of courtshipp, this week. He caressed the younge lady, and I complemented the mother, and understand she will consult Mr. Lightbrowne." Prays that Kenyon will speak in favour of Mr. Pigot to Mr. Lightbrown. *Seal of arms.*

WILLIAM ASSHETON to ROGER KENYON.

579. 1684, November 18. Manchester.—Yesterday, being in company with Dr. Cuerden, of Preston, he gave me an account of the Heralds' Office, and finding my good friend, Sir William Dugdale, principal King-at-Arms, and my fellow-servant, Mr. Gregory King, now Rouge Cross, Chief Pursuivant. I beg, at your leisure, you would please wait upon Sir William Dugdale and Mr. King, and beg their interest upon my account, in procuring me the now present Norroy's deputation to me, and my son Robert, for this county. *Seal.*

GEORGE KENYON to ROGER KENYON, M.P., at Westminster.

580. 1684, December 28. Manchester.—Information, given by Hartley, concerning fifteen coiners and clippers of coins, in Lancashire, Derbyshire, and Staffordshire. *Seal of arms.*

THOMAS MORCROFT to ROGER KENYON, at the " Sword and Buckler," in Holborn.

· **581.** 1684, —— 30. Ormskirk.—Begging Kenyon's interest on behalf of his son William, who is in want of employment, and " who went to London, about 3 months since, of his owne accompt, without aney knowledg of us, and, as it is said, concerning a yonge woman, whear some fixion was, as I am told, in the case."

THOMAS BRADDYLL to ROGER KENYON, at Peel.

582. 1684–5, February 3. Holborn.—"Considering the sad news we have here of the king's illness, you may in reason expect I should give some accounts of it, which I do as follows :—Yesterday morning, his Majestie, being about to walk out, was taken with an apoplecticall fit, so violently, that he fell down as he was drawing on his shoe. All means being used for his recovery imaginable, he was let blood, and after that, hot firepans were applied to his head, for all which he remained speechless for above 2 or 3 hours. But in the afternoon, having taken physick, as vomits, etc., which wrought very well with him, it was hoped his distemper was a working it self off. He also became sensible, and knew anyone that spoke to him. Betwixt 3 or 4 a'clock yesterday, he lay down to repose himself, but was not suffered to stay, they expecting a return of the fit, hoping, however, that if he continued to be better, the danger would be past. Yesternight he also continued to be well, and taking moderate rest; he was much better this morning. Just now I had news from a gentleman at Whitehall that (God be praised) the King continues in a mending condition. . . . . . My service to your fireside." *Portion of seal.*

THOMAS BRADDYLL to ROGER KENYON.

'**583·** 1684[–5], February 7.—"It pleased God the King was taken, the 2nd instant, with the fit of an apoplexy. Of the particulars, I suppose you have had from another hand ; but yesterday, about a quarter before twelve a clock, he died, and the Duke, according to the usual custom, was proclaimed King yesterday in the afternoon, with great solemnity." *Seal, broken.*

E. ASHTON to ROGER KENYON, at Peel.

584. 1684–5, February 24. London.—" I am advised and pressed by severall of my friends, to stand to be parlement man for Clitheroe, with Sir Thomas Stringer. The Duke of Albemarle, Sir Thomas, and Mr. Braddyl, promised mee last night to employ all their interest for mee. I cannot well refuse to use my endeavours, when I have the honour (I wish I did deserve it) to be taken notice of, as one capable to doe my country some service. I am sure I am very willing to doe it effectually at this time. But all this is to no purpose, unlesse you are free to give mee all the assistance you can, and, indeed, to manage the whole thing for mee. I have promis'd to desire this from you, and that with your best advice and interest you would befriend Sir Thomas Stringer and mee together. Pray tell mee sincerely, with all the freedome wee ever us'd, by the first post after this, what you thinke of all these particulars. Would you have mee stand ? How shall I manage it ? Should I come down myselfe ? About what time ? What service can my brother doe mee ? And, if you can guesse, whereabouts all this will cost mee ? " *Seal of arms.*

HENRY BROMPTON to MR. LEECH, Attorney-at-Law, in Manchester.

585. 1684[–5], February 26. Serjeants Inn.—I make bold to trouble you on behalf of a friend of mine, and one whom the Baron hath promoted to be master of the school of Repton, in the county of Derby. He informs me that Mr. Chetham, of Turton Tower, near Manchester, by marriage with his lady, hath a place like to fall suddenly, if not already fallen, to his disposal. It is called Etwall, the vicar whereof is dead or dying. It is usually joined to the place of master of the hospital of Repton. The person I desire you to speak for is one Mr. Doughty, a good divine, a great scholar, and not only loyal himself, but of loyal extraction. It may be, Mr. Robert [Roger ?] Kenyon would assist you in it. I do not question but the Baron will appear in it at the assizes, but Doughty was chaplain to Judge Charlton.

HENRY ROWE to ROGER KENYON.

586. 1684[–5], February. Wigan.—" Yesterday there came to this towne, a great many people out of Preston, to meete Mr. James Ashton, who brought the charter with him. Amongst the Prestoners there was Mr. Hodgkinson and several other aldermen of Preston." *Seal.*

R. Bradshaigh to Roger Kenyon.

587. 1684-5, March 4. ·Haigh.—He is commanded by Lord Derby to call a meeting of the gentlemen of Salford Hundred, to choose knights for the ensuing Parliament. *Seal of arms, broken.*

Roger Kenyon to " Thomas Sorocold, of Barton, William Hulme, of Daivehulme, and Peter Egerton, of Shaw, Esquires, and each of them."

588. 1684-5, March 5. Peel.—Lord Derby had written to Sir Roger Bradshaigh, to desire him to direct the "gentlemen of the county" to meet his lordship at Preston on Friday, the 13th instant, at 10 a.m., "to consider of fitt persons for knights of the shire and of burgesses for the ensueing Parliament." *Seal of arms, broken.*

Edward Rigby to Roger Kenyon.

589. 1684-5, March 7. London.—Having a command, from a great person at Court, to oblige Sir Edward Chisenhall from giving Lord Charles Murray an opposition at Wigan, and knowing Kenyon to be a member of the Corporation of Wigan, asks him to use his interest for such purpose. He knows Lord Charles Murray to be an honest gentleman, and firm for the Protestant religion. *Seal, broken.*

[Roger] Kenyon to the Duke of Albemarle.

590. 1684-5, March 10. Knowsley.—"I am very much troubled to find what I have done at Clitherow, at the instance of my Lord Derby, and other gentlemen, is disresented by your Grace. It was what I did believe was for the King and country's service, and could not have received so contrary a construction from your Grace. Your Grace, if times past may be remembered, never saw mee slack in service to you on like occassions, but I never before heard your Grace did insiste to nominate both burgesses to be chosen; and, therefore, preserving a place for one which wee did beleeve would be Sir Thomas Stringer, I thought, and so did those at whose instance I went, that the earlier application was made and more like to succeed. So, as time taken to consult your Grace would have been to let in others in the mean time, and our directions being to chose persons of untainted loyaltie, I thought, and still think, the gentleman proposed did, every way, answer that character." I never to this day heard that Mr. Stanley was proposed to stand for Liverpool. I went to Clitheroe after I received your Grace's first letter; it was a general meeting, to consider of all that were, or should then be, "pi opounded" to stand, which were: Mr. Stanley, Sir Edmund Ashton, Colonel Ashton, Sir Thomas Stringer, Mr. Warren, and Mr. Marsden. At my return home, I met with your Grace's later letter, and the next day came hither to acquaint my Lord Derby, who saith he hath no reason to believe his Majesty will be offended for his proposing his brother at Clitheroe, where many of the electors are his Lordship's good friends. Nor is it in my power to prevail with his Lordship, and Mr. Stanley, to desist. I am, in a particular manner, a servant to his Lordship, "nor can I so allowably, as perhaps in another way, expostulate with his Lordship." *Draft. Vide the Duke's letter. No. 594.*

The humble ADDRESS to the King by the GRAND JURY of the County Palatine of Lancaster from the Assizes held at Lancaster.

591. 1684-5, March 21.—" Since our wise God thought good to try your princely patience, in the want of so dear a brother, and our carriage in the losse of so gratiouse a soveraigne, the eye that pierces after this Providence, shews us his happy change in this translation, corrects our passion, stops our tears. It shows us, too, our duty and allegeance is changed to you, your person sacred to us, and lookeing up to you, your goodnes in your gratiouse declaration, anticipates our prayer of being governed by our established lawes in Church and State. What shall we doe to manifest our joys? We dedicate our lives, our fortunes, to you. Our constant loyaltie, in every act, shall speake our gratitude. May the King of Kings protect and preserve your Majesty long to raigne happy over your vast dominions, and in the hearts of all your people." *Copy.*

EDWARD RIGBY to ROGER KENYON.

592. 1684-5, March 24.—" My Lord Charles Murrey settes forward, upon Thorsday morning, post for Wiggon, for the election. Upon my owne accompte, I doe hartilie entrete you to give him as much satisfaction in the toune as you can (my frende Jack Asheton comes along with him), and I doe further entrete you to spend five pounds upon the out burgesses to drinke my Lord's heelth, and fevour me likwise to procure 50 ginys to offer my Lord, by Mr. Asheton, if he have occation, and I will pay the value heir upon sight." *Seal of arms.*

R. LEIGH to the EARL OF DERBY.

593. 1685, March 31. Lyme.—Has just received " our chancellor's " letter, which he quotes as follows: "Now for what my Lord Derby desires for my Lord Col[chester], nobody is satisfyed which is here, therefor I must not write such a letter as is desired, and I hope my Lord Derby will pardon me for not writing to Preston on my Lord Colchester's behalfe. All elections goes on most prosperously. Your countryman, Birch, is layd aside at Webley [Weobley], his oune toun, where he did beleeve no flesh liveing could receive any kindnes, but by his permission." Goes on to say that many of Lord Derby's friends were engaged for Colonel Ashton, before they knew his Lordship's brother would stand at Clitherow. " If your Lordshipp will please to let them at Preston know you are willing your brother should stand there, they will be glad on't, and he will have it without any trouble or charge. If the Preston election precede Clitherow, you will have two strings to your bow, and you doe extremely oblige Clitherow to serve you, whenever you command them." *Copy.*

The DUKE OF ALBEMARLE to ROGER KENYON.

594. 1684[-5], March.—" I saw, in a letter from Sir Roger Bradshaw to Robert Nowell, that att a meeting att Manchester, Mr. Stanley, my Lord Darby's brother, was one of those proposed to stand for Leverpool, and I perceive since, that by your meanes, in the name of the gentlemen att that meeting, he has, by you, beene proposed at Clitheroe to oppose the interest that I am endevouring to make their for Sir Thomas Stringer, and, by the King's direction, for Cornell Ashton, your kinsman. How I ought to take this from you, lett the world judge. When

M 2

you take soe much paines to concern my Lord Darby, and such a body of gentlemen against me, who of themselves had never thought of this but for you, I suppose you, who have occasioned this opposition, can be a meanes to put a stop to it, and prevent the clashing of the King's friends, at a time which requires soe much they should stand togeather. No doubt but Mr. Stanley may be chosen att Leaverpool, where he was first intended, without dividing an entrest, which is made by the King's direction, and which division, if it goe on, will be laid to your charge by every body that hears the story. I have directions still to push on the entrest, I first writt to, for Sir Thomas Stringer and (?) Cornell Ashton, which I must doe; and if you give us trouble, put us to charges, and divide the country against us, it will not be lookt upon here as a very considerable service to the King, but a very particqler disobligation to your friend, if you please, to serve you.—Albemarle." *Signed. Vide* No. 590.

" A DECLARATION " enjoined to be performed by JOSEPH HEYWORTH, and MARY, his wife, of the Parish of Hanmer, in the Deanery of Bangor and Diocese of Chester.

595. 1685, May 3.—The said Joseph Heyworth and Mary, his wife, shall be present in the Parish Church of Hanmer, upon some Sunday, in one of the months of June instant, or July next; and being in their accustomed apparel, in the time of divine morning service, in the presence of the whole congregation, then and there assembled; where, immediately after the reading of the gospel, standing upon a form or seat, before the place where the minister readeth prayers, they shall say after the minister as followeth :—" Whereas we, good people, not regarding or having respect to the good and wholesome laws and canons of the Church, have procured ourselves to be clandestinely married, without licence or publication of banns, contrary to the said good laws and canons of the Church, and thereby have incurred the heavy censure of excommunication, to the great danger of our own souls, and evil example of others; therefore, we are heartily sorry for the same, and desire Almighty God to forgive us both, &c."

The humble ADDRESS of the BOROUGH OF CLITHEROE to JAMES H.

596. [1685.]—" We humbly beg leave to expresse our great greife for the death of our late dread Sovereign and your Majestie's most dearly beloved brother. Wee blesse God for the preservation of your sacred Majestie and of your undoubted right to succeed him upon the throne of your royall ancestors. It is a just reward for all your sufferings, all your virtues, your steddy constancy to your friends and to your word, your mercy and forgivenesse to your enemies, the great example of your life in justice, temperance, patience, industry and integrity, your undaunted courage, so often tryed in the great varieties of your active life, your entire obedience to the King, your brother, and the strict regard you have allwaies had to our lawes. Your Majesty has been graciously pleased to promise you will still preserve them. May God Allmighty, who put it into your heart to make that gracious declaration, for ever confirme you in a sacred resolution to observe it. So may you live and reign, live long and happy, abundantly blessed with peace and plenty, blessed with a numerous progeny from your most illustrious consort, and may there never want one of this royall line to sway the scepter of these kingdomes. And may the people be never wanting in their allegiance to assist your Majestie, as wee do solemnly promise wee will with our lives and fortunes." *Copy.*

VOLUNTEERS to serve against the DUKE OF MONMOUTH.

597. [1685.]—Addresses to the Earl of Derby, Lord Lieutenant of Lancashire, from Manchester, and other parts of the county, setting out the readiness of the signatories to provide men and horses, to be employed in quelling Monmouth's rebellion. The address from Manchester is as follows :—" Wee whose names are hereto subscribed, his Majesties most loyall subjects of the toune of Manchester . . . true sons of the Church of England, astonished that the gracious declaration of our dread soveraigne, the King, should be requited with an horrid rebellion, and that, too, vailed under the pretence of that religion which most strictly enjoynes loyalty and allegeance, and forbids resistance and rebellion under the severest penaltyes, in detestation of this scandall laid upon it and us, and in perfect duty and fidelity to our gratious King (whom God long preserve with a prosperous reigne on the throne of his royall brother and ancestors), doe desire and humbly beseech your lordshipp that we may, during this most unnatural rebellion, list ourselves, our servants, or others, under your lordshipp as our captaine, to serve his Majestie in the war against the rebells, and goe under your lordshipp's conduct, at our own charge, with as much order, and as subject to discipline, as the souldiers in the militia are or any other. And this we subscribe to bring in, as well appointed as we can, as followeth ; viz :—

E. Mosley, two horses and men and two foot soldiers.
John Bland.
Joseph Yates, a horse and a man and a foot soldier.
Matthew Bootle, one horse and man and foot man.
John Lister, a footman with musket, compleat.
Samuell Lightbourne, a foot souldier, pike.
Thomas Shaw, a horseman and foot souldier.
Robert Illingworth, a horseman and armes and a footman.
William Drinkwater, a foot souldier, compleated.
John Byrom, a foot souldier well armed, pike.
·Joshuah Browne, a horseman, well accoutred.
Samuell Lesse, a foot souldier.
James Diggle, a foot souldier.
Samuell Brooke, a foot souldier.
Ellice Hey, in person, with his best armes.
John Winne, a musketeer.
Edward Chetham, a musketeer.
Joseph Slator and } a musketeer.
Thomas Herreck, }
Adam Gartside, a musketeer.
Miles Bradshaw, a musketeer.
Nathaniell Walker, a pikeman.
James Mosse, a pikeman.
John Hopwood, a musketeer.
Samuell Nash, a musketeer.
Abraham Holland, a pikeman.
Robert Thyer, a musketeer.
Francis Browne, a pikeman.
Joseph Stockdale, a foot souldier.
William Bowker, a musketeer.
Thomas Gartside, a musketeer.
Richard Whalley.
William Edmundson, a musketeer.
John Leadbeater, a pikeman.

Leonard Egerton.
Samuell Dickanson, a horse and man armed.
Francis Cartwright, a pike, in person.
Joseph Byrom, a musketeer.
James Baynton, a pikeman.
Thomas Dixon and }
George Loyd   } a foot souldier.
John Shelton, a musketeer.
Ralph Jaxkson.
Thomas Minshall.
Ellis Renshaw, a musketeer.
Henry Baley, a musketeer.
Oswald Mosley, a horse and man armed.
John Gilliam, junior, a horse and man.
John Lightboune.
George Curbesheth, a pikeman.
William Plungeon, a musketeer.
John Barton, tanner.
John Antrobus, a foot souldier.
Peter Maddock, a foot souldier.
Philip Oldfeild, a foot man.
Edward Bootle, a foot souldier, pike.
Thomas Drinkwater, a pikeman.
Thomas Radcliffe, a pikeman.
John Moxon, senior, a musketeer.
John Alexander, a foot souldier, pike.
John Gilliam, senior, a musketeer.
Thomas Bent, a musketeer.
John Widdowes, a musketeer.
John Werden, a musketeer.
Thomas Staynrod, a pikeman.
Gervase Staynrod, a pikeman.
Edward Byrom, a foot souldier.
Humphrey Marler, a pikeman.
James Radcliffe, one horse and man.
John Oldfeild and   }
Humphrey Oldfeild, } one horse and man.
Robert Alexander, two musketeers.
Joseph Sherwin, a pikeman.
Geffery Holcroft, a pikeman.
Joseph Bruckshaw, a musketeer.
Regnall Molyneux, a pikeman.
Robert Wilson, a musketeer.
Edward Greaves, a musketeer.
Charles Beswick, a musketeer.
Thomas Newby, a musketeer.
Edward Siddall, a musketeer.
Nathan Leech, a pikeman.
John Hollingworth, a pikeman.
Lawrence Gardnet, a musketeer.
John Booker, a musketeer.
Robert New, a pikeman.
John Barlow, a musketeer.
William Swarbreck, a musketeer.
Daniell Woolmer, a musketeer.
John Boardman and   }
William Hulme,   } a musketeer.

Michaell Pimlott, a musketeer.
Robert Sutton and } a musketeer.
Richard Worthington, }
Richard Hampson and } a musketeer.
Samuell Barlow, }
John Byron, a foot souldier.
Edward Radcliffe and } a pikeman.
Isaac Hyde, }
Jonathan Greene, a musketeer.
John Sandiford Mason, a musketeer.
Edward Scott and } a foot souldier.
Edward Holland, }
John Heywood, a pikeman.
George Grimshaw and } a foot souldier.
Peter Tickle, }
John Bradshaw, apothicary.
William Beck, a pikeman.
Joseph Bacon, a foot souldier.
Arnold Siddall.
Jonathan Runager, a pikeman.
Thomas White, a foot souldier.
John Watson and } a foot souldier.
Thomas Bowker, }
Edmund Travis, a foot souldier.
James Rodgers, a foot souldier.
William Crompton and } a foot souldier."
Thomas Buterworth, }

ROGER KENYON to the EARL OF ROCHESTER, "att his apartments in Whitehall."

598. [1685 ?]—Peel, near Manchester.—" From the great pleasure I read in our common newsepaper that your Lordship is comeing to be Lord High Treasurer of England, procedes the great presumtion of this, to offer my most humble and willing service in any office, in any part of England you will admit mee to serve you. I want neither health nor heart to do whatever you think mee fit for. I was trobled with a deafness at the beginning of this Parliament, [which] made mee not offer to come into it, but am now much better. My Lord, I have two sons, both bred to businesse ; if any or all of us be fitt for your Lordship's service it is the thinge I greatly desire and humbly aske. My eldest son presents you this; hee hath been at the barr four or five years. My other son is a diligent man and, if I may propperly say so, a good clerke. I can onely say of myselfe, that when I had the honour, in King Charles the Second's time, to serve your Lordshipp, and the rest of the Commissioners of the Treasury, I was very just and faithful, and so I will ever bee. I beseech your Lordship pardon this unwonted presumeing." *Draft.*

INFORMATION as to SEDITIOUS LANGUAGE used by GEORGE WRIGHT.

599. 1685-6, March 9.—Information by James Atwell, one of the constables of Bolton, that on the 1st instant he saw George Wright, of Leigh, carryer, on market day, go up to the top of the market cross at Bolton, " and there tooke off his hat and held it towards his mouth, and aloud said : ' Here is a health to the right King of England; the right King of England is alive.' " And three weeks before the informant heard the said George, in Little Bolton, "lying along upon his belly and drinking pudle water," say similar words, but did not name the late Duke of Monmouth. Other witnesses depose that said George went about the streets of Bolton crying " God bless the right James, the right King of England," and also cried " I hate all papists."

JOHN BRADDYLL to ROGER KENYON, at Peel.

600. 1686, April 24. London.—" I have sent you draughts of what fancyes are most usuall for the placing in gardens." Our countryman, Stamford, has made a great bussle in the City with his chapel; " but, being affronted last Sunday by your people, the King has this day sent a party of soldiers into the Citty, who are to guard him during his devotions tomorrow. Pennies [Penn's?] recantation is so ridiculous, that the papists, I think, will not proceede in it at this time." *Seal of arms.*

JOHN BRADDYLL to ROGER KENYON.

601. 1686, May 8. London.—I have given myself the best information which I could, as to the ornaments you most fancy for your garden, which you may imagine are made at several prices, from 15*li.* to 30*li.*; but, for 25*li.*, I believe you may have a pair of lions very well worked.

DECLARATION BY CHIEF JUSTICE HERBERT.

602. [1686, June.]—" Chiefe-Justice Herbert, on his giveing judgment for Sir Edward Hales, at the suit of Godden, declared that the Judges had resolved these five points in that case, for law :—

" 1. That the King of England is an hereditary, not elected, and an absolute soveraigne, not a limited prince.

" 2. That the lawes of England are the King's, and not the people's lawes, and that the construction of them belong onely to him.

" 3. That the King's prerogative is as much the law of England as that called the property or liberty of the subject.

" 4. That the King cannot by any concession, in or out of Parliament, separate from the Crowne any branch of his prerogative, necessarily incident thereunto ; but that the same instantly reverts againe to the Crowne.

" 5. That it is not in the power of a Parliament, though with the royall assent, to deprive the King of the service of his subject nor to limitt his choice, who shall and who shall not serve him, nor to impose qualifications upon the subject, whereby to disable him for, or make him incapable of, the service of his sovereigne, when he, in his discretion, thinks fitt to require it, and judges him serviceable to him." *Copy.*

JOHN BRADDYLL to ROGER KENYON.

603. 1686, July 27.—Our camp is quite lost now. The English have bravely, though unsuccessfully, fought at Breda (?). Out of twenty-three, twelve are killed and wounded ; amongst the latter is poor Mr. Bellasis, who is shot in the breast. They first mounted the breach, with other volunteers, and there, not being enough of them, nor well seconded by the infantry, they stood, a sacrifice to the enemy. One Mr. Wiseman, a very young gentleman, was fired upon ten times, but valiantly kept his post, till he was killed by a " cimeter." *Seal of arms.*

THOMAS BROUNE to ROGER KENYON, in London.

604. [16]86, November 23. St. John's, Cambridge.—Has sent a
bill of Kenyon's son's accounts for Lady Day and Michaelmas quarters,
1685, "and for the time that his name stood in the butteryes, after he
went doune:

	£	s.	d.
Due upon the bill of December 21, 1684 -	- 64	02	01½
His bill of March 25, [16]85 - - -	- 38	10	03½
His bill of June 24, [16]85 - - -	- 11	09	11
His detriments, &c., to June 24, [16]86 -	- 02	17	03½
Sum total	- 116	19	19½ (sic)
Received -	- 65	00	00
Rest due to me	- 51	19	09½ (sic)

The sum now due, you may please to order to be paid to Mr. Samuel
Smith, att the "Prince's Arms," in St. Paul's Churchyard, or leave a bill
with him, upon any in London." *Seal of arms.*

The EARL OF ROCHESTER to the CLERK OF THE PEACE for the
County of Lancaster.

605. 1686, December 1. Whitehall, Treasury Chambers.—His Majesty having been pleased to give fresh directions for the effectual prose-
cution|of clippers and coiners, I do therefore desire you to send copies of
informations or examinations against such offenders, unto Owen Wynne,
Esquire, Warden of his Majesty's Mint, in the Tower of London.

CLIPPERS and COINERS and their methods of coining.

606. 1686.—"An account of the coiners and clippers, discovered and
informed against, in the County of Lancaster and elsewhere, and of the
makers of stamps, stuff, and instruments to coin and clip with, and of
their factors, buyors, and vendors of clippings and of false money,
putters off, and of their agents, messengers, and persons employed in
this trade of diminishing or falsifying the King's coin, and of such as
furnish the clippers with fair money to be clipped for part of the gain."
A long list of persons indicted for coining follows, at the end of which
is an account of the manner in which the coiners proceeded:—

"The ingredient of the coyneing stuffe, call spawd, and the way they
make it.

"1. *Allumen plumosum*, one pound (worth 4 or 5 shillings). 'Tis a
light stuffe, in the forme of a feather, and is burned and bruised to
powder.

"2. Alabaster, burned and bruised to powder; about 6 pounds of that
to one of the *allumen plumosum.*

"3. *Bole armoniack,* burned and bruised to powder; twix a pound
and two of this, to the two former.

"All these to be searsed through a fine sive or searse cloth, mixed
well.

"4. *Sal armoniack*, dissolved in water; to which water, the aforementioned powders, so mixed and sifted very fine, when this stuffe is
to be used, are put and wrought like fine dough or past, and this
stuffe is not destroyed, nor much wasted by casting into, but becomes
both finer and fitter for the purpose, by usage.

" The materialls they have to coyne with, and the manner of useing them :—

" 1. Copper, whitened with white arsneck.

" 2. Silver, clipped off his Majesty's lawfull coyne. Two parts silver, to one parte whited copper.

" 3. A pair of flaskes, a casting pott, a pestell, all of iron. These flaskes are round or ovall, have a topp and a bottome made with pins in the topp, falling into holes made to fitt them in the bottom; that, when laid together, they fall fixedly and close all wayes even and alike. Then, in their bottom flask, laid upon a place for the purpose, they first lay their patternes, any pieces of money they will have counterfeited; and so, 7 or 8 half-crownes or shillings at a time, or more, as their flasks are in bignes; and these they cover with the stuffe called spawd, which they thrust and ramm hard downe with the iron pestell; and this leaves in that stuffe the impression of one side of the moneys to be counterfeited; then they turne this stuffe, which retaines the impression, out of the flask upon a smooth board and take out the patternes, which they then put, with the contrary side up, into the top flaske, and in like manner fill that with the same stuffe, which accordingly takes and retaines the impress of the other side of the money to be imitated, and then turne that allso out to take out their patternes, and then again putting these into their proper parts of the flask, with the smooth sides downe, they make, with a knife or other instrument, a hollow place in the stuffe lying in the flask, for the mettle to run in and come to the hollows, so prepared for the reception of it, into the moulds thus made; and thus, having fixed and prepared their spawd, as they call it, and closed their top and bottam flaskes, there is a little hollowed place comes out of their flask, into which, having melted their mixed metalls in their casting pott, they power the same, and presently take it, so cast, out of their flaskes, which comes out very black, and to alter that colour, they lay it upon a thin broad iron plate set upon a very red hot fire, which changes the colour to blew; and then they take it of the fire and boyle it in a tartar, bruised, which they call argoll, mixed with salt, and this makes it over white. Then they rub it in *sal armoniack*, which makes it somewhat black againe, and then they again rub it with clay, and after, wash of the clay with water, and when thus brought to the colour they would have it, they wipe away the clay and water with a cloth, and this makes it very passable; and this money, if cutt into, retaines it colour, as all silver."

Guicciardini Wentworth to Roger Kenyon.[1]

607. 1681, April 2.—Mr. Heywood went to Oxford the first day of the year, but what has become of him, I know not. Sir Robert [Carr ?] is not yet come home; he stays, I suppose, for Mrs. B———, who went down with him to her father's, and I fancy it will be suitable to his inclinations to bring her back. If he come home to-night, he and his son go on Monday to Newmarket. It is supposed the term will be kept at London. The City seem not to be appalled at the Parliament being rubbed off. Some say Fitz Harris' business was a main help to its being done. Soon my Lord of Oxford's regiment is brought and quartered round the City. It is, this morning, freshly discoursed that next week the Duke will be in London, that the Duke of Hanover is returning, and a match will be made with Lady Ann. Two nights ago, the Duke of Albemarl and Colonel Legg and divers others, supping together at Captain Skelton's, the Colonel told the Duke, with whom

---

[1] This letter has been misplaced.

ho had been discoursing, and grew hot, that he was a rascal, which was returned with a glass of wine in the Colonel's face, and had been followed by blows, had not the company interposed; some whereof immediately informing the King, command was sent them, upon their allegiance, not to stirr nor presume to fight, and there it stops. The quarrel began about Portsmouth, the garrison which the Duke had contracted for with the governor, which is Colonel Legg's. The mews is filled with horse and foot; what the issue will be God`knows; but to outward appearance, things are as still as ever in my life. *Seal of arms.*

L[EFTWICH] O[LDFIELD] to ROGER KENYON.

608. [1687,] April 10.—"Here is talk of some clashing among the grandees. For ought I can learn, the return made by the judges is as little satisfying as that made by the lord-lieutenant., which some argue, from the privicy of the matter, because against the nature of the thing, to have kept the *contra* secret. All is on the anvile before the Committees for regulating Corporations. The coffee newspapers say the Corporation at Oxford, resolves to defend their charter by law against the *Quo Warranto,* for the surrender whereof were but 2 votes, and 82 against the surrender. Here is talk of a fresh letter from Pentionary Fagell and another from Dr. Burnet to the Lord President, but the binding some booksellers to appear next term, stiffles the publishing such. It is said that Mr. Barker, Clerk of the Crown, a patentee for life, is suspended from his office, for neglecting to send down a *dedimus* with the commission of peace, and Sir Robert Clerk, of Lincoln's Inne, a Northampton-shire gentleman, put into the place The information and indictment on which the said office is to be adjudged forfeited (if found next term) yet is surely traversable. However, Sir Clerk (*sic*) at present takes the place upon him, and hath removed the office. If I mistake not, this said Sir Clerk marryed the Lady Ivy's daughter or daughter-in-law, who are both papists, and hee suspected to be gon over lately."

The humble ADDRESS of the PROTESTANT JUSTICES OF THE PEACE of the County Palatine of Lancaster.

609. 1687, July 12.—"We, your Majesties Justices of the Peace for this county, of the Church of England as by law established, do give your Majestie our humble and hearty thanks for the assistance your Majestie has been graciously pleased to give, by dispenseing with the `oaths and test, and so joyneing in the Comission with us, severall gentlemen of the Roman Catholique religion (persons of discretion and interest) by whose help and counsell, we doubt not but to be better enabled to preserve your lawes and the peace of this county, with which your Majestie has been pleased to intrust us; and we cannot but, in gratitude, make our humble acknowledgements for these and all the favours your Majestie has been pleased to conferr upon us." *Only two signatures. Copy.*

THE SAME.

610. [1687, July 12.]—A draft of the above address in the hand-writing of Roger Kenyon.

OBSERVATIONS upon the GOVERNMENT IN LANCASHIRE and the changes there.

611. 1687, August 27.—King James came to Chester; he there made the Lord Molineux, a popish rescusant convict, his Lord-Lieutenant of

Lancashire, and displaced the Earl of Derby. After this, the Lord Molineux made 12 Deputy-Lieutenants, which had the late King's approbation, viz.: Lord Braudon, Mr. Spencer, Mr. Girlington, Mr. Banaster, and Mr. Warren; all the rest, being convicted papists.

The EARL OF DERBY to ROGER KENYON.

612. 1687, December 10.—·I hope this will find you safe and sound at home, after a winter journey. Your saying my wife enjoined you to come hither, induces me to be the more earnest in the same thing; for perhaps you may give some light. I confess, if her carriage would surprise me, it would do now; but I shall say no more, referring matter enough against I see you, which I desire may be with all possible speed. *Seal, broken.*

FRANCIS MOLYNEUX to ROGER KENYON, at Peel.

613. 1687-8, February 25. London.—" Yours I received, and, in answer, shall receive your son upon likeing, and doe hope there will be noe reasons of objecticn on either side. Theire is one thing that my Lady Molyneux could not resolve me, that is, whether he hath had the small-pox, which is a distemper we are much afraid of, and must be expected, untill past, so that, if he is not past them, if any sumptoms appear, he must be removed, though I will see the same care, as att home; but for any other charge, except kitchin physick, wee doe nott allow; but if the distemper be apparent before he be removed, I will nott venture him, butt raither remove my owne children, for, as neare as I can, I will make the case myne and doe as I desyre myne may be dealt with. It is my desire to make all things plain, which avoids misunderstandings. I shall valew Sir John and my Lady's recommending me to be his master, and noething shall be wanteing in my parte for his good, but it must be his care to deserve encouragement and kindness before I shall allow it, which will be his owne advantage."

Following, is a letter from the writer's uncle, Sir John Molyneux, to the same, and of the same date.

" I have had a very severe fitt of the goute in both my feete, right knee, and hand, for six weekes, and could not write till this weeke, not wear my shooes till Thursday last. My nephew, Francis Molyneux, sent your owne letter with this, being he could not come see mee this night. I am sorry my cosen, your sonne, William, could not come up, before my wife and selfe went out of this towne, that I might have given him some good counsel. I am sure he will have a good mayster and mistress, if it bee not his owne fault. Therefore, I would advise him by all means to bee careful of what companions and acquaintance hee gets, and not to goe out of his mayster's house without lycence and command, and to bee sure hee goes not oft to his brother, lest hee make that a pretence and excuse for his absence; and pray doe you charge him not to bee too familiar with the footeboy in the house, who I doubte got noe good with being in the house with the other 'prentises who were turned away. I doubt not but both yourselfe and my cosen, his mother, and all freinds, will give him all the good counsell and advice imaginable, for this is a sad towne for youth, and greate complaynts are of them generally. And above all things, charge him against all gameing and goeing to the lottery, for my cosen's last prentise, being sent to pay 20*l.*, lost it the same day at the lottery, soe was sent to his parents into Yorkeshire the Munday after, for hee would not bee ruled. I shall bee most glad to heare hee doth well, and shall enquire after him. My wife talked to my neice about him alsoe, who is a very good woman and was much conserned. The two prentises did soe ill; they were both related to my nephew and niece, and if yours doe not well, they will never take any relation's children more, though they are much importuned already; they are very busye and . . . . his trade exceedingly encreases."

SERVANTS AND APPRENTICES.

614. 1687[-8,] March 23.--Minute of Justices of the Peace for the County Palatine of Lancaster, touching the settlement of servants and the apprenticing of poor children.

K. MOLYNEUX to ROGER KENYON.

614A. 1688, March 27. London.—"Accordinge to your desire, [I] have discourste Mr. M[olyneux] as effectuallye as I can, about your sonne, but can by no meanes perswade him to find cloathes, nor allowe anythinge towardes them, but promises to see your money warilye bestowed, that the charge may be as easy on that accompt as can be expected. Nor would hee, as he positively affirmes, find him with cloathes under 50*l.* more money, or neare it; and on those termes it is much better let it alone and find them yourself, for as much more yearely as the interest of the money comes too, will fitt very well for three or four of the first yeares, and about 8*l.* per annum afterwards; for soe much is the usuall allowance of masters to their servants (when they come to termes), though never soe good men's sonnes (I heare of none that goes higher), so that, accordiug to that computation, it were considerable loss to come to his termes. Mr. M[olyneux] and your sonne likes one another very well for this short time they have been together, and doubt not but it will continue; for I really thinke he could not have beene better placte in London (if to a shop trade), nor more hopefullye for preferment, for his master is a tyte fitt man for business as moste aboute towne, and has great trade, but his servants are exposed to as little hardshipp or servile worke as any man's; their employe is easye enough—dilligence and care are the onelye ingredients that is required to make them acceptable, and constitutes them capable and fitt for his employ. And I know it is the same with all considerable dealers, but then the difference is this : many such exposes their servants to great paines in carryinge burdens and many other waies; but heare they are put to no hardship at all, save removeing of cloath and liftinge it to and fro in the shopp."

WILLIAM B[ANKES] to ROGER KENYON.

615. 1688, April 16. Winstanley.—"I hear no newes, but only that the Bishop of Durham hath put some questions to the clergy of his diocesse, concerning their complying to take off the Penal Lawes, and those that refuse in so reasonable a request are to meet with the Oxford men's fate—suspension, &c. Our clergy conclude they must undergoe the same test, and expect to meet with the same kind usage. I hear they intend to consult one another betimes, and intend to give one and the same answer. The Wiggoners have refused to gratify their Mayor and new Aldermen, in not signing an addresse that was prepared to have been sent up to his Majesty, with their thanks in it, for the regulation; and, in it, promise to choose such members as would assist in so gratefull a work, as taking off those penall lawes would be." *Seal.*

The Earl of Derby to [Roger Kenyon].

616. 1688, April 19. Knowsley.—" I cannot but be concerned, not to see you before I leave the country, which I shall certainly do ere the sessions are ended." As to refusing to employ a papist as his "faulkener," and as to mapping out his estates.

Charles Hilton to Roger Kenyon.

617. 1688, May 24. "Fullers Rents."—" The news at present is slender; but there is come about, the Bishops' paper which was presented his Majesty on Friday last, and this is the true copy of the paper, viz.: ' I am not avers to the reading the K.'s declaration for liberty of conscience, for want of due tenderness towards dissenters, in relation to whom I shall willingly come to such a temper as shall be thought fit, when the matter comes to be considered and settled in Parliament; and the declaration being found upon such a dispenceing power as may lay by at pleasure all laws, ecclesiastical and civill, seems to me illegall, and did so to the Parliaments in 1662 and 1672; and, because it is a point of so great concernment, I cannot so far make myselfe party to it, as reading it in true divine service will amount to.' The names of the Bishops who subscribed this paper are Ely, Peterborough, Chichester, Bath and Wells, St. Asaph, Bristol. This is reported to be his Majesty's answer : ' My Lords, you have surprized me ; I did not expect such an answer from men of your principles, though 'tis no more, nor other, then what others have often told I might expect from you.'" The surrender of Alba Regalis is confirmed, with the several particulars.

Nathaniel Molyneux to Roger Kenyon.

618. 1688, May 24. London.—" I doubt not but you had an account from Mr. Molyneux, that your son was bound last Monday but one, to which I was a witness, and can assure you I never saw anything done with greater satisfaction and willingness, on both sides. I enclose a copy of the Bishops' address to his Majesty, last week. I have also sent you the King's answer, which came out in print yesterday, but is called in again ; it is a very severe thing, but short, he calls them trumpeters of rebellion, with many other strange sort of speeches, which I cannot now stand to mention. There is no other news at present, but things run so strangely high that there will in all probability be news enough, and too much, in a short time."

Richard Hatton to Roger Kenyon.

619. 1688, May 30. Dean.—" Although I have received noe command with the declaration, to annex any word of exhortation to the people to move their complyance therewith, yet I thought good to acquaint you herewith, and to send the declaration to peruse, if you have not seen it ; you may either returne it by the bearer, or send it, upon Friday, by Richard Farnworth. Sir, I humbly desire your opinion whether it be convenient to say anything at all to it, or noe. I would carry myselfe as inoffensive in this concerne as I could, that I might neither expose myselfe to be informed against by some busybody Romanist, nor to the censure of any Nonconformist, as if the meer publication of the declaration, did testify any concurrency therewith. I know not well what to resolve upon, but I am inclinable to think that the safest way will be to be silent. The clergy are injoyned (as you see, sir) in the declaration, to read it upon two Sabbath dayes, unless I mistake the sence of it, and that it does give a liberty to read it upon either day. I cannot well understand why it should be read twice. Sir, I cannot but acknowledge some particular kindnesse I have received from you; and above all, I am cordially thaukfull for your present countenance towards me. I have had a very great esteeme of you since I have understood your christian carriage and resolution against the takeing off the penall laws and test, notwithstanding the temptations you had to the contrary, from worldly respects, which, I am apt to think, would have prevailed with some others. I heartily love persons who are firm in their principles. Our poor distressed Church is hardly beset on every hand. I hope that God, in His due time, will give her a gracious deliverance. *Portion of seal.*

WILLIAM PATTEN to ROGER KENYON.

620. 1688, June 3. Gray's Inn.—" There is great news about our Bishops, and to tell you the whole trial, would take up almost a volume. But, in short, the Bishops, this morning, were found by the jury not guilty. Yesterday, upon the trial, Powell and Holloway were of opinion us the said jury gave their verdict, but the Lord Chief Justice and Justice Allabone, otherwise. The Court sat yesterday till after six, and began again at eight in the morning. So soon as the evidence was delivered to the jury, the whole hall loudly proclaimed huzzas. The jury gave not their verdict till after four this morning, and then privately to Mr. Justice Allabone, sealed up; and, about nine this morning, the verdict was recorded, the Bishops being present. All the four Courts near, sat, yet notwithstanding, the people, *alta voce*, gave several huzzas." *Seal of arms.*

LEFTWICH OLDFIELD to ROGER KENYON.

621. 1688, June 3.—" The clergy in this county [Cheshire ?], as far as I can perceive, generally agree not to read the declaration, notwithstanding the Bishops' monition, as well as order. For avoiding of schism, among other reasons, as I am told, they choose rather to follow the Metropolitan, accompanyed with soe many other Bishops of approved integrity and learning, with approbation of both Universitys, and the generality of the clergy of the kingdom, in the substantialls of the petition, then their own diocessan, dissenting from that nationall synodicall body (if I may so, in this case, call them), recconing it a strang task to be enjoyned, with their owne hands, to pull the Church fence; a *felo de se*, you know, can have noe benefit of clergy. Besides, they are jeallous lest their flocks should, like the doctors at London, when he began to read it, all goe out. How the Judges, the Commissioners Ecclesiastique, and the drummers, will thunder at this, in defence of the liberty and dispensing power, the fortnight promised probably will inform. The Bishops have, in my opinion, begun the intrenchment on a vantage ground. I am in paine till I know how some clergymen of your county acquitt themselves in this particular; it is a weighty matter, and will soe be found."

WILLIAM BANKES to ROGER KENYON.

622. 1688, June 12. Winstanley.—The seven Bishops are gone to the Tower, having refused the Lord Chancellor to be bound to appear at the King's Bench Bar, which, as they were Peers (thinking they might be questioned by the House of Lords), they could not submit to. His

Lordship asked then, whether they owned the petition; they all answered it was their own, upon which his Lordship replied it was a seditious one. A soldier that deserted his colours, was going the same day to be hanged, and a priest being earnest with him.to turn his religion ; but he told him he was a protestant, and would die so, so pulled his cap over his face and fell to his prayers. Just in the nick of time, a pardon came, without the priest's solicitation. This steadiness of the man, gave the Bishops great satisfaction. *Seal.*

George Kenyon to his father, Roger Kenyon.

623. [1688], June 14. London.—" I have been ill of the epidemicall distemper, but, I thank God, am perfectly recovered; it seises (like a giddiness in the head and a . . . . . and ague throwout the whole body. They say three parts of the City have had it. 'Tis now no news that there is a Prince of Wales, nor the committment of the Bishops. I was this day in the Tower to see them at prayers. People crowd so many to see them, that the soldiers are forced to keep all the gates shut, and, did they not, I beleeve the Tower would scarce hold the numbers that flock there. By good chance, I gott in after prayers; all the people kneeled in a lane to receave theyr benediction, and all the 7 layed theyr hands upon my head. Tomorrow, they are expected to appear in the King's Bench : if they do, I will write by Saturday's post to you." *Seal.*

George Macy to Roger Kenyon, Clerk of the Peace at Lancaster.

624. 1688, June 26. " Bow, near London."—" The occasion of this, is to desire you will send me a certificate, under your own hand, and to make oath of it before my Lord Chief Justice Wright, when he comes to Lancaster, that Thomas Lyon was brought, by *habeas corpus*, from Surry, and Robert Mollineaux from Essex, in August, 1684, and tryed for high treason, at your assize; the first executed, and the other transported. My Lord Chancellor was then their judge. For there is now estreats of 80*l.* come out against me, for not prosecuting them in the countyes where I apprehended them. Inclosed is your letter to me written concerning the proceedings at Lancaster Assize, at which time I was at Bristoll, prosecuting of clippers. I have acquainted my Lord Chief Justice with the trick that is put upon me. Thomas Higham, who broke the gaol at Lancaster, was seen lately here in London."

Thomas Parker to Roger Kenyon.

625. 1688, July 9. " Brewtholme."—The inhabitants of Colne Parish design to move the Justices, at the Sessions at Preston, for an order to cause the inhabitants of Admergill to contribute towards the relief of their poor; by what law or rule, the writer does not understand. They neither being in the same parish or county. Asks for Kenyon's favourable assistance to the inhabitants of Admergill. *Seal of arms.*

William Patten to Roger Kenyon.

626. 1688, July 10. Gray's Inn.—I cannot give you any more particulars of the Bishops' trials, for I was not in Court ; but, upon the trial, were very hot debates by counsel, on both sides ; and the Bishops' counsel were very smart and brisk, and Mr. Solicitor was so run down, that he was several times hissed. They talk as if the Bishops must be prosecuted before the Lords Ecclesiastical, but that is not certainly known to me. *Seal of arms, broken.*

THOMAS PARKER and CHRISTOPHER WILKINSON to ROGER KENYON.

627. 1688, July 12. Waddow.—On behalf of "Dr. Leeming, Practitioner in Physic and Chirurgery," long since licensed by the late Archbishop of York; who, by some misrepresentation, is committed to the Bridewell at Manchester, a prison for infamous persons.

LAURENCE RAWSTORNE to ROGER KENYON, at Ormskirk.

628. 1688, July 15. Preston.—" Hutton, one of the townes within the Parish of Penworth[am], is sore burdened with their poore, is not at all eased by the rest, notwithstanding they have no poore, some of them, and the rest not in any equality. The bearer can informe what would be tedious to express in writeing. If you think it feasible, pray you promote that the parish may be chardged mutually to contribute with it (as by law you know it ought) and it will be a great kindness to us, for the greatest share lyes indeed uppon me. I know you will advise them the best, and if it cannot be effected, tell them soe, and they will rest satisfied; better sit still then rise up to fall." *Seal of arms.*

ORDER touching HIGHWAYS in the HUNDRED OF DERBY, made at the General Quarter Sessions held at Ormskirk.

629. 1688, July 16.—" This Court, upon consideration of the great decay of the King's highways and the long neglects of the sufficient repaires thereof in this County, resolveing to make a thorrou reformation thereof in each towne and vill, doth hereby order, that all and every the King's highways, in each parish, towne, and place, within the Hundred of Derby, shall forthwith be put in perfect good repaire; that they be made so wide, so smoothed from little rockes, little hills, hollowes, slodds, and all unevenness, freed from boggie, sincking, soft, deepe, or founderous places, rid of all sorts of rubbish, and so sufficiently passable throughout, that coaches, carts, and carriages, may safely, in all places, goeing by the calsey, meet and pass each other. That all ditches which convey the water cross the highway, be soughed with wallstone, and well covered throughout, from one side of the lane to the other. That the ditches running on each side the lane be well scoured, and the earth or sand cast thereout, not left in heapes, but either spread to level the waye in low places, or removed out of the way. That all hedges on each side the lanes be cutt, and the trees lopped that in anywise anoy the highway, and the loppings removed out of the lanes. That all trees, underwoods, groves, bushes, broomes, brambles, gorses, and the like, be well ridd up and totally removed out of the said lanes; and that all the holes occasioned by ridding the same, as ailsoe all pits, slacks, and hollowes, little hills and heapes of stone, earth, and rubbish, be levelled and made even, and where the said wayes are cumbered with loose stones or other rubbish, or knotted and uneven calseys, that such calseys be pulled up and new paved, and the unnecessary stones and rubbish removed; and that all calseys be made of the full bredth of one yard and a quarter, of round stones and not of flags; and that all places where calseys are of flags, that if round stones may be had with a reasonable charge, that the flagged calseys be pulled up and new calseys, with round stones made in the place, or such other place of the lane, as may be more convenient, of the full bredth aforesaid, or a well gravelled way in lieu thereof; and that there be no channell paved for the water to be drained cross the calsey, except such draines be well soughed, covered, and paved over, and that it be so covered the full bredth of the calsey as may make it safe, by day and night, for horsemen to ride over. And all and every the overseeres of the highwayes within the said Hundred, are hereby required to see this·order duly and fully executed. And this Court, being of opinion that no gentleman will take it amiss to be intreated to promote and give his help to so publick and so good a work, hath thought fit to nominate for each parish within this Hundred of Derby, severall gentlemen, and to desire them, or any two or more of them, to call before them the respective overseers of the highwayes within each townshipp within the said parishes, and with them to inspect the severall highways, and, upon their view, to direct each overseer, within his particular precinct, what reformation, according to the Court's direction before herein specifyed, is to be made in all points, and how, and in whatt manner, the said overseer, with the aid of the inhabitants, shall proceed. And that the said gentlemen, or some of them, will please to have sometimes an eye to the said works, whilst they are in doing. And will, at the next sessions after Michaelmas next, certify this Court how this work is, in all or in part, performed, and which of the said overseers or inhabitants have been remiss or faulty, and how, or what part, of the wages or work, is neglected or omitted, and why, that the Court may, at the said next sessions, take such further course thereupon as the case shall require; and to these ends, the Court hath thought fitt to nominate for the said severall parishes, the persons following, viz. :—

"For the parish of Wygan :—Thomas Gerrard, Esquire ; William Standish, Esquire ; Philip Langton, Esquire ; William Bankes, Esquire ; Thomas Ashurst, Esquire ; Birtie Entwisle, Esquire ; Peter Holington, Esquire ; Mr. Thomas Ince, Mr. Peter Worthington, Mr. Robert Markland, Mr. Peter Catterall, Mr. Thomas Blackburne.

"Winwick :—Peter Legh, Esquire ; John Rizley, Esquire ; John Byron, Esquire ; Thomas Bretherton, Esquire ; Mr. John Lander, Mr. Jonathan Blackburne, Mr. John Widdowes, Mr. George Sorocold, Mr. Hamlett Woods, Mr. Legh Bowden.

"Prescott :—Peter Bold, Esquire ; John Byrom, Esquire ; Edward Ogle, Esquire ; Stephen Alcock, Esquire ; Mr. John Right, Mr. Peter Marsh, Mr. Edmund Taylor, Mr. Jonathan Care.

"Walton : — The Honourable William Molineux ; Edward Ogle, Esquire ; Stephen Alcock, Esquire ; Oliver Lyme, Esquire ; Silvester Richmond, Esquire ; Mr. Robert Breeres, Mr. Thomas Fletcher.

"Ormeskirke :—Sir Thomas Stanley, Baronet ; John Entwisle, Esquire ; Thomas Dod, Esquire ; Stephen Alcock, Esquire ; John Ashton, Esquire ; Mr. Samuel Andrewes, Mr. John Shawe, Mr. James Holland.

"Warrington :—Peter Bold, Esquire ; John Ashton, Esquire ; Robert, Lord Burlegh ; Mr. Richard Howorth, Mr. Thomas Chadwick.

"Legh :—William Hilton, Esquire ; John Rizley, Esquire ; Richard Stanley, Esquire ; Thomas Mort, Esquire ; Roger Kenyon, Esquire ; Mr. Alexander Ratcliffe, Mr. Rizley Brown, Mr. John Sorocold.

"Childwall :—Thomas Norres, Esquire ; John Harrington, Esquire ; Mr. Thomas Cooke, Mr. William Wainwright.

"Hyton :—John Harrington, Esquire ; Mr. Robert Roper, Mr. Henry Orme, Mr. Martin Willis, Mr. Henry Lathom, Mr. John Wright.

"Halsall :—Sir Charles Anderton, Baronet ; Robert Molineux, Esquire ; Mr. Thomas Bootle, Mr. John Tatlock, Mr. William Male, Mr. Peter Marsh, Mr. Robert Bootle, Mr. Thomas Lidiate.

"Sephton:—The Honorable William Molineux; Henry Blundell, Esquire; William Blundell, the younger, Esquire; Mr. William Byron, Mr. Thomas Bootle, Mr. Robert Breeres, Mr. John Johnson.

"Aughton:—Edward Stanley, Esquire; Mr. Alexander Hesketh, Mr. Roger Bostock, Mr. William Jameson, Mr. Thomas Lidiate, Mr. John Bamber, Mr. Roger Pye.

"Northmeales: — Barnaby Hesketh, Esquire; James Gorsuch, Esquire; Mr. Richard Formby, Mr. Nicholas Fazakerley.

"Alker:—Mr. Nicholas Fazakerley, Mr. Thomas Tickle, Mr. Thomas Bootle.

"And it is lastly ordered that the high constables of the Hundred of Derby shall forthwith issue copies of this order at large, to be sent to some of the said gentlemen herein named, of each parish within the said Hundred, to be communicated to the rest within his parish respectively."

[Similar Order, made at Manchester, on the 19th of July, 1688, for the Hundred of Salford.]

"Manchester:—Edmund Trafford, Esquire; Edward Moseley, Esquire; John Barlowe, Esquire; John Hartley, Esquire; James Lightboune, Esquire; George Pigot, Esquire; Joseph Yates, Esquire; Oswald Mosley, Esquire; Mr. James Chetham, Captaine Thomas Dicconson, Mr. Edward Bootle, Mr. William Ashton, Mr. Ralph Stopford, Mr. Ralph Worsley, Mr. John Newton, Mr. Henry Dicconson, Mr. Robert Lichford.

"Eccles:—Edmund Trafford, Esquire; Peter Egerton, Esquire; William Hulme, of Davyhulme, Esquire; Richard Stanley; Roger Kenyon, Esquire; Thomas Sorocold, Esquire; Mr. Francis Sherington, Mr. Edward Valentine, Mr. Richard Lightboune, Mr. Robert Edge, Mr. William Cooke.

"Flixton:—Peter Egerton, Esquire; William Hulme, Esquire; John Isherwood, Clerk; Mr. Roger Rogers, Mr. Henry Knight.

"Prestwich:—Sir John Egerton, Baronet; William Hulme, of Kearsley, Esquire; William Ashton, Clerk; Thomas Serjeant, Esquire; John Dantesey, Esquire; Rawstorne Lever, Esquire; Mr. Adam Gartside, Mr. Henry Colborne, Mr. Thomas Harrison.

"Dean:—The Honourable Hugh Willoughby; Sir Charles Anderton, Baronet, William Hilton, Esquire; William Hulme, Esquire; Roger Kenyon, Esquire; Mr. William Legh, Mr. Nathaniel Molineux, of Westhoughton, Mr. John Johnson, of Halliwill, Mr. John Johnson, of Westhoughton, Mr. Thomas Briggs.

"Bolton:—The Honourable Hugh Willoughby; Sir Charles Anderton, Baronet; William Hilton, Esquire; John Bradshaw, Esquire; James Chetham, Esquire; Thomas Lever, Esquire; Roger Kenyon, Esquire; Nicholas Starky, Esquire; Mr. Ralph Egerton, Dr. Grundy, Mr. Thomas Marsden, Mr. John Andrews, Mr. Thomas Smith, Mr. Nathaniel Molineux, Mr. James Crompton, Mr. Edward Richardson, Mr. Robert Roscoe, junior, Mr. George Smith, Mr. Thomas Briggs.

"Bury:—Thomas Greenhalgh, Esquire; Richard Holt, Esquire; Thomas Gipps, Clerk; John Lomax, Clerk; Mr. John Allen, Mr. Peter Holt, Mr. Richard Lomax, Mr. Edmund Bury, Mr. Thomas Nuttall, Nicholas Starky, Esquire; Mr. Robert Roscoe.

"Ratchdale: — James Holt, Esquire; Alexander Butterworth, Esquire; Henry Howorth, Esquire; Richard Entwisle, Esquire; Henry Pigot, Clerk; Mr. James Scholefeild, Mr. Richard Ingham, Mr. Samuel Hamer.

" Ouldham :—Sir Ralph Ashton, Baronet; Richard Ashton, Esquire; Joshua Horton, Esquire ; Joseph Greg, Esquire ; Isaack Harpur, Clerk.

" Middleton:—Sir Ralph Ashton, Barronet; Richard Ashton, Esquire; John Hopwood, the younger, Esquire; Richard Warburton, Clerk ; Henry Wrigley, Esquire; Mr. James Hilton.

" Ratcliffe:—Mr. Jervase Staynrod, Mr. Henry Coulborne, Mr. John Allen, Roger Walker.

" Ashton :—John Ashton, Esquire ; Mr. Jonathan Pickford, Mr. John Chadwick, Mr. Ralph Sandiforth, Mr. William Stopford, Mr. Ralph Stopford, Mr. Lawrence Right, Mr. Edward Roe, Mr. John Heywood."

ROGER KENYON to his father, ROGER KENYON, at Peel.

630. 1688, July 31. Cambridge.—" All our public papers are full of a speedy Parliament, and all possible care is taking here, by regulations, one after another, that such members may be elected that will remove these troublesome laws. All my little knowledge that way, teaches me that it was usually the business of Parliaments to enact and establish laws ; but I believe this will be the only one whose main end and design must be, to abrogate and overturn them. There was one piece of news, last post, which made me sweat, and, at the same time, think of you; it was [that] there is a design to have a general regulation of justices and clerks of peace, through the whole kingdom. This, though it is not altogether improbable, yet, for your sake, I hope it is absolutely false. . . . . . Dr. Gower (who, I think, is the only man you are acquainted with), was lately, upon the death of the divinity professor for the Lady Margaret, chosen by the University into that place." *Seal of arms.*

HENRY ROWE to " MR. KENYON."

631. 1688, September 6. [Wigan.]—I came into town before the election of the Mayor. The present Mayor went into Court at twelve, with Mr. Mollineux, Mr. Spencer, and several other gentlemen of their persuasion. The Court was called, the Jury sworn, and the charge given by Mr. James Anderton; after that, the Court was adjourned till three o'clock, with proclamation that the Mayor would go to election at two o'clock, and so rise to dinner at their coming to election. The Common Council, by whom he is to be chosen, were for Mr. Scott; but Mr. Mayor, and the others of his side, would not admit of election, but adjourned the Court till the 24th of this month, leaving behind him the staff, mace, and sword. And so the honest burgesses, I mean the Common Council men of the town, met together, after the Mayor was gone out of the town, and chose Mr. Alderman Scott to be Mayor, who was sworn by the Common Council with the greatest joy that ever was at the election of a mayor in Wigan. He was conducted to his house by Sir Edward Chisenhale, Mr. Bankes of Winstanley, and several other gentlemen.

THOMAS BRADDYLL to ROGER KENYON.

632. 1688, September 15. Portfeild.—Last night I received a letter from my son, stating that Mr. Preston of Holker, and Mr. Rowlinson of Carke, design to stand as burgesses for Lancaster. *Seal of arms.*

GEORGE ALLANSON to ROGER KENYON, at Peel.

633. 1688, September 25. [London.]—" Wee have scurvey newes here, that the Dutchy (*sic*) are out with a very great fleet and 23,000 land souldiers, and intend for England, which I hope not, if God keeps out the French." *Seal of arms.*

The EARL OF DUNMORE to [the EARL OF DERBY].

634. [1688,] September 25.—"The report of the Prince of Orange's landing, drives all thoughts of standing for Parliament out of my head. I do not know, as yet, what I shall be commanded. All officers are ordered to their quarters; great many companyes of foot and troopes of horse are raiseing. Here has beene the D[uke] of S[hrewsbury] with the King, and some other people of quality, about it. By the last express from Holland, there is now no doubt made but the designe is against us, which gives a very hot alarm, they being ready to saile." *Copy.*

The SAME to the SAME.

634A. [1688,] October 1.—"I received your Lordship's letters yesterday, by Mr. Corbett, and told the King of your readiness to serve him, which he was extreamely pleased with, and commanded me to tell you so, and that he would have you come up as soone as possible. I am sure you will receive all the markes of his kindness you can desire. I cannot help adding how much I was satisfyed with the King's obligeing way of receiveing your offers, which I assure you was very extraordinary. When you come up, you will find very different measures taken towards (*sic*) those practised, when you was last here, which is a great joy to us all. The particulars I cannot tell you, but some I will. The Bishop of London is restored. I am told Magdalene Colledge will be. The Bishopps that were in disgrace, have beene with the King, and are very well satisfyed of the assurances he has given them; but tomorrowe, they are to meet againe, and then wee shall know more particularly. Every post brings us newse of the great preparations are made in Holland for the invasion, but the wind has been contrary, which has hindered them from coming out, if they were ready, which I hear tonight they are not. Our forces are in so good order and so much encreased, that I believe they will find it very difficult, if not impossible, to compasce their designe, especially since there is a fleet out, which my Lord Dartmouth goes tomorrow to command. Other newes your messenger will inform you." *Copy.*

The COUNTESS OF DERBY to "MY LORD [DERBY]."

634B. [1688,] October 1.—"Last night I saw the King in the draweing roome. He came and told me you had offered your service, which he said he tooke very kindly, and thanked you for it." *Copy.*

The EARL OF DUNMORE to the EARL OF DERBY.

634C. [1688,] October 4.—"I have but just time to tell your Lordship that all those which wish you well here, are impatient to have you come up; for I am againe bid to assure you of all kindnesse imaginable from the Court. Things begin to change mightily, for the Church of England is wholly trusted; the Charter of London is restored, which will be followed, I believe, by doing the same thing to other citys. The Bishopps are every day with the King. Wee hear no more newes of the Dutch, the wind being contrary." *Copy sent to Roger Kenyon.*

635. 1688, September 28 to November 21.—" A DIARY or memorye [in the handwriting of Roger Kenyon] where my Lord Derby has been each day, with some observations of what he hath transacted on several accounts, and how corresponded, since the day before Michaelmas last, 1688.

"September 28. At Knowsley.—This day hee sent his servant, Mr. Corbet, post to London with a letter to the Lord [Dunmore], to make his complement to the King, haveing heard his Majestie was pleased to restore him to his leiftenancies; another letter to one of the seven Bishopps, to desire from his Lordshipp to be informed of the true state of affaires, and to have his advice.

" September 29. *Ibidem.*—[No entry.]

"September 30. *Ibidem.*—This day, his Lordship directed the Clerk of the Peace to observe what Popish justices came to the session, which were to begin at Lancaster the next day but one; what measures they took; what publick orders they made; and to give his Lordshipp an account.

" October 1. *Ibidem.*—This day, my Lord [Dunmore] writ to my Lord Derby that the King desired my Lord Derby to come up as soon as possible ; adding, that when my Lord did come, he would find very different measures taken towards those practized when my Lord Derby was last there, which was a great joy to them all, viz. : that the Bishopp of London was restored, that Magdalen Colledge would be, that the seven Bishops were much satisfyed with the assurances his Majesty had given them.

" October 2. *Ibidem.*—[No entry.]

" October 3. *Ibidem.*—This day, Mr. Corbet returned with letters *ut supra*, &c.

" October 4. *Ibidem.*—This day, my Lord [Dunmore] writ againe to my Lord Derby, all those who wish you well here, are impatient to have you come up; things change mightily, the Church of England is wholly trusted; the Charter of London is restored ; the like wilbe done to other cities and burrowes; the Bishops are every day with the King.

" October 5. *Ibidem.*—This day, his Lordship received a retorne from the Bishopp, and other letters adviseing him to come up ; and [that], at this time, the cuntry in generall were wonderously glad to hear his Lordship would be restored.

" October 6. *Ibidem.*—His Lordshipp was now preparing for his jorney ; and, this day, he received an account from the Sessions, &c.

" October 7. *Ibidem.*—This day, amongst other preparations, which he would not be unready with, at his waiteing upon the King, to deale dutifully and plainely with his Majestie, when, in secret, hee took a paper to this effect, amongst his remembrances.

" Things which much dissatisfy his Majestie's Protestant subjects.

" The removeall of officers without any falt charged upon them, both military and civil, and placeing men unqualifyed by law, in their roomes; and the illegall and maleadministrations of such officers.

" The extravagant methods practised by the new magistrates in the ancient loyall corporations, contrary to the expresse concessions in their charters, to the ruine of the burrows [and] destructive of the government thereof.

" That if his Majestie would please to have the cases truly stated, and sent up from Wigan, Liverpoole, and Preston, the retornes to be made by the displaced officers, and truly done at their perills.

" That the Protestant gentry will not, can not, joyne in Lancashire, in the execution of any office, with such as will not qualify themselves to act according to law

" That the popish clergie so bussie themselves in secular affaires, no
way relateing to their function, that they are grevvouse to his Majestie's
Protestant, and vexatiouse to his Romane Catholique, subjects.

" That these persons, and his Majestie's new made justices, have made
frequent adresses to his Majestie egregiously abusive, by false represen-
tations of things, quite contrary to the dispositions of the generality of
his subjects.

" October 8. At Sir Willowby Aston's house.—This day, his Lordshipp begun his jorney from Knowsley towards London.

" October 9. At Newport.—Thence he writes to have 2 pads bought,
to be ready at his retorne into Lancashire, haveing a prospect of his
much rideing.

" October 10–13 [blank].

" October 14. At London.—This being the King's birthday, and his
Lordship in mourneing, hee went not to Court.

" October 15. *Ibidem.*—This day his Lordship kissed the King's hand ;
his Majestie telling him he had sent for him to restore him to his
lieftenencies of Cheshire and Lancashire ; and after about an bower's
discourse, the King desired his Lordshipp to hasten his visits in town
and to see the King againe, so soon as those were over, and then, as
speedily to retorne. This day his Lordshipp was well welcomed to
town, by some of the Lords.

" October 16. *Ibidem.*—[No entry.]

" October 17. *Ibidem.*—This, and the two former days, his Lordshipp
made his visits to the lords, his relations and acquaintance in town,
who, understanding he was to be restored to the lieftenancies of the
countys of Lancaster and Chester, the one abounding with papists, and
both neer neighbors to Ireland, thought it a good hit to gaine that post
to out the two popeish Lords, and deemed it adviseable to act with that
caution as not to have his commission withdrawn, but authoritatively to
gaine and preserve a power to secure the quiet of those countyes, and
haveing raised the militia, who were eager to follow him, hee might
raise, upon occasion, those and the more northern countys; no man of
note to hinder him. Some of these Lords, then desired the Lord Derby
would correspond with the Lord Delamer. Whilst my Lord was at
London, the proclamation for restoreing Corporations came forth.

" October 18. *Ibidem.*—This day, my Lord Derby waited againe on
his Majestie, who received his Lordship with much respect, closetted
him for some time, but without one word of religion ; told him hee was
a Stanley, that his ancesters were ever loyal, that his Majestie had been
abused with false reports of him, that he did now restore him, and, that
no time might be lost, would have him presently on his jorney home-
ward, and that it should be his Majestie's care to speed his commission
after him, that it should be more large then any former had been, that
he expected his Lordshipp's great care to keep his two countyes in quiet,
and preserve the peace there. His Lordshipp told him hee would do his
utmost to do that, acting according to law. The same day, and next
morning, his Lordship revisited his friends, &c., and left London.

" October 19–23 [blank].

" October 24 and 25. At Knowsley.—[No entry.]

" October 26. *Ibidem.*—His Lordshipp, this day, writ to all his old
deputy-lieftenants that were able, and for Lancashire, to come to him to
Knowsley the Thursday, following, viz. *primo Novembris,* to prepare for
matters, after allmost 4 years discontinuance, many of the militia
officers being, by death or otherwise, removed.

" October 27. *Ibidem.*—This day, his Lordshipp received an Order,
with the Privy-Counsell's signatures affixed, signed by his Majestie's

own hand, and subsigned 'Sunderland,' stileing his Lordshipp lord-lief-tenant of the countyes of Chester and Lancashire, empowering him, as such, to raise the militia, all or part, with a large power, discretionarily to act for preservation of his Majestie's peace and the security and quiet of the 2 countys, to hinder any from raiseing officers, except by his Majestie's Commission. Note.—That before this ·time, Collonel Gage and his officers had Comissions, and had raised their cudgellery *(sic)* in Lancashire and Cheshire which were quartered in several townes in both countyes. Note, also that, as yet, his Lordshipp's Comission as lord lieftenant was not come to him.

"October 2&. *Ibidem.*—[No entry.]

"October 29. *Ibidem.*—This day, his Lordshipp's Comission for his Lieftenency not being comme, (which delay happened by my Lord Sunderland's being displaced before it could be ready, as was and is supposed) his Lordshipp sent Mr. Corbet againe, post to London, for it; with letters to the Lord Preston, then Secretary, and letters to the Duke of Ormond and Lord Rochester concerning the same.

"October 30. *Ibidem.*—This day, the Lord Derby sent to the Lord Delamer to desire a better correspondence betwixt them two, and to ask where, when, and how, they might meet. My Lord Delamer appointed to meet at Bold, the next day but one. This day, the Lord Derby sent by the post to Mr. Tench, the names of his intended deputy-lieftenants for both countys, to be approved of by the King and to have a Comission by his Majestie's direction to gentlemen in the cuntry to take his Lordshipp's oath, and for Mr. Tench to solicit these and send them down by Mr. Corbet.

"October 31. *Ibidem.*—This day, his Lordshipp writt to all those he had named in Cheshire for his deputy-lieftenants, to give him the meeting at Northwich in Cheshire, that day senight.

"November 1. *Ibidem.*—This day, the Lord Delamer met my Lord Derby at Bold, where they spent some time in secret discourse, and imparted to each their severall ways of acting, my Lord Delamer declareing his great satisfaction in that meeting; my Lord Derby haveing there told him more than he durst, at that time, do to his own deputy-lieftenants. This evening, my Lord Derby and his deputy-lieftenants for Lancashire, met at Knowsley.

"November 2. *Ibidem.*—His Lordship shewed these deputies the aforesaid order of the 19th of October. They were willing to serve him as deputies, but were all of opinyon, neither he ought to act till his Comission came and that hee had taken his oath, nor that they could act, till the King had approved them, his Lordship given them Comissions, and they taken their oathes. His Lordshipp then, that no time might be lost, directed them to enquire and informe him, from the majors of the severall regiments, and others, how many of the old officers were in being and fit and willing to serve, and to find fit persons to supply the vacancies of the rest.

"November 3. *Ibidem.*—This day, Major Farrington, Major Preston, and Mr. Copley were with his Lordshipp, to give names to supply vacancies. This day, Captain Oldfield was there, about their Cheshire concernes, for the militia of Cheshire. This day, Councellor Mort was there, sent for to advise how farr his Lordshipp might legaliy act, if occasion should be, before the Commission came. All resolve they would, if great occasion should be, act by it; but could not raise money for the militia, without the Comission. Mr. Bankes and R[oger] K[enyon] then there.

"November 4. *Ibidem.*—All the said company, save Captain Oldfield, this day took seale of his Lordship.

"November 5. *Ibidem.*—This day, the Prince of Orange landed at Dartmouth.

"November 6. *Ibidem.*—[No entry.]

"November 7. At Leftwich.—And this day, met the Cheshire deputy lieftenants at Northwich, whom his Lordshipp acquainted with what had been done, and that hee would send them deputations when his Comission came, which he dayly expected &c. and, that no time might be lost, that, in the meantime, they would consider and send him the names of fit officers to be comissionated (*sic*) by him, which they promised, but did not performe.

"November 8. At Knowsley.—This day, his Comission came to him, whilst at Leftwich; as also his Majestie's approbation of all the deputy lieftenants of both countys—29 in number; and a Comission to Lancashire gentlemen to take his oath. The Comission beares date the 25th of October. And by the laches of the Clerk of the Crown, the new Secretary, knowing nothing of it, had been so delayed.

"November 9. *Ibidem.*—This day, my Lord Derby was sworne Lord-Lieftenant of both countys.

"November 10–13. *Ibidem.*—These 4 days, my Lord's Secretary had 4 or 5 clerks, close at work, who made ready 29 deputations for the deputy lieftenants, and fixed his Lordshipp's large seale thereunto; all which, his Lordshipp, this day, signed, and afterwards gave comissions to, and swore 3 Lancashire deputy lieftenants, one lieftenant-collonel, and 3 captaines.

"November 14. *Ibidem.*—This day, the said deputations for all the deputy-lieftenants of Cheshire were sent and actually delivered to them, and they were at this time writ to, to speed the names of the militia officers for that county that were to be comissionated by his Lordship, and all his Lordshipp's men close at work, to make ready 80 comissions, with blankes, for the militia commission officers of both countyes.

"November 15. *Ibidem.*—This day, the deputations were accordingly sent to the rest of the deputy-lieftenants of Lancashire, and all of them were writ to that they, and all the comission officers of the Lancashire militia, would meet his Lordship at Preston, the then next Wensday, to receive their comissions and take their oath. This day, the Lord Delamer raised his tenants, and others, in Warrington, Manchester, and Ashton; and, to encourage them to rise with him, publickly did declare that my Lord Derby would go the same way. Which publication, hee knew, was against my Lord Derby's designe that that should be so soon known, for it did much startle severall of the deputy-lieftenants, and of the militia officers, in both countys, and rendered them, in Cheshire especially, very averse and backward in raiseing their militia.

"November 16. *Ibidem.*—The Lord Delamer was, with his new levies, at Boden Downes, in Cheshire. This day, Sir William Gerard sent to my Lord Derby the Lord Delamer's speech, which his servant had fixed on the crosse at Warrington. There was no secret in it, and to avoide the suspicion of confederacie, my Lord Derby sent it to the then Secretary, Lord Preston.

"November 17. *Ibidem.*—This day, my Lord Derby had an information in writing, and the informer sent with it from Wigan, that a soldier, sick and likely to dye, had declared to his landlady that his conscience durst not let him dye, without revealeing that there was a designe amongst the soldiers, against the Lord Derby, to take him prisoner, but hee feared to kill him; and that the soldiers were for this purpose, in the dead of the night, to march, without beat of drum, secretly, from Wigan to Knowsley, the next night. My Lord Derby hereupon set his tenants and servants to keep a strong guard in and about his house, and sent two of his servants, in the evening, with the paper to have the Mayor examine the sick soldier and the woman; and if they heard of any soldiers comeing, to be back before them and give notice.

"It was within night when my Lord's servants came to Wigan, and the guard took them and their paper at the guard-house; it was carryed to the collonels and captaines, and no examinations at that time taken upon it, nor till the sick soldier had been taught a new lessen, which was, that the soldiers, some of them, had said that if they thought my Lord Derby was in combination with my Lord Delamer, as my Lord Delamer had affirmed, that they would march to Knowsley and take or kill his Lordshipp; but true it was, the soldiers were up that night before day, and before sunrise did march out of town towards Liverpool, and on their way thither, were within a myle of Knowsley, and the common soldiers were heard to say (as it is probable they thought) they were going to Knowsley, though they did not come there at all. At this time, Collonel Gage's regiment had no arms, except one Captaine Moor's company, which was raised about London and sent down; but there were armes, about this very day, came to Chester for them, and were afterwards sent thence to them to Liverpoole. At this time, Captaine Ashurst, his foot company of the Militia, good men and well armed, were raised, and lay at Preston neer Knowsley.

"November 18. *Ibidem.*— This day, Collonel Gage, Captaine Tildesley, and other officers of that regiment, went to Knowsley, to dine with my Lord Derby and excuse themselves for not haveing waited on his Lordship sooner, and to beg his Lordshipp's beleefe that there was in none of their officers any ill-intention towards his Lordship. However, my Lord Derby was alarmed with the like report from Gage's soldiers, then at Liverpoole, and, to prevent danger, went that night to Winstanley."

"November 19. [At] Winstanley.—[No entry.]

"November 20. At Astley.—This day, my Lord sent commissions to the militia officers of the county of the city of Chester, and ordered the militia of the city to be forthwith raised and in readynesse for the defence of Chester Castle, if need were, there being a good understanding betwixt his Lordship and the governor. And this day, his Lordship writ to the governor, to meet him at Warrington the then next Friday. This day Lieftenant-Colonell Sir Richard Standish his foot company, were raised and quartered at Wigan."

"November 21. At Preston.—This day, his Lordshipp met all the deputy-lieftenants and all comission officers of the militia, who received their comissions and took their oaths; and now all the militia was ordered, forthwith, to be raised. This day, Captain Bold's troop was raised, and guarded my Lord into Preston. Captain Longworth's foot company raised and quartered in Preston; Collonel Rigby's regiment to be all forthwith raised, to lye, part in Lancaster, part in Preston; Collonel Nowell's regiment to go to Manchester; my Lord's own regiment of foot to be at Ormskirk, Prescot, Wigan, and two companys at Warrington which were ordered, if any force were heard of, to come against Dunham, to draw thither forthwith in defence of that house and family; and that speedy notice should be given to my Lord, who would follow them with sufficient force. This was somewhat beyond what the Militia Act appoints—that the force of one county do not march out of the county without the King's speciall order; wherefore, the aforesaid direction was probably given. The like direction was intended to be given at Manchester. Warrington is but 6 myles, and Manchester but 6 myles or 7, from Dunham, on each side it."

Dorothy Lagoe to Roger Kenyon.

636. 1688, October 11.—"The 3rd of August, John Digle, a callender man, one of the overseers of the highways, required a lay of mee for the higheway. I refused to pay it, and hee took a pewter dish out of my howse and said Mr. Kenyon could not bring mee off for this, if hee could for other layes." *Seal.*

Laurence Rawstorne to Roger Kenion.

637. 1688, October 16. Preston.—" The busines of this day has been a consultation of the Lord-Leivetenant and his deputies, and what the result of that is, wee poor inferiours know not; but the matter of your enquiry I suppose to be how the old deputy leivetenants came of. There was no more then Mr. Fleetwood, Colonel Rigby, and Cousin Preston, who, after they had dyned at [the] 'Mitre' together, came to resolve that they would waite on his Lordship and give this answer, (to wit) that in regard they had been formerly under the Lord of Derbye's command and that they understood hee was in the King's favour againe, they thought hee might comand their service, and they were ready and willing to serve his Majesty, in what capacity soever, to testifie their loyallty, but would not take commissions at present, till they heard from him ; with some other more pleasant words and expressions then I can give and would be tedious to relate, for I had it but at second hand and am imperfect in it. Cousin Preston had received his commission and returned it then, which my Lord said was strange, after acceptance ; his Lordship being in a jocose and pleasant humour, and Captain Greenhalgh had the same fate and sent his man with his, which was received. The conclusion was that hee dranke the King's health to them and wished, as they had been friends, they might part in charity. This small account accept, and for the news I suppose you have it, onely wee have 3,000 Scotch foot under Leivtenant General Douglas will be with us tomorrow, and wee hope will but stay one night." *Seal of arms.*

Nathaniel Molyneux to Roger Kenyon.

638. 1688, October 18. London.—"As to forraigne newes, and domestick alsoe, it is so various, that wee cannot tell what to creditt. Wednesday night last, and most of yesterday, it went for current that the Dutch was landed at Sole Bay, but proves a meere roman[ce]. The truest newes, and that which wee moste confyde in, is that . . . . . was appointed a publike fast throughout Holland to implore [God's] assistance and blessinge upon their designes, in the defence of the protestant religion, till which was over, the Prince resolved not to way anchor, or put to sea; soe that, it is concluded, they sayled not till today, or last night. It is sed, by all inteligence that comes from good handes, that the Prince has great forcses, both of foot and exelent horse, far more then our newes makes it, or the common report. Their navy consists (besydes an expectation, or rather an assurance, of 20 saile of Swedes ships) of 87 men-of-warr above . . . . . shipps and att leaste 400 flatt bottomes and good shipps that . . . . . them for carryinge men and horse. The great los that was said they sustained by the stres of wether, is a meere storye, all falce. Their navye is in excellent good order, and everything in good redines. Prince and all imbarke, but not one word sed there what their designe is, or whear their tradeinge voyige lyes. Our Dutch Embassador assures the Kinge they have noe designe against him, and pawns his head out, but if he forfeit yt, you know it is pretty secure, because hee is what hee is. I hope it will prove as hee ses, and that they are not so foolehardy as to atack us, who are soe strong, potent, and in such an equipage that wee are able almoste to blowe them home againe. The King (*laus Deo*) is in good health, and Prince of Wales alsoe, who was christened this weeke—Jacobus Franciscus Edwardus. The Pope and French King wear his godfathers, and Queen Dowager, godmother. There has been great pressinge hear of late, both for sea and land. A great army the King has, and in good equipage, and great preparations hee makes of wagons, and in all other respects, that such an ocasione requires for carryinge all warlike instruments to destroy theis fooles, forraigners, and strangers that cannot be soe wyse as to stay in their own countrye. And now, Sir, I thinke you have newes enough to fill, till theis madmen invade us, and then (if I continue hear soe long) will tell you both of their landinge and sending home again (if not well maunered)."

Postscript.—"Lord Derby is in *statu quo prius*—has his commission again of Lord-Leivetenant, as I am informed by a very good hand." *Seal of arms.*

WARRANT by JAMES II. to the EARL OF DERBY.

639. 1688, October 19. Whitehall.—" Whereas wee find it necessary, upon this intended invasion, that the kingdom should be in a posture of defence, Wee doe hereby authorise and require you, forthwith, to raise such part of the horse militia, as you think requisite, for preventing evill disposed persons to goe to the enemy, and for securing the peace and quiet of the country; leaving it to you, upon any exigency that may happen, to raise such part of the foot militia as you shall think necessary for the purposes aforesaid. And our further pleasure is, that in case you shall find that any person, of what quality soever, endeavoring to raise, without a comission from us, or doeing any thing else which may disturb the peace of our government, you forthwith give orders for seizing and securing the said persons, with their adherents and accomplices. And we doe also authorise and require you to doe what you shall further think requisite for our service and the security and peace of those parts, relying entirely upon your prudence and conduct." *Copy.*

WILLIAM B[ANKES] to ROGER KENYON.

640. 1688, October 23. Wigan.—" The Corporation here is going about this afternoon to place their old aldermen and officers. My sister, Betty Leigh, writes me a piece of news which looks strange, but I will venture it with you : that the Lord Sunderland and his Lady are said to be gone into Holland, and that our great Lord Chancellor would have a quicks (*sic*)." *Seal.*

THOMAS BRADDYLL to ROGER KENYON.

641. 1688, October 25. Portfield.—" On Saturday, we received the unwelcome news of the death of my little grandson at Connishead, who died on 19th instant, of convulsions. We have very good news of my Lord of Derby, that he hath a commission for Lord-Lieutenant of Lancashire and Cheshire, which rejoices the hearts of the generalities of the country, for the red-letter men talk very high. Young Townley, of Townley, is raising a troop of horse, and Mr. Holman, your acquaintance of London, is his colonel." *Portion of seal.*

DRAFT of a PETITION, giving particulars of a dispute between the EARL OF DERBY and LORD DELAMERE.

642. 1688, October to December.—" In October last, when the late King had apprehensions of the then Prince of Orange his preparations for coming into England, he, observeing he had put the lieftenancy of Cheshire and Lancashire into unserviceable bandes, thought fitt to restore them to the Earle of Derby; for, in that family, they had both been for many generations, some hundreds of years.

" The Earle of Derby, consulting with such as were promoters of the then Prince of Orange his interposing to redress the kingdom's greevances, they concluded it was very adviseable to reaccept the late King's comission for his lieftenancies, which the Earle of Derby himselfe had possessed 13 yeares; for, thereby, he would be enabled to secure those two countys, which were not onely most pestered with papists, but likeliest to be the inlets of the Ireish. The late King desired the Earle of Derby to go down to those countys, and sent him first a warrant to raise all or part of the militia for preservation of the peace, and after, a comission for the lieftenancy of both countys.

" 30 October, 1688.—The Earl of Derby, when in the country, kept an intimate correspondence with his freinds above, and being thence informed of the Lord Delamer's complyance, sent to desire a meeteing.

" 1 November.--These two Lords met, had secret discourse some howers, [and] imparted, each to other, diverse wayes to manage themselves. The Earle of Derby's part was to be acted with secrecie, least his comissions might be recalled; and in raiseing the militia, to comisionate such as might be relied on, or as time might work upon, and not to declare till things were riper.

" The Lord Delamer's undertaking was to rise so soon as newse came of the Prince's landing; of which the Earle of Derby was to take no notice, till the Lord Delamere was gone. The Earle of Derby, when the militia were raised, to quarter some near the Lord Delamere's house, with private intimation to secure it and the family.

" 15 November.—The Lord Delamere writt to the Earle of Derby that he was riseing.

" 16 November.—The Lord Delamere randevouzed his men on Boden Downes, and (perhaps to encourage them to come in) gave it out that the Earle of Derby would go the same way, which report alarumed his neighbouring intended deputy-lieftenents, and somewhat impeded their proceeding, haveing not yet been all acquainted with what was intended to be done.

" 19 November —Being but two days after the Lord Delamere's going, the Lady Delamer sent to Knowsley, the Earle of Derby's house, his Lordshipp being then abroad; her gentleman publickly told it there, that the Earle of Derby had promised to quarter part of the militia at Altringham in defence of Lord Delamere's house; which was a second publication of what was promised to be kept secret.

" 24 November.—The Earl of Derby met Mr. Shakerley, then governor of Chester Castle. who secretly corresponded with his Lordshipp to secure that castle; and the Earle of Derby then gave him orders to raise the militia of the city of Chester forthwith, for his assistance. The same day, the Earle of Derby sent, by Mr. Birlow, to the Lady Delamere to assure her of his constant care for her safety; that she had been, and should be, ever in his care, and that her house Dunham should be so, as much as Knowsley.

" 26 November.—The Earle of Derby sent severall foot companies to quarter at Warrington, five miles from the Lord Delamere's house, and one foot company at Manchester, within 6 miles of the Lord Delamer's house, who had secret orders that if any force were observed to draw towards Dunham, they should imediately march thither to defend it ; and himselfe, upon notice, would forthwith follow with his troopes.

"27 November.—Colonel Gage his Romish regiment, raised in Lancashire, before the militia was raised, grew uneasie (though they were not yet disturbed) of being in that county, and went to Chester ; and comeing thither in the night, the City militia being in armes, they were forced to be put and kept in the old town hall for that night, and not received into any quarters.

" Before this time, the Earle of Derby had comissionated 29 deputy-leiftenants, all Protestant gentlemen of best quality and interest in the two countyes, and comissionated fitt persons for militia officers in both countyes, and raised, besides the militia of the City of Chester, 4 good and great regiments of foot and 5 troopes of horse, all which, in convenient time, did unanimously declare for his Highness the Prince of Orange ; and the declaration proclaimed in the head of every troop and company.

"15 December.—All the country was greatly alarmed with the noyse of the Ireish Papists, burneing and killing all before them. The Earle of Derby thereupon, forthwith, with his own hand, writt and sent to the Lady Delamere to assure her that in this exigencie, she should assuredly find his particular assistance, and that he would send her what force she thought needfull to secure her person and house.

"16 December.—The Earle of Derby received a letter, which was sent open, or opened by the way, and copies taken before it came to his Lordshipp. It is the Lord Delamere's own hand in these words, viz :—

Superscribed.
' For the Earle of Derby at Knowsley in Lancashire.

' MY LORD,   December 10th.
 Had I foreseen how backward your Lordshipp is in doing your part, I should have told your Lordshipp that it was not worth the while to mention your name to the Prince ; for you cannot forgett you promised to raise the militia imediately, and to quarter Bucklow Hundred at Altrincham, and that if, in case the Papists comitted any outrage, or rose in armes, that then you would fall upon them and leave neither root nor branch. How farr you have made this good, your Lordship can best tell ; but I hear, that on the 3rd instant, no militia of Buckley Hundred was up, and, though the Papists made an attempt to burn my house, yet I don't hear of any resentment your Lordship has expressed against it. Your Lordship must think you cannot be esteemed by the Prince, or those with him, as a man that has given any assistance to the cause, and I beleeve the nation will have the same opinion of you. But God be praised, we need none of your help, or, if we be distressed, wee shall not seek to you for succor. Thus you have the opinion off,

Your humble servant,
DELAMERE.'

' Just now I hear you have suffered the Papists to possess themselves of Chester.'

" In this account, many matters done by the Earle of Derby are omitted, which perhaps in another, might have seemed meritorious ; but for the Earle of Derby to have deserved so ill of his great neighbour, the Lord Delamer, to be thus treated by him, and to add to his triumph, that the leiftenancy of Cheshire, which so many ages remained in the house of Derby, and the *Custos Rotulorum's* office, which the Earle of Derby held at his . . . . Majesty's accession to the Crowne, must be taken from the one, to be given to the other, it must be endured with humblest submission as to his Majestie; but whether, in honor, the Lord Derby could take one without both, is the humble question, and how accountable (so doing) he can be to his countrymen and freinds in both countyes, who have hitherto been allwaies united.

"To answer each part of the above mentioned letter: never were any Papist, or other, in all this time, near the Lord Delamer's house, to burne or harme it, nor was any manner of hurt done to it; nor did any Papist in either county, save those which were raised before the Lord Delamer's going, rise, or attempt to rise, nor did those who were before raised, committ anything, but were kept in awe after the militia were up, which were all up before the time in this letter supposed, nor did the Papists ever possess themselves of the government of Chester Castle or the city of Chester; they were only quartered there, one fortnight and 3 dayes, and might have been at any time, and then were taken prisoners by the governor, the city militia, and townsmen."

[———] to the EARL OF DERBY, at Knowsley.

643. 1688, November 13.—"Eight frigatts more are ordered to bee got ready with all speed, and his Majesty has sent to Trinity House, for them to provide him a thousand seamen. Yesterday, two batallions of the King's and one of the Lord Craven's regiment, marched, as also the Lord Churchill's troop of guards, and part of the Lord Dover's (?), and this day, the rest with the Duke of Northumberland's troop, and to-morrowe the Earl of Feversham's marches, and on Thursday his Majesty intends to goe for Salisbury to view the ground and order matters fit for the rendevous of his army, which will bee on the 28th instant. It will consist of 21,000 men; all old souldiers of the English, Scotch, and Irish, leaving the new raised . . . with some old ones, in garrisons, &c. A whole regiment is to guard the citty every night while the King goes for the west, but his Majesty will stay but 3 dayes there, att present. The western letters tell us that the Prince of Orange landed but 16,000 foot and 5,000 horse, and those were numbered by some persons of discretion; that the Earl of Shrewsbury, Earl of Macklesfeild, and Lord Wiltshire, came to Exeter on Wednesday, but the Prince of Orange did not come thither till Friday, and lodged himself at the Deanery. That his horse are pretty good, but the foot very ordinary, and much inferiour to ours; that some of his troops were advanced to Honiton, Tiverton, and other places, in order to go for Bristol; and that he had sent to bespeak 7,000 pair of shoes and 7,000 yards of cloath there. The Lord Colchester, lieutentant of the first troop of guards, Colonel Godfrey, Mr. Thomas Wharton, and 4 or 5 of that troop, and a brigadier, are absent, and supposed to be gone to the Prince of Orange, in calashes, last week. The Duke of Grafton came from sea last night. It is discoursed that one of the Prince of Orange's gunners has deserted and is come up, and gave his Majesty an account of their army, much to his satisfaction. On Sunday, the rabble got together to pull down the Popishe chapel at St. James', and broke the windows, &c., but the Lord Craven and guards coming, and promising to blow it up next day, they were dispersed; but yesterday, as the preists were removing their goods, they seized on two cartloads and burnt them on Holborn Hill and in Smithfeild; whereupon the guards were sent to suppress them, with orders to fire with bullet, which they did, and killed 4 or 5, and forced the rest to retreat." *Seal of arms.*

PETER EGERTON and WILLIAM HULME to ROGER KENYON, "at
Knowsley, or elsewhere."

644. 1688, November 14.—" You are very sensible we know what a
consternation the country is in, upon the account of the late potent invasion, and what a clatter the red-letter men make, and in what a readyness
they unanimously shew themselves to be to serve the King, upon that
occasion. Now, it is some surprise to us, that it should be thought
needless (by wise and thinking men) to put the country into as great a
forwardness for action as they. It is now some weeks agoe since we
had it from any good hands, that the Earle of Derby had received againe
his commission and was restored to his full power, as before, and we
have been in expectation of his calling the militia together every day.
Now, good cousen, we desire to be informed by you of the truth in that
matter, and what you doe conceive that his Lordship does design to doe,
for we doe apprehend the consequences of sitting still at this time to be
as fatal as those of doeing something; provided alwayes, that a man
have but the good luck to doe that little thing that he does, wisely ; but,
hit or miss, we are at his Lordship's devotion, and if we may but be
thought worthy to understand his mind, nobody shall be more ready to
the utmost extent of our power to serve him than we." *Seal of
Egerton armes.*

PETITION to JAMES II. by the Nobility and Gentry of the County of
York, City of York, and County of the same City.

645. 1688, November 17.—"We, your Majestie's most loyall subjects, in a deep sense of the miseries of a warr now breaking forth in the
bowells of your kingdomes, and of the danger to which your Majestie's
sacred person is thereby like to be exposed, and also of the distractions of
your people, by reason of their present grievances, do think ourselves
bound, in conscience of the duty we owe to God and our holy religion, to
your Majestie and our country, most humbly to offer to your Majestie
that, in our opinion, the only visible way to preserve your Majestie and
this your kingdome, would be the calling of a Parliament—regular and
free in all its circumstances.

" We, therefore, do most earnestly beseech your Majestie that you will
be graciously pleased, with all speed, to call such a Parliament, wherein
we shall be most ready to promote such councells and resolutions
of peace and settlement in Church and State, as may conduce to your
Majestie's honour and safety, and to the quieting of the mindes of
your people. We do likewise humbly beseech your Majestie, in the
meantime, to use such means for preventing the effusion of Christian
blood, as to your Majesty shall seem most meet."

[ROGER KENYON] to SIR WILLIAM [HULME].

646. 1688, November 28. Wigan.—The reports, you may believe,
were as surprising to me as they could be to any other ; but coming so
many ways, at sundry times, from divers places, and so sober persons,
though I am not apt to be too credulous, yet, pondering the circumstances
and discontents of some impatient to be anything but uppermost in everything, it seems as if such gave leave to their passions *per fas vel nefas*
to hurry them on to what they aim at by the most unaccountable
methods. The original reporters are professors of the Roman religion,
and seem rather religiously than maliciously to make the discoveries.
Minutest means are not despicable to detect conspiracies. *Draft.*

ROGER KENYON to the MAYOR OF WIGAN.

647. 1688, November 28.—" I heartily thank you for your intimation, though the matter of it, for those soldiers to demand of the militia some companyes to deliver up their guard is, I think, what ought not to have been done without pre-acquainting mee, who ordered the militia of your city (*sic*) to be at this time raised. You tell mee their entrance into your city, in the night, with light[ed] matches, put your town into a great consternation; and so it well might. If the thing is over, and all at quiet, I shalbe very glad; if otherwise, pray let mee forthwith hear from you againe, and I will readily contribute that power the King hath entrusted mee with to preserve your peace; and if you write againe, bee, I pray, as particuler as you can, that the remedy may not too much exceed the necessity of what aid is sent you, if occasion be."
Draft.

NEWS LETTER addressed to ROGER KENYON, at Peel.

648. 1688, November 29. London.—" In my laste, I tould you that the Lords Spirituall and Temporall were ordered to attend his Majesty, the effecte of which meeting hath produced a free Parliament; for, yesterday, the Lord Chancellor came to the severall Courts of Westminster Hall and declared his Majesty's resolution of a free Parliament, in all its cercomstances, being called immediately, and had given orders to the Clerk of the Petty Bagge to prepare the writts for passing the seales, and they will be issued out immediately. Three things, I am told, were agreed on in Council, viz., a free Parliament, a generall pardon, and commissioners to be sente to the Prince, who lay on Sunday night at Crakehurne, haveing hunted (?) in the Lord Pawlett's parke, and, on Tuesday, was expected at Sherburne, designed to lye at my Lord of Bristill's. His army marches three roads towards London, viz., by Sherburne, Marleborrow, and the Devizes We are advised from Birmingham that, on the 26th, the Lord Delameere, with severall other Lords, came to that place, with about 500 horse, well armed, and expected as many more in a few dayes. They marched to Edgbaston Hall, where they found a greate quantity of armes, which they seized. The Lord Danby, with severall other Lords, are still in Yorke; they have just sent parties of horse to bring in some companyes of foote which were marching southwarde, which, as soon as they met them, laide downe their armes and joyned the horse, declaring for a free Parliament and the Protestant religion.

" Nottingham, the 26th instant.—The Lord Devonshire, Sir Scroope How, &c., are going to Derby, with about 200 horse; severall stout fellows are there ready to mounte horses. One Cornet Gee, late of the Lord Arran's regiment, is gone to Liester, to raise men for Sir Scroope How. The Duke of Newcastle, having ordered the militia to meete him at Southwell, severall came, but had their armes seized; and partyes are sent out to seize the rest. All the Papists have there armes seized. In short, the generality of the people came into them, declareing for a free Parliament and the Protestante religion. The Lords Northampton, Gray of Ruthin, Manchester, and severall gentlemen, came to Northampton, the 26th, and marched towards Harborrow. Those in Oxfordshire are alsoe for a free Parliament, and severall gentlemen have joyned them. Yesterday, the Common Council of this City was chosen, being most of them Church of England men. The Kinge sente to the Lord Mayor that hee would not have them meete till he gave order. I am tould that the Commissioners that are to goe to the Prince of Orange are the Bishopps Ely and St. Asaph, the Lords Godolphin, Hallifax,

Nottingham, and Rochester. The Parliament is to meete the 15th of January. The Duke of Albamarle is dead, in Jemeca, and Dr. Oates dyed last Tuesday. It is said the Earl of Salsbury and Lord Milford are made Groomes of the Stole to his Majesty. Sir Nicholas Butler hath laide downe all his places."

J. Keeling to Roger Kenyon.

649. [1688, November.]—" Mr. Corbet and Mr. Ormeston are here; the occasion thus: one of our towne was tould by a soldier that our companies were to march out privately, this morning, and that some designe was against my Lord of Derby, which wee sent to acquaint Mr. Banks with, and hee, being at Knowesley, the person who heard the words went thither; upon which they came to inquire if there were anything in it; but, I believe, very little—only the jealousies, perhaps, of some Protestant soldiers, by reason of their sudden and private departure. Mr. Corbet was to order mee to send a messenger to you to let you know his Lordship's desires to see you today."

Postscript.—" If you have anything extraordinary of my Lord Delamore, pray let us have it. Pray let Dick give the messenger my handkerchief. The newes speaks little but that my Lord Lovelace is taken, with 13 of his horse (by the militia), goeing to the Prince of Orange. Severall killed on both sides. Hee intends to fortifye the line for his winter quarters. The Bishop of Exeter is made Archbishop of Yorke."
Seal, broken.

Thomas Preston to Roger Kenyon; to be left "att the three Legs of Man," in Wigan.

650. 1688, December 4. Lancaster.—" The officers are so clamorous I know not what to do with them; therefore, I desire you will not fail in sending me orders to receive the sum laid upon Lonsdale Hundred, and a discharge to the High Constables." *Seal of arms.*

The Earl of Derby to Roger Kenyon.

651. 1688, December 8.—" I am, I assure you, out of order, having been ill last night—much worse than I shall own. This may excuse me to the gentleman that designed to meet me; and, to tell you truly, I do not see any great necessity for it, my opinion being so well known for Lord Colchester and William Holt, for the King's proclamation removes all scruples, and I hope his carriage may take off the objection of a Court employment, so far am I from thinking it to his prejudice, as things go now." *Seal of arms.*

William Banks to Roger Kenyon.

652. 1688, December 9. Winstanley.—" Mr. Keeling had a letter, by the last post, from my Lord Ancrin [Ancrum]; it is more remarkable than any of his former, which makes Keeling impatient till my Lord [Derby] and you have had a sight of it." *Seal.*

Lord Delamere to the Earl of Derby.

653. [1688,] December 10.—Original of letter quoted in No. 642.

News Letter addressed to Roger Kenyon.

654. 1688, December 13. London.—" Yesterday, neare Wapping, my Lord Chancellor, in a seaman's habitt, was seized and brought before my

Lord Mayor, and from thence committed to the Tower. Lord Chief Justice Herbert [and the] Bishop of Chester are seized. Wright and some other of the Judges are fled. Prince George is alreddy come to Whitehall, and the Prince of Orange is expected tomorrow.

"Yesterday morning, severall of the Lords, Aldermen, and Comissioners, went in theire coaches and 6 horses to meet the Prince of Orange, to present him with a very complementall address, as, amongst others, that the King had left his people, and therefore prayed his highness to make hast to London to settle affaires."

MR. HAMMOND to ROGER KENYON.

655. 1688, December 13. Whalley.—"Mr. Parker, of Bradkirk, came to Clitherow, and, with his son, discoursed in the lawyer's behalf, who declared himself willing to serve in Parliament, if they should think him fit; he joins with none; several promised him their votes. Mr. Pudsay offers himself. Mr. Wilkinson, of Waddow, makes interest for himself or Mr. Waddall. Sir Edmund says little of it." *Seal.*

[ROGER KENYON] to the EARL OF DERBY.

656. 1688, December 18.—"Sunday last, his Majesty returned to Whitehall and was received with great joy. A Council was held and an express sent to Ireland to supersede the Earl of Tirconnel's Comission and to constitute the Lord Grenard in his room, who is to turn all papists out of comysion and disarm them. But the news of Tirconnel's being secured, proves false.

"Father Hall is comitted to Newgate, as is F. [Father?] Peters' brother and Sir Roger L'Estrange, for writing and dispersing treasonable papers against the government.

"The King's forces are marched out of town, to make room for those of the Prince of Orange, who entered on the guard att Whitehall last night, and the King has ordered the Duke of Berwick to deliver Portsmouth peaceably, &c.

"Major Littleton is killed by Captain Atherley, in a quarrel.

"The Lord Chancellour is writing a narrative in the Tower, and will discover all he knows. Wee are told he will discover something about the death of his late Majesty, and that he is much troubled in mind about his evidence concerning the birth of the Prince of Wales. His Lordship delivered the seal to his Majesty, and the writts for the Parliament to Mr. Chiffins.

"This morning, his Majesty went for Rochester, and some of the Prince of Orange's troops are his guard. The Prince of Orange has confined the Marquis of Hallifax, as some say, for advising a private treaty with his Majesty, and not in Parliament. And a guard is sett upon the Earl of Feversham and Collonel Oglethorpe, about some words of the Earl of Essex's death.

"The Bishop of London is Clerk of the Closet, and the Bishop of Durham turned out, and Dr. Hickman is made subdean of the Princess's Chappel.

"The Prince lay last night att Syon House, and this afternoon came to St. James's, being met by the Sheriffs and Aldermen in their formalityes, &c.

"Sir John Fenwick and the Lord Newburgh have layd down their Comissions.

"The Lord Mayor continues very ill.

"The Catholiques in Cheshire have layd down their arms.

" The tryall of the 7 Bishopps is now printing by order.

" The chusing Parliament men here, was putt off to-day by reason of the Prince's coming to town.

" Att Oxford Sir Thomas Clargis and Mr. Finch are chosen for the University, and Sir Edward Norris and Captain Berty, for the town ; but it is said Mr. Finch will bee made Lord Chancellour, and Sir John Powel, Lord Cheif Justice."

The DECLARATION of the Lord Lieutenant, the High Sheriff, Deputy Lieutenants, Justices of the Peace, Officers of the Militia, and other Protestant gentlemen of the County Palatine of Lancaster.

657. 1688, December.—"We being heartily and zealously concerned for the protestant religion, the laws of the land, and the liberties and properties of the subject, cannot, without being wanting to our duty, be silent under those calamities wherein late prevailing popish councils have miserably involved these kingdoms, and do therefore unanimously resolve to apply ourselves to his Highness the Prince of Orange, who, with so great kindness to these realms, so vast expence, and such hazard to his person, hath undertaken, by endeavouring to procure a free parliament, to rescue us, with as little effusion as possible of christian blood, from the eminent dangers of popery and slavery. And we do hereby declare that we will, with our utmost endeavours, assist his Highness in the obtaining such a parliament wherein our laws, liberties, and properties may be secured, the Church of England in particular, with due liberty to protestant dissenters, and, in generall, the protestant religion and interest may be supported and encouraged, to the glory of God and the happiness and reputation of the established government in these kingdoms. In the meantime, we will endeavour to preserve, as much as in us lies, the peace and security of this county, by taking care to disarm all papists, and to secure all Jesuites and Romish preists within the same. And if there be anything more to be performed by us for promoting his Highness' generous intentions for the publick good, we shall be ready, as occasion requires, to contribute our best endeavours."

The CONVENTION.

658. 1688.—" Remarques upon a free conference in the Convention."

Observations on LORD BRANDON'S LORD LIEUTENANCY and the State of the COUNTY OF LANCASTER.

659. [1688-1689.]—"That Lord Brandon, before the late King James his comeing to Chester and Holliwell, writ to the Lancashire Nonconformists, it being his post to introduce that party to complement that King, and on a large common, short of Chester, the Lord Molineux and his popeish sparkes standing on one hand in the King's way, and the Lord Brandon at the head of his tender holders-forth, some 16 or 17 of them haveing huds on, on a very hot day, and backed with a small mob of the same complexion, stood on the other hand to receive the late King.

" That the Lord Molineux was, at Chester, made Lord Leiutenant of Lancashire, who, thereupon, afterwards made 13 Deputy Lieutenants, 7 convicted papists and 6 reputed protestants; of all the 13, Lord Brandon was his first-named Deputy Leiutenant.

"January 22th, 1687-8.—Lord Derby put out from being *Custos Rotulorum* and Lord Molineux made *Custos*.

"11 April 1688.—Earl of Derby and 43 more of the Protestant Justices were turned out of the Comission of Peace, and 27 rejectors of the penall lawes and test came in, of which 16 were papists, the rest had the name of Protestants ; Lord Brandon one of these.

"May 1689.—Lord Delamer made Lord Leiutenant of the county of Chester. Lord Derby, whose ancestors had had it above 200 years, himself baveing been Lord Leiutenant 13 years, was turned out to give place to Lord Delamere. This, perhaps, was too much resented by Lord Derby, to find his freinds, who were the ancient Deputy Leiutenants and militia officers there, turned out, and thereupon he quitted the Leiutenancy of Lancashire too, so [that in]

"June 1689, Lord Brandon, who had been, within less then a yeare, a Deputy Leiutenant with the papists, was made, and is now, Lord Leiutenant of Lancashire. Lord Derby, who was before *Custos Rotulorum*, is laid aside for that too, and Lord Brandon in that place.

"Lord Brandon hath not, in Lancashire, ever qualified himself according to the Act of 25 Car. 2 for these places. *Quere*, if he have done that anywhere, and if he have not done. *Quere*, whether all the Comissions given by him, his being fallen, be not allso void, and then what a condition is the Lancashire Leiftenancy in, though the Deputy Leiutenants and militia officers did duly qualify themselves.

"The Lord Brandon was a regulator of the Lancashire Corporations, and very unaccountably removed the Mayor of Lancaster, the Mayor of Preston, the Mayor of Wygan, and other officers, sure that was an employment of trust under the late King and in those days he never qualified himself accordeing to the said law. *Quere*, if his disability be, or can be, restored, without an Act of Parliament.

"The Lord Brandon had diverse of the cheefe papists, in Lancashire, in prison, but so as in the townes of Manchester and Salford where they were, each had so much liberty as to choose his lodgeing, to remove at pleasure upon any dislike to any other lodgeing, to meet and dine together where they pleased, to converse without any restraint with any that came to them, together or apart, and some of them were frequently permitted to go to their own homes and to retorne upon paroll without any keeper, which gave them a much greater opportunity then they could have otherwise had, had they not been thus kept together.

"That a little before the election of this Parliament, to sweeten them for their interest, they were all discharged upon baile.

"That when the Lord Brandon came downe and set up his friend Sir Samuel Gerard to be chose at Lancaster, severall papists, which before absconded, came to give votes for his friend, Sir Samuel, his Lordshipp personally appeareing to manage that election.

"That some of the papists have owned a protection under the Lord Brandon.

"That there are now in Lancashire, many new companies, who have colours, drums, and armes, and frequently traine, formed into companies. *Quere*, by what Comission, they are not of the militia, viz. :—

"Captaine Right, Captaine Bootle, Captaine Hooper, Captain Browne, Captain Andrews, Captaine Crompton, Captain Sharples, Captain Rigby, Captain Willoughby, Captaine Clayton, Captain Astley, Captain Dorneinge.

"There are several others who have sometimes appeared in companies, but whether they have done of late, *Quere*, viz. :—Captaine Cross, Captaine Lever, Captaine Egerton, Captaine Birch, Captaine Hulme.

PETITION of WILLIAM RICHARD GEORGE, EARL OF DERBY, to
JAMES II.

660. ⌊1688.⌋—"I had not at this time in this matter appeared, when
your Majestie's troubles are too many ways multiplied upon you, but that
if oppertunities of this nature are slipped they are past retreeve.

"Your royall brother, King Charles the Second, was generously bounti-
full to the late Duke of Albemarle's father, for the doings of that brave
man, so eminently instrumentall in his Majestie's restoration, in con-
ferring upon him considerable estates in divers countys, which, I suppose,
by his late Grace his dyeing without issue, do revert to the Crown and
are now in your Majesty's disposition.

"Might I offer to your royall consideration in the other scale, my
grandfather's and father's sufferings, the consequences whereof have
sunk mee, comparatively to theirs, so low in estate (which, without
derogation, methinks I may mention, since by no prodigality, but by the
effect of faithfullest loyaltie, their losses came) that as I bear their
quality, which I would not eclipse, I have often chosen rather to
disapear then not support; I hope this may, with such proportion, weigh
in your compassionate thoughts, as in some degree to restore mee, if it
were but granting to mee and my family so much of that late Duke's
lands and estate as lye in Lancashire, where most of what remaines to
mee of my ancestors' estate is.

"To enumerate our losses (for theirs are now mine) would make it
too long for a petition, but by a moderate estimate, made 37 years ago,
they did amount to 209,000*l.*

"If I have sometimes failed in my attendance at Court, and suffered
for want of those influences which your benigne aspect hath enriched
others, which it hath never been my want of perfect loyaltie, but because
I was afraid to express my other wants. I have, I hope, no way
diminished my ancestors' character in these countryes where I live, but
if your royall heart shall incline by granting these lands to enable mee
to make a good figure abroad also, a much fallen family will, to ages to
come, celebrate your gracious Majestie's memory." *Draft, in Roger
Kenyon's hand.*

EDWARD CHIPPINDALL and JOHN WEBSTER to ROGER KENYON,
at Peel.

661. 1688-9, January 3. Cliderow.—They have received the Sheriff's
precept for the election of burgesses for Parliament. Not being sure
whether they ought to proceed thereon, or "new orders," have called a
"Hall" for the next Monday, "when we desire your company." *Seal
of arms.*

THOMAS GREENHALGH to ROGER KENYON, at Peel.

662. ⌈16⌉88⌈-9⌉, January 9.—"There was 2 men this day with mee,
the one lives in Bolton, the other on Tonge Moor, that were but a few
days since at the ale-hous on Hindley Common, when Mr. Langton of Loe
beinge gone out to look on the wall, the landlord begun the Earl of Derby's
health, which Mr. Langton hearing, broke the landlord's head with his
cane and threw him in the fyre. One of the witnesses blaming of him for
his abuse, he fell upon him, who threw Mr. Langton in the fyre; but
Mr. Langton goes and fetch't 4 more, soe that they being but .2,
thought it convenient to march off." *Seal of arms.*

J. Rowe to Roger Kenyon.

662A. 1688[-9], January 10. [Isle of Man ?]—"I have noe newes to send you hence in this great conjuncture, but can truely tell you that we are of one minde, unanimous, and of one true protestant religion, in this litle quiet nation; and if we have noe disturbances from abroad, we are assured of peace at home, not being (God be thancked) infested with Rome's incendiarys; yet we cannot but admire the suddaine and great revolutions, and with great eagernes expect to heare of the established peace of the three kingdoms. It would be too tedious to express here my earnest desire, for the welfaire of England to be restored to its pristine glory and happines."

[*Postscript.*]—"Captain Charles Christian gives his humble service to you." *Seal.*

R. Heywood to Roger Kenyon, at Peel.

663. 1688[-9], January 13. Castle Rushen [Isle of Man].—"I hope you and I may now drink a bottle of wine, without danger of our throats, by the sparks lately soe much in fashion . . . . We have been much amazed and distracted here, by the various reports wee have received of the affairs of England, not knowing what to believe; but of late we have received better satisfaction. . . . . . . There are severall of the Popish recognizances, forfeited 9 or 10 years agoe, yett uncompounded for, and you may please to remember I excepted them, and the remainder of Lever's fine, in the deed of conveyance to Tom Dod and his partner. If there bee any hope of getting any thing . . . I will come over." *Seal of arms.*

Viscount Colchester to Roger Kenyon.

664. 1688[-9], January 24.—"I have sent you the Prince's order to mee to seise horses of my Lord Branden's, or the Marquess de Miremond's regiment. I am informed there are, severall run into Lancashire. My request to you is that you will employ your people to seis such horses as they shall find did belong to either regiment, and send them to Wardly (?), and I will order Richard Lightborn to satisfy them for their expences." *Seal of arms.*

Justices for Lancashire.

665. 1688-9, January 29.—The names of the Justices of the Peace for the County of Lancaster. . . . .

———— to Roger Kenyon.

666. [1688-9 ?] February 2. Whitehall.—"The late King, as he is now stiled, has still a great party in the House of Lords, many being for calling him back, though it is declared by them, he has broke all the lawes and deserted the Government, as you may find by the votes, but we that se through it, are resolved to stick to the Prince and do not question our success at last." *Seal.*

George Allanson to Roger Kenyon.

667. 1688[-9], February 2. Temple.—The Lords begin to come pretty near a closure with the Commons, only they cannot agree that the Government is vacant, but the next week is supposed will settle that matter, by two or one crowned heads.

[William Banks to Roger Kenyon.]

668. 1688[-9], February 2. London.—There seems to be a difference in opinion between the Lords and Commons, about the vote sent up to the Lords relating to the vacancy, about which the Lords do not concurr; a conference is designed to be had on Monday. There are some sort of people that begin to threaten the Bishops, because all but two of them went against the vote, and, as I am told, their own house has a great many in it that would gladly have them only there as cyphers. It is said two letters were delivered this day to each house, one sent by the Lord Preston, and are supposed to come from the King. Neither house gave them reading, so that they cannot be certain who they come from ; they lie upon the tables, and I hear the Lords' house will look into them on Monday. " Two petitions were brought to the houses this morning, delivered by ten of the mobile; the substance of them was to have some one put into the throne, the King being gone. They report every one of the ten was deputed to this by 5,000 of the like, which, if not satisfied, will come themselves. These petitions were not read." This gang expressed their kindness to the Bishops, saying if they would deliver their chaplains, as they called them, into their custody, they would take care of them. *Seal of arms, broken.*

William B[anks] to [Roger Kenyon].

669. 1688[-9], February 7.—" After the Free Conference was over yesterday, the Lords, upon the return to their house, voted an agreement with the Commons as to the vacancies. About twelve this day, they sent them to us for our concurrence, but our Committee having not then drawn up all the heads judged necessary to be redressed and allowed by those who are to be set in the throne, they put off the consideration of the Lords' resolution till tomorrow." *Seal.*

Nicholas Starkie to Roger Kenyon, at Peel.

670. [16]88[-9], February 9. Gray's Inn.—Craves his " assistance and advice, which will be the most proper and best course to take, to get to be Attorney Generall of Lancashire," which place, he supposes, will be vacant, when the Prince is proclaimed King. He would not doubt of success, if he could make Lord Derby and Lord Colchester his friends. " I hear that Mr. Greenfield and Mr. Barty Entwisle, who are now in town, intends to make what interest they can, but through whom, I cannot learn. . . . . . . It is said that the Prince and Princess will be proclaimed King and Queen of England on Munday."

William Banks to Roger Kenyon.

671. 1688[-9], February 14.—Has spoken in his favour to Lord Derby. Lady Derby has been made, by the Queen, Groom of the Stole, a place of great profit, 1,000*li. per annum* at least, " and to take place of all Duchesses. This will let some people see there is merit in that person that hath been so neglected. The Lord Sunderland was seized at Rotterdam, in woman's habit. The Lord Chief Justice Wright was taken this morning in the Old Bailey and sent to prison. The King having chosen a council this day, they sat, and it is said that the great men will find it an easy matter to turn this Convention into a Parliament. I hear the lawyers engage to find law, so there is like to be a dull time for the poor alehouses that expected new treating of parties." *Seal.*

WILLIAM ASSHETON to ROGER KENYON.

672. 1688[-9], February 14. London.—The enclosed paper contains the substance of what the Convention has done since their meeting, and was perfected and concluded by both Houses last Tuesday night. That same night, the Princess of Orange came to Whitehall; she was met at Greenwich by the Prince and Princess of Denmark, and was received at Whitehall by the Prince of Orange himself. Yesterday, both Houses waited upon them both, in the Banquetting House, and, according to their resolution, at eleven o'clock they were proclaimed King and Queen. Their Majesties went to chapel at Whitehall the same day, and in the King's seat appeared his Majesty, with his Queen on his right hand and the Princess of Denmark on his left. The Bishop of London preached upon these words, "Neither circumcision availeth any thing nor uncircumcision, but a new creature." This morning I saw a list of the Privy Councillors, great officers of State, Judges, etc., but I am told it is imperfect; it is certain the Lord Delamere is of the Privy Council, but I do not learn that our good Earl is amongst them. *Seal*.

WILLIAM BANKS to ROGER KENYON.

673. 1688[-9], February 16.—The enclosed was their Highness' answer to the declaration presented by both Houses, in the Banquetting House, immediately after which they were proclaimed. Thanks was ordered to be returned them for their gracious answer. On Monday, their Majesties will come to the Lords' House, to which day we are adjourned. They had designed to have been there on Friday, but the Master of the Wardrobe to their late Majesties had laid the robes out of the way, so that they could not be found, therefore, new ones are to be ready for Monday. *Seal*.

WILLIAM BANKS to ROGER KENYON.

674. 1688[-9], February 19.—"Tomorrow we appointed to wait on my Lord Derby and Lord Colchester, the later of these I met with to day, gave him your service, and told him the contents of yours. He said he should be ready to do what lay in his power, when he was put in a way how to proceed. Mr. Starkey will direct him, I suppose, as to that. As to Vernon's place, I writ to you three or four posts agoe; there are several aiming at it, but no one yet hath a promise that I can hear. Mr. Hulme, of Urmstone, hopes for successe on my Lord Delamer's interest, having ingaged him at his first comming up, and his brother, Mr. George Booth, is made one of the Commissioners for the Customs, so that he stands in all likelyhood fair. My Lord Derby told me he had also desired the favour of recommending one, at the same time I put him in mind of you. When next I see him, you shall know more. The Lord Maxfield is made Captain of the first Troop of Guards, but it is believed his mind is not thoroughly satisfied with that command. His Grace the Duke of Ormond is first Bedchamber man (next to the Groom of the Stoole) if he pleases. This, if accepted on, it is hoped will let him in to greater preferment. I have inclosed you the King's speech and the Order for rectifying the prayers. To day we had designed to have considered his Majesty's speech, and accordingly had entered into a Grand Committee of the whole house, but the Lords sending us down a Bill to prevent and remove all doubts, questions, surmises, and difficulties, concerning the assembling and sitting of this present Parliament since February 13th, it was read, and ordered to be read again tomorrow, upon which the debate will be, whether we shall be a Parliament or not. To day, the King viewed in Hide Park about ten thousand of the Dutch forces, one half of which are to goe forwards tomorrow towards Holland, the rest are to follow, all but about 200 horse, which they call his Guard de Core." *Portion of seal.*

NICHOLAS STARKIE to ROGER KENYON.

675. 1688[-9], February 19.—Concerning his appointment as Customer for Liverpool, for which office several persons are applying. Lord Delamere has great hopes of getting one of his brothers to be a Commissioner of the Customs. This day the Convention have turned themselves into a Parliament.

WILLIAM BANKS to ROGER KENYON.

676. 1688[-9], February 21.—Lord Derby and Lord Col[chester] will deliver Mr. Starky's petition to his Majesty this night. As to Mr. Vern[on's] I find, by his Lordship, it is filled up, as he says, by a friend of Lord Delamere's, his brother George being made one of the Commissioners for the Customs. I can assure you I often remind him of you, but I know his slow way of proceeding so well that I must confess I was afraid he would let someone step in his way ; "for my part, I cannot hear that he hath opened his mouth for any soul living." However, Mr. Stanley was to-day made one of the Grooms of the Bedchamber, which I am glad of, but whether it was upon any motion of his, I cannot learn, "for his shy reserved humour sticks so close to him that I believe he will befriend but few." Joining Lord Colchester with him will make him more active. When William Ashton sees you, he will tell you more than I can well write, for I have told him all. The resolution of the Grand Committee yesterday was, that we were a Parliament ; the House agreed to it and gave the Lords' Bill a second reading ; it is committed, and will not be long, I suppose, before it be passed into an Act. There being several regiments of the Dutch forces ordered by his Majesty to return back into the States' service, there was a motion made in the House this day that his Majesty might be desired to bestow a donation on those forces that came over with him, that were now going back. It was agreed to, and the Lord Wiltshire ordered to present the desire of the House to his Majesty. It was also ordered that Sir Robert Howard bring in an account of all moneys issued out of the Exchequer to Burton and Graham, for prosecutions at law, etc., termed by some, blood service. Also, that he bring in an account of all moneys paid during the reign of King Charles II. and King James, for secret services. Last night, Lord Arran, Duke Hamilton's son, was set upon by six men, as he was going home in his chair, one of them ran the chair through and scarred his throat, but he got out, drew and defended himself, till his men got people together. He has several slight wounds in his hands and head. The men are not to be discovered, running away as his servant came up. This I had from one he told it to himself. They were English, and he heard them call him a "Papist dogg," though he is none of that religion. It is talked here that the Paptists in our country are inquiring who those were that pulled down or defaced their chapels. I can scarce believe they would be so silly at this time of day to act so imprudently.

NICHOLAS STARKIE to ROGER KENYON.

677. [1688-9,] February 28.—"The news here is, that the King is landed in Ireland with a great many French officers, and that Tarconnell (*sic*) is 70,000 strong, and 30,000 of them very well armed, and it is reported that they are very mutinous in Scotland. It is not certainly known who will be Judges Commissioners of the Great Seal, or Commissioners of the Treasury. The Commons have voted the king 70,000*l. per mensem* for six months, and are this day about setling the Revenue. It is doubtful whether for life, or from three years to three years, that there may be a tryennyal Parliaent."

The EARL OF DERBY to [ROGER KENYON ?].

678. 1688–9, February 28. Whitehall.—Being informed of the Popish meetings lately, in several places, and having acquainted the King with it, I am commanded by his Majesty to desire you and the rest of the Protestant gentlemen, to take such care as that they keep the peace, and also to desire that you will use your endeavours to suppress them, if they should attempt anything against the Government.

WILLIAM B[ANKES] to ROGER KENYON.

679. 1688[-9], March 9.—" The House hath had nothing before them these two days but the Bill for the Aid, which is to be read again on Tuesday next, and will afterwards be ordered to be ingrossed. All the Commissioners for each county are already added to it. The Councill is now, as I am told, putting the King in mind of filling the Commissions for Justices and Leiftenants. The Lords Leiftenants that were, and others of the members for each county, have delivered in lists of such as they think fit to serve, in order to it. You may guesse who did it for Chéshire. For Lancashire, my Lord Derby gave in one, but I am apt to think there might be some other papers delivered in besides, by others that pretend to as great interest there. After a while, when wee see who are the Lord Leiftenants, wee can easily guesse at the other commissions for all places, [which] I am told are ready. Reflections are cast on the Cheshire Deputies and officers as being persons of the least estates, least interest, and not liked by the souldiers, who are well affected, as they say, but I do not hear they will afford their officers so kind a character. You may guesse from whence this arises. I shall be glad to hear from you, after you have met Sir Ralph and Cozen Rawstorn. It is reported here, the Papists and others as disaffected, as themselves are very high in your parts, as though they had something in prospect."

[*Postscript.*]—" My Lord Colchester's Regiment is to march through our county to Carlisle. If there be any young fellows about you that will bring in horses of fiveteen hand high, he will take them into his troop. Richard Lightbound (*sic*) can tell you the certain time of the regiment's coming." *Seal.*

The EARL OF DERBY to ROGER KENYON.

680. 1688–9, March 14. Whitehall.—" I am very glad you have thoughts to come up, and I desire you will lose no time. I shall defer resolving upon a seal keeper until I see you. Roper has writ on behalf of two, but I tell him I am engaged to you, which I suppose will stop his mouth. Expecting to see you soon, I shall not mention the chancellorship nor anything else, only I showed the King Col : Rawstorne's letter; his Majesty is very well pleased with it. I trust now, in a short time, the lieutenancy will be settled, and that I shall be continued, notwithstanding the endeavours of some to the contrary." *Seal of arms.*

L. RAWSTORNE to ROGER KENYON, at the "Sword and Buckler," in London.

681. 1688–9, March 17. Preston.—Asks Kenyon to speak to Lord Derby on behalf of Capt. Bellingham, to procure him a captain's place in some regiment going to Ireland. *Seal of arms.*

S. RICHMOND to ROGER KENYON.

682. 1688–9, March 24. Liverpool.—Asking for Kenyon's influence to get his son the post "of one of the Lord of Derby's titular chaplains. It is generally observed that the Papists are as high and brisk as in King James' reign." Several of them abscond, which makes him apprehend they must have some pernicious design on foot, and now the soldiers are leaving the country and marching for Ireland, he could heartily wish that such a care were taken to secure them, that his Majesty's good Protestant subjects may be delivered from their fears and apprehensions.

[S.] RICHMOND to ROGER KENYON, in London.

683. [1689,] April 2. Liverpool.—Thanks him for his "friendly intercession" with Lord Derby on behalf of his son. "We have received nothing of late from Ireland. The . . . . opinion here is that [the] Protestants have little . . . . left but Londonderry, and should that place [be given] up by the Irish (with conveniencys for a siege) . . . . supplys reach them out of England or Scotland, the town must of necessity surrender; and then, farewell Ireland till a new conquest at . . . . must cost millions of treasure and thousands . . . . Our Papists are still very uppish and, it is said, some of the best of them are absconded, for what end, may be easily supposed. Pray God protect us from all their designs, and settle these distracted nations in peace and quietness." *Torn.*

LEFTWICH OLDFIELD to ROGER KENYON.

684. 1689, April 15.—"I am informed that my brother Tom—after having bin plundred and fearing wors usage—with som gents of considerable estates, made escape out of the River Shanon (many others, attempting the same thing, being taken), and is coming almost round Ireland, at last arrived at Plymouth, is now coming up to London. I hope he may come to find you in town; have therefore advised him to find you out (I hope the stationer in Gray's Inn Gate knows your lodging), because I tell him you will, as a true friend, direct and introduce him to my Lord and Lady Derby, and probably otherwaise to his hopefull advantage. He writes that King James landed, 13 March, at Kinsal with several French and Irish officers that escaped out of England, and that the Bishop of Chester is with them." *Seal.*

[The SAME] to ROGER KENYON.

685. [1689 ?] April 20.—"Here is terrible apprehensions of Northern disturbances; the imposing of oaths and necessary taxes to support new impositions, I expect will make divellish fractions. Every man is apt to stick to his purs, and not willing to part with it to everyone who bids him deliver. If the nation be measured by the rable, it will be found like recconing without the host. The division of the partys spoken of, threatens confusion. Many false steps and fatall omissions irremediable without wonderfull providence. The State proprietors and undertakers may answer, for sure they begin to find themselves out in their polliticks; but can falling all to pieces be avoided, when they come to determine and settle religion; that word imbroyleth (?) most part of the world at present, and raiseth . . . . that the thing itself is almost lost in the disputes. Many Babells are built upon that basis."

Postscript.—"The account of the King's landing in Ireland seems to agree with the Butler's letter to his mother in Wales. Here is report that he took 1,000, some say 10,000, hors with him, the Duke of Luxemburg, and many extraordinary officers." *Unsigned. Seal.*

THOMAS RISHTON to ROGER KENYON.

686. 1689, April 26. Greengore.—Asking for Kenyon's influence with the Chancellor, to have Mr. George Tounson made a Justice of the Peace, as he lives amongst a numerous neighbourhood of Papists in Chipping, Bleadale (?), Goosnargh, and Bolland, and he thinks there are some feuds betwixt him and them, as they are now strangely impudent in the country. The Papists here are so uneasily troublesome, they never carried themselves at a greater height and confidence than now, frequently and publicly libelling and rediculing the King and Queen and all such as side with them; they know at present they may do it with impunity, because there is nobody to complain to.

[THOMAS KENYON] to ROGER KENYON.

687. 1689, May 14. London.—The King went this morning towards Portsmouth, took with him 19,000*li.* to distribute amongst the sailors, who, it is said, behaved themselves very bravely in the late engagement. The Dutch fleet, consisting of 39 men-of-war and 10 tenders, joins the English to-morrow at Portsmouth, and will receive, it is believed, some private orders from the King, so that in a little time we may expect to hear of some signal action. Commissions for raising 50 regiments more will immediately be issued forth, five regiments arrived from England at Londonderry, and the garrison there has, in a late sally, entirely cut off the Royal regiment and most part of the Duke of Berwick's regiment of horse, and made a great slaughter amongst the rest. Sir Roger Strickland was killed in the engagement at sea. Colonel Lundy is committed to the Tower, and offers to impeach Colonel Richards and Cunningham of High Treason. The Parliament, resolving to set closely to the business of the kingdom, have ordered that no Private Bills shall be brought in during this session.

WILLIAM BANKS to ROGER KENYON, [M.P.].

688. [16]89, May 21. London.—"I received yours, and acquainted as many with it as I knew. For that purpose I staid in town last night. I have delivered the case to Sir Edward Chisbenall, who is very much your friend and takes a great deall of care in it; and because it is thought necessary to have more writ, I have desired him to imploy two or three scriveners to write out about a dozen off them, which we will distribute to such as we hope will make the best use of them for you. To-morrow, it will be brought before the House. I am forced to goe back this morning to Richmond, but will be here to-morrow to doe you the best service I can. I suppose you know who did you this dissarvice in the other House. Iff we can but gett it back to a conference (which will be all the tugg!) I hope it may goe well; we have a great many enymes in our House, because no other county hath the like . . . . .

The Dutch have joyned our fleet with seventeen men-off-war. Peter Shakerley is sent to the Tower, as the warrant is for treasonable practices . . . . Lord Derby is gone into Glostershire."

[LEFTWICH OLDFIELD] to ROGER KENYON.

689. [1689,] June 5.—"On the other side is, I believe, a prettie exact account of what passed this place. It would be a wild thing to say anything of reports how many passed Stockport, since we hear they came two or three days' march from or by Warrington, whence the most notable was a parcell of boys that mimicked granadeers and were very ready in their exercise; little exercising of any, either foot or horse, that I hear of, saving drawing up and saluting the lord with volleys, as he came nere them. Great thancks returned them, with money to the severall troopes and companies to drink, shouting and clawing one another. His lordship, they say, had pen and ink in his hand, and noted the names of the officers and number of their men, in his book, and the officers gave listes of them to his clerk, as is said. Great declaring of readiness, at his call, to fire and to die, as some say, but of any speech, petition, or address, can learn nothing to be relyed on. Some whispering or soft discourse passed between his lordship and the officers, when he came to them, and the largess given. Some companies had 20s., some 30s., some five or six half-crownes, as said, when the silver grew low, and afterward, the guineas went till all had some touch of the Generall's liberality. It is talked as if the Lancaster men designed a petition (if he pleased to undertake the delivery and redress) against Lord Brandon's being their Lord Lieutenant, but closly caryed. Some pretend to know, others do but guess at the growth of strawberries. This towne is now full of the retorning rout, for the rare-show ended Tuesday evening, but reports differ soe much about the gross number, that there is no ofering at an estimate—the difference being between five thousand and fourty thousand, besides spectators innumerable. The greater part mustered, are thought to be foreigners. I hear not of any man of note in Cheshire, save Colonel Legh; he brought in, as reported, 200 (not of the militia, but volunteers). Captain Low, of North . . . brought on Monday, foot, and on Tuesday, hors, but it is the other county-men are to mee most remarqerable, their principles considered, which you know better than I, and therefore I leave them to your further consideration. . . .

" I have, in all, a regard to our lord ; if, out of these broken hints you can spell any thing worth his notice, I have my end. I make noe comments and admitt noe gloss yet. Besides, I perceive by yours, it is dangerous writing. Mine to you have been with most freedom. I cannot imagine who should be sent for up, or who should be suspected. I have heard talk of an association at Chester; but, sure, it will prove noe more then making Mr. Leving an alderman by fair voting, though to the great dissatisfaction of the all-pretending party. And I would hope nothing wors can be charged or proved against P. Shakerley, and that the trick of putting him by, being restord [resorted ?] to, that government is att (?) the end on it.

"On Monday morn, at 3 o'clock, a pack of Ashton's foot, between two and three hundred, conductyd by Captain Wright, passed towards Bowden.

" At 7 o'clock another parcell, called Blakley Lyon, with two collours (with a lyon displayed in the said collours), about six score foot, lead by Captain Leaver, of Olerington, and Sam Dickinson, junior, with two drums and two pipers, and followed by about 40 hors, passed through this towne.

"About an hour after, Captain Parson-Duhurst passed, followed by about 80 hors, six abreast, all with drawn swords, but neither collours nor trumpeters, besides the parson, not above six carrying pistolls of the whole.

"A collours, with about 80 foot, from Radcliff, under Captain Seddon.

"Out of Salford went Birch of Ordsall, with a parcell of hors and a company of foot, very full and well armed.

"Out of Manchester, Captain Joshua Brown, with 60 hors, and Captain John Digles, with about 120 foot with armes and trophies, some trumpetts being sent in on Sunday by his Lordship, enquiring for Captain Brown.

"Egerton of Shaw, with others, passed at Barton, I hear.

"Monday night came into quarters at Manchester, Captain Cross, of Darwen, with about 50 hors, Lord Willoughby's second son with 72 foot, Captains Throp and Smith, of Bolton, with about 120 foot, all which marched out early on Tuesday morning for Bowdon, that being the principall show day.

"Same night came also to quarter in Manchester, a parcell of Cheshire hors, about 60 (with two trumpetts), from about Sandbach, conducted by one Cotton, a pettifogger, and nephew to Mr. Acton, of Crew. These had been at Bowden on Monday, where they had left their foot to ly all night in Bowden church, with a cart-load of Sandbach ale, brought thither for succour. The said hors returned to Bowden early on Tuesday.

"On Tuesday night, in their return from Bowden tumult, came to quarter at Manchester, about 60 foot in a company, from Saddleworth, in Yorkshire, headed by one Captain Bulkeley.

"It is said that old Colonel Dukenfeild undertook for a regiment of true old stagers." *Unsigned. Seal.*

SAFE CONDUCT.

690. 1689, June 6.—Safe conduct for Edward Henshaw, master of the ship *Dove*, of Dublin.

HENRY ROWE to ROGER KENYON, in London.

691. 1689, June 7. Peel.—"This is to give you an account of my travels (since you went for London) about the sheareing (*sic*) of the Justices that wold take their ooths. On Wednesday, after the receipt of the Commission of Peace, I went to Warrington, thinking to find there Mr. Bold and Mr. Risley. Mr. Bold was gone for London, Mr. Risley took his oath that night. I went to Liverpoole, thinking Dr. Richmond would have taken his oath, but he desired tyme till you come home, and would not then take it. I went on Thursday to Ormskirk, and Dr. Alcock gave me the same answer. I went afterwards to Preston to a general meete, where I thought I should have mett some gentlemen that were in commission, but there was none. Afterwards, I went to the assizes, and there I swore Judge More, Mr. William Kirkby, Mr. Cole, and one Mr. Fenwick. There was none that came beyond sands but Mr. Kirkby. Mr. More, Mr. Cole, and Mr. Fenwick appointed Quarty Sessions to be at Lancaster on Tuesday, the 11th of this month, and appointed me to be there . . . . Mr Kirkby, hereing of it, told me he would gett the gentleman in commission beyond sands, to meet two days after the Sessions at some place, and would give me notice, that I might come over and swere them. After the assyses were ended, I went into Blackborne Hundred, and first I went to Mr. Osbaldeston to have sworn him, but he lay upon his death-bed, and died the day following I met with Mr. Braddyll and he would not take it till you came home, saying, he had nobody to join with him but Mr. Holden, and he would joyne none with him. I went to Black-borne to see what Mr. Livesay would doe, and he desired to bee excused, being 81 years of age, and weeke and feeble." *Seal.*

CERTIFICATE OF THE ARRIVAL OF LUNT AND THRELFELL.

692. 1689, June 17.—Certificate, by James Crosfield and Henry Jaynson, that the *Lyon*, of Lancaster, came to Beathaven (?) from Ireland on that day, between 3 and 4 o'clock in the morning, and at that time her longboat put Lunt and Threlfell on shore.

TRAINED BANDS OF LANCASHIRE.

693. 1689, June 18.—Commission from Charles, Lord Brandon, Lord Lieutenant of the County Palatine of Lancaster, to Sir Richard Standish, Bart., as Lieutenant-Colonel of a regiment of foot of the trained bands within the County of Lancaster. *Copy.*

[The EARL OF DERBY] to ROGER KENYON.

694. [1689?] July 4.—" 1,000 foot and 1,000 horse are marching for Ireland under the command of Counte de Solmes. It is certain King James' affairs go ill, many of his own religion growing discontent[ed], and I am assured, from a very good hand, the gentlemen of best quality who are protestants, in and about Dublin, are at this time forced to beg their bread. I am sure I need not comment upon this to you, but I woud have others, if there can be such fools or knaves, to se what they must all come to if the late King should prevail." *Seal.*

[The EARL OF DERBY] to ROGER KENYON.

695. [16]89, August 13.—The Parliament is expected to rise this week, and, so soon as I have freed a friend, and a near relation, out of trouble, I resolve to go straight into Lancashire. By the informations and the letters, I find the Papists were in great expectation of the late King's and their great master's coming into Lancashire. I believe the Protestants will not envy their having such a one, and, for my part, I wish all popish governments had exactly the same for their heads. Their intelligence, I find, still fails them, for Ireland will certainly be very suddenly reduced, Kirk having at this time 15,000 men with him. I am very glad you have got those letters, I hope the authors will be found out. *Holograph, but unsigned.*

"MR. HIGHSHERIFF JOHN BIRCH's Order concerning the House of Correction at Preston in Amonderness."

696. 1689, August 26.—Ordering that John Willacy " do continue governour of the said House of Correction, as it appears that William Tomlinson, of Garstang, is a very disloyal and disaffected person to the Government, a great favourer of Papists, and did very much misbehave himself in the governing of the said House, formerly, and is not fit to be intrusted with so great a charge." *Copy.*

The Declaration of the Right Reverend Father in God, JOHN, late LORD BISHOP OF CHICHESTER, upon his death-bed.

697. 1689, August 27.—"Being called by a sick (I think a dying) bed, and the good hand of God upon mee in it, I take the last and best *viaticum*, the sacrament of my dear Lord's body and blood. I take myselfe oblidged to make this short recognition and profession, that whereas I was baptized into that religion of the Church of England, and sucked it in with my milk, and have constantly adhered to it through the whole course of my life, and now, if so be the will of God, shall dye in it, and had resolved through God's grace assisting mee, to have dyed so, tho' att a stake. And whereas that religion of the Church of England taught me the doctrine of non-resistence and passive obedience, which I have accordingly inculcated upon others, and which I took to be the distinguishing character of the Church of England, I adhere no less firmly and stedfastly to that and, in consequence of it, have incurred a suspension from the exercise of my office and expected a deprivation. I find, in so doing, much inward satisfaction, and if the oath had been tendered at the peril of my life, I could onely have obeyed by suffering.

" I desire you, my worthy friends and brethren, to bear witness of this upon ocation, and to beleive it as the words of a dying man and who is now ingaged in the most sacred and solemn act of conversing with God in this world, and may, for ought he knows to the contrary, appear with these very words in his mouth att the dreadfull tribunall."

" This Declaration was read and subscribed by the Bishop, in the presence of Dr. Green, the parish minister, Dr. Hicks, Dean of Worcester, Mr. Jenkins, his Lordship's chaplain, Mr. Powell, his secretary, and Mr. Willson, his emanuensis, who all communicated with him." *Copy.*

DANIEL FLEMING to ROGER KENYON, Clerk of the Peace.

698. [16]89, September 23. Rydal.—When they meet, he is ready to take such oaths as are appointed by law. " You may acquaint Judge Powell, that I am much his Lordship's servant; that the Clerk of the Peace for Cumberland and Westmoreland have been with me ; that I have taken the oaths for Justice of the Peace in those two counties, and that I shall doe the like for Lancashire." *Seal of arms, broken.*

LETTER from the LORDS OF THE TREASURY.

699. 1689, September 26. Whitehall.—Ordering the enforcement of the Act for the better securing the Government, by disarming papists and reputed papists. *Copy.*

A. RIGBY to ROGER KENYON.

700. 1689, October 12. London.—He has a great liking to a certain young lady, as well as to the excellent tempers of the father and mother ; otherwise, as he hopes to be saved, he can have a very fine young lady with 8,000*li*. " on the nail," with a prospect of much more.

The JUSTICES at MANCHESTER SESSIONS to the EARL OF SHREWSBURY.

701. 1689, October 18.—" Wee account it our humble duty to make his Majestie, by the favour of your Lordshipp's relation, acquainted that many of our Romann Catholique younger gentry, some of good quality,

have for some months absconded, though wee have assurance they
remaine in our cuntry. Wee have had diverse discoveries, by information, that their hath been some medelling of officers and men, preparatory to their hopes of an invasion or an insurrection, and after severall
too plaine [———] though not affecting us to that degree as to think
materiall enough to trouble your good Lordshipp with, yet the continuance of them, and the observation which spreads and becomes a
public remarque, puts us upon it to present your Honour the account
that, to some of the gentlemen now absconded, there hath been sent from
London, boxes with scarlet and loke pistolls, swords directed for safe
conveyance to protestants who knew nothing of them, and, by neglect of
the correspondents, unintentionally delivered as directed, and so discovered. That there hath been warr sadles bespoke and privately
conveyed to disafected persons, 5 or 6 months ago, that our gaoles are
full of Irish papists yet, we have frequent accounts of many others at
popish houses, and that which gives the occasion of this is, that the last
day but one, six new warr sadles, made by a popish sadler, were sent for
in the night by a popish gentlewoman, one Mrs. Cuthbert, a widow, who
hath three brothers now absconded. Wee have five persons in prison,
about them all papists, and the rumour so possesses the enraged rable,
that wee are more solicitouse to appease than afraid of what those male-
content restles gentlemen can do ; for wee, without aid, are sufficiently
able and vigilant to free our cuntry from danger. There are some
constables and others do deserve rewards for their extraordinary care.
What wee shall do with those offenders, with these sadles or with
others, upon like occasions, your Lordshipp's appointement, according to
his Majestie's good pleasure, will, with greatest humility and faithfull-
ness, be complyed with and obeyed."

Thomas Hodgkinson to Roger Kenyon.

702. 1689, October 23. Preston.—I went on Wednesday last to
Browsholme, to the christening of Cousin Parker's son and heir, where
the child was no sooner christened but the mother died, so that our
designed rejoicing was turned into mourning. *Seal of arms.*

William Banks to Roger Kenyon.

703. 1689, October 26. Winstanley.—Is sorry he disappointed him
to day at Wigan; he rose early intending to be off by eleven o'clock, but
Mr. Holt not being up, he was forced to stay till ten, before he came down,
after which Mr. Holt would not let him go without a breakfast equal to
a dinner; then they tossed off some "wooden cans" which took till half past
two. "We drank your health and a great many more that we took to be
no flinchers, and then, in hopes to have found you at Wiggan, I rid my mare
so as to get there before five. . . . . . . I must desire you will
deliver the enclosed to my Lord Derby ; it is only to pay my service to
him before I leave the country, and assure him I am the same man
(whatever he may think to the contrary) both to him and his family that
I always professed myself." *Seal.*

Richard Langton to Roger Kenyon.

704. 1689, November 21. London.—His affairs are in good posture,
which he ascribes to Kenyon's assistance. Lord Rawlinson chosen referee,
in the matter betwixt the Chancellor and clerks, who was of opinion " we
ought to be restored, and an order accordingly, last post, went from the

Chancellor to Preston for that purpose, and Tom White is to be removed, and I hope we are in a fair way for settling ourselves more steadfastly than heretofore. The Chancellor is very generous, and insisted not upon one penny more than our generosity would advance." *Seal of arms.*

WILLIAM BANKS to ROGER KENYON.

705. 1689, November 23. London.—I cannot yet learn who is to be our sheriff. Lord Delamere intends, I perceive, to top over our Chancellor, but who it is he hath recommended, time must only show. Last night, at a Committee, upon a full hearing, we voted his brother (though our sitting member) unduly elected for Dartmouth, so one Mr. Horne who opposed him, but could not have so much justice of the Mayor as to be returned, was voted into his place. We have no further account of Irish news but that they are gone into winter quarters; all former extravagant stories are contradicted.

- The EARL OF DERBY to ROGER KENYON.

706. 1689, November 24.—" I can more easily believe Lord Delamere designs that office for himself than you would imagine. I stood near half a quarter of an hour in the Court of Requests this morning, within four yards of Mr. Banks, who would not vouchsafe so much as to stir his hat; after this, I suppose, you will be of my mind." *Seal of arms.*

ROGER KENYON to his father, ROGER KENYON.

707. 1689, November 26. Cambridge.—" I must thankfully own your kind concern for me, in wishing my judgment (as you think mistaken) rectified, and indeed, sir, your thinking it so, were it a case where authority should prevail, would go a great way towards the setting it right, but authority seems there only to have place where reason is wholly at a loss and cannot direct, which is quite otherwise in the case before us, and I must confess, that of all those reasons made use of for the taking of the new oaths, not one appears to me forcible or convincing, but, on the contrary, there are a great many difficulties, which to myself are insuperable. This, I believe, will be the case with me on the thirty first of January.

"I have tried all our booksellers for the Oxford decree in '83, where the solemn dedication of it to the Holy Trinity is expressed at large, but cannot meet with it, though there is a late pamphlet, called the History of Passive Obedience, which gives some few of them, together with the doctrines of our Canons and Homilies, the judgments of our Universities, and the opinions of our divines in full, as to that case."

ROGER KENYON to his uncle.

708. 1689, December 7.—Our news here (as I suppose everywhere else) is very different, everyone telling his story according to his wishes and inclination, nor is it possible how to fix it. The Convocation, I believe, will consent to no alterations, for which reason they are already severely lashed in print, and what will be the issue of this great meeting we are yet to learn.

L[AURENCE] RAWSTORNE to ROGER KENYON.

709. 1689, December 18. Preston.—" This world, this degenerate age wee live in, is soe addicted to lyeing, that one can credit nothing beyond their owne knowledge. The storie of hideing armes at Sir Thomas Clifton's, when fixidly examined, amounts to nothing; the persons that should have proved it, denies flatly, they never saw armes, nor did any expressions ever come from them that they did. Mr. Rigby, of Riby, tould me uppon Monday last, that hee was urgent with theim to tell the trueth therein, but they know nothing of any such matter; this account I had from him on Monday last, and so could not write sooner. The countrey is troubled with the fears they lye under of the Irish Papists who are, under bail, at liberty, and it is thought many more appear under that pretext, which did not before. House-breakings and stealing of horses, and such rumors of misdemeanours are abroad, as are strange to hear; and yet not an information come[s] to mee about any. What such things will result in, I cannot define, but deme them presages of some ill consequences and effects; the Lord turne all to the best! I long to see you to conferre. The sessions will be too far of, if wee could with litle trouble doe it sooner, but I refferre that to you; the face of affairs has but an ill aspect, to say no more." *Seal of arms.*

Bond to Abstain from Excess of Drink.

710. 1689.—Bond by William Frankland, of Clare Street, in St. Clement's Inn, in the County of Middlesex, barber surgeon, to Nathaniel Molyneux, of Dez Hill, in West Houghton, in the County of Lancaster, gentleman, for 100*li.* to be paid to the said Nathaniel on the 6 May next, if the said William do, from the date hereof to the said time, drink any brandy, either entirely by itself or mixed with any other liquor or liquid stuff, or be drunk, or drink above one bottle of wine to his share, in any company. *Seal of arms.*

The Earl of Derby's Claim to Service at the Coronation.

711. [1689.]— The petition of William George Richard, Earl of Derby, to the Lords Commissioners of the Court of Claims, to carry before their Majesties, at their coronation, the sword called *Curtana*, by reason of his tenure of the Isle of Man. *Copy.*

Names of "Conformble Clergy" and of Chapels and Meeting Places in Lancashire.

712. [1689.]—"The names of our conformable clergy who have taken the oathes, within this County [of Lancaster] :—

Alcham—John Taylor, curate.
Ashton-under-Lyne—Thomas Ellison, parson.
Astley—John Battersby, minister.
Atherton—James Wood, minister.
Aughton—John Brownsword, rector.
Billinge—Nathan Golborne, minister.
Blackburne—Francis Price, vicar; Henry Walmsley, curate.
Blakeley—John Moreton, curate.
Bolton-by-the-Sands—Thomas Garforth, vicar.
Bolton-in-the-Moore—John Lever, vicar.
Broughton—George Sedgwick, curate.
Burneley—Thomas Kay, curate.
Bury—John Lomax, curate.
Caiton—Anthony Prockter, curate.
Cartmell—John Armestronge, curate; Rowland Johnson, curate.
Cartmell Fell—John Macdowell, curate.

Chipping—Richard White, minister.
Chorleton—Joshuah Hide, curate.
Chorley—Benjamin Edmunson, minister.
Church—John Barlowe, curate.
Cliderow—William Banck, curate. ·
Cockerham—Lawrence Shaw, vicar.
Colne—James Hargreaves, curate.
Coniston—John Byrkett, curate.
Coulton—Thomas Myers, curate.
Crossby Magna—John Waring, curate.
Crosshall—James Werden.
Crosston—John Ryley, rector.
Dean—Richard Hatten, vicar.
Denton—Roger Dale, curate.
Downham—Richard Wright, vicar.
Eccles—Thomas Hall, vicar.
Eccleston—Robert Linethurst, curate.
Ellinbrook—Myles Atkinson, minister.
Farneworth—Christopher Marsden, curate.
Flixon—John Usherwood, curate.
Flookebrough—George Bateman, curate.
Goosenargh—James Butterworth, minister.
Gorton—Robert Dewhurst, minister.
Gressingham—Richard Thompson, curate.
Hallsell—Nathanaell Brownell, rector.
Halton—Thomas Withers, rector.
Harwood and Lango—Edward Sheardley, curate.
Haslindean—John Duckworth, curate.
Hawkeshead—Thomas Bell, curate.
Heysham—Richard Taylor.
Holland—Roger Bolton, minister.
Hollenfayre—George Hatten, curate.
Hoole—Richard Foxcroft, parson ; John Battersby, curate.
Hyton—John Lowe, vicar.
Upper Kellet—Henry Batty, curate.
Kirby—James Muncaster, vicar.
Kirkham—Richard Clegg, vicar.
Lancaster—James Fenton, vicar; William Gregson, curate.
Leigh—William Barrett, minister.
Leyland—George Walmsley, vicar.
Lindall—Hugh Dobson, curate.
Lithom—James Threlfall, vicar.
Lowick—James Pickthall, curate.
Lun—Thomas Ryley, minister.
Maghull—Zachary Leach, curate.
Manchester—Dr. William Wroe, warden ; Francis Mosley, fellowe ;
   George Ogden, fellowe ; John Hinde, chaplaine.
Meales—Richard Hardy, rector.
Mellinge Church—Daniell Armstead, vicar.
Mellinge Chappel—Peter Dean, curate.
St. Michael's—Thomas Robinson, vicar.
Middleton—Richard Warburton, rector; Thomas Harcurt, curate.
Millam—William Wells, vicar.
Newchurch-in-Winwick—Thomas Willson, curate.
Newton—Samuell Leach, curate ; Edward Alanson, curate.
Ormkirk—Zachary Taylor, vicar.
Padiham—Richard Kippax, curate.

Pemberton—Peter Gregory.
Pillinge—Gabriell Dawson.
Poulton—Richard Harrison, vicar.
Prescott—Thomas Wells, curate.
Preston—James Bland, curate.
Prestwich—Archippus Kippax, curate.
Rachdale—Henry Pigott, vicar.
Ratcliffe—Charles Beswick, rector.
Ribchester—William Felgate, curate.
Ringley—Joshua Dixon, curate.
Rufford—Edward Atherton, curate.
Sallford—John Hide, minister.
Standish—William Heddock, parson.
Staveley—Robert Balfell, curate.
Tatham—Thomas Sharpe, rector.
Tunstall—Edmund Tatam, vicar.
Turton—William Richardson, curate.
Ulverston—John Crewdson, curate.
Urswick—Thomas Inman, vicar.
Walton-in-le-Dale—William Coulton, curate.
Walton-cum-Fazakerley—T. Pawlett, parson; Thomas Marsden, vicar.
Warrington—John Ward, minister.
Warton—Thomas Lawson, vicar.
Whalley—Stephen Gey, vicar.
Whittington—Thomas Bouch, rector.
Wigan—Peter Hadden, curate.
Winwick—Thomas Bennett, rector.
Wood Plumpton—Thomas Kirkham, curate.

" These following clergy who took the oathes, theyr benefices are not knowne :—

Thomas Ingham, of Burneley, clerk; Thomas Pendleton, of Manchester, clerk; John Usherwood, of Manchester, clerk; William Stones, clerk, supplyes the chappells of Darwen and Tockholes; Thomas Armetriding, clerk; William Woods, clerk.

" Presbiterian meeting houses not appropriated to any certain preacher :—

Richard Ingham's house of Little Harwood.
Thomas Dicconson's house of Stalmyn.
Robert Whiteside's house of Martin.
John Brook's house in Little Bolton.

" Meeting houses for Quakers within this county, certified and recorded, viz. :—

A house in Lancaster.
William Higginson's house of Yelland.
Thomas Wither's house of Kellet.
A house att Marsden.
A house in the forrest of Rossendale.
A house in Ouldham parish.
John Townson's house in Ratcliffe.
William Eccleston's house in Great Singleton.
Lawrence Coulborne's house of Freckleton.
Alexander Sailesbury's house at Wediker.
John Prockter's house of Dunishaw.
A house att Penketh, in Prescott parish.

A house att Hartshaw, in the same parish.
A house att Biccurstaff, in Ormkirk parish.
One roome in Manchester.
James Jamson's house in Preston.
Mathew Read's house in Mitton parish.
Thomas Dilworth's house of Bradley.
Certified by Henry Coward.

Swarthmoore Hall.
A new building upon Swarthmoore.
Colt House in Hawkeshead parish.
George Benson's house at Stangend, in Hawkeshead parish.
The Height, in Newton, in Cartmell parish.
John Gurnell's house att Spooner Close, in Hawkeshead parish.
James Harrison's house att Collingfield, in Cartmell parish.   Certified by Leonard Fell.
A chamber belonging to Ralph Ridgeway at the upper end of the Smithy Doore, in Manchester.
Henry Janney's house in Heaton Norris.
Certified by James Stretell.
Job Owen.

"The names of the Chappells in this County, certified and recorded, for meeting places for Dissenters :—

Shyreshead chappell in Cleeveley.
New chappell in Pendleton, for Thomas Jolly and his congregation.
Cleaveley chappell in Cleaveley, for Robert Waddington and his congregation.
Tockholes chappell in Tockholes.
Horwitch chappell in Horwitch.
Elswick chappell in St. Michaell's parish, for John Parr and his congregation.
New chappell in the Castle Hey in Liverpoole,
Toxteth Park chappell,
} for Samuell Augier and his congregation.
Rainford chappell in Rainford, for James Bradshaw and his congregation.
Birch chappell in Manchester parish, for Henry Finch and his congregation.

"Presbiterian parsons and theyr meeting places :—

Thomas Whalley—Christopher Parkinson's house in Chipping.
Charles Sagar—his owne house in Blackburne, William Harwood's house in Lower Darwen.
Thomas Jolly—New Chappell in Pendleton, his dwelling house, John Holkar's house in Read, Agnes Atkinson's house in Clayton-super-Moras, Abram Haworth's house in Haslinden.
Robert Waddington—Cleaveley chappel in Cleaveley.
Thomas Key—Thomas Livesay's house in Over Darwen, William Waddington's house in Alcham, Walton Hall in Walton-in-le-Dale.
John Parr—Elswick chappel in St. Michaell's parish.
Samuell Augier—New chappell in the Castle Hey, in Liverpoole, Toxteth Parke chappell.
Peter Aspinall—Eccleston's barne in Warrington.
Nathanaell Heywood—Bury's house in Ormkirk.
James Bradshaw—Rainford chappell in Rainford.
Thomas Risley—Richard Jackson's barne in Culcheth.

William Birchall—John Hasleden's house in Ashton-in-Makersfield.

Henry Finch—Birch chappell in Manchester parish ; his owne house in Manchester.

John Walker—John Hasleden's barne in Park Lane, in Ashton-in-Makersfield ; William Lathwait's barne in Wygau.

Henry Pendlebury—Oliver Nab's barne in Walmsley and Bast house.

Joseph Whitworth—Mr. Mathew Hallowe's house in Hundersfield.

Henry Newcome—an outbuilding in Dean's gate, in Manchester, belonging to the heirs of Thomas Stockton.

Robert Eaton—William Walker's barne in Pilkington.

Robert Constantine—an edifice of John Jackson's in Greenacres, in Ouldham parish.

John Lever—John Boardman's barne in Bolton.

Roger Baldwin—Mr. Roger's barne in Maunton, in Eccles parish.

Thomas Kinaston—William Broom's barne in Chorleton, in Manchester parish.

George Benson.

William Aspinall.

Jeremy Alredd.

James Naylor of St. Ellen's chappell, in Makersfield.

John Compton—Cockay chappell.

"Other meeting places for Presbiterians, certified and recorded, but appropriated to no particular persons, viz.:—

Meeting places certified by laymen, the preacher not named.

Mr. George Benson's house in Netherkellet.

Certified by { Richard Willson.
John Willson.
William Brathwait.

Augustine Greenwood,
Thomas Hodgson,
William Townson, } An upper chamber over a warehouse in Moor Lane in Lancaster.

Shyreshead chappell in Cleeveley.

Richard Dicconson's house in Whittingham.

Mrs. Mary Preston's house in Preston.

Bispham schoolehouse in Bispham.

Tockholes chappell.

Horwitch chappell.

Roger Kitchen's house in Wood Plumpton.

Robert Swarbreck's house in Rossiker.

Lawrence Livesay's barne in Upper Darwen.

Thomas Slater's house in Whittington.

Thomas Dugdall of Baery his barne in Whalley.

Ralph Walmsley's house in Tockholes.

Thomas Thomason's house in Edgeworth.

William Holder's barne in St. John's Wind in Preston.

John Sanderson of Hardhornend and Newton his house ; his barne belonging to the said house.

John Park, of Longton, his house ; his barne belonging to the said house.

Mary Collinge's house in Blakeley.

James Hardmans of Brodefield's house.

Ann Entwisle's house in Edgeworth, in Bolton parish.

Francis Beckett's house in Tatham.

Richard Jones' house in Caiton.

Nicholas Charnock's house of Barniker, in Garstang parish.

Mathew Hoole, of Martin, his house."

PETITION AGAINST THE SHERIFF OF LANCASTER.

713. [1689.]—Petition against the appointment of Mr. Birch as Sheriff of Lancaster, his quality not being greater than is fit for a high constable, and "instead of our dear and noble Lord Derby, who certainly had been fittest for our Chancellor, he knowing all men in our country, and who is fitt for the severall places, and would have placed men in them without being presented; but that my Lord Brandon should be pitched upon to succeed him in the Lieftenancy of Lancashire, one who, but a while since, was for takeing away our penall lawes and test, was a Deputy Lieftenant to the Lord Molineux, put in for a Justice of Peace when our Protestant Justices were turned out, and a late Regulator of our corporations. What interest can this worthy lord expect if he resort to his old acquaintance? It must be to papists and arch fanatiques. We did not oppose his being a Parliament man upon the account of his father; but it is severe to reject our old Lord Lieftenant who hath governed us and Cheshire, himselfe 13 yeares, and his ancestors time out of mind, whose services to your Majestie, when justly considered, have been inferiour to none, whose interest in the North is not to be vyed with, and we hope and beg you will not reject it him nor us."
Copy.

"A PARTICULAR of some LETTERS sent from the COUNCELL to the HOUSE OF COMMONS."

714, 715. [1689.]—" To Wm. Pigot, the King's own hand, but no name subscribed, purporting that the *Foster* was safe arrived, but had been in great danger. That care should be taken for landing the goods, but that it might do well to wait a convoy from the French fleet. Dated 8 June.

" To Mr. James Goodlad, same hand and same date, purporting that the writer would take care to send the goods, but desires to hear where they might be landed, unknown to the Custom House officers—adding that Londonderry still holds out.

" Another, the same hand, under the same cover, that he hoped ere long to be on their side of the water with them. That their good intentions and endeavours were satisfactory.

" To John Lane, merchant in Broad Street, London, same date. Informs 'tis dangerous passing to Ireland, but that, being got thither, he was well, and that what he asked the King was granted. That the person sent to the Lord Melford was not trusted, but kept in custody; that money wilbe sent by the way of France, for the Lord Walgrave is to pay 25,000*l*. per week till the whole be payed you.—C. POWELL.

" A printed paper, directed to the Convention in Scotland, inveighing against the illegall and unnaturall proceedings of the Prince of Orange, that he had fayled in making out the French league—the P[rince] of W[ales] being illegitimate or imposture, that the blood spilt and to be spilt would lye at their dores; that all the judges who condemned any person would be guilty of bloodshed, and that he desired they would chuse a President and proceed, &c. That he had sent to Dundee and Gorden. Dated 16 May, Dublin.

" To Mr. Abbot, subscribed W. B. Imports the security of his passage; that Londonderry is not taken. Kirk cannot land by reason of a bomb. Hopes to visit him ere long in some parte of England and bring the goods along. Dated 9 June.

" To Geo. Frogmorton, Esquire, at Hichin, in Hartfordshire, from W. B. Same date. Purporting the King is very well. Derry not yet taken ; that when he went down himselfe they fired at him, which caused a closer siege. Kirk at sea and cannot land. I have sent the commissions for Sir C. C. and Sir F. F., and hope, when F. F. comes, not to long from them. A blank commission undirected inclosed.

" To James Brig, at Charles Pigeon, Esquire, his chambers in Gray's Inn, from W. B., to the same effect of the former. If any letter be sent to you, subscribed C. Powell, it comes from a friend, Gooden, in White Heart Court, Lombert Street, [who] will pay the money when called for.

" These to be kept by the Attorney Generall." *Copy*.

LORD BRANDON'S LORD LIEUTENANCY.

716. [1689–1690.]—" It will not easily be fogott in Lancashire, that the Lord Brandon has had two pardens—one for murder, another for high treason—and that after the late Kinge had forgiven him, he was a violent asserter of that Kinge's dispenceing power to the highest degree, in that County, and in that raigne, when he was a Deputy Lievtenant to the Lord Mollineux, a grand papist. He was one that pressingly moved the people to promise to chuse men for the Parliament that would take away our penall lawes and testes. He was intimate with Father Leaburne, Father Goodon, and all the popish gentry. He was made a justice of the peace and never was soe before, together with all the grand papistes of that county, at the very time when forty-four protestant justices, firme to the Church of England, were all turned out of commission for noe other fault then for being soe. After all this, he was a colonel of horse for the late Kinge, and actually in armes till, and after, his abdication. His ancestors, and not very longe since, were dependents upon this Earl of Derby's ancestors, and the Lord Warrington's ancestors were Deputy Lievtenants to the Earle of Derby and his ancestors. In the late Revolution, this Earle of Derby acted his part, and was in his place much more instrumentall then any for the accession of their present Majesties to the Crown. There is no blott in his ancestors' escucheon ; they have borne the office of Lord Lievtenants of Lancashire and Cheshire above two hundred yeares, except in the time of the late horrid rebellion, in which this Earles grandfather, for his loyalty, lost his life, and a great part of his estate. And what has this Earle of Derby done soe much to demeritt, as to be turned out of these Lieftenencies ? The Lord Warrington is a minor and cannot personally execute the place of Lord Lieftenant of Cheshire. And as to the Lord Brandon, besides what hath been before observed of him, his actings may administer suspicion what his designes are, if these thinges were enquired into, viz.: what armes, besides the militia armes, of which every souldier keeps his owne, are stored up in Lancashire by that Lord, part at Hallsall, part at Liverpool Castle, and other partes elsewhere, in the custody of some dissentors. Sir Richard Standish said he believed there might be as many as would arme ten or twelve thousand men, and gave this account from whence they were had, viz.: some bought in and brought over from Irland, for which Sir Richard was asked, as he was a Deputy Leiftenant, to give a receipt, but he said he refused soe to doe, not knowing to what purpose they were brought over, for the Lord Branden, as was, two or three yeares agoe, informed to the House of Commons, had given commissions to a great many to be captaines &c., besides the captaines of the militia, all or most of them being dissenters—of which he could give noe good account. And it is not forgott that his Lordship summoned the Lancashire dissentinge ministers and their clan, to meet King James at Stocken

[Stockham ?] Heath, in Cheshire, at which place the Lord Branden, as their cheiftaine, presented them to King James. Besides these armes, all the old Lancashire militia armes, his Lordship tooke to himselfe, and sent down new ones from London, and made the countrey take them at his rates, and in sending down those, Sir Richard said he had an oportunity of sending down what greater number he thought fitt, and of storing up the overplus imperceptibly. Besides these, it is supposed his Lordship found a considerable stock of armes which were left at Liverpool Castle by the Lord Mollineux, layd up there by that Lord (who is a papist) when he was owner of that Castle and Lord Lieftenant of that County under the late King James. Besides all these, severall packes of swordes within this year or two have been pretendedly seized, carried from London by a Lancashire carrier, which, as it was given out, were goinge to some Lancashire papiste's, bot, when the swordes were disposed of according to his Lordship's order, noe farther inquiry was made after the party, whoever it was, to whom they were soe suppositiously sent. Sir Richard said there was a Lancashire man could cleanse armes who had a great deale of money owing by the Lord Branden, for dressing of all these armes. Sir Richard also told that the Lord Branden has now given protections to many of the great papists and other jacobites. His Lordship makes himself very busey in every corporation, soe often as there is occasion to choose any new Member of Parliament, soe much concerned as if he, as Lord Lieftenant, must govern the election, and in these he failes not to have the whole interest of papist and jacobite, tho' all that seldome makes his endeavours successfull; for the countrey, generally speaking, neither loves him nor feares him."

Order by RAPHE ASHTON, RICHARD STANDISH, JAMES HOLTE, HENRY FARINGTON, L. RAWSTORNE, L. (?) RICHMOND, and RALPH LONGWORTH, to the Bailiff of the Corporation of Wigan.

717. 1689[-90], January 11. Wigan.—" These are to require you, in their Majesties names, strictly to comand you, that you upon the twenty-seventh day of January instant, take to your assistance a competent nomber of such Protestant inhabitants as are well affected to their present Majesties' Government, and that you and they, the said 27th day of January instant, so soon as you can discern day, being well and sufficiently armed, repair to the houses of all Papists Recusants, or other houses, suspected secretly to harbour any absconded Papists which, in the late King's time bore arms or bore office, or to harbour any Irish, Scotch, or other popish Soldiers, or such as have harboured emissaries to the late King, since the Coronation of their present Majesties, or such as are reasonably suspected to keep to the use of any popish recusant, or for their assistance, any arms, armour, ammunition, horses fit for the warrs, warr saddles with furniture, or any other habiliments of warr whatsoever, and where you find any such absconded Papist, any Irish, Scotch, or other popish Souldiers, so secretly harboured, or any horses, arms, armour, ammunition, or other habiliments of warr, or you find any thievish, roguish, or other felonious or suspected persons to be robbers of houses or the like, that you forthwith seize and secure every such person's horses, arms, ammunition, or other habiliments of warr, and the master or owner of the said horses, where they shalbe so found, and them bring before some of their Majesties Justices of Peace in the said county, togather with this Warrant, to be examined, disposed of, and dealt with according to Law. And for as much as we are informed that several of the Irish, Scotch, and other popish souldiers, do lurk and hide themselves in the day time in woods, rocks, or other secret places, now, if any of the inhabitants of your town shall informe you of the places where they do so hide themselves and frequent, that then you fail not to search the said houses and places and to apprehend the said persons so lurking and hiding themselves, and bring them before some of their Majesties justices as aforesaid. And hereof· faile not att your perill." *Seven seals.*

SIR ROGER BRADSHAIGH to ROGER KENYON.

718. 1689[-90], January 19. Haigh.—"My cozen Shakerley is recommended to the Corporation of Wiggan by the Right Honorable the Earle of Derby, to searve for burgess of that town, in the roome of my cozen Banks, deceased. I hope you will favour that his Lordship's inclination." *Seal broken.*

JOHN ENTWISLE to ROGER KENYON.

719. 1689[-90], January.—Requesting a copy of the record of the conviction of Lord Molyneux as a popish recusant. *Seal.*

THOMAS KENYON to his Father, ROGER KENYON.

720. 1689[-90], February 5. Chester.—It was on Monday last I received the news of my Lord Derby's appointing Mr. Arthur Bennett (our Attorney Bennett's younger brother) his Deputy Bailiff Itinerant for Cheshire, allowing him, for his services, 30*li.* a year. We have little news now in Chester besides the adjournment of the Parliament till 22 April, and a great expectancy of seeing the King here, ere long, in his passage for Ireland ; whether it is real or a state trick to make soldiers come in faster, I must leave to wiser heads. *Seal.*

The EARL OF DERBY to ROGER KENYON.

721. 1689–90, February 8.—"My last gave you a short account of the parliament being dissolved, and this post will bring, dear Roger, the proclamation for calling another. We must now bestirr our selves, and I hope every one will do so ; I am sure I question not your endeavors. I intend to make what hast I can into the country. Major Preston writes to-night to the same effect. I did, the last, post to Mr. Holt. I hope all our party will unite and lay aside all animosities among one another. My Lord Colchester and my brother stand for Liverpool, which I hope will keep out Norris." *Seal of arms.*

ROGER KENYON to Various Constituents of Clitheroe.

722. 1689–90, February 12. Peel.—Asking for their votes for the next parliamentary election. Promises to serve the church, king, country, and borough. *Draft.*

THOMAS HODGKINSON to ROGER KENYON.

723. 1689–90, February 15. Preston.—"As to Mr. Highsheriffe's . . . am not much concerned further then to observe your kindnes and civility, which he ought to take more particuler notice of, if he rightly apprehended his owne interest. As to the other concern of Clitherow, I shall go to Cuerdall too-morrow and engage him, and *quantum in se* I do not expect to bee denyed. If I bee, I shall not take it kindly ; but do not much question what hee can do to the utmost. The mob here are mad and (I beleeve) that Greenfield will carry it, for one; whether the Chancellor will carry it or no, I know not, but it is reported he is coming down. I cannot say that his clearke has been over sedulous for him. However, I meddle none. I was summoned upon Thursday last (and only three more in this toune) to take the oaths before the Commissioners of the Tax, but did not appeare; the worst (as to that) is double charge. I am praying for the continuance of the last Parliament, having no prospect of a better." *Seal of arms.*

THOMAS KENYON to ROGER KENYON.

724. 1689-90, March 19. Chester.—" The ellection of members for the ensueing Parliament of this citty, began Monday morning last, and continued till near 7 att night, att which time, Proclamation beinge thrice made, by the common cryer of the court, that if any freeman of this citty were yet to vote, let them come forth, the Sheriffs would take their pole, otherwise the books would be closed; but, none answering, the Court adjourned, till 9 next day, to give judgment; about which hour, the court sat againe and the severall candidates attended, both sides having rakt together the small remainder of freemen which had not voted the precedeing day. Upon the first meeting, Colonel Whitley and Alderman Manwaring demanded the pole for some more of their party, which the said sheriff refused, answering, that haveing caused Proclamation to bee made the day before, as aforesaid, and none appearing, the Court was adjourned to this time and place to inspect the books and give judgment, pursuant to which he was resolved to take no more votes of either side, in whose Judgment Sir Thomas Grosvenor and Leeving (unwilling to give the Court further trouble, though they had as strong a party in readiness) acquiest. The other Sheriff (who is supposed to have been tampered with) resolving to make difference, protested his brother's proceedings, but being hastily asked again . . . . of them, and surprized for want of sufficient instructions what to say, was at a loss for an answer. By and by, a paper was put into his hands to read; but, not used much to writing, was consequently as unready as afore in speaking, but clapping it into a young clerk's hand at his elbowe, made him his deputy *pro tempore*, and desired him to read it for him, who instantly begins—the Protestation of Mr. Sheriffe's brother; at which the head Sheriff (Mr. Partington) commands him silence, who, not readily obeying, was forced from his standing by the Sheriffs officers. Sir John Manwaring (present at the election) takes the paper, together with his office, out of his hand, and gets up to read it, but the noise of the rable's continued shouting, prevented. Some time after, silence being made, the books were openly inspected, and the Sheriffe declared Alderman Manwaring, 457; Colonel Whiley (*sic*). 483; Mr. Leeving, 494; Sir Thomas, 498; and then adjourned to the pentice, to seale and signe the Indentures; which being accordingly done by the Mayor, Aldermen, &c., and affixt to the Chamberlain's mandate, indorsed with the Sheriffes returne, was by the head Sheriffe (the proper and usual officer) delivered into the seal keeper's hands, whose office it is to return, together with the Indenture, the Originall writ out of Chancery, before directed to the Chamberlaine with the Sherriffes answer to him indorst, affixed thereto; which was by him accordingly done and delivered to the hands of the chief member elect, by him to be retorned above . . . . Sir Thomas, Mr. Leeving (and I hear just now), my Lord Cholmondeley, are on their way already to London. The election for the county is not yet over, but I suppose may end to-night in disfavour of Sir Philip." *Seal broken.*

LAURENCE RAWSTORNE to ROGER KENYON.

725. 1689–90, March 24. Preston.—Captain Bellingham desires " horse," and " if he had a regiment with us now, they would be few (*sic*) enough to scour the countrey of the Irish disbanded souldiers, who are, by 2 at least, in some of our Papists' houses ; may be, 8 or 10 in a house, as they are of ability to receive theim. They alarum the country mightiely; but, in regard we have some foot companies here, our feares are the lesse. I signified so much to Cozen Bancks and wished he would impart it to my Lord, and his Lordship was pleased to write to me ; yet nothing of command how to behave our selfes in that case, and so wee are meerly passive, and hope they have not the spirit to attack us. I desired Mr. Patten, who by this time is with you, to put you in mind of our concerns with theim, which would make them a little more mute, and animate us to act more vigourously. You may set it a-work, now you are there. You knowe the way and means how to begin ; pray you omit not. It would be good allay to cook their brags."

THOMAS KENYON to ROGER KENYON.

726. 1690, March 29. Chester.—We have no newes from Ireland since the last account of 8,000 French that landed. Sir James Poole is already secured by order of Councell, and committed for high treason ; it is reported some others are in danger to undergoe the same fate. *Seal broken.*

WILLIAM HAYHURST to ROGER KENYON, M.P., in London.

727. 1690, April 1. Lancaster.—"Mr. Rowe and myselfe were, but a while agoe, before the Judge, upon a petition preferred against us by honest Richard Royd (?) ; the judge was a little brisk upon Mr. Rowe, and told him the words spoken against, were not indictable nor actionable ; and Mr. Rowe being something peremptory, hee grewe angry at him. Hee gives it out for law that no words are indictable, but such as touch the Government; though a man call you traytor and murderer, you cannot indict him . . . We had a very good charge, principally relating to an unity, and to lay aside animosities and distractions and to exhort the people to a hearty contribution to supply the King's occasions. There is a story of a plott in Lancashire for raising 3 troops of horse, discovered by one Dodsworth, a papist. Mr. Standish of Standish's house was besett, but I hear he escaped. Most of the principall papists are in it, and some protestants. This is a whispered thing ; some give it credit, some otherwise."

SIR RALPH ASSHETON to ROGER KENYON, M.P.

728. 1690, April 1. Middleton.—" Your unanimous agreeing to supply his Majesty, is extreame good news to us. Give what you will, so Ireland may speedily be reduced. I mension this because I know our enimies are still at worke, and, so long as the Frence have any hold in the aforesaid kingdom, we must expect it, to say no more. I am now to my part against those that would destroy his Majesty and our happy government." *Seal of arms.*

C. GREENFIELD to ROGER KENYON, M.P.

729. 1690, April 5. Preston.—The assizes ended on Friday. There is " a poll-bill in preparing, but the nomination of commissioners, I presume, will not be yet. If it should bee before I come up, pray name for this toune:—The Mayor for the time beinge; Laurence Rawsthorne, esquire; Edward Rigby, esquire; Chr: Greenfield; Law: Wall; Geo: Addison; William Lemon; Tho: Winckley (?); Jo: Kellett; Nath: Walmsley; Daniell Chadocke; Rich: V . . . ; Roger Sudell, junior; William Hebson; John Cockshull; [and] Tho: Greenfield." *Seal of arms.*

THOMAS WINCKLEY to ROGER KENYON.

730. 1690, April 13. Preston.—On Saturday last was sennight, two strangers, who had been in the town a day or two, were brought before Mr. Mayor and Col. Rawstorne; by their brogue they were discovered to be Irishmen. They pretended they were protestants, designing for Ireland to serve King William and Queen Mary, as volunteers in Duke Schombergh's camp. One says his name is Dore and the other, Burke. The first pretends he was sent out by the late King James with a detachment from Hounslow Heath to the Island of Bombay, as far as the River Euphrates, and returned to England about a year ago, knowing nothing of the revolution. The other came over from Ireland about Michaelmas 1688, being a corporal of dragoons to one Major Mathews, in Col. Butler's regiment, was wounded at Reading, and lay a long while in London. Upon being searched, letters were found on them to Sir William Creagh, Sir Rowland Stanley, and Sir James Poole, and the idle Mr. Molyneux; the contents had nothing extraordinary but recommending the bearers, with some hints of their usefulness. They are in the serjeant's custody, and copies of the letters have been sent to Lord Brandon. *Seal of arms.*

JO. HULTON to ROGER KENYON.

731. 1690, April 19.—"Since my last, wee have had our shipping returned from Belfast that went with the last recruites, by whom severall letters cam from persons in the Army to their freinds here. One of them, being more particular than the rest, I have sent you a coppy of it. I only tell you that our Irish gentlemen give great credit to it. If it should prove true, I am of opinion there will bee no action in the field. The Irish and French will get into strongholds and put our army on seiges, which will make tedious worke. Wee have a great many recruites of horse pas through this town for Highlake.

(Enclosure.)

" Dublin, April 12, 1690.—Our account of the French supplys are different. It is certain there are but four regiments, one red, one bleu, and two white, and the most they pretend is 1,600 in a regiment. The supplys of stores are, 1,000 barrells of powder, 10 feild peeces, 4 morters, with bombs, carcases, ball, and other necessarys for warr, as pistolls swords, &c., the number not knowne; they are 8 battalions, whereof 4 are Switzers, Walloones, and other strangers, and severall Germans, prisoners that are entertained, and about 300 English, Scotch, and Irish. That the Lord Hunsden had been at Corke neer two months with King James. He ordered the English, Scotch, and Irish, that came from France, into his regiments, but Lieftenant-Generall Loozon would not suffer him to have a man. That one of the French regiments are as far as Waterford, where they stay till they heare how we move. There is already shipt on board the French ships, five regiments of Irish, viz.:— the Lord Mountcashell's, Colonel Brown's, Colonel Cha: O'Brion's, Colonel Butler's, and Colonel Feilding's—all of foot. They say they force protestants on board—the Irish running away. Their eight regiments of dragoones are in a very bad condition, also four of the eight regiments of horse. Oates sould for 20s. per barrell, and but few to be had. Pease straw and other straw are their generall food, and the worke horses are so weak that carriages are not to be had. The Spring comes on apace about Dublin, and if grass can be had, their numbers will make them more formidable, but at present they are in a sad condition. On the 20th March, dyed the Governor of Drougheda; also Duke Mollass is dead. The force at Dundalke, Ardee, Cavan Castle, Blany, Drougheda are in a bad condition, dying in great numbers for want. Colonell Sarsfeild is come from the borders of Cavan, and Brigadeer Hamilton and Lord Galmoy are goeing to governe there. Sarsfeild is falne sicke since he came to towne. The [death] of Colonell Nugent is much lamented by the Irish. They lost a many brave men in that action with him at Cavan. The Duke of Berwick was there, and had his horse twice shot under him. He hath been heard to say he feares the Irish will never stand the English rebbles, as he calls them. This, a protestant gentleman at Dublin sent, by water, to the north; severall have soe made their escape of late from Dublin."

[THOMAS HODGKINSON] to his cousin, ROGER KENYON, M.P.

732. 1690, May 6. Preston.—" Upon Sunday last, I received a letter from Mr. Roper, wherein he desired an account what Colonel Mathews had done here, touching the papists, whereunto I recounted what I had heard, viz.: that Mr. Barlow and Mr. Harrington were taken, and sent to Lancaster, but do not hear that any other is apprehended. A detachment (of 42) of the Dutch troopers were sent from Lancaster hither, where they have quartred about three weekes and were sometimes (as I am tould) sent into the countrey to seize the old sinners, but returned *re infecta*. Colonell M. went from hence, upon Sunday morning last, towards London, and the Dutch troopers returned from hence, this morning, towards Lancaster, and this is all the account I can give, touching this affaire, whereof, I pray, acquaint my Lord Derby. I am mightily your debtor for your frequent letters. I have (according to your desire) burned your last, and did not think it prudentiall to communicate the same to any person, being morally certaine that noe certificate would have been sent upp by any sort of persons. More of this at our meeting. The gaole was broke upon Sunday night by the Irish soldiers, and onely three of them escaped. I tould you formerly that Edm : Threlfall's son was taken, but hath since made his escape, whilst his mother plaid at tables with his keeper. Nothing more here worth communicating."

. . . . WINCKLEY to ROGER KENYON, M.P., at Westminster.

733. 1690, May 9. Preston.—" On Wednesday, Sir Edward Chisnal came to towne, and has been here ever since. He seems not fond of petitioning. His reason is, that if there be either motion or petition for a short day, there wil be noe lesse then a moneth given the other side, considering the distance of place to attend and bring up witnesses, if any (as certainly some wil) move for reasonable time, and that Mr. Patten may not be surprised, liveing 160 miles from London, and before the moneths end, he supposes there will be a recesse. But Sir Edward is full of belief that, as this case happens, the House wil grant a new writ, and leave Mr. Patten to prosecute, or let fall his peticion, as he thinks fit; for, seeing my Lord Willoughby is removed to the House of

Lords, and soe noe longer a member of the House of Commons, there is a vacancy, as in case of death, and a writ to issue to elect another in my Lord Willoughby's roome; and, if Mr. Patten make good his peticion, then the person that succeeds his Lordship is removed, and Mr. Patten comes in; but if he fayle to procure his peticion, then the new member continues. How consonant or agreable this is to the rules and practice of the House, those that are the old members, can best tell; and he desires that you and Mr. Greenfield wil be laboring to informe your selves sufficiently in the thing, and if you see a fair prospect of obtaining such a writ, then to venture a motion; and I believe Sir Edward will be with you before the end of the next week. And by this post a short state of the case will be sent to Mr. Greenfield for you and him to advise upon with Sir Robert Sawyer, Mr. Finch, or such other eminent members as you judge most proper. It would be a great prejudice to us, if a day should shortly be assigned for hearing this matter, and a recesse happen, after a hurry up to London, and charges layd out, and all to noe purpose. Soe that we should have a fair prospect that the Parliament wil be sitting at the day to be assigned for hearing, or else we shal be spoyled, and not able to bear another journey. . . . . As to the petition concerning the gaol, I finde all here very cold in the matter; they think the castle will take up as much cost in keeping up and repaires, as building and maintaining a new gaol at Preston, which, being the middle of the county, wil save the country abundance of money, in carrying presoners as far as Lancaster, from your part of the county." *Seal of arms.*

THOMAS KENYON to his father, ROGER KENYON, M.P., at Westminster.

734. 1690, May 17. Chester.—Has received a letter from "Mr. Barton" stating that "My Lord" [Derby?] designed to wait on the King at Chester "as chamberlain of this county" and "for that end commanded me to get a new purse made, bearing their present Majesties' armes and cypher." Has consulted "the upholsterers here, and severall others [as to] the best artists in imbroydery, Chester affords, who unanimously agree that the old one is a peece [of work] not to be sampled in this toune: the goodnes of the worke . . . . richnes of the materiall, not being here to be met w[ith] . . . . Those frie[nds who have] seen the old one, and with whom I have advised, considering the work is but little decayed—except the ground upon which the motto is wrought—have perswaded me to have that took out, and a new one layed on, the which is very sensible, and with altering the cypher and setting new tassells to, will (it is not doubted) under the whole [look] very sumptuous and gay." Desires to know "his Lordship's" pleasure; if a new one is required, it must be prepared in London, "Chester not being able to afford it." . . . Its make "is the same with that carryed before the Chancellor of England, bearing the armes of England in embroydery and the cypher of their Majesties, viz.: XXX in the upper part; on one side the arms, and ℜ on the other side."

THOMAS RISHTON to ROGER KENYON, M.P.

735. 1690, May 17. Whalley.—"I have promised Sir Edmund Ashton to write to you, by this post, and it is to let you know his design of having a free plate, to be run for at Clitheroe, at such times as will be agreed to by consent. The contributers he has prickt down are a great many, and he thinks they will most of them willingly club with him. The town it self intends to make a joynt stock. He says he thinks he ought first to acquaint the burgesses and bayliffs." *Seal of arms.*

Robert Sclater to Roger Kenyon; M.P.

736. 1690, May 19.—We should be glad to hear that the Protestants would unite more than they do, to discourage the common enemy. The Papists make great boasts of our differences, and they and others disaffected, are at a great height. We would gladly know something of his Majesty's going for Ireland, which we hoped the last post, but had no letter from you. Sir Edmund Ashton laid his commands upon me to write to you, about a plate of 15 or 20*li.* to be run for at Clitheroe at midsummer. *Seal.*

Thomas Kenyon to Roger Kenyon, M.P.

737. 1690, May 19. Chester.—In my last, I had not time to give you an account of the taking of Charlemont, which was then spoken of, but since confirmed. It surrendered on Wednesday last, the garrison having suffered much for want of provisions, and constrained thereby to yield it up.

John Apulton to Roger Kenyon.

738. [1690, May?]—"His Lordship may be assured of officers that will stand and fall with him. I had the happiness to recommend Mr. Leiftwich Oldfeild for a captain of horse, whom I hope his Lordship was well pleased with. I do think Mr. Shakerley the fittest person in our county to bee a collonel of foot, and to make a good militia, in a short time, and I do not doubt but he will readily and willingly serve his Lordship, but I leave it to your consideration whether you think fit to propose him. On Sunday last, came a vessell to Highlake fr[om] D——, loaden with tallow and hides, her cockett was for France. Sir Cloudesly Shovell has secured all the men and put them on board severall vessells. The master pretends he made his escape, but that that gives mee suspition of him, is the relation hee gives of the affaires there. He says that the French were landed at Cork, but not above 3,000, and with very little ammunition or armes; that the Irish are very much dis[contented] at it, expecting much greater supply." *Much decayed.*

A Manchester News Letter.

739. 1690, July 5.—"On Thursday, in the afternoone, the Earle of Devonshire and Pembrooke were sent from Whitehall, in order to goe on board the fleete, as yet not known on what occasion, though various conjectures are made of it, though it is generally said, on complaint of some Dutch ministers, because my Lord Torrington did not releive the Dutch squadron, when they were soe warmely engaged, for we say here, he fought at too far a distance and might have come neerer the weather-gage. Our last advice from the fleet, left them of from Dunagence, on Thursday, in the afternoone, plying to the eastward, the French fleete tydeing it upon them within two leagues. Two Dutch disabled ships were left att Hastings, and haveing drawne them on shore, soe that the French could not get them of, who sent their boats on shore and burnt them. We are makeing our fleet towards the gunfleete, and it is believed that this day, both fleetes are seen of Dover. Expresses have been sent

to the Mayor and cheef officers of the ports, both of Sussex and
Kent.

" Since the before written, we have the following account (viz.) from
Dover, on the 4th instant, it is writt that the *Saldadoes* was sent
thither by the Lord Torrington for 40 or 50 pilots to cary the fleet
up the river, they making for the Downs. The Earle of Devonshire
and Pembroke were just arrived there and goeing to the fleet at
Rye, from which place they write, the 3rd instant, that our fleete came
to an anchor neare that place, and the French fleete followed, and came
to an anchor two leagues from them, haveing chased two Dutch men
of warr on shoare at Hastinges, from which place the weman and
children were sent, the 3rd instant, with what goods they could carry,
feareing the French should land, which they had not at 5 that afternoone, but had sett fire to the two Dutch ships, which were then
burneing, and that two other Dutch ships were on the sands by the
White Rocks, about a mile to the west of Hastings, at whom the French
fired, without much damage, about 60 guns, and the Dutch kept firing
at them from one of their ships, the other being left by all their men,
and in case they see no hopes of saveing them, they are resolved to sett
fire to them to prevent their falling into the French hands, who, it is
thought, will come up to them the next tide, which would be about
4 o'clock next morneing. The Dutch Vice-Admirall and his son are
buryed there, and about 250 sick and wounded were brought thither, and
to Battle. Severall gentlemen have been on the guard all this night,
feareing the landeing of the French, which as yet have not appeared,
and it is thought they have gone of to sea. The French sent five long
boats on shoor at Hastings, but were kept of that place by their greate
guns. Five of the French men of war came soe nigh, that they fired
severall guns on the sands. Al the pilotts, as well from Deale as Dover,
are sent to the fleet, and all the merchant ships that were in the Downes
are sent for back againe. Our Irish letters of the 26th past, say that
our army were in possession of Dundalke, that the enemy had drawne
their army on the south side the river Boine, where they were secureing
all the passes to hinder us from marching towards Dublin. All the
ships from Belfast are ordered to Highlake and Carlingford. The
Commissioners at Carrickfergus are ordered not to suffer any to depart
that kingdome, without his Majesty's pasport. By a vessel arrived at
Milford Haven, we are tould that the late King had drawne his army
towards Ardee, and left but one regiment in Dublin, the Protestants
being secured in the churches and colledges. The Parliament of
Scotland satt the 26th past, and agreed upon an Act to appoint Commissioners to visit all scholes and universities of learning, ordeineing all
the regents and masters to heighten the confession of faith and take the
oath of allegiance, and be assured that there principles be agreeable to
the present Government. The new Commission for the Privy Councel
was read this day, and all the present members took the oaths. By express from Plymouth, we hear that Sir Cloudesley Shovill, in the
Monke, with the *Experiment* and *Dover*, arrived, the 30th past, at the
Lands End, and were hourely expected at that place ; and from the Isle
of Wight they say that the fleet that came from Plymouth, being eleven
saile, were plying windward of that place, supposed to be as high as
Dunnese (?), the wind at east north east. Our Holland letters yesterday say that the Duke of Savoy had totally defeated the French army
and tooke Mounsier Callivate prisoner, but this merritts confirmation.
Sir, this is all the Bull's head post news in Manchester."

[P.S.]—" In Manchester her they be carrying a thing made like
the Pope, upon a man's shoulder, a long pole, rownd the towne, and

Q 2

a drum before it, and bonefires made, and ringing, for joy of the good newes last night out of Ireland of Dublin and Drocheda being taken, and King James fled away towards Kingsaile." ·

ORDER by the JUSTICES OF THE PEACE for the County of Chester to LIEUTENANT WILLIAM CHURCH and CORNET ROBERT LEE.

740. 1690, July 9.—" We, haveing receaved her Majesty's Order in Councel to secure all such papists and other persons whom we shall have reason to suspect to be disaffected to the Government, as may probably be active against it in case of an insurrection or invasion ; and for as much as Sir Philip Egerton, knight, Francis Cholmoley, esquire, and Thomas Minshall, of Erdeswick, in the said county, esquire, and Leftwich Oldfeld, of Leftwich, in the said county, esquire, have not taken the oathes to their present Majestyes, whereby they have rendered themselfs justly suspected to the Government ; these are, therefore, in there Majesties' names to authorise and require you, or ether of you, imediately to aperehend the said Sir P. E., F. C., and Tho. Minsh : and L. O., and convey them to the castle of Chester, and deliver them into the custody of Sir John Morgen, governer of the said castle, who is hereby required to receive and safely to keep the said persons there, until they shall be thence discharged by due order of law." *Copy.*

Note.—" There was likewise an order of same date, to the same persons, to search for and seize all arms in the houses or places of abode of the said Sir Philip Egerton, Francis Cholmondeley, Thomas Minshall, and Leftwich Oldfeld." *Copy.*

ORDER by the JUSTICES OF THE PEACE for the County of Chester to SIR THOMAS BELLOT and MAJOR JOHN DAVENPORT.

740A. 1690, July 21.—" We, having received her Majestie's order in Councell to cause all horses belonging to papists and persons disaffected to the Government, or who shall refuse to take the oathes to their present Majesties, to be seized, and forasmuch as the persons here undernamed are either known papists, or reputed papists, or persons disaffected to the Government, or have refused to take the oathes to their said Majesties, these are, therefore, in their Majesties' name, to authorize and require you, or either of you, imediately upon sight hereof, to make dilligent search for, and seize and take into your custody, all the horses of the said persons here undernamed, that you shall anywhere find in their possession, or in the possession of any others for their or any of their use or uses, and that you speedily give an account, unto us, of your doings, to the end that such horses may be disposed of according to order of law." *Copy.*

Schedule of names of recusants—viz. : " Tho : Holford of Newbrook, esquire, John Holford of Kinderton, Ger : Croxton of Ravenscroft, Ra : Walley of Stanthorn, gentlemen, Jer. Rooth of Twemlow, Leftwich Oldfeld of Leftwich, Tho : Minshull of Erdswick, esquires, Wm. Lownds of Overton, gentleman, Sir Phi : Egerton, knt., Francis Cholmondeley, esquire, Peter Yates of Church Hulm, innkeeper."

THOMAS KENYON to ROGER KENYON.

741. 1690, July 30.—The wind blows fresh from Ireland, and it is said the King resolves (if that gives leave) to set sail thence **to-night**. *Seal of arms.*

[LEFTWICH OLDFIELD] to the EARL OF DERBY.

742. 1690, July 31.—Recounting the substance of discourses with Sir John ―――― about the condition of Lancashire. "That the old divisions in these parts were well known, and the original thereof was Cavalier and Rounded. That we thought it not advisable to petition the King, not from any sullenness or disaffection, but lest it should be misconstrued by the same interpreters that sent us hither, complaining against the Queen, from whose order in Councell our committment is pretended to derive itself, as also the warrant for taking horses, and applications of that kind, if approved good manners would have directed that way, wherewith the King, in all likelyhood, would not at present interfere. That we were careful to avoid giving offence, and for any offence taken, or for anything acted, don, or said, or any just cause or reason of suspicion, by us or any of us given, for such dealing with us, we are ready to put ourselves, severally, upon God and the countrey, and to the ordinary cours, tryall, and determination of the laws of the land, with dutifull patience submit ourselves, hoping no more at the hands of our friends, then that they will oppertunely say and doe for us, what common justice and charity shall prompt. That the quiett enjoyment of our legall properties and liberty is all we desire, and that the harder dealing we find, and the longer causlesly held in durance, the harder will the reflection be, we conceive, upon those who take pleasure in our sufferings. That the root of animosities here, the old cause of new doeings, hath layn bare many years. Probably, we may never be mentioned, but if we should, or any questions should be asked, our friends should not differ in their accounts."

ORDER at a General Meeting of the JUSTICES OF THE PEACE for the County of Lancaster.

743. 1690, August 25.—Whereas, William Tomlinson, late Governor of the House of Correction at Preston, had been turned out of his place and one William Higginson, put therein, the said Tomlinson having been represented to his Majesty as one obnoxious to the Government, and in no way qualified for the said employment, the said Tomlinson petitioned that the charge might be examined, and, if innocent, he might be restored. It was thereupon ordered by Lord Nottingham, Principal Secretary of State, that the allegation be examined; and upon its examination, it was found that the said Tomlinson was a fit person to be Governour of the House of Correction. It is thereupon ordered that he enjoy the said place.

ORDERS at GENERAL MEETINGS of the JUSTICES OF THE PEACE for the County of Lancaster, held at Lancaster, &c.

744. 1690, August 25–1693, April 4.—Meeting held at Lancaster 25 August, 1690.—Whereas, upon the hearing of counsel on behalf of Nicholas, Bishop of Chester and Rector of Wigan, and on behalf of the parishioners of Wigan, and especially the inhabitants of Hindley, against John Greene, upon his tendering a certificate to the Clerk of the Peace, to record the Chapel of Hindley, in the parish of Wigan, as a place appointed to dissenting protestants for their religious worship, it was shown that in the year 1641 the said chapel was erected for the ease of the inhabitants that were above two miles distant from the parish church ; that it was built by the approbation of the then Bishop of Chester, and the first minister who settled there was conformable to the Church of England; and it was supplied by conformable ministers till they were turned out of their livings. And the nonconformist who got in was, at Bartholomewtide, 1662, put out by the Act, and a conformist restored, and it has since been possessed by conformists. That at communicating times, the inhabitants repair to Wigan to receive the sacrament, •owning thereby their dependence and subjection to the mother church. That the generality of the inhabitants of Hindley are very conformable. That this chapel is endowed with 22*li.* by the year, and upwards, besides the benevolent contributions of the chapelry. That the donatives of the endowment have been by persons of the Church of England, and one sum of 6*li.* by the year, which had been for some time withheld, was, in 1669, by the Duchy Court, decreed to be yearly paid to the minister of Hindley Chapel. That a very pious, orthodox minister is, about a month ago, dead; who had been long possessed of the place, and that another conformable minister had offered to come into the place, but had been kept out by the said Green on pretence that he, and some few other dissenters, are feoffees for the ground on which the chapel stands. The whole Court (the Honourable Hugh Willoughby excepted) were of opinion, and ordered, that the Clerk of the Peace should not record Mr. John Green's certificate, and that Hindley Chapel should not be used by dissenters for their pretended religious worship.

Meeting held at Ormskirk, April 11, 1692.—Whereas motion was yesterday made by Thomas Patten, Esqr., "counceller at law," for the recording of St. Ellen's Chapel for a meeting house for a congregation of dissenters from the Church of England; and upon hearing of counsel on behalf of Mr. Byrom and others of the Church of England, showing that the chapel is a consecrated chapel-of-ease within the parish of Prescott, which anciently was, and now of right ought to be, supplied with a minister of the Church of England, for the ease of the inhabitants within the parish aforesaid, particularly within the town of Hardshaw-within-Windle: Now, upon full hearing, the motion was lost by a majority of 26 to 1, and it was agreed that the said chapel be not so recorded, &c.

Meeting held at Lancaster, 4 April, 1693.—Whereas, upon reading the petition of Thomas Sharp, clerk, rector of Tatham, and other the parishioners of Tatham Parish, concerning Tatham Chapel, it appearing that the said chapel is an endowed ancient chapel, wherein the sacraments and prayers of the Church of England have been duly ministered and used, time out of mind, till, about two years last past, some of the dissenters living near the chapel, surreptitiously obtained the same to be recorded as a meeting place for dissenters, and, by colour thereof, have used the same; upon consideration whereof, the justices recommend it to the Justices of Peace, at their next Quarter Sessions, to order that the dissenters, for the future, shall not presume to meet and exercise their religion in the said chapel of Tatham, on any pretence whatsoever, &c. The recommendation was confirmed at a meeting of the justices on 25 April 1693.

At the General Quarter Sessions for Lancashire, held at Ormskirk, 20 July, 1693.—The petition was read of James Naylor, of Windle, clerk, shewing that by the Act for exempting their Majesties' Protestant subjects, dissenting from the Church of England, from the penalties of certain laws, the places of meeting are required to be certified at the next Quarter Sessions. In pursuance of this, the said James Naylor certifies that St. Helen's Chapel in Hardshawe, is intended as a meeting place for Protestant dissenters, and desires it may be so recorded. Upon the motion put, whether it be recorded or no:—Lord Willoughby,

Mr. Walmesley, Mr. Herle, and Mr. Samuel Crooke, for recording it; Mr. Bertie Entwisle, Captain Clayton, and Mr. Johnson, Mayor of Liverpool, against recording it. Therefore, ordered to be recorded.

Memoranda follow, dated 1 August 1696, as to the necessary steps to be taken by dissenters, for exempting themselves from penalties, and of the numbers of dissenting meeting places in Lancashire.

SIR RICHARD STANDISH and ALEXANDER RIGBY, Justices of the Peace for the County of Lancaster, to THEIR FELLOW JUSTICES.

745. 1690, September 17.—"Pursuant to your order, made at an adjornement of the last generall quarter sessions of the peace for this County of Lancaster, to the Sheriff's board at Lancaster, in the assize week, the 25th of August last, ordering that William Higginse be, for the reasons therein set forth, removed, and William Tomlinson restored to his place of Governer of the House of Correction at Preston in this County of Lancaster, and nominating and desireing Sir Richard Standish, Barronet, Alexander Rigby of Layton, Henry Farrington and Charlees Parker, Esquires, or any two or more of them, to put the said Tomlinson into possession of the said house and place: Wee the said Sir Richard Standish and Alexander Rigby, on Saturday the thirteenth of September instant, went to the House of Correction at Preston aforesaid, but found there the doors locked or bolted, which were refused to be opened to us; Higginson, in the said order enjoined to yeild obedience thereunto, not thinking fit to be seen, if he was in the house, nor then, nor ever since, to speak with us. Howbeit, some person imployed by him, a man unknowen to us, did come to the dore when wee demanded entrance, according to the said order, and that wee might restore the said William Tomlinson, in the order mentioned, to his said place; but the persons within, still kept the dores shut against us, and positively denyed to us entrance, one of them sayeing they had as good power to keep it as wee to demand it, and, as wee have since heard, they had then within the said house an armed rable to keep the house, and whilst wee were but a litle way gone from the place, wee heard a gun or guns go off in or about the said house."

HENRY ROWE to ROGER KENYON, M.P.

746. 1690, October 6. Wigan.—On Saturday last, Alderman Bancks, the town clerk, was chosen and sworn Mayor. "If you would be pleased to write two words to him, to desire him to take the oath of a justice for the whole county, I am sure he wold doe it, which would not be only a great service to their Majesties, but, I am sure, will be much to your advantage." *Seal, broken.*

THOMAS GREEN to ROGER KENYON.

747. 1690, October 6.—Having been sent to prison the previous year, on a charge of high treason, upon the information of one Kelly, a person he never knew, he begs Kenyon's assistance that he may be admitted to bail.

Enclosure.—Copy of a petition, by Thomas Green, to the Justices of Assize for the County Palatine of Lancaster, that he may be brought to trial.

R. LONGWORTH to ROGER KENYON.

748. 1690, October 7. St. Michael's.—Thanks Kenyon for his kindness in that "my good Lord Derby was pleased to honour my poor house with his presence." Hopes his letter will find Kenyon at the House of

Parliament. Commissioners [of the Peace?] are wanted for his part of
the Hundred of Amunderness, and he hopes the following names, or
some of them, may be added, viz.: —John Veale, Esq.; Mr. Richard
Longworth; Mr. Thomas Smith; Mr. Thomas Fiffe; Mr. William
Slater; and Mr. Richard Rivington, all living convenient for this part
of the Hundred. "When money is given, if I had the casting vote, it
shold be by a land tax, for certaynely it is the safest and readyest way
to raise money, and with the most equallity." *Seal of Arms.*

Edward Chisenhale to Roger Kenyon.

749. 1690, October 10. — " Pray give my serviss to all our Lancashire members that are com up. I wish they were all up to have heard
soe gratious a speech as the King has made, and especially in that all
accounts are redy to be layd downe before you—a suer way for his
Majesty to be supplyed by all of you, and, by all you represent, will be
most chearfully paid. Seeing our moneys fairely disposed, we think we
cannot pay too much, onely doe what you cann, that we may make money
of our land, as one way we want an Act to put downe all common bruers
in Norfolke and Suffolk, or that none shall be quallifyed to keepe inn or
victualling house, except they brue their one drink. All this inquire of
Sir William Cooke, farther; another, that theire may not be any undertakers to laye in the Kinge his beefe and swyne for sea, for by that the
country is beaten downe to theire owne price, and especially by having it
all bought at Smithfield, which is great charge to the farmer by driveing, and heats the King's beefe, but that the King would have his stores
at London, Bristoll, Hull, Ipswich and Dover, Chester or Liverpoole,
&c. This would be a vast advantage to the farmer, and better for the
King, and prevent a privatt running man forestoleing all the markett in
England, by drawing all to London."

The Earl of Derby to Roger Kenyon.

750. 1690, October 10. Kn[owsley].—Refers to his indisposition,
which, he thanks God, is much abated. It lies most in his head, and this
is the first day he attempted to write. There was an earthquake the
other night.

John Hulton to Roger Kenyon, M.P.

751. 1690, October 31.—"A relation of mine, that lives in Chester, was
lately at London, and lodged at Mr. Laurence Baskervile's; she has an
extraordinary art in cutting of paper, in imitation of point, and brought
some up with her, with design to present [it] to the Queen. Baskervile
understanding it, took her to the Lady Delamere, who was very fond of
it, and [told] her she would present it, but could not take her . . . .
this gave my kinswoman a jealousy that she would not perform her
promise, or, at least, tell her Majesty who did it; so that, a little before
she came out of town, she waited on the Lady Delamere to know
whether she had presented the Queen with that point. She replied, she
had not done it herself, but had given it to my Lady Derby, who had
given it to the Queen, and that she very much admired it. Now, a
friend of my kinswoman's writes her word that it is believed the point
was never given to the Lady Derby; and if the Queen has it, the Lady
Delamere presented it as from her daughter, or not from my relation.
I heartily beg the kindness of you that you would wait on my Lady
Derby, and know whether such point came to her ladyship's hand; if

so, we are satisfied. I have sent you, enclosed, a little for you to see, but this was her first work. That she took to London was ten times finer cut, and more in imitation of point. I should be glad to hear from you of your strength and procedeure in your House, and that, in a short time, you will call on our independent companies in Lancashire and Cheshire to account; for I take them to be as dangerous to our government as any enemy whatever. I suppose you have heard what industry is used by that party to make Cornet (?) Whitley mayor [for] this year, in this Corporation; he feasted the mob every day . . . . We have mayor and sheriff to our minds, and hope you will appoint us honest Commissioners for the monthly tax, for hitherto there has been the most impartial dealings in the world. I have paid twice as much as their adored coxcomb, Alderman Mainwaring, and, indeed, the fanatics in general, have paid little or nothing; they preserve themselves and purses for the good old cause! "

Robert Roper to Roger Kenyon, M.P.

752. 1690, November 11.—" I have this day given my Lord an account of the contents of Sir Vere Fane's paper, inclosed in your letter to me of the 1st instant, by which hee mentions 887*l*. 19*s*. 2*d*. to be already paid, in part of 1,730*l*. 10*s*. 7*d*., due at Michaelmas last. I have examined the receavor's accounts of the Isle of Man, and therein is charged 989*l*. 17*s*. 1*d*. paid to Mr. Greenwood, of Lancaster, by Alderman Bence's order, and for his use, which is 147*l*. 5*s*. 8*d*. more, and must bee in Mr. Greenwood's hands, if he hath not accounted for it. When it is seasonable, I know you will put my Lord in minde of this arreer, and also what is due to Mr. Stanley, upon the account of his rent charge; for I doubt my Lord will not bee able to stave off payment, noe longer then priviledge of Parliament doth continue, and when that is ended, these arrears will fall very heavy, unlesse, in the meane while, some course be taken for payment." *Seal.*

W. Hayhurst to Roger Kenyon.

753. 1690, December 5. Preston.—Making application for an appointment in Lord Derby's service. Lord Brandon has not thought fit to appear at the election. Mr. Buckingham, his gentleman, came up, on Wednesday, to Mr. Patten's, and went yesterday with Mr. Patten, and several of his party, to Mr. Mayor, to acquaint him that my Lord recommended Mr. Patten as the most proper person to represent them in Parliament. " I doe not hear, for certaine, of any indirect methods used of either side, though there is discourse of gold being offered by Buckingham, on behalfe of Mr. Patten. The comon method is for some two of acquaintence and interest to goe from house to house and ask their votes, and to drink them well. After the call book was called over and the defaulters, it was asked Mr. Patten's party if they had any more to poll, or if they could except against any that had polled for Sr. Edward, both which they did in a fewe, and were allowed to give Mr. P[atten] his due. Hee, carried beyond expectation, civill and willing to suppress any disorders. There was some fighting at the further end of the Court, but soon over. The Mayor and gentlemen of the town mett Sr. Edward into the town, with threescore and twelve horse, and ringing of bells. The Indenture was sealed in Court, and you need not fear any further appeales. Colonel Rawsthorne gave his vote for Sir Edward."

Thomas Hodgekinson to Roger Kenyon, M.P.

754. 1690, December 5. Preston.—"This day, our election began, about eleaven of clock, and continued until three this afternoon. There was never an election in this place managed with more calmnes on both sides, saving some few rude disturbances by Mr. Patten's creatures, but (indeed) against his inclinations. Sir Edward Chisenhale carried it by 57 votes, soe that you will have no further trouble, in the comittee of priviledges, about this corporation. Bee pleased to rectify my mistake to my good Lord Derby, for I have (by this post) given his Lordsbipp an account that wee outvoted Mr. Patten 60 votes, whereas (upon a more exact scrutiny) there only appeares 57, which mistake (though not very considerable) I thought fitt to correct, being sent to a person of that honnor and quality. Sir, I am now with Mr. Maior, Sir Edward Chisenhale, and many more of your friends, who have already drunke his Lordshippe's health, and are now remembering (their worthy friend) the sitting member ; unto whom they do owne themselves particularly obliged, in their late dispute in the senate . . . . . The company is pressing mee with glasses, and only give me time to tell you that I am, sir, your very affectionate servant." *Seal of arms.*

Army Accounts.

755. 1690, December 9.—The answer of Richard, Earl of Ranelagh, Paymaster-General, etc., " to soe much of the reporte, observations, and resolutions of the Committee for examining the accompts of the army," etc., as concern him.

Army Accounts.

756. 1690, December 9.—Remarks concerning the Report of the Committee for examining the Accounts of the Army.

The State of the Navy.

757. 1690, December 23. Admiralty Office.—An account of the present state of the ships of war of their Majesties' Royal navy.

The Earl of Derby to Roger Kenyon.

758. 1690[-1], January 15. Whitehall.—"We are every hour in expectation to go; all our coaches were ready this morning, the King resolving to set sail this afternoon, but the wind changed, not above three hours before, for last night it blew as [hard as] could be, so that we are all ready, upon an hour's warning. You will hear, in the public letters, of some persons taken who are lately come out of France ; they had letters about them which confirm very much what was my Lord . . . . . intentions." *Seal of arms.*

Nicholas Stratford, Bishop of Chester, to Roger Kenyon.

759. 1690-1, January 22.—Encloses the charge against Mr. Braddyll. Thinks Mr. Gey has "done the part of a good Christian and a good subject," and that " Mr. Braddyll, who has been so unfaithful, and abused his trust to so high a degree, deserves to be excluded, with some note of infamy, from any public trust for the future." *Seal of arms.*

John Barton to Roger Kenyon.

760. 1690[-1], January 22, Knowsley.—As to Kenyon's being the fittest man in Lancashire, if not too old, for the government [of the Isle of Man ?].

The Earl of Derby to Roger Kenyon.

761. [1691,] February 1. The Hague.—" It happens unfortunately for mee, that the Governor should dye whilst I am here; all that I need to say, I continue of the same mind I was of, when I last saw you; but that is not the thing I must now consider; it is sending someone to supply the place untill my return into England. I must first say I am sorry William Hayhurst is not gone, but that cannot be helped now. Yet I do not see any reason why he may not go still, for that instrument I signed for him, gives him greater authority than I have skill to dr[aw] here, for you or him, being directed to the Governor and the rest of my officers ; suche latter are obliged to give all the light they can, and hee may instruct them, by your advice, what is to be done in the meantime, onely keep the letter I writt to the Governor; and since I am out of the kingdome, I fancy you and the rest of my Commissioners may have power to graft an order to them in the Island, upon what I have signed and sealed to William Hayhurst, to bee of force untill they heare from mee. All things go as well here as I can desire, but, upon my word, I have very litle time for writeing, especially tonight, for I am to goe tomorrow morneing very early to Amsterdam. The gazette and the newse letters will be very full of the King's reception here, and the joy all people are in with the sight of him, which is not to be expressed, for I could not have imagined half so much, if I had not been eye-witnes." *Original and Copy, in Roger Kenyon's handwriting.*

Thomas Braddyll to Roger Kenyon.

762. 1690[-1], February 2. Portfield.—Desires a copy of the information, " or what you are pleased to call it," which " Cousin Gey " has laid against him to the Bishop of Chester.

Appended is the copy.

" T. B., esquire, a Justice of the Peace and a Commissioner in the severall Polls and 3*s*. Subsidy Act, who was a long time before he would take the oaths to the present government, dealt thus in his actings as Commissioner with the King and countrey in Whally, in the county of Lancaster, where he liveth.

" 1. Not one child in that township (though some scores taxable and taxed by the sworn assessors) would he suffer to pay, but struck them out of the assessment.

" 2. At the 2*s*. in the pound, an assessment was made up by the assessors, for 2*s*. in the pound only; but he causes his clerk to interline the other tax of 12*d*. in the pound, in that assessment, so that the King was cheated of the third part, through the whole town, and if enquired into, probably in many others.

" 3. His own demesnes of Braddyll and Brockall, and as it is believed, of Samsbury, to the valew of severall 100*l. per annum*, were clearly, by his procurement, left out of the tax, and not one penny paid for them.

" 4. In the review of the 1st poll, not a child in the town (though a great number) save his 2 daughters, the vicar's three children, and about 4 more, at most, put into the assessment, and his own wife omitted.

" 5. Numbers of papists of quality, freed by him (as it is presumed) because R. Grimshaw, esq., G. Talbot, gent., Justic Cotterell, Attorney at law, being doubly assessed, according to the Act, as professed papists were struck off by him, the 2 last, 40*l*. a peece, the 1st, a far greater sum.

"6. Servants, wages of whole townships (as it is believed) particularly the township of Osbuldalston, there being a great family in it, nearly related to him, by his means were wholly left out, and never paid [a] penny.

"7. Exclaimed on the vicar, telling him he deserved to be pulled out of the pulpit, for preaching against perjury, and pressing all concerned, to make just and true taxes, according to their oaths.

"8. Gave the countrey, in one assessment, no time to appeal, but instead of 14 days allowed by the Act, would have them pay within 4, and threatned and distreyned upon such as would not submit to his arbitrary commands, particularly the vicar of Whallay."

ROBERT ROPER to ROGER KENYON.

763. 1691, March 31.—"The bearer brings you a letter from my lord; and, this day, I have another from his lordshipp, wherein hee acquaints mee that hee hath appointed you Governor of the Isle of Man, but not to go over hither, untill his lordshipp's returne to England, and in the meanwhile, to appoint your deputy to stay in the Island about a moneth, and to bring his lordshipp an account how affaires stand there, and you and I to meet forthwith, to consider the affaires of the Island." *Seal.*

THOMAS GIPPS to ROGER KENYON.

764. [16]91, April 4. Bury.—"There is a gentleman at Manchester (one Dr. Buck) that designs to sett up, either at Manchester or at Warrington, in the practice of physick. He has a letter from some of your friends, recommending him to your favour and countenance to promote his interest, what in you lies." The writer has also one from a special friend and kinsman (a doctor in physic of the first rank in England) who gives a satisfactory character of this Dr. Buck. *Seal of arms.*

RALPH JACKSON to ROGER KENYON, at Manchester.

765. 1691, April 13. Middleton.—Has, for several years, been exercised in military affairs, "and does, in some measure, understand them," and, to satisfye any person that he is qualified for a commission, "will not onely performe the exercise before any commission officer whatever, but, at the same time, will undergoe the examination upon that account." Begs, therefore, Lord Derby's interest to obtain for him the King's commission. *Seal of arms.*

GENERAL GINCKLE to "MR. ROE, Comptroller of the Isle of Man."

766. 1691, April 29. Dublin.—"I am informed by Mr. Daniel Hayes, a merchant of this city, that the ship *St. Stephen*, of St. Sebastian, whereof John Lebarta is master, loaden at St. Sebastian with wine and brandy, and bound to this place, was, by distress of weather, in her voyage hither, driven to the Isle of Man, and there seized by your order, upon pretence of belonging to their Majesties' enemies. I can assure you that we have made it our particular care to encourage the trade of this distressed kingdom, in order to supply their Majesties' army with so necessary refreshments, of which we have great want. Therefore, I desire you will give him, in the release of said ship and her cargoe, the latter belonging to subjects, confederates to their Majesties, a friendly and impartial assistance, in order that their Majesties' army in this kingdom under our command, may have the benefit of those necessary refreshments in the field."

ADRIAN VENN to the EARL OF DERBY, at Ormond Gate, near Whitehall.

767. 1691, May 14. Harwich.—Has brought his lordship "two casts of Lenteners" from Antwerp. In the packet coming from "Helford Sluice," were 16 or 18 recruits for the Coreland (?) Regiment in Ireland, under the command of Colonel Shock. Some of the recruits took him for a spy, and, having no pass, he was brought before Justice Seamans, of Harwich, and one of the recruits swore that he was in the French army before Mons. Prays for his Lordship's intercession.

STEPHEN GEY to ROGER KENYON.

768. 1691, May 27.—When he got to Wigan, Lord Derby, with his whole family, went to Winstanley to dinner. Is a little amazed that he has not heard from Lord Derby nor Mr. Entwisle, but believes "that *per fas nefasque* he will continue to mischiefe me and mine, if possible, but I know God has a hooke in every manes nostrills."

The EARL OF NOTTINGHAM to the EARL OF DERBY.

769. 1691; June 4. Whitehall.—"I send your lordship enclosed, by the Queen's command, a warrant for releasing a Spanish ship called the *St. Stephen*, of St. Sebastian, driven into the Isle of Man by stress of weather, and there arrested, contrary to the constant practice everywhere observed in the like cases, and the provision made by the treaty between us and the Crown of Spain, for the security of the subjects of both nations against any such irregularity; and her Majesty is the more concerned to see the partys releived herein, in regard of the strict union and friendship, at this time, between us and Spain, and the benefit which accrues to this nation by the Spanish trade, which may be liable to suffer much, by such an example as this, if not timely redressed; and that this may be done the sooner, her Majesty has signed a duplicate of this order, which will be delivered to your Deputy Governour, and I do not doubt but your lordship will immediately issue such directions, on your part, as may prevent any delay in the execution of her Majesty's commands, in so just and necessary a cause." *Signed. Enclosed,* Warrant for release, signed "Marie R."

THE SHIP ST. STEPHEN.

770. 1691, after June 4.—Paper stating that the Queen's order of this date, touching the release of the *St. Stephen,* is based upon an entirely wrong supposition that she is a Spanish ship, manned by Spaniards, laden with goods the growth of Spain, bound from Spain to Dublin, on the account of the King of Spain's subjects, forced by stress of weather into the Isle of Man, and had not been guilty of any act of forfeiture; and setting out answers that will be "well proved" to each of these suppositions. The answers are to the effect that the vessel is "a sloop, built in New England" and that she had her name given her by Hilary and Peter Reneu—French merchants, living in London, but born at Bordeaux—"before she was ever at Spain." *Printed.*

The EARL OF DERBY to the EARL OF NOTTINGHAM.

771. 1691, June 7. Knowsley.—" I received your Lordship's letter this day, by the post, and also her Majestie's order, dated three days ago, for releasing a ship seized in the Isle of Man, pretending to come from St. Sebastian, in Spain, laden with claret and brandy. ' When I was with the King in Holland, my Governor of the Isle of Man died. I have appointed a new governor, who is going over, so soon as the wind will serve. This ship was seized by my officers of the Customs there, but that this ship was drove in by stress of weather, I believe is misinformation, and I am very doubtful whether, in truth, it be French or Spanish wine. A French merchant, one Mr. Renue, was divers times with me at London, and showed me a certificate from the Commissioners of the Customs, Sir Richard Temple and others, who, I am sure, never heard what my officers in the Isle of Man, who seized or stayed the ship, can say to this matter, and I suppose your Lordship will think it reasonable the whole truth should be known. This Mr. Renue would have sould me the claimer pretences (*sic*), I understood it to be his own, if I would have given him an inconsiderable sume in comparison of the real value, after he had showed me the Commissioners of the Customs discharge would have let the rest go; all these made me desirous to know the whole truth. My officers having done no wrong, I should not be blamed for their irregularity, and if the statute which prohibitts the importation of brandy into Ireland or the Isle of Man from any kingdom or place, under the penalty of forfeiting the brandy and the ship may be punished, I hope what is done, is not of very ill example. All I would, with all humility, beg of her Majesty, is that this strict order of delivery of this ship forthwith, may be dispensed with, till her Majesty and your Lordship may, so soon as the Governour, who lies at Liverpool, waiting for a wind, can goe over, by examination of the matter, be truly certified and fully informed. Or, if this may not be, I pray your Lordship's advice by the return of this post, for none shall more readily and humbly comply with all her Majesty's commands." *Copy*.

The EARL OF DERBY to ROGER KENYON, at Liverpool.

772. 1691, June 8. [Knowsley.]—Has received the Queen's order to deliver the ship and cargo now " stayed " in the Isle of Man. Has written to Lord Nottingham " to desire of her Majesty that order may be suspended, until due examination of all matters, in the Island, relating to the ship and goods, and that you have certified the truth of the whole matter under your hand, which I desire you to do with all care and speed, and so soon as I have heard from my Lord Nottingham, you shall hear further and receive my order, touching the said ship and goods, and in the meantime you are to keep the same in safe custody." *Signed*.

The EARL OF NOTTINGHAM to the EARL OF DERBY.

773. 1691, June 16. Whitehall.—" I have receaved your Lordship's letter of the 7th instant, about releasing the ship *St. Stephen*, of St. Sebastian, and had sooner returned you an answer, but that I was willing to acquaint the Queen with what your Lordship writ, and receive her directions. Before her Majesty signed the warrant which was sent to your Lordship, she referred this matter to the Commissioners of the Customs, upon whose report of the case, and upon consideration of the treaty with Spain, and the strict obligations of complying with it, her Majesty directed the immediate release of this ship, and I am now commanded to acquaint you, that her Majesty sees no reason to recede from her former orders, and does therefore expect your punctual complyance herein without any further delay."

C. WHARTON, SIR THOMAS TRAVERS, and WM. SACHEVERELL to the EARL OF DERBY, at Knowsley.

774. [1691,] June 22. Castletown, Isle of Man.—Upon the Governor's desire, they have been on board the seized vessel, and tasted three of the casks in her hold. They are of opinion that the casks contain "small French wines, and truly the growth of France." *Signed. Seal.*

INFORMATION of WILLIAM COOPER, of "Peeltown."

775. 1691, July 7.—"In April, 1689, one Mr. Jackson of the County of Downe, in Ireland, sent into the Isle [of Man] by one William Duglass, 82 tanned hydes and other goods, to save and secure them from the enemy ; being at that time when the Irish Protestants fled into the Isle for security." These were seized, because no cocket could be produced for the same.

EXAMINATION of "Mr. DAVID MURRAY, merchant at Douglas."

776. 1691, July 18.—He had received from his brother, Mr. Robert Murray, of Chester, the copy of a letter from Peter Renewe to Mr. William Clayton, merchant, of Liverpool, telling him of the seizure in question, stating the vessel—which was built in New England—was going from St. Sebastian to Dublin, and begging his aid in obtaining her release, &c. *Signed.*

EXAMINATION of JAMES CHENNEAU, taken before the EARL OF DERBY.

777. 1691, July 25.—Knows Stephen de Fernandis, who is a Spaniard; they, with two other Spaniards, sailed from London to St. Sebastian, in the ship in question, which was then called the *St. Stephen.* He was present at the lading of the said ship; the cargo was not taken out of any other ship, but was brought direct from the Custom House at London. Mr. Peter Renewe sent him with the ship and cargo to Spain. Hillary Renewe is Peter's brother and partner ; they are Frenchmen, born at Bordeaux. Believes that Mr. Hilliary Lesseur, who now lives at St. Sebastian with Mr. Stephen Cadroy, is nephew to the Renewes. The examinat was born at the Isle of Oleron, and does not know that he is a denizen of England, but Peter Renewe wrote to him, in the previous May, that he would send him his free denizenship, &c.

"The manner of his Lordship's [the EARL OF DERBY's] goeing to the Tinwall, from Castle Rushen."

778. 1691, July 30.—"About 7 of the clock in the morning, all persons who are to attend his Lordship from Castle Rushen to the Tinwall, to wit, the Governor, with his staffe of authority, all the officers and Lords Council (except such as are military, and except the deemsters and 24 Keys, who are to go before to the Tinwall, and attend there the Lord of Man's coming) all knights, gentlemen of quality, strangers and natives.

"At half an hour past 7 of the clock, the bell rings for half a quarter of an hour ; which done, the Constable of that Castle, with the other officers of that Castle, go forth of the Hall to the gates there, to order the guard, and to doe their obeysance at his Lordship's passing by.

" When the Governor hath notice that the guards are so sett, and his Lordship's horses and all things in readiness, he acquaints his Lordship therewith, who, thereupon, arises and commands the Governor, with his staffe, to goe, which he doth, walking barehead before him. Then followes my Lord, and next after him all the best gentlemen of quality that are strangers, and allsoe his Lordship's cheif servants, &c. When his Lordship is come out of the gate, the groomes stand ready with their horses, and whilst the Lord, the Governour, the persons of quality, &c. are mounting, the Constable of the Castle, with his guards, march forwards, with his Lordship's musick playeing before them; and when all are on horseback, then the Comptroller on the right hand, and the Steward of the Household on his left hand, rideing bare before the Governour. Then comes the Governour, allsoe rideing bare, before his Lordshipp, thorrow the towne, with his staff in his hand. Then the guards march, the musick playeing before them, thorrow the towne, all the best gentlemen of quality that are strangers, two by two, following next after his Lordshipp, and in like manner, his Lordshipp's cheife servants, and after them, the meaner persons accordingly.

" When his Lordship is about the middle of the town, the great guns from the Castle goe off, 5 at the least; and haveing marched thorrow the town, those footguards and musick take horse, and attend his Lordship, with the rest, to the Tinwall.

" When, in this order, they have passed the town, the Governor, &c. ride covered, till they come to the Tinwall feild, where his Lordship's guards, consisting of a thousand firelocks, are posted in great ordre. His Lordship, after he hath taken a view of them, passeth thorrow them on horseback, and in that passage is decently saluted by all the military officers commanding those guards. And thus his Lordship, the Governour, and persons of quality, &c., with him, ride on till they meet the Bishop and Clergy, the Deemsters, and the 24 Keys of the Island; the Clergy on the right hand, the other on the left.

" Then his Lordshipp alighteth, the Bishop, or in his absence the Archdeacon, or in his absence the Vicar-General, holding the right styrrup, accordeing to the ancient custome. When his Lordshipp hath saluted them all, they march; that is to say, the fower and twenty, in decent coates, and the Deemsters after them, in gownes, the Clergy in their habitts, and the Bishop after them. Then the Governor, my Lord, and after him all the gentry passing thorrow a guard, to witt, of Peele garrison, on one hand, and the garrison of Castle Rushen on the other hand, which make a lane to the church door. My Lord being thus conducted goes up into a chaire provided for that day, and then heares a sermon. The sermon ended, all goe forth of the church but my Lord, the Governor, the Lordes Councill, the Deemsters and twenty four Keys, the Secretarys, Clerke of the Rolls, and such as the Lord will comand to stay.

" If his Lordship have anything to propound to the country, he moves it to the Deemsters, and fower and twenty, who, debateing the matter, do agree thereunto, or give his Lordship satisfaction, by their sufficient reasons to the contrary. And if the Deemsters and fower and twenty have any request unto his Lordship, they move it themselves, in an humble manner. If my Lord approve thereof, he commands it to be inserted in the statute book, where it is mentioned as an humble request of the Deemsters and fower and twenty, on behalf of the country, setting all their names unto the same, as allsoe the Governor and all of the Lords Councill, subscribe; then my Lord confirmes the same with his own subscription, under these words :—' Be it enacted as it is desired'; but if his Lordshipp like not the motion, then he tells them that he will take it into consideration against another time.

" Note.—That when his Lordship intends to propound something that day, which he conceives may probably find some opposition, or require some long debate, to prevent an inconveniency, his Lordship appoints a meeteing some day the week before, where all things are well weighed and considered, to the contentment of all parties.

" When there is no more for his Lordship and the rest then with him to doe of themselves, his Lordship sends one of the Deemsters forth of the church into the feild, where the said Deemster comands the cryer to proclaime that if anyone have complaint to make, thoe it be against any of the officers, or any request by petition, or difference betweene party and party, he, or they, whoever they be, may come into the Church and be heard, and his Lordshipp will take order that right shall be done, accordeing to justice and the lawes of the land. Then such as have any business, present themselves before the table humbly, on their knees, and deliver their petitions to the Comptroller, who is there ready to receive the same and to read, when the Lord commands him; which being done, the Lord heares the matter, if he please, or appoints another day.

" All this being done, one goeth forth to cause the drums to beat ; then the people gather together expecting his Lordshipp's coming forth ; the souldiers stand to their armes, and then the Bishop and Clergy come into the church ; then the fower and twenty march, two in a brest, thorrow the guards up to the Tinwall hill, the Deemsters followeing them, then the Clergy, Bishop, &c., as before, two and two. The officers follow his Lordship, soe doe the gentlemen strangers and others, the Bishop and Clergy on the right hand ; the Deemsters and four and twenty, on the left, standing bare, make a lane for his Lordship to goe betwixt them up the degrees to the top of the hill, where, when his Lordship is arrived, he sitts in a chaire of state, with his face towards the east, the Governor standing or sitting on my Lord's right, and the Bishop on the left, the sword of state holden before his Lordship with the point upward, by whom his Lordship thinks fitt to honor therewith. The gentlemen strangers stand or sitt behind his Lordship ; the Deemsters and officers stand one degree below the Governor ; the Guards (to witt of the two garrisons) stand at the foot of the hill, with matches lighted, bullets in their mouths, &c. Then the people draw nigh to understand what is said unto them.

" The first busines on the hill is that the six Coroners or Sheriffs present themselves before his Lordship, with white rods in their hands, which were given to them at the late Tinwald, as markes of their office, to continue from that time for one year. They are to come one after another, on their knees, before his Lordship, presenting their staves which he receives and (haveing been but lately elected and sworn, and recommended unto him as able and honest men) he returns them their staves, being satisfyed that they are fitt persons for such a place of creditt, advantage, and trust. My Lord haveing a note of their names, and haveing comanded the Deemster to call them in order, he restores them their white rods, and each Coroner, as he receives the same on his knees, bowes towards his Lordship's feet, riseth, maketh his reverences as he retires to one side, his face still towards my Lord ; and, in like manner, all the rest.

" After this, if any new law be made, or old altered, it is proclaimed by the cryer, in Manckes, being read and dictated to him by the eldest Deemster.

R

" In conclusion, the Lord commands the cryer to lett the people know (in Mancks) that his Lordship continues his love unto them and his care of them, and prayes God to bless them.

" So, commonly, they crye aloud—' God allso bless his Lordship and all his,' and with a great huzzah and shout, concludes the business of that day."

EXAMINATION of ROBERT BURDETT, Junior, of Dublin, merchant.

779. 1691, August 3.—At the instance of Mr. Daniel Hayes, merchant of Dublin, he came to the Isle of Man to look after the ship [the *St. Stephen*] and mariners in question. Had no orders to " vend, retail, or utter " any of the wine, &c. on board, but " he was left at liberty, at his discretion, to have presented some of it to the Earle of Derby and Governour of the Island, if the ship had been released accordinge to her Majestie's order."

The EARL OF DERBY'S INSTRUCTIONS to his GOVERNOR OF THE ISLE OF MAN, his deputy or deputies.

780. 1691, August 4.—" That whereas many complaints have been made to me since my coming into this Island, against those persons, their actings here, who have been, by commission of the Commissioners of the Customs in England, sent hither to act, upon pretence for their Majesties' service, as surveyors of the Customs of this Island, and who have, contrary to law, as I am informed, taken upon them, in many particulars, very arbitrarily to act, to the great oppression of the people and with much contempt to me and my officers in the said Island; I do, therefore, hereby require you to have particular regard to these men, their demeanors and actings; and, whilst they behave themselves according to law for their Majesties' service, they, desiring your aid, that you very readily assist them, but when and where they otherwise act, that you, upon good proof of their misdemeanour, impartially put the law in execution against them : and for your so doing, I do hereby promise to indempnify you against any prosecution; notwithstanding their threats, insolencys, or the utmost they can do you. And I do expect your constant complyance to these my directions, with care and without timerity. And that in any case where any seizures are to be made, that you make seizures, and not permit them to make any seizures, or otherwise to act what is the part of my officers, properly to perform." *Copy.*

ORDER directing the release of the ship *St. Stephen.*

781. 1691, August 13. Whitehall.—Order in Council—made on the petition of Andrew de la Barthe, master of the *St. Stephen,* of St. Sebastian, belonging, with her cargo, to the subjects of Spain, seized in the Isle of Man by the Earl of Derby—directing the immediate release of the said vessel and her crew, or the attendance of the Earl of Derby and the master of the vessel, on 24 Sept. next.

Annexed.—Copy petition. Petitioner with his vessel, being forced by stress of weather into the " road of the Isle of Man," the vessel was seized by the Earl of Derby's officers, and carried into " a harbour " [Derby Haven] and Petitioner and his crew turned out of their vessel. Previous orders of Council, for restitution of the vessel, have been ignored by the Earl, &c.

An ACCOUNT of the EARL OF DERBY'S proceedings in disturbing the King's officers of the revenue in the Isle of Man.

782. 1691, August 13. Whitehall.—Order in Council stating that the Lords Commissioners of the Treasury had that day presented an account of the proceedings of the Earl of Derby and his officers in the Isle of Man, against the King's officers there, and directing the attendance of some person or persons, sent by the Earl, at the board to be held on the 24 September following, to give an account of the whole matter.

Appended.—" An account of the proceedings of the Earle of Derby, Roger Kenyon, Esq., Governor, and other his Lordship's officers in the Isle of Man, against the King's officers and other their Majesties' subjects :—

" It being apparent, since the death of the late Governor Haywood, that their Majesties' officers in the said Island do meet with strange interruptions, in the execution of their offices, by the said Earl of Derby, Roger Kenyon, Esqre., and other his Lordship's officers there, both to the prejudice of their Majesties' interest and other their Majesties' subjects as fall in there, by wreck or otherwise.

" 1st. That on 29th January, 1690, there hapned a vessell to be cast away upon the said Island, that had been in their Majesties' service, in the master's chest whereof, there was found by the said Earl of Derby's officers, an account that did discover a great abuse to the prejudice of their Majesties' interest; which account coming to the knowledge of Benjamin Dewy, the King's officer there, strange endeavours were used by the said Earl's officers to keep the said Dewy from a sight thereof, and although at last, with some trouble and charge, he got a copy of what had relation to the King, yet they would by no means part with the original, though it no ways belonged to them.

" 2nd. That General Ginckell's cornet, being one of them that was saved in the said vessel, who, with others, were going for England for recruits, with considerable sums, though it was known there was saved both money and goods of some value, yet the said Earl's officers, in whose hands it was, keeps the most part of it, whereby the said cornet was forced to go thence without money to bear his charges; and although he left a letter of attorney with the said Dewy, to take care of, and receive what should be found in his absence, and there being some goods taken up, which had been some small time in the possession of the said Dewy, yet the said Earl's officers came and took them away, never restoring them afterwards.

" 3rd. That in May, 1691, the said Dewy had an account that there was imported into the said Island, some goods without cockett, and the said Earl's officers, to baffle the said Dewy in this business, entred the said goods in an other man's name, then what the said Dewy had an account of, and before the said Dewy could find out the intrigue, the goods were conveyed away, and never after could be discovered.

" 4th. That in the beginning of June following, the said Dewy received an other account that there was lodged in one of the said Earl's officer's house, 1,100 yards of linen, imported into the said Island without cockett; he did not deny but he had the goods, yet would not suffer the said Dewy to have so much as a sight of them, of which the said Dewy complained to Mr. John Rowe, the Earl's comptroller, who declares he would not meddle therein.

" 5th. That on the 8th of April, 1691, there hapned, by contrary winds, to put into Darby Haven, a small vessel loaden with wine and brandy, the pilot whereof informed that he took in his goods at St. Sebastian, and [was] bound for Dublin, but the said Earl's officers first, and afterwards the said Earl and Governor themselves, against all law and precedent, stopt the said vessel, and still detein her, notwithstanding they have the Queen's order to release her. But the said Dewy, to prevent embezlement of the said goods, and not knowing but the same may more properly belong to the King, put a lock upon the hatches, till the business should be determined in England.

"6th. That the said Earl's officers when they first stayed the said vessel, declared that they only staid her, as being fallen into their Lord's priviledge, but yet about a month after, when required by some to know for whom they acted, the said John Rowe declared that he acted for the King, but being asked by what commission, to this he was silent.

"7th. That the said Dewy (as his duty was) made all the enquiry he could, to know what was the occasion that brought the said vessel into the Isle of Man, and cannot find but that what the said pilot pretended was really true, for that one Anthony Thompson, master of the *Lyon* of Lancaster, who was loaden with salt, and bound for Bristol, declared that he, being off of Wexford in Ireland, or thereabouts, met with this vessel, who followed him into Darby Haven, and could not, as the said Thompson informed the said Dewy, get Dublin, for that himself would fain have been there, as being a better outlet for Bristol than Derby Haven; and further, the said Dewy was informed that the said pilot, the same day, or the day after he came to an anchor in Derby Haven, not being willing to depend wholly upon his own judgment, was about hiring one Duncan McLoughlan for 50s. to pilot him to Dublin.

"8th. Also, after the said vessel had been in Derby Haven 6 or 7 days, the said Earl's officer, against the said Dewy's will, removed her, with the help of several boats, to Castle Town bourn, a very dangerous place, and, therefore, the said Dewy tould them that he would run no risque if she miscarried; to themselves be it.

"9th. That on the 17th of June, [16]91, the said Roger Kenyon, the Governor, landed at Darby Haven, and sending for the said Dewy (he being then at Douglas) to Castle Town, he attended him there the next day, and the said Governor told the said Dewy that he had an order from the Earl of Derby, to send him two bottles of wine out of each cask aboard the said vessel for a taste, which were 48 bottles in all, but the said Dewy scrupling it, the said Governor tould him he would break up the hatches if he did not open them; the said Dewy seeing no remedy, suffered the said 48 bottles of wine to be drawn off, which was sent into England, and owned to be received by the said Earl of Derby.

"10th. That on the 21st of June aforesaid, the said Governor sent his warrant, or token, for the said Dewy, who was then at Douglas, to come away presently to Castletown; according, he went thither; but because the said Dewy had not brought the key with him, to give some gentlemen (newly landed from England) a taste of the wine, the said Governor tells him, very angerly, that he would break up the hatches, and that he should have no key at all upon them, and further said that the King had nothing to do in the said Island, the laws of England was nothing there, neither had the said Dewy any power there, forasmuch as he knew who gave it him; and the said Dewy telling him that his business was to take care that the King's service received no prejudice, the said governor hastily asked, 'What King, what King?' The said Dewy tould him that he knew no king but one, meaning King William, to which the said Governor muttered some words, which the said Dewy could not understand, but by his fury in delivering them, they seemed to be dangerous.

"11th. That on the 22nd ditto, the said Dewy attended again at Castletown with the key, but because he did not open the hatches presently at the said Governor's command, he swore he would break them open, and that he would commit the said Dewy, and said that he should have no key at all upon them, and that he would take it away by force, in order to which, the said John Rowe, the comptroller, being present, and a very officious man against the King's officers, was sent out, to call in some soldiers, and had not the said Dewy complyed to open the hatches, and give those gentlemen a taste of the wine, he must have been committed by two soldiers which the said comptroller had got ready.

"12th. That the same day and the day following, the said Governor being gone to Peel Town, summoned Jonathan Antrobus, the other King's officer, before him, and, amongst other discourse, tould him that the King had no right in the Isle of Man, neither had his officers anything to do there, nor should they make any stop or seizure of any goods imported without cockett, and that the King had no more to do in the said Island than he had to do in Normandy or Gascony, and that he, the said Antrobus, should not presume to write to the Commissioners without first giving him an account of it, nor meddle with any goods there imported, but first make him acquainted with it.

"13th. That on the 3rd of July following, the said Earl himself landed at Darby Haven, and about ten o'clock the same night, gave order for the King's lock to be broken off the hatches, which accordingly was done, and the said John Rowe being present, together with one Beck, a cooper, which the said Earl had sent over some time before, and one Nicholas Harlowe, a very pernicious man in all this business, drew off some wine and brandy, and the said Earl never after would suffer the said Dewy to put a lock on for the King any more.

"14th. That on the 4th ditto, the said Dewy being at Castletown, was summoned by the said comptroller before the Earl of Darby, where he attending in the dining room of the Castle, in the presence of divers gentlemen, his Lordship asked the said Dewy how he durst meddle with this wine vessel, as being fallen into his right, and bid him, if he dared to give an account into England that the lock was broke off, which his Lordship owned to the said Dewy was done by his order, and further tould the said Dewy that he had nothing to do there, nor should not meddle with the staying or seizing of any goods imported into the said Island without cockett; 'I will humble you,' said his Lordship, 'I will make you know yourself, I will lay you by the heels, get you gone out of the room'; with several other expressions to this purpose, which the said Dewy cannot remember.

"15th. That on the 9th ditto, the said Earl of Darby, notwithstanding he had received the Queen's order for the releasing the said vessel, gave order to the Governor for the wine and brandy to be taken, from on board, into the Castle, of which the said Dewy and Antrobus having private notice, they, as their duty was, gave their attendance at Castletown, to take the account of what should be landed, and although they were often affronted by the said Earl's officers, yet the same day they took an account of 46 hogsheads of brandy, which was all that was then landed.

"16th. That on the 10th ditto, the said Earl's officers landed 13 pipes of wine out of the said vessel, which the said Dewy and Antrobus, and also one Mr. Robert Burdett, took an account of; after which, the said Dewy (having the Commissioners' leave to come to England) went for Douglas, to prepare himself for his voyage, leaving the said Antrobus behind, to take an account of the rest.

"17th. That on the 11th ditto, the said Earl's officers landed 7 pipes and 4 hogsheads of wine more, which the said Antrobus and Burdett took the account of, and thereupon, they were both immediately committed to prison, without any reason showed; and presently, a special messenger sent away with the Governor's warrant or token to Douglas, to fetch the said Dewy back to Castletown a prisoner, which said messenger was so severe, that he would not suffer the said Dewy to speak, or do anything out of his sight.

"18th. That the same day, the said Dewy being brought prisoner to Castletown, and so before the Governor, who asked him for his papers by which he had taken the account of the goods that were landed, demanding of the said Dewy why and for what reason he did so, and why he took men's names, and because the said Dewy tould him he had not brought the papers with him, the said Governor said he would commit him to prison, until he did produce them, there being all the while two soldiers to guard him. The said Governor further required the said Dewy to shew him the copies of all his letters to the Commission, about the said vessel, and to give bond to answer to what he should object against him; all which being so unreasonable, the said Dewy did absolutely deny him, and presently, thereupon, in came the said Earl of Darby, who only said, 'What this Dewy has to do to take the account of the landing these goods, I cannot tell; but I doubt not,' said his Lordship, 'but I shall find friends to disappoint them all,' and so went out; whereupon, the said Dewy, telling the said Governor that the papers signified but little, and that Mr. Antrobus had the same (who was still a prisoner), they being sent for, and nothing what was expected found therein, the said Dewy and Antrobus were both released, and ordered to attend the Governour again in the evening.

"19th. That the said Dewy and Antrobus appearing in the evening, according to order, the Governour only said, that as the said Dewy was to go for England, and Antrobus to stay in the country, he should not presume to write anything to the Commission, but first shew it him, nor meddle with anything, but first acquaint him with it."

PROCEEDINGS before the COMMISSIONERS, appointed under the Statute of 43 Elizabeth, entitled, An Act to redress the misemployment of lands, goods, and stocks of moneys, given to charitable uses.

783. 1691, September 8, Wigan.—The jurors present that there then was, and for time immemorial there had been, a consecrated chapel in Hardshey-cum-Windle, in the parish of Prescot, called St. Ellen's Chapel; and that the said chapel, about 70 years before, being old and decayed, and too little for the "auditors," was taken down, and a larger chapel was bnilt in the same chapel yard; and that divine service, according to the usage of the Church of England, had constantly, till of late, been used and exercised there, the sacraments administered, the dead buried, and all other ecclesiastical rites performed therein, as a chapel-of-ease, belonging to the parish church of Prescott. But of late, Thomas Roughley and others, trustees for the several gifts bequeathed for the use of a preaching minister at the said chapel, have brought in a minister of the Presbyterian persuasion to preach there, and have misappropriated the funds. It is therefore ordered by the Commissioners, that John Byron, of Parr, Nicholas Rigby, the younger, of Harrocke, and others, be appointed trustees, in the place of the said Thomas Rougbley, and others.

INFORMATION of THOMAS CORBIN, of Liverpool, mariner, taken before Thomas Brookbank, Esqre., Mayor of Liverpool.

784. 1691, September 14.—Was born in New England, and has been a seaman 16 or 17 years, during which time he was taken prisoner by the Turks, and carried captive to "Argiers," where he was kept four years, and learned to speak Spanish. On the Wednesday before

Easter last, he came from Drogheda in the ship *John and Anne*, of which Mr. John Bradshaw was master, into Derby Haven and there saw the sloop in question. One of the Frenchmen on board her was a very able seaman and had been first mate to Captain Wright, master of· a "transport ship," and after Captain Wright's death was himself master of her. The informant says he is hired to go with the ship *Barbadoes Merchant*, to Virginia, &c.

ORDER postponing the hearing of the cause concerning the ship
St. Stephen.

785. 1691, September 17. Whitehall.—Order in Council, consenting, at Lord Derby's request—his witnesses being unready—to the postponement of the hearing of the cause concerning the *St. Stephen*, to the 22nd of October next.

PETITION of the SHIPOWNERS of LIVERPOOL to ROGER KENYON, M.P.

786. 1691, October 23. Liverpool.—Pointing out that the shipowners, by constant victualling of their ships used in their Majesties' service, by supplying them with materials, and paying the poor seamen only so much as to keep alive their almost starved families, have so sunk under the burden, that, if not relieved, it will end in their ruin. They hope that supplies may be given, this session of Parliament, and a " branch" appropriated to the payment of these transport ships. Signed by Richard Houghton, the mayor, Thomas Brookbancke, William Williamson, Richard Windall, James Prescott, William Clayton, Peter Arberton, John Thomas, S. Richmond, John Molyneux, A. Norres, Thomas Johnson, senior, S. Richmond, junior, Thomas Johnson, junior, William Chantnell, Ed : Tarleton, Thomas Jumpe, William Roe, Daniel Chaddocke, Thomas Clayton, William Preeson, James Barton, Thomas Sneeling, Tho : Edwardson, John Sinkler, Thomas Reynolds, Jno. Rymmer, John Fells, William Webster, William Reynoldes, Thomas Bayly, and James Skinner, James Gourdon. *Attached are papers showing the comparative price of freight given by their Majesties and by merchants.*

WILLIAM PATTEN to ROGER KENYON.

787. 1691, December 20. Preston.—I have seen a letter from our good Lord Bishop, wherein he gives two reasons for not licensing Parson White to Wigan; one is, because it is a place of no certainty, for every bishop or new rector of Wigan, may displace him at pleasure ; and the other, because he is informed the parson has a great many children, and he is afraid that may prove a charge to the town. The latter reason cuts the poor parson to the heart ; and, considering he is not under these. circumstances, it grieves him that the Bishop should be misinformed.

CERTIFICATE of CAPTAIN PHINEAS PETT.

788. [1691.]—I having received orders to wait on the Right Honourable the Earl of Derby, at the Isle of Man, to transport his Lordship from thence to England in their Majestys' yacht *The Navy* (under my command), being present at the examination of Monsieur Cheveaux, who calls himself the pilot of the *St. Stephen*, of St. Sebastian, touching the reasons of their coming with that ship into the dangerous haven called Derby Haven, in the said Isle, to which the master (as he pretends) was forced by ill weather; observed [the] matter of fact to bee as followeth :—That coming, as he affirmed, from the southward, having passed the narrow between the Tuscar and the Smalls, that off of Arklee Head (which land they made and knew, as the said pilot himself says), they met with a hard gale of wind at S.W., whereupon the master (though he was bound for Dublin) bears away to the Isle of Man, for the safety of the ship and cargo, as is pretended. When I saw so great a fault in seamanship as this, I thought myself obliged to give my poor opinion in the matter, which is that none but a madman, or one that had no good design, would leave a weather shoare in a storm, to go to a place thirty-five leagues out of his way, to the manifest hazard of the ship and their lives, when he might, without any danger of weather, have kept the weather shoare on board, and, more than that, have got into Dublin (whither he was bound) at his pleasure, as the wind was, or, in great security, have kept sea, until better weather, as will be plain to any seaman which knows that coast, or to any body else that will give themselves the trouble to look on a chart of these seas. And I must further observe that there are many safe harbours which a good man might, with all the security in the world, have made use on, upon the coast of Ireland, where they were, and that there is not one in the whole Isle of Man which is not very dangerous in the fairest weather. All which I justify to be truth, and, therefore, give it under my hand. *Signed.*

"Mr. Graham's and Mr. Burton's Answers."

789 & 790. [After 1691.]—Answers to certain inquiries made by the House of Commons, concerning the Treasury accounts, principally relating to the cost of law suits. Among other things, that as to the charge against them for their exorbitant expenses in presenting the Lord Russell, Colonel Sydney, Sir Thomas Armstrong, Lord Brandon, Lord Delamere, Mr. Hampden, Mr. Cornish, Sir Samuel Barnardiston, Sir Patience Ward, Sir Thomas Pilkington, Mr. Bethell, Sir William Williams, Mr. Johnson, Dr. Oates, etc., the answer states that Lord Russell's trial came to but 18*li.* 17*s.* 6*d.*; Colonel Sydney's, to 51*li.* 3*s.* 5*d.*; Sir Thomas Armstrong's, to 10*li.* 14*s.* 2*d.*; Lord Brandon's, to 63*li.* 9*s.* 8*d.*; Mr. Hampden's trial, finding inquisitions, and seizing his estate, to 339*li.* 2*s.* 8*d.*; Mr. Cornish, as to his trial only, 30*li.* 15*s.* 6*d.*. As to the causes of Sir Patience Ward [and] Sir Thomas Pilkington, about the 100,000*li.* fine, these are not all brought to account, nor was the said Burton concerned in the same, nor in the causes of Sir William Williams, or Dr. Oates, otherwise than by paying 1,800*li.* to Mr. Hause, by the direction of the Lord Treasurer"; the said four causes being directed by the late king, when Duke of York, and followed by Mr. Swift, who was then his solicitor.

As to money paid to jurors, the answer states that, in cases of life and death, they never paid a penny to any juryman, or spent a farthing on them ; but, in all indictments of trespass, etc., they did as is usual, and the constant practice of the Court and not otherwise. Mr. Hause says he was recommended to the King by Sir Roger Lestrange, to be assistant to Mr. Graham and Mr. Burton, in the prosecution of Dr. Oates. As to Cragg's testimony, that Burton and Graham endeavoured to procure accusations against divers of the subjects, and solicited him to give information against the Earl of Macclesfield, with promise of a discharge, and 100*li.* to be paid him quarterly, which was refused, they say that after Cragg had given to his late Majesty an information (all of his own handwriting) of the invasion of the late Duke of Monmouth, Mr. Bridgeman, Graham, and Burton were directed to go to Cragg, in Newgate, to desire him to explain some passages in his information; but, as he gave no positive answer to anything, he was never called as a witness, nor was his evidence ever made use of. As to Aaron Smith's information, that they solicited against and prosecuted Stephen Colledge, and denied him a copy of his jury, they say that he had made his application to the Attorney-General and the Court, for a copy, before he came to them for it; and the same, being denied by the Attorney and the Court, it was not in their power to grant it.

The COMMISSIONERS OF CUSTOMS to the EARL OF DERBY.

791. 1691-2, February 19. Custom House.—" Wee have, not without some surprise, read your Lordship's letter to us of the 16th instant, whereby we presume your Lordship hath had our intentions represented, very different from what they are. Wee are so far from thinking to infringe your Lordshipp's rights in the Isle of Man, that wee have never soe much as questioned them, but, in all our proceedings, have desired the concurrence of your Lordship's authority, in secureing their Majesties' customs, and executing the laws of England. Your Lordship may also please to remember that, though complaints of no inconsiderable nature (and such as are proved upon oath) have lately been laid before the Council, wee have desisted from any prosecution thereof. And, in further deference to your Lordship, have placed another officer in the room of that person who seemed under your Lordship's displeasure, our end not being so much to vindicate the behaviour of any particular officer, whether discreet or not, as to obteyne those helps from your Lordship and your agents, as may best conduce to the performance of those instructions which are derived from an authority superiour to ours, and pursuent to the laws of England, and highly necessary for the security of the revenue of customs. We were in hopes your Lordship would have approved our proceedings in this matter, and complied with their Majesties' desire, signified in the late letter from the Lords of the Council. But, forasmuch as your Lordship seems resolved not to admit of any commission or instructions from us, to be obeyed in the Isle of Man, there remains nothing further for us to doe, but to report the whole matter to our superiors, as your Lordship is pleased to state it."

THOMAS KENYON to ROGER KENYON.

792. 1692, May 19. Chester.—It is probable you have had an account of the death of Mr. Bennett, late parson of Winwicke. The Dean, finding an inclination in himself to serve the house of Derby, and believing such a post not inconsistent with his deanery, begs you will be his assistant, by recommending him to my Lord. How far your interest might prevail with my Lord, I could not tell, since it is probable my Lord might expect other returns for such extraordinary favours than barely thanks. " He presently smelt out what it was I meant, and told me that, though it was contrary to his oath, and consequently to his conscience, to drive bargains beforehand, yet withall I might assure you in his name, and you his Lordship, that he never was ungrateful where he received kindness, nor would he carry himself in this, as unbecoming a gentleman or undeserving your friendship. I have sent two hundred and a half of asparagus for a taste."

ROBERT ROPER to ROGER KENYON.

793. 1692, May 20.—"My Lord [of Derby] being now in his bath, hath commanded mee to acquaint you that, this day, his Lordshipp hath receaved a letter from my Lord Rochester intimateing that, to prevent the report which Mr. Attorney-Generall must make to the Councell Board, touching the Isle of Man, it is necessary that my Lord doe, forthwith, signifie his mind to his agent in London, that hee doth comply with what is desired, touching those officers of the Customs sent thither by his Majestie's Commissioners; and his Lordshipp not knowing how farre you have proceeded heerin, doth therefore desire you to satisfye his Lordshipp in this point, by the bearer." *Seal.*

CHARLES HILTON to ROGER KENYON.

794. 1692, May 21. Gray's Inn.—"By an expres this morning, we have an account that on Thursday last, the two fleets engaged and fought for 12 hours incessantly, in which action the French lost 18 of their capitall shipps. And about noone this day, by another expresse, we heare they renewed the fight on Friday morning, and the French have since lost two of the Admirall's seconds. Severall of the French shipps were seen on fire, and for two leagues together, the sea was full of wrecks of shipps, and that, if the wind continued, it was not doughted but we shod make an intire defeate of their whole fleete." *Seal of arms.*

THOMAS TAUBMAN to ROGER KENYON.

795. 1692, May 24. London.—The French fleet are reduced to forty-two, the rest being sunk, burnt, and disabled, and the abovesaid remainder, divided east and west, are so closely pursued, that the Admiral is sure no one of them can escape. We have only disabled (not one lost) come in, the *Windsor, Hampton Court, Barwick, Sandwich,* and *Montague;* and killed, Carter, Hushings (?), Wheler, and Graydon.

"A full ACCOUNT of the late dreadfull EARTHQUAKE at Port Royall in Jamica, written in two letters from the minister of that place, from a board the *Granada* in Port Royall Harbour."

796. 1692, June 22.—"I doubt not but you will, both from gazetts and letters, hear of the great calamity that hath befallen this island, by a terrible earthquake, on the 7th inst., which has thrown down allmost all the houses, churches, sugar-works, mills, and bridges, through the whole country. It tore the rocks and mountains, and destroyed some whole plantations and threw them into the sea; but Port Royal had much the greatest share in this terrible judgment of God. I will, therefore, be more particular in giving you account of its proceedings in that place, that you may know what my danger was, and how unexpected my preservation.

"On Wednesday, the 4th (?) of June, I had been at church, reading prayers, which I did every day, since I was Rector of Port Royall, to keep up some shew of religion amongst a most ungodly and debauched people, and was gone to a place hard by the church, where the merchants used to meet, and there the President of the

Councell was, who acts in chief, till we have a new Governour, who
came into my company and engaged me to take a glass of worm-
wood wine with him, as a whet before dinner. He being my very
great friend, I stayed with him, upon which he lighted a pipe of tobacco,
which he was very long a-taking, and not being willing to leave him
before it was out, this detained me from going to dinner to one Captain
Rudens, where I was to dine, whose house upon the first concussion sunk
first into the earth, and then into the sea, with his wife and family and
some that were come to dine with him. Had I been · there, I had been
lost. But to return to the President and his pipe of tobacco. Before
that was out, I found the ground rowling and moving under my feet,
upon which I said to him—Lord, sir, what is this ? He replyed very
composedly, being a very grave man—It is an earthquake ; be not
afraid, it will soon be over. But it increased, and we heard the church
and tower fall, upon which we ran to save ourselves. I quickly lost
him, and made towards Morgan's Fort, which being a wide open place, I
thought to be there securest from the falling houses ; but, as I made towards it, I saw the earth open and swallow up a multitude of people, and
the sea mounting in over the fortification. I then laid aside all thoughts
of escaping, and resolved to make towards my own lodging and there to
meet death in as good a posture as I could. From the place where I
was, I was forced to cross and run through two or three very narrow
streets ; the houses and walls fell on each side of me, some bricks came
rolling over my shoes, but none hurt me. When I came to my lodging,
I found there all things in the same order I left them ; not a picture—
of which there were severall fair ones in my chamber—being out of its
place. I went to my balconey to view the street in which our house
stood, and saw never a house down there, nor the ground so much as
cracked. The people seing me there, cryed out to me to come and pray
with them. When I came into the street, everyone laid hold on my
clothes and embraced me, that, with their fear and kindness, I was
almost stifled. I perswaded them at last to kneel down and make a large
ring, which they did. I prayed with them near an hour, when I was
allmost spent with the heat of the sun and the exercise. They then
brought me a chair, the earth working all the while with new motions
and tremblings, like the rollings of the sea, insomuch that when I was at
prayer I could hardly keep myself upon my knees. By that time, I had
been halfe an hour longer with them. In setting before them their sins
and hainous provocations, and in seriously exhorting them to repentance,
there came some merchants to me in the place, who desired me to go
aboard some ship in the harbour and refresh myselfe, telling me they
had gotten a boat to carry me off. So, coming to the sea, which had
entirely swallowed up the wharf, with all these goodly brick houses upon
it—most of them as fine as those in Cheapside—and two entire streets
beyond that, I, upon the tops of some houses which were levelled with
the surface of the water, got first into a carol, then into a long boat,
which put me aboard a ship called the *Siam Merchant*, where I found
the President safe, who was overjoyed to see me. There I continued
that night, but could not sleep for the returns of the earthquake, allmost
every hour, which made all the guns in the ship to jarre and rattle.

"The next day, I went from ship to ship, to visit those that were bruised
and adying, and to pray with them, and likewise to doe the last office at
the sinking severall corps' that came floating from the Point ; which,
indeed, hath been my sorrowfull employment ever since I came aboard
this ship, with design to come for England. We having nothing but
shakings of the earth and thunder and lightening and foul weather, ever
since, and the people being so desperately wicked, makes me afraid to

stay in the place; for that very day the terrible earthquake was, as soon as night came on, a company of lewd rogues, whom they call privateers, fell on breaking open warehouses and houses deserted, to rob and rifle their neighbours, whilest the earth trembled under them, and some of the houses fell on them in the act, and those .audacious whores that remain still in the place, are as impudent and drunken as ever. I have been twice ou shore to pray with the bruised and dying people, and to christen children, where I found too many drunk [and] aswearing. I did not spare them, nor the magistrates neither, who have suffered wickednes to grow to so great a hight. I have, I bless God, to the best of my skill and power, discharged my duety in this place, which you will hear from most persons that came from hence. I have preached so seasonably to them in the church; I set before them what would be the issue of their impenitence and wickednes, that they have since confessed that it was more like a prophecy than a sermon. I had, I confesse, an impulse upon me to do it, and many times I have preached in this pulpit, things that I never premeditated at home, and could not, methought, do otherwise.

"The day when all this befell, it was very clear, afforded not the suspition of the least evill, but in the space of three minutes, about half-an-hour after eleven in the morning, Port Royall, the fairest town of all the English Plantations, [and] best emporium and mart of that part of the world, exceeding in its riches, plentifull in all good things, was shaken and shattered to pieces, sunk into and covered, for the greatest part, by the sea, and will, in a short time, be wholly eaten up by it, for few of these houses that yet stand, are left whole, and every day we hear them fall, and the sea daily incroaches upon it. We guess that by the falling of the houses and opening of the earth, there are lost fifteen hundred persons, and many of good note. I came, I told you, on board this ship, in order to come home, but the people are so importunate with me to stay, I know not what to say to them. I must undergo great hardship if I continue here—the country being all broken to pieces and dissetled.

"Ever since that fatall day, the most terrible that ever I saw in my life, I have lived on board aship, for the shakings of the earth return every now and then. Yesterday, we had a very great one, but it seems lesse terrible on ship-board then on shore, yet I have ventured to Port Royall no lesse than three times, since its desolation, among the shattered houses, to bury the dead and pray with the sick and christen the children. Sunday last, I preached to them in a hut, the houses that remain being so shaken that I durst not venture to preach in them. The people are overjoyed to see me among them, and wept bitterly when I preached unto them. I hope by this terrible judgment, God will make them reform their lives, for there was not a more ungodly people upon the face of the whole earth. It is a sad sight to see all this harbour, one of the fairest and goodlyest I ever saw, covered with dead bodies of people of all conditions, floating up and down without buriall, for our great buriall place, called the Palasidoes, was destroyed by the earthquake, and the sea washed the carcases of those that were buryed, out of their graves; their tombs were dashed in pieces by the earthquake, of which there were hundreds in that place. Wee have had accounts from severall parts of these Islands of the mischief done by the earthquake. From St. Ann's we . . . of above 1,000 acres of woodland changed into the sea, and carryed with it whole plantations, but no place suffered like . . . . so[me] were swallowed up to the neck and the earth shut upon them and squeezed them to death, and in that manner severall are found buryed, with their heads above ground; only, some heads the dogs have eaten, others are covered with the dust, by the people that live, to avoid the stench. Thus I have told you a long and sad story, and God knows what worse may happen. Yet the people tell me they hear noises and bellowings on mountains, and some think it is by fire. If so, I fear it will be more distructive then the earthquake. I am afraid to stay, and yet I know not how, in such a case as this, to quit my station."

The EARL OF DERBY to ROGER KENYON.

797. 1692, October 6   Lathom.—The day resolved upon for Bury, happens to be the very day of the month my poor grandfather was murdered, which I do not think proper at all to travel on, especially in those parts, for I suppose too, I must go through Bolton. Another day, the following week, must be taken.

R. STEVENSON to ROGER KENYON.

798. 1692, November 18.   Balladoule.—Thinks it would be better to have only one Deputy-Governour of the Isle of Man; if not, he prays someone else may be joined with Mr. Rowe, as their tempers do not agree. Thinks they should have free intercourse with the English markets. *Seal of arms.*

C. GREENFIELD to ROGER KENYON.

799. 1692, November 19.   Gray's Inn.—This day came on the *mandamus* about St. Ellen's Chapel. Nobody spoke in it but Mr. Finch and myself. All the Court declared their opinion, *seriatim*, that the return was a good return, that the justices may refuse certificates where church and property is concerned. *Portion of seal of arms.*

PETER SHAKERLEY to ROGER KENYON.

800. 1692, December 31.   Westminster.—There is like to be some difference concerning Lord Nottingham and Admiral Russell, the two Houses seeming to assist each their member. Yesterday, the Lords sent a message to desire a free conference, which is this day, at 11 o'clock, but the Admiral's friends here were not willing to come to that "touch," and so ceased to agree to the conference. The debate was taken up late; the House had sat till so dark, we could not see each other; few stayed in.

The HEADS of certain ACTS as to LINEN MANUFACTURE in the ISLE OF MAN.

801. [1692 ?]   " 1. That every farmour that holds a quarter of land, is to plant halfe an acre thereof either with flax or hemp, and soe proportionable to greater and lesser holdings.

" 2. That every woeman native, or maryed to a native of this isle, is to spin as much yarn as will make 12 yards of linen cloath, and to produce the same in yarn or cloth, at the Sheading courts, holden after May in every year, which is to be valued by 2 weavors; one chosen by the Governor and Officers for the Lord, and the other by the Deemsters and the great enquest for the countrey; and whosoever doth produce the finest yarn or cloath in a Sheading, is to have 20*s.* as a reward, besides the price of her yarn or cloath; and she that produces the finest in the whole island is to have 5*l.* (which is to be produced at the Tynwal), and if she be a maid or servant, she is to be freed from yarding or serveing, by a jury, while she lives.

" 3. That a workhouse be erected where all such flax and hemp as the country can spare (besides what is for their own use) is to be brought in, and a matron to be placed there, to teach all young girls, and a weaver to learn weaving, and other persons [to] dress flax and hemp ; to which workhouse, all vicious and debaucht persons, all loyterers, and vagabonds, are to be condempned ; and that all tenants are to give their assistance, by labour and carriages, to the erecting of the said house.

" The penalty for not planting flax and hemp according to the first parte of the Acte, is 3*s.* 4*d.* for every offence, and upon the seacond, for not spinning the quantity of yarn or cloath (after the firste admonition) to be fined and punished &c."

" For advancing value of money.

" 1. That all crown peeces are to passe at 5*s.* 4*d.* apeece.

" 2. That all half crown peeces at 2*s.* 8*d.* per peece, soe that they be of the new coyne called milned money."

" For non-residence.

" That all persons that have any promotions, places, offices or other liveings in this parte, to the value of 10*l.* *per annum,* or upwards, shall be obliged, after the 29th of September next, to reside in this Isle ; and live upon their promotions, and not otherwise, and in default thereof, they [are] to forfeit the 4th part of the proffitts of their liveings, which is to goe to the use of the workhouse aforesaid."

[ROGER KENYON to the BISHOP OF CHESTER.]

802. 1692[-3], January 6. Peel.—There is not any place for dissenters to meet at, in Hindley, nor was any ever asked to be recorded, by the Justices ; neither was the Chapel ever asked of the Justices, by any man, but John Green, who lives three miles from the Chapel. In Wigan, where they have two meeting places for dissenters, he and " his Mr. Whalley," who would be preacher at Hindley, have one, and there is another for dissenters, who do furiously dissent from each other. Mr. Green, I hear, talks very loud of his powerful friends in London, and mentions several I shame to name. " God grant King William may truly know who are his truest friends ; things would not be ordered in this country as they are." Mr. Green is very gracious with the Romanists about him ; he, indeed, has taken the oath to their Majesties, but for all the noise and clamour the dissenters make, very few of them have hitherto taken the oath.

C. GREENFIELD to [ROGER KENYON ?].

803. 1692[-3], February 16.—As to the Manchester petition about the linen manufactory, I have taken all pains possible in it. I find, by Mr. Mercer's letter, that their desire is to lay such an imposition upon French linen as may amount to an exclusion of it, viz. : 30*li. per cent.* Now, I have looked into the Bill, and find that the French goods are to be charged at 25*li. per cent.* (which is as near their desire as possible), and I have advised with the ancient members, upon the petition, and all tell me (indeed common reason tells us) that if we lay such a rate as will exclude them wholly, then the million given, by this Act, is so impaired, that the Act will not be worth a groat to the King. But this 25*li. per cent.* will set the English and the French upon an " even balance and foot of selling "; nay, it will be much better on the English side, and hurt no trade in England, that is sufficiently wretched already.

JOHN WOOD to ROGER KENYON.

804. 1692-3, March 3. Castletown.—" Haveing this optunatie of *The Wheele of Fortune*—David Christian maister and owner, now bound for Liverpoole, and Mr. Lesque, passenger, goeing to see you—I thought fit to aquaint you that all things here of yours are in good order ; onely the old oats consumed by rats and myse, but [I] preserves them as well as I can. The 2 hoddgsheads of beere and one of ale, that was brewed Christmas was twelvemonth, must bee made use of now this springe, or els the heat of this next summer will turn them sower. I have 12 boules of new malt, against your comeing, and will make more. I desire to know how many feathers for beding you will have bought ; I have layd out 3*l.* in feathers att 3*d. per* pound ; and what more I shall lay out, pray lett mee knowe. You have 4 bullocks, kept with best hay, and tended day and night, well, will bee good beefe. Make use of them when you please, besides the stoale-fed oxe, and 6 more, which will bee beefe soone, att grasse. Worthy sir, old Captain Robert Collcott is dead, commander of Darby Fort. Mr. Lesque, who has 2 souldiers places and the falkners place, and now [d]esignes to gett the command of Derby Fort and severall others, both to you and Governor Secheverell has write, as I am informed, but my dependance being wholy on your worship for some place here, desires if it lyes in your power, which I know it does, to procure mee a warrant either . . . . your Worshipp or my Lord. The sallary is 8*l. per ann*[*um*]." *Seal with device.*

NICHOLAS [STRATFORD], Bishop of Chester, to ROGER KENYON.

805. 1692[-3], March 16.—"A *mandamus* was sent, the last weeke, to Doctor Pope, to register Hindley Chappell. Mr. Greene's frendes here threaten him with such formidable eviles, in case he refuses, that the Doctor seemed to be in some fear ; but I thinke I have eased him of his feares, and fully satisfied him that he is in no danger. I intend to bring the *mandamus* down with me, and to have an answer drawn to it in the country, and returne it to London before the next terme. I wish the Comission for pious uses might be speedily prosecuted ; were the decree of the Comissioners once confirmed by the Chancellor of the Duchy, I hope that would put an end to all our troubles about Hindley Chappell."

FRANCIS BAYLY to ROGER KENYON, " one of the Pears of the Parliment House in London."

806. 1693, March 26.—" I presume the bouldness to write to your worship onst againe ; the ocesion of my writing is that the gelor hath hared that I have written to your worship, and he is mad at me ; wherein he hath poot a pere of irns on me, and locked me to a post, from morning to night, wherein he would not let nobody come to me, neither with meat nor drink ; and when he had done soe, he put me in the dungin all night. I continew there, and must be there, without your worship tack some ceare of me. And he hath torn my coat all to peses and hath abused me, that I am werey of my life. If I had born with him and not dis‐covered his rogrey, I should aben beter used. His draure, that fills the drink, tould me that he would have me to say nothing of his master, and it woulde be beter with me. Here is the tinker of Stretford has fallen to work again, for there is one of the prisoners did see him clip, in the pasag going in to the Chancery roome. There he sat, and his wife heled hur apron to kach the clipings as they fell from the shears. . . . . . I thought it fit to tell you that there is one Isrell Smith, who was in hear for clipping, [and] he sent to all the Justices fare and nere, and none of them would teak beall for this Isrell Smith, and Elison [the gaoler?] took 4*l.* of him and let him goe. . . . . I humbly beg that your worship would tak some cear of me to get the irns off me and [get me] out of the dungin, or els it will spoyle me, for I am very nesh (*sic*) and tender, for I shek and trimble every night when I goe to bed. I could wish meney a time that I wear dead. He tells some of the prisnors that I most not pech no mor." *Seal.*

PETER COLLIER to MRS. KENYON, at Peel.

807. 1693, April 12. Warrington.—Understands that "the school at Clethero" is vacant by the death of the master, that it is worth 40*l.* a year, and that Mr. Kenyon has an interest there. Begs, therefore, that Mr. Kenyon's interest may be used on his behalf. Is curate at Warrington. His allowance is but small, " and the people none of the easiest to please," which makes him " inclineable " to " take a school," that he might preach " seldomer." Would have applied in person, " but that we have two sacrament days, Good-Friday and Easter-Sunday, very near, besides praiers every day, till Thursday in Easter-weeke."

[The EARL OF DERBY] to ROGER KENYON.

808. 1693, May 13.—" My Lord Willoughby's locking up a chapple, I think, is very extraordinary; if you desire any assistance from hence, put it into forme, and I dare assure you I am able to do the Church some service, and to humble these uppish sparks." *Seal of arms.*

THOMAS WILSON to ROGER KENYON.

809. 1693, June 2. Knowsley.— " My Lord Strange had a letter from Mr. Archdeacon, who tells him that, the day he writes, he saw a lamb taken from the dam, with a head exactly made like a raven."

GUICCIARDINI WENTWORTH to ROGER KENYON.

810. 1693, June 6.—Begging Kenyon to use his influence on behalf of Mr. Bertie, for the Clitheroe election. *Seal of arms.*

" The account of ROGER KENYON, Esquire, of what hath been done by him, pursuant to his deputation from the Warden of the Mint, bearing date 23 June 1693."

811. 1693, July 8 to August 24.—An account of 30 persons in Lancashire and Cheshire taken up, or against whom warrants were issued, for clipping coins or issuing bad money.

JOHN LOMAX to ROGER KENYON.

812. 1693, July 8. Kirk Andrew [Isle of Man.]—No sooner was I landed on this dull solitary place, than several of your faithful servants and well wishers did passionately enquire after your health and return to the Island. When I assured them of your intention to visit them before the

Tinwell, they were transported with joy; but when Mr. Sacheveril arrived, and was sworn Governour, then I perceived their bright countenances were eclipsed by an " earthish dullness." *Seal of arms.*

ROGER KENYON to GUICCIARDINI WENTWORTH, Secretary to Lord Willoughby, Chancellor of the Duchy of Lancaster.

813. 1693, July 22. Manchester —" My last to you promised to be followed with a representation of the management of matters here, and of the parties managing; but though I have many things which I could freely and justifiably say to our w[ort]hy Chancellor, yet is my pen restrained by second thoughts, as convinced that such things are better said than writ.

" Things very unusuall are done, but who knows the intregues of State; for so it seems, when such things are acted, by such who are set to governe us. Could I, as secretly as the things are carryed, ask what can be the meaning of gathering armes, some thousands more then our militia ever uses? What can be the meaneing, if there be an order of councell in other countyes to disarme papists and nonjurors, that instead of that, protections are given here to such, that none shall molest them? When packs of swords, sent from London, and seized, are committed to the custody of the most violent and active dissenter in our country time after time? How comes our commission of the peace to be filled with justices of so many minds, that those whose office it is to preserve the peace are too often divided upon the Bench? So in separation that the solicitor knows his oppertunity who will befriend his motion; and thus things are done and undone by divided parties. Why should there be 206 places for the dissenters and religiouse meetings—as they call them— and not . . . . . but barely one hundred persons of all sorts of dissenters that have so qualifyed themselves as to be exempt from the penalties of the former laws, by doing what the late Act for such exemptions requires? Sure it is demonstration that either the dissenters do not give that satisfaction to the Government which the law requires, or that their party is not so numerous as they would be esteemed. It is obvious that our Magistraticall (*sic*) Dissenters bear themselves exceeding high as if it were meritoruouse, and the way to advancement to act so. We have had twenty-five Justices give an opinion one way, and but one dissenting Justice oppose them, and yet glory in the opposition. It is notoriously obvious, to want observation, that the Dissenters' chiefe favourers are, some of them, the same persons that, in thé late raigne, were as active in asserteing the dispenseing power, as forward to take away the penall laws and tests, and as busy in the then regulation—as they call it—of our Corporations, as they now are contenders for tender consciences. I give you these whispering hints, to be told to none but the Chancellor, but this is but that any reservednes may not be censured by his Lordshipp, when I say what perhaps I am full enough of, yet may be better said than writ. I have severall times sent to Clitherow, and have had two gentlemen of the Corporation with me, who tell me the warmest applications are on behalf of Mr. Fitton Gerrard and Mr. Weddall. For the assurance I have by your letter that the Honorable Philip Bertie, Esquire, whom I have heartily proposed, will go the same way my Lord Willoughby did, full willingly should he have all the votes I could make him, would those avayle him; but without some probable prospect of that, I thinke our noble Chancellor will give me leave, if not command mee, rather than lose both that are good by divideing . . . to push on his brother's appearance too far for it, without some seemeing assurance. I speake not this as an apology for my desertion of the worthy Mr. Bertie, nor without a beleef that it would bee much my own, as well as the kingdome's interest, and particulerly our burrough's, were I confident that it were in my power to do so acceptable a thing to him and the great personages his honor relates to. But considering how far Mr. Weddall got the start, and that his uncle, Mr. Wilkinson, who lives within halfe a mile of Clitherow, who is constantly intent and daily solicitous for him, and on the other hand, our potent Lord Lieftenent hath honored our little town with his great presence, two or three days together, and hath planted one of his gentlemen, some considerable time, curesseing the mobile, yea, more kind then were any of his predecessors, hath sent a regiment of the militia to exercise there four days, to the honour of the towne and advantage of the alehouses." *Draft.*

Roger Kenyon to Benjamin Overton, Warden of the Mint.

814. 1693, July 28. Peel, near Manchester.—Giving an account of his proceedings for the apprehension and commitment of coiners and clippers. *Draft.*

Guicciardini Wentworth to Roger Kenyon, at Peel.

815. 1693, July 29. [London.]—Encloses a warrant for a buck out of " Mierscoe." Is not certain how they should be directed, having sent no warrants thither, since the Revolution. " The Lord Warington is, in his patent, called master forester and keeper of the game, and, I am told, Sir Thomas Stanley is bow bearer, and you know there is no very good understanding between my Lord and T. P. (*sic*), who will perhaps lay hold of a wrong direction, to excuse the not serving it ; therefore, I have left the direction to you. My Lord and his brother are bent on this affaire, and desire you will carry it on as far as you may. The account of the last fight in Flanders is a very bad one, and seems not to mend, but the truth of all relations ridds on a lame post, which will bring more certainty of the affair then is at present known, or willingly believed. It is said there has been some action on the . . . . *Seal of arms.*

Enclosure.—1693, July 17.—Warrant by the Chancellor of the Duchy of Lancaster for the delivery of a Buck.—" These are to require you forthwith to deliver, or cause to be delivered, to the bearer hereof, one fatt buck of this season, fairly killed, due to me as Chancellor of their Majesties' Dutchy and County Pallatine of Lancaster." (Signed) " Willughby."

Ann Holland to Roger Kenyon.

816. 1693, August 14. Manchester.—Asking for a protection from quartering soldiers. *Seal.*

Nicholas, Bishop of Chester, to Roger Kenyon.

817. 1693, August 23. Chester.—" I again most heartily thank you for your constant paines and diligence in asserting and defending the just rights of our Church ; and I hope that I may, some time or other, be in a condition to return you more than bare thanks, though I cannot hope that I shall ever be able to make you a requital.

" Upon the receipt of your letter, I presently sent for Mr. Prescott, who told me that he had made a thorough search in the Registry, and could find nothing more than what he had already communicated to you, and I have no reason to question the truth of what he says, because I have ever found him faithful and diligent in his place. However, since the Lord Willoughby will not proceed to a tryall at the next Assises (as I find by your letter, you before suspected), I will myself make search in the Registry, and if I can find anything before the wares, which may be of advantage to our cause, I will not fail, in due time, to acquaint you with it. In particular, Mr. Prescott tells me that he can find nothing, either in the visitation books, or in the Acts of the Court relating to Mr. Johnson.

" I shall say nothing to that part of your letter in which Mr. Chancellor and Mr. Prescott are concerned, because the Chancellor tells me that he will return an answer to it under his own hand.

" I am told that my Lord Willoughby regrets that ever he set on foot this controversy, and that he would gladly retreat, if he could see how he might do so, with safty to his honour.

" P.S.—Since I wrote my letter, a paper of yours was brought to me, directed to Mr. Bridges or Mr. Prescott; in which you desire that several enquiries may be made relating to Ellenborough Chappel. I will therefore see that the Registry be again searched, and that thoroughly, and if anything can be there found concerning any of the persons or willes you mention, notice shall be given you thereof." *Seal of arms.*

GUICCIARDINI WENTWORTH to ROGER KENYON, at Peel.

818. 1693, August 28. [London.]—Is sorry Mr. Kenyon has had so much trouble in Mr. Bertie's affairs. "Your endeavours have made two Parliament men att Clitherow; and it seemed to me probable you might have sett faire for a third, but it may be *tempora mutantur.* There can be no room to question your friendship and justice to Mr. Bertie and mee; but I think there may be to yourselfe, to spend your pretious tyme and mony for another; the 5*l.* being only designed to bea[r]e that weeke's charge, to try whether there would have been room for the expence of 200*l.* or 300*l.* which I had order to employ for that service." *Seal of arms.*

THE CHARGE OF THE CIVIL LIST.

819. 1693, Michaelmas, to 1694, Michaelmas.—Customs :—The duties by the Act of Parliament determined at Christmas last past, were divided in three fourth parts, and one fourth part. The three fourth parts were constantly paid into the Receipt of the Exchequer, and applied towards the payment of the principal moneys borrowed, with the interest thereon. And out of the one fourth part, the Receiver-General paid so much of the charge of managing the customs as was payable by his hand, and the residue was applicable to the uses of the Civil List. The receipt for the year ending Michaelmas, 1694, over and above the debentures, discounts, and the charges of management, amounted to 406,987*li.* 16*s.* 7¾*d.*, besides 24,282*li.* 7*s.* 7½*d.*, which was not the real product of the Revenue, but money within the said year, advanced by the Receiver of the said fourth part.

Coffee and Tea :—These new duties were applicable to the Civil List. The net receipts thereof were 2,153*li.* 9*s.*, but these expired at Christmas last, and were not regranted by the Act newly passed.

Excise :—The rates of excise granted in fee, and those now enjoyed during his Majesty's life (which are called the hereditary or temporary excise), did produce (over and above the charges of management) 413,053*li.* 14*s.* 0¾*d.* Money borrowed by tallies amounted to

260,748*li*. 11*s*. 3*d*., besides which, it was charged with an old debt of 1,333,873*li*. 14*s*. 7¼*d*. due to several bankers and others or their assigns, for which Charles II. granted to them and their heirs, several sums amounting to 80,032*li*. 8*s*. 1*d. per annum* in the nature of perpetual interest, until they should be respectively satisfied. The principal and interest is in arrear for eleven years and three quarters, amounting to 940,380*li*. 14*s*. 11*d*. or thereabouts.

Low Wines:—The duties thereon amounted to 13,698*li*. 15*s*. 8¼*d*., and have no debt thereupon.

Letter Money :—The revenue from the Post Office, over and above the charges for management, amounted to 59,972*li*. 14*s*. 9*d*. There was a charge thereupon to the Civil List, of 21,200*li. per annum*.

Small Branches and Casualties :—Excluding the coinage, which was appropriated to the Mint, this branch of revenue amounted to 77,435*li*. 11*s*. 5¼*d*.

Charged, by Letters Patent or other special grants, on the Customs :— The Consul at Algiers, 600*li*. ; the Consul at Tripoli, 380*li*. ; the Controller of the Treasurer of the Chamber Office, 150*li*. ; the two Secretaries of State, each 1,850*li*. ; the Lord Privy Seal, 365*li*. ; Amias and Juliana Hext, 200*li*. ; Samuel Clerke, 300*li*. ; George Tuthill, 100*li*. ; Corporation of Lyme, 100*li*. ; Chancellor of the Garter, 570*li*. 5*s*.; Thomas Hyde, 50*li*.; Corporation of Berwick, 100*li*.; Corporation of Dartmouth, 40*li*.; Charles Fairfax, 100*li*.; the master of the otter hounds, 28*li*. 0*s*. 1½*d*.

Charged, by Letters Patent or other special grants, on the hereditary and temporary excise :—The Queen Dowager, 12,209*li*. 15*s*. 2*d*. ; the Prince and Princess of Denmark, 50,000*li*. ; the Duchess of Buccleuch (*sic*) 4,000*li*. ; the Duchess of Richmond, 1,000*li*. ; the Duke of Grafton, 4,000*li*. ; Duchess Dowager of Grafton, 1,000*li*. ; the Duke of Southampton, 3,000*li*.; the Duke of Northumberland, 300*li*.; Sir William Killegrew, 500*li*. ; Samuel Morland, esquire, 200*li*.; the Fishermen and Adventurers of Great Yarmouth, 160*li*.

Charged on the Post Office Revenue :—The Earl of Rochester, 4,000*li*. ; the Duchess of Cleveland, 4,700*li*.; the Duke of Leeds, 3,500*li*.; the Duke of Schombourgh, 4,000*li*. ; the Earl of Bath, 2,500*li*. ; the Lord Keeper, 2,000*li*. ; William Dockra, to the end of midsummer, 1697, 500*li*.

Charged on the 12*d*. per chalder on Sea Coals :—Sir Thomas Clarges, 500*li*.

Charged on the Alienation Office :—The Countess of Plymouth, part of her jointure, 1,000*li*.; Sir William Morris, 300*li*.; the Duke of St. Albans, part of 2,000*li*., 500*li*.

Charged on the Duchy of Cornwall :—The Earl of Bath, 3,000*li*. ; the Lord Keeper, 2,000*li*.; Sir Peter Killegrew, 300*li*.; the minister of Lostwithiel, 30*li*.

Charged on the Revenue of Wales :—Henry D'Auverquerc, 2,000*li*. ; the Duke of St. Albans, part of 2,000*li*., 500*li*.

Charged on the First Fruits and Tenths :—The Earl of Oxford, 2,000*li*. ; the Countess of Plymouth, part of her jointure, 2,000*li*. ; the Countess of Bristol, 2,000*li*. ; the Earl of Bath, 2,500*li*.; the Duke of St. Albans, part of 2,000*li*., 1,000*li*. ; Sir (*sic*) Samuel Morland, 600*li*.; Elizabeth Hamilton, 500*li*.; James and William Hamilton, 850*li*.

Charged on the Letter Rent:—Solomon Foubert, 500*li*.; Philip Howard, 400*li* ; James Grey, 400*li*.; Sir Gabriel Selvins, 300*li*.; Lady Armstrong's daughters, 200*li*.; Charles Killegrew, 200*li*.; Susanna Leighton, 100*li*ı; Jane Berkley, 200*li*.; Elinor Needham, 300*li*. ; Mary Fanshaw, 200*li*ı; Captain John Richards, 200*li*.; Sir Charles Slingsby, 40*li*.; Mallet Slingsby, 20*li*.; Elizabeth Slingsby, 45*li*. 12*s*. 6*d*. ; Colonel

Henry Ubank, 45*li.* 12*s.* 6*d.* ; Richard Sydenham, and Grace his wife, 40*li.* ; Ann Duke, 45*li.* 12*s.* 6*d.*; Captain John Baker, 36*li.* 10*s.*; Captain Hetleby's grandchildren, 36*li.* 10*s.*; Captain John Watkinson, 18*li.* 5*s.*; Ann Ashbary, 20*li.* ; Widdow Collins, 20*li.* ; Mr. Rosse's three daughters, 60*li.* ; Mr. Bass, 20*li.* ; Edward Duke, 24*li.* ; Colonel Vaughan, 300*li.* ; Dame Martha Cary, 20*li.* ; Dame Petronella Cary, 20*li.* ; Captain James Vosper, 20*li.* ; Captain Griffith Standon, 20*li.*; Ann Acton, 20*li* ; Anny Goldsbrough, 20*li.*; Elizabeth Hall, Jane Bell, and Margaret Pretty, each 20*li.*; Victoria Slingsby, 20*li.*

Charged on the Exchequer in general :—The Duke of Norfolk, 3,000*li.*; the Duke of Ormond, 2,500*li.*; the Duchess of Buckingham, 1,200*li.*; Ann Golding, 120*li.*; Nicholas Needam, 120*li.*; Catherine Gunter, 200*li.*; the Earl of Derby, and others, for poor ministers in the Isle of Man, 100*li.*; Rachell and Francis Wyndham, 400*li.*; Ann Lawton, 250*li.*; William Levett, 200*li.*; Dr. Nicholas Gibbon, 100*li.*; Robert Berty, 40*li.*; Lodowick Bray, 40*li.*; James Browning 60*li.*; Charles Dormer, 120*li.*; the Earl of [Kinnoull?] 120*li.*; Christ's Hospital, 370*li.* 10*s.*; the poor of St. Martin's, 100*li* ; the poor of Westminster, and King Charles I.'s Hospital there, 100*li.*; the poor of St. James', 50*li.*; the poor of St. Michael's, Cornhill, a perpetuity, 12*li.* 4*s.*; the poor of St. Magnus' parish, London, 21*li.* 4*s.* 8*d.*; the poor of St. Botolph's, 7*li.*; the poor of Walbrook, 7*li.* 13*s.* 4*d.*; the master of Southwell School, 10*li.*; Eton College, 42*lt.*; Emanuel [College] in Cambridge, 16*li.* 13*s.* 4*d.*; Reader of Civil law, 40*li.*; Reader of Physic there, 40*li.*; University of Cambridge, 10*li.*; Lady Margaret's profession at Oxford, 13*li.* 6*s.* 8*d.*; Reader of Civil Law there, 40*li.*; Reader of Physic there, 40*li.*; the Dean and Chapter of Lichfield, 10*li.*; the Vicar of Lichfield, 15*li.*; the Dean and Chapter of Westminster, for French ministers in the Savoy, 60*li.*; the Master of the Temple, 37*li.* 6*s.* 8*d.*; the Vicar of the Tower, 6*li.* 13*s.* 4*d.*; Sir John Cotton, a perpetuity, 5*li.* 6*s.* 8*d.*; the poor of the town of Hampton, 50*li.*; Thomas Lane, esquire, 60*li.*; John Rogers, and Ann his wife, 100*li.*; Rachell and Francis Wyndham, 400*li.*; Sir Thomas Wyndham, 600*li.*; Colonel Gifford, 300*li.*; Thomas Whitgrave, 200*li.*; Nicholas Yeates, 200*li.*; the four King's preachers in Lancashire, out of the rent of the dissolved monastery of Furness, 200*li.*

Various sums to officers of the household, and also payments for secret service, as follows :—*Per* Henry Guy, Esquire, 37,106*li.* 7*s.* 8¼*d.*; *per* the Earl of Nottingham, late Secretary of State, 3,000*li.*; *per* Sir John Trenchard, Secretary of State, 2,500*li.*; *per* the Duke of Shrewsbury, Secretary of State, 1,000*li.*

ROGER KENYON to ————.

820. 1693, October 25. Chester.—" It is now impertinent to attempt the discription of the partiality, precipitency, and fury, of the fanatick party, and particulerly of Sir William Williams, who presided as a judge, the Mayor being a party at the election. The votes on the one side were indeed made with as much courage, and the aldermen behaved themselves with as good resolution and constancy, as men in the right ought to doe. The Lord Warrington was there, on the other side; but scarce gave a word, save his vote as alderman, or looke, on behalfe of it. It was Williams his impetuosity, and the Mayor's partiality to himself, that carryed the matter violently against Alderman Allen, when it came to the last question about Mr. Hand's incapacity ; and if, in this time, my Lord Derby's presence and personall authority had interposed (having so great a majority of the Bench with him) it is beleeved it would have awed the unfaithfull and furiouse Recorder into regularity, justice, and manners. Mr. Shakerley's presence was of that satisfaction and service to the honest side, and they attribute that advantage very much to my Lord's letter to him; and now Mr. Shakerley is *statu quo prius* in their esteem, and by vertue of the majority by his vote, they succeeding in the election of a very honest man, for the first Sheriffe who is alwayes chosen by the Bench, for herein the 11 votes were admitted, though not in that of the Mayor. They hope for some redresse for a right so violated and abused. Sir Thomas Grosvenor and Mr. Shakerley seem now very sensible of the mistaken measures in the last business; for the *mandamus* taken out of the King's Bench, stopt that proceeding in Councell. As greater affaires stand for examination, I fear litle wilbe done in this, and that, at last, will almost ruine them in Westminster Hall to be rectifyed." *Draft.*

CHRISTOPHER WILKINSON, JO: LISTER, H. PUDSAY, THOMAS LISTER, EDWARD PARKER, HENRY MARSDEN, and ROBERT SCLATER to ROGER KENYON, at Peel.

821. 1693, November 25. Clitheroe.—"This day, Mr. Manwaring, with Mr. Gerrard and the greatest part of Mr. Gerrard's friends in town, finding the Moothall dore open for some workmen imployed there for some repairs, took possession thereof, and as it is reported, swore Mr. Manwaring bayliffe, who, with the High Sherriffe of the County, and the rest of the company, made proclamation for an election of a member to serve in Parliament, to be made on Thursday next. We therefore desire that you, with your son, would please to let us have your company here as soon as possible on Tuesday next, to meet us and other your brother burgesses, to consider what may be most expedient to be done for the Corporation's safety.

" P.S.—If possible bring Sir Richard Standish, Bart., along with you, to whom our service." *Seal.*

PROPOSAL FOR RAISING MONEY.

822. 1693, December 3.—"A Profitable Adventure to the Fortunate, and can be unfortunate to none; being a proposal for raising one million of money, by setling a fund of one hundred and forty thousand pounds *per annum* for fifteen years only, for it." *London,* "printed by F. Collins in the Old Bailey."

RICHARD EDGE to ROGER KENYON, M.P.

823. 1693, December 22. Peel.—"My mistress has tould me that you say I must be one to attend the Committee, about Cliderow election, on the 12th of the next month, which (though it be Preston Sessions) if I be alive and well, will certainly attend. . . . Mr. Warren has offered himself at Wygan, to stand for their representative, and has offered to build them a conduit in the market place and bring water to it, to supply it at his own charge. Mr. Richard Lightbourne went yesterday to Wygan, by my Lord Colchester's order, to offer and recommend to them Colonel Mathews as a fit person for the said service. Mr. Byrom stands very fair in the generallity of the townsmen." *Seal, broken.*

RICHARD EDGE to ROGER KENYON, M.P.

824. 1693, December 28. Waddow.—"I came this day to Cliderowe, where I find great preparations are making on both sides. I am told that Mr. Edmund Robinson his son John, the late Bayliffe Stockes, Tom Dugdale, Coleborne, the quaker, George Langford, and Madam Parker, sett out for London on Saturday next, on Mr. Gerrard's party. That Colonel Pudsay, Mr. Lister of Westby, Mr. Edward Parker, Mr. Robert Sclater, Mr. Oddy, the town clerke, Dr. Whittacre, and two or three more that can speake about bribes, will certainly sett out, about Tuesday next, on Mr. Weddall's party. But I am afraid we cannot get Bayliffe Lister up to London. I spoke to Mr. Oddy and Mr. Sclater, and they tell me they have informed themselves of every thing, as well as they can." *Seal of arms.*

Thomas Marsden to Roger Kenyon.

825. 1693, December 28.—It is a pity that a strong hand should prevail against justice, which I hope it will not do in the case of Clitheroe, you being upon the spot to manage the matter. Honest Mr. Preston will stick close to you, and toil for the public interest. Mr. Bootle is gone into the other world, and was, sometime before he fell sick, stripped of all relation to Mr. Mol[yneux]'s concerns. He was not, indeed, a good man, but had been good to the interests of Croxteth, without reaping any advantage from its service ; but so the devil uses to reward his drudges. " O ! what a loss have we of Sir Richard Standish ; I never heard that the dragooner who is recommended to succeed him was a man either for Christianity or Monarchy ; but, be he what he will, I hope he will not obtain at Wigan."

Richard Richmond to Roger Kenyon.

826. 1693, December 29. Walton.—I shall add a request that is, indeed, made to you by many others of your true friends, besides myself, viz., that when the time comes for nominating commissioners to act in the several subsidies and taxes, to be collected for the ensuing year, yourself, Mr. Preston (and such other Lancashire members as you confide in), would please to take care that we be not plagued at Liverpool with such fellows as Clayton, and a number of fanatics, from whom a churchman can expect little justice in his appeals. Mr. Byrom stands fairest to succeed poor Sir Richard Standish.

Major Richard Stevenson to Roger Kenyon.

827. 1693, ... [Isle of Man.]—"I have received your orders by Parson Lomax to send you over 4 or 5 of the oxen ; I had rather, for severell reasons, you would bring your family, and eate them here ; besides, I must acquent you that my Lord's orders to Governour Rowe is (as he sayes) that his honour is to have, this year, the full number of cattle (that is allowed) for his owne use ; so that if there be any above that, they will be seized on. . . . We have lately buried honest ould Deemster Christian, and, that which adds to the whole country's great greeffe, have no man therein that is fitt or capable to supplye his plase, unless it be given to his brother, who, with much perswasion, I and many more of his friends, have prevailed with to write to you to gett him that place, who will be boath lawgiver and speaker." *Seal of arms.*

Dispute as to a Monument to Colonel Birch.

828. 1693.—An account of a dispute between the Bishop of Hereford and John Birch, Esquire, concerning the erection of a monument, in the chancel of Weobly Parish Church, to the memory of Colonel Birch, and an inscription reflecting upon King Charles I. 5.

[RICHARD EDGE] to ROGER KENYON, M.P., at Westminster.

829. 1693[-4], January 2. Peel.—"Here has been a great falling out betwixt Lord and Lady W[illoughby] . . . the Warden of Manchester can give you the best account. It is reported . . . down the country, that the Warden has done some ill thing against . . . which he has since owned himselfe in fault, and begged pardon . . . say it is not true. I allsoe hear that my Lady had gott away a . . . deedes and writings, by getting a counterfeit key of my Lord's . . . his Lordshipp has since got them againe. They are all going into mourneing at Manchester for L . . . ."

MAJOR RICHARD STEVENSON to ROGER KENYON, at Peel.

830. 1693-4, January 4. Balladoule, [Isle of Man.]—Has previously sent him a letter by David Christian. "It is reported here we are to have a new controwler, at which the people are reddy, with one hart and voice, to sing *te Deum*. And as, in truth, it would be the blessing of peace to this people, so it would be the satisffaction of interest to our honourable Lord; for this accumulation of offices upon him, by his honour, hath put him past all equality with his fellow officers, so that he now despises, scornes, and quarrels, with all; and I humbly leave it to your judgement how it is possible his Lordshipp's concernes can be well managed whilst such hart burnings and differences remaine amongst his servants, and how the people can ever be thought to comply, in any reasonable termes, with his honour, whilst theire supposed (if not avowed) enemie is concerned! If you consider him in his naturall endowments, you will find him made of a complication of ill quallities; of a moroseness towards inferiors; of a disegreeable temper towards his equalls (if he hath the modesty to acknowledge any as such); and of pretending forwardness towards his superiors; dogmatically dictating where he ought to be but a pupil, mightily magnifying himself, in all company, of his great knowledge, both in the theorike and practicall parts of the lawes of England . . . much mistaken, in the metall, if, like gold, he refine upon the tryall, in his pretended . . . as a great statesman to serve his Majesty, he minds other people's business (beyond the duty of a christian) more than his owne, and measures their steps by the rules of his new geometry; prys like a pimp into all theire actions, with a malicious design to pick up some matter of complaint, which, whether he observes any outstepings or no, he wants not invention to feign he did; and, rather than be baffled in the fruit of his expectation, he will improve a mole into a beam, a mole-hill into a mountain, by his magnifying art of representation, &c. But now, upon consideration, I am a foole to give you a discription of the monster, who knows him much better than tis possible for me to describe him . . . Deempster Norris is dead; you would do well to remember your ould friend, Charles Christian." *Seal of arms.*

ABRAHAM ALLRED to ROGER KENYON, M.P., at Westminster.

831. 1693[-4], January 6.—"My brother James Allred's wife is dead, and the toune hath met about some concerns, and, amongst other things, the question was put whether he would continue to keepe ale, or to teache schoole; and, after some deliberation of the matter, he gave them his possitive answer, that he would leave off keepinge ale and continue teaching schoole, and designs to brew noe more." The writer, therefore, begs to be admitted tenant.

WILLIAM SHUTTLEWORTH to ROGER KENYON, M.P.,
at Westminster.

832. 1693[-4], January 9. Preston.—Finds himself daily less able to support his charges, and without prospect of receiving his just demands, "either of the King of Sweden" or of his father-in-law, Holt. Begs, therefore, that some "beneficiall place" may be bestowed upon him. *Seal of arms.*

GEORGE MACY to ROGER KENYON, at the "Blue Boar" in Holborn.

833. 1693[-4], January 10. Tower [of London].—Arranging an appointment with Mr. Overton, Warden of the Mint. *Seal, broken.*

ALICE KENYON to her husband, ROGER KENYON, M.P.,
at Westminster.

834. 1693[-4], January 12.—Fears he will suffer much in London from the cold weather; "pray thee, keep warm as thou can, and take something in thy pocket to the House, to supp off; thy age and weakness requires it." Hears that Mr. Nathaniel Hilton is dead, and that his body "comes along" with Lord Warrington's. . ·. . "Lord Willo[ughby] and his Lady are fallen out extreamly; they are the talk of the toune and country."

Postscript.—"Cosin Hilton was telling me he heard you are doeing something about clippers; hee says hee thinks the best way to lessen the number of them, would be to abate of the value of clipt moneys. He remembers it was so when he was a boy; a shilling went but for 9*d.*, and halfe-a-crown for 18*d.*"

THOMAS WILLSON to ROGER KENYON, M.P., in London.

835. 1693[-4], January 12. Knowsley.—Knows how zealous Mr. Kenyon has always been in serving the family [Lord Derby's] in which he "has the honour to live." The lieutenancy of Cheshire is vacant by the death of Lord Warrington, and Lord Derby is "pressed to think of regaining that place which he and his ancestors have so honourably managed for many generations"; thinks it right, therefore, to inform Mr. Kenyon of the fact, in order that he may take the necessary steps to promote Lord Derby's interest, his Lordship being no longer unwilling to accept a lieutenancy. "This is an opportunity, which will scarce ever be mett with againe," for Lord Derby to possess himself of both Lancashire and Cheshire, "since my Lord Brandon has often protested that he would resign that of Lancashire, whenever my Lord [Derby] would accept of it." *Original and copy.*

RICHARD RICHMOND and THOMAS MARSDEN to ROGER
KENYON, M.P.

836. 1693[-4], January 12. Walton.—They send a list of persons well qualified to act as commissioners "for the ensuing taxes" :—

For Liverpool.—Jasper Maudit, Mayor; Captain James Prescot; Alderman Richard Houghton; Alderman Thomas Tyrer; Alderman Thomas Johnson; Mr. John Barker; Mr. Thomas Johnson, junior; Mr. Alexander Norres; and Alderman Joshua Fisher.

For the neighbourhood. — Mr. Robert Roper; Mr. John Case; Mr. Jonathan Case; Mr. John Wright; Mr. James Ashton; Mr. John Layton of Whiston; and Mr. Thomas Cooke.

These persons the writers recommend to "the Honourable Master Stanley; Sir Edward Chisenhall; Sir Christopher Greenfield; Mr. Preston; Mr. Shakerley; and yourself . . . . May God's good providence crown all your endeavours for this church and state."

RICHARD WROE, Warden of Manchester, to ROGER KENYON, M.P., at Westminster.

837. 1693[-4], January 15 [date of receipt].—" I am glad that Sir Ralph Assheton designes to stand for Knight, which I think will do, not onely himself, but the county, a kindness, and hope he will find friends enow to make an unanimous vote, which I am confident he will have, in these parts of our countrey. Things look very well, too, at Wigan, whence I had an account yesterday, that Mr. Byrom's interest keeps firm and gets strength daily. It is said Collonel Matthews came as far as Warrington, but found no encouragement to goe nearer Wigan from his friends there, nor at Knowsly, whither I hear he went. If my wishes may contribute any thing to the success at Clitbero, I am sure you have them; and if it go well there, I hope the county will not change for the worse. My Lord Warrington's corps will be brought to Bowdon tomorrow, in the night, and a friend of his is to say something of him there on Sunday, which you may imagine I am at present very busy with, having an hard task, both through short warning and a very critical subject. I have writ, this post, both to our Bishop of Chester and Mr. Shakerley, about the Rectory of Aldingham in Fourness, now vacant by the death of Mr. Thompon, prebend of Chester. Mr. Shakerley, I suppose, will shew you his letter, where you will see my designe in writing to him, wherein I heartily beg your assistance."

THOMAS KENYON, to his father ROGER KENYON, M.P., "att the doore of the House, these."

838. [1693-4, January 20.] — About the death of Mr. Wilkinson. " On Tuesday, the writt for election att Wigan was delivered to Mr. Mayor, and on Wednesday, the day of election was proclaimed to be Wednesday next, when I designe to wait on Mr. Byrom; his intrest, I beleeve, may be but inaffectually opposed. The Scowes men are his with a *nemine contradicente*, and of the out burgesses, except three, all have promised him their votes. He has an equallity, if not a superiority, in all other streets, and from 5 to 10 guineas to one are offered on his side. Mr. Justice Warren importunes first him and then Bertie to decline it ; each puts him upon getting first the other's consent, and then bid him hope the best. In the meenetime, Mr. Byrome takes him along with him, and so, att halfe charges, makes merry with his friends, whilst he, poore gentleman, sees not what any tinker sees and laughs at." *Fragment of seal.*

JOSEPH YA[TES] to ROGER KENYON, M.P.

839. 1693[-4], January 20. Manchester.—Hopes for a reconciliation between Kenyon and himself. . " It is a generall rejoycing to hear that Sir Ralph Asheton will stand for Knight of the Shire, and not doubted but he will be elected unanimously . . . I was desired by letter from Lancaster, on Francis Bailey's account, to acquaint you that he brought his action against Elletson [Elliotson], the gaoler, for 20 ounces of silver, *videlicet*, a new cast-silver hilt and some bullion ; and when the action was to be tried, Elletson affirmed that he took them by order from the Warden of the Mint, and upon this pretence Mr. Mayor of Lancaster ordered the money (the goods being sold, as I understand) to be brought into Court till such time as he be satisfied of the truth of the matter; and, therefore, it is requested that you would satisfie Mr. Mayor, by letter, of the truth thereof, which I hope you will doe, for there is a generall complaint of his abuseing the prisoners, and suppose it will be as much as formerly to the full; for I understand that this year he gives 80*l.* for the place, and he will make it up if possible; and, indeed, I doe not see how any person can seaze a silver hilt or bullion in any person's custody, unless the bullion was known and proved to be clippings melted down by the same person. Your son Tom and I, drank your health yesternight, and was observing that you are not soe kind as formerly, in affording your acquaintance and friends your letters. He was very hearty, and very ready in his business in the Sessions, but unless you give me faire words, you may perhaps loose Manchester, for we are seldom above 2 on the bench, and I am one of them. For Bolton division, noe body appears, and our neighbour great ones are not well enough to sitt in the cold, and, alsoe, it is too far for them to come, and thus the country is served. But, indeed, the Friday and Saturday, we have constantly Cozin Horton's good company and assistance." *Seal of arms.*

ALICE KENYON to her husband, ROGER KENYON, M.P., in London.

840. 1693[–4], January 26.—" I fear thou art not kind to thy selfe in staying so long in the House everye day, without some refreshment. I pray thee, do not still neglect thy health so much. . . . . . . Yesterday, the Warden's lady was buried. . . . . . Cousin Byram hath carried it at Wigan. Judge Warren had but one vote; Cousin Byram had more, by halfe, in Entwistle, and a great many more than he made use of."

JOHN BYROM to ROGER KENYON, M.P., in London.

841. 1693–4, January 28. Wigan.—Was last Wednesday elected member for the borough of Wigan. Begs that his attendance in the House may be dispensed with for " some reasonable time," as his private affairs will take " some settling." *Seal of arms.*

JO: ELLETSON [ELLIOTSON] to ROGER KENYON, M.P.

842. 1693[–4], January 29. Lancaster.—Is much troubled with the insolence of Bayly and his wife [prisoners at Lancaster ?], who threaten him with " commenation " at the next assizes, for clipping and coining, crimes of which he is perfectly innocent. " Bayly hath a mind to begone, soe that I am obliged to sett a watch att his window every night, he having pickt out the morter and lossened some stones." Wishes they might be in custody, as here they are encouraged, by bad people, to be of bad-behaviour to their keepers. *Seal of arms.*

RICHARD ROWE to ROGER KENYON, M.P., in London.

843. 1693–4, January 30.—" I wish you better success about Clitheroe, in the House, than you had at the Committee ; and now that is partly over, I suppose this may come more safe to your hands then one, at least, of myne did formerly, which you told me you never received, but some body else did, for you, and sent down a copy of it into the country—not

out of kindness, you may imagine, but to pick quarrels, if it would bear
it; so that it was not without reason that I examined the post house
here, and hinted to you to take care lest somebody was too quick for you,
and got your letters before you, tho this of mine was said to be dropt in
Westminster Hall, but I rather think was found before it was lost, and
so dropt short of you. . . . I wish the heats that seem to be in
the house may be well layd."

J. HARTLEY to ROGER KENYON, M.P., in London.

844. 1693–4, January 30.—Believes the election at Clitheroe has
given him much trouble. Wishes his endeavours had been more successful.
It is seldom the House differs from what the Committee have agreed to,
as to elections. "We are, hereabouts, very unanimous as to the choosing
of Sir R. Assheton, for the Knight of this county." It is reported that
Sir Thomas Stanley designs to oppose him, and that "severall 1,000*l.*"
will be spent on his behalf. The election is fixed for next week. *Seal
of arms.*

THOMAS MARSDEN to ROGER KENYON, M.P., in London.

845. 1693[–4], February 4.—Mr. Richmond went yesterday to
Knowsley, but the Earl [of Derby], Lord Strange, and Mr. Wilson, had
gone to Lathom. Mr. Richmond wrote to the Earl, begging him to accept
"the thing, if offered." He described how far the honour of his lordship's house, and how far the welfare of the country was concerned
"in having the government of these countys turned into its old channel."
He will meet Lord Derby on the next Tuesday and take his "final
resolution." Thinks his lordship should "hearken with both ears" to the
advice given him; if he refuses, the writer is "bold to conclude him
felo de se. . . . What say you, but this post brings me Sir Cleave
More's desire to succeed the Lord Colchester at Liverpool, when the old
Earl turns off. His father, Mr. Edmunds, has also ticketed me, in order
to the same end. But I should hate myself if the notion of a landlord
should rob me of a principle of honesty. I shall not desert worthy
Mr. Bretherton for such an usless spark."

WILLIAM ODDY to ROGER KENYON, M.P.

846. 1693[–4], February 5. Clitheroe.—"Mr. Lister, of Thornton,
is coming up to London, and will give you an account of a letter, writt to
this town, to Mr. Bayliffe Lister, from a member of your country, which
tells us there is a bill preparing to disfranchise our corporation, and
make it fare no better than Stockbridge has done, and this occasioned by
the ryotts committed, or reported to be committed, since the first election,
which seems to be all false, no ryotts being committed. Mr. Lister has
entertained his friends nobly, both at Cliderow and elsewhere, and is
resolved, to the uttermost of his endeavour, to serve this corporation."
Fragment of seal.

DR. THOMAS WILSON to ROGER KENYON, M.P.

847. 1693[–4], February 6.—"My Lord is, I think, at last well
satisfied that you are still truly his friend; and, if you think fit, I could
wish with all my soul you would write to his Lordship, for, as I have all
the obligations imaginable of duty and gratitude to this family, so I
would not have it deprived of the service of one who, though now out of
favour, has the opportunity, as well as good will, of being yet more
serviceable." *Seal, broken.*

ALICE KENYON to ROGER KENYON, M.P., at Westminster.

848. [1693-4,] February 7.—"I am much pleased with your good news about the agreement between the King and Parliament, which I beseech God continue. . . . I hear Sir John Bland hath left you, and is come down; I would not have thee one of those runaways, but so soon as the great business of raising moneys is over, I wish thou would then get leave to come home, and, in the meantime, not sitt thy usuall long sittings in the House, but goe out and refresh thyself, as others do."

THOMAS MARSDEN to ROGER KENYON, M.P., in London.

849. 1693[-4], February 7.—Mr. Richmond went to Knowsley and " pressed the Earl to come up to you, notwithstanding the discouragement mentioned in yours. His Lordship determined to set out this week, and promised to assist you to his power, in the matter of Clitheroe. Sir, I remember you formerly told me all your letter saide of the armes, as related to you by Sir Richard Standish. One Woods, of Halsall, is the gun-smith, a tenant of the Lord Maxfield's, and, therefore, it will be more difficult to deal with him. That Lord ownes the having an armory in Leverpool Castle, and makes a shew of watching them there by an officer (a French-man), now and then resident in town, which will serve for a colour to blunt the edge of an information against him, on the score of arms-having. But how few of those many arms he hath somewhere, are there, we yet know not, but will enquire about it as well as we can. Sir Richard Standish being gone, I know not what gentleman in our county had head and heart enough, and will take pains enough, to hand about, and sollicit for subscriptions to, a petition. It is pity the Stanley family has not been careful to preserve a stock of such friends. For promoting such a thing amongst the clergy, in conjunction with the other, I know some that would attempt it. But this work must be done in season and, I conceive, not till the next campaign is over. . . . Clitheroe hath, I doubt, taken an imprudent course, as to the election on Friday last. By consenting they should sit in the Moot-hall, and take votes there for Mr. Gerrard, they seem to me to have spread a covering over all their irregularities and violences, and to keep the sneaking sheriff's neck out of a halter. Would they had took no notice of them, but as of paltry rioters, etc., so would they have been more liable to you." *Portion of seal.*

RICHARD RICHMOND to ROGER KENYON, M.P., at Westminster.

850. 1693-4, February 9. Walton.—" On Tuesday I waited upon my Lord of Derby with your letter, which he read, a[nd] afterwards I had some hours' free conference with him upon that subject. I omitted no argument that either my reason, or affection, could suggest, both with regard to the public good and the particular interest of my Lord and his family. I had a very kind audience, and could not perceive that anything I offer. . . . was ungrateful to his Lordship. On the contrary, I found him very inclinable to accept his old station, and desirous that his friends above should so represent it to his Majesty. But withal, his Lordship does not think it consistent with his honour to accept Cheshire alone, having before refused Lancashire, the place of his habitation. He told me (with some complaints of his friends) that he received no early notice of the Lord Warrington's death, and, therefore, inferred that they were not over-sollicitous for his restoration.

Particularly, that Master Stanley well knows what solemn engagements and protestations of honour the present Lord Maxfield lies under, to resign Lancashire when my Lord of Derby (to use his own words) was disposed to resume it, upon his Majestie's pleasure. And, that there being a present vacancy in Cheshire, as well as a prospect of advancing the Lord Maxfield to a considerable military employment, my Lord imagines this to be the critical time to address the King for both counties, as a motive to which, my Lord thinks his brother should signify to his Majesty the Lord Maxfield's promise. I dare say, sir, that my Lord of Derby is very hearty in what I have mentioned, and will warmly embrace the interest of their Majesties, both in Church and State. I would presume that when you communicate this to the Duke of Ormond, the Ladye Derby, Lady Dowager, and Colonel Stanley, they will unanimously address the King for both counties. I am told, my Lord Nottingham will do his utmost herein. And it is the opinion of more than myself, that if such Lancashire members as you know have a respect for my Lord, would jointly desire my Lord President's assistance, it would not be denied. To add weight to this, I am to assure you that my Lord himself moved this expedient, and will be ready to acknowledge my Lord President's kindness. And considering how great a point it would be to remove the Lord Maxfield, I cannot believe that great stateman will refuse this opportunity to support the Church of England's interest, so much discouraged in these counties by the new Lieftenancies, &c. Thus, sir, have I thus faithfully transmitted to you what was freely debated and concluded by my Lord, who presents you with his kind respects."

Joseph Yates to Roger Kenyon, M.P.

851. 1693–4, February 11. Manchester.—By this post, the writ and return "for Knight of our county" comes. No doubt "you will have a good assistant and partner of honest and worthy Sir Ralf Asheton, who was chose without any opposition." It was thought that "old Mr. Warren would put in," but he was discouraged when he came to Preston. Thinks that the "quarterly poll was soe very uneasy to the meaner sort of people, and looked upon soe unequall, that the renewing of it might be of ill consequence. What think [you] of a duty upon proceedings at law, for some few years, as was in King Charles the Second's time? And what think you of an imposition upon candles? for they that use most must pay most, as in the case of salt. These two ways, in my thoughts, would be the most easy to the subject." *Seal of arms.*

Thomas Marsden to Roger Kenyon.

852. 1693[-4], February 11.—I made bold, by letter, to petition the Earl of Derby to write to his friends, in favour of Mr. Weddall's ensuing election. I understand my Lord will now come out of his retirement, and show himself zealous both for Church and State, against dissenters and republicans, and "particularly against the clann."

The Earl of Derby to Roger Kenyon, M.P.

853. 1693–4, February 16. Knowsley.—Will not say much of his proceeding, since the Earl of Warrington's death, but is not disappointed in his expectation how little he is considered by his nearest relations, and how little he must depend on them. Resolves to hasten to London. *Seal of arms.*

ALICE KENYON to ROGER KENYON, M.P., at Westminster.

854. 1693[–4], February 17.—"Today Dick Edge was at Manchester; hee tells mee that the Justices' clarks have bin with my Lord W[illoughby] to desire him to stop thy fees for lycences; and that he says it hath never bin paid where hee had to do, and, therefore, his clarke shall take it. I think it might do well if thou would write to the Justices, if anything can bee done in Parliament to secure it. I suppose thou mayst make friends there. Dick says they are now settling the fees in other counties, which, when the bills are brought into the House, thou mayst easily get the same done for thy office. It would make you not so much slaves of the justices . . . . . Dick tells mee hee heard today that my Lord Derby is melancholy. I heard something of it three weekes agoe, but durst not mention it, lest it should come to my Lord's ear, and I know not what truth there is in it." *Cypher.*

ALICE KENYON to ROGER KENYON, M.P., at Westminster.

855. [1693–4], February 20.—"I like not the news by this post. I fear the House of Commons will sett us all together be the eares, and make the King di[s]olve them. I heartily wish thou could bee instrumentall in restoring my Lord Derby whilst thou stays." *Cypher.*

THOMAS MARSDEN to ROGER KENYON, M.P., in London.

856. 1693[–4], February 22.—" Several gentlemen were assembled at Clitherow (Mr. Pudsey, Mr. Lister, Mr. Marsden, &c.) when the letters I procured from the Earle of Derby, came thither, who,' by letter, returned his Lordship's thanks for them, which his Lordship took very kindly. The same day (viz. the 14th instant) Mr. Gerrard's party broke open the Moot-hall door, and George Stocks, the two Robinsons, and others, went in and swore Mr. Manwaring bailiffe, Mr. Gerrard having arrested the inn-bailiff for refusing to do it. Afterwards, the keys of the church-door being denied them, they broke that too, and rung the bells for their new officer. I acquainted the Earl of Derby with this, who thinks it ought to be represented in Parliament, and promises to give you what assistance he can, in order to the redress of such grievances. I only mention the history of their foul deeds, lest your letters from Clitherow may have been intercepted by your adversaries; for what will they stick at, that have ventured on such black work? The Earle sets out for London next week. God grant he may be well received there ! "

A. PUDSAY and JO: LISTER to ROGER KENYON, M.P., at Westminster.

857. 1693–4, February 23. Clitheroe.—"We suppose you have heard the irregularities acted here by Mr. Manwaring, who caused the Moot-hall door to be broken open, and himselfe to be sworne bayliffe, by private persons not quallifyed to administer an oath. And, at the same time, that Mr. Lister, the then bayliffe, was under arrest at Mr. Gerrard's suit. Notwithstanding which, on Monday last, we proceeded to an election of a new bayliffe in Mr. Wilkinson's stead, pursuant to a proclamation by Mr. Lister and severall burgesses made some dayes before, and the election fell upon Mr. Pudsay, the one of us who was presently sworne in Court. The same day Mr. Manwaring read the precept, by particular order from the high Sheriffe, which we both, in person, demanded from him, and he refused to deliver, as in the former election, but went into the hall, with severall of their party, and then appointed, and afterwards made proclamation, that this day at 12 o'clock they would go to an election of a member of Parliament, pursuant to the precept. Hereupon, we both joyned in a letter to Mr. High Sheriffe, to acquaint him of the strange proceedings above mentioned, and the several reasons why Mr. Manwaring was not quallifyed to be a bayliffe, to witt, his minority, and that he was never elected; and, therefore, to desire him to supersede the precept so delivered, and to make us a new one. Upon this, Mr. Shaw, who acts for the high Sheriff, came to this town and demanded the precept back from Mr. Manwaring, and Mr. Manwaring persisted in refusing to deliver it. This was all Mr. Shaw would doe, because, as he said, he thought it not justifyable, after a precept was delivered, either to supersede it or grant a new one.

"We therefore took this method, as most adviseable, to wit, to make a proclamation, in our names, to go to an election, and we appointed the same day and hour they had done before, and at the hour appointed, Mr. Manwaring went into the town-hall, a little before us. So soon as he was past, we followed in our formalityes; and then, that no disturbances might be made to the election, Mr. Lister, the one of us, called the hall, and Mr. Shaw, as a person indifferent, read the precept, and the town clerk made the proclamation. The town clerk was ordered to deliver a true copy of the call book to Mr. Shaw, and Mr. Shaw to call the voters. Mr. Morrice also gave him a list of voters, such as they had contrived; all persons in our call book, and in their list, were called without any disturbances. When any persons were excepted against, on either side, they were marked 'excepted against by those that tooke the poll.' The poll stands thus: for Mr. Gerrard, 46, 40 whereof were excepted against in open Court; for Mr. Lister, 43, 3 whereof only were excepted against. We, therefore, knowing the disquallifications of the voters excepted against, declared Mr. Lister duly elected, though, at the same time, Mr. Manwaring declared for Mr. Gerrard. We presently afterwards, with 24 burgesses, signed and executed an indenture in Mr. Shawe's, the Sheriff's agent's presence; we fixed it to the precept, it being endorsed by us two, and delivered it to Mr. Shaw, whom we hear has since allso accepted a return from the other party, and fixed it likewise to the precept, allthough theirs neither had the burrough seale nor a bayliffe's hand. We will take what care we can in the Chancellor's office, that this returne, which is now like to be a double one, shall come safe to the Clerk of the Crown, without any trick or miscarriage. This is a true relation of the matter of fact, and we hope that you and the rest of our friends will take care that Mr. Gerrard slip not into the House, by surprize, and doubt not but to justifye the fairness of our election, in case Mr. Lister, by the advantages of the returne, may not be admitted into the House without any further dispute."

RICHARD EDGE to ROGER KENYON, M.P., at Westminster.

858. 1693–4, March 2.—" Mr. Moody has not yett gott a coppy of Sir Richard Standish's commission for being Colonel or Lieutenant Colonel to the Lord Brandon, in the Militia, but has writ for it. I have searched our bookes carefully throughout this King's reigne, but doe not find Sir Richard ever tooke the oaths at the quarter Sessions. I rather think he took them at London, only I find he took them at the Bank, October '92, for his being Mayor of Wygan. I find the rest of the militia officers under his Lordship tooke the oathes in July '89, viz.: Ralph Longworth, Thomas Patten, Thomas Bradshaw, Henry Mallam James Starkie, Peter Rawstorne, Nicholas Rishton, James Holt, John Worthington, Sir Ralph Asheton, Richard Asheton, Laurence Rawstorne, William Worthington, &c. This July Sessions was the first Sessions kept in Lancashire, in this King's reigne. I was pressed for their Majesties' service att the door of our lodgeings, viz., Mr. Key's howse, and carryed to ' the Robin Hood ' over the way, by one Lieutenant Francklin, in Feb. 1691–2, though, at the same time, I told him I was a meniall servant to a member of Parliament who lay sick over the way, and 3 or 4 substantiall householders came to the officer and justified it; yet he would not release me before my mistress came herself, and begged pardon for me, for he told her I had talked saucily."

J. Weddell to Roger Kenyon, M.P.

859. 1693[–4], March 8. Waddow.—"I cannot furnish you with much news since the severai (as I was told) accounts sent you from Clitherow; only this may be materiall, that the noe Bailiffe, Mr. Manwaring, gave orders for the fixing of papers, to notifie the election of a member, on Monday only, immediately before Friday 23rd of February, which was the day of election, whereas notice ought to be given on the market day, and more warning than 3 or 4 days in our burrough, because of its out-burgesses. . . . . My opinion is that Oddy (the town clerk) and Mr. Farrer are witnesses enough to journey it up, who are ready to attend a summons when a day is appointed. We are very cheerfull in the burrough, and intend to keep a court tomorrow, in order to settle some matters." *Seal of arms.*

Richard Hutton to Roger Kenyon, M.P.

860. 1693[–4], March 9. Dean.—Is informed that Lord Willoughby intends, at the next assizes, to try the cause concerning Ellenborough chapel. Thinks this is probable, on account of the advantage he may promise himself in respect of the judges, the sheriffs, if not, the jury. Lord Willoughby will probably be at the assizes, and Kenyon should be there also.

Sir John Bland to Roger Kenyon, M.P., at Westminster.

861. 1693[–4], March 9.—Complains of gout. The country have made their assessments in most places. The Commissioners, in this county, act quite differently to what we do in our county; for they do not assess the tenants of papists, double. "And, for Mr. Trafford's estate, it is all assesst single, they pretending the estate is not in him, because of the Statute of Bankruptcy. These long sessions, I fancy, will incline a greate many to be for the frequent calling of Parliaments, that were against it formerly." *Seal.*

A. Pudsey and Jo: Lister, Bailiffs of Clitheroe, to Roger Kenyon, M.P.

862. 1693[–4], March 9. Clitheroe.—" On Saturday last, we made proclamation for our Burrowe Courte, and, according to custom, summoned an inquiry jury of burgesses and freemen, and none of Mr. Gerrard's freinds appeared. Wee have kept our Burrowe Courte, impanelled and

T

sworne an inquiry jury, and, as usually, they have proceeded [and] made some orders for the present affaires of the Corporation. Wee expected, as reported, to have had Mr. Manwaring here this day to have acted as Bayliffe, with some interruption, but mett with none. And this being the day appointed by severall Commissioners in the hundred for the constables of this towne to bring in assessors here for the four shilling in the pound aid, the time would have been elapsed and the burrow at a losse (Mr. Manwaringe, the pretended Bayliffe, not appearing), had not Mr. Pudsay been then present to joyne with his brother Lyster and Mr. Parker, the onely Commissioner there, and by that meanes the King's duty not timely paid. Wee hope you will be soe kind (as other members are) to comunicate the votes of the House to us, with your conveniency." *Seal.*

RICHARD EDGE to ROGER KENYON, M.P., at Westminster.

863. 1693[-4], March 9. Peel.—Lord Willoughby has been at the chapel, and he and his servants looked at the bell to find its age; and is, every day, tormenting and distraining upon the poor tenants, and felling timber. "Perhaps if you told my Lord Bridgewater of the Lord Willoughby's designing to make Ellinbrough Chapel into a barn, to conventicle itt, [it] might do goo service."

WILLIAM HULME to ROGER KENYON.

864. 1693-4, March 14. Hulme.—"Sum weekes since, I writt to you, and gave you an account of an impudent conventikel, held just by mee, having noe licence. I requested to know, whether, on the conviction, I may by warrant break the doors and enter and soe discover," and whether the bodies of those discovered, "for want of distress, may be teaken and imprisoned. I have certified to a Justice in Cheshire, Mr. Bradshaw of Marple, and sent my cleark; but he refused to sign the warrant . . If I misteak not, it is a hundred pound penalty of such justices as neglects." *Seal of arms, broken.*

CLITHEROE ELECTION.

865. 1693[-4], March 21.—The case of Christopher Lister, Esquire, as to his election and return for the Borough of Clitheroe.

ALICE KENYON to her husband, ROGER KENYON, M.P., at Westminster.

866. 1694, March 29.—"I fancy my Lord Derby is, as report says, not right in his mind; I wish he would so consider his actions as to become better. Thy carriage towards him must needs make him recollect his unjust usuage of thee, and perhaps ashamed, as he may well be. I hear there is likely to be a marriage betwixt Mr. Stanley and Mrs. K. Preston." *Cypher. Seal of arms.*

J. HARTLEY to ROGER KENYON.

867. 1694, March 30.—I am well pleased to see my name ranked among so many worthy gentlemen as are put out of the Commission of the Peace. I am sure I cannot make the complaint your old friend Judge Wilde is said to have made, when he was turned out from being Judge of the King's Bench, viz., that he was turned out with bad company.

J. Weddell and A. Pudsay to Roger Kenyon, M.P.,
at Westminster.

868. 1694, March 30. Lancaster.—"We find as little favour here,
as we did above at the Committee; for the High Sheriff, contrary to
our expectation, returned Mr. Manwaring and Mr. Lister, Bayliffes of
Clidderoe, upon which, I told the Judge that the Sheriff was mistaken
in his return, and that I came there to appear as Bayliffe of Clidderoe,
being legally elected and sworne, which Mr. Manwaring was not. The
Judge told me he was to take the Sheriffe's return, and not there to
decide titles, which was proper to be done in another court. Then I
desired my appearance might be recorded. He said by that he understood that I only meant to enter my claime, and it was a good one. It
is impossible for us to do any good, these Assizes, in the matter of the
riot, the Grand Jury being absolutely their friends; Mr. Bradshaw
kept Crook, and two of the Mandamus men being part of them." *Seal
of arms.*

Richard Rowe to Roger Kenyon, M.P., at Westminster.

869. 1694, March 30.—"Your concluding the money point with
a poll-bill, were it much more, far less troubles mee than the account
in yours to Mr. Hartley, this post, about our new justices; most of
which are of such a kidney as it is easy to smell the designe of putting
them in, and to foresee what kindness the poor Church of England
may expect from such Magistrates. But, as I dare say, somebody had
no hand in putting them in, so I am sure somebody as heartily wishes
them out. If a friend of myne waite on you with a small present
. . . a sermon on the Lord Warrington, I hope you will accept it,
though not for the worth . .. Mr. Bradshaw, of Bradshaw, is
buried this day."

Thomas Marsden to Roger Kenyon, M.P.

870. 1694, April 2.—"I have your description of some of our
new justices, and it is well our Lord-Lieutenant so frankly exhibites
his inclinations to undo, at least, our Church government. To place
such in power as are professed enemies to it, will justify the inference
I have made. We will keep our selves within the pales of the law,
and laugh at his new officers, till the Divine providence allow us a better
method for dealing with them. All our countrymen of quality, wisdom,
or virtue, will resent his management of things; and, at last, both
clergy and laity will unanimously petition to have a new governour,
which, whether it prove succesful or no, will get a brand upon his
honour. Oh! that Clitherow may prove victorious! That town, considering its cause and the managery of it, whilst Mr. Weddall stood
candidate, rather deserves additional honours, than to be disfranchised.
And it meant as well in the last choice; but, I know not, whether
things were ordered so wisely at that time, nor how they will be cooked
next week. An attempt now for the transport money, may smooth the
way against another session; but I hardly think it can, at present, be
accomplished. Sir, my last to you must look rough, till its meaning
was considered, which was to tell you what was talked aloud, with a
mixture of grumble and discontent. Give me leave to say once again,
the pole must be let to farm, or nought is done. Whalley, Mitton, and
Colcotes had not a child to be paid for, the last pole, and James Catteral
was neither atturney nor papist; and the like was seen in other places, and
will be again, unless that course be took. Why may not you be a doer
for Lancashire, to the publick good and your great advantage?"

ROGER KENYON to his mother, MRS. KENYON, at Stockport.

871. 1694, April 5.—Being by this new act taxed, God knows what for, for my fellowship, and not designing, as you know, any betterment to this government, by any good-will of mine, I am forced to flee for the same, and leave them to make it out as they can; for, by no consent of mine, shall they have one farthing. This is the true reason why this comes not dated from Cambridge, but from an honest, industrious farmer's, some distance from it, where I am very well employed in learning the art of husbandry, and courting my landlord's daughter, against the days prohibiting matrimony be over.

LADY STANDISH to ROGER KENYON, at Peel.

872. 1694, May 24. Duxbury.—I have sent you my case, drawn by Mr. Bagshaw, of Derbyshire, and Sir Cres[well] Levinz' opinion on it. "I have no great heart of this business coming to Manchester Sessions; I feare there is too meny of my Lord Willowby's faction there, and I have no reason to expect eny justice of that gang. We have a *cersorary* (*sic*) ready allowed by two justices, so that we can remove it; but in this I will be advised by you." *Seal.*

The INFORMATION of JOHN LUNT, gentleman.[1]

873. 1694, June 27.—"This informant, upon his oath saith, that when King James left the kingdom, upon the arrival of the Prince of Orange, in the year one thousand six hundred eighty eight, he, this informant, then went immediately after him into France, and, upon his arrival at St. Germans, was introduced to kiss his (the said King James') hand, in his closet, by the Lords Thomas and George Howard; that from thence he was, about the beginning of March then next following, ordered with the rest of his guards to go for Dublin; that immediately upon his arrival there, about the latter end of May, one thousand six hundred eighty nine, one Doctor Bromfield came there from England, expecting to meet his Majestie, and brought over with him an account of the condition and readiness of his friends, the Papists and Jacobites there, but more particularly in London, Sussex, and Kent, and in Staffordshire, Lancashire, Cheshire, and Yorkshire, and from them all desired of his Majestie commissions for the several persons of quality hereafter named, with blanks for their inferior officers, which accordingly his Majestie caused forthwith to be issued forth, both for England and Scotland. And because Bromfield was so well known, and it might be dangerous for him to come back himself, he desired the King to advise of a proper person, or persons, whom he might trust to bring them over, and distribute them here in England, according to his Majestie's orders.

"Amongst others, he, this informant, was recommended to him by my Lord Thomas Howard, who told him (the said King James) he would engage life for life for him, this informant, that he would not betray him in the service, and that if he were taken, would rather die upon the spot, etc. Upon which, this informant was sent for to my Lord Millford's office, where he found my Lord Thomas

---

[1] Printed, but with very material differences, in "The Trials at Manchester in MDCXCIV." Chetham Society, Vol. 28, p. 12.

Howard, Doctor Bromfield, and my Lord together in his closet, whither he was carried to them, and then and there they asked this informant whether he would venture to undertake to carry declarations, papers, and commissions, and other things, for his Majestie's service to England. They told him it was a hazardous thing, that he should think well of it, for if he should happen to be taken, his life was certainly gone, but if he would, and did escape, he would be sure of (and they promised him in the King's name) very great preferment and rewards when the King should come into England ; upon which he, this informant, undertook it, and my Lord Milford gave his Majestie an account of it; whereupon, to blind the business, and to take off any thought of his, this informant, being imployed or sent anywhere, my Lord Milford told him the King had thought fit to order this officer of the guards (who was a Frenchman) to cashiere him, and that he might say to any one that asked him the reason, that he knew none, but was resolved to get his pass as soon as he could, and go for England, etc. About a week after this, all things were got ready both for England and Scotland, and one Mr. Threllfall, of the Ashes, in Goosner, in Lancashire, gentleman, and this informant, were dispatched for England, and one Mr. Gourden (that was this informant's comrade, and cashiered as he was) went for Scotland. This informant and Mr. Threllfell brought with them declarations, commissions, and other papers, and landed at Cockram, within four miles of Lancaster, in or about the month of June or beginning of July, one thousand six hundred eighty nine.

" Upon our landing, we had like to have been wholly surprised by some custom house officers, but we escaped, and brought off the most material of our business, only lost some blankets and one of the King's declarations, four cases of pistols of this informant, that the King gave him, and some clothes of this informant's, etc. The commissions and most of the blankets and several bundles were saved, and this informant delivered them as fast as he could, one after another, as followeth, viz.: in Lancashire, to my Lord Molineux's son, William, a Colonel's commission for a regiment of horse, with blanks for all his interior officers, to be filled up as he should think fit; to Thomas Tildesley, esquire, the like for a regiment of Dragoons; to —— Dalton, of Thurnham, esquire, the like of Dragoons ; to —— Sherburne of Stonyhurst, esquire, the like for horse ; to —— Townley of Townley, esquire, the like for horse; to —— Girlington[1] of Girlington, esquire, a Colonel's commission; to —— Westby of Mobrick, esquire, the like for Dragoons. This informant further saith that he delivered Lord Molineux himself a paper of instructions, where, amongst other things, he was to be governor of Liverpool. And this informant took notice of it because my Lord Molineux and Doctor Bromfield both told him, this informant, so, and shewed it him in the paper, before they sealed it. Cheshire :— To —— Lee of Lyme,[1] esquire, a Colonel's commission with blanks for his inferior officers; to Sir Thomas Stanley[1] of Aldersay, the like for horse ; to —— Shumley[1] [Cholmondeley] of Vale Royal, the like for horse; to Sir Rowland Stanley, the like for horse ; to my Lord Brudnall a Colonel's commission for horse, with blanks for his inferior officers ; to Sir —— Throgmorton (?), the like for horse. This informant further saith that to these two gentlemen last above written, he delivered four other Colonels' commissions, for four gentlemen whose names he was not to know, because, as he did then conceive, they were protestants, for they told him, this informant, they were honest gentlemen, and protestants.

---

[1] Opposite these names, in the margin, is " protestant."

"Besides all these before mentioned, this informant delivered to one Mr. Jackson, in Castle Street, near the Meuse, two bundles of commissions, with a King's declaration, and two other papers sealed up with each, with orders to him to deliver one of them with a declaration and sealed paper, immediately, to my Lord Griffin, and the other to Sir William Penn, the quaker, which this informant supposeth he did, for in his sight he took coach and sayd he would.

"And besides all these which he, this informant, so as aforesaid delivered, Mr. Threlfall undertook to deliver several bundles of the same to several gentlemen in Yorkshire, viz. :—To my Lord Dunbarr, one ; to my Lord Preston, one ; to my Lord Fairfax, one ; to —— Strickland of —— one ; to Sir Thomas Gascone, one ; to Sir —— Stapleton, one ; to —— Tempest, esquire, one ; to —— Vavasor, one ; to —— Harrington, one. All these he, the said Mr. Threlfall, told this informant he delivered commissions to their own hands, and a great many more whose names this informant doth not at present remember, but has since been in the company of several of them and others (viz.), Lord Fairfax, Sir —— Strickland, Sir ——— Stapleton, Sir Thomas Gascone, ——— Harrington, esquire, —— Clayton, esquire, —— Ryder, esquire, —— Trappes, esquire, Sir——— Lawson, Major Morre, who, when they knew he, this informant, was concerned with Mr. Threlfall, owned they all had the commissions that he, the said Threlfall, brought over. This informant further saith that every Colonel with his commisson, had blanks for double his inferior officers, and that all the Colonels had the liberty to raise horse, foot, or dragoons, but horse were more especially recommended.

"This informant furthur saith that after the dispatch of these commissions, and other business, he had the ill luck to be made a prisoner for a considerable time, upon the accusation of the captain that brought him over out of Ireland. This informant further saith that during the time he was a prisoner under bayle, that is to say, about the beginning of the year one thousand six hundred ninety one, he, this informant, by the order of Colonel Tildesley, Colonel Townley, Colonel William Mollineux, Mr. Gerrard, Colonel Dalton, and others, listed here, in London, several men for soldieres, to serve as horse or dragoons, to be under the command of the said Colonels, or any other, as they should dispose of them. The names of several of the said soldiers so listed, and the money he, this informant, paid them, by the order of the Colonels aforesaid, to carry them to their officers, is as followeth." [Here follow the names of 75 men, with the amount of their conduct money.]

"This informant further saith that he listed for them, as by their order, before and since the said year one thousand x hundred ninety one, to the number of at least five hundred men.

"This informant further saith that, being discharged of his imprisonment in the month of November 1691, he, this informant, was desired by several of the gentlemen that he had delivered some of the commissions aforesaid to, viz. :—Lord Molineux, Colonel Molineux, his son, Sir William Gerrard and his son, Mr. Dickenson of Whrightington, John Harrington of Haytonhay, esquire, Colonel Townley, Colonel Tildesley, Colonel Dalton, and others, to go into France, to give King James an account in what condition they were, and to bring his Majestie's commands how they might be serviceable to him, which this informant did, and gave him (his Majestie) the said account. He, the said King James, commanded him to return for England, and then (amongst other things) that he, this informant, should tell them from him, that he did not doubt but, the spring following, to be in a condition to come for England; and at this informant coming away, he was ordered by my Lord Milford himself, to go to Captain Griffith, in the Meuse, as soon as he, this informant, should come to London, and deliver him, the said Griffith, a paper from his Lordship—it was sealed [so this] informant did not know what it was—and to advise and receive orders from him, the said Griffith.

" This informant saith that he arrived in London, about the latter end of December, 1691, and that he went imediately to Captain Griffith and delivered him the said paper; and the said Griffith read the same and told him, this informant, he did not question but this business (meaning that in the paper mentioned, as this informant then supposed) will be accomplished in a little time, and then he disclosed to this informant what it was he meant, which was the cutting off the Prince of Orange at some proper time when he should be a hunting, and then he put it to this informant whether he was willing to make one, and be concerned in it. This informant first desired to know the persons engaged in it; he, the said Griffith, then told him he was not to tell him their names, but he would at any time bring this informant into the company of several of them that were engaged in it. And about two days after, this informant came to him again, and went with him into the company of several gentlemen, at 'the Queen's Head,' in White Hart Yard, in the Strand, where and with whom the said Captain Griffith and this informant discoursed the method of doing it, and all agreed that it was to be the easiest done when he should be a hunting, or some time late when he went to or came from Kensington. This informant saith there was in company, at that time, about nine or ten; three or four or more of them this informant knew, three of which are now since dead. Captain Griffith then told this informant and the company, he had about sixty brave fellows engaged in the business, who he did not at all doubt but would one way or other effect it. Several of the principal of them, as Whitney, the highwayman, and several others, happened to be, some time after, taken and secured, which was the only reason that this informant knows of that it was not attempted.

" This informant further saith, that about the same time abovesaid, that he, this informant, came last out of France, viz., about the latter end of December, 1691, there came several English gentlemen of quality, viz. :— Lord Stafford, Mr. Stafford, Colonel Parker, Colonel Bartholomew Walmesley, a French Lieutenant-General (whose name this informant doth not remember), and others, with commissions, declarations, grants, and patents, for themselves and others, and for their inferior officers, from King James.' And this informant saith that a general meeting of several of the said gentlemen and others, to the number of about thirty or forty, in the month of February, 1691, viz —Colonel Townley, Colonel Tildesley, Colonel Dalton, Colonel Molineux, Mr. Dickenson, Sir William Gerrard, Mr. Gerrard, Mr. Stanley, Mr. Shultesworth, Mr. Tildeslsy of Stansacre, Mr. Langton, Mr. Chanerell, and others, at the house of Colonel Walmesley, called Dungenhall, in the county of Lancaster, where the said colonel then lay private, being lately come from St. German, as aforesaid. The said Colonel Walmesley produced to the aforesaid company, several of the said grants or patents, in the presence of this informant, of several gentlemen's esstates in that country, to and for several of the gentlemen that were then in the company, and others, viz. —To Colonel Tildesley, one for the estate of — — Patten of Preston, esquire ; to — — Stanley of Eccleston, to — - Tildesley of Stansacre, and Major Shuttleworth, one for the estate of Major Longwood ; to Colonel William Molineux, one for the estate of Sir Thomas Stanley, that married Mr. Patten's daughter; to my Lord Molineux; a grant of part to my Lord Dallamere's estate ; to Colonel Townley, one for ———. a Yorkshire gentleman's estate, of the value of 1,100*li.* per annum, and severall others, etc. At the same time, he brought others for the estates of several gentlemen of Yorkshire, to several of King James' friends there, and also for several imployments and places for several gentlemen, both in Lancashire, Yorkshire, and other adjacent countries (*sic*).

"This informant further saith that, in the latter end of the said month of February, or the beginning of March, he was at the house of —— Draycot, esquire, of Painsley Hall, in the county of Stafford, where there was the like meeting of about the same number of gentlemen of that country, and others, viz. :—Sir Richard Fleetwood, Mr. Rowland Fleetwood, —— Whitall, esquire, —— Cuny of Cuny, esquire, Mr. —— Cuny, —— Massey of Puddington, esquire, Sir James Simmons, Bazil Brooks, esquire, and others. There was produced several of the like grants or patents then lately brought over by my Lord Stafford (who they said was in the company, but this informant did not see him so as to know him), for several gentlemen, viz. :—To Sir James Simmons, one ; to Bazil Brooks, esquire, one ; to —— Cuny of Cuny, esquire, one ; to —— Whitall, esquire, one ; to Mr. —— Cuny of ——, one ; to Sir Richard Fleetwood, one ; to Mr. Rowland Fleetwood, one ; to Mr. Massey of Puddington, one ; and to several others that were there, whose names this informant (until he shall come at some papers that he yet has not) cannot yet mention. All or most of these grants or patents he, this informant, saw, and heard several of them read there, and then delivered to the persons to whom they were intended, by Colonel Walmesley, at his house, and at —— Draycott's by Mr. Stafford, my Lord Stafford's brother. This informant himself was also promised, by Colonel Walmesley, a grant of Justice Yates his estate at Chippin, in Lancashire.

" This informant further saith that amongst other resolutions that were then brought over by those gentlemen and then communicated at those two meetings aforesaid, for the encouragement of them and their friends that were and would engage, it was there publickly declared that the King did resolve, as soon as he should be -restored to the throne again, that he would, besides the traytors' estates, which he would dispose of amongst his friends, he would also take care and seize their children all under ten years of age, and have them brought up in the Catholic religion, and dispose of the fathers that lived to the Islands or Plantations.

" This informant further saith, that in the months of March and April, 1692, he, this informant, was imployed by, and was assisting, to one Mr. Whitfield, a cardmaker, to buy six or seven horses, arms, and saddles, which were presented to Captain Griffith and Captain Goodman from himself and his two sons-in-law, that is, Mr. Bassett, a goldsmith, at ' the Seven Stars,' in the Strand, and Mr. ——, the cutler, at Charing Cross, and one to this informant, with arms and saddles for two men and horses. And this informant further saith that Mr. ——, at ' the Red Lion' inn, by Charing Cross, did also furnish and provide four horses, arms, and saddles, and helped to buy horses himself : and that Mr. ——, at ' the George' inn, at the upper end of the Haymarket, did also furnish and provide four horses, arms, and saddles ; and that the said —— did buy for several gentlemen horses for the same service ; and that Mr. ——, at ' the Cheshire Cheese,' by Charing Cross, did furnish and provide three horses, arms, and saddles ; and that Mr. Pollards, at ' the Blew Posts,' in the Hay Market, did furnish five horses, arms, and saddles ; and that Mr. ——, at the ' Figure of Three,' over against the Tennis Court, in the Hay Market, was furnished with a horse and arms for himself and for two men, which he, the said ——, told this informant were provided by Mr. ——, a goldsmith, in Pauton Street ; and that Mr. ——, at the Great Tavern, in Bloomsbary, did buy, provide, and furnish, six horses, arms, and saddles ; and that Mr. Toogood, at 'the Griffin,' in Bloomsbury, did provide four horses, as aforesaid; and that Mr. Clarkson, at 'the Lancaster Castle,' in Red Lion Square, did provide for himself and one man, horses, arms, and saddles; and that Mr. ———, at 'the Hole in the Wall,' in Baldwens Gardens, where a club is kept, did provide and furnish three horses, as aforesaid, etc.; and that Mr. Vaughan, at 'the White Horse' inn, in Purple Lane, did provide and furnish three horses, as aforesaid, etc.; and that Mr. Eason, at 'the George' inn, by Holborn Bridge, did provide two horses, as aforesaid, etc.; and this informant saith that he, the said Eason, does usually buy horses for King James his service; and this informant saith that Mr. ———, at 'the Crown,' alehouse, in King's Street, in Bloomsbury, did provide and furnish one horse, and arms, as aforesaid, for himself to serve him; and that Mr. Cane, at 'the Royal Oak,' in Drury Lane, did provide and furnish three horses, and arms, etc., for himself and two men, he, the said Cane, to be a quartermaster; and that Mr. ———, at 'the Dog' tavern, in Drury Lane, did provide and furnish five horses, and arms, as aforesaid, and that he, this informant, did help him, the said ———, to buy part of them; and that Mr. Jolly, at 'the Black Posts' in Drury Lane, did provide and furnish three horses, and arms, etc., and that the said Mr. Jolly did present them to priests, to be disposed as they pleased; and that Mr. John Sharples, in the Hay Market, did provide and furnish three horses, as aforesaid, and that he, this informant, did help him, the said Sharples, to buy them; and that Mr. Rigby, in Covent Garden, and his son, did provide and furnish sevaen men, horses, arms, and saddles.

"And this informant saith that the said men, horses, and arms, as aforesaid, were provided and furnished, as aforesaid, for and towards the raising of the army that was then intended to be raised for the service of King James. And this informant saith that he, this informant, did either assist in the buying and furnishing of all the horses and arms, as aforesaid, or else that he heard the said partys, upon several occasions, at several meetings, own the same. And this informant further saith he, this informant, was told by the said persons that all the men, horses, and arms aforesaid were to be distributed under the command, or to be at the disposal, of the Lord Arundel, Lord Baltimore, Lord Griffin, Sir William Goreing, Colonel Tufton, Colonel Holman, Colonel Bernard Howard, Lieutenant Colonel Bancks, Colonel Porter, Lieutenant Colonel Griffith, Captain Goodman, Captain Nelson, Captain Tozer, Captain Spencer. And this informant saith that there were a great many more horses and arms so furnished and provided, as aforesaid, in and about London and Westminster, which he, this informant, believes, upon a little recollection, when he shall come at his papers, he shall be able to name and set forth.

"And this informant further saith that by the defeat of the French fleet, their designs of rising being wholly disappointed, they fell upon other measures. And this informant remained in several parts of this kingdom, and was at several of the like meetings, as aforesaid, until the last summer, and then about July, 1693, was desired, with some others, to go for France again. Several of the gentlemen that this informant has before mentioned to have delivered commissions to (that it is to say) in Lancashire, by my Lord Molineux, Colonel Molineux, Sir William Gerrard, Mr. Gerrard, Mr. Standis, Mr. Dickonson, Colonel Townley, and several others of that country, to give the King an account of the condition they were in, and to bring them back an account of what hopes, and when he thought he should be in a condition to come for England, and this informant went accordingly to St. Germans and spake with the King, and delivered him what he had in charge, from the gentlemen in England.

"And my Lord Milford being at that time with the King in his closet, bid him, this informant, go to Captain Griffith, who was then at St. Germans. The captain ordered him, this informant, to speak with Dr. Bromfield, who told him, this informant, when he came to him, that if he would undertake to carry a signet with him into England, and show it to such persons as he would direct him, this informant, to those that were concerned in a design, and would engage to make one with them in the same, he, this informant, should receive the same reward that was intended for them; which design he then told him, this informant, was to cutt off the Prince of Orange by any such way or means that the undertakers, amongst themselves, when they came together, should agree upon.

"Whereupon he, this informant, promised and engaged to them, the said Bromfield and Griffith, to make one in the business, and was then forthwith dispatched, with the signet and other matters, for England, where he arrived and landed at Dover in December last, and there he, this informant, mett with those that the said Dr. Bromfield and Captain Griffith had directed him to, which were, Captain Noell, Captain Walton, Mr. Pepper, Mr. Preston, and Captain Roberts, who were in the design of cutting off the Prince of Orange, as this informant was told   And that there were, in all, sixteen persons concerned, but there he, this informant, mett four of them only, who were as followeth :—Captain Noell, Sergeant of the Admiralty and one of the principall gunners, as this informant was told, who told him, this informant, hee had his son and two more ready for the occasion ; Captain Walton of Foulston, a Custome-house officer there, who told him, this informant, hee had six more engaged in the business, who with us together hee, the said Walton, was very confident, might, in a month or two's time, doe the business effectually with little hazard.   Mr. Pepper of Dover, a Custome-house officer, as this informant was told, or some place there worth about three hundred pounds *per annum*, and Mr. Preston of Feversham, one of the militia officers, were the other two of the foure before mencioned.

"This informant further saith that the said Dr. Bromfield and Captain Griffith did order this informant to assure the said Noell, Walton, Pepper, and Preston, from them, and in the King's name, that every one concerned in the action should have the reward of five hundred pounds *per annum* each, which was the same made to him, this informant, at St. Germans, by the said Dr. Bromfield and Captain Griffith.   And my Lord Milford told him, this informant, after hee had kissed the King's hand and was coming down stayres, that if that design, that Griffith and Bromfield had engaged him, this informant, in, tooke effect, the King would soon be in England ; upon this hee, this informant, came for England, and in travelling, being somewhat troubled in his thoughts with what he had undertaken, hee called upon severall priests that were his friends, acquaintance, and relations, in France, as hee came along, and did (though not in plain termes) acquaint them with what he, this informant, was engaged in ; some were possitively against it, as damnable, and others for it, as merritorious, which difference amongst themselves, gave him, this informant, more distorbance, so that, as soon as hee came into England, he resolved not to bee one in it, and to prevent it, if he could.   But this informant did not then resolve to discover it, until he was persuaded thereunto by a friend, by whom, after he had oftentimes discoursed the matter with him, he, this informant, was at length prevailed with to discover it.

" This informant further saith that, being at St. Germans in the months of October and November, 1693, the Lord Milford, Captain Griffith, and some others, then told him, this informant, that there was a designe layd by their friends, the Protestants, engaged with the Roman Catholicks there, for the seizing the Tower of London, Tilbury Fort, Sherness, the ports and coasts, etc. That some of the officers within the Tower, who were sure and firme to King James's interest (whose names this informant knoweth not, they being kept as a secret to the chiefes only), were to be ready to receive several gentlemen and others, who were to pass in as private persons, some in the babbitt of private gentlemen, with good private arms, others with the same babbitt as the horse-guards doe wear, and others in the habitt of foot soldiers, all armes accordingly, and some like plain countrymen, until there was a sufficient number, with the help of those within, to have secured the gate and bridge ; when, on a signal given, those without, who were in great numbers to have been lodged about the Tower Hill, St. Katherine's, East Smithfield, Thomas Street, and places adjacent, besides a great many that were to have been walking carelesly about the gates, upon the wharfe provided for that purpose, who were to have made to the gates, secured the gunns, and all within, by cutting them off and making them prisoners. And for Tilbury Fort, by the help of some within, much after the same manner. And that for Sherness, they did not doubt but to have secured by some officers of the Fleet ; and for the ports of Dover and Foulston (*sic*), and the coasts upon Rumney Marsh, those, they said, were undertaken to be made theirs by those officers of King William's that this informant hath above named, viz.: —Captain Noell and the rest, with the correspondents they pretended to have in those parts, and that Hull also, and all those parts in the North, were at the same time provided for in the like manner.

" This informant further saith that some time after his arrivall at London, which was in December one thousand six hundred ninety three, he was at a meeting at ' the Queen's Head,' in White Hart Yard, in the Strand, where was the Lord Griffin, the Lord Baltimore, and the Lord Feversham (but the Lord Feversham was gone before this informant came there), and Captain Tozier, Mr. Whitfield, Mr. Tasbrough, Mr. Kingsley, and some other gentlemen, told this informant they had consulted and agreed of the method abovesaid, with those lords, for the securing the Tower and the other places, and that there would bee noe doubt of accomplishing it, etc., with a great deale of ease. But still that they, the said lords and gentlemen, had a great dependance and assurance from those gentlemen and others in comision as aforesaid, for that they were well assured that they had an army listed, and officers, and ready, well armed and accoutred at all points, at twenty-four hours warning, to the number of at least thirty thousand horse, foot, and dragoons, in the North parts, besides those here in and about London and parts adjacent, which were under the command, care, and conduct, of Lord Feversham, Lord Griffin, Colonell Griffin, his son, Colonell Porter, Colonell Holeman, Colonell Sir William Goreing, Colonell Bernard Howard, Colonell Tufton, Lieutenant Colonell Bankes, and some others.

" This informant further saith that in March last, about the middle or latter end of that month, hee, this informant, was at a meeting at Lord Strangforde's, of about twelve or sixteen Protestants and Popish gentlemen, some of whom this informant knew, as Mr. Basteene of Dover, Captain Roberts, Dr. Clarke, Mr. Lee, Captain ———, that lives two miles from Sir Bazill Dixwell's. The meeting was to consider and agree to bee all ready for securing that countrey, and the ports and coasts there, upon any occasion, for the King's lauding or otherwise, and to compute what their strength they might depend upon, might amount to; and then it was agreed amongst themselves that they had between five and six thousand men, well armed and disciplined, besides what they might reasonably expect would come in upon their riseing, whose numbers they did not doubt but would bee very considerable, etc.

"This informant further saith that in his frequent passing too and again from the ports, to and from London, at his inn in Rochester, kept by one Hederman Crosse, of that city, hee was well known to him, the said Crosse, who several times and nights that hee has layne in his house, did introduce him, this informant, into the company of several commanders of the King's men of warr, who being by him, the said Crosse, satisfyed what this informant was, were extreamly civill and kind to this informant, entertaining him and inviting him on board their ships, and otherwise, and have been soe free in declareing themselves, that they have often, in the presence of this informant, pulled out King William's comissions, thrown them under their feet, trod upon them, and dranke King James' health, swearing they would venture all for his service, and they had sent to him, and would do, upon all occasions, to know how they might bee most serviceable to him, and to that purpose alwayes took as much care as possible to have Jacobites on board them, etc. And this informant saith that, in December last, hee did bring from my Lord Milford a paper, sealed, to that innkeeper; this informant did not see what was in it, but hee, the said Crosse, told this informant that it was for some honest gentlemen that did belong to the sea. This informant further saith that hee hath been told, both here and at St. Germans, by Captain Griffith (who was always in their secret counsells) and some others, the names of several persons of great quality, both Protestants and Papists, viz. :—Lord Feversham, Lord Arundell, Lord Carrington, Lord Salisbury, Lord Griffin, Lord Molineux, Lord Dunbarr, Lord Fairfax, Lord Huntington, Sir William Goreing, Sir Henry Tichbourne, Sir John Frend, Sir Thomas Stanley. Sir James Simmons and some others, that supplyed King James from time to time with money, and that have always a great banke here, and that they were those that made upp that summe, which was thirty thousand pounds, as this informant has been told both here and at St. Germans, and that my Lord Middleton carryed with him, and that they are the men that privately order money for payment of men.

"This informant further saith that, about six weeks since, Captain Tozier and Mr. Kingsley (a gentleman that then lately came from St. Germans) told him, this informant, Mr. Whitfield, and another, Mr. Kingsley being present, that since there was an account given there that the late Kentish designe upon the life of King William, was by some traytor or other, prevented, it was there resolved to try another way upon him, in Flanders, which was by causing several resolved gentlemen and others, of the English, Scotts, and Irish nations, and some French, of seeming quality, to desert from the French army in Flanders, as early this campaigne as they could, that would undertake to watch and take all and the first oportunity they could, in their severall posts, to attempt upon his life. This informant further saith that he is very sure that hee, this informant, can point to and carry any body to the very places (some, he believes, in or neer this town, but more particularly in several parts of Yorkshire, Lancashire, Staffordshire, and Cheshire, and other adjacent countreys) where theie were and, this informant is very confident, yet are lodged, secured, and kept, great quantityes of armes and warlike equipage of all sorts, with great numbers of horses fit for service. And this informant saith that if hee were authorized and impowered thereunto, he, this informant, would undertake to seize and secure them, etc. And this informant further saith, that in the year one thousand six hundred eighty nine, when hee, this informant, brought over the comissions aforesaid from King James, out of Ireland, which this informant delivered to the gentlemen in Lancashire, as aforesaid, this informant saith, by mistake, he hath, in the foregoing narrative, omitted one gentleman to whom he did at that time deliver a Colonell's comission for a regiment of horse, which was Sir Henry Titchbourne, a Hampshire gentleman, as this informant believes, but hee, the said Sir Henry Titchbourne, was then at my Lord Molineux' house in Lancashire, where he, this informant, delivered him the said comission.

"*Juratus* 27° *die Junii,* 1694, *coram me, J. Trenchard.*

"JOHN LUNT."

Copy.

The INFORMATION of GEORGE WILSON to the SECRETARY OF STATE.

874. 1694, June 27.—"This informant, upon his oath, saith that in or about the monthes of April or May, 1689, one Dr. Bromfield came to William Fitzherbert, esquire, of Wapra (?), near West Chester, in Flintshire, where he, the said Bromfield, ley concealed for some time, for a passage into Ireland, from whence he was recommended to this informant to assist him, who then lived near the sea-side, at a place called Redland, where, after the said Bromfield had stayed about a week, this informant did assist him in the buying of a boat of about 25 tunn, which said boat, being vitualled and ready to sail, was seized by Mr. Morston [Mostyn?], and Bromfield escaped to Mr. Crosbye's in Lancashire, from whence, by the assistance of Mr. Perce Morston [Piers Mostyn?], Mr. Wynne of Gop (?), Mr. Loyde of Greith, Mr. Robert Briarwood of West Chester, Mr. George Pennant, Mr. Pue of Pendrell, and this informant, afterwards gott over in a open boat.

"This informant further saith that being searched for by troopers from West Chester and other souldiers, and by the civil officers of the country, was forced to leave his house and family, and hide himself in the woods for many days, and could never returne to his house again, but gett into Lancashire, whither his wife and family followed him, where hee, this informant, was received and entertained by Lord Mollineux, Collonel Tildesley, Mr. Standish of Standish, Sir Rowland Stanley, Sir Thomas Poole, Sir William Gerrard, Collonel Townley, and others, sometimes in the house of one gentleman, and for some time at another.

"This informant saith, about Midsummer, 1689, he, this informant, and others, were ordered and directed by the gentlemen aforesaid, and others, to look out about the sea coast thereaboates, for any gentlemen that should come from Ireland, for at that time he, this informant, was told they expected some friends and news from Ireland, which hee, this informant, did. And about the beginning of July, 1689, Mr. Edmund Threlfall of the Ashes, in Goosener, and one Mr. Lunt, arrived at Cockram, and came imediately to Colonel Tilsdley, with several bundles of papers and other things in several cloackbaggs, where this informant then was attending their comeinge. This informant saith that upon their coming to the said Colonel Tilsdley, the said Mr. Threlfall and Mr. Lunt imediately opened their cloackbaggs and took out several commissions, declarations, blanks, and sealed papers, from King James to several persons and gentlemen of quality in that countrey, and

divided them; and those for Yorkshire Mr. Threlfall put up and
undertook to deliver, and had a guide imediately provided. The others
for Lancashire and Cheshire, Staffordshire and partes thereaboutes,
Mr. Lunt tooke to himself to deliver, and had this informant with him,
from place to place, to guide and assist him in the delivery of them, and
after they had left, and delivered to Colonel Tilsdesley his, for being
a Colonel (which hee, the said Colonel, recieved upon his knees and
kissed it), with the blankes for his inferiour officers they proceeded
and went to the Lord Mollineux his house, and delivered one Colonell's
commission to Mr. Mollineux his son, for a regiment of horse, with
blankes for his inferiour officers, hee, the said Collonell Mollineux,
immediately filling that blanke for the Lieuetenant Colonell, delivered
it in the presence of this informant, to Mr. William Gerrard, who was
with the said Colonell Mollineux when hee, this informant, and Mr. Lunt
came in.

"This informant further saith hee, this informant, was present and
did see Mr. Lunt deliver to —— Sherburne of Stonyhurst, esquire,
a Colonell's comission, with blankes, as aforesaid, for a regiment of
horse; to Townley of Townley, esquire, the like for horse ; to
Girlington of Girlington, esquire, a Colonell's comission; to Westby
of Mobricke, esquire, the like for dragoones; to Lee of Lyme, a
Colonel's comission, with blanks as aforesaid ; to Sir Thomas Stanley
of Aldersay, the like for horses; to Chumley of Vale Royall, the like
for horses; to Sir Roland Stanley, the like for horse, etc.; to Sir Robert
Throgmorton, the like for horse, etc.; to Sir Henery Tichbourn (hee
being then at the Lord Mollineux'), the like for horse; to Sir —— Giffard
of Chillington, the like for horse; to Sir James Simmons of Ashton in
Staffordshire, the like for horse. This informant saith that he alsoe
saw Sir Robert Throgmorton fill up a Lieuetenant Colonel's comission
to his own regiment, and deliver it to one Sir Charles Weale, who
accepted the same, and kissed it on his knees. And that hee, this
informant, also was present and saw Sir James Simmons deliver a
Captain's commission to Mr. William Fowler of St. Thomas, near
Stafford, and alsoe when Sir Thomas Gifford delivered a Captain's
commission to Mr. Augustin Gifford, and also to Captain Gowre, the like
Captain's commission, and to Bazill Brookes, esquire, the like Captain's
commission, and to Mr. John Pursell a Cornett's commission, and to
Thomas Pursell, a warrant for quarter-master, and to several other
inferiour officers, under the several Colonells aforesaid.

" This informant saith that all those Collonel's commissions, with the
blankes as aforesaid, were delivered by Mr. Lunt in the presence of this
informant; and this informant saith he knows they were such commissions, because he saw them, and heard most of them read at the end
of the delivery of them. And for the Lieuetenant Collonel's and other
inferiour officers' commissions hee, this informant, saw most of them filled
up by the superiours, and delivered to the inferiour officers, as aforesaid.
And this informant further saith that at the same time aforesaid hee,
this informant, saw the aforesaid Mr. Lunt deliver to my Lord Mollineux
a sealed paper which hee, this informant, saw him, the Lord Mollineux,
open and read, which, to the best of this informant's memory, was purporting a commission and instructions for the care and government of
Liverpoole. This informant also saith that hee was at a meeting at
Sir John Lawson's, in Yorkshire, about the month of March, then next
following, with Mr. Lunt, where were the geutlemen Mr. Lunt names
in his information (page the 6th), where hee, this informant, then heard
most of them publickly own that they had received comissions, by
Mr. Thriefall, some time before, from King James, and would there

have oblieged this informant and Mr. Lunt to have engaged with them the gentlemen of that country, etc.

"This informant further saith that about the beginning of the year 1691, hee, this informant, heard that Mr. Lunt was imployed in and about London to list men. And this informant saith that some short time after, several men came into Lancashire, as from London, and said they were listed by the said Mr. Lunt, and sent down to serve under the command of some of the officers aforesaid. And hee, this informant, saith that as fast as they came down, he was ordered by my Lord Mollineux, Sir Thomas Cliffton, Colonell Mollineux, Colonel Tildesley, Colonel Townley, Sir William Gerrard and his son, and severall others, the officers aforesaid, to take care of them and provide quarters or lodgings for them, which the informant did accordingly; and that at several times he, this informant, had and did receive money from my Lord Mollineux and Colonell Tildesley, Colonell Townley, Sir William Gerrard, and some others, to pay the said souldiers for their subsistance. And this informant saith hee did pay and distribute the money he soe received, amongst them, which this informant saith, in the whole, did amount to (to the best of his memory) about 3 or 400*li*. . . . . And this informant saith that hee is very well assured that the said Mr. Lunt did, at several other times, before and after, list a great many moore than these aforemencioned.

"This informant further saith that, about the month of February 1691, hee, this informant, was at a general meeting of several gentlemen att Collonel Walmesley's at Dungenhall, in Lancashire, many of whom he yet remembers, namely, Collonel Townley, Collonel Tildesley, Collonel Mollineux, Collonel Dalton, Sir William Gerrard, Mr. Gerrard, Mr. Dicconson, Mr. Stanley, Mr. Shuttleworth, Mr. Tilsdesley of Stansacre, Mr. Macy of Puddington, Mr. Langton of the Low, Mr. Gerrard of Ince, Sir Thomas Cliffton, Mr. Blundell of Crosby, Collonel Westby of Mabrick, Collonel Parker, and others. The said Collonel Walmesley being then lately came out of France, hee, the said Collonel, then produced publickly, in the said meeting, several comissions, declarations, grants, or patents, that hee had then lately brought from King James, of several gentlemen's esstates of that country, to other gentlemen there, that were King James' friends, as to Collonel Treldesley (*sic*), Lord Mollineux, Colonel Westby of Mobricke, Collonel Townley of Townley, Sir Thomas Cliffton, Sir William Gerrard, Collonel Mollineux, Mr. Gerrard of Ince, Mr. Langton of Low, and some others. This informant further saith that about a fortnight after, hee, this informant, was at the like meeting att Phillip Draycott's of Painsley Hall, in the county of Stafford, esquire, of most of the aforesaid gentlemen and others, as Mr. Bazill Brookes, Sir James Simons, Sir Richard Fleetwood and his sons, William and Rowland, —— Cuny of Cuny, esquire, and others, where were produced several of the like grants and patents, as aforesaid, brought over by the Lord Stafford, and there alsoe given out to those they did belong to.

"This informant saith that, at this meeting aforesaid, Collonel Parker being also there, and was then alsoe lately come out of France, hee, the said Collonel, did then publickly produce and deliver to one Captain George Penny (then in the company) a comission from King James for the said Penny to bee a Major of horse, which hee, the said Captain Penny, accepted of, with many thankes and promises to doe the King the best service with it hee could.

"And this informant further saith that at another time, being at a meeting with the said Collonel Parker, at the signe of 'the Starr,' an inn in Holywell, in Flintshire, and about twenty gentlemen, where hee, this informant, there saw the said Parker deliver one other comission from King James to one Mr. Pue of Pendrell, to bee a Captain of horse, and at the same time hee, the said Parker, delivered another comission, in the presence of this informant, to one Mr. George Davis of Treloughnell, and to several others, and that the said Parker did there, and at several others, as well as at the aforementioned meetings, order, direct, and desire, all the officers to take care to have their men ready at an hour's warning, with a pound of powder and ball, preportionable to each man, for that hee expected newes of the King's landing every day.

"This informant saith that about the beginning of the year 1689, hee, this informant, was ordered and imployed by Mr. Massey, Sir James Simmons, Sir Thomas Gifford, and Captain Fowler, to list as many men as hee could, in Staffordshire and North Wales, for King James and his service, under their command; and that hee. this informant, had money of the aforesaid gentlemen for that purpose. And this informant saith that hee did at that time (that is to say) within the space of three weekes, list about sixty men, whose names this informant has by him, ready to produce, as hee then tooke them.

"This informant alsoe saith that hee hath been since imployed to list men, several times, in the latter end of the year 1691, and in the beginning of the year 1692, by severall other gentlemen, as Collonel Walmesley, Captain Penny, Mr. Standish of Standish, Mr. Morston [Mostyn ?] of Delalery, and Captain Pennant of Baggall [Baghilt ?].

"And this informant saith hee did at those times, by the order and directions of those gentlemen last above mentioned, list about the number of six score, and had money of the said gentlemen, by the hands of Captain Pennent, for that purpose.

"And this informant further saith that hee did, severall times, after hee had soe listed the said souldiers, pay them subsistance money, by the order of Penny and Pennant, from whom hee had the same.

"And this informant further saith that hee has severall times seen great quantity of armes, in the houses of the gentlemen hereafter mentioned, in North Wales, .Cheshire, Staffordshire, and Lancashire, viz.:—in the house of Mr. Massy of Puddington, Captain Penny, Captain Pennant, Sir James Simmons, Sir Thomas Giffard, Mr. Fowler, Mr. Draycott, Sir William Garrard, Mr. Walmesley, Mr. Standish of Standish Hall, and in some other houses that hee cannot att present remember.

"In the whole, this informant verily believes that there were in the several houses abovesaid, that hee, this informant, saw armes for att least a thousand men, and that it is not above two years, at the most, since hee, this informant, saw them there."

REV. THOMAS WILSON to ROGER KENYON, at Peel.

875. 1694, July 7. Lathom.—"I cannot yet give you any certain account of my Lord's voyage. The yatch is come, a week since, to Liverpool; but we do not seem more in hast to be gone then we were when you were here. Colonel Vaughan is here too, and goes over Governor. My Lord Dunmore is come, with his family, to Ormeskirk, and designes for the Island, with my Lord Derby, if he goes this summer. As little time and room as I have, I must not forget to beg your pardon for a rudeness I committed, at your leaving of Knowsley; for, while you were at the bowling-green, I was suddenly sent for, and had neither time to leave word whither I went, nor to come back before you left Knowsley." *Fragment of seal.*

ROBBERY WITH VIOLENCE.

876. 1694, July 14.—The information by John Burch, of Manchester, linen draper, setting forth how he was attacked by four horsemen and robbed of 120*li.* in his money bags, and had a part of his tongue cut out.

GEORGE MACY to ROGER KENYON, at Lancaster.

877. 1694, August 21. The Tower of London.—" I came, accidentally, to my house in the Tower, this day, from my country house near London, where my wife lies dangerously ill of the small pox, and found your letter here, directed to Mr. Overton, who is also in the country (whether at the Bath or at Tunbridge, I know not), having not seen him since 3rd of August, when we were together at Kingston Assize. I have not left him nor my place here, but we are both cautious of laying out money, expecting satisfaction from the Sheriffs of London of what we are in disburse ; mine is many hundreds of pounds, haveing not received a penny for my last tedious and chargeable journey into your parts though I paid Mr. Hall, the apothecary of Manchester, his charges there, and have also taken Mr. Booth, of the Castle, in Chester, his account of charges being 30*l.* for carrying witnesses from place to place *ad testificandum.* My expectation is to be reimbursed from [the] said Sheriffs, against whom the King's tryall will go on, next terme, for what they have in their hands of clippers' forfeitures, to the value of 1,200*l.* or more. You are upon the same termes as myself, and I hope, in time, to receive mine as you will yours. So that I have thought it very necessary to answer your letter, in Mr. Overton's absence (who leaves all these affairs to me) concerning John Hartley, the old hardned, impenitent coyner, as you describe him. If he inclines to make a candid and ingenious, as well as thorough, discovery of all his accomplices, you may take it, and be expeditious in apprehending them ; but this fellow shall not play such tricks as Tom Bailey did ; let him rather receive his trial with utmost severity and proof you can make against him, and truly my opinion is that you hang them as you catch them, and not trust to their false discoveries." *Seal of arms.*

LADY STANDISH to GEORGE KENYON, at Peel.

878. 1694, September 11. Duxbury.—"Pray, sir, if you see your father, let him know that I have made some inquiry of the man called Lunt, but cannot yet here that he had a wife in our neighbourhood, nor that [his ?] family does not own that they know him ; but I will enquire farther after him, although I hope there will be no occation to fear him." *Seal.*

[MRS.] E. LEIGH to MR. KENYON.

879. [1694,] September 14.—"I doe beg the favor that you will make what inquiry you can of Brown. I thank God my son is in good halth, but so close confined that his wife and sisters was at the Tower to have sen him, and thay would not so much as permet him to loock out of the window to speke to them, nor his footman to tell them he was well, and he is put in the worst lodging in all the Tower, and in a rome but four yards square, and a warder leys by him ; but the pore warder is so sory for him that he cannot speke of him without tears in his eyes. We are petitioning the Queen that his wife may goe to him, but Lord Lucuus (*sic*) benders it all he can, to see if, by that mens, he can get his fees out of them. I think the prayers of our freinds were never more necessary then now to preserfe the inosent from falls wetneses, and shuer, the Parliment will thinke it hard to gife monny to mantane such a pack of hel-hounds that honts after the lifes and estats of inosent men. I pray God open the eyes of the King and Quene that they may deserne there frends from there foes." *Seal.*

THOMAS HODGKINSON to [ROGER KENYON].

880. 1694, September 29. Preston.—"About ten daies agone I received a letter from my worthy friend, Mr. Pigot, to enquire after the character of one Warring, who is supposed to be a witnes in the new plott, and saw your letter to Mr. Brooke, upon Wednesday last, touching the same matter. Since which time, I have made all the enquiries imaginable; and, although there be severall Warrings in Goosemargh and Whittingham, yet I cannot heare of any that can be imagined to bee a witnes in this prosecution; there being none (that I can hear of) that can speake to any point, save that of a spade, or a plow; and, therefore, cannot think there is any such witnes, in these parts, of that name."

GEORGE MACY to ROGER KENYON.

881. 1694, October 11. The Tower of London.—"I sent you, in a letter, last Saturday, the confession of Hartley and Hulme, and now I have received yours of the 7th instant, which doth confirm what I before imagined, that Elliotson came up on the business of Hartley, and that guineas are not spared to be disposed of, if they could accomplish their ends. I could do no less then send you those papers, because my Lord Chief Justice Treby desired it; though I believe it will come to nothing. I perceive that Elliotson did not only compliment you, but your son too, with the offer of guineas; he hath often muttered to me in the same manner (after that he found I guesst right the cause of his comeing up) how well I should be rewarded if I would not hinder the proceedings, but he found me very cool to accept of any such proposals, haveing experienced, when I was last at Lancaster, that no bribe would take with me. *Caveats* have been entered in both the secretaries' offices here, to prevent any pardon for Hartley, which he hath found to be so; and, therefore, came to me yesterday, declaring his dispair in the matter, and of his resolution of going this day out of town, and at last spoke out that he had 20 guineas to present some person, for his favor and assistance. I askt him why he did not do it to Mr. Pierce, my Lord Treby's gentleman; he answered that was done already, and was very sorry he had spent so much of the poor fellow's money, with so little success. If you desire it, I doubt not but a warrant may be had from the Queen, both for Hartley's and Hulme's executions, though, perhaps, it would nettle my Lord Chief Justice Treby. I know that your cheif design is that they should both discover all their confederates, without reserve, and if you will put me in way how to frighten them into it, you shall speedily have it, but as I wrote you formerly, that their bounceing, at Lancaster, how easily and speedily they could get a pardon because that gold was plentiful, was no more than common breath. It would have been more prudent for them to engage those on their side that could hinder their proceedings, than barely to make friends towards the procuring a pardon. Pray give my humble service to Mr. Justice Yeates. I thank him for his kind lines, and when he sees this, will find that no care is wanting here to prevent clandestine contrivances to the

King and country's damage, and I hope, when he comes to London, that he will honour me with his company at my house in the Tower, and I can expect no less from yourself, because you have often promised me so to do. My opinion is that Hartley's estate, both real and personal, ought to be enquired after, lookt into, and secured for their Majesties' use, persuant to the authority you have, by virtue of the privy seal, even to the very guineas that have been given Elliottson to dispose of. In order to which, do send me the names of such persons that you can learne have any effects of the said Hartley's in their possession or disposal, and I will send you down *subpœnas* out of the Exchequer, to be speedily served upon them, returnable the first of next term, which proceeding will abate the courage of Hartley and bring him to a thorough confession, or that he do prepare himself for the gallows. The rogues have got a new way here in London to acquit themselves, when charged with clipping or coyneing; at the time when they are brought before a judge or justice, to swear that such persons who came to apprehend them and search their houses or lodgings (not spareing the constables and the warden's officers) to have robbed them of moneys, plate, &c., thereby not only to lessen the evidences, but put them on tryals for their lives. Thus, I have written you a large letter in testimony of my zeal in promoteing good and public services."

ELEANOR BUNBURY to ROGER KENYON, " by the Church Gate," Manchester.

882. [1694,] October 12.—"Let me know when these great trials against our countrey gentlemen begins at Manchester. I hope God will preserve them, for I hear they have a company of sad witnesses against them. It will be an act of merit to protect them against false swearing. Pray God, make you and other good men useful to them as you have been to me." *Seal of arms, broken.*

INDICTMENT of SIR ROWLAND STANLEY and others.

883. 1694, October 17.—Indictment against Sir Rowland Stanley, Sir Thomas Clifton, William Dicconson, Philip Langton, and William Blundell, for treason and rebellion in receiving commissions from James II. to levy soldiers, and treating with Louis, King of France, for the invasion of England.

R. B[ROOK] to ROGER KENYON.

884. 1694, October 18.—Is glad Lord Strange "layes hold of so considerable an opportunity of reading men; a very useful part of learning at this time a day. And you will joyne with me in opinion that his Lordship is as capable to make observations as most gentlemen of his yeares."

SPEECH of the JUDGES to the JURY at the Trial of LORD MOLLYNEUX and others for High Treason, at the Manchester Assizes.

885. [1694, October 20.]—"Gentlemen, we must acquaint you that these five prisoners at the barr stand indicted for high treason, imagining and designing our most gracious King and Queen's death ; also that they accepted comissions from King James, for levying a warr here against us.

" The next thing is that they did adhere to their Majesties' enemies without this Kingdome, being an open and notoriuus act of rebellion. That they held correspondance with the French King, adhereing to that party.

" One part of their indictment is that they imagined and designed to depose their Majesties, King William and Queen Mary, from their regall Crown and Government, and to bring them to death and other destruction.

" Another part of their indictment relates that they imployed one Mr. John Lunt as their agent into France, which said Lunt, being discarded by King James in Ireland, came over into England, and that he then knew none of these gentlemen, but was conducted to their houses. He tells you that these gentlemen sent him as their messenger into France, and haveing received commissions from thence, delivered them to these gentlemen prisouers, who, upon their receiveing of them, kissed them, and drunk King James' and his Queen's and the Prince of Wales' health upon their knees; that they gave him about five pounds apiece. Afterwards he went to London, and listed about 60 men for soldiers, and provided a great quantity of armes, amounting to the value of 50*li.* or thereabouts, and that these armes were sent into the countrey, in severall boxes, and they were allowed of by these five gentlemen. He tells you that these armes were sent to Standish Hall; he also saith that he was directed by these gentlemen to goe for France, to acquaint King James of their proceedings in England, and that the said King James bade him tell his friends in England, that he would be ready for them the Spring following, viz., 1690, and this he did positively swear.

" One George Wilson evidenceth that he was to goe to the waterside, to wait for some friends that were to come over sea, with commissions from France.

" Colonel Bruerton, he onely relates that he had some moneyes given him, to bee assisting to these five prisoners for preparing an army. You have also heard what the rest of the witnesses have said, to witt, Mr. Baker, &c. But now on the other side. That, that is most materiall against the aforesaid witnesses for the King. is that of one Parsons, who tells you that one of them offered to tempt him with the reward of 150*li.* if he would assest him against some of these gentlemen prisoners. You have heard it sufficiently proved that they have indeavoured, at severall times and places, to tempt men with large rewards to assist them in their treatrous designes against their Majesties of this Kingdome. And when that would not take effect, they turned enemies to these prisoners, and tempted several men to assist them against these prisoners, witness Mr. Parsons aforesaid. Also for Colonel Bruerton, there are witnesses enough who doe confirm that this Bruerton, being in a poor condition, complained much against Mr. Liegh of Lyme, and Sir Rowland Stanley, who, because they would give him little or nothing, swore he would be revenged on them, if ever time served.

" Soe that if you doe believe that this is a perfect contrivance of Lunt, Wilson, Wombell, Bruerton, Baker, and the rest, whereby to discreditt these gentlemen at the barr, and to inhance themselves by their estates, hopeing to compass a third part of them at the least, as these witnesses have proved it against them, then these prisoners are more innocent, and the fault will lye more upon their accusers, soe that this is a great mystery of iniquity contrived by one of the two partyes. We give you what time you please to bring in your verdict."

The prisoners were brought in not guilty.

ACCOUNT, in the handwriting of ROGER KENYON, of the TRIAL of SIR ROWLAND STANLEY and others, at Manchester.

886. [1694, October 20.]—"The two Lancashire Justices writ to by the Secretary to assist Captain Baker in takeing up the prisoners, were the Lord Willoughby and Mr. Norres, the first made, by the Commission of Oyer and Terminer, one of their Judges, the latter reserved for foreman of the Grand Inquest. The persons joyned with the Judges in that Commission were, three of them, viz., the Earl of M[acclesfield?], the Lord W[illoughby?], and Sir E[dward] M[oseley], strenuous asserters of the late King's dispenseing power, each of them subscribeing or declareing their consents to take away the penall lawes, [and] tests, and none greater with the Lancashire prisoners then they were. Sir William Gerrard, who was first arraigned, prayed hee might have a copy of the indictment; the Judge, Sir Gyles Eyres, told him that was not allowable by law. The rest of the prisoners, in their turn, prayed the like, which in like manner were denyed. Captain Baker, a captain in Munmouth's insurrection, now commanded a Dutch troop to guard him, with his prisoners, to London, to make them a spectacle in all countyes and townes thorow which they were carryed. Mr. Aaron Smith, the furious phanatick, so styled in the raigne of Charles the Second, sent down, in great pomp, to manage these tryalls. The Lord Molineux, upon his arraignment, presented a petition to the Judges that, in regard of his deafnes and of the defects of his memory, hee might have councell or a solicitor to assist him at his tryall. Sir Gyles Eyres said it could not be allowed. Sir Rowland Stanley, Sir Thomas Clifton, William Diccon (*sic*), esquire, Philip Lawton (*sic*), esquire, and Mr. Blundell, were all indicted in one bill, and the first tryed, and the Court proposeing to try them together, if they, in all, would but challenge 35 peremptorily. They did accordingly consent, and being bid to prepare for their tryalls the next morneing, they were took from the barr, and so soon as they were gone, it was ordered, upon Mr. Aron Smith's motion, that the Sheriffe was ordered forthwith to summou at least 40 freeholders more, to attend these tryalls the next day, though hee had then allready retorned a pannell of 76 summoned for that service, besides the 24 retorned upon the Grand Jury. The reason of this was apparent the next day, for the King's Councell, with[out] shewing any cause, challenged 20 of the cheefe gentlemen reteyned. Query—how this sudden short summons accorded with the Act of 4th and 5th of this King and Queen, that jurors for tryalls of issues should have six days' notice, &c. Before any evidence was given, the prisoners petitioned that the witnesses against them might be examined apart, but that was not thought fit by Sir Gyles Eyres. John Lunt, the first witnesse, being bid by the King's Councell to look upon the five prisoners, and asked if he knew them all, hee answered hee did know them all; and Sir Rowland Stanley desireing Lunt to shew which was Sir Rowland Stanley, Lunt pauseing upon it, Sir William Williams said, Why do not you shew which is Sir Rowland? Lunt thereupon pointed at Sir Thomas Clifton, saying that was Sir Rowland, which mistake causing a lafter and a noyse, the Judge, Sir Giles Eyres, bid Lunt take one of the officer's white staves and lay it upon Sir Rowland's head. Lunt, taking the staff, layd it upon the head of Sir Thomas Clifton, and poynted after at Sir Rowland, and said that was Sir Thomas Clifton. After this, Sir Gyles Eyres, the Judge, asked Lunt if ever, before the time of giving them those commissions, hee had seen those two gentlemen; hee replyed hee had not. Upon which, the judge said there was no such mighty matter in the mistake, for being

310

told that those were the two gentlemen, in diversifying their names, takeing the one for the other; and though Lunt after this, swore that Sir Rowland Stanley gave him 5*l.*, viz., two guineas, and the rest in silver, and that about February, 1690, Sir Thomas Clifton at his house, Lithom, had given him ten poundes to buy armes for him, and that before that time Lunt had been with Sir Rowland Stanley, who had given Lunt 4*l.* to buy armes with; that about July or August 1691, Lunt was at Standish with Sir Rowland Stanlow (*sic*), Mr. Dicconson, Mr. Blundell, Mr. Lameton (*sic*), *et aliis*, and by them sent into France to acquaint King James with their forwardnes; that at his retorne hee acquainted Sir Thomas Clifton, Mr. Legh, and the rest, that King James would be in readiness the Spring following. By all which, besides Lunt's positive affirmance what sort of moneys Sir Rowland had given him, hee the said Lunt tells, two severall times and different places, that hee had seen Sir Thomas and Sir Rowland severally and not together before their being at the tryall, yet the Judge did not think fit to correct the excuse hee had made for the mistake. When Colonel Brereton gave his evidence that hee had received of Sir Rowland Stanley moneys for the service of King James, but for his own use, it was asked him what summes. Hee replyed small summes, five or ten or twenty shillings at a time, but not ready at telling what it was; for the Judge helped him with an answer, saying it might be for subsistence money."

MRS. E. LEIGH to ROGER KENYON.

887. [1694,] October 25.—Thanks Kenyon for clearing the innocent. Lady Mollyneux said she never expected him to be a friend to the Roman Catholics. Despairs of anything being done for the Church party, because the Commonwealth party fills the Council Board and all the great places. She prays the King's eyes may be opened, and that he may not be ruined, as Father Peters ruined King James. *Seal.*

"The following ACCOUNT of LUNT is what hath been attested by particular witnesses, not otherwise worth the reading, but as an index, if turned to, to show from the circumstances of times and places, what construction may be made as to the truth or improbability of his evidence, with some deviations observable to the same purpose."

888. [1694, October.]—"*Anno* 1666, the year when London was burned, Lunt, who sets the crountryes where he comes, in combustion, was borne at a place called Crooked Yard, on the edge of Maclesfield Forest, two myles from Maclesfield town, in Cheshire, and christened at a little ale-house near Hassop, in Derbyshire, son to a bungling bookbinder, who ther pedled with pamphlets and ballads, and now keeps a common ale-house in Nottingham. His father is a protestant, his mother was a papist, who, in the sickness whereof she died, recommended her son's education to the piouse care of a popeish priest, to be brought up in her religion. The holy father (so soon as the youth was grown old enough to go on errands) got him into the service of Mr. Smith of Quinyburrow, in Leicestershire, where, after some years' stay, the stripling (grown so sawcie as to pretend love to his master's doughter), hee was presently packt from that place.

"*Anno* 1680, Lunt's next service was with Captain Walter Hastings, at Plumptree, three myles from Nottingham, who kept him as footboy and waiter.

"*Anno* 1682, Lunt went to serve the Lord Oswaldston as postilion and under-groom. When his Lord or Lady went abroad with their coach and six, hee was postilion, and when in town, but with two horses, hee sometimes drove the coach. In that service, after some weeks' stay, hee cut out and sold the rich lineing of his Lady's coach, for which hee was stripped of his livery and sent to Bridewell, in Westminster, and there lay very poor and almost naked, for a considerable time, without any releefe but what Bridewell afforded, except what he found from an old laundresse, one Bety Langley, who said shee was his wife.

"Lunt, after he came from Bridewell, for some short time served a shoomaker, and, about Whitsunday, 1684, hee went to live with Collonell Staples at his house, 'the Iron Balcony' in St. Alban's Street, St. James's, and there, till August following, served him as footman and groom.

"In August, 1684, Lunt went to live as under-groom and postilion to Sutton Lodge, the Lord Carrington's house in Warwickshire; hee sometimes there (tho' not good at it) drove the coach, and stayed in that service about nine months.

"In June, 1685, Lunt retorned to the service of Collonell Staples, in St. Alban Street, whence, after about two months' stay, he was turned out againe.

"In or about October, 1685, Lunt went to live with Captain Talbot, and abode with him about a quarter of a year.

"In or about January, 1685[-6], Lunt went to serve Captain Ucworth (?), son-in-law to Collonell Staples, who then lived with the Collonell at his said house in St. Alban's Street, and in that service, on Thursday, June 3rd, 1686, John Lunt, in Knightsbridge Church, by the minister of the place, was marryed to Ann Tatham, widow, Collonell Staples his kinswoman and servant, and thence they retorned to their respective services, where, for a considerable time, though marryed, they continued as servants.

"On or about the 10th of June, 1688, John Lunt, with his said wife, kept a publique house, at the signe of 'the Golden Square,' near Golden Square, in St. James's, and Lunt, whilst hee there lived, was a frequent companyon of Pour, Neland, and Fetherston, the three notoriouse theeves of that time for breaking and robbing of houses. The same year Lunt got himself listed a horse granadeir in the late King's guards under Captaine Guy, and in that post went that year in the expedition to Salisbury, to oppose the Prince of Orange after his landing.

"At Christmas, 1688, Lunt crowded in amongst the Lord George Howard's retinue, and so came to King James' forces in France, England being scarce safe for him, considering the company hee had kept, and about the 12th of March, 1688, Lunt, in King James' army, landed in Ireland.

"In Aprill, 1689, Lunt, who never wanted confidence, claymed a right to ryde in King James' lifeguard in Ireland, boldly affirming to the King himself that hee had been of the lifeguard in England, but upon search of the muster-roll, it appearing that Lunt in England was no more but a horse granadeer, hee being detected of telling the King a lye, was casheered and sent away, not in pretended, but in reall disgrace.

"On or about the —— day of ———, 1689, Dr. Bromfield, as they call him, being sometimes an apothecary in Warrington in Lancashire, and there turned quaker, and sometimes since goes by the name of Berkley, a broad, fat, well-complexioned man, of a midle stature, aged about 50 years, in a blacke or sad-colored suite, came to one James Williamson's, an alehouse in Great Crosby; his man's name, as he called himselfe, was Morgan, a slender man in plaine habit. At that alehouse they left their horses, and there hyred an open boat to carry them, as they gave it out, into Ireland, but as is supposed, it carryed them along the sea-coast till they came unto Mr. Edmund Threlfall, who had a small ship ready for them in the rever of Lune.

"On Tewsday, May 14th, 1689, the *Lyon* of Lancaster, a small brigue, Charles Cawson, master, sayled out of the river Lune about two in the morning. Shee had then in her the master and five marriners, a boy, with Mr. Edmund Threlfall and two other passengers unknown. Shee went without cocket or certificate, and without fraight at her going off, pretending to stand for the Isle of Man, but when at sea, made straight for Dublin, and on Saturday, May 18th, 1689, that ship came to anchor in Dublin Bay, and there continued till the 10th of June following, waiting Mr. Threlfall's retorne, who had hyred her thither and back.

"On Sunday, June 9th, 1689, Collonel Mathews his regiment of dragoons began to take up the cheef of the papists in Lancashire, and that day, Richard Townley of Townley, Esquire, and his brother, Mr. Charles Townley, were taken at Townley and brought prisoners to Preston.

"Munday night, June 10th, 1689, there was brought on board the vessell that waited for Mr. Threlfall, one tun and an halfe of iron pots, halfe a tun of iron barrs, and nine barrells of beef, the same master and ship's crew, the same Mr. Threlfall, after his stay of three weeks and two days in Dublin, and with him onely one other passenger, called Mr. Lunt, who pretended he was going to an uncle of his in England. How Lunt (whose wits had been at worke how to get a passage to England) became acquainted with Mr. Threlfall, doth not appear; hee, at his comeing on board, was an absolute stranger to all the ship's crew, and perhaps not till then acquainted with Mr. Threlfall. The vessell set saile that night. Whether Lunt, in their passage, might pump from Mr. Threlfall, by his insinuations, a discoverie of Mr. Threlfall's errand, or how hee knew, it is uncertaine.

"On Thursday morning, June 13th, 1689, Mr. Threlfall and Lunt with him were set on shore near Cockeram, about a league from Lancaster, at a place called the Crooke, on the south side the river by the Cock Boat, and as the boatmen were rowing back towards the vessell, Mr. Lunt called after them (perhaps by Mr. Threlfall's bidding) and said hee had left his two lethern bags in the hold of the vessell, and desired them to bring them to him to Cockeram. It was observed by the seamen that these passengers had two case of pistolls and one sword, a hair port-mantle trunk, and two lethern bags. The trunk, being heavie, was bid so soon as might bee, after they came on shore, and so continued, till, by a dog's scratching to it, where it was covered with earth, and gnawing the skin that covered it, it was found, and when opened, there were found in it six case of large pistolls, marked J. R., an old campaign wig, two pair of old stockens, some sully linnen, which was all—no papers; but in the bags left in the ship were all their papers—·King James' declarations and commissions, and many papers printed and written. They had no paquets to divide on shore, nor commissions to carry to Croxteth; but that morneing, so soon as those papers which they brought over were, by the custom-house officers, seised in the ship, Mr. Threlfall, observeing the boat coming towards the shore, hee and Lunt with him fled, and at a place called Thurnham Mosse, betwixt Thurnham Hall and Cockersand Abby, they lay hid under a hedge till night came, and then going some myles together, Mr. Threlfall, who well knew the country, got Lunt a guide to bring him to Mr. Tildsley's house-lodge, and so Threlfall and Lunt parted. What Lunt's pretence to go thither was, being an absolute stranger, wee know not, but Mrs. Tildsley, who is since dead,

her husband being then from home, sent, as is said, one John Nickson
forthwith to bring Lunt the sand-way to Ince, where the Lady Tildsley,
who is since also dead, then lived. Nickson took with him a horse, on
which both Lunt and hee rid over the sand, and Friday, June 14th,
1689, at 2 afternoon, Nickson brought Lunt to Ince from Cockeram.
Where Threlfall and Lunt landed is nine myles to Lodge, and from
Lodge to Ince 22 myles. In going that way, no such person as George
Wilson was with them, nor did any person, either at Lodge or Ince, ever
see Wilson, as they say. Lunt stayed at Ince two nights.

"Saturday, 15 June, 1689, at night, Captain Brereton, with a party
of dragoones, took the Lord Molineux a prisoner, at Croxteth, and set
soldiers to guard him whilst they searched the house; at which time, his
Lordship being very ill of the gowt, prevayled with the Captain that the
Lord Brandon might be acquaynted, who was then at Preston, that the
Lord Molineux was not then able to remove, and upon his honor promised, if able, hee would come when required. The Captain thereupon,
for that time, let his Lordship remaine.

" On Sunday morning, June 16th, 1689, the same party of dragoons
which had been at Croxteth, came to Garstwood, Sir William Gerard's
house, and there took up Sir William, and that day brought him prisoner
to Preston.

" The same 16th of June, 1689, another party of Collonel Mathews'
dragoons went to Lithom, Sir Thomas Clifton's house, above 30 myles
from Croxteth, and there took up Sir Thomas Clifton and brought him
prisoner to Preston.

" The same Sunday, June 16th, 1689, Lunt haveing stayed two nights
at Ince, and haveing by some meanes got a bay nag, supposed to be one
of the horses left by Dr. Bromfield with James Williamson of Great
Crosby, hee was guided from Ince by Edward Parker, the Lady
Tildsley's servant, to Runcorn boat, and so passed, without calling
at Croxteth, or anywhere else, into Cheshire, on his way to London.

" On Monday, June 17th, 1689, one Lieftenant Isherwood, with
another party of dragoones, took up Mr. Dalton and carryed him from his
house, Thurnham, to Garstang, and the next day prisoner to Preston,
and at the same time were taken up, many more of the popeish gentry,
and brought prisoners to Preston.

" The same 17th of June, 1689, the Lancashire Militia were raised,
and came to their Lord Lieftenant, Brandon, at Preston.

"On Tewsday, June 18, 1694,[1] an account of what papers, commissions,
declarations, &c., that were seised in the ship were, by Mr. W. K——
certifyed to the Commissioners of the Custom-House, London, and
shortly after, they were all sent up to the Principall Secretary of State,
by a special messinger.

" On Thursday, 20 of June, 1689, Lunt lodged, by the name of Benet,
up two pair of staires over the gatehouse at the ' Cock and Dolphin ' Inn
in Gray's Inn Lane. Hee there stole a case of pistolls belonging to a
gentleman that then lay at that Inn, and William Hopkins, the then
chamberlain there, for not paying the value of the pistolls, lost his
place. The said Hopkins saith Lunt came thither on a bay nag.

" The popeish gentleman brought prisoners to Preston were afterwards
thought fit to be removed, and June 24th, 1689, the order following was
made, directed to the Constables of Manchester :—These are to will and
require you to receive and take into your custody all such persons as
shall be brought to you by Captain Stanley, Captain Penington, and
Captain Norres, or any under their command, and that you place such

---

[1] *Sic.* In another copy 1689.

persons in such protestant houses, that they may not conferre or discorse together, and that you see that guards of the militia be set upon their severall and respective lodgings, the better to secure them. Given under our hands and seales the 24th of June, 1689. C. Brandon, L. Rawstorne, R. Longworth, T. Patten.

" June 25th, 1689, the aforenamed prisoners, with many more, were, by a part of the militia soldiers appointed thereunto, carryed to Manchester, where two of them dyed. The rest, all save Sir Thomas Clifton, who was left at Preston, were kept in custody at Manchester, till January following, save that two or three had leave to go to their houses, on extraordinary occasions, for a day or two, but went with a guard of soldiers to bring them back. They were lodged as followeth :—At ' the Bull's Head ' :—Mr. Sherburne of Stonyhurst (he dyed at Manchester), Mr. Dicconson of Wrightington, Mr. Stanley of Preston, Mr. Barlow of Barlow. At Peter Tickles' :—Christopher Carns of Halton, Esquire, William Anderton of Euxton, Esquire, Mr. Robert Bryers [and] Mr. Roger Bryers of Walton. At Mr. Swartbreck's :—Sir William Gerrard, Richard Townley of Townley, Esquire, Mr. Charles Townley, his brother, Robert Dalton of Thurnham, Esquire, William Blundell of Crosby, Esquire. At the ' Rose and Crown ' :—Doctor Thomas Worthington, Mr. Thomas Lancaster, Mr. Christopher Anderton. At ' the Wheatsheaf' :—Thomas Worthington of Blanisco, Esquire, Mr. Richard Worthington, his son, Richard Chorley of Chorley, Esquire, Mr. William Clifton, brother to Sir Thomas, Mr. James Clifton, another brother, Mr. John Blundell.

" The Lord Molineux, after some days that Captain Brereton had left him at Croxteth, too unfit to be removed, was a second time sent to, to be brought by Sir Thomas Stanley, a militia captain of horse, but being then also unable to bee removed, hee was, after a litle longer stay at Croxteth, a third time, by Sir William Pennington, another captain of horse of the militia, sent for, with positive orders to bring him, and then, his Lordship being utterly unable to ride on horseback, and haveing no coach at home, Major Generall Kirk, who then lay at Leverpool, lent his coach, and therein, on Sunday, 30th June, 1689, the Lord Molineux came to Manchester, in Major Generall Kirk's coach, and was there made a prisoner with the rest; but two days before that time, viz., June 28, 1689, the order following was made at Manchester :—' Whereas there are severall prisoners in custody at Manchester, this is to authorize you to deliver them into the custody of Captaine Dicconson, them to keep untill hee shall receive further order from me. (Signed) C. Brandon. To the Constables of Manchester.'

" The forenamed gentlemen were not discharged till January following. In January, 1689, they were all set at liberty without any impeachment, either for the crimes, whatever they were, which they were taken up for, or for whatever could be charged upon any of them by what was found of Threlfall or Lunt's bringing over, and even the absconders which could not be taken when the rest were, did then shortly after appeare to vote at the election of Members of Parliament as the great man would have them.

" Digression :—Wilson swears Threlfall and Lunt landed at Cockeram in the beginning of July, and that hee, after Lunt's coming to Mr. Tildsley's house, called the Lodge, went thence with him to Croxteth, and there saw him deliver commissions from King James. It is therefore observed that none of those gentlemen could then be found at Croxteth, and if Lunt had come to Croxteth after his landing, as it is plain he did not, how fit a man was the Lord Molineux to be then drinking healths on his knees.

" But to retorn to Mr. Lunt, whom wee brought, 20 June, to ' the Cock and Dolphin ' inn, in Gray's Inn Lane. Whilst hee stayed at that time in town, hee continued at that inn, and on or about Saturday, 29th of June, 1689, Mr. Lunt, in a hackney coach, called at his wife's dore, who then lived at the sign of the Golden Square, near Golden Square, in St. James's. Shee saith that, at her first comeing to him, shee did scarce know him; hee had so blacked his eyebrows to disguise himselfe. That he then took her in the coach to the ' Cock and Dolphin ' inn, in Gray's Inn Lane. That at night shee returned to her house, and that the next day shee and her brother Burges came againe to the said Inn to see and take leave with Mr. Lunt, who was then, as hee said, to go a jorney northwards.

" Whilst Lunt lay at that inn, one Mr. Thomas Stafford, a famed highwayman and an old companyon of Lunt's, being newly come out of [the] New Prison, became Lunt's bedfellow at that inn, about two nights before Lunt and Stafford went thence northwards. On 5 July, 1689, Lunt and Stafford were committed to gaol at Coventry, on suspicion of being persons disaffected to the Government. In August, Lunt was, by order of the Council, committed to Newgate, but in November he was released on bail.

" In December, 1689, Lunt went down to Mr. Threlfall's house in Goosenargh, in Lancashire, and stayed there, by the name of Jackson, until towards the end of January following.

" In Hillary term, 1689, Lunt, appearing at the Court of King's Bench, was thence, at the instance of Mr. Aaron Smith, bound over to the then next Assizes at Lancaster, but whatever Mr. Smith meant by it, there was no prosecution.

" March 31st, 1690. Upon Lunt's appearance in court, he was committed, and though there was no prosecution, he was continued in prison there, until the August Assizes following.

" 24 August, 1690. Mr. Edmund Threlfall (with whom Lunt came out of Ireland) was buryed.

" At Lancaster Assizes, in August, 1690, Lunt, though there was no prosecution, was but discharged upon bail, himself bound, by the name and addition of John Lunt, of the parish of St. James, Westminster, in 500*li.*, Peter Bradshaw of Scale, in the county of Lancaster, in 250*li.*, —— Mercer of Lancaster, in the county of Lancaster, in 250*l.*, on condition that John Lunt appear at the then next Assize, and, in the meantime, be of good behaviour.

" On or about the 6th of September, 1690, Lunt came from Lancaster. His friend, Mr. Threlfall, was dead. He had then no gentleman of his acquaintance to go to. His sureties were the common bail for many popish recusants that then were bound over, so he then came againe to John Wilson's house, a linnen weaver, and then was called Mr. Lunt.

" At Lent Assizes at Lancaster, 1690-1, Lunt appeared, and was discharged, and thence came and stayed at Isabel Burton's house in Chippin, and sometimes at John Sharples his house in Lagrum, and continued in that part of the cuntry till May following. Lunt, in this month of May, before hee left Chippin, being in an house with Cuthbert Wilson, desired Wilson to walk with him into a field, and there moved Wilson, saying he was a strong man, to go with him to rob upon the highway, telling Wilson it was a very merry way of living.

" August, 1691. In Bartholomew Fair time, Lunt came to his wife at ' the White Hart,' in St. James's parish, and stayed with her somewhat more then a month, save that two or three nights in that September he lay at Mr. Whitfield's house in Bear Street, in Leicester Fields, at which time Lunt told Mr. Whitfield that hee had that summer lived near Hull, in Yorkshire, and that whilst hee was in that cuntry, a French man-of-warr had taken some ships that belonged to Hull. Though he told them not, at Chippin, whither hee was to go, yet he then told Mr. Whitfield where he had been.

"October, 1691, Lunt being about to leave London, hee told his friend, Mr. Whitfield, hee had then to pay for his mare's keeping for a month and nine nights, in Bloomsbury.

"In October, 1691, Lunt came again to Chippin, in Lancashire, and ther stayed, till about Christmas following. Where Lunt was, from Christmas till 29 January following, appears not; but what hee had been doing, the next paragraph but two sheweth.

"Friday, 29 January, 1691 [-2], Lunt was at Robert Clerkson's house in Chippin.

"Wednesday, 3rd of February, 1691[-2], Lunt lay at 'the White Bull' in Bilsburrow, and stayed two nights.

"Friday, 5 February, 1691[-2], Lunt lay at Thomas Plant's house in Myerscough, Lancashire, and there stayed ten days, at which place,

"Friday, Febuary 12, Cuthbert Wilson being in Lunt's company, Lunt took him to the stable to shew him two horses, and asked Wilson what he thought of them, who answering one seemed a broken bellyed horse fit for the cart, Lunt thereupon replyed that that horse, about a fortnight agone, had carryed him off 200*l.* upon the pad, and brought him with it, 50 myles in one day. After such an exploit, Lunt could scarce have come to so safe a retirement as Chippin, it being in an obscure part of the cuntry, scituate betwixt the great forrests of Bowland and Wyersdale, in a boggie, mossie, neighborhood. And Lunt, who had no estate, no trade, nor other way of getting money, being out of service, but this, save selling a horse which, perhaps, hee never bought; though hee came often, after he had found it, to that retirement, yet hee never stayed long at any one house there.

"Wensday, 17 February, 1691, Lunt lay at John Anderton's house, an inn in Walton, where hee was so sick as hee sent for a ghostly father.

"On Thursday, 19th, being better, he took horse to go, as he said, towards London, but went to Mr. Richard Wood's house in Ormskirke, and there lodged three or four days, till he got Mrs. Ann Wrennall, in mind to go to London with him, as his wife.

"The next account we have of Mr. Lunt is that, in the beginning of March, 1691-2 Lunt lodged three or four nights at Mr. Whitfield's house in Bear Street, in Leicester Fields, and told Mr. Whitfield hee had brought a gentlewoman out of Lancashire, whom hee had promised to marry, that hee had laine with her all the way up. At this time of Lunt's lodgeing there, one night after Mr. Whitfield was gone to bed, Lunt, sitting by the fyer with Peter Rogers and Mathew Turner, two of Mr. Whitfield's servants, who had then ended their day's work, said to them, he wondred that they, being strong men, would so toyle and drudge for a livelyhood, as they dayly did, since much more might be easier got another way; as for him, hee would rather adventure to be shot, padding upon the highway, then take such paines. And haveing so said, hee took out of his pocket and shewed them the instruments which hee said hee used in his way of getting money, which were a dark lanthorn, a wax candle, gags and cords to bind and gag the persons robbed; but they telling him they contented themselves in their own way of liveing, after that Lunt urged them no further, but put up his tackle, saying no more upon that subject.

"28 March, 1692, being Easter Munday, Lunt was marryed by Mr. Lacy, the Spanish Embassador's priest, to Ann, relict of Richard Reynolds, who had been an Ireish exciseman, and dyeing so, had owing to him from King James' Exchequer in Ireland, two or three hundred pounds. She it was which Lunt brought from Lancashire. The bride, on the wedding night (they haveing before had their fills of love) went to lodge with her sister, Taafe, at Mr. Taafe's house in St. James' Street, in the parish of St. James', Westminster, and after some days, Lunt, the bridegroom (who had another forsaken wife and three children, then liveing in that parish), came to Mr. Taaf's said house, calling himself Captain Widrington, and told Mr. Taaf he was marryed to his wife's sister. Lunt lay with this woman after they came to town, but before the wedding, at a little alley near Long Acre, and after that, removed to an alehouse in the Savoy, and Mr. Widrington, when he came to St. James' Parish, to which his first wife and children were then a charge, hee was there known to bee Lunt, and his lodging in the Savoy being found, 4 May, 1692, Lunt was taken before William Bridgman, Esquire, Justice of the Peace, charged, *ut per* warrant, with suspicion of going away and leaveing his wife and children to the charge of the parish; and for want of suerties for his personall appearance at the next Sessions, and to answer the same, hee was committed to the Gatehouse prison, Westminster, where hee lay untill 20 December, 1692. Lunt was discharged by the same Justice and Justice Tully. Whilst Lunt lay in prison in the Gatehouse, there were brought in thither, his three theeving companyons—Pour, Neland, and Fetherston ; and Pour, foreseeing his doom (for they all three, after the then next Sessions, dyed at Tyburne), gave Lunt a blew cloke by which hee was known a great while, and likewise left him halfe a crowne.

"In December, 1692, Lunt being got out of the Gatehouse, came not to his true wife and children, but having taken up above 30*l*. in hand off Mr. Whitfield, secured by the assignement of a collusive, fraudulent bond, under which cheating security Lunt was also to receive from Whitfield ten shillings a week for some time. Lunt, thus furnished, took his new wife, who was then with child, to lodge at one Mrs. Cooke's house in King's Street, in Southampton Square, calling himself then, Mr. Jackson, and hee had from Mr. Whitfield his 10*s*. a week untill May 15, 1693 ; Mr. Whitfield being then informed that the bond assigned to him, which was from Lunt's brother-in-law, a supposed preist, was a meer contrivance for a fund of credit, and released at the same time it was made ; and the cheat being discovered, Lunt's weekly allowance ceased. Then Lunt lived by running on the score, where hee could, and selling his wife's apparell, and at last, put beyond all his shifts, in the midle of July, 1693, Lunt went to Highgate, and was there employed as a day laborer by one Mr. Bridges, from that time till the midle of September, 1693, to wheel gravell and sand to make ponds to hold water for a constant supply of the water conveyed by pipes to London. In this month, Lunt informs the Secretary hee was sent by the Lancaster gentleman to King James, to let him know their readines to serve him, and to know when they might expect his landing.

"Lunt's true wife hearing of his being at Highgate, went thither, with a warrant from a justice of the peace, but he got away, and coming to his other wife, hee had a project to black her and there child, and to go as gipsies, and tell fortunes, but that wife being faire, or conceited, would not be blacked.

"Lunt, after this, compelled by necessity, adventured to go again to Mr. Whitfield, and with too many asseverations that Woodward, the priest's, bond was a good bond, and not released nor assigned to any but himself, and telling Mr. Whitfield of a new way by which hee had hopes to get 700*li*., as he called it, owing to his new wife's former husband, by King James, which, when got, should pay all that Lunt owed to Mr. Whitfield. This so took with Whitfield that hee, like him that shootes a second arrow to find a first that was lost, was prevayled with, and, 17 September, 1693, Mr. Whitfield let Lunt have the further sum of three pounds six shillings, and with that supply, 19 September, 1693, Lunt went with his new wife and child from London towards Flanders, his said wife haveing a sister at St. Clare's nunnery, in the town of Ayre (?), and thither comme, Lunt left his wife and child for some time to be provided by her sister there, and went, as hee said, into France begging or gipsying to St. Germain, to try if hee could get from King James any of the money due to Richard Reynolds, his said wife's former husband, and at his returne to Flanders, hee told that he had got 30 pounds, but said he was robbed of it coming back, and that helped his pretence to beg by ; but wherever hee had been, or however hee had sped, hee came back to St. Clare's nunnery as pore as hee went.

"In the midle of December, [16]93 Lunt, with his wife and child, comeing back, landed at Dover.

"The 21st of that December, having stayed some days at Dover, they thence came towards London, and Mr. Lunt, having forgot to pay his reckoning at Dover, was overtaken and arrested at Canterbury. The debt and charges being under 20s., some gentlemen drinking in the Inn where Lunt was arrested, did contribute three or four shillings apiece to discharge the traveller, which Lunt afterwards ill requited, as hee also did his old friend Mr. Whitfield, putting their names amongst those hee informed against as plotters.

"In the beginning of Christmas, 1693, Lunt came to London and went to Mr. Whitfield.

"January 6th, Lunt's said wife and child lay at Mr. Taaf's house in Bury Street, St. James', unto which place, near a fortnight after, Lunt also came.

"In the third week of that January, Lunt, by the name of Johnson, lived chamberlain at 'the George' inn, in Holburne. Hee stayed not there full three weekes, for whilst there, hee severall times borrowed a sword and a peruke, and went out in the nights, which his master, not endureing, turned him away.

"In the midle of February, 1693[-4], Lunt lodged at a little court in Exeter Street, and there, by the name of Smith, lay about three weeks. At the first week's end, in March, 1693-[4], Lunt removed into Duck Lane, in the Savoy, and there stayed till the latter end of that month, in which time, being at 'the Royal Oak' in Drury Lane, and told Mr. Whitfield was there, Mr. Lunt sent to speak with him. Mr. Whitfield, asking who was with Lunt, was told Lunt was drinking in the kitchen with Gray and Woodman, two reputed highwaymen. Mr. Whitfield hearing that, went not, but Mr. Lunt went up to him, asking why he would not come down, who answered, because your companyons are no company for mee. Lunt huffingly told him that though hee did, indeed, then owe him money, hee was now in a way to be able to pay him. The plot was then ahatching, and Mr. Whitfield was one that was after informed against.

"In April, May, and June, 1694, Lunt lodged in Greyhound Court, in Milford Lane, near the Temple, in which time, viz., April 6th, 1694, Lunt was sworn to his examination before Mr. Baron Powell, in the cause concerning lands given to superstitious uses.

"22 June, 1694, publication passed in the cause about lands given to superstitious uses.

"Wednesday, 27th of June, 1694, Lunt gave his information upon oath to Sir John Trenchard, then one of the Principall Secretarys of State, concerning his plot.

" Munday, July 9th, 1694, Lunt, with Captain Baker and the rest of the informers and witnesses, lay at Dunstable.

" On Thursday, July 12, 1694, that company lay at Manchester at severall inns, and severall of them by borrowed names, Captain Baker by the name of Harris, Mr. Taaf by the name of Johnson, Lunt by the name of Captain Smith, George Wilson by the name of Mr. Brown, and there stayed till Munday following.

" Munday, 16 July, Lunt went with Captain Baker, etc., to Worsley Hall, the Lord Willoughby's house in Lancashire, to meet the four messengers that were sent down, Morisco, Clerk, Sutton, and Heaward, to be ordered how to divide and proceed the next day, with severall parties of Dutch troopers, to the severall gentlemen's houses, that were to be taken up. And it was thought fit and necessary that the informers should be sent with the messingers and their guards, whereby the informers might see and learn to know those against whom they had informed, and to enable them to give an account of their seats, as well as of their persons, when they should be called to give their evidence against them.

" Tewsday, July 17th, 1694, Lunt went with Clerk, the messinger, and 14 Duch troopers, to Mr. Legh's house [at] Lyme, to which place they came betwixt six and seven in the morning ; the messinger, with three or four Duch troopers, apprehended and carryed Mr. Legh, in his morneing gown, from his dressing room to his closset, where Mr. Lunt stood with three or four more Duchmen, and Lunt searched amongst Mr. Legh's papers, from 7 till 12, and put up what he pleased. Mr. Legh afterwards was taken to a parlor, and there a guard set upon him, whilst Lunt and the rest searched every room and place where they pleased, in that great house, for armes, which gave Mr. Lunt oppertunity sufficient to know both Mr. Lee and his house. The armes they found were a case of pistolls and a carbine, which were in Mr. Legh's closset. Mr. Legh had a fine horse, and the more by him vallued being the legacy of a dying kinsman, which Mr. Lunt seised, and set his own sadle upon him, and thus (leaving Mr. Legh to be brought by forraigners to the common gaole of the county, Chester Castle), hee, better mounted then hee came thither, retorned into Lancashire, a thoroughly instructed informer against Mr. Legh.

" Friday, July 20, 1694, Lunt, at Wigan, in Lancashire, seeing Symon Arrowsmith, who theretofore, when under gaoler at Lancaster, had had Lunt in custody, he then invyted Symon to drinke ; Symon replyed, ' How come you to know mee here, who would not know mee the last week at Manchester when I saluted you by your name, Mr. Lunt ? you then turned away from mee saying I was mistaken, your name was Smith.' To which Lunt replyed, ' Your calling me Lunt there might have spoyled the project I was then upon, being the King's informer.'

" From Wigan, Lunt went into Blackburn Hundred, and at one Peele's house, two myles from Blackburn, hee endeavoured, by large promises, to inveigle Mr. James Parkinson to turne informer and to swear, as Lunt should instruct him, against the prisoner. Thence Lunt, for a week or more, went up and down the cuntry seiseing horses ; in the Hundred of Blackburne, at Mr. Catterall's and other houses ; in Amoundernes Hundred, at Mr. Tilsley's and other houses ; in the Hundred of Loynsdale, at Mr. Dalton's and other houses.

" Munday, July 30th, 1694, Lunt, with Wombwell, Ellis, and three messengers, were at the hall of Crosby, in Derby Hundred, seiseing of horses and searching the house for armes. There Wombwell, instead of armes, picked up money, the sinues of warr, which some of the company were ashamed of, and for which Mr. Marisco made amends.

"Munday, 27th August, 1694, John Lunt, at the generall Sessions of the peace held at Hicks Hall, in St. John's Street, in the County of Middlesex, was indicted for marrying Ann Tatham at St. Martin's in the Fields, in the County of Middlesex, widow, on the 3rd of June, 1692, and afterwards, that the said John Lunt did, on the 30th day of Aprill, 1694, *anno* 4 William & Marie, at the parish of St. Gyles in the Fields, in the County of Middlesex, marry Anne Reynolds, widow, the afforesaid Ann Tatham, otherwise Lunt, being then living, against the forme of the statute, &c.

. "The —— day of September, 1694, John Lunt, by a warrant pursuant to that process upon that indictment, was taken up by the Constable of ———— and carryed before ————, and bayled by Mr. Aaron Smith."

INSTRUCTIONS for the EXAMINATION of LUNT and others.

889. [1694, October.]—Instructions to counsel as to the examination of Lunt, Wilson, and others.

REV. THOMAS WILSON to ROGER KENYON, at Manchester.

890. 1694, November 11. Knowsley.—Desires Lord Derby should "goe to Parliament," since "his duty, honour, and interest oblige him to it." As to the progress of the "Leverpooll affair," Lord Derby is "hearty" for Mr. Brotherton, which gives great satisfaction to the Liverpool aldermen, who, on learning it, "swore" the writer "free of the town." Mr. Arthur Bold will vote as Mr. Byrome directs him. *Seal, broken.*

THOMAS MARSDEN to ROGER KENYON.

891. 1694, November 18.—"You have already heard how zealous the Earle of Derby was for our friend, against Mr. Maudit, and how zealously the body of the dissenters acted for the contrary interest, together with a deal of inconsiderate churchmen, draun in by crafty insinuations and confirmed in their opposition by a letter from the Lords Rivers and Macclesfield. It is most evident it was not the single concern of Mr. Maudit, as a private person, that was transacted, but that of the mis-called good old cause. After Mr. Mayor had demanded the freeman to say who they were that stood candidates for the vacant burgesship, and it was answered Mr. Maudit and Mr. Brotherton, and no other, he ordered the oaths of the Mayor and freemen to be publickly read by the town clerk, and added that he could not admit a poll for Mr. Maudit, who, as coroner, could not appoint a deputy, nor could be sent away from the town without the violation of its priviledges, or words to that effect. And to convince us that the matter, indeed, so stood, he caused also to be read Sir Francis Pemberton's opinion to that purpose. This done, the Mayor also told our people, if they would name any qualified person against Mr. Br[otherton], he would willingly admit them to a poll. But nothing would serve our opposites but a poll for Mr. Maudit; their cry and clamours being thick and loud for that end. After the aldermen and gentlemen upon the Bench had declared for Mr. Brotherton, the Mayor pronounced him to be elected, dissolved the court, and went away. I leave it to them that were then personally present, to acquaint you with the mobbish rudenesses our opposites were guilty of, in court. This I will only mention, that Mr. William Norres of Speak, and apothecary Molineux of Leverpool (*fanaticorum caput*), enraged the people against us by their own very unmannerly example, and the Recorder vaunted a flood of canker upon Mr. Brotherton, which he overcame by a generous silence. We want the utmost of your interest and industry to enable us to keep our ground, and I am sure we shall not misse of it." *Seal with crest.*

LADY H. WILLOUGHBY to Mr. KENYON, Burgess of Clitheroe, at the House of Commons.

892. [1694,] November 23.—"I thank you for your civility in calling, and those other kindueses you offer my most unhappy condition, to which it is the highest agrivation to find myself disapointed where I might have had the greatest hopes of a friend to do me that justice my sad case requires, and which he solomley ingaged to performe, before our marriage, which infidelity wold have an ill reflection on the wholl sex, but that it is to be hoped some are better then others, as farr as wit and good parts excell those that want them, of which you have a competent share, which makes me hope that good Judge Powell and you may find out some way, sence itt is such a publick grevance to the common people that they have given that villan Blacksmith's house towards Islington, the name of the English Inquisition, and to my knowledge there was a discours of the mob rising and pulling itt downe, and there being noe less than aleaven affidavides taken by Justice Gorge Evens of Surry, some of which contains murders dun in that house. I remember one old gentlewoman, Mrs. Rackliff, that was beat to death there, which Parker, a manservant to Newton, swears, and was privatly buryed, it is sayed, in his garden at Clerkenwell, where was a heap of earth att one end, like such a place. As for myself, I can easely prove that he was to have had two hundred pownd to dispatch me in eight months' time, besides five pownd a weeke for my diet and lodging, and that I had poysonous powders given me, unknowne to me, in my spoone meat, to make me mad, but that I timely discovered itt, as God wold have itt, that sent me a friend, good Lady Littleton, Sir Thomases mother, of the House of Commons, to healpe me to the benifitt of the lawe, which so frighted my enemeys, that they, rather then there villany shuld be discovered in Westminster Hall, imediately drew up private articles with an Ant of mine, to bring me out, otherways I had bin in my grave before this, and my son also, that they might have the estate which Massey told me they sent to inquire of him the value of, soon after Sir William Egerton's death, which showes what there hearts were sett on. And now, if yet liveing, there is three young heirs in Sir Thomas Willis, Barronett, Sir Richard Fanshaw, and one Mr. Collett, not mad, but to be destroyed for the same cause.

"Now, sence these horriable oppressions are a publick grevance, and made knowne to the Government, I suppose they ought to be redrest, upon a publick account. For my part, since I am deneyed it other ways, by this ungratefull, falce, and covitious person, who is now my husband, I must demand that justice of the Government which belonges to me as a subject of England and the Perrage, and desire you, as a christian and gentleman, to assist me what you can in the obtaining of it, which will be in ittselfe so merritorious an act as will engage the prayers and highest esteeme of all, perticulerly those that shall be delivered out of that lyon's den of distraction."

[P.S.]—"I have written the judge, on the same account, and desire your good assistance when you writ, direct to the Wardens to Mrs. Heap, but put not my name on itt. Praye let me heare if there be any hope." *Seal of arms.*

EXAMINATIONS taken before the HOUSE of COMMONS in connection with the LANCASHIRE TRIALS.

893. 1694, November 23, to 1694–5, February 5.

23 November, 1694.

".   .   .   .   . stake you I thinke you say you   .   .   .   .   . June or July last?

Mr. [Aaron] Smyth.—In July.

Mr. Speaker.—You say you were sent for to the secretary's, and he delivered you some bookes?

Mr. Sm.—3 books of Examinations.

Mr. Sp.—And directed you to abridge them?

Mr. Sm.—Yes, and I have the abridgement here.

Mr. Sp.—Then you had these men under your own examination?

Mr. Sm.—Yes, but that was not till after the gentlemen were seized. I think it was about 3 weekes before the tryall.

Mr. Sp.—When were they first seized?

Mr. Sm.—I cannot tell, but I suppose they might bee seized the latter end of July or beginning of August.

Mr. Sp.—And then after they were seized, were the witnesses brought to you, in order to take their evidence and prepare for their tryall?

Mr. Sm.—Yes, to distinguish their evidence as to the severall persons.

Mr. Sp.—Have you any other papers to deliver to the House but those papers the secretary delivered to you?

Mr. Sm.—None but those and the examinations of Kelley, which was in confirmation of their evidence as to some parts of the fact they had given evidence of.

Mr. Sp.—I apprehend that you make use of the discovery in Flintshire, and Bromfield's going into the hireing the boat by Muwson, and the examinations in Worcestershire, and of the other examinations to induce the discovery of the gentlemen in Lancashire. Have you a list of them?

[Mr. Sm.]—They are all marked   .   .   .   .   .   . of them Dowdsworthy   .   .   .   .   .

[Mr. Sp.]—Have you anything to say   .   .   .   .   .   . these gentlemen in their bringing up, or carrying down, or the proceeding at their tryall?

Mr. Sm.—I was not present at their tryall, for I was taken very sick, in Court, and was foiced to withdraw. I heard noe part of this tryall.

Mr. Sp.—Can you say anything relating to the proceedings to the tryall?

Mr. Sm.—Noe, otherwise than the takeing their informations from their mouths and giving them to the King's Councell, and their consulting about them; and then a comission was taken out, upon which they were tryed afterwards.

Mr. Sp.—How many papers in number have you?

Mr. Sm.—Here are 31 papers in number, that I have here.

Mr. Sp.—Besides the 3 bookes?

Mr. Sm.—With the 3 bookes.

Mr. Sp.—Have you the Examinations you tooke yourselfe?

Mr. Sm.—I have the Examinations I tooke myselfe here. The 3 bookes are as I had them from the Secretary, save that I have made a figure of the outside of them.

Mr. Smith withdraws.   Mr. Leigh Bankes brought in.

Mr. Ba.—Supposing that Taffe and Lunt had been people to trapan me, ou Monday I went and tendred it to my Lord Chiefe Justice.   I told him I had conversed with a villan.   Hee said he did not think it propper to take it then, but would take time to consider of it till 4 a'clocke and (*sic*) the aforenoon.   Hee then told me it would not bee proper then, but he thought it would bee serviceable to the gentlemen, in case they should be tryed.

Mr. Sp.—This was before the tryall?

Mr. B.—·This was the 28th.   The 27th I was with Taffe ; the 1st of October I tendered the Afidavid to my Lord Chiefe [Justice], and I think the gentlemen went down on the 9th or 10th.

Mr. Sp.—Have you a coppye of the Affidavit you tendered to my Lord Chiefe Justice?

Mr. B.—I left it in the countrey.   There was one of Mr. Beresford's, a second of Mr. Bagshaw's, my own was the third.

Mr. Sp.—Did you give this information upon the tryall of the gentlemen, in Lancashire?

Mr. B.—I gave very little but my own there.

Mr. Sp.—Was you examined as a witness there?

Mr. B.—Yes, and I gave the evidence there that I have given here.

Mr. Sp.—Did you tell any other circu[mstance]   .   .   .   you doe now here?

Mr. B.—I doe not remember any now.

Mr. Sp.—You say the coppeys of those affidavits that you offered to my Lord Chiefe Justice, are in the countrey?

Mr. B.—Yes, I left them with Mr. Pigott, a lawyer in Lancashire. Hee hath mine and the declaration I made, after I had been conversing with Taffe.

Mr. Sp.—Did Mr. Berresford goe with you to my Lord Chiefe Justice?

Mr. B.—Mr. Beresford and Mr. Bagshaw went both with me to my Lord Chief Justice.

Mr. Sp.—You say you heard from severall persons that Mr. Taffe could discover the villiany?

Mr. B.—Mr. Beresford lay at my chamber and sayd it would be dangerous for us to goe about to detect, etc.   Mr. Taffe's wife went to Mrs. Dickonson; she related it to one of the gentlemen in the countrey ; she sayd she never saw Mr. Taffe himself, but his wife had come crying, several times, and said she was sorry for her landlord.   Mr. Dickonson, says she, my husband can descover a great part of the villiany if any gentleman—

Mr. Sp.—Did you hear it from any other person?

Mr. B.—Mrs. Dickonson told me to the same effect, for Mr. Beresford had it from her.

Mr. Bankes withdraws.   Mr. Bankes brought in again.

Mr. Sp.—I am commanded by the House to ask you severall questions.   First, how long have you been acquainted with Mr. Taffe?

Mr. B.—I had noe acquaintance with Mr. Taffe before the tyme I met him about this buisness.

Mr. Sp.—When was the first time?

Mr. B.—The 27th Sep., when the prisoners came to Coventry.   I went down to meet them to pay my respects to Mr. Lee, and I dined at the same house the witnesses did, and I knew him when I saw him again.

Mr. Sp.—This discourse you speake was after they were brought to town?

Mr. B.—Yes, within 9 or 10 days of their going down. I knew him, and he knew mee again, and he asked me if I did not come as a spy at Coventry.

Mr. Sp.—What did you answer?

Mr. B.—We heard there was a parcel of King's evidence at Coventry, soe I and some gentlemen went to dine with them out of curiosity. I did not see him afterwards till September.

Mr. Sp.—Had you any discourse with Mr. Taffe at Coventry?

Mr. B.—Noe, only there was a merrey gentleman with me, and he asked him a great many of questions.

Mr. Sp.—Who was that gentleman?

Mr. B.—His name was Mr. Milward, clarke to my Lord Lovelace's troop. I went down from hence to Coventry. I came on Sonday, and went away again on Monday morning.

Mr. Sp.—Did hee come backe with you on Monday?

Mr. Ba.—No, I left him there; he was about his concerns there, paying of quarters.

Mr. Sp.—You say you heard some of the King's evidence were in a house and you went to see them?

Mr. Ba.—Mr. Milward knew the house. I designed to dine with Mr. Lee and the rest of the prisoners, but at night, we asked what a number of people was there. They sayd there was a parcell of Captain Baker's servants, soe wee supposed they must be good men, and wee went among them to dine with them.

Mr. Sp.—Who did you meet at dinner?

Mr. Ba.—There was Mr. Milward, the only man I knew, the landlord of the house, Mr. Taffe, and 4 or 5 scoundrell fellows.

Mr. Sp.—Did you or Mr. Milward ask any questions relating to the evidence against the gentlemen?

Mr. Ba.—Yes, Mr. Milward did, but Mr. Taffe, taking us to be strangers, was very shy in answering of them. I sayd very little to them, but laughed at them.

Mr. Sp.—Why did you looke upon Mr. Taffe as a dangerous man?

Mr. Ba.—I saw his name in a certain pamphlet directed to my Lord Chiefe Justice Holt.

Mr. Sp.—Was that letter printed before 27th?

Mr. Ba.—Yes, a considerable while before.

Mr. Sp.—What evidence did you give at the tryall, concerning Lunt's having told you that, as soon as these gentlemen were taken off, there would be a further prosecution against severall other gentlemen?

Mr. Ba.—I forgot to tell you that upon Lunt's reading his narrative, that a vast number were concerned. I asked him how it came to pass that soe few were taken up Says bee, it is noe matter, for that, for after wee have cut off 3 or 4 of these, we shall run through the body of England; there is not a county of England shall escape us.

Mr. Sp.—But was this all you said upon this head when you gave your evidence at Manchester?

Mr. Ba.—Yes; I do not remember anything more that I said. I remember one thing more, but I do not know that I did say it at Manchester. Hee said he delivered a commission to one Lee, of Lime. and one Shalcross, and Beresford. I asked him what Beresford sayes. Is he not a tall black man? He said he was a tall black man, and knew him very well, and Mr. Beresford is a middle sized man and weares a flaxen wigg.

Mr. Sp.—Had you any coppye of the narrative?

Mr. Ba.—Hee said, at our next meeting, I should have a coppye of the narrative, and some forged commissions from King James. I asked him how hee would have King James' hand, and I understood he had King James' hand.

Mr. Sp.—Did he read over all the narrative?

Mr. Ba.—I was then under an apprehension of their being all rogues, and did not take much notice of it. Mr. Taffe read it. I know not whether Lunt can read or noe.

Mr. Sp.—Did Taffe tell you?

Mr. Ba.—Mr. Taffe said Lunt would have brought him to be witness, but Mr. Taffe told him he did not care to swear himself, but he would bring him some other persons.

Mr. Sp.—I am to ask you what you know concerning some warrants issued out against any persons for suborning witnesses against the King's evidence.

Mr. Ba.—I know nothing of that, only the common report that there were warrants against some, for suborning persons to descredit the King's witnesses. I had a caution given me by some of my friends. I heard they were against me and Mr. Beresford. I heard it from a woman, but it might bee only her feares.

Mr. Sp.—You say you looked upon Mr. Taffe to bee a dangerous man, and the reason was because you found his name in a libell; had you noe other reason?

Mr. Ba.—That made me the more to enquire what he was, and I heard hee was a runagate priest. I heard hee was a chiefe evidence in this plott, but I foud him very just, after he did pretend to discover this matter.

Mr. Sp.—When you mett Lunt and Taffe, who shewed it you?

Mr. Ba.—Mr. Lunt pulled it out of his pocquett and he gave it to Mr. Taffe. Wee stood in a cluster, and I looked upon it and said it was a good handwriting. Mr. Taffe read it.

Mr. Sp.—How much did he read of it?

Mr. Ba.—I think he did not read it all.

Mr. Sp.—How much?

Mr. Ba.—I cannot bee positive.

Mr. Sp.—What was the subject matter of the narrative; can you remember the names of the persons mentioned in it?

Mr. Ba.—Noe; but it named the persons in custody and some others. I found very few captains, but there was a pretty many colonels and leiutenat-colonels.

Mr. Sp.—In the narrative Mr. Taffe read, there were severall persons named to bee in the conspiracy, besides those gentlemen that were tryed. I aske you now to declare as many of those persons' names as you can.

Mr. Ba.—Really, at that time, I thought only of Mr. Lee, he being a near relation; not thinking but I should have another opportunity, I tooke notice of very little but that.

Mr. Sp.—Cannot you remember none of the names?

Mr. Ba.—Noe, indeed, sir, I cannot.

Mr. Sp.—You were speaking of Lievetenant-colonels?

Mr. Ba.—He named Mr. Lee as Colonel of Horse, and Mr. Shacroft as Lievetenant-colonel, and Mr. Beresford as Captain.

Mr. Sp.—You said there was Commissions to bee writt over, &c. How was it that you came to understand that Lunt had something under King James' hand?

Mr. Ba.—I asked him how he would get King James' hand, and how he would counterfeit it, unless he had some of King James' handwriting, and I understood him that he had a commission of King James in his pocket, for he said he would doe it effectually. Mr. Taffe and he afterwards went to the window, and he pulled out an old parchment; what it was I cannot tell.

Mr. Sp.—You said Mr. Taffe asked you whether you were not a spy, when you were at Coventry; where was that question asked you?

Mr. Ba.—When I met him, the 27th September, at one Barns his house in Brownlow Street, in Drury Lane; that was the day I mett Mr. Taffe.

Mr. Leigh Bankes withdraws. Called in again.

Mr. Sp.—I am commanded to ask you, when he went to my Lord Chiefe Justice and tendered him those affidavits, what reason did he give why he would not take them?

Mr. Ba.—My Lord said it was not proper at that time, and he thought he would not take them, and he would take it into consideration, and he desired me to come again at 4 in the afternoon, and accordingly I did come, and then he said it was discursing the King's evidence, and it was not proper, but in case the gentlemen should be tryed, it would bee of service to the gentlemen.

Mr. Sp.—Did my Lord Chiefe Justice direct you to goe to any other person?

Mr. Ba.—Noe. I prayed my Lord Chiefe Justice to advise me whether I might proceed with safety any further with these fellows, and hee told me I knew my own business best, he could not advise me.

Mr. Sp.—You were pleased to say, when you mett Taffe and Lunt there was an appointment to meet him on the Saturday after, and that you and Mr. Beresford did advise about going to meet him, and that you did not thinke fitt to meet him any more. The House hath commanded mee to aske you who you advised with?

Mr. Ba.—If I must give answer to it, it was Sir Bartholomew Shower.

[Mr. Sp.]— . . . . . made a proposall to you of swearing [to] some things, as he should direct you, wer you to swear the whole narrative, or some particular point? He made a proposition to you of swearing a falsity; what proposall did hee make you of a rewarde for it?

Mr. Ba.—All he said was that if I did him service, I should be plentifully provided for. I told him it was a shrewd temptation, and I should doe him what service lay in my power.

Mr. Sp.—Did you ask him how much?

Mr. Ba.—Wee were not come to bargain, for on Saturday after, I was to have received further instructions.

Mr. Sp.—Well, hee did not propose to you any particular sume, or any estate?

Mr. Ba.—Noe, sir, hee said I should bee plentifully provided for, and I seemed satisfied with it.

Mr. Leigh Bankes withdraws. Called in again.

[Mr. Sp.]—I am commanded . . . . questions. When . . . . again on Saturday yo . . . . . . was to goe to the Secretary's . . . you had had it under his hand to goe to the Secretary, and clear these gentlemen. Why did you not meet Lunt on Saturday, according to appointment?

Mr. Ba.—I and Mr. Beresford advised about it, and we thought it might be dangerous to the gentlemen.

Mr. Sp.—Why did not you goe to the Secretary's and discover what you had already found out, for you had sufficiently found out that this was a conspiracy and design against the gentlemen, by what discourse you had with Lunt and Taffe?

Mr. Ba.—I acquainted my Lord Chiefe Justice with it, and I thought he was fitter to represent to the Secretary than I was.

Mr. Sp.—How long was it after the Saturday ?

Mr. Ba.—On Monday morning after, about 10 o'clock . . . . .

24th November, [16]94.

[Mr. Taffe brought in.]

Mr. Sp.—Pray, Mr. Taffe, where is your house; where do you live ?

Mr. Taffe.—I live in Berry St., by St. James'.

Mr. Sp.—When was it that Lunt came to you first?

Mr. Ta.—A little after Christmas, I tooke noe note of it. It is easily known, because he hath given an information, to the Secretary of State, of the very time.

Mr. Sp.—What doe you mean by a little after Christmas ?

Mr. Ta.—I believe it might be a month or 6 weeks.

Mr. Taffe withdraws. Brought in again.

Mr. Sp.—I am commanded by the House to ask you severall questions, which most part of them do arise from the narrative that you have made to the House, and they expect you should explain it. You say your house is in Berry Street. How long have you lived there ?

Mr. Ta.—I have lived there a year and halfe at Christmas.

Mr. Sp.—But where did you live before ?

Mr. Ta.—In St. James' St., next street to it.

Mr. Sp.—How long there ?

Mr. Ta.—Since the Revolution.

Mr. Sp.—What do you mean by since ?

Mr. Ta.—From the begining.

Mr. Sp.—Did you know a gentleman called Count Taffe ?

Mr. Ta.—I never saw him.

Mr. Sp.—What Count Taffe is it you know ?

Mr. Ta.—I know him that was killed at the Boyne.

Mr. Sp.—Where did he lodge when he was here in town ?

Mr. Ta.—He lived in Wild House, and was sent Embassador into Germany, and then he went to France and thence to Ireland, [to] the Earl of Carlingford.

Mr. Sp.—Did any person under the name of Count Taffe lye at your house ?

Mr. Ta.—Noe, sir, never.

Mr. Sp.—Did my Lord Car[lingford] lye at your house ?

Mr. Ta.—Noe.

Mr. Sp.—Did any letter come to your house directed to Count Taffe ?

Mr. Ta.—Not as I know of.

Mr. Sp.—Did any letter come enclosed to you directed to any person called Count Taffe ?

Mr. Ta.—That could not be, for Count Taffe, in Germany, is a man I never had corrospondance with, and as for the Earl of Carlingford, I never saw him since he went into Germany; the reason was, I was of the Church of Rome, and changed my religion; the Bishopps were sent to the Tower, and I have had noe correspondence with them since.

Mr. Sp.—Did ever any letter that was directed to you, either by mistake of direction or any other wayes, come to the hands of Count Taffe ?

Mr. Ta.—Noe, not as I know of; but there was a yonge man, some tyme last yeare, that received a letter, directed to me by the penny post; the penny post that brought my letter asked for one Taffe, and they directed him to the King's Head, and he opened it, and came and beged my pardon, and sayd there was a letter soe directed, but it was not to him; but it was a letter of no consequence.

Mr. Sp.—What was in that letter?

Mr. Ta.—I cannot tell, but it was a letter of no consequence.

Mr. Sp.—Did you inquire who the yonge man was; did you know him?

Mr. Ta.—Noe, truly, I do not thinke I do.

Mr. Sp.—Have you the letter?

Mr. Ta.—I threw it upon the table, I know not what is become of it.

Mr. Sp.—Did Lunt goe down in a borrowed name?

Mr. Ta.—Yes, by the name of one Smith. I asked Captain Baker why he would bring the witnesses down; he sayd he had a particular reason, but would not tell it. Then I asked Mr. Lunt. Sayes he, you must know I do not know these houses, and soe I goe to them, that I may know the place and people, and, sayes he, I have fixed upon a matted roome or matted gallery. And; sayes he, I will sweare to that place, for, in my narrative, I have not put it down the particular place, but I will put it into my information, when I come to London.

Mr. Sp.—When was this discourse?

Mr. Ta.—It was at Wigan.

Mr. Sp.—Who was present when you discoursed this with Lunt?

Mr. Ta.—Noebody, for I called him aside to discourse with him.

Mr. Sp.—Had you noe time to aske Lunt this question, till you came to Wigan?

Mr. Ta.—It never came into my mind till then. The countrey people said, that those people that were come to take them up are to be witnesses.

Mr. Sp.—What do you know of any articles for dureing of the gentlemen's estates, that were thus prosecuted?

Mr. Ta.—There are a great many articles. I know not the contents of them. There were articles made between Mr. Wybraham and others.

Mr. Sp.—How many articles doe you mean?

Mr. Ta.—There were several gentlemen that made articles with the undertakers, about begging their estates of the King.

Mr. Sp.—When were those articles made?

Mr. Ta.—There have been severall, since these 4 yeares. Some articles were between the Marquis of Winchester and Mr. Samd(?) and Mr. Wybraham, and between Sir Scroope How and Sir J. Guise.

Mr. Sp.—When were these articles made?

Mr. Ta.—Some tyme the last yeare. The articles are in being, if this House desire them to be produced.

Mr. Sp.—You speake of articles. Doe you know of any articles that you are a witness to?

Mr. Ta.—Noe.

Mr. Sp.—How do you know that there were articles?

Mr. Ta.—I know nothing but what they told me. There were articles between Mr. Wybraham, Goddard, and Hall. I saw them in Wybraham's hand and Captain Baker's hand. They were left at my house once.

Mr. Sp.—Did you read them?

Mr. Ta.—Yes, sir.

Mr. Sp.—Why were they left at your house?

Mr. Ta.—Mr. Wybraham went out of town, and he left all his writings, to keep for him in my scrutore. There was a noise they were in trust for the witnesses. Says I, I will have nothing to do with them.

Mr. Sp.—Why did you looke into them?

Mr. Ta.—He gave me leave, and we read them together.

Mr. Sp.—Why did you deliver them to Mr. Baker, without Wybraham's leave?

Mr. Ta.—There was a report that these articles were in trust for me, because in my custody, and to shew they were not, I delivered them to Captain Baker, for he was undertaker of the whole matter.

Mr. Sp.—Were you to have noe share?

Mr. Ta.—Not as I know of. They told me when the business was done, they would reward me very well.

Mr. Sp.—What doe you know of articles about their estates in Lancashire?

Mr. Ta.—I know of noe other. It was the estates of 2 or 3 gentlemen at Manchester, for setting their estates to superstitious uses.

Mr. Sp.—Pray tell mee what was your share?

Mr. Ta.—I do not know. They never specified to me anything in particular, but said I should be well rewarded.

Mr. Sp.—Who is your trustee among all these men?

Mr. Ta.—Truly I have none at all.

Mr. Sp.—What were you to doe?

Mr. Ta.—I was to be rewarded for making a discovery.

Mr. Sp.—Were you examined as a witness?

Mr. Ta.—Yes, in the Exchequer, upon the Commissions of Inquiry, in the countrey.

Mr. Sp.—When you were here last, you acquainted the House that Captain Baker tooke you along with him, to assist him to take the gentlemen in the countrey; I ask you whether you did see the list of the gentlemen that were to be taken up?

Mr. Ta.—Yes, I saw the list in Lunt's narrative, and warrants against them.

Mr. Sp.—I ask you if you saw any list in Captain Baker's hands, or any other person's hands, of the persons to bee taken up?

Mr. Ta.—I did not see it at that tyme, but I saw it before, when they were writeing, when Lunt brought the narrative to Mr. Leigh Bankes.

Mr. Sp.—When; who was writeing of them?

Mr. Ta.—When? Captain Baker's clarke and he himself.

Mr. Sp.—Had you ever any coppy of them?

Mr. Ta.—Noe, sir; I had a list of them, but I cannot tell what has become of it.

Mr. Sp.—Can you remember any of their names?

Mr. Ta.—There was my Lord Molineux, Garrard, Stanley, Clifton, Dickinson, Standish, Girlington, Blundell, Langton, Jackson, Wood, Wilson, Lee, Townley, Gerrard, and Esquire Molineux.

Mr. Sp.—Did you see any of the warrants?

Mr. Ta.—Yes.

Mr. Sp.—Were there warrants against all those?

Mr. Ta.—Yes.

Mr. Sp.—Were they all taken up?

Mr. Ta.—Noe, a great many got away; Standish and Esquire Molineux made his (sic) escape.

Mr. Sp.—You saw Lunt's narrative. Did you read it over?

Mr. Ta.—Yes.

Mr. Sp.—Can you remember the names that were in that narrative?

Mr. Ta.—I can remember some of them. Most of the gentlemen that I have named were in. In the first narrative, there was the Marquis of Carmarthen, Lord Hallifax, Sir John Manwaring, Ashby, Lord Nottingham, but they broke the list, for they asked mee my opinion of it, and I told them if they accused those gentlemen, they were soe much for the government, they would not be believed.

Mr. Sp.—Who shewed you this narrative ?

Mr. Ta.—Lunt was the chiefe. There was Captain Baker. I thought it to be a reall thing then. Says I, I know not but they may be guilty, but you will not be believed.

Mr. Sp.—Where was it ?

Mr. Ta.—In Captain Baker's office.

Mr. Sp.—Now I ask you, was the narrative that Lunt produced when Mr. Leigh Bankes and you and Lunt were together, was that the same narrative ?

Mr. Ta.—Noe, that narrative was the narrative when the plott was perfect ; upon that they grounded it.

Mr. Sp.—Did they make any more narratives but one, before they made that ?

Mr. Ta.—They have made severall broken papers—rough draughts—but I never saw any other in forme, that was approved.

Mr. Sp.—You read over the narrative, did not you ? Pray give an account to the House, of the names of the persons that were named and mentioned in the narrative.

Mr. Ta.—As far as I can remember, there was my Lord Mollineux, Sir William Gerrard, and all that were taken up, and one Symonds.

Mr. Sp.—Was there any there in any other countyes than Lancashire and Cheshire ?

Mr. Ta.—Yes, there was one; I thinke Wilson named Symonds.

Mr. Sp.—I ask you whether there were any other gentlemen that you know of, of any other countyes, named in that narrative ; not what Wilson told you ?

Mr. Ta.—Truly, to the best of my remembrance, I thinke there were some Yorkshire gentlemen. I think my Lord Dunbarr was there, Sir John Lawson, but I am not positive, because I am not acquainted with those gentlemen ; and severall of the men taken up in Kent, that were to murder the King, I think were in it.

Mr. Sp.—Doe you know any particular county in England, one more than the other ?

Mr. Ta.—Lancashire.

Mr. Sp.—Was there any more you have not named in Lancashire ?

Mr. Ta.—Not that I remember at present.

Mr. Sp.—You were speaking of Roger Dickonson, and sayd that when you and Lunt and he were together, you sayd Lunt turned you out of the room ?

Mr. Ta.—They desired mee to goe out of the room, soe I went down stayres.

Mr. Sp.—What did they say to you when you came up ?

Mr. Ta.—That they had agreed an appointment to meet in the after-noon.

Mr. Sp.—Doe you know Mr. Dickinson ?

Mr. Ta.—Hee said he was a Roman Catholic, but was brought up in the Church of England.

Mr. Sp.—When was the first time that you and Mr. Bankes met together ?

Mr. Ta.—Sir, I cannot call to mind at present, but it was about a month or 3 weeks before the tryall.

Mr. Sp.—When did you meet the first time ?

Mr. Ta.—It was in Russell Street, at one Mr. Banister's house, where Mr. Dickinson appointed mee to meet him. I am not positive it is Russell Street. I was never there before ; it is in Bloomsbury.

Mr. Sp.—Who was with you besides Mr. Bankes ?

Mr. Ta.—There was noebody but hee and I.

Mr. Sp.—Who was it told you he was to meet you there ?

Mr. Ta.—Mr. Dickinson.

Mr. Sp.—Were you there first, or Mr. Bankes ?

Mr. Ta.—I thinke I was there first.

Mr. Sp.—Who brought Mr. Bankes into the room to you ?

Mr. Ta.—The woman of the house ; shee knew we were to meet there.

Mr. Sp.—What was the next time ?

Mr. Ta.—The next morning.

Mr. Sp.—Where was that ?

Mr. Ta. -- Att his chamber in Gray's Inn.

Mr. Sp.—Who was with him there ?

Mr. Ta.—Mr. Beresford and another gentleman.

Mr. Sp.—Was there any more in the company but you and Mr. Leigh Bankes and Mr. Beresford and the other gentleman ?

Mr. Ta.—Noe, sir.

Mr. Sp.—When was the next time you and Mr. Banks mett ?

Mr. Ta.—That very afternoon.

Mr. Sp.—Where was that ?

Mr. Ta.—At the 'Ship' alehouse, in the Butcher Row, without Temple Barr.

Mr. Sp.—Who mett you there ?

Mr. Ta.—Mr. Lunt and I came there first, and when wee had been there a little while, Mr. Leigh Banks and Mr. Beresford came in and took a room and sent for mee. They were loth to speake with Mr. Lunt, but I perswaded them to speake with him. Mr. Beresford went away, and I brought Mr. Lunt to Mr. Banks, and wee were all three together.

Mr. Sp.—Was there any other persons at that meeting but Mr. Lunt and you and Mr. Leigh Banks and Mr. Beresford ?

Mr. Ta.—Noe, but Mr. Beresford did not speak to Mr. Lunt.

Mr. Sp.—When was the next time you mett with Mr. Leigh Banks ?

Mr. Ta.—I saw him very often, almost every day.

Mr. Sp.—When was the next time you and Mr. Leigh Banks mett ?

Mr. Ta.—I came to his chamber next morning again, and then found him shy of mee, because they had had some lawyer's advise, and I went to see if he had got another man to goe with him, and then I went to Mrs. Dickinson, and then I found Mr. Roger Dickinson.

Mr. Sp.—After the meeting you had in the Butcher Row, was there any other appointment between you and Mr. Leigh Banks and Mr. Beresford to meet ?

Mr. Ta.—There was noe meeting between Mr. Lunt and Leigh Banks and mee, afterwards, but wee appointed, that night, to meet next morning, but Mr. Leigh Banks would not come.

Mr. Sp.—Where ?

Mr. Ta.—Wee did not fix on any particular place then, but I was to give Mr. Lunt notice of it.

Mr. Sp.—What was the meeting you talked of ?

Mr. Ta.—We were to meet somewhere thereabouts, and then to goe into the Savoy and counterfeit comissions. The reason wee were to goe into the Savoy was because Mr. Lunt would goe to noe place but some priviledged place, for he was afraid to bee taken up.

Mr. Sp.—When did you come to Lunt to tell him of this meeting in the Savoy ?

Mr. Ta.—I was to come to him the next morning.

Mr. Sp.—Did you goe to Lunt first, or Mr. Leigh Banks?

Mr. Ta.—I was to goe to Mr. Leigh Banks first, and accordingly did goe to him first, but Mr. Banks was shy, and instead of bringing Mr. Leigh Banks, I brought Mr. Roger Dickinson.

Mr. Sp.—What house were you in at the Savoy?

Mr. Ta.—Wee never were there.

Mr. Sp.—Where was it that Lunt was taken by the constable?

Mr. Ta —Att a little coffee house in Fetter Lane.

Mr. Sp.—Who was there at the time when he was taken?

Mr. Ta.—None but he and I.

Mr. Sp.—Where was it that Mr. Banks went away?

Mr. Ta.—It was at that coffee house. He came with Mr. Dickonson and Mr. Beresford, but hearing of a constable, they went of. Mr. Banks did not see Lunt there.

Mr. Sp.—You say Capt. Baker writt a letter to you into Lancashire, and that you answered that letter again?

Mr. Ta.—Yes, sir.

Mr. Sp.—Have you that letter that Capt. Baker writt to you?

Mr. Ta.—Yes, I have it in my pocket. It is directed to an attorney that it might the better come to mee. [He read the letter at Barr.] Mr. Barrow was the attorney that was employed for the Comission below, and he had layd out some money, and I wrote to Capt. Baker to get him paid.

Mr. Sp.—You say you had severall discourses with Mr. Smith and Capt. Baker. Pray how many meetings had you with Mr. Smith?

Mr. Ta.—I had noe meeting ever with Mr. Smith, but by chances; when Mr. Lunt was taken up by a constable, he then came to goe with him before my Lord Mayor. That was the time I had most discourse with him.

Mr. Sp.—How long since is it that you knew Mr. A[aron] Smith?

Mr. Ta.—I never had familiarity with that man, but he used to come often to Capt. Baker's office. But when I came out of the countrey, I went to him about an horse I had hired. Mr. Baker directed me to Mr. Smith, and he sayd he had noe order to doe any such thing. That was the first time I spoke to him and had any conversation with him. The second time hee came to baile Mr. Lunt, and then hee called me aside, and said it was a sad thing, he was an ill man; and he desired me to goe to my Lord Mayor's, and because I told him Lunt had two wifes, he turned me off.

Mr. Sp.—You sayd you had some offers of money by Mrs. Dickinson?

Mr. Ta.—They did not offer mee money, but they asked me what summe I would have and name my summe, and I should have what I pleased, for they had resolved, if I had named any summe, they would not have taken any notice of me, and when I told them I did not do it for reward, they thought I was reall.

Mr. Sp.—But how did you know this before?

Mr. Ta.—I knew it but since; they told mee soe.

Mr. Sp.—Have you had any money since?

Mr. Ta.—I have had money to bear my charges up and down.

Mr. Sp.—Have you had money from those gentlemen?

Mr. Ta.—Yes, I had 6l. to bear my charges down, and post. And when the tryalls were over in Chester, Mr. Beresford, that payd the charge of the witnesses, asked me if I wanted money for my charges, soe he gave me 20l. I told him I had been there a fortnight.

Mr. Sp.—Who paid you the 6l.?

Mr. Ta.—It was sent to mee by Mr. Leigh Banks.

Mr. Sp.—Have you had any more money?

Mr. Ta.—Noe, sir.

Mr. Sp.—You say you went down with Lunt and Capt. Baker into those countreys. How instrumental were you now to Capt. Baker or Mr. Lunt? What hand had you in seizing of horses?

Mr. Ta.—I had noe hand in it; there were 4 messengers and they toke 4 parts, and I went with one when hee tooke up Sir William Gerrard, and was at Standish Hall when that was searched, and was then about seizing of horses and seaching for armes.

Mr. Sp.—What other service did you doe?

Mr. Ta.—That is all.

Mr. Sp.—But it is pretty strange that Capt. Baker and Lunt should carrey you into the countrey and you should not bee more servicable than this?

Mr. Ta.—The reason was, Capt. Baker did not care to trust him soe far with these men, and he was willing to have my advice.

Mr. Sp.—And you did advise from time to time?

Mr. Ta.—Yes, I gave him my advise as well as I could.

Mr. Sp.—What way of living have you in this town?

Mr. Ta.—I have an house and let lodgings. I have a pension from the King; the King allowed me 100l. a yeare.

Mr. Sp.—How long have you had it?

Mr. Ta.—About 3 or 4 yeares.

Mr. Sp.—Upon what account had you that pension?

Mr Ta.—My Lord Bellamont introduced me to the King, and spake for me, as I had been a sufferer in King James' time and had noe estate to live upon.

Mr. Sp.—What sufferer were you in King James' time?

Mr. Ta.—When the seven Bishops were sent to the Tower, I changed my religion. I was a clergyman of the Church of Roome, and asked to say mass at the Pope's Nuncio's, and after, came into England and had a designe to change my religion, and thought I could not have a better time for it than when popery was in its height, to shew the world I did not doe for interest, and soe the day the Bishopps were sent to the Tower, I recanted before Mr. Tenison, and afterwards I was trapanned and put into prison, and lay there 28 days. I had a knife to cut my victualls, and with that cut through the bricks and got out and leaped into the garden, and then put on my clothes and got a ladder and got atop of the wall, and leaped into the street and broke my leg, and lay there a good while. There was an acquaintance of mine, a Roman Catholic; I thought if I could get to his house, he would save mee, so I went as well as I could to his house, and he received mee, and keept me till I was pretty well, and lent me his horse and clothes and sent me to Dunkirke, and came over at that time King James went to Salisbury Place, and my bookes, my writings, and clothes, were all taken from my lodgings. I cannot say the pension was granted particularly for that, but Lord Bellamount had some business in the countrey, and desired me to goe along with him, and when I came home, he spake for mee to the King, and said I was very serviceable.

Mr. Sp.—What were you to doe for my Lord Bellamount?

Mr. Ta.—This was one reason. Wee went into the country to follow one Shynner that was gone into Ireland. My Lord Bellamount was sent to examine him.

Mr. Sp.—How many pentions have you received?

Mr. Ta.—It is about 3 or 4 yeares.

Mr. Sp.—When was the last payment paid you?

Mr. Ta.—At our Lady day last.

Mr. Sp.—What, are you in arrear then?

Mr. Ta.—Noe more but from that time.

Mr. Sp.—Were you paid it yearly, half yearly, or quarterly ?

Mr. Ta.—Every halfe yeare.

Mr. Sp.—How much is due to you now ?

Mr. Ta.—3 quarters at Christmas.

Mr. Sp.—Have you demanded what was due ?

Mr. Ta.—Yes, my wife has.

Mr. Sp.—From whom ?

Mr. Ta.—-From my Lord Portland's secretary. The first time she went, he told her it would come in two days, then she went and he put her off till next Monday.

Mr. Sp.—You say you never saw Lunt till after Christmas ?

Mr. Ta.—Noe, I doe not say soe, but I say he came to my house, at that time, to acquaint me of the plott ; but I have known him 2 years before that time.

Mr. Sp.—How come you to bee acquainted with Lunt, and how long have you been acquainted with him before Christmas last, and upon what occasion ?

Mr. Ta.—I cannot possitively, but the year is remarkable ; it was when the French were beaten by Admiral Russell. The Easter Monday before la Hogue buisness, he came to my house in St. James', and told me he was newly come from Lancashire, and that he had married my wife's sister. I asked him what name, and he said Capt. Witherington. Says, I, what is your religion ? Says he, a Roman Catholicke, and I would faigne goe to King James. Says I, if you would goe to King James, I will have nothing to do with you. Hee delivered a letter of recomendation to Mr. Walmsley, in France. Afterwards, he was taken and comitted to the Gate House, and I never saw him afterwards, till after last Christmas.

Mr. Sp.—When did you carry Mr. Lunt to my Lord Bellamount ?

Mr. Ta.—It was a little after Christmas last.

Mr. Sp.—About what time, doe you thinke ?

Mr. Ta.—As I told you before, it may bee a month, or 6 weeks, or 3 weekes ; I cannot tell.

Mr. Sp.—Had hee been with the Secretary before you carryed him to my Lord Bellamount ?

Mr. Ta.—It was after, for my Lord Bellamount spake for him to the Secretary of State.

Mr. Sp.—Is there any relacion betwixt you and Mr. Lunt ?

Mr. Ta.—He told me he marryed my wife's sister, but he had a wife before, soe it was but a cheat upon her.

Mr. Sp.—Did you see the passe that Mr. Lunt had from my Lord Melford ?

Mr. Ta.—Yes, Mr. Lunt has it, I suppose.

Mr. Sp.—Did you see it in Lunt's hands ?

Mr. Ta.—Yes, I read it, and it is in French.

Mr. Sp.—When did you see that passe first ?

Mr. Ta.—The first day he came to mee.

Mr. Sp.—Did you see it at any time afterwards ?

Mr. Ta.—When I brought him to my Lord Bellamount, he shewed it to him and severall people, to Capt. Baker.

Mr. Sp.—You mentioned some money that was given to witness. Pray, by whom was that money given, and what money ?

Mr. Ta.—I was never at the payment of any considerable summe, but Capt. Baker payd them money, and Aaron Smith at other times, as they told mee.

Mr. Sp.—Did you see any money payd ?

Mr. Ta.—I doe not remember I was present at any payment, but I have seen them come with summes of money from Capt. Baker and Mr. Smith, and shewed me they have had guinneas.

Mr. Sp.—Did Capt. Baker ever tell you that he had paid money?

Mr. Ta.—Yes, he said there was 50 guinneas, and that Mr. Lunt and he had divided it. Capt. Baker said he had only 10 of it.

Mr. Sp—Did Aron Smith ever say that he gave any money?

Mr. Ta.—Noe, I do not remember he did.

Mr. Sp.—For what was this money?

Mr. Ta.—It was to maintain the witnesses and encourage them, and that Mr. Lunt might goe among his friends and see whether they would come in with him and confirme what he said. Wilson, that had not bread to eat before, was tempted with soe many guineas.

Mr. Sp.—What doe you remember of the narrative that Mr. Lunt drew out when Mr. Bankes was there? What doe you remember, besides the names of the persons?

Mr. Ta.—I remember he declared he followed King James into France, and from thence into Ireland, and that he was introduced to King James by my Lord T. Howard and George Howard, and they told him he was a very trusty man, and that he was sent with one Melford to carry comissions, and that they landed in Lancashire, and had delivered comissions to the severall gentlemen in custody, and how they kissed the comissions, and drunke King James' health, and gave them money.

Mr. Sp.—Have you any coppye of the narrative?

Mr. Ta.—I had a coppye of some of it, but I can't tell what has become of it.

Mr. Sp.—What is Capt. Baker's office?

Mr. Ta.—A place they call his office.

Mr. Sp.—Why doe you call it an office?

Mr. Ta.—It is a name they gave it. It was appointed to examine what money the dissenters had payd in King Charles' time.

Mr. Sp.—Who was that divided among?

Mr. Ta.—I cannot tell.

Mr. Sp.—You were saying Mrs. Dicconson was very much concerned to know the witnesses' names?

Mr. Ta—Yes, sir.

Mr. Sp.—Was that concern of Mrs. Dicconson and that discourse you had with her, before you spake with Mr. Leigh Banks, or after?

Mr. Ta.—Before, sir.

Mr. Sp.—How long before?

Mr. Ta.—I thinke it was about a fortnight or 10 dayes. It was at the beginning, when my wife spake to her.

Mr. Sp.—I need not ask you what religion you are of?

Mr. Ta.—I am of the Church of England.

Mr. Sp.—You were giving an account to the House, of Mr. Leigh Banks his going to my Lord Chiefe Justice. Pray, who was in company when he went to my Lord Chiefe Justice?

Mr. Ta.—I doe not know, for I did not know of their goeing till afterwards.

Mr. Sp.—Who told you of it afterwards?

Mr. Ta.—Mrs. Dickinson told mee first, and afterwards I asked Mr. Banks, and hee told mee he was there, and he told mee there was Mr. Leigh Banks and Mr. Beresford; I know not who else.

Mr. Ashton brought in.

Mr. Sp.—What countrey man are you?

Mr Ashton.—Lancashire; I lived at the 'Three Tunns,' in Bread Street.

Mr. Sp.—How long since?

A.—A matter of 6 weekes. I came out of Lancashire, and lost my place in going there.

Mr. Sp.—With whom did you live in Bread Street?

A.—Mr. Wright, I thinke they called him. I lived with him a month or 5 weeks.

Mr. Sp.—In what quality did you live with this gentleman?

A.—I was under-chamberlain.

Mr. Sp.—What doe you know of the proceedings against severall gentlemen that were indicted and tryed in the County of Lancaster and Chester?

A.—I doe not know that ever I knew any thing against them.

Mr. Sp.—What doe you know of the proceedings against them?

A.—Why, there was one Wombell, a carrier, and I was a carrier. I asked him how he lived, and he said he was the King's messenger. I asked him if he could doe me any kindness in that concerne, and he said he did not know, but he might. He asked me to come to his lodgings, and I came and lay with him, and he said he did not know but he might helpe mee to a place, in a short time, and said if I could swear that I had carryed armes for such and such a gentleman, hee would helpe mee to a place, or money to maintain me. He named Mr. Legh of Lyme, and ————. Hee said he would help mee to 50*l.* a year or 27*s.* a weeke. I told him I knew nothing of it.

Mr. Sp.—Was you at Manchester?

A.—Yes.

Mr. Sp.—Were you examined as a witness there?

A.—Yes, I gave that evidence there.

Mr. Ashton withdraws.

28 November, 1694.

Capt. Baker, after he was withdrawn, being called in again.

Mr. Sp.—I am commanded by the House to ask you severall questions upon the narrative you have made to the House, that it may be the better understood. You were pleased to say that you searched Mr. Standish's house yourself, and that you tooke some papers there; have you those papers about you?

Capt. Ba.—Yes, sir.

Mr. Sp.—What papers are they?

Capt. Ba.—There is a paper relateing to the tryall of some pyrates, the other is called Rules for Exercise. I thinke the other is a paper that I marked. I tooke it to be heads for a declaration upon the intended insurrection.

(He delivered in the papers, and that importing heads of a declaration was read by the Clarke.)

Mr. Sp.—You should acquaint the House with the matter of this paper. Did you thinke this was a paper fitt to make a declaration out of? It is fitt to be burned, and not produced to the House. Where did you find these papers?

Capt. Ba.—I found them at the house of one Mr. Standish, called Standish Hall. I found them above staires in a bed chamber.

Mr. Sp.—You say Lunt went down along with you into Cheshire; I am commanded to ask you by what name did he goe down with you?

Capt. Ba.—He went mostly by the name of Smith.

Mr. Sp.—By what other name?

Capt. Ba.—By the name of Lunt.

Mr. Sp.—Did he pretend to know any of the gentlemen that were to be taken up?

Capt. Ba.--Yes, sir, he pretended to know Mr. Leigh of Lyme.

Mr. Sp.—What house did Mr. Lunt go to, in Lancashire and Cheshire for [which] you had the warrants?

Capt. Ba.—Sir, I sent him to noe house in Lancashire or Cheshire, but only to Mr. Legh of Lyme.

Mr. Sp.—Did he obey your commands in that, or goe to any other?

Capt. Ba.—I know not that he went to any other; I gave noe warrants to Mr. Lunt, or any other but the King's messengers.

Mr. Sp.—You were speaking of Mr. Taffe, that when he returned from Cheshire and Lancashire, that he came to you for a reward, to satisfye him for his journey, and afterwards he desired you to goe along with him to Mr. A. Smith; that you did not goe with him that morning, but he went afterwards by himself, and you said you were told Mr. Taffe was angry, and threatened revenge?

Capt. Ba.—I did soe.

Mr. Sp.—Who was that person?

Capt. Ba.—There was one Dibidderon that told me he talked of revenge, and there was one Wybraham that was one in the lobby, when I came into the House.

Mr. Sp.—Where is the other?

Capt. Ba.—I doe not know where he lodges, but I believe I can find him, in a day or two.

Mr. Sp.—By whose order did Mr. Lunt goe down?

Capt. Ba.—By the Secretary.

Mr. Sp.—What Secretary?

Capt. Ba.—Both of them.

Mr. Sp.—For what reason, to what purpose, did he goe down?

Capt. Ba.—I doe not know the reason; I suppose there was cause and reason in the information before them.

Mr. Sp.—In your information to the House, you made mention of one Wilson, that I thinke you say you met at Manchester?

Capt. Ba.—I mentioned one Wilson that was taken up for high treason, among the rest; he was carryed down to Manchester, among the rest.

Mr. Sp.—Why was not he made use of as a witness?

Capt. Ba.—I cannot answer that reason, but he was upon the briefe, and the councell pressed to call him.

Mr. Sp.—Which of the King's councell did you speake to, to call Wilson?

Capt. Ba.—Sir, it was Mr. Napp that told mee hee had received hard language for pressing him to be called.

Mr. Sp.—Who was the King's councell?

Capt. Ba.—There was Sir William Williams, Serjeant Gould, and Mr. Hawles.

Mr. Sp.—But you say you spake to some of the King's councell, yourselfe?

Capt. Ba.—Yes, I did speake to Mr. Sergeant Gould and to Mr. Ball and some of the managers.

Mr. Sp.—When you pressed that hee should bee called, what answer was given to you?

Capt. Ba.—None at all.

Mr. Sp.—Did you hear the King's councell give a repremand to Mr. Napp for pressing the calling him for a witness?

Capt. Ba.—Noe, sir.

Mr. Sp.—When you were at Mr. Standish's house, you came into the lady's chamber, and the lady told you you came too late, for that she

Y

had an information, some time before, of your coming into the countrey, and since that time, you said you came to understand how the intelli·· gence came to be given?

Capt. Ba.—I did say I thought there was some reason to believe how. I believe it came from Mr. Taffe's wife, who is godmother, &c.

Mr. Sp.—You say you had money for dischargeing your expenses; pray, what money, and from whom?

Capt. Ba.—From the Secretary.

Mr. Sp.—From both or from whom?

Capt. Ba.—From both.

Mr. Sp.—Was it one summe from both, or severall summes?

Capt. Ba.—It was a summe from each, 100*l.*

Mr. Sp.—You were saying there was some discourse of Mr. Taffe's, that he should say he could serve Mr. Legh. Now, the House desires to know who it was that told you soe.

ˑCapt. Ba.—It was one Mr. Wybraham.

Mr. Sp.—What did he tell you?

Capt. Ba.—He told me he was walking with Mr. Taffe, and that he told Mr. Taffe that such a one did wonder he would be concerned in the matter. Why, says hee, why does he wonder? I am noe evidence. But, says he, there is evidence that will certainly goe to the lives of every one of them, it is soe clear. But, says he, Legh of Lyme is Protestant; for the rest, he did not care if they were hanged. He asked if he knew him, and sayd he wished he could come to some relation or friend of his, for he could put him in a way to save his life, but there was noe comeing to Lee of Lyme, for he was in the Tower.

Mr. Sp.—You say Mr. Lunt was examined; before whom was he examined?

Capt. Ba.—He was examined before the Secretary.

Mr. Sp.—Was he examined before any other person?

Capt. Ba.—They were together.

Mr. Sp.—Was he examined before any other person?

Capt. Ba.—I believe my Lord Keeper was at the Secretary's at that time; they did all ask him questions.

Mr. Sp.—Was he examined by any other persons than them 3?

Capt. Ba.—Not that I know of.

Mr. Sp.—You were speaking of some warrants that were delivered to you, when you went into the countrey?

Capt. Ba.—Yes, they were soe.

Mr. Sp.—Were the warrants all filled up when they were delivered to you?

Capt. Ba.—Every one of them, all but the directions, all but the messengers' names; the body of the warrants were all full.

Mr. Sp.—Were the persons' names inserted in the warrants against whom they were issued?

Capt. Ba.—Yes, they were.

Mr. Sp.—Were there any blanks?

Capt. Ba.—Perhaps for a Christian name, not otherwise.

Mr. Sp.—Had you any blank warrants?

Capt. Ba.—Not one. They were directed to blank such a one, messenger to their Majesties in ordinary.

Mr. Sp.—You did inform the House that about August was 12 months, you were employed in the buisness concerning finding out lands given to superstitious uses?

Capt. Ba.—I was employed to execute a comission in the countrey.

Mr. Sp.—Doe you know of any articles for dureing those lands, in case they should be discovered and found out?

Capt. Ba.—The lands were to be the King's. I never was in any articles.

Mr. Sp.—I aske you whether you know of any articles that were made, concerning the devision of such forfeited lands?

Capt. Ba.—Sir, I have heard of an order of the Lords of the Treasury, for inquireing after such lands, and that, for recovery of such lands, there should be a third parte for the undertakers, and did hear there were some persons did enter into articles to bear the charge, and that when they were recovered, they should have them amongst them, soe and soe.

Mr. Sp.—Doe you know of the undertakers' names?

Capt. Ba.—I have heard there was one Goddard Stepkyn.

Mr. Sp.—Who employed you in the comission?

Capt. Ba.—I was employed by one Docwra of London, and severall other gentlemen.

Mr. Sp.—Please to name them.

Capt. Ba.—My Lord Monmouth was one, Sir Scroope How, Sir. J. Guise.

Mr. Sp.—Any other person that you can remember?

Capt. Ba.—Not that I remember.

Mr. Sp.—Is there any determination of the matter in the Exchequer?

Capt. Ba.—Noe, sir; there is an information, but the answers some are in and others are out.

Mr. Sp.—It is still in procecution?

Capt. Ba.—Yes, sir.

Mr. Sp.—What other comissions doe you know of?

Capt. Ba.—I have heard of one in Lancashire.

Mr. Sp.—What proceedings upon that?

Capt. Ba.—There have been proceedings to the examininge of witnessees.

Mr. Sp.—What witnesses were examined in the last comissions?

Capt. Ba.—A great many. I cannot remember all their names. Mr. Taffe was examined, and one Nevill, and De la Gard, Barrow, and some others.

Mr. Sp.—Has Lunt been examined?

Capt. Ba.—Yes.

Mr. Sp.—Has Wombell?

Capt. Ba.—As to the credit of the witnesses, noe otherwise, that I remember.

Mr. Sp.—Was Wilson ever tryed?

Capt. Ba.—Wilson was never tryed.

Mr. Sp.—Were you at the tryall at Manchester? Were you there when the Grand Jury did appeare?

Capt. Ba.—Yes, sir.

Mr. Sp.—What did you observe? Did you observe there was any alteration to the pannel of the Grand Jury?

Capt. Ba.—Noe, sir; nor I believe there was none.

Mr. Sp.—There was noe names aded nor none struck out?

Capt. Ba.—Noe, sir, that I know of.

Mr. Sp.—Was you there when the prisoners were arraigned?

Capt. Ba.—I was soe, sir.

Mr. Sp.—Did you observe that the pannel of the Petit Jury was either altered or any added to it?

Capt. Ba.—The pannel of the Petit Jury there was an edition to it, and the reason was because it was supposed to be too small, for there was not above 65, soe there was an edition to 112, or 114, or 120 at the most.

Mr. Sp.—Was there any Act of Parliament or Statute read concerning pannells?

Capt. Ba.—There was a Statute read, but I cannot charge myself what Statute or to what purpose. It was something about Grand Jurys, as I remember.

Mr. Sp.—What was done upon it?

Capt. Ba.—I know nothing that was done upon it; the Grand Jury was impannelled and sworne.

Mr. Sp.—What was the occasion of the reading of it?

Capt. Ba.—Upon some speach the Judge made, they called for the booke and ordered it to be read.

Mr. Sp.—What did he say upon the reading of it?

Capt. Ba.—I cannot tell; it did not concerne me.

Mr. Sp.—Was there any declaration made by the Judges, relateing to the law upon the point whether a pannell might be altered?

Capt. Ba.—I believe there was something said that the law was soe and soe, but I cannot remember particularly what it was. The Statute that was read was not relateing to the Petit Jury, but the Grand-Jury.

Mr. Sp.—The House have been informed of an office that you keep, in the Temple?

Capt. Ba.—I am ready to give an account of those chambers they call an office. It was upon this occasion: about 2 or 3 yeares agoe, there was an order issued to some gentlemen, who had made a proposal to make a discovery of great summes levyed upon dissenters, and not paid into the Exchequer. The people that undertooke that, made some progress in it, and thought fitt to make choice of some chambers near the Exchequer office, for the purpose. They discovered 3,000l. upon Sir Thomas Jenner, and he pleaded it. Severall great summes were discovered, to the value of 20,000l. I was not one of them, but a well wisher to them, soe they called me to their assistance, I haveing laid in goale almost 2 yeares for the service of my countrey and the Protestant religion, as I tooke it, at that time. They tooke these chambers, and I lodged in them ever since they have proceeded to tryall, and there are severall summes of money paid into the King's receiver.

Mr. Sp.—Who are the undertakers?

Capt. Ba.—There was a brother of mine in it, Mr. Dockwra, and one that belonged to Sir William Godolphin.

Mr. Sp.—You say there have been examinations of witnesses upon a comission into Lancashire; has there been any indictment against any of those witnesses for perjury? And what doe you know of any *Certiorari*?

Capt. Ba.—Never that I heard. Mr. Lunt and Mr. Taffe were both witnesses, but I know of noe *Certiorari* in that matter.

Mr. Sp.—When you went down into the countrey was there any horses seized?

Capt. Ba.—Yes, a great many.

Mr. Sp.—Of what value?

Capt. Ba.—Some were worth 50l., 40l., 10l. 7l., but the lowest, I believe, was worth 7l.

Mr. Sp.—From whom were they taken?

Capt. Ba.—From a great many persons. I suppose Mr. Smith hath given in a memorial whose horses they were. I seized none. I believe a great many was returned. I believe 30 that I thought barely within the Statute. They were seized by virtue of warrants.

Mr. Sp.—How could you direct the returning of them?

Capt. Ba.—Advised it.

Mr. Sp.—Were any taken, under the value of 5l.?

Capt. Ba.—None that I know of but was returned.

Mr. Sp.—Pray, how were they disposed of?

Capt. Ba.—According to the orders I received. I believe there are a matter of 30 at Coventrey. I thinke all the rest are at London.

Mr. Sp.—Who did you give an account of these matters to?

Capt. Ba.—To the Secretary of State.

Mr. Sp.—I thought you sayd to Mr. Smith?

Capt. Ba.—I suppose he communicated my letters.

Mr. Sp.—Doe you know of any warrants that were issued against any persons to be used as witnesses for the prisoners?

Capt. Ba.—Noe, sir; there were warrants, I believe, against Mr. Taffe. I know none against any body else, nor heard any talk of it. One thing I had forgot. When we were searching at Standish Hall, after a great deale of searching, comeing into the lady's chamber, putting by the hanging by the chimney side, says the lady—Why do you put it by? upon my honour there is nothinge there in the bricks. He put in his hands, and pulled out a matter of 10 yellow swords blades and scabbords, such as the soldiers wear now.

Mr. Sp.—I thinke when you were here before you mentioned a silver chalice and a silver hilted sword that Mr. Taffe had?

Capt. Ba.—There was soe at Standish Hall, and Mr. Taffe threw by his own blacke hilted sword. I did not then contradict him, but afterwards it was sent backe because it was sould away, and caused a fowling peece to be returned, which she said was her son's.

Mr. Sp.—If you found Mr. Taffe such a filching fellow as to rob instead of searching, perhaps if you had not returned it, you might have been in danger of robbery?

Capt. Ba.—I did not take the sword to be robbery, because it looked like armes; it was seized as armes; but I did take the chalice to be robbery. I did injoyn them to goe into noe chappell.

Withdraws. Called in again.

Mr. Sp.—You have delivered a paper in here to the House, that was found at Standish Hall, that was read while you were here. Have you kept that paper ever since yourself?

Capt. Ba.—Noe, sir.

Mr. Sp.—Who did you deliver it to?

Capt. Ba.—To Mr. Aaron Smith.

Mr. Sp.—How long did he keepe it?

Capt. Ba.—I believe he might have had it for 10 days or more.

Mr. Sp.—When did he deliver it to you again?

Capt. Ba.—I believe a weeke or 10 days agoe.

Mr. Sp.—You cannot say whether he showed it to any person?

Capt. Ba.—Noe.

Mr. Sp.—Why did not you carrey it to a Secretary of State?

Capt. Ba.—I believe Mr. Smith did.

Mr. Sp.—Was there any agreement of the prisoners that they should take but one challenge for all, and they all should be concluded by that challenge?

Capt. Ba.—I know not of such agreement.

Mr. Sp.—This was in open court?

Capt Ba.—Noe, sir, I doe not remember any such agreement; but they did talke to one another and mind one another.

Mr. Sp.—You were saying there was some adittion, upon the reading of the Statute, to the pannell, which was at first about 65. Had the prisoners a coppye of the first pannell of the 65?

Capt. Ba.—I believe they had.

Mr. Sp.—Was the addition made after the coppye of the pannell was delivered to the prisoners, or before?

Capt. Ba.—I cannot tell that, for I had not the manageing of that part, nor had nothing to doe with the pannell.

Mr. Sp.—I only asked you if you observed that matter. Can you give an account to the House what the Judges said, upon the adding to the pannell?

Capt. Ba.—I cannot give you any other account than that the Judge sayd he must make a full pannell, and that he would not make it less than 120; but I thinke they did not amount to soe many at last.

Mr. Sp.—You say that Mr. Lunt gave information that Walton was a dangerous man. Why was not he seized?

Capt. Ba.—I believe he was seized. I thinke I saw him once in Newgate when I went to visit one of the prisoners.

Mr. Sp.—But why was not he seized immediately, as soon as he was found out? How long was it after that, that you saw him in Newgate?

Capt. Ba.—I believe it was 2 months and more; but I heared he was seized that very day we went out of ——.

Mr. Sp.—How long was that, after you saw him in the Temple?

Capt. Ba.—I believe a fortnight or 3 weekes.

Mr. Sp.—Doe you remember the time when the pannell of the Petit Jury was altered? Was it when the prisoners were present?

Capt. Ba.—I believe they were present.

Mr. Sp.—You were speaking concerning one Wybrand; was he a party to the articles that were made for deviding the estates given to superstitious uses?

Capt. Ba.—I believe not.

Mr. Sp.—Was he to have any part?

Capt. Ba.—Not that I know of.

Mr. Sp.—Doe you know of any affidavits offered and tendered to my Lord Chiefe Justice?

Capt. Ba.—In what matter?

Mr. Sp.—Concerning the information here, and the conspiracy?

Capt. Ba.—Noe, sir; I never heard of any affidavits that were offered to him.

Mr. Sp.—Did Mr. Aaron Smith ever tell you of any affidavits that were tendered to my Lord Chiefe Justice?

Capt. Ba.—Not that I know of. I believe he did say that. Mr. Taffe or some body had offered affidavits in the countrey, or just going out of town. I believe he or Mr. Ball told me soe.

Mr. Sp.—Has Mr. Taffe and you held any correspondence by letters?

Capt. Ba.—Sir, I have told you how, and how long the acquaintance, and upon what occasion I sent him 2 or 3 letters, upon executeing the comission he went down about.

Mr. Sp.—Give an account of persons meeting you at Dunstaple.

Capt. Ba.—Mr. Parsons is brother-in-law to Mr. Taffe, and lives within a quarter of a mile of Standish Hall. I thought it an odd thing that Mr. Taffe should meet him at such a time.

Mr. Sp.—You were speaking of the money exacted upon dissenters, and that the money was paid to the receiver. Did he account to the Exchequer, or any other person?

Capt Ba.—He had an express Privy Seale to receive the money and give discharges.

Mr. Sp.—To whom was he accountable?

Capt. Ba.—To the Exchequer, I believe.

Mr. Sp.—You said you were ill-used in the late reignes, and was a prisoner for the Protestant religion. What was you a prisoner for?

Capt. Ba.—I was first taken up for treasonable practice. Atterbury tooke me up, and I lay all that while upon the King's account. I was charged upon other accounts, but, as soon as I had a pardon for that, I superseded the other, or else they withdrew, and I was discharged.

Mr. Sp.—You could not be charged while in Atterbury's hands?

Capt. Ba.—I was, by judgment of the Court, commited to the King's Bench for a fine.

Mr. Sp.—Did you observe the prisoners desired that the witnesses might be examined apart?

Capt. Ba.—I cannot tell; I doe not remember any such-thing was insisted on.

Captain Baker withdraws.   Mr. Wybrand called in.

Mr. Sp.—Doe you know one Mr. Taffe?

Mr. Wybrand.—Yes.

Mr. Sp.—How long have you known him?

Mr. Wy.—Three or four yeares.

Mr. Sp.—Have you had any discourse with Mr. Taffe concerning Mr. Legh of Lyme?

Mr. Wy.—Yes, I had some in the Temple, a little before the prisoners went into the countrey.

Mr. Sp.—What discourse?

Mr. Wy.—He pressed me severall times, whether I knew any one that was a particular friend of Mr. Lee's of Lyme, for that he could put him in a way to save his life, and he was sure, if he did, he should make his fortune by it. I asked him, how can you save his life when you said the evidence against him was enough to hang him? Ay, says he, but I have a way to doe it, for all that.

Mr. Sp.—Upon what occasion was this discourse?

Mr. Wy.—Why, sir, being acquainted with Mr. Taffe, a gentleman that was an acquaintance of mine said he heard such a one was an evidence against Mr. Legh of Lyme, and, says he, I wish he was not, because there is one Legh of Lyme, a Protestant and an honest gentleman. I went to him, and he sayd he was not a witness. I pressed him again as to Mr. Legh, and upon that occasion he told me there was evidence enough to hang them all, but there was some disgust; he sayd they did not use him as kindly as he ought to be, and upon that occasion he sayd he would put them in a way to save Mr. Legh of Lyme's life.

Mr. Sp.—Did he complain of ill usage?

Mr. Wy.—He said he was not rewarded well enough for his journey. They would not give him money enough.

Mr. Sp.—Did you see this matter any further, for it seems you were spoken to by a friend of Mr. Legh of Lyme's?

Mr. Wy.—Noe, sir.

Mr. Sp.—That was pretty strange, when he told you he could doe Mr. Legh any service. Did you acquaint him with what Mr. Taffe told you?

Mr. Wy.—Noe, I never saw the gentleman or him afterwards, till I saw him in the lobby.

Mr. Sp.—Doe you know of any articles made by any persons concerning the dividing the forfeited estates that were to be superstitious uses?

Mr. Wy.—Yes, I doe know of articles.

Mr. Sp.—Between whom? Doe you know of one Stepkins? Doe you know of any articles with him?

Mr. Wy.—There are some articles I have with him myself, upon the comission that was sent into Lancashire. He was to have such a share for being at the charge of speeding the comission.

Mr. Sp.—Who was to have a share?

Mr. Wy.—I was to have a share.

Mr. Sp.—What share?

Mr. Wy.—1 can't particularly tell you the articles. I thinke 100*l.* for every 1,000*l.* that came to their share.

Mr. Sp.—What power had Mr. Stepkin to make the agreement?

Mr. Wy.—He said he had a power from the Treasury.

Mr. Sp.—Were you a trustee for any person, or concerned in your own right?

Mr. Wy.—Only for myself.

Mr. Sp.—You have those articles, have you not?

Mr. Wy.—Noe, I have not, but I can have them. Really, I cannot tell very well, for Mr. Taffe asked me one day for them, and I doe not know whether I had them out of his hands since.

Mr. Sp.—Why did you deliver them to him? How was he concerned?

Mr. Wy.—Hee and I was friends, and had been concerned in this buisness, and I used to leave severall of my writeings at his house. I asked him severall times for them, and he would not give them me. I suppose he hath them.

6 December, [16]94.

Lunt at the Barr; after he had told his story.—

Mr. Sp.—Let me ask you 2 or 3 questions. You gave evidence at Manchester against the prisoners; you did observe there, I suppose, that Mr. Legh Bankes gave evidence for the prisoners?

Mr. Lunt.—Yes.

Mr. Sp.—You observed likewise that Mr. Dicconson was a witness for the prisoners?

L.—Yes.

Mr. Sp.—And that Mr Taffe was also examined there?

L.—Yes.

Mr. Sp.—Well, you heard them tell a long story concerning you, of procureing witnesses for the King against those gentlemen. Now, I would ask you, why did not you clear yourself to the Judges and the Jury, and answer those severall objections against you?

L.—I was willing, but they stopped me and bid me hold my tongue.

Mr. Sp.—Who bid you hold your tongue?

L.—The King's councell, till they had done, and after they had done I was never asked. I had severall witnesses that were not examined; I know not the reason.

Mr. Sp.—Who interrupted you?

L.—I doe not know them if I saw them again.

Mr. Sp.—Doe you not know the names of the King's councell that were there that examined the witnesses?

L.—Sir William Williams, I thinke it was.

Mr. Sp.—Why did not you desire to be heard, after the evidence was done, to clear yourself, for they gave very strange evidence against you, as wee understand, for they say you went about London to get witnesses to swear falsly against these gentlemen.

L.—I never did. I will tell you all that I know of Mr. Legh Bankes and Mr. Dicconson. I will give you a just account, as I hope to be saved.

Mr. Sp.—You are now at full liberty to say what you please, as you would have done at Manchester.

L.—If it pleases your honour, Mr. Taffe came to me. Sayes he, did not you know one Captain Howard. Noe, sayes I, I never had much acquaintance with him; there was one Howard in la Hogue buisness, and should have been an officer, but I had noe acquaintance with him. Sayes he, what will you say if he will come in, and evidence for the King; he hath a comission in his pocket. Says I, if he would, it would do a good deal of service; you know how to take him to the Secretary as well as I. But, says he, he hath a great mind to see you. Sayes I, with all my heart. Says he, I would have you tell Mr. Smith of it. That there is such a person, says he, you may take my word, aud I believe he knows a great deale, as much as you almost. Sayes I, it may be he does. Sayes I, I will meet him at any time. This passed on for a fortnight. Afterwards, Mr. Taffe comes one morning. Sayes he, you must goe out to see the gentleman, and bring me to 'the Ship' ale house in the Butcher's Row, where I sat, and he went out. I admired he left me in that manner. At last he comes. Sayes he, he is come; let you and I goe above. When I came in, there was a gentleman sat. Sayes he, I beg your pardon, I am in drinke; I am not fit now, but if you will met four a'clocke, I shall bee glad to see you. Mr. Taffe would have been faign putting on what I had to say to the gentleman, in Lancashire. Sayes I, I know not the meaning. Sayes I, is this the gentleman you pretended to have a comission? Noe, sayes he. I told him I had nothing to say to him, and never saw the man afterwards till he came to be an evidence against me. Monday after this I was a little angry with Mr. Taffe. Sayes I, what in the name of Jesuss is the meaning of it, to bring me into such a man's company to make a fool of me? Sayes he, he knew a great deale, but he had dranke soe much he knew nothing of it. On Monday after, sayes he, we shall meet with Mr. Howard as tomorrow. The morrow I came, according to my promise, and saw noebody but Mr. Taffe. He sayd he was engaged with a Jacobite club, but he would meet me next day. Sayes I, I doe not desire to see any of them. On Monday he takes me to meet him, and there I met a gentleman which, if it was Mr. Dicconson, my eyes were not well my own. Mr. Taffe, when he came, he went to the staires. Sayes he, it may be you may have some buisness. Well, sayes he, I will but just goe to the wall; calls in for a pint of mum. Sayes he, I hear you are going to be evidence against some Lancashire gentlemen. Sayes I, who told you? Sayes he, Mr. Taffe. Sayes he, I believe I know and can prove as much as most can, but would not willingly have my name known. Sir, sayes I, if you please, I will send for a gentleman that will take your information what you can say, and I believe it will be kept private. But, sayes he, I can't stay now, but I will meet you in the after-noon. Sayes I, if you please, let it be between 2 or 3 a'clock, and then the gentleman will be within, and I will send for him. I payd for the mum and we parted, and that was all that was sayd upon it, one way or other, in that gentleman's company. Insted of meeting at 3, Mr. Taffe came to my lodging and there dined with me. His wife, Taffe, and I, went to meet him at 2 or 3 a'clock, and I never saw him afterwards.

Mr. Sp.—Mr. Lunt, you heard what Mr. Taffe sayd against you at Manchester, and the other gentleman. How long have you been acquainted with Mr. Taffe?

L.—This 2 yeares and upwards I have known him.

Mr. Sp.—Did you never tell Mr. Legh Banks and Mr. Dicconson they shoud have good rewards out of those gentlemen's estates, if they would swear against them, and they were couvicted?

L.—Never since I was born.

Mr. Sp.—Did you never tell Mr. Legh Bank and Mr. Dicconson that you would make a plot of your own?

L.—Noe, never in my days, as I hope to be saved.

Mr. Sp.—Did you never tell him you would carry the plott through all the countys of England, if you could convict these men?

L.—I never said any such thing in my dayes.

Mr. Sp.—What a company of people these are; they have told this House you did say soe.

L.—I cannot help it if they threw 1,000 aspersions upon me.

Mr. Sp.—You say you bought armes, severall times, for these gentlemen in the country; where did you buy them?

L.—I bought some in Middle Row, in Holborne. I bespake above a 100 swords and sword hilts, for they had blades, in the country.

Mr. Sp.—Who paid for them?

L.—Mr. Whitfield.

Mr. Sp.—You bought armes at other times; where did you buy them?

L.—Some armes I bought at Chearing Cross.

Mr. Sp.—You were in Ireland and in France, and have been, after, in prison; you were a prisoner and gave bayle. Who were your baile?

L.—Mr. Whitfield, Mr. Burgees, Mr. Rogers another.

Mr. Sp.—You have been employed by the late King in England, and my Lord Melford employed you; what money was given you? who maintained you?

L.—The Lancashire gentlemen allowed me money in prison, and gave me money when they received comissions of me, and tooke care to maintain me. And when I was at St. Germans, the King gave me money to bring me backe. He gave me 100 livers and 15 pistolls, and another time 200 livers.

Mr. Sp.—Was this all the reward you were to have?

L.—As soon as I came into England, I was to have some forfeited estates.

Mr. Sp.—You had great hopes of these forfeited estates in England?

L.—If King James had come, I should have been sure of it.

Mr. Sp.—You have given your information before some magistrate; before whom was it?

L.—Before the Duke of Shrewsbury and Secretary Trenchard.

Mr. Sp.—Were you sworn to that?

L.—Yes, they were all true; I am sure there is noe person can prove anything false.

Mr. Sp.—What money have you had for bearing of your charges, since those examinations, and for your going down into Lancashire and Cheshire?

L.—I have had in all (but then Sir John Trenchard employed in buisness, sending me down into Essex, that cost me a great deal of money), I believe I have had three score pounds. I have not had four score pounds in the whole world.

Mr. Sp.—But Mr. Taffe sayes you were to have a great share of the estates of those gentlemen in Lancashire, if they were convicted.

L.—Noe, I did not doe it for that; I did it to serve the Government.

Mr. Sp.—You say you have a paper, and you can produce severall witnesses to prove a great many particulars, and to verifye the depositions and your information. What is your paper?

L.—That is a paper of evidence; names that can prove a great deal of what I say, to be true.

Mr. Sp.—Is there only their names?

L.—Their names and what they will speake to.

(Lunt delivered in the paper.)

L.---Here is my pass I had from my Lord Melford, at my coming over last.

(Which he delivered in.)

Lunt withdraws. Called in again.

Mr. Sp.—In this paper you delivered in, it is that William Cooper and Robert Dandy can prove Mr. Walmesley to be in Lancashire, about the time you have mentioned in your information; were these 2 persons at the assizes at Manchester?

L.—Yes, they were there.

Mr. Sp.—Were they examined in Court?

L.—Noe.

Mr. Sp.—Were they in town then?

L.—Yes.

Mr. Sp.—You say the King's counsell omitted to call severall persons that were in their breviates. Did you see their breviates?

L.—These evidences were at Manchester, and waited' to be [called, but] they were not called.

Mr. Sp.—Who ordered them to attend there?

L.—They were subpœnaed in.

Mr. Sp.—You are shure they were subpœnaed in?

L.—I am sure they were; 2 or 3 came in of themselves, and the rest were subpœnaed.

Mr. Sp.—When these men were there, and your evidence soe confronted by these evidences that appeared against you, why did not 'you desire that these men should be called in, to justifye your credit?

L.—I expected those that managed the King's affairs would have called them.

Mr. Sp.—When you came out of France, had you a signall or a signet?

L.—Noe, a seale.

Mr. Sp.—When you came over to Dover, you met 4 men there. At what house?

L.—Why, they tooke me to their own house, Captain Noell's house. Capt. Walton lives 7 miles off. Captain Walton came to me to his house, and Preston came there and Captain Roberts.

Mr. Sp.—What house is Captain Noell's?

L.—It is a private house. I was there a weeke. He was Sergeant of the Admiralty, under King William.

Mr. Sp.—What was the day you came over to Dover?

L.—I cannot tell just the day.

Mr. Sp.—What time in the yeare?

L.—In December last.

Mr. Sp.—Was it the beginning, or end, or middle of the month?

L.—Towards the latter end, I thinke.

Mr. Sp.—What was the signet you brought over?

L.—It was the Binkes (?) head.

Mr. Sp.—And what was writt upon the paper?

L.—There was a seale upon 'the paper. I was to shew it Captain Griffith's lady, who then lodged at Pepper's, in Newgate Street.

Mr. Sp.—You said you were advised by a particular person to disclose this matter. Who was that person?

L.—Mr. Taffe knew of my comeinge over out of France because of his wife, and he introduced me to my Lord Bellamount.

Mr. Sp.—Did Mr. Taff induce you to discover it?

L.—My Lord Bellamount did.

Mr. Sp.—When you were examined at the tryall at Manchester how many places there did you mention that you did buy armes at?

L.—I mentioned Middle Row, Charing Cross, Drury Lane, and the Citty.

Mr. Sp.—Where, at Charing Cross, did you buy the armes?

L.—I am not certain of the place. I was taken down to Charing Cross, and Mr. Whitfield brought me into his company, at the ' Cheshire Cheese,' soe that I was not at his shop. He said he would furnish me, and he had furnished for the north parts. In London, he took me to the ' Swan with Two Necks,' and there came a man that sayd he would provide any armes whatsoever, as pistolls, &c., but I was at none of their shopps but in Middle Row. In Drury Lane, he came to the ' Royall Oake ' to me; where he did live, I know not.

Mr. Sp.—You delivered me a paper of the names of witnesses; were any of these examined at the tryall?

L.—Not in the Court.

Mr. Sp.—Were they examined by anybody else?

L.—They said they were examined by somebody.

Mr. Sp.—You sayd, at the tryall, that you did deliver comissions to Sir Rowland Stanley and Sir Thomas Cliffton. Were you ever at Sir Rowland Stanley's house?

L.—I have seen his house; was never at it to lye all night. I was once at it, but I delivered his comissions at my Lord Mollineux'.

Mr. Sp.—Were you acquainted, before the tryall, with Sir Thomas Cliffton?

L.—I had seen him twice; once at his own house, then in his night dress; and at his own house it was, he desired me to buy some swords. Another time I saw him at Standish Hall.

Mr. Sp.—How long before the tryall?

L.—Two or three yeares. I see him once after, at Dungan Hall; I but just see him.

Mr. Sp.—Were you in Court when the gentlemen were arr[aigned]? Remember, you were asked the question which [was] Stanley and which Sir Thomas Cliffton.

L.—Yes; they asked me a question very hastily. I tooke a stick and mistooke, but I meant Sir Rowland.

Mr. Sp.—How came you to make that mistake?

L.—As soon as I tooke the sticke again, I layd it upon every one there; they never told me when they gave me time. I am a little short-sighted.

Mr. Sp.—What religion were you of, when you discovered the plot?

L.—I was a Roman Catholicke.

Mr. Sp.—What religion are you of now?

L.—I did not change my religion; the King does not desire any man to change his religion.

Mr. Sp.—You say you were to have noe reward for giving your evidence against these gentlemen, at Manchester. What made you, then, discover this matter, when you were to have noe reward for the evidence that you gave against these gentlemen, when you were to have soe great a reward if the plott went on?

L.—I was satisfied, by severall priests of the Church of Rome, that it would have been a notorious and bloody murder.

Mr. Sp.—When you came over from Ireland, where did you land?

L.—Att Cockermouth (sic), within 4 miles of Lancaster.

Mr. Sp.—-You speake of a trunke, wherein were papers and comissions ?

L.—Wee tooke those out, and left the trunke in a ditch.

Mr. Sp.—Have you any of those comissions and papers by you, that you did save at that time ?

L.—Noe, I have none by me now ; I had a comission that I had at that time, but at my last comeing over from France, I was surprised by some persons, and my wife had them and delivered them to ——— Taffe.

[Mr. Sp.]—When you spake of the 4 persons, I think you named 5, you mett at Dover ; there was 16 in all. Can you name the names of the rest ?

[L.] [No]e, I cannot. Capt. Floyd said he would engage his son, and Capt. . . . lcot sayd he had 6 more.

[Mr. Sp.]—You have been at Dungan Hall, Mr. Walmesly's house ?

L.—Yes.

Mr. Sp.—You came there in February, [16]91 ?

L.—Yes.

Mr. Sp.—And brought comissions along with you ?

L.—I ? noe ; Mr. Walmesley.

Mr. Sp.—Did you observe Mr. Legh of Lyme to be there at that time ?

L.—Yes; he was there at that time.

Mr. Sp.—Was you ever at Mr. Legh of Lyme's house ?

L.—I was there in 1689.

Mr. Sp.—Was Mr. Legh of Lyme then at home ?

L.—Yes.

Mr. Sp.—Did you ever tell Mr. Taffe that you were not acquainted with Mr. Legh of Lyme, or knew his house ?

L.—I never told him soe, nor he asked me such a question.

Mr. Sp.—What occasion brought you to Mr. Legh of Lyme's in [16]89 ?

L.—I was ordered by the King to deliver a comission for a collonel of horse.

Mr. Sp.—And you did deliver it him ?

L.—Yes.

Mr. Sp.—Was anybody by ?

L.—Yes, there was one Wilson by, that shewed me the way, and he delivered a comission, forthwith, to another that was there.

Mr. Sp.—What time was it you were there ?

L.—About June it was. Upon my arrival, the gentlemen in Lanca-shire, upon those blank comissions that were taken in the boat, were taken up.

Mr. Sp.—What was the day you landed out of Ireland ?

L.—I cannot exactly tell the day. I thinke it was Thursday. I beli[eve] the Mayor of Lancaster, that brought up the comissions, [can] give an account of the day.

Mr. Sp.—You sayd you went to Croxteth; how long did y[ou stay] ?

L.—I came in the night and went before day. I cam[e] . . . . to Tildsleye's, and thence to Croxteth, and thence to Tow[nley's].

Mr. Sp.—That was 3 dayes ?

L.—Not in 3 dayes, I went as fast as I could.

Mr. Sp.—How long did you stay at every one of these places ?

L.—I went away the night, or next morning. I humbly beg of this honorable House I have not had a bed these 3 dayes.

Lunt withdraws. Called in again.

Mr. Sp.—Mr. Lunt, I am commanded by the House to ask you some more questions; if you can remember what day of the week you went to Croxton [Croxteth?]

L.—I cannot tell truly. I did not keep an account of the day.

Mr. Sp.—Can you remember what day of the weeke you went to Townley?

L.—Noe.

Mr. Sp.—Was Mr. Townley at home then?

L.—Yes, I am sure he was at home; he received a comission from me.

Mr. Sp.—Well, you were acquainted with Wilson?

L.—Yes.

Mr. Sp.—How long have you been acquainted with him; he that mett you when you came out of Ireland?

L.—I had been once at his house before that.

Mr. Sp.—What is his name?

L.—George Wilson.

Mr. Sp.—What time did he come to you, at your landing?

L.—He was at Esquire Tinsley's [Tildesley's], of the Lodge. Hee was ordered to wait for our comeing.

[Mr. Sp.]—Where did you part with him?

L.—He went away with me from the Lodge to my Lord Molineux's to shew me the countrey.

[Mr. Sp.]—Did he goe with you to all the places?

[L.]—All, till I came to Sir Roland Throckmorton's, and there I [par]ted with him.

[Mr. Sp.]—[Yo]u say you delivered a comission to Mr. Lee of Lyme, in 1689?

L.—Yes.

Mr. Sp.—In what part of the house did you deliver the comission to him?

L.—It was above staires. I did not take a particular account of the roomes that I delivered the comission in, but it was matted, a kind of a gallery.

Mr. Sp.—Did you take notice of anything else, besides that it was matted?

L.—Noe, indeed, not I.

Mr. Sp.—Who was in the room when you delivered him the co-mission?

L.—There were severall.

Mr. Sp. —Can you name them?

L.—There was Mr. Shallcross; he delivered him a comission to be lieutenant-colonel.

Mr. Sp.—Was there any other person there?

L.—Some gentlemen; I doe not know their names.

Mr. Sp.—Did he open the comission?

L.—Yes, he did, and delivered it to him.

Mr. Sp.—Was there any table in the roome?

L.—I did not see any table; he signed it in the window.

Mr. Sp.—What, did he call for a pen and inke?

L.—There was a pen and inke.

Mr. Sp.—Was Wilson there?

L.—Yes, Wilson was there at the same time.

Mr. Sp.—Was Wilson acquainted with Mr. Legh of Lyme?

L.—I know not whether he was or noe.

Mr. Sp.—It was a strange thing that you should carry comissions, which was a secret thing, and carry a man, that was a stranger, from house to house; how came you to carry Wilson up staires to Mr. Lee of Lyme ?

L.—Hee went with me everywhere . . . . I was to give an account to the King . . . . recomended Mr. Wilson to me . . . . might trust my life.

Mr. Sp.—What reward had you from Mr. . . . . .

· L.—I had 5 guineas.

Mr. Sp.—Had Wilson anything ?

L.--Not that I saw.

Mr. Sp.—Did he make you drinke ?

L.—Yes, he downed on his knees and drank King James' health, and kissed the comission.

Mr. Sp.—Did you deliver any more comissions there besides that ?

L.—Noe.

Mr. Sp.—Did Mr. Lee deliver any other comissions?

L.—I saw him deliver 2 or 3, but did not know their names; they were captains' comissions.

Mr. Sp.—Were you not to give King James an account of the comissions ?

L.—Yes, I delivered none but collonells' comissions, and they were to make their under officers.

Mr. Sp.—You were in Lancashire along with Capt. Baker; what horses were taken by you or him, in the County of Lancaster ?

L.—I cannot give an account of them; the messengers can, I thinke, they had the Secretary's warrant.

Mr. Sp.—What became of them ?

L.—They are all in being, I suppose.

Mr. Sp.—How are they disposed of ?

L.—I know not, I have none of them.

Mr. Sp.—Of what value were the horses ?

L.—They were good horses and fit for service.

Mr. Sp.—Were they all above 5l. ?

L.—If I had had money, and occasion for horses, I would have given 5l. for the worth [worst ?] of them.

Mr. Sp.—There was a mistake, it seemes, at your pointing out Sir Thomas Cliffton and Sir Rowland Stanley. Did you mistake any other of the prisoners at the barr ?

L.—Noe, Sir.

. . . . Langton and Blundell ?

. . . .

. . . . the one and the other ?

. . . . Langton for Blundell.

. . . . . know Mr. Beresford ?

[L.]—I have noe acquaintance with Mr. Beresford; I have heard of such a man.

Mr. Sp.—Have you seen him ?

L.—I cannot tell, by his name, whether I ever saw him or noe.

Mr. Sp.—Where are Cooper and Dandy ?

L.—They were in Lancashire.

Mr. Sp.—Are they there now ?

L.—Yes, and have estates there, indifferent good estates.

Mr. Sp.—Why were they not made use of at the tryall ?

L.—I doe not know.

Withdraws.

5th Feb., [16]94[-5].

Oliver Peirson at the Barr.

Mr. Speaker.—Oliver Peirson, I think your name is?

O. P.—Yes, sir.

Mr. Sp.—Do you know Mr. Wombell?

O. P.—Yes.

Mr. Sp.—How long have you known him?

O. P.—I have known him 20 years.

Mr. Sp.—Were you at any time a servant to him?

O. P.—Yes.

Mr. Sp.—How long agoe?

O. P.—A matter of halfe a year ago I came from him.

Mr. Sp.—How long did you serve him?

O. P.—A matter of 2 years and an halfe.

Mr. Sp.—Dureing that time of your being his servant did you goe along with his horses into the countrey?

O. P.—Noe, I went sometimes. I was his husband-man at home.

Mr. Sp.—Did you use to come up to London with his horses?

O. P.—Never, but 2 or 3 times.

Mr. Sp.—Where did he use to inn, in town?

O. P.—At ' the Castle,' in Wood Street.

Mr. Sp.—Doe you know of any armes that were brought to ' the Castle,' in Wood Street, to carry down into the countrey?

O. P.—Yes, I know of armes that were carried down into the countrey.

Mr. Sp.—Do you know of any armes brought to ' the Castle,' in Wood Street?

O. P.—There was pistolls and kettle drumms; there might be other armes, but I never saw none else.

Mr. Sp.—Did you open any of the packs that went into the countrey at any time?

O. P.—Yes; I will tell you our misfortune. As I went to meet my master, there was the young lord of Standish and my old lord of Standish a-drinking, and, in Wigan Road, my master had a mare down and fell, and with much adoe wee got her out, and as soon as we came home we opened the pack to see if any damage. In the meantime came my young lord of Standish, and asked for my master. He sayd he had some goods directed to one Lightboune, and had such a marke, and desired the goods home that night. My master broke open the goods, to see what they were, and they proved to bee pistolls. On Saturday or Sunday night, he and I saddled two horses, and put the kettle drums on my head, and went to Standish, and delivered them to the steward, on the bowling green.

Mr. Sp.—When was this?

O. P.—This is 2 years ago, as well as I can remember.

Mr. Sp.—Well, you packed up these armes again?

O. P.—Yes.

Mr. Sp.—Did you carry a year together with your master?

O. P.—I was his husband-man at home. He kept 2 men besides me. I often went out with the goods when they came home.

Mr. Sp.— How many packs did you see?

O. P.—I never saw any armes but those, but I went severall times with goods to the same place, that were expected to bee armes.

Mr. Sp.—Well, you say you helped to open the armes at Standish Hall?

O. P.—I opened no armes at Standish Hall but what I brought there.

Mr. Sp.—Did you help to open them there?

O. P.—Yes, I delivered them to the steward.

Mr. Sp.—At the opening them there, who did you see? Did you see any but the steward?

O. P.—I saw the steward and some of the servants; most of them were gone to bed. It was between 12 and 1 on Sunday night.

Mr. Sp.—What did the steward with them?

O. P.—I did not see where he carried them.

Mr. Sp.—How many packs of goods can you remember that went there?

O. P.—I cannot tell you. Hardly ever came down but there went less or more goods thither.

Mr. Sp.—Doe you know Mr. Walmesley?

O. P.—I was going by Lightbourne, and called to drink a pot of ale, and there was some gentlemen drinking in another roome, and I inquired who such a one was, and they told me, one Walmesley, and about 3 years after, I met him about —— and some 3 men along with him.

Mr. Sp.—Did you know him before?

O. P.—Noe. About 3 years after, I mett the same man, three quarters a mile of Dungan, a place they called Chester parish; there was two or three men along with him.

Mr. Sp.—What sort of a man was Mr. Walmesley?

O. P.—He was a gentillman, a young man.

Mr. Sp.—What size?

O. P.—A middle sized man.

Mr. Sp.—What complexcion?

O. P.—A blacke complexcion, I think he was.

Mr. Sp.—Did he wear his own hair, or a peruque?

O. P.—He had a peruque.

Mr. Sp—Did you see any man in his company that you knew?

O. P.—Noe.

Mr. Sp.—Who told you it was Mr. Walmesley?

O. P.—Some woman in the house, when I went to drinke a pot of ale.

Mr. Sp.—What quantity of armes do you know Woombell carryed?

O. P.—There came, every time almost, goods directed to one place, and went to another.

Mr. Sp—Name the places?

O. P.—I cannot name the places, but I remember they were directed to other places; the reason was wee thought they were armes.

Mr. Sp.—Therefore, name the places.

O. P.—There was goods to Blackbourne and to Standish Town, and they went to the Hall and other places. I did not goe along with them.

Mr. Sp.—Did you see any other goods opened, besides the pistolls?

O. P.—No, never none but those.

Mr. Sp.—Did Woombell tell you he had armes?

O. P.—He told me he mistrusted such things were armes, though I doe not know whether he saw them or noe. If it please this honorable House, I will tell you somethinge more. One Thomas Clayton was a carrier at the same time, and he was gotten fuddled, and he said he would hang my master for carrying of armes, and Thomas Smith, belonging to the same inne, bid him hold his tongue, for he would undoe himself, and others too.

Mr. Sp.—Where was this?

O. P.—In Wigun Lane, at one Thomas Smyth's.

Mr. Sp.—How long agoe?

O. P.—A matter of 2 years, or somewhat more, agoe.

Mr. Sp.—Can you inform this House of anything more?

O. P.—Yes. My master used to bee often at Standish Town; and being there late, I used to watch him home, and coming along, he told mee he had been with a deale of gentlemen, and how they had concluded to give him something, and my Lord of Standish stepped up amongst them, and said hee would not have them trouble themselves, for hee had rewarded him himself.

Mr. Sp.—What did my Lord of Standish doe for him?

O. P.—Nothing at all. He was in a very good way of trading, and well beloved among the gentlemen. His horses never stood nor prospered, after he began to carry armes.

Mr. Sp.—Did he name the persons to you that were there?

O. P.—I believe he named them all.

Mr. Sp.—Can you remember their names?

O. P.—There was Mr. Townley of Townley, and severall other gentlemen. .

Mr. Sp.—Did he use to be among these gentlemen?

O. P.—Yes, no [it was?] great day of bowling but he went up still.

Mr. Sp.—What reputation had he among them; you say he was very well beloved of all the countrey?

O. P.—Yes, he was.

Mr. Sp.—What occasion made him fail and breake?

O. P.—I cannot tell. He broke for a small matter, at first. He broke, at first, for the summe of 20*l*., and they promised to raise him a place to pay it.

Mr. Sp.—Who did?

O. P.—The Lord of Standish.

Mr. Sp.—How much?

O. P.—I cannot tell. Hee told me he was to have money of him, but I doe not know that ever he had any.

THE WAR ON THE CONTINENT.

894. 1694, November 26.—A document relating to " the quotas, which the confederates and allies do severally furnish."

GEORGE KENYON to his father, ROGER KENYON., M.P., at Westminster.

895. [1694,] December 1.—" If I could have given you any satisfactory account in the business of Lunt, I had done it long agoe. Mr. Threlfall's widow cannot, or will not, take upon her to remember the week, month, or year, her husband came from Ireland; Mr. Winckley continues to say it was the 13th of June. Mr. Patton, nor no others in Preston, can give an account when the Papist gentlemen were brought prisoners, nor when discharged. But, as to the buisiness of Hartley, he took time, as he said, to recollect himself, and now does offer, if I will go over to Lancaster, that he will give me an information against a very great number in Staffordshire, Shropshire, and Worcestershire, and will undertake, upon pain of his life, if I will follow his directions, to instruct me how to take a very great many, actually at work. I have appointed Wednesday next to take his information, and, if you think fitt on it, and I can be empowered and incouraged from above in it, I will take a journey on purpose into those counties, and doubt not to secure them " [the coiners?]. *Seul of arms.*

CHARLES RIGBY to ROGER KENYON, M.P., in London.

896. 1694, December 4. Lancaster.—Encloses Hartley's information, by which he will stand or fall. He always said that he and Richard Allen of " Wallesie " could discover " a vast number, in severall countys, and thinks Allen would readilly joyne with him, if he was apprehended." Though pressed, he denies knowledge of the "robbery." Encloses a certificate by James Crosfield—one of the Custom House officers that pursued Lunt, when he landed—which gives, from a memorandum in his pocket-book, the time. Jaynson was witness of the chase.

J. HARTLEY to ROGER KENYON, M.P., in London.

897. 1694, December 4.—" I doubt not but a greate many honest gentlemen are well pleased with what the King said, as to the witnesses produced at the trialls in Lancashire; and whether Lunt, or who else was concerned, ought not to give account who should have been tooke up, had the business succeeded, by virtue of those blancke warrants, after their names had been inserted." *Seal of arms.*

JANE HOWORTH to ROGER KENYON, M.P., in London.

898. [16]94, December 6. Parkhead.—Finds Mr. Bradyll " eagerly seeking for seats in Whaley church." Entreats Kenyon's assistance in " breaking with the Bushopp, and who ellse may be conserned therein," if he can do anything, on her daughter Oldfield's behalf, either for the two seats next the chancel " which my father might, in his time, have had, or my mother's own seat, with that next before it, in exchange for part of two seats behind." *Seal of arms, broken.*

DR. RICHARD ROWE to ROGER KENYON, M.P., in London.

899. [16]94, December 7.—The account of the election at Liverpool is dull. " If the Bill for a new Parliament goes on, perhaps both [members ?] will wish they had spent less money; and, if what some very honest men say, be true, it is no great matter which of them carryes it." Finds Monday's vote about Kitson and Coachman variously construed ; hopes the whole mystery will be discovered, and looks for the account of Wednesday's examination. Wishes the Archbishop " be no worse disposed on that you mention, though he be young enough."

WILLIAM HAYHURST to ROGER KENYON, M.P., in London.

900. 1694, December 7. Preston.—" Wee have a report there are Irish witnesses come over, to corroborate the testimony of Mr. Lunt; that place used to be very fruitfull of such creatures, which will seldom fail to help a lame dog over stile. I pray God direct the councills of the nation ; so that, hereafter, it may bee safe for an innocent man to follow his own business with safetie." The Lords of the Treasury have appointed him (the writer) Receiver-General of Lancashire, Westmoreland, and Cumberland; and he has given 1,000*l.* security for the due execution of his office ; but the auditor, Mr. Marriott, "makes my place as uneasy and unprofitable as he can. He has sent a messenger, one of the King's messengers, [as] a spy, along with mee ; and, though the Lords have appointed mee, hee has appointed this messenger, Mr. Boddison, to receeve the best rents (pretending them to bee purchased by the Duke of Leeds), and I am only to receive the small ones." Begs that Kenyon will speak on his behalf, to the Treasury. *Seal of arms.*

The EARL OF DERBY to ROGER KENYON.

901. 1694, December 7. Knowsley.—The last year, Sir Christopher [Greenfield] took, or rather bought, the office of Bailiff of this Hundred, in my name. He has agreed with Ned Darbishire about it, and I am to consign it over by a deed. "Now, my objection is, that by my doing so, it obliges me to take the oaths and test, for which I shall hardly do, after refusing a more considerable thing. Pray let me have your thoughts upon it, for your judgment, as it ever has been, must be esteemed by your most affectionate, faithful friend,—DERBY." *Seal, broken.*

LADY STANDISH to ROGER KENYON.

902. 1694, December 14. Duxbury.—My adversaries, upon receiving the news, from London, that their indictment had not that success which they designed, have set another inquisition, privately, at Bolton, before lawyer Leaver and lawyer Starky, and yesternight, when we least thought of it, they brought the under-sheriff, Valentine, and a great deal of the mob, armed with "pikforks" and other offensive weapons; they broke the doors and locks of the mines and have put in their men, so that now they and the water are in possession of the mines. I caused the wheel to be stopped, so that they will be drowned out before to-morrow morning.

THOMAS PIERCE to ROGER KENYON, at the "Blue Boar," in Holborn.

903. 1694, December 15.—Mr. Hartley solemnly declares he can make no further discovery. "My Lord has signed a warrant for his execution; and, I think, it was delivered to Mr. Sergeant, who, I presume, sent it down, last post, to the High Sheriffe of Lancashire." *Seal, broken.*

WILLIAM HAYDOCK, "the parson of Standish," to ROGER KENYON, M.P., in London.

904. 1694, December 16. [Standish.]—"My poor Lady Standish has met with a great disturbance, notwithstanding my Lord Chief Justice Treby's order, &c. . . . pray use your interest (?) for her. She designs honestly, and I hope that right will take place." *Seal of arms.*

LADY STANDISH to ROGER KENYON, M.P., in London.

905. 1694, December 16. Duxbury.—"I hope, by this time, you have my other letter, with the account of Mr. Shaw's proceedings about the lead mines; in short, the water has put both them and me out of possession, for they are quite drowned up . . . I hope you will not blame me for letting you know who is Clerk of the Peace now, in Lancashire; it is Mr. Morton, an attorney in Bolton. I suppose he expects thanks for easing your family of the trouble of that office, and I hope you will not forget that he is rewarded. Sir, if this be mallice in me to put you in mind that you are affronted, as well as myself abused, I hope God will pardon it, for I think it is for the public good that these people be made to know themselves . . . I find there is nothing but punishing their purses can procure my peace. Your son advises me to pay them in their own coyn, and indite all but the Sheriff himself." *Seal.*

ALICE KENYON to her husband, ROGER KENYON, M.P., at Westminster.

906. 1694, December 18.—"Thy friends begin now to wish for thy return. I hope when you have finished the great business, that of the moneys given to his Majesty, thou may then get leave to come home. I am sure thine own family wants thee much. I pray thee, in what part of the world is my Lord Derby, and what is he doing? The drum is beating here for soldiers for Col. Stanley, but he gets few. I pray thee, buy me 'The Art of Patience,' written by the author of 'The Whole Duty of Man,' and when thou art alone, read it: thou wilt like it well." *Seal of arms.*

WILLIAM DICCONSON to ROGER KENYON, M.P.

907. 1694, December 21.—"You need not begg excuses for your man bringing mee, or others, a draught of the tryalls, for it was my own request to him soe to do . . . I hope, if it be proper, some of our friends will move that the witnesses who have been examined, may be discharged from any further attendance of the House, for the charge will be very great as it is; soe I hope they will not spitefully increase it. Methinks the Court party itself cannot refuse the reasonableness of this; they should, indeed, rather, in honer, make us some amends for our great charge, wrongfully sustained; and, *usque* wee have runn of our lives, exempt us, who were tryed, from dubble taxes for 7 years; but I doubt they will scarce consider us soe farr."

EDMUND HORNBY to ROGER KENYON, M.P.

908. [16]94, December 22. Foulton.—"About ten this evening, I received a warrant (but with some mistakes) from the Attorney-General, to make copy of the indictments against Sir Rowland Stanley, and the other 4 gentlemen tryed with him at Manchester, which my inclinations, as well as profit, would readily have prompted me to, if my (perhaps causeles) apprehensions that some trouble might ensue thereon, had not discouraged me from. But, if that copy be designed to be read in your house, it is naturall enough to believe that the opposing party in that matter, will presently enquire how, or by whom, it was made. If answered, by the Clerke of the Crowne, upon the Attorney-Generall's warrant, and by any considerable part of your great and honourable body objected that that cause being taken notice of by, and now depending before that great counsell, nothing on record relateing to it ought to have beene copyed without their order, it is probable enough that I may be put to the charge of a journey, to shew my warrant, and answere that account, if noe further. To obviate which, and render me easy and safe, I humbly beg your direction; and that the House may (if in your better judgment it be thought proper) be moved to make their order that the Attorney-Generall may send his warrant to us, to make a copy, and that we, thereon, may make one. I made my clerk transcrible (*sic*) this, and have sent the same to Mr. Shakerley, this post. I beg you will please to consider whether the warrant of the Attorney-Generall for the kingdom or for the county, shall be more proper to be sent to us." *Seal of arms.*

RICHARD TOWNELEY to "CAPTAIN BERISFORD, at Mr. Legh's, in Legh Street, near Red Lion Square, in Holburn."

909. 1694, December 23. Towneley.—"In complyance with your desire, I have here sent you what I have found was noted down by others, as well as myself, about the times you mention. And first, that on the 9th of June, 1689, I was apprehended here, and, by a partie of dragoons, that night carried prisoner to Preston. I was, by virtue of a warrant (if I remember right) from Col. Rocthern and Mr. Patten, [at] once called before them and some other justices, else, for the most part, confined to my chamber, under a guard, till the arrival of the then Lord Brandon, who was, [on] the 14th, pleased to see me, and that night tooke off the confinement to my chamber. On the 16th, I find it noted down that Sir William Gerard and severall others were that day brought in prisoners allso, to Preston, where wee remained till the 25th, when wee were all, under a guard, carried to Manchester, where wee continued prisoners till the 2nd of January following; during which time I was never at home but twice. The first time was on the 1st of August, when I was allowed, with a guard, to go to Towneley, to assist at the buriall of Mr. Kennett, who, not many months before, had married a daughter of mine. The particular time of my being secured, besides its being written down, was remarkable, and not to be forgot, because on the 13th of the said June, my daughter Towneley was brought to bed of her eldest sonne, and a servant was dispatcht to me at Preston, with that pleasing news, and besides, my sonne then absented himself from home, upon the score of his being on the same warrant that I was apprehended by; and by these circumstances, all the familie remember that they tooke notice of everie person that came to the house, and assure me that Lunt came not hither about that time, for had he bene here, he would then have bene particularly remembered, since he had before that, by lettres, made clame, and pretended to be contracted, to a cooke maid of mine, and the yeare following, hereabouts, made a great bustle about her, even after she was married; the clame he made caused a servant of mine, the year, as I take it, before, to enquire of him, meet him, and found he lived with another woman, who was esteemed, and owned herself, his wife ; and upon this account, when he afterwards came into these parts, and made these stirs, and came hither, he was always looked upon as an idle and ill man; insomuch, that my sonne would not be seene by him. As for Sir Thomas Clifton, I can give you no satisfactory account, for he was not a prisoner with us at Manchester, nor, that I remember, in the same condition as we were at Preston, if there; but answered for, and under, Mr. Patten. But particulars I cannot remember. However, I hope you will take in good part what I have been able to recollect." *Seal of arms.*

CHARLES RIGBY to ROGER KENYON, M.P.

910. 1694, December 25. Lancaster.—Sending a list of persons against whom Hartley (who had been reprieved) had informed :—

Christopher Carus, Esquire ; Taken prisoner in his own house, on 24 June, 1689, by three or four soldiers of Lieutenant Huddleston's (then Sir William Pennington's) troop of militia. Was carried, the same day, to Lancaster and Garstang ; next day to Preston— there kept two days—and thence to Manchester, where he found Mr. Dalton, Mr. Sherburne of Stonyhurst (who died there), and several others. He continued a prisoner there till the latter end of the January following, when he had leave to go home; he fell sick, and did not return to prison, as soon after Candlemas, "a releasment came for them all."

Mr. Dalton was apprehended at his own house, on 17 June, 1689, by Lieutenant Usherwood and his men, and taken, about midnight, to Preston, where he found Sir William Gerrard, Mr.

Dickinson, "two Mr. Tounleys," Mr. Chorley, Mr. Stanley, Mr. Blundell of Crosby, Mr. Worthington of Bleciskow (?) and his son, Mr. Andrew Mores, and some others. He was kept at Preston 4 days, in the custody of Captain Etogh (*sic*), and thence carried to Manchester, by Captain Ralph Egerton. There, Mr. Dalton and Mr. Stanley were kept prisoners at Mr. Newcome's house, with two men to guard them, to whom they were forced to pay 1/- a day each. Mr. Dalton continued a prisoner at Manchester till the beginning of February following. The other prisoners then at Manchester were :—

Lord Molyneux, "who lay at Mrs. Byrom's."

Mr. Dickinson and Sir William Gerrard, at Captain Dickinson's house.

Mr. Townley, his brother Charles, and Mr. Blundell, "at Newton's, the clerk."

"Two Mr. Worthingtons" and Mr. William Clifton, "at a private house in Millgate."

Mr. Anderton, Mr. Robert Bryon and Roger, his son, at a house near the bridge end.

Mr. Carns, at Lieutenant Ashton's.

Richard Cher of Atherton, nailer.

Richard Houghton [Stoughton ?] of the same.

Thomas Allen of Smallbrooke, "lives at a place called the Mault House" near Newcastle, Staffordshire.

William Lathom of Hartington, Derbyshire.

George Hulme of Langnor, Staffordshire, drov[er].

Francis Stealy of Yeograve, near Hartington.

John Sherbotham of Hulton Hey, near Norton, Staffordshire.

Samuel Nuttall of Yeograve.

Richard Foxley of Buxton, Derbyshire.

Richard Allen of Wallasey, Cheshire.

Ralph Crompton of Tongue-fold, near Bolton.

Ralph Brotherst of Megg Lane, near Maxfield, Cheshire.

Simon Hurst of Deanchurch, Lancashire.

"Two brothers, surnamed Sparrows," betwixt Newcastle and Nantwich.

Elizabeth Redfearne, near Langnor.

"Thomas Allen lives at an house called Malt house, near Weston Cony, near Newcastle, in Staffordshire; Randle Bagnell lives near Allen. They work in Allen's house, in a roome on the second flore; there being a ladder which goes up out of a ground room, on the right hand of the first room [on] entering the house, up into the working room, w[here] there is an hole in the wall of the room where [they] hide their work. They are weekly supplied by Joseph Hoyle, near Uxeter [Uttoxeter ?], for keep, with clippings; he hath a wodden legg." *Seal.*

SIR WILLIAM GERARD to ROGER DICONSON, at "the Barber's Powle in Fullwood Street, neare Gray's Inn."

911. 1694, December 28.—" I finde that I was caried to Preston prisoner, by the dragoons, the 16th of June, [16]89, where I found Mr. Towneley in custody. Wee staied there about 10 daies, and then I and old Blundell went by Wigan, where we staied all night, to Manchester, and wee kept there untill February after. Now, the Militia had then been raised severall daies before, so that there was no likelewood of meeting at others houses. Robert Molineux is here now, and says that Lunt was with him at Mosbrough, about Midsummer in 1690, and then, told him, severall times, that he then never had seen my Lord Molineux nor me, and desired him he would begg some relief of . . for him, and that Lunt came hither once in hopes of meeting him, and that he would get something for him ; but Lord Molineux not coming, hee got nothing, nor did see me then, nor ever else, at any time that I know of, for I never as yet spoke with him or saw him, that I know. My coachman tells me that at Coventrie, in his journey home, he met Bandy, who was well acquainted with Roger, Sir Thomas Clifton's coachman, and there Bandy protested to them that he knew nothing against any of the prisoners. I should think it would be much to clearing of your (?) prisoners, and the lessening of the r[epu]tation of Baker, if Woods of Wigan and W . . . Jackson did declare how often they were tempted by Baker and others, to become evidence against us, and doubtless, no man can thinke that there had been listed above 500, as Lunt and Wilson sweares, but that some of them made (*sic*) have appeared. How should anyone think that so many regiments of horse could have been raised here when, in King James's raigne, all our interest, backed by his authority, could not raise one regiment of foot! I doubt not but all reasonable men will be easily satisfied of the false oathes of our adversaries, and all parties concerned will be ever obliged to you for your great paines and labour you have undertaken for the publick." *Seal.*

ROBERT DALTON to ROGER DICONSON.

912. 1694, December 29. Thurnham (?).—"In answear to yours, John Carson's ship came into our port the 13th of June 1689; and it was sayd that Threlfall and Lunt arive[d] in that shipe. I was not then a prisoner, but upon suspicion that they might bee att my hous, which they were not. That night, about 10 of the clock, Sir John Bloud, with a party of hors, came to search my hous and seas me, which they did, and I being much out of order, lett me remayne all night att my owne hous, upon my parole that I would go to them att Lancaster the next day, which I did, and there was bound, in 500*li.* to apeare upon summons. Upon the 20th, Livetenant Ussherwood came allso, about 10 o'clocke att night, and searched agayne, and tooke me away to Preston that night, whither we arive[d] next morning about 5 o'clocke. There I was delivered to the Militia souldiers, and there kept untill the 26th of June, on which day I was conveyed, with severall other gentlemen, to Manchester, by Captin Ralf Egerton, with a party of the Militia hors. If you see my Cousin Kenion, you may give him this account, for itt iss exacter than that I gave lawier Rigby, who came, with his Secretarie, about itt."

CHARLES RIGBY to ROGER KENYON.

913. 1694, December 30. Lancaster.—Giving an account of the confession of Hartley, the coiner, who had been condemned, and was reprieved upon giving information against other coiners and clippers. " But the trouble, at this time, is to acquaint you with Hartley's complaints against Mr. Elletson, the goaler, since he hath reliéd on the discovery he hath made for procureing his pardon, and hath left of feeding the gaoler with monye. He says the gaoler, soon after the Assizes, had a considerable sum of money of him, in order to procure his pardon, and, though he effected nothing, yet keept his moneye. Hartley allso gave 12*l.* more, or upwards, to keep the yrons of him; but this notwithstanding, the gaoler now threatens him with grievous ill usage, — unless Hartley will weekely pay him his owne demands, which are very large; and not only so, but this day the goaler threatned that he would, by this post, write some things of him that should do his worke, which makes Hartley fear that because the goaler cannot have his end of him, he will endeavour; by some false story, to incence you, or others, against him. Hartley therefore desires that, since he is resolved to deal ingeniously in his discovery, that he may not be discouraged in it by the goaler, who hath no ends but his owne private gaine." *Seal, broken.*

ACCOUNT of the ARREST and IMPRISONMENT of MR. LEIGH, of Lyme House.

914. 1694.—The 17th of July, 1694, " Mr. Clark, the messenger, and Mr. Lunt, together with 14 Dutch troopers, came to Lyme, between 6 and 7 of the clock in the morning. That the messenger, with one Oldham, who was their guide, with two or three Dutch troopers, came up the great stairs in Lyme House, and apprehended Mr. Leigh in his night-gown; and the messenger charged him with a warrant for high treason, and carryed him, the said Mr. Leigh, out of his dressing roome to his closett, where stood Mr. Lunt, with two or three Dutchmen, and then all went into the closett. The messenger and Lunt searched through Mr. Leigh's papers from 7 till 12, and Lunt, when he mett with any paper that pleased him, putt it in his pocket. And from thence they carryed Mr. Leigh downstairs into the parlour, and there sett two Dutchmen to guard him whilst they searched every roome and place for armes, finding onely a case of pistolls and carrobin in Mr. Leigh's closett, which they carryed away. And that night, they took Mr. Leigh from his house and carryed him to Knutsford, guarded by the messenger and 12 Dutchmen. That Lunt seized one of the best horses Mr. Leigh had, sett his owne saddle upon him, and carryed him quite away. That they carryed Mr. Leigh to Chester Castle the next day, where he remained till the last day of August, or the first day of September. Then he lodged ther with ———— were carryed from Chester to London guarded by 4 messengers and 21 Dutch troopers, comanded by Captaine Baker in person, and at St. Giles Barr's house, committed to the hands of the messengers, and there kept three dayes, and then brought down to the Secretary's office, Duke of Shrewsbury, principall Secretary, who examined Mr. Leigh and remanded him back to the messengers for three dayes more, and then committed to the Tower. Whilst Mr. Leigh was in the Tower, and in the worste roome in all the Tower, [he] had very hard usage; that his lady, at the first, was denyed either to see him or heare him speak. That old Madam Leigh came under the window where Mr. Leigh lodged, and asked her sonn, Mr. Leigh, how he did; and [the] sentinell, with his gun cockt, said, if she spoke another word, he would shoot her. That he had notice to prepare for his tryall at Chester Castle in fourteen dayes, and within six dayes after, was removed out of the Tower and carryed down to Chester, guarded by a party of horse, the gentleman porter, and the gentleman gaoler of the Tower, and each two warders, and committed to the Constable of Chester Castle, after which, he was onely called to the barr, and discharged without tryall."

Account of the Arrests of Philip Langton and Mr. Blundell.

915. [1694.]—27 July, 1694.—"Philip Langton, when gone to Wapra, in Flintshire, to the buriall of his sister-in-law, was there taken up by Marisco, the messinger, alone, and the same day taken to Chester Castle, and there kept till Thursday the 30th of August, and then brought by Captain Baker and his Duch Guards to London, upon Wensday, 5th of September. And there, at one Beak's, a messinger's house in Warwick Street, near Golden Square, in St. James's, was kept with Sir Rowland Stanley, Sir Thomas Clifton, and Mr. Legh, till Tuesday the 11th, and that day brought before the Duke of Shrewsbury ; and the next day, September 12th, carryed to Newgate, where he remained prisoner with Mr. Blundell, but in different rooms, till Wednesday the 10th of October, and there was then brought down to be tryed with the rest of the gentlemen, at Manchester.

"30 July, 1694.—About half [an] hower past five in the morning, three of the King's messengers, Francis Clark, Richard Heward, and Peter Moriscoe, together with John Lunt, John Wombell, and Christopher Ellis, came to the hall of Crosby, to take up Mr. Blundell; and young Mr. Blundell, being the first person the messingers there met, which Clark and Heward, with pistolls in their hand, asked if Esquire Blundell was stirring, hee told them hee thought hee was not. They then required him to bring them to Esquire Blundell's chamber, which forthwith he did, and called of his father, who arose and unlocked his door ; then Haward, the messinger, went into the roome, desiring the other messinger, Clarke, to go down the stairs to call up some more of their company, who went accordingly, and young Mr. Blundell followed him down and went away. The house was then very strictly searched, and a case of pistolls, two swords, one birding piece, seaven horses, and two hackney saddles were taken, and brought to Captain Baker at Wigan, But the old gentleman, Esquire Blundell, who for more than thirty years huth been very lame, when they saw what a man hee was, they did not think fit to carry him with them. And at young Mr. Blundell's return, his horses, though of small value, being taken, he went (in hope of his aid to get his horses agane) to his neighbour Mr. Norris, who committed him to the care of Mr. Mawdit, then Mayor of Levepoole (now Mr. Norriss's brother-burgess in Parliament, for Leverpoole), with whom Mr. Blundell must stay till Captain Baker's comeing thither the next day, and then hee, instead of his father (as the likelyer man of the two, though he also is very lame), was then sent to Chester Castle a prisoner, and thence, with the rest of the prisoners, taken to London."

Note, in the handwriting of Roger Kenyon, of the arrest of Sir William Gerrard.

916. 1694, ———.—"Sir William Gerrard taken up on Tuesday 17th of June, 1694, about 7 in the afternoon, at Garsewood, his own house, by Marisco, the messenger, accompanyed by Mr. Taaf and John Womwall (*sic*), and attended by eight Duch troopers. They suffered Sir William to tarry at his own house that night, and the next day, the messenger, with four Dutch troopers, carryed Sir William to Chester Castle, where he was kept prisoner six weeks and one day, and, the 30th of August, taken with the rest, by 30 Dutch troopers or thereabouts, towards London, whither they came the 5th of September, and then Sir William, for a week, was kept at Morison's house in Dartmouth Street, Westminster. No other gentleman was there, except a Frenchman, upon some other account. Six days after Sir William's being first in that house, hee was taken before the Duke of Shrewsbury, and a few questions asked. He was after that remanded to the messenger's house, and, the 12th of September, at night, brought to the Tower, and after a month's stay there, brought thence by Major Hawley and the gentleman gaoler, sixteen of the Tower warders, and 32 of the Earl of Oxford's troop, to Coventree, and thence by a party of Dutch horse, commanded by the Tower Major, Major Hawley, who brought them to Manchester, and there delivered to the Sheriff of Lancashire on Teusday, 16 October, 1694."

The CASE of PETER LEIGH of Lyme, in the County of Chester.

917. [1694.]—"Peter Legh of Lyme, in the County of Chester, Esquire. Hee hath allways lived in the communion of the Church of England, free from any factiouse hankering, either towards Rome or Geneva. A gentleman of a plentiful estate, under no necessitouse exigencies to induce him to a change for the bettering his conditions. A man of great moderation and temper, both in his words and in his actions; so far from being a busie body, that hee never had nor sought for any office. Hee was, in the reign of King [Charles] the Second, a Member of Parliament, and on that occasion onely tooke the oaths of allegiance and supremace, and never els, till of late, being subpœnad a witness, on his now Majestie's behalf, did he, in all his life, take any oath.

" His case and usage. On the 17th of July, 1694, betwixt 6 and 7 in the morning, in his morneing gown, just come from his bed, hee was seised in his dressing room at Lyme, by Mr. Clerke, one of the King's messengerrs, accompanied by John Lunt, the informer, guarded by a party of Duch troopers, charged with a warrant for High Treason; his house ransacked for armes and papers from 7 till 12 o'clock, but nothing to their purpose found. Hee was, that day, by the messenger and 12 Duch troops, taken to the market town of Knutsford, and thence, the next day, to Chester Castle, the common gaol for that county, and there kept prisoner 6 weeks and 2 days; and thence, by about 30 Duch troops, commanded by Captain Baker, carryed to London, and for some time kept a close prisoner at a messenger's house in Barwick Street; and, after, by the Duke of Shrewsbury's warrant, committed to the Tower of London, and had there a bad room and ill usage. His wife was denied to see or speak to him, but she obtained the Queen's order to be kept with him. His mother, though under his window, was denied the satisfaction to hear him speak to her, and after one month's endurance there, hee was, with other prisoners, taken by the Tower officers and a numerouse guard of troopers, exposed as a show, through the streets of London and through the severall countys and townes in the road, from thence to Chester. And when thither comme, kept in gaol there till the comeing of the Judges, at whose sitting in Court, he, together with Sir Thomas Stanley, being by the gaoler brought to the barr, they were without any impeachment, arraignment, or anything layed to their charge, discharged. But Mr. Legh, in fees and payments under his several confinements, and in preparation for a tryall for his life, his charge of witnesses and counsel, and in his expenses at those chargeable places for himselfe, his wife, and their attendants, besides the hard usages, the indignity and reproaches he sustained, at least the charge of [   ]. Such as sit at the helme seem not yet at leisure to think how disagreeable such usages are to our civil constitution; that our English laws—*leges Angliæ quas nolumus mutare*—should endure such sufferings, remediless of relief.

" Do our English laws authorize a Minister of State, by his arbitrary warrant, to empower any common person, that hee will style the King's messenger, to break and enter into any man's house, all England over, to search for and seize armes, commonly shewed at musters, or armes usually worn by the maister and servants, park guns, or fowling or birding pieces, or to break into and ransack and search every room, cabinet, and drawer, chest, trunk or box ; break locks, bolts, and barrs, to come to everything -jewells, gold, silver, plate, evidences, bonds, bills, bookes of accounts, letters of a man's most important and secret correspondencie, and to take away what he shall judge fit to be seised, and to seise and carry away with him the master of the house, from his house and from his county, supposing him a criminall; may he be carryed quite away from that county where the fact is supposed to be done, and is onely tryable, and carryed into a far remote county, to the great minister by whose warrant he is seised; and to be committed close prisoner to no known prison, but to a messenger's private house, and there kept day by day, nor friend, nor servant suffered to see him; and, after that, sent to the Tower of London, to be there kept some weekes, in order to be sent to his tryall at Chester, from which county he was first sent for, and when thither brought, on pretence to bee tryed, after all, neither prosecutor nor witnes appear there against him ; nor more to be done, but pay the fees demanded and go home ?

" But the thing done—if pretending to be a legall prosecution—was not more unusual than was the manner of doing it; for the laws of England establish to us known officers, judiciall and ministeriall, in the Crown Office, or Court of Pleas; wee know none by the name of King's Messenger. However, his coming might be more formidable by being accompanyed by an armed power of aliens, never naturalised nor made denizens, and by his associate Lunt, more dangerous and dreadfull than them all.

" It was, sure, an extravagant apprehension possessed the Minister of State, that he durst not rely upon the *Posse Comitatus*, to bring Mr. Legh, if a criminall, to the propper tribunall, to receive his doom. It is, by our English laws, a part of the civil magistrate's oath, when he takes his office, not to send his warrant against any man to be taken up and abridged of his liberty, directed to the party upon whose information, or at whose instance, the man is to be apprehended, but to direct it to such indifferent person as will do right. Now that Mr. Lunt, upon whose information Mr. Legh was to be taken up, must be one to take up Mr. Legh, and one to go through his house, which he had never seen before, and have the perussall of his study and papers, from 7 o'clock till 12, and make his observations upon the person of Mr. Legh, whom, though he had sworn against, hee had never, till then, seene. This, one would think, may pass at least for a peccadillo, when our laws are consulted on the case.

" And surpassing were the unparalleled preparations for the management of the ensuing tryalls. Mr. Aaron Smith, solicitor of the Lords of the Treasury, who, to the fame of their choyce, had in the late reign stood in the pillory, in regard of his parts, was, with a good purse, sent in state with his coach and six, first to Manchester, a trading town in Lancashire, where never an assize had been before kept, to appear great there, where the tryalls were to be begun, as principal solicitor against the prisoners; who, after he had convicted there (for nothing less than convictions were thought on) eight red-letter criminalls, he was to take Chester in his way home, to do Sir Thomas Stanley and Mr. Legh's businesse there, both gentlemen of the Church of England.

"But some months before this, Captaine Baker, who, in the late raigne, had received a harder sentance than the pillory, though he escaped the execution, he was not so soon acquainted with Lunt, as Mr. Smith was; but he, after he had licked into forme Lunt's, Wilson's, and Wombwell's informations, and introduced those informers to a great Minister of State, hee was thought fittest, before Mr. Smith, to be dispatched into Lancashire and Cheshire, with a purse, to take down 4 messengers, and more informers, with letters to 2 Justices of each County to assist him, and a power to command a party of Duch troopers to take up and carry the gentlemen, in the messenger's warrants, first to Chester Castle, and after, together, to London, which, when hee had performed, hee againe came downe at their returne to be tryed, his chiefe charge being then to take care of the witnesses, hee having most reason to know best how to manage his own creatures.

"The two entrusted Justices, writ to in Lancashire : — one was made one of the commissioners of Oyer and Terminer, and sate as Judge; the other, reserved for . . . . of finding the bills, to be foreman of the Grand Jury. The bills, being long and of unusuall forme, they were brought down ready drawn. And, least the Clerk of the Crown of Lancashire, whose office it is, by the King's letters patent, that hee, or his sufficient deputy, sit under the Judges to dispatch the business of the Crown in that County Palatine, least they should not manage to Mr. Aaron's mind, hee brought down one Winter, from the King's Bench, who did officiate, and, which was more than usuall, went from the Court to read the bills to the grand jury. Mr. Boyd, another King's Bench practiser, came down as a second-rate solicitor, with briefs to instruct and inform the King's counsell. No lesse than 5 lawyers were brought down, to be of counsell for the King and Queen. 137 gentlemen, from all parts of the County of Lancaster, were summoned for Jurors, and with 4 of the Judges (duble the number of our circuiters) sate, and 4 other great persons joyned with them in the commission of Oyer and Terminer. No person that could be any way usefull, was unbrought. Nothing was omitted to agrandize the solemnity of this session !

"The first tryall was against 5 of the prisoners, indicted together in one bill:—Sir Roland Stanley, Sir Thomas Clifton, Mr. Dicconson, Mr. Langton, and Mr. Blundell, against whom were produced 8 witnesses, who severall of them gave a full evidence against the five. But, when all that evidence was over, the prisoners called 34 witnesses, by whom the said former witnesses were so disproved and detected, that the Judge said it was a great mystery of iniquity on one side, saying to the Jury, if the first witnesses be believed, there is a plaine proofe of a great contrivance to bring in the French King, and raise a rebellion here; but if you believe that Lunt and the rest have contrived this way to ruin the gentlemen, and take away their lives and estates, in hope to enrich themselves, then the falt will lye more upon the accusers. Then the gentlemen are innocent; you must acquit them. The Jury, without going forth of Court, sayd they were agreed of their verdict. And being called to give their verdict, and demanded to each of the prisoners whether guilty or not guilty, they gave their verdict to each apart, not guilty. After which the Lord Molineùx, Sir William Gerard, and Bartholomew Walmsley, Esquire, the other prisoners there, being on Monday brought to the barr, and the Jury to trye them, sworn and charged, and the indictment opened to the Jury, no witness appeared against them, so the Jury, to each of them apart, gave their verdict not guilty. Whereupon, Mr. Justice Eyre said: 'Gentlemen, you that are acquitted, you have a very pregnant instance shown to you that the Court refuses to give credit, or so much as an ear, to what the witnesses on Saturday have sworn to; and since there are none to accuse you (for the witnesses were sent away), I do not condemn you.'

"The assizes, for the tryall of Sir Thomas Stanley and Mr. Legh, being appointed to be two days following, at Chester, viz., on Wensday, 24 October, 1694, the Judges were thither comme, but Lunt, Wilson, Wombel, and Bruerton, the four principle witnesses, being vanished, there was none found to swear to the bills against Sir Thomas Stanley or Mr. Legh; and no bill being found against them, there was nothing to try, nor to do, but dismisse them; the cryer's proclamation being far from so loud as the acclamation of the people.

"Now, as to Mr. Legh, of whom particularly this paper is intended to give an account, it may very truly be said hee is a gentleman well known, and as well beloved, who never did a thing offensive to the government hee lived under, and as seldom as any to anybody in it. A gentleman who avoyds disputes, meddles not in the controversies of the time, it may perhaps be hard to find one to whom this character is so truly due; and can this his case and usage, were the lawes of England had in due execution, lye long unremembered, or, when remembered, remaine unresented? Would it not beget at least a hard thought, if not a sensure, which should by no means be suffered towards our government, which hath enemies too many, that would be too ready to improve it, being that which cannot by reason be justified. It is from no disafected wish to pray that justice and right may be done; for it is justice doth establish the throne!"

Depositions of Edward Beresford.

918. [1694.]—"Edward Beresford of London, gentleman, maketh oath That Mrs. Dickenson, wife of Mr. Dickenson, now in custody, having several tymes desyred this deponent to meet, or procure some one to meet, one Mr. Taffe, who told her that he had some things to say of importance, relating to the service of the Cheshire and Lancashire gentlemen now in prison, and that he desyred very much to meet any one that he might declare his mynd to. That this deponent, having noe inclynation to meet or converse with him, had put it off for above a weeke, during which tyme, as the said Mrs. Dickenson told this deponent, the said Mr. Taffe, or his wife, had severall tymes prest to have some one to meet him. At last one Mr. Bankes, of Gray's Inn, did consent to meet the said Taffe, saying he would hear what the gentlemen had to say, and thought there could be noe danger in it, and accordingly did, as this deponent beleeves, meet the said Mr. Taffe on the twenty seaventh day of September last in the afternoone. That on the twenty eighth of the same month, in the morning early, the said Mr. Taffe came to Mr. Banks at his chambers in Gray's Inn, where this deponent alsoe then was. That after some complements past betwixt Mr. Banks and Mr. Taffe, the said Mr. Taffe tooke occasion to say that he was very much concerned for those gentlemen that were prisoners, meaning those of Cheshire and Lancashire, as this deponent beleeves.

"That he was noe witnesse himselfe, nor any wayes concerned, but that there was one Lunt, *alias* Smith, who, he said, was a witnesse against them, in relation to a plot against the Government, and that he reposed an intyre confidence in him, the said Taffe. That he, the said Lunt, had often read to him his narrative of the said plot; that he was a loose, extravagant talking fellow, and would expose and reveal himselfe at first sight to any one or more that he, the said Taffe, recommended, or to that effect. And farther said that

Lunt was a great rogue; and he, the said Taffe, proposed to recomend someone to his acquaintance as a certayne means to detect him, or to that effect. That what he proposed was in respect to the Government as well as truth. That he had great obligations, and was zealous for the interest of the Government. That he began to have a distrust of the plot, and in particular of Lunt's testimony, upon the said Lunt and a messenger going lately to seize young Mr. Blundell of Crosby, now a prisoner, against whom Lunt was a witnesse, as the said Taffe declared; that he, the said Lunt, met the prisoner, Mr. Blundell, and askt for Esquire Blundell, and the prisoner showed them upp to his father and then left them ; upon this accident the said Taffe said he began to conceive a bad oppinion of him and his evidence because he knew not the man against whom he had sworne, or to that effect.

"That Lunt had often complayned to him that he wanted a man or two—as this deponent supposed, to be evidence in his plot ; but he desired one of credit, that was a protestant and lookt like a gentleman or an officer, and had often prest the said Taffe to helpe him to some such, according to his promise. That Mr. Taffe farther sayd that yf some gentleman woud consent to see him upon his, the said Taffe's, recommendation, he questioned not but upon the first or second tyme of seeing him, he, the said Lunt, would give the said gentleman what he would have him to swear, in wryting, relating to his plot, as this deponent beleeved. He, the said Taffe, prest his method very much, and said he beleeved it the only way to discover the rouges, whereupon Mr. Bagshawe of Gray's Inn, who was then by, consented to meet him, the said Taffe, at the 'Ship' alehouse, by Temple Barr, at three of the clock in the same day, the said Taffe undertaking to bring the said Lunt thither.

" Thereupon, Mr. Taffe instructed Mr. Bagshawe what to say and how to behave himselfe, and so Mr. Taffe went away. Mr. Bagshaw afterwards, upon further thought and reflection, was unwilling to goe till hee had further consulted what was adviseable and safe, and it was agreed that Mr. Bankes and this deponent should go to the place named, and disappoint the meeting by telling Mr. Taffe the reason of Mr. Bagshawe's not coming, which this deponent did, upon which Mr. Taffe seemed very much concerned that he must disappoint Lunt, who was very eager, he said, and would not stay to be sent for, as was agreed, but would come along with him. And the said Taffe was particulerly concerned that Mr. Bagshawe would not come, because, he said, he was mightily taken with his countenance. Mr. Taffe was very urgent with Mr. Bankes or this deponent to stay, though it were only to drinke a glasse of ale with Lunt, and nothing of business should be talked of. Thereupon, Mr. Bankes consented to stay, and this deponent imedeately left him and Mr. Taffe together, and went to the 'Rainebow' coffee-house, to Mr. Bagshaw. About an hour afterwards, or something more, Mr. Bankes came to this deponent and Mr. Bagshaw, and all three imediately went into Lincoln's Inn walks, where Mr. Bankes gave a relation to this deponent and Mr. Bagshaw of what passed at the 'Ship' alehouse, betwixt him, Mr. Taffe, and Mr. Lunt."

LANCASHIRE PLOT.—DEPOSITIONS OF LAURENCE PARSONS and JAMES PARKINSON.

919. [1694].—Laurence Parsons, of Shavington, in the parish of Standish, in the county of Lancaster, dyer, deposes that in May last, he met Lunt in London, and that Lunt promised, if he would swear that they together did deliver commissions from King James to gentlemen in Ormskirk and other places, that he should receive 150*li*. and be entered into Capt. Baker's office and have the King's pay of 20*s*. a week. And Lunt told him that he should soon have a commission from the Secretary of State and Privy Council for seizing of horses and arms in Lancashire, and requested deponent to join with him in the execution thereof. Deponent afterwards travelled to Manchester with Lunt, Taaffe, John Woombell, Captain Baker, Christopher Ellis, and George Wilson.

James Parkinson, of Carhall, in the county of Lancaster, gentleman, deposes that one Ellis, servant to Captain Baker, and one of the King's messengers, had seized two of his horses, and deponent sent his wife to try if she could prevail on Ellis and his company to restore his horses, and his wife informed him that John Lunt, who was with Ellis, said he had matters of consequence to impart to deponent. And deponent went to Lunt, who asked his assistance in giving evidence against Lord Molyneux and other gentlemen in the county ; to which deponent said, " I know nothing against them "; to which Lunt replied, " You know as much as I do "·; and added, " We have taken Lord Molyneux and Sir William Gerrard; if we could but take Master Molyneux and Esquire Gerrard we would let the Lord Molyneux and Sir William Gerrard go."

DEPOSITIONS of WILLIAM WHALLEY concerning the LANCASHIRE PLOT.

920. [1694.]—" I doe remember that on Saturday, the 20th of October, 1694, I was on the jury that tryed Sir Rowland Stanley, Sir Thomas Clifton, William Dickonson, Esqre., Philip Langton, Esqre., William Blundell, Esqre. Att which tryall John Lunt was produced as an evidence for the Kinge and Queene, and swore that, att Dunkenhall (which to the best of my remembrance as to the time) he affirmed to be in the yeare 1691, in his presence, Mr. Walmsley did then and there deliver to Mr. Dicconson, of Wrightington, a comission from Kinge James to bee a Lieftannant Collonel of Horse, and that Mr. Dickonson did then and there take and receive it att his hands.

" I doe alsoe remember, at the same tryall, George Wilson was then and there produced as an evidence for the Kinge and Queene, and swore that hee was in the company of John Lunt att Croxtath, and there found the Lord Mollineux, Sir Rowland Stanley, Sir William Gerrard, and others, mett together, and that hee was present when John Lunt att Croxteth did, with his owne hands, deliver to the Lord Mollineux a comission under or from Kinge James, that made him Governor of Liverpoole. And that hee was present alsoe when John Lunt did deliver, then and there, to Sir Rowland Stanley a comission, from or under Kinge James, to make him a Collonel of Horse ; and alsoe when John Lunt did then and there deliver to Sir William Gerrard a comission under or from King James to make him a Collonel of Horse (and this to the best of my remembrance as to the time) Wilson swore to bee in the month of June or July, 1689.

" I doe alsoe remember, att the same tryall, the said Wilson swore that hee was present at Dunkenhall, and that Mr. Walmsley did then and there, in person, with his own hand, in the presence of him, the said Wilson, deliver to Mr. Dickonson a comission in writinge, under and from Kinge James, to make him, the said Mr. Dickonson, a Lieftennant Collonel of Horse, and that Mr. Dickonson did then and there, in his presence, receive and accept the same att his hands, and this, to the best of my knowledge (as to the time) Wilson affirmed to bee in February, 1691.

"I do alsoe remember that John Wombell, at the same tryall, was produced as an evidence for the Kinge and Queene, and swore that hee came to Standish Hall with armes, and then and there found and saw Mr. Dickonson, Mr. Blundell, and others, present and mett together, and that hee then and there saw great quantity of armes to be divided, and that a certain part of the said armes to be shared and distributed between Mr. Dickonson and Mr. Blundell, and that Mr. Dickonson and Mr. Blundell did, in his sight, take their share of the arms soe divided, and this to the best of my remembrance (as to the time) Wombell swore to be about December, 1691.

"I do alsoe remember the said Wombell, att the same tryall, being asked by Mr. Blundell whether hee was not att Crosbie with the Kinges messengers, att the search for arms. Hee answered, hee was there. Mr. Blundell asked him whether he knew anything of any moneys taken there by any of the company, and whether none was found about him, being searched, who answered, no money was found about him butt his owne, which as I remember hee said was about 12s. *Copy.*

[*Depositions to same effect made by Hugh Holme.*]

NAMES of those appointed to make arrests, and of informers.

921. [1694]—"The names of the persons employed to take up persons impeached, as also of the informers, with an account of who and what they are or have been."

The NAMES of the Gentlemen informed against by LUNT.

922. [1694.]—In all, there are the names of 103 persons, viz.:—
"Lord Thomas Howard, Lord George Howard, Dr. Bromfield, the Earl of Melfort, Mr. Edmund Threlfall (dead), Mr. Gourden, the Lord Molineux's son, Thomas Tildesley, Esquire, Mr. Dalton of Thurnham, Mr. Sherburn of Stonyhurst, Mr. Townley of Townley, Mr. Girlington, Mr. Westby of Mowbreck, the Lord Molineux, Mr. Legh of Lyme, Sir Thomas Stanley of Aldersley, Mr. Cholmondeley of Valeroyall, Sir Rowland Stanley, Sir Thomas Clifton, my Lord Brudenall, Sir ——— Troogmorton (?), the Lord Dunbar, the Lord Preston, the Lord Fairfax, Mr. Strickland, Sir Thomas Gascow, Sir ——— Stapleton, Mr. Tempest, Mr. Vavasour, Mr. Harrington, Mr. Clayton, Mr. Ryder, Mr. Traps, Mr. Lawson, Major Moor, Sir William Gerard's son, Mr. Dicconson of Wrightington, Capt. Griffith, Whitney the highwayman (dead), Mr. Stanley, Mr. Shuttleworth, Mr. Tildsley of Stonesacre, Mr. Langton, Mr. Chantrell, Colonel Walmsley of Dunghall, Mr. Dracot of Pansley, Staffordshire, Sir Richard Fleetwood, Mr. Roland Fleetwood, Mr. Whital, Mr. Cuny of Cuny, Mr. Stacy of Reddington, Sir James Simons, Mr. Bazil Brook, the Lord Stafford, Mr. Stafford, the Lord Stafford's brother, Mr. Whitfield, Mr. Basell, Capt. Goodman, Mr. Pollard of 'the Blue Posts' in the Haymarket, Mr. Towgood at 'the Griffin' in Bloomsbury, Mr. Clarkson at 'the Lancaster Castle' in Red Lyon Square, Mr. Vaughan at the 'White Horse' inn in . . . . . , Mr. Eason at 'the George' inn by Holborn Bridge, Mr. Carre at 'the Royall Oak' in Drury Lane, Mr. Jolly of 'the Black Posts' in Drury Lane, Mr. John Sharples in the Haymarket, Mr. Rigby in Covent Garden, and his son, the Lord Arundell, Lord Barimore (?), Lord Griffin, Sir William Goreng, Colonel Tufton, Colonel Holeman, Colonel Bernard Howard. Lieutenant - Colonel Bankes, Colonel Porter, Lieutenant - Colonel Griffith, Captain Goodman, Capt. Nelson, Captain Tozar, Captain

Spencer, Mr. Standish, Captain Noell, Captain Walton, Mr. Pepper, Mr. Preston, Captain Roberts, the Lord Feversham, Mr. Tasbrough, Mr. Kingsley, Colonel Griffin, Colonel Tufton, Lord Strangfort, Mr. Basteen, Mr. Clark, Mr. Loe, Alderman Crosse of Rochester, Lord Carrington, Lord Salisbury, Lord Huntington, Sir Henry Tichburn, Sir John Friend. *In the handwriting of Roger Kenyon.*

DRAFT SPEECH, probably to be delivered to the House of Commons by ROGER KENYON.

923. [1694.]—"Wee are now to consider the present posture and condition of the nation, and this our resolution being published, the eyes of our countrey are upon us, and makes them hope for and expect redress of those grievances under which they labour. You had some of them hinted at the other day, under the heads of false evidence, forrainers in our councells, and an unequall burthen of the warr upon us. But the first of these is that which most sencibly affects mee and my countrey, where the blackest of vilanyes has been most plainly detected, and the thoughts of it strikes all men with horror and amazement. Gentlemen of peaceable dispositions (but, indeed, they had good estates, and that was their greatest crime) were under Dutch guards, to the great expence of their fortunes and hazard of their lives, hurryed from their own house to Chester Castle, thence to the Tower and Newgate, thence down again to the countrey, and there arraigned and tryed for high treason, but, God bee thanked, acquitted. I happened to bee at the tryall, and shall, by your permission, give you a short account of some transactions I there observed, the legality of which I shall not take on myself to determine, but sure I am, most people thought they were very great hardships. A power was avowed, in open court, that the judges might put into, and put out of, the pannell of the Grand Jury what persons they pleased, and that in cases of high treason. The Judge, in his charge, passed his censure upon the gentlemen before any bill was preferred against them, telling the jury that the occasion of their coming armed with that commission was the treachery of their own countrymen; but this was also accompanyed with a side blow at the Church of England, hee adding that those countrymen of theirs were Protestants and Papists: 'Protestants,' sayes hee, 'of the Church of England, as they call themselves, who mingle with Papists, as the iron and the clay at the feet of Nebuchednazer's image.' The Lord Mollineux, upon his arraignment, put in a petition, that, by reason of his great age and infirmityes, hee could neither see, hear, nor understand, soe prayed that councell might bee assigned him, but this the Court very truly told him could not be granted by law; yet Barron Powell, one of the judges, in tender compassion and commiseration of his condition, said that if he had a friend or two to stand by and assist him they would connive at it, but this the judge who managed the Commission opposed, and sayd it must neither be granted nor connived at. Five of the gentlemen being put into one indictment, and a coppye of their pannell given them, the Court terryfyed them, telling them that if they would not wave their seperate challenges and consent that one of them should challenge for the whole, the Court would proceed to try one of them presently. Whereupon they waved their right, given them by law, and consented; which being done, and they withdrawn under their guards out of Court, the judge ordered 40 more to bee added to that pannell, which was accordingly done. Tenn gentlemen of quality, some of them members of this House, some of them deputy lievetenants, but all of them justices of the peace for that county, were all excepted against by the King's councell, without cause shewn, by direction, as was reasonably supposed, of Aron Smith, and not one gentleman of note was allowed to serve on that jury; soe the foreman was an ordinary tradesman and the landlord of the house where the judges lodged. The prisoners desired that the evidence against them might be examined seperately and apart, but this was denyed, the judge saying it would cast a reflection upon the King's evidence. Lunt, .the first evidence, said he knew the prisoners very well, that he had been often in their companyes, done business for them, and given commissions to them, but being demanded which was Sir Rowland Stanley, he pointed to Sir Thomas Cliffton and called him Sir Rowland Stanley, and pointing to Sir Rowland Stanley and called him Sir Thomas Cliffton, which caused some just muttering against him by the people in the Court. Therefore, to rectifye this his mistake, hee was bid to take the cryer's staffe and lay it upon Sir Rowland Stanley. Hee tooke the staffe and layd it upon Sir Thomas Cliffton, and again called him Sir Rowland Stanley, and Sir Rowland Stanley he again called Sir Thomas Cliffton. Now, to help this lame evidence out of this ditch, which the cryer's staffe was not stronge enough to doe, the judge asked him if those were the two knights for whom hee had done busness and to whom hee had delivered commissions, to which leading question the profligate wretch could easily make an affirmation, and soe he said that they were. 'Why then,' sayes the Judge to the Jury, 'gentlemen, you are not to lay any stress at all upon his mistaking of one for the other, nor is it to weigh anything with you.'

" These, sir, are some of the hardships I observed at this tryall, but how the evidences were confronted and their perjurys manifested, and how it was made to appear that had those knights of the post succeeded in this first essay of their plott, they would have caryed it on to the gentlemen of the best estates in England, and where and by whom an office is kept, where informers are listed into pay, I hope other gentlemen who were there and have better memoryes than I have, will acquaint you. And then I hope you will not only pass your sensure upon the wrong-doores but that you will also by some good bill or bills " [*ends abruptly*].

In the handwriting of Richard Edge.

EDWARD FINCH to ROGER KENYON, at Manchester.

924. 1694, " Friday, 9th." Winwick.—" We expect my Lord Derby here to day, whom I beleive I shall perswade to go up to parliament earlier than he used to do. I shall meet the Chester coach at Whitchurch next Monday night, and go up to London in that. I have so many things to confer with you about, that it would be in vain to attempt it by letters, in so short a time as I have to stay in the country. But thus much I think I ought to hint to you, viz. that I hear the wittnesses are clapped up and ordered to be prosecuted for perjury. I hope your illness will not hinder your early attendance in parliament, and the rather because what you are able to make out concerning our sham plott's being built upon Dodsworth's, will be so verry material that it may be a means effectually to prevent the game which I apprehend they will endeavour to play, because it was what they did do in Admirall Russell's business—voted him first the thanks of the House for his courage and conduct in beating the French fleet, and thereby precluded themselves from examining into my brother Nottingham's papers and orders, which were sent down to our House from the House of Lords, and sent back again, without examining or suffering them to be on the table, as usual in such cases, whereby it would plainly have appeared that had it not been for Admiral Russell's mismanagement and disobedience to positive and repeated orders, he had wholly destroyd the French fleet. Just so, I suppose, they will convict these people of perjury, to stop higher inquiry; vote Trenchard, Shrewsbury, Willoughby, and Norris (and for ought I know Baker and Judge Eyre) the thanks of the House for their watchful care of the Government, in his Majestie's absence, so that their scandalous grafting upon Dodsworth's plott will be looked on as a pardonable over-forward zeal. The wittnesses being pilloried, all is done that can be; for shall the House find fault with the same people they thank ? This they will urge as a ridiculous thing to appear in our votes. By all means possible hasten your own journey to London, and the rest of our Lancashire members, for I wonder to find that severall of them that were present at the tryalls, intend to stay so long in the country. If they cry ' whose first' (as the saying is), we come upon a disadvantage, and a very great one." *Seal with crest.*

CUTHBERT HESKETH to [ROGER KENYON].

925. 1694[-5], January.—"I have seene John Wilson, who was a prisoner at lardge, and accused for to bee guilty of the late plott, and have discoursed him, and desyred him to lett me know how farre he was moved to bee a witness against Mr. Walmesley of Dunkenhalgh; and hee tells me that Aron Smith, Captayne Baker, and Lunt, did much solicite him to sweare that Mr. Walmesleye was att Dunkenhalgh about three years since, to which hee did say, and is ready to testify, that hee never knew or saw the said Mr. Walmesley till hee saw him att Manchester Sessions, in October last, nor was ever at Dunkenhalgh in his lyfetyme. Upon which, Aron Smith, Captayne Baker, and Lunt, did threaten him that, if hee would not testify the same, hee should bee indicted and hanged for being guilty of the plott. Wilson says he was never a prisoner in Newgate, but was still kept a prisoner with the messenger that apprehended him. Hee was lykewyse moved by Aaron Smith, Beaker, and Lunt, to bee a witness against severall other gentlemen in this county, upon the same score, three of which were Mr. Towneley, Mr. Warren, and Mr. Walmesley of the Hall, against whome, or any of them, hee neither could at that time, nor now, say anything in that business, being (*sic*) hee never had any acquaintance with any of them. Hee further sayes that hee heard the said Aron Smith, Beaker, and Lunt say at the Sessions att Manchester, that if the buisiness against the gentlemen at that time did not take effect hee would have another way for it."

JOHN ASSHETON to ROGER KENYON, M.P.

926. 1694[-5], January 10. Clitheroe.—"The death of the Queen was a great surprize to us, whose death is by all here very much lamented . . . . . The known experience of your readinesse to assist us, and your repeated promises, incouraged us to crave your help in relation to our burruogh and county in particular. The poore of these parts mostly employ the winter in spinning flaxen yarne, and formerly made advantage thereof; which forreigners seeing, have undermined us, buying the best of flax and imploying their owne poor to spin, about Hamborow, etc., where they live cheap and send us the yarne, which we must either take at their rates or bee content with the worst sort of flax, litle else now comeing ; by which meanes, our poore complaine they cannot get for their yarn what their flax cost, and must either turne beggers, or worke to no purpose. And soe the poore are ruined, and the better sort sore layne upon to relieve them, which might be remedied were a smart duty (the *quantum* we dare not prescribe) layd on forreign yarne, and to promote that is our request, wherein wee are seconded by many other burroughs, our neighbors, to their representative. It meets here with soe generall approbation, that wee cannot find any inconveniency, publicke or private, to object thereto, and therefore hope you will find the lesse opposition, in soe generall a good worke. The advantage will be further in the advance of his Majesty's revenue, and, being in nature of a subsidy bill, it perhaps may bee seasonably moved at this time when you are cons[idering] the poore, to whose act this may bee added. Your thought and advice herein, with your assistance, is earnestly entreated."

Joseph Yates to Roger Kenyon, M.P.

927. 1694[-5], January 14.—Our great surmise in the country is, (1) Will the King go into Flanders, or no ? (2) Why did Parliament desire, "with that strictness," all members to attend, on Thursday last ? and (3) "What will be the event of the Parliament's enquiry after the Manchester trials ? . . . . . In my mind, an imposition upon perri-wiggs and topp-knotts would be easier to the poor sort of people, then that proposed of leather ; but doe begg your pardon in presuming to mention any of these things, which chiefly concerne your honourable assembly." There is talk in this town of new county justices, "not to adorn (?) the church," viz. : Mr. Worsley of Platt, Mr. Nathaniel Gaskell, Mr. Joseph Hooper, Mr. Richard Percivall, and several others of this town and near it. Other justices are to be "put out," because "not brisk enough against the prisoners." *Seal of arms.*

Thomas Wilson to Roger Kenyon.

928. 1694[-5], January 18. Lathom.—On Wednesday last, my Lord Derby went to Preston, in order to promote an address to his Majesty upon the death of the Queen. His Lordship was met at the town by the High Sheriff and a handsome appearance of gentry, and, in the town, met with a very welcome reception, offered an address, which was kindly and unanimously received and signed, and will be signed by most of the gentry of this county in a few days. From all which, it is manifest that the hearts of the people are yet very much towards his Lordship. This address his Lordship designs to send up to Colonel Stanley, who is the fittest person in the world to represent it fairly to the King. To this purpose, his Lordship writes this post to his brother to know his thoughts and resolutions. In the meantime, I desire this favour of you, that you will take an occasion to discourse with Colonel Stanley upon this subject. *Seal of arms.*

Charles Rigby to Roger Kenyon, M.P., in London.

929. 1694[-5], January 18. Lancaster.—"Upon the receipt of yours of the 6th instant, I pressed Hartley to recollect with himselfe for a further discovery, assureing him of the want of your friendship, whilst there was reason to believe hee consailed any of his associates; and for this purpose I gave him two days to consider in, but when I came to him again, he still protested he had not missed one that he could remember to be liveing, or that had not been tryed. I then shewed him your letter, and to the persons named therein he gives this answer : that as to Murrean, the Scotch pedler, he was acquainted with him before his owne goeing into Ireland, but since his comeing back, he heard that about seven years agoe the pedler was tryed at Shrewesbury and acquitted, but was so frighted then, that he believes he never medled since. And that himselfe had a young wife who used to come with him to Hartley, but neither hath she medled since her husband's tryal, that he knows of. He averrs he never knew either Laith or Steward on any account; that Smith, *alias* Buffer, is the same in the last information named *alias* Chamber; that John Goulton hath been dead above 15 years : that it is 20 years since he had broad moneys from Samuel Bromley, but believed him dead, not having dealt with him since; that Leek never clipped, that Hartley knowes of, nor he never worked at Leek's house; that Wheck was hanged soon after Jo : Thomasson was robed; [and] that he hath sent to his brother, in order to make what discovery he can of that robbery. Sir, what I wrote of Hartley being bailed till the Assizes, though under sentence of death, is not without president, for Sir Walter Rawleigh was (when under the sentence of high treason) let out of the Tower, and entrusted with a commission beyond sea, in the King's service, and after that executed (*ut vide Cros. jur.* fol. 495), and there resolved the King might make use of the service of any subject in that condition, and yet it should not be any dispensation of former crime. I never meant that Hartley, whilst unpardoned, should be evidence against any; but might, with assistance, apprehend the persons accused, which he still sais he can do, either at baile or under such circumstances as will be strong proofes against them. Sir, if you please to signifie my Lord Cheife Justice Treby's sentiment of the last information, together with your commands, I will, to my power, observe them. Hartley sais Mr. Élleson, the gaoler, had ten pounds from him to keep the yrons of[f] him, and eleven pounds to bear his charges up to London, which is all the moneys he hath had of him, except for his dyet. But Hartley lodged a greater sum, he sais, in a frind's hands of Ellesson, which he should have had, if he had proved his pardon. And Elleson, hearing that Hartley had a watch in a watchmaker's hand, in this towne, by dilusion got it into his hands, after the warrant came down for Hartley's execution, and still keeps it.

"Last Wednesday I was at Thurneham (?) with Mr. Dalton, he being returned from Parke Hall. He shewed me his book, wherein he sets down not only his travels, but the remarkeable passages of his life. He there sais on the 13th of June, 1689, he was apprehended in his owne house by Sir John Bland, then an officer quartered in Lancaster, and he sais, he does remember they searched his house for Thelfall and Lunt, and he believes they did land near Cockerham that morning, and I am induced to believe they were that night entertained at Thurnham, though he does not say so, and that the certificate I sent you mistakes the day." *Seal of arms.*

ALICE KENYON to her husbànd, ROGER KENYON.

930. 1694[–5], January 20.—Mrs. Marcer was here to-night, and tells me there is to be many new justices such as never was made justices :— Mr. Edward Boodle, Hilton of Willingrave, Jo : Diggle, "a calendar man," and young Gaskill; she says it is thought Lord Willoughby is the cause of their being put on. *Seal.*

The EARL OF DERBY to ROGER KENYON.

931, 932. 1694–5, January 22. Knowsley.—I cannot forbear thinking of, and owning, how much I am beholden to your eldest son and my seal-keeper, in following so well the steps of their father. I am not able to imagine what should be the cause that my wife never wrote one word to me, nor James, since the Queen's death; though letters and condoling, and inviting down here, have not been wanting. If you do, or can, know anything what should be the matter, an account of as much as is fit for a letter, will be very acceptable. *Seal.*

W. DICCONSON to ROGER KENYON, M.P.

933. 1694-5, January 25. Wrigh[tington].—"Pursuant to directions, I have this day sent for Jo: Wilson; hee is very weak in health, and I fear much whether hee will bee able to perform his journey, at least it will be to morrow seavenight before he can reach the 'Blew Boar' in Holborn, whither I have directed him. Hee has his brother with him, who goes on fott, and is not willing to leave alone because of his illness. If hee goes on to London with him, hee may perhaps bee of use too as a wettness to testify Luntt's acknowledging that hee had robbed on the highway; butt I know that is not needful now, soe I did not send him, and if hee accompanys his brother quite thorough, it is on his owne accord. For my part, I could not find Jo: Wilson's testimoney very materiall as to my judgment." *Seal of arms.*

WILLIAM HAYHURST to ROGER KENYON, "a member of the honourable House of Commons, at Westminster."

934. 1694-5, January 26. Preston.—"As for the precise day laid in the indictment, we have not usually such a particular regard to it as to observe to laye it the very day, but suppose it good enough though laid after the day; and where it relates to severall facts, wee lay one day with a *diversis aliis diebus et vicibus tam antea quam postea.* And so for the place, wee doe not much regard it, if it bee in the same county. The record against Darlington is at Lancaster, so I fear cannot come to you in time. Mr. Walmsleye's neighbours suppose that if he came to Dunkenhalgh when Mr. Lunt swore hee did, that hee rid upon Paccolett's horse, or that hee came over in a flying coach, either of which will as soon bee believed as that hee was there; but when I reflect of the certain reports of troopes of horse exercising underground, wee may easily believe the former. I pray God direct you, that are the protectors of the liberty of the people of England, so to determine matters, that innocent men may not bee run down by false accusers, and that it may not bee judgd a crime to have a good estate." *Seal of arms.*

T. WINCKLEY to ROGER KENYON, M.P.

935. 1694[-5], January 27.—When Threlfal and Lunt left the ship they forgot something like a saddle-bag, which fell into the customs officers' hands at Lancaster. *Seal of arms.*

LADY STANDISH to ROGER KENYON, M.P.

936. 1694[-5], January 28. Duxbury.—"I wish you all health, and safe into Lancashire. If I consulted my own intrest, I should wish to send my Lord Willoughby to the Parliament and fetch you home, but for the publick it is beter ordered. He is almost as great a plauge to me as he is to his wife and her maids, for my Lord, feighting with my Lady's woman, she has broak his shins with a brass candle stick, and he is a criple." *Seal.*

INFORMATION by SIR EDWARD WARD, Attorney-General,
against JOHN LUNT, for perjury.

937. [1695,] Hilary Term.—Reciting the indictment against Sir
Rowland Stanley, Sir Thomas Clifton, William Dicconson, Phillip Langton, and William Blundell, and that, upon the case coming on for trial,
before Sir Giles Eyre, Sir John Turton, Sir John Powell, and Sir
Samuel Eyre, 'at' Manchester, the said Sir Rowland Stanley, and the
others, pleaded not guilty. And at the trial, one John Lunt, late of the
parish of St. Martin's in the Fields, in the county of Middlesex, labourer,
swore that in February, 1691[-2], he was present at "Dunginhall," the
dwelling house of Bartholomew Walmesley, Esquire, in the parish of
Whalley, with the said Walmesley, when he, the said Walmesley, delivered
to William Dicconson a commission from James the Second, late King
of England, as lieutenant-colonel of horse ; whereas the said Walmesley
was not at "Dunginhall" at any time within the month of February,
1691[-2], nor did he deliver such a commission to the said Dicconson,
and thereby the said Lunt committed wilful perjury. Also a like information against George Wilson.

J. HARTLEY to ROGER KENYON, M.P.

938. 1695[-5], February 1.—"Noe doubt there are pressing
reasons of state for these very great taxes; and I doe not thinke any
Englishman but would willingly pay what he is asked, if that would
prevent it, rather then this nation should bee made the seate of war.
The inequality of the taxes is the greate thing complained of. For,
you will owne, it is very hard for some to pay above halfe as much for
30l. per annum, singly taxed, as others for 200l. per annum, in the
same parish." Seal of arms.

CHARLES RIGBY to ROGER KENYON, M.P.

938A. 1694[-5], February 19. Lancaster.—As to proof that Captain
Clent supplied his soldiers and officers under him, with his own moneys,
and sold his plate and jewels for that purpose, we can produce the testimony of persons that heard him on his death-bed say, and it was well
known to his relations, that he was, at his last going into Ireland, rich
both in that and clothes, and returned "very ordinary," and his colonel
knew him to be " a civil and a frugal brave man." Hartley is advised by
his friends in the castle to apply for a pardon, and, for that purpose, has
written to Mr. Pears, the Lord Chief Justice's secretary, with whom he
has held a close correspondence all along. He expresses a true service
to the government, and promises, when at liberty, to discover all or most
of the clippers in Staffordshire.

" And now, sir, as to the time of Lunt's landing, though, in answering
yours in the order it is writt, I postponed this to other buisness, yet it
hath been the chiefe of my endeavours to learne the true time for your information. In the first place, yesterday morning I went to Mr. William
Kirkby (who is now in this towne, and presents you with his service).
I told him of the matter, and after a searche in his booke, wherein he
transcribes coppys of his letters and takes account of his travells, he
found that on Tuesday the 18th of June, 1689, he came to Lancaster,
and the same day, being informed by Mr. Jo: Foster, then collector of
the Customs here, that Carson's vessel was come in from Ireland, he,
the same night, wrote up to the Commissioners of the Customs above,
and in his letter, finds that he tells them of Carson's vessell coming in,
and for the rest referrs to the collector, Mr. Foster's letter ; but whether

Mr. Foster's letter was wrote the post before, or no, he remembers not, nor any more thereof; but he thinks amongst the letters kept by the Commissioners above, of that month of June, 1689, Mr. Jo: Foster's letter may be found, which acquainted them of the landing. Wee after went together to Mr. . . . . , now our Mayor, who, though not then concerned in the Custom House, did business for Mr. Jo: Foster. He remembers letters wrote to the Commissioners, but no particulars. We then went to the Custom House, but can find no letters or coppys of letters about it. Charles Carson, the master of the vessell that brought them over, as allso one Peter Gourden, who was then bailiffe of this towne, and was the man that was sent up with the informations (as I have, or ought to have, wrote to you before), are both dead; nor hath Mr. Sherison, who was then Mayor, and tooke Carson's information, any coppyes or other papers relaiteing thereunto, in his hands, nor can he remember anything of particulars; but this afternoon he tells me old Mr. Cole, who joyned with him in taking Carson's information, did keep coppyes of them, and believes his son may find them, and if so, be assured you shall have them by the next post. I am sensibly troubled that I have not yet been able to answer your expectation in this matter, but to recount the contradictions I have mett with in my enquiry, would almost breed distraction; however, I will not desist till I can send you such account as you may depend on."

INFORMATION of OLIVER PIERSON, of Wigan Lane, in the Parish of Standish, carrier.

939. 1694[-5], February 23.—Concerning the bringing of pistols and kettledrums to Mr. Standish, at Standish Hall.

JOHN HEYS (?) to ROGER KENYON.

940. 1694[-5], February 26.—John Breers believes that Lunt was at his house at Lathom in February, or at the beginning of March, 1691-2. The death and funeral of Sir Thomas Stanley's lady, at Preston, has so busied Dic. Woods, of this town, and his wife, that I am at want of an opportunity to discourse them upon the point. There is a well-founded report that there will be a great alteration of Justices of the Peace in this county. Those to be "outed" are Cornet (?) Mawdesley, Mr. Farrington, Mr. Blackburn, Mr. Nicholas Starky, and some others. Those to be put in "are of meane qualitys, none being of the degree of a gentleman, save the two Pattens. . . . . These alterations make honest gentlemen's hearts very heavy." *Seal of arms, broken.*

THOMAS MERCER to ROGER KENYON, M.P.

941. 1694[-5], March 12.—Sends him, from Colonel Stainbuck (?), an account of what is due to the innkeepers, of Manchester and Salford, from the " Dutch troops, from 18th August last, 778*l.* 6*s.* 6*d.*" Difficulty experienced in obtaining payment of accounts, in the past. *Seal, broken.*

WILLIAM PATTEN to ROGER KENYON, M.P., in London.

942. 1694[5], March 12. Preston.—My brother Patten readily shewed me the information he took about Threfall and Lunt's landing. There were 3 of the ship's crew gave informations, but Henry Knowles gave the fullest. About 5 weeks before the taking of the information, they sailed from the Lune for the Isle of Man; but, before

they came there, Threlfall desired they might go for Dublin. They
sailed there and stayed 3 weeks, and then the master, and Threlfall,
"and a stranger, whoe was called Mr. Lunt," came to the ship, and they
sailed back to England and landed near Cockerham, on the Thursday
morning before the taking of the information. When they landed, the
crew gave Threlfall out of the ship "his haire portmantu truncke," and
afterwards, Lunt called to them that he had left his two leather bags,
but he would call for them afterwards. Immediately after this, the
Custom House boat came and seized Lunt's two bags, wherein were
several printed and other papers. This information was taken 18 June,
1689.

DR. RICHARD WROE to ROGER KENYON, M.P., at Westminster.

943. 1694-5, March 12.—The sudden death of Mrs. Noel has
carried away your good family to-day to the funeral. The talk of a new
set of justices revives again. A pleasant bench we are like to have ; but
probably "the timing of the Assizes to begin on Good Friday portended
some unusual and strange alteration, since some here say that it never
happened so since Pontius Pilate sat judge."

JOHN ASSHETON, Bailiff of Clitheroe, to ROGER KENYON, M.P.

944. 1694-5, March 14. Clitheroe.—"Nothing could bee more
acceptable to this burrough then a duty uppon forrin (?) yarne, as
Hambro, &c. . . . The motion you have made has given no small
sort of satisfaction to the common sort of people, whose livelyhood much
consists in spinning ; and, indeed, is well taken by all." Describes
the funeral of Mistress Townley, at Whalley, who recently married
Mr. Nowell. Believes Kenyon's letters are opened before they come to
"our" hands. "The seale seemed to be a wax impression."

CHRISTOPHER (?) NORRES, Mayor of Liverpool, to ROGER
KENYON, M.P.

945. 1694-5, March 16. Liverpool.—"The two great heads (representatives of our poor burrough) are laid so close togather that none
but P———, and their party, must be obliged with the votes of the
House ; the Mayor and bretheren must depend on good Mr. Kenyon, or
some other worthy member, to make up that misfortune, and I am sure
the honest part of the towne will be very thankfull, if I may judge by
the last you sent me. The two parsons of Walton, all the aldermen,
and many more, desired me to give you their humble service."

ROBERT WHITFORD to [ROGER] KENYON, at the "Blue Boar" Inn,
in Holborn, near Red Lion Square.

946. 1694-5, March 19.—Promising to bring "Mrs. Lunt" for an
interview "one of these mornings." She "goes from her kepeing to
night, and then will be at libertie."

JO: HEYS to ROGER KENYON, M.P.

947. 1695, April 2.—"I have made it my purpose to go unto and
send for Mr. Breers to this town, to examine him to the points you
desire. And all that I can gather from him is that about the middle of
February, [16]91-2, Lunt was at his house, went to Ormskirke, and
Mr. Breers' neice with him, to buy linnens, which they did. Mr. Breers

does not remember how long before that tyme Lunt was at his house, but referred himself to a more particular account he says he has already given to Mr. Dicconson, of Wrightington, a copy whereof, he says, you may have at your command next week. Your son George and I have agreed to discourse some things, in order to the tryalls of perjury, next assizes, against Womball, and the rest of his gang. Mary, wife of Richard Wood, of this town, says she dare depose that Lunt was at her house the 17th, 18th, 19th and 20th [of] February, 1691-2." *Fragment of seal.*

THOMAS FLEETWOOD to ROGER KENYON, M.P., in London.

948. [16]95, April 3. Nottingham.—I, this morning, went down to old Lunt's, but the old fellow was very ill in bed; his wife gave me this account :—Lunt was born in Manfield [Mansfield]; his godfather's name is Blunt, a papist gentleman that lives 3 miles from here, worth about 200*l.* a year. "She told me many of his rogerys, too long to writ, whilst he was young. His first master was one Mr. Hastings, with whom he stayed not long; then went to the Mr. Smith you mention, and he, beginning to beare up to his daughter, he turned him off. Hence he went to London, and one of Smith's servants, that was in love with him, followed him to London and put him prentice to a shoemaker, where he stayed 2 or 3 years, and then fell out with his master and listed himself a soldier. His godfather being a papist, I presume he was christened by a Romish priest, and then you will find no register; but, if any be to be found, it must be at Manfield [Mansfield]. This is the best account I can get you. I return you thanks about my bill, and desire you will see it pass when the King comes to the House. . . . . I have bin in the fens in Lincolnshire, and have vewed all their works and ingens, and have found out the ablest man in England for my purposes, who is not only rich, but has the caracter of a very honest man."

——— NORRES, Mayor of Liverpool, to ROGER KENYON.

949. 1695, April 5. Liverpool.—As to the charter, by which now we govern, it is that granted in King Charles II.'s time, whereof we have an exemplification by King William and Queen Mary, at the charge of my Lord Colchester (now Earl Rivers) ; for King Charles II.'s charter was lost, by the negligence of Alderman Clayton, senior. There is no endorsement on the exemplification, but the learned in the law tell us that we are safe in acting by it, because a confirmation; and all conclude the Duchy seal is of validity sufficient, and that in that office a record may be found.

MARGARET, LADY STANDISH, to ROGER KENYON, M.P., "to be left at the loby door, Westminster."

950. [1695, April 10.] Manchester, "11 a'clock, Sunday night."—
" I received your letter this morning, and though it was Sabath day, I went to the parsonage, having but few friends to advise with; and Mr. Hadock was so kind [as] to go along with me to Manchester. We waited on my Lord Willowby ; he declared he had nothing to do with the thing, further then as a trusty [trustee] . . . . He seemed to be a little heated when he saw the petition, and said he would be ready to answer it, so I have signed it and sent it up." Mr. Cheetham advises me to prevail with Lord Derby to do my son the honour to be called his guardian, and, in his name, to employ workmen, and to bring a petition

in Lord Derby's name. Mr. Cheetham thinks this might be a short way to get into possession, and keep the works going.

Postscript.—" I have sent up two letters, one from Sir John Ardern to my Lord Chumley, another to my Lord Cornbury. Though these Lords sit not in the House, they may influence those that do. . . . My Lord Willowby passionately said, he was sure nobody durst present this petition to the House of Lords."

PETITION of MARGARET, LADY STANDISH, widow of SIR RICHARD
STANDISH, to the HOUSE OF LORDS.

951. [1695, April 11.]—Sets out that Peter Shaw and George Smith were in possession, under a wrongful title, of a lead mine, lately open in the manor of Aulezargh, in Lancashire, which was settled towards the petitioner's jointure. To recover possession, she caused an action of trespass and ejectment, to be brought in the name of Thomas Morris, upon several demises of the petitioner, and John Abbot, to whose father the land, in which the mine lay, was anciently leased for a term of years, yet enduring. Shaw and Smith were duly served with copies of the declaration in that action, and they—" to shelter and cover the possession, by and under a mortgage made to one Thomas Wadington" by Sir Richard Standish—agreed with the said Wadington to assign over the mortgage, in trust for them, to Lord Willoughby of Parham. At the time the said Shaw and Smith should have defended their title in the said action, they offered a rule, in Lord Willoughby's name, to make him defendant; but the plaintiffs' attorney refused it, " in respect of his Lordship's privillege of parliament." At the last assizes at Lancaster, the plaintiffs moved for judgment against " the casual ejector," for want of a proper defendant. The Judge—on hearing afterwards that Lord Willoughby, after the action brought, disowned that he had any title, and that if his name was made use of, it was only in trust—refused to give judgment till the House of Peers determined how far Lord Willoughby's interest was really concerned.

Prays, therefore, that—as Lord Willoughby is no ways concerned in this cause, but as trustee—privilege may not obstruct the petitioner and the said Abbot, in prosecuting their rights. *Draft.*

Order on the above, referring it " to the Lords Committees for priveledges," who were to meet in the House of Peers on the 22nd of April, at 4 o'clok in the afternoon; Lord Willoughby to have a copy of the petition, and to give or send his answer, at or before the above named day and hour. *Copy.*

THOMAS KENYON to his father, ROGER KENYON, M.P., "att the
doore of the House of Commons att Westminster."

952. 1695, April 12. Manchester.—" I had like to have forgott to tell you, that Simon Arrowsmith, and another bayliffe, haveing a warrant from the Sherriff, against James Rogers of this towne, upon an execution, last night, about 10 a'clock, arrested him in the churchyard, neare his owne house there, and struggling together, Simon had him downe; but whilst he was so, Mr. Rogers drewe a bayonett from under his coat and stabbed him in three severall places in the lower part of his belly; one of which wounds, being searched by the Coroner, was found to be two inches deep and very wide. Of these wounds, Symon, halfe-an-hour after, dyed; but the other bailiffe, and Mr. Betton (?), who came in a while after, secured Mr. Rogers, and he is prisoner now, as well upon that execution, as upon the Coroner's warrant for murder. His bayonett is found all bloody, though he threw it away, and two pocket pistolls taken from him, loaden. The like accident happened the other day at Preston; a gentleman, Mr. Walsmisly by name, borne at Bury, and then a gager att Preston, was murdered basely, by a Dutchman at Preston, who is committed to Lancaster." *Seal.*

J. LEIGH to PETER LEIGH, " at Lyme, by Poynton Lane end, near Disley, Cheshire."

953. 1695, May 18.—" It is not easy to find what is pardoned but by observing what is, or is not, excepted as to treasons; there are exceptions of all prisoners of warre, synce June, 1689; all prisoners under bayle, synce 29 April, 1695; all persons in the French King's dominions, or employed in his service, or of King James; all treasons committed out of England, since 13 February, 1688; all treasons committed upon the high seas, and generally all treasons and offences, whereby any indictment is depending, or was, att any time within two years next before the assembling of this Parliament. I doe not see that you can be brought within the exceptions, or any of them, and [you are] consequently pardoned. There is a particular exception levelled against Mr. Standish, thus :—An exception of all persons against whom there was published any proclamation, synce the 27th of April, 1694, and before the 29th April, 1695. The miscreants who have beene the occasion of soe many gentlemans' trouble, are cccepted thus :—' And alsoe excepted out of this pardon, all offences of perjury and subornation of wittnesses, and endeavouring or conspireing to bribe or corrupt any person to give false testimony,' etc. Soe that as they are excepted and open to a procecution, it is surely safe to have them procecuted vigourously, and the rather, synce other prosecutions against them for perjury of another kind, have received interuption; and it is to be feared this may be so too, in case any occasion be given by a neglected procecution. They have pleaded, and the records, if you will give order, shall be sent downe by *Nisi Prius,* to be tried next Lancaster assises, by which tyme (or the sooner the better) it is safe and prudent to be provided of witnesses, to make out the matters wherin the perjurys are assigned." *Portion of seal.*

LADY STANDISH to ROGER KENYON.

954. 1695, May 23. Duxbury.—Is removing her family to Preston. Will be glad to receive his commands to wait upon him, " when your business will permit you to loose halphe a day, in hearing an impertinent woman talk." Can never express her obligations to him.

THOMAS HODGKINSON to ROGER KENYON.

955. 1695, June 24. Preston.—Asking for his interest with Lady Derby to procure a scholar's place in the Charterhouse, for the son of young Mr. Osbaldeston.

LEIGH BANKES to PETER LEIGH, at Lyme.

956. 1695, June 27. Gray's Inn.—" It is high time to think of our late friends L[un]t, W[ilson], and Wombell; for, Lancaster assizes drawing near, it will be necessary to find out proper persons that can remember what was given in evidence at Manchester. I trouble you of this, because I do not find any one else takes either care of their persons or the publick, and, though the storm is over at present, yet slothfullnesse in these cases may cause a relapse. I am apt to beleeve that these villayns will never appear; however, after they are once convicted, the foundation of their contrivances is totally destroyed."

Jo: LEIGH, Junior, to [MRS. KENYON].

957. 1695, June 27. [London.]—Does not know where certain papers, required by Mr. Kenyon, are, but they are not material for the trials at Lancaster. The assizes are on the 7th August. Cannot leave "the town" so early, nor take a journey into Cheshire, till he has been "att the Bath or Tunbridge."

J. LEIGH to ROGER KENYON, M.P., at Manchester.

958. 1695, July 4. [London.]—The Informations against Lunt, &c., are brought on behalf of the King by the Attorney-General. The venue is laid at Manchester, the perjury being committed there, and the trials must be at Lancaster. "As for your Attorney-Generall and Clerke of the Croune, neither of them have anything to doe in this businesse; their power and jurisdiction is only of such matters as purely arise, and are depending, in their oune county." I never heard of an Assignment of perjury in an Information, in English; for, as it is laid in Latin, it may easily be proved, and doubt not but you will find apt and proper witnesses who can doe itt." *Seal.*

ROBERT ROPER to ROGER KENYON.

959. 1695, July 5.—His Lordship commands me to acquaint you that he brings on a trial the next assizes at Lancaster, for the manor of Broughton-in-Furness, wherein, if his Lordship have good success, he will bring ejectments for all the lands in Bury and Pilkington which were sold by his father, because these lands and Broughton do depend upon the same title.

MARGARET, LADY WILLOUGHBY, to MR. KENYON.

960. 1695, July 10.—"Being at present indisposed, I have sent you the inclosed, which I suppose will, in most perticulars, raise your admiration, as itt has dun mine, to see my cozens great partiallity to others, in acquiting the guilty and accusing the innocent, so contrary to truth, and what I might expect from him; but, as I have sayed, this Whitchurch plan has made up all there mouths. I sopose you can very well make out what you told me of the waste that has been made, notwithstanding all is saye[d] in the inclosed to the conterary; and for his vindication of Masterson, you yourselfe are a witness how false that is, being you heard him take the other side in all company is against me, so not like to be my friend. Since things are thus, I have noe reason to reliey on my cosen Bromley, noe more then his .brother-in-law; he is not the man I have taken him for. There is a great league betweene him and my Lord, and he payes so great an obsequeousness to him, that he sends him coppyes of what he writs to me. All the good he did me, is that Jack will be sent into Warwickshire, and now I must, as advised, get an address for myself to my Lord-keeper, in which I desire your assistance, that we may part; for I can safely sweare, that I goe in danger of my life of him, since he once attempted to choack me with both his hands att my throth (*sic*), and will not let me have one servant I can trust, which shews some ill designe, and deneyes me that healpe and advise for my health, which I so much neede for the rectifieing of my blood, by those persons I can trust, and talks of goeing to London this winter ; but I must be a prisoner in this countrey, out of which I must not stir by his good will, and he not affording me better usage, nor being willing to a faire parting, plainly shewes he has some wicked desine, and my death ; clearing all his accounts for wast. And the hopes of a fortune in the City with money, and one he may have children by, makes him in hast to be a widower, to which his haveing the advantages of haveing married one of quality and estate, will the more recommend him. For God's sake, give me your advice which way I may get well rid of him. For my case is as desperate as his wicked desines, in the opinion of the best judges as . . . owne that know more of him then the world will beleeve . . . trouble."

JOHN FENWICK to ROGER KENYON.

961. 1695, July 13. Burrow Hall.—Desiring to know by whose means he was turned out of the *quorum.*

J. LEIGH to ROGER KENYON, M.P., at Manchester.

962. 1695, July 18. [London.]—I believe Lunt, Wilson, and Wombell, will not oppose at the Assizes ; but, as they have pleaded, you may proceed to try them. The warrant for their commitment to the King's Bench was made by the late Mr. Justice Giles Eyre, and I have applied to the Marshal for a copy, but he refuses it, as he has "directions to the contrary." As for their being bailed, it was done by Mr. Justice Samuel Eyre. He being gone circuit, I cannot give you the names of their bail, for the bail-piece is with him, and was not filed in the Crown Office. *Seal, broken.*

WILLIAM PATTEN to ROGER KENYON, at Manchester.

963. 1695, July 29. Warrington.—"I am free and forward to remember those villouns, as any one," but cannot call to mind that Lunt swore he saw the Lord of S——— at Dungkinhall, or Mr. Walmesley. *Seal, broken.*

THOMAS ASSHETON to ROGER KENYON, at Manchester.

964. 1695, August 1. Staple Inn.—As to the trials of Lunt and others, for perjury, Mr. Cheshire has retained me for the King ; so I shall be at Lancaster on the evening of the 7th instant. I was with Captain Rigby at Portsmouth on Tuesday. *Seal with crest.*

ROGER KENYON to JOHN ASHTON, Bailiff of Clitheroe.

965. 1695, August 28. Manchester.—I received, from London, this advertisement, that the more knowing persons there do talk as if we should soon have a dissolution of this Parliament, which, to my real belief, is not very probable. However, since if it should be so, it will be of the greatest importance, perhaps, that ever befell this kingdom.

THOMAS WHALLEY to ROGER KENYON.

966. 1695, September 13. Sparth.—"As to Mr. Walmsley's confinement, it was thus : On Sunday, the 15th of July last, aboute 7 in the morninge, the messenger Hopkins, with 2 or 3 constables, and some others, came to his lodgings att Mrs. Procer's house in Southampton Street, and there served him with a warrant from Sir John Trenchard, for high treason, and from thence caryed him to Hopkins' own house near Charinge Crosse, where hee stayd not above an houre, in respect of the inconveniency of the lodginge, but was caryed to the house of one Kidson, another messenger, in Barwick Street, where hee stayd till the 31st of the same month, and that day was caryed with Kidson, the messenger, to the Tower, where hee continued till, with the other prisoners, hee was sent downe into Lancashire to be tryed, which is all the account that I can have now, in his absence."

[Charles] Rigby to [Roger Kenyon].

967. 1695, September 17. Lancaster.—As to the prospects of Preston election, " Sir Christopher " has little hope, the majority seeming to be with Sir Thomas Stanley and "my cousin M." If Sir Edward Chisnell will strike in time, I believe it will be Sir Thomas and him. Yesterday, Mr. Foster and I rode to Sunderland, to enquire for James Crossfield, one of the Custom House officers who signed the certificate I formerly sent you, of the *Lyon* of Lancaster coming to anchor at Cockerham, with Lunt and Threlfall, on 17 June, 1689 (?). He " stuck " to that day; but says, after he had given the certificate, Mr. William K—— took the book from him, wherein he entered a memorandum of the day and hour of the ship's coming to Sunderland. " I believe the fellow hath had very severe rebukes from Mr. K—— about it, and, therefore, cannot be got to discover further. I find Mr. Justice Sheirson as unwilling to discover the truth as the other."

Sir Alexander Rigby to his cousin, Roger Kenyon, at Peel.

968. 1695, September 24. London.—"You have often assured me of being my friend, on any occasion, but particularly in the affaire of Parliment man ; I now have need of your performance, for [I] am encouraged to stand for Wiggan. Who I shall oppose, I am not certaine of; but I hope, bee it who it will, that your kindness will not bee lost for sake of any other person. . . . I do not sett up on any particular party. I will always bee true to the church and my country. Lord Derby has assured me of his friendship, under his hand, and the Lord Lieutenant is resolved to do what he cann."

Thomas Wilson to Roger Kenyon.

969. 1695, September 24. Knowsley.—My Lord [Derby] presents his services to you, and desires to know your thoughts, in relation to Clitheroe. My Lord has some intimation that you will be chosen for Newton ; if you have any thoughts that way, his Lordship would propose a colleague to Colonel Pudsey. The gentleman whom he would propose to you, is Sir Godfrey Copley, a Yorkshire gentleman, of a good estate, and, they say, of an extraordinary character.

Roger Kenyon to Charles Rigby.

970. 1695, September 30. Manchester.—The gentleman you mention, is my fellow member, and our House is not yet dissolved; though words should happen to be scattered, yet, whilst boys are under the lash, school tales are not to be told. Our rules in Parliament are to give nobody a hard word, much more not to write it of any, for the *vox audita perit, in littera scripta manet.* I say not this for fear that I ever have said anything that I cannot justify. *Draft.*

[Dr. Roger Kenyon] to "Madam Kenyon, at her house near Stockport, in Cheshire, England."

971. 1695, October 5.—You will be content by this, only to know that I am very well in all circumstances. Be pleased to write to me, as if you wrote to a neice, and send it undirected, but under cover, to Madam Boile, Prioress of the English Convent, called Spiliken, at Brussels; only ask her to direct and send it to Mr. Charles Lee, who will take care of it for me.

W. Blundel, Junior, to Roger Kenyon, "at his house in Manchester, post paid, 2*d.*"

972. 1695, October 11. Crosby.—James Williamson can give no account of Dr. Bromfield or his man, Morgan. Believes they were at his house in April, 1689. The doctor took an open boat at Wallesey (not at Crosby), and went direct to Ireland.

PETER LEIGH to ROGER KENYON.

973. 1695, October 20. Lyme.—Is sorry to think there is a chance of Kenyon losing his seat at Clitheroe, in the "new Parliament." "I was sollicitied by Sir J. Arden, sometime agone, to stand for Newton." Believes Sir John is "what you say : true to the church, monarchy, and the old laws"; but his (Leigh's) "unfortunate circumstances" prevent his complying with the request. *Seal.*

THOMAS WILSON [to ROGER KENYON].

974. 1695, October 28. Liverpool.—I had my Lord's commands to write to you about the election at Liverpool, and to desire your company there, on Friday next. We have the whole Presbyterian party, to a man, engaged against us, and, unless the country burgesses come in, we are in some danger of losing our point. There is one Hugh Brobbin, of Street Gate, who must be secured for us by your, or your son's, solicitation. I am also desired to write you to get Mr. Hulm, of Deaf (*sic*) Hulm, to stay at home if he will not be for us.

J. LEIGH to ROGER KENYON, at Manchester.

975. 1695, October 31. [Furnival's Inn, London.]—Lunt, Wilson, and Wombell, upon their own affidavits, have moved the court for a new trial, on your informations against them, upon a pretence they had no notice of the trial. Due notice was given, as is shewn by the book in the Crown office, and notice was also given to Mr. Winter, their attorney, who now denies he was ever retained for them. "I discovered this disposition in the court, that, in case Winter swears that he was never employed by the defendants, nor anyone els, on their behalf, nor ever acted for them, a new tryall will be granted." Winter will swear anything. "I will continue to do all I can to prevent a new tryall." Our counsel are Mr. Attorney General, Sir William Williams, Sir Bartholomew Shore, Mr. Northey, and Mr. Harcourt. If a new trial be had, "I doubt not that they [the defendants] will be readily convicted; but, as it is a matter of great charge and trouble, it is very mischeevouse."

ROGER KENYON to JOHN LEGH, "at his chambers in Furnivall's Inn, in Holborne."

976. 1695, November 10. Manchester.—"Mee thinks this extraordinary strugling to evade the convicti[on] and punishment of these infamous purjured knaves, looks as if fools would not rest it so low as upon these only; for that which has appeared will allwayes be manifest, and the more it is storred in, the more will come out. If I aright remember, one of your former letters told me that the three sparkes, Lunt, &c., had made application to the Lords-Justices to have obtained an order from them to stay the last tryalls; that, mee thinks, is an indication that they had notice of them . . . . . . At our assizes at Lancaster, before those tryalls came on, all ways and means that could be, were attempted to prevent the tryalls; this was not the work of Lunt, Willson, or Wombell, but of severall who would not care what becomes of them, if they looked no further; and, if anything occasion the carreying of this matter further, such may thank themselves for being so needlesly busie, when the whole is laid open by the further ripping up the sore." *Seal of arms.*

THOMAS KENYON to his father, ROGER KENYON.

977. 1695, November 16.—My Lord[1] is uneasy under his disappointment, and quarrelsome with everybody that is concerned with him.

JO: LEIGH to ROGER KENYON, at Manchester.

978. 1695, November 22.—"As to Lunt, Wilson, and Wombell, the Court of King's Bench hath thought fitt to grant them new tryalls, not withstanding it was opposed by Mr. Attorney-Generall, Sir Bartholomew Showre (?), Mr. Wortley, Mr. Harcourt, and Mr. Chesshyre. But—Wilson's and Lunt's bail not being willing to stand any longer, but prayed to be discharged, and they not able to find further bayle—they were committed to the Marshal of the King's Bench, where they now remain prisoners. As to Wombell, he continues at liberty, on his former bayle." Application was made to the Lords-Justices and Council for stopping the trials. *Seal of arms.*

RICHARD EDGE to ROGER KENYON, in Manchester.

979. 1695, December 15. "Blew Boar in Holborne."—Mr. Legh considers that the verdict, given at the last Assizes against Lunt and the others, cannot be exemplified nor given in evidence. It is not known who will be "our sheriff"; if the King names him, it will be Mr. Norres. Who the Chancellor names, is not known. Mr. Pudsay votes with the Court party, "but they like him not, saying, it is only to make his election sure, and when that is over they will loose him." Meantime, he has lost his interest with the other party. The Scots have got an Act passed by "our King" touching their trade to the East Indies, "which very much distastes both our Houses of Parliament. They have addressed him in it, and he has answered: he is ill served there, but will remedy the greevance as soon as he can."

SIR JOHN BLAND to ROGER KENYON.

980. 1695, December 31. Soho Square.—"The last night was the first time that there was any tryall of skill betwixt court and country, at

---

[1] Lord Derby.

the Committee of Elections this session, and it was a very full Committee.
The petitioners were my Lord Orrery and Spencer Compton, brother to
my Lord Northampton; the sitting members were Sir Thomas Dyke
and Mr. Conyers, the former of which, you remember, always behaved
himself very honnestly and like a lover of his country, all the last
Parliament. At his election, he met with all the opposition the c[ourt]
party could give him, and they did not forget to call him 'Jacobite,' and
toold the town, if he was chose, and 60 more of the old members
of his principles, they would be turned out of the House.

" Sir Thomas Dyke was elected by the burgesses, and they insisted the
right of election was in them and the inhabitants togeither. There was
2 questions put; the first was, whether it was in the burghesses alone, or
in them and the inhabitants, and there was in that division 198 and 129.
But before the latter question was put, it was one o'clock, and the
numbers were then 168 and 113 to the court party, and somebody else
was disappointed.

" The Act about coinage, which the House of Commons have put to
the Lords, and the Proclamation about mony, hath had this effect, as to
put a stop to trade; but, at the same time, it hath, in some measure,
opened some peoples eyes, and in the west of England they regret it
very ill. The flying post will let you see we are apprehensive of the
French visiting our costes, and if the accounts be true which we have,
that the French are 67 at Tholonn, and Admirall Rooke but 38 sayle,
it will be an easy matter for them to passe the streightes. There is a
great many projects for mony, and glasse windowes, it is thought, will be
one of them. Guinneyis is now come to 30s. again, but half-crowns are
now condemned quite, and it is the goldsmiths' trade to buy them at an
underworth. Shillings and sixpences do passe pretty well, though not
worth 2d. a peece, except at the markett."

Mr. Taaffe's Discovery.

981. [1695.]—" A copy of Mr. Taaffe's discovery of the practices
and contrivances against the gentlemen of Lancashire and Cheshire, late
impeached for high treason, and sent prisoners, some to the Tower, and
some to Newgate, and from thence sent to be tryed for their lives, some
at Manchester and some at Chester, which, his discovery, was prefaced
with a dedication to the King."

" The gentlemen tryed at Manchester were the Lord Mollineux, Sir
William Garrard, Sir Rowland Stanley, Sir Thomas Cliffton, Barronets,
Bartholomew Walmisley, William Dicconson, Phillip Langton, Esquires,
and William Blundell, gentleman. The gentlemen sent prisoners to be
tryed at Chester—Sir Thomas Stanley, Barronet, and Peter Legh,
Esquire.

" Sometime after Christmas last, 1693, John Lunt came to my house,
and told me he had a discovery of great consequence to make to the
government, but was unwilling to comunicate it to any, except some
man that had an interest at Court. Whereupon, I acquainted the Earl
of Bellamount with it, who desired me to get Lunt to set down in
writeing what he had to say; and then, said his Lordship, I will intrc-
duce him to the Secretary of State. I went and told Lunt what my
Lord said, and he accordingly brought me a paper importing, to the best
of my remembrance, that himself and one Bromfield were sent from
France to murder King William, and that severall others were to joyn
with them in the attempt; which paper I carried to my Lord Bellamount,
who acquainted Secretary Trenchard with it. The Secretary desired to
speake with Lunt, who accordingly waited . on him severall times.

I cannot say whether the Secretary believed him or not, but I remember Lunt told me this : he was sure the Secretary was a Jacobite, for that he seemed to take little notice of him, and gave him but five guineas.

Then the said Lunt desired me to bring [him] acquainted with Captain Baker, for that the said Lunt knew a great deal concerning the estates given to superstitious uses. I brought him to Baker's office, where he was entertained as a witness, receiving a sume of money in hand, besides a pension of twenty shillings a weeke. Lunt and Baker were alwayes together, till all the witnesses were examined, who pretended to know anything concerning those estates; after which, Captain Baker, having nothing to doe, resolved upon another project, which was to sue all the English gentlemen, then in France, to an outlawry, in order to which, he desired Lunt to give him the names of some of the gentlemen then in France. Lunt names Mr. Walmesley, promising to prove him there. Baker acquaints Mr. Aron Smith with the matter, who was very glad to hear of the forfeture of soe considerable an estate as Mr. Walmesley's, and desired Baker to keep his witnesses private, and to get some person of quality to beg that estate, and bargain with him for a third part thereof, to bee divided betwixt Aron Smith, Captain Baker, Lunt, and the rest of the witnesses.

" Captain Baker came to me and told me the discourse he had with Mr. Aron Smith, and desired me to speake to the Lord Portland, to beg the estate, and I should come in for a share with them. I answered, I was sure my Lord Portland was a man of more honour then to meddle with any such thing, that his Lordship was upon his journey for Flanders, and that it was reported Mr. Walmesley was returning for England with his Majesty's pass. This surprized Baker a little, who thereupon bethought him of another designe, which was to go on with Lunt on his first discovery of murdering King William, and still Aron Smith was consulted, who was never backward to any of Baker's projects, finding them very useful for getting good estates for himselfe and his 'fellow-sufferer,' for soe he called Captain Baker. Wherefore they gave Lunt considerable sumes of money, till they had got his narrative in writing. Mr. Aron Smith gave it to Mr. Ellis to coppye it over fair, he haveing first corrected it (Mr. Ellis was their clerk), who was to deliver [it] to Lunt, to be got by heart, for which service, the said Ellis had ten shillings a weeke. Captain Baker and Lunt shewed me, from time to time, what they had done, asking my opinion or approbation, which I freely gave them, believing, at that time, what Lunt said, to be true.

" They brought into their plot a vast number of nobility and gentry, viz.: Carmarthen, Hallifax, Notingham, Devon, Sir John Mannering, Sir Willoughby Ashton, Sir Ralph Dutton, Mr. Norris, of Sprake, and Mr. Rigby, &c. I told them I did not know but these Protestant gentlemen might be guilty, but my opinion was, that if they accused them before they made out the truth of the plott, noebody would believe them. Wherefore, they resolved to begin with the Nonjurants and the Papists; and Lunt's narrative being at length compleated, Captain Baker and Lunt told me they were advised by Aron Smith not to bring the matter before the Privy Counsell, for that some of the Counsell was guilty, and that they should get some gentleman, who was a Parliment man, to prevaile with her Majesty to let noebody be acquainted with the thing but my Lord-Keeper, and the Secretaryes, for which I then thought they had good reason, but now I am convinced it was because they thought it easier to impose on three persons then the whole body of the Counsel. Not long after this, I went on vigorously with their plot.

"Aron Smith gave them great sumes of money, which Baker and Lunt divided between them, and bought such fine cloathes with the money, that I scarce knew them. In the meantime, Lunt had pickt up one Wilson, a fellow that made the beds for the guestes· at the 'Bear and ·Ragged Staffe,' in Smithfield; and whilst I was in Lancashire, Captain Baker wrote to me to bring up one Womball, a broken carrier, who pretended he could make a discovery of armes, sent by him into the countrey. On the road, I asked the said Womball what he knew concerning the plott. He protested to me severall times he knew nothing of it, more than that he once carried swords into Lancashire, but knew not to whom they belonged. He then alsoe denyed he knew Lunt. When we came to London, I shewed Lunt to him. Womball said he had never seen him before; but when he came to Baker's office, and had two or three dayes conversant (*sic*) there, my carryer knew both Lunt and the plott, as well as any man in England; and haveing got a spill of money, grew soe elevated, that he threatened to bring all into the plott that he owed money to, in case they asked him for it. After this, I desired Lunt to give me some account of Wilson, when and where he became acquainted with him; who answered, he was a gentleman that came from near Preston, in Lancashire, to whom Mr. Aron Smith had given ten pound to bear his charges to London.

"After this, they passed the time merrily, for most commonly they went to the tavern every night, where they used to instruct one another, even in my presence, sometimes, but telling me that if I discovered them, they would swear treason against me, soe that I was forced to wait an oportunity for the unravelling this piece of villany. After this, all things being ready, they went into the countrey [with] what warrants, messengers, and whatsoever was necessary, for seizing men, armes, horse, &c. Captain Baker told me if I would go along with him he would bear my charges, and be oblieged to me for my company, for he did not like Lunt's nor Willson's. Upon his saying soe, I made bold to tell Captain Baker I doubted they did not, in everything, speake truth. The Captain replyed, whether they speake truth or noe, I am sure to make out a hainous plott, for if these witnesses fail, Aron has more in store, and, if armes and horses can be found in the hands of the Papists, we will certainly make a plott which shall goe over all England, and make a thorough reformation, pull down Bishops and their cathedrall law; for, says he (the said Captain), 'we shall never be happye whilest there is any bishoppe or priest of the Protestant religion in England.' This, and a great deal of discourse, was to this effect. I consented to goe for sundry reasons; first, because I feared they would doe me some mischief if I refused; secondly, they would not trust me more, and that then I should loose an oportunity of discovering their mass of villany, and be deprived of an oportunity of serving the government, as I was oblieged to doe.

"Should I give you a description of their impiety on the road, and tell you their atheism, swearings, blasphemie, and all their many different sorts of prophaness that was acted amongst them, you could not read it without a thousand teares, and as many blushes. They made it a capital fault to say grace, or goe to the church on Sundayes, or any other dayes, and allthough they were all arrived to a tollerable piece of villany, that Captain Baker did much excell them all; he was arrived to the very Tenarife of villany. He did always exclaime against bishops, and the religion, as well as clergy, of the Church of England, and for the truth of this, I appeal to the people of all the houses they lodged in; vizt., at the 'Bullhead,' in Manchester, the 'Eagle and Child,' in Wigan, [and] the 'Golden Lyon,' in Warrington. Captain Baker did often say that he thought the time was now come to pull down all ecclesiastical law, and that he thought God had preserved Aron and himselfe to be the Church of England's ruin. He said he had not soe great an animositie against the priests of the Church of Rome as against those of the Church of England, because they were for monarchy and hierarchy. He wished for Old Oliver again, saying the kingdom was never soe happye as under him. With these, and such like sayings, the Captain entertained us, Wombell confirming, with bloody oathes, his worship was in the right. When we came to Lancashire, and all things were in readiness for seizing the horses and armes of the Roman Catholickes, Captain Baker had gotten together a company of the greatest rakehells that the countrey could afford, who minded nothing but rapeing and plunder. Wherever they came, they used to search houses and seize upon horses, without constables, and sell them again to the owners for five or ten shillings a horse. Sometimes they would bring the horses to Captain Baker, who kept and restored what he pleased, though I never heard he restored any without money. I told him of the irregularities of such proceedings, because when he first invited me down, he said he would be advised by me, but he would be advised by nobody.

" The messengers were used to curse and say 'God damm Taaffe; he would perswade Captain Baker to return, for that if he did, they should never have such an oportunity of getting money.' Soe I let them goe on to their own ruin, being very uneasie in my mind for want of somebody to whome I might reveale the matter. I gave some hints of it to the parson of Newton, but he, seeing me in such company, would not trust me; soe I thought it my best way to goe to London and to find out some meanes to acquaint the government with it, but Mr. Aron Smith did so threaten all who contradicted him, that I durst not doe it. It was his custome to come to Captain Baker's office and instruct and cross-examine the witnesses against the tryall, and sometimes he would assure them that, in less then halfe a year, he would have the lives of five hundred persons. In short, I knew not what to resolve upon, till the quarrells of Wilsone, Womball, and Lunt, gave me oportunity of detecting their unpararleled villany, which I hope will be acceptable to your Majesty.

" In short, I must confess, I knew not what to resolve on, till the quarrels of Lunt, Wilson, and Womball gave me oportunity, as I thought, of doing good to the gentlemen, my countrey, and selfe; to effect which, I thought it necessary to find out Wilson, which, when I had done, I invited him to dinner, that I might learn of him what the matter was between them. Wilson told me Lunt had cheated him of money that was given him to bear his charges out of Lancashire, from whence he made the Secretary believe he came, though he dwelt in Smithfield. Wilson told me the sume given him to bear his charges up was ten pound, which Lunt and Baker did divide betwixt them, except five shillings which they gave to him. Then I asked Wilson how he would doe if he should disobliege Lunt, since Lunt was the first man that taught him his lesson. It is true, says Wilson, Lunt first taught me my lesson, but now I am acquainted with Mr. Aron Smith and Captain Baker, who looke upon me to be a soberrer man then Lunt, and they will teach me what to say. Moreover, said Wilson, John Wombell and I agree very well; but besides myself and Wombell there is one Dr. Dandy, and Peirson, kept on purpose by Captain Baker, at Coventry, to swear, and after we have hanged the gentlemen in custody, we will turn off[f] Lunt and employ Dr. Dandy and Peirson for evidence over the whole kingdome. He told me this, and a great deal more to the same purpose. The day following, I went to Lunt to enquire what was the matter between him and Wilson. Lunt answered, Wilson and Wombell were a couple of ungratfull rouges, because they expected to have as much as he, though he was the chiefe evidence. After which, he said, 'I wish with all my heart that I had to doe with some gentleman.' He alsoe said to me, 'if you, Mr. Taaffe, would swear with me, I would introduce you to the Secretarys of State, and would have nothing to doe with those fellowes, Wilson and Wombell.' I answered, 'I would not doe any such thing myselfe, but I would make it my buisness to find out some gentleman to swear him.' 'Then,' said Lunt, 'Mr. Aron Smith tells me that, unless I produce some commissions, I cannot doe my buisness soe well. Wherefore,' saith Lunt, 'Mr. Taaffe, if you will write them, I will gratify you very largly.'

"Mr. Aron Smith told me he would procure a warrant to search in what house I pleased, where I may drop the commissions myself, and get the messengers to find, and swear these were the very commissions I brought from King James. Lunt and I parted, and then I went to severall of my acquaintance, to desire them to help me in the discovery of a piece of rougery, but nobody would concern themselves with it, lest Lunt and Wilson should swear something against them, and I myself was apprehensive that if I went to the Secretary he would not believe me, but looke upon me as a man not well affected to the government. Whereupon, I thought it my best way to find out some persons who would pretend to swear with Lunt, and counterfeit the commissions he desired, and then goe to the government and acquaint them they were imposed upon by a parcell of villans. . I was very uneasie to thinke that soe many innocent gentlemen should suffer by the evidence of men whom I knew perjured, fearing both for the gentlemen and myself, that [if] I did not discover the villany of the plotters, that not only they, but most of the nobility and gentry in England would, in a short time, have followed their fate, it being the designe of those plotters, by their false evidence, to take away the lives of most of the prime nobility and gentry in England. For myself, I was afraid of endangering my own life by endeavouring to preserve theirs, and on the other side, I was afraid, that if I did suffer these gentlemen to dye innocently, I thought their blood would be required at my hands, and therefore bethought me on what means I might most conveniently doe it.

"Once I thought that if I did acquaint some of the prisoners' friends, they would soon find out somebody to list himselfe with Lunt, but I was unwilling to have anything to doe with the prisoners' friends that I knew were reputed Papists or Jaccobites ; yet finding the day of tryall drawing on, and Lunt impatient to drop his commissions, and Aron Smith very eager to hasten his worke, I resolved, rather then fail, to send to some of the ladyes, whose husbands were in custody. My wife undertooke the thinge and went to Madame Dicconson, who, after severall meetings, prevailed with one Mr. Legh Bankes to give me a · meeting. I told that if he and some others would goe to Lunt and tell him they wanted money, and that, if he could put them in a way to get money, they would be oblieged to him and doe what service he could. Banks said he would consider on it, and desired to meet next morning, and there I went to him and found him with two other gentlemen. The gentlemen who were with Mr. Legh Bankes liked the project, and promised to meet him at 4 o'clocke in the afternoon. In the meanetime, I went and acquainted Lunt with the thing, who was overjoyed to have gentlemen swear him, and swore a great bloody oath he would turn off Wombell and Wilson, and them to returne to their old employment. Lunt and I went to the place appointed, which was the 'Ship' ale-house, in Butcher Row, without Temple Barr, where the gentlemen came and sent for me, and told me they would willingly put off the thing till next day, but I told them if they put it of, Lunt would mistrust something, and such arguments, that Mr. Bankes was perswaded to speake with Lunt.

"As soon as Lunt saw him, he complemented him, saying, he thought himself very happy to be concerned with a gentleman, for that he had to doe with a company of machenick fellows that knew nothing of the plot but [what] he told them, and that he would turn them off if Mr. Legh Bankes would joyn with him in the discovery, and swear what Lunt would have him swear. Mr. Legh Bankes seemed very modest, and pretended to have been in company all that day, and would be glad to get money, but was not prepared at that time to undertake a busness of that consequence, yet he then desired Lunt to give him some insight into the matter. Lunt immediately draws out his narrative in very good form, writ by Captain Baker's clerk, and gave it us to read. 'I know nothing of this matter,' said Mr. Bankes, 'therefore, pray, Mr. Lunt, tell me what I must doe.' Lunt answered, 'Sir, you must swear you know all this to be true. I am,' said Lunt, 'upon counterfeiting commissions, and you must have a commission, and you must swear you had it from one of the gentlemen in custody.' After this, says Lunt, 'But, sir, can you write a good hand? for if you doe, you must write the commissions yourselfe, because we must not trust too many in our affaires.' 'I doe not write well,' sayes Mr. Legh Bankes, 'and if you intend such a thing, how can you counterfeit King James' hand?' 'I have,' replyes Lunt, 'an old commission in my pocket, and have likewise my Lord Milford's hand, and I will have all the commissions signed by King James, and we must drop a bundle of them in some house, and when Mr. Aron Smith sends to search the house, the messenger will find the commissions and wee will swear they were the same King James sent by me to the gentlemen in custody and to severall others, for,' sayes Lunt, 'I intend to goe all over England with my plott if you will but joyn heartily with me, and bring some friend along with you that will swear the same thing with us. And,' Lunt said, 'I was to be of Dodsworth's plott, but I refused, resolveing to have a plott of my owne making and not of another's.' Mr. Legh Bankes replyed he had a friend of his that understood these things better then himself, and therefore he desired him to meet him the next day.

"Lunt consented freely to it, and soe we parted for that day. Next day, some lawyers perswaded Mr. Legh Bankes to acquaint my Lord Cheife-Justice with what he had done, unknown to me; wherupon, I found Mr. Bankes a little shy of me, and he would not tell me the reason, upon which I went to Mrs. Dicconson and desired her to find out somebody to goe to Lunt, according to Bank's promise, or I was sure the buisness was ruined. As I and Madam Dicconson was talking, Mr. Roger Dicconson came in, and his sister did noe sooner propose the thing, but Mr. Roger freely offered himselfe, and he went along with me to Fetter Lane, to a little coffee house next the 'Globe,' where I left him, and went for Lunt, who was not at his lodgings, but as soon as he came home he ran to us where we were, and made this excuse for his absence—that Mr. Aron Smith sent him to John Wilson, the prisoner, [for?] two shirts, for that they intended to make him a witness. In short, Dicconson and Lunt fell upon their buisnes. Lunt asked Dicconson what his name was. Dicconson answered, 'Howard.' Lunt asked again which religion he was. Dicconson said he was of the Church of England. 'Then,' sayes Lunt, swearing a great oath, 'you must have a commission under Lee of Lime, for he is of that religion.'

" Then Dicconson began to swear as hard as Lunt that he would doe anything to get money, but that he was not acquainted with any of the gentlemen in custody, and that he must know them before he could swer against them. [Lunt replyed,] he would shew them to him and give in writing what he would have him swear. Then Dicconson said he was acquainted with one Roger Dicconson and all the rest of the Dicconsons. In a short time, Captain Howard replyed he would help him to swear against Roger Dicconson in particular, but that he was unwilling to swear without considerable reward. ' We shall have,' sayes Lunt, ' the third part of all those gentlemen's estates, and then will goe all over England and hang up whom we please. I will turn off Womball and Wilson, and deal with none but your friend. I will likewise turn off Aron Smith and Baker, for they doe not give us the whole sume that is allowed us; we will goe to the Secretary ourselves and have the whole credit of the busness. We must,' sayes Lunt, ' counterfeit commissions, and you shall have a captain's commission under Mr. Lee of Lime, and you must swear you had it from his own hand. In the meantime, you must swear,' sayes Lunt, ' to be true to me, and not to discover me.' Upon this they desired me to goe out of the room, and after they had been together awhile they called me in again, and told me they had agreed together to meet at 2 a'clocke in the afternoon and go to the Savoy, or over the water, to get the commissions counterfeited, upon which we parted, and at 2 a'clocke, according to our appointment, Lunt and I came to the aforesaid coffee house, into which we were noe sooner entred, but in comes one of Lunt's wifes with a constable, and makes him prisoner.

" Lunt immediately begins to mistrust Captain Howard, *alias* Dicconson, and I myselfe knew not what to thinke of it, till saw Mr. Dicconson and Mr. Lee Bankes, who, hearing there was a constable, began to mistrust that was a trick put upon them, soe they got away. and I followed them into the street and told them what the matter was, at which they seemed to be concerned. I returned to Lunt again and stead with him till Mr. Aron Smith came, who hectored Lunt's wife at a strange rate, and threatened what he would doe to her for takeing up the King's evidence. Then Mr. Aron Smith called for a coach, saying he would give bail for Lunt's appearance, and desired me to goe with him in his coach. As we were goeing, he swore he did not know what to doe in relation to Lunt, and asked my advice. I answered I believed Lunt to be an ill man, and that I knew he had two wifes, at least, upon which, he fell into such a passion, that I thought he would have cast himself headlong out of the coach, upon which, Aron said I must not goe with him before the Lord Mayor, least his Lordshipe should examine me and I should be such a fool as to tell the truth of Lunt, for that he intended to make my Lord Mayor believe Lunt was an honest man, and that it was but a trick of the Papists to take him up, because he was the King's evidence. Then Aron desired me to go home, which I very freely did, for I began to be weary of his company.

" In the evening, I called at Captain Baker's office, where I found Lunt giving an account of what happened that day, but soe little suspecting the designe we had to discover the rougery, that, on the contrary, he desired me to goe to Captain Howard and tell him he would meet him next morning, but, notwithstanding, Lunt thought himself secure in his plot as ever, yet. Aron Smith found out, that very night, either at my Lord Chiefe Justice's, or at some other place, that we were sufficiently prepared to expose their sham plott, and accordingely gave notice of it to Lunt and Baker, who kept Lunt out of the way till the tryall. In the meanetime they threatened what they would doe to me. But notwithstanding all their menaces, I was resolved to be soe just to my King and countrey as to become a sacrifice myselfe to the fury of these conspirations rather then have the raign of soe great and good a King sullied with the innocent blood of so many nobles and gentlemen. Baker sent for me the night before he went out of town, and asked me who that Captain Howard was. I answered, he was one of Lunt's acquaintance, and therefore I desired him to ask Lunt, upon which he perceived I did but banter him. Whereupon, he began to threaten me, saying the law was very severe against all men that went about to put tricks upon the King's evidence. I answered, ' I had not offended against the law, and therefore the law would not meddle with me; and,' said I, 'Mr. Baker, if you will goe with me before the Secretary of State, I will justify myself.' ' If the Secretary of State saw you,' replyed he, ' he would commit you.' When I heard that, and next morning they went out of town, saying nothing, but taking my saddle and bridell away with them, whereupon I tooke post and went to Manchester, wher I was informed by severall, how Lunt, Baker, and the messengers, had reported in that countrey that they had left me in Newgate, for endeavouring to corrupt the King's evidence.

" My intention [is] here to give any account of the tryall, whereof the reader may better informe himself from those many able lawyers that were present, only I must not forget to acquaint the world how Aron Smith, as soon as he had heard the names of the gentlemen's witnesses in court, feigned himself sicke; knowing very well that, when I was called, I could discover the mistery of his plot. I call it his plot— though since the miscariage of it, he was willing to cast it on me— for I have severall arguments which doe demonstratively shew the plot to be his; first, because he furnished the evidence with large sumes of money to carrye it on; secondly, because it was he that fashioned and formed their depositions ; thirdly, he bailed Lunt, and made the Lord Mayor believe he was an honest man. It was he, in fine, that threatened to have me punished for striveing to detect the villany of his witnesses; in a word, he is so well known, that I need say noe more."

RICHARD EDGE to ROGER KENYON.

982. 1695[-6], January 4. London.—The Council is not sitting. In the list, are Mr. Richard Fleetwood, Mr. Robert Mawdesley, and one Mr. Dionisius Byron. The Lords and Commons cannot yet agree about the Coin Bill, but have appointed another conference on Monday next. The King has answered the Commons that he will issue out his proclamation for receiving the clipped standard money, as they desire.

RICHARD EDGE to ROGER KENYON, at Manchester.

983. 1695-6, January 7. London.—" No sheriffe for our county yet pricked. Taaffe is at liberty, upon bayle, to appear in the King's Bench. The House of Commons did nothing yesterday, and to day only called over the House." *Seal.*

P[ETER] SHAKERLEY to ROGER KENYON, at his house in Manchester.

984. 1695[-6], January 8. Westminster. —" I am under som straights on account of the designes of my enemies against mee, at Wigan, which they are verry industrious in forming and suiteing their evidence to ; whilst my friends there are too slack in finding out what the intended objections and evidence against mee are · . . . . . .

I have noe friend in all that county to whom I can committ this great trust, or hope to procure the great favour from of putting this affair into order, besides yourself. And, considering that your Quarter Sessions at Wigan is to be next week, where it is possible you may be, I begg you will be pleased to give yourself the trouble to stay there som few days. to make enquirey what the objections intended against mee are, and the persous designed to proove the same, and put all that into one breviate. I am under another misfortune, that I cannot, with safety, write any letter on this affair, or any other, by the way of Warrington, because you know who is the postmaster there, and who it was procured him to be soe. Therefore, I pray, doe not you send anything that way, concerning the premises; and I beseech you mannage all this matter with great secrecy and caution . . . . and what charges you are at in staying at Wigan, to make enquireys and putting matters into method, I will thankfully repay you."

RICHARD EDGE to GEORGE KENYON, at Manchester.

985. 1695–6, January 9. London.—Commences with private business matters. "I have no forreigne news to tell you both, but a peece of domestick newes which comes in time, and will mightily help the Sessions; for it is to-day resolved that all clipped money, which is silver, though of a coarser alloy than the standard, shall pass in payment of taxes, and that all persons, whatever, shall so take it in payment; that any person may pay his next yeares tax, to the 4s. in the pound, at one intire payment in clipped money; that all Commissioners to be appointed, shall be sent into all countyes of England, to disperse the new coynd money and receive clipped money for it. Here was such a decay of trade and such a work about it that caused the House of Commons to sitt *de die in diem*, about the coyne, and come to this resolution, which is generally well pleaseing. The Sheriffe of Lancashire, I hear, [is] to be pricked to-night."

RICHARD EDGE to ROGER KENYON, at Manchester.

986. 1695–6, January 11. London.—"On Thursday night last, Mr. Norreys, of Speake, was prickt at Kensington, by the King, for our High Sheriffe. I am privately told that the Chancellour went to wait upon the King, on Wednesday, at which time, the King wished him to strike out one of his 3 names returned, and put in Mr. Norres. You may guess how things go by that. This day the Commons passed the bill for preventing charge and expense in elections, etc. . . . By all our forreigne posts, we have advice that the French fleet will pass the streights this year, if they can."

JOHN HARTLEY to ROGER KENYON, at Manchester.

987. 1695–6, January 15. Lancaster (?).—Is sorry he could not discourse with Mr. Kenyou, during his last visit. Finds it was a "designed thing" on the part of the gaoler, who set persons to drink with the writer, lest his (the gaoler's) "rogurys" should be discovered. *Endorsed* "John Hartley, Esqre."

RICHARD EDGE to ROGER KENYON, at Manchester.

988. 1695–6, January 16. London.—Sir John Bland is gone into Yorkshire. Lady Moseley is well; a letter will find her at her lodgings, in Soho Square. Has waited on Sir John Leveson-Gower. "You-bid me tell you how the Cliderow members go, in Parliament; they go with the Liverpoole members perpetually. I think I need say no more than that."

RICHARD EDGE to ROGER KENYON.

989. 1695[-6], January 18. London.—I received your last long letter by the post, which was not sealed with your own seal; therefore I reckon it had been opened by the way. There are some rascals who do frequently open letters, and these are called "secret friends to the government." All this preparation the French are making at sea, seems to be designed on our foreign Plantations, to ruin them We shall have an army of 140,000 in the Netherlands, the next campaign, and the discourse there is of our besieging Dunkirk. The Lords will pass the Coin Bill on Monday or Tuesday, and then they will begin coining; our coin is to be as good as it was. There is already brought into the Exchequer 1,700,000*li.* in clipped coin.

RICHARD EDGE to ROGER KENYON, at Manchester.

990. 1695-6, January 21. London.—"This day the King came to the House of Lords and passed four publick bills (besides private bills), *videlicet :*—the treason bill, the coyn bill, the bill for preventing expenses in elections, and the bill for continuing duties upon spirits, etc. The House of Commons have ordered in the bill for preventing and punishing of perjury before the sheriffes, at the elections of knights, at the county court; that a forme of an oath be brought in to be taken by the freeholders, which will hinder the Jacobites from voteing, which some say will be thrown out. The report about the Scotch East India Company was likewise to day made; that it was guilty of a high crime and misdemeanour; and resolved that the English and Scotch subscribers to that company, resideing in England, shall be impeached of high crimes and misdemeanours. Some people dread the ill consequence of this. You know these votes are not printed till to morrow morning, and are not written. I have them allwaes from a freind, which is no member. I know not how safe it is to give such account, but I presume you have the same in written news letters, which I have not seen in any place, since I came to town, for in the coffee houses are no letters, but printed. Some of our printed news letters say the French will have 95 men of war in a line of battle, 50 of them to go from Brest, Port Louis, etc., and to joyn the Thoulon fleet, which 50 will saile in a fortnight. And this is sworn to by a prisoner, come from Brest, before our Commissioners of the Admiralty. Others say it is false; some few ships are ordered to transport men from Catolonia into Piedmont, against the Duke of Savoy. Others say that a great many private persons, in France, are concerned, and furnish the fleet at their own private charge, to go upon some enterprise. The King of France is to have a third part of what they gett. Some say our Lords of the Admiralty have not behaved themselves as they ought to do; that our shipping is not in so great forwardness as it ought to be. Some say it is in greater forwardness than ever, but I observe Sir Jn. Louther, of Whithaven, is getting off. I forgett to tell you that the House of Commons go to morrow to wait upon the King, with an address against the Lord Portland, who had thought to have been Prince of Wales. One Mr. Price made a very learned speech against his Lordshipp, and, as Mr. Shakerley told me, left nothing unsaid. I cannot yet learne when Cliderow election comes on, for I avoid seeing **either side.**"

PETER SHAKERLEY to [ROGER KENYON].

991. 1695[-6], January 23. Westminster.—Would have him keep the "breviate" as long as necessary. The petition now stands, according to course, not to come on or be heard before the 10th or 12th of March next, and it is possible it may be April before it comes on. We have much business to do, and it is possible Committees may be frequently adjourned; however, it is best to be prepared. The first preparation must be fully to answer all objections which you can possibly learn are intended to be made; and the next thing is to recriminate upon the opponent, in such substantial objections and proofs as will stick fast upon him : " but those should not be too levious ; such as his caresses of the woman, which will not signifye any thing. But if, in kissing of them, hee hurryed guinneas into their mouths (as was done at one place), that will be to purpose, provided it is proved; and that hee used that sollicitation to gett, and that hee did thereby gett, their husbands to vote for him."

RICHARD EDGE to GEORGE KENYON.

991A. 1695-6, January 23. London.—The House of Commons has nipped the Prince of Wales (who should have been) in the bud, and waited on the King yesternight with their address. At the Admiralty Office, they are taking care to send a re-inforcement to Sir George Rooke, and a squadron, as some say, to block up Dunkirk. *Seal.*

P[ETER] SHAKERLEY to ROGER KENYON, at his house in Manchester.

992. 1695[-6], January 25. Westminster.—"I thank you for your continued care in my affair; inclosed is Mr. R——'s petition, which is very dark, as are the intended objections against mee. I under-stand the petition was concerted with Mr. Mountague, who brought it in, and it is timed so that I conceive it is intended to come on towards the end of the Session, when the House is thiner, for it stands now to be about the 10th or 12th of March, though noe time is yet appointed for it, nor has it yet been read in the committee. Mr. Harvey and Mr. Tattlock are made Commissioners for the Land Tax, so is Mr. Harvey's father, Mr. Brown, Mr. Ralph Markland, and Mr. Wells. Inclosed I send you the Act about clipped and counterfeit money, which please to communicate to Mr. Warden, who will allso communicate to you three other Acts I send to him this post, viz., the Act for trial of treason, the Act for preventing expenses at elections, and an Act about . . . . and annuities. I doe perceive that Mr. R——'s designe is onely to make my election void, and not to come in himself but by a new election. I am informed they intend to charge me with som words, said to be spoken by mee, but what they are, where, when, or before whom spoken, I cannot learn. The condition of our navy is very deplorable ; and had I not seen a peece of one of the great shipps, I could not have believed it possible that the worm could have made such great and soe many vacuitys in the sound heart of oak. God Allmighty preserve ould England from a French conquest !" *Seal.*

RICHARD EDGE to ROGER KENYON, at Manchester.

993. [1695-6, January 28 ?] London.—Commences with family matters. "I cannot yet tell you when Cliderow election comes on, nor concerne myself in that matter. The House of Commons were to-day in a comittee for trade, and came to severall heads, which will be reported on Friday next. The House of Lords have been all this day about our East India Company, and divided about it, and carried by 22 that there shall be an East India Company established by Act of Parliament, and carryed on by a joynt stock. I hear allso that there is to be an imbargo laid upon Scotch East India ships which are fitting out in the river of Thames. *The Royall Soveraigne*, a ship of 104 guns, is burnt, as some people say, by an accident of a snuff of a candle, and some say done a purpose. Our fleet at Cadiz will be all careened in a three weekes, and then will put to sea, which will be as soon as the Thoulon fleet can go to sea. The squadron at Spitthead, which waits for a fair wind to joyne our fleet, are to be doubled in the number which was so lately ordered. A great overgrown French man-of-war mett with one of our cruisers in the Straits and sunk him. But all honest persons conclude that all our men-of-war are in good order and will be ready to sail eearlier than in any spring before. I mett with a Jacobite yesterday (a great rogue I beleeve) and he tells me the Thoulon fleet is out allready; that they have taken one of our cruisers in the Straits, sunk another, and sent another, ragged and shattered, into Cadiz; that the French fleet may goe where they will, for a great many of our great ships in England will not be fitt to saile this year, nor scarce ever; that we shall have no money presently, but guineas, which are coined, a great deal of them, in Holland; that what milled money is made, or making, must be all sent to Holland; and that there can be no circulation of the milled money this six months; and a great deal more of these roguish stories, which I would give no ear to. I will take care to buy you an almanack, but you writeing so late that I have not yet mett with such a one as you use[d] to have; and if I bespeake it they will excise me. The word excise putts me in mind of proposalls offered to the House of Commons for a penny a peck upon bread, and allso duties proposed to be laid on periwigs, comodes, swords, and a great many things more, which I cannot name."

P[ETER] SHAKERLEY to ROGER KENYON, "at his house in Manchester."

994. 1695[-6], February 1. Westminster.—"Yours, dated the 26th instant, came to my hands but yesterday, but in such a condition that 1 cannot possibly read it, and is all dirt and daub even on the inside, where it is impossible that such dirt could com but by opening it, and daubing it so on purpose. The post mark on it, viz., the Generall Letter Office mark, when it came hither, is January the 31st, and your other letter, dated the 28th January, has allso the same mark, and they both came together yesterday. Therefore, I pray, inquire of your postmaster at Manchester, how long the said letter dated the 26th of January, did lye in his hands, and how and when hee did dispose of it, viz.: (1) whether he sent it away immediately there? (2) whether it was so besmeared and daubed before hee sent it? (3) whether he sent it sealed up in his bagg? and (4) whether his bagg was opened at any place before it coms to London, and where? When he has answered to these questions, if hee is clear and innocent in the matter, I desire hee will make affidavid of it that hee did send the said letter sealed up in his bagg, without blemmish, &c., and send the same to mee, I pray you, by next post. I perceive the superscription is Mr. Tattlock's handwriting; therefore, to trace this matter right, know of him in what manner, when, and to whom, he delivered it? And I desire you will have his affidavid of it and send it up to mee immediately, with the postmaster's affidavid. Wee had a long debate yesterday about the Oath, [as] I writt to Mr. Warden, which was at last, upon a division, rejected; Sir Thomas Stanley, Sir Ro.-

Bradshaigh, Cozen Preston, Mr. Puddsey, Mr. Brotherton, Leigh Banks, and myself, were together in the division; all the Foleys were also with us."

Postscript.—"Since I writt this, I hear that other letters in that packquett were all used as mine. . . . Wee have this day carryed, by ballotting, all the Commissioners of Accompts."

P[ETER] SHAKERLEY to ROGER KENYON, at Manchester.

995. 1695[-6], February 4. Westminster.—"Dick Edge was with mee last night, just after the election for Clitheroe was determined in the comittee, for Mr. Pudsay against Mr. Stringer, which was soe cleer a case that it was rather a *nemine contradicente.* Our success in carrying, by ballotting, all the seven Commissioners wee named for the publick accounts, was very good, and therefore I will give you their names and the names of the other seven who came next to them, and seemed to be competfitors :

Paul Foley, Esq., Speaker - - - -	238
Henry Boyl, Esq. - - - - -	228
John Granville, Esq. - - - •	227
Sir Thomas Dyke - - - -	185
Mr. Bromley, of Warwickshire - - •	200
Robert Harley, Esq. - - - -	243
Francis Gwynn, Esq. - - - -	188
Sir Thomas Pope Blunt - - ' ·· -	178
Sir John Thomson - - - -	160
Sir William Ashurst - - - -	163
Mr. Mouldsworth - • - - - -	118
Mr. Norris - - - - - -	134
Mr. Booth - - - - -	131
Sir Edward Abney - - - -	155 "

Postscript.—"Aron Smith was called to our bar this day, for having received nineteen thousand pounds and refused to give accompt of it to our Commissioners. Hee has tenn days time to make his accompt in, and if hee does not in that time, you will hear of him in custody."

RICHARD EDGE to ROGER KENYON, at Manchester.

996. 1695-6, February 4. London.—"I was with Mr. Shakerley yesterday, and [he] shewed me a letter from you, but it had been in some bottom of a ditch, for neither your letter, nor the inclosed, was legible; it was so all dirt. I am sure no stranger could have read it. Here and there it was plain, and I, knowing your hand, guessed at the rest, and have since transcribed it for Mr. Shakerley. . . . . As I observe, all that they can pretend to is that he [?] is a Jacobite, an enemy to this government, and I cannot see that can make an election void; it is the first, if such thing be done. But they are mistaken, the Committee is not so much a committee of affections as they think. Collonell Granvill is the Chairman, an ingenious, honest, bold gentleman, and vallues nere a courtier of them all. The Committee for Cliderowe was last night, who, after heareing councell and witnesses on both sides, never debated, but put the question whether Mr. Pudsey was duely elected and returned. It was carried in the affirmative; I think, *nemine contradicente.* Sir Thomas Powis [and] Sir Bartholomew Shore, councell for Mr. Stringer ; Mr. Dormer [and] Mr. Dobbins, councell for Mr. Pudsay.

" The Committee sate till 12 at night; there was a pretty full Committee. I crept into the gallery above, to avoid being seen. I think all our Lancashire members attended, save Collonells Stanley and Kirkby. Mr. Molineux asked a question in favour of Mr. Pudsay, so did Mr. Brotherton, and so did Mr. Preston, And Mr. Norris, who is a violent man, but speakes well, asked half a dozen questions in favour of Mr. Stringer, whose councell opened the cause, and pleaded that he had the same case as Mr. Gerrard, which was (they doubted not) remembered by a great deal of the members in this Parliament. They agreed that, as the poll was taken at the day of election, they had a minority of votes by 12, but had 15 freinds, who had a right to be found by the ceremonial inquiry jury, and were ready to have given their votes; that the present bayliffes obstructed the calling of a jury, and that the sitting member, Mr. Pudsay, had, by his agent, given a bribe of 30s. to one Nowell (one of Mr. Stringer's friends, but not found freeman) to keep out of the hall at the time of election; and that the House declared in favour of such cases at two former committees. This was the substance of their allegations. They made it out by 15 Cliderowe witnesses, the chief of which were Tom Dugdale and John son of Edmund Robinson. Mr. Pudsay's councell answered they had the majority of quallifyed voters; moreover, that they had freinds of the same number, 15, which would have voted for Mr. Pudsay had they been found, and had the same qualificacons as Mr. Stringer's, but the present bayliffes refused to call a jury after the test of the writt for either side, that if such thing were done, which was never known, it would brake a constitution of the burrough and consequently be pernicious.

" Besides, Mr. Pudsay made it appear to the Committee that the 15 freinds of Mr. Stringer never demanded to be polled, which was looked upon by Mr. Stringer's freinds in the House to be a great omission of his agent, Troy, who was called to answer to that point. One of the members asked him his profession; an attorney in London, he answered. Some members comented upon him, saying what did you go into the North 200 miles to sollicit at an election, so that he was not well heard. Mr. Pudsay called Mr. Sclater, Ned Farrer, and Dick Wilson, who are now three thorrow paced Committee witnesses, and made out what Mr. Pudsay's councell had asserted, and called one Nowell to disprove his own brother, about the 30s. bribe, who, with two others, did it with effect, and affirmed he drew ale and beer (the word beer smelled of London discipline) before the election, and Mr Pudsay's voters drunk as much as that came to, and his agents paid the reckoning. Nowell, that had the bribe, was called againe to confront his brother, had gott some brandy into his noddle, and said with a loud voice that his brother was a lyer, and the greatest that did come there. The Chairman was hearty for Mr. Pudsay, and Mr. Pudsay had got all his friends there, and cryed withdraw, withdraw, half an hour together, and then put the question as before. Paul Folie, Esquire, Collonell Granvill, Mr. Harley, Mr. Boyle, Mr. Bromley, of Staffordshire (who brought in the petition against Lord Portland), Sir Thomas Dike, and —————— are the Commissioners for the publick accounts. None of them had the nomination from the Court party, so that I reckon it is as good a choice as the Pope has made of Cardinalls, and both alike to me.

" This day Mr. Aaron Smith was called into the House, and ordered to give in his accounts in 10 dayes to the Commissioners, or incurr the displeasure of the House of Commons. This good man has something in hand, and now on the anvill, against the stiflers of the Lancashire plott. Now we have an account from abroad that the French fleet will not be equipped before the latter end of March; that our Lords of the Admiralty have given positive orders to the commodore of the squadron, designed for the reinforceing of Sir George Rook at Cadiz to be in areadiness to sayle the first fair wind ; that there has been a great buzzle at Amsterdam about a placart for a tax upon burialls; that the mob risse three dayes together against the governours, but after hanging of half a score of them, the matter was appeased, and all now quiett. Here is a rumour here as if there were some disturbances in Scotland, but I think it is but a story, for commonly one post contradicts another."

RICHARD WROE to ROGER KENYON, at Manchester.

997. 1695–6, February 6.—" My last told you that the Capitation Bill was a long one, and I believe you will think so by the enclosed abstract, which Mr. Shakerley has franked for you, and had sent you one if I had not prevented him. It was given for four millions, but Mr. Montague informed the House yesterday, that it would not raise above three millions, so that they have yet 1,800,000*l.* and 500,000*l.* for the Civil List to raise, and were yesterday upon ways and means, but without any certain resolution. It was talked of 2*s.* more per pound upon land, and the Plate Bill was voted to pay 6*d.* per ounce, for all plate under three ounces value, or weight, which, it is concluded, will passe. They have been this day upon prohibiting East India silks, Bengalls, calicoes, but I know not the issue, though, it is said, it will passe. However, some say it is a giving up our East India trade to the Dutch. They that pretend to know news from Court, say that all the preliminaryes of the peace are adjusted, and that it will certainly be concluded, which some believe and others take for a jest ; but the news that more concerns us is better, I mean in relation to the business I came hither upon.

Yesterday, being a day of great business in the Exchequer, we moved to deferr judgment in our case till to-day, because it would be long in giving, as it proved full two howers ; every baron giving his opinions and the reasons of it, with answers to all the arguments that had been urged on the other side, and every one of them was clear in their opinion for us, that the lease was expired six years since, being onely for 21 years and 99. Their resolution seemed very clear and satisfactory to the whole Court, and even to Mr. Trafford's counsel and atturney, who attended there, and who told me afterwards that they would acquiesce in it without bringing any writ of error, which is the onely remedy they have ; and on Weddensday next, judgment is to be recorded, and then we shall know what costs they will allow, which I hope will be favourable, and for the mean profits, we are left to our action at law, if Mr. Trafford will contest it, and not compound fairly with us. Pray communicate this, with the enclosed, to Mr. Yates, with my respects, not having any other news for him nor time to transcribe this, having stayed long and late at Westminster ; and if you please to be so kind as to let my niece know the successe of our business, you will further oblige mee, having nothing more but my health to acquaint her with. Mr. Preston's corps set out on Munday or Tuesday, but privately, that no notice may be taken of it. I was with our bishop yesterday, but shall have more time to acquaint him with yours on Weddensday, when his tryall about Hindley Chappel comes on." *Seal of arms.*

RICHARD EDGE to ROGER KENYON, at Manchester.

998. 1695–6, February 8. London.—" The House of Commons have this day agreed to the Lords' amendments to the bill for recovery

C C

of small tithes. A petition was made and presented to lower the extravagant price of guineas; it was referred to the Committee for the second coinage bill, but since withdrawn. They have resolved that no plate shall be used in the publick houses after the 4th of May, except spoons. The tryall *de novo* of Lunt, Wilson, and Womball, which should have come on this terme, is putt off to the next. Some sayes Sir George Rooke has orders to go to sea immediately, and some say not till 18 Dutch joyn him; and that the squadron designed heare to reinforce him are countermanded. But it is certaine that 51 great men-of-war at Thoulon are ready to sayle. . . . . I hear Mr. Shakerley has, upon Mr. Rigby's promiseing to withdraw his petition, writt to the mayor of Wygan to tell him that he will sollicit no more to be chosen there, which I think (but a fooll's boult is soon shot) is the meanest thing he ever did in his life."

RICHARD EDGE to ROGER KENYON, at Manchester.

999. 1695-6, February 10. London.—"In a weeke or two, in this town, there will be no silver to be had. I was with Mr. Legh, to take a copy of the *postea* about Lunt, Wilson, and Womball's verdict. He tells me it was never returned to him, in regard that verdict was sett aside, and the three gents are as clear as before that assizes. I see Capt. Baker frequently conversing with great men. Saturday's votes will tell you of Aaron Smith's being sent for, in custody; I did not hear that he is taken up, as yet. There is no news, for we have had no foreign mailes. Admirale Aylmer is to command 8 men of-warr that are to go in quest of Du Bart. We have an account how that one man (with his accomplices) in Derbishire, have allready made, coined, and counterfeited, to the likeness of the new milled money, 700*l.*, and is now in custody for it. Guineas are current here, but at 27*s.*, and silver growes very scarce." *Seal.*

The SAME to the SAME.

1000. 1695-6, February 11. London.—"I was at Mr. Legh Banke's chambers this morning, but he has not been there this two nights, and am told that he lodges sometimes with Sir Thomas Stanley in Pell Mall; but I very well remember one morning I went to Mr. Banke's chambers, there was this taylor Barnes, which has arrested me upon Mr. (*sic*) Thomas's account. Had I not mett with him there, he had not known that I was in town. I forgott to tell you that the sume I was forced to pay was 4*l.* 1*s.* I beg, if Mr. Thomas be in Lancashire, you will please to order him to remitt it me hither, for I cannot move till I have it, for the landlord will not let the horse stirr till he be paid, and my acknowledgment besides. . . . . Yesterday the House of Commons ordered the election of Cliderowe to be reported tomorrowe. I cannot tell what the House has done today. The resolutions of the House are ordered to be kept more secret, for the printer's sake, and [I] could not meet with any of the members tonight. I doe not yet hear that Aaron Smith has given in his accounts. The news from Flanders is that the French seem to talke of opening their campagne with the seige of Namur; that their fleet at Thoulon is allready careened and the guns on board, yet one account sayes they are takeing off their guns; that Admirall Rooke is very vigilant in observeing the French fleet's motions, and has got most of his ships new careened; that the French King has transmitted a great sume of money to the grand Seignior with 300 [or 3,000] officers and engineers, to carry on the war against the Emperor, and that he will be 40,000 stronger in Flanders than last year. Guineas are lowered in their price to-day 2s., but Thursday is the day to regulate that matter."

RICHARD EDGE to ROGER KENYON, at Manchester.

1001. 1695-6, February 13. "Westminster, 9 o'clock at night."— "This day the King has been here and passed the three publick Acts. . . . . The House has been in a grand Committee about guineas, and is so still. . . . . Here is a mighty full house, and all the halls, painted chamber, Speaker's chamber, and the lobby and coffee houses, full of people, watching the result the House will come [to] about guineas. The House had an account from the Mint that 700,000 guineas have been coined, since Candlemas 1694-5. The Court party are for lowering them to 27s.; the other party, for keeping them at 30s. Lancaster assizes to be the 25th of March; Nevill and Turton [the] judges. If the House come to any resolution before the post goes out, I will write."

The EARL OF DERBY to [ROGER KENYON].

1002. 1695-6, February 13. Knowsley.—"I have thought it a long while since I saw or heard from dear Roger; the last time the seal keeper was with me, I enquired how you did, and I think he then said you had the gout upon you, so that you could not stir; I had-els desired your company to have advised about my trial again, this next assizes, which I design to bring on; and in order to it, there are 24 to be named by each side, out of the freeholders' book, which I send you, that you may consider who they are I can most depend upon, and to send me the names in writing, as, I take it, the 21st is the day appointed for the prothonotary to strike the names. This, you must be sensible, is of great moment to me, as I shall look upon your assistance to be in this affair; for I do think this preliminary is of great consequence. But I shall not enter into particulars; you know them so well, and I so little."

PETER SHAKERLEY to ROGER KENYON.

1003. 1695[-6], February 13.—Advising him, if he has any guineas at 30s., to part with them forthwith, as a vote is passed in Committee that they should not go for more than 28s., and the Court party pushed hard to have them at 26s.

GUICCIARDINI WENTWORTH to ROGER KENYON, at Manchester.

1004. 1695[-6], February 15.—"And now I must acquaint you with an affaire which allarums us much. There is, as I am well informed, a Bill ready (upon leave) to take away the Dutchy and County Pallatine and annex them to the Exchequer, and this is in the hands of Mr. Norris' brother, of Speake. Who the setlers (?) are I know not, nor the suggestions of the Bill. It is yett a secrett; but, plowing with the heifer, I found out the riddle. Wee want your assistance in this affaire very much, and must, in behalfe of the Dutchy, and all others concerned, begg itt att your hands with what speed you may; and that you will be so kind to send us a copy of that colection relating to the Dutchy, you made when last this matter was on foot, which, with som few coments on it, by your hand, will, I question not, but be artillary sufficient (if well managed) to stem this tyde. Please you to write to mee under cover to Sir Gervas Elwes, or Mr. Preston; it will com safe." *Seal of arms.*

C C 2

Postscript.—" I remember Thomas Killegrewe was for goeing to
Manchester, to heare news; and though you do not want it, yett I cannot
forbeare to tell you that Admirall Rooke is makeing the best of his wey
home ; his brother beeing killed for a little familiarity with a Spanish
lady.   The French are makeing vast preparations by sea and land, and
have, as it is said, as good as concluded a peace with Spaine.   The
affaire of guinies gives great disturbance.   A committy to that affaire
have stated them att 28*s.*, but the House has not yet past it into a vote.
Divers angry questions seem prepared, ready against an opportunity.
I doe not see any likelyhood of compromising that matter with the
Spanish ambassador; but he is like to depart in a huff.   There be that
think Sir John Somers will survive the Lord Keeper."

Roger Kenyon to " Mr. George Macy, an officer relating to
the Mint, at his house in the Tower of London."

1005. 1695[-6], February 20. Manchester.—Has heard of him by
his letter to one Ralph Thompson, "a scandalouse fellow," in the gaol
at Lancaster, "which letter shews mee my great mistake in your
acquaintance. . . . You tell Thompson of 7*li.* which Mr. Charles
Rigby had of Hartley for writeing to mee.   I am sure hee writ nothing
to mee but one or two letters with long informations which Hartley, as
he said, desired him to take against many persons, to be transcribed to
mee.   I no sooner received them, but immediately waited with them
upon my Lord Chief Justice Treby, who thereupon thought fit further
to reprieve Hartley; and his Lordship gave or sent those papers, I think,
to you.   Mr. Rigby, [who] is a lawyer, lives next house to the Castle in
Lancaster, was sent for to do a public good, tooke those informations
without asking or expecting anything for his paines, and Hartley sent
them away by a special post to mee.   After the man's returne with a
reprieve, Hartley sent Mr. Rigby forty shillings as a gratefull present,
which, as Mr. Rigby saith, was alltogether unexpected, and all he had
upon that account.   Mr. Rigby had before that, as councell at the
Assizes, when Hartley was convict, a fee of 20*s.* to move upon the
Habeas Corpus Act, that Hartley might be tryed or not kept in prison ;
and hee had, the last Assizes, as councell for Hartley, 10*s.* to move the
Judge in Court, upon your petition, that Hartley might be bayled, for
the Judge ordered it to be moved in Court.   These are all the summes
Mr. Rigby ever had from Hartley, which are but halfe 7*l.*, and this is
an answer to the account you say you had from your correspondent,
Russell.   Had it been 7*l.*, I would not descant upon the implication.

" Your letter mentions your 20*s.* charge of post letters from your choyce
correspondents, two wretched gaole birds, Thompson and Russell ; I
thinke neither your choyce nor your charge is envyed by any.   You
tell your intimate, Tompson, in that letter, you are to be trobled no
more, but Hartley must imploy his gaoler, or els Mr. Kenyon.   Mr.
Macy, I am not wont to be so cupled, nor so imployed.   Your next
lash is: Mr. Kenyon, without your knowledge [. . . . your leave],
got Hartley a reprieve.   You know the fellow was to have dyed on
Saterday forenoone.   The letter I had, came to mee in Parliament at
12 o'clock the Tewsday before ; I carryed it forthwith to my Lord Chief
Justice, which I thought my duty.   The matter admitted of no delay.
I never asked in that for any reward, nor any way disrespective to you
then, or since.   Thus I leave you, in the word of your letter, to your
study to serve Mr. Tompson, and to dispose yourself charitably in
releeveing that ingeniouse gentleman.   You betake yourself to . . .
by postscript, with a secret, which none els must know; that no pardon

will this circuit, nor the circuit after, go into the north; and yet your special confidant sends your letter abroad. Sir, after all, I do tell you, and I think whilst you have time, you have, I think, done an unkind thing to your own reputation, if Hartley have not his pardon this Assizes. Nor is your letter, meethinkes, kind to Mr. Pierce. When the Judges see it, with one you writt to one of them, the last Assizes, their Lord-shipps' construction will be known. In the meanetime, I am uneasy under your sensorious pen, not that I am unable to do myselfe right, but because meethinkes Mr. Macy is not that Mr. Macy to whom I , have often very heartily subscribed, &c." *Copy.*

RICHARD EDGE to ROGER KENYON, at Manchester.

1006. 1695–6, February 27. London.—Does not hear that any Bill is yet brought in to "destroy the Duchy"; weightier matters are in hand. "I very well remember I writt, at the time you were sick, two bookes about the Duchy; the first draught is in my keepeing, but the fair one, and which has more in it, is in your keepeing amongst your papers, if Sir Gervase Elwes had it not. . . . I beseech you not to mention those three rascalls in any of your letters to me. I hear Captain Baker, who is a gentleman of great reputation and affection to the Governement, officiates in the roome of Mr. Smith, who is under confinement because he will not come to account. I cannot tell you more than you will hear by the printed papers, of this horrid plott (yet there are some infidells make light of it); the person that discovered it, desired his pardon, that he might not be an evidence, nor that his name should be known, which the King, out of his wonted clemency, consented to; that there were 60 readye to do it; and that [the] Duke of Berwick was in town, ready to head his Majesty's and the nation's enemyes; that King James and Boufflers, with 20,000 men, lay ready at Callice, and other places on those coasts, to invade this kingdome, upon a signall to be given from Dover, when the King was assassinated, which signall was ordered to be given by the Earl of Rumney, he being ready there to receive those rogues, by his Majesty's orders. That Amirall Russell, haveing first impressed seamen enough out of 600 merchantmen that lay in the Downes, is sailed, or ready to sail, with 48 ships of war. That . . . . is off the Isle of Wight with 15 French men-of-war. That Chasteau Renaut is off the Isle of Hieres, with part of the Thoulon fleet, so that we are in hopes of some sea action, and doubt not of success, being in greater readiness to receive them than they think we are.

"There are about 100 non-associators in all in the House of Commons; I told you who the Lancashire were, in my last. The ring-leaders are Mr. Finch, Sir Edward Seymour, Mr. Harcourt, Lord Digby, Lord Norres, and his brothers, Mr. Bromley, Collonel Granvill, who is the Chairman of Privilidges and Elections. I cannot particularly name them, and, as I heare, in the Lord's House [there are] about 30 that will no[t] subscribe—Marquis Halifax, Marquis Normanby, Lords Nottingham [and] Rochester; nay, I heard, but I beleeve not, that the Duke of Leeds, etc.; I cannot justly name them. I heard Mr. Norres made a speech, that the House would vote that the French King and the late King James were the promoters of this wicked designe against the King; but the courtiers did not think well of that, because it had not yet appeared so to the House, and Mr. Berty and Sir Richard Atkins, two great courtiers, stood up and opposed that, and so there was an end of Mr. Norres' speech. I have but things by hearsay, and I dare not write, for fear they should be Jacobites that tell me anything." *Seal.*

RICHARD EDGE to ROGER KENYON, at Manchester.

1007. 1695-6, February 29. London.—"I have, but with no small difficulty, gott the copy annext. I am told the Lords' association differs from the Commons; that the whole purport of it is, that King William is lawfull King, and that the late King James and the pretended Prince of Wales have no right to the Crown. We have severall accounts that the late King James was at Callice; that there were severall men-of-war in that port and ports adjacent, and a great many transport vessells, and that they had imbarqued severall thousands of men with all warlike amunition, in order for an invasion upon us, but was beleeved they had got advice that they were discovered, and so the men were deimbarqueing. But fresher advice tells us, they are begun to imbarque againe, but it is certaine that Admirall Russell is now upon their skirts; for on Thursday last, at 4 in the afternoon, he was saluted from Dover, and had then under his command 48 men-of-war, besides a great many tenders, and steered with a fair wind directly for Callais. We have an account that 12 of the traytors mentioned in the proclamation are allready taken, but not the Duke of Berwick.

"I saw a printed paper to-day that mentions the association and the justness and reasonableness of it, and that the address presented formerly by the present Earle of Macclesfeild, signed by 28,000 persons in Lancashire, was the same in effect, which I will assure you is a great peece of honor to our county of Lancaster; and for that reason, the King and parliament, sure, will never take away our Duchy, the very quintescense of loyalty haveing appeared in us so early, before the rest of the kingdome. I am told the Earl of Chesterfield has since signed, and that, though the Duke of Leeds spoke against it, yet he signed at the latter end. I am allso told that there are more members which have not signed, neither will signe, which were absent on Tuesday."

RICHARD EDGE to GEORGE KENYON, at Manchester.

1008. 1695-6, February 29. London.—"I have sent my old master a list of the non-associators [see previous letter], by which you will see that it is my sad fortune to deal with Jacobites." Describes events, as in previous letter to Roger Kenyon. *Seal.*

MARGARET OSBALDESTON to ROGER KENYON, at Manchester.

1009. 1695[-6], March 3. Preston.—The Countess of Derby is willing "to assist our design," though she said "that her interest, since the Queen's death, was diminished," and that she did not see the governors so frequently. Dr. Brabant will also assist "our cause," between this and All Saints, "in which time, it is soposed, will be two elections of scollers." *Seal of arms, broken.*

RICHARD EDGE to ROGER KENYON, at Manchester.

1010. 1695-6, March 5. London.—"The conspirators will not be tryed till the next week; Newgate is so full of them that the City train bands guard them day and night. We have no news from Admirall Russell, but what the publick prints mentioned by the last post, which were that he hoped to give a good account of 14 French men-of-war that lay in Flemish road near Dunkirk, if they creep not into Dunkirke. . . . . . . The ships mentioned in my last to be taken by our grand fleet was a mistake, they being taken by Guernsey privateers."

RICHARD EDGE to ROGER KENYON, at Manchester.

1011. 1695-6, March 7. London,—"Prothonotary Foster went hence yesterday for Lancashire, and told me from his master, Sir Gervase Elwes, there was no danger of anything being done against the Duchy of Lancaster, this sessions. Our great fleet is still off Gravelins, on the coast of France, with at least 90 men-of-war; but not yet able to make any considerable attempt on the enemy, for want of bomb vessels and fireships, which are here ready to saile, but the wind is in their teeth. Charnock, Keyes, and King, three of the conspirators mentioned in the proclamation, will be arraigned on Wednesday next, upon indictments (as is said) allready found against them at Hicks Hall, and will be allowed the full benefitt of the late acts for tryalls of treason, etc. I would fain come out hence; for every day, either pressmasters or the Kinges messengers, are laying hold on me." *Seal.*

The SAME to the SAME.

1012. 1695-6, March 12. London.—Has been with Mr. Ayleffe to enquire about any lands alienated from the Duchy. He states that the Duchy borroughs are as follows: "the county and burroughs of Lancashire"; the boroughs of Monmouth, Thetford (Norfolk), Higham Ferrars (Northamptonshire), Stockbridge (Hampshire), Newcastle-under-Lyne (Staffordshire), Sudbury (Suffolk), East Grinstead (Sussex), and Knaresborough, Ripon, Bourroughbridge, Pontefract, and Alborough, in Yorkshire. "Yesterday, Charnock, King, and Keyes were tryed at the Old Bailey, and upon a clear, fair, and full evidence, found guilty, and sentence past upon them; and I believe will be executed on Wednesday next. I was there, but could not come near euough to hear. The tryall will be printed, and you shall have it. Ferguson, who has been in all plots, is in this, and [is] in prison. I hear a great many warrants are signed and sent down to take up persons in Lancashire. The good news of the Earl of Athlone, with a great body of men, haveing burned the great provisions of the French, laid in at Givet, is confirmed; it is said there was as much as would have kept 50,000 horse, three months. They intended to have used it at the seige of Namur this year, at the same time the late King should have invaded England; but they are happily prevented. The bill for suppressing hawkers and pedlars is ordered to be engrossed, which will please the shopkeepers. [The] Duke [of] Wertemburgh is with the King, at Kensington, but the forces he brought, will be sent back and never come ashore." *Seal.*

GEORGE MACY to ROGER KENYON.

1013. 1695[-6], March 14. The Tower.—Touching a pardon for one Hartley, a coiner and clipper of coins. Regarding the proposal for four mints in the country, besides the one in the Tower, viz., at York, Exeter, Chester, and Norwich. The number was reduced to two, and this week, the Lords of the Treasury have resolved that one shall be at York and the other at Exeter.

RICHARD EDGE to ROGER KENYON, at Manchester.

1014. 1695-6, March 21. London.—Commences with family matters. "This day, at Hicks Hall, bills of high treason were found against Sir John Freind and Sir William Perkins, in order to be tryed on Monday and Tuesday; but I hear since, they will not then be tryed, for they would both squeak and make discoveryes, if the King would

pardon them. This day, the Earl of Aylesbury was committed to the
Tower, for high treason; and it is now sayd that far greater men are
concerned in the intended invasion. The three assassinates (*sic*) that
were executed on Wednesday (as the last post would tell you) confessed
the fact, but, by their equivocateing words, would seeme to clear the
late King and the body of the Roman Catholicks; but nobody of sense
beleeved that part. The burrowes within the Duchy of Lancaster,
mentioned in my last, all send two burgesses, except Higham Ferrers,
which sends only one. Mr. Ayloffe either cannot, or will not, tell me
what is paid from the Crown to the Duchy officers. I cannot tell you
who are our new Lancashire Justices. I hear Mr. Foster, the sub-
prothonotary, is to be one. Our printed news letters say that the
Lancashire gentlemen in the late plot are in this, and most of them in
custody." *Seal.*

RICHARD EDGE to ROGER KENYON, at Manchester.

1015. 1696, March 28. The "Blew Boare in Holboune."—
"Mr. Shakerley's antagonist was introduced into the King's presence by
the right honourable the Earle of Macclesfeild, and was knighted.
Sir John Freind and Sir William Perkins are to be hanged on Wednesday next. The Sessions at the Old Baily is adjourned to the 22nd of
Aprill. The Commons have passed the bill for the bringing in of plate to
the Mint, and sent it to the Lords, in which is enacted that no clipt
money (except sixpences) shall pass in payment, after the 4th of May
next, and guineas to pass at 22*s.* I hear the Lords have thrown out
the bill against hawkers and pedlars. I hear Captain Porter has confirmed that part of Mr. Wombell's evidence, of carrying vast quantityes
of armes into Lancashire to Standish Hall." *Seal.*

PETER SHAKERLEY to ROGER KENYON, at Manchester.

1016. 1696, April 9. Westminster.—"I writt, last post, to Mr.
Warden, and I think I desired him to thank you for the account you sent
mee of Mr. Shar (*sic*), but whether I did soe or not, I cannot well tell,
neither can I remember well what I did write, for I must own to you
I had that day som of my fellow-members [to] dine at my house, and upon
such an occasion, you know a little libberty of transgression is allowable.
. . . . . The bill for better preserving his Majesty's person
and Goeverment went up yesterday to the Lords; it is a smart one. It
enacts that persons refusing to take the oaths shall incur the pain and
penalty of Popeish recusant convicts; that all persons in any civill or
millitary employ, and every member of a future parliament, shall subscribe the association; that persons refuseing to take the oaths at any
election of Members to serve in Parliament, shall have noe voice in that
election; and for any one to declare by writeing, printing, preaching,
or adviceing, speaking against the King's right, it is a præmunire, and
there are som few other things in the Bill which I cannot well remember, but these are the chief. A duty is layd upon tobacco-pipes and
earthenware, viz., 12*d. per* gross upon the first and 10*d. per cent. ad
valorem* on the latter; therefore I advice you and Mr. Warden to stock
your selves well with pipes and piss-potts presently, because this duty is
to be perpetuall."

EDWARD KENYON to his father, ROGER KENYON.

1017. 1696, May 7. London.—"Upon Tuesday last, I got hither,
where, at my arrivall, I found the King and Collonel Stanley gone.

Next day, I went to Cosin Molleneux, who was soe kind to write and send his man along with me to Mr. Charles Stanley, who, though I could not meet with, yet there I heard of the Collonel's agent, to whom I went, who told me that the Collonel, at his departure, said there were two Lancashire gentlemen to follow him over, and named me for one. . . . . .What it will cost is uncertaine, but Cozen Moleneux's brother's was betwixt 4*l*. and 5*l*. . . .

"Upon Tuesday, the King sailed from Sheerneest, and it is believed is in Flanders ere this."

[ROGER KENYON] to "MR. MACY."

1018. 1696, June 13. Manchester.—"The cuntry is in so great distresse for want of current money, that without some speedy supply, all traffick will cease. Our markets cannot be continued. The poor have been, in severall markets, tumultuously murmuring; and we are, I think, in great danger of greater unquietnes. I write to you, to acquaint the worthy Warden of the Mint who will, perhaps, think fit to let the Lords of the Treasury, or who he thinkes most proper, if possible, to helpe us." *Draft.*

WILLIAM PATTEN to ROGER KENYON, at Manchester.

1019. 1696, June 20. Gray's Inn.—" I have, these ten dayes, forbore writeinge to you, according to my promise at Wigan, in expectation of having some newes worth writeing, but no newes as yet comes from Flanders, of any action or intended speedy action, that I heare of, and in this towne, lonne and tradinge are at a great stande, by reason of the scarsity of money; litle newe money is to be seen, where I goe, and noe old moneys goe, but such as was never clipped, let them have never soe many letters to be seene. I this daye sawe a shillinge refused that out-weighed a millde shilling, and you cannot exchange an hundred shillings of old money, though it be not much clipped, under 25*s*. or 30*s*. in ex-change, and how those will at the last end, God knowes! but there is great murmuring about it. Yesterday Sir John Feineicke was examined by the Lords Justices at Duke Shrewsbury's office, and afterwards sent to the Tower, and one Webber (?), an attorney of Furvivalls Inne, whoe was taken in the company of Sir John, and who was solicitor to the late General who dyed for the plott, is sent to Newgate. I question not but you have in your common newes letter an accompt of the tryall betwixt the Earles of . . . and Montague, which lasted 27 bowers, and a verdict given in favour of the latter; they are to have another tryall at the King's Bench barr on Thursday."

EDWARD KENYON to [his father?]

1020. 1696, June 25.—"Upon the 25th of May, I came to the camp before Gaunt; and the day following, I met with the Colonel, who received me with abundance of kindness and, according to promise, gave me my commission, the 18th. All the officers express a great deale of kindness, esspessially Captain Fleming (the gentleman I spake of, when with you), whose guest I have been ever since. Dear sir, before this, I had not the opportunity of writing, or else would not thus long have been silent (noe post goeing from hence), but att this time I am forced to give you a further trouble, which is the paying of a 20*l*. bill to Mr. John Morden, upon 4 days' sight; the reason why I trouble you is that the buying a horse to ride, a horse to carry my trunk, a tent bed, with other necessaries, not to be avoided, myself being not able to foot it, by reason of my weakness. That I have not been any way extravigant, the Colonel will witness for me."

"A REPRESENTATION of the TRADESMEN in MANCHESTER."

1021. 1696, June.—" A true representation of the case of the tradesmen of Manchester ; for the want of currant coyn, not beeing able to employ the many families that depend upon them for work ; and [the] miseries of those that know not how to buy bread at present, for the want of their wonted employments.

" Wee, therefore, being sensable of our great miseries at present, and of more we are in danger of for the future, if wee have not seasonable releif, thought it nesesarie, and our duty, for the releife of the poor and the peace of our country, to represent our condition to the worshipfull Justises of the Peace, at there meeting upon the 20th day of June, 1696.

" Wee have been labouring sume time under the dificulties of trade, by the scarseness of currant coyn, and have, to our utmost, improved our credit and intrest to supply the nesesities of the poor ; but are not able to proceed, unless some speedy cource bee taken as to the state of the coyn, to enable us to keepe the poore with work, and to prevent there starving, and the many mischeifs that may ensue.

" The number of the poor that are employed in the manufactures of Manchester, by a modest computation, are above fourtie thousand.

" Wee, whose names are hereunto supscribed, doe earnestly desire your Worships' consideration :—

" Joseph Scott, William Scholes, Joseph Leeth, John Deggles, Rich : Worthington, Edm : Traves, Edw : Scott, Edw : Syddall, James Moss, Tho : Moss, Miles Bradshaw, Tho : Bradshaw, John Walker, Tho : Buerdsell, Jno. Wroe, Jno. Browne, James Bayley, Edw : Bootle, Ralph Worsley, Samuell Pendleton, Josiah Walker, Richard Taylor, Will : Holme, Thomas Hartley, Sam : Worthington, Francis Cartwright, Diniss Cass, Edm : Johnson, Sam : Tinney (?), John Dickanson, Richard Davenport, Jos : Byrom, Mich : Pimlott, Samuell Brooke, Charles Beswicke, R. Percivall, Joseph Hooper, John Hewood, Joseph Slater, Joseph Sherwin, Dan : Woolmer, Geo : Lloyd, Samuell Clowes, Samuell Wharmbye, Ralph Poole, William Crompton, Jonath. Nicholls, James Travez, Ralph Hall, Peter Wagstaffe, John Schoales, Michaell Stockton, Joshua Crompton, Cha : Broster, Joseph Walker, Samuel Haward, Samuell Drinkwater, John Collier, Chr : Lancashire, Tho : Collier, Jno : Lancashire, James Both, Fran : Davenport."

INDICTMENT of JOHN LEEDS, of Manchester, at the Sessions of the Peace held at Lancaster.

1022. 1696, July 14.—That John Leeds, of Manchester, chapman, on 30th June, in the 8th year of this King, at Manchester aforesaid, did maliciously publish these words : " The Book of Common Prayer ; the afforesaid book, meaning nothing but masse in English. The Book of Common Prayer ; the afforesaid booke meaning now used in the Church of England, was popery, and that whosoever prayed by that booke, their prayers never prevailed. That the service of the Church of England was diabolical, and no true divine worship, and not pleasing to God Almighty."

GUICCIARDINI WENTWORTH to ROGER KENYON.

1023. 1696, September 10.—The names of the Justices of the Peace for Lancashire, thought fit to be turned out :—William Farrington, P. Shakerly (under the last name was subscribed Maclesfield), Ralph Ashton, Roger Kirkby, William Norrice, Thomas Moulyneux, Jasper Mauditt, Christopher Lister, and Ambrose Pudsie.

ROGER KENYON to GUICCIARDINI WENTWORTH.

1024. 1696, September 13. Manchester.—"Yours gives (which I thank you for) what the certificate of a noble peer, and seven of our members, did certify, for the turneing out of severall of our Justices of the Peace, who might be largely certified for, were true lovers of the present government to appearance in all their demeanars, neither non-jurors nor non-residents ; but most of them of that quality, as their ancestors had born the same office for generations past, and these very gentlemen of great acceptation in their cuntry.

"I do truly thinke, though perhaps it is not seasonable for mee to say so, that most of the members that did so certify, if it were demanded of them to tell the falts of these gentlemen they have certifyed against, must say either they do not at all know them, or do not of their own knowledge certify any one misdemeanor that can look like a disafection to King William or to the Governement ; but this was done at the instance of the noble Lord, as some of them were told, who would take it kindly, &c. Now, sir, can it be for the service of the Governement to have such gentlemen turned out without being told why ?

"The carriage of him that is cheefe of this in the late raigne is not forgotten, and the King was very kind if it bee forgiven.

"As to those formerly put in, who have not taken their oaths, two of them are by name Roughley—I think the father and son; the grand-father, as I have heard, was a collier-banksman at a colepit belonging to Mr. Bold. The house they dwell in is certifyed to the Quarter Sessions for a place for Dissenters to meet at, and allowed by the Justices for their way of worship, as they call it. Molineux, of Liverpool, is an apothecary, as I am told ; Johnson, a shopkeeper there ; Mathew Holles, a trader with Rachdale baise, or some cloth; Radcliffe Scofield, you may remember, was Mr. Jessop's man, and of late a preacher at con-venticles ; hee, when holding forth, was inveighing, as it is said, against top-knots ; his text was about the strait way, and if heaven was so strait, hee would have it considered how top-knots would get thither, and was, as is said, answered, though strait, it was high enough overhead. Another of your new Justices was one Gaskell ; there are two brothers of that name, tradeing men, and it being told that one of them was in the Commission of the Peace, they going together to the last Assizes save one, at Lancaster, the elder brother, supposeing it was hee, desired his younger brother to let his bags be laid upon his horse, who did so, but comeing to the Assizes, it proved the younger brother was the Justice, and, retorneing, he said to his elder brother his horse should carry their bags home. These are none of them sworne, but these are placed in the same Commission with the Lords of the Councell, and called as Justices, fellow Justices, with them, and no doubt but they had before now been sworn but for the snake in the grasse ; they will not come to church to receive the sacrament, so [long ?] as the sting in the Test Act, the 500*l.* forfeiture, keeps them in awe. Now some other of the Dissenters, rather then be kept from their office, for a time will come to receive the sacrament, though they never come to church againe, unles upon a like occasion for some other office. This is enough

at this time on this subject, but [not] all that might be said of it, if
things were narrowly looked into, but I . . . to tell you of the
three new Justices who lately have taken their oath. Edward Herle,
esquire; he is an ancient, though no eminent lawyer, not well to passe
in the world, though hee hath beene much better; his wife is a constant
Conventicler, and he uxoriouse. The next is Mr. John Walmsley, who, I
doubt not, but you may remember; hee was Henry Roe's clerk, and after
served Sir Richard Hoghton, who had a doughter married to a rich
man who dyed and left his wife very rich, but stone blind. Mr. Walmsley
was since called to the barr, and haveing carryed himselfe so long since
as to be well liked by that lady, shee hath since marryed him. She
is a constant Conventicler, and hee also uxoriouse. The third is
Mr. Crocke, a young unmarried man, and no housekeeper. His father
dyed rich, was a fustian man, and bred him to the University; his
mother and freinds, most of them Dissenters. Colonel Sawrey, who was
a major in Cromwell's own regiment, and a tub preacher, was another of
our great Lord's putting in, before these, but never swore for the reason
aforesaid." *Draft.*

Sir Charles Greenfield to Roger Kenyon, at Manchester.

1025. 1696, October 15. Ormskirk.—" Coming through Ormskirke,
I mett with a most heavy complaint, that a captaine here (a Scotch
man) takes upon him, just like the town of Royston case, to exact and
demand 3s. a weeke from everye private centinell, and soe proportionable for every officer, else to make good their quarters. This is soo much
against the lawe of England [that] it cannot be putt upp. Worthy
Mr. Charles Stanley hath been so kind [as] to assert the illegality, and
take notice of the boldness of this impudent action." *Seal of arms,
broken.*

The Earl of Derby to [Roger] Kenyon.

1026. 1696, October (?) 24.—" I send, dear Roger, a letter enclosed, the contents of which the bearer, Mr. Serjeant, is able to informe
you, and so will save me that labor. I freely tell you it is a thought of
my own, which I shall be proud of, if it is approved of. I am sure I
mean it well ; and if it is rightly managed, I will venture to say it will
do our whole county justice, and, perhaps, produce good effect in what
you will easily gues at." *Seal of arms.*

William Aspinall to Roger Kenyon, at Manchester.

1027. 1696, December 8. Haslingden.—Desires that some one else
may be put in to gather the tolls, as he grows old, and cannot stand the
cold. There is now at hand " a sort of faire or meeting, on St. Thomas,
at Colne, which is very little but hides and flesh, and nothing but peneyes
to be gathered ; which, for my part, I do not understand how it can be
gathered, for to stand to weigh everyone's money is a thing the
time will not permit. Besides, the people will not suffer their broad
money to be weighed, and will be so tedious in their change that, for my
part, I doe not understand how it can be gathered, except you be pleased
to take money, iff it hath not beene clipt, though it want of weight."

Sir John Fenwick.

1028. 1696.—The reasons of the Lords against the attainder of
Sir John Fenwick.

R[OGER] K[ENYON] to his sister, ANNE KENYON, at Stockport.

1029. 1696-7, January 25. Venice.—This town is in the height of its frenzy, and one would almost despair to see it reduced to reason again ; man, woman, and child go masked, so that nobody is known, and I perceive it is only from fear of one another that keeps us ever sober. It would be a sort of madness now to be wise. *Seal.*

ROBERT WEDDELL, Warden of the Mint at Chester, to ROGER KENYON.

1030. 1696[-7], January 25. Chester Castle.—Asking for information concerning one Ferdinando Croudson, a coiner. *Seal of arms.*

RICHARD WROE to ROGER KENYON.

1031. 1696-7, January 26.—" Though I have not the same opportunity that you had when in the House, of giving an exact account of proceedings there, yet what I can learn, I am very glad to communicate. The capitation bill is now the great point, and goes on, though not well liked either by the court or country party, but must pass, as it is said, rather than a general excise. They talk today of tacking to it the bill for qualifications of elections, which was thrown out by the Lords on Saturday ; but others say that cannot be and is unpresidented. Sir John Fenwick will certainly dye on Thursday, and the late Bp. of Peterborough, Dr. White, is allowed to be with him to prepare him for it. Sir Ralph Ashton's bill will now pass easily without opposition, the Collonell and he bring agreed, as he told me this day."

RICHARD WROE to ROGER KENYON, at Manchester.

1032. [16]96-7, January 30.—" Yesterday the King passed the Capitation Bill, which it is said staines 100 sheets of paper, without Commissioners' names. I am told the Earl of Macclesfeild has already named those for our county. Our Cheshire Members have brought in a Bill to make the river Dee navigable, and perswade themselves it will be effected. The enclosed shews you how little Sir Jo: Fenwick thought himself concernd to repent of his Jacobitisme; he would faine have had a reprieve till this day, in hopes to have been reckoned a martyr too." *Seal of arms.*

ACCUSATION against DR. RICHARD WROE.

1033. 1696-7, January.—Informations of various persons, taken at Manchester, that John Leeds, of Manchester, chapman, did, at the inn called " the Swan with the two necks," and at other places in Manchester, say that Doctor Wroe, Warden of Manchester, was a papist, and knew " of the late assassinations against the present King William."

DR. RICHARD WROE to ROGER KENYON.

1034. 1696[-7], February 4.—Mr. Preston died on Sunday last; he is to be buried at Cartmell. He has left his lady and his daughter his executrices; he has made an addition to his lady's jointure of 100*li.* *per annum,* so that she has now 300*li. per annum.* His daughter's fortune will be worth near 30,000*li.*, and, you may imagine, she will not want looking after. I received a message yesterday from Colonel Stanley, by Mr. Wilson, to pump what I knew of her concerns, but at an unlucky place, being at Mr. Shakerley's. It is said here Mr. Fitton Gerrard puts in for Lancaster; I wish Mr. Charles Rigby would stand.

Great complaints were made yesterday in the House that several dyes and stamps were conveyed out of the Tower, chiefly by one Rotiere (?), and they talk of disfranchising the Mint from being a Corporation, and to oblige them to work more briskly. They seem resolved, too, to bring the Bank to rights, which made the discount fall yesterday from 19 to 15; but this day it is 17 again. Great expectation of the Commissioners for the grand capitation, who, it is said, will be named on Saturday under the great seal.

MAJOR RICHARD STEVENSON to ROGER KENYON, at Manchester.

1035. 1696–7, February 9. Douglas [Isle of Man].—" Last month, I writt to Mr. Edge, wherein I desired him to give you an account of my late suspension from all offices whatsoever, under my honorable Lord, without any offence or fault by me, to my own knowledge or, by what I can learn, from any other. I was in very easy [   ] under my dismission, having the example of so worthy and honourable a person as yourself, who, by my Lord's permission, first made me an officer, and indeed, since you left the Isle, never enjoyed it with true contentment; but since I have been prossecuted (I may say persecuted) by the Governor and all the officers for erecting a miln upon my own estate. My ancestors have had that privelige above a hundred years, and were never before disturbed or molested. I have been likewise required to pay for all the puffins I have had since my father's death (which was always paid to him ever since the surrender of the Calfe Isle to Earle James), and since his death to myself. In which particular you were, as also all the Governours that were before you, since Earle James' time, well satisfied when I shewed you my papers; and notwithstanding I showed the same to the present Governour and that I have his refference to my petition to make my application to my honourable Lord, yet this day had I been at home my pawnd should have bein taken for the value of them, though there be more money due to me for my sallery than the price of the puffin comes to, for they would not let me stopp any of my sallery in my office account, but made me cleare those books immediately. And on Thursday last, att a Chancery Court, I had herring of the premises, where I had scarce leave to make my own defence, by reason I was disturbed with scandalous reflections from the Governour, such as were never heard in these Courts before, insomuch that the whole Court was amased at it. The words he used and called me was (besides some others) a rascall, a villain, and a scoundrell; all which I patiently tooke in respect to his office, and for fear of disturbance amongest the people, who were highly displeased, &c. Now, deare sir, you cannot but imagine this to be a great trouble to me and all my relations and friends, that I am thus abused, and I have not a friend in England whose advice I would desire in this weighty affaire before your own, wherein I hope you will not faile . . . . I have writ to my Lord, and given him an account thereoff, wherein I have begged his leave to come for England, that the whole concerne may be heard before himself." *Seal of arms.*

Appended.—A letter from Richard Wroe to Roger Kenyon, expressing the hope that justice may be done to the writer; and the draft of the latter's letter to Lord Derby, which is as follows :—

1696–7, March 19. Manchester.—" The account upon which this comes is very unwonted, and not very willing from me at this time, who am always afraid to write to your Lordshipp under any umbrage of a doubtful acceptation : *sed si crimen erit, crimen amoris erit.* With all humility I presume to acquaint your Lordshipp that I am, by my old friends in the Isle of man, particularly Major Stevenson, desired to intercede with your honor that he may by your Lordshipp's leave have accesse to your honor in England, and to lay his causes of complaint of his hard and ungentlemanly usages, both in words and actions, before your honor, to whose justice hee humbly desires to appeale. If it be as related to mee, I am sure there is cause for it; and I more than thinke it cannot be a disservice to your Lordshipp and family to keep the hearts of your Islanders, by such administrations as they may always naturally, chearfully, and unanimously discharge their utmost duties to your honor; without their doing which, I am farr from saying one word on any of their behalfes. An appeal to your justice you will never deny, least the complaint, if just, should be carryed higher and be made more general than you are aware of. I could much better discourse than write more on this subject." *Draft*.

RICHARD WROE to ROGER KENYON, at Manchester.

1036. 1696–7, February 11.—The trial about Hindley was heard yesterday before the Chancellor, Lord Chief Baron, and Judge Turton, and lasted nearly four hours, but all on a single point, which was the exception to the decree. It was begun by Jo: Green's counsel, because—if for them —they thought the whole point was determined, namely: whether the erecting an oratory or chapel was within the power of the Commission for Charitable Uses, "which we, [who] had learned distinctions between charitable and pious uses, as well ridiculed." After all the "bandying," the judges took time to consider till Tuesday next. Must stay and "arm" for Mr. Trafford's writ of error, though he does not much fear it; for "we have already the opinion of five judges in twelve for us, and I doubt not but I can secure the Lord Keeper for our interest." *Seal, broken*.

THOMAS WILSON to ROGER KENYON, at Manchester.

1037. 1696[-7], February 20. Whitehall.—" My Lord [Derby] has yet had no positive answer from my Lord Nottingham; his Lordship is at present out of towne . . . This day, the Lords were in a committy about the East India Bill; those who were against it gott a clause put into it, which they say will certainly be the occasion of flinging it out. Lord Portland has a Blew Ribon given him. This day the Commons were making enquiry into the loss of the 25 ships which Du Rarl took lately, but I cannot tell what resolutions they made." *Seal, with Lord Derby's arms*.

PAPER relating to MAJOR STEVENSON'S PETITION.

1038. 1696[-7], February.—"My appeal, shewing that notwithstanding your honour was pleased, the last Chancery Court day, to refer the detirmination of the difference touching the puffins, to our right honourable Lord, yet now your appealant is committed into Castle Rushen, for not delivering a pawne to answer the demands of the comptroller for the value of the said puffins for many years past, although there was always allowance took for the same in the accounts, and these accounts never questioned by our honourable Lord; whereupon your appealant conceived himself to be greatly aggrieved, and therefore appeals from the proceedings here unto our most honourable Lord. Humbly beseeching that this his appeale may be accepted and sufficient time given to your appealant to make his address to his Lordshipp, and his releasement granted thereupon."

"At Castle Rushen, the 13th February [16]96-[7].—The Honourable Governor having sent unto us the above appeale to certifie him whether the first part thereof, *videlicet*, that his honour referred the detirmination of his differences touching the puffins, to our right honourable, be true, we do hereby declare that we heard his honour say, that although he had allowed Major Stevenson to make his application to his Lordshipp, yet he declared at the same time that he would not interfere betwixt the complainant and his duty.—W. Sacheverell, J. Rowe, T. Huddlestone."

"Being present in Court the same time, I also heard the honourable Governor express himself as is above mentioned; and his honour desireing my opinion touching the acceptance of this appeale, I say that since the said Major Stevenson hath suggested a falles allegation therein, as is within certified, that his honour need not to accept of the same for that reason.—Jo: Raw.

"The words of the Governor's answer to Major Stevenson's petition about the puffins.

"Castletowne, Feb. 4, 1696-7.

"I allow the petitioner to make his application to my honourable Lord.—N. Sankey."

PETER SHAKERLEY to ROGER KENYON, at Manchester.

1039. 1696[-7], March 6. Westminster.—"The Bill for incloseing of commons would allso have inclosed forrests, &c., out of which large estates might have been carved for forraigners, but the evill consequences of it appeared soe vissible, that, upon the second reading, noe one movved for the committing it; therefore the question passed for rejecting it. We have now a very thinn House; it is near eleaven o'clock in a morning before 40 be gott together to make a House. The weather is very faire. Cozin Preston and her daughter are gon down into the country (I supose to pass fines, &c., at Lancaster Assizes). Mr. Lowther, I am told, is the person must have her."

THOMAS MATHER to [ROGER KENYON?].

1040. 1697, March 30. Manchester.—"I humbly make bold to write to you, accquainting your worshipp of the trouble I am brought in. First, that I got a kay made at Boulton for a man that said he came out of Durham (?) There was severall by, when the man delivered the patten in clay to mee, in Bolton, and at the delivery of the kay to him the same day. And within a short time, it happened the kay was found in a doore, and two men was there, and was seased by some other men that lay in waite, and by reason I gott the kay made, those two persons swore I was one of the men, and they never saw mee till after it was done, in their lifetime, but upon that I was committed; and I, knowing something of the charges if I was imprisoned, besides I was tould Mr. Plumer, goldsmith, had put the bonde in suite which he had against mee for twenty pounds, and would lay it upon mee as soon as the Assizes were over, and likewise I being much afraid your worship would not be my friend, concerning the ould business, I made my escape and went away, but not that I was anything afraid, but onlye of that which I know, if you were my adversary, my life was gone. And now, since I went away, they have apprehended mee and a neighbour of mine, upon suspition of staleing a horse and some fustian, upon Wednesday night last, and wee have produced severall witnesses to the men that wee were in Stockport all that night, which hath satisfyed the persons that wee were not there at any such thing ; but for all this, they have sent us to the House of Correction here in Manchester, because Lord Willoughby was not at home to have a hearing of the business. So, sir, I humbly beg your worshipp's advice herein, I not haveing any other I dare trust or confide in for good counsell ; for if I must dye this minute, I dare take it upon my death I am not guilty of any such thing as is laid to my charge. However, before I would be imprisoned to my utter ruine, both I and the man that is with me, are free and willing to serve the King under your sone before wee goe before Lord Willoughby, if your worshipp may thinke it convenient ; for if wee goe before him, wee are afraid hee will send us to Lancaster, soe wee humbly beg your worshipp's answer tonight. Sir, if you please, wee will serve faithfully, but are not free to goe with anyone else save your sone."

J. THORNTON to ROGER KENYON, at Manchester.

1041. 1697, April 3. Preston.—" The bearer, it seems (one Edward Kenyon, a clothier, and a very honest man), has a pack of cloth detayned and searched at Chorle by the allnigers (one of which, he is informed, is Mr. James Edge, formerly your servant), who, with others, has a commission to search cloth, whereby to see that it be right sealed. If it lye in your way to doe him any kindness in it, whereby to help him to his cloth, I begg you doe it."

ROGER KENYON to the BISHOP OF CHESTER.

1042. 1697, April 7. Manchester.—" Your Lordshipp has been so kind, not long since, to preach to us at Ellenbrook Chapel. Your Registrar hath in his book a copy of a decree exemplified *octavo Elizabethæ*, 1565, 132 year ago, evidenceing it at that time a very ancient chapel, before the Reformation; and to it, ever since, they of the chapelry, who are numerouse, and far from any other church, have constantly come to hear divine service. The parish church is three myles from it. The parish hath never [had] another chapel of ease but this, and is accounted 20 myles in circuit.

" Our Lord Willoughby, whose lady's house is not much above a myle from the chapel, and his Lordship, I think, the only nonconformist of anything that hath the name of a gentleman in our country, hath, by undue means, possessed himself of the key of the chapel dore, and locks out Mr. Atkinson and any sent by him, and puts in to preach there one Cheney, who, as is said, never saw an university, but has been a justice of peace his clerk, and, proveing a guifted brother, used to preach at all the conventicling barns about him, and now frequently uses so to do.

" I was, my Lord, for more then thirty yeares together, with a greater family then ever my Lord Willoughby yet had, a constant comet (*sic*) to that chapel. I am one of the feoffees for that small endowment it hath, which is but, besides contribution, about 33*l. per annum*. Mr. Atkinson has been our minister, I think, at least a dozen years, and his local licence was exhibitted and allowed at your Lordshipp's late visitation, as it had often been before ; but hee now saith hee is willing to resigne when your Lordshipp and the minister of the parish and the feoffees have a parson such as they approve of. ready for the place. I have been sent to, and I suppose the other feoffees, to order the payment of the minister's wages to Mr. Cheney. My Lord Willoughby pretends not to be patron, and I think the Conventicler hath no licence from your Lordshipp. I humbly beg your Lordshipp's direction what I shall do. I consider it is a time that such as truly wish well to the present government should suffer, [rather] then create such a disturbance as a violent opposition of these encroachments might occasion ; but, on the contrary, the sufferance of such is a reproach to the government. I shall, my Lord, if your Lordshipp soe advise, be very willing to refeoffe (*sic*), and much rather do so then apply the wages, which should go to an orthodox minister, to this (Mr.) Cheney.

" Wee were seaven feoffees, but one of the seven never yet acted, and three of them are lately dead. There are enow gentlemen of quality, who have good estates within this chapelry, [who] might be added to make up the old number, and such as well love the government, but would not be well pleased with Mr. Cheney for their minister." *Copy, in Roger Kenyon's handwriting.*

N[ICHOLAS], BISHOP OF CHESTER, to ROGER KENYON, at Manchester.

1043. 1697, April 14.—" I received your letter by Mr. Warden, in which (as in many others I have received from you) you give ample testimony of your kind affection to our Church, and your readiness upon all occasions to promote its interest. I should highly deserve to be blamed, should I not readily concurr with you, and employ that little power I have to prevent those encroachments which its adversaries daily endeavour to make upon it. I am satisfyed, by what you have formerly told me, that the Lord Willoughby has no title to the Chappel of Ellenbrough, and, consequently, that a clerk of his nomination cannot, upon that account, justly challenge the profits which belong to it. Mr. Cheney has no licence from me, and you may rest assured that he never shall have one. I think it most advisable that you proceed, with all convenient speed, to fill up the places of the dead feoffees (?), in the choice of whom you must observe the directions given you by the decree in Chancery. I leave it to Mr. Warden to tell you my thoughts more fully upon this subject." *Seàl of arms.*

THOMAS MATHER to ROGER KENYON.

1044. 1697, April 21. Lancaster Castle.—Begs Kenyon to procure his liberty, and, if it can be obtained, he will list under Kenyon's son. " The execution-day was this day, being the 21 of this instant Aprill ; there was executed six men ; there names were : Edward and his brother Henry, Brearly, and Robert Clegg, [who] were executed for cliping and coyninge of new moneys. There was Edmund Barlowe, and John Bury, for robbings on the high-way. The others was John Hill, for taking money out of a house in Ratchdale. John Dixson was condemed, but was the tops-man to them all."

RICHARD EDGE to ROGER KENYON.

1045. 1697, June 2. Liverpool.—" We came to •Knowsley [on] Wednesday last, at which time I delivered your letter to Mr. Willson. My Lord Derby askt where you were, whether at Peele or Manchester. We staaid at Knowsley till Monday last, and now we are ready the first wind, [and] have a ship ready bound for the Island. My Lord and Lord Strange are at Knowsley, keepe a very few servants, and no gentlemen come there whilst we staid, onely Mrs. Lime one day, and Parson Richmond, another day. My Lady will be in the country after midsumer. My Lord's youngest daughter is named Elizabeth. My Lord Rochester, godfather, the Dutchess of Somersett and Marchioness of Halifax, godmothers. The Bishopp of St. Asaph christened it. Major

Stevenson, who has been in close prison, is at liberty, but is yet under my Lord's displeasure. Collonel Sancky, the governor, has a mind yet to do his buisness, that is, to do him all the hurt he can. The Major writes to Mr. Willson, who seemes to speak much on his behalfe to my Lord. My Lord Derby did intend to goe himself for the Island, but is off that, because of the danger of the sea, and the many privateers who are now in St. George's Channell, waiteing for the ships that will come to Highlake for Chester fair. There is there a man-of-warr waiteing to convey the Lords-Justices to Ireland, who came to Chester Thursday last, and will saile the first fair wind. Mr. Sacheverell is in England, at his father's house in Oxfordshire, but whether ever he returnes to the Island, I know not. Mr. Huddleston hath all Major Stevenson's planes. The Major, by Mr. Willson, has promised to lay all his papers before my Lord, and put himselfe wholly at his mercy, when his Lordshipp has seen his writeings. I observe my Lord is considering of my Lady Westmorland, and his mother's, petitions, either to pay them what due, or how to avoid it. But I doe not heare that he is inclineable ever to be freindly with Master Charles Stanley, who brought his mother's petition to the House of Lords, meeteing my Lord in the Painted Chamber, and not saying a word of it. Mr. Willson has promised to write to you, and then you will have account of all matters.

Postscript.—" Mr. David Murray is this day gone to Knowsley, to petition his Lordship, in his own cause, being sued by the officers of the Isle for 500*l.*; in the matter where Mr. Cholmondley is concerned [he] has taken advice at London, and, if my Lord will not dismiss him, resolves to remove it before the House of Lords, and wholly give up his concernes in the Island. I hear Collonel Sankey has 200*l. per annum* sallary [as] Comptroller; though [he has] a great many places, yet a pension besides, and so hath Deempster Parr. Your horses are at Lathom, onely two left. The black-eyed mare's colt dyed of the stackers. The wind is now fair. I hope to goe off this afternoon. The Marquess of Winchester, Earl of Gallaway, and other persons of quality, went to sea, Sunday last, in a man-of-warr, from Highlake, for Ireland, but the ship run upon a sand, so they were forced to go in another ship to Holyhead, but I since hear the man-of-warr is gott off again without damage."

Thomas Marsden to Roger Kenyon.

1046. 1697, June 14. Walton.—I purpose to set forth to-morrow towards Furness, where I shall, for some time, officiate as King's preacher. If the confederacy crumble, who forbids the French King to become Emperor of the West ? If no peace this year, what will become of us the next ? If war cannot be waged without money, we shall shortly leave it off.

H[onora, Lady] Willoughby, [of Parham,] to Roger Kenyon.

1047. [16]97, June 16.—" I had written one letter before this daye too you, but he (*sic*) found itt and took itt by forse from me ; he so much fears his villany coming to light, as I trust it will in time. The contents were onely to give you and Mrs. Kenyon thanks for your kind enquiry after me (?) when you were at Peale, and how uneasy it is for me to be neare such good neighbours and engenous company as yours and nott enjoye itt ; as allso to lett you know the great and heavey oppressions I suffer under in being so horridly abused and keept a prisoner by him, and denyed all meanes for my health, as Dr. Banne, if he dare speake truth, very well knows, when hee, as our butler told me, had pen and paper to write to me, and was not suffered to give me any advice. (I thought he had bin coming, and bloted my paper.) I was forst to borrow money of the chaplain to give, last sacrament. So I leave you to judge if my usage can bee indured. Hee is such a devil, noebody can live with him, and one of the greatest cheats that ever were, and marryes only to rob and plunder all he can, and then, if he could, wold sett them goeing, to be at liberty to cheat somebody else, and get, if he could, by the help of this match, one with money in the City, which he is in hast of, and, therefore, tryes all meanes to sett me goeing, because I escaped the poyson I was so longe sicke of att Manchester, as Dr. Leeds sayed; and the winter following, another dose by his house-keeper, that confest she could poyson in butcher's meat, for which she was soon turned away, and the doctor I then had, advised me to fa . . . . . . and knowes it very well . . . . . shall not outlive him, which shows . . . . . . against my life, and also his strange usage of me, and endeavouring to posses the world that I am mad, when all see the conterary, and that all he can doe cannot make me so, though oppression is the way; and such as was never heard of to be kept thus a prisoner from my only son that so much wants a mother's care, and may lose his life for want of itt, for I doe not yet heare anyone is gon to the Bath with him, but his man, that I can put no confidence in, and not fitt for so great a trust. He wold not let me have money to send him till I sent to my friends, or he shold not have last time, which has opened my relations' eyes, so that I am in great hopes of assistance by them; and if you. as a kind neigh-bour, wold writ in my behalf to my good unkle that is trustee for the children, now, this next post, with John Parkinson, the testimony of a Parliament man wold doe me a kindness under this oppression, for I am now locked up in my chamber for writing to you and noe soule with me, which pray let my unkle know that I cannot live long at this rate, and direct your letter for the Honorable Charles Leigh, at his house in Leighton, in Bedfordshire; I know not if by Brickhill bag, and be so charitable to doe this."

Postscript.—" He says he will complain of you in Parliament if you encroach upon his prerogative." *Seal of arms.*

WILLIAM PATTEN to ROGER KENYON, at Manchester.

1048. 1697, June 17. Greye's Inn—"I have no news save that the Parliament is prorouged to the 22 July; and that Dr. Baynard yesterday buried his daughter at Barne Elms, wherre shee died of a consumption, got by over much studdy."

H[ONORA, LADY] W[ILLOUGHBY, of Parham,] to ROGER KENYON.

1049. 1697, June 23.—" I am much obliged to you for your redyness in affording me your charitable assistance now, in this great oppression I suffer under, being kept prisoner in my owne house, and every night loocked into my chamber, as fast as any in Lanchaster Jayle, and run down for a mad woman, by a villan that tells me will sell my life, and dares doe anything too my children, and twice deneyed me money to send my son to the Bath, who might have perisht, but that I sent a messenger on purpose to my friends, and by delayes, made him loose the spring season in May, as the doctors advised, and denys me all advice, as I writ you word, for my owne health; all which plainly showes his desines on our lives, and that, haveing robed us of all, he thinks, by the healp of this match, to get one with redy money in the City, and so purchase land of inheritance, and have one to have children by (perhaps not his owne); and too excuse his ill usage of me to the tenants, tells them that my relations writ to him to lock me up, and to be very strict with me, which he would soon doe, were it so; but they are so farr from that, that my unkle has lately, in all their names as his own, desired we might part, and offers to joyne my brother in security; but he is one so governed by people, not my friends, that as he acts not in his own concernes, will not be prevailed with to ingage in any business, being not skilled in it. Now, if you could get me any kind neighbour to joyne with my unkle to be my security, he says I shall have my liberty, and I doe faithfully promise you and them, on the parole of honour, that they shall never be any way damaged by itt; if either the good Bishopp, or Sir John Bland, or any other charitable person you can think of. And allso I entreat the favour of Lord Darby, by your mediation, to give James clearly (?) his Lordshipps protection; for this divill, rather then man, threatens him very much, and I wold not have him lye att his mercy."

H[ONORA, LADY] WILLOUGHBY, [of Parham,] to ROGER KENYON.

1050. 1697, July 13.—"The bearer hereof, Alce Leigh, that served [me] very faithfully and well, is turned away only for her good nature and charity to my missirable condition, which this is an instance of the horriable oppression I suffer under, when I am so inhumanly denied all conversation with my friends, that it is as bad as treason here for a servant but to carry a letter for me, which was all her crime. So I beg of you and Mrs. Kenyon to doe her all the kindness you can, to any friend that wants a servant; she is very desirous to serve you, and can tell you how villanously and barbourously I am treated by him, that by his denying me all advice for my health, nay, necessary food, as she can tell you he did lately; and also she heard him tell me that he wold chain me to the bed-post, and set a keeper on me, and feed me with bread and water; all this she can witness to be true, if called to itt. So I beg of you, as you are a gentleman and christian, that you will do all that is possible to procure me my liberty, or I am a dead woman, for there is no subsisting under such a loade, and that I may be sent for by an order from the King and Councell, to be tryed by my Peares if I be a mad woman; and then his villanous lyes will apeare. If you wold writ to Lord Darby and get him to speak in my behalfe to Lord Shrowosbury (*sic*) to writ for me, when he writes to the King, itt wold be dun, and a handsom peece of plate shuld be att Mrs. Kenyon's service."

R. BRADSHAIGH to ROGER KENYON.

1051. 1697, July 18. Haigh.—At a privy session held at Newton on the 12th instant, Mr. Entwisle and others, of Wigan, made an order for settling William Balshaw, a shoemaker, in this township of Haigh. His settlement ought to be at Wigan, for he has not been in Haigh more than five or six months; but Mr. Entwisle insisted on the fact that Balshaw was made a sidesman in Haigh, which was, however, done contrary to the election of the inhabitants. "I think I need not mention here the ill will Mr. Entwisle bears to everything which concerns or relates to Haigh. . . . The thrusting this Balshaw, with a wife and likely charge of children, into this town, I take to be a great oppression upon my tenants. . . . I humbly conceive this office of sidesman, thus obtayned, shall not be adjudged a good cause of settlement." *Seal.*

1052. 1697, July $\frac{20}{30}$.—Proceedings at a Court Martial at the camp at . . . . . before Brigadier Thomas Fairfax, President, upon the complaint of John Reddish, Henry Hayes, Thomas Cooke, Thomas Parsons, Stephen Penicuick, and William Holliday, Captains in the Honourable Colonel James Stanley's regiment of foot, against the said Colonel. Judgment of the Court, that Captain Thomas Cooke shall be cashiered from his Majesty's service; that Capt. Henry Hayes, Capt. Thomas Parsons, Capt. William Holliday, and Capt. Stephen Penicuick, shall be suspended during his Majesty's pleasure.

Appointment of GEORGE and THOMAS KENYON as gamekeepers to PETER SHAKERLEY.

1053. 1697, August 1.—Appointment of George Kenyon, of Peel, and Thomas Kenyon, of Manchester, as gamekeepers to Peter Shakerley, for his manor of Shakerley, in the county of Lancaster.

JAMES STANLEY to ROGER [KENYON]

1054. 1697, August 12. Kockelberg (?).—" Your young spark heir is verry well. You may be shure I shall be glad when it is in my power to doe him a kindnesse. The King left us mutch sooner this yeir then he used to doe, which made us thinke of peace, which we are thorrowly perswaded heir is as good as don, and we hope the buisness of Barselona will be no hinderang to it. I hope, when this hurleburle is over, I shall goe and see my frends in Lancashire."

1055. 1697, August 25.—Address of the Justices of the Peace of the County of Lancaster to the King, concerning the encouragement to Dissenters, who have lately certified, as meeting houses, several ancient chapels-of-ease, and have threatened the Clerk of the Peace with actions, if he do not record such certificates, although the Justices of the Peace disallow them. *Draft.*

P. SHAKERLEY to ROGER KENYON.

1056. 1697, October 2. Wigan.—" This comes to acquaint you that my cousin, Robert Penington, the bearer's son (Mr. Nicholas Penington), takes his bachelor of arts degree at Brasenose, in Oxford, at Midsummer, 1699, and intends to stand then candidate for one of Captain Holmes' scholarships. I desire you will assist him therein by your interest with Mr. Ashton, the parson of Prestwitch, and that you will, in order thereto, make speedy application to him. Since writing, the election here is concluded for alderman : Harvey, Mayor, and your son George, Recorder."

RICHARD EDGE to ROGER KENYON.

1057. 1697, November 16. " The Blue Boar," in Holborn.—" His Majestie landed on Sunday last, about 11 a'clock in the aforenoon, at Margret, came that night to Canterbury, last night to Greenwich, where this morning most of the great officers and persons of quality in the town, waited of him, and about two this afternoon made his publick entry into the citty; came through Fleet Street about 4, and so went to Whitehall. The ceremony was thus, as near as I can remember : ringing of bells, the streets lined with the citty trainbands, here and there a conduit running with wine. First, a company of granadeers, a troop of the royall dragoons, next 3 of the King's coaches, with several persons of quality in them—Collonel Stanley I saw in one of them;

next was the messengers on horseback, next the Citty trumpetts and waits, next the serjeants of the counters, next the Common Councell on horseback, next the Aldermen on horseback, next the Lord Mayor, carrying the sword, on horseback, then the heralds, all bare, then the kettle-drums, next the yeomen of the guard, then the King's coach, very fine, in which was the King, who looked very brisk, and made his compliments to each side the street, and the Prince of Denmark and Earl of Rumney, next Prince George's empty coach, then a troop of the life guard, then the Archbishopp of Canterbury, then the Lord Chancellor, then the Duke of Leeds in his coach besides his grace the Earl of Pembrooke, then the Duke of Norfolke, then the Duke of Devonshire, then several dukes' coaches, then severall earls and lords, amongst which I saw the Earls of Macclesfeild and Warrington, then severall bishopps, amongst whom was the Bishopp of Chester, then all the judges' coaches, then severall persons of quality's coaches ; all the coaches before had six horses each, and footmen and laques going by.

"The Prince of Conti has left Poland, and taken 4 of their ships; but the Poles have gott three times as much of the French effects. The Elector of Saxony is now absolute King of Poland, the Saxony troops haveing taken severall of Prince Conti's attendants, his coaches, and his plate, the French ambassador narrowly escaping to sea ; all the nobility of Lithuania haveing forsaken the French. The Emperor has gott all Bosnia. When the souldiers came before a fine citty called Serraglio there, they sent a trumpeter to them to surrender, who they put to death, at which the souldiers were so enraged they sett fire to it, burnt 6,000 houses, and 150 mosks or temples.

"The people in the streets here are makeing bonfires, throwing of squibs, and ringing of bells; all persons, as the King came by them, huzzaed."

PETER SHAKERLEY to ROGER KENYON.

1058. 1697[-8], January 6. Westminster.—Concerning the enclosure of Walkden Moor. "Whitehall is burnt down, except the banquetting house ; it was a dismal sad spectacle to see the flame and the silly weak methods used to stop the fire, such as no boys at school but would have given and followed better directions Had it not been for the Duke of Leeds, I really believe all Westminster had been burnt, but he came at last and ordered them to pull down all the wainscoat and pluck up the boards in the stone Gate house, by the Cock Pit, and to throw them out of the windows ; and so the fire (not having wood to work on) stopped there."

"THE HUMBLE ANSWER" made to the KING by the MAYOR, BAILIFFS, ALDERMEN, and principal inhabitants of Wigan.

1059. 1697-8, January 13.—Touching the revenues of the borough, and complaining of Mr. Entwisle, who was "intruded" on the Corporation as Recorder, under "a pretended" charter of James II. *Draft.*
Written in the margin :

> "To the women he does send raisins
> To make up their Christmas pies,
> To the lawyers he does send florins,
> That they may support him with lies."

SIR R. BRADSHAIGH to GEORGE KENYON.

1060. [16]97[-8], January 15.—" I have had very good encouragement from the King that he will confirme you the Recorder of Wigan, and I hope in a short while it will be done. Sir Alexendar [Rigby] is sensible of it, or at least fears the interest I have made with the King, so has delivered another petition into the Council, signed by as many hands, as well those that were burgesses as those that were none, to make it seeme as if it were the general desire of the town to have a new charter and their old Recorder. . . . . I desire you will goe speedily to the Mayor of Wigan, and advise with him and some other ancient burgesses what answer they can best return, which I would have you put into a method and get it signed, first by Mr. Mayor, and then let it be delivered to Charles Lee and Mr. Sumner, to goe about the towne and get all the hands, as well free-men as burgesses. Let it be drawn on a large role of parchment to hold a great many hands." *Seal, broken.*

Dr. Richard Wroe to Roger Kenyon.

1061. 1697–8, February 1.—I prevailed with the good Bishop of Chester to go with me to Kensington on Sunday evening, to present our address, where we were fortunately introduced to the King, in his bed-chamber, by the Lord Chancellor (who, by the way, refreshed his memory of the Warden and Fellows of Manchester's case, and his promise), and our address was very graciously received, but with few words—the King's usual way.

Dr. Richard Wroe to Roger Kenyon.

1062. 1697[-8], February 8.—On Thursday last died old Mr. Rigby, of Layton, and it is said that his last words were that his son's un-kindness had broken his heart; it is the great subject of discourse amongst all that knew him, and little to Sir Alexander's reputation, who, if he were as little valued at Wigan as here, I think might save himself the labour of putting in for the town. Tomorrow, the Lady Macclesfield makes her defence, and the most say it will be a good one, and that the noble peer says that if he cannot carry his point, he will leave England, and then, alas! what will become of us in Lancashire?

R. Bradshaigh to ———.

1063. 1698, May 12.—" I am just now come from Councell, and have onely time to tell you that his Majesty has been pleased to nominate George Kenion, Esq., your Recorder, so wishing both you and him much joy of each other."

John Harvey to George Kenyon, at Bolton.

1063A. [16]98, May 25. Wigan.—" By the bearer, you receive Mr. Shakerley's last letter, with instructions for the afidavids hee mentions in his. Now, if Jack Byrron be a Master in Chancery, and Mr. Lawson commissioned to take afidavids in the King's Bench, that will doe; if nott, we desire to be informed of you. Our leet court is adjourned a month longer. I am just takeing horse for Chester; I will be back, by the grace of God, tomorrow."
Enclosure.—May 24, 1698.—" Then, at the house of Charles Leigh, in Wigan, were demanded of the present Towne's Clerke of Wigan aforesaid, viz., Mr. Ralph Bankes, all the records, papers, and parchments, belongeing and relateing to the said Corporation, by Mr. Maior, viz., Ja: Harvey, and the present Bailiffs, viz., Robert Hollingshead and Roger Browne, in order they might be now, as the case stands, nott

onely of use to their Councell concerned in the High Court of Chancery, butt alsoe to their Councell in the King's Bench, in matters then dependinge. His answer was, 'Noe, noe,' twice togeather. 'But,' says hee att last, 'if any person will come and copy them over—soe, if nott, I will not part with them out of my handes,' says hee, 'I being the fittest man to keep them. Therefore,' says hee, 'as I have told you before, I will not parte with them.'"

PETITION against the infringement of the rights of the Palatinate of Lancaster.

1064. 1698, May.—Petition of the High Sheriff, Justices of the Peace, and Grand Juries, assembled at the Quarter Sessions, against the infringement of the rights of the Palatinate of Lancaster, by the practice of transmitting of causes out of the Chancery Court of the County Palatine into the Court of the Duchy Chamber at Westminster.

PETER SHAKERLEY to GEORGE KENYON, Recorder of Wigan.

1065. 1698, July 7. Westminster.—I hope by this time you are "perfect Recorder," and easy in that station I wish you and the town much comfort and long peace and amity. "I presume you will goe to church Sunday next, in your Recorder's gown, and Sir Roger in his Alderman's gown. I am tould here that James Anderton is, by Lord Maxfield, made Deputy *Custos Rotulorum* of your county, and that this is done to nip (?) you of some proffitts, by his having the records of our county and of our estates in his hands. This is what I think all the gentlemen there should highly resent, and should remonstrate by petition to the King and Councill." I think Lord Derby, and Lord Rivers, and Lord Bridgewater, &c., should be well and speedily informed of this matter.

POLL AT WIGAN ELECTION.

1066. 1698, August 5.—Poll of the Wigan election, taken by Ralph Bankes, Town-Clerk. The result of the poll was as follows :—Sir Roger Bradshaigh, 96 votes ; Sir Alexander Rigby, 73 votes, Orlando Bridgeman, Esquire, 73 votes ; James Anderton, Esquire, 25 votes ; Mr. Sharkerley, 1 vote ; Sir Edward Chisnall, 1 vote ; William Bancks, 1 vote, Mr. Bald, 1 vote.

JAMES HARVYE (?) to GEORGE KENYON, Esq., "at his house in Bolton."

1067. [16]98, August 20. Wigan.—"The affairs of the Corporation necessarily require your presence here. Till I have had some hours' talke with you, I cannot proceed to keep the Court Leet tomorrow at ten a clock, with safety, for, on Monday last, immediately after the adjournment of the Court, Sir Alexander [Rigby's] party, in a tumultuous manner, headed by John Green, went up into the room above, and elected both Aldermen and Burgesses, and design to tender them to morrow to be sworn." *Seal, broken.*

ORDER FOR RETURNS OF THE POOR.

1068. 1698, October 28.—Order to the Constables of the parish of Hanmer, in the County of Flint, to send in returns of their poor, according to the Statute, 40 Elizabeth.

The METHOD for SETTLING the POOR, taken at KANVAIR(?), in the County of Flint.

1069. 1698, November 23.—"1. An exact account was taken of all the begging poor of the parish, by the curate; with an account of their condition, the age of each of them; in all about 80 persons.

"2. Severall of them were struck out, who were either able to. maintaine themselves, or whose parents were able to maintaine them; whereof some were bastards, who were fixed upon their parents, though alwaies before mantained by begging; in number, aboute 15.

"3. The allowed poor were divided into 3 classes:—(1) Persons of age, able to worke. (2) Children fit for service. (3) The impotent poor, disabled by youth, old age, or any other disability.

"4. Towards the imploying of the working poor, a tax of 15*l.* was laid upon the parish, and, although so moderate, has imployed hitherto all the working poor, without being any way burdensome; and have not yet laid out a third part of the stock, though the poor have beene imployed neer halfe a year

"Now that these poor being once imployed, it appeared they either found themselves work, or were otherwise imployed by the parishoners, so that they were seldome obliged to stick to the publick work, which was given them for their support onely when they were otherwise out of imployment, from whence it may be inferred that a much smaller stock will serve to sett the poor att work in any parish then is usually imagined, and will be found so, whoever makes the experiment. The working are aboute 25.

"The children fitt for service, aboute 20 in number, were divided among the parishoners as followeth:—

"First, the parish was divided, according to the parishoners, into so many parts as we had poor children, the next neighbours always together; then wee putt each child's name in a hatt, like so many valentines, and put a child to draw them, one by one, for each division, till all were drawn; and to what division soever any child fell, those persons were obliged to take him. By which meanes, all the children were provided for and imployed, the persons who were to mantaine them takeing them week for week, or otherwise, as they agreed among themselves.

"Not that the parishoners were easier brought to this method then by fixing each of them upon one parishoner; for, by that meanes, some must bee excused, and but few bear the burden, which would not well take among men for the generality of equal state and condition.

"The impotent poor were also quartered among the parishoners, each in his own neighbourhood, the parish being divided, as before, into as many parts as there were impotent poor, and some places into larger divisions, where 2 or 3 poor are to be quartered together.

"As it sometimes happened, where more than one impotent poor were in the same family (*sic*), none of the impotent poor are to wander out of their limits, but are to be mantained wholly in their own quarters, and to be imployed in anything they are capable of, by their benefactors.

"By this means the parishoners find some service done them, even by many of the impotent poor, and more then they had before from all the numerous company of beggars putt together The impotent poor are about 20."

SIR ORLANDO BRIDGMAN to "the REVEREND MR. SUMNER, att Wigan, near Warrington."

1070. [16]98[-9], March 7.—"The petition stands now for the 24th of this month, but it will be yett postponed, so that I believe you need not begin your journey til! Monday the 20th, for there is two, petitions for breach of priviledge to be heard before it, so that, in course, it will not come on till the 29th. If the Town-Clerk refuses to bring up the charters, &c., it is a contempt of the order, and I will take care he shall be punished for it; but if he only refuses upon the account of expence, the chairman sayes he must be att the charges ; therefore, pray give the necessary orders as above."

AGREEMENT TO SUPPLY MEAT.

1071. 1699, April 21.—Agreement between George Kenyon, of Peel, in the county of Lancaster, and James Hilton, of Manchester, butcher, that the said James shall supply the said George, his servants and others, with "beef, mutton, veal, pork, neats tongues, suet, tallow, or any other shambles meat," usually sold in the shambles at Manchester, at $2\frac{1}{2}d.$ the pound, excepting "beeves heads, calves heads, sheeps heads, and swines heads, brawn, and lamb," upon condition that the said George deals at no other butcher.

ROGER KENYON, [Junior,] to his sister-in-law, "MRS. KENYON, Junior," at Peel.

1072. 1700, July 16.—I have yet heard nothing of Mr. Nightingale, but I suppose I shall, ere long. I am extremely concerned for what you tell me of Sir Fr : Leister, but I hope my mother's enmity to tobacco and drinking makes her complain of him though but in a small degree; for, of all men alive, I should the least have suspected Sir Fr: to have been much guilty that way. I have a very great friendship for Sir Fr : and would have him without blemish, because he may be so, nor do I know any difficulty I would refuse to serve him in.

ROGER KENYON to his mother, "MRS. KENYON, Senior," at Peel.

1073. 1700, October, 10. Paris.—"It is a filthy life to have to do with English men, where they know nothing of the language of the country they are in. Honest Ned Berisford is not ten years old in this country, and when he will come to his age is hard to say ; a man ought to love talking wondrous well that has six people to answer for, especially in a place where impertinent questions are very much in fashon. We ran away from poor Ned once, and he was lost for one day and a night. You would wonder what a world of French he gott in that time ; it did him abundance of good, and the history of it was pleasant enuf.

"Such sort of divertisements as these, are all this way of life will afford; but I have assured all my company that, if they cannot get French enuf to do their own business, I will sell them, every one, when I get near a seaport town. Jack Warren is with us still, and I doubt whether I shall be able to make a market for him without his perceiving it; if I can, he and Ned Ber[esford] may go for a pretty considerable sum, which may be of good use to us; they both send you all their most affectionate service.

"It is our last day here, and I am not a little busy; for, without laughing, I am forct to run the errands of everybody into the town, as well as do their business. I am sure you never wished more that Dol : Ashton would hold her tongue, than I do that any of these creatures coud speak."

The EARL OF DERBY to —————.

1074. 1700, December 12. London.—"For some perticular reasons, I must desire you will not faile to keep a court at Manchester on the

27 instant; and that you will give express notice to the clarks and officers to attend you at that time; and that you give me an account who are absent." *Signed*.

Roger Kenyon to Mrs. Kenyon, Junior, at Peele.

1075. 1701, September 7. Paris.—On Monday, it was in everybody's mouth that King James was dead; but yesterday assured us that it was false, though he had been, and was still, dangerously ill. A few days will let us see what is like to be expected of that, though the news of last night was that he was much better.

R. Bold to George Kenyon.

1076. 1702, April 2. London.—Having served for the county of Lancaster in the two last Parliaments, makes me venture a third time to offer myself.

Sir Thomas Hanmer to the Rev: Richard Hilton, Vicar of Hanmer.

1077. 1702, April 7. London.—"I fear the next election for the county and town of Flint will not be made with that quiet which I could wish, and which, indeed, I did expect If Sir John Conway will not be content to be out of Parliament once in ten years, when other gentlemen require to have their turn of serving, it must be disputed with him. I doe not find he is in any such temper of resigning; but, on the contrary, I believe he is forming an interest against that which Sir Roger Mostyn and I shall joyntly prosecute on our own behalfs. The county, I shall appear for; and Sir Roger, for the burrough; both mutually assisting one another, and so I desire you will understand our interest to be united . . . . that in both you will take all the pains you can to assist us."

Roger Kenyon to his sister-in-law, Mrs. Kenyon.

1078. [1702 ?] May.—"It is the best convenience of this country that, in the boats by which wee pass from one town to another, everybody has the liberty of diverting themselves with reading, writing, playing, talking, or any other way they can think of to pass their time better. I, for my part, take them all in their turn, and, whether you will or no, I am resolved you shall make one voyage with us. I am now going betwixt Utreckt and the Hague, which will be about 11 or 12 hours, and the company is as various as that in Noah's Ark, for you must know we live here without any manner of respect or disposition. There is a Dutch parson, and his wife, half a dozen market-women, a great Doctor, who is making speeches over his pots and plasters, one of the Lords of the States Generall, a fellow with a lottery, and two young gentlewomen of the country, who are prodigiously hansome, and by whom, betwixt you and I, I have plact myself. They are two sisters who speak French very well, and they tell me they take it very ill I can find no diversion but in writing.

"We have had abundance of disputes about this letter, and the knotting has been twice laid by, upon condition I would throw away my pen; but you see how much you are obliged to me. I have assured them it is to the woman in the world I love best, and that she had obliged me, when I left England, to write to her from the place where I thought myself in the most agreable company which

I could have in this country, so, at last, the peace is made and they both send their humble service. This freedom is not much of the scoll of this country, for the women are generally sleepy enuf, and keep a good distance, especially from strangers; but these two good Christians are indeed of the best sort, and with the French whicht they have learned perfectly, and which they love to speak, much rather than their own language, they have gott a little of the French air, and have more life and easiness than is common in this country. The grave, sage parson, who sits over against me, says he has seen me in the College at Utrecht, and we are got into a very weighty discourse of the history of learning, for you must know that Latin, which is the language we conver-e in, is a very untoward one for jest and drollery. He tells me the major criticks are almost finish[ed] of at Amsterdam; that Grevins (?) is very busy in his *Thesorus*, and that we are to have a mighty auction shortly at Leyden, where, if I do not appear, I doubt I shall forfeit all my pretence to letters. It is very well, good brother, but what care I for all this? Well, good sister, believe me, I care no more for it than you, and yet I am forced to hear it, and so shall you too, I am resolved of that, like it as little as you please. To keep my hand in in all the languages, I had no more grace than to ask a fellow who sits near me, a question or two in Dutch, and he has put me into a cruel swett with a hideous long story, or else is telling, and ot which, God knows, I understand not half, for, though I can converse daintily in short sentences, when they stray into large discourses, I am quite lost.

"My good women have just opened their basket of cake and provisions, and we are makeing collation; for it is thus I always trust to providence, without tak[ing] care for myself. And, as good chance will have it, here is a fellow lately come into the boat with a bottle or two of wine; he says he has been in England, and has learnt the language, but the other fellow's Dutch was much more intelligible. However, be his language what it will, his wine is very seasonable to our cake, and he pays me very well for lying, and saying I understand him. You see how gloriously we live in this country, and yet I warrant you, think all this nothing to the diversion of Stockport! Well, we will not dispute that at present. I find I am at the end of my paper, and must bid thee farewell."

The Poll at Wigan.

1079. 1702, July 28.—The poll at Wigan election. Candidates :— Sir Roger Bradshaigh, Sir Edward Chesenhall, Sir Alexander Rigby, and Mr. Bridgman.

REASONS humbly offered by HENRY JONES, Esquire, for building a Mould or Harbour in Whitsand Bay, at the Land's End, in Cornwall.

1080. 1702.—Estimated cost of the work, 30,000*l*. The place will, for the future, prevent our merchant ships being taken by our enemies, as they were during all the last war, this being a place of safety for them, and where our cruisers, of betwixt forty and sixty guns, may, on all occasions, have re:ourse to. Hence, I gave the Admiralty a list of about forty sail of ships retaken, and a greater number preserved by a fishing boat, for which service the Admiralty Board ordered the boat's master a commission and a medal. Reasons 9 to 12 are as follows:—

"(9) It is observable that when the wind is east on land, it is always (off the Land's End) E.S.East in the South Channell, and

E.N.East in the North Channell, by which it happens, ships ·from the northward cannot, so far, weather the Land's End, as to get into the South Channell, neither can those from the south get into the North Channell. And on the 9th of December, 1693, by a storm, shifting from east to westward, one hundred sail (under convoy of *the Prince of Orange* and *Quaker*, ketch), being off the Land's End, were, for want of harbour in Whitsand Bay, driven back into the North Channell, and above seventy sail of them wrecked. And I believe the ships lost by storms, and taken by the enemies during the last war (for want of such an harbour), came little short in number with those lost on all the coast of England besides.

"(10) By all the above it is likewise further manifest that even in times of peace there hath not nor can be secure trading 'twixt St. George's and the British Channels, or anywhere to the westward of the Land's End, without this proposed mould, and that, for want of it, there hath been and may be more ships lost (yearly, besides the men's lives) than three times the value of what would erect the same. Hence, the Leverpoole merchants, during all the last war, possessed those who trade from London that their ships might come safer north about Ireland, unload their effects at Leverpoole, and be at charge of land-carriage from thence to London, rather than run the hazard of having their ship taken by the enemy, or wreckt, by reason of the great dangers of Scilly, the Land's End, Mount's Bay, Lizzard, and all the South Channell to London, which hath proved an unspeakable detriment to all the trading seaport towns that border upon the British Channell; which evills would effectually be prevented were there an harbour and lighthouse at the Land's End of England.

"(11) It is apparent the thirty thousand pounds proposed will not be money lost or hazarded, but entirely applied in employing of poor labourers, and three years' time may finish the proposed mould or harbour. And further, that the most eminent merchants and commanders of ships belonging to London, Exon, Topsham, Dartmouth, Plymouth, Looe, Fowey, Penzance, St. Ives, Barnstaple, Bideford, Bridgewater, Bristol, Trinity House of Hull, and ports adjacent, are well satisfied by certifying their opinions, that an harbour in Whitsand Bay would be an advantage to England and greatly encourage trade and navigation.

"(12) The charges of building the said mould will be very small, and easy to the publick, but the benefit being greater than I can express, refer to Mr Hautecourt and Mr. Mitchill, engineers, who with Mr. Tuttell, his late Majesty's hydrographer, did survey the western coasts, and approved of this place as the most convenient receptacle for shipping, being the in and out-let of the kingdom and opposite to Brest."

An ADDRESS, signed " W. S.," to JAMES, EARL OF DERBY, in which the writer proposes certain new laws for the Isle of Man.

1081. 1702–36.—For the better maintenance of the clergy. As " most men love religion best when it costs them lest," the burden to the people should be as light as possible. " The likelyest way for this, it is suggested, will be to assign the clergy some land, say 100 acres, and accustom the people to manure it for them, and let no man be suffered to meddle in his own husbandry till he has performed this service for the minister, as suppose every man was obliged to give him a week's labour either with his team or person, according to his ability. This would be very little burden to the people, and yet of great advantage to the minister."

For the erection of schools in every parish, where parents should be obliged to send their children, from 8 to 12 years of age, where they should be taught to read English, say their prayers and catechism, so that they may be confirmed at 12. The eldest son only to be left with the parents, and the rest to undergo 7 years apprenticeship in husbandry, fishing or weaving, etc.

In every town, to have a "matronlike woman" to teach girls to read, spin, and do needlework, to whom parents should be obliged to send their daughters.

To encourage public diversions to render people more civilised, "as particularly for the service of Sunday, the parishes being wide, I would have the younger sort to be in church an hour before divine service, where the person who teaches the children should catechise them carefully." After morning service, the whole parish to dine together in a public booth, where the better sort should send what provisions they could spare, and the poor be entertained, "and the whole parish kept together in reading and laudable conversation untill the evening service. Holidays to be spent in the same manner till after dinner, when all sorts of martial exercises should be performed by the youth, and the evening spent in dancing."

A proposal also that "an honest history" should be placed in every church, that those who desired to read might do so

That "a company" be established which shall manage all the trade of the island; that no man subscribe more than 1,000*li.*, or less than 100*li.* to it; that the Lord Derby coin to the value of 10,000*li.*—one half silver and one half brass; and that the company be divided into separate committees to supervise the different trades.

That encouragement be given for the immigration of strangers, and that waste lands be allotted them

That the population be increased by encouraging persons to marry by 25 years of age; when, if they are not bred to a trade, that 100 acres of land be allotted to them.

That manufactures be thus encouraged; that every woman, without distinction of quality, be obliged to spin a small quantity—such as 20 pounds—of wool or flax every year, and deliver it to the company at a set price; and that those who spin the finest and make most cloth in every parish, should be rewarded with a spinning-wheel; and if any young woman gained the prize twice, the magistrates should be obliged to offer her a suitable husband, or some reasonable reward towards her fortune, "which would be a great encouragement."

That the breed of cattle be improved.

That persons having estates in the Island, be obliged to live there at least 6 months in the year.

That a public workhouse be erected for the punishment of criminals, so that nothing but murder, blasphemy, and rebellion should be punished with death.

That a public register be kept, and no title or security to be good in law that is not entered there.

That a town be built, where all persons having 1,000 acres of land, and 600*li.* stock in the company, be obliged to build houses, and that there be public fairs and markets granted to the town.

A PAPER about the CHARACTER and DEEDS of LORD DERBY.

1082. [1702 ?]—"In publick and laudible undertakeings, he that has the prospect and prudence to see and keep his way, and art to avoyd the dangers he may passe in attaineing the ends, and manages these with resolution, effect, and successe, is weighed in an unequall scale of consideration if his performances passe not in some measure for meritoriouse.

"If the Lord Derby's doings were had in remembrance, his detractor must confesse he acted the part he undertooke ; he raised four regiments of foot and five troops of horse, and these he did without noise, censure, or the complaints of any ; he made the adverse party submissively send in what they were charged with by law, and made them then submitt to those lawes which till then they had made so much ado to suppress. In his charge, care, and attendance of that business, he never spared the expence of his time or his money ; his life was diverse times threatned to be taken away, his house to be burned ; night after night, and messenger after messenger, he had expresses to advertise him of parties to be drawn out against his house and to surprize his person ; letters were intercepted going to the late King to certifye his Lordship's adherence to the Prince's party and to render him to the utmost obnoxiouse to that King. And besides his hazards by the machinations of the aforementioned, had the enterprize miscarryed, the sequel must certainly have been this Lord's attainder, which must have cost him his estate, his honor, his life, and put a period to one of the most ancient, noble families in England, which comparatively transcends the adven‧ ture that person could make that doth traduce him; for where severall hazard all that they have, he hazards most that hath most to lose.

"The undertaking pretended to, was the preservation of our property, our liberty, our fundamentall lawes, and our religion by those lawes established. To have defended these by force without conduct, had been fortunate beyond beleefe ; to attempt it by art without visibility of force, all former successeless essays had shewed was hopeless. But to accomplish it by an appearance of force without useing it, was the well useing his well timed endeavours with providentiall successe. If the lord we are mentioning acted this part to convince gainsayers without detriment, to keep complyers within the bounds of moderation when successfull, the conduct was not so despicable ; but if it merited no more, it might seem thanksworthy.

"But consider the detractor. If the obtaineing what we pretended to be not our reward, our contending for more seemes to bespatter our pretensions as if the project of the warr were not more for the victory then the pillage. When such desires are let loose the designes are limitless, and he that lyes upon the catch grasps att all he can gett without distinction, whether it was the spoyle of an enemy or the property of a friend ; to such, all's fish that comes to the net, and all must come that can be hooked or drove in. To do this he bids fair for outdoing posture John, in signalizeing himselfe in such sundry shapes ; he is now, haveing jusled out his neighbour, displaying the banners of his selected militia ; anon, he is mustered in buffe in the head of another neighbour's regiment. The next shape he assumes is his tufted gown upon the Bench—*cedant arma togæ*. From thence he struts into the Treasury for his diversion, to lord it there. Anon, yee hear of his speecheing in the Supreme Court, and thence, for his universality of notions, promptness of parts, profundity of judgment in the secrets of the empire, he is wooed to be one of the Privy Councell."

EDWARD KENYON to his brother, GEORGE KENYON.

1083. 1703, May 20. "Cabu Corsu Castle, on the south side of Africa."—"Aprill the 23rd, I landed here, and the same day was put into possession of the castle. On the 14th of May, the proffits of the seller was given me (it is to sell liquor to the officers and soldiers of the garrison, besides some other sort of provisions), which, would the Company continue to me by a commission from themselves, is a better post than e're a factor on the coast, who is not a cheife. If my friends will take pains to ask it of them heartely, by the name of the Lieutenant of the Castle, it is not to be questioned, but it will be granted if none other be already sent over. If that should happen, then my humble petition is you will endeavour to get me made factor, for, without one of the two things, it is impossible to live here; all eatables and drinkables, as well as wearing cloaths, being sold at least 200 *per cent.* above their prime cost in England. The gentlemen that first engaged me in the Company's service may further the thing a great deale, but Sir —— Master (?), though none of the Company, if he could be brought to undertake it, would certainly succeed. I may be authorized, if one of the two things happen, to see England in a few years, possessed of a competency to live on; if otherwise, to live miserably here; the income of the post I came over in, not being enough to buy food fit for man to eat, not recconing drink or cloathing To let you judge of the whole by part:—a cow, not larger than a 3-months old Lancashire calf, is sold at 12 pound; fowl, like wild pidgions, 3 for a crowne; 5 pound for an ordinary sheep, and English flower, 1*l.* 10*s. per* hundred-weight; cheese, four pounds for a crowne; beere 1*l.* 10*s.* per dozen bottles. But enough of this. From Gambia, I writt to you; the conclusion of which letter was like most of my others, viz., begging. But, least Mr. Frenchman has mett with it, it was for a few necessaries to wear, such as shoes, thread stockings, and a few callicoe shirts; but, rather than by asking too much I lose all, pray doe not forget belly-timber, and the maine supporter of life —good beere. I doe assure you when your lowest seller comes into my mind, which it never fails to doe when I goe into my own, I break a commandment. My teeth waters, too, when Mr. Moody, of the Bank, also is remembered. This castle is well built, being founded on a rock; seventy odd guns well mounted, thirteen of which are cannon mounted on a platform which commands the rode the shipping rides in; the others placed for commanding the country. I have noe news, except our loseing a briganteene by an hurricane, where a great number of my fellow passengers lost all their goods, all the men, except one, lost, and the Company, above 2,000*l.* worth of effects. The . . . man-of-war, sails this day for England, in which comes this. Enclosed is a ring made in this country; pray give it my sister, and desire she wear it for the sake of her sincere well wisher."

C. Lyttleton to "Doctor Roger Kenyon, at the corner of Lincoln-Inn-fields, on the garden side, the end of Great Turn Stile."

1084. 1703-4, February 5. Hagley.—"I thank you for the skech you give me of your thought of the present affaires, which I think very just, and there is no remedy for, in the age we live, wherein every one resolves to keep what he has and get what he can; and which puts me in mind of my old Lord Herbert of Cherburye's answer to Jack Henham, upon a time when King Charles 1st sent him of a message from Oxford to the Parliament, bidding him tell him that he as little expected he woud have left him as anybody, for he knew he had obliged him, and had made the greatest professions of returns of personal love and kindness, which my Lord replyed to, pray tell his Majesty, so I have, as much as any man can, that intends to keep his estate! This was told me, upon a like ocasion, by a very great man in this Lord's time . . . . . . I have as good appetite as ever, but a

E E

very weake digestion; but what is that, after 74, which is now gone. You are very kind in your offer to my sons, and it will be a mighty inducement to venture one or both into this wide world under so good advice and conduct, and which I may some time put upon you. Thom : is so grown that you cannot imagine, and big withall. Charles is well grown too . . . . . . You will have the goodness to excuse these blots of a septuaginarian shaking hand . . . . . . The Presbyterians (?) and Whigs are very busy to make votes against a new parliament, with us."

Thomas Fleetwood to "Mr. Keynion."

1085. 1704, October 3. Bank.—"The persons under named, I hear, stands indited for keeping greyhounds and guns, through a mistake of the constables; they being my tennants, and the greyhounds and guns are mine, and kept by them for my use, being obliged by their leases. Whose names I desire you to take out of the inditement and acquitt them from any further trouble or charges:—

Edward Blackledge in Bretheton.

Ralph Withington ⎫
Henry Dobson ⎪
William Dobson ⎬ Tarleton.
Henry Leadbetter ⎭

If this be not practicable, I will try whether I am qualified or not; so that insolent bailifs may not come to my house to inquire, for the future, into such matters."

R. Bradshaigh to George Kenyon.

1086. 1704-5, February 8.—I am writing to all the freeholders about Lancaster, and beyond the sands. Perhaps, taking notice of them in that manner may oblige them. I find most gentlemen will be determined, as my Lord Derby recommends, and that I am sure of, and [I] hope he will go down, as soon as possible. He can settle his matters after matrimony, which is either concluded or very near it, to a fortune of sixty thousand pounds.

[Rev.] Jo: Sumner to George Kenyon.

1087. 1704[-5], March 20.—It is said, with assurance, that my Lord Derby will forthwith be declared Chancellor of the Exchequer, and that he laid down his colonel's commission. He assures Sir Roger [Bradshaigh] for the county election, and says he will be down soon. Shakerley, they say, is out of his government, and my Lord Cholmonderley has it.

W. Delaune, Vice-Chancellor of Oxford, to ————.

1088. 1705, September 21. St. John's [College, Oxford].— " Whereas Mr. [Samuel] Wesley, rector of Epworth, in Lincolnshire, has made known the deplorable condition he is brought into, by the inveterate malice and persecution of the Dissenters, for his vindicating the Church of England from their scandal, and detecting their villanous practices in their schismaticall schooles and seminaries, set up in opposition to the Church, and prejudice of the Universities, we thought fitt to recomend this, his pressing case, to all the members of our University, as a great object of their charity and compassion, and such as requires speedy releif to deliver him out of prison, and the calamitous sufferings he at present labours under."

Appended.—" A copy of Mr. Wesley's letter:—On my printing a poem on the battle of Blenheim, I was sent for to London by a person of quality, in January last, the Duke of Marlbrough haveing promised me a chaplain's place in one of the new regiments, and another honourable person greater favours. I had writt two books against the Dissenters, at which they were very angry. The person who sent for me told me I must drop that controversy, and, at last, that I must publickly, and in print, recant or palliate what I had writt against the Dissenters ; he added, that those people expected so many friends in the next House of Commons, more than they had in the last, that when they came to sitt they had resolved to call those to account who had affronted them ; this had a contrary effect to what was expected. I left my fortunes in God's hands, and resolved to act according to my conscience. And as soon [as I could] I came into the country, to use what little interest I had in our election, to serve those who were not likely to be partial to the Dissenters; but before I would act, I was so nice as to write to Collonel Whitchcott, because there had been some intimacy between us, giveing the reasons why I thought myself obliged to vote against him. This letter he exposed, and his friends reported there was treason in it. After which I gave copies of it. They likewise threatned to write up against me, and throw me out of my chaplaine's place which the Duke had given me, and throw me into gaol ; all which, I thank them, they have fully effected. I writt to London to know why I was turned out without knowing my accusation. My Collonel Lepel answered that a person of the greatest quality told him it was for something I had published which was not approved of at Court, and for haveing concerned myself too much in some other matters.⸴ The first must be my books against the Dissenters, the latter my acting in the election for my own country, which I thought I had as much right to do as any other freeholder. God be praised, these two crimes were linked together. After this the friends of the new candidates, the Dissenters, and their adherents, charged me with preaching treason, and reported I was distracted; where then was their mercy ? But at last were content to throw me into prison, according to their promise, for no great debt, to a relation and zealous friend of one of the new members. They knew it was sufficient to do my business, I haveing been thrown behind hand by a series of misfortunes; my parsonage barne was blown down e're I had recovered the takeing my liveing; my house, great part of it, burnt down about two years agoe; my flax, great part of my income (now in my own hands), I doubt, wilfully fired and burned in the night, whilst I was last at London ; my income sunk, about one half, by the low price of grain ; and my credit lost, by the takeing away my regiment. I was brought to Lincolne Castle, June 23 last past. About three weekes since, my very unkind people, thinking they had not yet done enough, have, in the night, stabed my 3 cowes, which was a great part of my numerous family's subsistence, for which God forgive them."

The Lords of the Council to James, Earl of Derby, *Custos Rotulorum* of Lancashire.

1089. 1705, November 29. St. James'.—Requesting him to raise recruits in the County of Lancaster.

The Same to the Same.

1090. 1706, March 25. Kensington.—" It being highly requisite for her Majesty's service, in the more speedy manning and maintaining a powerfull fleet at sea against the common enemy, that all possible ways and means be used for the supply of the Royall Navy with seamen and other able-bodyed men, for which purpose her Majesty has likewise issued out her royall proclamation, bearing even date herewith, and an Act of Parliament (a copy whereof is herewith sent you) having been lately past by her Majesty, entituled 'an Act for the encouragement and encrease of seamen, and for the better and speedier manning her Majesty's Fleet,' the successe whereof cheifly depends upon the care, diligence, and zeal of yourself, and of her Majesty's justices of the peace, in finding out and impressing such seamen and able-bodyed landmen and prisoners for debt, as are intended by this Act for her Majesty's Fleet, her Majesty has thought fit to command us, on this extraordinary occasion, most earnestly to recommend to your Lordship and the justices of the peace the vigorous execution of the said Act, so far as is incumbent on you and the said justices; and in order to so great and important a service, we cannot but hope your dutifull regard to her Majesty and her Government will make you resolve to improve every opportunity, and to agree immediately so to distribute yourselves that no part of your county may want the number of justices required by the said . . . And for the more effectual carrying on this work, [dir]ections will be likewise given to the officers of her Majesty's navy to be ready, with the least trouble possible to the said justices, to receive such seamen and able-bodyed landmen and prisoners for debt as shall be raised and procured in pursuance of the said Act of Parliament. This being a service so necessary for carrying on the war, and consequently most acceptable to her Majesty, we cannot doubt of a ready and hearty complyance with these directions. And we are further to acquaint you that it is her Majesty's pleasure that, besides the severall particulars directed by the Act, you take care to send up an account, to be layd before her Majesty in Councill, of your proceedings herein, and of the number and names of such seamen and able-bodyed landmen and prisoners for debt, respectively, as shall be raised and procured as aforementioned. We are likewise to recommend to your Lordship, that all possible care be had that no person be taken up and delivered to the officers of her Majesty's navy who are boys or aged persons, or unfitt for her Majesty's sea service by infirmities or otherwise."

The Lords of the Council to James, Earl of Derby, *Custos Rotulorum* of Lancashire.

1091. 1706, April 4. Kensington.—" Whereas the Lords Spiritual and Temporal in Parliament assembled have, by their humble address, acquainted her Majestie with severall instances of the very great boldness and presumption of the Romish priests and papists in this kingdom, together with their humble opinion that, for the safety of her Majesties royal person and government, a more watchful eye should be had over them for the future, and for that purpose that a distinct and particular account should be taken of all papists and reputed papists in this kingdom, with their respective qualityes, estates, and places of abode. We do therefore, in her Majesties name and by her express comand, hereby pray and require your Lordshipp to cause all the Justices of the Peace of the County of Lancaster to assemble together, and, being so assembled, there to agree on the most propper manner to subdivide themselves unto severall subdivisions for the more effectuall performing the said service within such subdivisions, where they are to take a distinct and particular account of all papists and reputed papists within the same, with their respective qualities, estates, and places of abode, above mentioned; and it is her Majesties further pleasure that, at such generall meeting, an account be taken, distinctly, of the names of the severall Justices of the Peace designed for the said several subdivisions, and that the said Justices of the Peace do, under their hands, returne unto you a particular account in writeing of what they shall perform in the said severall subdivisions, which account you are thereupon to returne to her Majesties Privy Councell, together with the names of every one of the Justices of the Peace who shall neglect or refuse to performe their dutys in relation to that service."

R[OGER] K[ENYON] to MRS. KENYON, Junior.

1092. 1706, May 25.--" The Dutchy of Lancaster has changed its face a little since my last, or, at least, I have heard of the change since then. My Lord Gower gave up the seals to the Queen this day sennight, and my Lord Darby generally understood to be his successor, though I have not heard that the latter is actually in the place, as yet. This change, I hope, may be of some service to my brother, in securing at least one point he has great reason to wish done. If there be any other place my brother could wish himself possest of, I sopose his personal knowledge with my Lord Darby may be his best way of applying, and the sooner the better; for the other thing, it may not be amiss to let my lord settle in his place, ere it be moved. I saw Sir R—— Br—— the midle of this week; he shewed me a letter from T. Kenyon, who had cut him out work enuf, but the thought about it will not, I sopose, disturb Sir R's rest; he made great professions of his willingness to serve my brother upon this change, if my brother would instruct him ; . . to ask, and, if my brother thinks it will be of any significance, I sopose he will not let him dye ignorant. Well, rain or fair, high church or low, it is much at one with me, my hopes or fears are not exercised either way; and, excepting a few smiles to see the merryment of the world and the different countenances of winners and losers, it gives me no more concern than a game att all-fours."

JOHN SUMNER to GEORGE KENYON.

1093. 1706, June 18.--" The Queen being altogether at Winsor, Sir Roger is obliged to be there often to expedite the coming out of his commision, and ordered me, if he did not return to town this evening, to write to you that you would, with all hast, send an address to him, with the town's seal only affixt. He desires he may receive it Fryday sennit, without fail, for he has a perticuler reason why he shoud, by all means, present it the Sunday following; he would have it as short as may be, and if you think fit to take notice of my Lord Peterborough in it, he would have you also to mention my Lord Galway, by no means omitting the Church being out of danger. I hope to be in Lancashire the beginning of the next week, whither Sir Roger will hasten as soon as the commissions come out, which will be now very soon, my Lord Treasurer having delayed halfe a year Munday next, and thereby saved the Government forty thousand pound. We have no news but what you will find in your prints, nor pamphletts worth sending. My Lord Rivers' expedition is mighty secrett; no one here does know where it is intended. It is rumoured Mr. John Howe is to be removed."

Postscript.—" The Government has ordered forty thousand flambeauxs for my Lord Rivers' expedition. I have spoke about your [debt?], and he will pay you part of the principall and the interest att his coming down."

John Sumner to George Kenyon.

1094. 1706, June 20.—I think Lord Derby really designs to come to Manchester, and bring my Lady with him. Great William is to be a captain in his regiment. " He has swopt his commission with one Wallis, who had got a commission in Sir Roger's."

The Earl of Derby to George Kenyon.

1095. 1706, September 4.—" I have heird from severall hands how much I am obliged to you in the opposition we are like to meet with at Preston, which I beleve you think, as well as my self, very unaccountable. I beleve you have found the Dons very stiff, but ye shall find me as stiff as themselves. I know, when you goe that way, you may doe good service, for which I shall alley endeavour to shew my gratetude, as soon as an oppertunety offers. I have written to severall gentilmen in and about Preston, which I hope may have good success. I beleve they industriously spred it about as if I would not stand it out, but they shall find themselves much mistaken."

Christopher Parker to Roger Kenyon, at Manchester.

1096. 1706, October 31. Clitheroe.—Upon the death of Col: Stringer (my uncle), there being now a vacancy here, I expect a new election very soon. I have offered myself to the town, and should be very glad to serve as their representative, in his room. *Seal of arms.*

The Earl of Derby to George Kenyon.

1097. 1706, October 31. London.—Offering him the post of Vice-Chancellor of the Palatinate of Lancaster.

Alexander Rigby to George Kenyon.

1098. 1706, November 12. Westminster.—" I am just come from my Lord Derby, and he tells me he has made you his Vice-Chancelor, at which I demonstrated my great satisfaction, both as you are my kinesman, a good lawyer, and one that nothing can byass, where friendship and equity is in the scale. I layed hold of this opportunity, humbly to throw in my mite in favour of your brother, at Manchester. I hope now, sir, it will ever be our fortune to drawe together; our anchestors did. My Lord is certainely one of the best men that lives upon God's earth. I was very endeavouring to gett in Brenaud, as pittying the errors of youth, considering him of a brisk temper, of a good presence, voluble and dilligent, related at Preston, &c., but my Lord, who is eagle-eyed, resolute in being served by honest men, and informed fully of every minute passage in Lancashire, stood in a clearer light, and hath so convinced me why he past by Brenaud, that I am under the greatest admiration of his Lordship's goodness and wisdom immaginable. I am sure you will not think that I knew till now that my Lord aimed at my couzen Kenyon. I did not so much as dreame of it, because that you are Clerk of the Peace. It is very unkind in the people at Preston to give my Lord so much trouble, and I doubt not but you will use all your force to make them sensible. Mr. Maynwaring is such a sorte of person that, in my lifetime, I never mett a greater man of sublime witt and judgement, are what renders a mortall most to be admired. I wish you saw a letter he writt last week to Mr. Wrickley; that paints him better then any thing I am able to express.

" Pray, sir, if ever you see my old friend Mr. Luca, of Parke-hall, be so kind as to give him my service. I wish you would bring him under my Lord in the malitia. He is brave, he is honourable, a sincere freind where he takes, and everybody knows he is a man of substance; he is also your neighbour.

Postscript.—" The towne is full of a peace between the King of Sweden and the King of Poland, and it is the more admired at for that Stanislaus is to be over Poland, and Augustus is to returne to Saxony; if so, hee is a poor spirited blockhead. The Hague letters mention all this, and the Swedish envoy tells it.

" Duke Marlebro' comes over with the first faire wind."

The Earl of Derby to George Kenyon.

1099. 1706, November 16. London.—Expressing pleasure at Kenyon's acceptance of the post of Vice-Chancellor of the County Palatine, to which he has joined the Stewardship of Salford. *Seal of arms.*

John Harrisson to George Kenyon.

1100. 1706, November 20. Clitheroe.—" I hope you will pardon this trouble, which comes att the request of Mr .Lister, Mr. Pudsay, Mr. Sclater, and other gentlemen in this neighbourhood, to desire the favour of your vote and interest for Major-Generall Harvey, the Duke of Mountague's nephew, this next election. Mr. Parker (notwithstanding the endeavours of many of his own well-wishers to the contrary) is resolved to oppose him, but we hope you, sir, will joyn with the rest of the gentlemen to assist Mr. Harvey, and free the town from such arbitrary proceedings as have too much of late prevailed in it."

Nicholas Starkie to George Kenyon, at Manchester.

1101. 1706, November 30.—The 20*l.* bill received. Mr. Wolfe has promised to get your patent passed, so that you may not lose the benefit of the next court. · They tell me that if the warrant the Queen should sign be for life or years certain, it will not pass; they have known such rejected, and that no such grant has been made since the Revolution, except Lord Derby's as Chamberlain of Chester, which had been usually granted for life. Your cousin, Charles Rigby, has his late father's gown, which you may either borrow or buy, on easy terms. " I shall top a justice of peaceship upon you before I leave the town." *Seal of arms.*

The Earl of Derby to George Kenyon.

1102. 1706, December 5. London.—" Mr. Maynwaring will be at Preston, Wednesday next; your company at that time will be very acceptable, as well as usefull. · No stone must be unturned in order to bring it to a good effect, otherwise, I am shure, we shall be scoft at, which must be prevented, if possible. I am shure no one knows the method of it better then yourself. I shall be in pane till I know how matters are like to goe."

C. Z. Stanley to George Kenyon.

1103. 1706, December 9. Preston.—" I had a letter yesterday from my brother Derby, that he had writ to you by that post. This is, therefore, to let you know that I belive Mr. Manwering wil be at Wigan on

Wedensday next; therefore, I think it wil be absolutely necessary for you to be their that day. I hear the High Sherrif has said, if he knew when Mr. Mauwering will be down, he would meit him at Wiggan ; if he should be at home, I think it would do wel to feil his pulce. I do not mein for him to bring his spear-men with him."

The Earl of Derby to George Kenyon.

1104. 1706, December 10. London.—" I send you, enclosed, the warrant for Vice-Chancellor. I shall be glad to be informed by you how Mr. Maynwaring likes his reception, and what you think of the election. Mr. Starkie set out yeisterday in the Warington coche, and, I beleve, will be with you on Sunday, if his consiens will give him leve to travel that day. I should be glad to here that the Chancery clarkes have repentyd, for there sakes as well as my owne."

John Watson to Rev. John Sumner, at Wigan.

1105. 1706, December 19. London.—Acquainting him that, at the Hague, coming to England, the " Lord Duke" thought fit to put another chaplain in Sumner's place, one Mr. Durrell, brother to Colonel Durrell, " aid-de-camp to his grace," by reason of his not giving attendance.

John Sumner to George Kenyon, " att the Great House in Bromley Street, near Drury Lane."

1106. 1706[-7], February 11. Wigan.—Has previously written to him about procuring the discharge of " one Richard Whalley, a soldier in Brigadeer How's regiment, in Captain Johnson's company." Dr. Wroe " has preach't an extrordinary reformation sermon here, this day. Pray be sure to remember the written sermons I desired you to procure . . . . . Pray remember the arms of the crucifix." *Seal.*

Richard Wroe to George Kenyon, " at the Great White House in Brownloe Street, in Drury Lane."

1107. 1706–7, February 23.—Speaks of living " in such a place and post as Chester is, since Wigan is actually given from it." Has " been moved by one good friend, if I would have made use of my friends for the Bishoprick, to see if the wardenship might be held with it, as it has been twice before—by Bishop Stanley, of the house of Derby, and Bishop Chadderton ; and are consistent enough, though the advantage would be but small, not much above 100*l. per annum*, which is yet half as much as Wigan brings in, clear ; but this I onely mention to you, as suggested to mee, without any designe to attempt it, nor need you mention it, save onely in discourse with friends, as from yourself."

Thomas Martin to George Kenyon, at Salford.

1108. 1706[-7], March 17. Wigan.—" Being lame of the gout, I was not at church, [and] there came the Rector, the Dean of York, Mr. Boyer, Mr. Hindley, and Mr. Smith, to see me. . The Rector told me there was one John Leyland come to Winwick, to desire his admittance to be the church-clerk of Wigan, [and] told him he was chosen by the Jury, according to the ancient custom of the town ; [and] if he was not pleased, he (Leyland) would try with him, this Assize." The Rector is uneasy, and desires it " composed " without a law suit.

ROGER KENYON to his sister-in-law, MRS. KENYON.

1109. 1707, September 13, [St. Germains.]—"By a letter I saw from Lancashire, not long since, I perceive there was another dispute at the Assizes, besides the Lord Derby's, in which I fancy my brother was concerned ; and that was about the parish clerk of Wigan, which, it seems, Mr. Finch has recovered into his own power again. This honest gentleman will revive their diversicn again at Wigan, which was got so much before on one side, that it grew dull."

Postscript.—" My lady master is near me, and bids me wish you all happiness from her."

DECLARATION by the CORPORATION OF WIGAN, of the Title under which they hold the Fair, Markets, and Leet, in Wigan.

1110. 1708, April 8.—" Whereas, by an Award made by Sir Orlando Bridgeman, Knight, then Lord Chief Justice of the Common Pleas, between the Right Reverend father in God, George, Lord Bishopp of Chester and Parson of Wigan, the said George Lord Bishopp being then Parson and Ordinary there, of the one part, and the Mayor, Bayliffes, and Burgesses of Wigan, on the other part, bearing date the twenty-eighth day of September, in the fifteenth year of the reign of our late Sovereign Lord King Charles the Second, *annoque Domini,* 1663 ; it is, amongst other things, therein and thereby declared, ordered, and awarded, that the then Parson of Wigan and his successors, parsons of Wigan, should for ever, as in right of their Church of Wigan, have the Assention Faire, the Munday Markett, and the Easter Leet, within the said towne of Wigan, with the proffitts of the same.

"But for the establishing peace between the Parson and the Corporation, hee did award that the then Parson of Wigan, and his successors, should execute a lease for the tearme of one and twentie years of the said Faire, Market, and Leet, to the said Corporation, under the yearly rent of five markes, payable at Christmas and Midsummer yearly, by equall portions, and that upon the expiration of the said lease, by surrender, effluxion of time, or otherwise, the Parson of Wigan, for the time being, should at the request and cost in law of the said Corporation of Wigan, make a new lease, by Indenture, of the premises for the terme of one and twenty yeares, under the like reservation of rent of five markes yearely, dureing the said tearme. And that upon the makeing of every new lease, the counterpart thereof should be delivered to the said Parson, under the seale of the said Corporation, as by the said Award, relation being thereunto had, may appeare. Which said Award was confirmed by the patrons of the said Parish Church. And whereas, since the makeing of the said Award, the Corporation of Wigan have constantly held and enjoyed the said Faire, Markett, and Leete, from the successive parsons, under the yearly rent of five markes, pursuant to the said Award. And whereas the late Right Reverend Father in God, Nicholas, Lord Bishopp of Chester and Rector of Wigan, did execute a lease of the premises to the said Corporation, for the tearme of one and twentie yeares, and dyed before the expiration of that tearme, notwithstanding which the Corporation did hold the last Easter Leet, and received the proffitts of the last Assention Faire, before any application was made to the Honourable and Reverend Edward Finch, then and now Parson of Wigan.

" And whereas, the said Corporation, in owneing of the Parson's right, have this day requested a lease, to bee by him executed, of the premises, and likewise offered to deliver a counterpart of the said lease from the Corporation, pursuant to the said Award, which said lease the

Parson has consented to execute, upon their owning that they did not hold the said Leet or receive the profitts of the last Assention Faire, by any other claime or title whatsoever, but under the said Award. We therefore, the Mayor, Bayliffes, and Burgesses of the said Corporation, doe declare that wee did hold the said Leet and receive the said profitts in submission and obedience to the said Award, and by noe other claime or title whatsoever. And the said Mayor, Bayliffes, and Burgesses, for themselves, and the said Rector of Wigan, for himself, doth hereby. mutually agree and declare that they will now, and at all times hereafter, on their respective parts and behalfes, in all things observe and performe the said Award."

Lord Gower to George Kenyon.

1111. 1708, April 18.—" The occasion of my writing to you is to beg your assistance to my friend, Mr. Bridgman, in his election at Wigan. I know your obligations to my Lord Derby are such, that on his account you will serve Sir Roger Bradshaw in the first place ; and therefore, I only beg your second vote and interest for Mr. Bridgman ; you must allow me to press you to this in such a manner, as to tell you that I shall not take any excuse or refusall well from you."

R[oger] Kenyon to his brother, George Kenyon.

1112. 1708, June 1.—I perceive, by Mr. Starkey, that you have been busy in your county amongst the Roman Catholics. I know none of them, but if you could do any favour to Mr. Oldfield I should be glad of it, for the relation his lady stands unto some friends I love very well. *Seal.*

Repair of Chester Cathedral.

1113. 1708, October 4.—The case for the repair of the Cathedral Church of Chester.

George Kenyon to ————.

1114. 1708[-9], March 4. Salford.—Giving the bounds of a seat in [Wigan ?] Church, viz. :—on the north, by the reading desk ; on the west, by the clerk's desk ; on the east, by a seat claimed by Richard Bolton ; and on the south, open to the middle aisle. Length 2½ yards, breadth 2½ yards.

Sir R. Bradshaigh to George Kenyon.

1115. 1709, June 16. London.—Lord Derby is gone into the country for these holidays. I have left the papers and grant of the gallery in Winstanley's hands, to be delivered to yourself when required; they are sealed up. I hope the Bishop will think the gallery at the west end of the Church [of Wigan ?] to be the proper place for the organ ; if so, and that our seats may be erected again at the rector's charge, I believe the money which may be spent in law-suits had better be applied towards the organ, if the town and parish thinks fit to consent to it, and that upon a full hearing of the matter before the Bishop, it be done by his direction. You know best what to say in this matter, and I doubt not but you will push everything to the utmost, to prevent the organ being put upon our gallery floor.

Roger Kenyon to his sister-in-law, Mrs. Kenyon.

1116. 1709, August 2.—" I was yesterday to make a visit to the Palatines, as we call them, who are encamped, to the number of six or eight thousand, upon Blackheath, near Greenwich. They are all poor as may be, and a good many sick, as a great many more will soon be, if some means be not found out to put them into houses and other conveniences of living. What freak brought these poor creatures hither, is not easy to guess; but it seems there has been some bookes sent among them (by whose means I know not) with flattering descriptions of Caroline (*sic*), and they are mad to go thither. This account Dr. Hobart (?) gives me, who is in the very country they come from, which is not the Palatinate, but on the other side of the Rhine, at some distance from Mayence, and most of them where under Protestant princes; so religion, or a persecution upon that account, was not in the case. Upon whose motive they were encouraged to come hither, and what they are to do now they are here, is out of my reach."

JOHN SUMNER to GEORGE KENYON, at his house in Salford.

1117. 1709[-10], January 8.—"The Rector will certainly be here this week; his maids and provisions are already here. It is talkt among his people, with great assurance, that the organ will be soon up, so that it is expected a vestry notice will be given on Sunday next, and, pray, after you have notice of it come forthwith hither, though it should be a day or two before. Mr. Bancks having been abroad, and not yet returned from Preston fair, I sent last night for some of those in this town, chiefly concerned in the linnen affair; they were glad to hear you made any enquiry how that matter proceeded, and desired me to acquaint you they were resolved to try the matter, let the success of it be what it would. They have been at Leverpoole about it, and sent to York, and are not without encouragement from both places: I find, by them, they think their greatest discouragement proceeds from what you have given, both as to your talking too heartlessly, and by your delaying to draw the petition to be signed by the Websters, and which has hindered some subscriptions, which, however, they doubt not will be retrived, when the petition is tendered to be signed. This week, they will send for all the money already collected, and would be glad you would appoint some place to meet them, which pray do, and I will come along with Mr. Bancks and them. I was coming to Peele on Wednesday, to have seen you, as you said you would be there this Christmas, but meeting your letter by the way, I took up at Heelen's. Ral[ph] Winstanley and William Glazbrook are ordered by Sir Roger . . . will appear in Mr. Warmisley's room. Pray direct me in a . . . line or two, as soon as possible, how that matter is to be done; because Mr. Warmisley is very uneasy, if they are to sign any instrument. Pray send it drawn, or order them to meet you to do it. I have not seen William Green since I had yours, but will bring him over to you when you appoint. The linnen men say they have already collected, in divers places, a considerable sum, and are resolved nothing of that kind shall be wanting. Pray send or step to Captain Leigh and deliver him the enclosed; it is concerning a man to be rendered in Leiuftenant-General Steward's regiment, in the room of a servant of Bayliff Acton's, for which Sir Roger prevailed with the Leftenant-General to give him a furloug, and after promised him a discharge, upon promise Sir Roger would render a man in his room. Sir Roger has ordered me to treat with the Captain about it. Pray use your intrest with the Captain to take two guineas, or less, and then, perhaps, a man may get one to his pockett, but a man must forthwith be rendered, or Sir Roger forfeits his honour. Pray write to me by the first opportunity. I wish you a happy, merry new year." *Seal.*

R[OGER] K[ENYON] to his sister[-in-law], MRS. KENYON.

1118. 1709[-10], January 14. [London.]—" The great amusement of this town is the affair of Sacheverell, about which all companys squabble and box, as they find themselves inclined. For my part, I look on with calmness enuf, and if one cannot but observe, on one side, that there are some inconsistencys in the Doctor's sermons, yet the moderation (which has been the word so long) of the other side is admirable. But let them go on as they please ; my rule is that whatever happens is best." *Seal of arms, broken.*

The SAME to the SAME.

1119. [1709-10,] February 28. London.—" I am just come from the baiting of Dr. Sacheverel. It is past seven o'clock, and I have not eat one bit all day. Yesterday, the inditement was read, and a little opened. To-day, the managers of the House of Commons have brought the two first articles, the first of which relates to passive obedience, which was mauld (?) to purpose. The other related to the toleration, and what was said about it. They having low voices who spoke, I cannot so well tell you the whole of the matter. If one may be allowed to guess at these gentlemen's meaning, [it] is to establish some new oath or declaration against passive obedience, and to affirm the righteousness and lawfulness of all the steps of the revolution. The Doctor has yet said nothing for himself, but stands it very well, with all shews of resolution and modesty."

CHARLES RIGBY to GEORGE KENYON.

1120. 1710, May. 5. Lancaster.—" This application is on behalf of my near kinsman, Sawney Rigby, who is the top of my kin, by my father's side, as he is yours by the mother's ; but it is not that consideration which moves me to this, so much as the service or dis-service that he may do the house of Derby, as he shall be obliged or disobliged. It was some time before this last assizes that Sawney had the compliment from Colonel Stanley that he should be put into the Commission of the Peace ; but he not being found in this last Commission, it has been some disgust to him. I believe his wife (who is a discret woman) wishes him in, for no other reason than it may estrange him from some very mean associates of his, and ashame him out of an idle habit of profane swearing. It can have no ill to the government, and will be a lasting tie upon him to my Lord's interest." *Seal.*

J[AMES] H[ILTON] to GEORGE KENYON, Vice-Chancellor of the County Palatine of Lancaster.

1121. 1710, July 20. Gray's Inn.—" I should be very glad to hear from you often, especially in these bustling times, wherein Whig and Tory is the only conversation, but the Tories talk the loudest now in the coffee houses, and it is agreed of all sides that the judgement of the Court is against the Whiggs ; the only dougt is whether there must be a *cœffal execuco* (?) against them or noe. Some say that upon that, the Whiggs have promised to mend, which they have roome enough to do. *Quere*, if they are to be trusted ? My Lord Rivers has an interest in the Middlesex freeholders, as Constable of [the] Tower, which he gives to Smithson and Ba[r]tie, Tories ; *quære*, under the rose, if this will not mend Wigan ? I am afraid I have quite lost Mr. Okeley and my Lord Anglesey, who has a place of 6,000*l. per annum ;* for, since the time that I refused to be concerned against you, they seem not to speak to me so freely as formerly : howsoever, if it were [to] do again, I would doe it, for I always be true to my friend, whatever happens. Notwithstanding this, if affaires turne, I believe I have a good friend remaining who will be of service to me in the matter of an office, but I have the hard fortune to be such a naked gull, that I am so far from having cloaths fit to appear in and money in my pocket, that I have scarcely so much as pockets left to put it in, if I had any. I hear my brother is to receive, by the hands of Jack Phim, who is my friend, 200*l*. out of Ireland ; if so, this sum would come very opportune to make interest for an office with, or if that faild, I could put it to such advantage as never to troble my relations, which is the thing I do heartily abhorr. My brother H[ilton] has given my other brother, besides making him master of everything, 700*l*. upon the bankers' buisness."

———— to his cousin, GEORGE KENYON.

1122. 1710, September 19. Gray's Inn.—This day, the officers of the Duchy waited upon the Lord Berkeley of Berkshire, as Chancellor of the Duchy. He has a very good character, was a younger brother, and educated to the law, and is an ingenious man, and commended for his mildness and temper. He is of the same party with yourself, that is, a churchman ; though you have seemed to act another part of late years. It is said the Parliament will be dissolved on Thursday. My Lady Anglesea is with child, and so Arthur Annesley does not take upon himself yet the title of Earl. It is said Sir Thomas Pois, Baron Price, and Mr. Ettrick, will be Commissioners of the Great Seal. . . . It is thought the Tories will have a majority in the elections, though some say the City will be but indifferent, by reason of the Bank and Companies.

ROGER KENYON to his sister[-in-law], MRS. KENYON.

1123. 1710, October 7.—It is not impossible but I might find somebody who would mention the matter you speak of to Lord Berkeley, if it be true that he is indisposed to keep the old officers, but then it will undoubtedly be expected in these elections, and especially at Preston, where the Courts are held, that the Chancellor and his Vice-Chancellor should be on the same side. I have heard that the present Chancellor has recommended Mr. Ansly for member there, having formerly served for that place, and if Mr. Manwaring give up all thoughts of appearing, as it is likely he will, and the measures my brother may think fit to observe with the late Chancellor, will allow him to appear for Mr. Ansly, who in truth is a very honest gentleman. I do not doubt but I can engage him to move my Lord in my brother's cause. My poor Lord Kilmorey, after the small-pox was all gone off, died the 20th day for want of strength to spit up what fell upon his lungs, he being inclining to a consumption before he fell ill. *Seal of arms, broken.*

RICHARD EDGE to GEORGE KENYON.

1124. 1710, October 30.—" It is ten to one you had the newes yesterday that Sir George Warburton and Mr. Cholmondeley carried it for knights for Cheshire, by a great majority, but perhaps you have not heard yet how yesterday morning, about two, they sett the bells on ringing at Manchester, and rang till service time for joy thereof." *Seal.*

SIR R. BRADSHAIGH to GEORGE KENYON.

1125. 1710[-11], March 6.—" As to sending you some wine to Bolton, it will so much exceed the price you mention, that, unless you require it in your next, I shall not venture to send any. Florence is sold here at 4s. 6d. per flask, new French wine at 6s. and 7s. a bottle, nothing of Spanish wine worth drinking, under 2s. 6d., so that I believe you might be better and cheaper fitted from Chester or Liverpool. The Lottery Bill passed the Royal assent this day, and how it will fill is yet uncertain, but the advantage is much greater than in the last, which, though it may be a means to raise the money at present, yet at long run it will help to increase the debt of the nation."

Sir R. Bradshaigh to George Kenyon.

1126. 1710[-11], March 24.—"You may assure yourself I used my endeavours to have put your money in the Lottery, but it was impossible to do it, though I was very early that morning in the City, and a vast number of persons was disappointed as well as myself. It is thought there may be another Lottery. As for buying up any of the tickets, I cannot tell how to advise you, such advantage is made of them by the stock-jobbers. As to our business with the Rector [of Wigan?], counsel believe if we cannot carry it to have the gallery put up in the old place, that we shall so far prevail as to have a proper place given us in the room of it, and that the organ will not be allowed to be set up there, and that we shall be considered for the damage done in pulling it down. As to a *Quo Warranto*, which you hear the rector intends to bring against the town, I do not fear any motions that way. *Seal of arms.*

Sir R. Bradshaigh to the Rev. Mr. Sumner, in Wigan.

1127. 1711, March 31.—"It will be verry materiall to know how the Corporation came to sitt in those seates where the Rector's servants now sitt, and whether they had not a right to them, but I understood always that the Rector's seate was the place where they used to sit, before the gallery was built; likewise, how they came to leave the north isle, and what right they had to that seate, and what title they have to it, who enjoy it now. It will be very necessary to prove titles to all or most of them seates where the Rector calls the Old Chancell, for their councell said Bishop Brigman built the present chancell, which was an addition to the church, for that the lenth of the church was no ferther than the Maior's gallery, which I must owne I cannot believe, because my chancel must have been built at the same time, and I beleive it is as old as any part of the church; but pray informe yourself about it. They have got an old book of Bishop Brigman's which they intend to give as evidence, and in the beginninge of it, the Bishop calls God to witness the whole contents of it to be true. Remember the old man in Scarsbrick."

C. Z. Stanley to George Kenyon.

1128. 1711, April 5. London.—There is a bill before the House of Commons for qualifying justices. It is proposed 300li. a year to be the qualification. "We are now in a vein for building churches; I do not know why you may not have as much reason to desire help as others. If it is thought proper, I shall be very glad to do what you think may promote the same good for yours that is in my power." *Seal.*

R[oger] Kenyon to his brother, George Kenyon.

1129. 1711, April 7.—You are so much a college man still, that I dare say you will be concerned to know that we have lost Dr. Gower at St. John's, who died about ten days ago. His place, indeed, is very worthily filled by Dr. Jenkins, who was a part of our family in Brownlow Street, 2 or 3 months since Christmas. He is likewise chosen Margaret professor.

SIR R. BRADSHAIGH to GEORGE KENYON.

1130. 1711, May 5.—The qualification for Justices of the Peace for our county is an hundred pounds *per annum*, which is less than other counties, except Wales. As to the new lottery, it is not yet settled, but nobody can subscribe less than an hundred pounds.

PROCEEDINGS in a SUIT between RALPH BANKS and others against the Honourable and Reverend EDWARD FINCH, Clerk, Rector of Wigan, and others.

1131. 1711, May.—The suit relates to the church of Wigan. The respondents claimed that the two chancels—called by the names of the upper and lower chancel, the old and new chancel, and sometimes the bishop's and parson's chancel—belonged to the rector of the said church, but the appellants contended that in reality, notwithstanding the several names, there was only one chancel, and that part of the church called the old chancel was, upon the fall of the rector's chancel, borrowed from the parish, and was part of the nave, and in that part of the said church was the gallery, wherein the Mayor, Bailiffs, and other officers of the Corporation of Wigan used to sit, and that the parishioners paid for the repair of the said old chancel. It appears that the rector collected a fund for erecting an organ in the old chancel, for which purpose the gallery, where the Corporation sat, was pulled down, and no provision made for the Corporation. The appellants said that the said fund was insufficient to maintain an organ in repair, or to pay an organist, and in that part of the church called the old chancel, are divers vaults and burial places belonging to several families in the parish of Wigan, where the parishioners have immemorially buried, without leave of the rector; that there was particularly a vault pertaining to the estate of Gorse, formerly belonging to the family of Lowe and then to the family of Rigby, and another to the family of Ashurst, of Ashurst, and that over the same vaults were pews or seats belonging to the same families; that the only old and proper chancel, now called the easternmost chancel of the Church of Wigan, being ruinous or fallen down before the time of Bishop Bridgeman, late Bishop of Chester, the same was, in part only, rebuilt by the said Bishop upon the old foundation, and that the "ranke or range" of single pillars in the old chancel was of the same figure and size with the rest of the pillars in the middle aisle, and the place called the old chancel was separated from the easternmost chancel by two double hollow bulky round pillars, which were fluted and worked in small rounds down to the bottom, and upon a view, it would appear that the said two pillars could not be placed there but as bounding or flanking a passage into some more easternly building.
Depositions in support of above allegations, 22 *pp. brief.*

R[OGER] K[ENYON] to his sister[-in-law], MRS. KENYON.

1132. 1711, October 27.—" I saw Mr. W. Shippen, who told me he had received a letter from the head of Brazen-nose, who said he would favour what he could Mr. Entwissle's pretensions, but he added that the young man, he finds, was a Whig, which was against the present humour of the College. In truth, unless the young man's learning distinguish him a good deal, I doubt not the party he is of will be some prejudice to him, for our Colleges, like all other places, get into parties. You have a new scene among you, the courting of Mrs. Walmesley; there seems to be a great deal of knight errantry in it." *Seal of arms.*

ROGER KENYON to his sister[-in-law], MRS. KENYON.

1133. 1712, July 10.—"We have news to-day, by an express from Dunkirk, that we are in full possession of the town and citadel, etc., and now whether our allies will come into the peace or continue the war by themselves, is no very great matter, in my opinion. Certain it is the war is at an end as to England, unless our allies will needs have us against them. The guns of the Tower have gone off this morning, upon this account."

The SAME to the SAME, at Salford.

1134. 1712, September 6.—"I met Sir R. Brads[haigh] a day or two ago; he intends to be in the country, as he says, about a fortnight hence, and though I do not always give him credit, in this matter I do, because he is pretty watchfull about his elections, and who is chose Mayor this next term, may probably serve for the election the next sumer; accordingly he told me his brother is chose Alderman, and is designed for next Mayor. I tell you that, if he should not have acquainted my brother with it before, my brother may have begunn to think whether it be altogether safe to trust so near a relation of Sir Roger's with a power of being partial, if he pleases, and how near soever the time seems, yet nobody can well foresee what alterations of partys and interests may happen by that time.

"Lord Rivers' will is very much blamed for forgetting his legitimate daughter, in favour of his natural one. It is probable some disputes may arise about it, and I sopose Lord Barramore is got into Lancashire to get possession of all he could; it may happen to be of some use if my brother went to wait of him."

LORD BERKELEY to [GEORGE KENYON].

1135. 1712, October 23.—"Since you cannot, at present, think of any body soe proper for the office of Sherif as Mr. Valentine, I am very willing he should have it, having noe objection to him, but what I told yon in my last of the apprehension I had, that he would not be thought soe impartial as were to be wished in a Sherif, in case of any tryals in the great cause wherein he was concerned, but by what you tell me of him I do not doubt but he will behave himself like an honest man, and I desire you will let him know that I will offer his name to the Queen, when the time comes for pricking of Sherifs, and that you will send me his christian name. I have been very much pressed from Preston to send the name of the gentleman I intend to recommend att the next election, because Sir Harry Houghton and Mr. Fleetwood have declared they would stand, but besides that, the gentleman I have a mind to is out of town, and the distance to the election. I have some other reasons that make me unwilling to recommend soe long beforehand. I will acquaint you with them when you come to town, which you gave me hopes would be before Christmas, for your advice in that, as well as in other things, will always be much esteemed."

SIR R. BRADSHAIGH to GEORGE KENYON.

1136. 1712, November 15.—Duke Hamilton and my Lord Mohun fought this morning in Hyde. Park, and both died before they were brought home. The quarrel was about their law suit.

F. CHOLMONDELEY (?) to his cousin, [GEORGE KENYON].

1137. 1712, November 15.—" This evening I saw the good Doctor [Kenyon], who, betwixt some city patients and suburb attendances, is fully employed. This day, the death of Duke Hamilton and Lord Mohoun, both killed, is all the noise of the town. They met in the Park this morning. Hamilton killed Mohoun at the first thrust, and Mohoun's second, Macarty, killed Hamilton as he was getting into his coach, and after he had run his sword through him, hit him as he stood on the step of the coach, down right butchering with his back on him all the while. As yet he his not taken, but I hope he will be. Mr. Manering died on Thursday last, and the town reports he hath left his daughter (?) Oldfield, the player, twenty thousand pounds, following Lord Rivers' example."

SIR R. BRADSHAIGH to GEORGE KENYON.

1138. 1712, November 18.—" Last Sunday, my Lord Willoughby and I dined with my Lord Berkley; he has promised to write to Mr. Walls, of the Moore Side, he has interest with him to engage him. My Lord Berkley and I have had a good deale of talk about your standing the next Parliament, and you may depend upon his friendship, as likewise what service he can doe with whomsoever is made our Lord Lieutenant to engage him immediately. It is thought my Lord Cardigan will be the man, but this is onely surmise att present. I do not doubt but we shall doe well enough with my Lord T——, and, the first opportunity, will mention it to him, and nothing else shall be wanting. The Bishop of Chester is not in towne, but will see him when hee returns out of the country. I think the death of D[uke] H[amilton] is no loss to us, for he had no great mind you should be chosen att Wigan, if he could have found out means to hinder it. Mr. Fleetwood has lost a friend of him, for he was endeavouring to have sett him up att Preston as the Chancelour's man. I received Mr. K——pe's letter to Mr. S——r last post ; the contents are a little extraordinary, but I do not doubt we shall manage matters well enough. I will let you know what passes when I have seen my Lord B——re [Barrymore ?], and if I find him resolved to stand, I will lose no time in securing that T——r and all other persons here. Nobody can tell yett how matters stand betwixt the two lords, as to the Yorkshire estate, but I believe there is like to be some difference, so I shall take proper measures as I see occasion offers."

A SCHEME FOR RAISING MONEY.

1139. 1712.—A scheme for raising 1,800,000*li.* upon standing orders in the Exchequer, payable, in course, out of a fund of 168,003*li. per annum* for thirty-two years ; with a certain increase of principal and interest, according to several classes, in the same manner as the two million classes were last year; and in this scheme there are 1,800 premiums or prizes, which make the premiums or prizes just one to nine over and above the certain increase of principal and interest in every class. *Printed by John Barber.*

R[OGER] K[ENYON] to his sister[-in-law, MRS. KENYON].

1140. 1712–13, January 3.—Recommending her to send his godson to Westminster School, where there are houses at which boys (at least those no older than his godson) pay but 20*li.* a year for boarding, and the schooling but 5 or 6 guineas.

F F

PETER SHAKERLEY to GEORGE KENYON.

1141. 1712[-13], January 20. Westminster.—"If you find you shall meet with oposition at the next election of a member to serve for Wigan, in the room of my cozen, Henery Bradshaigh, deceased, give due notice to my cozen, John Booth, ironmonger, in Warrington, to his brother, Laurence Booth, esquire, at Tremlow, in Cheshire, and to Doctor Fogg and Mr. Callis, at Chester, and they will com and vote for you. I could not see Parson Walls, of Sanbach, nor Mr. Brayon, but I spoke to cozen Swettenham, and hee will stay at home. I could not prevail with Tom Cowper, of Chester (Mr. Callis, his son-in-law), neither to vote for you nor to promise to stay at home, but I am tould you will not meet with opposition.

"Last night Sir Roger shewed me your draughts of petitions from Wigan and the Fylde country, for makeing Douglas navigable, but the first petition for leave to bring in the Bill, should have been from the Justices and Grand Jury at the Quarter Sessions at Ormskirk, Preston, or Wigan. I doubt it is now too late for that, therefore, inclosed is such a draught of petition as I conceive will be propper enough for leave to bring in the Bill, it being signed by such Justices of Peace, gentlemen, and freeholders, as have estates adjacent to the said river, from Wigan to Hesketh Bank."

R. BRADSHAIGH to GEORGE KENYON, "att his house in Manchester."

1142. 1712[-13], March 21.—Captain Lee, who sets out for Lancashire this afternoon, will give you a full account of what passed. I think "the Lord" has tied himself down not to oppose you, if you stand; "this should not be talked on, least it putt somebody els upon the thoughts of standing; which Mr. Vernon told Captain Lee, Mr. Brigman intended. But my Lord B[arrymo]re says quite otherwise. I hope you will be in towne as soone as possible after your election; I shall want you about the River Act, and other matters of consequence, not proper to write about." What is Lord Willoughby doing, and "how do you stand with him, since his coming down? He is in bad health, and does not intend to live at Shaw Place."

RICHARD LANGTON to GEORGE KENYON, M.P.

1143. 1713, May 8. Preston.—The news of Mr. Southwell being lately elected as a member for Tregony, in Cornwall, has made great alarm amongst us here, and though, to all thinking people, it is no reason but that gentlemen may serve for this place in the next Parliament, but our adversaries make use of it as an argument to the ordinary people, that they are discharged from their promises to him. *Seal of arms, broken.*

RICHARD LANGTON to GEORGE KENYON.

1144. 1713, May 15. Preston.—I believe Mr. Southwell's friends have already spent 100*li.* amongst his voters here, and their bellies and pockets are as empty as at the beginning; and further expenses are necessary to establish an interest (if possible), but to name a sum I cannot tell how, for the expense will be uncertain. If you please, you may hint to the Chancellor, or Mr. Southwell, that letters of compliment from one of them to Mr. Aldermen Sudell, Lemon, Gruddell, and Lamplugh, and also to Mr. Rawstorn, Mr. Foster, Dr. Farington, and Mr. Thornton (which two last are useful and zealous friends) might be of good service.

Ralph Assheton to George Kenyon.

1145. 1713, May 17. Preston.—Mr. Houghton, of Ormskirk, died on Friday, and Mr. Eyre was with me yesterday and desired I would procure a writ *de coronatore eligendo* from you. He tells me he intends to offer himself to the county, as coroner. Sir T. Stanley died about half an hour before Dick Houghton. *Seal.*

William Bradshaigh to George Kenyon, M.P., "to be left at Sir Roger Braidshaigh's house, in Frith Street, near Soho Square."

1146. 1713, May 22.—"I received both your letters, the latter of which I shewed to the Corporation, who are very well pleased with the tender of your service to represent us [in] the next Parliament." Since I am at the head, I will answer for the body that they think you most capable of serving them, in conjunction with my brother. Captain Shakerly is very much in your favour. I thank you for sending me the Votes. *Seal of arms, broken.*

Dr. R. Wroe to his brother-in-law, George Kenyon, M.P.

1147. 1713, May 24.—"I am very heartily glad, by yours, of the right understanding between Sir Roger and you, the doubt of which gave your friends no little uneasiness. If Lord Bar[rymore] has already trickt you, you have less reason to expect very faire play for the future. It is said he hopes to unqualify you, in point of estate, which is another proof of his disingenuity, and I mention it as such, not that I think it can hurt you, nor that his interest can be considerable, if your friends stick by you, as I hope they will. I have writ to Mr. Pigot, Mr. Shaw, and Mr. Blackburn. I met Mr. Pigot yesterday at the funeral of Mr. Newcome, of Middleton, who very freely promised his vote, and presence if need be, though he would not do so for Sir Roger, unless on my account. Mr. Shaw says (as formerly) that he never promises, but I doubt not but you may depend both on him and Mr. Blackburn. I have not yet writ to Chester, because I think to be there shortly, but would have you get Mr. Shakerley's letter to his friends there, which will much prevaile with them. If the Parliament end as you mention, it is well that it is with a thanksgiving. The Treaty is not yet come down that I hear on, and if you could strive to send it, it will be acceptable. I am sorry your indisposition returns, and wish you could vote all your members free from the gout and all other ill humours. I am glad to see, today, that the Yorkshire bill for enclosing commons for the benefit of poor vicarages and chappels, is like to pass. I hope we shall have the like in other places."

John Sumner to George Kenyon.

1148. 1713, May 31.—"I thought it most adviseable to have had all the burgesses together at Serjeant Langshaw's, but he enclined to go from house to house to them, so I let him have his mind. You were saying you had a mind to oblige Ralph Ashton, so the last week, I told him that if three or four pound would do him a kindness, I did believe I could prevail with you to lend it him; it will engage both him and his son, but it must be done soon. Tho: Mullineux has promised me to vote for you, and I believe will. I have reason to think Bayliff William Brown will vote for you and Sir Roger. My Lord Barrymore's steward was in town, drinking, Thursday and Friday last, and Calvert keeps drinking continually; he is much at Randle Crooks, and Randle will, I believe, be for my Lord, in hopes of great shotts, unless Mr. Mawsdesley can get a promise from him for Sir Roger and you. Mr. Mawdesley makes him Bayliff of the Hundred, and Mr. Mawsdesley being now at home, on this side, it would do well for you to write to Mr. Mawsdesley to send for Randle and get a .positive promise from him, or threaten to turn him out of his place, otherwise he will be lost, and perhaps giving his place to another (if he will not promise) may get another vote—but do it forthwith. There should be some money ordered to be drunk, at times, with halfe a dozen or halfe a score burgesses ; it is what they expect, and Calvert gives drink to all that came to him. I have spent all I could shift for. I have told the two Langshaws I will contrive some way to get them in serjeants, at Miclemas ; there is no other way of keeping them from going over to my lord."

RICHARD LANGTON to GEORGE KENYON, M.P., "at his lodgings at the White House, in Brounlow Street, near Drury Lane."

1149. 1713, June 12. Preston.—"I have inquired of Mr. Stanley, Governor of the House of Correction, concerning Johnson, the landwaiter, named·in your letter, who tells me that Johnson is under a very dull and melancholy distraction, and, in all probability, never likely to be restored so farr to his senses as to be capable for business. He keeps him very close, and so tyed or chained, that he cannot do himself any mischief, for he has attempted to cut his own throat since he came into the House of Correction. Mr. Stanley says that Mr. Smith, the Collector at Leverpool, told him that he onely intends to continue Johnson in his place till his halfe yeare is up, which ends in the latter end of July next. We are all under great expectations what the House of Commons will do upon the Articles of Commerce and Trade. There is a great many severall sortes of trades and manufactures to be considered. I wish these points well setled. . . . . . I hear that the Judges in the Queen's Bench will, next week, give their opinions about a petty-bagg in the Chancery here, and that there is hopes we shall have their judgment for it, notwithstanding the great opposition and struggle made by the other side. . . . . . Pray, will it not be proper to acquaint the Chancellor with the design against the jurisdiction of the County-Palatine, and the pains and charge hath been to maintain the point about a petty-bagg ? I wish his Lordship would be prevailed with to grant me transmission orders out of Court; for g . . . . ing them upon petitions has been of no long standing, and is of very pernicious consequence, and oftentimes detained upon false suggestions, on the petitions, and without hearing both sides." All this was provided against by recently drawn rules, which, however, he cannot get signed by the Chancellor and officers.

JOHN SUMNER to GEORGE KENYON, M.P., at "the Great White House," in Brownlow Street, London.

1150. 1713, June 14.—Advising him to pay certain expenses at his election at Wigan. Lord Willoughby went to London on Friday ; they say Bland, the late lord's gentleman, came down for him.

RICHARD WROE to GEORGE KENYON, M.P.

1151. 1713, June 19. [Manchester.]—"I am got so far at liberty from the gout as to be free from paine and able to ride out as far as Nev on, but dare not yet attempt a journey to Chester, but have not been wanting to do you what service I can there, by writing, and do not find there they have any great opinion of Lord Bar[ymore]. However, some of them, I ′believe, will be for him. Mr. Knipe is now at Wardley, where Mr. High Sheriff was with him on Weddensday, as hee told mee yesterday, and says hee does not seem so confident as hee was, nor can I learn that he has done any great feats at Wigan, and would do less, if either Sir Roger or you were present, or at least some one for you to warm their memoryes; and, perhaps, if neither of you can be there, it might be a proper time at the Thanksgiving Day, to help on the rejoyceing, and promote your own interests. I onely give the hint, and leave it to your thoughts, supposing Mr. Knipe may be busy at that time. Mr. Serjeant, of Stand, is to be buryed on Monday, said to be dead very rich. I heare much of a poem called, I think, *The Fable of the Birds;* ′if worth while, pray send it in a post letter. Give service to all friends in your house."

JOHN WALMESLEY to GEORGE KENYON.

1152. 1713, June 23. Wigan.—"I have received from Sir. H. Houghton a request for my vote for Sir R. Bradshaigh and yourself, at the next election. "Sir, it is not my temper to make myselfe busey, and yet I have a desire to acquaint you with townes-talke, on confidence you will suppress it. That through the rector's and Mr. Bridgman's interest, and a disgust that some burgesses have taken against Sir R. B., it is believed the Lord Barrymore may make a prity strong intrest. As to yourself, I hear not any personal dislike, but only that Sir R. should assume •upon himself to impose one, without the town's consent." *Seal of arms.*

"THE ENGLISHMAN; OR, A CHOICE SPEECH AT THE ELECTION OF A SPEAKER, ETC."

1153. [1713.]—"Since you are now upon the choice of a Speaker, give me leave, as an Englishman, to acquaint you that her Majesty, the last session of the last Parliament, at which time I had not the honour to be a member of this House, promised to lay before us the Treaty of Commerce, which treaty, I beg leave to say, is demonstrably against the interest of Great Brittain, and for that reason I cannot but highly applaud the proposall made you for supplying the Chair with so honorable and worthy a member as Sir T[homas] H[anmer] must be allowed to be. I think I am not irregular in nameing him, since the Speaker is not in the Chair, nor would I, gentlemen, take this liberty, but that I find it impossible to omitt this oppertunity of doing an honour to Sir T[homas] H[anmer] by publickly asserting that Dunkirk is not yet demolished. And now I am upon the affair of Dunkirke, permit me, sir, to say I shall never be satisfied till the House of Han[ove]r shall think fitt to give the same assureance of a good correspondence betweene them and this Crown, which her Majesty hath been pleased frequently to give us. And this I say out of the profound respect I have for her Majesty, and the duty I owe to the house of Han[ove]r, and therefore I cannot but again repeat that I entirely concurr with that worthy gentleman who thought fit to propose Sir T[homas] H[anmer] for their Speaker. But at the same time, I must affirme that had I been to name you one, it should not have been this gentleman. I hope this is no reflection upon Sir T[homas] H[anmer]. The House, out of their candour and great temper, I am persuaded, will not think it one, when I say that I would not have named the same person which the worthey member has named you. I must confess, Mr. Jod . . el, the qualifications which I should have regarded should have been such as, in my humble opinion, are absolutely necessary to qualifie a person for this great employment. I would have proposed to you, sir, one who had thoroughly applyed himselfe to the perusall of ' The Crisis,' a book lately published, the perusall of which will, I believe, more certainly make him who shall think fitt to study it, a good Speaker, than him who wrote it, a good member. I find gentlemen are diverted with what I say; I acknowledge the honour this day done me in their great desire to hear what I had to say, and in their just reception they have given to what I have said. But, sir, to come to the purpose, I will demonstrate the Bill of Commerce to be a bad bill, and therefore I hope that we shall agree upon Sir T[homas] H[anmer] for our Speaker. Those gentlemen who are not of my opinion will, I hope, in this debate, confine themselves to the subject; and as to that gentleman whom I rise up to answer, I hope, if I have offered anything irregular, that he will consider I am but a new member, and that as I came much later into this House, I may chance to get much sooner out of it. *Servetur ad imum qualis ab incepto.*"

ROGER KENYON to MRS. KENYON.

1154. 1713–14, February 9.—"I fancy, with all my skill, I could not invent a tale which would surprize thee more than what I am going to tell thee, with great truth, that I was this day marryed. The times, you see, are calm and promise great security, so that for the prudence and seasonableness of it, in that point, you cannot doubt; and for the rest, all that I can tell thee at present is, that her name was Cotton, daughter to Sir John Cotton, of Huntingdonshire; in stature and fattness not much different from myself, about as good a Jacobite, and in every other quality and circumstance a great deal better. When you come to know her more I will let you judge for yourself, and I make no doubt but you will love one another very well."

MR. STEELE'S SPEECH upon the proposal of Sir Thomas Hanmer for Speaker of the House of Commons.

1155. 1713–14, February 16.—"At the close of the last session of Parliament, her Majesty was graciously pleased to declare from the throne, that the late rejected Bill of Commerce between Great Britain and France should be offered this House. That declaration was certainly made that every gentlemen who should have the honour to be returned hither, might make himself master of that important question. It is demonstration, that Bill ought to be taken notice of, and no man can have so great meritt to this nation att this time, as his by whose weight and authority that Bill was thrown out. I rise up to do him honour in some measure, and distinguish myself by saying I wish him our Speaker for that his inestimable service to his country."

PETER SHAKERLEY to GEORGE KENYON.

1156. 1713[–14], March 6. Westminster.—"By the resolutions of the Committee of the whole House this day made (who were, by order of the House, to take into consideration the Act for quallifying members to sit in Parliament, and which resolutions come with this), you will see how plainly they are levelled against you, in particular. They were brought in ready cooked (pockett questions) by Mr. Ward, for Newton, and the time proposed for giving in rent rolls, &c. was to have been but ten days from the time of reading the petition, which was Wednesday last, so that you would have been an offender, for want of due notice of the order, for it will be Tuesday next before the House can have agreed to these resolutions, the House being adjourned to that day; and if the House do agree to them, it will be Wednesday before they come out in print, and Thursday before they can be sent by the post to you. I opposed these unfair proceedings, and, upon debate, instead of 10 days, 15 days was incerted. So that you are now to suppose the worst, which is that the House, upon the Report, Tuesday next, will not allow a longer time then fifteen days from Wednesday last.

" Therefore, send up forthwith such paper, fairly written, signed by you, as the said resolutions require, and, least one should miscarry, send one to Sir Roger and another to me, both signed by you."

[George Kenyon to Peter Shakerley ?]

1157. 1713[-14], March 10. Manchester.—"There is an objection against one of the petitioners (Mr. Bridgman) which I think wee ought to have advantage of, and which Sir Roger was acquainted with, but what time is most proper to try the House's sence in it, I submitt to you. The matter is this. At the election, it was demanded that all the candidates should take the oaths prescribed by the Act. Mr. Bridgman, who was absent, has, as I believe, never taken them yet, and the Act declares such a one's election to be voyd, if he refuse or neglect to take them before the returne of the writt of election. I therefore hope he can be no legall petitioner, and, if so, I further hope Lord B——— [Barrymore ?] joyneing in petition with him and makeing it but one petition, will destroy that likewise. To this I know but one answer, that wee have not personally demanded of Mr. Bridgman to take the oath, which was occationed by his perpetuall absence, and I presume, if he had been out of England, it would not have been intended wee should seeke him out, especially since, by his petition, he takes upon him to be apprized of what was done and demanded all the election."

Election Petition.

1158. 1713[-14], March.—Petition of James Barry, Earl Barrymore, in the kingdom of Ireland, and Orlando Bridgman, Esquire, to the House of Commons, against the election of Sir Roger Bradshaigh and George Kenyon at Wigan, they not having estates of the annual value of 300*li*. to qualify them to serve as members.

Receipt for a Salver, and for engraving the same.

1159. 1714, April 9.—Receipt, given by Thomas Beech, of " the ' Blackamoor's Head,' in Cheapside," to Dr. Kenyon :—

" A salver at 6*s*. 2*d*. the ounc, weing 28 oz. 7 pe.	- 8*l*. 15*s*. 2*d*.
For graving the salver - - - - -	- 0*l*. 2*s*. 6*d*.
	8*l*. 17*s*. 8*d*."

George Kenyon to his wife.

1160. 1714, June 5.—" The Princess Sophia is dead, and of an appoplexy, as it is said. The Exclusion Bill was read yesterday a first time, and ordered a second reading on Monday, without a division upon that point, though many speeches. Lords Bull——ke [Bollingbroke], Angl——y

[Anglesey], and Abington, amongst those for the Bill; Lord Nott[ingham] with those against it. There was a division about hearing council against the Bill, and carried against it 72 against 66, which was a full House, and may perhaps show the fate of the Bill."

1161. 1714, June 15.—ESTIMATE for FUNERAL CHARGES, given by PHILIP MORRIS.

	£	s.	d.
"For a leaden and elme coffin covered with fine cloth, sett off with the best guilt worke - - - -	8	0	0
A herse and 6 horses, at 1*l*. 2*s*. 6*d*. *per* day - - -	6	10	0
Two mourning coaches and six horses ditto - -	13	0	0
Velvet covering for herse and horses - - - -	1	10	0
Seventeen plumes of feathers for herse and horses -	2	10	0
Twenty four buckram escutcheons for herse and horses	2	8	0
12 shields and 6 chapperons - - - - -	2	5	0
12 large pencells and 36 small pencells - - -	3	0	0
A pall—the journey - - - - - - -	1	0	0
12 silk escutcheons for the pall - - - -	3	0	0
A lid and feathers for the top of the corps - - -	1	0	0
3 horsemen, and [to] bare their own charges, at 9*s*. *per* day - - - - - - - - -	5	8	0
6 footmen to attend the herse to the stone's end - -		15	0
12 escutcheons for the pulpit - - - - -	1	4	0
5 yards cloth for the pulpit at — *per* yard; a hatchment for the house - - - - - - -	3	0	0
4 gentlemen's cloakes, at 5*s*. apiece - - - -	1	0	0
12 pair shamy gloves, at 3*s*. 6*d*. a pair - - -	2	2	0
12 hats (?) at 3*s*. 6*d*. apiece, for gentlemen - - -	2	2	0
6 scarves at 10*s*. apiece - - - - - -	3	0	0
12 hatbands for servants, at 2*s*. apiece - - -	1	4	0
12 pair gloves for coachmen, at 1*s*. apiece - - -		12	0
12 pair gloves for servants, at 1*s*. 6*d*. a pair - -		18	0
19 yards of bayes for the chancell, [and] bayes for the life and deth - - - - - - - - -		19	0
12 paper escutcheons for the chancell - - -		12	0
	66	19	0

" This 15 June, 1714, I agree with Roger Kennyon, Esquire, to perform all the articles above recited for the sum of sixty four pounds."

ROGER KENYON to his brother, GEORGE KENYON.

1162. 1714, July 29.—" The quarrels at Court, indeed, are ended, but it is by the rout of the Lord Treasurer. Yesterday, or the evening before, his staff was taken from him, and the Treasury is to be [in] commission, for some time, at least. Lord Bolinbroke, and the Chancellor, are to rule the world, and it is said they will be swingeing Torys, and not a Whig left in place a month hence ; however, I do not find that the Court will have many more removes in it, either from their own affection to quitt with the Treasurer, or the Court's aversion to them. The City seems so unconcerned at this work, that I do not find the stocks to alter one bitt upon it. It has one present ill effect, that it furnishes an excuse to let poor Mr. Bedford (?) lye where he is, and when they will come to themselves upon that head, I know not."

R[OGER] K[ENYON] to his brother, GEORGE KENYON.

1163. 1714, August 12.—The event of the Queen's [death] was generally expected to be attended with confusion; nothing like it has occurred. Everything is in tranquillity, and the stocks rise upon the bettering of the times. Indeed, to tell the truth, the Queen and her Ministry seem very clear of the charge some people made against them, of endeavouring to bring in the Pretender. Whatever thoughts she had upon that subject, she is gone to answer for to Him who only can judge of thoughts. *Seal of arms.*

The EARL OF DERBY to GEORGE KENYON, at Manchester.

1164. 1714, September 14. London.—" When I came hither, which was within few days after the Queen dyed, my sister, Colchester, gave me a letter from my Lord Baramore, by which he desired the same thing you did some time after. I did not then believe you would have stud (*sic*) at Wigan, so I made no difficulty to let h[im] know I should be glad it were in my powre to serve him. I thought I could doe no less, sins I had refused him last time; you haveing spoken to me furst, l hope you will think this a suffitiant excuse." *Seal of arms.*

JOHN SUMNER to GEORGE KENYON.

1165. 1714, September 19.—" On Friday last, John Rigby (steward to the late Lord Rivers) came to me and, after some talke about the election of Mayor, and the differences that were in the town, told me it was in my power to make peace. I said I wisht it were. ' Yes,' says he, ' you may '; and the expedient he offered was that I would propose to you to desist, and he would undertake my Lord should repay all the expence you have been at. He pressed me mightily, and made me promise to propose this to you and to meet him at Betty Bolton's, in the Scoles, on Tuesday next, and give him your answer. I therefore send the bearer over on purpose, and desire you will, by him, let me know in a line what answer, and in what manner, I must give Rigby ou Tuesday. I have good reasons to think that he was ordered to make this proposall; Knipe was then in Wigan, and Rigby would gladly have sent for him to us, but I would not suffer him."

[GEORGE KENYON to JOHN SUMNER.]

1165A. [1714, September.]—" I wonder you should entertain a proposition of that sort from that quarter. I hoped you had more discretion than to suffer yourself to be amused with it, from so unlikely a hand too, which I looke upon no other than an artifice to draw off some of my friends by it. You may be sure I will give no manner of answer to it, nor would I have writt, but in respect to yourself. Now to speak to yourself. You must be witness I have allwayes declared that to the reall quiett and settlement of the towne I would be a willing sacrifice; and if I be the Jonas that keeps up the storm, that you throw me overboard. You say you have not acquainted Sir R. Bradshaigh with it, which I much wonder att. However my own inclinations stood, I will not move the least step in that affair without his." *Draft, on back of preceding letter.*

JOHN BERESFORD to his brother.

1166. 1714, December 21.—" I could exchange a sheet of storys with you, but have lost the pleasure on't; since, by gradation, they gott to the top of villany at Derby, which was to make about 92 more burgesses of the Duke, and Lord James' tenants, sent for out of Scarsdale (in all about 200). The wonder is over, and talke ceases. The last account is from the King's Bench, where attachments were granted, in extraordinary manner, upon bare motion of the Attorney-Generall, against five or six gentlemen, in and about the towne of Derby, to appear and traverse without any notice of the information or summonce, to shew cause why attachments should not goe out; and all the while, the Lord Chief Justice seems to bee sorry, and wonder at the violent proceedings of the Corporation, though the cheife manager (Tom Gisborne) has letters from him every weeke. Some applications have been made (as I perceive by Tom Bagshaw) to give disturbance in the county, but I do not find they take. Wee have now got a Sheriff, which releives us of some fees, and gives some hope as to jurys, upon proceedings that may happen in his yeare. The man lives in Derby, and hath been offered Tom Gisborne's friendship and interest to gett him off for a summe of money which . . . . Tom thought the covetous wretch would readily swallow, by which hee might gett both the bribe and his owne ends; but the man generously refused his friendship, and though his father, Mr. Burton, of Weston, was sheriffe but nine years ago, hath taken, and goes on with the office, which animates our Derby friends in some measure."

The AFRICAN COMPANY.

1167. 1714.—The case for and against the African Company. *Various printed papers.*

WIGAN ELECTION.

1168. [1714.]—Depositions of William Low, of Wigan, in the County of Lancaster, labourer, who says that " the night before the last election of Parliament men for Wygan, he, together with Matt: Turner, a comon bayliff, arrested one John Bullock, att the suit of Mr. Boyer, and the same night gave notice of the said arrest to the said Mr. Boyer and Mr. Alexander Leigh, the attorney, who were both friends, and the said Mr. Leigh an agent or manager . . . . was commonly reported to be for the Lord Barrymore, att the said election, whom he found in the great room att the 'Cross Keys,' a publick house in Wygan, with a great deal of company, amongst whom was . . . . whom this deponent was then told was Lord Barrimore. That thereupon, the said Mr. Boyer, Mr. Leigh, and the rest of the company, very much presst this deponent to carry the said Bullock forthwith away to Chorley, which is six miles distant from Wygan, but it being then very late, this deponent desired to be excused, as fearing the prisoner might escape in the dark. And this deponent further saith, that the said bayliffes had then, warrants against Mr. John Sumner, Ralph Langshaw, James Leyland, and other Burgesses of the said burrough, which, he conceives, were then intended to be made use off to prevent their voteing att the said election, for that the said Mr. Leigh and the Lord [Barrymore], and others there present, did appoint this deponent and Alexander Horrocks, servant to the said Matt Turner, to watch at the town hall of Wygan that night, and that if any of the before named persons, against whom they had warrants, did attempt to come into the said hall that night, this deponent and Horrocks should seize and carry them away; and that this deponent and the said Horrocks did watch all or most part of the said night accordingly, and Mr. Leigh and the said company ordered them to call for what drink they had a mind to, and he would take care it should be paid for, and this deponent and the said Horrocks had what drink they pleased, accordingly. And this deponent further saith that he was imployed the next day, being the day of election of members of Parliament, by the said Mr. Leigh. together with Matthew Turner, William Turner, and other bayliffs and assistants, to arrest the said persons before mentioned, as they came to vote; and by direction of the said Mr. Leigh, this deponent and others, the said bayliffes placed themselves upon and att the foot of the said hall-stairs, that being the oncly passage into the said hall, with intention to arrest the said persons accordingly, and carry them away as they were severally arrested . . . . And this deponent further saith that he heard the said Lord, together with Mr. Robert Holt, of Wygan, and the said Mr. Leigh—who was likewise, as this deponent has heard and believes, a manager or agent for the said Lord att the said election—speake to and encourage Thomas Mitton and John Barrow, hatter, and others, to get their friends together the next day, and to stand true to each other and to knock down, or words to that effect, and beat such Haighmen as should appear in the town, and that they would bear them out in so doing; and that the said Mitton and Barrow thereupon declared to their companions below stairs, the said encouragement, and accordingly, with multitudes of their friends armed with clubs and staves, they assembled the next day. And this deponent further saith that he very well remembers that the said Mr. Sumner, Ralph Langshaw, and (he beleeves) James Leyland, did publickly appear and were seen abroad in the town of Wygan, without any manner of absconding, for severall months before the said day of election for members for Parliament, and he beleeves there was no attempt in that time to arrest them, and that from and after the said day of election for members of Parliament, they likewise appeared publickly in town; and this deponent had no orders, and beleeves no other person upon the said warrants had orders, to arrest them untill the day or near the time of choosing a Mayor for the said town, which was upon the third day of October then following."

The humble ADDRESS of the MAYOR, BAILIFFS, and BURGESSES of the CORPORATION OF WIGAN, in the County Palatine of Lancaster, presented by Sir Roger Bradshaigh.

1169. 1715, March 27.—" Dread Sovereign, we begg leave to condole with you the death of her late Majesty, whose memory ought to be dear to the present generation, and whose reigne will be esteemed glorious and happy to the latest posterity, glorious in tryumphs of war and carrying the reputation of the English armes to a height unknowne to former ages; happy in seeing that warr terminate in a generall, solid, and beneficial peace for her people, herself being the arbitress thereof.

" Give to us leave, as the first fruits of that happy peace, to congratulate your Majestie's quiett accession to the Imperiall Throne of these kingdomes. Your Majesty's consummate prudence in government, knowledge and abilities in warr, gives us confidence; your piety and virtues gives us assurance; and your royall issue gives us a prospect of the long continuance of all the blessings that a gratefull and dutifull people can wish for.

" We take this opportunity to return our thanks for your Majesties gracious assureance of protecting the episcopall churches of England; this, with your being in full communication with that church, must make you dear to all the members thereof. We cannot but please ourselves with the hopes that, by the establishment of your family amongst us, the favourable conjuncture which has been so long wished for is now come, to extend the episcopall government to the reformed churches abroad, which, as we believe the only foundation possable to unite the Christian world upon (if ever it must be so happy), so it must render you, above all things, glorious to the whole reformation, by being the happy instrument of so universall a benefitt.

"Upon all these hopes and prospects we are tyed, as well by our interest as the principles of our holy church, to pay you our allegiance in an inviolable manner, and pray that after a long continuance of a prosperous reigne here, you may be translated to one eternall hereafter."

"Conic" Lamps.

1170. 1715, June 25.—Receipt for 5s. given to Dr. Kenyon by Richard Post, collector, for the use of "the Proprietors of the Conic Lamps."

Registration of Papists' Lands.

1171. [after 1715.]--There are particulars of the lands in the county of Lancaster, of the following Papists, viz. :—Hugh Bulling, of Lathom, yeoman ; Humphrey Orrell, of Parr, in the parish of Prescot ; Thomas Johnson, of Downholland, in the parish of Halsall ; William Bradshaw, of Burscough ; Lawrence Wilson, of Ormskirk ; Margaret Assheton, of Abram, widow ; Francis Farrar, of Downholland, in the parish of Halsall ; Richard Moor, of Downholland ; John Boardman, of Ashton, in the parish of Winwick, linen webster ; John Fletcher, of Windle ; and Richard Cropper, of Burscough.

P (?) Kenyon to Mrs. Kenyon, at Gredington.

1172. [1715-16,] January 10.—We have just received an express, dated Dumfries, January 3, which gives an account that the rebels were then at Glasgow, where they are raising a large contribution in cloth, linen, stockings, tartan, bonnets, and cash to a considerable sum. They are not yet joined by the rebels in the north at Perth, Dundee, Aberdeen, etc. Part of General Hawley's army has got to Edinburgh, and the rest expected in a day or two, so far our letter. As to Manchester, they are ready to pull one another's eyes out, and the country is full of thieves and rogues.

Voting on the Triennial Act.

1173. 1716, April 24.—An exact and correct list of the members of the House of Commons who voted for and against the Bill for repealing the Triennial Act. Also of the absent members, which makes this a compleat list.

T. Stafford to "Captain Martell, of Colonel Stanhope's Dragoons, or, in his absence, to Captain Deleuze (?), of the same regiment."

1174. 1716, October 16. Dumfries.—"The misfortunes, disapointments, and ingratitude, I have met with in this vile world, are soe many and great, that I cannot longer bear them, therefore have thought fit to retire, beleiveing it better to dye than to live miserable, which I have already done too long. I beg you will order sentrys on my room and stable, that the people of this town and country may have nothing to doe with my person nor effects. The bearer brings you my writing box, the key of which is here inclosed. In that part of the box that holds the pens and ink, you will find my purse with 29 guineas; in the other, my pockett book relateing to paying the regiment, &c. I beg you will pay my landlord, Gripton, about 40s. for some hay and corn I had of him; my servant about 3l. or 4l. due to him for wages; what you think fit, for burying me; and the rest of the money I desire may be returned to my wife, by bill or otherwise. You may please to direct to Mrs. Stafford, att Mr. Congreaves, of Stretton, in Staffordshire, by Wolverhampton bagg, *per* London, and represent my misfortune as favourably as you can to her. And if you please to write to my father, Thomas Stafford, Esq., at Maxfield, in Cheshire, I desire you would condemn his severe usage of me, as you will see he deserves by the inclosed letters, though I might very reasonably have expected better, considering I have paid severall thousand pounds for him. The books and accounts of the regiment are in my trunk, the accounts and vouchers sealed up in a canvas bagg marked Stanhope, No. 6, where you will find the vouchers for all, except the 14l. 18s. 6d. continjencys, and the 41l. 10s. 0d. I have charged myself with for paying the regiment, which the colonel will please to order, as he thinks fit. This tragicall action has been thought of for some time. I am sorry it has hindred me takeing care of your troop, and doing my duty in the regiment I ought, but hope that will all be forgiven, since it was my misfortune, not my fault ; for it was wholly out of my power to alter my dismal temper, nor could anything divert my melancholy, it was soe deeprooted. If the major and you, secure my horses and effects to be disposed of by auction in the regiment, I hope they will be sufficient to answer anything that I may be charged with by Mr. Bourn, &c., for I would not have Colonel Stanhope suffer the loss of a farthing on my account, nor any officer in his regiment. I hope, and doubt not, but you will have hat reguard to a dead friend, and the rest of the choar to a brother officer, as to insist upon a decent buryall, and in such place as you shall think proper, notwithstanding the clergy and their creatures may object against it. I have ten thousand pardons to ask for giving you this trouble, and many others, but when I consider it will be the last, I readily ghess it will be forgiven. I wish all happiness, glory, and conquest, may ever attend you."

Postscript.—" I beg you will take your fine new hat again, it is in the top of my trunk, but has never been worn. I am very sorry you put yourself to that expence for soe miserable a creature as I am. . . . . . I desire you would accept of my little gun, to keep for my sake. Part of my linen is at wash with Radclyff's wife, of your troop. . . . . . It will be very kind in Colonel Stanhope if he will get my wife in upon the widows' list."

ANTHONY BARLOW to GEORGE KENYON, " at his house in Salford."

1175. 1716, November 18. Stopford.—Is it necessary for me to come to Salford to-day, in order to make a new will to-morrow, for the benefit of my estate and children " before I am any way convicted "? For I think I was told by a lawyer that, by the Act of Parliament " made about the time they pulled downe meeteing-houses," any person summoned by Justices to appear before them to take the oaths, upon a refusal was immediately convicted. And shall be apprehensive it will prove so, unless you send me word to the contrary, and that I have longer time to make my will in than to-morrow, unconvicted.

PETER SHAKERLEY to the MAYOR and MAGISTRATES of the
Corporation of Wigan.

1176. 1717[-18], January 23. Hulm.—"My desire was, and is, that
you might take possession of the west end gallery in Wigan church, the
2nd of next month, at which time, I am tould, the interest of those who
rent seats therein, expires; and I writt to Sir Roger Bradshaigh a good
while since to take effectuall care that not any seat therein should be
disposed of from that time, which hee writt to me hee had don by
giveing a caution thereof to the clerk, who had the disposall of those
seats.

"Last post, I received a letter from Mr. Prescott, the Register at
Chester, to whom I writt before Christmas last, and sent him your
Recorder, Mr. Kenyon's, objections (which hee sent to Sir Roger) for
. . . . the title to be the purchaser of the said gallery. This
inclosed is in answer to it, which I desire you forthwith to communicate
to Mr. Kenyon. I am entirely a stranger to the methods of the Ecclesiasticall Court, and hope I shall always continue soe. I am ready and
willing to pay you the 100*l.* I promised, for the purchase of the said gallery
for you and your successors, haveing good and sure title made to it; but
if there is any debt to workmen or others for building it, or otherwise,
that must be paid out of the 100*l.* purchase money, for every estate
must be freed from debts, &c., to a purchaser."

[DR. ROGER KENYON] to his sister-in-law, MRS. KENYON.

1177. 1718, May.—"I am now removing from Paris; two days
more will be all my stay in it, and where my next to this will be dated,
is hard to say—Flanders or Holland, for I shall go through them both,
in my way home. I could not but be sensibly touched for my relations
in their loss for so good a man as the late worthy warden.[1] As death
is the lot of every man, so is the history of it the subject of all times
and all countries. Saturday last, about 7 in the morning, dyed the
Queen of England, at St. Germains, of a pleurike (*sic*) fever, after 4 or 5
days' illness. She was a lady of great virtues and great sufferings. The
worldly blessings of this life are surely of small esteem in the eye of
Providence, or its ways are very impenetrable to us, or, what is as true
as either, there is another time and place where all accounts will be
most justly stated. Her enemies, too, will dye, and if they have caused
her sufferings wrongfully, I do not envy them their success." *Seal of
arms.*

The SAME to the SAME.

1178. 1718, September 6 (N. S.). Amsterdam.—"You do well to
visit Peel sometimes and keep it in repair. When there are a great
many good fires in it and a great deal of good company, Peel is not an unpleasant place. It is now almost three weekes since I came to this pious
town of Amsterdam, a place of little mirth, but busy enuf, in a country
where scarce anything grows but where everything abounds, and yet, in
this abundance, where they eat and drink, themselves, the worst things
they have, and send the best abroad; in short, where the whole pleasure
and bent of their mind is to get together a great heap of money, and
make very little use of it when they have done. An idle person is one
of the greatest raritys in the country, seems out of his place and in their

[1] Dr. Wroe, Warden of Manchester.

way; so I will even leave them where I found them, and where, I beleive, the last day will find them—in the search of wealth, with all the powers of body and mind. They do, however, say their prayers, and in great variety of languages and all sorts of forms; but the petitions in which they are most devout, I fancy, have a view towards this world."

The SAME to the SAME.

1179. 1718–19, March 17.—"The end of this week, or the beginning of the next, I intend to go down to Cambridge, and design to lodge in the College, where they have promised to get me a room; or, if anything alters that purpose, I shall be found at the 'Bear Inn,' which is one of the best houses in the town, but more convenient, it may be, for me than my brother, being, as he knows, at a small distance from the College, but very near to Mr. Thomkinson. The 'Sun,' or 'Queen's Arms,' are nearer to St. John's, but what sort of landlords they have at present I am too much a stranger there to know. We abound here in reports of, I know not what invasions from Spain. That they are frightened in Exchange Alley is certain, but what projects Cardinal Alberoni may have in his head is [out] of my reach, and whether they will . . . here [or] where, though we do well to take our precautions . . . I fancy, as yet nobody is very sure."

The SAME to the SAME.

1180. 1719, June 9.—"Rumours abound here, as with you, and truth is so mixed with falshood that it is most difficult to separate them. It is, however, no longer doubted but that the Princess Sobiesky is at Rome, and Lord Mar stopt at Geneva, whither K[ing] G[eorge] has writt to thank them for their zeal in his cause; will take a little time to consider what to do with him, but in the mean time, would have him well used. I have heard nothing spoke yet of the deeds of our [vice kings, unless some debate they had about sending a squadron to the Baltick, which the majority of them, being against Mr. Crags, produced an order from his Majesty that one should be sent of 12 men-of-war. For the rest, people seem to wait for some great matter with very curious ears, but upon what ground I know not, I believe they neither."

EDWARD BERESFORD to DR. KENYON, " at his lodgings, number 31 in Gloster Street, near Red Lyon Square."

1181. 1719–20, January 17. [Stockport.]—I have such a great sensibility and soreness in the "joyning" of my head, that I cannot bear the touch of a light wig, but almost always wear a thin silk cap, yet without ever getting cold. What methods are taken to advance a subscription in other parts, this and the neighbouring counties, or in the kingdom in general, I know not; but undoubtedly an application might be made, which would turn to very great account. You are very generous to our design of a new school.

CHURCH SEATS.

1182. 1719[–20], February 20.—Case and opinion of counsel, upon the validity of a grant of a seat in the body of the parish church of Manchester, made by the Bishop of Chester, in 1630, to Sir Alexander Radcliffe.

Information as to Treasonable Language.

1183. 1720, August 31.—Information of Henry Harris, a soldier "in his royal highness George, Prince of Wales', own regiment of Welsh Fuzilleers, commanded by Major General Sabin, now quartered at Manchester," taken before George Cheetham, esquire, Justice of the Peace, that on the 30th August, at ten o'clock at night, he heard John Whiteley, of Manchester, yeoman, say, "I am the man that says, downe with the Rump, and downe with King George, and be damned."

Rights over Tonge Moor.

1184. [1720.]—Statement about rights over Tonge Moor, in the township of Tonge, claimed as belonging to the owner of the capital messuage called "Hall of Wood, in Tonge."

George Kenyon to Mr. Moss.

1185. 1720[-1], February 17. Salford.—"Charles Beswick was with me yesterday, with orders from Mr. Egerton, Mr. Chetham, Mr. Ratcliffe and Parson Ashton, and to-day again from Mr. Warren and Mr. Arderne, all trustees for Manchester Schoole, to tell you they doe noe way intend to oppose your [Navigation] Bill, but that they expect the Schoole Mills to be effectually secured." They suggest a clause, relative to the mills, to form part of the bill; this recites that the revenue of the mills "is an antient charity, founded for the maintenance of a free schoole" within Manchester, and enacts that nothing in the bill shall be taken to give power to the "undertakers" to construct any works which should obstruct the free working of the mills. *Copy.*

Dr. Roger Kenyon to his sister-in-law, Mrs. Kenyon.

1186. 1721, November 2. — "I affirm nothing, but every body talks of a new Parliament. Whether my brother has any sort of intention to busy himself about it, either upon his own account or anybody's els, I know not; but I heard, by Mr. Masters, that he was lately at Wigan, and that Sir R. Br[adshaigh] intends for himself and son. If my brother is of that side, I hope he will put himself to no charge about it, for whatever Sir R. may be in other respects, he is certainly as bad a member of Parliament as can be had. Yesterday, it being moved in the House to lessen the forces, being now in an universall tranquillity, and it being much prest on one side that if it was not now done, a standing army and a land tax would be perpetuated without one word of answer, though desired to say somewhat, the question was called for and carryed, to continue the army, by 99 against 40."

Thomas Robinson, curate of Mottram, to "Mr. Kenyon, counsellor-at-law, living in Salford."

1187. 1722, December 6. Mottram.—"A purchase is proposed for the augmentation of Mottram; and, therefore, the Bishop of Chester desires me to lay before you an abstract of all the writings belonging to the estate, and to ask your opinion. I have sent your fee *per* bearer."

Benjamin Grosvenor to "the Rev: Mr. Wood, in Chowbent."

1188. 1722[-3], February 18. Hoxton Square.—"This comes to desire you to send up an account of your labours at the late rebellion, your dangers and hazards, your expenses and charge, your sufferings and damages, and what you are yet out of pocket. Make it appear as much for the King's service as it really was, and, I believe, it will be an hundred pounds in your way; for, as far as 100*l*. goes, we have a prospect of procuring it for your reimbursement. You are also to send up a letter of thanks (after we have the money secured) to a certain great man, whose name you shall hereafter know. Be as quick as you can. If your former account had been a little more particular, I do not know but it might have been two hundred, instead of one. I leave it to you to *servare modum*. Between tediousness and dryness be a little distinct, but do not be long, and touch it up so as to make the representation as advantageous as you can. God be with you, and give you such success as is hoped for."

Postscript.—"Something about the state of the country about you, how affected; and if you can, suggest anything for the King's service. Direct yours to Mr. Holding, merchant in Fenchurch Street, Fan Court, London."

EDWARD HULTON "to the FEOFFEES of the FREE SCHOOL at Manchester."

1189. 1723, May 17. Manchester.—"These lines are occasioned by some apprehensions of hard usage, which I have met with, relating to my concern with the school, upon the death of the two masters, a year ago; for upon the demise of the late Mr. Barrow, one of the body engaging me to do the office of a school-master there till the patron had filled up the two vacancies, promised, before Mr. John Kay and the steward, that I should be very well satisfied for my diligence during service in that trust. Notwithstanding which, it has happened otherwise with me, as I hope will appear to you by the following account. From the death of Mr. Barrow, March the 4th, to April the 26th, inclusive, are seven weeks and 3 days, for which time's service there was due to me, according to your own allowance of a guinea and a half *per* week, 11*l*. 0*s*. 0*d*. and upwards; instead of which sum, I have only received six guineas, to wit, one month's payment, which falls a great deal short of the first sum. And further, since you were pleased to assign me half a guinea *per* week, as a recompence for my care of Mr. Thompson's school for the said 7 weeks, I apprehend that if I really desired such a consideration upon that account for that term, I did also for all the time besides it, which, besides the 3 weeks 3 days already intimated, includes in its account the time from February 17 to the said 4th of March; for upon February 17, Mr. Gray deserted the said school. This is the state of the most material of my present grievances, though I doubt not but most of you are sensible that I have reason to complain of severe treatment in other respects, though at the same time, justice requires that I should acquit the gross of the worthy body, which I accordingly do, hoping that your generosity will engage you to give me satisfaction in what I have chiefly here insisted upon, which will oblige me to a behaviour towards each and all of you, suitable to the dignity and merits of such worthy gentlemen."

Following is a copy, attested by Roger Bolton and J. Richards, of a receipt, as follows :—

"April 9th, 1722.

"Received of Mrs. Thompson the sum of ten pounds, as a gratification for my assistance of the late Mr. Barrow, in teaching the free school.

"As witnesseth my hand,

"EDWARD HULTON."

R[OGER] K[ENYON] to MRS. KENYON, "at her house at Salford."

1190. 1723, July 25.—"You are like, I perceive, to have your old parson at Peel; the lay-brother has complied and taken the oath, to the great disappointment of some good Protestants, who had prepared themselves to bid for his estate, when it came to be auctioned. Poor man, I believe it was a bad morning's work with him, but I must own I was not a little pleased to find they were all disappointed. These new Acts of Parliament will possibly revive old doubts and disputes, and bring some gentlemen in the neighbourhood to a resolution who have wavered, as I hear of late; in truth, I am sorry for them either way. . . . . The lottery is almost at an end."

ROBERT BROMLEY to GEORGE KENYON, "or his clerk, Mr. Banks."

1191. 1723[-4], February 18. Warrington.—The bearer comes to know whether (sic) the last Quarter Sessions was, and whether it stands now adjourned, in order to give the Roman Catholics who have not already registered their estates, an opportunity of doing it, betwixt this and Lady-day.

SETH BROXUP to "the WORSHIPFULL FEOFFEES at the Free Schoole in Manchester."

1192. 1724, June 30. Manchester.—"Most worthy patrons and my noble benefactors, upon the 17th of this instant, which was the first time that I heard you had a design of displacing me, it was surprising and amazing unto me, and I was almost sunk down with horror and despondency; but my sorrow was soon alleviated when Mr. Richards informed me you would continue me in my place until the 25 of March next ensueing, which comfortable news brought great serenity to my mind and filled me with transports of joy; moreover, a worthy friend of mine told me that you would allow me a hansome maintenance for my life, which added a greater degree of satisfaction unto me, inasmuch as in a manner (under God) you have given a new being unto me. If you please to continue me in my station after Lady Day next, I shall be glad to serve you and the town; but if otherwise, I shall confide in your generosity and the bounty and provision you make for me. I have taught at the free school in Manchester ever since the year of our Lord God, 1688, and am 68 years of age, and begin to feel myself to decline. I hope you will be kind unto me for my father's sake, who lived in the town many years, in good credit and esteem: he suffered very much in the times of the late usurpation and was a true Royalist. I myself was born in this town, and had my education in it. I rely upon your innate principle of goodness that, if I am removed, you will grant me a handsome donation that I may live comfortably in the world, amongst my townsmen and acquaintance: my abode cannot in all probability be long here, therefore I desire you would continue your favours and compassion unto me, who am a poor object of your bounty and charity."

PETITION of SETH BROXUP, "late Under-Master of the Free School of Manchester," to the FEOFFEES of the said School.

1193. [1724, after June 30.]—"Your humble petitioner, having been Master of the Lower School ever since it was builded, and your honours knowing my (sic) being superannuated and uncapable either to serve your honours or my self, humbly begs leave to informe your honours that my circumstance is very deplorable, and unless your honours will please, not only to consider my condition, but grant me something yearly, I shall certainly want common necessaries of life. My thanks and gratitude for your kindnesses received since I have left the School, are sincerely acknowledged."

CATALOGUE of the PUPILS [" *discipulorum* "] of JOSEPH HOBSON, [at Manchester].

1194. 1725, June 7.—Charles Hobson, John Leigh, Samuel Davenport, Burton Brace, Thomas Seddon, Daniel Pollit, John Renshaw, John Hobson, John Walker, Thomas Raffold, John Adams, Henry Lees, William Barlowe, Robert Bradshaw, William Barrow, Thomas Robinson, John Baker, Noah Hallows, Thomas Boardman, Peter Tickel, James Clough, Samuel Oakes, Henry Gore, William Crompton, William Tomlinson, Thomas Gothard, William Heywood, Thomas Tinsley, John Jones, Samuel Goodgear [Goodyear ?], John Goodgear, Hugo Whittle, Richard Thorpe, John Bell, James Somister, James Barlowe, Daniel Mode, George Hulton, John Hulme, Peter Heywood, Joseph Bancroft, Samuel Kinder, John Whitley, James Rowe, James Berry, James Jonson, Thomas Stretch, James Crompton, John Pemberton, Robert Adcroft, James Hall, John Smith, Thomas Gathorne, John Warmingham, Thomas Ashley, James Priestnal, Richard Brookes, William Barlowe, John Thorpe, Charles Hadfield, Henry Tonge, Nathaniel Winterbotham, John ;Redford, Thomas Hudson, Samuel Wolmore, John Wadsworth, James Bradshaw, Thomas Hibbard, James Holden, Samuel Lees, James Heywood, James Birchall, James Wagstaff, Robert Aspinal, Robert Philips, James Heys, Thomas Kyrke, Charles Heywood, Jeremiah Gothard, James Ridley, Thomas Barrow, Thomas Chadock, Alexander Holbrooke, and Thomas Haworth.

THOMAS GELLYBRAND to GEORGE KENYON.

1195. 1725, June 14. Leigh.—" I make bould to retorn you thanks for your former kinness to me and my poor wife, who continus in a wacke condishen, in so much that she is not abell to help her self, without one or two to help her, and the town will not do nothing towards her relife, unless she and I will ware the bag, which she is unwilling."

SIR R. BRADSHAIGH to GEORGE KENYON.

1196. 1727, July 10. Haigh.—Asking for his vote at the election of members to represent the Borough of Wigan. *Seal of arms, broken.*

RESIGNATION OF THE SECOND MASTER OF MANCHESTER SCHOOL.

1197. 1727, September 15.—" I, William Purnell, second master of Manchester School, do by these presents resign any right of succeeding which may be granted me by the statutes or ordinances of the Free Grammar School of Manchester, upon the death or departure of any head master, for the next turn, upon the following conditions (viz.) : to have the arrears for the three last years, and the money that I laid out upon my house, and to have my house either rebuilt or repaired." *Draft.*

SAMUEL, BISHOP OF CHESTER, to REV. MR. OLDERSEY, Rector of Wigan.

1198. [1727.]—Enclosing the draft of an address from the Bishop, Dean, and Prebendaries, of the Cathedral Church of Chester, to George II., upon his accession. *Seal of arms, broken.*

"Count Sinzendorf, Chancellor of the Court of his Imperial and Catholic Majesty, to Monsieur de Palm, the Emperor's Resident in the Court of Great Britain."

1199. 1727[-8,] February 20. Vienna. — "His Imperial and Catholick Majestie judges it indispensably necessary, upon the step which has been lately taken in the country where you are, to send you, in the dispatch here annexed, a memorial which you are to present to the King of Great Britain, and to publish afterwards, that the whole nation may be acquainted with it, whilst answers are prepareing to certain pamphletts, published before the opening of the Parliament.

"It is easy to see that the speech was made for no purpose but to excite the nation to a rupture and open war with the Emperor and with Spain, and to make the Parliament approve the precipetate and burthensome measures which the Government has taken for private ends, but too well known. Not only unwarrantable inferences and pretences have been made use of, but manifest falsehoods have been boldly advanced for indisputable facts, a proceeding never seen before among Powers who ought to respect each other, when in the most flagrant wars, from whence it ought to be presumed that the King, whose sacred mouth ought to be an oracle of truth, must have been himself abused by the suggestions and false reports of those who have the honor to possess his confidence, and who think it their interest to inflame, by these meanes, both the Prince and the nation, for their own private views and personall preservation, without any regard to the honour of the majestie of the throne, or to the evils which may result from hence to their own country, and to all Europe.

"For these purposes they establish a foundation, and lay down, as a certain fact, that there is a positive article in the Treaty of Alliance, between the Emperor and the King of Spain, to place the Pretender on the throne of Great Britain, and to invade that kingdom with open force, and this they do, a few dayes after the Minister Plenipotentiary of the Catholick King had, before his departure from London, in a memorial presented in the sacred name of his master, publickly and in the most authentick manner, disavowed these imputations, which sufficiently prove the Emperor's disavowall of the same, since the pretended article was equally imputed to the two Powers, and one of them could not have stipulated anything in the same treaty, without the other. Besides which, it is to be considered that 6 months ago, upon the first reports of these false suppositions, the Emperor and King of Spain, in order to silence them, proposed a formall *de non offendendo*, into which all the allies, on one side and the other, might enter, and which would effectually have secured the peacable possessions of each of the Powers contracting, either in the Treaty of Vienna or that of Hanover, till such time as it had been possible, by one generall treaty, to remove and quiet the complaints of all sides. But these proposalls were rendered ineffectual by the same views of those persons who chose rather to hinder the peaceable effect of those just designs, by attacks and open hostilities.

"It is further known, and it is ever notorious by the solemn comunication made to the King of Great Britain by the treaty of peace concluded at Vienna between the Emperor and the King of Spain, that the treaty of the Quadruple Alliance, made at London the 2nd of August 1718, has been laid down as the unalterable basis of their peace, and that all the articles of this Quadruple Alliance are therein confirmed and corroborated, as if they had been inserted anew. How, then, can it bee supposed, and even given out as a matter of fact, that by another secret treaty, signed on the same day, conditions have been established and engagements taken, entirely repugnant to the same.

"Such a thing cannot be advanced without insulting and injuring, in the most outrageous manner, the majesty of the two contracting Powers, who have a right to demand a signall reparation and satisfaction, proportioned to the enormity of the affront, which equally interests their honour, and that faith (?) which ought allwaies to be respected amongst Sovereign princes.

"But if those who endeavour to avail themselves of such feigned recriminations, and to excuse themselves from the blame which their rash and turbulent measures deserve, imagine that this unjustifiable conduct may at last oblige the Emperor and King of Spain to repell force by force, and to defend themselves, by all those meanes which God has put into their hands, from the mischeifs with which they are threatned, and from the insults and attacks which have been actually made use of against them, so far that it has been even attempted to engage the Ottoman Porte in these unparelleled designs, at least, ought they not to publish, as antecedent facts, those things which they have reason to apprehend may bee the consequence of a war into which they will have forced these two Powers to enter, in their own just defence.

"The Emperor and King of Spain hope, however, from the Divine goodnes, and from the wisdom of persons less prejudiced and less passionate, that more mature and serious reflections will be made, in order to restore amicably the publick tranquility, and to save all Europe from the misfortunes of a war, stirred up by motives so trifling and groundless, which can tend to nothing but the distruction of the subject, of his estate, and of his countre.

"Their Majesties, the Emperor and the King of Spain, ardently desire the blessing of peace, and to observe their treaties with all their allies with the strictest fidelity. But, as a mutuall contract can subsist no longer on one side then while it remaines unbroken on the other, the evill consequences of a rupture, if that should happen, ought to be imputed to those alone who have been the authors of these instructions.

"I have the Emperor's express order to write this to you, in his name, that you may be able to destroy the falshoods and calumnies which have been charged on the high contracting parties of the Treaty of Vienna, who have no other view but that of making peace between themselves without hurting any one else." *Copy.*

Appended.—The representation made, according to the foregoing instructions, by Monsieur de Palm. *Copy.*

A PROTEST.

1200. 1729.—The protests of the Lords in Parliament. *Printed.*

ELECTION ADDRESS.

1201. 1733, October 12. Dunham.—Address by Lord Warrington to his tenants, and other freeholders, in the county of Chester, in favour of the election to Parliament of Mr. Cholmondeley, of Vale Royal, and Mr. Crew, junior. *Copy.*

GEORGE PARRY to the REVEREND ————.

1202. 1735, October 21. Holywell, [Flintshire].—Sending the translation of a grant by Queen Anne, dated 20 January, in the second year of her reign, to Sir John Egerton, baronet, of a market, to be held every Friday, in the town of Holywell, and three fairs there every year. A question seems to have arisen as to the right of taking toll.

PETITION of JANE ARROWSMITH, widow, to the FEOFFEES of the Manchester Free School.

1203. 1736, April 5. Manchester.—"My son, John Arrowsmith, now at Oxford, some time since officiated in the free school of Manchester for the space of twenty-three weeks, at the request of the town, upon the account of Mr. Richards' indisposition, the late head-master. My son was desired by several persons to assist in the school, who proposed to make contributions in return for his time. The late Mr. Foxley collected a sum in order for him, but being told by Mr. Purnell that the worshipful trustees would pay him, occasioned Mr. Foxley to return the collected sum; so I humbly desire your worships will take this affair in consideration."

PETITION of JOHN ARROWSMITH "to the worthy gentlemen concerned for the Free School in Manchester."

1204. [1736, April.]—"The humble memorial of John Arrowsmith, born in Manchester, late a scholar of the free school there, sheweth—

"That he was lately nominated by Mr. Richards, master of the said School, to go to the University of Oxford (where he now is), hopeing to make a good use of the improvement he has received in Manchester. Your petitioner being informed there is an allowance to be given to the scholars going from the said school to Oxford, humbly hopes he may, towards his encouragement, be admitted to a share of such benevolence, his present dependance being only on a mother, who is a widow, with many children to provide for."

JAMES OLDHAM to GEORGE KENYON.

1205. 1736, July 27. Manchester.—Mr. Egerton desires counsel about Holywell affairs, before Kersall Moor Races, where he hoped to have seen Mr. Kenyon. *Seal with crest.*

CROSTON CHURCH.

1206. 1739, October 8.—Petition from the Justices of the Peace for the County of Lancaster to Philip, Lord Hardwicke, Lord Chancellor, for Letters Patent for a collection to be made for rebuilding a portion of the Parish Church of Croston; the foundations of the church being weakened by the overflowing of the River Yarrow, so that the pillars and arches which support the middle aisle must be rebuilt. *Copy.*

ORDER MADE AT LANCASTER SESSIONS.

1207. 1740, July 15.—The Justices at Lancaster desire the justices at Preston, Ormskirk, and Manchester, to direct what rate or allowance *per* mile, or otherwise, shall be made, for "passing" vagrants, according to the late act. "The gentlemen at Lancaster think 8*d.* a mile sufficient for one vagrant, if conveyed on horseback; if two vagrants, 6*d.* each; and if more, in proportion, accordingly." The justices at Preston agree; but they recommend that vagrants should pass on foot, where practicable, and they suggest the allowance of 6*d.* each *per* mile, or 4*d.* each, if more than one is passed. The justices at Ormskirk consider " the passing of Irish vagrants out of Cheshire to the House of Correction at Manchester, is contrary to the act, Park Gate being the next port." Draft table of rates for conveying vagrants to Ireland follows :—

"For passing vagrants from Liverpool to Dublin, to

the master - - - - - - -	2s. 6d.
For maintaining while on board - - - -	1s. 0d.
From Liverpool to Cork, or to the north part of Ireland - - - - - - -	5s. 0d.
For maintenance - - - - -	1s. 6d.
From Liverpool to the Isle of Man - - -	2s. 6d.
[For] maintenance - - - - - -	1s. 0d.
For maintenance whilst in port, till they can be shipped, not exceeding, *per day* - - -	0s. 6d."

ROBERT TAYLOR to GEORGE KENYON.

1208. 1741, April 23. Nantwich.—Was in hopes not to have troubled Mr. Kenyon more, about his affair with Mr. Manley, but hears he intends to go to law. "He is a very ignorant countryman, and I find is advised by a very ill man, though, I am sorry to say it, a clergyman, one Mr. Wright, of Hazlington, who gets more by being concerned in law than by preaching. [He] keeps his chambers at this town and Sandbach every market day, and takes any thing in hand; draws the person on he is concerned for, just comes to tryal, and then generally persuades them to agree. No question but you have heard his character."

The SAME to the SAME, "near the old church in Manchester."

1209. 1741, May 28. Nantwich.—As to the procedure in the Court of Chester. "Mr. Willett desired I would let you know they have 6 weeks from the filing of the declaration to plead in." According to the rules of that Court, "all the rules there are 6 weeks." . . . I see the fourth edition of Collins's Peerage is reprinted; "if you would have them (*sic*), I shall be very glad to serve you with them."

R. MOLYNEUX to GEORGE KENYON.

1210. 1744, "May-day." Preston.—It has been confidently reported in our coffee-house that you, as clerk of the peace, have received a letter from the Duke of Newcastle, directing you not to return the convictions into Chancery, and ordering you to send them up to him at his office at Whitehall, and furthur, that the Duke wrote you word that the justices for this county were the only justices in England that had proceeded so far against the papists. I should be extremely glad to know the truth of this account, as I think it is very extraordinary, and, therefore, beg the favour of a line by the return of the carrier (or otherwise) to clear up this affair, and if you have any such letter, I should be very much obliged to you for a copy of it. *Seal of arms.*

N. PARKER to GEORGE KENYON.

1211. 1744[-5], February 21. Chancery Lane.—To-day the report has again got about of Mr. Fazakerley being Chancellor, as soon as a place is found out for Lord Edgecumbe, whose temper is said to be much altered by being very good natured to the late minority, insomuch that a new Commission of the Peace, it is said, will be made out at the next assizes; this I cannot think, but perhaps it may be, against the summer assizes, if this Lord keeps this place.

R———— Y———— to GEORGE KENYON, at Peel.

1212. [1745,] July 1? Manchester.—There was, on Sunday, a Gazette extraordinary, which . . . . . in your own paper, but I had not heard of it when your servant . . . . in to-day's Gazette is an account of the loss of the English, Hanoverians, and Hessians [at Fontenoy], which, in the whole, amounts to 4,930—English, 2,100; Hanoverians, 2,500; and Hessians, 300—the odd numbers, I forget. Above a thousand horses killed, &c.; seven pieces of cannon lost, and some things belonging to the artillery. No account yet of what the Dutch and Austrians have lost. They say the French have 6,000 wounded, and leave us to guess the number killed; but I believe it is all guess work. Two of the Duke's [the Duke of Cumberland] Aids-de-Camps are prisoners, and several officers of note, wounded or prisoners, not in the first list. The French King is (sic) at the Commanderie, where the battle was fought, and Saxe at Hoesfelt. Lowendal is to be sent somewhither with a detachment, but his design uncertain. Prisoners on both sides are released, except officers. It is said a new camp is marked out for the Duke, I think Gronvelt, or some such name, is the place. The Duke is providing the army with such things as are commonly lost in a battle, as the Gazette gently expresses it, though it is thought the single word baggage would have been the properest term. An article from Marseilles, in the Gazette, says the Genoese are going to be bombarded, which will soon oblige them to capitulate; and another, from Rotterdam, mentions a report of Belisle's having met with a repulse at Ventriuolia, but neither of them seem to be very authentic, as there is no news from the General or our resident there. So far the Government is pleased to go, and as to other news, I suppose your *Evening Post* will inform you as well as I, though we have no mails this post. I fancy you must have heard that Captain Barlow has written to his friends. He fixes the loss in his regiment at 160 killed, &c., which does not exactly tally with the Gazette. His own company lost 22, himself slightly wounded. He says it was a very bloody and desperate action, and continued 4 or 5 hours. He writes that all the foreign troops behaved ill, but afterwards, in a postscript, has a saving clause for the Hanoverians, which occasions much speculation here. I fancy you will be diverted, as well as we have been, with a strange piece of Irish in Sunday's Gazette, about the village of Val, which, it is there said, was taken and retaken several times, after which immediately follows—that the English, &c., entered it five different times and the French but once. How it could be taken and retaken several times, and the French enter it but once, is an enigma which we cannot unriddle; and it puts people in mind of the story of an angry tutor's scolding an idle pupil of his and telling him that he came down stairs half a dozen times for his going up once! We have no pamphlets stirring but one, called "Cry aloud and spare not," which they say is very bitter, but I have not yet seen it. When I shall do myself the pleasure of waiting upon you at Peel I cannot tell, for our youngest child has just begun with the small-pox, but we hope is in no danger.

SIR H. HOUGHTON to GEORGE KENYON.

1213. 1745, October 18. Walton. — I hope, as you promised Mr. Molyneux and me at Chorley, I shall shortly have an account that you have recorded the convictions. You owned that you were not a judicial but a ministerial officer, which is certainly true, and, as such, are obliged to observe the plain direction of the Act of Parliament, which I and several of the Justices of Peace have often called upon you to do; it will not be sufficient excuse to say you are advised to the contrary, or that it has not been done in other counties; neither can justify you in such neglect; there was not such a tenderness shewed to the popish interest, the last rebellion, and as the expectation of the rebells now must be from the support they expect from the popish interest, there is the same reason and necessity to record the convictions now as there was then.

T. BOOTLE to [SIR H. HOUGHTON?].

1214. 1745, November 2.—"I troubled you with a letter, some time ago, concerning the conviction of the papists, to which you have not thought fit to give me any answer.

"When I was last in the country, I acquainted you and many other justices of the peace, that to carry the proceedings against the papists upon the last proclamation to a complete conviction, would be wrong. That convicting them would not disable, but rather exasperate, and be a means to drive them into rebellion, or at least furnish them with a plausible pretence for taking so desperate a step. That tendering the Oaths and Declaration, and upon their refusal, to take from the refusers their horses and armes, would be complying with the proclamation and doing all what you were required to do. That it was not the design of the proclamation, nor of the Administration, that the justices of peace should take upon them to judge of the expediency or fitness of carrying it to a final conviction, but that was to be left to the judgment and discretion of the Privy Council. With this, every justice of the peace with whom I conversed (who were many) was perfectly satisfied, as was also my Lord Derby, the Lord Lieutenant, with whom I also talked upon this subject; and I do not hear but that every justice in the county, save yourself and Mr. Molyneux, continue in the same mind. But, to my great surprise, hearing that you by a menacing letter to the Clerk of the Peace were for forcing him to return into Chancery all the convictions which have been returned to the Quarter Sessions, I thereupon acquainted several of the Privy Council with what you were doing, who, I take the liberty to tell you, do not approve of your conduct. That before a final step of that kind be taken you should have certified what you had done under the proclamation, to the Council, to the end they might judge of the fitness of doing or not doing it. And that you may see that that is so, I have inclosed to you the proclamation. And therefore, the first step to be taken, in order to a final conviction, is for the justices to certify to the Council what they have done under the proclamation, which, I understand, they have not; and when that is done, the Council will judge and direct whether it be proper at this time, or not, to have the convictions recorded in one of the Courts above. If it is right, to be sure they will direct it, and then it may be done; but if not proper, then they will let them remain in readiness, as in every other county of the kingdom, to be recorded when they shall see just occasion.

"I believe that none can doubt but that my zeal for his Majesty, his family, and his Government, is equal to any justices' in the county; and, did I think that convicting the papists would tend to disable them, or add the least security, strength, or safety, to the Government, I should be as forward as any man in the kingdom to have it done immediately; but as I am convinced it will have quite a contrary effect—instead of disabling, it will irritate and provoke, and make them the more desperate—it is from that cause, and that only, that I thus interpose. While they are quiet (as I do not hear from any quarter but they are), let us not, from a mistaken zeal, do anything to provoke them and give them a handle for disturbance or drive them into rebellion, and give them ground to say you have done your worst, and so make them desperate. I shall only add that, by the Act of Parliament, the justices of peace have nothing to do in the return of the convictions into the Court of Chancery or King's Bench; they are only required to certify them to the Quarter Sessions, and when that is done, their power of intermeddling is at an end, and what is further to be done, wholly rests on the Clerk of the Peace." *Copy.*

[FREDERICK THE GREAT to PRINCE CHARLES EDWARD.]

1215. [1745.]—"I can no longer, my dear friend, deny myself the satisfaction of congratulating you on your safe arrival in France; and, though the connexions I have with the reigning family did not permit me to rejoice too openly at the progress of your arms, I can assure you, with great truth, that I was sincerely touched with your misfortunes, and under the deepest apprehensions for your person. All Europe was astonished at the greatness of your enterprise; for though Alexander, and other heroes, have conquered kingdoms with inferior armies, you are the only one who ever engaged in such an attempt without any. My friend Voltaire, who is perfectly well acquainted with my sentiments for you, is, more than any body, indebted to your Highness for having at length furnished him with a subject worthy of his pen, except an happier event. However, though fortune was your foe, Great Britain, and not your Royal Highness, is a loser by it, as the difficulties you have undergone have only served to discover those rare talents and virtues which have gained you the admiration of all mankind, and even the esteem of those amongst your enemies, in whom every spark of virtue is not totally extinct. The Princess Amelia, who has all the curiosity of her sex, is desirous of seeing the features of a hero of whom she has heard so much; so that you have it in your power to oblige both her and me, [by] sending us your picture by the Count de ———, who is on his return to Berlin; and be assured I shall esteem it the most valuable acquisition I ever made. You are frequently the subject of my conversation with General Keith, whom I have had the good fortune to engage in my service; and though, besides his consummate knowledge in military affairs, he possesses a thousand amiable qualities, nothing endears him to me so entirely as his entertaining the same sentiments with regard to your Royal Highness. Was I differently situated from what I am, I would give you more essential proofs of my friendship than mere words; but you may depend on any good offices I can do you with my brother the King of France; though I am sorry to tell you, that I am too well acquainted with the politics of that court to expect they will do any solid services, as they would have everything to apprehend from a prince of your consummate abilities and enterprising genius, placed at the head of the bravest people in the world. Adieu, my dear Prince, and assure yourself no change in your fortune can make any alteration in my esteem." *Copy.*

GEORGE KENYON [to SIR H. HOUGHTON ?].

1216. 1745[-6], January 4. Manchester—"I received the favour of yours, dated the 25th of November last, at Manchester, when I was going with my family into Wales, for fear of our late visitors, and am but lately returned back, which has prevented my answering you sooner. I left your letter with Mr. Bootle, and desired him to communicate it to the rest of the justices in Manchester, for their advice and direction; but he leaving the town likewise, in the hurry, forgot it. As to the method you have taken by the direction of Mr. Bootle, and of the noble Lord, etc., mentioned in yours, I suppose they thought it the most prudent way, and I could have been glad the Privy Council would have given their orders, which would have been a justification and direction for you to act. If they do not think fit to take that step, I see no way I have to do but to follow the plain directions of an Act of Parliament, and not to take upon me to be wiser than they. I had no other view in delaying the return of the convictions, but the application of Mr. Bootle, who told me it would be the most for the interest of the Government to delay it, and that it was neither the intention of the Proclamation nor of the Privy Counsell to have the convictions returned to the K[ing's] B[ench] or C[hancery], and made use of some great names to justify his opinion; but as this has not been satisfactory to the justices below, and I have been a good deal blamed about it (though I have heard nothing from them since the convictions were sent up) I cannot think it prudent for me, who am only a ministerial officer, to stand in the gap in an open breach of an Act of Parliament, to screen others from the law, without some legal or competent authority to justify me in so doing. You may communicate this to Mr. Bootle (if you please) and send me his thoughts about it; but if nothing more is to be expected from above, I should think it the prudentest way to record them. I desire your answer, and that you would let me know whether any other clerks of the peace have recorded the convictions, or no." *Draft.*

The SAME to ————————.

1217. 1745[-6], January 5. Peel.—"Our confusion has been so great here, by the rebels marching through this county, that I have been forced to fly into Wales with my wife and children, for fear of them; and the roads have been so bad, and the weather so severe since, that I am but just reached home."

ORDER by the JUSTICES OF THE PEACE for the County of Lancaster.

1218. 1745[-6], February 3.—"We whose names are hereunto subscribed (who act in the Commission of Peace for the County Palatine of Lancaster aforesaid) think it proper, especially at this time, when there [is] a most unnatural rebellion against his Majestie's person and Government, that the convictions of the papists, reputed papists, and nonjurors, which were returned to the Quarter Sessions by some of us and other Justices of the Peace of the said county, in the year 1744, and which have been hitherto neglected by the Clerk of the Peace, or by some others who have been employed for him, be without delay returned to the High Court of Chancery or King's Bench, by the Clerk of the Peace of this county, in order there to be recorded, according to an Act of Parliament in that case made and provided." *Copy.*

R. JENKINS to [GEORGE KENYON].

1219. 1745[-6], February 15. "Salop."—Mr. Wright greatly approves of Mrs. Kenyon's choice of nectarines, plums, and peaches, and recommends the following pears:—Jargonelle, St. Michael, Bury du Roy, Crasan, and Colmar.

THOMAS THEODORUS DEACON to his father, Dr. DEACON, at Manchester.

1220. 1746, July 29. London.—"Before you receive this I hope to be in Paradise, not that I have the least right to expect it from any merit of my own, or the goodness of my past life, but meerly through the intercession of my Saviour and Redeemer, a sincere and hearty repentance of all my sins, the variety of punishments I have suffered since I saw you, and the death which I shall die to-morrow, which, I trust in God, will be some small atonement for my transgressions, and to which I think I am almost confident I shall submit, with all the resignation and chearfulness that a true pious christian and a brave loyal soldier can wish. I hope you will do my character so much justice (and if you think proper make use of this) as absolutely to contradict that false and malicious report which has been spread only by my enemies, in hopes it might be of prejudice to you and your family, viz., that I was persuaded and compelled by you to engage contrary to my own inclination. I send my tenderest love to all the dear children, and beg Almighty God to bless you and them in this world, and grant us all a happy meeting in that to come. I shall leave directions with Charles to send them some trifle whereby to remember me. Pray excuse my naming any particular friends, for there is no end, but give my hearty service and best wishes to them all in general. Mr. Syddall is very well, and sends his sincere compliments, but does not choose to write. He behaves as well as his best friends can wish. My uncle has behaved to me in such a manner as cannot be paralleled but by yourself. I know I shall have your prayers without asking, which I am satisfied will be of infinite service."

Extract of a letter from the clergyman who attended upon Mr. Syddall and Mr. Deacon.

1220A. [end of July 1746.]—"Their behaviour at divine worship was always with great reverence, attention, and piety; but had you, sir, been present, the last day that I attended them, your soul would have been ravished with the fervour of their devotions. From the time of their condemnation, a decent cheerfulness constantly appeared in their countenance and behaviour, and I believe it may be truly said that no men ever suffered in a righteous cause with greater magnanimity and more christian fortitude, for the appearance and near approach of a violent death, armed with the utmost terror of pains and torments, made no impression of dread upon their minds. In a word, great is the honour they have done the Church, the King, yourself, and themselves, and may their example be imitated by all that suffer in the same cause. This short and faithful account of our martyred friends, I hope, sir, will yield great consolation to yourself and poor Mrs. Syddall. Poor dear Mr. Charles bears in a commendable manner his great loss and other afflictions, and behaves like a man and a good christian, in all his actions."

DYING SPEECH OF ROBERT LYON.

1221. 1746, October 28.—The last dying speech of Robert Lyon, M.A., presbyter of Perth, which he read at the place of execution at Penrith, in Cumberland.

DECLARATION BY JAMES BRADSHAW.

1222. 1746, November 28.—"It would be a breach of duty in me to omit this last opportunity of doing justice to those who stand in need of it, and I think it incumbent upon me, the rather because I am the only Englishman in this part of the world who had the honour to attend his Royal Highness in Scotland.

"When I first joined the King's forces, I was induced to it by a principle of duty only, and I never saw any reason since to convince me that I was in the least mistaken, but, on the contrary, every day's experience has strengthened my opinion that what I did was right and necessary; that duty I discharged to the best of my power, and as I did not receive the reward of my service in this world, I have no doubt of receiving it in the next. Under an opinion I could do more good by marching with the army into Scotland than remaining with the Manchester regiment at Carlisle, I obtained leave to be in my Lord Elcho's corps, for I was willing to be in action.

"After the battle of Culloden I had the misfortune to fall into the hands of the most ungenerous enemy that, I believe, ever assumed the name of a soldier—I mean the pretended Duke of Cumberland and those under his command, whose inhumanity exceeded anything I could have imagined, in a country where the bare mention of a God is allowed of. I was put into one of the Scotch kirks, together with a great number of wounded prisoners, who were stripped naked, and there left to die of their wounds, without the least assistance; and though we had a surgeon of our own, a prisoner in the same place, yet he was not permitted to dress their wounds, but his instruments were taken from him, on purpose to prevent it, and in the consequence of this, many expired in the utmost agonies. Several of the wounded were put on shore at the Island of Leith, and there died in lingering tortures. Our general allowance while we were prisoners there, was half a pound of meal a day, which was sometimes increased to a pound, but it never exceeded it, and I myself was an eye witness that great numbers were starved to death. Their barbarity extended so far as not to suffer the men who were put on board the *Pean* to lie down, even on the planks, but they were obliged to sit on large stones, by which their legs were swelled as big almost as their bodies. These are some of their cruelties exercised, which, being almost incredible in a christian country, I am obliged to add my asseveration to the truth of them, and I do assure you, upon the word of a dying man, as I hope for mercy at the day of judgment, I assert nothing but what I know to be true.

"The injustice of these proceedings is aggravated by the ingratitude of them; for the El[ector] of H[anove]r's people had often been obliged by our prince, who allowed his prisoners the same allowance of meat as his own troops, and allways made them his particular . . . .; that all the wounded should be carefully dressed and used with the utmost tenderness. This extreme caution to avoid the effusion of blood, even with regard to . . . . when his own safety made it almost necessary, and his surprising generosity to his enemies, without distinction, certainly demanded different treatment, and I could not think that an English army under English . . . . tions, could possibly behave with such unprovoked barbarity.

"With regard to the report of his Royal Highness having ordered no quarter should be given to the enemy, I am persuaded in my conscience it was a malicious lie, raised by the friends of usurpation for an excuse for the cruelties committed in Scotland, which were many more and greater than I have time to describe, for I firmly believe the Prince would not consent to such orders, even if it were to gain the three kingdoms.

"I would gladly enter into the particulars of his Royal Highness's character, if I were able, but his qualifications are above description ; all I can say is, he is everything I could imagine, great and excellent, fully deserving what he was born for—to rule over a free people.

"I die a member of the Church of England, which I am satisfied would flourish much more under the reign of a Stuart than it does now, or has done for many years. The friends of the House of Hanover say they keep out Popery ; but do they not let in infidelity, which is almost become (if I may so say) religion established ?

"I think it every man's duty, by all lawful means, to live as long as he can, and with this view I made a defence upon my trial which I thought might possibly do me service. All that the witnesses swore in my behalf was strictly true, for I would much rather die than be the occasion of perjury. After sentence, my friends petitioned for my life, and if it had been granted I should have been thankful for it, but as it otherwise happened I patiently submit, and have confident hopes, upon the whole, it will be better for me, for I suffer for having done my duty. What I expected, soon happened upon my trial, Mr. Maddox perjured me, and I am afraid that he is so immersed in wickedness that it would be difficult for him to forbear it. Lieutenant Moore swore he was acquainted with me at Manchester, but I declare I never was in his company till we met at Inverness. I should think it a great reflection upon any government to encourage any officer to lay by his sword and become an informer. I forgive both them and all my enemies.

"I am convinced that these nations are inevitably ruined, unless the royal family be restored, which I hope will soon happen, for I love my country, and with my parting breath I pray God to bless it. I also beseech Him to bless and preserve my lawful sovereign, King James the Third, the Prince of Wales, the Duke of York, to prosper all my friends, and to have mercy upon me." *Copy.*

BRIEF for the defendant in the suit of the KING *v.* WILLIAM FOWDEN.

1223 & 1224. [1746.]—Copy of Indictment :—" The jurors for our present Sovereign Lord the King, upon their oath present that Thomas Walley, late of the town of Manchester, in the County Palatine of Lancaster, gentleman, and William Fowden, late of the same place, merchant and chapman, being subjects of our said present most Serene Sovereign Lord George the Second, by the grace of God, of Great Britain, France, and Ireland, King, Defender of the Faith, and so forth, not having the fear of God in their hearts, nor having any regard for the duty of their allegiance, but being moved and seduced by the instigation of the Devil, as false traitors and rebels against our said present Sovereign Lord the King, their supreme, true, natural, lawful, and undoubted Sovereign Lord, entirely withdrawing that cordial love and that true and due obedience, fidelity and allegiance, which every subject of our said present Sovereign Lord the King should, and of right ought to bear, towards our said present Sovereign Lord the King, and also devising (as much as in them lay) most wickedly and traitorously intending to change and subvert the rule and government of this kingdom, duly and happily established under our said present Sovereign Lord the King, and also to depose and deprive our said present Sovereign Lord the King of his title, honour, and royal estate, and of his imperial rule and government of this kingdom, and also to put and bring our said present Sovereign Lord the King to death and final destruction, and to raise and exalt the person pretended to be Prince of Wales during the life of James the Second, late King of England, and so forth, and, since the decease of the said late King, pretending to be and taking upon himself the stile and tytle of King of England, by the name of James the Third, to the crown and to the royal state and dignity of King, and to the imperial rule and government of this kingdom, upon the twenty ninth day of November, in the nineteenth year of the reign of our said present Sovereign Lord the King, at the town of Manchester aforesaid, in the County Palatine of Lancaster aforesaid, with a great multitude of traitors and rebels, against our said present Sovereign Lord the King, to wit, to the number of three thousand persons (whose names are as yet unknown to the said Jurors) being armed and arrayed in a warlike and hostile manner (to wit) with colours displayed, drums beating, pipes playing, and with swords, clubs, guns, pistols, and divers other weapons, as well offensive as defensive, with force and arms, did falsely and traitorously assemble and join themselves against our said present Sovereign Lord the King, and then and there, with force and arms, did falsly and traitorously, and in a warlike and hostile manner, array and dispose themselves against our said present Sovereign Lord the King, and then and there, with force and arms, in pursuance and execution of such their wicked and traitorous intentions and purpose aforesaid, did falsly and traitorously prepare, order, wage, and levy, a public and cruel war against our said present Sovereign Lord the King, against the duty of their allegiance, against the peace of our said present Sovereign Lord the King, his crown and dignity, and also against the form of the statute in such case made and provided.

"Note. The said Fowden and Walley were, on the said twenty ninth day of November aforesaid, Constables of the town of Manchester, in this county."

"The indictment as to Thomas Walley was found *ignoramus*, and there was found a true bill as to Mr. Fowden."

The prisoner's case. "The rebels in Scotland, about the latter end of the year 1745, to the number of seven or eight thousand men, penetrated into England and took the city and castle of Carlisle, advanced forwards to Penrith, Kendal, Lancaster, Preston, and Wigan, and the vanguard of them reached Manchester on Thursday, the twenty eighth of November, the main body of the army following them the day after. They halted in Manchester till Sunday, December the first, when they marched out for Macclesfield, and from thence forwards to Derby, and on Monday, the 9th of December, returned to Manchester, in their way back to Scotland. In the several towns through which they passed, they compelled the Mayors, Bayliffs, Constables, and other head officers and Magistrates to appear in their formalities and assist in proclaiming the Pretender, in billeting their troops, in providing horses, carriages, hay, straw, and whatever else they wanted, under pain of military execution, and the Magistrates were obliged, and accordingly did, in general, comply with such orders, for fear of having their houses fired or plundered, and to preserve their own lives and their families, and not only the Magistrates, but even private persons, were obliged to pay them money, provide hay, corn, &c., and where their orders were disobeyed, they sometimes imprisoned the persons, plundred their houses, and offered and attempted to fire their houses, and by such means forced the parties to a compliance; and, in general, it was observed that where persons had left their houses they were hardlier and more roughly dealt with.

"The prisoner, Mr. Fowden, is a Protestant of the Church of England, has taken the oaths to his Majesty, and is a person well affected to the present establishment. He has lived upwards of . . . years in Manchester or Salford, and during all that time, and always before his coming hither, behaved himself quietly and orderly and peaceably, and lived in good reputation with all his neighbours, never was suspected of having any disaffection to the Government. About Michaelmas, 1745, he was elected Constable of the town of Manchester, at the Court Leet there. Upon hearing that he was designed for that office, he applied to all his friends then upon the Jury, and he offered a considerable sum of money to fine off, instead of serving the office, but being told the fine was arbitrary and that they would compel him to serve it, he was forced to submit, much against his inclination. When news came to the town of Manchester that the rebels were advancing that way, and how they had behaved in other places, the Constables thought it prudent to apply, and accordingly Mr. Walley, the other Constable, with the privity and consent of Mr. Fowden, did apply, to the Justices for their directions how they should act, in case the rebels came forward to Manchester, and Mr. Chetham, a Justice there, then told Mr. Walley that if the rebels forced them to do anything, they were like to submit, but that he advised them to do nothing for them but what they were forced to, which direction they determined to follow, and accordingly did.

"Upon the vanguard of the rebels coming into Manchester, on Thursday, the 28th of November, about 9 o'clock at night, Mr. Fowden kept himself private in his own house with some few friends, and, being sent for, at first ordered himself to be denied, but afterwards a party of the rebel officers came to his house, armed with swords, pistols, &c., and the prisoner being obliged to appear, they took him down by force to the 'Bull's Head' where the commanding officer then was. The prisoner then demanding by what authority he was sent for, the commanding officer drew his sword and sayd, 'Damn you—by this'; and then told the prisoner he must obey all orders of their Prince, as they called him, on pain of military execution. The next day, about 11 o'clock, Mr. Fowden was brought a prisoner to the 'Saracen's Head,' where was six or eight rebel officers with their pistols and swords drawn, and the commanding officer then told him, 'Sir, I charge you in Prince Charles's name to obey all our commands; if you refuse any of them you are a dead man, and we'll lay your house in ashes and take your family prisoners. The first is, you are to read up Prince Charles's proclamation at the market cross, and to search for arms, and swear the inhabitants wherever you go.' To which the prisoner replied, 'I have taken the oaths to King George and cannot do it.' The rebel officer made answer, 'If you mention George of Hanover in my presence, I'll stab you dead.' And the prisoner was often afterwards taken and kept prisoner by the rebels, and they often threatned to take away his life, burn his house, &c., if he did not comply with their orders, as will appear in the course of the evidence; and if it should be objected that he did more than the other Constable, it was because his house standing very near to where the Pretender then lodged, he was the person they could most readily apply to, yet in general, it will appear he did nothing but what he was under an absolute necessity and constraint to do."

"As to the billeting the rebels, Mr. Fowden billeted none, the rebels doing it themselves, till about Saturday, the 30th November, some of the townspeople complaining that they had a great number of the rebels and others of their neighbours none, the rebels commanded the Constables to go through the town to ease the houses that had too many quartered upon them. As to proclaiming the Pretender, the Constables were sent for to the Pretender's lodging, under a guard of armed rebels, and thence, about 3 o'clock in the afternoon of Friday, November 29th, guarded down to the market cross, where a rebel officer tendered the proclamation unto Mr. Whalley, who absolutely refused to read it, and it was then tendered to the prisoner, Mr. Fowden, who gave a like refusal, but, upon being pressed, he told them he could not see without his spectacles. Then Mr. Whalley, being demanded to repeat the proclamation after one of the rebel officers, said he had a hesitation in his speech and could not, upon which they obliged Mr. Fowden to repeat after them, which he did very unwillingly and in great fear.

" As to providing or paying for corn, hay, &c., an order was signed by the Pretender's secretary, Murray, addressed to the High Constable, to provide forage for their troops on Friday, 29th November, which order the High Constable, or his clerk, being then under guard of the rebels, was obliged to comply with, under pain of military execution, and accordingly made an order upon the Constables of Manchester, amongst the rest, for their proportion of such forage, &c. This order was brought to Mr. Bowker, Deputy Constable of the said town, then under a guard of the rebels at the ' Saracen's Head,' in Manchester, who was obliged by them to make under-warrants to the petty Constables of the inferior hamlets, and to put thereto the names of Mr. Walley and the prisoner, as is usually done to all warrants issued out from the Constables of Manchester under the High Constable's precept. This order is now in the custody of the Duke of Newcastle:

" Mr. Fowden was obliged to pay a bill to one Oaks, for corn which the rebels took out of his shop. Mr. Fowden provided no drums ; but it is presumed they will call one Shelmerdine to this point. This Shelmerdine was formerly a drummer in the King's service, and, at the time of the rebels coming to Manchester, kept the ' Rose and Crown,' in Manchester, and the rebels having lost their drummer, went to Shelmerdine's house to oblige him to drum for them. Shelmerdine, meeting with Mr. Fowden, acquainted him with the rebels' demand, and asked his advice, upon which Mr. Fowden said he could not tell how to advise him, for the sword was drawn against them, and he was forced to do many things against his will. Shelmerdine is a bad character, and has expressed great inveteracy against Mr. Fowden.

" As to providing men for casting bullets, Mr. Fowden was brought down, under a guard of armed rebels, to the house of one William Middleton, a plumber, to oblige him to assist in making bullets, which he refused to do, and Mr. Fowden never advised him to do it. But one Thomas Tipping, a Presbyterian, advised the said Middleton to comply with their demands to make bullets. Mr. Fowden was also taken to other places for the like purpose.

" As to seizing or searching for guns, or other arms, for the rebel army. The prisoner, Mr. Fowden, did go to several houses to search, but always under a guard of rebels.

" As to impressing, or ordering carriages, or horses, to draw the rebels' artillery, &c., they were generally provided by order from the High Constable. If it should be proved that the prisoner provided any, it will appear that he did so, guarded by the rebels.

" As to directing the rebels over fords, &c., Mr. Fowden was made a prisoner by the rebels, and forced either to find a man or to go himself as a guide, to shew the road leading to Cheadle Ford, &c. He provided one John Ratcliffe, but gave him directions to steal away as soon as he could.

"It will fully appear that, upon the rebels marching to Derby, and before any accounts of their retreat, two or three of the stragglers were picked up by the country people, and there being no Justices of the Peace in the town or neighbourhood of Manchester, the prisoner and his fellow constable committed them to the House of Correction, in order for their prosecution. Upon the return of the rebels towards Manchester, news being brought that a small party of them were intending to steal into the town before the rest, the prisoner ordered the watch to observe what house they went to, and immediately surround it and take them prisoners. Further, one Mr. Furnival, agent or steward to Lord Harrington, coming with dispatches from the Duke's army, and applying for horses to the prisoner, and the prisoner, thinking him to be a friend to the rebels, at first said there was no such thing to be got, but upon the said Furnival's telling him he came from the Duke, he then told him he would get horses immediately, and accordingly provided two horses for Mr. Furnival, in a very short time.

" If it be objected that the prisoner should have left the town upon the rebels' approach, it was apprehended by the inhabitants of the town in general, that if all the principal inhabitants had left the place, it would have been in very great danger to have been plundered. And as to the prisoner in particular, he had a great quantity of goods, some time before, bought in, and then in his warehouse in Manchester, which he apprehended would have been plundered and destroyed, if he left the place, and it was upon these considerations only that the prisoner was induced to stay at his own house.

" Mr. John Wilkinson and others of Preston, and Mr. Robert Bower of Stockport, will be called to prove that at Lancaster, Preston, and elsewhere, the rebels obliged the magistrates and others of the Corporations, to billet the rebels, attend at the proclamation of the Pretender, and provide hay, corn, &c., under threats of burning their houses and military execution, and that such commands were everywhere obeyed through fear.

" Mr. Thomas Walley will be called to prove that on the 26th of November, three days before the rebels came to Manchester, he applied to James Chetham, Esqre., and another justice of the peace, for directions how he and the prisoner, his fellow constable, should conduct themselves, in case the rebels came to Manchester, and Mr. Chetham said they must do whatever the rebels commanded.

" Mr Thomas Walley will be called to prove also, that on the 27th November, 1745, Edward Chetham, esquire, an eminent lawyer in Manchester, sent a letter to the witness, desiring that if all private houses in the town must necessarily have part of the forces that were expected, he would use his endeavours that none should be quartered in Mr. Chetham's house but such as were likely to behave well, and adds that, though he was going from home, he had ordered them to be accommodated as well in all respects as if he were present.

" Mr. Thomas Walley and Mr. Benjamin Bowker (who was Deputy Constable to the prisoner) will be called to prove that they and the prisoner had a meeting, to consider how to conduct themselves in case the rebels came to Manchester, and that at such meeting it was resolved that none of them should do anything for the rebels but what they were forced to do. They stayed in Manchester when the rebels came thither, by the advice of the substantial inhabitants of the town, in hopes to save the town being plundered and destroyed by the rebels, a report then prevailing at Manchester that the rebels had done much more damage, in the towns through which they had passed, where persons deserted their houses, than to the houses of persons who stayed at home.

"Mr. John Clowes and Mr. John Smith, the former of whom was High Constable for the Hundred of Salford, and the latter his clerk, will be called to prove that they were forced by the rebels to issue out their precepts or warrants to the petty constables, to press carriages for the rebels' use.

"N.B.—It is given out that the prosecutors intend to offer in evidence that the prisoner made interest to be elected Constable, in order, as is supposed, to favour the rebels. Mr. John Harrison and Mr. William Thackeray will be called to prove that the prisoner made all the interest he could to avoid the office.

"Matthew Lilly will be called to prove that his house was fixed on by the rebels for the quarters of the officers of the guard of the artillery, it being adjacent to the artillery ground. That on the 30th of November (the day after the entry of the main body of the rebels into Manchester), the military guard was relieved, and orders were given to have a number of men, the next morning (being Sunday) with picks, mattocks, and other instruments, to repair the ways for their better passage. He will prove that the rebels were so peremptory in their demands that no one dare disobey them.

"Mr. Josiah Nichols and Mr. John Lees will be called to prove that the former was compelled to pay the land tax, and the latter the window tax.

"Mr. Adam Parrin and Mr. J. Dickenson, junior, will be called to prove that the prisoner was, on Friday, the 29th November, 1745, brought down a street in Manchester, called Market Street Lane, by a great number of rebel officers, armed. That, as the prisoner came up to the 'Star and Garter' in the same street, he made a step sideways to speak to a person, which was not immediately observed by the rebels, who walked forward, but, looking back, they commanded the prisoner to go forward with them to the Market Cross, to proclaim the King, as they called him.

"William Oakes will be called to prove that a rebel officer, quartered at the house of one Mr. Richard Oliver, in Manchester, having bought corn from this witness for the rebels' horses, drew a bill upon the prisoner for the money payable to this witness. The prisoner refused to accept this, and the witness applied to the rebel officer, who ordered the Constable to be found out, and, meeting with the prisoner, cursed him, and told him that if he did not immediately pay, he would shoot him and plunder his house. That under these threats the prisoner paid witness the money.

"Elizabeth Hepworth will be called to prove that one of the rebel officers, who was called commissary, and others, sent from her house messengers, several times to the prison   ) attend them, and on his not coming upon their sending three   ., the commissary sent a fourth time, acquainting him that if }   .d not come forthwith, he should be put to military execution. That thereupon he came, and upon his coming before the commissary, the prisoner trembled and appeared to be in great fear. That the commissary commanded the prisoner to supply hay and corn for the Prince's use.

"William Hardwick will be called to prove that he told one Robert Shelmerdine that this witness had been informed that the said Shelmerdine had made oath before Mr. Duckinfield, a Justice of the Peace, that

Mr. Fowden ordered the said Shelmerdine to drum or beat up. Shelmerdine denied to this witness that he had made such oath, and said if any such thing was done it was Duckenfield's own doing.

" George Platt and Edward Bibby will be called to prove that the said Shelmerdine, after his having been at Lancaster, the last assizes, to give evidence to the indictment against the prisoner, declared he had been at Lancaster as a witness against the prisoner, and would go again and hang Fowden, if hemp would do it.

" The witness James Evans is subpœnaed by, and it is supposed will be examined on the part of the King; if not, he will be in Court, and upon his being called, will prove that he is a plumber and glazier in Manchester. That on Friday, the 29th November 1745, about 10 o'clock at night, seven armed rebel officers came to his house and asked how many men he had, and whether he had any bullet moulds. He answered that he kept no men, nor ever had any bullet moulds. That they thereupon told him they would find him moulds, and he must find men to cast the bullets. He told them it was impossible, at that time of night, to find men to assist him. They thereupon said they would apply to the Constables and force them to find men, and accordingly, two of them went from this witness's house to go to the Constables. The other five stayed with this witness, who desired they would excuse him making bullets, and let some of their own make them, whereupon they threatened to kill him, and oblige him to cast bullets the remainder of that night. That about 10 o'clock the next forenoon, ten or more townsmen came to assist this witness to make and file bullets, which they continued to do till Sunday morning, but he knows not by whom they were sent. That he never had any directions from the prisoner to cast bullets. That after the retreat of the rebels, one Samuel Taylor, a dissenter in Manchester, sent to this witness to examine him, who gave directions to cast bullets, and understanding he was not paid for the bullets so made, the said Taylor told the witness he thought he could assist him to get his money, and asked the witness if the Constables did not employ him to make bullets. Witness answered, no. Taylor then shook his head and said he was afraid he could get him nothing. Taylor afterwards asked witness again if the Constables did not employ him, and said that if they did he could help witness to get his money. Witness answered that they did not employ him.

" William Middleton, plumber, will be called to prove that on Saturday, the 30th of November, 1745, two Scotch rebels, who called themselves captains, came to this witness' house and asked him to work for the Prince, and upon his telling them he had no lead, one of the rebels brought the prisoner to witness' house, upon whose coming in, one of the rebels said, ' This is the man we want to work for the Prince.' The prisoner seemed very much surprised and frightened, and said, ' I can't make him go, gentlemen, if he won't go.' One of them replied, ' If he will not go, and you will not oblige him to go, we'll execute military law upon you both and burn both your houses.' That thereupon, one Mr. Thomas Tipping (a near neighbour to this witness) came into the shop, and being acquainted with what had passed, he advised the witness to go. Witness then went and worked for the rebels till he found means to escape, and never afterwards during the stay of the rebels saw the prisoner.

" James Williamson will be called to prove that on Saturday, the 30th November, 1745, a rebel officer and two other armed rebels, with bayonets fixed on their muskets, came to this witness' house and obliged him to swear, and then examined him as to arms. Witness told them he had a musket, which they made him produce. That upon their going away, the prisoner told the witness, privately, that he would not have come upon such an occasion, but that he was forced to. That the rebel officer, in this witness' hearing, commanded the prisoner to go with them to the house of one Pass, a militia-man, to search for arms.

"Mrs. Martha Cookson will be called to prove that on the same Saturday, a number of rebels came to her house to inform several rebel officers billeted there that they had been at the prisoner's house, and that the prisoner had refused to go with them to search for one Pass' gun, saying he was not well. Thereupon, the rebel officers ordered a captain of the rebels to go at the head of a party to the prisoner's house and bring him to this witness' house, dead or alive, and if he refused to come, to blow up his house. That thereupon they went, and after some time, brought the prisoner to the witness' house. That in a short time, the rebel captain commanded the prisoner to go with him, and in about half an hour they returned. That one Parkes, a new-listed rebel, brought with him a gun, which he told witness was Pass' gun. That the prisoner was again ordered into a room, and guarded by the rebels, on pretence they wanted him to search for arms in the parsonage in Manchester, where he was confined for about an hour, and then, the guard having left his post, the witness helped the prisoner to escape through a back door.

"Elizabeth Lancashire will be called to prove that on the same Saturday, the rebels brought the prisoner, under guard, to search for arms at the house of Francis Clay, in Manchester, and that the rebels, in their retreat from Derby, came to the said Clay's house to search for arms.

"Hurst will be called to prove a command to the prisoner, to provide a number of arms, by a certain time fixed by the rebels.

"Robert Smethurst will be called to prove a command to the prisoner to send to Wigan for arms, which he refused to do.

"Elizabeth Fletcher will be called to prove that . . . Pass declared that she would have no scruple in swearing the prisoner's life away. She also told witness that the prisoner came twice with rebel officers to her house to search for arms, and that the prisoner, by order of a rebel officer, took out a book to swear her.

"Ralph Ryder will be called to prove that he asked the said Pass why she shewed such malice against the prisoner, and the said Pass answered that it would make anybody spiteful to come to swear her for her husband's arms.

"William Thomas will be called to prove that, soon after the Lancaster Assizes, the said Pass told him that if the prisoner desired that she should not have appeared against him, he should have given her a fee.

"George Seddon will be called to prove that Samuel Maddox, one of the rebels, who, it is said, will appear against the prisoner, came with the prisoner to demand guests' horses at this witness' house, on Saturday, the 30th November, 1745. That the prisoner seemed uneasy at being under a constraint to attend Maddox.

"James Lord will be called to prove that two or three days after the rebels marched from Manchester towards Derby, and before any notice of their retreat, William Baynes and Robert Lever, both of Preston, came to Manchester; one of them having a sword, and they being strangers, and not giving a satisfactory account of themselves, the prisoner and his brother constable ordered them to be confined under a guard, and they continued in this witness' custody till the next day, when, having satisfied the prisoner and Mr. Walley, they were dismissed.

"John Barry will be called to prove that on Saturday night, 30th November, 1745, a rebel officer, armed, came to the prisoner's house, and commanded 12 or 14 carts to be in readiness at 8 o'clock the next morning, on account of drawing the artillery, &c.

" Mr. Thomas Furnivall will be called to prove that, being steward to Lord Harrington (a stranger to the prisoner, who came to Manchester as an emissary from the Duke of Cumberland, to give notice of the motions of the rebels), on his applying to the prisoner for horses, on the evening the rebels left Manchester in their retreat, that the prisoner, apprehending the witness was a friend of the rebels, told him he could not possibly procure any horses for him, but when witness told the prisoner the horses were for the Duke's service, the prisoner, with cheerfulness, told witness if there were two horses in town the witness should have them.

" William Greenhalgh will prove that he was upon the watch, as one of the watch of the town of Manchester, on the Saturday night before the rebels came to Manchester, in their retreat from Derby, and this witness and other persons upon the watch, having notice that some few of the rebels were upon the road between Stockport and Manchester, witness came to the prisoner and acquainted him therewith; the prisoner thereupon ordered the witness to follow any of the rebels who came to the place, and surround the house where they alighted and take them prisoners.

" John Ratcliffe will be called to prove that, being sent as a guide to the rebels, he was privately ordered by the prisoner to leave them as soon as he had an opportunity. That witness was likewise procured and sent by the prisoner as a guide, with part of the Duke's army towards Wigan and Preston, and the prisoner then gave him directions to do all he could for the Duke's army, and showed great zeal and desire to do anything in his power to serve the Duke's army.

" N.B.—It does not appear that the Government is in any way concerned in the prosecution of the prisoner at the bar, or that the same is carried on at the Crown's expense."

OPINION of SIR EDWARD NORTHEY and LORD FORTESCUE to the LORDS OF THE TREASURY, touching waste committed by Lords and others awaiting their trial for High Treason.

1225. [1746.]—" We have considered of the letter of Lord Viscount Townshend to your Lordships, and inclosed to us, acquainting your Lordships that the stewards, bailiffs, and other officers of those lords and gentlemen who were taken at Preston, are useing their utmost dilligence to raise what money they can from their estates, by collecting all arrears of rent and fines, cutting down wood, and by all such other methods as they can devise. And your Lordships having commanded us to advise the most proper methods to be taken to prevent the wastes, spoils, and ill practices therein complained of, we do most humbly testify to your Lorships that, by the law, the Crown is not intitled to the real estate or profits thereof of any person guilty of high treason till such person shall be legally attainted thereof by judgement or outlawry ; and that when such judgement shall be had, although the same will relate (in order to intitle the Crown to the land of the person so attainted) to the time mentioned in the impeachment or indictment on which they shall be attainted, when the treason was committed, yet as to the mean profits thereof, the Crown will be intitled only from the time of the judgement given. Therefore, such offenders may, until attainder, receive the profits of their real estates for the support of themselves and their families. But upon conviction, by verdict and confession, such offenders forfeit all their goods and chattels, which will extend to the arrears of rent grown due.

And therefore, as to the Lords convict by their own confession, notice may be given to their tenants to desist payment of such arrears of rent; and if they do pay the same to the Lords, they will be obliged to answer them again to the Crown.

"As to the goods and chattels of persons guilty of high treason, not convicted of the same by confession or otherwise, they may dispose of the same to the maintenance of themselves and their families, until conviction, and before conviction no seizure can be made for the same, but voluntary and unnecessary gifts and dispositions of their personal estates after treason committed, will be fraudulent against the Crown, and not prevent the forfeiture thereof, when they shall be convicted. As to the felling of timber, if it be not out of necessity for the support of the offenders and their families, we are of opinion the same ought not to be allowed, though before conviction, and where there is a conviction, the trees, when severed, will become personal estate and be forfeited by the conviction, and therefore, the removal of such as are felled may be stopped, and directions given not to fell more. Where there is no conviction, we think it proper that notice be given that the timber and personal estate be not disposed of but for the necessary support of the offenders and their families, and that if they should be otherwise disposed of, that an account thereof will be expected by the Crown, after conviction."

PETITION to the MEMBERS OF PARLIAMENT for the County of Lancaster.

1226. [1746.]—"We hope it will not be thought improper nor unbecoming to apply ourselves to you, the representatives of our county in the sitting of a Parliament, and in a matter of greivance and heavy oppression we labour under, and therefore, without more apology, we presume to lay the case of our hardships before you.

"There have been quartered within the towns of Manchester and Salford, from near the time of the action at Preston, which is now four months since, one regiment of foot and one of dragoons, making nine hundred men in both the towns, for they lie contiguous and appear but as one town, but have indeed distinct constables and are differently taxed. There are not above six inns that can entertain any number of horses, nor more than twenty public houses of any sort that can receive more than two horses apiece, the town being no throughfare, nor upon any public road for travellers, nor place of public resort other than for their own trade only, so that one single regiment of dragoons quartered upon the public houses would fill them all, so as not to leave one bed for a guest in their houses, nor room for one traveller's horse in any public stable in the two towns.

"The officers therefore have forced the Constables, though against law, to billet both themselves and their soldiers upon the private houses, and not only so, but have compelled them to follow their directions therein upon what persons to billet and whom to excuse, and this by threats of commitment, of stabbing and beating, and one of the officers upon this occasion drew his sword upon one of the constables and struck him therewith, in the presence of his wife, who was then great with child. Some officers likewise have demanded more billets than they have had soldiers, and by taking the billets into their own hands, have excused such houses as they pleased from quartering soldiers, and have made private advantage to themselves thereby.

"At their first coming to town, there were not more than three or four officers that were quartered at any public house, nor would they suffer the Constables to quarter them there, and five parts in six of the officers and above six hundred private soldiers are still quartered upon the private houses. Besides the soldiers, there are near two hundred and fifty women and children belonging to them in the two towns. For a considerable time after their coming to town, besides the regimental horses, there were belonging to the officers of dragoons and of the foot, and to several private soldiers, other horses not regimental, equal at least in number to the horses of the regiment, and great numbers are still continued, many officers having two or three apiece, some five, six, or more, and some near twenty horses, that are not regimental.

"The women and children and most of the horses are likewise forced upon private houses, the women and children entirely upon free quarter, and the greatest part of these horses the same, though, by law, all horses not regimental ought to pay sixpence a night for hay. The better to colour their illegal billeting upon private houses, and to make it specious as if done by consent of the people themselves, they have provided the Constables with a form of a billet, which is thus :—By consent, upon A. B. so many men and so many horses, from thence insisting that the Constable does not force any person, for he only draws his billet in case the party consent; and the officer or soldier, they say, forces nobody, for he comes there by their consent, as is plain from their receiving him. Notwithstanding this pretence of consent, yet when the people seemed averse to it, they demanded the names of all such as refused; they gave out they would be committed to the gaol or taken prisoner to the guard, and that they had a commission to do so at discretion; others that refused they threatned to be sent for to London by messengers and others, to be plundered.

"There fell out two very flagrant instances of plundering in the neighbourhood, both yet unpunished, and one with circumstances very suspicious upon some of the officers. There happened likewise, many instances of persons committed to the guard, and one of very severe usage there to a tradesman of substance in the town, who, without any offence charged upon him, was tyed neck and heels till blood sprung out of his eares. The apprehensions of these things, therefore, have made the billeting generally complied with, except only some dissenters who have stood upon the privilege of the subject, and have found favour beyond their neighbours.

"But to take off all pretence to this implied consent, such as it was, whether for fear or for peace sake, we beg leave to give an instance or two of their dealing with those that withstood them. One was an attorney, who, being a young man, a bachelor, and haveing only two lodging rooms fitted up, one for himself, the other for his sister, and a stable for his own horse, had a dragoon and two horses billeted upon him, and he refuseing to admit them, an officer of the dragoons ordered the soldier to break open the stable and to make his quarters good, which he did, put in the two dragoon horses and turned out the attorney's, for the stable would but very inconveniently hold two horses, and hath compelled the attorney to fit up a lodging for him and to entertain him. Another is of a tradesman, who having no stable, and having two dragoons and their horses billeted upon him, offered to entertain the dragoons, provided he might be freed from the horses, as having no stable; whereupon the dragoons, as they were ordered, took the horses into his parlour, and kept them there two days, till such time as he otherwise provided them a stable.

"It was expected, where they quartered upon houses not compellable by law to receive them, they would be the more punctual in the payment of those quarters. Yet for some time after their coming to town, neither officers nor soldiers in general paid anything at all. A great many officers and several soldiers have paid nothing to this day. Methods have been taken that some have had not only their hay but their corn provided. The dragoons who do pay, yet pay only eight pence a night for themselves and their horse ; the foot soldiers who pay highest, pay two shillings a week, some twenty pence, some eighteen pence, some less, and some nothing at all. Though the pay of the dragoons, by Act of Parliament, is nine pence a night, and for the foot soldiers two shillings and four pence *per* week, and by law expresly, the quarters ought to be paid before any subsistance is given either to officer or soldier, if any of the quarters dare to insist upon nine pence *per* night they are threatned to be made much more losers in their hay than that comes to, and yet they are forced to give receipts in full for the subsistance.

"A further hardship the Constables of the town suffer under is by being compelled to provide and pay rent for guard rooms, for a hospital for the sick rooms, for the tents and baggage of the soldiers, and likewise to provide coals and candles for the guard rooms and hospital, and bedding, linnen, washing and other necessaries for the hospital, which at the first, and for the cold season, cost three pounds a week, besides ten or fifteen pounds in fitting and preparing them, and does yet and is like still to continue to be thirty shillings a week, a charge which, as it cannot be assessed upon the town in a tax, by law, so, considering the other sufferings the inhabitants have undergone by quartering soldiers, is not likely to be voluntarily contributed to by the town, and if it must fall upon the Constables, will unavoidably ruin them. Now to estimate the damages, though far short of the truth, the penny a day for nine hundred soldiers, if all was paid to it, is three pounds fifteen shillings a day, and one thousand three hundred and sixty-eight pounds fifteen shillings a year short of the allowance of the Government; the women and children, at four pence *per* day, is four pounds three shillings and four pence *per* day, and one thousand five hundred and twenty pounds thirteen shillings and four pence a year. The charge of the non-regimental horses, we conceive should be six pence a night, but where there has been anything at all paid for them, it has not exceeded four pence by the highest officers.

"We will not compute, nor can we state, what the free quarter of the officers and soldiers will amount unto, because they may allege that though they have not yet paid, yet they do design to pay at last, but we beleive these two articles do much exceed all the other.

"By these hardships the town hath already suffered very much, and in a short time must be entirely ruined, several having already given up their houses, and a great many more families preparing to break up and leave the town ; the revenue of excise—though by the addition of nine hundred soldiers it might be expected to be exceedingly advanced —does hardly keep up to its former rate, and the returns by the trade in the town, by computation, are already found to have sunk a thousand pounds a week.

"We will not presume to judge of a reason for quartering so great a body of men upon us, when there are near half a score considerable market towns in our county and in Cheshire, within twelve or fourteen miles of us, that have not a soldier amongst them, but we humbly hope we may enjoy the benefit of the laws of England, and if there be any necessity for keeping so great a body of men together, either upon us or in any one place, more than there is convenient quarters for by law, that barracks or other conveniences may be provided at the charge of the Government ; that we may be maintained in our rights and pro-properties, so long as the law continues them to us.

" We applied to Mr. Wills, whilst in town, and more especially concerning the women, children, and non-regimental horses, and were promised to be freed therein. We have applied to the commanding officers since, and likewise to the civil magistrates, for releif, but can obtain none, nor any hopes thereof, nor can we hear of any time the burden is likely to be removed. The people's patience is tired out thereby, the Constables are in danger to be torne to peices by actions on that account, the inhabitants are leaving the place, and the trade does visibly decline every day, and this without the least charge of crime or disaffection to be fixed upon any one person of substance in the town, after the most strict and diligent inquiry.

" We therefore humbly beg your direction and assistance for redress, in the most proper legal and dutiful method, that the towns may not be burthened with more soldiers than they are able to quarter, and that those may be placed in the public houses, with reasonable convenience to them ; that the officers and soldiers may be removed from the private houses or from such as are not willing longer to continue them; that we may be freed from the quartering of women, children, and non-regimental horses ; that the officers and soldiers may be obliged to pay their quarters and to the full subsistance, as allowed by law, and that the extraordinary expenses and rent for guard rooms, hospital, and the other charges above mentioned, may be repaid and, for the future, discharged by the Government. We will make good in proof every allegation charged, with much more if it be insisted on, as shall be directed by you, and will, with all thankfulness, pursue your orders herein." *Draft.*

George Kenyon to George Gibson.

1227. 1746[-7], January 31. Peel.—I have sent up to you, by Mr. Chadwick, the convictions of the popish recusants in our county, in the year 1744. The convictions were sent up about a year ago to the late Mr. John Kay of Furnival's Inn, with directions for him to get them certified into Chancery or the King's Bench, but Sir Thomas Bootle interposing, and applying to the Lord Chancellor and some other of the Lords of the Privy Council, an order was, on 3 March, 1745, issued for suspending, all proceedings upon such returns. I need not tell you how disagreable these delays were to some of our Justices, and how much I was teased, bullied, and threatened, though I was quite innocent and passive. I was in hopes, when the Privy Council had taken the matter into their own hands, our Justices would have waited the resolutions of that august assembly ; however, I find it otherwise, for last Saturday, at Manchester, after the business of the Sessions was over, and I was gone home, the Justices adjourned their Sessions to an alehouse that evening, at which adjournment Mr. Chetham of Smedley (as I am informed) produced a letter from Sir Henry Houghton, with a draft of an order, ordering the Clerk of the Peace, before the 1st March next, to certify into the High Court of Chancery or King's Bench, the names of all such persons as were convicted, in pursuance of an order of Council to put the laws in execution against papists, reputed papists, and non-jurors, bearing date 24 February, 1743-4. I desire you, therefore, to wait upon Sir Thomas Bootle and acquaint him with what has happened, and tell him I hope he will not take it amiss if you should proceed to certify the convictions in Chancery or the King's Bench (as I desire you would) in case the Lords of the Privy Council shall not please to give other directions.

GEORGE GIBSON to GEORGE KENYON.

1228. 1746[-7], February 14. Inner Temple. — Sir Thomas Bootle has been so much engaged, that he has not had time to apply to the Chancellor to stop returning the convictions, but promises me to do it directly. I have also spoken to Mr. Westby, the Duke of Norfolk's steward, and others, to apply for the same purpose, and hope they will be able to make interest to prevent the designs of that persecuting dog, Sir H[enr]y [Hoghton], and his wicked accomplices.

PETER LEIGH to GEORGE KENYON.

1229. 1746[-7], February 26. — Sir Roger Bradshaw died last night, and Mr. Clayton is gone down to offer his service. He is a good sort of a man, and I will venture to ask your vote in his favour. *Seals.*

ORDER by the LORDS OF THE COUNCIL.

1230. 1747, April 3. Whitehall.—Whereas by order of this Board of the 3rd of March, 1745, it was directed that the several returns or certificates made by the *Custodes Rotulorum,* Justices of the Peace, Mayors, &c., in pursuance of his Majesty's late Proclamation and the Orders of this Board for putting the laws in execution against papists and non-jurors, should be taken into consideration upon that day month, and that all proceedings upon the said returns or certificates should be for the present suspended. And whereas three petitions have been presented to his Majesty, at this Board, from the County of Lancaster, "all which petitions relate to the recording in the Courts of Chancery or King's Bench the names of those persons who neglected to appear before the said Justices, or who have appeared and refused to take the oaths; It is hereby ordered in Council that the Orders of this Board, issued to the Justices of the Peace of the County Palatine of Lancaster on the 24th of February, 1743-4, and 5th of September, 1745, together with the returns or certificates made thereto by the Justices of the Peace of the said county, and also the three before mentioned petitions (copies of all which papers are herewith annexed) be referred to his Majesty's Attorney and Sollicitor General, to consider thereof and report to his Majesty in Council what may be done by law, either for proceeding upon the said returns or certificates, or for staying proceedings thereupon absolutely, or for such time as his Majesty shall think proper, and likewise to report their opinion upon the whole. And it is hereby further ordered in Council, that all proceedings on the said returns or certificates be, in the meantime, suspended and stayed." *Copy.*

ROBERT ESCOLME, Clerk to George Gibson, to GEORGE KENYON.

1231. 1747, May 5. London.—"Herewith, by Mr. Gibson's order, you receive the Orders of Council which have come to my hands, but the last could not [be] got, Mr. Westby being very much troubled, having lost, as I am told, his wife."

GEORGE GIBSON to MR. MORT, Deputy Clerk of the Peace, at Ormskirk.

1232. 1748[-9], February 16. Inner Temple.—"By this post, I have sent to Mr. Kenyon, at Peel, an order of the Privy Councill to stay the proceedings on the convictions against Dr. Deacon, etc., and to refer them to the Attorney and Sollicitor-General, in the manner the former were. If your outragious Justices continue troublesome and make any more orders, I fancy they will be left out of the Commission of the Peace, for the Lords of the Privy Council are very angry at them."

J. Kenrick to Lloyd Kenyon.

1233. 1750, November 14. Brazenose College, Oxford.—"It is true, as you observe, that we in college here are not absolutely obliged to pursue our studies, but then there are so many restraints laid upon us, that they almost put it out of our power to avoid it. For, if we appear out, we are in danger of being taken by the Proctors, or of being branded by names of loungers; besides, we have duties in our college to attend, all which we consider make our confinement here as great as at school, but far from being so disagreeable, for you may suppose that we can employ some part of the day with a great deal of pleasure in our private chambers, exclusive of all obligation.

"That you may the better understand the method we go upon, I shall divide our lectures into public and private. First, then, with our private tutor, we are lectured in Plato's Dialogues and logic, whenever he pleases to call upon us ; for our public lectures in the hall, we have particular days in the week, which consists of Xenophon's *Memorabilia*, and Horace, by two different lecturers, one of whom is Mr. Mather, a very ingenious man, whom, I dare say, you have heard of   As for our exercises, they are disputations, three times a week, besides a declamation every term. I must now, since you desired me, give you some account of my examination for admission.

"My tutor first of all tried me in epics and Horace; the next day the Principal sent for me, and put a Horace into my hand, and then Virgil, and lastly Sophocles, where I read half a dozen lines . . . , and to conclude the farce, he gave me a theme to make. But I must not omit telling you that I came on to dispute last week, a work which I do not like much as yet, though I chop logic pretty fast. I was last night at Frederick's room, when he had just received a letter from Thelwall, who is the only person that sends us any country news. He tells us that all they that make any figure at school now, are to be up at Lent, and guess what a wretched place it must be then ! The daring Baronet has left school long since, in a great pet, and is now the hero of Beaumaris' school ; the reason of his elopement again was a correction given him for a criminal intrigue with Robert Jones, of 'the Raven's,' daughters. . . . The freshmen at Cambridge tell me they like their situation vastly ; if you should chuse to write to them, you will find Jones at St. John's College and Thelwall at Catherine Hall."

George Kenyon to his cousin, Lloyd Kenyon.

1234. 1750, November 16. Oxford.—"I do not wonder at all that Kenrick sent you so very different an account of Oxford from mine. It is indeed a very different place to different persons. The gown a man wears excuses him from many exercises, as a lower gown obliges him to them. Besides this, he has got an office that obliges him to attend morning, noon, and night, so that he can never be away six hours together. This, you allow, is confinement indeed, and no wonder he should prefer school to it. However, he will be eased of this in a little time. The only exercises we have to do is to repeat a passage out of a classic; every day at dinner, when it comes to our turns, to dispute in turns ; to make a theme once a week and a declaration once a term, and to read the lessons in chapel, when we are a year's standing, in turn. Most of these, you see, come to us one after another, so that we are not often plagued with them, and the rest, if a man will, may very easily be slubbered (*sic*) over."

GEORGE KENYON to his father, GEORGE KENYON.

1235. 1750[-1], February 27. Oxford.—Giving an account of his studies. He hopes his affair with Mr. Clayton is in a likely way to end well, but he knows his father would not have him sit tamely and lose his reputation.

WARRANT to impress carriages to convey the baggage and stores of General Woolf's regiment from Lancaster to Burton.

1236. 1751, September 19.—Warrant from James Fenton, Doctor of Laws, one of the Justices of the Peace for the County of Lancaster, to the constable of Heysham, to impress six carriages within his township, each carriage to consist of an able horse and cart, with an able man to attend the same, to be at the Town Hall, in Lancaster, on the 21st September, by five o'clock in the morning, to convey the baggage and military stores belonging to General Woolf's regiment of foot, from Lancaster to Burton, in the County of Westmoreland. *Signed.*

J. KENYON to LLOYD KENYON.

1237. 1752, February 12.—"Mr. Hanmer intends to build a tower so high that he may see over the Welsh mountains into Anglesea and to the Irish seas, so I hope when I go up there I may see you running about the streets at Nantwich, which will be a more pleasing object to me."

BRIDGE OVER THE RIBBLE.

1238. 1752, October 9.—Specifications for the masons' work in a bridge over the Ribble near Preston.

1239. 1753, May 4. Wigan.—An address from "a disinterested Burgess of Wigan" to the Burgesses of Wigan, concerning the candidates for election to Parliament, and calling attention to the bribery and corruption committed by two candidates, Sir J———— S———— and Mr. Serjeant P————. The two other candidates are the Hon. Richard Barry and Sir William Meredith, Bart. *Printed.*

GORTON CHAPEL.

1240. 1753, October 11.—Petition of the minister, chapel wardens, and inhabitants, of the township and chapelry of Gorton, in the parish of Manchester, to the Justices of the Peace for the County of Lancaster, praying that their case for Letters Patents, to authorize them to ask and receive charity to enable them to rebuild the said chapel, may be recommended to the Lord Chancellor.

The petition sets out that the chapel of Gorton is a very ancient building, and that divine service and the sacraments were performed therein in the reign of Queen Elizabeth (as appears by the register of the said chapel) but, through length of time, it is become ruinous and in decay, and in so great danger of falling that the inhabitants cannot assemble therein, without danger to their lives. They have been at great expense in repairing the pillars, posts, and supporters of the roof, which is chiefly of timber covered with heavy slate. That the chapel is not large enough to contain the increased number of persons who resort to the township to be employed in the manufactures there. That the walls of the chapel, being sixty feet in length and forty in breadth, are so cracked and bulged that they must be wholly rebuilt. That the estimate for the charges of taking down and rebuilding the said chapel is computed at 1,171*l.* and upwards, over and besides the old materials, which the inhabitants, of themselves, are unable to raise, the said township being small, though populous, and a considerable part thereof consisting of cottagers and labourers, and common workpeople in the linen and cotton manufactures, who are not able to contribute much thereto. *Signed.*

JAMES TOMKINSON to LLOYD, afterwards first LORD KENYON.

1241. [17]55, March 22. London.—"As your stay in town will be, at your first coming up, short, it may perhaps be as well for you to take lodgings, and you may then determine, yoursef, with more satisfaction as to chambers. But, in my opinion, you cannot prudently avoid having chambers in Michaelmas term. I find that the Society of the Middle Temple is esteemed equal, if not preferable, to any other, and, soon after my return home, I will solve all your enquiries, when I shall be glad to see you at Nantwich. You will be so good as to give Jemmy (?) the inclosed letter; if his learning shorthand will not interfere with his other business, and it is thought he may acquire by Christmas a tolerable knowledge of it, I have then no objection to his attending Dr. Byrom."

BILL OF MORTALITY for the towns of MANCHESTER and SALFORD.

1242. 1755.—Total number of christenings, 744; of burials, 706; and of marriages, 287. The greatest mortality was of children under 2 years old. Consumption was the most fatal disease, carrying off 204 persons.

R. KENYON to his brother, LLOYD KENYON, at Gredington.

1243. 1756, April 15. Nantwich.—"Mr. Tomkinson's weakness prevents his going to the meeting at Northwich to-day, but it is supposed Mr. Cholmondeley will meet with no opposition, as Councillor Wilbraham has great influence over Lord Dysart, and I am told has advised him to drop all thoughts of setting up his son, Lord Huntingtower."

JANE KENYON to LLOYD KENYON.

1244. 1757, May 6.—"I believe you have heard of a cocking that was to be at Hanmer on May-day, at which Tom Puleston was victor. Mr. Probert was here yesterday, but would not own his loss, said it was more than he ever lost at once, or ever would again; and as for Puleston, I believe, if he will reckon his bad chances with the good ones, he will not find himself much enriched, for they say he was above forty pound loser at Wellington."

CHURCH SEATS.

1245. 1757, August 18.—Acknowledgment by John Ryder that though he and his family sit in a seat in the parish church of Leigh which adjoins a seat belonging to Mr. Shackerley, and stands in the north aisle of the said church, which seat belongs to George Kenyon, yet he, the said John Ryder, claims no right or interest therein. *Signed.*

Like acknowledgements by Mary Battersby and Joseph Eckersley, under the same date. *Signed.*

R. KENYON to LLOYD KENYON.

1246. 1758, February 25.—Lord Dupplin is resolved to part with no places belonging to the Duchy or extend the present grants, "as the office had been scandalously stript already. . . . Captain Clive has remitted three bills, value 57,000*l.* each, and also 40,000*l.* in cash, by way of Holland; and writes word he has sent 140,000*l.* by his wife, whom he hopes to follow soon with as much more, an amazing sum for one man, and this is, it seems, all his own. Sir John Glynne has speeched it away last week in support of the Triennial Bill, and they say pretty sensibly, but the notion was rejected again by a great majority. Pitt had got the gout and did not attend, and Beckford is much blamed for making the motion at so improper and unexpected a time. Jones sets out to-morrow on horseback, I believe, as does Dunning, on the Western circuit. The *Habeas Corpus* Bill is ordered to be brought into the House, but much opposition was given by Mr. Solictor and Norton, till Pratt undertook them, who answered the former, and cut through the latter very severely."

The SAME to the SAME.

1247. [1758, March —.]—"Mr. Tomkinson has given up his application and assigned his votes to Mr. Wilbraham, so that the dispute will now lie betwixt Bob Gorst, Mr. Wilbraham, and Tom Davenport, and it seems most likely Mr. Wilbraham will have it; and if that happens, wise Tommy talks of leaving Germain Street and going to Chester, to be his brother's secretary. . . . .

"The *Habeas Corpus* Bill was read a second time on Friday, and hot work ensued. Wilbraham made a speech above an hour long against it, in which he enumerated a happy situation, and many blessings he enjoyed in a dutiful son and daughter, with other things as pertinent to the question! But Mr. Pitt soon cut down this old apple-woman, and handled him most severely. Pratt opposed the Solicitor, and Beckford roared out loudly that the writ was a writ of right, and of too much consequence to be denied at the option of a folish or time-serving judge, many of whom were incapable of judging when it should be granted, and others so audacious and arbitrary, that he had heard they had not scrupled to shew their lust of subverting our freedom by breaking in upon the institution of juries and exhorting a verdict, in direct opposition to their conscience (meaning the late trial of the *Monitor*), and though some of the jurymen had signifyed their doubts, and refused to find it, they had been several times sent from the Bar with this memerable order: 'that they must find the defendant guilty.' In all probability the act will pass through the lower House; but for the other, I much question it."

The SAME to the SAME.

1248. 1758, November 9.—Has been shooting on Bettisfield Moss with "Champion Dymock and Bob Powell."

"Nabob Clive's father, Brother Clive of the Styche, Squire Broughton, and Johnny Alcock, arrived at Whitfield's the day we were there. I suppose they have pretty near cleared the country."

R. KENYON to LLOYD KENYON.

1249. 1759, June 25. Peel.—" The behaviour of Sir J. Glynne raised my indignation not a little, though from what he said on Wednesday was three weeks at Mr. Price's birthday, I had no expectation of hearing any good of him. He is, I find, a great condemner of Mr. Pitt, and little better than a chattering caff (*sic*). You do not say whether his motion was granted or not."

———————— to GEORGE KENYON.

1250. [1759, September.]—" The account in to-day's paper is that Captains Brett and Douglas were arrived express from General Towns-hend, with an account that on the 16th of September, General Wolfe attempted to draw the French out of their trenches by sending a body of four or five thousand men up the country to destroy their shipping and provisions, but this did not succeed. On the 17th, the General determined to attack the French army by scaling a ridge of rocks on the north side of the town, which the French thought impracticable, and consequently had placed no sentry in that part. That on the 18th, three or four thousand men, with the General at their head, went to the attack. That General Wolfe and the other general officers were the first that got to the top of the rocks, and the troops followed them, being handed up by one another unperceived by the French. That as soon as the troops began to form they were discovered, and attacked by the French and Canadians. That the action continued not above twenty minutes, when the French were totally defeated, and the town was surrendered immediately. The loss on our side is only 45 men killed, amongst whom is General Wolf, who was killed at the first fire; and 500 wounded. The French had 1,400 killed. Mons. Montcalm and the three or four next in command are dead."

GEORGE KENYON to his father, GEORGE KENYON.

1251. 1759, November 3.—" General Haddick is arrested and sent to Vienna to answer for his conduct, and his army has joined Daun, who seems determined to attack Prince Henry, and the Prussians likewise seem to expect a battle. The King of Spain sailed, the 6th of last month, from Italy, and the morning before he went, declared his third son King of Naples. The French ministry is entirely changed, and Belleisle is quite out; D'Estrées succeeds him, and Broglie is to command the army. The French fleet is sailed into the road of Brest, and Hawke has sent word that he expects they will come out and fight him, but there seems to be no great dependence on this. There is no further account of Thurot."

THOMAS PERCIVAL to ————————.

1252. 1759, November 16. Royton, near Rochdale.—" For my own part, though I am enlisted amongst the men of speculative learning, I would have all my relations and friends enrolled amongst the men of business, and have every one of them aspire to be at the top of his profession. It is but, as Lord Somers said, a man making a resolution he will be Chancellor of England and he will be so. By resolution, he means endeavours, as well as inclination, to be so; and therefore I advise you, as a friend, to make that resolution in time, for the sooner you make it, the more likely you will be to obtain it. The glorious success of this year I ascribe solely, and under God, to Mr. Pitt; for you must know that I have a most despicable opinion of the heads and hearts of the *junto*, and often reflect with anguish on those psuedo patriots at White's. As old Harley said formerly, he feared that set would ruin the nation, so I am so very much of his opinion that I could almost wish to act one winter in the commission of peace, to rout them; for I much fear they will contrive to sell what they could not obtain by their own councils."

R. KENYON to LLOYD KENYON.

1253. 1760, June 17. Gredington.—The judicious Mr. Heber has undoubtedly given an account of Prees races, where there was but little diversion or company, and Tom Bycott and Mr. Pytts are stewards elect. Our Rowdee races are to be the 3rd and 4th July, and a considerable subscription, I am told, is made. The expectation of these last must undoubtedly have hurt Whitchurch races very materially.

THOMAS PERCIVAL to —— ——.

1254. [1760,] November 20. Royton.—"A gentleman of good estate in Ireland and Lancashire, Mr. Matthews, of Brandelsholme, about three weeks ago, went from Parkgate to Dublin, in order to his election of member for Kilkenny, and is said to be lost at sea, the vessel stranding he was aboard of. The King of Prussia's victory will, I hope, set him beyond the power of Austrian malice, as I presume money, the sinew of war, is not very plentiful at Paris and Vienna. The worthy clergy of the diocese of Canterbury are very pompose in their address; and if his Majesty will follow the advice of that learned reverend body, without reserve, I doubt not but the everlasting crown they promise him would be such a one as Laud provided for Charles the First. I am sincerly for the good of the Church of England, but I freely own I think the clergy ought not to be concerned in state affairs, for they always make blundering work of it, their politics being more calculated for the meridian of Madrid or Lisbon then that of London or Westminster. In the meantime, if they can flatter the present King into good measures, I will say they have, for once, done well. But what are we to say to the address of the London clergy? They seem to be as much too low as the Canterbury folks are too high. Now, I draw from these addresses this inference: Secker thinks his interest at court is rising, and Sherlock thinks his over, in that pious place. You will say I judge harshly; but remember, whenever you want a key to a priest's conduct, that interest is his ruling motive."

"SIR WILLIAM MEREDITH's CONFESSION OF FAITH, with the last speech and dying words, to a gentleman in London."

1255. 1761, January 2. Chester.—"You are so kind as to mention an objection that has been made to me as if I was suspected to retain principles of disaffection to the Government. In the universal abolition of those opinions it is hard that I am to remain under so odious a distinction. On the most diligent recollection of my actions it seems impossible such a notion can be founded on any one event of my life. It is true I had a grandfather a nonjuror, who had been educated in the Court and enjoyed some preferments in the reign of Charles the 2nd and his brother, for which reason he refused to take any oath to another King. How does that affect me, otherwise than to teach me, as far as example can, the same religious observance of the oath I have taken to this King that he did to the Stuarts? If I can receive conviction from the feelings of my own heart, there was not a man took up arms with a firmer resolution than myself, to venture his life against the very interest I am supposed to adhere to, had any attempt been made, or should one be made, in its favour. But to think me insensible of the blessings this nation may expect from a King born and bred amongst us, of the same religion, the same sentiments of liberty that every honest man feels, and as much private virtue as ever man possessèd, and that I wish to change such a King for a foreigner, a papist, and an unhappy man whose actions almost destroy the compassion one would naturally feel for the misfortune of his family. I say whoever harbours such an opinion of me, must either imagine I have a very weak head or a depraved and wicked heart. There is no report so foolish and absurd as not to make an impression on some minds, but I did never think to hear myself called a Jacobite. I do not wish to know either the author or retailers of such an aspersion. I have said too much on a subject that deserves so little notice, but was desirous to shew a regard to anything you mentioned." *Copy.*

THOMAS PERCIVAL to [LLOYD KENYON ?].

1256. 1761, April 18.— "I am afraid poor Kitty is still in a worse state than me. She is now at Buxton. The doctors have sent her thither, perhaps to lay the blame on the waters rather than on their own skill. In the meantime, I must say I have hopes of the best, but I fear the worst. These dismal thoughts naturally put one in mind of preparing for all events, and, as you are a lawyer, I beg you will put me into a proper way to settle an annuity on Juba, my black boy; as he is an alien, there must be some care taken in it, and I fancy you have cases of that kind occur sometimes in London; whether it is possible to do it, I own it is to me a doubt, without trusting some friends absolutely, and I would choose to avoid that if I could, and I know no one more capable in directing me than yourself. Surely, somebody besides me have had a friendship for an alien; and if so, where would they apply for advice but to the Temple? At your leisure, favour me with your thoughts hereon."

W. STARKIE to GEORGE KENYON.

1257. 1761, September 29. Manchester.—As to a meeting which Mr. Richard Assheton suggests should take place at "Dangerous Corner," in Manchester, at "ringing ten a clock," as it is "Mr. Parker and Mr. Londsdall's way into town, and near the colleges."

FRANCIS FILMER to LLOYD KENYON, at Gredington.

1258. 1761, December 19.—"The day you went out of town, the Parliament met in the Middle Temple Hall, and, after chusing Mr. Morris their speaker, resolved on a call of the House, and Mr. Wood, the Serjeant-at-Arms, was commanded to give personal notice to all the members then in town. The session continued during the remainder of vacation commons, and, as I hear, for I never attended the House, came to several resolutions of great importance. But as the votes are not published, I know not the particulars, further than that they sat very late, the last day of their session, upon a motion for impeaching the worthy president of the bar-mess of high crimes and misdemeanours, pretended to have been committed by him during the last term, in violation of the rights and privileges of the commons. The debate was long, and maintained with great obstinacy on both sides, but at length the worthy gentleman's friends so far prevailed that he, who attended pursuant to summons, was allowed to make his defence in his place, much to the satisfaction and entertainment of all parties, not excepting his most violent opponents. The chief speakers in this and every other debate of consequence were Messrs. Dunning and Hotham, whose eloquence has been much applauded. These gentlemen attended that service with the greater assiduity, as they were excluded from the gallery of the other House of Commons by an order expressly prohibiting the admission of any but the sons of Members or Peers of Parliament. You see the Chief Justice of the Common Pleas is dead, and probably to night's Gazette may declare his successor; it is generally thought Mr. Attorney will be the man, though it is said Bathurst makes a push. If the Attorney takes it, Mr. Sollicitor will, of course, succeed him, and then the contest for Sollicitor, it is imagined, will be between Norton and De Grey."

The Rev. R. Wroe to George Kenyon.

1259. 1763, September 16. Radcliffe.—"You were so good to desire me to consult you, upon any little emergency, by letter. My friend Smethurst plays his old game ; he has sowed his grain in so many different fields, that he has in some of them only nine riders (a rider is ten sheaves), in others nineteen, and so on. Another litigious fellow has bound up all his oats into nine large riders. They will say corn has usually been set up in riders in this county ; but if I do not gather it of these people in the sheaf, I am precluded from receiving tithe. Shall I demand every tenth sheaf in form, or make my observations only, and wait till the harvest is closed ? "

William Hulton to George Kenyon, at Peel.

1260. 1763, November 20. Hulton Park.—I cannot perceive the confusion in Manchester without being a little, myself, surprised at Mr. Clayton's conduct; so I make no doubt but you are apprehensive of the consequences, [and] inconveniences, to which the town and neighbourhood may be exposed by his obstinacy. The expected lapse to the Government will undoubtedly be attended with a total expulsion of the honest men in Lancashire from the Collegiate Society of Manchester. This, you are well satisfied, may not only effect both you and myself, but each landed man in the county, and more especially those who have connections in the parish. The intercession of you, for whom Mr. Clayton has expressed often a great regard might, perhaps, prevent his character from being . . . . into, the constitution of Manchester Church from being overturned, and the child yet unborn, cussing (*sic*) the day of Mr. Clayton's birth. It is very possible some composition might be made, though I cannot answer for any. The Warden stands Mr. Assheton's friend, purely, I believe, through principle and regard to the town. He, I believe, expected Clayton would not have falsified his word, but, according to his promise, would have joined Mr. Assheton. Mr. Clowes has little expectations, and is to go for Cambridge to-morrow. If he had the chaplainship and St. Mary's, would not that be sufficient to keep a worthy man in the county and pave a road to his future preferment ?

Reginald Heber to [George Kenyon].

1261. 1764, January 19. Oxford.—"You may depend upon my best endeavours to do your brother all the service in my power, who, I believe, is very deserving. I hope he will soon be able to return to college, where his residence will be proper, some time before the election."

RICHARD HEBER to GEORGE KENYON.

1262. 1764, January 21. Westminster.—Has received his letter, and has lost no time in applying to his brother in Manchester in regard to the contents of it. Finds his brother is ready to serve Mr. Robert Kenyon [as applicant for the librarianship at Manchester College?], but is doubtful if he will have a vote.

GEORGE KENYON to THOMAS BANKS.

1263. 1765, December 3. Peel.—I left them much engaged at Manchester about a new navigation intended between Macclesfield, Stockport, and Manchester. It is to come to the top of Market Street Lane, and to have no communication with the Duke's, which makes his Grace oppose it, but the old navigators seem to be for it, at least, do not seem willing to be at the expense of opposing it. The undertakers are Sir George Warren and the Macclesfield people.

ACT for making the Mersey and Irwell navigable from Liverpool to Manchester.

1264. [1765.]—An Act for making the rivers Mersey and Irwell navigable from Liverpool to Manchester, in the County Palatine of Lancaster. *Printed.*

ROGER KENYON to GEORGE KENYON, at Wigan.

1265. 1768, April 26. Penylan.—"If your candidates can boast of their dissipation, ours may of their parsimony; the representative for this county was chaired by his own servants, and the whole expense, I am told, amounted not to ten pounds, five of which was squeezed out of him, with prodigious reluctance, towards a ball for the Denbigh ladies; and small as this expense may seem to you, the member for our borough of Flint managed still better. Such of the voters as came out of Maylor Hundred (and I think there were only 4 of them) had an allowance of a pint of ale apiece, but were obliged to pay for their supper and breakfast themselves, and, it is supposed, all charges together (including ringers) could not amount to 40s., save the fees paid to the returning officer. I rejoice much at Mr. Barry's defeat, as well as at that of Lord Strange, but rather suspect the latter will petition (if the present Ministry stands) and carry everything before him. If Lord Rockingham comes in (which with us is generally believed) I suppose they will . . . . warn him out of the Dutchy Court . . . . . . Your letter to me had not been opened at the Post Office, but there certainly are strange abuses all over the kingdom in that department, both with regard to over charging letters and sending them a roundabout way, and it is great pity but some examples were made."

The DUKE OF PORTLAND to LLOYD KENYON, "Essex Court, Temple."

1266. 1768, July 10. Charles Street, Berkeley Square.—"Poorly as the enclosed may express the sense of the gentleman concerned in the Cumberland and Carlisle elections, as well as my own, custom must apologise for such an offer, and your own kindness and zeal for the cause will, I hope, represent to you the sentiments we entertain of the services you rendered to the cause. We have only to beg the continuance of your assistance in the completion of this work, when Mr. Fletcher's petition comes on to be heard."

W. W. Tomkinson to ——————.

1267. 1768, November 10. "At Mr. Mackenrots, Pall Mall."— "This day was presented, by Lord Strange, the petition of Sir Henry Hoghton and Colonel Burgoyne, complaining of a false return and partiality, in the late election for Preston. There is another petition from the inhabitants, setting forth that they were rejected by the Mayor, etc., and were deprived of their right, under the last resolution of the House and the statute made in confirmation thereof; and the 29th of this instant is fixed for the hearing of the petition . . . . Colonel Burgoyne, I understand, gives out that he hath engaged Govern-ment on his side and is sure of success. This idea seems pretty general, but no pains will be spared to defeat them, although we are told it will be to no purpose, and that the rights of a very respectable borough is to be left to a Ministerial vote, guarded in such a manner as to be taken up anew, and determined according to the humor of future Tories."

G. Byng to ——————.

1268. 1769, February 25. North Audley Street.—"In the Committee last night on the *Nullum Tempus* Bill, we had a division whether we were to have prospect as well as retrospect, and beat the administration hollow; our numbers, 205 to 124. I thought you would be glad to hear of so good a bill meeting with so great a support in the Commons, and that it is likely to carry equal good to posterity as to ourselves, and that ministerial power has not, in this instance, as yet prevailed. I hope it will meet with no diminution in the Lords."

George Kenyon, Junior, to his father, George Kenyon, at Peel.

1269. 1769, February 28. Swinley. — The defeat of Lord Strange, mentioned in Mr. Byng's letter, was upon the following occasion. "Upon the hearing of the complaint against Harris for a breach of privilege, he asked pardon of Sir William Meredith, and was dismissed. But Sir William forgot to move (as is usual) that Mr. Harris might be obliged to pay the expense of all the witnesses, &c., who had been ordered to attend upon the occasion; upon which Mr. Tarleton and Phillips (the printer of the Liverpool newspaper) petitioned the House that Sir William might pay their expenses himself, and the petition was to have been delivered in by Lord Strange. But at the first mention of the thing, the House took it up so warmly that my Lord Strange durst not go on with it, and was treated so roughly that he did not appear in the House for some days after." Lady Sarah Bunbury has eloped with Lord William Gordon; they went from Sir Thomas's house, in Suffolk, to the young Duke of Dorset's, in Kent.

The Same to the Same.

1270. 1769, March 24. Swinley. — Yesterday, the information against Burgoyne came on at six o'clock in the morning, and lasted thirteen hours, when Burgoyne and several other of the defendants were found guilty. " I had a letter from Hotham, who tells me he took some pains to have that clause altered in the Militia Act, which is so extremely severe upon the clerks of the peace, and that Sir George Saville employed his endeavours to the same purpose, but they found all the rest of the committee unanimous against them, which, I suppose, was through my Lord Strange's influence. . . . . An indictment was tried at Lancaster against one of Burgoyne's mobbers, for plundering Jackson, the linnen-draper's, house, and forcing him to deliver up his money on his knees. Jackson swore positively to the fact and the person, and there was other evidence; but two witnesses were produced for the defendant, who swore he was never in the shop, but was at that time in bed at a public house, upon which he was acquitted. His counsel afterwards moved to have a copy of the indictment, and that the Judge should certify the prosecution to have been malicious, but the Judge refused it, and said, if he must speak his own opinion, the man was fortunate to come off as he did."

R. Bradley to George Kenyon.

1271. [17]69, May 9. Leigh.—"This morning, Sir Joseph Yates, after a very pathetic and proper speech, wherein he laid it on very hard upon the Colonel, pronounced the judgment of the Court, viz., fined Burgoyne 1,000l. but no imprisonment, and the fine was paid in Court. Wilson, the grocer, Captain Harrison, and Winnall, the horn-blower, 100l. each and three months' imprisonment. The three sergeants and drummer six months' imprisonment, but no fine, being poor. I do think they should have sent the Colonel to keep Mr. Wilkes company as well as the rest, and then every body would have been satisfied; most people think that part was wanting to make the sentence complete."

R. Kenyon to Miss Kenyon, at Peel.

1272. 1770, September 7. Overton.—"Our jubilee week at Wynnstay is at last over. We had a grand oratorio at the opening the new organ at Ruabon Church, on the Tuesday, where several solos were performed by Mr. Paxton, the first violoncello, and Signior Giardagni, the first singer in the kingdom. The company were all invited to Wynnstay to dinner, and a grand entertainment we had. About nine o'clock, we all went to the puppet show, where a handsome theatre and good music were exhibited; but as to Punch, I have seen him much more entertaining for a penny, and never crucified four hours more stupidly in my life. It would have done you good to see how many grave senators were entertaining themselves with the old history of [the] Babes in the Wood—Lord Grosvenor, Mr. Kynaston, Mr. Middleton, were amongst them. . . . . The whole must have cost Sir Watkin a couple of thousand at least, and was meant to please every body, but whether calculated rightly for that purpose, or to answer any good end, I much doubt."

Lord Thurlow to Lloyd Kenyon.

1273. 1771, May 15.—"I want to look after the legality of granting a ministerial office in the Court of Justice in America, for more than one life, and I remember two cases upon that head: one of Trelawney against the Bishop of Winchester; the other of the Register of the Admiralty, in which Bellers was concerned. Can you help me to a note of both or either?"

Lloyd Kenyon to Mrs. Kenyon.

1274. 1771, December 10.—"I told you in my last of the success of the Duke of Portland's cause. I am now to inform you that the Shrewsbury *mandamus* cause has been equally successful. It was tried on Friday last. The evening before, and that morning, we had no hopes of success, but the prospect grew better as we proceeded, and, owing to Mr. Dunning's abilities, which were exerted on this occasion to the astonishment of all parties, a verdict was given against the Corporation."

LLOYD KENYON, Junior, to his father, LLOYD KENYON.

1275. 1772, May 7. [London.]—"You used to like to know what my gains were in my profession. I have cast up my last year's book, and it comes to 2,487*l.* 17*s.* 6*d.*, besides some fees unreceived, which would increase it, I believe, to at least 2,500*l.* It appears to me a vast sum indeed, and much more now than I have merited or than I expected. . . . . Yesterday Mr. Tomkinson's youngest son was married to Miss Marsden. It is a match which has been a long time in agitation, but since her mother (who was widow to William Tomkinson) has married a third husband, she has quarrelled with her daughter, and Mr. Tomkinson has been against the match. As she was under age, they could not have a licence, and did not like to go to Scotland, and therefore were asked in church. This could not be in the parish where they resided for fear of a discovery, but they were asked in two or three different churches in the city and borough, and passed muster without suspicion, and though that does not comply with the meaning of the Act, yet, when it is over, the marriage is good."

LLOYD KENYON to his father.

1276. 1772, December 9.—"Mr. Fletcher wrote to me the other day to inform me that a ticket I bought for his mother was come up a prize of 20*l.* . . . He also sent me a commission to lay out his mother's prize in the purchase of another ticket, as she has still a mind to have a chance for the 20,000*l.* I have accordingly bought another ticket for her at the large price of 17*l.* 10*s.* 6*d.* . . . . . . I went on Saturday with Mr. Dunning to Putney, and stayed there till yesterday morning, when I walked home, about six miles. I hope he gets better, though he is not yet well; you will see by my *frank* that his hand is pretty steady. Lord Shelburne and other considerable people called on Sunday to pay him a morning visit, and Lord Shelburne desired he would bring me to dine with him some day. I drank tea with him on Saturday at Mr. Pulteney's."

The SAME to the SAME.

1277. 1773, January 19.—"The number of bankruptcies is immense. Some of the greatest houses in town are talked of very suspiciously. It is well to be of a trade where one can scarcely contrive to be bankrupted. I have now got considerably more than ever I have got on so early a day in the year. . . . . . . I was lately, for several nights, with Mr. Dunning; he is cheerful, very clear headed, and pretty well; but I hope the Attorney-General and I have prevailed on him to refrain coming to the Hall during next term. By that means he will increase his vacation till April."

The SAME to the SAME.

1278. 1773, February 16.—Last Saturday's Gazette contained 15 bankrupts. "I am very creditably informed that the state of credit in London is worse than it is remembered to have ever been. Some of the principal houses are upon the brink of bankruptcy. It is as much as the richest can do to take care of themselves, without attempting to help their neighbours. The distress is understood to be much, owing to the expensive manner of living, which exceeds all bounds."

MARY KENYON to —————

1279. 1773, February 29. Hulton Park.—" Mrs. Hulton has given me a description of many places she saw abroad, and, from what she says, Nice (in Italy) must be one of the most delightful situations, in winter, in the world. She got there the 7th of January, which is their depth of winter as well as ours, and found the gardens in high beauty; ripe oranges upon the trees, and the finest carnations, in full blow, that ever she saw, and all the necessaries of life (house rent excepted) are very cheap. They bought a quarter of lamb for sixpence, and two pounds of butter for ninepence. The air was as warm, Mrs. Hulton said, as it usually is with us in June; and she met with a great many English there, which, had she stayed, would have made it very agreeable. She does not seem to admire Marseilles at all, and says she would never recommend it to any sick person. . . . . . . They have ploughs in France so constructed as to go without holding, except when the horses turn; then the man that drives puts it in the proper place, and has no further trouble till he gets to the other side the field."

LLOYD KENYON to [his father].

1280. 1773, May 11.—" Yesterday, the important business of the Indian plunderers came before the House of Commons. . . . . . You can hardly conceive what satisfaction almost every person one meets with expresses to-day at the event of yesterday, and at the hopes they entertain that justice will at last overtake these enormous offenders. My Lord North, I am well informed, cut and shuffled excedingly, and was at last brought about to concur in what was right, by finding from my friend, the Attorney General's, speech that he was likely to be left in the lurch if he proceded to screen the culprits. I am told that Lord Clive's friends look wonderfully crestfallen. I met Sir Roger Mostyn and Mr. Curzon yesterday morning, and cautioned them to take care of the public interest. Sir Lynch Cotton has not, I believe, yet been able to attend the House. I find Mr. Hulton's body is at last deposited in Dean Parish."

LLOYD KENYON to his father, at Gredington.

1280A. 1773, May 25. London.—" I am quite out of temper with all politics. Ten days ago I was in hopes Lord Clive and the other Nabobs would have been brought to justice for their peculations, but on Wednesday last, the House of Commons thought good to acquit him, by a large majority. The whole Rockingham party joined in his favour. Before this sample of their virtue, I had a better opinion of them than of any other party, but now my opinion of them is very much altered, and some of their leaders know it. I cannot forbear suspecting that some lacs of rupees have been employed in obtaining this victory. My friend, the Attorney General (Thurlow), behaved nobly upon the occasion, Lord North very shamefully, and I hope to have an opportunity of voting against Baldwin at the next Shropshire election. He spoke (as well as he could) and voted as stoutly as anybody for Lord Clive. This acquittal of Lord Clive, I am afraid, will discourage all honest men from pursuing the more petty Rajahs."

LLOYD KENYON to ——— ———.

1281. 1773, June 8.—"When I last wrote to you, I believe I was in hopes Lord Clive would have been obliged to disgorge some of his ill-got riches, but the House of Commons took a sudden turn and let him off. The upshot of this business is to be imputed to the Rockingham party, who, for reasons best known to themselves, all in a body, took part with Lord Clive, with a view, I suppose, to add him and his friends to their number. I thought much better of them before than I shall ever do again. Mr. Baldwin, the member for Shropshire, spoke and voted for Lord Clive, in hopes, I fancy, to have his interest in the next election. I shall be very glad to see him opposed and turned out for his pains. I am in treaty for a house in Lincoln's Inn Fields, and hope to agree for it this week. I believe the terms, &c., will be very high, but the airyness of the situation is worth a good deal to one who has no time to use proper exercise."

LLOYD KENYON to his father.

1282. 1773, July 6.—"My profits in my profession continue to increase so much, that I have now got more money since the beginning of the year than I had when I left town, the latter end of last July. When half the year closed, at the end of June, I had got about 2,060*l.* What with buying the lease of my house, and furnishing it, I shall not be able to make any very large purchase with this year's savings, though I hope to be something in profit."

The SAME to the SAME.

1283. [1773,] "Sunday evening."—"I dined yesterday with my friend Mr. Dunning, who looks better than when I saw him at Stafford, but I think is yet far from perfectly well. . . . . . . The Committee of the House of Commons about the India affairs are going on with their inquiries, and, from some talk which I had yesterday with the Attorny General, I fancy Lord Clive is likely to cut but a bad figure."

ALLEN, SEDGWICK, & CO.'S BANK.

1248. 1774, September 3.—Draft letter, unsigned and not addressed, concerning the partnership deeds of the bank of Allen, Sedgwick, and Co. Certain additions recommended, subject to the approval of the house in London, viz:—That the bank be continued in the firm of Allen, Sedgwick, and Co., during the present co-partnership, and upon the decease of Mr. Peach, Mr. Allen and Dr. Sedgwick, their respective shares to be vested in their wives or children; any of their sons may commence as a partner at the age of twenty-one, in the room of his father.

MARY KENYON to her mother.

1284A. [1775,] October 30. London.—Describing her new house in Lincoln's Inn Fields, she says, "The entrance is a broad lobby, well lighted by a window over the door, and a staircase window. It is wainscot, painted white as far as the arch turned at the bottom of the staircase. On the left hand is a sweet pretty parlour, stuccoed and painted white—marble chimney piece and hearth; two windows, and, at the lower end of the room, two pillars, on which stands a mahogany sideboard. On the one side stands a *garde du vin*, on the other side a chair, which I think must be displaced and a small table set there. On the side, where the door opens, which is a long way from the window, stands our dining table, with one chair on one side, near the pillar. Between the windows is a very pretty round glass, ornamented with gilt paper-mache, in great taste, two chairs on each side the fire, a handsome cistern of mahogany, with brass hoops, &c., under the sideboard, and a Turkey carpet. The back room has only one window, which looks into a little flagged court, twelve of my steps long and six steps broad, but quite entire and not overlooked by any window but our own, a marble chimney piece and hearth, a stove grate, the same to the other parlour; [it] is wainscot, painted white, has a larger dining table for great days, a ward-robe from Chambers for Mr. Kenyon's clothes, a wash-hand stand, a little closet, dark, but shelved very conveniently, and four chairs, the same as the dining parlour. The room behind that is white wainscot, has two windows, is as large as the little drawing room, but has nothing at all in yet. There is a fire-place with a marble chimney piece; but that and all the back-rooms are common fire-places. Behind that is the back staircase, and beyond that a butler's pantry with a dresser that has two drawers and a cupboard under it, shelves over it for glasses, &c., a lead cistern and pipe with water.

"So much for that floor. The front staircase is a very good one, with a neat mahogany rail to the top of the house. I must tell you, before I proceed further, there is a very handsome glass lamp in the passage, another upon the landing, and a third by the dining room door. The dining room is 21 feet and a half long, and 17 feet wide, has [a] marble chimney piece and hearth, a handsome steel grate, &c.; [it] is to be new papered, this week, and have the furniture all in order; it is quite ready when the paper is put up. The paper is to be a blue small patterned flock; I will send you a bit of it. The back room has, at present, a bed in it, which is to be removed on Wednesday morning, and that room is to have the old blue flock paper we found in it, blue moreen curtains, chairs, a toilet, and a book-case—will not that be a nice breakfast room? In the little room behind that, which is wainscoted and painted white, is a blue moreen bed, a little chest of dressing drawers, and two chairs; then comes my little store room, which is about as large as half the little drawing-room, has two rows of shelves, a table across the end with drawers and cupbords under. In this place I keep china, glasses, and all my stock of groceries; the plate chest is to be kept there too, when it arrives. Through this closet is the water-closet, very convenient and sweet; it is over the stable.

"Up the next story is our lodging room, over the dining room. It is hung with a green flock paper, has green moreen bed and window cur-tains, a large chest upon [a] chest (so high, that I must have a step-ladder to look into the five top drawers), a dressing table and glass in one pier, a small chest of dressing drawers in the other pier, a night table, a wash-hand stand, and eight chairs. The back room is wainscoted, and is to have the bed from Chambers in. A maid's room behind that, and, over my own store room, another pretty closet with a linnen press, and a light large cupbord or small closet through it. The two back garrets have servants' beds in. The front is a landing. All the garrets have flat roofs, and are in every respect as good rooms as those below."

FRANCIS BULLER to LLOYD KENYON, "Oxford Circuit, Stafford."

1285. 1778, March 21. Upton.—Yesterday morning, a midshipman was tried at Exeter for murder. He and some sailors were sent by the Lieutenant to examine the fishing boats as they came into Torbay. The midshipman put a sailor on board of one sloop and ordered them to go to the tender, to be examined by the Lieutenant; but the master, instead of going to the tender, put out to sea. The midshipman took another fishing sloop and chased for 3 hours, during which time he fired several musket shots to make the master bring to, saying, if he could only get his sailor back again, the master and his men might go to hell, and he would chace no further. Struggles between the master and his crew and the sailor were seen during the chace, and they expected to see the sailor thrown overboard. When the midshipman got within 60 yards, he said, if the other sloop did not bring to, he would fire at the man at the helm, and, whilst they were in the act of bringing to, fired and killed the master. "Baron Perryn was of opinion that this was wilful murder, abused the practice of the navy in firing balls, asked if it was usual for one fishing sloop to fire on another, said the subjects of this country were in a calamitous state, and [that] the expression 'he might go to hell' (which in a seaman's phrase, I take it, only means he might go about his business), shewed malice, and reflected on four silk gowns being concerned for the prisoner. However, he dropt a hint that we might have a special verdict, which, under all the circumstances of the case, we thought it prudent to take. In stating that, he took wonderful care to put all the facts against the prisoner in the strongest terms; and it was with great difficulty that we could get a few facts, which were proved on the part of the prisoner, inserted at all, because he did not think them material: such as that firing in the case was according to the usage of the navy to bring ships to; that it was for the purpose of hitting the sails; and that the struggle seen between the sailors and the deceased. However, at last, all that was inserted. It was proved that the midshipman fired and the deceased was killed. Perryn directed the officer of the Court to take down, as the minutes of the special verdict, that the prisoner levelled at the deceased; however, that, at last, was altered. There have been some heavy complaints of severity on the Crown side before, during this circuit, but whether deserved or not, I cannot say. . . . . . . The name of the midshipman is Phillips, and [he] is a neighbour of yours."

R. KENYON to MRS. LLOYD KENYON.

1286. 1778, August 16. Cefn.—" Our Denbighshire squires are trying to kick up a dust against our Chief Justice, for permitting a felon (after the Grand Jury had found the Bill against him) to enlist in the Liverpool volunteers (I believe the Manchester regiment had completed their number of thieves before) without puting him on his trial. A flaming advertisement has been inserted by the High Sheriff, in the Chester paper, to call a country meeting to consider of this breach in the criminal justice of the kingdom. It is not likely to come to any thing against the Chief Justice, as the affair was with the consent of the Attorney General and the prosecutor, but it will vex Mr. Morton greatly, which I am sorry for, as he is (with all his roughness) a very excellent judge."

The SAME to the SAME.

1287. 1778, October 8.—The sale at Iscoed has continued for this last week. Thinks the prices fetched were very low, the day he was there, but was told they advanced greatly afterwards. "The large picture in the saloon, of Peter denying Christ, was bought by Mr.

Curzon, as a present for an altar piece at Malpas Church,[1] for twenty-nine guineas and a half, but few of the paintings exceeded a couple of guineas."

W. LEYCESTER to LLOYD KENYON.

1288. 1778. Buxton.—" I cannot give you any hopes of tolerable accomodation at the Hall,[2] which is quite full ; not a room empty, and many bespoke. But you may be very comfortably accommodated at the Grove Coffee House, within 200 yards of the Hall, where you may either dine with the company, which seldom consists of more than 12, or you may have a private parlour for half-a-guinea a week, if you like that better. You will meet here with several of your acquaintance— P[epper] Arden, Bower, Mr. and Mrs. Joddrell, Parker, Coke, Mr. and Mrs. Erskine, Miss Bolds, [and] Miss Biffins."

T. STANLEY to GEORGE KENYON.

1289. 1780, January 18. Crosshall.—Offering himself as a candidate for election to Parliament, in the place of the Hon. Mr. Stanley, deceased, and asking for Kenyon's vote.

EDMUND BURKE to LLOYD KENYON.

1290. 1780, March 6. Charles Street.—"Mr. Dunning made me very happy this day in telling me that you did me the honour of approving the principle and chief provisions of my Welsh Bill. A Court opposition is stirred up against it with great industry, and though those who are inveigled into that opposition are utterly ignorant of the grounds they go on, they are as rancorous as if they had had some cause of discontent ; but little politicks are at the bottom. As I had not the happiness of any legal assistance in preparing the Bill, I daresay that my meaning is inartificially and unaptly expressed. Mr. Dunning assured me that you would be so obliging as to look over the Bill and correct it. May I beg, then, that you would do it as soon as possible, for I am much pressed for it. I beg, too, that you will exercise a further discretion, and add and alter as you please, preserving (as you will) the principle." *Holograph.*

ROGER KENYON to ⸺ ⸺.

1290A. 1780, March 30. Cefn.—The sinking the vaults at Gredington (which was done by contract) has taken up more time than I expected. It is a very considerable marl pit, I assure you, but now quite finished, and the bricklayers busy at work. We found a framing of old timber in the middle of the old kitchen walls, which was quite decayed, and proves that end to have been originally built of timber and plaister, and   of the walls within were divided by soft tiles laid edgeways, of the dimensions of those in the little house floor.

MARY KENYON to MRS. KENYON, at Peel.

1291. [1780, June 3,] " 4 o'clock.'—" Mr. Kenyon is just come in, and says the Attorney-General was very active last night in endeavouring to save the chapel, and was in great darger from the mob ; they were so perverse, they would not help to work the engines to prevent the fire spreading ; that if Mr. Graham Midford, and some

---

[1] This picture, still in Malpas Church, is by Hayman.
[2] The Old Hall Hotel, Buxton.

other gentlemen spectators had not assisted, most likely great mischief might have been done; and [that] the guards (who were sent for) were heard to say of the mob, 'great fools, why did they not pull down the building; fire might hurt their neighbours.' Fine times!"

MRS. LLOYD KENYON to —————.

1292. [1780], June 3. Lincoln's Inn Fields.—"Least my dear friends at Peel should be under any apprehension for us, on account of this mob, I will write to day to tell you we neither suffered fright nor danger by it, though they were very noisy all night, and there still is a continual crowd about the Sardinian Ambassador's. I do believe there were very many thousands of people assembled yesterday in St. George's fields, who afterwards went to Westminster Hall, but did no sort of harm there further than crowding the Hall and making it hot, and sometimes shouting at the people they did not like as they passed. Lord George Gordon was seen by Mr. Leycester haranguing the crowd, with his hat off, for a considerable time, and misleading an unruly ignorant set of people in St. George's fields. He afterwards came to them out of the House of Commons, and said he could get no answer as to the repeal of the Roman Catholic Act, and advised them to attend every day in a body, till their petition was granted. They then vowed they would destroy all the Roman Catholic chapels, and, as it was a very hot day, took care to get drunk in good time, and as soon as it was dark, began to attack our neighbourhood, though till we went to bed, at eleven, they seemed not to do any mischief.

"They waked us between 12 and 1, with noise and shouting; we got up to look, and saw a great crowd, but knew nothing of fire till this morning; as you know, the chapel is in Duke Street. We sent Hewett to look at it; he says they have taken all the images and every thing within the chappel that they could find, and pulled all to pieces and burnt before the door; broke the windows, and burnt the frames and doors of the chappel. But, by the help of two engines, all the houses, etc., were preserved, just one window in the Sardinian Ambassador's house broken. Mr. Kenyon is provoked beyond measure at Lord G. Gordon; says he is mad, and should be confined, and wishes some spirited conduct may be pursued to suppress this first lawless outrage. Eight of these poor fellows are taken up, who little knew what they have been about. They say there are three more Roman Catholic chappels that have suffered the same fate. Mr. Filmer called this morning to know what disturbance we had met with. I see the papers say there were 50,000 people in this square. I saw them twice, and Mr. Kenyon two or three times, and there were not, as I think, even so many as two hundred, at one time, in this square. . . . . Do you hear that Lord Surrey has renounced the Roman Catholic religion, and Sir Thomas Gascoigne likewise? Mr. Wallace told Mr. Kenyon so, and said Lord and Lady Surrey were to meet yesterday at their house, at the desire of both parties."

The SAME to MRS. KENYON, at Peel.

1293. 1780, June 6. London.—"Do not be uneasy if you should not hear of us by every post; for, notwithstanding the accounts in the papers, I hope we shall be just as safe in this place as anywhere. We are happy in our neighbourhood; all are equally disposed to be quiet, and though we have, till to day, had continual tumults and noises, day and night, in this square [Lincoln's Inn Fields], they have not molested any creature in it, except the chaplain of the Sardinian Ambassador.

We were waked last night, about twelve or near one, by a great light which proceeded from a fire in Great Wild Street, just behind Clare market. The mob set a tallow chandler's in a flame, who had assisted to take one of the rioters on Thursday night, and pulled another house to pieces in Little Queen Street, which belonged to a currier who had offended in the same way, but there they did not burn anything. From there they went to Sir George . . ., but he soon got guards, [so] that they only broke windows and doors, and were beat off. To day, I fear they will attend at the House, but Mr. Kenyon has promised me to come home before they sit. Some of the members talk of complying with the repeal of the Roman Catholic Act. . . . . . If it is not soon repressed, many innocent people must suffer, for the love of mischeif exceeds all bounds. They say these people are most of them Methodists, but there are bad enough of all religions to make a sad bustle here, and I dare say do not care a straw what is done, if they can plunder, destroy, and level all distinction. What a blessing it is to have an able and kind protector at such a time. My Mr. Kenyon is now as cool, composed, and compassionate to all parties, as a sensible and good man can be. . . . My sister and my sweet lads are in a place of great safety, where we shall certainly join them if there is the least hazard of danger or alarm, from living here. I do not believe half the stories I hear, but am grieved to hear of the fright and apprehensions of other people. The account of the Bishop of Lincoln in the papers, was very true, and my Lord Mansfield was forced to escape on Friday, by water, in a green coat and bob-wig. Many of the members of both Houses were affronted, but I have not yet heard of one life being lost. I drank tea with Mrs. Walker yesterday; she is furious against Roman Catholics, and thinks it a sad thing to grant them any indulgences. One of their chappels was destroyed in Moorfields on Saturday night, and the poor priest's house ransacked and burnt, as well as two or three empty ones adjoining. What do people say in the country on this subject? I hope they will not follow our wicked example. Mr. Kenyon came safe home, about two o'clock, but said there was a great crowd gathering, and two regiments of guards drawn up in the Park, and a regiment of light horse [brought?] down to the Parliament House. How this day will end, God knows! Mr. Burke, they say, was in great danger this morning. He took up two . . . . himself, and went to ask the mob what they would have; 'if you want me,' he said, 'here I am; do what you will; but never expect I shall vote for a repeal of the Act I supported.' They all cried out, ' he is a gentleman, make way for him.' Lord George Gordon, it is said, has decamped. That old hall has stood many a brush; I hope it will withstand this."

JOHN DUNNING to " the HONOURABLE LLOYD KENYON, Esq., Chief Justice of Chester."

1294. 1780, August 11.—"Be assured you have not a friend who more sincerely rejoices than I do, in any good that happens to you. I could not, therefore, but receive with pleasure the account you have favoured me with of your appointment to an office [the Chief Justiceship of Chester] which it was so natural for you to desire. . . . . I congratulate the Principality of an event, not less important to them for being new— their being treated as men who have lives and fortunes to be preserved, and I am glad, for the Chancellor's sake, that he has made an appointment which does him credit. When the sun scorches, as it does at present, I feel it pleasant (without a metaphor) to live in the shade ! "

The Poll at Wigan.

1295. 1780, September 11.—The poll, with the names of burgesses who polled, taken at Wigan, The candidates were Henry Simpson Bridgeman, 70 votes; Horatio Walpole, 44 votes, and Sir Richard Clayton, 24 votes.

Lord George Gordon to Lloyd Kenyon.

1295A. 1780, November 22. The Tower.—"Lord George Gordon presents his most respectful compliments to Mr. Kenyon. As something has occurred since the message delivered to him by Mr. Wallis, Lord George would be very glad to see Mr. Kenyon, whenever he finds himself disengaged."

Edmund Burke to the Same.

1296. 1782, January 4 (?). Beconsfield.—"You have done so much more for me than I had any sort of reason to expect from anything but your extraordinary good nature, that I do not know how to thank you for it sufficiently. I should hope that in stating Mr. Story's business to the Chancellor, that it might be made to stand on the reason of the Union, and the equity of giving the object rather to thirty years' service than to any sollicitation. The Chancellor is a man very much made to listen to a plea of that kind. If he were not, I do not know upon what pretence I could ever have gone to him with any recommendation. I am additionally obliged to you for not mentioning my name." *Holograph.*

Peter Davies to the Same.

1297. 1782, April 14. Broughton.—"I now address myself to you as a senator. About twenty-five years ago, it was under consideration of Parliament to enact a law for the appointing of an office in each county, for the regestering of bonds and mortgages. For some reason the Bill was rejected. A most shocking affair which has lately been discovered in the counties of Denbigh and Flint calls aloud for such an office to protect the properties of the ignorant and incautious. If you could, by your interest and abilities, carry such a Bill through the House of Commons, you would procure a most essential and [lasting] blessing, not only to those counties over which [you] preside as Lord Chief Justice, but also to every county in England."

M. H[anmer] to Mrs. Kenyon, in Chester.

1298. [1782,] April 16. Bettisfield Park.—"Arden is said not to give general satisfaction; he is in too great haste, and hurries things over, so as not to please some people. My cousin complains he cannot keep him in order as to forms; that he walks away from Barrington, gets before Mr. Kenyon, and runs among the mob in his red gown. You know how absent he is. It is just like Pepper; but there are things one must not comment upon, only between friends."

Charles James Fox to Lloyd Kenyon, Attorney General.

1299. 1782, April 26. St. James's.—"Mr. Secretary Fox presents his compliments to Mr. Attorney General. He troubles him with a letter he has received from Monsieur Cavalli, the Venetian Resident, and will take it as a very particular favor if Mr. Attorney General will let him know the state of the business relative to Monsieur Pizzoni, the former Venetian Resident, that he may return an answer to Monsieur Cavalli, who is lately recalled." *Holograph.*

WILLIAM [afterwards SIR WILLIAM] JONES to LLOYD KENYON.

1300. 1782, April 30. Lamb's Buildings, Temple.—" I cannot forbear troubling you with a few lines on a subject extremely simple in itself, but deeply affecting my happiness. My happiness does not depend on being appointed to fill the vacant seat on the bench at Calcutta—which I have been four years hoping to attain, by the favour of the Chancellor, to whom I never personally applied, for fear of giving offence—but my happiness entirely depends on being removed from a state of suspense, both painful and ruinous, in a degree not to be described. I am not conscious of having given offence to the Chancellor, nor ever had an idea of obtaining the appointment, except by his sole patronage; yet, if I had insulted or injured him, I could not be more severely punished than by ruin in my profession, where I had begun to prosper, and by a total disarrangement of all my domestic plans, for so many years, at the most important period of my life. Chambers, who was then above three years older than I now am, and whose prospects here were not superior, perhaps not equal, to mine, deliberated four months about accepting an appointment, which I have been four years soliciting, without being able to obtain even a negative; and, next to the appointment itself, the highest obligation I could now receive would be a speedy refusal. All England knows your weight with the Chancellor, but I do not even request you to exert it in my favour; all I pant for, all I solicit, is an answer, favourable or unfavourable, and (though I would not have the Chancellor know that I am so importunate) yet you will greatly add to the obligations under which you have already laid me, by your attention and friendship, if you will endeavour to put me out of suspense by informing me, as soon as you know, either that the vacancy is not to be supplied, or that, whoever may supply it, I am not to be the man, or that no arrangement whatever will take place this year."

CHARLES JAMES FOX to LLOYD KENYON, Lincoln's Inn Fields.

1301. 1782, St. James' Street.—" I ought to make you many apologies for the liberty I am taking in venturing to press you to stay in town tomorrow; but I understand your reason for going is a supposition that Lord North is actually out. Now the fact is, that though I believe he is certainly to go out, yet it is of infinite consequence that the question should be carried tomorrow, for the purpose of forming an administration who shall have the real support and confidence of Parliament. I am the more encouraged to take the liberty of troubling you upon the occasion, because the motion was not fixed for tomorrow till I had heard from Mr. Dunning that you were not to leave town till Saturday, and tomorrow was preferred to this day for the making of it, owing to what you hinted to me, on a former day, of Thursday being always an inconvenient day to you for attending the House." *Holograph.*

LORD THURLOW to ————— —————.

1302. 1783, January 4.—" Your Lordship calls upon me to state my objections to the patent proposed for the Duke of Manchester, and I am happy in the opportunity of referring myself to your Lordship, because I have the most unfeigned confidence that you have still less disposition than myself to establish an abuse in so an important a branch of the public revenue, and much more firmness to resist it. The proposed patent imparts a grant of Collector outwards of the Customs in the Port of London, with a variety of other duties specified in it, to hold to the grantee, his executors, administrators, and assignees, for three lives, including his own.

"The great extent of the duty and importance of the trust, which your Lordship is more familiarly acquainted with than I am, are the only good reasons why so profitable an office should exist at all; and these seem to militate with equal force against an appointment which may, according to the natural course of events, call into a situation of great confidence, women, children, and other description of persons, who may prove neither competent to the office, nor responsible for the abuse of it. Nay, considering the many and various accidents to which men of the most proper description are liable, it seems stranger that such a trust should be reposed irrevocably, even in any single person; and I remember, in this very office, an instance of misbehaviour springing purely from the duration of it, which embarrassed the Custom House for a great length of time. The wisdom and moderation of the Duke put an end to their trouble at length; but it was impossible to observe, without regret, the arrangement of so great a public concern depend on the personal qualities of the actual possessor of an office, when so many accidents might any day throw it upon persons neither wise enough to take so proper a part, nor capable (as in the case of executors and trustees) to make such concessions as might be eventually necessary to the public interest. No instances occur where private men (whose attention is more awake to their own interest) appoint their stewards, bailiffs, and other agents, to hold for their lives, and still less to their executors, administrators, and assigns.

"In the public revenue, however, the abuse is not new; many old statutes have been provided against it, and, so far as I can trace the matter, these had the effect to prevent the mischief done in the reign of Charles the Second. That period was pregnant with too many abuses to serve as a sanction to-day. Under the cover of that precedent, however, it has been renewed. But I have thought it indispensable to state these samples to your Lordship, in the present hour, when in articles much less important, reformation has been called for so loudly and promised so solemnly. Upon the whole, I submit it to your Lordship, that it would be proper to refer this matter to his Majesty's Attorney and Sollicitor General. The propriety of the measure (except so far as it makes an ingredient in the question of its legality), will not come under their consideration, and to that extent your Lordship will readily refer it, because I am perfectly satisfied, that neither your Lordship would suffer, nor the Duke of Manchester wish, the King's favour to be surprised (?) in prejudice to the laws or interests of the country."

LORD GEORGE GORDON to LLOYD KENYON, Attorney-General.

1303. 1783, January 14. Welbeck Street.—Enclosing the original of a libel, left at his house on the 2nd, by "the penny post," commencing :—"To Lord George Gordon, Welbeck Street.—Your insolent letter to Lord Shelburne I have seen. How dare you boast of family, when your silly father ran about the Continent with your coarse and vulgar mother, like a fool!" *Printed in the "Public Advertizer" of the* 14th *January,* 1783.

MARY KENYON to MRS. KENYON, at Chester.

1304. [1783,] January 20. London.—" Since last Saturday, I
have done nothing but think of clothes, and written on no other
subject. My own gown was so much admired at Court; I was so
much flattered as was possible for me to be, in any article of dress. I
wish I could have exhibited myself to my dear mother, if it had only
been for one minute, to repay all the faddle I went through. It was
much the pleasantest Court-Day I ever knew. Lady Ashburton asked
me to go with her, which I did. Lady Yates met me by appointment,
[and] was very attentive and pleasant. [The] Lady Mayoress
(Mrs. Newnham, who presides as Lady Mayoress for her brother)
saught my protection. My Lord Chancellor came across to shake
hands with me and wish me joy of the children's recovery. In short,
I was quite as conceited as I am likely ever to be by nature and
attention. Our neighbour, Lord Willoughby, is always very civil, and
Sir Thomas Egerton was there, but I did notice that she was not. The
dresses were very fine, and great profusion of diamonds.

" The two Princesses were charmingly dressed, and would be called fine
young women if they were of low rank, and the Prince [was] very handsome. . . . Lady Yates took me to see the little children in the Queen's
drawing-room, which was a charming sight. The Princess Elizabeth was
the only one spoke, and she acquitted herself as well as anybody could
have done, in point of address; the two younger princesses, Mary and
Sophia, were in the room, and Prince Octavius, in his little buff coat and
blue sash, like my Lloyd's picture, was running about and eating hard
biscuit. . . . . Have you heard what a fine way great people
have got of disposing of old things, or turning the penny? At Lady
Harrington's, this winter, she said we must have a pool at Commerce,
and you shall play for a gown I had got from abroad, which cost me
16 guineas, and as I am in mourning, I cannot wear it; so 8 of you put in
2 guineas apiece, and it will just do. They obeyed; and she is not singular
in this style of entertainment. At another house they played for fine
muslin; at a third, I hear the lady proposed half-a-guinea apiece towards
some black lace, but one lady said she would measure it first, and see if it
was the quantity promised; it proved two yards short, so then the lady
said, well, if you don't like that, I have some more blon (*sic*) lace
that I am sure will do. Did you ever hear anything so completely
wrong? Woe be to sideboards and husbands' property, if this becomes
fashionable. There is no reason why all the furniture in the house
should not be staked at Commerce."

SIR WILLIAM JONES to LLOYD KENYON, Attorney-General.

1305. 1783, January 27. Lamb Building, Temple.—" The Lord
Advocate, who takes the lead in India affairs in the House of Commons,
having announced a new arrangement in India, both executive and
judicial, I beg leave to claim your friendly attentions to my interests in
that quarter, on the success of which my speedy marriage and, of
course, my happiness will depend. My anxious wish is that you
would take some convenient opportunity, some *molle tempus fandi*, to
place me in a favourable light with the Chancellor. I wish him to be
persuaded of a plain truth, that I never conceived the idea of the
appointment to the long vacant judgeship residing anywhere but with
his Lordship, but was deterred from applying for it to him through a
fear of incurring his displeasure. As to my politics, which he has
heard much misrepresented, his Lordship may be assured that I am

no more a republican than a Mahomedan or a Gentoo, and that I have ever formed my opinions from what appeared to me, on the calmest inquiry, the true spirit of our constitution."

R. P. ARDEN to LLOYD KENYON.

1306. 1783, April 1. Lincoln's Inn.—"Mr. Pitt resigned the Seal of the Exchequer yesterday, at the Levée, which was delivered to Lord Mansfield. Every thing last night was totally unsettled, but it is universally believed that the coalition must be accepted. Indeed, I believe all other attempts have been given up. What will be the event, the Lord knows! but there is a great discontent in the House, and, I believe, much regret at Pitt's going out. That is almost the universal language, both within doors and without."

The SAME to the SAME.

1307. 1783, April 8.—"Yesterday, the Chancellor resigned the Great Seal, which is given to Lord Loughborough, Mr. Justice Ashurst, and Baron Hotham. They have not yet received the seal, but I signed their commission last night, whilst I was dining at Lord Thurlow's, who had just come from St. James'. You have, by going out of town, left me a very disagreeable office, that of signing the dismissal of my friends. The Chancellor received his letter of dismission from Charles Fox. I have not yet learnt for certain who are to succeed you and me, but it is generally understood, Wallace and Lee. Charles Fox was elected without a poll, but with a great deal of hissing and noise. There is great dissatisfaction in the House of Commons, but what it will end in, no one can tell. For my part, I am heartily sick of politics, and should be very glad never to set my foot in the House of Commons again."

LORD NORTH to the SAME.

1308. 1783, April 13. Whitehall.—"I have his Majesty's commands to acquaint you that, it being his Majesty's intention to replace Mr. Wallace in the office he formerly held, of Attorney-General, he has no further occasion for your services in that department."

R. P. ARDEN to the SAME.

1309. 1783, April 14. Lincoln's Inn.—"I received, this morning, a letter from Lord North, informing me that it is his Majesty's intention to replace Mr. Lee in the situation he formerly held, of Solicitor-General. I take it for granted you had a letter of a similar nature, with respect to Wallace. . . . I am very well, in good spirits, and appeared in the House of Commons in boots, in the character of an independent country gentleman. Lord Thurlow has already growled in the House of Lords; and, I fancy, does not mean to be quiet, if we may judge by his beginning."

SIR ASHTON LEVER to ——————.

1310. 1783, May 29. Leicester House.—"All his Majesty's subjects that have visited my collection having expressed their wish that it should be kept together in this kingdom, the following plan is submitted to the consideration of Government. At present, there being no fund for the support of the establishment of the British Museum, and Parliament being frequently called upon for that purpose, it has been in contemplation to put a price on admission, which idea was given up on the report of some of its officers that the receipt would not amount to five hundred pounds a year. The receipt at Leicester House has been encreasing every year, and last year it amounted to two thousand two hundred and fifty three pounds. There is room in the British Museum for my collection to be added; and rather than it should be broken up and sold by auction, I am willing to take a sum much less than its intrinsic value, and to receive it in any mode that may be thought consistent with the present economical plan. In this case, when joined to the collection now in Montagu House, and the admission for the whole made half-a-crown, there is not the least doubt but it would produce a sum which would enable the trustees to collect, preserve, and pay its establishment for ever. Should his Majesty's Ministers disapprove of this plan, I humbly request that I may be permitted to dispose of my collection in one lot, dependant upon the national lottery as my *dernier resource*, to keep it together." *Signed.*

LORD THURLOW to LLOYD KENYON.

1311. 1783, May 31.—"I have offered Scott a seat in Parliament for Weobley. He hesitates. As I know his delicacy, I am apprehensive that he fancies it is likely to fetter him; you know my sentiments on that subject perfectly well. If he were embarged (*sic*) in any of these confederacies, by which knots of men propose to struggle in a body for places, &c., I do not think he would do well to take this, or, indeed, be at liberty to do so. On the other hand, it would be an impudent thing to propose such a circumstance as a place in Parliament to a man of sense and honour, as the price of acting for another man's opinion against his own. I could not enter into this sort of explanation with him, because it seemed to be indelicate even to suppose that there was any thing to be explained. And all I aim at now is, that, if you converse with him, you should make him understand that there is nothing to explain in the matter." *Holograph.*

MARY KENYON to MRS. KENYON, at Gredington.

1312. [1783,] December 5. Peel.—"At Lancaster, Sir George Warren is opposed by Lord John Cavendish, and we did hear Mr. Reynolds would be turned out by Lord Archibald Hamilton, but whether that be true, I cannot say. The Lancaster people are very angry with Mr. Reynolds for selling the borough to Sir George, which they say he certainly did, when they offered to bring in any body he would recommend, thinking he would bring in his own son. At Preston, all sides are very warm; Sir Frank's friends say he is before, by fifty votes; but it is much . . . if Lord Strange does not get the better. He keeps open house at this time, and has a great mob on his side; so have the other side, and a violent one too. The other day, when he was in the street, [he] received a great blow on the breast from a brick, which knocked him down, at which he was so much enraged that when he went to his own house (where the mob followed him) he ordered his servants to fire among them, which they did both with ball and shot. The ball went over their heads, as I suppose it was intended to do, but the shot peppered some of them terribly. Everybody's windows are broke and patched with paper, as well as they can, till the bustles are over. At Liverpool, they have been worse than anywhere. Mr. Gildart's brother Richard opposed Mr. Penant, but has given up, Mr. Pennant being too well backed by Sir William Meredith, and, as some say, by a Ministerial purse, which there is no contending with. I am very sorry for Mr. James Gildart's family, who have suffered much by the mob. They have broke the house to pieces; all the windows, shutters, and even iron bars are broke; and [they] cut the window curtains with cutlasses all to bits, tore up and destroyed the palisades and wall before the house."

R. P. ARDEN to LLOYD KENYON, Attorney-General, at Marsh Gate.

1313. 1784, January 3.—" Mr. Pitt is very anxious that you should write to such persons as you wrote to before, and such as you can properly address upon the subject, to inform them how important it is that every independent gentleman should be in the . House, without fail, upon Monday the 12th; and to beg they will by no means be induced to pair off. I give you joy of being returned for Hindon. Our friends here say everything goes on very well. The great difficulty is to get our friends to be punctual to the day, and Fox will be sure to have his troops in order."

The SAME to the SAME.

1314. 1784, January 9. —" The Chancellor is very indignant at the auditor's answer to you, and thinks it a gross insult on the public. . . . Those who ought to know, tell me that things wear a very favourable aspect. I was sorry to find that Charles Robinson's chambers are not ordered to be got ready, and that his laundress does not expect him till the term. I am sure it arises from his not knowing the pressing necessity of an attendance on Monday. . . . I have had a letter from Sir Thomas Egerton, who will be in town tomorrow. Sir Robert Cotton has written a letter to Pitt, which does him much honour, in my opinion, and will certainly be here. . . . My constituents are so perfectly satisfied with my conduct in Parliament, that they have unanimously re-elected me. I wish that other gentlemen who have vacated their seats could boast of the same."

The SAME to the SAME.

1315. 1784, March 26. Lincoln's Inn, 12 o'clock.—" Mr. Pitt and I are, this instant, returned from Cambridge, where, as far as can be judged from a thin University, he has had a very successful canvass. We left Cambridge in the middle of the night, and not having been in bed."

WILLIAM PITT to the SAME.

1316. [1784,] March 29. Downing Street.—"I have received the King's pleasure for the warrant to be made out for your appointment as Master of the Rolls; and it will be desirable, if it is convenient to you, that you should kiss hands for it on Friday." *Holograph.*

DAINES BARRINGTON to [LLOYD KENYON, Master of the Rolls].

1316A. [1784,] July 5.—"I am as much obliged to you for your kind permission to make use of the Rolls' garden as if the experiment was to take place there. Kegan, however, and I reconnoitred it, after I had written my note to you, and found it would answer admirably well, except that it was impossible, from the narrowness of Chancery Lane, to introduce two poles of 60 feet long through the arch. On account of this objection, I have applied to the Duke of Devonshire for Devonshire garden, which being granted, I will give you notice of time and

place, and will take care to secure two tickets of admission for yourself
and Mrs. Kenyon, should you choose to see the experiment. Kegan
himself will not give out more than 50 tickets, so that the rest will be
left to the Duke. You will be so good as not to mention this to any,
as the experiment is intended to be as private as possible."

DAINES BARRINGTON to LLOYD KENYON.

1316B. 1784, July 9.—" I have just received a letter from the Duke
of Devonshire, in which he wishes that his garden may not be made use
of for the balloon. The reason which at present weighs with him (as
I know by conversation I have had with his Grace) is the fear of giving
offence by inviting a few of his acquaintances and not inviting all, his
garden being so large. May I therefore beg that you will permit
Kegan to have the use of the Rolls' garden, and he will wait upon you
tomorrow before nine, to receive your directions. I should conceive
that, with your permission, he might give 60 or 70 tickets to those who
have patronised him. The rest will be those whom you and Mrs. Kenyon
may invite to see the sight, and I will take the liberty of begging that
Mr. Haworth may be one of them. Most of the spectators will certainly choose to be in the garden. Kegan has reason to expect the
Duke and Duchess of Devonshire, as also the Duke and Duchess of
Richmond, will honour him with their presence. The less is said about
this matter the better. *P.S.*—As the poles cannot otherwise be got into
the garden, they must be cut in two and fastened afterwards by irons."

F. NORTON to the SAME.

1317. 1784, July 10. Edinburgh.—" The Scotch judges have petitioned the King for an increase of salary, of which, to say the truth,
they stand in great need, and their petition will probably soon be laid
before Parliament. As I am much interested in the success of this
application, give me leave to request, as a very particular favour, the
assistance of your influence, both with the Ministers and the House of
Commons. It may be necessary to acquaint you that the English Baron,
besides the Scotch salary which he receives in common with the other
judges, has always, since the constitution of the Court of Exchequer, had a
separate warrant for 500*l.* *per annum*, but this warrant has never been
considered, in any degree, to affect or interfere with his Scotch salary,
which was originally the same with that of the other judges, and has
always been augmented at the same times and in the same proportions
with their salaries."

WILLIAM PITT to the SAME.

1318. 1784, July 20. Downing Street.—" If you could have the
goodness to call here for a quarter of an hour, in the course of this
morning, I shall be much obliged to you. I wish to talk a little more
about the India Judicature, and to beg you to take an opportunity of
talking to the Chancellor about the alterations in question. If you
should be engaged this morning, and can see the Chancellor before we
meet tomorrow, it will answer all the purpose." *Holograph.*

THOMAS PENNANT to SIR LLOYD KENYON, Bart.

1319. 1784, August 8. Buxton.—" If there is a possibility of getting
a clause into the Franking Act, to empower members to frank printed
papers and prints, under a cover open at both ends, it will be no small
use to litterature, as well as an amusement to private life, which will be
greatly taken away by the necessity of the abolition of the privilege."

MARY KENYON to MRS. A. KENYON, at Chester.[1]

1320. [1782,] December 24. [London.]—"I feel a little tired with the bustle, but more with the anxiety of my Mr. Kenyon's situation, for he is once again made Attorney-General. Mr. Pitt wrote to him this morning. Mr. Kenyon went, and told Mr. Pitt he would much rather not accept the place, would support his administration as steadily out of office as in, and should not think himself neglected if he was left where he was. Mr. Pitt said it was impossible to go on without him. Everybody says he must have it, but neither Mr. Kenyon nor I like such popping in and out every month, nor this place, at any rate. I am afraid, too, it will drive us to the Rolls, but this you must not say, nor would Mr. Kenyon accept that place but to escape from the Attorney-General's."

WILLIAM PITT to SIR LLOYD KENYON, BART.

1321. 1785, March 20. Putney Heath.—"The enclosed paper with which I trouble you, contains a sketch of the Bill which I shall move for leave to bring in on Wednesday, and which I am anxious to submit to your consideration. I trust the plan guards against the principal objections hitherto suggested, either with respect to arbitary disfranchisement, or to introducing further innovation. The idea of transferring a certain proportion of representation from boroughs to counties (which is limited by the impossibility of more than a certain number being ever conveniently chosen by counties), and of providing that the boroughs which must continue to elect shall be those best entitled to it, seems to include all the amendment which our constitution can admit in the frame of Parliament, unless some new principle were to be admitted, for which I see no reason. If, upon casting your eye over it, there occurs to you anything which you wish explained, I shall be happy to see you, or to hear from you, any time before Wednesday. You will, I am sure, excuse the trouble I give you on a subject on which I am, for so many reasons, anxious." *Holograph.*

R. P. ARDEN to the SAME.

1322. 1785, September 21. Pepper Hall.—"I know you will have the goodness to excuse the trouble of this letter, which is to satisfy myself, beyond all doubt, respecting the power of the feoffees of the school at Manchester to convey a part of the school estate to a purchaser, in fee, under an annual rent, to be issuing for ever out of the premises conveyed, and the buildings to be thereupon erected. . . . The terms are one penny halfpenny a square yard, the common terms upon which ground near Manchester has been granted out for building leases."

J. PEMBERTON to the SAME.

1323. 1785, December 13. Halifax, Nova Scotia.—"We lost no time in sending dispatches to different parts of this province, and to the adjoining provinces, making our arrival known, and giving such information as we thought necessary for expediting the business in which we are employed [and] of the manner in which we intended to proceed. The Colonel, my colleague, and myself took a small house for ourselves, and another, not very distant, for our office. In a fortnight's time we entered upon business, and we have gone on with so much dispatch that we have been forced to stop for want of parties being prepared, or coming in from the country, more than once. . . . I am not apprehensive that the indulgence shewn by Parliament, in allowing new

---

[1] This letter is misplaced.

claims, will be productive of any great trouble to us, or of expense to the nation. Of those which we have already received, we shall not retain for examination, above one in ten. The numbers are very small at present. . . .

"The loyalists whom we have conversed with appear highly sensible of the generosity of the British Government, and express their gratitude in the warmest terms for this mark of attention which has been shewn them, in giving them an opportunity of having their claims heard abroad; and, indeed, had not this been done, many of the poorer claimants must have given up all hope of any sort of compensation. This you may well imagine, from an instance which I can give you of what passed to-day. We had before us a case where there was a fair claim, but yet we could not allow more than 30*l*. sterling. Claimants of this description could never have procured money to defray their expences to England, or if they had, notwithstanding the allowance which would have been made them for their expenses, they would have returned poorer than they came, and their new settlements would have been, perhaps, during the time of their absence, neglected and uncultivated. I do not know enough of the new settlements in this and the adjoining provinces to give you a satisfactory account of them.

"The principal settlement of which we hear the most promising report is that of New Brunswick, on the other side the Bay of Fundy, on St. John's River. The next to it is Shelbourn, in Rosway Bay, on the Nova Scotia coast. The number of settlers in each of these places is very considerable, and increasing; the number of buildings is astonishing, and, indeed, has been one cause of the poverty of the inhabitants, for they spent, many of them, what money they brought, in building handsom houses. There is said to be a spirit for trade beginning to exert itself in these places, and, in the interior parts of this province, great advances are made in the cultivation and improvement of the lands. I cannot but think favourably of this climate, from what I have hitherto experienced. We had a month of November much pleasanter, probably, than it was in England; fine chearful weather with a clear unclouded sky almost the whole of the time. We had one or two days when the cold was very sharp and piercing, but quite pleasant and enlivening, as I thought. They tell me, however, that I must wait till after Christmas before I think of judging of a Nova Scotia winter.

"This town is well situated on an easy ascent from the harbour, is extensive, but very ill-built. Several of the houses (amongst which is our own) command fine prospects of the harbour, and the coast on each side of it. The soil in this neighbourhood is craggy, and incapable, I should think, of being made very fruitful, different from most of the interior parts of the province. At present there is hardly any intercourse between this place and the United States, which is in great measure stopped by mutual prohibitions, but such, however, as are not strictly attended to, and they are not general in all the United States against British ships, though, in these provinces, I believe, generally, there are prohibitions against American vessels."

Thomas Hughes to Sir Lloyd Kenyon, Abbey Street, Bath.

1324. 1785, December 26. Windsor.—"I had in my mind to ask your opinion upon a subject that concerns my brother and sister, when you were in town, but some way or other it escaped me. My sister has been entertaining some scruples, which only make my brother and myself laugh, with respect to the validity of her marriage, because it was not registered in the Mayor's Court at Madras. You probably know that the ceremony of marriage in India is generally performed at most of the out settlements, where there is seldom or never a chaplain, by the chief of that settlement, and in a thousand instances, with still less sanctity, by any officer, civil or military; and my brother and sister were married at Granjam in October, 1778, by Mr. Smith, the chief, and they have a written attestation of this marriage, signed by him, and witnessed by Mr. Smith and a Mr. Dangly, at whose house they were married. When they removed to Madras, in 1779, they offered this paper to the secretary (I think he is called) of the Mayor's Court, to be entered amongst their records. But he said it was not usual to make an entry of any marriages in the out settlements ; and there the matter rested, and has never been thought of since. Half the people married in India are exactly in the same predicament, and this fact is at least a ground of presumption that those legal forms which are required in this country are not required abroad. All that I therefore would wish to ask is whether any possible inconvenience may arise from the informality of such marriages, in the case of litigated property, or of anything else that might concern the children? If any inconvenience in future is possible, may it be prevented by any steps to be taken in present; and if any steps are to be taken, are they to be taken in this country or in India?

" It is generally presumed here, that as the birthday is put off to the 9th of February, on account of Princess Charles' death, the King will not remove to town till the day before the meeting of Parliament. I should not be surprised if, after opening the session, he should slip his cables and come down here for another fortnight, if he can possibly put off his Monday levées ; for I have heard him declare lately, that if it were in his choice to live either in London or Calcutta, he should prefer the latter, though he hates warm weather. We had the honour of a visit yesterday, in the Equerry's room, from the Prince of Wales. He was come to condole with the Queen, and I thing (*sic*) his countenance had more of the doleful cast than ordinary. But of this there may be other assignable causes. I never saw his Royal Highness so sedate and so rational. The world will have it that he is meditating that which is not very rational, though it may be very sedate."

R. KENYON to his brother, SIR LLOYD KENYON, at the Rolls House, London.

1325. 1786, January 3. Cefn.—"The Wynnstay plays were not so well attended as formerly, though crowded on some of the nights. The performers behaved as well as usual, and Mr. Bridgeman is particularly clever. The elegant ticket of the last year admitted on the present occasion."

WILLIAM PITT to the SAME.

1326. 1786, February 21. Downing Street.—"The question to-morrow, respecting the fortifications, in itself is important, and so much relied on by [the] Opposition, that you will, I am sure, excuse my expressing a wish that your engagements may allow you to attend. May I also beg the favour of you to furnish me, as soon as you conveniently can, with your opinion respecting the Bill I troubled you with, as the time will soon press." *Holograph.*

HENRY DUNDAS to the SAME.

1327. 1786, April 14. Wimbledon.—"When we met at [the] Lord Chancellor's, he expressed a wish that I would pay attention to the laws which restrain the residence of British subjects, unlicensed, in India. I have done so, and send you some clauses upon the subject. I hope to learn from you when there could be an opportunity of meeting with you and Mr. Bearcoft and Mr. Scott, finally to settle all this business."

WILLIAM PITT to SIR LLOYD KENYON.

1328. 1786, July 8. Downing Street.—"It is necessary that we should soon have a meeting with the rest of the Commons, appointed by the act of this session for the reduction of the national debt. Our business, at first, is probably little more than form; and it will, perhaps, answer the purpose in you doing me the favour of dining here on Tuesday, if you will come half-an-hour before dinner." *Holograph.*

J. PEMBERTON to the SAME.

1329. 1786, July 11. Halifax, Nova Scotia.—"I continue to find my situation in America not comfortable only, but pleasant and agreable. The spring was scarce perceivable, and we got at once, almost, from winter to summer. I do not find the heat of the summer at all oppressive; though the sun is powerful, yet the heat is so tempered by cool sea breezes as hardly ever to be oppressive. But the present state of the country does not allow me to say much more in commendation of it; all that I can say is that it appears to have great natural advantages, and in a course of years, perhaps ages, when well cultivated, may prove a very fine and rich country. We have made a considerable progress in our business, and, as we have given up our whole time to it, should probably have made still greater advances, could we have procured claimants from the other provinces, or even the distant parts of this, to have attended us. We hope to have finished most of the business of this province in the course of two months. We shall go to New Brunswick in the month of September next, and stay there all the next winter. In the summer following, we shall visit Canada. At present, popularity attends us, but I suppose we must lose a good deal of it when the loyalists find how much many of their claims are curtailed (as they well deserve), and how many new claims are rejected, though we are as liberal in the admission of them as we think the last Act of Parliament can possibly admit. A report has arrived here, that an offer would be made me of the Chief Justiceship of this province."

LORD SYDNEY to the SAME.

1330. 1786, August 2. "St. James, 4 o'clock."—"A woman has attempted to stab the King, but has not wounded him at all. We are assembling a Council to examine her. We wish much for your attendance."

LADY KENYON to MRS. ALICE KENYON.

1331. 1786, October 30. London.—"Mr. Wilson seems very happy in his promotion to the bench; is to kiss hands as soon as the Chancellor can present him. Mr. Bearcroft desires Sir Lloyd will not make any resolution against the place of Chief Justice. Some days Lord Mansfield seems just sinking and others, all alive, his head clear as possible, but his nerves bad. Some say he will not attempt to sit again, but most agree they only conjecture the Lord Chancellor is better. You must prepare your mourning for the Princess Amelia; she is very bad; they say an inflamation has taken place in her bowels."

ROBERT KENYON to ——————.

1332. 1786, December 13. Bank.—" I have no objections to Sunday Schools in Salford, provided they are properly regulated, and the children are brought duly and constantly to church; otherwise you are teaching the children this false and wicked principle, that for the sake of learning to read and write, or other worldly advantages, it is lawful to neglect the public worship of God. But I am convinced, in my own mind, that regular charity schools are much more useful institutions, and had not my ill state of health prevented it, it was my fixed purpose and intention, the last spring, to have solicited your kind assistance, as well as that of the trustees of the different charities in Salford, in establishing two regular charity schools, one for fifty boys and the other for fifty girls."

WILLIAM WILBERFORCE to SIR LLOYD KENYON.

1333. 1787, May 3. Palace Yard.—"Knowing how your hours are engrossed, I cannot be surprized that the little Bill you had the goodness to undertake for me has not yet made its appearance in the House; at the same time, I flatter myself, you will allow for the anxiety with which I wait for it, being afraid lest the lateness of the session should prevent its being gone through with, this year, and I should be reproached by the Mayor of Leeds for having disappointed his wishes of introducing good order and regularity into that populous town, during his mayoralty, which expires in October or November. He is, besides, so worthy a man, and so warm a friend of mine, that public opinion and private motives concur in making me extremely desirous that his good intentions should not be frustrated." *Holograph.*

LORD CAMDEN to the SAME.

1334. 1787, May 4. Hill Street.—"I came home yesterday from the Cockpit, very much dissatified with our conversation upon Maclaghan's cause; for, although that Mooting did produce several matters that are new and not stated in the printed cases, yet the confused discourse of counsel, judges, and solicitors, did so cloud my understanding that I had almost forgot the great outlines of the cause, at the close of it. And I could wish that my friend Lord Grantly would not be quite so hasty in disclosing his opinion, for that discovery throws the [court] at once into a general conversation, and then we get into an altercation upon the separate bills and parcels of the clause, and, oftentimes, being confounded from such confusion of talk, one is apt to forget the great merit of the business. My Lord Grantley has great knowledge and excellent judgment, but his patience is not equal to the other qualities. I mention this to you, my dear sir, only as a hint, and in confidence to ourselves, and to hope you will assist me when there shall be occasion to check our friend's hastiness, which I would always attempt in the gentlest way, taking care to give not the least offence in the manner of doing it. I have appointed next Wednesday for our meeting upon this business."

G. HARDINGE to SIR LLOYD KENYON.

1335. 1787, June 29.—"I have a serious disagreement with my dear Lord Camden, whom I love and revere with more than filial affection; but, though in offending him I have made a painful sacrifice to public honour (as I feel the demand of it), I cannot repent of my firmness. If you should think I have done right, and would intimate your sentiments to Lord Camden, you would restore him to me. He has pressed me to supersede an able and useful officer who is Registrar and Marshal, for the sake of a new appointment in favour of a person recommended by him. Usage in modern times (to the honour of them, be it said) is uniform against any such removals. The last and present Chief Justice of Chester, Beard, Hayes, and Barrington, have been. quoted by me in vain, and proof adduced as to the last three. I have consulted Scott and Plumer, men of sound judgement. I asked Pool today what he thought of it. All these have said, without one dissenteint voice, that I am right. But Lord Camden will compare it with his Common Pleas and Court of Chancery, where this usage admits and justifies an immediate sweep of the old officers. To say the truth, if usage could justify it upon my circuit, I would not act upon it, but would endeavour to begin a usage the other way."

LADY MARY ELEANOR BOWES.

1336. 1787, Michaelmas Term.—Articles exhibited by Mary Eleanor Bowes, commonly called the Countess Dowager of Strathmore, wife of Andrew Robinson Bowes, of Streatlam Castle, in the county of Durham, against the said Andrew Robinson Bowes, her husband, and Edward Lucas and others, she being in fear of death, or of receiving some great bodily harm.

The articles recount the ill-usage received by the said Lady Bowes from her husband and the others, who carried her into Scotland, and tried to compel her to make certain settlements.

PHILIP YORKE to SIR LLOYD KENYON.

1337. 1788, January 7. Erthig.—"I should have been ashamed of breaking in upon any part of your Lordship's precious time, had you not expressed some wish and pleasure (when I had last the honour of being with you at Gredington) in collecting the MSS. opinions of old lawyers of rank in their profession; as such, I send the two enclosed for your Lordship's acceptance, and if I should find any more, I will venture to send them also. It seems not a little singular that these should be the opinions on the same case of eminent lawyers, both dismissed from great employments, one before, the other at, the Revolution; and both returning to their practice without the Bar (Pemberton, I believe, Williams, certainly) and giving common opinions, as in the present case. I remember the late Mr. Charles Yorke repaired Lord Chief Justice Pemberton's monument at Highgate, and that Charles the II. turned him out, upon Lord Russell's trial. I recollect none such good symptom in Sir William William's case. I wonder whether Burnet is well founded in saying that Pemberton got all his law in jail; I believe Serjeant Davy, of later times, certainly did."

Enclosures.—Original opinions of Sir William Williams, dated 17 February, 1691, and Sir Francis Pemberton, undated, on a question concerning the Dymock property.

MARY, LADY KENYON to LADY HANMER.

1337A. 1788, February 16. London.—"What a pleasant day we had yesterday, at Westminster Hall; the sight is far more magnificent than even the Abbey, and we were in a charming place. The Chancellor sent to ask how many tickets we would have (I will send you the two notes and beg you will lay them by for me, for I am very proud of them). I asked for four. My sister Jane, Sir Thomas, and I went in with them. This box is placed near the throne, just behind the Duchess of Gloucester's box, and at the end of the Peeresses', which enabled us to see all the great ladies. The Peers were all robed, and came in two and two. The room fine, beyond description, and very full, to hear Mr. Burke, who is a wonderful speaker, though, I fear, a very malignant man. I declare the impression his speech made on me was that I would as soon choose to be the criminal, Mr. Hastings, as the accuser. He seemed to dwell with such pleasure on every thing that was harsh and cruel. We met with Mr. and Mrs. Hay in their box, which holds 24 people. Lady Grose and Mrs. Pepys were in the Chief Justice's, just behind us (for one box is raised behind another to the top of the hall). and behind us sat the Duchess of Gloucester and the Princess Sophia, her daughter, and many more, partly behind the throne, but in a good place to see was the Duchess of Cumberland and Mrs. Fitzherbert, in the same box. The Duke of Gloucester's son, Prince William, walked in state, immediately after the Chancellor, followed by all the four princes —Cumberland, Gloucester, York, and the Prince of Wales. After it was over, we were taken into the Chancellor's room, till our coach cam e."

WILLIAM WILBERFORCE to SIR LLOYD KENYON.

1337B. 1788, February 29. Palace Yard.—Perhaps you are not aware that I have been long confined to my house by indisposition, and am still a close prisoner, wholly unequal to such little business as even this that I am now engaged in; add to which, my eyes are so bad that I can scarce see how to direct my pen, so that on all accounts I must be very brief. I have long wanted to include in our society for carrying the Proclamation into effect, the name of Mr. Scott, having a real respect for him, but when I have seen him he has always been busy, and lately, when the matter has pressed, I have been myself laid fast. Could you mention it to him, and that to-day; indeed, it is possible that doing it to-day may be essential, because I believe the list is to be made out for printing, to-morrow, at 9 o'clock. Nothing is to be announced to the world of a society, only that the gentlemen mentioned have felt the necessity of attending to his Majesty's call, and have agreed to assist in carrying the Proclamation into effect.

WILLIAM PITT to the SAME.

1338. 1788, April 11. Downing Street.—"I find from Lord Stanhope, that he has communicated to you his Bill for a register of freeholders in the different counties, with the alterations lately made in it, which he thinks you approve; and I flatter myself, from what I hear of it, that it is not likely to meet with much objection. If, upon consideration, you should think it unexceptionable, and should have no objection to take a part in introducing it into the House, your authority would give it great weight, in every respect, and particularly as it is connected with legal questions. I consider the object itself of diminishing the expense and trouble of election as a very important public object, if it can be obtained; and this will, I hope, be my excuse for venturing to give you this trouble, and for requesting that you would allow me an opportunity of talking with you on the subject whenever it is convenient."

LORD STANHOPE to the SAME.

1339. 1788, April 14. Mansfield Street.—"Lord Stanhope presents his compliments to the Master of the Rolls, and (by Mr. Pitt's desire) takes the liberty of sending him, herewith, the Election Bill, for his perusal. As it is the House copy, he begs the favor of the Master of the Rolls to make any remarks in pencil on the margin." The Bill will be too late for the next General Election, unless it be passed this session of Parliament."

LORD MANSFIELD to SIR LLOYD KENYON.

1340. 1788, April 14. "Kenwood."—"Lord Mansfield is not able to wait on the Master of the Rolls, and therefore is forced to take this method of saying to him, that he thinks he owes it to the great respect and personal regard he has always had for the Master of the Rolls, to send him the first communication of his resolution to resign next term. Except Mr. Justice Buller, to whom Lord Mansfield is bound by many ties, there is no man in Westminster Hall by whom Lord Mansfield had rather be succeeded than by the Master of the Rolls."

WILLIAM PITT to the SAME.

1341. 1788, June 5.—"You will receive to-day from Lord Sydney the formal signification of his Majesty's intention to advance you to the peerage, for which his Majesty means you would kiss hands to-morrow. You will have the goodness to let Lord Sydney know what title you wish to take. Allow me only to add my sincere congratulations." *Holograph.*

SIR R. P. ARDEN to LORD KENYON.

1342. 1788, June 18.—"I have kissed his Majesty's hand, and, much against my inclination, been knighted. Mr. Pitt tells me that he has written to the Chancellor. After what has passed, I really know not what to do. Whatever the Chancellor would think the most respectful, I would do, for I shall never be wanting in that point towards him, let him treat me as he will."

THE LORD CHIEF JUSTICE'S GOLD COLLAR.

1343. 1788, June 21.—Receipt given by J. Way, on behalf of Lord Mansfield, for 147*l.* 3*s.* 3*d.* received of Lord Kenyon "for the debit to Lord Mansfield on his late chamber in Sergeant's Inn; and also the sum of one hundred guineas for the gold collar of office, as Chief Justice."

WILLIAM PITT to LORD KENYON.

1344. 1788, November 15. Downing Street.---"I sleep tonight at Mr. Dundas' at Wimbledon, but return to town some time tomorrow. It would therefore suit me equally well to see you, either at Wimbledon or Marsh Gate (if you intended going into the country), or otherwise in town, and I beg you will have the goodness to name whatever hour or place is most convenient to yourself."

MARY, LADY KENYON to MRS. A. KENYON, at Chester.

1345. 1789, January 17. London.—"Last night, in the House of Commons, they sat till two o'clock; the division in favour of restrictions in the Regency Bill gave a majority of 70. Another division, proposed to know whether those restrictions should be for a limited time or not, was carried, against limited time, by above 60, but it [is] so certain now where the power will be lodged, that many will go over daily; the 'Rats,' as they are called, are all on the watch. Everybody speaks highly of the Chancellor, on all sides. The Opposition say Mr. Pitt has been personally uncivil to the Prince. I do not believe it. That party have done all they can to throw blame on him, and, in this examination of doctors, on the Queen. The last night, the leaders of their party thought it prudent to say every thing fine of her; all they pretend to blame her for is that she wishes to have the kingdom believe that the King will get well again. Is there any crime in a wife wishing this, when she is daily told by 5 out of 6 of the physicians that they have not a doubt he will recover? She is teazed and harassed to death, but this Regency Bill will now soon be settled, and another empowering the Queen to take care of the King's person, which gives her the command of the household, physicians, &c., [so] that even the Regent cannot remove or alter any body in places about the King's person. They have coaxed and courted the Chancellor every way, and by every person, but he will not gain them (sic) [written in error for 'they will not gain him' ?]."

LORD THURLOW to LORD KENYON.

1345A. 1789, January 31.—" I am sorry Mr. Pitt did not shew you my answer to the paper from the Cabinet. The object is [to] get a Regency, in the only way, I presume, wherein a Regency can be appointed, by Act of Parliament. That Act may be passed three (sic) ways—by general commission to the usual persons to assent or dissent, or by such commission to the Prince, or by general commission to pass that Bill, directed to the usual persons or to the Prince, or by address to pass it in the name and on the behalf of the King, or to direct a commission to be issued for that purpose. When passed in any of these ways, the Act will be good, the enrolment in Chancery being the original record."

WILLIAM WILBERFORCE to the SAME.

1346. 1789, February 12.—" You cannot imagine how insipid and vapid our debates are without Fox. They serve us up the same tasteless mess day after day, till one loathes the very sight of it. Your Lordship's old favourite, Powys, tried his hand yesterday. I understand Mr. Francis is to be one of the head cooks today."

LADY KENYON to MRS. A. KENYON, Chester.

1346A. 1789, March 11. London.—" I long to have all my dear sisters here just now, to see how fine we look in this square, all lighted up as brilliant as possible. Mr. Lee has ten candles in each window, four more than anybody else, to make amends for the want of joy within. I think I have made this house pretty; there is a large candle in each large payn and a small lamp in the little ones . . . . Mr. Abbot's is the same, I believe, and we light five stands. The town will be beautiful, for there are more devices than ever I saw. Lord Mansfield's house has ' G. R.' in little lamps on the outside his house. Many have (at the other end the town) a crown and ' G. R.'; some the word " Rejoice." Over the gateway at the Rolls there are 300 lamps to form the crown and ' G. R.'; always a touch extraordinary there. Lord Chesterfield's house, they say, is covered with Scripture phrases. I should like to drive about to look at these things, for Jane's sake, to whom all this is new; but there will be so many people out, I dare neither go nor leave my candles at home. Coaches are flying about at a great rate, and by and by I expect squibs and crackers. Lord Kenyon is dining at the Duke of Richmond's. He was at Kew on Sunday, found the King vastly well; stayed with him above an hour, was

most graciously received, and entrusted with as many of his private papers as Lord Kenyon could lift into his coach. The King spake with the highest approbation of the Queen's conduct, spake of the Duke of Gloucester with affection, of Cumberland with compassion, of some of the 'Rats' with contempt, but saying they had done as he expected they would if ever they found an opportunity; some of them will be turned out of their places, and I hope honester men put in. . . . .
"It is expected the Prince will make a speech to-night in the House. It is well if he does not expose himself. I dare not write all I could tell you about his party, but am thankful I am not nearly connected with any of them. Lord Kenyon goes again to Kew on Friday. . . . . There was a sad riot at the Opera House on Saturday; Lady Bromley and Miss Curzon were there, and the latter in tears, with fright. Colonel Phipps and his brother were two of the ringleaders, with three other gentlemen, all very drunk." (*Extract printed in Life of Lord Kenyon, by Hon. G. Kenyon, p.* 220.)

LORD CAMDEN to LORD KENYON.

1347. 1789, March 24. Hill Street.—" I have sent you the Marine Treaties, but I am not able, at present, to find Douglass' reports, though I am persuaded the book is in my study; but such is the litter in this disorderly room, that it will require more time to search for it than I can spare at this moment as I am going to Cockpit to hear Plantation causes."

JOHN SCOTT to the SAME.

1347A. 1789, June 28. East India House.—"Having procured a copy of the question which was referred by the Lords for the consideration of the Judges, I have discovered, to my infinite astonishment, that it is drawn up, throughout, upon false grounds, an error into which their Lordships have fallen, from giving credit to what fell from one of the managers in Westminster Hall. The inclosed paper is very accurately drawn up by me, from a strict examination of all the documents. I have taken the liberty to send it, and your Lordship will at once see that the second error (where the Lords affirm certain facts to be in proof, which have really no existence) is owing to their giving credit to Mr. Burke for having truly stated that question which Mr. Hastings brought before the Council on the 11th May, 1778."

WILLIAM PITT to the SAME.

1348. 1789, September 18.—" I am very sorry to have been prevented answering sooner your Lordship's letter, enclosing one from Mr. Vaughan, respecting the Lieutenancy of Merionethshire. The circumstances which your Lordship mentioned would have given great weight to Mr. Vaughan's pretensions, but immediately on the death of Sir Watkin Williams, I promised to recommend whatever appointment would be most acceptable to his family, and before I received your Lordship's letter, it had been agreed that it should be held, for the present, by Mr. W. Williams."

PETER WHITEHALL DAVIES to the SAME.

1348A. 1789, November 21. Broughton.--" The very high price of corn in this and the adjoining counties, so very soon after the harvest, alarms us much, and if we are not supplied from abroad long before the next harvest, dreadful consequences probably will ensue, for the colliers threaten to rise again; if they should, I am much afraid the populace will join them, and there is no military force near enough to protect the lives and properties of his Majesty's subjects. Fatal outrages are much easier prevented than remedied. The high price of corn appears to me to proceed from the following causes :—The great scarcity of it before the harvest and the last wet summer, which has made the quantity produced only as two to three of the usual produce. The constant heavy rains which have fallen the last two months have so much prevented the sowing of wheat in this neighbourhood, that I believe not one tenth part of the usual quantity has been put into the ground. Potatoes, the great support of the poor, are also very dear; if they could be imported at a cheap rate they would relieve them much. I send your Lordship this intelligence that, if you think it necessary, you may communicate it to the Lord Chancellor, Mr. Pitt, and the rest of his Majesty's Privy Council, that every thing possible may be done to supply the common people with necessary food."

THOMAS PENNANT to LORD KENYON.

1349. 1789, December 1. Downing.—"I am highly honoured and pleased with the effect of my letter. An inundation of corn has been suddenly poured into Liverpool, and as suddenly engaged. I cannot but suspect the destination, and therefore again humbly suggest the necessity of compelling the collectors at the port, and also the common officers, to be most rigorous in their demand of the highest bonds the law will admit for landing the corn in the places they clear out for. It is also my opinion that correspondence should be kept between the port of clearance and the port of landing, in order to prevent collusion, as, in that case, smuggling can be carried on in only very small vessels, and the officers should attend to the little creeks. Before it was in the papers, I knew— but forgot to mention to your Lordship—that the French had offered premium for importation. This is a critical time. It is not inhumanity to wish to see them pinched. It will prevent domestic evils here, and effect political good there. Three or four of us have ordered a ship load of barley to this country, to be sold at prime cost; and I hope our example will be followed."

SAMUEL STRONG to the SAME.

1350. 1790, February 27.—"The Duchess of Kingston being supposed to have died intestate, with respect to her property in France, Mrs. Strong, with four other cousins, being the next of kin, were advised to send over a proper person to make enquiries, &c., on their behalf; but a Mr. Glover, who stood in a more remote degree of relation to the Duchess, got the start of us, and went to Paris to claim the whole for himself. After disposing of all the property he could get into his hands, and taking every other step he could devise to injure the succession, he began to fear that the issue would be against him, and therefor threw out a proposal to the next of kin that if they would formally relinquish all their claims in his favour, he would enter into a bond to pay them 4,500*l*, clear of expenses, except the part that we had incurred by agency. Rather than suffer the whole to be spent and embezzled, we closed with this offer, and the bond was executed accordingly, and made payable to Sir Henry Oxenden, in trust for the next of kin, his lady being one of them. The bond, with one year's interest, becomes due next July; but I have just now heard that Mr. Glover is returned from Paris, and, pretending that he is a great loser by this business, requests that, on his defraying our expenses, which amount to 1,500*l.* between the five parties, he may have the bond cancelled. This after the treatment we have received from him appears unreasonable in the highest degree, and we are unanimous in refusing to listen to it. But as Mr. Glover may possibly sell his estates in England and quit the kingdom before July, the questions I presume to ask your Lordship are these : Whether the relinquishing of our claims to the Duchess of Kingston's effects in France, in favour of Mr. Glover, as above stated, would be deemed a legal consideration ; and, if so, what steps (if any) can be taken to prevent him from evading the payment of the 4,500*l.* under the bond ? "

Sir William Pulteney to Lord Kenyon.

1351. 1790, April 1. London.—" I have long wished to have it in my power to give your Lordship some small proof of the value which I put on your friendship, and of the high regard which I entertain for your talents and character. I have been able, at last, to contrive it so that I can now make you an offer of recommending any respectable independant gentleman, in whom your Lordship interests yourself, to a seat in Parliament, without his being put to any expense. I am sure I shall be happy to connect myself with any one who has the good fortune to enjoy your Lordship's good opinion. As I have been obliged to refuse many applications by letting it be understood that my arrangements were made, I trust that your Lordship will let this pass as an old engagement, and that the gentleman you recommend may understand it in that way."

James Tomkinson to the Same, at Lincoln's Inn Fields, London.

1352. 1790, June 18. Bath.—" The election here is to come on next Monday, but the conclusion is already known, having been fixed at a meeting of the Corporation yesterday. Lord Bayham and Lord Weymouth are the fortunate candidates. Owing to Mr. Grenville declining, his votes went to Lord Weymouth, which gave him a majority over Mr. Watson, who resigned yesterday, and Mr. Morris, it is supposed, will follow his example, as he has not, I find, the least chance of success."

Sentence of Excommunication.

1352a. 1790, July 22.—Petition to Lord Kenyon of Mrs. Roe and Mrs. Bush, " two poor helpless women that has experienced a long and painful imprisonment of three years, by virtue of an *excommunicato capiendo* writ from the spiritual court, for being publickly married in the meeting house at Calverton, seven miles from Nottingham, in the same publick manner and form as quakers do." They pray that, as they have neither committed theft nor injured anyone, though they may perhaps be thought to have infringed some laws of man, that Lord Kenyon will look on them with an eye of pity, as Pharoah did to his chief butler, and restore them to their former station. What makes their affliction harder is that they and two small children have to sleep in one bed, and have to pay the jailer four shillings a week.

The Bishop of Ferns to Lord Kenyon.

1353. 1790, August 14. Dublin.—" As the election of a Lord Mayor for the City of Dublin has created much clamour and perhaps engaged attention on your side of the water, I enclose to your Lordship two papers, one of which I am told gives an authentic account of the Lord Chancellor's defence of the Privy Council in the House of

Lords; the other, the reprobation of that defence by the Whig Club. I
see that some of the English papers have reprinted these, but if an
authentic copy should not fall into your hands, the inclosed, perhaps,
will not be inacceptable. No unlearned man who reads the 33rd of
George II., which regulates the election of the Chief Magistrate, can
suppose it possible that Alderman James could be duly elected; but I
am not accustomed to the construction of Acts of Parliament. The
point, however, is now so far given up, that Alderman James has
resigned his pretensions, and Howison (?) has been sent down, by the
Board of Aldermen, to the Commons for this approbation. I cannot but
be glad of the concession, as even with the colour only of right, factious
men can at all times create discontent in this country."

Charles Dundas to Lord Kenyon.

1354. 1790, September 2. Barton Court, near Newbury.—" Your
Lordship having, on a late occasion, publicly declared the opinion of
the Court of King's Bench on the subject of meetings held for the purpose of fighting and boxing matches, which of late have been so frequent
and disgraceful in this kingdom, I trust you will forgive the liberty I
am now taking of addressing you on a case of this nature, in which the
High Sheriff of the county of Berks and myself have endeavoured to do
what we could to follow the line pointed out by your Lordship, but
which is now beyond the limits of this county. For some time before
the 30th of August, it was declared by newspaper paragraphs, etc., that
on that day a battle would be fought at Newbury, between a Mr. Hooper
and a Mr. Bryan (two great characters in the art of boxing). The stage
was erected on barges, in the bason of Newbury Wharf, and an immense
crowd assembled, from places above an hundred miles distant. The
Sheriff and myself attended at 8 o'clock in the morning, for the purpose
of preventing this fight. Immediately the alarm was given, the com-
batants, with their supporters, were secured. Speenhamland, where
we were, is surrounded by several different districts, in none of which my
warrant could have effect, without the endorsement of the Justices belonging to them (viz., Hampshire, Wiltshire, Oxfordshire, and the
Borough of Newbury) and in the three first, the magistrates resided at
a distance.

" On my promise that no advantage should be taken of the parties
by detaining them if they appeared voluntarily, some of them came
before the Sheriff and myself. We endeavoured to persuade them
to be bound over not to disturb the peace of this county, which was
agreed on, when, by the accidental arrival of Mr. Bigge Wither (who
acts as a Justice of the Peace for Berks, Wilts, and Hants), he insisted
on their promising not to offend in either of the other counties. They
left Newbury soon after, very hastily, with above a thousand of their
attendants, declaring they were going to Oxfordshire; but when they
reached Chapel Row, about nine miles from Newbury, they began their
fight in this county. A warrant, signed by Mr. Wither and myself,
followed them there, but their numbers prevented the constable from
doing his duty. By the declaration of Lord Barrymore (who appeared
to be their director), this contest is to be renewed at Doncaster during
the races, it being now said to be undecided, for the purpose of collecting a greater mob on that occasion. Having stated these circumstances,
I hope your Lordship will excuse this application. The objection made
by these people to their being bound over was the dread they had of
the example being followed by other counties; and we could not (con-
sistently with our promise) lay hold of them to bind them over generally.

"The warrant is now in search of them in this county, but they are not residents here. They may be indicted at the next Quarter Sessions, when the Bench warrant would issue against them, which would have effect beyond the bounds of the county; but before that time, their intention of fighting at Doncaster will be executed. This being the case, if the Sheriff and myself dare with propriety ask your Lordship's directions, we will act accordingly. Considering it as a public good to keep the peace, we trust we are not guilty of either impropriety or indelicacy to the high station of your Lordship, when we lay this matter before that power which extends over the whole kingdom. If, personally, I may be allowed to offer a further justification of my conduct, it is that, having had the honor of moving at the Sessions at Reading that the peace officers within the county should be ordered to suppress these tumultuous meetings to the utmost of their power, I was then unanimously supported by fifteen of the most respectable magistrates of this county, several of whom have called on me, on this occasion, to exert myself in preventing this declared breach of the peace in my own neighbourhood."

The Rev. W[ILLIAM] J[ONES], of Nayland, to the Honourable George Kenyon.

1355. 1790 (?), November 13.—Thanks him for a promised present of books. "This nation seems threatened with the approach of terrible times; so that they who are ready to depart with age and infirmities will be taken from evil that is to come. All I can do now is to watch and to pray that no hour nor moment may find me unprepared. Yet my mind will ever be running on the times, and the Church, and the poor distracted condition of the best religion we have amongst us. My heart is divided between sorrow for myself and the Christian world; both seem equally hastening to a dying state. But God will always have a remnant. I have by me in MS. a little sort of another *Tom Bull*, upon religion; but I know not what to do with it. I have likewise a piece which I call an *Essay on Man, as he is described to us in the Scripture;* this has been written out fair above 30 years, and perhaps might do some good, but, alas, my agent is getting old and indolent, like myself. Our next coach comes out on Friday morning. When once I get the next parcel (if I live to get it) I will depend no more on Rivington." *Seal.*

Postscript.—"The books are come (Keith on *Prophecy,* &c.), but letters cost me so much trouble that I cannot afford to throw even a false one away, so you must let me speak as a fool."

Robert Barclay to [Thomas Steele ?].

1356. 1791, March 21.—"An event has just happened which, as it may materially serve the interest of this house, compels me to request the favour of your interest with Government, whose influence will be in some degree affected by it. The fact is simply that Mr. Walker, the Marshal of the King's Bench, is dead, and his place is in the gift of Lord Kenyon, whom we wish so far to influence the intended successor to Walker, as to take his supply of porter from this house, whose predecessor, Mr. Thrale, served it until it was burnt by the riots, 1781; since which, Calvert (a decided friend of the blue and buff interest) has had the supply of it. But a change of Marshal creates a change of interest, and, in case of a contested election, it has been found of use to our cause to have his interest united to our own, which you can vouch honestly to have been on all occasions actively exerted on behalf of the present administration. I feel more difficulty in asking, even through you, any personal favour; but as not only in the addresses of the Regency business we were chief instruments, but have been recently active [and] successful in returning our old Members, as well as were the first to take up Captain Finch (for the county) in this borough, I hope you will be able to obtain Lord Kenyon's own interest direct, or through either of the Judges."

WILLIAM WILBERFORCE to LORD KENYON.

1357. 1791, March 23.—Mr. Henry Thornton called on me this morning, to consult me respecting an application which has been made to him by Mr. Barclay, the great brewer in the Borough. After some little consideration, I advised him to mention the matter to your Lordship; but though I did not say a syllable to him which could give him an idea of my troubling your Lordship on the occasion, yet, reflecting on the kindness your Lordship had always shewn me, being ignorant how far the subject of his request is altogether proper, and that if there be any impropriety in it I am in some degree *particeps criminis*, I have thought it only right to take up the pen. I will only add that my friend, Mr. Henry Thornton, is one of the worthiest of men, and that on this account, added to our having been from our childhood in habits of closest intimacy and affection, I am happy, in introducing him to your Lordship, bearing my testimony to his character.

THOMAS STEELE to the SAME.

1358. 1791, March 23. Pay Office, Whitehall.—"Your Lordship having lately appointed a successor to the late Marshal óf the King's Bench, I am earnestly requested to apply to you . . . . to request that he may be desired to authorise the house of Mr. Barclay, under the name of Thrale & Co., in Southwark, to supply, from time to time, the porter which is required for the consumption of the inhabitants of the King's Bench. Mr. Calvert's house has lately been employed in this ·service, and will naturally endeavour to obtain a continuance of it. They are inveterate enemies to the present Government. Mr. Barclay and his uncle, Mr. David Barclay, are the best friends that any government ever had, and we are bound, in gratitude to them for past services, to strain every nerve for the purpose of accomplishing this point, which they have very much at heart."

SAMUEL HORSLEY, Bishop of St. David's, to the SAME.

1359. 1791, April. Bulls Cross.—"I take the liberty to beg your Lordship's perusal of a short bill, which has been drawn upon a principle suggested by me, for the relief of the Scottish episcopalians. Your Lordship knows that these people now pray for their King and royal family, and take the oath of allegiance. But many of their clergy scruple the oath of abjuration, as containing a retrospective denial of the right of the abdicated family, which they hold to have been indefeasible so long as that family subsisted, though they now consider it as extinct. For they think the only remaining representative of that family, the Cardinal York, has incapacitated himself by the oath of submission as a churchman to a foreign sovereign. But the particular hardship that they labour under is this, that by the 9th clause of the 19th of George II. c. 38, notwithstanding that they were to take the oaths, they would remain subject to the penalties of that Act. The operation of the bill which I enclose will be nothing more than to do away that cruel hardship, and relieve such of them as can persuade themselves to take the oaths, from the penalties which by that Act would still hang over them. It leaves the delicate question of the validity of their orders quite untouched, and in the same state of ambiguity in which it was left by the statutes of Queen Anne. The relief it extends to them will be very considerable. . . . . . . I think they are deserving of the indulgence of Government, as by praying expressly for the King (which they now do), and recognising his title, they have contributed much towards the extinction of Jacobitism in Scotland."

George Rose to Lord Kenyon.

1360. 1791, May 10. Old Palace Yard.—Mr. Pitt means to recommend Mr. Vaughan, a neighbour of yours, to the King, for a baronetcy. "I shall be very much obliged to your Lordship if you will tell me whether you happen to know if Mr. Myddleton, the member for Denbigh, is in determined opposition, or whether the complying with a request he has just made to Mr. Pitt would have any chance of conciliating him."

Sir W. Pulteney to the Same.

1361. 1791, May 12. London.—As to a bill for enlarging the term of a patent granted to James Turner "for his invention of a yellow colour for painting coaches." Thinks Mr. Turner has been cruelly defrauded of the benefits of his first patent. He is a remarkable chemist, and a person of good character. Lord Dundonald and the Bishop of Llandaff, who are skilled in chemistry, have a good opinion of him. "I do not agree with those who think that patents for inventions are hurtful; I think they have been one of the great causes of the important discoveries which in this country have so much improved our manufactures and trade."

William Pitt to the Same.

1362. 1791, June 25. Downing Street.—"I was very much obliged to your Lordship for your friendly suggestion respecting the Jersey Commission, which I have endeavorde (*sic*) to make use of, without mentioning your name. The business originated last year at the Council board, and all the papers respecting it were then communicated to the Chancellor; and, indeed, I thought the draft of the commission had been likewise. The gentlemen who were thought of to be joined to Mr. Grant, are Mr. Partridge and Mr. Nicoll." *Holograph.*

Francis Plowden to the Same.

1363. 1791, August 4. Adelphi—"I have, this morning, understood from the Soilicitor General that your Lordship had done me the honor of mentioning me to him; and, from what I could collect from him, it appeared to me that a sort of specimen or trial would be expected from me, before the heads of the law would choose to recommend me as a proper person to undertake the revision and compression of the statutes. I have already published one tract upon the point of alienage, and have by me a manuscript draft of a bill which is adapted to the subject matter of that tract. I have also published a tract upon the inrolment of deeds and wills, with a draft of a bill upon that subject. I should hope that these two publications would enable your Lordship, and any other person, to form a conclusive judgement of the competency of the writer of them to handle other legal topics, especially under the advantages of the previous directions and subsequent revision of the law officers of the Crown. But, as the intended plan will comprise much constitutional and political, as well as legal, matter, I am very ready to undertake to give a specimen or trial of my abilities, should it be wished, upon that topic."

LORD ERSKINE to LORD KENYON.

1364. 1791, August.—'I have left you Burke's pamphlet, which, though perfidious to his friends by imputing sentiments to them which they never held, in order to disgrace them, has yet in it some very splendid passages."

POEMS.

1365. 1791, September 1. Bury St. Edmunds.—Poems by Reverend William Jones, of Nayland: (1) "A character, by lover of truth"; (2) "On seeing some pigeons sitting on a meeting-house."

BARTHELEMY, the French Minister Plenipotentiary in London, to LORD KENYON.

1366. 1791, December 28.—" A person named Charton (?), one of the many unfortunate persons who are victims of the troubles which have happened in France, is a prisoner for debt, in the King's Bench. He has been strongly recommended to Mr. Franchlyn, of Welbeck Street, by a gentleman of rank and character in Paris, as an honest, though an unfortunate, manufacturer, who has been imprisoned here for a debt contracted in France. It appears by the enclosed letter, which Mr. Franchlyn has received from him, that he has paid for a chamber, which he fitted up at some expence, and where he hoped to be able to maintain himself well, from the produce of his industry or the assistance of his friends, till he might be enabled to regain his liberty. As he is a stranger both to the laws of this country and to the language, it is not improbable he may experience some hardships, which, if he could explain himself to the marshal, he would avoid. Will your Lordship forgive my taking the liberty to request you would be so good as to make this man's situation known to the marshal, by any of your officers, or by transmitting the man's letter."

LORD BATHURST to the SAME.

1367. 1792, May 1. Apsley House.—"Permit me to trouble your Lordship with the inclosed Bill which, I trust, will tomorrow be brought up to our House. Your Lordship is well acquainted with the misconduct and various grievances of county courts. The Bill is to substitute a less oppressive and less expensive administration of justice in my court, which takes in near a sixth part of the county of Gloucester. It is with the general approbation of the Justices and all persons concerned. I got the Master of the Rolls and the Attorney-General to peruse and model it in the Commons, and will be obliged to your Lordship for giving me your opinion of it." Any of Lord Kenyon's suggestions will be adopted.

WILLIAM PITT to the SAME.

1368. 1792, May 16. Downing Street.—" I shall be much obliged to your Lordship if you can allow me ten minutes' conversation tomorrow, at any time that will interfere least with your engagements, and whenever is most convenient to you." *Holograph.*

Note at foot, in Lord Kenyon's handwriting.—" In consequence of this letter, I called on Mr. Pitt, who told me he wished to inform me first, that in consequence of the Lord Chancellor's opposing his measures, he had stated to the King that one must go out, and [that] the Chancellor was to go out."

WILLIAM PITT to LORD KENYON.

1369. 1792, June 1.—" I should be much obliged to your Lordship, if your engagements will allow you, to let me have the honour of seeing you for a few minutes any time before four to day, except from two to three, when I shall be obliged to be at St. James'." *Holograph.*

Note, in Lord Kenyon's handwriting.—" I went to Mr. Pitt, in pursuance of this letter, on Friday, 1st June, 1792, when he asked me if I would accept the office of First Commissioner of the Great Seal, on Lord Thurlow's resigning. I told him it was impossible I could take it, and perform the duties of my office as C. J. of the King's Bench. He then conversed with me about the proper persons to make commissioners, and desired he might talk with me again."

The REV. WILLIAM JONES to the SAME.

1370. 1792, December 2. Nayland.—" And now, my Lord, I must inform you, in confidence, that I am in a great bustle, under the character of *Thomas Bull*. By the blessing of God (for such I account it) I have hit upon a mode of address which has gained the ear of my countrymen, and may be of great use at this critical time. Ten thousand of these papers are already dispersed, and their influence is increasing. In consequence of this, some other matters are under consideration, and I have a summons, in such terms as I must not resist, to attend a meeting on Thursday, at London, where nothing effectual can be done without me. We of this place can witness that the cry of ' No King ' comes universally from the Dissenters ; and some of my neighbours are considering how to conduct themselves, so as to turn a few of them into public examples."

WILLIAM PITT to the SAME.

1371. 1792, December 12.—" I trouble your Lordship with a copy of the speech which his Majesty will deliver tomorrow. Under the present circumstances, I flatter myself we may trust to your Lordship having the goodness to sit as Speaker."

LORD GRENVILLE to the SAME.

1372. 1792, December 16. St. James's Square.—" The motion for thanks to Lord Cornwallis stands for Monday ; and my wish is to bring in on Wednesday a bill about foreigners residing in this country."

PETER WHITEHALL DAVIES to the SAME.

1373. 1792, December 19. Broughton.—" I take the liberty to trouble your Lordship with another letter, in which I have inclosed an *assignat*, made payable at Bersham Furnace, endorsed ' Gilbert Gilpin ' ; I am informed he is the first clerk of Mr. Wilkinson, whose sister married Doctor Priestley. With what view Mr. Wilkinson circulates *assignats*, is best known to himself. It appears to me that good consequences cannot arise from their being made currant, and that very pernicious effects may. Mr. Wilkinson, at his foundry at Bersham (where, I am informed, he has now a very large number of cannon), and in his coal and lead mines, employs a considerable body of men. They are regularly paid every Saturday with *assignats*. The Presbyterian tradesmen receive them in payment for goods, by which intercourse they have frequent opportunities to corrupt the principles of that description of men, by infusing into their minds the pernicious tenets of Paine's *Rights of Man*, upon whose book, I am told, publick lectures are delivered to a considerable number in the neighbourhood of Wrexham, by a methodist. The bad effects of them are too evident in that parish."

Note in the handwriting of Chief Justice Kenyon.—"This letter occasioned the Act of Parliament, passed in January, 1793, for preventing the negotiation of French paper money in England."

WILLIAM PITT to LORD KENYON.

1374. 1793, January 2. Downing Street.—"We have been under the necessity of deferring the report of the Bill respecting aliens, till Friday, but I have very little doubt that on that day we can both report and read it a third time. I hope it may be possible for your Lordship to sit for half an hour on Saturday, in order to receive the Bill, as the amendments made may perhaps make the Lords wish to reprint it, which, in that case, could be done before Monday, and the Bill might then receive the royal consent on Tuesday. I will take the liberty of sending you a copy of the Bill as now amended, as soon as it is printed, which will probably be to morrow evening or Friday morning." *Holograph.*

R. RICHARDS to the SAME.

1375. 1793, January 23. Lincoln's Inn.—"Your Lordship knows that Sir William Scott is a candidate for the University of Oxford. Mr. Hall, who used to go the Chester Circuit, has a vote, and will, as I have reason to think from his expressions of the sense which he has of the obligations he owes your Lordship, be very glad of an opportunity of voting in a manner agreeable to your Lordship's wishes. I should not have presumed to take the liberty of troubling your Lordship with this information if academical delicacy had not, in Mr. Solicitor-General's opinion, made it improper for him to mention it to your Lordship."

LORD GRENVILLE to the SAME.

1376. 1793. January 24. St. James' Square.—"I take the earliest moment in my power to apprize your Lordship that the King has signified his intention to deliver the custody of the Great Seal to Lord Loughborough, as Lord Chancellor, and that he will take his seat on the Woolsack on Monday, when the House meets again."

The SAME to the SAME.

1377. 1793, January 26. Whitehall.—"His Majesty being out of town today, the Great Seal cannot be delivered to Lord Loughborough till Monday; and I am, therefore, under the necessity of requesting your Lordship to sit as Speaker on that day."

SIR JOHN SCOTT to the SAME.

1378. [17]93, June 17.—"The bit to cure blunders in the bill for issuing Exchequer Bills, and the opposition to the Farnham Hop Bill—which is a bill to compel the impropriater of that parish to take 20s. an acre, where the tithe is worth 50s., for three years, to the intent to punish him, and terrify others, in like cases offending—may detain me beyond your Lordship's dinner hour. If they do, I presume to hope your Lordship will excuse me."

WILLIAM WILBERFORCE to LORD KENYON.

1379. 1793, June 28. London.—" The respect I bear your Lordship, and the sense I entertain of the kindness with which your Lordship has always regarded me, impose a debt(?) of obligation on me to transmit your Lordship a copy of the case which, with its documents, I am sending to Mr. Dundas. I conceive there can be no impropriety in so doing, when the judicial proceedings are at an end. I am not conscious of any unfair statement; and, if there be any inaccuracy, your Lordship will do me the justice to believe it is not intentional. I shall be very happy to shew your Lordship any of the other documents referred to, and to explain any part of the case which may require explanation. I need hardly say that this case is not fit matter of general communication."

JUSTICE GROSE to LORD KENYON, at Gredington.

1380. 1793, August 7.—"Through all the counties I passed, the wheat was fine, and in many, standing ripe and fit to be cut down, but wanting reapers. There are no hands to get the harvest in. The Portuguese fleet are at Spithead, and make a very respectable figure."

LORD BATHURST to LORD KENYON.

1381. 1794, January 4.—" The state of the Carmarthen Circuit is this: the two seniors meaning to quit, have declared to Mr. Douglas that they do not wish to succeed him. Mr. Williams is next in seniority, but I am assured that Mr. Douglas and Mr. Plomer (who has just left the circuit) would give their testimony in favor of Mr. Philipps; and I submit to your Lordship's judgement whether it be not for the advantage of the district that their Attorney-General should reside much among them."

The REV. WILLIAM JONES to JAMES BOSWELL.

1382. 1794, January 4. Nayland, Suffolk.—" As a biographer of the first character, you have preserved Dr. Johnson to us as a living lecturer upon life and manners; and I consider your work as a complete antidote to the letters of Lord Chesterfield, under the advantage of which, this nation ought to be wiser upon some subjects than any other in Europe. As a very small and inadequate return for the pleasure I had received, I formed the design of communicating to you a few anecdotes relating to Dr. Johnson, and drew up the following letter, with an intention to shew it first to my excellent friend the late Dr. Horne, Bishop of Norwich; but he being unfortunately taken from us before he had seen it, I laid my papers aside and forgot them, till a passage in your last edition brought them to my mind, and encouraged me to transcribe them for your own inspection. . . . . In the earlier part of my life, I took up and cultivated indefatigably, for some years, certain ideas of nature, not agreeable to the received notions of what is called natural philosophy; and as soon as I thought myself competent, I threw out a philosophical essay, to clear the ground, and try my strength upon it.

" In consequence of what I had done, a friend of Dr. Johnson's was desirous that he should see me, and a friend of mine was desirous that I should see him, knowing that he had read my book, and would probably have something to say upon it. He was therefore invited to spend an evening at my friend's house, and came accordingly. After he had seated himself, he sat for a long time musing and looking at his shoe buckles; at length he began to open, upon such subjects as came in the way, and soon convinced me that his mind was as great as his gestures were singular. The subject of natural philosophy, with long practice, was so familiar to me, and the ground I was upon had been so scrupulously examined, that I was under no apprehension of being driven out of my strongholds by the force of his words. I had heard, and I need not inform you of it, that it was too much the manner of this great man to assume a sovereignty over all understandings, and to contradict rather than be silent. My lot, therefore, was common with that of most strangers who fell into his company. But still I thought there were some subjects on which I had a right to exercise the liberty of speech.

"So when the subject of nature, on which I had been writing, came forward (as I suppose some body took care it should do), finding I was not likely to have a friend in Dr. Johnson, I endeavoured to defend some of my principles with civility and good manners; and when I say this, I speak the truth to the best of my recollection. You will believe me, when I add, that my adversary, who could admit of no opposition, soon raised his voice, till he roared like a giant; and I being neither able nor willing to answer him in the same tone, the discourse on that subject was dropped. I freely confess how much I was disgusted with his manner, as Mrs. Boswell also was. His other excellencies would, I make no doubt, have prevailed against all the prejudice I had conceived, but the opportunity, which I never sought, never happened. His report of me afterwards, as I heard from the worthy Mr. Allen of Bolt Court, was more favourable than I had any reason to expect; but his judgment of what I had published in philosophy was very severe, and such as I must understand to have been incompetent and unjust; for in this line Dr. Johnson was but as one of the people, and had the safe and easy task of holding the popular side of the question. 'Sir,' said he, when I had left the room, 'he supposes authors to contradict one another, who all mean the same thing. Sir, it is disingenuous to take advantage of their expressions; sir, you may depend upon it the book will be answered.' To this a gentleman replied, 'Dr. Johnson, if you think it a matter of importance to the public that they should be guarded against the ill effect of the work, you would do well to answer it yourself.' 'No, sir, I shall not answer it; but the book will be answered.' In his prediction Dr. Johnson was not right; my book never was answered, as he said it would be. It was illiberally railed at and totally misunderstood in a monthly review of that time, and many ill names were laid upon the author, of which I never thought it worth my while to complain to the public; but this was not what Dr. Johnson meant by an answer. The book, sir, never was answered, nor ever will be, not because I am a powerful writer, but because its principles are those of fact and nature; and he who shall confute them effectually must be able to make a new world.

"My first essay for settling of principles was very much condemned. . . . . . However, the ill words I had met with being unmerited, and the prejudice against me being rather popular than rational, I resumed my subject with little discouragement, and went on with it through a large quarto . . . . . and as the whole of the edition, consisting of 750 copies, has been disposed of, and the work for a considerable time past out of print, it must have found many readers. But, wonderful to relate, I do not remember that a single copy was purchased at Cambridge, or that more than one was purchased at Oxford, which went into the hands of the ingenious Dr. Wall, a very respectable physician of that place. . . . . The principles of Newton being mathematical, mathematicians are naturally attached to them; their fame lies in that quarter; and their reports are generally of great effect, because their science is in few hands, and the public at large is not qualified to scruple their decisions. This was the reason why my first essay found no reception in Ireland. The whole Irish edition lay dead in the hands of the bookseller, there being in the University of Dublin some leading mathematicians who kept guard for the old system of attraction, more severely than Newton himself did, and would not suffer an heretic to land upon their coast. In Scotland, my last work has been much attended to; and I suspect that the bulk of the edition went northward. A learned gentleman informed me that it had also found its way to the East Indies, where it was taken for the work of my learned and ingenious namesake, Sir William Jones; but some persons disputing this, supposed it rather to be a posthumous work of his father.

" During a literary evening spent in Dr. Johnson's company, " one of his observations made a great impression upon me; it was delivered in the true Johnsonian style . . . . A question was started, by somebody in the company, about the original of the word *satyr* (*sic*) in the sense of a *sarcastic* composition. When some had guessed one thing, and some another and Johnson approved of none of them, I ventured to hazard an opinion of my own, that it was from the Hebrew verb *satar* to hide; such compositions having always been conceived in obscure expressions, for many reasons, and that the *satyrs*, those fabulous beings which were feigned to hide themselves in woods and forests, were of the same family. Here I had the honour of meeting with Dr. Johnson's approbation. 'He is right,' said he, 'it is certainly derived from *satar*, to hide.' The weight of his [Johnson's] pen, exposing the false wit and chastising the vanity of scepticism, would have been felt by friends and foes, and might have done good as a preservative against the evil times which were approaching. The late Mr. Allen of Magdalen Hall, who was a priviledged person, and could say what he pleased to him, addressed him once very freely upon the subject. 'Johnson, if you really are a christian, as I suppose you to be, do write something to make us sure of it.' But I presume he was not very conversant in ecclesiastical history, and that he was a better critic on the sense of Juvenal than on the style of the Bible, on which considerations he was not forward to pit himself against an infidel. I found myself much interested in what you relate of Mrs. Williams, whom Dr. Johnson, with singular benevolence, took under his protection; I once knew her well. . . . . . I had also much of the confidence of her father, Zachary Williams, the author of a magnetical theory which is now lost . . . At this period of my life, I was a school-boy at the Charterhouse. Some time afterwards, Mrs. Williams and her father fell into distress; and I being then unable to relieve it, either by my pocket or my interest, I became shy of making visits."

Lord Thurlow to Lord Kenyon.

1383. 1794, February 8.—"I enclose you Lord Loughborough's answer to my account of the business causes depending in the House of Lords. I do not thoroughly understand his ideas of Home and Lord Camden; but if it is to be a ministeral business I shall not attend it, for I do not wish to spend my breath in a vain opposition, and still less do I desire that either House of Parliament should manifest any signs of disloyalty to his Majestie's Ministers, even by doing justice, contrary to their commands."

Lord Grenville to Lord Kenyon.

1384. 1794, April 12. St. James's Square.—"I understand your Lordship entertains some doubt whether a new clause may not be necessary to be added to the Alien Bill, in order to prevent the evasion of that Act by collusive arrests. As the question was considered by the Attorney-General, when the Bill was before the House of Commons, I should be much obliged if your Lordship could find time to converse with that gentleman upon the subject; and if your Lordship's doubts should still remain, I should be desirous of proposing to add to the Bill (which is now before the House of Lords) such a clause as may answer the purpose designed."

RICHARD BRINSLEY SHERIDAN to LORD KENYON.

1385. 1794, May 12.—"I must trust to your indulgence to excuse the liberty I take in troubling you with a few lines, respecting the appointment of the next day of sitting for the trial after tomorrow (Monday). I would, by no means, wish a single hour to be lost in the week; but if it be intended to miss one day, and, as I am informed, that Tuesday is the least convenient day for the attendance of the Judges, I have presumed to suggest that, from particular circumstances, it would be a material accommodation to me to speak on Wednesday instead of Tuesday, and my reply will certainly be confined to that one day. I have only again to apologise to your Lordship, not meaning to be in town tomorrow, for directly addressing myself to your Lordship, as I apprehend any other mode of application might be too late." *Holograph.*

WARREN HASTINGS to LORD KENYON.

1386. 1794, May 27. Westminster Hall.—"I have been within a few hours since informed that Mr. Burke intends to solicit the Lords to adjourn my trial over to another year, for the purpose of affording him time to prepare his concluding reply. This is an occasion in which I think myself justified in praying every one of my own judges to interpose his authority and influence to repel so gross and atrocious a wrong; and I do most earnestly beseech your Lordship to give your attendance, and to afford me your good offices for this end."

JOHN SINCLAIR to LORD KENYON.

1387. 1794, July 24.—"At the desire of the Board of Agriculture, I have the honor of transmitting to your Lordship a paper, drawn up by John Robinson, Esq., Surveyor-General of the Woods and Forests, respecting the laws now in being for the division of waste lands, commons, and common fields, with suggestions for rendering such divisions more easy and less expensive in future. As this is one of the greatest objects to which the Board can possibly dedicate its attention, it was resolved to send a copy of this paper to the Judges, requesting their remarks upon it, with which we hope to be favourd, as soon as their other important avocations will admit of it. Permit me, at the same time, to request that your Lordship would have the goodness, in the course of the ensuing circuit, to collect as much as possible the opinions of the active magistrates in the different counties, and of other intelligent persons, upon this great subject, and to take any opportunity that may occur of explaining the advantages which may result from the attention that is paid by the Board of Agriculture to this and other great sources of national improvement."

REV. WILLIAM JONES to LORD KENYON.

1388. 1794, September 20.—"I intended to go down to Bath, for which purpose I went up to town, and did actually set forward, but found myself not well enough to proceed. By this accident, I was at London during the riots, and was walking down Holborn while the mob were in possession of the street, and doing as much harm as they were able. A man in the crowd, who seemed to be an acting member, cast his eye upon me and said, ' Hah, what are you there, old Churchman ? You are a *passive obedience* man, I suppose, you look as if you were of that sort.' If I had recollected myself soon enough, I should have told him I was a dissenting minister, which might have drawn something more out of him, but I only told him I was one of those plain people that do not love mischief. What this fellow had said seemed to indicate that the tumult, which aimed ostensibly at the Crimping Houses, had, to those who were in the secret, a farther and greater object in the Church and the Government."

MARY, LADY KENYON to the HONOURABLE GEORGE KENYON, at Oxford.

1389. 1794, December 3. London.—I believe Lord Fitzwilliam is to go to Ireland, but should not think it will be so soon as the papers say, for I know Lord Westmorland had not given any orders for any of his houses to be got ready for his family in England, a very few days ago, and two suns cannot shine in the same hemisphere. . . . It has been rumoured here that one of the Cleavers would be Primate; some said the Bishop of Chester, others his brother. . . . . Thelwell's trial is going on, and much stranger things are expected to appear against him than those . . .; but whether enough to convince a London jury, time only can shew.

CHARLES JAMES FOX to LORD KENYON.

1390. 1794, ————.—" Understanding from Mr. Taylor that your Lordship wished to know how far I should be able to go on with the business of the impeachment tomorrow, I take the liberty of troubling you with this, to let you know that I can go on tomorrow if neccessary, but that I am still indisposed, and that a later day would be more agreeable to me if, as I suspect from the present state of the session, this small delay would not be likely materially to affect the final conclusion of the trial." *Holograph.*

GEORGE III. to LORD KENYON.

1391. 1795, March 7. Queen's House.—"The question that has been so improperly patronized by the Lord Lieutenant of Ireland in favour of the Papists, though certainly very properly silenced here, yet seems not to have been viewed in what seems to me the strongest point of view—its militating against the Coronation oath and many existing statutes. I have, therefore, stated the accompanying queries on paper, to which I desire the Lord Kenion will, after due consideration, state his opinion in the same manner, and should be glad if he would also acquire the sentiments of the Attorney-General on this most serious subject." *Holograph.*

Enclosure :—" The following queries on the present attempt to abolish all distractions in religion in Ireland, with the intention of favouring the Roman Catholics in that kingdom, are stated from the desire of learning whether this can be done without affecting the constitution of this country; if not, there is no occasion to view whether this measure, in itself, be not highly improper.

" The only laws which now affect the Papists in Ireland, are the Acts of Supremacy and Uniformity, the Test Act, and the Bill of Rights.

It seems to require very serious investigation how far the King can give his assent to a repeal of any one of these Acts, without a breach of his coronation oath and of the Articles of Union with Scotland.

"The construction put on the Coronation Oath by the Parliament, at the Revolution, seems strongly marked in the Journals of the House of Commons, where the clause was proposed by way of rider to the Bill for establishing the Coronation Oath, declaring that nothing contained in it should be construed to bind down the King and Queen, their heirs and successors, not to give the royal assent to any bill for qualifying the Act of Uniformity, so far as to render it palatable to Protestant Dissenters, and the clause was negatived upon a division. This leads to the implication that the Coronation Oath was understood, at the Revolution, to bind the Crown not to assent to any repeal of any of the existing laws at the Revolution, or which were then enacted for the maintenance and defence of the Protestant religion, as by law established.

"If the Oath was understood to bind the Crown not to assent to the repeal of the Act of Uniformity in favour of Protestant Dissenters, it would seem to bind the Crown full as strongly not to assent to the repeal of the Act of Supremacy, as the Test Act, in favour of Roman Catholics.

"Another question arises from the provisions of the Act limiting the succession to the Crown, by which a forfeiture of the Crown is expressly enacted, if the King upon the throne should hold communication, or be reconciled to, the Church of Rome. May not the repeal of the Act of Supremacy, and the establishing the popish religion in any of the hereditary dominions, be construed as amounting to a reconciliation with the Church of Rome?

"Would not the Chancellor of England incurr some risk, in affixing the great seal to a bill for giving the Pope a concurrent ecclesiastical jurisdiction with the King?

"By the Articles of Union with Scotland, it is declared to be an essential and fundamental article that the King of Great Britain shall maintain the Church of England, as by law established, in England, Ireland, and Berwick-upon-Tweed.

"The bargain made by England in 1782, by Yelverton's Act, gives rise to the question whether the repeal of any of the English statutes adopted by that Act would not be a direct violation of the compact made by the Parliament of Ireland with Great Britain." *Holograph. Seal of Royal arms.*

THOMAS PENNANT to LORD KENYON.

1392. 1795, March 8. Downing.—On Friday I attended the meeting respecting our internal defence. In respect to the Yeomanry-Cavalry, nothing was done, and I rejoice to think that nothing can be done, for it will cost more than double the remaining part of our stock. "My reasons against Yeomanry-Cavalry are inclosed. I may, to your Lordship, add another, which is, that our worthy Dean is warm for it, and would be real commander of this civil-military, as he is, wonderful to relate, of the ecclesiastical government of the diocese."

MARY, LADY KENYON to the HON. GEORGE KENYON, at Oxford.

1393. 1795, May 25. London.—" I need not caution either of you to keep out of the way of entering into election disputes or scrapes; it is a time that calls for great circumspection and conduct, in talking as well as acting, and yet, when one feels very anxious for or against, it is a difficult thing to keep clear of offence. We have nothing riotous or troublesome yet, though Horne Tooke and Mr. Fox are busy canvasing, whether together or separate, I cannot tell. Tooke lodges at Hardy's, near Covent Garden—the man that was tried. This can never help him to good votes, one would think. Harry Tomkinson called here yesterday; [he] says Sir Robert Cotton has give up in a pet, for being refused some little place he had asked for, for a Cheshire man. ·He has given great offence by doing it so suddenly. The other members have not had time to canvas; this has made Lord Grey give up, and I fancy poor Cholmondeley will come in, owing to this sudden resolution, which makes Lord Stamford's party very angry. There are five candidates for Liverpool. Thelwell, we hear, is gone down to stand for Norwich. Martindale, who deals at all the Faro tables, and one Philips, who keeps a gaming house in St. James's Street, are likewise trying to get into Parliament, but I cannot tell you for what places. There is a violent opposition at Grantham, I fear, against Mr. S. Yorke; Sir William Manners is the opponant, very rich and so tumultuous. He has already destroyed some houses, and threatens to pull down the market place, and remove the market to his own land in the town. At Preston, there will be an opposition. The county is safe for the two old members; so, I fancy, Chester will be, but H. Tomkinson says Lord Grosvenor encouraged Cholmondeley to stand for the county, for fear he should be troublesome to him in the city. He likewise said there had been a deal of money lost at Chester races by gaming, but as we never asked by whom, neither heard of winners or losers, we were sorry to hear there had been any. There are sad stories of the Prince's behaviour to his wife; so much, that a seperation is talked of, but how that can be I do not know. It is his, Lady J[ersey's], and Mrs. Pelham's amusement, to tease, ridicule, and torment her all day. This is what is said, but one would think he could never be such a brute. Mr. (sic) Kenyon must finish at Guildhall to day, because they want the hall for the election."

MARY, LADY KENYON to LORD KENYON.

1393A. 1795, July 16. London.—"I feel quite sorry for poor Mr. Burke, and do not wonder at his retiring from the world.

"We had no riot last night at all, but the night before, they were very violent, wanted to get to Mr. Pitt's house to pull it down, but were kept off by the military. The Duchess of Gloucester was in great danger, returning from the circus; she was pursued by the mob, crying no Royalty, no Pitt, till she got very near to her own house."

The SAME to the SAME.

1394. [1795.]—"I met Miss H[annah] More, and her sister, today, and thanked her for her book; she says she has sold 10,000 copies; what a deal!"

SIR F. BULLER to the SAME.

1395. 1796, March 11. Salisbury.—As soon as the circuit is finished, I shall endeavour to get a little rest and take Bath water, but quiet and horse exercise are most likely to prove efficacious; "that the leisure of the Common Pleas will [not] fully admit of. And, therefore, though I shall quit your court with great reluctance, I must try the effect of the other; for though I have been a judge 16 years, I dare not yet ask the rude *donatum*, and I cannot live without it. If I get through the summer well, it may set me up for 6 or 7 years longer; but if not, I shall hardly sit in the Common Pleas for a greater length of time than Yates did."

Rev. William Jones to the Hon. Lloyd Kenyon.

1395A. 1796, July 16. Nayland.—Asking for Lord Kenyon's interest for a prebend.

William Pitt to Lord Kenyon.

1396. 1796, July 31. Downing street.—" On receiving your Lordship's letter, I took the earliest opportunity to apprise the King of your wishes, respecting the lieutenancy of Flintshire in case of Sir Roger Mostyn's death, and have received, as I had no doubt I should, the strongest assurances of his Majestie's readiness to comply with them. It might possibly, however, prevent some embarassment, that the appointment should be given to yourself, rather than to your son; and, on that ground, I have his Majesty's commands to propose to you that it should be so arranged."

Lady Kenyon to the Same.

1397. 1796, November 11.—" The Dean had a little lash at you, for ommitting the usual style of address, in the middle of his speech; but concluded with a high panegeric on you and your son. I am sorry you find trouble in your new honours, but as this is, I fancy, rather an unusual thing, and you asked for it, I would not give it up too hastily; it will keep these turbulent spirits in order. . . . . . There is a sad story, Mr. Davies says, a duel (*sic*) between Mr. Puleston, Mr. Owen, and Mr. Dodd, of Edge. But things are so much afloat . that, Mr. Davies said, it is quite dangerous to talk about it, for fear of making bad worse, so that I could get at no particulars."

Thomas Pennant to the Same.

1398. 1796, November 16. Downing.—" The faction exults highly on the neglect of your Lordship's agent in not producing to the sheriff, on the day of election, the certificate of Sir T. M.'s birth. Mr. Kenyon was advised to it by myself, at Wrexham, and he promised to do it. . . . . . In these days, so notorious an affront to the laws and constitution should not pass unnoticed; your Lordship's conduct in putting it in a train, by the offer of your son, had the applause of all good men, and it is to be hoped you will proceed with the perseverence and dignity worthy of yourself. The advertisement of thanks by Sir R. W. in this day's paper, is certainly the Dean's, by the bad stile and impudence. That profligate man has been the origin of all the mischief, and merits the most exemplary punishment. He had fair warning, by his trial. By the manner he has past his probation from that time to this, convinces every one of his incorrigibility. I inclose words attributed to him last year. One man of character would swear to the words; I think two. But such is the profligacy of many, that several, I fear, would take a false oath and explain them away. I am sorry to say that the Bishop, seduced by the Dean, has taken a great part in encouraging the unhappy young man to persevere in standing, unqualified as he is. It is in vain to talk to the prelate, for he has an implied faith in all the Dean says. If there is a possibility of calling up that worthless wretch, for his dialogue, to judgement, as is asserted in Mr. William Jones's letter, it would be a happy thing. The tenor of his whole conduct, from his trial in 1784, will be a full vindication of the proceedings."

M M

Thomas Pennant to Lord Kenyon. .

1399. 1797, January 8. Downing.—"We have gone through the greater part of the supplementary militia business, and that with perfect good humour. I am glad to find it reduced to two battallions, one of which my son will be happy to command. I imagine that Sir Thomas Mostyn will take the other. Everything is at present quiescent. . . . . . Within about a week, our worthy Dean had a quarrel with a man about a pig, which he said had trespassed on his land. A quarrel arose; the Dean levelled his gun and shot the man in his face and hands, for, perceiving the attitude of the dignitary, he put his hands up to save his eyes. Enraged, he ran after the divine with his spade, but could not overtake him. I am told the affair was made up with a sum of money."

Thomas S. Champneys to Nathaniel Jeffereys, M.P., . 57, Pall Mall, London.

1400. 1797, February 27. Orchard Leigh, Frome.—"The consternation at Bristol, on the reports from South Wales of the French having landed, is not to be described. I am just called out to head a Volunteer Corps of almost all the inhabitants capable of bearing arms in Frome."

W. D. Shipley, Dean of St. Asaph, [to Lord Kenyon].

1400A. 1797, March 4. Bolton Street.—"Many respectable gentlemen and yeomen in that part of the county of Flint which is situated at the extremity of the Vale of Clwydd are desirous of arming themselves and their dependants in support of the Government they live under, and for the more immediate purpose of protecting their families and their property from any predatory incursions that may be attempted by the enemy, on that coast. I am commissioned by them to solicit your Lordship's advice and assistance, as lieutenant of the county, upon the proper measures to be taken for carrying their design into effect. Whether your Lordship's authority is sufficient, or whether application must be made immediately to the Crown, and in the latter case through what channel.

"It is proposed to muster about fifty cavalry, if each man could be supplied with a sabre and one pistol; and here another difficulty occurs, as to how these are to be procured. Your Lordship's commands upon the subject shall be immediately communicated to the country."

D. Pennant to the Same.

1400B. 1797, March 9. Mold.—"In reply to your favor which followed me to Mold, where I have performed my duty with much satisfaction from the orderly behaviour of the men, I can only thank you for the honor of seeming to consult me on the purport of the Dean's letter. It seems to confine itself to the neighbourhood of St. Asaph, unconnected with the association at Holywell, of which my father is chairman, and your Lordship will consider in these times whether advantage should not be taken of the influence even of bad men, if their self interest coincides with the public good. Sir Edward Lloyd has certainly offered himself to take the command of the Holywell Volunteers. If a corps is raised nearer Pengwern, I think he had better act with that, and allow me to say at the same time that if it can be done with honour, and my country equally well served, I should be glad to exchange a militia duty, which may carry me far from home, for a service more congenial to domestic life, but not till the militia have gone through their exercise."

THOMAS PENNANT to LORD KENYON.

1400C. 1797, March 27. Downing.—"Do not let your Lordship be surprized when I say that my opinion is much changed as to volunteer corps in general. Our corps was to be formed by the manufacturers, tradesmen, and country people, in the neighbourhood. A most respectable head of our cotton manufacturers set the plan first agoing, and he and friends subscribed near a fifth of the money and twenty men. A sudden jealousy seized the trading part of the town and some others, who, on hearing I intended to nominate Mr. Smalley, the cotton manufacturer, as lieutenant, declared they would take their names out of the list. This forebodes such want of subordination and such want of respect to their old friend and neighbour that I sincerely hope that there will be a lack of arms, and so we may be dissolved quietly. Certainly the exercise of two afternoons in a week will never form soldiers. I think Government perceive it, and possibly are wisely damping the spirit of excess of armament; *entre nous*, a certain gentleman is arming without permission, and that with pikes; which, if left in the country people's hands, may, in cases of riots, be turned against ourselves."

The SAME to the SAME.

1400D. 1797, April 26. Downing.—"I return with ·thanks the enclosed; then, with great joy, congratulate your Lordship on the suppression of the mutiny of the Portsmouth Fleet. No calamity during the whole war affected my spirits to that degree. Had it been democratical, ruin inevitable must have followed. What could have hindred myriads of Gallic banditti from pouring in on us?"

LORD THURLOW to the SAME.

1401. 1797, June —.—"Counsel are to be heard for the general body of the surgeons against the bill on Friday next; but the Bishop of Bangor supposes that your great objection against the bill had been softened, and that you have altered your opinion that the surgeons are a part of the City of London. If that be so, and you mean to take no more notice of it, I wish you would give me your bill, with the notes upon it. I have some general prejudice against it, arising from the quarter·which I imagin originated it; but more seriously, I think the placing the whole corporation, consisting of 300, in the present circumference of seven miles, or 500 in the proposed one of 10 miles, under the management of 21, is too much. Perhaps the popular administration of so many would be inconvenient, but I think a select body of 50 or 100 would be a council to select superior officers, and that they should be elected annualy. . . . I think separating them from the City of London may not be wrong, but it should be so declared, and a new body, of a more general description, be appointed."

THOMAS PENNANT to the SAME.

1402. 1797, July 13. Downing.—"From a strange mistake of the volunteers imagining that they had martial law impending over them, we had a defection of near two thirds of the Holywell part. It was a wicked report, studiously inculcated. Yesterday, they all returned true penitents, except one, who knew he ought not to be received, another, whose health would not permit his return, and a third, who got well thrashed, and his cockade burnt by his fond wife, who would not suffer him to incur the dangers of war! My son is arrived and is indefatigable. The mutiny I allude [to] was founded on a republican, levelling principle; I inclose the infamous hand-bill circulated. The authors were ashamed, and it was soon drawn in. A friend writes me word that it may be a design of government to give volunteers opportunity of continuing themselves; it will certainly be a prudent measure, even should peace be concluded, for the inveterate enemies of order will exert every nerve to disturb and destroy our excellent constitution."

Lord Thurlow to Lord Kenyon.

1403. 1797, July 14.—" The surgeons bill comes on Monday next. I expect it will take up no time. . . . The Bishops and Chancellor are shaken ; a single jog, even your presence, would dissipate it."

Lady Kenyon to the Same, on the Oxford Circuit.

1404. [1797,] August 3. Peel.—" This country is so covered with smart new houses, all the way from Prescot to this place, it is quite astonishing. St. Helens was a poor little place when I passed through it, 30 years ago, and now is a very neat, pretty country town; the roads all as good broad pavements as can be."

Thomas Pennant to the Same.

1405. 1797, August 25. Downing.—" The volunteers of Holywell and Whiteford gratefully acknowledge their many obligations to your Lordship for procuring from Government numberless favors. We received, this week, 100 stand of arms, ammunition, &c., &c.; and an army of taylors will put the volunteers in full feather, in less than a fortnight. Still, I must lament that our rulers are deaf to our application for a quantum of officers . . . We really and truly cannot do without five officers. We shall have 100 privates besides non-commissioned officers . . . . We have two pair of colours, to be carried occasionally, besides the other duties of officers to perform; three officers cannot perform them."

The Rev. William Jones to the Hon. George Kenyon.

1406. 1797, September 2. [Nayland.]—" I have left off my doctor and my medicines, for some days . . . It is happy I got well, for I have enough to do in making one house answer the purpose of two, my neighbour, Whitaker, having taken the adjoining house to his own use. The room over the kitchen is now filled on every side with books. . . . It seems there is a son of the Bishop, a nephew of Lord Thurlow, who, by Tom's description of him, would suit so well with us, that if there should be any chance of his coming, I would put aside every other application and keep one place open for him. If you know of any such thing in the wind, let me know of it, privately. . . . . It is a matter of indifference to me whether I take another pupil or not.

"The case is this: my friend and pupil, Reginald Cocks, has questioned me about a son of Lord Lyttelton's, at whose house he now is. Do you know the young man, or does he know him? because, for your brother's sake, and my own comfort, I shall be very tender what sort of person I take into my family. Reginald, if he knows the lad, would not deceive me. He is now at Rugby School, a seminary not upon a level with Cheam, in my opinion, as a preparation for my house . . . . Now I talk of pupils, I can tell you that, since your brother went home, I have had a female pupil of a very unusual description. In the first place, a Quaker; in the next place, one of the finest and most amiable young women I ever saw; allied to the first Quakers in the kingdom, and the admiration of them all. Robert Barclay, the famous apologist of the Quakers to Charles the Second, was her grandfather. Pupils I have had, some of whom have been, to be sure, very extraordinary, but none more so than this young woman. When I thought her sufficiently instructed, we made her a christian, by baptism, in Nayland Church, and next week, to my great surprize, our William is to make her his wife. Things are to be well or ill in this world, according to God's blessing, and not without; so of this, I can only say that it appears well. Her name is Margaret Lindoe, and your brother Tom dined with her at my table, together with two presbyterians who introduced her here, when I knew nothing of what was approaching. . . . .

"So you met with the little obsolete first treatise on philosophy; I was a bold man to publish it, and lost the gift of a degree from the University by it, together with some favour and reputation from the world, but—*floreat veritas, ruat cœlum*—there is a fine prospect which deserves to be opened upon the world by some man more able and more popular than the curate of Nayland. If you would understand that first work better, it should be compared with the introduction to the Physiological Disquisitions. I wrote an Hebrew letter once to your elder brother; but of philosophy, the best piece, in my judgment, is yet behind, written in a series of letters to your friend Reginald, which he has never yet seen."

Lord Thurlow to Lord Kenyon.

1407. 1797, December 28.—"Since I sent you my last note, I have been commanded to dine with the Prince to morrow, which you courtiers have settled must be obeyed. Give me leave, therefore, to hope for the pleasure of seeing you and the family some other day."

Rev. William Jones to the Hon. George Kenyon.

1408. 1798, May 13.—"A gentleman wrote to me a while ago, from Oxford, whose name is the Honourable Pearce (*sic*) Meade, and promised me a copy of Lord Clare's speech, in answer to Lord Moira; which, as I understood, was to be sent to me through your hands, Mr. Meade himself not knowing the conveyance. But it is not yet arrived, and I am disappointed, for I wished to see it, Ireland being now the chief point to which our attention is turned. It is now evident to me that an Irish insurrection and massacre was to have been the French introduction, and that they have been waiting about their coasts in expectation of it; but the plot has appeared bottom upwards, a little too soon. God send the government may see an end of it, for it is a perilous business. Providence seems to have been with us as in the old powder plot, and the picture of the eye looking out of the cloud upon the dark lanthorn of Guy Fawkes, often recurrs to my mind, which was greatly delighted with it when I was a child. Thank God, we are as well here as we can expect. I sometimes remember what Lord

Kenyon said of old Lord Camden, who took his declining years with impatience, and am under some anxiety for myself, lest I should not go down the hill of life with any degree of dignity or prosperity. I have, therefore, good reason to say, in the simple words of Sternhold and Hopkins :

> ' Refuse me not, O Lord, I pray,
> When age my limbs doth take,
> And when my strength doth waste away,
> Do not my soul forsake.' "

The Rev. William Jones to Lord Kenyon.

1409. 1798, July 1. Nayland.—"I have just now parted with that fine young man, the son of Lord Lyttelton. From the first of his appearance in this house, your son and I were afraid of him, though it was impossible not to admire him. . . . . . . Of late, we have been among so much of the higher pursuits of Greek, Hebrew, and philosophy, that we are fallen somewhat behind in common Latin."

The Same to the Hon. George Kenyon.

1410. 1798, November 30 [Nayland].—"The *Anti-Jacobin* is in earnest, and will have the encouragement of the whole honest party, who are now a very great majority. . . . . I wish the Government would lay such a tax on circulating libraries as would amount to a prohibition ; they are among the chief engines of Jacobinism, and do a great mischief; we have now got one in this paltry place, undoubtedly set up by the Dissenters. . . . I like squire-soldiers better than parson-soldiers, of which sort, however, I believe my son is one of the best in the kingdom, and his corps the best disciplined. . : . I rejoice with you at the punishment of the booksellers. Johnson, for years past, has kept the grand shop for heresy, schismatology, and rebellion, and I hope Wakefield will follow in order. That fellow is one of the learned ruffians of the age. If learning does not humanize, it turns man into a demon, and adds him to the pedants of pandaemonium. I am not yet firm enough to think with pleasure of a journey to London. My touchwood will never be turned into timber, till the resurrection, when all things shall be made new. How I lament that we are never more to see Brother Horne's *Apology*, but in the little extracts I have from it in his life ! I then wished that it might be republished, but my wishes have been abortive, and I am not quite master of the reason, for I am still persuaded it must do good."

Postscript.—"I open this letter to reassure you that Dr. Horne's *Apology* and *Case* will soon be out. Brother Stevens sees a new dawn in the hemisphere, and acts accordingly, with hope and spirit. You see I am detected as an author, but I hope I shall not be subject to a prosecution with G[ilbert] Wakefield. Pray ask Lord Kenyon what he thinks of my case; for they have put me in for ' Tom Bull ' and ' Church and State.' I am now in for both ; nothing wanting now but a prosecution to make me as great as Horne Tooke."

George Hill to Lord Kenyon.

1411. 1799, June 15. St. Mary's College, St. Andrews.—"We have observed in the newspapers that Hugh Moises, plaintiff, was non-suited in an action for slander which he brought against Dr. Thornton, who had called him a quack, and that on the 8th of this month, the court, in which your Lordship presides, refused to grant a new trial. So long as the private cause was in dependance, we thought it highly improper to interfere, any further than as we were called upon by the plaintiff, at whose desire we subscribed our names, in presence of a commissioner whom he sent from London for the purpose of authenticating the subscriptions, which, on the 13th of April, 1798, we had adhibited to the diploma by which we created him Doctor in Medicine. But now that the private cause is disposed of, we hope we shall not be thought presumptuous if, with a grateful sense of the handsome manner in which your Lordship was pleased to speak of the character of the University, when you gave judgment in that cause, and from an earnest desire to sustain the good opinion of a person whom all good men must honour, we take the liberty of submitting to your Lordship, merely as a matter of historical importance, a simple account of the manner in which this University confers degrees in medicine." [The account is appended.]

LADY KENYON to the HON. GEORGE KENYON, at Peel, near Manchester.

1412. 1799, July 4.—"The Chief Justice is still in great danger. . . . Would you believe it, the Master of the Rolls sat for the Chancellor yesterday, that he might be drilled as a light horseman in the morning."

JOHN WALTER to LORD KENYON.

1413. 1799, July 6. Teddington Grove.—"I am impelled by gratitude to return your Lordship my sincere thanks for the favourable opinion you entertain, and reported as due to my character, and I defy any man, separate from political opinion, which has no doubt created me many enemies, to accuse me on any act but what will appear to my credit in upwards of 40 years commerce with the world. I received the public thanks of a meeting held of the body of the coal trade, when I resigned being their chairman, after 25 years. I pursued that business, though I raised it at the envy of those I was a competitor with. I was 12 years an underwriter in Lloyd's Coffee House, and subscribed my name to 6 millions of property; but was weighed down, in common with above half those who were engaged in the protection of property, by the host of foes this nation had to combat in the American War. . . . . I paid all my private creditors what was due to them, before I stopped payment.

"I did not resort to false credit; for such was my character, that I could have raised any sum on my credit, when I stopped payment. . . . . Neither a single note, bond, or any security, were exhibited under the commission, but the policies of Lloyd's Coffee House. My creditors were my friends. I lived at that time in Queen Square, Bloomsbury, in the house Sergeant Adair left, when he went to Lincoln's Inn Fields. No messenger was put in my house, as usual under the Bankruptcy Laws. They made me a present of all my household furniture, plate, and effects, which it contained, gave me my certificate the very day of the third meeting, appointed me to collect in above 20,000l. due to my estate, without taking any security, with a *per centage* for collecting it, made me a present of a freehold share of the Coal Exchange, which had been raised under my directions. With 6 children growing to maturity, I was left to begin the world again; when, from the large scope of business I had been concerned in, I might reasonably have expected an easy fortune to have had the enjoyment of life with. It was difficult for me to establish myself. A memorial was presented to the Minister, stating my case, signed by 12 of the most respectable merchants of the city of London, for his appointing me to some official situation. I was personally introduced to Lord John Cavendish, the Chancellor of the Exchequer, by Mr. Dent, the banker, and Mr. Robert Palmer, of Great Russell Street, who were trustees for the Duke of Portland, and afterwards by Lord John to him, who made use of the handsome expression, 'That he would endeavour to clear the cloud from my brow.' But nothing happened worth my acceptance, during the short time he continued in administration.

"Among many other projects which offered to my view, was a plan to print logographically. I sat down closely to digest it, and formed a fount which reduced the English language from 90,000 words which were usually used in printing to 1,500, by reducing all compound words into simple, and by keeping a separate case for particles and terminations. By this means, I was enabled to print much faster than by taking up single letters. I first printed a pamphlet dedicated to his Majesty, which was presented to him by the Duke of Portland, the day before he quitted the administration. I was advised to get a number of nobility and men of letters to espouse it, among whom was Lord Mansfield, then in your situation, to patronize the plan, to which his Majesty was to have been the patron. But happening, unfortunately as it turned out, to correspond on the subject with Dr. Franklin, then Ambassador at Paris, whose opinion I wished for, his name was among my list of subscribers, and when it was given, among near 200 more, to the King's librarian, and a fount of the cemented words had been sent there for his Majesty's inspection and acceptance, I found an increasing coolness in the librarian, and afterwards a note from him, saying the King had viewed it with pleasure, but, there being no room in Buckingham House, he desired I would send some person to take it away. Thus ended royal patronage, and when it [the invention] was used by me in business, the journeymen cabaled and refused to work at the invention, without I paid the prices as paid in the common way.

"Thus all the expence and labour I had been at for some years fell to the ground. In the course of conducting the printing business, I was advised to publish a newspaper, as my acquaintances were numerous. I succeeded in establishing it, and kept consistent to my opinion to defend the administration during the Regency, when the other papers veered round to the rising son. (sic), though many temptations were made me by individuals of the opposite party. I was accustomed to receive communications from the Treasury, with a private mark, by direction of one of the Under Secretaries of State; by the insertion of one of them, I was prosecuted at the instance of the Prince of Wales, at the suit of the Treasury, for a Treasury offence. Expecting remuneration, I gave up no author, and suffered a long and painful imprisonment, under a delusion of being soon released, though it lasted 16 months; and after all the promises made me from time to time, years, months, and days, have passed without any appointment to print for Government or any other remuneration, and I now despair of it, though had I disclosed the authors and their employers, I might have escaped prosecution myself, and proved it on others.

"Now I am brought into a very disagreeable predicament, from an incautious insertion of my eldest son, on whom I have for several years committed the guidance of the paper. The long confinement I underwent, and want of exercise, produced a corpulence of habit, and I was frequently attacked by fits of the gout. About 4 years since, I gave up the management of the business and retired into the country, intending to enjoy the few years I have to live in *otium cum dignitate*.

The Act made last session of Parliament, has disturbed my quiet, and involved me in difficulties. I cannot help observing, that it was unwise in its formation, as it subjects innocent individuals to punishment without intention of guilt, as the law was laid down on the trial against me, who was utterly ignorant of the paragraph complained of, till I read it in the ' Times.' The Act has bound the proprieters, who frequently have no concern in its conduct, and left free the only two persons who are culpable, and should be amenable to the law—the *Author* and *Editor* of a newspaper. In this case the Act is unjust, and ought at least to be amended. I never knew, before the late trial, that a person, totally ignorant of a fact could be tried criminally, and that a jury would find a man guilty of wickedly, wilfully, and maliciously, doing an act, of which it was admitted I was wholly ignorant and unconscious. Thirty years ago, I was frequently on special juries, and remember many actions brought civilly against principals, for the acts of their servants, by which injury was sustained, but never criminally; otherwise, I should never have submitted to a general, but have given a special verdict, as, on my oath, I should have conceived it contrary to every principle of justice and common sense.

"As for the insertion of the paragraph, it never was my idea to defend it; but when I am accused falsely by the inuendos of the declaration, I considered it right to clear my character from such aspersions. And there was another strong circumstance which did not appear before the court, on which I mean to apply, next term, for an arrest of judgment, which my counsel were instructed to represent, but it past by, and I hope it will have its force; but from motives of delicacy for your high station, it would be improper to mention, till it comes before the court. I believe there are few advocates at the Bar who would have advised the friends of Lord Cowper to have pursued the present vindictive prosecution." Concludes by stating the circumstances which led to the insertion of the paragraph of which Lord Cowper complained.

J. KYNASTON POWELL to LORD KENYON.

1414. 1799, September 10. Hardwick.—"I have taken the liberty of enclosing the Curzon case. . . . I possess volumes of papers, now properly scheduled; but I do not wish to trouble your Lordship further than to request your opinion, whether there is ground for me to prosecute my claim to the barony in question. My grandfather was oppressed by Sir Robert Walpole, and by ill health. He petitioned in 1731. The petition, and the counter petition of the Curzons, were referred, as usual, to the Committee of Privileges. The Committee heard evidence, and then adjourned by order of the House—first from week to week, and then by fortnights, to the end of the session of Parliament. My grandfather did not renew the petition, and the Curzons could not, as their claim was in abeyance."

The SAME to the SAME.

1415. 1799, September 18. Hardwick.—"I feel myself highly obliged by the indulgence granted me of leaving the papers. By that, I do not wish to give any unreasonable trouble, but to request your Lordship's opinion, whether my claim appears to be such as to justify the prosecution of it—that is, that I may not throw away my time, or, what is more valuable to me, *my money*, on a fruitless or wild scheme. Government will not, I trust, cast delays or obstacles in my way, as Sir Robert Walpole did against my grandfather. I shall ask them but for justice, and to allow me to stand on equal terms with my opponents (if I have any), so that alliance, wealth, and great connections, may not weigh down a country gentleman petitioning for what he conceives his birth-right."

GEORGE ROSE to LORD KENYON.

1416. 1799, October 24. Old Palace Yard.—"The second Spanish frigate is taken; the two have, I really believe, more than 800,000*l.* worth of silver. It comes very opportunely."

HENRY CLIVE to the HON. GEORGE KENYON, at Clifton, Bristol.

1417. 1800, June 23. London.—"Did not Erskine's apology, for his defending Hatfield, make you smile ? What stuff to say he shewed his loyalty and affection to his sovereign best by complying with the prisoner's request; I believe he could not refuse. Hatfield has not shewn any symptoms of madness, I think, in chosing one whose eloquence can touch the feelings of a jury, and another whom we must allow to be best in his profession."

LADY KENYON to LORD KENYON, on the Home Circuit.

1417A. 1800, July 19. London.—Referring to the rain, she says :— " We had a deal here, but luckily not to incommode Lady Gray and me in our visit to St. James's. She was so good to send the coach at half-past one. I called for her, and she brought me back to this door at 10 minutes past 3. The King asked where you was (*sic*), how you did, and whether you had not altered the places on the circuit this year. I told him you never thought it right to do so, but wished to keep to settled rules. ' That is right, that is right,' [he said]. He likewise asked how Judge Buller did. The Chancellor was surrounded with black gowns. . . . Mansfield looked well pleased, and is to set out for the circuit to-day. His Honour says he has been in a great fidget about it, but seems satisfied at last. Sir Richard Arden dines here to-day ; he called this morning, and stayed some time. He tells me Sir John Scott's title is Lord Eldon ; the one he had fixed on, we heard, gave offence to some noble family it had formerly belonged to—Lord Derwentwater's, I think he said—and Eldon is Sir J. Scott's own property in Durham, and can offend nobody. Lord Carlton, of Ireland, Sir William Scott, and the Master of the Rolls, were all at Court, so were the two Lady Elgins. . . . . ."

THOMAS ERSKINE to [the SAME].

1418. 1800, October 15. Hampstead.—"I have heard of some desponding expressions which fell from you, most naturally, in the moment of affliction, which pointed towards retirement. You may remember that you consulted me, many years ago, before you became Chief-Justice, when I was less your friend, because I knew you less, and when I was less capable, from years and experience, to advise you. I now give my advice unasked. Let nothing (whilst your health remains) induce you to quit your station. The sudden transition from great activity to retirement, unless as vigour ebbs and calls naturally for ease, ever has been, and ever will be, mortal to mind and body. You have, besides, great duties to perform. You are perfectly right in the view you have taken of the evils arising from the high prices of provisions, and of the law which visits and corrects them. I have looked at the subject since we met, and am sure of what I say. The war, undoubtedly, and the vast circulation of paper, increases the public suffering ; but, depend upon it, the whole system of trade in provisions has been entirely changed. There are now only great landholders (the farmers) and great merchants with great capitals, in lines which were not formerly considered as the occupations of merchants. They sweep the whole country before them, in the purchase of the necessaries of life, and they command the markets. I have talked with Fox, who thinks all this is visionary (taught, I suppose, in other days, by Burke), but who has not, in the least, convinced me. I have not found a case, almost, in which I have been consulted, that the common law will not reach; and perhaps that is one of the evils attending the repeal of the statutes; they served at once as helps and as qualifications of the common law, in cases where its principles might have reached too far. . . . . We have always differed, my dear Lord, upon political questions, and, above all, upon that grand one, which I am afraid, if not attended to, will materially affect us all—I mean this ruinous war. But I have always been steadily your friend, from a thorough conviction that you act from your conscience and feelings in all things, and from the recollection that you have never ceased to be mine."

WILLIAM WILBERFORCE to LORD KENYON.

1419. 1801, January 9. " Near London."—" Some words which dropped from your Lordship, as the newspapers reported, intimated that you conceived it not impracticable to impose and enforce a maximum price for corn. I own frankly, and I have made no secret of my opinion, that I think it would be a perfectly just measure, but I fear it could not be carried into execution. Ever since I heard of your Lordship's declaration, I meant to request your Lordship to be so kind as to open to me a little on this subject, and I still should be happy to hear your Lordship's sentiments."

The KING to the SAME.

1420. 1801, February 13. Queen's House.—" The King judges that, the term being over, Lord Kenyon probably has a day or two of leisure, previous to his sittings; should that be the [case], his Majesty would be desirous of seeing Lord Kenyon here to-morrow. But if that is inconvenient, on Sunday, at one." *Holograph.*

LORD ST. VINCENT to the SAME.

1421. 1801, February 15. Mortimer.—" I have many apologies to make for waiting upon your Lordship at so late an hour last night, but my time is so much occupied (as you may imagine) at present, I cannot command it. The principal object of my visit was to inform your Lordship that I am extremely desirous to name my near relation, Mr. Thomas Jervis, to succeed Mr. Percival at the Admiralty, and I only wait your Lordship's sanction, as to his fitness for the office, to do it."

LORD LOUGHBOROUGH to the SAME.

1422. 1801, February 26.—" It appears to me a possible case, that, in the administration of justice upon the ensuing circuits, a case may occur which would extremely embarrass the several Judges. There are Acts which, being passed for a limited time after the commencement of the next session, may possibly be contended to have expired during the time of the assizes; and the question, as it seems to me, will turn on the point, what constitutes the commencement of a session, or, as in the present case, of a session of Parliament. This may either be (1) the day at which, by the writs of proclamation and summons, the Lords and Commons are ordered to be at the place to which they are called; or (2) the day on which the House of Commons, by virtue of the King's approbation of their choice of a Speaker, is formed into an active body; or (3) the day on which, by the King in person opening the causes of calling the Parliament, both Houses are constituted deliberative bodies, and each, according to ancient form, proceds to what is stiled opening the session by reading a Bill.

" I have only to state the question, and to refer your Lordship to all that I know relative to it, which is in Mr. Hatsell's Book, vol. ii., p. 288, and to what your own memory will suggest, at the unhappy period of November, 1788. I submit to your judgement, whether it would not be right to apprize the Judges of the possibility which I forsee, of this question arising when they are separated, and of the propriety of their holding some communication upon it, that an equal rule may (if it can) be observed in all places. My constant zeal for the public service dictates this address to your Lordship. It is no neccessary function of that station from which his Majesty was graciously pleased to permit me to retire, but with which, unfortunately, I still remain charged, and shall, under the most trying circumstances, continue to execute on all necessary points, as long as it is the will of God that I should be so committed. I should have equally troubled you with this notice, had I been entirely and officially discharged, from the zeal I shall ever entertain for the honour of that profession which has ever been so kind to me above my deserts."

Postscript.—" I shall send to Lord Eldon and to the Lord Chief Baron, a short note to the same effect."

LADY KENYON to Mrs. KENYON, at Chester.

1423. 1801, March 2. London.—"Poor Pepper looks sadly; had been very ill the night before, but was better. He has lost his own self-approbation by not exerting [himself] in this great point against Pitt, who has behaved in the most shameful way; and almost everybody says so, when they dare speak out. But such mincing, foolish things are said to paliate for Pitt's going out, as disgrace people one never suspected being wrong in so material a point as religious support. My dear Lord is worth a host of them, and has made many look about them by his plain, open-spoken reproof. Do not expose poor Pepper. Leycester is in the same paliating mood, and thinks an oath should be made to suit Pitt's coming in again, I believe. I have never named this even to Lord Kenyon. Let people get right if they can, and Pitt stay out till he learns to know the value of such a King as he has forsaken, in a most perilous moment. Abbott (would you believe it?) is to be Secretary of State for Ireland; live here during Parliament, and in Ireland the rest of the year. . . . ."

" Young people can hardly guess how far they may be forced to mix in the world. Who would have thought little Abbott would have been a Secretary of State ! "

PERIGRINA KENYON to the SAME.

1424. 1801, March 9.—" . . . . . I am more shocked at the loose faith and want of right principles in this kingdom, both in Church and State, than I hoped had been in our Christian Church. I pray God support us steadily in it, and the sooner we get out of this world the better. . . . . Thank God, my brother is firm and right as anything can be, and not afraid to declare it, in an open, positive manner, that does him honour; says Mr. Pitt has behaved vilely (which he has), and is the most ungrateful, unfeeling man that ever was born. But when he deserts his King of Kings, no wonder he forsake[s] his earthly one. Poor Pepper is so wavering, and Pitt bitter, that he frets and wearits (*sic*) himself that I should think his health will give way. He knows it is wrong, and yet worldly interests, and [the] uncertainty which turn things will take, make him net at all know what to do or say.

"Now do you know that [the] opposition are rejoicing in the King's recovery, for they have found out that the Prince of Wales was determined to keep Mr. Pitt in as Prime Minister, as so good a friend to the Roman Catholics. . . . . They have had a great many meetings, and Pitt and many of them would have been glad the poor King could have been proved mad, that there might have been a Regency. But, thank God, the King's recovery puts an end to this. This day the doctors would have been summoned to give an account, but now he is known to be so much better, they will wait. I supose the Marquis of Buckingham and his Lady have been very violent for this imancipation; so much so, that my brother was told from the first authority, that at Court, when Lady B. should have thanked for the title the King had given her and her eldest son, she would not speak to the King. But do not name this to any one, that it should get out, as you know where it came from. . . . .

"The account to day was not so good; again it was the high fever returned in the night, and was not yet subsided, so what they will do yet, heaven only knows. I hope he will get well, and Pitt keep out. Sure abilities may be found with good Church principles. His letters and arguments were so positively wrong, you would have no patience; but be sure do not betray me. I shall be hanged for telling, and the good master, though steady to what was right, spoke with so much kindness and sorrow to part with him, that he was a hard, unfeeling mortal. You would have thought by his stile that he was the master and the other the inferior. Mr. Abbot is to be Secretary for Ireland; but the papers will soon tell you what they are to be, and who will come in."

Margaret, Lady Hanmer to the Hon. George Kenyon.

1425. 1801, Good Friday. Bettisfield.—"I should be glad to hear our good King had been to pay his usual Easter visit to my dear uncle; when the weather is fit, going to the sea, I should think, would help to re-establish his health. . . . . . I dare say the Marquis of Buckingham is too great and grand to think as I do; but to me it appears as if the family of Grenville had much to regret that he had married a Roman Catholic, however delightful and charming she may be, as I have always understood she is; perhaps the more to be regreted, in consequence, from that very reason."

Lord Eldon to the King.

1426. 1801, May 5, 9 a.m.—"The Lord Chancellor, tendering to your Majesty his most humble duty, offers also Lord Kenyon's, Sir J. Mitford's, and his own most grateful acknowledgements for the testimony of regard, which they learn from the communication, transmitted through Mr. Strong, it is your Majesty's gracious purpose to bestow, by appointing them trustees of part of your Majesty's property. They all hope that your Majesty will find, in a conscientious discharge of their duty as such, a proof of their earnest desire to manifest their gratitude.

" Your Majesty's Chancellor presumes to add, that, highly as he should have thought himself honoured under any circumstances by such a testimony of your Majesty's regard, he cannot but feel particular satisfaction in being associated in this trust, with persons whose advice and assistance he knows to be highly valuable, with one from whom, in the course of his professional life, he has received marks of kindness almost parental, and with another with whom he has long lived in habits of brotherly regard, and of both of whom he can most truly represent to your Majesty that, in private life as well as in public, their conduct has been uniformly and strongly marked by a dutiful, anxious, affectionate, and loyal attatchment to your Majesty.'

Mary, Lady Kenyon to the Hon. George Kenyon.

1427. 1801, July 11.—"I asked Leger (?) how the Chancellor and Lord Alvanley were liked in their courts; he says the first is very great in his manner of doing business. His summing up is very instructive and great, but takes too much time, as he gives his full reasons for his judgement, in all cases, which can never get on, and he complains he finds it hard work. Lord Alvanley does extremely well in his business, but talks to the jury and witnesses so much, it lets down the dignity of the court, and as this is more publick than the Rolls, it is much to be lamented."

The Hon. George Kenyon to Lady Hanmer.

1428. 1801, November 8. Lincoln's Inn.—Mr. F. Filmer was one of the callers; he pointed out to me an excellency in his coat, which I should not have discovered (it looked as other coats do), that it was waterproof; and said that there was a method used by a man at Chelsea which would make muslin or the thin bank note paper waterproof.

Mary, Lady Kenyon to her sisters.

1429. 1801, November 29. London.—"I was most kindly received on Thursday. The King asked how my dear Lord did, hoped business was of use to him, said he was doing all he could to keep these forestallers in order, and thought they would feel it; seemed pleased with what he had done about Waddington. . . . . . I never felt Court so oppressive and unpleasant as this week."

M. Lee to the Dowager Lady Kenyon.

1429A. 1805, September 20. Staindrop.—By the death of Sir William Pulteney, 40,000l. *per annum* devolves on our neighbour, Lord Darlington, and since, that excellent Miss Lowther, after a long and most severe suffering from a cancer, is released, and she has left Lady Darlington 40,000l. Lady Darlington is at a hunting place near Doncaster. She is said to be better than she was last year, but I am afraid she is in a very delicate state of health. Hears that Lord and Lady Darlington intend to fit up, each year, two rooms in their venerable old castle; "this year they have fitted up a drawing room and a bedchamber and dressing room, the former in the Chinese stile, the latter, I suppose, the same as the furniture, in chintz; the bed has something the appearance of a Persian tent. This appartment is stiled 'the Prince's,' and is not to be used until his Royal Highness has occupied it, which, it is said, he means to do next summer. In the bedchamber are an arm chair and sofa; in the dressing room, a sofa and a small chair, the back upright (this is called a dressing chair), and I think there is a stool or two. The drawing room is so full of various articles, painted glass, transparent lamps, china, furniture, etc , that there is no describing it; the paper is India, the curtains blue (chintz they call it), with scarlet drapery, the carpet plain mulberry cloth, with a scarlet cloth, about a yard wide, with a small pattern black border, laid over the carpet, loose both length ways and across ways ; the *toute ensemble* is certainly very handsome. I hope, however, they will not entirely adopt this newly adopted eastern stile, but will fit up some of the apartments in what seems to old fashioned folk the true taste of that Pile Gothick."

LORD KENYON to LADY KENYON.

1430. 1806, May 28.—". . . . . I am not sure, however, that I shall feel justified in leaving town before the case of Miss Seymour is considered, I feel so extreme a horror at the Prince's intentions on that subject." I met at dinner at Mr. Percival's, Mr. Leycester, "who brought me home in his carriage as far as Pall Mall. We were talking all the way about Lord Melville's case, about which he is quite a partizan. I am afraid there are but few persons in the House who intend to endeavour to do strict justice in that business. I do not expect that there will be a perfect acquital, though I am not sure whether that may not turn out to be the only mode of not doing injustice. From the framing of the articles of impeachment, I understand people will endeavour to drive conscientious persons away, by including a good number of charges in different articles, and persuading folks they cannot justly vote not guilty, without being convinced that there is no ground for any charge. I for one will not be so bamfoozled (*sic*). If they choose to reduce it to distinct charges, that a vote may take place on each ground, which in itself may constitute a charge, I shall be very well satisfied to vote guilty to a certain extent ; but if they will not do that, then I shall not hesitate to vote 'not guilty,' as nothing can be more unjust than to drive away those voters who do not allow of the charges to a high extent, by mixing up the articles. I think that there can be no question but that if you do not think a person guilty of the article to the extent alleged in it, that the just course is to vote that he is 'not guilty' of it. That, at least, is my perfect conviction on the subject."

The SAME to the SAME.

1431. 1806, June 1. London.—"I have had a long and very pleasant walk to day with Mr. Illingworth, in Kensington Gardens, and saw all the extreme crowd there about 3 o'clock, and between that and 4. The most conspicuous figure was Mr. Skeffington, with Miss Duncan leaning on his arm. He is so great an author that all which is done is thought correct, and not open to scandal. To be sure, they looked rather a comical pair, she with only a cap on, and he with his curious whiskers and sharp sallow face."

The SAME to the SAME.

1432. 1807, March 6. 'Warrens.'—"The Prince of Wales was at the concert on Wednesday, [and] looks extremely altered, and it is said is really in a very bad way. Lord Curzon was there, looking very well; said he had that morning seen the Prince's apothecary, Mr. Walker, who said he did not drink a drop of wine. Lord C. told him that would not do, after all his full habits; he said it would. . . . He and the Chancellor have completely quarrelled."

LORD KENYON to LADY KENYON.

1433. 1807, March 21. 'Warrens.'—Is coming to Shropshire, but fears his stay will be short, as he must be in London again to attend Parliament "if they try to pass the R[oman] Catholic Bill. . . . . I hear Sheridan says he has heard of people running their heads against a wall, but never knew, till now, of people making a wall to run their heads against!"

ROBERT HOWARTH, of the 95th "Rifle Regiment," to his father.

1434. 1807, September.—"I shall give you an account of what has happened since I left England. I embarked on board the *Urania*, transport, at Harwich, on the 25th of July, and remained in harbour till the 1st of August, when we set sail and arrived safe on the coast of Denmark, on the 9th, and anchored close under Elsinore Castle, one of the strongest places I ever saw in my life. We remained there till the 16th, when we landed within a few miles of Copenhagen and marched up the country. Early the next morning, the 17th, we came within about two miles of the city, when we were ordered to halt at some small villages to get some refreshment. About two o'clock, our regiment was ordered to advance upon their outposts, which were about one mile from the town. We marched down upon them without firing one shot; but when they perceived we advanced, they began to fire upon us with their artillery very smartly, but without effect. We gained our position within one mile of the city and remained there till the 21st, during which time the enemy kept up a brisk fire from their battery upon us, and we had severe skirmishes with their outposts and piquets; but early in the morning of the 21st, our regiment was ordered out to drive them all into the town if possible. We marched down upon them with as little noise as possible, and was (*sic*) ordered not to fire till we came close to them, when we fired a few shot at them. When they perceived us, they gave way, and we took up our position over the first drawbridge, and drove them over the second.

"On the 25th, the whole of the army was ordered under arms, about two o'clock in the afternoon, and received orders to advance upon the town. We all thought that we were going to make the grand attack, but we only drove them all from their batteries, and made them to fly into the city, the only place left them to go to, for we had the possession of the suburbs, and the action lasted about two hours, during which time the enemy lost a great number of men, killed, wounded, and prisoners. Our regiment had only one man wounded and none killed, for we have always the best chance, although we are always in front of the rest of the regiment, being riflemen. On the 26th, the light brigade, consisting of 9 companies of our regiment, the 43rd, 52nd, 92nd, and two brigades of artillery, with four troops of the German legion light dragoons, was ordered to the rear of the army to attack an army of the enemy that we heard was coming to attack our army in the rear; their strength was reported to be between 8,000 and 9,000. We marched three days, and could hear nothing of them till late on the 28th. On the 29th, we marched early in the morning to a town called Kiöge, where we were informed the enemy was. About ten o'clock we came in sight of the town, where we halted, and sent the artillery and light dragoons in front of the town. When the enemy perceived them, they began to fire on them from their batteries. We were then ordered to fall in, and marched up to the town. Our 5 companies of the first battalion, which I belong to, were ordered out to the front of the other regiments. The action began a little before eleven o'clock and continued till about five in the afternoon. When we began to advance upon the town they fired very smartly both great and small guns. When we came within 50 yards of the enemy, our five companies, that were in front, were ordered to the rear of the other regiments to let them charge, but they would not go, so we gave three cheers and charged them ourselves, with three companies of the 92nd and two troops of light horse. We drove them all out of the town with great loss on the enemy's side. We pursued them for two or three miles into the country.

" When all was over, we found ourselves in possession of 9 pieces of cannon, besides a great number of ammunition and provision waggons, and fifteen hundred prisoners. That day, and the two following days, their own account of their killed, wounded, and prisoners, are, 840 killed and wounded, and 3,100 prisoners. On the 6th of September, the city of Copenhagen surrendered, after being burning two days and nights, and the same day there was a great quantity of money taken that they were sending away. The whole amount of money taken is twenty one millions and some thousands, but you will hear more in the papers than I am able to tell you in a letter. Do not write again, as we expect to leave this place in a short time, as we have nothing more to do here, and British soldiers must not lie idle at this time." *Copy.*

JOHN GIFFORD to LORD KENYON.

1434A. 1807, October 18.   Penge Cottage, Bromley.—I have, for some time, been busily engaged with the political life of Mr. Pitt, which I have undertaken to finish by the month of April. The task is a laborious one, and requires constant attention. Mr. York had originally engaged to write one half of it, but after some months, at a time when I thought he was considerably advanced in the work, he declined to write it, and the whole burden was thrown upon myself. I am pretty far advanced in the second volume (it is to extend to four), but the difficulty I have experienced in obtaining information, even from some of Mr. Pitt's bosom friends, has rendered the task extremely irksome to me ; indeed, nothing but the prospect of pecuniary emolument could have led me to persevere in it under such dispiriting circumstances. You will scarcely believe that the Bishop of Lincoln refused to give me the smallest information respecting the last moments of Mr. Pitt, or even to assign the motives for his conduct. Lord Chatham, too, never answered the letter which I wrote to him on the subject. On the other hand, the Marquis Wellesley, Lord Melville, and Mr. Charles Long have been as friendly and communicative as I could wish them to be.

LORD ELLENBOROUGH to the SAME.

1434B. 1811, November 7.   St. James' Square.—" The writer of the inclosed letter is entirely a stranger to me. I find he has written a similar letter to several of the judges, in respect to which they all think as I do. I shall not answer him myself nor, perhaps, should have noticed his application at all, if it had not been for the mention he has introduced of your lordship's name. As I feel an anxiety, second only to that of your lordship's, that so delicate and important a subject as the writing of the history of the life of my virtuous and very learned predecessor should not be committed to any but the most able, judicious, and respectable hands, I am induced to request that your lordship will pause, and inquire very fully respecting the fitness of the proposed biographer for the work he is desirous of undertaking, before he receives any more avowed countenance from your lordship on this subject. Your lordship may recollect how very little Lord Mansfield's celebrity was advanced by the indiscreet life of him by Holliday. I am not aware that Mr. Blagdon is at all likely to perform his task better. The lives of the most distinguished persons in the law contain little of interest for the world at large. Their history is best to be found in their judgments and in the other recorded memorials of the courts in which they sat. If, however, your lordship should, from motives the most respectable, still incline that a life of your excellent father should be published, I am sure your lordship will forgive me when I suggest the propriety of considering well the description and character of the person, his talents and means of knowledge upon such a subject, before he is handed forth to the world as the authorized biographer of the late Lord Kenyon."

H. Hanmer to his father.

1435. 1813, June 22. Salvatierra.—"Yesterday was gained one of the greatest victories of our country and one, perhaps, of more importance in its consequences than any hitherto in the Peninsula. The battle of Vittoria, will ever be esteemed another proof of British superiority, and a lasting monument of the talents of our great general. Vittoria is situated in a valley about four miles in breadth but the ground is uneven and intersected with ditches. The hills on our right are considerable and woody; on the east is an unfordable river protected also by hills. The enemy had taken up an excellent position, their right on the river, their left on the heights. Our army advanced in three columns—the right commanded by Sir Rowland Hill, the left by Sir Thomas Graham, the centre by Lord Wellington. The action was begun [by] Sir Rowland Hill attacking along the heights, and the enemy, though retiring, fought resolutely for some hours, especially in the village, which was charged and carried by the light division. Owing to some impediments in the roads, General Graham's column was an hour or more behind its time, which caused some loss to General Hill. However, it came up about 11 o'clock, and immediately attacked and turned the enemy's right; now the action became general.

"We advanced by the great centre road and the enemy retired to their second position, suffering immensely from our artillery. This they maintained but a short time, and after driving them through Vittoria to their east, it became a complete rout, and nothing but night saved them from annihilation. Though the longest day in the year, we thought it too short for our successes, and never saw the sun go down with such regret. The progress of our brigade I have marked with red ink, in the hasty plan I have sent you of the battle, though in the midst of the enemy. Neither their Imperial Guards nor infantry would wait our charge, but fled immediately at our approach. We lost some horses by the cannonade, but, fortunately, had only one man wounded. The distance we drove the enemy during the action was upwards of three leagues. We have taken 132 pieces of cannon, all they had but two howitzers, the military chest, containing an immense treasure, the whole of King Joseph's baggage, plate, diamonds, carriages, and other valuables, together with that of all the other generals and officers of that immense army. The number of prisoners I have not yet heard. Our loss has been considerable, upwards, I fear, of 3,000.

" We are now following up our successes, and shall inevitably cut off two more corps of the enemy that were coming to support the defeated army. Marshal Jourdan commanded, but his dispositions and arrangements were overruled by the King, who thought himself quite secure in his position, and bears now all the blame of the defeat. It is the opinion that Spain will be entirely liberated from the French in three months. I can only add that I am quite well, and that the brigade obtained the approbation of Lord Wellington, for its behaviour and activity in all parts of the action."

LADY KENYON to her Son, at Christ Church, Oxford.

1436. [1814,] November 17. Marlborough.—"Now for my journey, but it is well you do not name any difficulty to your father, as I have not yet told him, nor mean to do so, in full. We set out at ½ past 6, with William Thorpe's two horses, and John to drive, and the . . . . mare for Charles ; us three in the chaise. We left London in such peaceful repose it grieved one to think what a tumult it might be in, in a few hours. We went on well, met a large party of ' Blues ' going to town, and before we got to Cranford Bridge, our poor horses smoked and sweated so sadly (with over feed, I fancy) I feared they would not do well. There we got hay and water, and got to Salt Hill at ½ past 10 and stayed two hours, and got well to Reading before five. We met another strong party of soldiers before we got to Maidenhead, which were sent for to quell a riot at Iver and Slough, about corn. . . - I never left your father with so much regret as now. I thought there was danger of riot from so full a meeting as was expected at Westminster ; but, thank God, all was quiet at 4 yesterday, and [I] trust remained so."

REV. W. ALLEN to LORD KENYON.

1437. 1815, April 22. Bolton.—" As for Mr. Jones, I am sure that our venerable establishment never had a firmer friend than he was. The very name of ' Nayland Jones ' makes all the Unitarians and Methodists tremble."

ROBERT SOUTHEY to ――――――.

1438. 1816, November 12. Keswick.—"I am glad to hear of your safe return and of your good progress on the Continent. Lord Kenyon has sent me one of your letters (that from Yverdon, Aug. 1), and I am looking with some eagerness for another, which is to tell me concerning Pestellozzi. Do not fail to let me see your correspondence with the French authorities, and all the minutes which you have made upon your travels. You know how much these (?) things interest me, and the knowledge may be made useful. We have had Mr. Nash with us during the summer—the artist who was our fellow traveller in the Low Countries and made my Waterloo drawings. If when you return to town, and are in the neighbourhood, and will call at No. 6, George Street, Hanover Square, he will show you a drawing of the twins, with which you will be pleased,' and sundry other memoranda of this house and its inhabitants. The Beaumonts were also in Keswick, but the birds of passage have all taken their departure now ; premature winter has set in, and I am settled to my desk for the dark season, with little heart to stir from it, or set foot beyond my own threshold, for there is an end to my morning walks. My spirits carry a fair outside, and are, indeed, as well as they will ever be; nor do I, nor ought I, to complain of them. Not an hour passes in which I do not feel the change. Scarcely a circumstance occurs that does not bring it home to my heart; but the result is a composure of mind, a livelier faith, and an habitual aspiration after that state of existing in which our enjoyment shall be permanent.

" Part of that paper upon the lower classes, which you are pleased to commend, came from my own immediate feelings. If it was the system of our Church to admit volunteers, I should gladly become one. And I am inclined to think that something of the kind would be the best means of preventing her overthrow. Very easily might she have Methodists of her own; all of them would else be enlisted against her. But I think seriously of girding up my loins for an arduous undertaking—that of writing upon the present state of things—fully, unreservedly, and with my whole heart. What I have done in the *Quarterly* has been by piecemeal, and has generally suffered something by repression on my part, and much afterwards by the editor's mutilations. But knowing as I do what has been in the world and seeing, as I believe, farther before me than most of my contemporaries, it may be in my power to produce such an estimate of the wants as might possibly avert great danger, or lead to great benefits; and, if I have the power, the sin of omission would in this case be a heavy one. Another month or six weeks will clear off immediate business and provide for my ways and means. Meanwhile, these thoughts will ferment and ripen. All here desire their love. Believe me, my dear sir, most truly and affectionately yours." *Holograph.*

Christopher Wordsworth to Lord Kenyon, at Gredington.

1438A. 1816, December 5. The Rectory House, Lambeth.—"So far as I understand Mr. Southey's views, from the partial disclosure contained in his letter, I apprehend his inclination leads him to set about the giving an estimate of the religious, moral, and, perhaps, political (in the more elevated sence of the term) state of the country, particularly with regard to the deficiencies in these several respects, and to such remedies as might be suggested. The term 'estimate,' used by him, leads me to suppose that he may have had in his thoughts what was done by Dr. Brown, something more than half a century ago, in his 'Estimate of the Manners and Principles of the Times.' To a work of this kind Mr. Southey would come with more singleness of aim, and with incalculably more talents, than Dr. Brown did. And, judging from the paper on 'The Poor,' in the *Quarterly Review*, which is evidently written from the heart, I doubt not he would produce a very interesting and impressive work. Still, unless Parliament are likely themselves to buckle to the difficulties of the times, in good earnest, and especially to treat [the] most important of all objects, the provision of an increased number of churches, I can hardly feel a wish even that Mr. Southey's pen should be engaged. If nothing is to be done, the most impressive appeal would only increase our national responsibility, and further tend only to render us callous and insensible. If we are to act, then I would say, 'O for a tongue of fire and for a prophet's voice.' But if Government will not act, then I would rather have the friends of the Church, and even the moving eloquence of Mr. Southey, to be silent The doing nothing, in the midst of so many moving cries, begets a habit of despair, even in the best disposed, and a kind of lurking feeling that there must be something of unseen lurking (?) difficulty, some kind of fatal necessity, against which it is vain to struggle. The only help the Church wants is fair play and more churches; but, while dissenters are at liberty, and the Church, by its connection with the State, completely tied up and handcuffed by the very increase of population, things must grow worse and worse, and the activity, even of the most able advocates of the Church, inevitably tends to the increase of the malady. Their appeals increase the aggregate of religeous feeling; but then the Church has no receptacle for that feeling, and the very animation of those appeals increases the vigilance and zeal of the enemies of the Church, who have no such impediments and bars to their proceedings as we are shackled by.

"The Methodists studiously conform in, the service in the numerous chapels which of late years they have erected, to a resemblance in form and substance with the service of the Church of England, which is a decisive proof that the people would have the Church service if they could get it. Nay, the very alterations which the Methodist introduces into the liturgy are not so much from principle, as to enable them to open their chapels under the plea of dissent, which, if they avowed themselves to be Churchmen, they could not open. After all, anything that they can do, and anything that all the other sects of dissenters can do (even if it were free from all other objections), is, and will be utterly insufficient to the supplying to the people at large, the opportunity of public worship and public instruction, in places of public worship, on the Lord's day. Here then, is the field which Parliament ought to occupy, and they ought to do it in connection with the Church; for one reason, among others, that they will not let the Church do it for its self. Who can wonder that there should be faction, bloodshed, and rebellion, where there is no religion; and how can there be religion when, amid thousands of temptations to evil, the great bulk of the people, especially in the metropolis and in large towns, are living in a state of excomunication and necessary separation from all religious exercises and religious instruction? We are doing well with respect to schools; but, unless churches are added, nothing will be effective. Nay, schools themselves would be much larger and more numerous then they are, had we any possibility of giving them accommodation on Sundays. In one word, my Lord, I think the religious responsibility of the legislature and the government of this country, at this time, is tremendous. If they would permit us, I think we might be a religious and happy people."

MEMORANDUM by LORD KENYON.

1439. 1821, February 5.—"The Bishop of Salisbury (Dr. Fisher) has just left me; he mentioned to me the following instances of conversations which took place at the table of the Princess of Wales, the Princess Charlotte sitting between her and Sir W. Drummond. Sir William Drummond told Princess Charlotte he understood she was reading history, and asked what history it was that most interested her; without waiting for her reply, he went on, and said that he had latterly been in the habit of reading Oriental history, as the most amusing, and added, as to what is called Scripture history, I can assure your Royal Highness there is nothing in it, it is all an allegory, and nothing more. The next time of his being by Princess Charlotte, he brought forward several of Paine's objections against Christianity, which she met and confuted, and Lady E. Lindsay said she never saw any man in her life so completely thrown on his back. The third time of their meeting, Sir William Drummond was beginning again in the same style, by saying that the education of the nobility and of all ranks, even the highest in this country, was on a very bad plan, all in the hands of priests; and, addressing her Royal Highness, he said, you know that priests have always been the most corrupt and contemptible of mankind. She replied, ' Sir William, you are now for the third time so good as to be giving me instruction in the same way; I do not know what your object can be; you seem to be an Atheist, or at least a Deist, and I must beg to refrain from holding any more such conversation with you. I will, therefore, take my leave, and have only to thank you for the pains you have been so good as to take to enlighten my darkened understanding,' and so withdrew." The anecdote is marked as " communicated to the Bishop of Salisbury by Lady E. Lindsey and Lady de Clifford, and confirmed by the Princess Charlotte, then about 14 years old. The Bishop informed the Prince, and the intercourse was lessened."

" K———, an English gentleman," [LORD KENYON?] to the EARL OF LIVERPOOL.

1440. 1821.—" As a gentleman of England, I am inclined to request, for a few moments, the attention of the Prime Minister of my Sovereign. Were that minister not an Englishman, I should neither waste my time nor his in so doing; were he not a Minister, in my judgment sincerely attached to the welfare of his country and to its constitution in Church and State and imbued with true English feelings, I should not intrude myself on his notice; were a certain noble Marquis in his lordship's place, I should despair of producing the slightest impression on his all Irish mind.

"My Lord, I much regret that my King is again quitting the British shores. After the convulsive state in which the public mind has been for the last 15 months, at least after the happy change which the coronation, for a short interval, appeared to produce, I cannot but think that the returning spirit of loyalty and affection in Engand well deserved the fostering smile and encouragement of royalty. The selfish, insidious huzzas of Irish popery, industriously stimulated by the pure promoters of the Irish Union, by the celebrated invention of the two stringed bow, are not—never can be—to a monarch with a truly British heart, such as, we doubt not, beats in the breast of George IV., of a tenth part the value which must be attached to the genuine affections of honest John Bull, by the general and generous attachment of the gentry, yeomanry, and population of England.

"My Lord, it is much to be regretted that the King could not be dissuaded from visiting Hanover this year. It will be deeply to be regretted if, in addition to Hanover, in which kingly duty and attachment have some part, his Majesty should visit Vienna and Paris. The interests of the British Empire can nowise be promoted by the King of England travelling *incog.*, and forming personal attachments to foreigners or to foreign manners. Nothing contributed so much to fix George the Third in his people's hearts as his being altogether English; of him it could justly be said, as of Nelson,

' O thou, in whom no thought of self had part,
But thy lov'd country filled up all thy heart.'

" The visit to Ireland will soon lose all its grace, if other visits for pleasure's sake become the royal habits. The most popular of actors, though known as such, and valued as an imitator only, in time loses his popularity by his frequent appearance. I should regret that my Sovereign should (by making it be thought he affected popularity rather than followed the gracious dictates of his heart) lose that attachment of his subjects, which, coming from their hearts, should be worn in its newest gloss, and not capriciously be forgotten for newer and valueless applause.

"Our country, my Lord, is in a state of great delicacy and danger. The loyalty of the yeomanry I trust will never fail, but their distress is very far greater than your lordship knows, or will believe; the prevalent opinion that great official characters, like the Jews of old, wish that there should be told to them 'smooth things, and that there should be prophecied deceits,' prevents your lordship's hearing and knowing the truth.

"My Lord, the mass of landlords are now in debt for interest, to the extent of from one quarter to one half of their incomes; and the mass of tenants are at least one half of their rents in arrear, and have greatly reduced their capital, to enable themselves to be more so.

"My Lord, be pleased to inquire, from those who have honesty to tell you the truth, if this be an exaggeration respecting tenants at rack-rent, or who have taken leases within the last ten or fifteen years. Be pleased, then, to look forwards. If foreign corn be imported in November or February next, what will be their condition, and what must their feelings be as to warmth of attachment to the Government? My Lord, the sympathy of the great has deep effect on the distresses of their more humble countrymen. What then will be the effect of the supposition that there is no feeling of sympathy towards them, that foreign gaities, pageants, feastings, and perhaps cabals (for the author of 'the Union of Ireland' is there), possess the royal thoughts, and England, the source of his power and glory, is—forgotten I will not say—but deserted.

"My Lord, we live in times that no one can say what a day may bring forth; the day of the Queen's funeral brought forth rebellion in the metropolis. Is the spirit crushed? My Lord, it is not dead, and some question whether it even sleepeth. No one can say when the aid of Parliament may be wanted; and that George IV. may be excited to hallow his blessed father's memory by treading in his steps and applying all his thoughts and energies to promote his country's welfare, is prayed at your lordship's hands."

LADY ELEANOR BUTLER and MISS SARAH PONSONBY[1] to LORD KENYON.

1440A. 1822, January 1. Llangollen.—"Most sincerely and most fervently do we pray that many and many happy years may dawn upon your lordship with intelligence equally gratifying to your feelings as that, with which you have honoured us by this morning's post, has been to ours. We intreat you, dear Lord Kenyon, to accept a thousand, thousand thanks, and to believe that, important as such an addition of income will be to our comfort—and there are circumstances which, indeed, make it most materially so—its value is more than doubled, in our estimation, by being indebted for it, solely and entirely—as we must ever gratefully acknowledge—to the interest and friendship of a nobleman whose character, conduct, and principles stand so high in our esteem and respect, and whose kindness has such claim upon our affection. We can only repeat our earnest hope that our obligations may be repaid with the most abundant interest, by the amiable persons who, as we calculate, at this moment surround the best of fathers. We truly rejoice in the report you indulge us with of their good health, mingled with some fear that, if you could have accompanied it with one equally satisfactory of your own, it would not have been withheld from those to whom it would have been so infinitely acceptable.

---

[1] The Ladies of Llangollen.

"We return the two letters so kindly entrusted to us, without a moment's delay, but cannot do so without offering additional acknowledgments for a favour of which we are so deeply sensible as that of the manner in which, under your representation, Lord Sidmouth has been pleased to express himself on our subject. It is appreciated much beyond what, had his lordship been in the Minister's place, we can have no doubt he would have granted us, through your lordship's patronage. But, with that, and the good opinion of such a character as Lord Sidmouth, we hope that we can truly acknowledge ourselves more proudly content than we should be with treble the pecuniary emolument obtained through a different protection."

MARY ANNE KENYON to Mrs. KENYON, at Peel.

1441. 1826, May 30. P[ortman] Square.—"I sit down to give you an account of our evening on Saturday at the Haymarket, where we were very much amused with Liston, who acted in two very droll things—*Quite Correct* and *Paul Pry.* . . . . Paul Pry is a regular busybody, who just 'drops in' at every house he goes by, and says, 'I hope I don't intrude,' and then begins asking all sorts of impertinent questions. . . Lord Stowell went with us, and enjoyed it very much."

ERNEST, DUKE OF CUMBERLAND, to LORD KENYON.

1442. 1832, November 3. Kew.—"Naturally, both the Duchess and myself have been in the greatest misery about our darling boy, who originally met with an accident, about two weeks ago, and give (*sic*) himself a violent blow on the left eye, which occasioned him much pain; but he perceived no consequence from it for the first 24 hours, and made light of it, nay, he even went out and shot a rabbit, and wounded another; but towards the evening of the 2nd day, he lost the vision of his left eye. . . . . . . We all go, in a few days, to Hastings, and I trust, by the aid of that salubrious air, and under Divine Providence, whose mercy is so great, that he will take pity of our beloved child, and restore him the blessing of sight—the greatest blessing of all. Though he is my child, yet, I must say, never did I see any one bear his misfortune with greater patience or resignation. Never has he uttered one single murmur, and, knowing him as you do, his activity of mind and body, you must own it is a severe trial." *Holograph.*

ROBERT SOUTHEY to LORD KENYON.

1443. 1834, July 16. Keswick.—"The condition of this distracted country is such that, at this time, I know neither what to expect, nor what to wish. That any Conservative administration could go on with the present House of Commons, seems impossible. A new election might throw out many Whigs, but they would mostly be replaced by Radicals. I do not say this would be casting out devils by Beelzebub, because it is difficult to say which of the two parties is worst. Perhaps Lord Althorp might be the best Premier that could, at this juncture, be chosen. His tried and proved incapacity would draw more disgrace upon a set of men who could find no better head; and, if it be not the will of Providence to punish us by such a revolution as we most righteously have deserved, nothing is more likely to avert it than the continuance in authority, for a little while longer, of men who have no pretensions to talent, and are fast losing all pretension to character.

It is far better that they should go on bringing contempt and odium on themselves than that we should see a pseudo-Tory administration treading in their steps, and thereby deserving both." *Holograph.*

Robert Southey to Lord Kenyon.

1444. 1835, May 20. Keswick.—" The enclosed letter is for Mr. Bamford, if you see nothing to disapprove in it. The temper in which his notes were written has been my reason for entering so fully into the character of our late friend. If you had seen his papers, you would clearly perceive how desirable it is that I should endeavour to bring him to a better man (?), and this seemed the best, or, at least, the most inoffensive way in which it could be attempted. You may believe that I have written with extreme care and caution.

" I have heard from Mr. Cook, who expresses a disposition, on the part of the Edinburgh Trustees, to be guided by Murray's opinion ; but he had not heard from Murray, neither have I received the farther communication which the bibliarch promised. I will rub up his memory in a few days." *Holograph.*

The Same to the Same.

1445. 1836, January 11. Keswick.—" Yours was the first greeting that reached me at the opening of the New Year, and I am fully sensible of its kindness. Seasons of festivity become seasons of melancholy when those with whom we formerly enjoyed them are removed from us by distance or death. This I was made to feel early in life, and expressed, in consequence, reflections in a New Year ode, two and forty years ago, which are brought home to my heart now.

" A man of great, but crazed, genius, whom I was once well acquainted with, chose to cast my nativity. He promised me, on the faith of the stars, great good fortune, either at Berlin or Algiers, and pronounced that I possessed, according to my horoscope, 'a gloomy capability of walking through desolation.' Were he alive, he would probably say that I have lost the good fortune by not going to look for it where it was to be found. But if he had known me as well as I know myself, he would not have predicated gloominess of one who has no such ingredient, either extant or latent, in his nature. God has left me with a cheerful and contented spirit, and lays on me no burthen which He has not given me strength to bear. I have enjoyed a larger portion of happiness than falls to the lot of most men. Whatever may be the complexion of my remaining years, they cannot be many, nor can they be miserable, while I am capable of employing myself, and retain that faith of which nothing can deprive me.

" 'The printers are pressing on me at this time. In the course of a few weeks, I hope to work my way to some leisure, which will be employed in bringing up the arrears of other business and in beginning new. My motto is *In Labore Quies.* I borrowed it from the Spanish historian Garibay." *Holograph.*

The Same to the Same.

1446. 1836, January 22. Keswick.—" I take the liberty of enclosing a note for Davies, in reply to a letter of his, received this morning. You will see by it that Professor Haldane has written to me, and the substance of my answer. I am glad to hear that the Madras College at

St. Andrews is going on prosperously, but the University (thanks to Sir John Campbell) was probably never before in so distracted a state, except during the storms of a religious revolution." *Holograph.*

LORD ELDON to LORD KENYON.

1447. 1836, September 3. Encombe.—"After again reading the King's Speech, I am still to say that there is nothing in it. The papers intimate that he read it well. I was once joked by George III.; whilst unrobing after a speech, in the House of Lords, he said to me, ' I hope I read it well.' My answer was, ' Yes, sir.' ' That,' replied he, ' is not sincere. How could I read well what had nothing in it?'"

ROBERT SOUTHEY to the SAME.

1448. 1836, September 21. Keswick.—"If no mishap should intervene, I hope to leave home on Monday, the 17th of October, and to reach Gredington on the Wednesday following; Friday, to pay my respects to Mr. Parker, and on Saturday to halt with my son-in-law's parents at Crickhowel (?) We are bound for Bristol and the West of England. I wish to show my son what no one else can show him— the scenes of my childhood and youth, and to introduce him to a few old and dear friends, whom it is most likely I may never again visit in this world, and whom hereafter he will be glad to have seen. To lay up stores for memory, is the next best thing to laying up treasures in heaven." *Seal of arms. Holograph.*

The SAME to the SAME.

1449. 1837, December 5. Keswick.—"In my case, a deliverance from what might truly be called ' the body of this death,' was to be desired, when it became no longer possible to entertain a hope of mental restoration. Yet, when the separation took place, I felt how verily we had been one, during the far greater part of our lives, and, consequently, how great a change has now taken place in my own condition. My dear Edith had been so long the chief object of my thoughts, as I had been of hers, that it seems as if I had lost part of myself. But all losses will be restored in God's good time. It behoves me to be thankful for a greater portion of happiness than falls to the lot of most men, and for the unusual length of time that I was permitted to possess it. And it is with thankfulness alone that I would recall the past, if it were possible to exercise a complete control over our own thoughts." *Holograph.*

EXTRACTS FROM A MEMORANDUM BOOK, IN THE HANDWRITING OF VARIOUS DATES.

A News Letter.

f. 1. [1588.] The names of the writer and of the person to whom it is addressed, do not appear. The first part is torn away.

"Some saye the King of Spain's fleete was at sea three weeks past, but our 106 shippes that then were owt with the Lord Admyrall and Sir Francis Drake, colde heare of none, though they, against wynde, byd forthe on the Coaste of Brytaine 7 daies, but now are at Plommouthe [Plymouth] and readie to goe out with 14 more, and vyctualled till the last of Auguste. The Lord Henry Somerset feared them muche when hee ryde afore Graveline with 36 greate shippes, till my Lord your father, att the great entreatie of the Commissioners for the King of Spaine, wryte hys letter to the Lord Henry that they were well used, yet desyred him to departe, which he presentlie did, with protestation if the Earl Darby or the Lord should not be well used, hee wolde returne and batter their towne on their beades.

"From thence hee wente to Dunkirk and shewed the like force, and from thence before Slewse, to shew her Majesties readiness to defend them. The forces at home are now called to be readie, for that her Majestie will staunde upon her garde and have sea . . . army with officers apointed forthwith to resist invasion.

"The Erenche King, as is reported, is agreed with the Duke of Guise by artycles [to] the King's dishonnoure, the certaintie not yet knoune which by the ne . . . . . sende.

"Mr. Bodlye, sende to him, returned with great thankes, since Sir Thomas Layt[oun] . . . . . to him and returned this morninge, leaving the King at Rowan and the . . . . . . Paris.

"Daniel Rogers going to condole the death of the King of Denmarke and a messenger . . . . . the Emperoure of Muscovia, who is Doctor Fletcher. And one Folkes to be there residente for the marchaunts, as her Majesties Agente.

"So with my humble dewtie to your Lordship tyll the nexte, when your . . . . . more and more particuler.

(*Postcript.*)—"Since the wrytinge hereof, this more is knowen unto me, which . . . . . amisse to lette your Lordshipe know. Sir Thomas Laytoun brings . . . . . hathe of the King, and that shee hath done more than all the Princes . . . . . which he hathe unfaignedlie protested, he to requite in like to h . . . . . and that he will not put upp the injuryes the Duke of Guise offers . . . . . .

"The Spanish fleete sett owt, as is said, 500 shippes, the fyrste . . . . . . the 20 of Maye after our accompte, and are at a haven in Biscaye . . . . . Zarmin's dyrections, the haven called Calbone.

"The resolutions heare, that 2,000 souldiars shall come out of the Low country . . . with ther leaders to be her Majesty's garde.

"The shippes are to sea and all the forces on the costes to be . . to be tended.

"The noblemen and Bishopps, by Letters from her Majestie, for to enforce . . . . . . with horses and men, to withstande the invacion.

"The pensioners send for all to . . . . . . with horse and armour.

"A newe bande of horse of all her Majesties servauntes, ordinarye and extraordinarye, to attende att Courte.

"The Lyetennants to have ther force in all readines to marche.

"To assure Scotland to be at her Majesties devotion by money, to that end privie seals to be out of a losane [loan ?].

"The cytye of London to be full mustered and to have ther 6,000 men to courte at . . . . . . dies warninge and they to garde the cytye . . . . . . for a reall army to be appointed by her Majestie.

"The chief recusants to be to [the] Tower, and a new constable thereof, and the seminaries and practizers, with other persons, under a garde.

"A proclamation to putt doun all letters or bookes to seduce the people to rebellion.

"The Commissioners to returne, if the season be not to ther desyre, and all other thynges.

"f. 1d. The namys of them that commytted the disorder in Burye, on Sondaie, beinge the xiiijth daie of June."

" Of *Leeze* [Leeds].—Paul Ogden, Thomas Travis.

" Of *Oldham*.—James Tayler, Peter Bexwicke, William Hall, the son of Robert Jackson, the wife of Edmund Greave, Alice Taylor, Alice Tetlawe, Margaret Hopwoode, George Tetlawe.

" Of *Chatterton*.—[E]llis Whitaker, Richard Thorpe, four daughters of John Goddard [names torn away], Henry Whitaker, of Oldham, one Bowtree, one Nylde, and the eldest son of John Whitaker, all of Hollinwoode."

E[DMUND] H[OPKINS] to ————.

f. 2. 1588, July 21.—On the 14th, being Sunday, "there was, by certain of Oldham parishe, in tyme of divine service, gallowpinge of horses in the streete of Burye, showtinge and pypinge, with other fowle disorders, in the forenone of the same daie, a lamentable spectacle in the place of preachinge ministerye, of all good men to be pytted and reformed." Hopes the offenders may be apprehended and punished.

WEAVING.

f. 2d. The Vycare of Leedes sente for Rauf Mathewe, who ys very skelfull in all thinges apperteyninge to his trade of clothinge.

"Instruments:—Wheels, cardes, combes, leades, swinginge, combe stocks, loomes, sheares, handles, tassells, tenters.

"Threescore persons are thus to be devided:—xii for sortinge, dressinge, and lyttinge the wolle; xxx^tie for spinninge and cardinge; xii for weavinge and shearinge; the odd vj persons to helpe the reste, as to goe to the myllne and tourle, &c.

"Syx stone of undressed woole will make ij dossens, or a whole clothe, contayninge xxiij yardes in lengthe and vij quarters in bredgthe.

"Twelve stone woolle will serve lx persons in a week.

"Four gallons of cyvill [Seville ?] oyle will serve to xij stone of woolle, and looke what the wool doth cost after the maner of makinge clothe at Leades, the cost wilbe as much more before it can be converted to good and perfect cloth.

"One stone of woole spinninge, xxd.; weavinge a dossen, iijs. iiijd.; walking a stoke, viijd.; shearinge and dressinge, xd.; and this after the use of Leades, where only brode clothe is made.

"Threscore persons are thus to be devided:—Sorting and dressinge, vj; spinninge and cardinge, xl; weavinge, viij; sheremen, vj; whereof ij maye be to helpe the rest.

"Two stone beinge xxviijli. will make xviij yardes, yarde broade.

"One stone spinninge, ijs. iiijd.; weavinge a peece, xxd.; walkinge, iijs.; burteing, ijd.; dressinge, xd. And xl spinners will spinne in the weeke xx stone. One gallon cyvill [Seville ?] oyle will serve to iiij stone of white woolle.

"The woole about Sciptoun (Skipton) will make no carsies, excepte it be very pure white; and at Hallifax there is no clothe made, but yearde broade carseis.

"If the stuffe that is to be bought for lyttinge were cheape and easie to be gotten, brode clothe were the beste kinde of clothe that is to be made aboute Sciptoun, bycause it is course woolle.

"Hallifax men occupie fyne wolle most owt of Lincolneshire, and there corse wolle they sell to men of Ratchdeall (Rochdale).

"To beginne this trade, some persons must be broughte from Leeds or Hallifax, or from some other towne of that facultie, for the teachinge of all these particular offices appertenginninge to it.

"There lawes and customes for punishinge of offendours are none other than the statutes and lawes of this realme allowes of, and appoincts, savinge that [at Hali[faxe] there ancyente custome of beheadinge such as are taken with . . . . . . seemethe to be raised of necessitie in the beginninge of there . . . . . . which without treuth woulde not stande, neyther in that rude place time . . . . . . were so good meanes of justice as nowe the lawes afforde."

"The DUKE OF NORFOLK's submission to HER MAJESTIE."

f. 3. 1571, September 10.—"O my deare and dreadfull Soveraigne Lady and most gracious Majestie. When I consider with myself howe farre I have transgressed my dutie towardes your moste excellente Majestie, I dare not once presume to looke up, or hope of your gracious favoure. I confesse myself so farre unworthye thereof; but againe, when I looke unto your Highness' manyfoulde mercies and moste pitefull nature, of the which so manie have so abundauntlie tasted sithence your Majesties moste gracious raigne, I am emboldened with a moste penitente and sorowefull harte to make this my tremblinge hand offer unto your Highness my most humble and lowlie submissione, havinge no other meanes to ease myne oppressed minde. I am, for my sinnes and disobediences, to aske pardone, that ys of the Allmightie God and of your moste excellente Majestie, with a newe harte and full minde of amendement, aud doubte me not, but, asking mercye, to receave yt, accordinge to the Scripture, hee that knockethe at the doore shall have yt opened unto him. Nowe doe I at your moste Highnes graces (sic) feete offer my poore children and all that I have, hopinge more in your Majesties moste gracious clemencie then in mine unadvised desert. I seeke to excuse myself no waie, but whollie to submitte myself to what beste yt shall please your most mercifull harte.

"O moste gracious Soveraigne Ladye, manye men have runne astraie who, fyndinge mercye, have afterwardes, with good service, redobled ther former follies. O noble Queene, yt ys in your moste gracious hande to make of my wretched moulde what yt pleasethe you, my bodie beinge allreadie your humble subjecte and prisoner, by due desartes. I dedicate my harte and minde for ever as yt shall please your Majestie to dyrecte. I doe not seeke favoure at your Majesties bandes for former true service. I confesse my unduetifullnes nowe hath blotted the same, nor I dare not remember, which heretofore was my greateste comforte, bycause I deserved [no]t that honoure, which was, that yt pleased your Highnes to accompte me your (indeed unworthye) kinseman; woe worthe the daie that I entred into that matter w[hich] hathe made suche alteration of your most gracious favoure unto me, and h[ath] heaped unto myself these untollerable troubles.

"O unhappie wretche that I am, which, in all the daies of my lyffe, coveted nothinge but a quiet lyffe, I take God to wytnesse, whatsoever, and yf yt please your Highnes, some have judged of me otherwise. I was unhappy to give eare to that whiche hathe done and ever was lyke to bringe me to this . . . . . . O, I dare not presume too longe to trouble your excellent Majestie with my harty repentable and pytiefull lamentation, but I shall not cease to make my most humble praier to Allmightie God that yt woulde please him of his most mercifull goodnes to put into your [heart] most gracious clemencie, and then, I doubt not, but my service in time comminge shalbe suche as your Highnes shall have no cause to repente your mercy extended unto me; and so most humblie prayinge God to continue your Majestie longe to raigne over us, yf yt be his will, to Nestor's yeares, with all felicitie and prosperitie, with an overwhelminge harte and watered cheekes, gyven most lowlie upon my knees, I most humbly take my leave. From your Highness' woefull Tower. By the bandes of your Majesties servant and moste sorowfull prisoner.—T. N[orfolk].

The Taxation of Middleton Parish.

f. 3d. 1590, April 20.—Document setting out that there had been, heretofore, disagreement between the inhabitants of the parish of "Mydleton and the toune and hamelles" of the same, as to the repair of the parish church of Middleton, taxes for furnishing the Queen with soldiers, the repair of bridges, &c., the fifteenth, when granted by Parliament, only excepted. The said persons have caused the said parish to be "measured and throughly surveighed"; and according to the "quantity and goodness of every towne and hamell," have agreed— with the consent of Richard Assheton of Middleton, Ralph Assheton of Great Leaver, Francis Holt of Gristelhurste, Edmund Hopwood of Hopwood, Esquires; Edward Assheton, parson of Middleton, Robert Holt of Asheworthe, Owen Radcliffe of Langley, and Thomas Ainsworth of Ainsworth, gentlemen—that from henceforth "all taxes, galdes, and laies" should be made as follows:—For every "taxation, galde, or laye of 40s., levied on the whole toune, hamells, and parish, Middleton hamlell to pay 6s. 2d., Hopwood hamell 6s. 6d., Thurnham hamell 6s. 7d., Pillsworthe hamell 5s. 3d., Ainsworth hamell 4s. 8½d., Byrkle and Camford (?) hamell 4s. 6¼d., Ashworth hamell 3s. 4d., and Leaver hamell 2s. 11d.," and so in proportion for smaller or larger taxations.

"The manner of the Scottishe Queene's deathe, owt of a lettre wrytten by Mr. Doctor Fletcher, Deane of Peterboroughe."

f. 4. [1586–7, February 8.]—"Shee was verie confident and resolute in deathe, uppon Wednesdaie, beinge the viijth of Februarie, beinge forewarned ij or iij daies before. Shee was broughte downe into the greate halle of the castell, where was sett upp a schaffolde thre foote highe and xij foote square, all lade and covered with blacke,—stoole, pillowe, blocke and all, aboute x of the clocke in the forenoone, where, after the commissione redde, I was appoincted by the Lordes Commissioners to speake to her, they syttinge upon a stage; but assoone as I begane shee cried, 'Mr. Deane, trouble me not, I will not heare you, I am resolved in the Romaine Catholique faithe.' I stryved to have proceeded, but shee cryed out againe vehementlie, and woulde not suffer me to proceede. Soe the Lordes Commissioners, viz., Therles of Shrewsburie and Kente, seinge shee refused obstinatelie to praye with us, willed me to goe on, soe I prayed for her, and the rest repeated; all which time shee, upon her beades, babled aloude, in Latine, to drowne me and the reste. Praier beinge doone, shee kneeled downe, and, havinge a crucifixe of a spanne longe betweene her bandes, shee praied often to yt, kissinge the foote of yt. Her praier was chiefile that God would give her pardone for her sinnes, for her sonne, for the Queene's majestie, and, so rysinge, was by the executioner disrobed. 'I was not woonte (quod shee) to have my clothes plucked of by suche groumes,' and so standinge in her peticote, barenecked, shee blessed her owne companie and badde them farewell, kissed her women, and badd them not lamente for her, and then verie boldlie and without all feare, shee kneeled downe towardes the blocke, and one of her women put a napkine, wroughte all with golde, aboute her face, her piriwigge and white coife remaininge on, then shee saide the psalme, *in Te Domine confido*, in Latine, and so laid downe her heade; one of the executioners holdinge her downe, thother strok harde, and yet cutte not halfe of, yet did shee move neyther bodie, hande, nor foote; so hee stroke againe. All her owne people cryde out uppon the hangeman, and yet yt hunge by the skinne; beinge quyte off, hee helde yt upp out of the periwigge and clouthes (?), yt was a greaye powlled heade like a boyes heade, newe powlled, save two lockes, at each eare one, and [he] cryed— 'God save the Queene,' and all the people aunsweared, 'Amen.' I added, 'so perish all thy enimies, O Lord,' &c., and againe they shoutted 'Amen.' Then the Earle of Kente spake and saide, 'this be the end of all the enimies of the ghospell and her Majestie'; and they cryed againe, 'Amen.' No man was suffered to touche her bloude. Certaine bloudie clothes, with the blocke, were burned, and the hangeman not suffered to have so muche as a pinne, nor there owne aprons, till they were washed. His rewarde was in money. Shee confessed in her praier to be saved onlie by the bloude of Christe, and yet praied all the Saintes in heaven to praie for her, and added shee woulde sheede her bloude at the feete of the crucifixe. The daye beinge verye fayre did, as yt were, shewe favoure from heaven and commended the justice. The viijth of Februarie, that judgment was repayed home to her, which the tenthe of the same monethe, xx yeares paste, shee measured to her husband, &c."

"The EARLE OF ARUNDELL's lettre to the Queene's Majestie."

f. 4d. 1585.—"May yt please your moste excellente Majestie. As the displeasure of a prince ys a heavier burthen to beare then the harde conceipte of a meaner and inferioure persone, so yt ys not lawfull for any, and lesse conveniente for them, to settell ane oppinione of mislike, before eyther there appeare some cause suffyciente to procure yt, or there be a faulte commytted worthie to deserve yt. I speake not this that I doubte of your Majesties disposition or that I feare you condempne me without juste and evydent proofe. For yt agreethe with the honoure of your estate, and I can wytnesse yt hathe bene the manner of your proceedinges, to knowe the cause before you give your censure, and to heare the matter before you condemne the persone, but I speake with all humilitie that I maie receave this favorable and indifferent dealinge at your Majestie's bandes, because as I am moste desirous to conserve your gracious and good opinione, soe am I most carefull to remove all impedimentes that maie hinder or withdrawe the same.

"And besides, for that manie actions at the firste showe maie seeme to be rashe and unadvised which, after rype and suffyciente consideration of the cause, doe appeare to be juste and necessarie, and in allowinge me this, which ys no more then your Majestie's place dothe requyre you to bestowe upon the meaneste subjectes and the graciousnes of your nature hathe allwaies moved you to grante unto every sutter, your Majestie shall doe a thinge whiche ys pleasinge in the sighte of God, and honourable in the eyes of the worlde; you shall take a course which ys worthie of yourself, and doe that justice which pertainethe to your estate. To be shorte, I doubte not but by this meanes bothe your Majestie shall reste satisfied in seinge a true and full defence of my dealinge, and I remaine happy at beinge delivered from all feare and suspicion of your displeasure.

"And bycause the course of my former lyffe maye, in some parte, expresse the reasons of my present faite, I moste humblie beseeke your Majestie that, by your favour, I maie put you in remembraunce howe, since my firste cominge to the Courte, which is ix or x yeares paste at the leaste, yt hathe bene my cheifeste care to please your Majestie and my greatest desire to perfourme that which I thoughte mighte moste contente you ; howe I have bene allwaies readie and ever willinge to doe you that service which eyther ductie requyred at my handes, or the smalenes of my abilitie woulde permitte. And for proof heerof, I will [not] appeale to anie other judge but yourself, thoughe I coulde justlie call a great parte of your realme to wytnesse heerin. And soe bappie was I before some yeares to have your Majestie to accepte my service in gracious parte and to conceave a favourable opinione of mine actions, as I accompted my laboure I tooke, a pleasure, and all the paines I sustained, a comforte, I made myself a stranger to mine owne house, to be a continuall wayter uppon your Majestie, and liked better to lyve, in a sorte, at the Courte then to lyve in the best sorte at home ; for I thoughte myself most happie when I was most neere unto your Majestie and my time best employed when I bestowed yt in doinge of your service.

" But at the laste, whether the mallice of my adversaries, by reasone of your Majesties good countenance towardes me, begunne to be greater then yt was, or their credytte with your Majestie (for my mishappe) did growe to be more then in times paste yt hathe bene, I knowe not, but I found, by litell and litell, your good oppinione decayinge, and your favoure, as I thoughte, somewhat estraunged from me. I harde, from time to time, howe your Majestie, in wordes, tooke exceptions to manie of my actions, and howe yt hathe pleased you daylie in your speeche to bewraie ane harde and evill conceipte of me. I sawe that suche as you had ever moste misliked in your harte, and those whome before you had never favoured, did enjoye your Majesties good countenaunce, which (till that time) they coulde by no meanes obtaine, and besides that, received protection and assistaunce from your Majestie, in all their actions againste me, presentlie after they had offered me wronge and were become my adversaries; notwithstanding all this, I, knowinge my conscience to be cleare, came at convenient times to doe my dutie to your Majestie, and thoughe yt pleased you at sometimes to talke with me, yet your Majestie never charged me with the leaste faulte or offence to you, and those adversaries of mine which did barke behinde my backe, durste never accuse me or open there mouthes to my face, soe as I accompted my hap verye evill in that I was wrongfullie accused. But muche worse, because I could at no time be charged, wherby I mighte have had a fytte occasione bothe to have shewed mine owne innocence [and] to have satisfied your Majesties suspicion. For, firste seinge your Majestie to countenaunce my adversaries in my owne sighte of purpose to disgrace me, and that you woulde manie times, in there presence, not vouchsafe so muche as once to bende your eyes to the place where I did stande.

"Secondlie, fyndinge them e[nga]ged to doe me injurye, manie waies, by the helpe of your favoure, and that I was unhable to defend myself anie waies by the reasone of your displeasure.

"Lastlie, perceavinge by your Majestie's open disgraces, which all men did note, and by your bitter speeches, whiche moste men did knowe that I was generally accompted, naye, that I was in manner poincted at as one whome your Majestie did leaste favoure and moste disgrace, and as a persone whom you did deeplie suspecte and speciallie mislike, I knewe this smoke did bewraie a fire, and I sawe those cloudes did foretell a storme; therefore, I prepared myself, with all patience, to endure whatsoever yt was that the will of God, by the meanes of your Majesties indignation, should laye uppon me, beinge assured that my faultes towardes you were none, though my offences againste Him were manie. And havinge thus resolved to endure whatsoever shall happen, I contynued some monethes in these deepe disgraces, withowt eyther knowinge what was the grounde of your Majesties displeasure, or hearinge what shoulde be the ende of my owne misfortune, till at laste I was called, by your Majesties commaundement, before your Councell at two soondrie times, wherin manie thinges were objected againste me, and some of them suche triffles as they were ridiculous, others of them soe unlikelie as they were incredible, but all of them soe untrue as no one of them coulde be justified. And yet, notwithstandinge that my innocence did soe evidentlie appeare by my answers, as my greatest enimies coulde not reprove me of the smalleste offence or unduetifullnes towardes your Majestie, I was commaunded to keepe my howse, wherfore I sawe yt was resolved by the course of this dealinge, that howe cleare or manifeste soever myne innocencie was, mine adversaries shoulde receave the triumphe of the vyctorie, as havinge what they woulde. And I feele that disgrace of my owne misfortune, induringe that which I had no waie deserved. And myne enimies to maintaine there doinges by some coulorable showe, since they coulde not justifie there accusations by any sufficiente proofe, procured your Majestie to sende some of your noble Councell, iiij daies after my restrainte, to examine againe of newe matters that were of greate weighte and importaunce but as improbable as the former, and I discharged myself as clearly of them as of the other before mentioned, soe as my innocencie did more plainlie appeare, althoughe my restrainte did still continue, for after this, which was my last examination, I remained in the same state xv weekes at the leaste, no man charginge me with the leaste offence, nor my conscience beinge able to accuse me of the smalleste faulte.

"And, at the laste, when eyther my adversaries coulde not, for shame, longer contynewe in theire unconscionable proceedinges, for that your Majestie was enformed by some of my friendes that I had too longe endured this undeserved punishmente, I was restored to my former libertye, withowt eyther hearinge any juste cause of your Majesties harde conceipte, or any suffyciente reasone of my longe restrainte, naye, withowt eyther understandinge any good collor why I was commytted, or but the shadowe of a faulte wherwith I mighte be touched, wherfore, after I had safelie escaped these stormes, and when I was clearlie delivered from all my troubles, I beganne to remember the heavie sentence which had lighte upon those thre of mine auncestors which immediatelie wennte before me.

"1. The firste beinge my greate graundfather, who was so free from all suspicion and showe of anie faulte as, bycause they had no color of matter to bringe him to his triall, they attainted him by Acte of Parliamente without callinge him to his aunsweare.

"2. The second, beinge my graundfather, was broughte to his triall, condempned for suche triffles as amazed the standers by at that time, and ys rydiculous at this daie to all that heare the same ; naye, hee was soe faultles in all respectes that, as the Earle of Southampton that then was, beinge one of his greateste enimies, fearinge leaste his innocencie woulde be a meanes to save his lyffe, toulde Sir Christopher Haydon, beinge one of the jurie, beforehande, that, thoughe hee sawe no other matter weightie inoughe to condempne him, yet yt was a suffycient reasone to make him saie guiltie, for that hee was an unmeete man to have in the commonewealthe.

"The laste, beinge my father, was arraigned accordinge to lawe, and condempned. . . . . . God forbide I shoulde thinke but that his triours did that wherunto there cons[ciences] did leade them. And yet give me leave, I moste humblie beseeke your Majestie, to saye thus much, that howsoever hee mighte be unwittinglie and unwillinglie drawne into greater daunger then himself did eyther see or imagine, yet all his actions did plainlie declare, and his greateste enimies must of necessitie confesse, that hee never caryed any disloyal minde to your Majestie, nor entended any unduetifull a[ct] to his countrie; and when I had . . . . . sorte, bothe fullie and throwlie considered the fortune of these iij which was paste, I called to minde mine owne, which was presente, and did thinke yt impossible, by the showe of this roughe beginninge, but that I might as well followe them in there fortune, as I had succeeded them in there place, for I considered the greatnes of mine enimies' power to overthrowe me, [and] the weaknes of my abilitie to defende myself. I perceaved by my late trouble, howe narrowlie my lyffe was soughte, and howe easilie your Majestie was drawen to carrye a suspicious minde and a harde opinione of me. I sawe, by the example of my auncestours, and by my passed daunger, howe innocencie was no suffyciente warrante to protect me in safetie.

"I knew myself, and, besides, was charged by your Counsell, to be of that relligioue which they accompte odious and daungerous to your State. Lastlie, but principallie, I wayted in what miserable and dolefull case my sowle had remayned, yf my lyffe had bene taken awaie, as yt was not unlike in my former troubles; for I proteste, the greateste burthen that rested in my conscience at that time was bycause I had not lyved accordinge to the prescripte rule of that which I undoubtedlie did beleeve, and assuredlie persuade myself to be the truthe, wherfore, beinge somewhat induced by all these reasons, but chieflie moved by the laste argumente, I thoughte that the not perfourminge of my duetie towardes God in suche sorte as I knewe woulde please him beste, woulde be a principall occasione of my late punishmente. Therfore I resolved, whiles I had opportunitie, to take the course which mighte be sure to save my sowle from the daunger of shipwracke althoughe my bodye were subjecte to the perill of misfortune ; and ever since the time

I followed and perfourmed this good entente of mine, thoughe I have perceaved somewhat more daunger to my estate, yet I humblie thanke God I have founde a greate deale more quyette in my minde. And, in this respect, I have occasione to thanke my mortalleste enimies as my cheifeste frindes, naye, I have juste occasione to esteeme my passed troubles as my greateste felycitye, for bothe of them were (thoughe endirectlie) the meanes to leade me to that course which ever bringethe perfecte quyette and onlie procurethe eternall happines. And being resolved rather to endure any punishmente then willinglie to decline from the good beginninge I had made, I did lende myself whollie, as neare as I coulde, still to contynewe in the same, without yealdinge to anythinge that mighte danger my sowle, or doinge of any acte that was repugnaunte to my faithe and professione, and by meanes hereof, I was compelled to doe manie thinges which mighte procure perill to myselfe and be an occasione of mislike to your Majestie.

"For, the first daie of this Parliamente, when your Majestie, with all your nobilitie, was hearinge a sermone in the cathedral churche of West-minster, above in the chaunsell, I was dryven to walke by myself alone belowe in one of the yles. And one day this Lente, when your Majestie was hearinge another sermone in the chappell at Greenwiche, I was forced to staie all the while alone in the presence chamber. To be shorte, when your Majestie wente uppon Sundaie or holidaie, to the greate clossette, I was enforced eyther to staie in the privie chamber or not to wayte uppon you at all or elles presentlie to departe assone as I brought you to the chappell. These thinges, with manie mo, I coulde by no meanes escape, but onlie by suche an open and plaine discoverie of myself in the eye and oppinione of all men, as the true course of my refusall coulde not longe be hidden, althoughe for a while yt were generallie noted and observed; wherfore, since I sawe that, of necessitie, yt muste shortlie be discovered, and withall remembred what watchfull and jelous eye was carryed over all those which were known to be recusauntes, naye, callinge to minde howe all ther lodginges were contynuallie searched, and to howe greate daunger they were subjecte yf anie Jesuite or seminarie prieste where founde within there howse, I begann to consider that eyther I could not serve God in suche sorte as I had professed, or elles I must encurre the hassarde of greater punishmente then I was willinge to endure. I stoode resolute and unremovable to contynue in the firste, thoughe yt were with the daunger of my lyffe, and therfore did imploye my minde to devise what meane I coulde for avoydinge of the laste.

"Longe I was in debatinge with myself which course to take, for when I considered in what continuall daunger I did remaine here in Engla[nd], both by the lawes heretofore established, and by a newe acte nowe latelie made, I did thinke it my safeste waye to depart owte of this realme and abide in some other place where I mighte lyve without daunger to my conscience, withowt offence to your Majestie, without the servile sub-jection to mine enimies, and without this dailie perill to my lyffe. And yet I was drawen by so forcible persuasions to be of another opinione, as I could not easilie resolve on which parte to grounde and settle my determination, for, on the one side, my natyve countrie, my frindes, my wyffe, and my kinsfolkes, did invyte me to staie; on the other side, the misfortune of my house, the power of my adver-saries, the remembraunce of my former troubles, and the knowledge of my presente daunger, did haste me to goe; and in the ende, fyndinge no middle course, but eyther I must ventre to lyve in extreame povertie abroade, or be faine to remaine in continuall daunger at home, I regarded more the hassarde of myself wherein I stoode, then the perill of my state, and I rather soughte the preferringe and preservinge of my lyffe then the possessione of my lyvinge. Wherfore, after I had wayed as manie daungers as I coulde remember, and was persuaded that to departe the realme was the safeste waie I could devise, I did resolve to take the benefyte of a happie wynde to avoyde the violence of a bytter storme, and knowinge by experience that the dealinges of all suche as goe beyond the seas are hardlie enterpreted, thoughe there intentes be never so good and duetifull, I presumed to wryte this letter unto your Majestie, and in yt to declare the two reasons and causes of my departure, bothe to remove all occasione of doubte and suspicion from your Majestie, which otherwise the sodaine departure of mine might peradventure procure, and allso to seeke, asmuche as lyethe in me, the retayninge of your gracious and good oppinione, which as I have bene ever moste desirous to enjoye, so will I be moste willinge to deserve.

" And because mine adversaries maie not take this as a fytte opportunitie to bewraie there owne mallice and to kindle your Majesties indignation againste me, I moste humblie beseeche you to aske those which you thinke doe hate me moste, whether, beinge of that religione which I doe professe, and standinge every waie in that state and condition wherin I did remaine, they woulde not have taken that course for safetie of ther sowles and dischardge of there consciences, which I did, and eyther they muste tell you directlie that they woulde have done the same, or elles plainlie acknowledge themselves to be meere atheistes, which, howsoever they be affected in there hartes, I thinke they woulde be lothe to confesse with there mouthes. And when they have satisfied your Majestie in this poincte, whiche ys the firste, I beseeche you aske them of the seconde, which ys the laste, whether, havinge had there howse so fatallie and successivelie touched, and fyndinge themselves to be of that religione which was accompted odious and daungerous to the presente state, whether, havinge bene hardlie handled, longe restrained, and openlie disgraced, heretofore, for nothinge, and mighte nowe justlie be drawen, for there conscience, into greate and continuall daunger, whether, havinge some in cheifeste creditte with your Majestie there mortall and professed enimies, and standinge suspected persons in your Majesties oppinione, bothe in respecte of my father, who was taken awaie in your time, and of myselve, who have bene since manie times wronged and injuried, and besides for beinge of that relligione which your Majestie dothe moste deteste and of which you are moste jealous and doubtfull.—to be shorte, whether, havinge had one of there auncestors taken awaie, withowt anye shadowe of faulte, but onlie for this cause, that hee was thoughte ane unmeete man to lyve in the commone wealthe at that time; knowinge myselve to be soe reputed att this time, of those which nowe doe beare moste swaie in your Majesties governmente.

" Lastlie, whether, not beinge able to doe any manner of acte or duetie wherunto there religione did bynde them, withowt incurringe the daunger of felonie, by a newe Acte latelie made, they would not have departed owt of this realme as I have done ; and eyther they muste saie that they would joyfullie have runne·uppon there owne deathe and hedlonge have throwen themselves into open and ymynent daunger, which ys repugnaunte to the lawe of God, contrarie to the lawe of nature, and, as I thinke, flatlie againste there owne conscience ; or elles they must acknowledge that they woulde have soughte the same meanes which I have used for escapinge. . . . . And then I hope your Majestie will not hardlie conceave of this my dealinge . .. . . leste enimies, yf they speake not contrarie to all truthe and reasone, muste . . . . confesse to be juste, conveniente, and necessarie; besides, to confirme your Majestie . . . . of mine innocence heerin, yourself maie beste remember howe . . . . departed longe before this time, yf I had bene guiltie of anye cry[me] . . . . stond to the uttermoste triall [and ex]amination of all my dealinges, and thoughe I have tasted all the time, since my laste restrainte, your Majesties open and publique disgraces, bothe dailie and howrelie, withowt any hope or likelihoode of ever reservinge your favor and good opinione. And yf my protestation, who never toulde your Majestie the leaste untruthe, maye carrye any credytte in your oppinione, I heare call God and His aungelles to wytnesse that I woulde not have taken this course, yf I mighte have staied still in Englaunde withowt daunger to my sowle and perill to my lyffe.

" Wherefore, as yt ys the true token of a noble minde, and hathe all-waies bene noted for a certaine argumente of your Majestie's gracious disposition in that that yt hathe ever pleased you to take pitie of those which are in miserie, and to respecte with the eye of your favor all afflicted persons, soe can I not be broughte anye waie to feare your Majestie will make me the firste example of your severe and rigorous dealinge, in layinge your displeasure uppon me who am enforsed to forsake my countrie, to foregoe my frindes, to leave my lyvinge, and to loose the hope of all worldlie pleasures and earthlie commodities yf eyther I will not willfullie consente to the certaine destruction of my bodie, or willinglie yealde, to the manifeste endaungeringe of my soule, the leste of which are intollerable for any Christian man to endure, as I hope yt can be thoughte no unduetifullnes in me yf I seeke, by good and lawful meanes, to avoyde soe great an inconvenience. And thoughe the losse of temporall commodities be so grievous unto fleshe and bloude as I could not desyre to lyve yf I were not comforted with the hope of eternall happines in an other worlde, and with remembrance of His mercye, for whom I endure all this, and who endured ten thousande times more for me; yet I assure your Majestie that your displeasure shoulde be more unplesaunte unto me then the bytternes of my other losses, and more greater grief then the greateste of all my misfortunes. Wherefore, remayninge in assured hope that myself and my cause shall receave that favourable conceipte and rightfull construction att your Majestie's bandes which I maie justlie challenge, bothe bycause the triall of my good dealinge heertofore hathe suffycientlie deserved the same, and allso for that the confessione of my mortall enimies att this time muste needes acknowledg my innocencie heerein, I doe humblie crave pardone of my longe and tedious letter, which the weighte of the matter enforcethe me unto, and beseeche God, from the bottome of my harte, to sende your Majestie as greate happines as I wishe to mine owne soule."

RICHARD HOLLAND to RICHARD ASSHETON, JAMES ASSHETON, and EDMUND HOPWOOD.

f. 7. 1590, March 30.—The Lord Lieutenant of Lancashire has commanded him to see that "diligente watche be laide in places likelie thoroughout these partes of the shire" for the stay of those persons, described in an enclosure, whom Lord Scroope states did on Sunday, the 22 inst., "break" Mr. Myddelton's house in "Carleile," and took from him 300l. in money. A general search for strangers is also to be made.

[Enclosure.]

" The markes and notes of the men and there horses and apparell.

" Firste, Christopher Mydletone ys of a middle stature, and a slender man, of the age of xxiij yeares, withowt any heare on his face, the beare on his heade somethinge longe. Hee hathe a newe vyolette sadd coloured frisado jerkine, gathered in plaites upon the backe, and the sleeves cutte downe all alonge the overside of the arme and tyed with a silke lace; and rydethe on a baye horse.

" John Webbe ys a man of small stature, blacke heare, bothe of his head and beard, the heare of his heade somethinge longe, and of the age of xxx^{tle} yeares, and wearethe a blewe coate, beinge my Lorde Scroope his lyverie, and bathe for his cognoscentes a Cornishe choughe. Hee rydethe upon a blacke nagge, and hathe a hole in his eare to hange a pearle.

" William Allan ys a man of reasonable tall stature, and somethinge grosse made, his heare blacke, and bathe a hole in his eare to hange a pearle att, his cassocke of russette clothe. Hee rydethe upon a graye geldin, and ys of the age of xxxi yeares. His cassocke hathe broade buttons upon the breste, with a lace upon the same cassocke.

PROFANING THE SABBATH.

f. 10. Undated. Presentment that in Bury parish, William Key, of Elenfield, had an " alle and minstrells " who " plaied uppon the Sabbothe daye."

THE SAME.

f. 10d. 1588, April 15.—Presentments within the parish of Rochdale. " Adam Stolte, gentleman, uppon the Sabbothe daye, in the eveninge, beinge eyther the last Sundaye in December or the fyrste in Januarie, had a minstrell which plaied uppon a gythorne a[t] his howse, with a greate number of men and women dauncinge."

The wife of Lawrence Collendge " had a minstrell playinge uppon a gythorne at hys (sic) howse, uppon a festivall daye in Christenmas laste, in the eveninge, and many yonge folkes dauncinge."

Presentments follow of persons suspected of keeping disorderly houses.

Names of the Jurors for Manchester: Thomas Byrom, Henry Hardy, Ralph Haughton, Richard Nugent, John Dawson, Ralph Jephson, Robert Kenyon. Those for Oldham, Ashton, Eccles, Dean, Bury, Rochdale, Middletoun, Radcliffe, Prestwich, and other places appear.

These Juries are to present assults, or those who keep " wakes, fayres, markettes, bearebaites, bull baites, greenes, alles, maye games, pypinge and dawncing, huntinge and gaminge, uppon the Sabothe daye."

The names of those who absent themselves from church in Eccles are:—The wife of Hamlet Nollcroft, gentleman, in Woden in Barton; the wife of Ralph Slade, yeoman, in Clifton; Mrs. Worsley, dwelling at Wardley; Mrs. Ellen Holland, widow, in Clifton; the wife of George Latham, gentleman, in Ireland; the wife of Thomas Holden, of Eccles, husbandman.

ABSENTEES FROM CHURCH.

fo. 11d. 1588, April 15.—Presentment by the churchwardens for Manchester. For negligent absence from church for a month or more, none. " For causing a bayre to be bayted upon Sundaie, beinge the xviith of March 1587[-8] att the bullringe neere the conduyte in

Manchester, William Radcliffe of Manchester, gentleman, Robert Radclif, James Radcliffe, Thomas Radcliffe, William Batesonn, Edward Prescot, George Wollsencrofte, John Lees, smith, Robert Bridghowse, Rychard Moreton, the younger, with diverse others wee know not." Several persons presented for being in alehouses, or in the street, during service or sermon time on Sundays. Presentments follow of the names of all the alehouse keepers in Manchester and Salford, and in Ashton and Oldham parishes.

JUSTICES OF THE PEACE FOR LANCASHIRE.

fo. 16. A.D. 1595.—"The names of all justices of peace within this county of Lancaster resydent."

Blackburn hundred.

Thomas Walmersley, one of the Justices *de banco ;* Thomas Talbot, esquire, now sheriff; Ralph Assheton of Whalley; Nicholas Banester of Altham; Edmund Towneley of Royle.

Derby hundred.

Sir Edward Fitton, knight; Sir Richard Molyneux, knight; Peter Leigh, esquire; Richard Bolde, esquire; Cuthbert Halsalle, esquire; Henry Eccleston, esquire ; Thomas Tyldesley, esquire; Thomas Ireland, esquire; Barnaby Kytchen, esquire.

Amounderness hundred.

Richard Houghton, esquire; Thomas Hesketh, esquire; Edward Walmersley, esquire; Edmund Fleetwood, esquire; Thomas Barton, esquire.

Lonsdale hundred.

Thomas Preston, esquire; Francis Tunstall, esquire; John Bradley, esquire ; William Fleming, esquire; Miles Dodding, esquire.

Leyland hundred.

Edward Standish, esquire; William Farrington, esquire; Richard Fleetwood; James Anderton, esquire; John Wrightington, esquire; Thomas Lathom, esquire; John Cuerden, esquire.

Salford hundred.

John Byrom, esquire; Thomas Holcroft, esquire; Richard Assheton, esquire ; Richard Holland, esquire; Richard Brereton, esquire; James Assheton, esquire; Edmund Hopwood, esquire; Alexander Redditche, esquire; John Bradshaigh, esquire; Henry Radcliffe, esquire; Thomas Leigh, esquire.

LANCASHIRE PLACE-NAMES.

f. 17. Names of all the vills within the hundreds of Lonsdale, Amounderness, Blackburn, Leyland, West Derby, and Salford.

EDMUND ASSHETON.

f. 19d. Memorandum that Edmund Assheton of Chadderton, esquire, died at Hopwood on Wednesday, 19 August 1584, *" circiter horam noctis sexta."*

RICHARD HOLLAND to the CONSTABLES of the town of Middleton.

f. 21d. 1592, May 20.—The Earl of Derby—by the advice of the Bishop of Chester, Sir Richard Molyneux, knt., and other justices of the peace for Lancashire, for the good keeping of armour and weapons provided at the charge of the county, " for the furnyture of 600 trayned souldiers and 700 selected souldiers " for the Queen's service in the north parts and in Ireland, and also for the repair of beacons, and watching the same in time of danger—has ordered a general taxation throughout Lancashire, for raising 260*l*. : 47*s*. 11*d*. of this sum is imposed upon the town of Middleton, which sum the constables are directed to collect, and bring or forward it to Holland, or his deputy, " att the parishe churche of Manchester," by 10 o'clock in the morning of the 10th of June following.

" A GUYLDED TWELVPÈNCE."

f. 22. 1594, September 7.—Memorandum that " John Nowell of Ardsley, in the countye of Yorke, husbandman, commynge to Burie fayre, and buying a yoake of oxen of an unknowne man, delivered in parte of paymente, a guylded twelivpence in leawe of a royall, and havinge annother peece of goulde, seeminge to bee an angell, payed the same to the same man in parte of paymente for the sayd oxen . . . . . asked where he hadd the guilded shilling, sayeth hee hadd yt of one Thomas Hill of Broughton in Craven, in a litle toune called Adwaltoun, about six weekes ago, in exchange for a mare, receyved the same peece for tenn shillinges." . . . Robert Bradley confessed that Nowell " showed him a peece of goulde seeminge to be a guilded twelvepennce," and advised him to return it " where he hadd yt, yf possiblie he coulde."

PAPISTS IN LANCASHIRE.

1595, October 28.—Entry of an unsigned letter, commencing, " The love you bere (Righte Honourable and my especiall good Lord) for the furtherance of Christe his glorious gospell, the most comfortable tydinges of our salvation, with the honourable and manifold favors you ever have vouchsafed mee in regarde to the same." The writer states that there are many abuses in Lancashire which require redress, an account of which he sets out in an enclosure. A copy of the enclosure follows :—

In the parishes of Garstang and St. Michael's " are as many farmers, notorious recusanttes, as will make two graunde jureys "; the names of such should be given to the churchwardens of these parishes, who should see if they attended the parish church according to the law, and if they did not, would give them warning to reform, at their dwelling houses, once in six weeks at the least. The writer also advises the prosecution of " all of them knoune to be riche (and not havinge manye children) accordinge to the statute of 20*l*. a monthe ; and the pourer sorte, accordinge to the statute of *anno primo*, for 2*s*. everie Sondaie and holidaye." If such a course were taken in every parish in Lancashire for the space of two years, it would discover the number " of obstinate and maskinge subjects, as also take awaye all colourable and cunninge dealinge from the churchwardens, which, for the moste part, are infected withe papistrie, or placed by papistes, or their favorites of the baddeste sorte."

There are in the same parishes the following gentlewomen who are recusants :—

Elizabeth Tyldesley, widow, late of Merscoe [Mierscough ?], and sometime residing at Morley or Entwistle.

Dorothy, wife of Thomas Brockeholes, esquire, of Claughton.

Anne, wife of Mr. Travers, of Natbie.

Jane, wife of Mr. Twinge, of Kirkeland, when he lives in Lancashire ; he has a house near York.

Anne, wife of Walter Rygmayden, esquire.

Anne, wife of Henry Butler, esquire, of Rowcliff.

Elizabeth, wife of William Butler, son and heir of the said Henry.

Isabel, wife of William Kirkby, esquire, of Rowcliff.

The husbands of these persons attend church, perhaps not so much as monthly. The churchwardens of Garstang and St. Michael's should warn them to conform once a month. If they still remain obstinate, "then the gentlewomen, withe their husbandes, should bee removed to the severall howses of gentlemen knoune to be well affected, and resolute in [the] religion established, there to be honestlie and well used with all pleasures and recreations conveniente during their obstinancie"; so shall they neither "frequente shryvinge, massinge, nor releve papishe preestes or seditious seminaryes, to the perill of their soules, great danger of theyr husbandes, and utter spoyle of their husbandes simple seduced tenants and neighbours."

Since 1592, many who submitted themselves before the Justices of Assize for Lancashire, "refrayne" from church, except "for one Sundaye or two before the Assizes," whereby they "shadowe their hypocrasie." If the clerk of assize was to deliver the names and addresses of such "submitters"—so that they were, in the end, given to the churchwardens of the different parishes—a report might be made as to the attendance of those persons at church, and their behaviour at service.

The writer then recommends as commissioners for carrying out his proposals:— Richard Shuttleworth, the King's Justice of Chester, Thomas Hesketh, esquire, the Queen's Attorney-General for Lancashire, the sheriff for the time being, Edmund Fleetwood of Rossall, William Farrington of Werden, Richard Fleetwood of Penwortham, James Anderton of Clayton, John Wrightington of Wrightington, Nicholas Bannister of Althome, John Bradshaigh of Bradshaigh, and Edmund Hopwood of Hopwood, esquires.

If James Anderton, Nicholas Bannister, or John Bradshaigh (assigned for the hundreds of Derby, Leyland, and Salford) "follow affection or zeale more than sounde judegment or reason, Mr. Anderton wyll moderate their hote humors"; Mr. Farrington would do the like for the remainder of those named above, who were to act for the hundreds of Blackburn, Amounderness, and some part of Lonsdale.

The writer suggests the arrest of such as are suspected of being messengers or carriers of letters amongst recusants, and concludes:—
"I dare not geve my voyce to any commissioners, concerninge takinge of preestes and seminaryes, &c., excepte Edmund Fleetwood, Nicholas Bannister, John Bradshaigh, John Wrightington, and Edmund Hopwood; and I am in conscyence perswaded that everie peculier of theise would spende all the buttons att their doublettes to purge Lancashyre from idolatrie, papistrie, seditious seminaryes, and theyr favorytes."

A CONVERSION FROM POPERY.

fo. 24. 1595, November 24.—"This bearer, right honorable and my verye good Lorde, was fyrste broughte into Lancashire by an olde preeste called Laykin, *alias* Knylye, and was, for the space of twentye yeares, an obstinate recusant, and of great credytt amongste that crewe, tyll yt pleased God Almightie to call him to the knowledge of His truthe, whiche he no sooner professed but they cried 'crucifice,' by meanes wherof hee was glad to leave those partes, and place himselfe with a sonne-in-lawe of myne, to teache his children playe and

singe, and to reade service upon Sondayes and holidayes at a lyttle
chappell, within two myles where I dwell. And for his sincere conversion, I can saye of knowledge, that suche papistes as are in some sorte
my deare famyliares, greeve and frett when they heare speeche of hym, a
stronge motyve to perswade mee to thinke the dearlier of hym. And
further, this last Assize at Lancaster (where I was fyrste acquainted
withe hym) hee prosecuted, in the face of the cuntrye, by waye of in-
dictmente, one Charneleye, for rescuinge a semynarie preeste from hym
this last somer. And this is the messenger I unfeanedlie love and truste,
and have sent to enforme your honor of some few particulers, and
humblie to crave your lordship's directions concerninge my letters of
the laste October."

LANCASHIRE FREEHOLDERS.

ff. 25–33d. 1578.—"The freeholde booke for Lancashire." This
contains the names of the free tenants within the hundreds of Lonsdale, Blackburn, West Derby, and Salford.

INHABITANTS OF MANCHESTER.

ff. 34–37. 1571.—Return of the payment of a subsidy in the hundred
of Salford. The following is the return for Manchester :—

Edmund Prestwiche	in lands		13l.
Mary Staundishe	„		10l.
Dorathie Brewrtoun	„		100s.
John Marler	„		40s.
Thomas Willote	„		60s.
William Radcliffe	„		40s.
Robert Holme	„		60s.
Robert Clayden	„		4l.
John Gregorie	„		41(?)s.
John Chethome	„		40s.
The heirs of Ralph Culchethe	„		20s.
Thomas Trafforde	„		40s.
Thomas Hyde	„		40s.
George Byrche	„		3l.
Lady Elizabeth Byroun, widow	„		3l.
Anne Bocke	in goods		3l.
The wife of William Edge	„		3l.
Frauncis Pendletoun	„		100s.
William Baggerley	„		100s.
Humphry Houghton	„		7l.
George Pendletoun	„		6l.
John Houghton	„		6l.
Christopher Graunt	„		4l.
George Travis	„		4l.
James Rydellsonne	„		4l.
Mylles Willsonn	„		100s.
Richard Fox	„		3l.
Ralph Prowdeloofe [Prowdlove]	„		3l.
Robert Langley	„		3l.
John Davie	„		4l.
Richard Gee	„		100s.
Robert Marler	„		4l.

John Radcliffe	-	-	·	in goods	-	-	4*l.*
Hugh Shaclocke	-	-	-	,,	-	-	3*l.*
James Chowtertoun	-	-	..	-	-	3*l.*
George Worall (?)	-	-	.,	-	-	3*l.*
George Prowdlove	-	-	,,	-	-	4*l.*

SUBSIDY.

ff. 38–43d.—Sums of money levied by subsidy. [No names of persons.]

PERSONS CHARGEABLE FOR HORSE AND ARMS.

ff. 44–47. 1569.—Return by a Jury of persons chargeable with the maintenance of horses, armour, and weapons, within the hundred of Salford.

SABBATH BREAKING.

f. 47d. 1574, April 21.—Orders taken at Manchester by eight of the justices of the peace for Lancashire. Amongst them is one which directs that "every churchwarden, cunstable and sworne man shall, everye Sondaye and holydaye, take the names of suche persons as doe walke in places ordeyned for divine service, in the time of sermons or divine services "; the names of such, or of those who go out of church before the end of the services or sermons, are to be presented to the justices.

ARCHERS IN LANCASHIRE.

f. 49.—The appointment and taxation of 200 soldiers, all archers, levied within the county of Lancaster, to serve the Queen; under Sir Robert Worsley and Edward Tildsley, esquire, in 1556 ; every archer had 10*s.* allowed to him besides "his furnyture": and the taxation of 300 men (whereof 78 were archers) within Lancashire, in 1559, to serve the Queen at Berwick, under Sir John Sowthworth.

SOLDIERS IN LEIGH.

f. 49d.—Soldiers appointed to serve the Queen at Leigh, in 1559, under Thomas Butler, esquire :—Soldiers, 200 ; pioneers, 267.

ARCHERS FOR IRELAND.

1567.—The taxation in Lancashire for 50 archers for Ireland. "Memorandum, that everye of the said archers was furnished with a cassocke of blewe clothe, garded with two small gardes of white clothe, a view bowe, a sheaffe of arrowes in a case, a skull in a redd cappe, a jerkin of a stagge or bucke skinne, sworde and dagger; and everye one in hys purse had in redye moneye 13*s.* 4*d.*, besides 4*s.* to everye of them, delivered for their coate and conducte money, at their cominge to Chester. And for the furnishinge of the said souldiers, the countrye [county ?] was taxed at the rate of 60*s.* for everye the said archers or souldiers."

SOLDIERS FOR IRELAND.

1574, Feb. 13.—Taxation of the county for sending 100 soldiers ("archers, byllmen, and qualyvers") into Ireland. Every archer to have a bow, a sheaf of arrows, "a stile cappe or a skull," a sword and a dagger. Every billman to have "a byll, a coat of plate, a sallette, a sworde, and a dagger." Every "caliver" to have "a caliver furnished morrian, or burgonette, a sworde, and dagger." Every man to have in his purse, besides his "furniture," 16s. 8d. For the "furnishing" of every archer 3l. 10s. 8d. was levied, for every billman 3l. 16s. 2d., and for every "caliver" 4l. 10s. 10d. "Aliso the Queen's Majestie did allowe for conducte moneye to everye souldiare, a half penie a myle from the hundred where they dwelled unto the toune of Lyverpoole, and 2s. a peece for their transportinge."

TAXATION OF LANCASHIRE.

f. 50. 1575.—A taxation, within Lancashire, for the "levyinge, makinge, and setting furthe" thirty labourers and soldiers to serve in Ireland; from each hundred, one of the men is to be a "smithe." They are to be at Chester on 10th May; each is to have for his "whole furni. ture," 30s. "There coates are to be redde, of 6s. 8d. the yarde, gascoine fashion, tyed under the arme with whitte incle,[1] everye one to have a sworde, dagger, and gyrdle."

THE SAME.

f. 50d. 1576, June.—Taxation made within the same county for "makinge of 6 masons, 6 carpenters, and 12 labourers," to be sent into Ireland. A note states that these never went. 33s. 4d. was to be levied towards their "furniture," with which was to be provided for each man "doblette, hose, showes, dagger, and a coate of whytte clothe made of the fashione of a cassocke, garded with two laces of conles [?], the one of the coller of redde, and the other grene."

PAROCHIAL ARMOUR.

f. 51.—List of "common armour" delivered to the several parishes in Salford hundred; the articles are chiefly "coarslettes," "morrianns," "flaxboxes," "moldes," and "calivers."

COST OF SOLDIERS' OUTFITS.

f. 53. 1577, January 30.—Taxation of Lancashire, made at Ormskirk, "for the making readye of 300 men within one houres warninge." The cost of "furniture" for an armed pikeman was:—

Hys dublette of white homes (sic) fuscion - - -	6s.	8d.
Hys hose of watchet kersaye, venisioned fashione, 2 yardes and a halfe - - - - -	5s.	10d.
Thre quarters of whyte kersaye netherstocke - -		18d.
Two yards and a halfe of course canvas for lynninge -		15d.
One yard and half a quarter of flaxoun, for straite lyninge - - - - - - - - - -		15d.
For makyng hys hose - - - - - -		8d.
Hys shyrte - - - - - - -	3s.	4d.
For hys showes - - - - - - -	2s.	
Garters and poincts - - - - - -		6d.
Hys coate of watchet, fashione gascoine, of Yorkshire broade clothe, one yarde and three quarters - -	11s.	8d.
Yelowe or redde broad clothe for two gardes about the coate, two gardes doune the hose, two fingars broad, one quarter and a halfe - - - - - -	2s.	6d.

---

[1] A sort of tape.—*Bailey.*

Hys corslett furnished - - - - - - 33s. 4d.
Pike - - - - - - - - - 2s. 8d.
Hys swode and dagger, and sword gyrdell - - - 8s.
Moneye in hys purse, over and besydes suche moneye as
her Majestie shall allowe for coate and conducte
money - - - - - - - - - 10s.

"Furniture" of a billman :—

f. 52d.—For hys apparell, armoure, byll, sword, dagger,
money in hys purse, and in all sortes as the pikeman - 4l. 11s. 2d.

"Furniture" of an archer :—

Hys apparell, allowed as a picke, vew bowe - - - 5s.
Hys sheaf of arrowes and a case to the arrowes - - 3s. 4d.
Hys coate of plate - - - - - - 13s. 4d.
Hys skull and Scottishe cappe to cover the same - - 3s. 4d.
Hys swode, dagger, and swode gyrdell to the same - 8s.
Hys shootinge gloves, bracelette, and stringe - - 12d.
Money in hys purse besides hys conducte monye, as her
Majestie shall alow, ys - - - - - - [blank]

The "furniture" of a pioneer :—

Hys cassocke watchette, 1 yard 3 quarters - - - 8s. 9d.
Hys shyrte - - - - - - - - 2s. 9d.
Hys doublette, whytte - - - - - - 5s.
Hys hose of whyte, two yardes - - - - - 5s. 4d.
Makyng and lyninge - - - - - - - 16d.
Hys showes - - - - - - - - 2s.
Garters and poincts - - - - - - - 6d.
Hys sculle cappe - - - - - - - 3s. 4d.
Hys sword, dagger, and sword gyrdell - - - 8s.
Mony in hys purse over and besides suche money as her
Majestie shall allowe for coate and conducte money - 10s."

LANCASHIRE HUNDREDS.

f. 55d. 1582, April 5.—A "divisione" of the hundreds of Lancashire, taken at Wigan.

PIKEMAN'S DRESS.

"The pike's" coat was of "broade blewe" at 8s. the yard, each coat
containing one yard and a quarter. The billman's "jacke or coate of
plate" cost 13s. 4d., and the bowman's "shootinge glove, bowe stringes,
and braselettes" cost 16d.

THOMAS PRESTON to the JUSTICES OF THE PEACE within the Hundred of Salford.

f. 59. 1584-5, January 9.—Has received the Privy Council's directions for "ellectinge" 50 soldiers to be employed in Ireland, out of the
200 before appointed by the Queen's letters of 16 August last. The
50 men are to be at Chester on 15 February, furnished and sorted as
follows :—20 with "calivers," 10 with "corslettes and pykes," 10 with

bowes and arrows, and 10 with "halberts or good black bills." He therefore desires the Justices to direct the Constables to bring before him, at Preston in Amounderness, on the 21st January, all the 200 soldiers, that he may select therefrom 50), according to the order given him, "and withall, to have the monye ther readie, accordinge to the rates sett doune att the time, for their furniture and allowance for the fourthe parte of the said 200 men being then sessed."

Suggestions for reforming " the Enormities of the Saobothe," signed by Henry, Earl of Derby, and Sir Francis Walsingham.

f. 63d.—" Wakes, fayres, markettes, bayrbeytes, bullbaytes, ales, maygames, resortinge to alle bowses in time of divine service, pypinge and daunciuge, huntinge, and all manner of unlawfull gaminge.

" The meanes how to reforme the same.

" 1. To give charge, att the publique Quarter Sessions, to all mayores, bailiffes, cunstables, and other civill offycers, churche wardens, and other offyceres of the churche, to suppresse, by all meanes lawfull, the said disorderes of the Saobothe, as allso to present the said offendours at the Quarter Sessions, that they maye be dealt with for the same, so farr as lawe will beare. And for the present time, to apprehende the minstrelles, bearewardes, and other suche lyke cheif authores of the said disorderes, and them to bringe imediatlie before some justice of peace, to be punished att ther discretion.

" 2. That the churchwardens and other churche offyceres be enjoyned to appeare at the Quarter Sessions, and ther to make presentmente of all that neglecte divine service upon the Saobothe daye, by absence or otherwise, that they may be indycted upon the statute which imposethe a penalltie of xij^d for every suche offence.

" 3. To abridge the immeasurable multitude of allehowses to the poincte of the statute.

" 4. To take order that the allehowses shall utter a full quarte of alle for a pennye, and none of any lesser sysse.

" 5. To bynde the allehowse keepers by speciall terms in the condition of ther recognizaunce, for receiptinge (sic) any that are chief maintainers, partakers of thafforsaid disorderes of the Saobothe, as sellinge alle and other victualles, in time of dyvine service.

" 6. That cunstables and other civill offyceres, and churchwardens and other the churche offyceres, be enjoyned, at the Quarter Sessiouns, to make presentmente to the justices of the peace of all those allhowse-keepers that have broken the condition of ther recognizaunce, and the justices to take orders with the clarke of the peace, or otherwise, for the further presentinge of the said forfaitors, accordinge to the righte course of lawe.

" 7. That the saide officeres be enjoyned to make presentmente allso att the Sessions of all those that sell alle, havinge therto lyceaunce.

" 8. That your worshipps woulde take order amongste yourselves that no lycence be given to any to keepe allehowse, but onlie in publique Sessiouns.

" 9. That your worshippes would enjoyne the aforesaid offyceres of the churche and comone wealthe that they make due presentmente att the Quarter Sessiouns of all bastardes borne or remayninge within ther severall precinctes, and that, therupon, a straite course be taken for the due punishmente of the reputed parenntes, according to the statute, as allso for the conveniente keepinge and relief of the said infauntes. And allso for vacaboundes, according to the statute.—Henry Derby, Francis Wallsingham."

Suggestions for the Reformation of Defaults of Lancashire Freeholders and others, signed by the abovesaid Earl of Derby and Sir Francis Walsingham.

f. 64d. No. 6 reads :—" Concerning justices of peace, yt were conveniente·that a sermond should allwaies be had, at everye quarter sessions, and att a conveniente howre of the daye, whereat the presence of justices of peace, and other offycers of that courte, were especiallie to be requyred, wherefore yt were good they endeavoured to come to the place of justice sette betime of the daye." No. 8 reads :—" To the end they may more willinglie bestowe their continuall attendaunce in this so necessarye a service and so properlie belonging to their charge, the Chauncler will take order they shall enjoye the allowance owt of the fines and issues for the ease of ther chardge, according to the statute." It is considered expedient that the sessions should begin at Manchester and thence proceed to Wigan or Ormskirk, then to Preston, and end at Lancaster, "which rightlie maye falle owt for the conveniente placinge of the records of all proceedings before hadd in the severall sessions, as beinge a place generallie assigned therunto."

The COUNCIL to the SHERIFF and JUSTICES OF THE PEACE for Lancashire.

f. 75d. 1584, August 17. Oatlands.—"Wheras the Quene's Majestie, at this presennte, sennte her letters unto you, for the levyinge of 200 able men in that County of Lanncaster for her service in her warres in the realme of Yrelaunde, albeit ther ys suche truste reposed as that you will, with all your indeavoure, further suche service, yet to thintente ther may be noe defaulte therof, wee have thought good to recomende the same unto you, upon conference amongste yourselves, howe the same nomber ys to levyed in every particuler divisione of that county, to have an especiall care that choise be made of able personns meete for this service, and that the furniture of them be suche as maye not by the captaine, or any other that shall have the view and charge of them, uppon juste cause, be misliked, so as the said nomber be in a readiness to marche towardes Chester by the xth day of September, as you shalbe dyrected by us, there to be imbarked ; againste which time wee have allreadye given order that conveniente shippinge shalbe provided for ther transportation.

"And wher heretofore information hathe bene given, bothe to her Majestie and us, that in suche lyke services, by reasonne that the men were in this realme, or in Irelaunde, commytted to straunge captaines, who for the moste parte have not used ther souldiours with that love and care that appertained, ther was not so good choise made of them as was fytte ; and allso the furniture of the shire never returned, so as the souldiours have bene therby greatlie discouraged in the services, and the countrye wher the levyes have bene made, more burdened ; and yet wee have done what wee can for the redresse of ther disorder, thoughe our care therin hathe lytell or nothinge prevailed : her Majestie, therfore, for the avoydinge of the lyke inconvenience hereafter, and for the benefytte of that countrie and encouragemente to the souldiaurs, hathe thoughte good that some gentlemen of that countrye and shyre shoulde be the captaine under whom they shoulde serve, and not to have them committed to any other straunger, neyther here nor in Yrelaund ; and for that purpose her Majestie hathe, by her letters, recommended unto you the eldeste sonne of Edmunde Trafford, knighte, to whom her pleasure ys you shoulde signifie so muche as to make him privie to your saide choise and levie of men, changinge suche of the men and furniture as he shall, uppon juste cause to be shewed unto you, mislike and desire to have yt altered, so as hereafter hee maye have noe excuse or exception, yf defaulte shalbe founde to the contrarie.

" It ys allso thoughte conveniente that yf the said nomber of souldiars shoulde be certified, with ther severall kindes of weapons, as ys prescribed in Her Majestie's said letters, and that they shoulde be furnished with swordes and daggers, and lykewise conveniente doblettes and hose, and allso a cassocke of the same motley or other sad greene color, or russette, and lykewise, upon the deliverie of them to the said captaine or his lyvetenaunte, to be [by] hym or hys lyvetenaunte conducted to the seaside, and so over into Yrlaunde: which wee thinke meete to be done by true perfytte byll indented betwene you and the captaine specified, bothe names of the men, and the manner of ther furniture, wherof the one copie to be sente unto us and the other to remayne with you, and the third with the saide captaine. It ys allso thoughte requisite, and so wee praye you procure, that there maye be delivered unto hym, for every souldiare beinge harquebussed, two poundes of good powlder, with conveniente matche and bullette, for use of hys peece. And lykewise, for every souldiar, v' of mony, to provide a mantell for him in Yrelaunde, besides hys lyverie coate, when he shalbe ther arived. Wee praye you allso, upon the computation of the myles, to cause so muche mony to be delivered to the said souldiaurs as shalbe conveniente for ther journey, the charge of whiche coate and conducte monye, accordinge to her Majestie's usuall rates, shalbe repaied by the maior ther to suche as you shall appoincte to receave the same.

" Finallie, wheras upon the vew of the late certificate of musters of that countye wee doe not finde the same furnished with suche proportion of armoure, especiallie of calivers and corslettes with pickes, as wee thinke were conveniente for her Majesty's service and defence of this realme; so as yf any parte ther shoulde be sennte owt for this presente service yt woulde growe therby the worse furnished, wee therfore thinke yt beste ther shoulde so muche mony levyed within the said county as maye suffice to provide the calivers and corslettes for the nomber appoincted ther to be levyed, for which purpose wee have caused a certaine proportion of bothe corslettes and calivers to be sente to the porte of Chester, which, before wee sennte them downe, wee appoincted certaine of skill to view the same, to see them good and servicable, havinge allso agreed with the owner of the said armoure to be uttered and delivered to the captaine at the rates contained in the scedule enclosed."

The COUNCIL to [the SHERIFF and JUSTICES of Lancashire].

1584, August 27. Oatlands.—"Wheras the Queenes Majestie hathe occasione, for this presente service in Yrelaunde, to sende certaine horsmen into that realme and understaundinge that ther be within your county certaine gentlemen and others that [are] recusantes, who, notwithstaundinge that in poinctes of relligion they do not shewe themselves so conformable as appertainethe and her Majestie most earnestlie desyrethe, yet in all ther matters, when they are chardged with undewtifullnes, they doe professe all dewtifull affection unto her Highnes, so farre furthe as to adventure bothe ther lyves and goodes in Her Majestie's service ; shee therfore, beinge desirous, upon this occasione, to make some profe therof, hathe thought meete that those whose names wee send you here, which are contayned in a scedule subscribed by us, shoulde by you be dealte withall in that behalfe, and for that purpose shee hathe comaunded us that wee shoulde dyrecte you to repaire to the places wher the recusantes doe reside, takinge with you two of the commissioners for musters or any two justices of peace within the said countye neere to the residentes of the said parties; and, after you have acquainted them with the contentes of these our letters, to requyre them, in her Majesties name, as so dyrected by us, that they give order owt of haunde for the preparinge, by the xvth daye of September, so manie horse or horses as are taxed upon eche of ther names, in suche sorte furnished as ys contained in the said scedule, lettinge them understande that, in case her Majestie shall finde them conformable in that behalf, they shall give her cause to use them with more favoure, and to qualifie some parte of the extremitie that otherwise the lawe dothe laye upon them; and for that wee doubte that they maye not so convenientlie, and within the time apoincted, provide the men and horses furnished, accordinge as in that scedule ys expressed, you shall offer unto them that on paymente of xxiiij^h, which ys the leaste some that maye be to serve that proportion, to be paide within tenn daies after knowledge given to them by you of her Majestie's pleasure, that then you will see them dischardged. And in case any of them shall refuse to doe eyther one or other, then yt ys her Majestie's pleasure that you shall cause the parties soe refusinge to sett downe under ther baudes the causes of ther refusall and to certifie the same unto us, as allso to deliver into our handes so manie of them as by this notice shall dewtifullie assente or yealde therunto; to the end that therupon wee may take such order therin as shalbe thoughte meete." *The Schedule :*—

"The names of suche personns as are apoincted to fynde lyghte horsemen within the countye of Lanncaster, every one to be furnished with a good, large, and servicable horse or gelldinge, a lyghte horseman's staffe, a jacke, a burhonette, scleeves of male, a case of pistolettes, and a cassocke of suche a color as shalbe here-after signified from the Lordes of her Majestie's moste [honourable] Previe Counsell, or elles to paye so muche money as shalbe suffy-ciente for the furnishinge of the same.

> Alexander Barlowe, j.
> Sir John Sowthworthe of Sainsbury, j.
> Thomas Clifton, j.
> John Talbotte of Salebury, ij.
> Rychard Blundell, j.
> William Orrell, j.
> Thomas Singleton of the Tower, j.
> William Thornborough, j.
> Thomas Assheton, j.
> William Haydock, j.
> Albaine Butler, j.
> John Westby of Molebrigge, j.
> William Hesketh, j.
> John Rygmarden, j.
> Peter Stanley, j.
> Robert Blundell, j."

JOHN BYRON to ————————.

f. 76d. 1587-8, February 20. Knowsley.—Has received letters lately from the Earl of Derby, "her Majesties lyvetennaunt of these partes, to Sir Richard Sherborne and me dyrected," stating that "a gentleman, an experensied souldiaure of credytte, shall presentlie come downe into this Countye of Lancaster, by apoinctmente of the Lordes of her Majestie's moste honourable Privie Counsell, by her Highness' speciall comaundemente, to take a full and perfecte viewe in what redines he fyndeth all the forces, aswell horsmen as footmen, within this shire furnished.   These are, therefore, forthwith, with all speede possible, to requyre you and every of you the justices of peace and gentlemen, with the freholders within the Hundred of Derby, to put in a readines all your forces, aswell demilaunces, lyghte horses as footemen, with your tennantes and folowers, furnished with armoure and weaponne, to serve her Majestie as staundethe with your credyte, so as you have them all readie to be showed within these viij daies nexte cominge, yf need so requyre.   Thus hopinge hereof you will not faile to use your best diligences as you tender her Majestie's service and your owne credytte."

The Council to Lord Straunge, the Bishop of Chester, the Sheriff of Lancashire, and the Justices for the County.

f. 77. [Undated.] Requiring improvement in the system employed by churchwardens in levying and bestowing penalties for not attending church ; " the said churchwardens being in manie places (as wee heare) men of meaneste qualitie."

Instructions as to taking Musters.

ff. 77d–80. [Undated.] Instructions, given at the Queen's command, by the Council to the Commissioners for taking the general musters in Lancashire; one of the instructions is that " none suspected in religion have the chardge of any nomber of soldiaurs."

Further Instructions as to the Same.

ff. 81–83d. [Undated.] Instructions, given at the Queen's command, by the Council to the late Commissioners appointed for taking musters in Lancashire.   They commence, " Her Majestie's clemencie ys not to charge the poore."

" Orders howe every personne that shalbe trained, shalbe taught to handle hys peece."

f. 84. " Fyrste, that every harquebushire, utterlie voide of the knowledge of the use of hys peece, be instructed in maner and forme following :—

" Imprimis, that every such personne be instructed how to handle and carrye hys peece, flaxe, and touche boxe.

" Then to teache him how, in handsome maner, hee shall charge hys peece, and after, how to laye yt on hys cheike ; and beinge once acquainted how to charge them, to teache him to carrye and to shoote off hys peece att raundome, and afterwardes to be taught to shoote at a marke certaine, the same to be distaunte the uttermoste levell of the peece.   Item, after beinge, at the two fyrste meetinges, experieuced how to handle and charge hys peece and to shoote at a marke, att the laste meetinge, they are to be trained further how, uppon a small staye, either in marche or in skirmishe, they maye moste readilie shoote and speedilie chardge and dischardge ther said peeces.

" Item, att every daye appoincted in the instructions for ther trayninge, that the gentlemen appoincted to this chardge shall give order that the private personnes appoincted to be trained shall not use any disorderlie shootinge, but discharge and shoote off hys peece att suche time and in suche order as hee shalbe comanded so to doe ; provided that att every suche time of meetinge hee shall not shoote above tenn shootes of the comon allowaunce of bullettes and powder allotted unto him by the charge of the countrye.

"Item, that the peeces, before there traininges, be vewed by gentlemen to be good and meete for the purpose, and not suche as are lyke to breake or doe any harme.

"Item, good care to be hadd and greate charge to be given, that in the time of the skirmishe or exercize at ther last meetinge, no peece be laden with bullettes, or otherwise to be shotte of, wherby any personn may be maymed or put in hassard of lyffe or lymme.

"Twentye bullettes for the caliver of the Tower ys juste a pounde weighte, and one pounde of powder will make xxv^{tie} shootes, allowinge three quarters weighte of powder to every bullette, and the overplus, after that rate, ys fyve shoote more, which ys for tuche powder; so that, in the whole, xx^{tie} bullettes are to be made of the pounde, and thirtye shootes to the pounde of powder, whereof fyve allowed for tuche powder."

THE WOOL TRADE IN ROCHDALE.

f. 86d. 1588, June 26. An order taken by Sir John Byron and Edmund Hopwood, esquire, at Rochdale. Recites that sundry informations have been exhibited in the Court of Exchequer against sundry the inhabitants of Rochdale (and process was served upon them to appear at the Easter term last past) for dealing in wool, contrary to the statute 5 Edward VI. Supplication was thereupon made by the writers, and other justices of the county, to the Master of the Rolls, "signifyinge that yf the same statute were executed in this countrie, where the poor clothier ys not able to go to the grower of the wooles, neither the grower able to come hither, ther were thousandes of poore people utterlie undone." The matter was considered and referred back to the writers to see that there was no forestalling, regrating, nor engrossing, "neyther that the wooles were sold oftener than to buy yt of the grower and sell it to the maker of clothe, which libertie the men of Hallifax have." The writers, therefore, order that no man inhabiting in Rochdale parish shall buy wool therein and sell it again, nor use any forestalling, regrating, nor engrossing of wool, neither sell it, except in the market town there; and that none buy wool to sell it again except of the grower, nor sell it except to the cloth maker. "Provided allwaies that the northren men shall have libertie to sell woolle in the toune of Ratchdall to any person or persons which will buye the same, bycause he knowethe not the clothe makers. But let the same buyer be well advised he sell not the same again, but converte it into clothe."

AN "EASTER BOOK."

ff. 93d–97. 1569.—The "Easter booke" of the hamlets of Middleton, Hopwood, Thurnham, and Pilsworth, gives the names of the inhabitants, and the tax on "house, hay," &c.

EXAMINATION OF MYLES ROSSE AND JOHN BRINDLEY.

f. 97d. 1595.—Notes of the examination of Myles Rosse of Manchester, goldsmith, and John Brindley, "tinker or plummer." Rosse says that John Brindley, a "tynker," showed him certain "lytell portions of plate," and that he afterwards bought of him the "bottome of this silver tunne, now shewed him," and other small portions of plate, to the value of 3 ounces of silver, for 13s.

Henry, Earl of Derby to ——————.

f. 98d. 1589–90 (?), February 20.—By means of the death of sundry gentlemen and the departure of others out of the county, "upon the troubles latelie fallen owt in this shire," he is forced to alter, in some places, the first rate for furnishing the 25 (?) demi-lances specially required. *Copy.*

The Same to the "Gentlemen of Sallford Hundred."

f. 100. 1590, June 2. "New Parke, my house."— "By letters which this laste nighte were delivered me from there lordships of her Majestie's most honourable Privie Councell, I understand of an attempte entended againste Lancashire, Cheshire, and Anglesey, wherupon I am straitelie required to put in a readines, and see presentlie furnished with armoure and weapon, my whole lyvetenancie. These therfore, are, on her Majestie's behaulf, to chardge and comaunde you that, accordinge to the tenor of my late letters, you presentlie (for her Majestie's service and your owne defence) see furnished with sufficiente armoure and weapon, yourselves, servauntes, tenantes, and followers, in suche warlicke maner as, upon an hour's warninge, you and they dare and will adventure to withstande any and all attemptes that shalbe proffered or made, eyther againste these two (*sic*) shires or any other parties of this realme. Hereunto faile not, but have suche regard as standethe with your duties towardes God, her Majestie, and the realme."

Richard Holland to Richard Assheton, Richard Brereton, and others.

f. 100d. 1590, June 4. Heaton.—"For better preparation and warning of the country againste some newe entended invasions upon these partes, especiallie as by my Lord Lyvetenante his letters, which herewithall I have sente you, maye partlie appeare, and for the enterceptinge and discoverie of suche intelligences or devices as in this dangerous time may be sente from one lewde persone to another,—his lordshipe hathe comaunded that presente order be taken for watchinge of the beacons in every place throughout his lyvetenancie, and in like maner, for straite watche and warde to be kepte in places usuall and of moste importaunce. These maie be, therfore, in her Majestie's name, to requyre you, with all speed and dilligence, to [see] the same his lordship's order and comandemente fullie accomplished within your severall divisions, untill suche time as you shall be warned to surceasse or forbeare the same. And withall, that you comaunde all and every the cunstables that, in there watch and warde, no suspitious or unknowne person be suffered to passe eyther by daie or nighte, untill suche time as hee hathe rendred a lawfull and due accompte of his order of lief and the presente occasione of his travell, before you or suche discrete person as in every place of watche and ward you shall appoincte for better assistinge of the cunstable in that behaulf, where suche assistaunce shall seeme requisite."

Richard Holland and E[dmund] Hopwood to the Bishop of Chester.

f. 101 1590, July 19.—The bearer, Ralph Holland, by order of the Bishop and other the Queen's Commissioners, "hath done all his penance, saving the inninge (?) of his bodie prisoner to the castell of Chester, certaine daies," which he is ready to do, as by certificate of the vicar of Rochdale appears. He is bound by recognizance to perform the order, and "not frequent the woman's companie hereafter, by whom he had the bastard childe." The woman is a bad character, and if, hereafter, she should "wrongfullie father a childe upon him, and hee, by reasone of this former offence not able by the lawe to purge himselve thereby (though in no faulte), should forfaite his recognisance." The writers, therefore, beg the Bishop to accept his abjuration and cancel his recognizance, and—after being for one day and one night in the castle—to discharge him; particularly as Holland "hathe worne papers in Ratchdall markette, which never none did heretofore to our knowledge, althoughe this be his first offence."

——————— to LORD BURGHLEY.

f. 102. 1590, September. Wigan.—Miles Gerrard, esquire, of Ince, was lately indicted for fourteen months absence from church, and is "estreated into the Exchequer, without any tryall of jury," though he traversed and pleaded for the same. The "commone voice of his country" imputes this to the negligence of his attorney. The truth is, he was most part of the time "so extreame sicke that he was, nexte under God, preserved by drinkinge of goates milke," and for rest of the time too weak to "come aud abide one houre in the churche." The writers certify that the said Miles, under ordinary circumstances, is a regular attendant at church.

Oliver Carter, "preacher, of Manchester," Edward Fleetwood, "parsone of Wygan," William Leighe, "parson of Standishe," Edward Assheton, "parson of Mydleton," Peter Shawe, parson of Bury, Edward Welshe, "vycar of Blakeburne," William Langley, "parson of Prestwiche," John Buckley, "preacher att Manchester," John Hill, "preacher at Prestwiche," Thomas Hunte, "preacher at Oldham," and Richard Mydgley, "pastour of Ratchdall," to the Archbishop [of York].

f. 103d. 1590, October.—At the Archbishop's late visitation, they were commanded by "Mr. Doctor Gibson" to appear before the Bishop [of Chester], at Manchester, and give evidence as to their conformity. This they did, and were enjoined to make answer to the Bishop, by November 1, as to their future action with regard to conformity. As they understand that this action originated with the Archbishop, and as it is to "receive its end" before him, they think it their duty not only to return their answer to the Bishop, but also to send it to the Archbishop, and beg he will require no "more particular" answer than that set down, because none of them, so far as they can perceive, were presented at the said visitation for not using "the commone booke," or for refusing "to weare the surpleasse att any tyme, beinge duelie tendered unto us," or for preaching "againste the commone booke or any parte thereof"; and, moreover, because it "woulde requyre a more particular consideration of all poinctes in the common booke then the tyme lymited unto us" would afford.

They ask the Archbishop—in considering their actions—to remember "the generall state of the people amongese who wee live, standinge of two sortes: the obstinate papists and the zealous professours of relligione. The one sorte beinge (as St. Paule speaketh of the Athenians) in all thinges too superstitious, and therefore make every ceremonie of our churche, but especiallie that of the crosse, as an idoll of their churche; the other sorte, so farre carried into scandall at those thinges which so greatlie are drawen into abuse by the papists, that plainlie many of them woulde in sondrie places leave us and our ministration, yf wee shoulde be broughte under the power of the same, whome to grieve in any thinge of that kind, it maye seem no small matter to such of their pastours, especiallie by whom they have been reclaimed from poperie and broughte to the ghospell, in respecte of bothe; which, howsoever otherwise they may be thoughte lawfull and toillerable ellswhere, yett assuredlie in these partes of our country, they may seem lesse expediente then in any other parte of the realme."

The Archbishop is also reminded that, for many years, the writers have been called—both by the Ecclesiastical Commission, "when it was," and by the civil authority, since the former has ceased—to make presentment of the "papists" amongst them, by which means many have been reformed, but the greater part "styrred up in rancour and mallice againste us"; these persons, taking advantage of the present "proceedings" against the writers, and thinking "all protection to be taken from us," begin "to make revenge of our former dutifull ymploiments againste them by bringinge us in questione att the Assizes and sesses, for these matters of inconformite." The writers also feel "a grievous smart" at their prosecutions, by those "whom wee bould for reverend fathers and protectours."

Consideration of all this has hitherto led their own bishop to deal favourably with them in such matters, and they do not doubt that, "of himselfe," he intends to continue so to do; they also presume that like considerations have drawn similar favour from the Archbishop himself and his predecessors; therefore, as their latter dealings have not altered from their former, they trust to receive similar favour to that which they have before received, by which they "doubte not but your lordshippe shall finde a farre greater blessinge to the good reformation of our country from the grosse idolatory and heathenish prophanations which yet contynue with many amongste us, then yf a more strycte course were taken in these smaller matters of inconformity in the preachers." In this behalf they have requested Mr. Hopwood, a justice of the county, one of the Ecclesiastical Commission, and "an earneste favourer of the preachers and the worke of the mynesterie," to attend the Archbishop with the present letter, that the Archbishop may be by him more fully informed of their doings.

Postscript.—For satisfaction of the Archbishop's order proposed to the writers in the College of Manchester, on September 2, their joint answer is, that they have "heretofore generallie used the commone booke in all dyvine service and none other; and in all other thinges which concerne our public mynistery have so peaceablie carried ourselves, as well in practyze as doctrine, that the adversaries of religione amongeste whom wee live are not able justlie to charge us to have bene contemners of authoryty or recusauts of any thinge by lawe prescribed, [and] so wee meane (by God's grace) hereafter to contynue."

—————— to ———— BUNNY, forwarding the foregoing letter.

f. 105. 1590, November 14. Staincliff.—"I receaved upon Mundaye laste this letter, dyrected to my Lord Archbishop, and beinge acquainted with his purpose to wryte to our bushoppe, and hopinge his Grace will, the xvj[th] or xvij[th] of this instante, be in Yorke, I thoughte yt my duety to sende this bearer to you, entreatinge you to deliver' the same to his grace, yf hee be in Yorke; yf not, then helpe this bearer, and I praie that you will deliver them to my Lorde of Yorke.

"I have delivered to Mr. Fleetwood that his Grace woulde, att the returne of Dr. Gybsonne (which in fewe daies, hee expected) wryte to

the Bushoppe of Chester his pleasure concerninge the letters receaved by me, and that his Grace charged me, in his name, to desire
them to be carefull of themselves and not give their adversaries cause to
rejoyce by withdrawinge ther dueties from ther gratious Prince, in
matters of endefferencie, but rather of ther owne accordes to take some
time betwixte this and nexte Candlemas to put on the surpleasse, eyther
by themselves or ther curates, and yf any of them did thinke yt not
a matter endifferente, that then they would take ther. journey to
Yorke, and conferre with his lordshipp, who was in good hope to
persuade them to conformitie, as all the preachers within the diocesse of
Yorke are, excepte one onlie man.   And this is the effecte of my
speache from my Lord his Grace to them.

"You knowe, Mr. Bunye, his Grace's respyte was till our Lady daye
in Lente, but I have not acquainted any therwith, excepte Mr. Fleetwood, bycause I would have them to come on speedilie in this action,
and I meane, this nexte Christetyde, to admonishe all and every of them
which have not then done as ys required and desired, to be mindfull
of his Lordshipp's milde dealinge towardes them, and yf this course
have no goode effecte, I will, *Deo volente,* nexte Candlemas, chide with
them severelie, and yf that take no good successe, I will, before our
Lady daye in Lente, exclame and in sorte braide against them.   And
now, Mr. Bunny, yf I might, by your good meanes, be so boulde with
my Lord Archbishop as to begge att his Grace's handes the enlargeinge
of this tolleration for one syx weekes longer then our Ladye daye in
Lente, then woulde I frame myselve to deale by all courteous
persuations with them, as att the fyrste I begunne, and yf then I cannot prevaile, I wil leavel them to taste the fruites of there owne
humoures."

Postscript.—"I praye you deale earnestlie with my Lord Archbishop
for the tolleration for one syx weekes, bycause some of them have bene
planters or founders of religion in these partes, contynuall well users of
ther lyberty so many yeares enjoyed, and therfore yt behovethe me to
use all goode meanes I maye, that this corner of my country mighte
still enjoye them, excepte they shall endirectlie cutte of themselves, and
I feare none of them more then your and my old friend, that moste
honeste natured gentleman, Mr. Langley; and for the ould vycar you
knowe I doe not knowe what to saie, but leave him to Jesus Christe."

JOHN, ARCHBISHOP OF YORK, to [EDMUND HOPWOOD].

f. 108d. 1590, December 7. Cawood Castle.—Upon conference with
Doctor Gibson, he understands that the order taken with the preachers of
Manchester deanery was taken with others in his visitation "where the
like occasion was offered." Nearly all those who signed the letter sent to
him, were presented for not wearing the surplice; their conduct on that
point was "evydent" and "complained of." They allege that they did
not speak against the common book, but their "actions and exemplers"
are witness to the contrary. "Yf any doubte aryse in the common
booke, the preface of the same doth apoincte an order for the resolution
thereof, so yt be not contrarie to the booke." In their other allegations,
he sees no reason for breaking the "order of the churche, established by
authority, and not being contrary to God his worde." He, therefore,
requires that divine service be celebrated in their churches according to
the order of the common book, and "the sacraments administered in a
surpleasse." If any of them desire conference with him, "they shalbe
moste hartilie wellcome." Desires to know what is done herein. · ' ' '

EDMUND HOPWOOD to the ARCHBISHOP OF YORK.

f. 112. 1590–1, January 15.—Has signified the Archbishop's pleasure to the preachers above referred to. Perceives that some of them will "repaire to your grace" for conference. If they do not, before the end of the next February, he will certify what he thinks of every of them in particular. Sends a note of the "enormities of the Saboathe, used in these parts," and suggests means for repressing them. "Wee have in our service booke, thirteen daies appointed for fastinge, but no frequentinge of publique praier, service and sermone, upon those daies." If the Archbishop could "procure" that yearly on those days, "or some twoe or three of them," all or the greatest part of the householders dwelling within two miles of their parish church should send on each of those days "one person of their particular families" to such services, and—"for want of a discreet preacher"—to hear one of the homilies "distinctely and plainlie read"; this would be a good means to work a "continuall and holly sorrowe for our sinns." Asks favour for Mr. Hunt, curate and preacher at Oldham[1]; does not know what is "enformed againste him," but hopes the Archbishop will find him a "discreet, peaceable, and honeste man;" begs that, so long as he seeks the peace of the church, he may continue in his ministry.

ARTICLES TO BE OBSERVED BY THE CLERGY IN THE DIOCESE OF CHESTER.

f. 109. 1590–1, January 22.—"Articles to be observed in every churche, chapell, and parishe, throughoute the diocese of Chester, by the persons, vycars, curates, and churchwardens."

(1.) The names and addresses of those who absent themselves from church are to be returned by the churchwardens of the different parishes, and fines for non-attendance are to be given towards the relief of the poor.

(2.) The clergy are to use all diligence to reclaim such as be "recusants or non-communicants," as they shall think best.

(3.) Every parson and vicar having two benefices, or being absent from his benefice by dispensation, or that is impotent, or that will keep any curate to assist him in his church, is, before the next midsummer, to provide "suche a learned preacher or other sufficiente minister" to serve in his said church and parish, as the Bishop or his officers shall allow. None to be appointed till they have received the said Bishop's authority.

(4.) The inhabitants of every chapel[ry] of ease—other than such as have a curate found by the parson or vicar of the parish—are to provide either a learned preacher or sufficient curate to serve in such chapel; such person to be examined and allowed, as aforesaid.

PROVISION OF SURPLICES.

f. 110. 1590–1, January 22.—Directions by the Bishop of Chester, *inter alia*, that all churchwardens shall provide, at the charge of their several parishes or chapelries, before the following Lady Day, for each of their parish churches and chapels, "two surpleasses, the one to be made in decente, usuall, and comely manner, of whyte lynnen clothe, the pryse thereof to be 2s. 6d. the yard at the leaste, for the parson,

---

[1] Hunt is one of the signatories to the letter to the Archbishop on the subject of conformity.

vycar, or curate, of that churche or chappell to weare in the administration of comon praier, of the sacraments, and other rytes and ceremonies of the Churche of England; and the other to be for the clarke of everye churche or chappell aforesaid, to be made of whyte lynnen clothe allso, the pryse whereof to be att the discretion of the said churchwardens in their severall churches and chappells." The churchwardens are also to make quarterly returns, stating if the surplices are used in accordance with these directions.

THOMAS RYCH, dean of the deanery of Manchester, to " MR. MIDGLEY, parson of Rochdale," and all Curates and Churchwardens of the same parish.

f. 111. 1590-1, January 26.—Commanding them to attend at the church of Bury and learn the directions imposed on them by the Queen, Privy Council, and Archbishop of York.

The BISHOP OF CHESTER to [the CLERGY and CHURCH OFFICIALS of his diocese].

1590-1, January 22.—Urging diligent enquiry after recusants, and the dealing with them " by learned, wise, and gentle enstructions, exhortations, admonitions, and reprehensions, and partly by ecclesiastical censure."

[EDMUND HOPWOOD] to [the ARCHBISHOP OF YORK].

f. 112d. 1590-1, February 23.—" Your honour doeth knowe how destitute Lancashire is of preachers, and therefor I will spare the dis.coverie thereof; but bycause the harvest ys greate and the labourers too (?) fewe, I beseche your Lordship, in Jesus Christe crucyfied, to finde out some good meanes to relieve these moste greate and pytiful wantes." Two preachers should be continually resident in Lancashire—one at Liverpool and one at Preston in Amounderness ; the first place being a " haven toune " and the other " a very great markette toune as any within Lancashire, and is within 10 myles of the sea coaste." Liver. pool is " a chapell belonging unto the parishe churche of Walton." The parson there is Alexander Mollyneux, uncle to Sir Richard Mollyneux of Seiphton [Sefton ?], " a yonge gent not inferiour to any of worship in Lancashire," but he is unlearned, and not used to " say service or administer sacraments." Suggests that he might bestow 20l. a year on a preacher. Preston is an impropriation belonging to the Queen. The farmer is " Mr. Houghton, or his mother, Mrs. Houghton, who is a recusant of seven yeares standinge." The vicar is " an old grave man of simple persuatione in dyvinity and one that in his youthe hath used sondrie callinges, and now at laste settled himself in the ministery." Suggests that Houghton or his mother should yield 36l., and the farmer of the vicarage 4l. a year, to support a resident preacher at Preston; knows no place in Lancashire " more fytter for a weekly lecture."

The " enormoties " of the Sabboth, in Lancashire, which require suppression are these :—" Fayres, marketts, wakes, ales, maye-games, pypinge and dauncing, bear-beates, bull-beates, resorting to ale-howses in tyme of dyvyne service, huntinge, hawkinge, and all manner of unlawfull gaminge."

The " charitable and honourable respite your Grace did give " to the
preachers in " this corner of Lancashire," has not wrought the good
effect desired, as neither they nor their curates use the surplice.

REFUSERS OF THE SURPLICE.

f. 113d.—Memorandum about those who refuse to use the surplice.
Amongst these are " Rychard Mydgley, vycar of Ratchdall, a contry
scholler, yet discrete, sober, and very peaceable, the only first planter of
sounde religion in this corner of our contrye, in her Majestie's tyme,
and sythence his first entraunce, hath not used the surpleasse in his
churche; yet hath used his mynistrey very peaceablie, and had at his
monethlie communions above eighte hundred communicantes that
zealouslye cryd 'Thy kingdom come.'" The writer of the memorandum
[Edmund Hopwood ?] continues that he thinks this vicar will conform
" or elles peaceablie give over his ministery and praie for the simplesete
in authority." Continues with several quotations from " Bishopp
Jewell, of blessed memorye," and concludes by setting forth that the
then Bishop of Winchester, when Bishop of Lincoln, preached and printed,
in the year 1580, sermons against the "fryndes and favourers of the
Churche of Rome," in one of which he says :—" As for the controversie
of apparell, as ther ys in yt some diversitie of judgment, so ys there
no seperation of Christian faithe and charity; for sure I am, that
neyther they that doe refuse the appointed apparell doe condemne us
that wear [it]—I speake of them that be learned—neyther we, that at
the Prynce's order receave yt, doe hate them that, of conscience for
certain consyderations, think they may not safelie use it, although in this
matter wee wishe that they would do as we doe."

The ARCHBISHOP OF YORK to [EDMUND] HOPWOOD.

f. 115. 1590-1, February 26. Bishopthorpe.—Thanks him for his
friendly letters. Has good hope the preachers will conform ; will welcome Mr. Fleetwood and Mr. Leigh, who are " Godlie learned men."
Bishop Jewell, in the passages quoted by Hopwood, " dothe not condemne the orders of our churche, nor maketh the use of them ungodlie ;
the opinione of that singular man in those points ys very well knowne."

The SAME to the SAME.

Ibid. 1591, September 12. Bishopthorpe.—Hopes the ministers
about him have conformed. Has been rebuked by the authorities for
" slack dealinge " with regard to these matters.

[EDMUND HOPWOOD to the ARCHBISHOP OF YORK.]

f. 119. Undated.—Answer to the foregoing. Did not think the
Archbishop expected further answer than that made by the writer on
February 23. " Our preachers and ministers here contynue the same
course they did when I attended your Grace att Cawood. I have
sondrie times signified to suche of them as I thoughte not affected to
the conformity requyred, that yf all or any of them were desyrous of
conference " they would be welcomed by the Archbishop. Is sorry his
—the Archbishop's—" mylde proceedings " have not wrought better
effect.

RICHARD SHERBURN and RICHARD HOLLAND, Deputy Lieutenants of Lancashire, to SIR RICHARD SHUTTLEWORTH, RICHARD ASSHETON, RALPH ASSHETON, CHRISTOPHER ANDERTON, EDMUND HOPWOOD, and JOHN BRADSHAW, Esquires.

f. 117d. 1591, May 24.—The Privy Council has informed them that the King of Spain "hath a navy allready come to the seas, uppon the costes of Brytaine," and therefore required the due watching of beacons, reviewing of the county forces, and the placing under arms of the "tenaunts, servants, and wellwishers" of those addressed in this letter. A postscript mentions that "Mr. Asheton, of Leaver, doe dwell neerest unto the beacon upon Ryvington Hill."

——————— to the BISHOP OF ———————.

f. 120. 1591, October 6. Middleton.—Last year, Mr. Henry Stanley, "of good accounte and of the best estimation in our countrie," died intestate and seized of certain tithes in Ireland; he left no issue. His wife is entitled to a reasonable third part of his possessions, and to obtain this has sent her brother, Mr. Richard Southworth, into Ireland, she being unable to travel. Begs the Bishop to be to him "a sure friend," whilst in Ireland.

The EARL OF DERBY to ———————.

f. 123. 1591-2, February 7. Lathom.—In order that the same course be held in the execution of the Queen's commission as to recusants in Lancashire, lets him know the plan already adopted and to be followed "upon Wednesdaye nexte," which is that all who persist in their recusancy —"knightes' and esquires' wives and daughters only excepted"—shall be committed to gaol and not only have the oath tendered to them as set down in "the instructions," but also answer certain questions, now enclosed, which only concern allegiance, and not religion or conscience; "to all which, what the two Blundells and Lathom of Misseberowe (?) have answered, whome I have comytted, I have now sende you for your better satysfaction." The persons above excepted are to be "removed from ther dwellinges and to be comytted to the keepinge (att there owne charges) of some gentleman, their kinsman, or other well given in relligione, ther still to be furthcoming, tyll further order be taken;" such as conform are to undertake the continuance of their conformity.
Questions enclosed :
(1.) "Doe you thinke her Majestie lawfull Queene of these her dominions, or no ?
(2.) "Do you thinke, and be fully assured, that she hath as much power over the person and goodes of all her subjectes as any kinge christened (*sic*) hathe ?
(3.) "In case of warres betwixte her Majestie and the Pope, or Kinge of Spaine, for any cause or quarrell whatsoever, whose parte would you take ?"

RECUSANTS IN SALFORD AND BLACKBURN HUNDREDS.

ff. 124-126d. 1591-2, January 26.—The names of persons in Salford and Blackburn hundreds, presented at Bury as obstinate recusants, with a memorandum of such as have produced proof of their conformity. The return for Manchester is "*bene*," but the following persons were in the Fleet there :—"John Lee, gentleman, and Mary his wife, Christofer Hankes, preste, Rauffe Scott, preste, William Willsoun, preste, Raphe

Walker, scholemaster, Umfraye Cartwright, master in arts, Luce Siges-wike, Catheren Marshe, [and] Ellyn Chaunce." Throughout the list, many men and women are shown to have been committed to prison for "obstinacye."

COMMISSION TO ENQUIRE AFTER RECUSANTS.

ff. 127–129d. 1590, November 23.—Copy of the Queen's Commission concerning the diligent enquiry after recusants, and of the articles thereto annexed "for the further instruction" to the Commissioners, how to proceed in the execution thereof. One of the questions to be put is, "Whether have you bene att Rome, Rhemes, or in Spaine, at any time within these fyve yeares?"

RECOGNIZANCE OF CONFORMITY.

ff. 130d–135. 1591–2, February 9.—"The recognizance of con-formity taken at Burye," and forms of warrants to gaolers, for receiving convicted persons, to church-wardens, and others.

The COUNCIL to [the EARL OF DERBY].

f. 135. 1592, March 25. Whitehall.—They commend his late zealous public proceeding as to recusants, and also the steps taken by himself, "privately, in refermation of your oun tenauntes, for their wyllfullnes in not resortinge to ther parishe churches," and refusing to assist in the general reformation of Lancashire, "which was allmoste overflowed" with obstinate persons.

RICHARD HOLLAND to RICHARD ASSHETON, High Sheriff of Lancashire.

f. 141. 1593, October 26. Manchester.—For answer to the late letter from Council touching the execution of the Act for the relief of aged and maimed soldiers, states that the sum directed was duly rated on the different parishes, but that, as yet, no soldiers have come to demand the benefit of the Act, with proper certificates from the "generalls or captaynes" under whom they served, though divers soldiers not so furnished have applied for relief.

The COUNCIL to RICHARD HOLLAND, of Denton, and others in the Commission of the Peace for Lancashire.

f. 145d. 1595, August 5.—Upon petition lately exhibited to them by "the shermen" of Manchester and Salford, they referred to the Chancellor of the Exchequer and the Master of the Rolls the hearing of a matter in controversy between those persons and the "traders and clothiers of those partes," concerning "the cottoninge of all cottons, rugges and fryzes, made within the county of Lancaster." Certain orders were thereupon drawn up, which the Council now desire those addressed to see properly executed. A joint complaint was also made by the said clothiers and traders against the searchers of London, concerning a seizure, lately made by them, of a great quantity of cotton, supposing the same to be . . . . being "fryzes" and, as they thought, not sealed. At the hearing by the Chancellor of the Exchequer and Master of the Rolls, above referred to, bond was taken of the traders to stand by such award as the Council, the Lord Treasurer, and the Chancellor of the Exchequer, should make; for the better understanding of the matter, the "know-ledge" of those addressed is now requested.

The Award referred to in the Foregoing.

f. 146. 1595, August 1.—" Whereas upon the petition exhibited to the Lordes of her Majestie's most honorabell Privie Counsell by William Sorocold, for and in the names of the shermen of Manchester and Salford on the one party, and the traders of Manchester, Bolton, and Bury, on the other party, yt pleased their honors (by their honors' letters) to committ the hearinge and examination of the cause to the right honorabell Sir John Forteskew, knight, Chauncellor of Her Majestie's Court of Exchequier, and the Right Woorshippfull Sir Thomas Egreton, knight, Master of the Roles.

" The saied Committees havinge hard and examined the cause, this first day of August 1595, they have, with the assent of the sayed parties, set downe these articcles as notes of orders which they thinke convenient to bee established, touchinge the same, viz :—

" 1. Whereas the saied Sorocold, in the names of the said shermen, demaundeth the cottoninge of all such cottones, rugges and fryzes, as are used to bee within the County Palantine of Lancaster, the said tralers affirming against yt that yt would bee greate hurte to the makers thereof in the countrey, beinge the greater number, yt ys agreed by both the saied parties, and thought good by the saied Committees, that suche order shalbe sett downe therein as might redownd to the releive and contentment of the greatest number of peopill that live thereby, to thend the most store or quantetie thereof might bee vented or saved for theire benefite.

" 2. Therefore yt ys thought meet by the saied Committees, and consented unto by the sayed Sorocold, and those parties that answere for the saied traders, that the trade or occupyinge of cottons, rugges, and fryzes, shall still go forwarde (as ys accostomed) till further order be taken therein, to thend the poore peopell shall not exclaime for want of woorke.

" 3. Also yt ys thought good by the saied Committees, and agreed unto by the saied parties that appeared beefore them, that in consideration the cottones fittinge for London might comonly [be] rowed as they were accustomed before this complaint made, the shermen shall have eightpence a peece for the well rowinge and burlinge of everie peece thereof to be done by them, in respect they neyther shere them nor cotton them as they doo other cottons fittinge for forraine trade beyonde the seas and elswhere, as the partyes desire to have them.

" 4. Also yt ys thought convenient by the saied Committees that, for the oversight of this rowinge and burlinge to bee done for the good of the cloth, there shalbe appoincted and chosen in Manchester and Salforde yerely, from yeare to yeare, twoo persons of judgment and knowledge therein, to bee vewers and overseeres thereof, the one a trader, thother a sherman, and the lyke in everie other towne where suche other clothe ys made, to the end that suche as fynde themselves greived that theire clothe shall not bee well wrought as yt ought to bee, maie complaine to the said overseeres of the parties not doinge theire dutyes in theire woorke, and that the offendours maie receyve punishment accordinge to the qualety of theire offence, and the saied overseeres to bee appoincted by Mr. Richard Holland, Richard Assheton of Midleton, Ralph Assheton of Lever, and Edmund Hopwood, esquires, or any one of theym.

" 5. Also yt ys thought meet by the saied Committees that no trader useinge to buy clothe within the saied county to carry or cause to bee carryed out of the same, shall or maie rowe, pirche, shere, or cotton the same within his owne howse or elswhere, eyther by himselve or any other by his procurement, but shall cause the same to be rowed, shorne, and cottoned, by suche shermen or woorkmen as the owner of the cloth shall bee thought fitt and woorthie to have the doinge thereof, in respect of theire good woorkmanshipp, and shall bee so accompted of by the twoo overseeres afforesaied, respectivelie, in the places of their office and charge. For that yt ys thought there be diveres who, for the tyme, use to take into theire howses suche persons as they neyther give' meate nor drinke unto, and but very small wages for the present tyme."

Further, whereas by a petition exhibited in the names of the clothiers and traders " of the County Palantyne of Lancaster, complainte was made of the searcheres of London for that they had made seazure of a greate quantetie of cottones, rugges, and fryzes, whereby the saied traders were prohibited there ordinary markett in London ; these searcheres pretend-inge a forfeyture of the moste parte of the saied cottones, affirminge them to be fryzes and not sealled (as they ought to bee), neyther by the owners nor the awlnager.

" To which pretence yt ys answered and affirmed, on the behalve of the snied traders, that they are cottones, and sealled accordinge to there nature, bothe by the owners and the awlnager, and so shall be prooved by the makers and owners thereof, for that they differ nothinge in sub-stance, spinninge, weavinge, mylninge, nor any other woorkmanshipp, neyther in waight nor length, but onely in cullour, which cullour was lately deceased for the greate good of the countrey and releive of the poore therein ; for the trade of the oulde sorte of cottones which were sent into France, Spayne, and other places, was cleane overthrowne, by reason of warres and trobeiles that happened in those countryes where they were usuallie vented and soulde, so that these graye colloured cottones (beinge fitt for England) were putt in use and made, to the great good of many peopell and releive of greate nombers of familyes and howseholdes in the countrey, which otherwise had [been] given to greate wante and misery yf the cullour had not bene altered and devized, as nowe yt ys used.

" Uppon the hearinge of this cause betweene the saied traders and searchers by the sayed Sir John Forteskew and Sir Thomas Egerton, as afforesaied, It ys ordered that the saied traders and clothiers shall put in suerties, to bee bound in fower hundred powndes, to stande to the awarde and judgmente of the Right Honorable the Lord High Thresorer of England and of the saied Sir John Forteskew, touchinge the saied matter and controversie that for theire Honors' better information therein, reporte or certifficate shall bee made from the worshipful justices of peace, Mr. Richard Holland of Denton, Mr. Richard Assheton of Middleton, Mr. Ralph Assheton of Lever, and Mr. Edmund Hopwood of Hopwood, which justices shall trie and certefy, from the clothiers and makers of the countrie where the saied cottones and frizes are made, wether they bee cottones or fryzes that bee in controversie as aforesaied. For that the saied traders affirme that they have fryzes made in the countrey, accordinge to the statute provided for them ; but that these graye cottones are cottones in waighte and length,. accordinge to the forme of the ould sorte of cottones made in the same cuntrey, accordinge to the statute in that behalve. And therefore, the awlnager and seallers do continewe theire seallinge as they were accus-tomed, untill furder order be taken in the cause."

A SUBSIDY.

ff. 148–152. Undated.—"The whole subsidie for landes and goodes in Derby hundreth " in Lancashire. A long list of names.

A Subsidy.

ff. 152d.–156d. 1591, September 26.—A similar return for the hundreds of Blackburn, Amounderness, Leylond, and Lonsdale.

Memorandum of the arraignment, at Newgate, of William Hacket, of Northamptonshire, for high treason.

f. 159d. 1591, July 26.—There were two indictments found by the great inquest against him. (1) For these traiterous words against the Queen: "that her Majestie was no longer Queene of Englande, but deposed and deprived by the spriritte and the dyrector of the crowne of Englande; the same spiritte referred to the absolute disposicion of the saide Hackett," and that he "did trayterouslie debruze and deface her Majestie's armes in one Kaye's house, by London Bridge, inveighinge then and there bytterlie againste her Majestie, in most trayterous and despite-full manner." (2) Plotting with Coppinger and Ardington for the "pretended reformation of the abuses of the Churche of Englande," and determining to carry out their resolution by force of arms. Hackett was to "usurpe the name of the highe prophette, participatinge the nature of the Almighty Sonne of God," and Coppinger and Ardington were to be his "prophetts to preparre his waies; the one of them to be called the prophett of Justice, the other of Mercye." These two were to "preache repentance in the streets of London, of purpose that the bretheren of the faction coming together in tumulte, mighte possesse themselves of the Cytie of London" and then proceed to depose the Queen. Ardington and Coppinger began their preaching "at the Blacke Fryers, throughe the high streets in London, and continuing ther course untill they came to Cheapside," announced the day of Judgment to be at hand, and that confusion was present upon all, unless they repented.

"Having reached Cheapside, and the people being gathered to hear them, they went into a cart "and then and there did bytterlie inveighe againste the present government, the Lord Archbishop of Canterbury, and the Lord Chancellor of England, as traytours to the state and the churche, advising the people to undertake to themselves the reformation of those abuses and the restitution of christian purity." Besides this, Hackett, seeing the Queen's picture in Kaye's house, "did, with an iron instrument, villainouslie and trayterouslie deface the pycture, and especiallie that part of the picture which represented her Majestie's harte, raylinge most traiterously againste her Majestie's personne." To the first indictment he pleaded guilty, "swearinge most horriblie, and blaspheminge the name of Allmightie God, in most odious maner, to the great terror of all that harde him." When asked to answer to the second indictment he answered the Court "in gybinge manner," that "they were wise inoughe to know what they had to doe withowt his advise, and therefore he would not direct them." At last, when pressed to answer, he pleaded not guilty. The Clerk of the Crown thereupon asked him if he would be tried by God and the Jury, and he answered "that he would be tryed by the Jury onlie, utterlie, in plaine tearmes, renouncinge Allmightie God in such damnable manner as ys unfiytt to be repeated."

"Upon this the Court purposed to have found him guilty of default of answer; but "Mr. Attorney Generall—perceivinge this pollicie, that to the indictment which only touched his traytrous speeches which he had uttered before sundrie of her Majestie's privie counsell and divers others, he pleaded guilty," and that to the other indictment, "wherein was contained the very ground of this treasone, he would not directly confess it," but answered " in such scoffing manner as though he were then franticke "—intreated leave, " for satisfaction of everye man, and that the matter shoulde not be carried awaie in the cloudes—with this apparante exception, that in all appearancie Hackett was franticke, and therefore his confession, or not answering, on conviction to others that are questioned in the same cause—that he mighte make it evydente to the worlde uppon what grounde and ententione this presente action had been undertaken and performed by the saide Hackett and his fellowe traytours."

This obtained, the Attorney General pointed out that any " franticke humours lately contrived " should have no influence upon this conspiracy, which was very carefully planned, so as to obtain from the Queen by " plaine strengthe, what they could not obtain by their trayterous petycons," in proof of which he urged :—

(1) That Hackett, Coppinger, and Ardington, were as " inward and familiar " with Cartwright, Wiggington, Udall, and Newman, as any other " of that faction."

(2) That on Cartwright's imprisonment, Hackett and the others " procured a solemne meetinge in a woode, where great consultation was had concerninge the deliverye of ther restrained bretheren."

(3) That Coppinger, in the previous Hilary term, after the said conference, wrote to Udall " then and nowe in Newgate," who had been convicted, the year before, of felony. At that time Coppinger was not suspected of lunacy, but " had as good accesse to some nobles of her Majestie's privie counsell as any person of his qualitye had," the tenor of the letter being as follows:—" As far furthe as I coulde note yt, being redd by the clarke of the crowne, Right Reverend Saint in the Lord, my forbearinge to visit you and the reste of our bretheren, who suffer for righteousness' sake, mighte give you just cause to suspecte that I should have forsaken my first love to our cause; but you are endowed with the guifte of discerninge spiritts, and, therefore, may easilie understaunde that my coming unto you mighte procure me more daunger then yt coulde pleasure you, notwithstandinge assuring you and the reste of our bretheren, of my settled contynuance in the faithe, these are to entreate your brotherhood to joine in praier that yt wolde please the Lorde to blesse the labors of me and others who have taken another course for the furtheraunce of the common cause, that ys the building up of Syon and destruction to Babell, &c." Udall received this letter and concealed it, and afterwards, upon search of Wiggington's chamber, copies of divers letters and pamphlets were found, to the purposes following :—(1) Copies of 200 letters were dispersed on July 13, two days before " the action in the streets," directed to divers brethren, " but especiallie to the sisters of that faction, as to the weaker vessells," signifying that the brethren of their church had undertaken a course of reformation to which they must put " their helping handes," which action was " prentlie " to be put in execution. (2) Printed pamphlets, to the number of 1,000, in bundles, to be sent to the brethren in Warwickshire, Northamptonshire, Essex, and Hertfordshire, of which some are already abroad, to satisfy the brethren " in the reason of this course taken for reformation." In these pamphlets the doctrine of predestination was grossly abused, to this purpose, that the saints of God were pre-elected and pre-destined to join in this action, and therefore, the doing of it was warranted and not to be refused, because they were forechosen by God's providence for accomplishing His

pleasure. A second sort of printed pamphlets for the laity were in rhyme—in this manner :—

> " Yf you in youthe will learne
> A courtier for to be,
> Then must thou first come knowe
> Thy lessen true of me :
> A christian trew, althoughe he be a cloune,
> Shall teache a prince to wear his scepter and his crown."

There was also printed an order to the privy council and all the Queen's officers, not to leave their houses during the tumult, in order to appease it, till Hackett and his confederates had possessed themselves of the city ; in return for which favour it was promised that the rioters would "not proceed to the question of her Majestie's lyffe or of any her privie counsel's," though there was "never a good man amongest them." There was, however, to be "some personall correctione, as well of her sacred Majestie as of her honorable counsellors " as a precedent, for fear of "a relapse thereafter." The printer of these pamphlets died, "for sorrow," two days after his arrest.

The Attorney did not go into the rest of the evidence, as it concerned others not as yet impeached, and as he considered that brought out sufficient to prove treason.

"Mr. Sollicitor" then followed with "a most excellent discourse," saying that "no treason was so dangerous to the estate as that proceeding from so base puddelles shaddowed with the glosse of a pretended holliness, forasmuche as yf a nobleman rebell, his meaninge ys onelie to usurpe the Crowne, not impayringe the governmente ; but ther can be no means to these peasants to accomplishe ther purpose, excepte by the absolute extirpation of all governmente, magistracy, nobility and gentrye, with the utter subversione and ruine of all lawes that should suppresse these ther trayterous actions." This he exemplified with the rebellions of "Cade, Taylor, and them of Norfolke " in the reign of Edward VI., but "the verye paterne of this conspiracy, Mr. Sollicitor remembered in Sleidon's (sic) comentaries, and practysed in Westphalia by one John Leydone, the Archana baptiste, who with his adherency, by this very practize, surprised ther the most famous cytye of Mounster, as I thinke hee named yt ; and no difference in the worlde betwene that action and this conspiracie. And, therefore, most plainlie and evidentlie, yt was never complotted by men possessed with frency or lunacies. And, further, Mr. Sollicitor protested, to his comforte, that howsoever there was some questione in the churche of Englande for ceremonies and other unnecessary mattres, yet a true christian mighte have the free and whole practize of his christian religione in the churche now established, and therefore noe occasion to any good subjecte to mutine againste this her Majestie's most absolute and blessed government."

After Hackett's default of answer had been recorded, Mr. Recorder pronounced sentence of high treason, and Hackett was accordingly executed in Cheapside on the Wednesday following, being the 28th of July, "continuing, to his laste breathe, his blasphemous course of raylinge."

" The mannar how my LORD LIEUTENAUNTE and GOVERNOUR GENERALL proceded in his jorny for the victuallinge of the Forte of the Lesse, and so to divers other places."

f. 162d. 1599, May 9.—" Uppon the nynthe of Maye, his Lordship advanced forwardes from the Castell of Dubbline towardes the victuallinge of the forte of the Lesse, being attended with many honorable personages, gentlemen, and souldiars. The armye lodged this nighte at the Nasse.

10th.—" This daye, the armye remooved. His Honor lodged at Castell Martyn, and part of the armye was quartered in severall townes there adjoyninge.

11th.—" This daye, the armye marched to Kilrusshe, where the generall rendevous was appointed; the wholle force then beinge mett, his Honor appointed the vawwarde (sic), the battell, and rearegarde of bothe foote and horse; all which beinge advaunced forwardes, intelligence was broughte that the enemye was in his lordship's waye before hime, whereuppon hee sent forthe his lesse shotte and pitche uppon eyther syde of his battelleres. They were 100 in number, but at the firste chasinge of our men, they runne awaye. The army lodged, this nighte, a myle shorte of the bridge of Athey, at which place the Lorde of Ormonde came unto his lordship and broughte with hime Vicomte Mumgaratt, who was leifetenaunt to Terrone of all his forces, and the Lord of Clare, bothe which had been in this rebellione. They, uppon theire knees, submitted themselves withowte conditione.

12th.—" This daye James Fitz Pearce, a rebell, havinge a castell upon the bridge of Athey, delivered the same unto his lordshipp, submittinge himsellfe withowte conditione, and also delivered upp the howse called Woodstorkle, which was neare adjoyninge, at which place the army lodged that nighte.

13th and 14th.—" These dayes the armye removed not, but my Lord [1] lodged those nightes at Captain Lea his howse. Uppon the 14th, the rebells neare to his howse offered skyrmishe to us. My Lord Graye, goinge contrarye to my Lord of Southampton's comandement, hee beinge General of the Horse, was that night comitted to the Marshall.

15th.—" This daye, the armye removed; my Lord lefte in the Castell of ——— [2] and Castle Woodsuche, souldiars, 50 apeece. In our march towardes the Blacke Forde, the rebells offered skyrmishe, but would not stand, but fled before us. This night, wee encamped at Stradburye, neare Cosbie's howse.

16th.—" This daye, the armie removed. My Lord victualled the forte of the Lesse, knighted Sir Fraunces Rialie (?), Captain of that fort of Lesse, added unto his number 500 solldiers more, and soe retourned to the campe, which was neare unto a howse of Sir Thomas Coldouphes(?), not fare from which place the rebelles likewise encamped in our sighte. Onye Macke Rorie was there chieffe comaunder. Hee sent challenge to my Lord to fight 100 to 100, which by his Honor was excepted, but in the morninge the villaines would not performe it.

17th.—" This daye, the armye marched throughe the ——— of ——— were the rebelles fought with us; Captain Boswell and Captain Gardener were slaine. Boswell had no comaund. My cossen, Heugh Dove, behaved himselfe valliauntly, slew a rebell and hurt another, and made the hole retret. 3 or 4 of our men were slaine, 13 hurt. Of the rebells, ——— slayne. We encamped this night at the market towne. 30 rebells set uppon our quarter-maister, who whas but ———. The rebelles slayne, amongest whom Donell Knagge, a chiefe man sent thether by Terrone, was slaine. Mr. Bushell, one of the gentlemen ushers, only hurt. The rest of the enemies fledd. Nedd Hidde was in this companie.

18.—" This daye the armye removed, and my Lord sent 1,000 men, under the commaund of the Marshall, in the morninge before the camp,

---

[1] " My Lord Gray, leader of all the valiant gentlemen."
[2] Blank in original.

dislodged to possesse a passe neare adjoyning, which wee after marched throughe with some light skirmishe, and came to the Castell of Ballie Raggac, wich was my Lord Vicont Mountgrivalie's, where my Lord Leeftenant placed a garrison of 100 men under the comaunde of Captain Folliot, and that night the army lodged within ij milles of Killkennye. My Lord Leeftenant laye with my Lord of Ormaunde that night.

19.—"This daye the armye removed and lodged at Killaghe, but my Lord Leeftenant stayed at Killkennye, at which the Lord Rotche (?) beeinge a rebell, submitted himselffe."

"The copie of a lettre sent from the Quene's Majestie unto Sir Amias Powlette, governoure and keeper of the Queen of Scotes, wrytten with her Majestie's own hande."

f. 136d. Undated [1586, August].[1]—"Amias, my most carefull and faithfull servaunte, God reward thee triple fould in the double, for thy most troublesome chardge, so well discharged. Yf you knewe (my Amias) how kindlie, besides duetifullie, my gratefull harte accepts your double labours and faithfull actions, your wise orders and safe regardes, perfourmed in soe daungerous and craftie a chardge, that would ease your travaile and rejoyce your harte, in which I chardge you carie this my most juste thought, that I cannot ballaunce in the weighte of my judgment the value I price you att, and suppose no treasure to countervaile suche a faithe, and shall condemne myselve in that thoughte which yet I never commytted, yf I rewarde not such rewardes, yea, lette me lacke when I moste neede, yf I acknowledge not suche a merytte with a rewarde *non omnibus datum*. Lett your wicked murtheresse knowe howe, with hartie sorowe, her vile desertes compell these orders, and bid her from me, aske God forgivenes for her treacherous dealinge towardes the saver of her liefe, manie yeares, to the intollerable perill of her owne. And yet not contente with so manie forgivenesses, muste falle againe so horriblie, farre passinge a woman's thoughte, much lesse a prince. Insteede of excusinge whereof, not anye can salve yt, beinge soe plainlie confessed by the aucthores of my guiltles deathe. Lette repentance take place, and lette not the feind possesse her soe as the better parte be loste, which I praie with handes lyfted upp to Him that maye bothe save and spill. With my lovinge adewe, I praie for thy longe lyfe. Your assured and loving soveraigne as harte by good desert endued. To my faithfull Amias.—Eliz. Reg."

TRIAL AND EXECUTION OF BABBINGTON AND HIS ACCOMPLICES.

f. 164. 1586, September 13.—By virtue of a commission of oyer and terminer, a precept was directed to the Lieutenant of the Tower, commanding him to have the bodies of "Anthonie Babingtone, esquire, Cheadyoke Tychburne, esquire, Thomas Salsburie, esquire, Robert Barnewell, gentleman, John Savage, gentleman, and John Ballard, clerke," before the commissioners. It was decided to arraign Savage first, "forasmoche as hee medled firste in these mattres."

The account of their trial is given as it appears in Howell's "State Trials." The account of their last confessions and executions is as follows:—

"The Confession of Barnewell.

"Firste, hee praied in Latine, and beinge willed of Dr. White to confesse his faulte, and aske forgivenes of the Quene, hee said, I aske

---

[1] *See* State Papers, Scotland (Mary Queen of Scots), vol. 19, No. 55.

the Quene and all others whom I have offended, forgivenes; and said hee would not dyssemble, for I was drawen into this action, as Mr. Babington before this time hathe declared, but I did it not for any worldlie comoditie, but for my conscience sake. Then Mr. Shereif Topclyff damaunded of him why hee concealed the matter so longe; and hee said hee thought it to bee an offence to bewraie a catholique, and said hee wished aswell to the Quene as to his owne soule, and praie she mighte be converted to be a catholique, and desired all catholiques to praie for him. Then the shereif asked him whether hee were att the Courte of Rychmonde, walkinge in the grene, and that there the Quene's Majestie espied you, so that yf others had had knowledge as well as her Majestie, your daies had bene shorter. But att that time I had no suche pretence, for I had matters att the Courte for to dispatche, and so praied that God woulde grante him patience in that agonie. And said other praiers in Latine, and so ended his lyffe. The rope did slippe so sone as hee was turned off the ladder.

"The Confession of Tychbourne.

"First, hee praied in sorte aforesaid, and said, O my good countrymen, you looke for a large discource of me, beinge a badd orator and havinge a worse texte, but lette me, beinge a yonge man, be an example to all *precertim generosis adolescentibus*. I am sorie I have offended the Quene, and I have offended more then I shall receave punishment for, and yet I never entended the death of her Majestie, but I was privie to all there actions; and so proved that olde proverbe true *qui tacet consentire videtur*, for I will not make the faulte lesse then yt ys. Yt was Mr. Babington, my deare friend whose heade here standeth, that made me privie of all these matters. I maye very well compare the state of Mr. Babington and myselve to the estate of Adam before his falle, to whose subjection all thinges were obediente, onlie the tree of lyffe forbidden. So wee havinge the world at will, were accompted the happiest that were ever dwellinge 'or abidinge in London; no place forbidden us, no one thresholde to stoppe us, the streetes as we passed by admired us; only her Majestie's lyffe was the tree that we oughte not to have towched. Adam, with a lytell lycourousnes, was brought to offende his Lord, and so procured his owne destruction. Wee, I knowe not for what consideration, have wroughte our owne overthrowe. Adam, after his sinne was discovered, soughte to hide himselve in the garden amonge the trees, but all in vaine, for he coulde not escape from the sighte of the Lord. We endeavoured to harbour ourselves in woods, but the carefull and vigilant watchmen of her Majestie's true subjectes had espied us. The griefe we sustaine ys no lesse then the griefe of Adam; but these yearninges of sorowe proceedinge from me, ought to move teares of joye aboundantlie to distill from you. Praie for her Majestie, all true subjectes, for she loveth you well, and I perfectly knowe shee ys no nyggarde of her mercye; but the quallitie of mine offence deserveth yt not. What thinges att any time heretofore did enter into my heade lesse then matters of estate. I am descended from an house which was 200 yeares before the Conquest; there bloude was never stained before now. But my deare wiefe (O Lord), yf I shoulde thinke on earthlie thinges, shee woulde grieve me more then I can speake of. But lette me not deceave you; I have offended, and am a true catholique, and now cannot chaunge. I expected some favour, althoughe I deserved none. I lefte a note of my debtes with my wiefe. I beseche you that it maie be paid. And then he spake to one Mr. Fulwell, one of Sir Christopher Hatton's, gentlemen, that he woulde commende him to all his fellowes, and aske them all forgivenes. And lette not these my unnatural dealinges be any waie offensive unto them, and thoughe yt maye be said that one of Mr. Vice-chamberlaine's men had attempted her Majestie's destruction, yt can be no sclander to them that be free from yt. I desire his honoure to forgive me. Yf yt please the people to praie for me, I am willinge.

"Dr. White willed him to saie the Lorde's praier in English, and hee saide hee woulde firste saye yt in Latine and then in Englishe, that you may all knowe that I understande the Latine. And then they were somewhat hastie with him, and hee willed them to staie, not that hee feared deathe, but that hee might thinke on God, as hee said, and said manie praiers in Latine and so ended his lyffe. Hee hanged longe, and yet was alyve when they rypped him.

"The Confessione of Tillney.

"Hee firste praied as afforesaid, with manie crosinges said : For my owne parte, I am come not to argue, but to dye. Dr. White willed him to aske the Quene forgivenes, and hee said, I aske the Quene and all other forgivenes whom I have offended, and desire all catholiques to praie for me, and said hee trusted to be saved in the bloudsheade of Jesus Christe. Dr. White willed him to acknowledge his offences to God, and so beganne to praie in Latine, and ended his lyffe very obstinatelie. After hee was turned off the ladder, the rope brake or hee slipte, for hee hanged never a whitte."

"The Confessione of Ballard.

"Praie for me, I beseche you. I desire all those that came with me to saie the Creede for me, for that ys a speciall meanes to strengthen our beliefe. Dr. White willed him to acknowledge his faulte, and confesse his sinnes. Then hee said, For the matter for the which I was condemned, I am guiltie. Dr. White willed him to aske the Quene forgivenes. Then hee said, Yf I have offended her I aske her forgivenes. Dr. White would have had him made a confessione of his faithe, but hee said, I have allreadie talked with you aboute that matter. And so desired so manie as were of the catholique churche to praie for him, for I hope, said hee, within this halfe houre, to be with the angelles of heaven. Then the Shereif of London asked whether hee was guiltie of that matter for which hee was condemned, and hee said, I am justlie condemned. And Dr. Whyte willed him againe to make a confessione of his faithe. Then hee said, There is not one poincte of the catholique faithe, but I confesse yt. And then said his praiers in Latine, the most parte privatelie, and so ended his lyffe.

"The Confessione of Babingtone.

"Firste, hee kneeled on the ladder, and praied privatelie to himselve, crossinge him and knockinge himselve manie times on the breaste. Since yt bathe pleased God to bringe me to this, that my offence ys suche that nothinge can satisfye yt but the sheadinge of my harte's bloude, I protest that my entraunce into this action was not for any temporall promotion, but for matter of religione. Dr. White willed him to aske the Quene Majestie's forgivenes, and hee said, I aske forgivenes of all those I have offended, especiallie all those of the catholique churche. And so desired his debtes might be paide, and said hee lefte a note thereof with Sir Owen Hopton, and said hee had a poore man in the easte country whom he meant to imploie in the trade of merchandize; hee ys att wante of manie thinges. I have a wyffe and child and knowe not howe theye are lefte, but her friendes are righte nought. I woulde humblie desire that favoure mighte be shewed them.

And then did requeste all his friendes to praie for him, bothe att this presente and after his death; and then the people murmured att that, and hee said, I am sure you will confesse that these praiers after I am dead can doe me no harme. And then he begane to praie in Latine. But Dr. White willed him againe to aske the Quene forgivenes, and hee said, I aske God forgivenes and the Quene, and I praie that my death maye doe her good bothe in bodie and soule; and praied in Latine, privatelie, and departed.

"The Confessione of Savage.

Firste, he praied in Latine, kneeling on the ladder, as Babingtone did, and said, I muste confesse I was guiltie of this treasone for which I am condemned, and I did yt not for any worldlie benefyte, but for resolution of my owne conscience. Dr. White willed him to aske the Quene forgivenes, and hee desired all catholiques to forgive him, and said that hee had done the Quene good service for his owne persone, but all that I have offended by my weaknes I aske forgivenes. White willed him to confesse his faithe, and hee said, I believe in the catholique faithe. And so praied in Latine, and then was turned beside the ladder, and when his bowelles were in cuttinge furthe, hee cried, Lorde have mercy on me.

"The Confessione of Sallesburie and otheres, att their execution, the xxjth of September 1586.

"When Sallesburie wente uppon the ladder, hee beganne with his ancyente countenance, but his voyce somewhat altered, in sorte followinge: Yt hathe pleased God to call me that I shoulde ende my lyffe here, and therfore I thank the Lord God; firste, that hee hathe redeemed me, and secondlie, that hee hathe ellected me and chosen us. I confesse I have grievouslie offended her Majestie through ignoraunce. I beseche her to forgive me for the same, and I counsell all catholiques to laye no violente bandes on her Majestie, but to beare patientlie this cross of tribulation. Then said Dr. White, Sallesburie, call to God for mercie, for hee ys mercifull and readie to forgive. Then said Sallesburie, I hope in his mercie, and I doe penitentlie confesse I am a grievous sinner, and I praie all catholiques to praie for me, and I beseeche God from my harte to blesse her Majestie and all her Counsell. And then hee said his praiers in Latine, and crossed himselve. Then said Dr. White, Whoso ys ashamed to confess God before men, God will be ashamed of him in his kingdome. Wherefore doe not dallie with the world for any vaine ostentation, but cleave unto God with a true faithe. Then said Sallesburie, I have lyved a catholique, and so will I dye. And the hangman thrust him off the ladder, where he hanged till hee was allmoste utterlie deade, and cutt then, accordinge to his judgmente, and so ended his lyffe, as yt seemed, penitentlie, accordinge as his religione woulde permitt him.

"The Confessione of Dunne.

"Nexte unto Sallesburie proceeded Dunne, who was condemned the second daie with Sallesburie. First, when he came to the schaffold, hee kneeled on the ladder and said his praiers softlie to himselve; then he ascended the ladder, and with a black visage, for so was his countenance, a cheerfull and a sorowfull minde, hee demaunded whether the people expected anythinge, and answeare beiug made that they did, hee uttered these speaches: No soule more sorowful then my soule, firste unto God, nexte unto her Majestie, and thirdlie, unto all, for that I have offended all, and I confesse there lyveth not one man more sinnefull then myselve. Allso, I beseche all catholiques to beware howe they attempt anythinge againste the Quene, whom I beseeche God from the bottome of my harte to blesse. Then one that stood on the schaffold saide, yf thou meane Quene Elizabethe and none other, God blesse her. Then hee said, Yes, her and none other, and I beseeche God to blesse her. Then Dunne proceeded and said, I lyved here joyfullie and pleasauntlie under her Majestie, and ten weekes agoe I mette with Anthonie Babington, who toulde me of all his treasons and devises, and urged me thereunto to give my consente, but I refused him, and disswaded him allso. Then hee toulde that I was one whom hee loved well, and so urged me againe, and, to confesse a truthe, I said I woulde doe the beste I coulde, and consented. And afterwardes, when Babington grewe rype in these treasons, hee made me privie to all, and I said that I woulde doe nothinge but that which shoulde be to the glory of God. Dr. White then said, Why, dideste thou think that murther of the Quene would be to the glory of God? No, no, said Dunne, I never thoughte yt woulde be to the glorye of God. Then Dunne proceeded further and said, I owe some money and am endebted, and I knowe not howe to paye yt. I beseche them moste hartely to forgive yt me. But I professe I came endebted by reasone of others, and by others' procuremente. Thirdlie, I am sorie—I am noo more sorowful, more soroweful then ever I was in all my lyffe—for Mrs. Bellamie's house, whome Babington hathe brought to this, for hee never rested till hee had gotten us entertaignement when wee fledd. Laste of all, I hartilie aske my prince forgivenes, and I praie that shee and you all may be eternized with eternall blessednes. Then Sir Frauncis Knowelles desired him to saie the Lordes praier in Englishe, that all the people mighte praie with him; but Dunne aunsweared, I have bene allwaies of this religione and broughte up in yt, and therfore I beseche you pardone me in that, but I will saye yt in Latine, for I understande yt, and so saide yt in Latine; and when hee had done hee said, *Domine miserere mei, Domine miserere mei*, and so was throwen off the ladder, where hee hanged till hee was thoroughlie deade, and so humblie (exceptinge his religione) and bouldlie finished his tragedie. Hee was of a milde [*sic*, middle?] stature, a broad visage and broade blacke eyes, and blacke beard which grewe somewhat thicke; of speache hee had reasonable good deliverie, and was of melancholy complexione as yt seemed.

"Jones, his Confessione.

" When he had ascended the schaffold, after some speaches passed betwene those on the schaffold, which was Sir Frauncis Knowles, Sir Rychard Knightley, Sir Drew Drurie, the Shereiffes, and him, hee said, I will confesse a truthe as I shall answeare att the dreadfull daie of judgemente. I will conceale nothinge; howe farre I was of myselve from commyttinge these treasons, God doth knowe, for I was prepared to have gone into Flanders when my Lord wente, and I was readie, and my horses were in the towne. Then he spake in blame of my Lord of Leycester for not payinge 15 hundred poundes, which hee shoulde have had to have kepte him, and one that was on the schaffold aunsweared, retorrninge the blame upon Sallisburie himselve. And Jones said, Well, I knowe not in whome the faulte ys, but yf yt had bene as yt was, wee had not come to this. Furthermore, said hee, two daies before I was taken, I was readie to have gone into Scotland, eyther of which thinges yf had happened, I had escaped this ende. Then hee said, *Agnus Dei, qui tollis peccatum mundi, miserere mei*, and said so thrise; and then said in English, O lambe of God, that takeste awaie the sinnes of the worlde, &c. And so hee wente up the ladder and spake louder then hee did before, for his speache on the schaffold fewe coulde heare, and said, I am come hither for to dye, beinge adjudged for to dye, and therefore nowe muste I speake truthe, for in this worlde I speake no more.

"In Trinitie terme laste, some speache was passed betwene Babington and others; myselve was conversante amonge them, but I proteste they durste not make me privie or acquainted with yt, nor call me to counsell, onlie Sallesburie mentioned unto me the deliverie of the Quene of Scottes, desiringe my ayde, and I tould him yt was Babington's badd minde onlie, and praied him to refraine his companie. Att laste hee even urged me, and I said, Well, Tom, thou maieste comande anythinge. Herein I have offended her Majestie, and beseche her to forgive me, and I beseche God with all my harte to blesse and preserve her. And when Sallisburie came to his countrye to keepe him att home, I kepte house anewe, havinge kepte no house before, onlie to keepe Thomas Sallisburie att home, meaning to bringe him from his former lyffe and make him leade a settled lyffe. Allso because myselve would lyve quietlie. I made meanes to Mr. Secretarie that I mighte have conference, bycause I woulde not be obstinate, and I had bene with Mr. Goodman of Chester, and I was prisoner with Sir Edward Frytton (sic). I confesse, I concealed these treasons, and when a note came to my sighte that Babington, Sallesburie, and others were soughte for, as they that would have killed the Quene, then I thoughte that even hee, Thomas Sallesburie, woulde be my destroier. And then hee wepte, but recoveringe his former alacritie, hee proceeded, and said hee (meaning Sallesburie) came to my house att midnighte, and takinge a candle owt of one of my men's handes, hee came to my chamber where I laye, and said, Ned, howe doest thou? Then I tould him that hee was soughte for, pytyinge his case. But hee said there be manie catholiques that be as deepe in these actions as myselve. Thus farre have I offended. But sithence I was a catholique I allwaies bare a loyall minde to her Majestie, and I proteste here that shee ys the onlie prince that hathe righte and tytell to this crowne and realme. And I proteste before God I would have spente my lyffe in her Majestie's service against Frenche, Spanish, or whatsoever. I aske her Majestie forgivenes, then you all. And with you, Sir Frauncis Knowlles, I have lefte a note of all my debtes. I owe thre hundrethe threscores odde poundes, whereof I owe to my [brother] Pype 40l., for when hee had my sister, yt was concluded that eyther hee shoulde have certaine landes convayed unto him, or elles so muche money; and I have borowed of my mother 300l. The debtes owinge me, whosoever seekethe shall finde a greate rablemente, and some of them by bill paye, saving 40s., 3l., or suche like. The summe that ys owinge me ys a thowsande 'six hundrethe and odde poundes. And I beseche her Majestie my debtes maye be paide. And I praye you that some man of conscience maye have the accompte of my goodes, for a greate deale of my landes ys mortgaged landes, and that onlie by worde of mouthe. [I] beseche you yf they pay the money yt may be redeemed.

"And then, beinge moved to saie his praiers in Englishe, hee said, I understande the Latine, and I will saie nothinge but that which shall be to the glorye of God. My professione was a catholique that acknowledged my duetie to my prince, and I beseche all catholiques to praie for me. Then hee said the Lordes praier in Latine, and then in Englishe, and that finished hee said, *O Jesu, esto mihi Jesu, O Jesu esto*, &c., *non secundum peccata nostra, sed secundum misericordiam tuam.* Then spake Mr. Whyte, willinge him to laye houlde of salvation by Christe Jesus alone. And Jones said, I confesse my carcasse can doe nothinge. Yt ys a lumpe, a piece of claye, not able to doe anythinge; I believe, withowt a true faithe, I can doe nothinge. And then hee said, *Agnus Dei, qui tollis peccatum mundi, miserere mei,* and said yt thrise, and then in Englishe thrise, and then after, *Propitius esto mihi peccatori,* and said so thrise, and then in Englishe thrise, Be mercifull unto me a sinner. Laste of all he said, *In manus tuas, Domine, comendo spiritum meum,* and then was throwen off the ladder and hanged till hee was deade, and then quartred accordinge to his judgmente. And so dyed penitentlie and pitifullie to the behoulders, and as one that was more faithefull to his friende then provident for himselve, and one that was rather misled by the ambitious minde of others, then caried headlong by his owne bad nature.

" The Confessione of Charnocke.

" When hee came uppon the ladder, hee beganne and said, *Ave Maria, gratia plena.* Then Sir Drew Drurie answeared, What can Mary doe ? shee cannot heare thee. And White said, O Charnocke, when Mary was alive this was but a salutation, and nowe when shee ys deade, when shee cannot heare thee, what can yt bee nowe ? Then said Charnocke, I besecche all catholiques praye for me. Then answeared Dr. White, Wee be all true catholiques. I beseche you all pray for me, and then said, *Pater noster,* in Latine, and then said, *Ave Maria, gratia plena,* &c., againe. And being moved to aske her Majestie forgivenes, hee said, Yf I have offended her I desire her to forgive me. I muste confesse I concealed these treasons when I knewe them. Then Sir Frauncis Knowlles said, Therin thou didste offende againste her, and commytted highe treasone. Then said Charnocke, I beseche her to forgive me. And then Dr. White, movinge him to beleve in Jesus Christe alone, hee said, I beleve in Jesus Christe, and I truste hee will save me. And then arysinge, hee said, *O Jesu, esto mihi Jesus, O Jesu, esto mihi Jesus.* And so was throwen off the ladder and hanged till hee was deade, and afterwardes used as the others, and so dyed fearfullie and obstinatelie in his relligione. Hee had bene a good souldioure and a talle fellowe, and onlie drawen to playe the butcher, as yt seemed, in these actions ; for so yt appeared by his arraignement. Hee was a proper man in his apparell, somewhat talle and verye stronge, his visage somewhat wanne and pale, a lytell bearde hee had, betwixte blacke and browne, his skinne appeared to be scurvie and scabbie, hee had a foule botche in his lefte legge, whether of a wounde or of some badd disease I knowe not, onlie this, that hee lived like a hardy souldioure and dyed like a fearefull tratoure.

" The Confessione of Travis.

" As for Travis, his superstitione was so greate as nothinge more was whatsoever said unto him hee neglected, onlie hee seemed to regard his idolatrous opinions ; for before hee came to the ladder hee ceased not continuallie to crosse himselve. Then Dr. White, movinge him to crye upon Jesus Christe onlie, hee said, I crye on Jesus in faithe. And when hee had ascended the ladder hee said hee was never guiltie of any treasone in his lyffe. And when they on the schaffold shewed invincible argumentes to prove his guilte by confessione voluntarie of his companions, hee gave no eare, but was whollie given to his owne willfullnes, onlie hee said, I doe dye a true catholique and doe beleve all that the true catholique churche dothe. And then hee said his creede in Latine. Then Dr. White bade him aske her Majestie forgivenes, but hee regarded yt not, but besoughte all catholiques to praie for him. And when Dr. White toulde him that all were true catholiques that were there, hee fell ymediatlie to his *Ave Maria gratia,* and that donne, hee beganne, *Omnes martyres,* and then *Signum crucis est necessarium omnibus corporibus nostris.* And hee was fallinge besides the ladder, and Dr. Whyte prayed God to deliver thy soule from the errors of poperie. So hee hanged in all men's sighte till hee was deade, and when the hangman had his harte in his hande, yt leapte and panted. Even this concluded the laste parte of this obstinate fellowe, who had fullie purposed, as yt was to be conjectured, to lyve a seditious persone, and resolute to dye a papisticall traytour.

" The Confessione of Gage.

" Gage came hartilie and willinglie to the ladder, and when they moved him to aske forgivenes of the Quene for his offence againste her, hee answeared, I aske all forgivenes whom I have offended. And when Mr. Shereife toulde him this was the fruicte of their religione, to comytte suche abominable treasons, hee with vehemente and woonderful earnestnes replied, O Mr. Shereife, said hee, condemne not the whole religione for a fewe bad men; and when yt was tould him howe muche his father was behoulden to her Majestie for speciall greate favoure, hee answeared, I confesse shee has bene as gratious a prince and mistress to my father as ever was any. Then Sir Frauncis Knowlles would have proved his offence to be accordinge as hee was adjudged, but hee hastelie interrupted him, sayinge, O Sir Frauncis, take me with you; when I wente awaie with Babington I knew nothinge of these treasons, but afterwardes hee toulde me therof, and after that time I soughte occasions to escape from them, and when I was taken, I was out of there companie. Then Topcliffe, a justice of peace, toulde him hee had confessed that a prieste came unto him and said yf anythinge be to be done lette yt be done quicklie, after that Ballard was taken. I confesse this [he said], but yt ys no argumente to prove me guiltie. And when yt was suffyciente to prove his treasons, hee answeared, Why then I confesse I am guiltie in that sence. And when yt was objected hee attended on Ballard as his man, when Ballard wente into the northe to move rebellione, hee answeared, I did so, I will waite on anie suche prieste in the world. I did yt, saythe hee, and I confesse yt. And I confesse further, when Ballard came furthe of the northe hee wryte certaine letters into Fraunce and desired me, because I wryte a fayer hand, to wryte yt fayrer, and I did so, but the superscription or subscription I sawe not, but yt was some greate name, for this worde gratious was in, but nowe yf yt be treason to keepe companie with traytours, then have I commytted treasone; but I proteste, as I shall dye, I never had malicious mind againste her Majestie. Then he fell to his praiers in Latine, *Ave Maria gratia plena,* &c., *Sancta Maria, ora pro nobis,* with such like rablementes, insomuche that Sir Francis Knowlles said, Hee knowethe not what hee sayethe, and yet will not bee advised. Last of all, hee concluded, *Averte faciem peccatis meis.* And so was thruste off the ladder and permitted to hange till hee was deade. His hearte did leape in the hangman's hande, and so dyed.

" Gage—resolute, obstinate, and altogether unlearned; of personage hee was a proper man, talle and sclender, but yonge in years and yet rype in abhominations; of visage somethinge a pale countenance and a prowde looke. To conclude, his personage required farre better actions, and his actions deserved farre greater punishmente.

" Bellamie's Confessione.

" Hee talked with the Shereif and others upon the schaffold, concerninge his guilte. Hee expressed his offence by ignoraunce that hee knewe not they were traytoures. Then hee ascended the ladder and desired Mr. Shereife to shewe him some favoure. Dr. Whyte answeared, Aske mercy of God, and hee and they will shewe thee favoure. Then Bellamie said, I have bene a catholique, and I desire all true catholiques to pray for me. Whyte: Beseche all true christians to praie for thee, for here be no suche catholiques as you meane. Soe he desired leave to saie his praiers, and when yt was graunted hee praied privatlie with himselve. Laste of all he was throwen of the ladder to abide the covenaunte of deathe, and there hanged till he was deade.

"Hee was a bigge man, broade sette and talle, of mightie limmes; the colour of his skinne was dunne, broade visaged, a brownishe bearde, which grewe withowt curiositie. And when hee was deade, his countenance was wonderfull blacke. Finallie, he semed rather to have bene wearied with houlding the plowe then overlabouringe with studyinge of a booke; and rather to have bene nurced in papistrie by others, then able to maintaine his erronious opinions by his owne wysdome or learninge."

EDWARD GLOVER and others, described as "inhabitants of Manchester and Salforde," to Dr. JOHN DEE, Warden of Manchester College.

f. 182d. 1597, April 5. — "The uncharitable and malitious proceedinges of Mr. Palmer against oure godlie and learned preacher, Mr. Heaton (Right Worshipful) have beene so many and manifest, as well by open invectyves in the pulpitt as by secreate practyzes otherwise, and that (as wee are fullie perswaded) withowt any occation given by him, that wee can no longer endure the same, and therefore are in conscience mooved to joyne together in this oure earneste and instant requeste that, for the glorie of God and generall good of this people and place, you will vouchesafe to laie to your healpinge hande, or rather to use your lawfull auctoritie to represse the contention likelie to ensue, and take suche speedie order, that eyther Mr. Palmer maie bee broughte to the sighte, acknowledgement, and reformation of his disorder (which were to bee wished), or, if youe find him wilfull and incorrigible, which wee greatelie feare, that then you will judiciallie proceede and remoove him, that oure preacher maie be no more molested, nor his godlie travayls hereafter, by suche ungodlie courses, impeached. Soe shall youe doe a deed beseeminge your callinge, righte acceptable to God, moste necessarie for the quiett of this place, and shall bande us theereby to a thanckfull acknowledgement of your tender consideration of our estate, where otherwise wee shall bee enforced to complaine further, as not myndinge to see or suffer his godlie endevours thus crossed, or the man himselfe, for his good will towardes us, thus grossley abused amonge us."

COMPLAINT TO THE COUNCIL BY AN ANONYMOUS PREACHER.

f. 183. [Undated.]—"Imprimis, Maiester Pagett hath sundrie tymes, openlie, in the pullpitt at Barnestaple, termed your Majestie's injunctions, the dreggs of poperie, and those Statute Protestants, who like such raggs of Rome and tayles of Antechriste.

"Item, hee constantlie affirmed in the hearinge of dyvers persons of sufficient creditt, that your Majestie commaunded idolatrie and superstition, and that hee would prove the same by the booke of common prayer.

"Item, where the people, being sore devyded by his meanes, have beene perswaded to dewtifull obedience and christian charitie, hee hath, in the pullpitt, called that doctrine unitie with a mischeife and unitie with a verie vengeance.

" Item, one of his adherentes, one Bryan, parson of Pairecombe, in lyke sort impugned the doctrine of obedience, and grew verie farr that, in effect, hee compared your Majestie with Pharao, Nabucodonezer (*sic*), Darius, and other persecutors, affirminge that because yt was lawfull for there subjectes to disobeye them then, thearefore your Majestie might in lyke sort bee disobeyed of us nowe.

" One Robert Dillon, gentleman, came into the parish churche of Barnstaple aforesaid, and there brake and spoiled the organes, and the next day abused the Maior in his owne howse, puttinge him in greate feare, so that the whole towne was forced to rise to his reskewe, and thereby great occation given of upprore amonge the people, and murder lyke to have ensewed.

" These, with divers other articcles, are to bee proved and vouched by the Maior, Aldermen, and inhabitantes of the towne of Barnstaple, who feare (withowt speedie reformation) further inconteinence by theese meanes then, of themselves, they shall bee able to redresse."

The EXAMINATION, at Rochdale, of ROBERT HOLT, servant to Sir John Byron, Knight, before CHARLES HOLT and EDMUND HOPWOOD, Esquires, Justices of the Peace in the county of Lancaster.

f. 184. 1588, July 3. — " Yesterdaie, in the morninge, beinge att breakefaste att Badger Yate, in Marchden, in the Countye of Yorke, in the companie of James Marchden, hys hoste, Thomas Butterworth, and Anthonie Hamer, the saide James Marchden asked of them what newes ; wherunto the said Anthonie saide that there was a man which did over-take him and the saide Butterworthe, and one Thomas Chethame, there neighboure, aboute 2 myles from Barnsley, as they were cominge from the markette the daie before, who seemed to be of acquaintaunce with the saide Chethame, but hee was a straunger to the saide Anthonie, which man saide to the said Thomas Chethame, after salutations had betwene them, these wordes, or the lyke in effect : — Yt ys reported that the Earle of Derby ys turned from us, or shrunke awaie from us; and that the saide Anthonie and Thomas Butterworth answeared, By the grace of God yt was not soo, neyther ever woulde be soo. And that the said straunge man then saide hee trusted yt was not so ; but yet suche newes were tolde abroade."

" Thexamination of the said Anthonie Hamer, the daie, time, and at the place afforsaide.

" The said examinant deposethe and saithe, that as this examinant, Thomas Chethame and Thomas Butterworth were coming from Barnesley afforsaide, upon Wednesdaie laste, in the afternoone, ther overtooke them a straunge man, abowte two myles from the said Barnsley, who, takinge acquaintance to the saide Chetham, after some talke passed between them, asked the said Chetham, what newes in Lancashire. The saide Chethame said, none but good ; and then the saide straunger saide that yt was reported that the Earle of Darbye was turned from us, or shrunke awaie from us (meaninge from hys country, as this examinant then tooke yt), to whom the saide Anthonie saide, Yt ys not so, by the grace of God. So I truste, said the said straunger, yet yt ys so reported, suche newes are tolde abroade. And the said straunge man then saide, Roberte Holte, your neighboure, ys behinde you. And this examinant further saithe that the examination of the

saide Roberte Holte, as yt ys before sette downe in these presents, ys
true; and further saithe, that when the speaches were uttered, as they
were at breakefaste, at Rdger Ynte, as afforsaide, that the saide Roberte
Holte said he knewe the said straunge man very well, and that hys
name was James Barneby, servaunte to Mr. Barneby, of Barneby, in
the county of Yorke, Esquire.

"The said Thomas Butterworthe deposethe and saithe as the saide
Anthonie Hamer hathe before saide.

" Item, the said Robert Holte beinge examined howe hee knewe the
said straunger's name, saithe that the man which hee mette in Barnsley
towne feilde was James Barnebie, seryaunte to Mr. Barnbie,
and that the saide James Barnby did then ryde uppon a graie nagge,
withowt any bootes; and because the said Anthonie and Thomas Butterworthe told this examinant that the said straunger saide that he was
behinde them, and that the said stranger saide hee had lefte hys nagge
uppon a common, neere where they mette with the said straunger,
therfore, the said Robert Holte takethe yt to be the said James Barneby,
bycause he mette him as afforsaid, and mette not any other man to hys
remembraunce.

"The said Roberte Holte, beinge examined what speaches passed
betwene him and the said James Barneby, in Barnesley towne fielde,
uppon Wednesdaie last, saithe that the said James Barnesby offered
this examinant hys nagge to sell, and said that hys master had forty
stone of woolle which hee woulde sell to this examinant, and sette the
same at 7s. the stone. And further speaches passed not betwene them at
that time."

SYDALL MOOR.

f. 184d. Undated.—Memorandum as to common rights, &c., on
Syddall Moor.

"The CONFERENCE or COMMYSSONE between the Quene of Scottes
and the Lordes, concerninge her examinacion."

f. 196. 1586.—" Upon Wednesdaie, the 12 of October, the Lordes
Commissioners for hearinge the Scottishe Quene came to the Castle of
Fotheringhey, in the County of Northampton, aboute nyne of the clocke
in the morninge, at which houre, in the chappell of the said castle, the
Deane of Peterboroughe preached before them. From the sermone, they
wente to Councell, in the Counsell Chamber of the same house, and from
thence sente Sir Walter Myldmaye and Sir Amias Pawlette, Governoure
of the house to the Scottishe Quene, to knowe whether shee woulde appeare
or no. There was also delivered unto her a letter from her Majestie, to
that effecte. After which summons shee refused to appeare, and stoode
all that daie, beinge oftentimes required therto by some of the Commissioners sente in unto her. Upon Thursdaie there wente unto her, in
her lodginge, the Lord Chauncelor, the Lord Treasourer, the Earles of
Oxforde, Shresburie, Kente, Worcester, Viscount Montague, the
Lordes Zouche, Graye, Lumley, Sir Raphe Sadler, Sir James Crofte,
Mr. Vicechamberlaine, Sir Amias Pawlette, the two Chief Justices of
England, Doctor Dale, and Doctor Forde, Barker, and Wheler, notaries,
who remained with her allmoste the space of two houres, signifyinge
unto her that yf shee woulde not come furthe before the Commissioners
they woulde proceede againste her accordinge to ther Commissione.
That whole daie was spente in Councell and sendinge unto her.

"In the morninge, upon Frydaie, shee resolved to appeare, and so
aboute 9 of the clocke came furthe into the presence chamber, which

was prepared and hanged with clouthe of state in the upper parte and downe alonge bothe sides. There were formes covered with grene for the Earles and Lordes on the righte side, and for Barons on the lefte side. Somewhat below the middle of the chamber was a barre sette, and within the barre a fourme for the Knightes of the Privie Counsell, and before there fourmes was a chair with a quishione and a foote carpett, for the Quene of Scottes, dyrectlie againste the seate belowe. In the middle of the chamber was a table, wherat sate the Quene's Attorney and Sollicitor, the Quene's Sergeaunte, the Clerkes of the Crowne, the two notaries, directlie above the table. In the middeste of the chamber were two fourmes, wherupon sate, on the righte side, the Lord Chief Justice of England, the Lorde Chief Baron, Doctor Dalle, Doctor Forde. Over againste them sate the Lord Chief Justice of the Common Pleas, Justice Pieram; belowe the barre sate suche gentlemen as came to see the action.

" On the righte side were these lordes :—

[On the left side.]

The Lord Chauncelor		The Lord Aburgaveny
The Lord Treasourer		The Lord Zouche
Earle of Oxford		The Lord Morley
Earle of Shrewsburie		The Lord Stafford
Earle of Kente	Sir James Crofte	The Lord Graye
Earle of Derby	Sir Walter Mildmaie	The Lord Sturton
Earle of Worcester	Sir Raphe Sadler	The Lord Sandes
Earle of Rutlaund	Sir Frauncis Wallsingham	The Lord Wentworth
Earle of Cumberland		The Lord Mordant
Earle of Warwicke	Mr.Vice-chamberlaine	The Lord St. John of Bletso
Earle of Lincolne		The Lord Compton
Earle of Penbrooke		The Lord Chenie.
Viscounte Montague		

" The Lordes beinge thus sette and all thinges readie, the Quene of Scottes was broughte in, havinge a waie or a lane made with halbardes from her lodging doore, which was in the lower corner of the chamber. Shee was in a gowne of blacke velvette, covered over with a white vaile of lane, a very bigge woman and talle, beinge lame, and supported by the one arme with Melvine, her gentleman, and by the other arme with her phisician. One of her women curyed up her traine, three other attainded her, one of her servauntes broughte her a chayre covered with crimsone velvette, and another broughte a quishione of the same. A lytell before her coming her chaire was removed from the bottome of the chamber to the upper parte bellowe the state, and set, as yt were, cornerwise towardes the side of the lordes barons.

" Scilence beinge made, the Lord Chauncelor stoode up, and, beinge uncovered, spake to this effecte :—

" Madame, the Quene, beinge stronglie enfourmed of sondrie practizes made by you againste her, hathe caused this our meeting, as hathe bene signified unto you. You have reade the Quene's letters certyfyinge the same ; and I muste saie thus much unto you from her Majestie's mouthe, that havinge borne soe manie thinges att your handes, shee cannot forbeare any longer but proceede againste you, not for the perills which may befalle her, for God, she trustethe, who hathe ever defended her, will still deliver her from them; but there dependethe more upon yt. Shee saith that you are the foundation of all practizes againste her, and yf shee shoulde neglecte yt, shee shoulde forgette the cause of God, and beare the sworde in vaine. Yt ys not mallice, Madame, nor regarde of her persone, that causethe her to doe yt, albeit shee mighte doe otherwise and proceed againste you, that you shoulde not be hard speak for yourself.

" The Quene answeared to this effecte, by waie of protestation, that shee was a free prince, borne a quene, not subjecte to any but to God, to whom shee muste give accompt, and, therfore, her appearinge should not be prejudiciall to other kinges or princes, nor her allies, nor her sonne. And thereupon desired an Acte to be made, and required her owne people to beare wytnesse of yt.

" The Lord Chauncelor againe protested againste that protestation, and said in nowise yt should be prejudiciall unto the Quene's Majestie, nor to the Crowne of Englande, and that they all, on the behalf of her Majestie, required it to be enacted.

" Then Mr. Poole, Clerke of the Crowne Office, did reade the Commysyone, grownded upon the Statute of *anno* 27.

" The Quene answeared, I proteste that this lawe is insuffycient, and, therfore, I cannot submit myselve unto yt.

" The Lord Treasourer avouched and justified the lawe to be suffyciente to proceede againste her.

" To whom shee answeared, that that law was made against her.

" The Lorde Treasourer said, wee have commissione to proceede, and yf you will not heare and answeare, wee will therin proceede againste you.

" Then shee said, I will heare and answeare yt.

" Then arose Sergeaunte Gawdie, and declared firste the Statute, and then enferred ₜbhaₜ the Quene of Scottes, there presente, had offended againste bothe the branches therof, viz., that shee had bene bothe privie to the conspiracie of killinge the Quene's Majestie, and allso had herselve practized and compassed yt, and so rypped the whole matter complete, from Ballarde's cominge into the realme. When the Sergeaunte · said that the Quene was bothe a mover and a compasser, she bowed her bodie and smiled.

" Her firste letter to Babington, to renewe the intelligence, was reade.

" Then Sergeaunte Puckeringe perused the reste of Babington's letters unto her, and her answeare to him againe.

" To the which the Quene answeared that shee had never seen Babington, nor ever had speache with him, nor ever receaved letters from him, and that shee coulde stoppe noe man's goinge beyond the seas ; but lette any man in Englande come and saie that I did ever any- thinge againste the Quene's lyffe.

" Then Sandes, Clerke of the Crowne, reade Babington's confessione, and Sergeaunte Puckering opened the poinctes.

" The Quene said that, beinge kepte from intelligence of her friendes, and of her sonne, yt mighte be shee desired intelligence, but yf any other man have done or practized anythinge, yt ys no matter to this purpose ; ther be some that send me letters, and I knowe not from whence they come nor what they are.

" The Clerke of the Crowne reades againe Babington's confessione.

" The Quene said againe, I wote not of any suche letter.

" Then was reade againe her letter to Babington.

" To the which shee said, Yf Babington said yt, and all the world, they lye in yt. I will see my owne handwrytinge. And to Babington's letter to her, shee said, I never sawe that letter, nor ever harde of yt.

" The Lord Treasourer proved the receipte of Babington's letter.

" So the Sergeaunte shewed an answeare to Babington's letter from her by the same cypher, by a servinge man in a blewe coate, and so opéned the poinctes of her answeres to Babington. When mention therin was made of the Earle of Arundell, she wepte and blobered out, sayinge, Woe ys me, that your house hathe suffered so muche for my sake.

"And after weepinge a time, shee said, Yf ever I made any suche device againste the Quene, my sister, I praie God I never see God in the face. I have written, I confesse, aboute my deliveraunce, as any prince kepte captive as I mighte doe, but never againste the Quene. I confesse I have sente for the catholiques deliveraunce from persecution, and I will worke ytt, yf I coulde, with my bloude, to save them from destruction. I wolde, and yf yt maie be soe, I praie you laye yt upon me ; and therwith wepte accordinge to her guise.

"The Lord Treasourer said, Madame, the Quene puttes none to deathe for ther conscience ; but they mighte enjoye the libertie of there conscience yf they woulde lyve as duetifull subjecte ; and therefore, Madame, reforme your opinione therin.

"The Quene of Scottes said shee had reade yt so in a booke.

"The Lord Treasourer said, They that doe wryte so, Madame, wryte allso that the Quene of Englande ys no Quene.

"Then pyked shee a quarrell againste Mr. Secretarye, that hee had bene her sore enimie, and her sonne's, and practized with certaine persons againste hir. But, Mr. Walsingham, I thinke you are an honeste man, and I praie you saie, in the worde of an honeste man, whether you have bene so unto me.

"Mr. Secretarie rose up, and came to the end of the table, standinge in the middeste before his seate, and said, Madame, I am charged by you to have practized somethinge againste you. I call God, and all the worlde, to wytnesse I have done nothinge, as a private man, unworthie an honeste man, as a publique person unworthie my callinge. I pro- teste before God that, as a man carefull of my Mistress' safetie, I have bene curious, and yf Ballard had offered me his service, I proteste I woulde have used him, and yf hee had done service, I woulde have re- warded him ; but yf hee were practized with by me, why did hee not pleade yt for his liefe.

"Here, againe, shee wepte, and protested shee would not make shipp- wracke of her soule in conspiringe againste her good sister, and that these spies whom Mr. Secretarie had sette over her, were spies for her againste him, and had likewise toulde her things of him.

"The Quene's Attorney proves that the Quene of Scottes was privie to the conspiracie, and gave the enstructions to her Secretarie to wryte by ; her Secretarys, not constrained, not imprisoned, wrote copies of the originall, upon theire oathes, some in cypher, some translated, by her dyrectione, into Englishe. Her Secretaries were Jaques Maw [and] Gilbert Carle.

"The Sollicitor proves bothe the poinctes of the Statute, agreinge with the poinctes of the Commissione ; firste, and that shee was privie to the conspiracie, she receaved Babington's letters wherin the conspiracie was contained to kill the Quene. Shee givethe answeare to yt, diposed by her Secretaries, who, besides ther othes and voluntarie confessione, did sette downe, accordinge to ther memorie, the contents and poincts of Babington's letters to the Quene, and her answeares to Babington, wher especiallie shee remembred the poinctes of the conspiracie, particularlie by Babington, before hee was apprehended and att large, when he had thought to have executed yt, and have bene advaunced by yt, shee shewed her letters and her answeares to Ballard, Savage, and Tychburne, as they confessed yt.

"Secondlie, he proves that shee herselve did compasse and conspire againste the Quene, for besides the provinge of Babington's plotte, shee addeth in a letter of her owne, for the maner and order of the execution of the designment, &c.

"The Secretaries, at the viewe of her letters, doe wryte thus: *per le expres commandement de la reigna ma Matressa*—at the expresse commandmete of the Quene my mistress. Maw and Carle.

"Shee beinge asked whether yt were ther handes, shee confessed shee knewe yt to be ther bandes, and that Carle ys an honeste man, but shee would not be judged by him; and that Maw was the King's Secretarie of Fraunce, and that bee had bene Secretarie to the Cardinall of Loraine.

"When shee said shee knewe not Babington nor Ballard,

"The Lord Treasourer said: Madame, I will tell you whome you knowe; you knowe Morgan that hyred Parrie to kill the Quene, and after you knewe yt you gave him pension—you gave pension, madame, to a murtherer.

"Shee said, hee lost all for my sake, but you gave pensions in Scotland to my sonne againste me.

"The Lord Treasourer said, The Quene, bycause the reveneue of the Crowne of Scotland ys diminished, givethe a benevolence to the Kinge, her kinsman.

"The second daie, att her first cominge, shee renewed her protestation, sayinge, I am a sacred and anointed Prince, and oughte not to be judged by the lawe. I am a free prince, and owe no more to any prince then they doe to me. I come hither for the justification of my honoure, and that which ys laid to my charge againste my sister. Her oration was very longe here, and of manie thinges. Shee said the Quene was so dealt with when the matter of Wyatte was laid to her chardge, and yet not founde guiltie of yt. I like not to take this course, thoughe I desire the catholiques deliverance from ther persecution. I had rather play the part of Hester then Judith, to deliver my people. God forbidd I shoulde deserve to be denied of Jesus Christe before his Father.

"They gave yt owt I was of no religione, for ther was a time when I tendred myselve, but then cared not for my soule. But my Lordes, when you have done all that you can, and have put me from that I would have, yet shall you not obtaine your cause for Mary Stuarte.

"And here shee wepte and blobered, that they coulde not conceave her speach. I desire, said shee, that another Assemblie maie be called, where I may have my Counsell. I appeale to God firste, who ys the wise judge, and to princes my allies.

"Here the Lord Treasourer said, Wee have, Madame, sett downe your protestation under a notaries hand, and againe wee have protested that your protestation be not prejudiciall to the Crowne of Englande.

"The Quene said, Indeed, my Lord, you take no Commissione but what shall serve your turne beste; you have done the worste you can. I have ofte offered, yf I mighte be att lybertie, that I woulde doe all dueties and laboures to quenche the troubles that are made, and I coulde not be harde. I was made to beleve that I shoulde be att lybertie, and I promised hostiges for my securitie, my owne sonne and my cosine Guise' sonne.

"The Lord Treasourer said it was true that the Quene was contente, and so was the Counsell. You offered hostiges as you saie, and yt ys as true that the Lords of Scotland woulde not consente that the Kinge shoulde come.

"The Quene of Scottes: I toulde you yf I were att lybertie I woulde effecte yt.

"Madame, said the Lord Treasourer, the Quene shall sette you att lyberty, and you shall seeke her destruction, for all this practize of your enlargemente was nothinge elles but a plotte againste the Quene, for even then, when this was doinge, your man Morgan hyred Parry to kill the Quene.

"My Lord, quothe shee, you are my enimie.

"No, said my Lord Treasourer, I am enimy unto the Quene's enimies.

"Was yt not said, saythe shee, that the Quene shoulde never be free from practizes untill I was sette att lybertie; therfore I desired that the occasione mighte be taken awaie.

"Then was reade a letter to Mendoza, the Spanishe Embassador in Fraunce, wherin shee promisethe to give the Kinge of Spaine the king-domes of England and Scotland, yf her sonne woulde not be reclaimed from that beresie wherin shee sayed hee was misled.

"A letter allso to Doctor Allen, wherin shee callethe him reverente father in God, and dealethe with him aboute the invasion, and his letter to her.

".Theire was likewise reade, her letters to the Lord Pagette and Sir Frauncis Englefield, wherin to everyone shee saith that shee hathe given dyrectione to the catholiques on this syde to dispatche her.

"Shee beinge pressed with truthes of the conspiracie, bycause her owne man had sworne yt, shee said that shee thoughte no conscience of an oathe given to them.

"Wherat the whole house murmured. Concerninge the givinge awaie the Kingdome of Englande to the Kinge of Spaine, wrytten to Mendoza, shee advisethe him thus:—Lette not this be knowne, for yf yt shoulde, yt would be in Fraunce the losse of my dowrie, in Scotlaunde the breach with my sonne, in England my totall and utter destruction. Here the Sollicitor remembred the Lords that yf a forraine prince had the Kingdome as shee woulde assigne yt, what should become of ther dignities and estates.

. "Madame, said the Lord Treasourer, the successione of the Crowne, whosoever hathe yt, cannot give yt to a strainge prince, yt muste goe by the lawes of the realme. Your enimies in Scotland threatned to kill you, and her Majestie said shee would then revenge yt, and so your lief was assured.

"Att her risinge first upp, shee talked longe with the Lord Treasourer, cominge to him to his seate, after to Mr. Vice-Chamberlaine and to Mr. Secretarye, excusinge herselve unto them, and like a serpente to winde herselve unto them. Shee said unto the Earle of Warwicke that shee hard hee was an honourable gentleman, desiringe him not to beleve all thinges that hee hard of her, desiringe him to comende her to my Lord of Leycester, sayinge that shee wished him good successe in all his affaires.

. "To the judges and lawiers shee said, I praie God blesse me from you, for you have sore handes over them that come under you; and to Mr. Phillipps, thou never readeste any good thinge towardes me.

· "And so the Lordes brake upp on Saturdaie, att one of the clocke, and adjorned the Commissione to the Starre Chamber, the xxij[th] of the same monethe."

INDEX.

H

Y Y

LONDON: Printed by EYRE and SPOTTISWOODE,
Printers to the Queen's most Excellent Majesty.
For Her Majesty's Stationery Office.

HISTORICAL MANUSCRIPTS COMMISSION.

Date.	—	Size.	Sessional Paper.	Price.
				s. d.

1870 (Reprinted 1874.)	FIRST REPORT, WITH APPENDIX - -
	 Contents :—
	    ENGLAND. House of Lords; Cambridge Colleges; Abingdon, and other Corporations, &c.
	    SCOTLAND. Advocates' Library, Glasgow Corporation,. &c.
	    IRELAND. Dublin, Cork, and other Corporations, &c.
		f'cap	[C. 55]	1 6

1871	SECOND REPORT, WITH APPENDIX, AND INDEX TO THE FIRST AND SECOND REPORTS - - - - -
	 Contents :—
	    ENGLAND. House of Lords; Cambridge Colleges; Oxford Colleges; Monastery of Dominican Friars at Woodchester, Duke of Bedford, Earl Spencer, &c.
	    SCOTLAND. Aberdeen and St. Andrew's Universities, &c.
	    IRELAND. Marquis of Ormonde; Dr. Lyons, &c.
		,,	[C. 441]	3 10

1872	THIRD REPORT, WITH APPENDIX AND INDEX - - - - -
	 Contents :—
	    ENGLAND. House of Lords; Cambridge Colleges; Stonyhurst College; Bridgewater and other Corporations; Duke of Northumberland, Marquis of Lansdowne, Marquis of Bath, &c.
	    SCOTLAND. University of Glasgow; Duke of Montrose, &c.
	    IRELAND. Marquis of Ormonde; Black Book of Limerick, &c.
		,,	[C. 673]	[Reprinting]

1873	FOURTH REPORT, WITH APPENDIX. PART I. - - - - -
	 Contents :—
	    ENGLAND. House of Lords; Westminster Abbey; Cambridge and Oxford Colleges; Cinque Ports, Hythe, and other Corporations, Marquis of Bath, Earl of Denbigh, &c.
	    SCOTLAND. Duke of Argyll, &c.
	    IRELAND. Trinity College, Dublin; Marquis of Ormonde.
		,,	[C. 857]	6 8

1873	DITTO. PART II. INDEX - - -	,,	[C.857i.]	2 6

1876	FIFTH REPORT, WITH APPENDIX. PART I. -
	 Contents :—
	    ENGLAND. House of Lords; Oxford and Cambridge Colleges; Dean and Chapter of Canterbury; Rye, Lydd, and other Corporations, Duke of Sutherland, Marquis of Lansdowne, Reginald Cholmondeley, Esq., &c.
	    SCOTLAND. Earl of Aberdeen, &c.
		,,	[C.1432]	7 0

,,	DITTO. PART II. INDEX - - -	,,	[C.1432 i.]	3 6

Date.	—	Size.	Sessional Paper.	Price.

Date.	—	Size.	Sessional Paper.	Price. *s. d.*
1877	SIXTH REPORT, WITH APPENDIX. PART I. - Contents :— ENGLAND. House of Lords; Oxford and Cambridge Colleges; Lambeth Palace; Black Book of the Archdeacon of Canterbury; Bridport, Wallingford, and other Corporations; Lord Leconfield, Sir Reginald Graham, Sir Henry Ingilby, &c. SCOTLAND. Duke of Argyll, Earl of Moray, &c. IRELAND. Marquis of Ormonde.	f'cap	[C.1745]	8 6
1879	DITTO. PART II. INDEX (Reprinted 1893)	,,	[C.2102]	1 10
	SEVENTH REPORT, WITH APPENDIX. PART I. - - - - Contents :— House of Lords; County of Somerset; Earl of Egmont, Sir Frederick Graham, Sir Harry Verney, &c.	,,	[C.2340]	[Reprinting]
	DITTO. PART II. APPENDIX AND INDEX - Contents :— Duke of Athole, Marquis of Ormonde, S. F. Livingstone, Esq., &c.	,,	[C. 2340 i.]	[Reprinting]
1881	EIGHTH REPORT, WITH APPENDIX AND INDEX. PART I. - - - Contents :— List of collections examined, 1869–1880. ENGLAND. House of Lords; Duke of Marlborough; Magdalen College, Oxford; Royal College of Physicians; Queen Anne's Bounty Office; Corporations of Chester, Leicester, &c. IRELAND. Marquis of Ormonde, Lord Emly, The O'Conor Don, Trinity College, Dublin, &c.	,,	[C.3040]	8 6
1881	DITTO. PART II. APPENDIX AND INDEX - Contents :— The Duke of Manchester.	,,	[C. 3040 i.]	1 9
1881	EIGHTH REPORT. PART III. APPENDIX AND INDEX - - - - - Contents :— The Earl of Ashburnham.	,,	[C. 3040 ii.]	1 4
1883	NINTH REPORT, WITH APPENDIX AND INDEX. PART I. - - - - Contents :— St. Paul's and Canterbury Cathedrals; Eton College; Carlisle, Yarmouth, Canterbury, and Barnstaple Corporations, &c.	,,	[C.3773]	[Reprinting]
1884	DITTO. PART II. APPENDIX AND INDEX - Contents :— ENGLAND. House of Lords, Earl of Leicester; C. Pole Gell, Alfred Morrison, Esqs., &c. SCOTLAND. Lord Elphinstone, H. C. Maxwell Stuart, Esq., &c. IRELAND. Duke of Leinster, Marquis of Drogheda, &c.	,,	[C.3773 i.]	6 8
1884	DITTO. PART III. APPENDIX AND INDEX - - - - - Contents :— Mrs. Stopford Sackville.	,,	[C.3773 ii.]	1 7

Date.	—	Size.	Sessional Paper.	Price.
				s. d.
1883	CALENDAR OF THE MANUSCRIPTS OF THE MARQUIS OF SALISBURY, K.G. (or CECIL MSS.). PART I. - - - -	8vo.	[C.3777]	[Re-printing]
1888	Do. PART II. - - -	,,	[C.5463]	3 5
1889	Do. PART III. - - -	,,	[C. 5889 v.]	2 1
1892	Do. PART IV. - - -	,,	[C.6823]	2 11
	Do. PART V. - - -	In the Press.		
1885	TENTH REPORT - - - - This is introductory to the following :—	,,	[C.4548]	0 3½
1885	(1.) APPENDIX AND INDEX - - - The Earl of Eglinton, Sir J. S. Maxwell, Bart., and C. S. H. D. Moray, C. F. Weston Underwood, G. W. Digby, Esqs.	,,	[C.4575]	[Re-printing]
1885	(2.) APPENDIX AND INDEX - - The Family of Gawdy.	,,	[C.4576 iii.]	1 4
1885	(3.) APPENDIX AND INDEX - - Wells Cathedral.	,,	[C.4576 ii.]	2 0
1885	(4.) APPENDIX AND INDEX - - The Earl of Westmorland; Capt. Stewart; Lord Stafford; Sir N. W. Throckmorton, Stonyhurst College; Sir P. T. Mainwaring, Misses Boycott, Lord Muncaster, M.P., Capt. J. F. Bagot, Earl of Kilmorey, Earl of Powis, Rev. T. S. Hill and others, the Corporations of Kendal, Wenlock, Bridgnorth, Eye, Plymouth, and the County of Essex.	,,	[C.4576]	3 6
1885	(5.) APPENDIX AND INDEX - - - The Marquis of Ormonde, Earl of Fingall, Corporations of Galway, Waterford, the Sees of Dublin and Ossory, the Jesuits in Ireland.	,,	[C. 4576 i.]	[Re-printing]
1887	(6.) APPENDIX AND INDEX - - - The Marquis of Abergavenny, Lord Braye, G. F. Luttrell, P. P. Bouverie, W. Bromley Davenport, M.P., R. T. Balfour, Esquires.	,,	[C.5242]	1 7
1887	ELEVENTH REPORT - - - - This is introductory to the following :—	,,	[C. 5060 vi.]	0 3
1887	(1.) APPENDIX AND INDEX - - H. D. Skrine, Esq., Salvetti Correspondence.	,,	[C.5060]	1 1
1887	(2.) APPENDIX AND INDEX - - - House of Lords. 1678-1688.	,,	[C. 5060 i.]	2 0
1887	(3.) APPENDIX AND INDEX - - - Corporations of Southampton and Lynn.	,,	[C. 5060 ii.]	1 8
1887	(4.) APPENDIX AND INDEX - - - The Marquis Townshend.	,,	[C. 5060 iii.]	6 2

Date.		Size.	Sessional Paper.	Price.
				s. d.
1887	(5.) APPENDIX AND INDEX - - - The Earl of Dartmouth.	8vo	[C. 5060 iv.]	2 8
1887	(6.) APPENDIX AND INDEX - - - The Duke of Hamilton.	,,	[C. 5060 v.]	1 6
1888	(7.) APPENDIX AND INDEX - - - The Duke of Leeds, Marchioness of Waterford, Lord Hothfield, &c.; Bridgwater Trust Office, Reading Corporation, Inner Temple Library.	,,	[C.5612]	2 0
1890	TWELFTH REPORT - - - - This is introductory to the following :—	,,	[C.5889]	0 3
1888	(1.) APPENDIX - - - - The Earl Cowper, K.G. (Coke MSS., at Melbourne Hall, Derby) Vol. I.	,,	[C.5472]	2 7
1888	(2.) APPENDIX - - - - Ditto. Vol. II.	,,	[C.5613]	2 5
1889	(3.) APPENDIX AND INDEX - - - Ditto. Vol. III.	,,	[C. 5889 i.]	1 4
1888	(4.) APPENDIX - - - - The Duke of Rutland, G.C.B. Vol. I.	,,	[C.5614]	3 2
1891	(5.) APPENDIX AND INDEX - - - Ditto. Vol. II.	,,	[C. 5889 ii.]	2 0
1889	(6.) APPENDIX AND INDEX - - - House of Lords, 1689-1690.	,,	[C. 5889 iii.]	2 1½
1890	(7.) APPENDIX AND INDEX - - - S. H. le Fleming, Esq., of Rydal.	,,	[C. 5889 iv.]	1 11
1891	(8.) APPENDIX AND INDEX - - - The Duke of Athole, K.T., and the Earl of Home.	,,	[C.6338]	1 0
1891	(9.) APPENDIX AND INDEX - - - The Duke of Beaufort, K.G., the Earl of Donoughmore, J. H. Gurney, W. W. B. Hulton, R. W. Ketton, G. A. Aitken, P. V. Smith, Esqs.; Bishop of Ely ; Cathedrals of Ely, Glouces-ter, Lincoln, and Peterborough ; Corporations of Gloucester, Higham Ferrers, and Newark; Southwell Minster; Lincoln District Registry.	,,	[C. 6338 i.]	2 6
1891	(10.) APPENDIX AND INDEX - - The First Earl of Charlemont. Vol. I. 1745-1783.	,,	[C. 6338 ii.]	1 11
1892	THIRTEENTH REPORT - - - This is introductory to the following :—	,,	[C.6827]	0 3
1891	(1.) APPENDIX - - - - The Duke of Portland. Vol. I.	,,	[C.6474]	3 0
	(2.) APPENDIX AND INDEX - - - Ditto. Vol. II.	,,	[C. 6827 i.]	2 0
1892	(3.) APPENDIX. J. B. Fortescue, Esq. Vol. I. -	,,	[C.6660]	2 7

Date.	—	Size.	Sessional Paper.	Price.
				s. d.
1892	(4.) APPENDIX AND INDEX - - - Corporations of Rye, Hastings, and Hereford. Capt. F. C. Loder-Symonds, E. R. Wodehouse, M.P., J. Dovaston, Esqs., Sir T. Barrett Lennard, Bart., Rev. W. D. Macray, and Earl of Dartmouth (Supplementary Report).	8vo.	[C.6810]	2 4
1892	(5.) APPENDIX AND INDEX - - - House of Lords, 1690–1691.	,,	[C.6822]	2 4
1893	(6.) APPENDIX AND INDEX - - Sir William FitzHerbert, Earl of Ancaster, &c.	,,	[C.7166]	1 4
1894	(7.) APPENDIX AND INDEX - - - The Earl of Lonsdale.	,,	[C.7241]	1 3
1894	(8.) APPENDIX AND INDEX - - The First Earl of Charlemont. Vol. II. 1784–1799.	,,	[C.7424]	1 11
	FOURTEENTH REPORT. This will be introductory to the following :—			
	(1.) APPENDIX AND INDEX. The Duke of Rutland, G.C.B. Vol. III.	*In the Press.*		
	(2.) APPENDIX. The Duke of Portland. Vol. III. -	,,	[C.7569]	2 8
	(3.) APPENDIX AND INDEX. The Duke of Roxburghe; Sir H. H. Campbell; the Earl of Strathmore; and the Countess Dowager of Seafield.	,,	[C.7570]	1 2
	(4.) APPENDIX AND INDEX. Lord Kenyon - - - -	*In the Press.*		
	(5.) APPENDIX. J. B. Fortescue, Esq. Vol. II. - -	*Ditto.*		
	(6.) APPENDIX AND INDEX. House of Lords, 1692 - - -	*Ditto.*		

Lightning Source UK Ltd.
Milton Keynes UK
UKHW022256011218
333216UK00008B/366/P